THE OXFORD HANDBOOK OF

ANGLO-SAXON ARCHAEOLOGY

THE OXFORD HANDBOOK OF

ANGLO-SAXON ARCHAEOLOGY

Edited by
HELENA HAMEROW,
DAVID A. HINTON,
and
SALLY CRAWFORD

OXFORD
UNIVERSITY PRESS

OXFORD
UNIVERSITY PRESS

Great Clarendon Street, Oxford OX2 6DP

Oxford University Press is a department of the University of Oxford.
It furthers the University's objective of excellence in research, scholarship,
and education by publishing worldwide in

Oxford New York

Auckland Cape Town Dar es Salaam Hong Kong Karachi
Kuala Lumpur Madrid Melbourne Mexico City Nairobi
New Delhi Shanghai Taipei Toronto

With offices in

Argentina Austria Brazil Chile Czech Republic France Greece
Guatemala Hungary Italy Japan Poland Portugal Singapore
South Korea Switzerland Thailand Turkey Ukraine Vietnam

Oxford is a registered trade mark of Oxford University Press
in the UK and in certain other countries

Published in the United States
by Oxford University Press Inc., New York

© Oxford University Press 2011

The moral rights of the authors have been asserted
Database right Oxford University Press (maker)

First published 2011

All rights reserved. No part of this publication may be reproduced,
stored in a retrieval system, or transmitted, in any form or by any means,
without the prior permission in writing of Oxford University Press,
or as expressly permitted by law, or under terms agreed with the appropriate
reprographics rights organization. Enquiries concerning reproduction
outside the scope of the above should be sent to the Rights Department,
Oxford University Press, at the address above

You must not circulate this book in any other binding or cover
and you must impose the same condition on any acquirer

British Library Cataloguing in Publication Data
Data available

Library of Congress Cataloging in Publication Data
Data available

Typeset by SPI Publisher Services, Pondicherry, India
Printed in Great Britain
on acid-free paper by
CPI Antony Rowe, Chippenham, Wiltshire

ISBN 978–0–19–921214–9

1 3 5 7 9 10 8 6 4 2

Contents

List of Figures x
List of Tables xvii
List of Contributors xviii
Preface xxi
Acknowledgements xxvi

PART I ANGLO-SAXON IDENTITY: ETHNICITY, CULTURE, AND GENES

1. Overview: Anglo-Saxon Identity 3
   C. Hills

2. The Ending(s) of Roman Britain 13
   S. Esmonde Cleary

3. Migration and Endogenous Change 30
   B. Brugmann

4. Anglo-Scandinavian Identity 46
   J. D. Richards

5. The Ending of Anglo-Saxon England: Identity, Allegiance, and Nationality 62
   D. Griffiths

6. Anglo-Saxon Migration and the Molecular Evidence 79
   R. Hedges

7. Dress and Identity 91
   G. R. Owen-Crocker

PART II RURAL SETTLEMENT

8. Overview: Rural Settlement 119
   H. Hamerow

9.	Anglo-Saxon Timber Buildings and Their Social Context H. Hamerow	128
10.	Settlement Hierarchy K. Ulmschneider	156
11.	Local Churches in the Anglo-Saxon Countryside R. Morris	172
12.	Late Saxon Settlements M. Gardiner	198

PART III MORTUARY RITUAL

13.	Overview: Mortuary Ritual T. M. Dickinson	221
14.	Mortuary Practices in Early Anglo-Saxon England H. Williams	238
15.	The Mid Saxon 'Final Phase' †M. Welch	266
16.	Late Saxon Burial Practice D. M. Hadley	288

PART IV FOOD PRODUCTION

17.	Overview: Rural Production D. Hooke	315
18.	Woods and the Wild N. Sykes	327
19.	Food Plants on Archaeological Sites: The Nature of the Archaeobotanical Record L. Moffett	346
20.	Animal Husbandry T. O'Connor	361

21. Anglo-Saxon Fields — 377
    S. Oosthuizen

PART V CRAFT PRODUCTION AND TECHNOLOGY

22. Overview: Craft Production and Technology — 405
    G. Thomas

23. Raw Materials: Sources and Demand — 423
    D. A. Hinton

24. Anglo-Saxon Crafts — 440
    K. Leahy

25. Style: Influences, Chronology, and Meaning — 460
    L. Webster

PART VI TRADE, EXCHANGE, AND URBANIZATION

26. Overview: Trade, Exchange, and Urbanization — 503
    G. Astill

27. The Fate of Late Roman Towns — 515
    M. Henig

28. Britons and Anglo-Saxons — 534
    C. Loveluck and L. Laing

29. Markets, *Emporia*, *Wics*, and 'Productive' Sites: Pre-Viking Trade Centres in Anglo-Saxon England — 556
    T. Pestell

30. Coinage in its Archaeological Context — 580
    M. Blackburn

31. *Burhs* and Boroughs: Defended Places, Trade, and Towns. Plans, Defences, Civic Features — 600
    R. A. Hall

PART VII THE BODY AND LIFE COURSE

32. Overview: The Body and Life Course — 625
    S. Crawford

33. Childhood to Old Age — 641
    N. Stoodley

34. Diet: Recent Evidence from Analytical Chemical Techniques — 667
    B. D. Hull and T. C. O'Connell

35. Gender and Gender Roles — 688
    S. Lucy

36. Disease — 704
    C. Lee

PART VIII THE ARCHAEOLOGY OF RELIGION

37. Overview: The Archaeology of Religion — 727
    J. Blair

38. Sacred Spaces and Places in Pre-Christian and Conversion Period Anglo-Saxon England — 742
    S. Semple

39. The Archaeology of Paganism — 764
    A. Pluskowski

40. The Material Culture of the Anglo-Saxon Church — 779
    E. Coatsworth

41. The Archaeology of the Anglo-Saxon Book — 797
    R. Gameson

42. Christian Sacred Spaces and Places — 824
    H. Gittos

PART IX SIGNALS OF POWER

43. Overview: Signals of Power — 845
    M. O. H. Carver

44. Social Transactions, Gift Exchange, and Power in the Archaeology of the Fifth to Seventh Centuries — 848
    C. Scull

45. Image and Power in the Early Saxon Period — 865
    M. Gaimster

46. Crime and Punishment — 892
    A. Reynolds

47. What Were They Thinking? Intellectual Territories in Anglo-Saxon England — 914
    M. O. H. Carver

PART X THE PLACE OF ARCHAEOLOGY IN ANGLO-SAXON STUDIES

48. Historical Sources and Archaeology — 951
    J. Campbell

49. Literary Sources and Archaeology — 968
    J. Hines

50. Place-Names and Archaeology — 986
    †M. Gelling

51. Anthropology and Archaeology — 1003
    C. Gosden

52. Anglo-Saxon Archaeology and the Public — 1025
    S. Marzinzik

Index — 1043

List of Figures

	Map. Places referred to in more than one contribution	xxviii
5.1	Greensted Church, Essex	72
5.2	Limestone grave slab from St Paul's Churchyard, London	75
7.1	Reconstructions of early Anglo-Saxon female dress	99
7.2	Three types of masculine dress	102
7.3	Male and female dress	104
7.4	Pagan belief on dress accessories	107
7.5	Christian belief on dress accessories	108
9.1	An Anglo-Saxon house with entrances and lines of symmetry indicated	129
9.2	Suggested chronological development of Anglo-Saxon earthfast timber buildings	130
9.3	Superimposed plans of three early Anglo-Saxon buildings from Mucking	131
9.4	Building A from Steyning	133
9.5	Building 9150 from Renhold Water End	135
9.6	Cowdery's Down Building A1	137
9.7	Late Saxon long halls from Cheddar, Sulgrave, Goltho, and Bicester	139
9.8	Plans of four Late Saxon long halls superimposed	142
9.9	Late Saxon narrow-aisled halls from Portchester, Faccombe Netherton, Raunds, and Ketton	144
9.10	A probable barn from Higham Ferrers	145
9.11	Reconstruction of a *Grubenhaus* as a sunken-floored structure	147
10.1	The settlement at Mucking	158
10.2	The seventh-century royal site at Yeavering (Phase IIIc)	160
10.3	Cheddar: the early tenth-century royal complex (Period 2)	166
11.1	Kirk Hammerton, North Yorks	173
11.2	Map of Worcestershire from Thomas Badeslade's *Chorographia Britanniae* (1742)	175

11.3	Earl's Barton, Northamptonshire: architecturally elaborate early eleventh-century tower-church (extended later) co-located with ringwork	179
11.4	Coin of Edward the Elder (899–924) bearing image of a structure that suggests features in common with aristocratic towers of a century later	180
11.5	Spofforth, North Yorks	182
11.6	Stonegrave, North Yorks	187
11.7	Appleton-le-Street, North Yorks	188
11.8	Middleton-by-Pickering, North Yorks	190
11.9	Open fields and rural resources at Weston-by-Welland, Ashley and Sutton Bassett	191
11.10	Extracts from geomagnetic survey in the Vale of Pickering, North Yorks	192
12.1	Enclosures around settlements at North Shoebury Hall and Whitehouse Road, Ipswich	201
12.2	Enclosures with gates at Steyning and Little Paxton	202
12.3	The development of the enclosures at West Cotton	204
12.4	The development of the manorial site at Goltho, Phases 3 to 5	205
12.5	Peasant farmsteads at North Elmham and Stratton Biggleswade	209
14.1	Artist's impression of a wealthy late sixth-century cremation ceremony	244
14.2	Cinerary urn with bossed decoration and artefacts found in grave C23 from the mixed-rite early Anglo-Saxon cemetery at Worthy Park, Kingsworthy	247
14.3	A wealthy sixth-century grave of an adult female from Butler's Field, Lechlade	251
14.4	Adult male aged between 40 and 50 years of age interred with a spearhead and knife from grave 83, Worthy Park, Kingsworthy	252
14.5	Artist's impression of the Finglesham cemetery	256
15.1	Diagrammatic 3D reconstruction of Prittlewell burial	270
15.2	Eccles Grave 19 buckle, front and back views	272
15.3	Milton Regis gold cross pendant and other pendants	274
15.4	Riseley grave group pendants	282
16.1	Plan of the late Anglo-Saxon cemetery excavated at York Minster	289

xii   LIST OF FIGURES

16.2	A coffined burial in a cemetery dated to the tenth/eleventh century at Swinegate in York, possibly associated with the 'lost' church of St Benet	292
16.3	Late Saxon burials from York Minster	293
16.4	Iron hinge straps, stapled hasps, and locks found during excavations at Ailcy Hill, Ripon	298
16.5	Organic remains at Barton-upon-Humber	300
16.6	Plan of a cemetery dated to the eighth to tenth centuries excavated at Addingham	303
17.1	Estate linkages in the West Midlands	320
18.1	Variation in representation of wild mammals on Anglo-Saxon sites of different type	329
18.2	Variation in representation of wild birds on Anglo-Saxon sites of different type	330
18.3	Anatomical representation of red and roe deer remains from elite sites dating to the mid Saxon period	335
18.4	Anatomical representation of red and roe deer remains from elite sites dating to the late Saxon period	340
20.1	Relative abundance of the three main domesticates in the Anglo-Saxon assemblages discussed in this chapter	366
21.1	The putative extent of irregular open-field systems in England	378
21.2	The distribution of common-field systems in England	379
22.1	Seventh-century composite disc brooch from Harford Farm, Caistor St Edmund	408
22.2	Slotted iron tool with holes of uneven diameter, from Tattershall Thorpe Length 114 mm	410
22.3	Iron file, with remains of wooden handle	411
22.4	Lead-alloy brooch from London	416
24.1	Reconstruction of the ninth-century water mill at Tamworth, and Anglo-Saxon wood-working tools	442
24.2	Textile production	446
24.3	Ironsmithing	450
24.4	Metalwork production	452
25.1	Beginnings (late Roman style)	462
25.2	The fifth-century Quoit-Brooch style	464
25.3	The fifth-century Saxon Relief style	466

25.4	The later fifth and sixth centuries: Style 1	468
25.5	The later sixth and seventh centuries: Style 2	473
25.6	The later seventh and eighth centuries: Christian art, new influences and directions	477
25.7	The eighth century: the emergence of a Mercian style	481
25.8	The ninth century: the rise of Wessex, and innovations of King Alfred's reign	485
25.9	The tenth and eleventh centuries: the 'Winchester' Style	488
25.10	The tenth and eleventh centuries: Anglo-Scandinavian influences	492
27.1	Plan of Verulamium and surrounding area in the fifth and sixth centuries	518
27.2	Roman baluster shaft (note mouldings at the base) with incised Ogham inscription, found in a well in Silchester	521
27.3	Fragment of a gold tremissis, struck in the late fifth century, found in Canterbury	523
29.1	The location of the principal *emporia*, *wics*, 'productive', and other sites, plotted against the navigable extent of rivers c.1750	558
29.2	Metal-detected finds from the high-status site at Bawsey	564
29.3	*Lundenwic* and *Gippeswic* in their wider landscape settings	567
29.4	*Hamwic* and *Eoforwic* in their wider landscape settings	568
29.5	The rewards for an emergent elite: gold and garnet pendant, and composite disc brooches	571
29.6	The environs of *Venta Icenorum*, Caistor St Edmund, showing the relationship between the 'productive' site, settlement area, and the surrounding cemeteries	572
30.1	(a) Early penny, Series Q, East Anglia c.725–40; (b) Offa of Mercia, penny, London, c.780–92; (c) Egbert of Wessex, penny, London, 829–30	583
30.2	Histograms reflecting coin loss at particular sites, 600–1100 (a) Hamwic; (b) Lincoln; (c) London	588
30.3	Iron obverse die for Sword St Peter penny from 16–22 Coppergate, York	594
31.1	Anglian York in the seventh to mid ninth centuries; a speculative interpretation, superimposed on the modern plan	603
31.2	Composite picture of a sunken-floored building constructed at Hungate, York, c.970, incorporating timbers from a boat built in southern England ten to fifteen years earlier	612

31.3	Minting-places in 975 and 1066 as guide to urban places at those dates	616
32.1	Adult-artefact pathways into the archaeological record through child agency	629
33.1	Mill Hill, Deal: Distribution of age categories	647
33.2	Blacknall Field, Pewsey: Distribution of age categories	652
33.3	Norton: Distribution of age categories	657
34.1	Map indicating the available stable isotope evidence for Anglo-Saxons	672
34.2	A plot showing the average animal and human isotope values for the sampled sites	674
34.3	Stable isotope results for $\delta^{15}N$ plotted for male burials with and without weapons	676
34.4	Stable isotope results for Anglo-Saxon cemeteries and Weingarten, Germany	680
34.5	Stable isotope results for East Anglia categorized by phase	682
35.1	Grave 1 from Westfield Farm, Ely	690
35.2	Male and female Anglo-Saxon costumes	698
35.3	Concentrations of textile equipment at Bloodmoor Hill	700
37.1	Catholme: liminal burials in relation to the boundaries and enclosures of the Anglo-Saxon settlement	730
37.2	Yeavering: grave AX in relation to the axis of the great hall A4	731
37.3	Bishopstone, late Anglo-Saxon occupation next to the minster church: excavations in progress, 2003	734
37.4	A Saami shrine, pictured by the early ethnographer Johann Schefferus in his *Lapponia*	737
37.5	A modern example of a 'wooden tomb in the form of a little house having a hole in one wall': the grave of Klaudia Fomin (d.1990) at Nilsiä, eastern Finland	738
38.1	A landscape view of Harrow-on-the-Hill, Middlesex, London	746
38.2	Detail showing a stylized rocky cleft as a place of torment or entrance to hell	747
38.3	Avebury from the air	752
38.4	Yeavering: an aerial view	754
41.1	Knives associated with writing figures depicted in a cross-section of Anglo-Saxon manuscripts	801

41.2	Ink-holders associated with writing figures depicted in a cross-section of Anglo-Saxon manuscripts	804
41.3	Quill pens associated with writing figures depicted in a cross-section of Anglo-Saxon manuscripts	807
41.4	Düsseldorf, Universitätsbibliothek, A.14, fol. 119v. Pauline and other Epistles: early ninth century	809
41.5	Canterbury Cathedral Archives and Library, MS Add. 172. Pauline Epistles and other texts: late eleventh century	815
45.1	Style I decorated brooch of gilt silver from Vedstrup, Zealand, East Denmark	868
45.2	C-bracteate from Funen, Denmark; Øvre Tøyen, Norway; Sletner, Norway	872
45.3	D-bracteate from Finglesham, Kent	875
45.4	Reconstruction of two-strand necklace from Finglesham, Kent	878
45.5	Reconstruction of two-strand necklace from Gudme, Funen, Denmark	879
45.6	Design on embossed mounts of tinned copper alloy, decorating the helmet from Sutton Hoo, Mound 1	883
46.1	Distribution of excavated execution cemeteries in England	900
46.2	Plan of the execution burials at Stockbridge Down	903
46.3	South-facing view of execution burials at Meon Hill	905
46.4	Prone burial 159 with the hands tied behind the back from Guildown	907
46.5	Double burial S441/S442 (upper) and triple burial S432/S433/S434 (lower) from Staines	908
47.1	Cemetery evolution at Wasperton, fourth to seventh centuries	920
47.2	Changes of alignment: distribution of artefacts that occur at Wasperton in the earlier sixth century	921
47.3	Location of Sutton Hoo by the River Deben in Suffolk	924
47.4	Plan of the Sutton Hoo cemetery, sixth to tenth centuries	925
47.5	Monastic geography: the Portmahomack excavations	927
47.6	The Tarbat peninsula	929
47.7	Plan of Stafford town, showing the sites of excavation to 1990	931
47.8	Stafford Ware	932
47.9	Four territorial mosaics for Britain	936
47.10	Late Saxon pottery distributions, tenth and eleventh centuries	939

47.11	Iron Age pottery zones, sixth to fourth centuries BC	940
47.12	Architectural preferences in Anglo-Saxon churches, tenth and eleventh centuries	942
48.1	Silver-gilt head, late tenth/early eleventh century from Winchester	963
49.1	Artefacts from the Prittlewell, Essex chamber-grave	981
52.1	The visitor centre at Sutton Hoo	1030
52.2	A re-enactment tableau featuring the seventh-century hanging bowl from Oliver's Battery	1031

List of Tables

20.1	Comparandum NISP data from Anglo-Saxon sites, with sources	365
33.1	Age groups	646
33.2	Children at Mill Hill, Deal: details of graves	648
33.3	Youth at Mill Hill, Deal: details of graves	649
33.4	Adults at Mill Hill, Deal: details of graves	650
33.5	Infants/Children at Pewsey: details of graves	653
33.6	Youths at Pewsey: details of graves	654
33.7	Adults at Pewsey: details of graves	655
33.8	Infants/Children at Norton: details of graves	658
33.9	Youth at Norton: details of graves	659
33.10	Adults at Norton: details of graves	660
34.1	Stable isotope results plotted by region (mean) for humans and animals	679

List of Contributors

Grenville Astill, Professor, Department of Archaeology, University of Reading

Mark Blackburn, Keeper, Department of Coins and Medals, The Fitzwilliam Museum, University of Cambridge

John Blair, Professor of Anglo-Saxon History and Archaeology, The Queen's College, Oxford

Birte Brugmann, Free-lance archaeology and heritage consultant, Mannheim, Germany

James Campbell, Professor and Emeritus Fellow, Worcester College, Oxford

Martin Carver, Professor of Archaeology and Editor of *Antiquity*, Department of Archaeology, University of York

Simon Esmonde Cleary, Reader in Archaeology, Institute of Archaeology and Antiquity, University of Birmingham

Elizabeth Coatsworth, Senior Lecturer, Department of History of Art and Design, Manchester Metropolitan University

Sally Crawford, Honorary Research Associate, Institute of Archaeology, Oxford

Tania Dickinson, Senior Lecturer, Department of Archaeology, University of York

Märit Gaimster, Finds specialist, Pre-Construct Archaeology, London

Richard Gameson, Professor of the History of the Book, Department of History, University of Durham

Mark Gardiner, Senior Lecturer in Medieval Archaeology, School of Archaeology, Queen's University Belfast

†Margaret Gelling, Honorary Senior Research Fellow, School of History, University of Birmingham

Helen Gittos, Lecturer in Medieval History, University of Kent

Chris Gosden, Professor of European Archaeology, Institute of Archaeology, University of Oxford

David Griffiths, Reader in Archaeology, Department for Continuing Education, University of Oxford

Dawn Hadley, Reader in Historical Archaeology, Department of Archaeology, University of Sheffield

Richard Hall, Director of Archaeology, York Archaeological Trust

Helena Hamerow, Professor of Early Medieval Archaeology, Institute of Archaeology, University of Oxford

Robert Hedges, Professor of Archaeological Science and Deputy Director of the Research Laboratory for Archaeology and the History of Art, University of Oxford

Martin Henig, Fellow of Wolfson College, University of Oxford and Honorary Professor, University College London

Catherine Hills, Senior Lecturer, Department of Archaeology, University of Cambridge

John Hines, Professor of Archaeology, Department of History and Archaeology, Cardiff University

David A. Hinton, Emeritus Professor of Archaeology, University of Southampton

Della Hooke, Editor of *Landscape History*, and formerly Research Fellow, Institute for Advanced Research in Arts and Social Sciences, University of Birmingham

Bradley Hull, Post-doctoral researcher, Oak Ridge Institute for Science and Education, Virginia

Lloyd Laing, Associate Professor, Department of Archaeology, University of Nottingham

Kevin Leahy, Finds Adviser, Portable Antiquities Service

Christina Lee, Lecturer in Viking Studies, School of English Studies, University of Nottingham

Christopher Loveluck, Associate Professor and Reader, Department of Archaeology, University of Nottingham

Sam Lucy, Cambridge Archaeological Unit, University of Cambridge

Sonja Marzinzik, Curator with responsibility for the early medieval collection of the British Isles, Department of Prehistory and Europe, The British Museum

Lisa Moffett, Regional Advisor for Archaeological Science, English Heritage, and Institute of Archaeology and Antiquity, University of Birmingham

Richard Morris, Head of the Institute of Medieval Studies and Professor for Research in the Historic Environment, University of Leeds

LIST OF CONTRIBUTORS

Tamsin O'Connell, The McDonald Institute, University of Cambridge

Terry O'Connor, Professor, Department of Archaeology, University of York

Susan Oosthuizen, Senior Lecturer and Associate Director, Institute of Continuing Education, University of Cambridge

Gale Owen-Crocker, Professor of Anglo-Saxon Culture, Department of English and American Studies, University of Manchester

Tim Pestell, Curator of Archaeology, Norwich Castle Museum and Art Gallery

Julian D. Richards, Professor and Director of the Archaeological Data Service, Department of Archaeology, University of York

Aleks Pluskowski, Lecturer, Department of Archaeology, University of Reading

Andrew Reynolds, Professor of Medieval Archaeology, Institute of Archaeology, University College London

Christopher Scull, Honorary Visiting Professor, Department of Archaeology and Conservation, Cardiff University

Sarah Semple, Lecturer in Early Medieval Archaeology, Department of Archaeology, University of Durham

Naomi Sykes, Lecturer, Department of Archaeology, University of Nottingham

Nick Stoodley, Research Associate, Department of Archaeology, University of Winchester

Gabor Thomas, Lecturer, Department of Archaeology, University of Reading

Katharina Ulmschneider, Senior Research Fellow, Worcester College, Oxford

Leslie Webster, formerly Keeper, Department of Prehistory and Europe, The British Museum

†Martin Welch, Senior Lecturer, Institute of Archaeology, University College London

Howard Williams, Professor, Department of Archaeology, University of Chester

Preface

The term 'Anglo-Saxon'—a ninth-century construction in origin—has come to be used as a convenient label for a characteristic material culture, the geographical area within which it is found (broadly corresponding to modern-day England), and a chronological period defined by historical events, namely *c*.410–1066. The purpose of this volume is to review the role of archaeology in creating an understanding of the seven Anglo-Saxon centuries.

The very long tradition of scholarly study of surviving Anglo-Saxon texts, which offer a compelling picture of the chronology, history, and significant social, political, economic, and religious events of the period, has now been augmented by systematic excavation and analysis of physical evidence—settlements, cemeteries, artefacts, environmental data, and standing buildings. Antiquarian recognition of Anglo-Saxon remains, surviving either as churches or as features in the landscape such as embankments or barrows, were traditionally interpreted in the light of written sources and culturally-defined assumptions about the Anglo-Saxon past; the florid portrayals of noble but ignorant barbarian ancestors by Victorian novelists represent the popular, and to some extent enduring, public face of such interpretations.

Analysis of artefacts, followed by systematic excavations in the 1920s and 1930s, at first of cemeteries and then of settlements, began to show that archaeology confirmed some readings of the Anglo-Saxon literary and documentary sources and challenged others. In the second half of the twentieth century, large-scale open-area excavations both in towns and in the countryside put archaeology onto a new footing. The application of computer methods to large bodies of data, new techniques for site identification such as magnetometry and ground-penetrating radar, new dating methods such as dendrochronology, and new means of metallurgical, geochemical, x-ray, and mineral investigation, have affected archaeology in general, including that of the Anglo-Saxon period.

This volume demonstrates how the study of Anglo-Saxon society through its material remains provides new insights, as well as contextualization, support, and qualification of our readings of the written sources. The archaeology of Anglo-Saxon England has also provided an important testing ground for new theoretical approaches, notably those that seek to bridge the gap between archaeology and history. The Anglo-Saxon world's position at the interface between the historic and prehistoric provides a fruitful body of evidence for evaluating new approaches within the archaeological discipline.

Many studies of Anglo-Saxon England have of course been made, but it is over thirty years since the last multi-author compendium of its archaeology appeared (Wilson 1976); we are grateful to several of the contributors to that book for their enthusiastic support for the production of this one. Many of the chapters in this Handbook pay tribute to this predecessor, using it as a starting-point for their discussions. A key difference is that we have asked for discussions as much as for syntheses of current knowledge. Authors were encouraged to highlight current approaches and debates in order to stimulate and support further research, while the writers of 'Overviews' were asked to explore key themes and arguments running through individual parts. Like others in the same series, this volume is not intended to be a practical handbook or an encyclopaedic compendium but rather to concentrate on those aspects of Anglo-Saxon life and culture which archaeology has fundamentally illuminated. Topics at the forefront of research in the 1970s, such as ceramics, sculpture, and manuscript art, are here not presented as separate chapters, but are embedded within thematic considerations of style, identity, craft, economy, and the broader world of Anglo-Saxon material culture. Constraints on space (the volume in its present form contains over fifty contributions), as well as principle, have determined the structure and contents of the volume; in particular, the wider European—notably Irish, Welsh, Scottish, and Scandinavian—context would ideally have received more extended treatment (for which see Graham-Campbell 2007). It is a testament to the flourishing state of Anglo-Saxon archaeology that even a volume of this size cannot cover every aspect of the subject.

That flourishing state stems partly from discoveries made in the last thirty years. Remarkably, the location of the trading sites at both London and York, attested in documents, had not been revealed archaeologically by 1976 (Pestell, Hall, this volume). Interest in the redevelopment of urbanism has been greatly stimulated by such work, most of it caused by modern pressures and much of it on a large scale—Planning Policy Guidance 16 has been fundamental in changing access to and financing for excavations. The quantity and scope of the archaeological evidence emerging as a result of PPG16, for example through excavation of sites where gravel extraction is practised, have changed the scale of our observations, as larger slices of the Anglo-Saxon landscape are revealed. Research excavations have been less prominent over recent years, however, as the cost of excavation and conservation, particularly of early cemetery sites, have soared: the emphasis is on preservation *in situ* unless a site is threatened.

The growth of the metal-detecting hobby has also transformed the range and quantity of evidence coming to light. Some doubts may remain about the reliability of reporting and the number of unreported objects, but the recording of objects found has immeasurably improved as a result of the Portable Antiquities Scheme.

The quantity of finds emerging from sites which do not fall within the previously recognized distributions of settlements and cemeteries are demanding significant reinterpretations (e.g. Loveluck and Laing, this volume), and will continue to do so as the numbers of metal-detected artefacts increase. In regard to this subject and others, this volume presents current questions and ideas about Anglo-Saxon archaeology, not definitive answers.

The term 'Anglo-Saxon' has the disadvantage of hinting at ethnic specificity, as though excluding from consideration other constituents such as indigenous Britons. Its convenience and common usage, however, give it more currency in defining much of the archaeology of this period than, for example, terms such as 'post-Roman' or 'Dark Age', or even 'early medieval'. The creation of an Anglo-Saxon identity, and the problems in using the term 'Anglo-Saxon' to define the groups of people who used a particular material culture in particular places and times, has generated much recent interest; these issues are addressed by the contributors to Part 1 of this volume.

Part 2 considers the changing nature of rural settlement, including the extent to which the settlements of Anglo-Saxon England were the forerunners of later medieval villages. It might be thought that a section on 'landscape' would form an obvious corollary to the section on rural settlement. What is striking, however, as evidenced in the contributions to this volume, is that landscape—considered a new and distinct area of study in the 1970s (Rowley 1974)— is now integral to the study not only of settlements, but also of burials, the geography of belief, and economic systems.

The graves of the dead provided antiquarians with the first evidence of a distinct Anglo-Saxon material culture, and grave-goods still yield the most abundant source of information about the early Anglo-Saxons. New approaches to understanding mortuary ritual and religion—both pre- and post-Conversion—as well as to the body and life course are presented in Parts 3, 7, and 8. The abundant evidence which excavation has yielded for food and craft production forms the subject of Parts 4 and 5, while Part 6, on trade, exchange, and urbanization, emphasizes the sophistication of the Anglo-Saxon economy, something which has only recently— thanks in part to metal-detector use—been fully appreciated. The use of archaeology to reveal mentalities of power and changing expressions of authority is an important new research trajectory, the potential of which is explored in Part 9.

One of the most important developments in Anglo-Saxon archaeology since 1976 has been the exploration and application of theory (Gilchrist 2009). The contributors to Wilson (1976) did not think it necessary to define their theoretical positions. Since then, however, the application of theory (largely derived from anthropology and sociology) to the interpretation of Anglo-Saxon archaeology has become widespread, and many of the papers in this volume reflect the influence of theoretical approaches on the discipline.

Since 1976, the progress made by science-based archaeology has been little short of revolutionary, notably in biological and botanical research (O'Connor, Sykes, Moffett, Hedges, this volume). Dating of the Anglo-Saxon period has traditionally been dependent on documentary sources of variable reliability, in part because other methods, such as radiocarbon dating, have been notoriously difficult to apply to the Anglo-Saxon period with close precision. Recent developments in radiocarbon dating, Optically Stimulated Luminescence, dendrochronology, and other science-based dating methods are allowing us to date new kinds of materials, and to date with greater precision, thereby providing new and more nuanced readings of the Anglo-Saxon past.

Archaeology has fundamentally altered our view of Anglo-Saxon England, in some cases revealing entirely new aspects of its society and economy, in others radically altering long-held views based entirely on written sources. Because the period effectively began in prehistory, passed into what could be described as proto-history, and ended within a fully historic period, it lends itself to interdisciplinarity. In practice, however, research has tended to reflect a divide between 'archaeological' and other approaches. The final part of this volume therefore explores the complex, potentially fruitful, yet sometimes still uneasy relationship between archaeological, historical, anthropological, and literary approaches, as well as the importance of public engagement with the past in ensuring that the next thirty years of research into Anglo-Saxon archaeology will be as fruitful as the last.

* * * *

At almost the same time in July 2009 as the editors met for the final time before submitting the papers for this volume to the Press, a metal-detectorist in a field in Staffordshire was unearthing the first pieces of what has turned out to be an extraordinary hoard of Anglo-Saxon gold and silver, indeed the largest ever found. It will be many years before all the implications of the hoard can be discussed; it certainly demonstrates that there was as much wealth in Mercia as in Kent or East Anglia, at least at one moment in time, for whether it represents the spoils of battle, the payment of a ransom, or a wergild compensation, it signifies the transitory nature of success in the early Anglo-Saxon world, with the accumulated treasure staying 'useless to men' in the ground, like the dragon's hoard in *Beowulf*.

Sally Crawford, Helena Hamerow, David A. Hinton

REFERENCES

GILCHRIST, R. (2009). 'Medieval archaeology and theory: a disciplinary leap of faith', in R. A. Gilchrist and A. Reynolds (eds.), *Fifty Years of Medieval Archaeology*. Society for Medieval Archaeology Monograph 30. London: Society for Medieval Archaeology, 385–408.

GRAHAM-CAMPBELL, J. G., with VALOR, M. (eds.) (2007). *The Archaeology of Medieval Europe*, Vol. 1: *Eighth to Twelfth Centuries AD*. Aarhus: Aarhus University Press.

Rowley, T. (ed.) (1974). *Anglo-Saxon Settlement and Landscape*. BAR British Series 6. Oxford: British Archaeological Reports.

WILSON, D. M. (ed.) (1976). *The Archaeology of Anglo-Saxon England*. London: Methuen.

Acknowledgements

The editors are grateful to Hilary O'Shea, Tessa Eaton, and Dorothy McCarthy for initiating and patiently overseeing the production of this volume, to Malcolm Todd for his efficient and skilful copy-editing, to the contributors for their patience during what has inevitably been a protracted editorial process, and to Nathaniel Donoghue, Julia Schlozman, Devon Sherman, and Liz Strange for their invaluable assistance in checking and collating the texts.

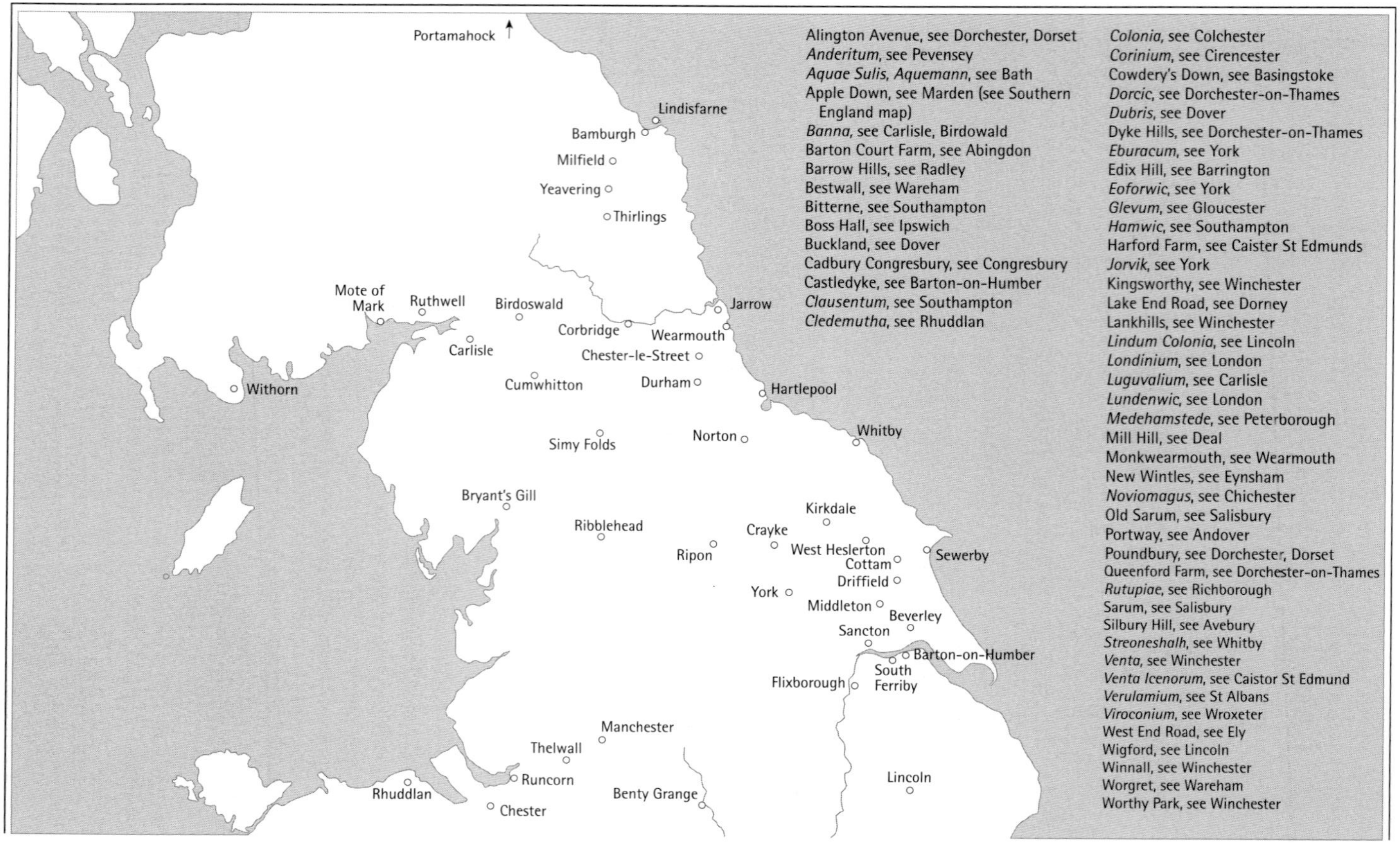

Alington Avenue, see Dorchester, Dorset	Colonia, see Colchester
Anderitum, see Pevensey	Corinium, see Cirencester
Aquae Sulis, Aquemann, see Bath	Cowdery's Down, see Basingstoke
Apple Down, see Marden (see Southern England map)	Dorcic, see Dorchester-on-Thames
	Dubris, see Dover
Banna, see Carlisle, Birdoswald	Dyke Hills, see Dorchester-on-Thames
Barton Court Farm, see Abingdon	Eburacum, see York
Barrow Hills, see Radley	Edix Hill, see Barrington
Bestwall, see Wareham	Eoforwic, see York
Bitterne, see Southampton	Glevum, see Gloucester
Boss Hall, see Ipswich	Hamwic, see Southampton
Buckland, see Dover	Harford Farm, see Caister St Edmunds
Cadbury Congresbury, see Congresbury	Jorvik, see York
Castledyke, see Barton-on-Humber	Kingsworthy, see Winchester
Clausentum, see Southampton	Lake End Road, see Dorney
Cledemutha, see Rhuddlan	Lankhills, see Winchester
	Lindum Colonia, see Lincoln
	Londinium, see London
	Luguvalium, see Carlisle
	Lundenwic, see London
	Medehamstede, see Peterborough
	Mill Hill, see Deal
	Monkwearmouth, see Wearmouth
	New Wintles, see Eynsham
	Noviomagus, see Chichester
	Old Sarum, see Salisbury
	Portway, see Andover
	Poundbury, see Dorchester, Dorset
	Queenford Farm, see Dorchester-on-Thames
	Rutupiae, see Richborough
	Sarum, see Salisbury
	Silbury Hill, see Avebury
	Streoneshalh, see Whitby
	Venta, see Winchester
	Venta Icenorum, see Caistor St Edmund
	Verulamium, see St Albans
	Viroconium, see Wroxeter
	West End Road, see Ely
	Wigford, see Lincoln
	Winnall, see Winchester
	Worgret, see Wareham
	Worthy Park, see Winchester

Portamahock

Withorn

Mote of Mark

Ruthwell

Carlisle

Cumwhitton

Bryant's Gill

Rhuddlan

Bamburgh

Milfield

Yeavering

Birdoswald

Lindisfarne

Thirlings

Jarrow

Wearmouth

Chester-le-Street

Durham

Corbridge

Simy Folds

Ripon

Ribblehead

Thelwall

Runcorn

Chester

Manchester

Hartlepool

Norton

Whitby

Kirkdale

Crayke

York

West Heslerton

Cottam

Middleton

Sancton

Driffield

Sewerby

Beverley

Barton-on-Humber

South Ferriby

Flixborough

Benty Grange

Lincoln

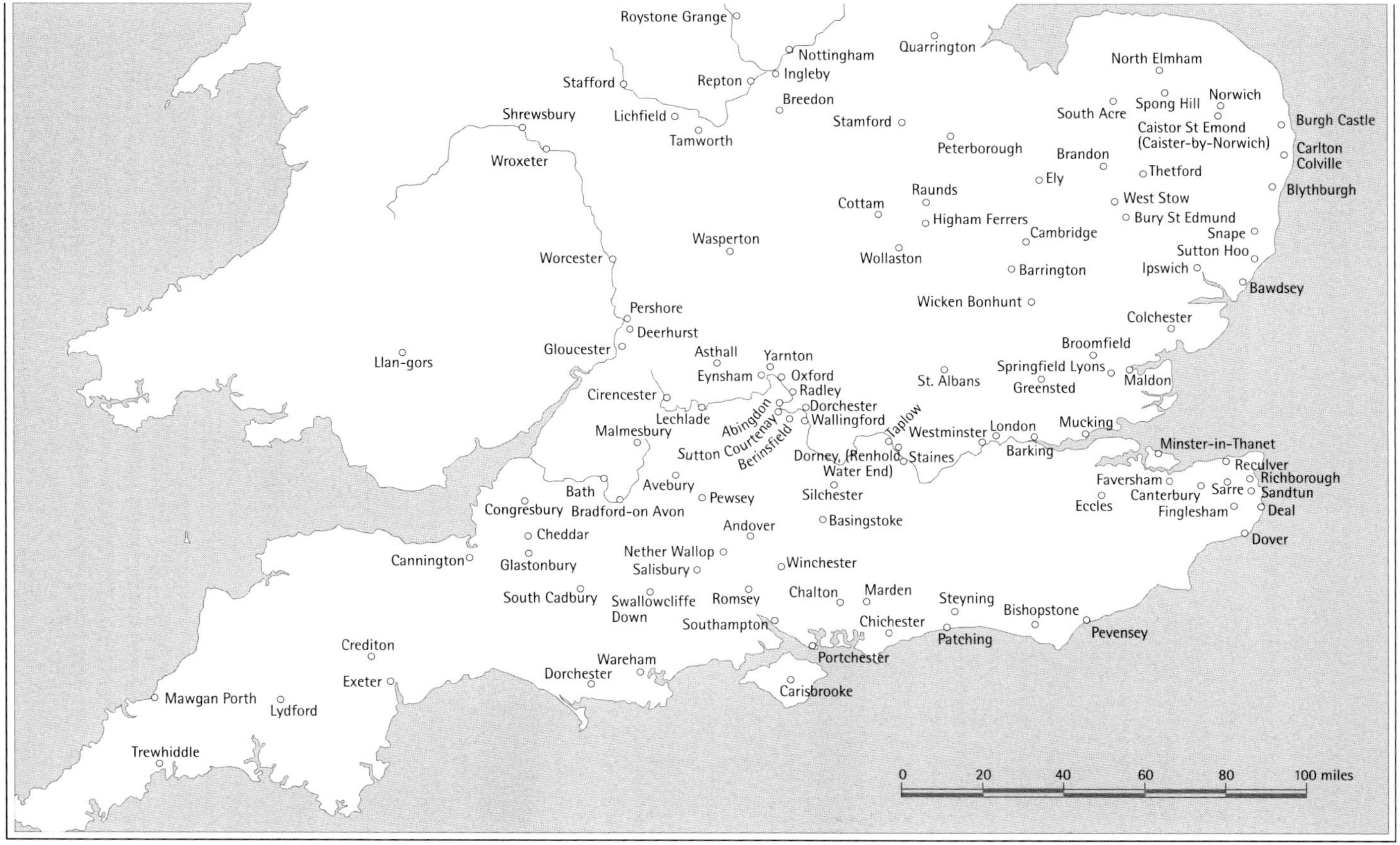

Map: places referred to in more than one contribution.

PART I

ANGLO-SAXON IDENTITY

Ethnicity, Culture, and Genes

CHAPTER 1

OVERVIEW: ANGLO-SAXON IDENTITY

CATHERINE HILLS

The archaeology of identity is a subject which has attracted increasing interest in recent years (e.g. Diaz-Andreu *et al.* 2005). To some extent it is a blanket term, including a range of topics previously dealt with separately such as ethnicity, religious affiliation, status, age, and gender. This is because of the realization that individuals and groups have multiple interconnected identities which can change over time, and also because 'identity' seems a more neutral term than some of the others listed above, with less immediately obvious political overtones. Most of these topics have been of concern to Anglo-Saxon archaeologists for many years, especially in relation to burial archaeology. The extent to which burial reflects the age, status, religious belief, wealth, or gender of the individual buried has been extensively investigated in relation to Anglo-Saxon burial, especially burials of the early Anglo-Saxon period where a wide range of grave-goods and osteological evidence allows sophisticated analysis. These topics are addressed in this Part. The authors, either implicitly or explicitly, apart from Owen-Crocker, focus mainly on ethnicity. What did it mean to be 'Anglo-Saxon' and how does archaeological evidence reflect this aspect of the identity of the people who lived in southern and eastern Britain in the second half of the first millennium AD?

Because group identity, including ethnicity, is defined most clearly in opposition to the identity of other groups, the question of ethnicity becomes most hotly contested in times of stress and conflict. The papers in this section reflect that, in their emphasis on periods of interface—between the Anglo-Saxons and Britons, Scandinavians (Vikings) and Normans—rather than on periods such as the seventh and eighth centuries when identity seems to have related less to an overall Anglo-Saxon ethnicity and more to membership of family or tribe, Christian or pagan, elite or peasant.

On a daily basis these are the identities which usually matter most, locating the individual in the context of the small groups, family, community, age, gender, and workplace within which we operate on a daily basis. Dress is a key element in the construction of this kind of identity. All of us, consciously or unconsciously, represent ourselves to the world through our choice of dress and bodily ornament. That choice is constrained by what is available, what we can afford, and what is deemed appropriate by our society for persons of our age, gender, and status—even a deliberate statement of non-conformity in appearance only has meaning if there is a norm from which to deviate. The Anglo-Saxons, as Owen-Crocker shows, were no different. Her chapter on dress and identity addresses the wide range of identities displayed through dress in the Anglo-Saxon period. The evidence of pictures and surviving textiles, mostly small fragments on the back of dress fasteners, has been assembled to give a detailed picture of how Anglo-Saxons chose to represent their identity as individuals or members of groups.

It is important to remember that 'the Anglo-Saxons' were no more homogeneous than we are. The most visible identities would have been, as now, age, gender, and status, especially wealth. It would have been immediately obvious whether individuals were young or old, male or female, rich or poor, warrior or peasant. Amongst women, marital status would probably also be indicated. After the arrival of the Christian church, members of the clergy would also have been recognizable by their appearance. Beyond that, the key identity would have been local. Which village, region, or tribal grouping you belonged to would have been apparent on at least a local basis, archaeologically discernible mainly through variation in dress fasteners but originally through hairstyles, and colour and detail of clothes. While individuals within communities would have been known to each other, it would have been important to signal what kind of person you were when meeting strangers. Most people may not have thought of themselves as Anglo-Saxons at all, but as the people of a region or descendants of the followers of a leader, as preserved in the names of the Tribal Hidage (Brooks 1989).

However, it is the question of broader identity which has occupied, and continues to dominate, both academic and popular discussion of this period. To what extent were the Anglo-Saxons separate from the British? Did invading Germanic settlers displace and/or destroy the existing British population of the eastern part of Britain during the fifth and sixth centuries AD? Or did the existing population take on a new culture under the influence, peaceful or forcible, of a small incoming group of Germanic leaders? Why is this question still of interest, and why has it not yet been conclusively answered?

The last question relates more to the politics and scholarship of recent centuries than to the Anglo-Saxon period. The British Isles, like other parts of Europe, has modern national identities which derive from real or constructed histories of the period when the western Roman Empire disintegrated, leaving fragmented territories which eventually became the modern nation states of Europe (Moreland 2000; Geary 2002). The process through which this happened has been interpreted variously according to changing political circumstances, and this formative period has been described and studied from varied perspectives. The very names given to the period show this by their choice of dominant theme: Migration Period, Late Antiquity, Dark Ages, Early Medieval. Even the name 'Anglo-Saxon' is not contemporary with the migration period (Foot 1996). Germanic peoples may be regarded either as honoured ancestors and founding fathers or as hostile aliens. They may have arrived en masse, completely replacing the previous population, apart from a few enslaved women, or, instead, a few charismatic foreign leaders may have inspired local chiefs to take on Germanic clothing and weapons and change the names of their peoples. Much of this is based on interpretation of limited historical sources which were not written as modern objective histories. These stories became part of the bedrock of nineteenth- and early twentieth-century nationalist political history, to be deconstructed or defended from assorted post-colonial, post-modern, or nationalist perspectives. For the British Isles, the key issue still seems to be whether the English are descended from invading Anglo-Saxons, and are therefore a different people from the Scots, Welsh, and Irish, descended from native Britons. Alternatively, 'the Anglo-Saxons' were simply those Britons living in the parts of Britain which came under the control of leaders descended (or claiming descent) from invading Germanic chieftains. In that scenario, the peoples of the British Isles have much ancestry in common, although all regions have been affected by migration and invasion on different scales at different times. It is not an accident that the Scots, Welsh, and Irish favour the first interpretation and indeed often seem to regard it as incontrovertible and unproblematic, whereas within England we are more often torn by doubt, having moved from an apparent knowledge of our superior difference to an uncertainty as to who we really are.

Study of the fifth and sixth centuries AD has had as one of its goals the provision of some certainty. Yet successive academic focus in recent decades on the detailed analysis of historical texts, archaeological evidence, and now genetics, in the light of ever more sophisticated technical and theoretical analysis, has so far failed to give closure to the debate. Modern scholarship has demonstrated that the early medieval texts which purport to recount the early history of different peoples—the Franks, Lombards, Goths, or Anglo-Saxons—are complex compilations of information and tradition from different sources, shaped to suit the political imperatives of those who produced them (Goffart 1988). Some of the accounts are based on facts: but which are factual is difficult to decide. It seems clear that claims that the Franks were descended from Aeneas of Troy, or that Aeneas' son Brutus was an early king of Britain, are myths relating to a wish to claim equality or even priority over Rome—a city also purportedly founded by Aeneas. Hengist and Horsa, however, have managed to retain more credibility than Aeneas, as Jutish chieftains who conquered Kent in the fifth century. This is partly because the claim is less far-fetched, but also because archaeological evidence has lent some support to the story. There are artefacts of Jutish origin in Kent.

Another problem is that written sources are concerned with leaders, and their immediate followers. Early writers were seldom concerned with the ethnicity of peasants: the people of East Anglia or Essex had rulers with Anglian or Saxon genealogies but they could have ruled over populations of mixed ancestry. A minority of the people in Roman Britain or Norman England had Roman or Norman ancestry. The archaeological evidence may also tell us more about the upper sections of society than its base, and brooches and weapons in early medieval graves may have been intended to convey messages about power and status, rather than ethnic origin (Moreland 2000).

In the 1960s and 1970s, as confidence in the literal truth of the historical accounts ebbed, it seemed that archaeological information would replace them and provide an alternative means of writing the stories of the Migration Period. The continuing European tradition of collection and classification of archaeological artefacts has resulted in the publication of many volumes of catalogues of artefacts, mostly from cemeteries, from all parts of Europe and from Britain. The artefacts have been classified and mapped, showing chronological development over time and geographical distribution in space of different types of brooch, sword, or buckle (Hines et al. 1999). This is essential basic information and what has been achieved so far by recent generations of archaeologists is very impressive. The major problem confronting us is, however, how to interpret the patterns we can see. It used to be seen as self-evident that geographical patterning of archaeological material reflected 'cultures' (Childe 1929: v–vii), which were often equated with 'peoples'. Changes in material culture meant the arrival of new people. Plotting of 'Saxon' or 'Angle' brooches would show where the Angles and/or Saxons themselves were at dates determined by the dates of the artefacts. You might even be able to trace the career of individuals, Hengist himself for example (Myres 1969: 96–7), and certainly could trace the movement of invaders/settlers across Britain. The only argument would be how representative the recorded assemblage might be of the original distribution and how precise the dates could be.

Archaeological interpretation has however undergone as drastic a phase of rethinking as historical. More anthropological awareness amongst archaeologists has cast doubt on the idea of 'culture' and has shown that ethnicity is a very complex concept. It is no longer seen by anthropologists and archaeologists as a straightforward objective definition of individuals and groups in terms of shared ancestry (Lucy 2005) although that interpretation still has much popular currency. Ethnicity involves perceived relationships which do not necessarily remain constant, and which are not, in the present, always related to material culture, thus throwing doubt on the reflection of ethnicity in archaeological evidence. Material culture is often (but not always) a key aspect of the definition of groups of people, by themselves or others, but the relationship is not always obvious or easy to understand. Multiple processes can lead to the distribution of objects far from their original source: economic, political, religious, social. The large-scale movement of people is not the only mechanism for change in material culture. We understand this in modern terms: Tesco has not arrived in Budapest as a result of invasion by Britain but due to recent changes in politics and economics in central Europe, a similar process to that traced by Härke in Russia (Härke 2007). We have to be aware of this also in the past: as Lethbridge pointed out as long ago as 1956 in his discussion of the Anglo-Saxon settlement of East Anglia, there is 'no proof that people...did not obtain their ornaments from some source quite outside the district in which they lived' (Lethbridge 1956: 113–14).

A further complication is that we have given objects ethnic labels on the basis of the historical sources whose literal truth we have come to doubt. Maps of objects in different parts of Europe have been labelled 'Frankish', 'Lombardic', or 'Anglian' because they date to the time when the historical sources claim those peoples were in that region. So the archaeological maps inevitably seem to support the historical sources. But a map of belt-buckles or brooches is actually just a map of the surviving examples of a type of object. These might have been worn by all members of one ethnic group—or, instead, those of a certain rank, gender, or occupation in that region, whatever their ancestry. Fifth-century weapon burials in northern France might be burials of invading Franks—or of a militarized aristocracy of local and/or mixed origin.

The complexities of the arguments about Anglo-Saxon migration cannot be understood unless the scholarship itself is put in its historical context. Different interpretations have been put on the same evidence because of the different intellectual backgrounds of the scholars who have studied it. The specialist literature is not easily approached without an awareness of the history of this research, as traced by Brugmann here. Nineteenth-century certainties about the equation between ethnicity and material culture, and of the superiority of the Anglo-Saxon ancestors of the English, have given way to modern reappraisal of both theoretical and material foundations of the discussion. The fifth century is key: the evidence must be reconsidered without preconceptions. Application of modern migration theory has also clarified the issues without as yet allowing consensus. Identity is and was a complex and fluid phenomenon, not always easy to understand in the present, and extremely difficult to explore in the past through the medium of incomplete surviving material evidence.

Realization of these difficulties has led to disillusion with archaeological evidence amongst some historians and has made it more difficult for archaeologists to present an agreed account. A new way of answering old questions seems now to have emerged with the considerable expansion of genetic research. Scientific evidence seems to many people, both academics and general public, to have more validity than history or traditional archaeology. If pottery and belt buckles don't really prove Hengist existed, perhaps genetics will. The application of genetics to the study of the origins of the populations of Britain has been reviewed recently by Richards *et al.* (2008), and in this volume by Hedges, who also discusses other molecular evidence, explaining why we do not yet have clear unambiguous conclusions. This is a fast-developing field which is contributing much to our understanding of prehistoric and historical demography, but a number of problems remain to be overcome. Some provisional conclusions have had overexposure in popular media, leading to confusion when apparently contradictory results have been achieved. Several studies, based on modern DNA samples, have shown a difference between the populations of western and eastern Britain. Dating and explaining the origin of this distinction is still debated. The original human re-colonization of Britain after the last Ice Age, the arrival of Neolithic farmers, or the Anglo-Saxons have all been canvassed. Similarity between East Anglian and Frisian Y-chromosomes, identified in other studies, has been argued to represent replacement of British men by Frisian, thus confirming traditional accounts of violent invasion. But there are problems in accepting this conclusion, not the least being the difficulty of distinguishing between fifth-century Anglo-Saxons (and Frisians) and ninth-century Danish Vikings. The relationship between populations around the North Sea has a long and complicated history, which makes it a more difficult problem to unravel than it might at first seem.

Another technique uses the analysis of isotopes from ancient skeletal material to show whether individuals had grown up near where they were buried, or had come from elsewhere. Results are on too small a scale for generalization, but this approach does hold out the promise of some very specific accounts of lives of individuals buried with an apparently 'Anglo-Saxon' identity.

The identities of the peoples who lived in Britain in the past varied regionally and chronologically. This was true in the prehistoric and Roman periods as well as later. Esmonde Cleary in his chapter emphasizes this: '"Roman Britain" was not a monolithic entity'. Late Roman Britain was even officially divided into four provinces. The transition from Roman to Anglo-Saxon which is visible in material culture took different courses in different parts of Britain. A fundamental underlying process was the disintegration of the Roman Empire in the west, and its replacement by small territories. Many explanations for the end of the Roman Empire have been given: 210 according to Ward-Perkins (2005: 33), very roughly divided between external and internal. Did collapse come from the inside, from internal conflict, bureaucracy, or Christianity, or from the pressure of external enemies, the barbarians who took over? Without resolving this debate, it is clear that Britain during the fifth century ceased to be part of a large empire and that here the collapse of the infrastructure of the Roman period seems more complete and possibly more sudden than in other parts of that empire. Esmonde Cleary explains this in terms of state collapse.

The removal of Roman military, economic, and administrative support caused fragmentation into a series of small territories and the disappearance of economic systems and specialist skills. Different regional histories resulted from the extent to which these territories renewed pre-Roman Iron Age identities, retained connections with the rest of the Roman world, or fell under Germanic control. Esmonde Cleary also points out that much of what we see as 'Roman' related to the way of life of the elite. The removal of those elites, or their transformation into native chieftains, had a disproportionate effect on the archaeological record. The material culture of the underlying peasantry may not have differed much from the Iron Age to the end of the Anglo-Saxon period. They are visible when using mass-produced Roman pottery—and when burying their dead with grave-goods according to early Saxon practice—but can otherwise be all but invisible. Even at an elite level the wealth of structures and artefacts which can be made of perishable materials which do not survive into the archaeological record is sometimes forgotten. Not just wood, leather, and textile, but metal objects can disappear completely from the record: recycled into new objects, rusted away, melted down. The occasional survival, like the Oseberg ship burial, reminds us of what has been lost.

The detail of change in the fifth century remains unclear because of the difficulty of attributing material culture of any kind, in any part of Britain, to this period, with the exception of some continuing Mediterranean imports to the south-west. Considerable change in all aspects of material culture did take place between AD 400 and 500, but while we can see either end of the process, the crucial central part of the fifth century remains elusive. The perception of the sudden death of Roman Britain soon after AD 400 results from the disappearance of dated coins together with inscriptions, the basis on which the chronology of Roman Britain has been built. But the buildings, institutions, and artefacts—and the people who used them—did not all vanish at once just because coins ceased to arrive to pay troops and administrators. Much 'late Roman' material must have continued in use into the fifth century. At the other end of the century, dating used to start from historical accounts which put Anglo-Saxon migration to Britain in the fifth century, therefore the earliest Anglo-Saxon artefacts found in Britain were attributed to that period. Typologies of artefacts whose earlier phases are found on continental sites in the late fourth and fifth centuries furthermore suggest that the later phases, found in Britain, belong to the later fifth and sixth centuries. Despite considerable effort by archaeologists starting from both ends of the century, it remains unclear whether there was a gap in identifiable material culture during the fifth century or not, and how much overlap can be seen between 'Roman' and

'Saxon'. It is clear that there was much regional variation, and that identity may have been understood more in terms of local affiliation than membership of an overarching 'British' or 'Anglo-Saxon' people.

From the end of the fifth century these varying regional identities are partially visible in the archaeological record. In the south and east many burials contained distinctive jewellery, pottery, and weapons. In the west such burials are lacking and it is in fact difficult to characterize the material culture of this region. This distinction has always been taken as indicating the divide between Briton and Anglo-Saxon. Within the Anglo-Saxon areas there are further divisions, often equated with the political geography suggested by Bede. He located the Angles in East Anglia and further north, the Saxons in the Thames valley and to the south, and the Jutes in Kent and the Isle of Wight. These broad divisions do seem to be reflected in different types of jewellery, dress fasteners, and pottery, which suggest distinct regional identities. But they cannot be understood as simply as Bede explained them, as relating to the ancestral culture brought over by the Angles, Saxons, and Jutes, because many of the components of the package did not exist in the putative homelands (Hills 2003: 104–7). New identities were created in Britain. The recorded kingdoms of Anglo-Saxon England did not originally correspond to a neat threefold original division either: many small territories existed which were gradually incorporated into the few larger kingdoms of Bede's day in the early eighth century.

The impact of Scandinavian attacks and settlement in the ninth and tenth centuries raises some of the same questions as those relating to the Migration Period. Is it possible to determine the scale of settlement or to understand the nature of the interaction between native and Scandinavian? To what extent have Scandinavian incomers left material traces in Britain? Richards reviews the archaeological evidence and shows that it indicates interaction between native and Scandinavian at all levels, and in all aspects of society. The result was new identities, created within Britain, drawing on both local and Scandinavian roots. The dress ornaments and sculpture labelled 'Anglo-Scandinavian' are not simple hybrids but new developments within England, drawing on local and Scandinavian traditions. The pottery characteristic of the Danelaw, some of it wheel-thrown and even glazed, uses technology familiar neither in Scandinavia nor in pre- Viking England, but in Carolingian Europe. The opportunity for this new production may have been created by the entrepreneurial climate of Anglo-Scandinavian England, where towns and trade also flourished, but it is not 'Viking' pottery.

Regional divisions remained important. The England created by Alfred of Wessex and his successors in the tenth century was not a 'reconquest' but a new creation, taking over control of territories from Scandinavian rulers which had not been part of Wessex in pre-Viking days, a process reviewed by Griffiths in his chapter. The differences of identity between regions, especially between the north and south-east, the borders with Wales and with Scotland, and the far south-west, remained to cause trouble for William of Normandy and many later English rulers, and have not been eradicated to this day.

As for Roman Britain, there was not one ending for Anglo-Saxon England but many. What ended with the Norman Conquest was the Anglo-Saxon or Anglo-Scandinavian elite. With this conquest the historical and archaeological evidence is clearer than for the other transitions. Imposition of a new elite, with new priorities which they were free to impose in terms of control of land and construction of architecture, created a new and very visible Norman identity for the elite. But at the level of everyday life, the archaeological evidence does not show a change of identity: most of what has been seen as 'Medieval England' was in place long before the Conquest. The villages, towns, parishes, and shires were created as part of Anglo-Saxon England, and the people went on using the same pottery, living in the same houses (at least those not destroyed by Norman soldiers) and burying their dead in the churchyards by the parish churches built by Anglo-Saxon thegns and priests. The official identity of England and its rulers may have changed after 1066, but the majority of the people in this new country were descended from those who had lived in the old, as Anglo-Saxons. The question we still have not definitively resolved is whether those Anglo-Saxons had prehistoric native British ancestors, or were Germanic immigrants.

REFERENCES

BROOKS, N. (1989). 'The formation of the Mercian kingdom', in S. Bassett (ed.), *The Origins of the Anglo-Saxon Kingdoms*. London and New York: Leicester University Press, 159–70.

CHILDE, V. G. (1929). *The Danube in Prehistory*. Oxford: Clarendon Press.

DIAZ-ANDREU, M., LUCY, S., BABIC, S., and EDWARDS, D. N. (eds.) (2005). *The Archaeology of Identity*. London and New York: Routledge.

FOOT, S. (1996). 'The making of Angelcynn: English identity before the Norman Conquest'. *Transactions of the Royal Historical Society*, 6th Series, 6: 25–49.

GEARY, P. J. (2002) *The Myth of Nation: the Medieval Origins of Europe*. Princeton and Oxford: Princeton University Press.

GOFFART, W. (1988). *The Narrators of Barbarian History*. Princeton: Princeton University Press.

HÄRKE, H. (2007). 'Invisible Britons, Gallo-Romans and Russians: perspectives on culture change', in N. Higham (ed.), *Britons in Anglo-Saxon England*. Woodbridge: Boydell, 57–67.

HIGHAM, N. (ed.) (2007). *Britons in Anglo-Saxon England*. Woodbridge: Boydell.

HILLS, C. M. (2003). *Origins of the English*. London: Duckworth.

HINES, J., HOILUND NIELSEN, K., and SIEGMUND, F. (eds.) (1999). *The Pace of Change: Studies in Early-Medieval Chronology*. Oxford: Oxbow Books.

LETHBRIDGE, T. C. (1956). 'The Anglo-Saxon settlement in eastern England: a reassessment', in D. Harden (ed.), *Dark Age Britain: Studies presented to E. T. Leeds*. London: Methuen, 112–22.

Lucy, S. (2005). 'Ethnic and cultural identities', in Diaz-Andreu *et al.* (eds.), *The Archaeology of Identity*, 43–66.

Myres, J. N. L. (1969). *Anglo-Saxon Pottery and the Settlement of England*. Oxford: Oxford University Press.

Moreland, J. (2000). 'Ethnicity, power and the English', in Frazer, W. O. and Tyrrell, A. (eds.), *Social Identity in Early Medieval Britain*. London and New York: Leicester University Press, 23–51.

Richards, M., Capelli, C., and Wilson, J. F. (2008). 'Genetics and the origins of the British population', in *Encyclopedia of Life Sciences* (ELS). Chichester: John Wiley and Sons Ltd.

Ward-Perkins, B. (2005). *The Fall of Rome and the End of Civilization*. Oxford: Oxford University Press.

CHAPTER 2

THE ENDING(S) OF ROMAN BRITAIN

SIMON ESMONDE CLEARY

'ENDING(s)': the bracketed final letter reminds us straightaway that what we know as 'Roman Britain' was not a monolithic entity and it did not come to a single, clear-cut stop on a particular date and for a particular cause. For the people at the time there were multiple experiences of a whole range of changes taking place and consciously or unconsciously they recorded their experiences of these changes in the creation of the archaeological records that are our concern in this volume. Equally, these records have given rise to a series of competing modern analyses and narratives of the period according to the specialisms, standpoints, and agendas of modern workers, influenced by the datasets available at the time. This contribution needs to be situated in its own context: that of a work concerned essentially with the 'Anglo-Saxon' period, to which the ending(s) of Roman Britain form a 'prequel'; in a way what this contribution is required to do is to get rid of the archaeology of Roman Britain in order for something new to be created. It will therefore necessarily privilege those aspects of a massively variable archaeological record which may provide some context for the initial Germanic settlements in Britain: different narratives could be written if there were different purposes in view. It will also concern itself principally with the archaeology of the fifth century.

The gross differences in the archaeological record between the later fourth century and the later fifth century are very marked, indeed one of the most marked 'mass extinctions' in all the archaeological record of Britain, and deserve some characterization. In a nutshell, the archaeology of the later fourth century is plentiful, very varied, and very visible to the archaeologist: the archaeology of the later fifth century is much less plentiful, biased towards certain areas of expression, and often difficult to detect. The archaeology of the later fourth century was created by a society with considerable command over the mobilization of economic resources, with social formations that were complex both 'vertically' in terms of hierarchy and 'horizontally' in terms of the specialization of functions and groupings, with complex cultural traditions and expressions in a variety of aspects of life and death, including religions. These all resulted in material correlates that were equally complex in their structures, materials, and expressions. By the later fifth century the economic, social, and cultural complexity of the populations seems to have undergone massive simplification, with much reduced mobilization of resources, a severe flattening of the social hierarchy and of social specialization and complexity, with concomitant huge reductions in the range of markers for cultural variability and expression. This applies across the board, whatever the ethnicity we ascribe to the inhabitants of the various areas of the country and their material cultures. It also helps explain the low visibility of these populations in both absolute terms and relative to a century earlier, a low visibility which has tended to privilege the more visible and more easily comprehended periods of the fourth and sixth centuries.

This contribution will seek to depict and analyse these gross changes, concentrating particularly on the massive alterations to the creation of the archaeological record visible in roughly the first half of the fifth century and on to the end of that century. Given the focus of this book, the main geographical area of discussion will be roughly what is now England, though even that area was a large entity and as we shall see we need to be sensitive to regional variations, which could be quite marked. It cannot seek to treat of every aspect of the archaeology, rather it will seek to give a chronological structure and an explanatory framework: starting by characterizing the nature of the archaeological record for the later fourth century and the ways in which this expressed 'Roman-ness'; then outlining the changes in the record produced by the 'ending(s)' of Roman political, military, and economic systems in Britain along with the related collapse in the cultural systems materialized in the archaeology; then considering the much less visible archaeological record for the mid to later fifth century, which will be theorized using a version of the modern category of 'failed/collapsed state', a model which may also help explain the magnitude of the collapse in the archaeology. The implications of this for the incoming Germanic peoples and the ways in which they and the Britons constructed their identities will conclude this contribution.

The archaeology of the core areas of fourth-century Roman Britain is in its general outlines tolerably well-known (cf. Esmonde Cleary 1989: ch. 3; Faulkner 2000b: chs. 3, 6), with its suite of highly visible settlement, burial, and artefact types, be they forts, towns, villas, temples; cemeteries and burials with or without grave-goods; pottery, coins, metal goods large and small. Rather than rehearse them all here, the approach will be to ask what they signified in terms of the frameworks within which those who made, used, and deposited them operated. The evident answer is that these aspects of the archaeology are immediately expressive of the integration of Britain within the political, military, economic, social, and cultural structures of the later Roman Empire, in particular for those sections of the population who needed to express that integration visibly.

The most obvious group is the servants of the late Roman state, principally the army but also the bureaucrats serving the military, administrative, and financial organs of the state and listed in the *Notitia Dignitatum*. The needs of those state organs, both internally to Britain and more widely across the Western Empire, led to a significant part of the mobilization of resources noted above as characteristic of the period. This took various forms, but was particularly linked to the fiscal cycle of the raising of revenues either in precious metals or in kind, in Britain destined principally to supply the army but also capable of being transported to the Continent to be disbursed or distributed there as the state wished. The archaeology of the military systems within Britain, principally Hadrian's Wall and its hinterland commanding the northern approaches to the Roman diocese and the forts of the 'Saxon Shore' around the eastern and southern coasts, is well known, if not always well understood, a case in point being whether the Saxon Shore installations were designed purely for defence (against whom?) and/or to facilitate passage of supplies to the Continent (cf. Pearson 2002: ch. 6). Likewise, artefact types and distributions can be read as reflecting the impact of state-induced movement of goods, most obviously in the supply to Britain of coins from the state mints, in gold and silver reflecting the fiscal cycle of taxation and payment, or in copper alloy in order to buy in the precious metals, but also visible through fittings from the state factories (Swift 2000: esp. ch. 6) or more locally the distribution patterns of regional potteries such as Dorset, Oxfordshire, or East Yorkshire (cf. Tyers 1996).

Mobilization of resources was also part and parcel of the behaviour of the other important group in creating the familiar, visible archaeology of late Roman Britain, the elite, a *rentier* class deriving their wealth from land. What these people (especially the men) had in common was that there were strict codes in the later Roman world about how such status was to be displayed, encompassing such archaeologically visible arenas as house types, decoration, and dress along with others, less visible but still crucial, such as education, speech, and social networks. These were intended to mark the gradations in a complex, hierarchical society with its competing structures of inherited and acquired means, 'old' landed money or military officers and imperial officials. The study of the archaeology of late Roman Britain has long been dominated by the epiphenomena of this class: the large urban residences ('town-houses') that make up so much of the building stock of the major towns, the villas, particularly the larger and more elaborate ones, the mosaics and wall-plaster that decorated them (cf. Scott 2000) and the furniture, fixtures, and fittings such as silver plate or elaborate glassware that attested simultaneously to the owner's wealth, taste, and education (cf. Leader-Newby

2004, esp. ch. 3). The evidence of great country residences such as Woodchester, Bignor, or Keynsham shows that the British elite was closely in contact with the display architecture and culture of the wider late Roman aristocracy, including new developments in that culture such as the adoption of Christianity and its outward manifestations (cf. Petts 2003). But it shows also that the gap between richest and poorest in late Roman Britain was very wide indeed and that the former lived to a large extent an existence removed from the majority experience.

The demands of the state generally, of the army in particular, and of the aristocracy helped create a wider economy characterized by the movement of raw materials and of finished goods, particularly in the south and east of the island, resulting in the familiar proliferation of objects, especially pottery, but also of materials such as animal bone, which must stand proxy for less visible but very common materials such as textiles and leather. This mobilization and redistribution of resources was very probably aided by the growing presence of a low-value, base-metal coinage, with episodes of counterfeiting to cover periods of shortfall in central supply (cf. Reece 2002: chs. 4, 5). Again, this is not the place to rehearse this in detail. The important point is that the military, economic, and cultural formations of the Roman world did bring about the creation of an archaeology that for the Roman period is far more plentiful and visible than for preceding and succeeding periods, albeit that this was the archaeology of a minority of the population.

The majority of the population, the peasantry, have been the object of less concerted field-work, research, and analysis, yet will be central to our concerns here. In the north and west of Roman Britain it has long been realized that outside the forts of the army with their attendant civil settlements (*vici*), there was little other than this element of the population (cf. Hingley 1989: ch. 9), one that set no great store by the trappings of Roman culture. The archaeology of these people is dominated by field-systems or enclosures and tracts of undivided land associated with enclosed settlements with stone or wood circular structures probably housing nucleated or extended families, depending on size. In the south and east of Britain, regions which were to become the centres for Anglo-Saxons, it is now clear that the majority of the rural population lived in timber-built farmsteads of various forms (cf. Hingley 1989: ch. 8) which in their structures and material culture showed a lower level of engagement with Roman-style material culture than did the more familiar villas. This is not to say that they were divorced from that material culture: pottery, some coins, and metalwork of the same types as are found on urban and villa sites all come from these rural sites, showing that there were economic and cultural commonalities. It should also be remembered that these sites and people were ultimately the producers of the agricultural and manpower resources on which the state and the *rentier* class depended. Thus they were not isolated from the wider economic, social, and cultural currents of the time, simply less involved in and, crucially, less defined by such trends and their archaeological markers.

The preceding survey cannot but be very summary, but it does serve to make an important point: the intimate relationship in late Roman Britain between status, cultural norms, and the creation of the archaeological record. To put it another way, most of the features of the settlement, burial, and archaeological record that to modern eyes define 'Roman' Britain were linked to the behaviours of a small fraction of the population, though it should not be forgotten that they also impacted more widely on areas such as the agrarian regime as manifested in the environmental record. The corollary of this is that the most archaeologically visible 'ending(s)' of Roman Britain need only have affected this small but important and visible class.

Again, the general outline is tolerably clear. Starting in the later fourth century there is a perceptible quantitative and qualitative decline in many of the most characteristically 'Roman' features of the archaeological record in Britain. This has been particularly well charted for those most Roman of sites, the major, administrative towns. In the earlier fourth century these had contained many 'townhouses', the urban residences of the elite, where power was increasingly exercised and displayed in the private sphere rather than in old-style public buildings. But from around the middle of the century these declined in number and extent (Faulkner 2000a; 2000b: ch. 6), with a rise in smaller, simpler structures (nevertheless betokening continuing manufacture and commerce); at the turn of the fourth and fifth centuries came the final implosion, with very few urban buildings datable far into the fifth century. A similar pattern seems to hold good for villas (cf. Gregson 1988), with a peak in construction and embellishment visible around the turn of the third and fourth centuries. Thereafter there seems to be a numerical decline, but there is some evidence that this affected more the middle- to small-sized establishments, with the really large ones being sustained late into the century, possibly indicating continuing concentration of wealth and power into fewer hands. At both towns and villas the phenomenon of 'squatter occupation' has long been recognized: occupation of residences taking the form of ephemeral, timber structures, hearths, occupation deposits, installed in once-grand rooms with, for instance, mosaics. Formerly thought of as re-occupation of abandoned buildings it is now more generally perceived as the latest-phase occupation, in considerably reduced circumstances. A similar pattern seems to hold good for military installations in the north (cf. papers in Wilmott and Wilson 2000), with occupation from the start of the fifth century becoming more sporadic and often with simpler timber structures in the place of the larger, stone buildings of the second to fourth centuries. So in terms of building types at those sites most conspicuously implicated in the Roman system, the later fourth century was generally seeing a process of simplification of plan and materials, or to put it another way, they were converging with the building types of the rest of the population.

A major bugbear in charting and calibrating the 'implosion' at the beginning of the fifth century has always been the lack of good dating evidence. The supply of low-value coin of the type that tended to enter the archaeological record ceased after the issues of 395–402, a date-bracket that of course represents the minting period of these issues and thus acts only as a *terminus post quem* for the deposits in which they were included: the problem is how long *post* the *terminus*? The poor definition of the surface detail on many of these coins of the House of Theodosius suggests either 'wear' or slovenly production. If it was wear, this suggests that they had either passed through many hands in a short time or had remained in less intense circulation for a longer time, suggesting there has been 'bunching' of dates too close to the minting dates for the latest coins. This would in turn affect the dating of the latest pottery, dated of course by its associations with coins, suggesting it also might have to be 'stretched'. Some supporting evidence may come from the silver coinage, where the practice of clipping the edges of coins in order to obtain silver, probably for the production of counterfeits, whilst maintaining the original coin in circulation, probably dates to after the cessation of effective Roman politico-legal and fiscal control of the island in the 410s (Guest 2005: ch. 7), thus at least the second decade of the fifth century. The probability that previous analyses of this period (including mine) have over-compressed the dating is growing stronger and a lower date for the winding-down of Roman-style archaeology should be envisaged: into the third decade of the fifth century and possibly later, though it becomes increasingly difficult to demonstrate any such later dates.

On the other hand, it has often been pointed out that whereas in the fourth century periods of shortage of official supply resulted in local counterfeiting, there is comparatively little evidence for this after the cessation of official supply after 402, suggesting that coin-use was already in decline, with implications for the nature of the economy. There also remains the possibility that 'wear' on the latest bronze issues results from poor minting rather than prolonged use. Important work by Hilary Cool (2000; 2006: ch. 19) has identified trends in pottery and glass forms and appearance characteristic of the later fourth century and later: for pottery the dominance of jar forms, for glass beakers and cups, both probably betokening changed eating and drinking customs. Also there was a changed colour preference, in favour of objects in certain colours such as orange, green, and black. These are presumably the artefact suites that go with the longer date-bracket provided by the evidence for the persistence of the use of coinage some way into the fifth century. Nevertheless, this material culture horizon is the latest one recognizable in the Romano-British sequence and does not develop further, and as has been remarked, the Romano-British material present on Anglo-Saxon sites from the mid fifth century onward is a hodge-podge of types and dates, suggesting the inhabitants of these sites were not in contact with a continuing, Roman-derived material culture suite. It is possible that glass may be an exception to this, with the continental glass-houses still supplying British as well as Anglo-Saxon users with the cup forms characteristic of the fifth century, underlining the growing importance of glass rather than pottery as a dating medium in the fifth and sixth centuries both in Britain and on the Continent.

This new evidence in turn feeds back into the debate about the date and nature of the latest occupation of Roman-style sites, particularly the larger towns, since these coins and other artefact types are precisely what date the latest stratigraphic sequences, making it entirely possible that the final-phase Roman occupation at the majority of these towns can now be sited in the first half of the fifth century. At a number of urban sites there is evidence for long stratigraphic sequences indicating activity well after the arrival of the latest datable artefact suites. One of the most famous of these, Verulamium Insula XXVII, has recently been re-dated (Neal 2003), pushing the late Roman town-house back into the late fourth rather than early fifth century, but the later phases must still extend into that century. More recent work on Silchester, Insula IX, has also shown continued occupation of Roman urban buildings into the earlier fifth century, with some later, less-well-defined activity suggesting continued use of the site, but what the nature of that use was and, crucially, whether it was 'urban' is far from clear (Fulford *et al.* 2006: 267–80).

Later activity at some other towns can be detected. For instance, Gerrard (2007) has re-examined the sequence in the temple precinct at Bath, dating the deliberate destruction of the monumental structures to the late fifth century, closing a sequence of fifth-century use of the precinct. At Bath the stone was left *in situ*, whereas at Exeter the civil basilica was demolished and removed in the course of the fifth century (Bidwell 1979: ch. 6), as was the baths basilica area at Wroxeter, with the basilica itself being demolished in the earlier sixth century (Barker *et al.* 1997: 129–38). In both these cases the stone was re-used elsewhere. For what? On the Continent it would be for those staples of the late-antique urban landscape, walls and churches. New excavations or re-assessment of old ones at a range of towns will presumably show sequences into the first part of the fifth century, though equally there will be others that end earlier.

Logically, since the same artefact suites are present at them also, other classes of site, particularly villas and military sites, should also now be datable in their latest phases to the first part of the fifth century. The remnant magnetism dating of the latest phases of the Whitley Grange (Salop) villa show what might be the case, with evidence for 'squatter occupation' and other activity through the fifth century (Gaffney and White 2007: 95–142), or Frocester Court (Glos), with good evidence for a series of fifth-century phases (Price 2000: Part B, ch. 6). For forts, one might point to sites such as South Shields (Bidwell and Speak 1994: 45–7) and York (Phillips and Heywood 1995: 184–91) in the north or Portchester on the Saxon Shore (Cunliffe 1975: ch. 14), where the stratigraphic sequences suggest continued occupation down into the first half of the fifth century, though whether this betokens still-functioning garrisons (cf. Böhme 1986) may be doubted since the fiscal and supply infrastructures necessary to sustain a standing, Roman army had broken down. Perhaps more likely is the privatization of military force by local warlords, a version of the *bucellarii* attested on the Continent in the fifth century (Whittaker 1994: ch. 7).

The question that arises from the likelihood that Roman-style occupation should sometimes be pushed later into the fifth century than has often been allowed is whether this changes our perspective on the nature and causality of the 'ending' of the Romano-British archaeological complex, or whether it simply pushes the same problem later in time but leaves its essential nature and causality unchanged? I would argue that it shifts the timing rather than the fundamental understanding of the events. The chronological coincidence between the cessation of Roman imperial power in the island and the ending of the Roman-style archaeological complex in the island is still close and can reasonably be taken to imply a causal coincidence. In seeking to understand and explain the coincidences, I intend to draw on the emerging concept and characterization of the 'failed state', or its more extreme version the 'collapsed state' (cf. Rotberg 2002) in the modern world (cf. the definitions offered by the Fund for Peace – www.fundforpeace.org), adapted for the ancient context.

States exist and existed to provide, consciously or unconsciously, certain fundamental frameworks and systems to make life more bearable than it would otherwise be; chief amongst these are security, both internal and external, a legal and judicial system, a political structure, civil administration. With these frameworks in place, other activities, economic, cultural, religious, can take place so long as they do not conflict with the state's well-being or ideologies. In return, the citizens of the state at least acquiesce in its continued existence—for it provides a measure of personal security and the ability to make their way in life—or even actively promote the interests of the state. Of course, the benefits of the state are not distributed equally across its citizenry, but in a functioning state these disparities and tensions can be managed so as not to imperil the state's existence or activities. In a 'failed' and on into a 'collapsed' state, a categorization arising from contemporary experience in countries such as Afghanistan, Somalia, or Zaire, the state no longer guarantees these fundamental frameworks and the consent of the governed is withdrawn, to be replaced by something far more unpredictable and bloody. The roots of failure generally lie in unsustainable internal dysfunction, with the oppression of one group by another, sometimes on a class basis or on ethnic or religious grounds. Another cause is a heightened form of this oppression: the organs of the state become perverted to serve the will of a dictator or oligarchy who regard the state essentially as a personal fiefdom to be exploited at a whim: the 'kleptocracy'. In either case the state and its actions become increasingly arbitrary.

Failure is usually brought about by internal tensions that overwhelm the ability of the institutions of the state to function: the borders of the state can no longer be guaranteed and internal security breaks down, the civil administration becomes ineffective or even oppressive, the judicial system ineffective or unacceptably corrupt. The result is the collapse of the frameworks provided by a functioning state, the end of the state monopoly on force, the de-legitimation of the state, its agents, and its ideology. Usually their replacement is a series of competing 'warlords', using force to impose their rule. In the train of the collapse of civil society comes a collapse of the other activities made possible by a functioning state; with economic dislocation and a reversion to the simplest of productive and commercial modes, usually with a collapse of the currency and a reversion to non-monetary exchange; cultural and educational collapse; collapse (often enough literally) of the infrastructure and destruction of settlements and buildings either directly through warfare or indirectly through neglect. Another regular characteristic is large-scale, unregulated movements of people into or out of the affected areas.

The general relevance of this to the late Roman state as manifested in Britain and the particular consequences for the island in the fifth century should be clear enough. The empire provided external and internal security, a political system and structures at several levels, a judicial system operating the laws that distinguished 'Roman' from 'barbarian', a civil administration based in London but extending into the localities. It also espoused religious and political ideologies aimed explicitly at legitimizing the state and the emperor as divinely ordained, thus binding the empire together and promoting its values above neighbouring peoples or powers. In pursuing these it also created important economic frameworks (cf. Wickham 2005: chs. 3, 11), including a currency, whose major impact on Britain and its archaeology we have already considered. The ideological and cultural structures inherent in the Roman system, particularly as they affected the ruling classes and their self-representation, we have also already seen to be crucial to the structures of the late Roman period in Britain and thus to their archaeology.

The chronological link between the collapse of the Roman imperial system in Britain early in the fifth century and the collapse of Roman-ness in Britain and hence of Roman-style archaeology has always been clear. The problems have lain in how to articulate cause and effect. The articulation between imperial collapse and economic collapse has been traced, but the reasons for the width and depth of the collapse as exhibited in the archaeology and encompassing all aspects of life and death including settlement and building archaeology, funerary archaeology, and the production and use of material culture, have been less easy to comprehend (e.g. Esmonde Cleary 1989: chs. 4, 5; 2000a). But the model of a 'failed/collapsed state' is clearly relevant here. It may start before the fifth-century collapse with contradictions internal to late Romano-British society. It was noted above both that the late Roman state was exploitative in order to sustain itself and that there was evidence for growing disparity between a small group of 'haves' and the majority of 'have-nots' (oppression along ethnic or religious grounds cannot be demonstrated), so the breakdown could have been violent and swift.

The *de facto* end of imperial government seems to have come with the inability of the Western Empire to re-impose military and political control after the suppression of Constantine III in 411 and the absence of any new authority powerful enough to impose its writ, as happened for instance in Ostrogothic Italy. This entailed the collapse of external and internal security as what was left of the army disintegrated (as in the oft-quoted, near-contemporary parallel of St Severinus in Noricum). Presumably the financial, civil, and judicial administrations also broke down as their ultimate underpinning of state-sanctioned force disappeared. If there was already a developing crisis of legitimacy, then the agents and also the ideology and symbols of the state could well have been rejected. Given the dependence of the insular elite on the Roman state for position and power and also for the cultural context of the expression of that position, it is not surprising to find that it is they and their archaeology who were most traumatically implicated.

In place of a centrally organized governance of the Roman part of the island there would presumably have developed a shifting pattern of competing 'warlords'. The modern experience suggests that this dissolution of civil society would also have resulted in economic collapse as the preconditions of personal and commercial security disappeared, disabling the mechanisms of access to materials, craft specialization (along with transmission of techniques), and mercantile activity on which the richness of structures, decoration, and material culture characteristic of much of late Roman Britain depended. Other features of ordered civil society such as education or cultural interaction would also have suffered gravely. Of course, this would not necessarily have come about instantaneously and undoubtedly there would have been attempts to maintain the *status quo ante*, especially in the immediate aftermath of 411 and by those accustomed to rule and who had most to lose. But gradually, and probably increasingly rapidly, it would have proved impossible to maintain the forms of the imperial system.

If the 'collapsed state' gives us a model for thinking about Britain in the first half of the fifth century, how well does this map onto the archaeology? As argued above, recent re-examination of the material culture of 'final-phase' Roman Britain now suggests that settlements, structures, burials, and artefacts of the Romano-British sequence continued in use through the first third of the fifth century. The social, economic, and cultural norms of late Roman Britain had enough vigour and momentum to maintain themselves for a while beyond the termination of direct imperial rule, perhaps for a generation or so. This would help explain the late occupation sequences at some towns, forts, and villas as well as phenomena such as the striking of copies of the latest imperial silver coinage and the possible late circulation of the copper coinage or the latest phases of pottery use. But as posited above, the re-assessment of the dating postpones rather than cancels the final disappearance of Roman-style activities and hence archaeology, for ultimately disappear it did. The breakdown did come and is marked by the ending of the great majority of sequences at classic Romano-British site types such as towns, forts, and villas, with at the major towns the disuse then or earlier of major cemeteries such as at Colchester (Butt Road), Dorchester (Poundbury), or

Winchester (Lankhills, Victoria Road), suggesting the end of the towns' role as a focus. It may also be marked by regional phenomena such as the spate of precious-metal hoard-deposition in East Anglia or silver coin-hoards in the Cotswolds and neighbouring areas (Hobbs 2006: 51–9, fig.14).

It remains the case that there is still little recognizable, non-Anglo-Saxon archaeology of the mid to later fifth century in what is now England. This has made it very difficult to identify the nature of the populations of this horizon, since they lack a distinctive archaeological 'signature', especially when compared with late Roman Britain or the early Anglo-Saxon settlers. Here an outline of what there is will be sketched, in order to try to draw some general conclusions about this archaeology and what it may mean and thus what it may tell us about frameworks for interactions between indigenous populations and incoming Germanic settlers from the middle of the century.

To start at the general scale, the environmental evidence (cf. Dark 1996) does not suggest any sudden, overall drop in the amount of open countryside in the fifth century. There is regional variation, with the zone around Hadrian's Wall showing the most marked drop in open land, possibly linked to the cessation of military demand, and there was probably also a certain amount of retrenchment and re-balancing of the agricultural regime consequent upon the disappearance of the demands of the late Roman state and elite. The important message from this is that the landscape must still have been peopled and worked, otherwise it would have reverted to woodland. It may be that there was population decline also, since another feature of a 'failed/collapsed state' scenario is demographic decline consequent upon warfare, bringing famine and death and a decline in reproduction and replacement of the population.

The long-standing problem has been how to recognize these post-Roman but non-Anglo-Saxon people since their archaeology is so slight, a problem accentuated by the hugely visible archaeology of late Roman Britain and the visibility of Anglo-Saxon sites and material, particularly cemeteries. Nevertheless, the continuing, painstaking accumulation of data is beginning to yield an archaeological 'signature' for them, visible in a variety of types of evidence. Settlement sites remain the most fugitive, and when one looks at the material remains of a site such as Poundbury (Dorset) (Sparey Green 1987; cf. Esmonde Cleary 2001: 93–6) or Crickley Hill (cf. White 2007: 170–1) one can see why. Other sites with more substantial stratigraphy, such as the Wroxeter baths-basilica (Barker *et al.* 1997) tend to be found by accident and have an artefact suite that could easily be taken to be standard late Roman in composition and date (cf. Cool 2006: 231–5). The presence of round-houses of an Iron Age/Romano-British tradition on the early Saxon settlement of Quarrington (Lincs) may be a variation on this theme, attesting to the continuing influence of indigenous practice alongside 'Anglo-Saxon' material culture (Taylor 2003). It is only towards the end of the fifth century with the appearance of (re-)defended hilltop sites, particularly in the south-west of England (cf. Alcock 1995), that something more substantial appears in the record, interestingly suggesting the importance of warfare. Warfare may also be demonstrated by the major linear earthworks such as Bokerley Dyke and Wansdyke, hard to date but which may well originate in the latter part of the fifth century. This is also the horizon with evidence for renewed contact with the Roman Mediterranean attested by imported ceramics.

Burial should in theory be an area where these people become visible, since their corpses would need to be disposed of. But it needs to remembered that archaeologically-visible burial was only ever a minority option in Roman-period Britain (Philpott 1991: ch. 31; cf. Esmonde Cleary 2000b: 127–8) and this, combined with the extreme penury of datable fifth-century artefacts, has made identifying burials of the second and final thirds of the fifth century very difficult. Nevertheless, it is clear that there was a continuing tradition of inhumation burial deriving from late Romano-British practice (cf. Rahtz 1977), as for instance at the Queenford Farm cemetery near urban Dorchester-on-Thames (Chambers 1988). A bit more common are rural sites, also starting in the later Roman period but running on into the fifth and sixth centuries, such as Cannington (Somerset), quite possibly associated with the neighbouring hillfort (Rahtz et al. 2000), and presumably representing a population of British origins. Somewhat different is the cemetery of Wasperton (Warks) (Scheschkewitz 2006), apparently originating as the burial-ground of a Romano-British rural settlement, but where burial continued through the fifth and sixth centuries with the later burials coming to be made with Anglo-Saxon objects, presumably attesting more to a change of identity and self-representation amongst an indigenous population rather than its replacement. More nebulous but still of interest is the possibility of continuing influence of late Roman burial practices in the layout of some early medieval (generally sixth- or seventh- rather than fifth-century) cemeteries, in particular the use of rectangular enclosures to bound and define certain graves or burial plots (cf. Webster and Brunning 2004), and it should be noted that all the cemeteries referred to here are inhumation cemeteries, the preferred late Romano-British rite (Philpott 1991: ch. 12). Different again, but occurring to some extent in the fifth century was the use of non-funerary Romano-British sites for burial (Bell 2005: esp. ch. 4), suggesting a continuing importance of such sites for the succeeding population. It is to be hoped that future work on such sites will not only make more use of advanced dating techniques such as AMS to gain as many and as reliable dates as possible, but will also employ techniques of stable isotope and DNA analysis to try to pin down the likely geographical origins and the descent of the people represented (see Hedges, this volume).

At present, the best, albeit very imperfect, pointer to the presence of fifth-century activity remains certain classes of artefact. The most plentiful and diagnostic is the complex of objects in the 'Quoit Brooch' style (Suzuki 2000), brooches, belt-fittings, and some other material whose decorative style developed out of that on late Roman material, particularly official-issue belt-fittings. The distribution of this material, as has long been recognized, is principally south of the Thames, essentially in the modern counties of Kent and East and West Sussex. This would seem to argue for a population to whom an identity linking them to the trappings of Roman power was important, as may have been links across the Channel to north-western Gaul where similar material is present. It is interesting to note that the only hoard of later-fifth-century coinage, the Patching hoard (S. White *et al.* 1999), comes from this area, and its closest parallels lie in Gaul. It is also of note that some Quoit Brooch material comes from the earliest 'Anglo-Saxon' cemeteries in East Sussex, Bishopstone and High Down. It may be that something similar is beginning to appear for Lincolnshire (Leahy 2007), with its remarkable concentrations of late Roman and later metalwork of types related to the Quoit Brooch material and its antecedents and their relationship to fifth-century Germanic metalwork from the county.

If Quoit Brooch metalwork is the most visible marker for fifth-century activity, there are also other classes of metalwork that can be placed in the same general time bracket, such as Fowler (1960) Type G penannular brooches or long, decorated pins. These tend to have a distribution further to the west, in the south-west and the west Midlands, an area which also shows a marked concentration of fourth-century and possibly later metalwork related to official-issue, Roman fittings (cf. R. White 2007: ch. 7). So it may be that we are beginning to recognize regional groupings to whom a vocabulary of material culture derived from Roman antecedents was important. The re-use of Roman structures for burials (Bell 2005) may be another version of this. Pottery, so central a tool for the archaeologist and so abundant in the Roman period, becomes very, very scarce. Simple fabrics (such as 'grass-tempered' wares), often handmade and in a restricted range of forms, are known from some areas and more sites with such material continue to be recognized (incidentally affording the hope that thermoluminescence or other analytical techniques may help fill the dating gap). In due course this will add to the evidence for the post-Roman artefact horizon, whilst still attesting to the massive drop in the overall level of material culture and of production and exchange in the first half of the fifth century.

So an archaeological 'signature', or rather 'signatures', for the British population of the mid to later fifth century are beginning to emerge. It should be remembered that the numbers of sites and quantities of material concerned are minuscule compared with the archaeology of the mid to later fourth century; by concentrating too much on what there is (a natural response) we can too easily forget how much there is not. The concept of 'collapsed state' may again be of use here. As noted above, one of the features of state collapse is a concomitant collapse in manufacture and commerce as conditions become so fluid and dangerous that staying alive becomes much more important than craft specialization and the personal safety and social networks for commerce can no longer be guaranteed. Another frequent feature of this scenario is large-scale population movement, and of course a mobile population is one far less likely to invest in activities which leave a durable and visible archaeological record.

What we are probably seeing is the characteristic pattern of the 'collapsed state' where warlordism predominates, with ever-shifting areas of influence depending on the rise, success, and failure of a succession of 'big men'. For fifth-century Britain it is increasingly clear that one vocabulary of power remained, namely that deriving from or appealing to the memory of the Roman empire and its outward displays of power. We have seen this for the area south of the Thames and for the Cotswold/Marches area. Another area may have been across the Thames from the Quoit Brooch province, in the Chilterns/Essex area (Baker 2006), where there is evidence for a patchwork of groupings, some deriving from late Roman origins, others from across the North Sea. Other groups may have rejected the vocabulary of Roman power and appealed to other ideal communities, but they are next-to-invisible to us. It is very possible that Christianity played some part, perhaps as part of the Roman-derived nexus (as maybe at Saint Paul-in-the-Bail, Lincoln), perhaps developing its own identity; it is just that for much of the fifth century there is not as yet a 'signature' for the archaeology of Christianity in what was to become England since we lack demonstrable church sites and the concept of 'Christian burial' is now recognized to be an anachronism before the seventh century.

The relevance of the 'failed/collapsed state' model for the circumstances of the settlement of the Anglo-Saxons is evident. At one level they could be seen as part of the phenomenon of uncontrolled population movement, internally or from outside, that is a regular feature of such situations. But they could also be seen as another group exploiting the collapse of civil society to make their own way, another group of warlords and their followers, but one whose cultural identity was strong, expressed through mediums such as language, but also through dress, material culture, structures, and burial rites with their very visible impact on the creation of the archaeological record. In the longer term they were able to establish dominance over the competing war-bands of the core areas of the old Britannia, probably absorbing many of them as these replaced their 'British' identity with an 'Anglo-Saxon' one.

References

Alcock, L. (1995). *Cadbury Castle: the Early Medieval Archaeology*. Cardiff: University of Wales Press.

Baker, J. (2006). *Cultural Transition in the Chilterns and Essex Region 350 AD to 650 AD*. Studies in Regional and Local History Volume 4. Hertford: Hertfordshire University Press.

BARKER, P., WHITE, R., PRETTY, K., BIRD, H., and CORBISHLEY, M. (1997). *The Baths Basilica Wroxeter: Excavations 1966–90*. English Heritage Archaeological Report 8. London: English Heritage.

BELL, T. (2005). *The Religious Reuse of Roman Structures in Early Medieval England*. British Archaeological Reports British Series 390. Oxford: Archaeopress.

BÖHME, H.-W. (1986). 'Das Ende der Römerherrschaft in Britannien und die Angelsächsische Besiedlung Englands im 5. Jahrhundert'. *Jahrbuch des Römisch-Germanischen Zentralmuseums Mainz* 33: 468–574.

BIDWELL, P. (1979). *The Legionary Bath-House and Basilica and Forum at Exeter*. Exeter Archaeological Reports Volume 1. Exeter: University of Exeter Press.

—— and SPEAK, S. (1994). *Excavations at South Shields Roman Fort*, Volume 1. Newcastle-upon-Tyne: The Society of Antiquaries of Newcastle-upon-Tyne with Tyne and Wear Museums.

CHAMBERS, R. (1988). 'The late- and sub-Roman cemetery at Queenford Farm, Dorchester-on-Thames, Oxon'. *Oxoniensia* 52: 35–69.

COOL, H. (2000). 'The parts left over: material culture into the fifth century', in Wilmott and Wilson (eds.), *The Late Roman Transition in the North*, 47–65.

—— (2006). *Eating and Drinking in Roman Britain*. Cambridge: Cambridge University Press.

CUNLIFFE, B. (1975). *Excavations at Portchester Castle*, Volume 1: *Roman*. Reports of the Research Committee No. 33. London: Society of Antiquaries of London.

DARK, S. P. (1996). 'Palaeoecological evidence for landscape continuity and change in Britain *ca* A.D. 400–800', in K. R. Dark (ed.), *External Contacts and the Economy of Late Roman and Post-Roman Britain*. Woodbridge: Boydell, 23–51.

ESMONDE CLEARY, S. (1989). *The Ending of Roman Britain*. London: Batsford.

—— (2000a). 'Summing up', in Wilmott and Wilson (eds.), *The Late Roman Transition in the North*, 89–94.

—— (2000b). 'Putting the dead in their place: burial location in Roman Britain', in J. Pearce, M. Millett, and M. Struck (eds.), *Burial, Society and Context in the Roman World*. Oxford: Oxbow Books, 127–42.

—— (2001). 'The Roman to medieval transition', in S. James and M. Millett (eds.), *Britons and Romans: Advancing an Archaeological Agenda*. CBA Research Report 125. London: Council for British Archaeology, 90–7.

FAULKNER, N. (2000a). 'Change and decline in late Romano-British towns', in T. R. Slater (ed.), *Towns in Decline AD 100–1600*. Aldershot: Ashgate, 1–50.

—— (2000b). *The Decline and Fall of Roman Britain*. Stroud: Tempus.

FOWLER, E. (1960). 'The origins and development of the penannular brooch in Europe'. *Proceedings of the Prehistoric Society* 26: 149–77.

FULFORD, M., CLARKE, A., and ECKARDT, H. (2006). *Life and Labour in Late Roman Silchester: Excavations in Insula IX since 1997*. Britannia Monograph Series No. 22. London: Society for the Promotion of Roman Studies.

GAFFNEY, V., and WHITE, R. (2007). *Wroxeter, the Cornovii and the Urban Process: Final Report on the Wroxeter Hinterland Project 1994–1997*, Volume 1: *Researching the Hinterland*. JRA Supplement 68. Portsmouth, RI: Journal of Roman Archaeology.

GERRARD, J. (2007). 'The temple of Sulis Minerva at Bath and the end of Roman Britain'. *The Antiquaries Journal* 87: 148–64.

GREGSON, M. (1988). 'The Villa as Private Property', in K. Branigan and D. Miles (eds.), *The Economies of Romano-British Villas*. Sheffield: Department of Prehistory and Archaeology, University of Sheffield, 21–33.

GUEST, P. (2005). *The Late Roman Gold and Silver Coins from the Hoxne Treasure*. London: British Museum Press.

HINGLEY, R. (1989). *Rural Settlement in Roman Britain*. London: Seaby.

HOBBS, R. (2006). *Late Roman Precious Metal Deposits c. AD 200–700: Change over Time and Space*. British Archaeological Reports International Series 1504. Oxford: Archaeopress.

LEADER-NEWBY, R. (2004). *Silver and Society in Late Antiquity: Functions and Meanings of Silver Plate in the Fourth to Seventh Centuries*. Aldershot: Ashgate.

LEAHY, K. (2007). 'Soldiers and settlers in Britain, fourth to fifth century – revisited', in M. Henig and T. J. Smith (eds.), *Collectanea Antiqua: Essays in Memory of Sonia Chadwick Hawkes*. British Archaeological Reports International Series 1673. Oxford: Archaeopress, 133–43.

NEAL, D. (2003). 'Building 2, *Insula* XXVII from *Verulamium*: A Reinterpretation of the Evidence', in P. Wilson (ed.), *The Archaeology of Roman Towns: Studies in Honour of John S. Wacher*. Oxford: Oxbow Books, 195–202.

PEARSON, A. (2002). *The Roman Shore Forts: Coastal Defences of Southern Britain*. Stroud: Tempus.

PETTS, D. (2003). *Christianity in Roman Britain*. Stroud: Tempus.

PHILLIPS, D. and HEYWOOD, B. (1995), *Excavations at York Minster*, Volume 1: *From Roman Fortress to Norman Cathedral*. Ed. M. Carver. Royal Commission on the Historical Monuments of England. London: Her Majesty's Stationery Office.

PHILPOTT, R. (1991). *Burial Practices in Roman Britain: A Survey of Grave Treatment and Furnishing A.D. 43–410*. British Archaeological Reports British Series 219. Oxford: Archaeopress.

PRICE, E. (2000). *Frocester: A Romano-British Settlement, its Antecedents and Successors*. Kings Stanley: Gloucester and District Archaeological Research Group.

RAHTZ, P. (1977). 'Late Roman cemeteries and beyond', in R. Reece (ed.), *Burial in the Roman World*. CBA Research Report 22. London: Council for British Archeology, 53–64.

—— HIRST, S., and WRIGHT, S. (2000). *Cannington Cemetery*. Britannia Monograph Series No. 17. London: Society for the Promotion of Roman Studies.

REECE, R. (2002). *The Coinage of Roman Britain*. Stroud: Tempus.

ROTBERG, R. (2002). 'The new nature of nation-state failure'. *The Washington Quarterly* 25(3): 85–96.

SCHESCHKEWITZ, J. (2006). *Das spätrömische und angelsächsische Gräberfeld von Wasperton, Warwickshire*. Bonn: Rudolf Habelt.

SCOTT, S. (2000). *Art and Society in Fourth-Century Britain: Villa Mosaics in Context*. Oxford: Oxford University School of Archaeology Monograph No. 53.

SPAREY GREEN, C. (1987). *Excavations at Poundbury*, Volume 1: *The Settlements*. Dorset Natural History and Archaeological Society Monograph No. 7. Dorchester.

SUZUKI, S. (2000). *The Quoit Brooch Style and the Anglo-Saxon Settlement*. Woodbridge: Boydell and Brewer.

SWIFT, E. (2000). *Regionality in Dress Accessories in the Late Roman West*. Monographies Instrumentum 11. Montagnac: Éditions Monique Mergoil.

TAYLOR, G. (2003). 'An Early to Middle Saxon Settlement at Quarrington, Lincolnshire'. *Antiquaries Journal* 83: 231–80.
TYERS, P. (1996). *Roman Pottery in Britain*. London: Batsford.
WEBSTER, C. and BRUNNING, R. (2004). 'A seventh-century AD cemetery at Stoneage Barton Farm, Bishop's Lydeard, Somerset and square-ditched burials in post-Roman Britain'. *Archaeological Journal* 161: 54–81.
WHITE, R. (2007). *Britannia Prima: Britain's Last Roman Province*. Stroud: Tempus.
WHITE, S., MANLEY, J., JONES, R., ORNA-ORNSTEIN, J., JOHNS, C., and WEBSTER, L. (1999). 'A mid-fifth-century hoard of Roman and pseudo-Roman material from Patching, West Sussex'. *Britannia* 30: 301–25.
WHITTAKER, C. R. (1994). *Frontiers of the Roman Empire: A Social and Economic Study*. Baltimore and London: Johns Hopkins University Press.
WICKHAM, C. (2005). *Framing the Early Middle Ages: Europe and the Mediterranean, 400–800*. Oxford: Oxford University Press.
WILMOTT, T. and WILSON, P. (eds.) (2000). *The Late Roman Transition in the North*. British Archaeological Reports British Series 299. Oxford: Archaeopress.

CHAPTER 3

MIGRATION AND ENDOGENOUS CHANGE

BIRTE BRUGMANN

How many migrants are needed to explain the fifth-century cultural changes generally understood as marking the transition from late Roman Britain to early Anglo-Saxon England? Answers have varied from almost none to a total replacement of the population. The subject of migration and endogenous change in fifth-century Britain from an archaeological perspective has been debated for over two centuries, and the debate reviewed by a number of scholars (e.g. Scull 1995; Hamerow 1997; 1998; Lucy 2000: 155–73; Härke 2003; Hills 2003; Prien 2005: 53–88). Most archaeologists have used a framework of historic, linguistic, and/or biological evidence for their interpretations of the archaeological evidence; it would in fact be impossible to understand the archaeological debate out of its historical context, while it is less dependent on the linguistic evidence, which has mainly been used to strengthen or refute archaeological arguments. Biological data, first on skulls (see Cummings 2007), then mainly on stature (see Härke 1998), and most recently on DNA (Thomas *et al.* 2006; see Hedges, this volume), have also played a role. It is important, however, to remember that other disciplines are no different from archaeology in that interpretations are not cast in stone and are often used uncritically outside the discipline which generated them. Interpretations that draw on more than one discipline can create pseudo-facts which are difficult to identify as such and even harder to dismantle, such as circular arguments embedded in dates applied to fifth-century artefacts. I will focus on interpretations of material culture changes from 'late Roman Britain' to 'Anglo-Saxon England' and outline how approaches to the archaeological material have changed over time. I will then offer a few suggestions for further research.

'THE CORNER-STONE OF OLD ENGLISH ETHNOLOGY'

For some 150 years, archaeological finds had the air of 'hard evidence' about them, the source of 'scientific data furnished by archaeology' (Baldwin Brown 1915: 26): cremation pots and grave goods gave a touch of reality to early medieval accounts of an invasion that shaped 'Anglo-Saxon' England, first and foremost Gildas' *De Excidio Britonum* and Bede's *Historia Ecclesiastica*. While Gildas is mostly valued for his (sixth-century) dramatic tale of the decline of Roman Britain and of the role that raiders and invaders played in it, Bede is famous for the spin that the story receives in his eighth-century account, 'the corner-stone of old English ethnology' (Baldwin Brown 1915: 566), which bears the hallmarks of an origin myth:

In the year of our Lord 449... the race of the Angles or Saxons, invited by Vortigern, came to Britain in three warships and by his command were granted a place of settlement in the eastern part of the island, ostensibly to fight on behalf of the country, but their real intention was to conquer it. First they fought against the enemy who attacked from the north and the Saxons won the victory. A report of this as well as of the fertility of the island and the slackness of the Britons reached their homes and at once a much larger fleet was sent over with a stronger band of warriors; this, added to the contingent they already were, made an invincible army. The newcomers received from the Britons a grant of land in their midst on condition that they fought against their foes for the peace and safety of the country, and for this soldiers were also to receive pay.

They came from three very powerful Germanic tribes, the Saxons, the Angles and the Jutes. The people of Kent and the inhabitants of the Isle of Wight are of Jutish origin and also those opposite the Isle of Wight... From the Saxon country, that is, the district known as Old Saxony, came the ... Saxons.... From the country of the Angles, that is the land between the territories of the Jutes and the Saxons, which is called *Angulus*, came the... Anglian tribes. *Angulus* is said to have remained deserted from that day to this.

It was not long before hordes of these people eagerly crowded into the island and the number of foreigners began to increase to such an extent that they became a source of terror ... the fire kindled by the hands of the heathen executed the just vengeance of God on the nation for its crimes ... there was no-one left to bury those who had died a cruel death. Some of the miserable remnant were captured in the mountains and butchered indiscriminately; others, exhausted by hunger, came forward and submitted themselves to the enemy, ready to accept perpetual slavery for the sake of food, provided only they escaped being killed on the spot: some fled sorrowfully to the lands beyond the sea, while others remained in their own land and led a wretched existence, always in fear and dread, among the mountains and woods and precipitous rocks.

(*HE* I.15: Colgrave and Mynors 1969)

Bede's account tells of a migration in three phases which largely correspond to the phases Roland Prien (2005) has defined for early medieval migrations, drawing on sociological migration theories: an 'exploration' phase, in which migrant mercenaries employed to protect the resident population assess the environmental and political conditions for further migration; a second 'migration' phase dated to AD 449, in which larger contingents of warriors follow and take control of the land; and an 'establishment' phase implied in Bede's statement about the origins of the tribes inhabiting England in the eighth century. According to Bede's narrative, which draws on Gildas', this establishment phase included prolonged fighting against an organized British resistance. The mention of a deserted *Angulus* (presumably roughly corresponding to Angeln in North Germany) suggests that at least in regard to this region there was no fourth phase in which contacts between the original and the new homeland were intensified.

The first phase, as described by Bede, represents a 'specialist migration' (migrants filling a certain role in the resident society); the success of the military campaigns that followed suggests that the specialist migration transformed into an 'elite migration' (the newcomers controlling or replacing the resident elite). That this was followed by a 'mass migration' (i.e. at least half of the population living at the destination after the event are newcomers) or at least by the migration of a cross-section of a population is, again, implied by Bede's mention of *Angulus desertus* and his statement about the ethnicity of the eighth-century population of Anglo-Saxon England. Bede's description of the forced migration of parts of the British population and the fight against the Saxon newcomers based on Gildas gives the impression of a mass migration, although neither Gildas nor Bede specify how many Britons stayed and fought, how many fled, and how many died in the process. The chronology of fifth-century events is by no means as clear as it appears in the written sources, nor are the details of the story irrefutable (see Campbell, this volume).

The existence of a Germanic military presence in Britain prior to a mass migration that may or may not have taken place has never been doubted, and since the 1960s much work has been devoted to identifying these migrants and their continental background in the form of late Roman military belt sets associated with mercenaries, and Germanic brooches ascribed to their womenfolk (see Welch 1993). Drawing a clear line in the burial record between the controlled migration of mercenaries and their families (*foederati*) and the influx of uninvited migrants or an acculturation process has, however, proven impossible, as too much depends on the dating of the archaeological material and historical events (see Prien 2005: 69–71) as well as the theoretical framework used for the interpretation of the archaeological evidence.

If the distribution of fourth- to sixth-century types of grave goods and burial practices on the continent and in England are anything to go by, Bede's tidy tribal geography oversimplifies a much more complex situation that involved not only contacts between the areas described by Bede—apparently Denmark and northern Germany—but also connections to Frisia and Frankia, and beyond. These patterns can be read as the sum of small-scale migrations (see e.g. Gebühr 1997 and Bode 1998 on cruciform brooches). Those who have tried to find clearer indications for migration or endogenous change in the settlement evidence have found signs of both continuity and innovation in house-building traditions (see Hamerow 1999; 2002: 48–51) and palaeobotanical studies indicate that by and large the fifth-century landscape remained open. Social and economic reasons for continuity and changes in land use are again a matter of interpretation rather than direct proof of migration or endogenous change (see Härke 2003: 16–17).

The enormous increase of archaeological finds, especially over the past thirty years, has confirmed patterns in the record that are now unlikely to change, such as the overall distribution of Anglo-Saxon cemeteries, but has also demonstrated that generalizations based on a single cemetery or settlement site can be misleading and that landscape studies and metal-detector finds do not always correspond with what excavations suggest about a particular region. The motor of the migration-versus-acculturation debate, however, has been a clash between traditional culture-historians advocating a mass migration, and processualists arguing for an elite migration triggering endogenous change (for an overview of this debate see e.g. Scull 1995: 71–2; Härke 2003: 15–16). In this debate, largely the same archaeological material has been used to argue quite different cases. The following outline concentrates on a few authors whose work is quoted to convey the zeitgeist.

'But how do you know they are Anglo-Saxon?'

The idea of an early medieval mass migration that led to the 'Origins of the English' has been deeply entrenched in English culture since the seventeenth century (see MacDougall 1982), but it took until the mid nineteenth century for Anglo-Saxon archaeology to become popular. While enthusiasts like James Douglas and Bryan Faussett, who systematically excavated about 750 mostly sixth- and seventh-century barrows in east Kent in the second half of the eighteenth century (Faussett 1856), were few and reliant on private collections, 'Anglo-Saxon' cemetery archaeology became 'all the rage', as Sonia Hawkes (1990: 20) put it, in Victorian England.

Two of the most influential books on early Anglo-Saxon archaeology were published in the early twentieth century: E. Thurlow Leeds' *Archaeology of the Anglo-Saxon Settlements* (1913) and G. Baldwin Brown's *The Arts in Early England* (1915). The two authors differed in their approaches but largely came to the same conclusions. Baldwin Brown (1915: 4) declared in his introduction to the volume that 'A good part of what follows has for one of its main objects the establishment of our national autonomy in the art in the early medieval period', while Leeds' aim was to 'put forward the problems of early Anglo-Saxon archaeology in a connected form' (Leeds 1913: 3).

At the time, not a single settlement had been excavated and Anglo-Saxon archaeology relied entirely on graves, producing a regionally varied but on the whole remarkably uniform material culture in the form of grave-goods. Leeds (1913: 24) had no doubt about the identity of those buried with these objects and outlined the reasoning behind this in his chapter on archaeological methods: 'In the last chapter it was assumed that the graves in question were those of Anglo-Saxons, and of the earliest period. It might seem superfluous to refer to such an assumption at all, but, as the writer once had the question put to him, "But how do you know they are Anglo-Saxon?", it is perhaps only right that all doubt on that score should be removed.' John Kemble had been the first to demonstrate close links between Anglo-Saxon material culture and finds made in northern Germany (see Williams 2006: 7–8). The main arguments Leeds (1913: 24–5) put forward were the distribution of the 'Anglo-Saxon' graves in question within the regions outlined as Anglo-Saxon in written sources, the dating of some of these graves through Roman coins with *termini post quos* in the late fourth/early fifth century, and the 'examination of the skull-types' believed to prove northern German origin.

Leeds (1913: 25–6) recommended 'methodical comparison and correlation' and 'the purely typological method' for dating 'an initial occupation by one tribe and its eventual dispossession by members of another, owing to the variation in the types of objects used for similar purposes among the different racial elements of which the immigrating Teutons were composed'. It has been pointed out more than once that the idea of material culture reflecting ethnic identity was not Leeds' idea but an approach that was considered to make perfect sense at the time. Baldwin Brown in fact played the role of an *advocatus diaboli* not only on the matter of British survival after the *adventus saxonum* but on the migration as a wholesale event:

> If the result of the conquest were expatriation rather than massacre then the British women would doubtless accompany their menkind into exile. Supposing on the other hand there had ensued a peaceable settling down side by side of the two races... intermarriages between the two races might be expected to follow, and such unions would have some material traces in the cemeteries.... the modern craniologist might now conceivably sort them apart, while the antiquary was finding a racial difference in their grave-goods.
>
> (Baldwin Brown 1915: 50–1)

Baldwin Brown's dismissal of the intermarriage theory combines the concept of material culture as an ethnic marker with the idea of cultural superiority:

> It must be borne in mind that the Romano-British population was in matters of art more advanced than the Teutonic immigrants, and if British ladies had exercised rule in the new homesteads they would certainly have introduced their own style in trinkets and ornaments. Anglo-Saxon art would in this manner have taken on a decided Roman or Late-Celtic tinge, and had any appreciable number of the women sprung from the British race their personal belongings would certainly have been of a less pronounced Germanic type than those of the men. As a matter of fact this difference is not apparent.
>
> (Baldwin Brown 1915: 51)

A 'typology of migration' based on the concept of superior and inferior cultures was first published in 1913 and in a revised form in 1925. The sociologist Henry P. Fairchild (1925) had developed an ethnocentric typology that defined an 'invasion' as a migration that constituted an attack of a 'lower' on a 'higher' culture and a 'conquest' as the reversed situation. He called the peaceful migration of a 'higher' culture a 'colonization', and 'immigration' a situation in which two cultures are on the same level. In these terms, however, the *adventus* constituted a somewhat muddled case. Although Anglo-Saxons were 'barbarians' at a time when Romans were considered superior, those considered one's own ancestors could be romanticized along the lines of Rousseau's 'noble savage'. Romano-Britons had a somewhat difficult stand as not-quite-Romans, and Baldwin Brown described them as 'in matters of art more advanced' rather than as outright superior. Despite the bloodshed described by Gildas and Bede, Baldwin Brown seems to have been quite happy to consider the possibility of a peaceful Anglo-Saxon immigration, which raised the interesting question of marital acculturation, but could not quite imagine Romano-British material culture sinking without a trace if there had been any Britons to hold it up.

Not only Baldwin Brown, who set out to do so, but also Leeds (1913: 95) came to the conclusion that early Anglo-Saxon material culture, though thoroughly 'Teutonic', had its own distinctive features, to an extent that it backfired on Anglo-Saxon England as a textbook case of a migration traceable in the archaeological record:

> The whole culture of the Continental homelands is clearly of earlier date, and not only is this so, but so scarce are the actual links connecting it with that of England, that it is difficult to bring the two into immediate connexion with one another... There seems to be lacking an interval of some kind, probably quite brief, during which the culture of the invaders reached the stage of development which characterizes its first appearance in England... If... the migrations started direct from North Germany and Holland, then the process of evolution at work in the culture of the invaders must have been unusually rapid, and finally a large number of the settlements must have come into being considerably earlier than any historical documents will warrant.

What Leeds and Baldwin Brown had expected to find were graves of migrants who left their homelands as Angles, Saxons, and Jutes and were buried as such in

England. This first-generation-overlap, however, turned out to be less substantial in the archaeological record than expected.

The image of the barbarians who were believed to have come from northern Germany and founded the English nation suffered over the First World War (see e.g. MacDougall 1982: 129; Brugmann 2005). It seems however that Leeds' attitude towards the 'children of nature' who had followed 'the prompting of their own sweet will' (Leeds 1913: 23) was first and foremost sobered by settlement finds made since 1922. Leeds (1936: 21) seemed quite aghast about the features he had excavated at Sutton Courtenay, Oxfordshire, and interpreted as 'hovels', and though he conceded that 'it may seem unfair to generalize from such meagre material' as it was at the time, he had little hope that more than simple farmsteads would ever be found. As it turned out, excavations not only at other sites but also at Sutton Courtenay (Hamerow et al. 2007) have demonstrated that housing in the Anglo-Saxon period was more respectable than he realized. His disappointment, however, may have prompted him to turn back to grave goods, and to look for the 'survival of a native substratum in Anglo-Saxon culture' (Leeds 1936: 3).

While the archaeological 'material has changed but little, and indeed, is not likely to change', Leeds (1936: xii) believed 'that certain aspects of Anglo-Saxon archaeology have been insufficiently explored' and his aim was 'a truer estimate... of the relationships between the English material and its continental analogues' by 'constructing a relative chronology for the remains of pagan Saxondom, as the first step towards establishing their absolute chronology'. He considered 'commercial relations' as an alternative to objects indicating the movement of people, and defined chronological phases for Kentish grave-goods. This allowed Leeds to reject T. D. Kendrick's theory that some sixth- and seventh-century Kentish disc and composite brooches, 'certain recognized masterpieces found in Kentish graves of the early Anglo-Saxon period were the work of purely British craftsmen... and that the Jutes could lay claim only to certain classes of jewels of a humbler and less intricate kind'. Kendrick's attempt to date these brooches to the fifth century clashed with Leeds' idea of a typological sequence of the 'material [Kendrick] so curiously rearranged from its natural order to arrive at his theory of an epoch of Arthurian brilliance' (Leeds 1936: 41).

That more recent research (see Brugmann 1999) has backed up Leeds rather than Kendrick is almost beside the point in the present context; what makes Kendrick's approach particularly interesting is his attempt to carve space for Britons in an 'Anglo-Saxon' environment. Kendrick (1933: 451–2) not only reassigned material culture that had previously been firmly put into Anglo-Saxon hands to British craftsmen and interpreted it as 'the influence of the British cloisonné on Jutish craftsmanship' but also saw signs of Britons buried in 'Anglo-Saxon' cemeteries of 'federal Teutons (probably Angles, Saxons and Frisians)... mercenaries from the continent' who 'founded settlements that perhaps included a substantial British population'. If Kendrick's interpretation of the archaeological evidence was based on theories about educational acculturation derived from sociological or anthropological research, he did not indicate this, and it seems quite possible that it was intuitive and reflecting general ideas of the time such as the notion of 'superior' British culture adopted by 'inferior' cultures in British colonies.

Leeds (1945: 2), however, criticized Kendrick's interpretation of the archaeological evidence in this particular case, not the search for signs of a mixed population as such. He argued 'That the regional character of ornament among less advanced peoples is a commonplace of archaeology and ethnology' and that the distribution of brooch types and pottery over time could therefore be used to trace patterns of migration and consolidation. He conceded however that:

Hardly anyone credits nowadays the possibility of total extermination: in the worst and most devastating invasions this accusation has never been wholly true. In early England, even though it might apply in a large measure to the male portion of the older population, it is certain that many women must have been spared to become the slaves, concubines, or wives of the invaders. Here again the story of extermination differs in veracity according to the region to which it is applied; for it can be clearly demonstrated that in some districts an element, possibly quite considerable, of the earlier woman-folk must have survived.

(Leeds 1945: 4)

'THERE IS NO PROOF WHATSOEVER'

It seems appropriate that a spirited article which broke with the research tradition of interpreting material culture in ethnic terms was published in Leeds' posthumous *Festschrift* (Harden 1956). In T. C. Lethbridge's approach the production of objects and trade took centre stage:

Because a large number of ornaments are found in a series of graves and it can be shown that the origin of the style of ornaments lies in some continental district or other, is it any proof that the people in those graves were descended from those in the land in which that style of ornament was formerly common? Of course it is not. There is no proof whatsoever that the people in the graves did not obtain their ornaments from some source quite outside the district in which they lived.... It will be seen that this problem lies at the back of any attempt to use archaeological study to interpret the character of the Anglo-Saxon conquest of Britain.... No one could prove that the wearers of these ornaments were Saxons, or Angles, or Romano-Britons or a mixture of them all.... Brooches could be carried by pedlars for many miles without difficulty; other things in the graves were certainly carried thousands of miles.

(Lethbridge 1956: 113–14)

Lethbridge's arguments for endogenous change previously interpreted as a change in population are more complex than can be given justice here. It is, however, worth pointing out that finally British women could lie next to British men in Anglo-Saxon graves and that Lethbridge (1956: 119) outlined a concept which later became better known as an element of the 'elite-dominance model' (see Renfrew 1987: 131–3):

It is even possible to question whether they [Leeds' tribes] and the little kingdoms with which they are more or less associated, present tribal districts formed by Anglo-Saxons.... Anglo-Saxons no doubt provided the rulers, the moving spirits and the large farmers, replacing their bankrupt or murdered predecessors; but the tribal boundaries remained more or less as they had been for five hundred years.

(Lethbridge 1956: 119)

The focus in the present context is on Lethbridge's re-interpretation of tribal areas as sellers' markets rather than cultural identity:

We have evidence here of a trade in cheap, mass-produced jewellery.... we have no picture here of the itinerant jeweller wandering from place to place, but every indication of established firms catering for somewhat barbaric taste on a large scale.... It may merely be a question of salesmanship. Here and there in many areas something of a type, which could be disposed of in numbers in another district, would only harden into custom after many years. Taste in itself could have been at first the work of a single dealer, who took to a particular area the goods that he believed the people ought to like, and repeated his success year after year.

(Lethbridge 1956: 121)

Lethbridge did not offer an explanation for the 'somewhat barbaric taste' of the customers and the acculturation process it implies. His idea, however, raises the question whether it would be possible to explain the material culture change from late Roman Britain to Anglo-Saxon England in terms of an elite migration combined with a specialist migration of metalsmiths. Lethbridge's functionalist approach in any case broke with culture-historical traditions and put economic factors to the foreground.

While Lethbridge's ideas were largely ignored, C. J. Arnold (1984: 124) is well known for his interpretation of the archaeological evidence as an elite migration, arguing that only a small minority of the population was buried in Anglo-Saxon cemeteries: 'If the Anglo-Saxon cemetery evidence is taken literally, there can have been few people in fifth-century England and it is tempting to extend this to account for the very small number of known settlements.' The argument seems somewhat inconsistent, however, considering that Arnold (1984: 123, 133) was willing to take the *c.* 25,000 known Anglo-Saxon burials he had counted at face value, while finding reasons for the Roman-period population estimated at 3 to 4 million at its peak being represented by only 19,000 graves. Again, British women appeared in Anglo-Saxon cemeteries, in Arnold's case on the basis of anthropological data on age and human stature from small samples. He argued for 'the influx of larger proportioned Germanic males, whose presence eventually affects the whole population' and suggested 'that the numbers of migrants were very small, predominantly male, and quickly settled in isolated farmsteads' (Arnold 1984: 139, but see Härke 1998: 110–12 and Thomas *et al.* 2006).

Arnold's attempt at explaining the changes from late Roman Britain to early Anglo-Saxon England in terms of an elite migration is generally considered to mark the beginning of a relatively late reception of processual archaeology, with its dismissal of migration as an explanation for cultural change, in Anglo-Saxon archaeology (see Scull 1995). Nicholas Higham's arguments for an elite migration published eight years later show additional influence of contextual archaeology, interpreting material culture not as a reflection of, for example, ethnic identity, but as an active element of social expression. Higham (1992: 15) explored 'the possibility that Germanic immigrants comprised only a small proportion of the population of Anglo-Saxon England' and concluded that 'The lack of British influence on Anglo-Saxon material culture need occasion no surprise.... the incoming range of goods was adopted by communities ranged in social hierarchies within which Britons of low rank were keen to make upward progress. In so doing, they found it necessary to look and sound like Anglo-Saxons' (Higham 1992: 233). Higham's interpretation of the evidence has been disputed by scholars who argue that the elite-dominance model fails to explain convincingly the 'radical change in material culture and cultural practice' (Scull 1995: 79).

If Gildas and Bede had indicated an acculturation process taking place in the wake of an elite migration—a lament by Gildas about Britons lining up their fairest maidens for the invaders in the hope of negotiating peace, for example, and a tweak to Bede's story to the effect that Angles, Saxons, and Jutes carved up Britain to rule as their own barbarian-style 'provinces' which soon rose above their homelands and became powerful kingdoms—could Baldwin Brown and Leeds have found convincing ways of interpreting the archaeological evidence accordingly? Both authors might have argued that if Roman Britain required few dyed-in-the-wool resident Romans to use and produce the material culture of a Roman province, there was no need for an Anglo-Saxon takeover to be much different. Instead of having to wrestle with a weak first-generation-overlap and intermarriage as a form of acculturation, Leeds could have concentrated on the rise of the Anglo-Saxon kingdoms and on ways of explaining why the original homelands should have gone downhill so soon after. Britons being the better Angles, Saxon, and Jutes would have made a respectable origin myth that would have withstood the twentieth century easily. The typological method would probably have remained the same, but it seems likely that archaeologists would have tried harder to draw out the overlap between continental and insular Anglo-Saxon material culture in their absolute chronological frameworks.

In this parallel universe, culture historians might have tried to demonstrate that not only Saxon mercenaries had returned home and been buried with their military belt sets in Lower Saxony (see Böhme 1986: 495) but also British soldiers who, against popular belief, had made it home from the unfortunate campaigns of the early fifth century described by Bede (*HE* I.12–13), some bringing back Germanic wives. Processual archaeologists may have felt compelled to test whether it could be argued that mass migration played an important role in the formation of Anglo-Saxon England after all, and developed mass-migration hypotheses instead of being content not to have to move too many people (see Chapman and Hamerow 1997: 3–9), possibly along the lines of Everett S. Lee's migration theory (Lee 1966: 52), e.g.: 'if the push factors in one region correlate with the pull factors in another region, migration takes place'. Post-processual archaeology could be busy testing sociological acculturation models and theories about the brain-drain effect of an elite migration on the original homelands. And last but not least, feminist archaeologists might have ended the plight of all those British women enslaved, raped, or married and dressed by Anglo-Saxons by arguing that women in Anglo-Saxon graves tend to be better equipped with grave-goods than men (see e.g. Arnold 1988: 154) because the female heirs of Boudica regained social power after the Romans had left, and before they lost it again to Christianization.

Where does this leave research on migration and endogenous change in 'late Roman' and 'early Anglo-Saxon' England in our universe? It would seem wise to heed Simon Esmonde Cleary's advice to study the fifth century as a time of change within a period rather than as a seam between two periods (Esmonde Cleary 2001), and to make a start with going back to basics for the material culture of the fourth and fifth centuries, which is crucial to any archaeological evaluation of culture change during this time. While our understanding of the fourth to sixth centuries in Britain has moved beyond Gildas' and Bede's narrative, much of the archaeological research on the period is still based on a chronological framework which has hidden roots in the notion that Romano-British material culture cannot date much past AD 410, that Anglo-Saxon finds as such cannot pre-date AD 450, and that types which seem to be an insular development rather than an import cannot pre-date the late fifth century, a framework that is bound to create an image of a drastic material culture change, leaving little time for Anglo-Saxon material culture to evolve and no room for an overlap with Romano-British material culture other than in the shape of 'heirlooms' or 'curated objects'. Recent chronological studies based on continental chronological frameworks suggest unconventionally early dates for some Anglo-Saxon grave-goods (e.g. Penn and Brugmann 2007), and it seems that correspondence analysis is also a promising tool for analysing Anglo-Saxon cremation pottery (see Høilund Nielsen in Ravn 2003: 101). It seems quite possible that an overhaul of conventional dates for fifth- and sixth-century Anglo-Saxon material that ignores historical dates as *termini ante/post quos* can substantiate the overlap between late Roman and early Anglo-Saxon material culture outlined by Böhme (1986) although it becomes increasingly clear that not only late Roman burial practice made relatively little use of grave-goods but also Anglo-Saxon practice in its early stages (see e.g. Stoodley 1999; Penn and Brugmann 2007).

Another aspect worth pursuing seems to be a conceptualization of archaeological migration hypotheses in terms of migration and acculturation classifications developed by sociologists, anthropologists, and others (see Chapman and Hamerow 1997), such as attempted by Prien (2005). Questions that arise from mass-migration hypotheses are the push- and pull-factors involved (see e.g. Gebühr 1998; Zimmermann 1999), the logistics of the migration itself, its timescale and sustainability at both ends, and settlement patterns created in the process (see e.g. Moore 2001). Elite-migration hypotheses rise and fall with explanations offered for acculturation processes, most of all the plausibility of a 'barbarian' elite successfully governing a collapsed complex society rapidly transforming to emulate its masters. A quite constant theme in discussions on acculturation processes has been intermarriage, which seems to cover a wide range of concepts, from a euphemism for sexual enslavement enforced by a dominant culture, to intermarriage as a late stage in the assimilation process of two cultures interacting on equal terms (see e.g. Dohrenwend and Smith 1962). Anthropologists and sociologists however seem to consider acculturation and assimilation an even more difficult subject than migration, which is mainly approached in the form of case studies (for overviews see Rudmin 2003; Han 2005). This suggests that common-sense approaches risk making it into the curiosity cabinet of the history of archaeological research as products of their time but also warns against a hasty integration of models or theories into archaeological thought.

The interpretation of biological data derived from current populations in terms of an 'apartheid-like social structure' in early Anglo-Saxon England (Thomas *et al.* 2006: 1) defined as 'Reproductive isolation and differential social status along ethnic lines' may form a case in point. Social sciences seem to understand the term 'apartheid' primarily in its historical South African context while in international law it appears to be conceptualized as a general term that describes institutionalized discrimination based on racism. In the Rome Statute of the International Criminal Court of 2002 (Art. 7, § 1j) '"The crime of apartheid" means inhumane acts of a character similar to those referred to in paragraph 1, committed in the context of an institutionalized regime of systematic oppression and domination by one racial group over any other racial group or groups and committed with the intention of maintaining that regime' (Art. 7, § 2h). Paragraph 1 lists murder, extermination, enslavement, forcible transfer of population, and sexual violence amongst others as crimes against humanity. Historians, sociologists, and lawyers among others seem to agree that apartheid is based on racism, which raises the question whether using the term 'apartheid-like social structure' in an early medieval context may be misleading. Charles Hirschman (2004: 389) among others has argued that racism, other than ethnocentrism, is a concept that in Europe post-dates the early medieval period: 'The distinction between ethnocentrism and racism does not hinge on the presence of antipathy, the often observed outbreaks of mass slaughter of "others", or the degree of domination and exploitation. Racism is a structure of belief that the "other community" is inherently inferior and lacks the capacity to create a society comparable to one's own.' This view seems to be supported by Patrick Geary's analysis of early medieval society (Geary 2004).

This is not meant to say that modern history and politics are of no interest to the study of earlier periods. Once Pandora's Box is opened, aspects of migration and assimilation appear that make Thomas *et al.*'s calculations of 'intermarriage rates' between Anglo-Saxons and Britons in the 'apartheid-like social structure' look tame. The Rome Statute of the International Criminal Court (2008) lists among the crimes against humanity 'Forced pregnancy', which 'means the unlawful confinement of a woman forcibly made pregnant, with the intent of affecting the ethnic composition of any population...' (Art. 7, § 2f). If Thomas *et al.*'s computer simulations are re-interpreted in such a vein, Gildas and Bede with their tale of murder and mayhem seem to have been right all along. Bede's account, however, is followed by a chapter that may foretell a better fate for the Romano-British population in research to come and allows this outlook to close on a happier note: 'When the army of the enemy had exterminated or scattered the native peoples, they returned home [*domus reuersus est*] and the Britons slowly began to recover strength and courage. They emerged from their hiding-places and with one accord they prayed for the help of God that they might not be completely annihilated' (*HE* I.16 after Colgrave and Mynors 1969).

Acknowledgement

The author wishes to thank Chris Scull for lively discussion and for suggestions that helped to shape the final version. Responsibility for all opinions expressed remain the author's alone.

References

Arnold, C. J. (1984). *Roman Britain to Saxon England: An Archaeological Study*. London and Sydney: Croom Helm.
——(1988). *An Archaeology of the Early Anglo-Saxon Kingdoms*. London: Routledge.

BALDWIN BROWN, G. (1915). *The Arts in Early England: Saxon Art and Industry in the Pagan Period*. London: John Murray.

BODE, M.-J. (1998). *Schmalstede: Ein Urnengräberfeld der Kaiser- und Völkerwanderungszeit*. Urnengräberfriedhöfe Schleswig-Holsteins 14 = Offa Bücher 78. Neumünster: Wachholz.

BÖHME, H.-W. (1986). 'Das Ende der Römerherrschaft in Britannien und die angelsächsische Besiedlung Englands im 5. Jahrhundert'. *Jahrbuch des Römisch-Germanischen Zentralmuseums* 33(2): 469–574.

BRUGMANN, B. (1999). 'The role of continental artefact types in sixth-century Kentish chronology', in J. Hines, K. Høilund Nielsen, and F. Siegmund (eds.), *The Pace of Change: Studies in Early Medieval Chronology*. Oxford: Oxbow, 37–51.

——(2005). 'Von Piraten zu Reichsgründern?', in M. Knaut and D. Quast (eds.), *Die Völkerwanderung: Europa zwischen Antike und Mittelalter*. Sonderheft 2005 der Zeitschrift Archäologie in Deutschland. Stuttgart: Konrad Theiss, 73–9.

CHAPMAN, J., and HAMEROW, H. (eds.) (1997). *Migrations and Invasions in Archaeological Explanation*. British Archaeological Reports International Series 664. Oxford: Archeopress.

COLGRAVE, B., and MYNORS, R. A. B. (1969). *Bede's Ecclesiastical History of the English People*. Oxford: Clarendon Press.

CUMMINGS, C. (2007). 'Human remains'. *Novum Inventorium Sepulchrale: Kentish Anglo-Saxon Graves and Grave Goods in the Sonia Hawkes Archive*, July 2007, 1st Edition, <http://web.arch.ox.ac.uk/archives/inventorium/osteology.php>. Accessed 1 October 2007.

DOHRENWEND, B. P., and SMITH, R. J. (1962). 'Toward a theory of acculturation'. *Southwestern Journal of Anthropology* 18(1): 30–9.

ESMONDE CLEARY, S. (2001). 'The Roman to medieval transition', in S. James and M. Millett (eds.), *Britons and Romans: Advancing an Archaeological Agenda*. London: Council for British Archaeology, 90–111.

FAIRCHILD, H. P. (1925). *Immigration: A World Movement and its American Significance*. New York: Macmillan Company.

FAUSSETT, B. (1856). *Inventorium Sepulchrale: an Account of some Antiquities in the County of Kent, from A.D. 1757 to A.D. 1773*. Ed. C. Roach Smith. London: printed for subscribers.

GEARY, P. J. (2004). *The Myth of Nations: The Medieval Origins of Europe*. Princeton, NJ: Princeton University Press.

GEBÜHR, M. (1997). 'Überlegungen zum archäologischen Nachweis von Wanderungen am Beispiel der angelsächsischen Landnahme in Britannien'. *Archäologische Informationen* 20(1): 11–24.

——(1998). 'Angulus desertus?', in Häßler (ed.), *Die Wanderung der Angeln nach England*, 43–86.

HAMEROW, H. (1997). 'Migration theory and the Anglo-Saxon "identity crisis"', in Chapman and Hamerow (eds.), *Migrations and Invasions in Archaeological Explanation*, 33–44.

——(1998). 'Wanderungstheorien und die angelsächsische "Identitätskrise"', in Häßler (ed.), *Die Wanderung der Angeln nach England*, 121–34.

——(1999). 'Anglo-Saxon timber buildings: the continental connection', in Sarfatij, Verwers, und Woltering (eds.), *In Discussion with the Past*, 119–28.

——(2002). *Early Medieval Settlements: The Archaeology of Rural Communities in Northwest Europe 400–900*. Oxford: Oxford University Press.

—— Hayden, C., and Hey, G. (2007). 'Anglo-Saxon and earlier settlement near Drayton Road, Sutton Courtenay, Berkshire'. *Archaeological Journal* 164: 109–96.

Han, P. (2005). *Soziologie der Migration: Erklärungsmodelle, Fakten, Politische Konsequenzen, Perspektiven*. 2nd edition. Stuttgart: Lucius & Lucius.

Harden, D. B. (ed.) (1956). *Dark-Age Britain: Studies Presented to E. T. Leeds*. London: Methuen.

Härke, H. (1998). 'Briten und Angelsachsen im nachrömischen England: Zum Nachweis der einheimischen Bevölkerung in den angelsächsischen Landnahmegebieten', in Häßler (ed.), *Die Wanderung der Angeln nach England*, 87–119.

——(2003). 'Population replacement or acculturation? An archaeological perspective on population and migration in post-Roman Britain', in H. Tristam (ed.), *The Celtic Englishes 3*. Anglistische Forschungen 324. Heidelberg: Winter, 13–28.

Häßler, H.-J. (ed.) (1998). *Die Wanderung der Angeln nach England. 46. Sachsymposion im Archäologischen Landesmuseum der Christian-Albrecht-Universität, Schloß Gottorf, Schleswig, 3. bis 5. September 1995* (Studien zur Sachsenforschung, 11) Oldenburg: Isensee Verlag.

Hawkes, S. C. (1990). 'Bryan Faussett and the Faussett Collection: an assessment', in E. Southworth (ed.), *Anglo-Saxon Cemeteries: A Reappraisal; Proceedings of a Conference held at Liverpool Museum 1986*. Stroud: Alan Sutton, 1–24.

Higham, N. (1992). *Rome, Britain and the Anglo-Saxons*. London: Seaby.

Hills, C. (2003). *Origins of the English*. London: Duckworth.

Hirschman, C. (2004). 'The origins and demise of the concept of race'. *Population and Development Review* 30(3): 385–415.

Kendrick, T. D. (1933). 'Polychrome jewellery in Kent'. *Antiquity* 7: 429–52.

Lee, E. S. (1966). 'A theory of migration'. *Demography* 3(1): 47–57.

Leeds, E. T. (1913). *The Archaeology of the Anglo-Saxon Settlements*. Oxford: Clarendon Press.

——(1936). *Early Anglo-Saxon Art and Archaeology*. Oxford: Clarendon Press.

——(1945). 'The distribution of Angles and Saxons archaeologically considered'. *Archaeologia* 91: 1–101.

Lethbridge, T. C. (1956). 'The Anglo-Saxon settlement in Eastern England. A reassessment', in Harden, *Dark-Age Britain*, 112–22.

Lucy, S. (2000). *The Anglo-Saxon Way of Death: Burial Rites in Early England*. Stroud: Sutton Publishing.

MacDougall, H. A. (1982). *Racial Myth in English History: Trojans, Teutons and Anglo-Saxons*. Montreal: Harvest House.

Moore, J. H. (2001). 'Evaluating five models of human colonization'. *American Anthropologist* 193(2): 395–408.

Penn, K., and Brugmann, B., with Høiland Nielsen, K. (2007). *Aspects of Anglo-Saxon Inhumation Cemeteries: Morning Thorpe, Spong Hill, Bergh Apton and Westgarth Gardens*. East Anglian Archaeology Report 119. Dereham: Suffolk County Council.

Prien, R. (2005). *Archäologie und Migration: Vergleichende Studien zur archäologischen Nachweisbarkeit von Wanderungsbewegungen*. Universitätsforschungen zur Prähistorischen Archäologie 120. Bonn: Habelt.

Ravn, M. (2003). *Death Ritual and Germanic Social Structure (c. AD 200–600)*. British Archaeological Reports International Series 1164. Oxford: Archeopress.

RENFREW, C. (1987). *Archaeology and Language: The Puzzle of Indo-European Origins*. New York: Cambridge University Press.

INTERNATIONAL CRIMINAL COURT (2008). 'Rome Statute of the International Criminal Court'. <http://www.icc-cpi.int/library/about/officialjournal/Rome_Statute_English.pdf>. Accessed 4 March 2008.

RUDMIN, F. W. (2003). 'Catalogue of acculturation constructs: descriptions of 126 taxonomies, 1918–2003', in W. J. Lonner, D. L. Dinnel, S. A. Hayes, and D. N. Sattler (eds.), *Online Readings in Psychology and Culture* (Unit 8, Chapter 8), (http://www.wwu.edu/culture). Center for Cross-Cultural Research, Western Washington University, Bellingham, Washington USA.

SARFATIJ, H., VERWERS, W. J. H., and WOLTERING, P. J. (eds.) (1999). *In Discussion with the Past: Archaeological Studies Presented to W. A. van Es*. Zwolle: Stichting Promotie Archeologie.

SCULL, C. J. (1995). 'Approaches to material culture and social dynamics of the Migration period in eastern England', in J. Bintliffe and H. Hamerow (eds.), *Europe between Late Antiquity and the Middle Ages: Recent Archaeological and Historical Research in Western and Southern Europe*. British Archaeological Reports International Series 617. Oxford: Archaeopress, 71–83.

STOODLEY, N. (1999). *The Spindle and the Spear: A Critical Enquiry into the Construction and Meaning of Gender in the Early Anglo-Saxon Burial Rite*. BAR British Series 288. Oxford: British Archaeological Reports.

THOMAS, M. G., STUMPF, M. P. H., and HÄRKE, H. (2006). 'Evidence for an apartheid-like social structure in early Anglo-Saxon England'. *Proceedings of the Royal Society* B doi:10.1098/rspb.2006.3627.

WELCH, M. G. (1993). 'The archaeological evidence for federate settlement in Britain within the fifth century', in F. Vallet and M. Kazanski (eds.), *L'armée romaine et les Barbares du 3e au 7e siècle. Actes du Colloque International org. par le Musée des Antiquités Nationales et l'URA 880 du CNRS (Saint-Germain-en-Laye, 24–28 février 1990)*. Mémoires de l'Association Française d'Archéologie Mérovingienne, 5. Rouen: Association Française d'Archéologie, 269–78.

WILLIAMS, H. (2006). 'Heathen graves and Victorian Anglo-Saxonism: assessing the archaeology of John Mitchell Kemble'. *Anglo-Saxon Studies in Archaeology and History* 13: 1–18.

ZIMMERMANN, W. H. (1999). 'Favourable conditions for cattle farming, one reason for the Anglo-Saxon migration over the North Sea?', in Sarfatij, Verwers, and Woltering (eds.), *In Discussion with the Past*, 130–44.

CHAPTER 4

ANGLO-SCANDINAVIAN IDENTITY

JULIAN D. RICHARDS

The scale of Scandinavian raiding and settling and the contribution of Scandinavians to the creation of Anglo-Saxon identity have been much debated. In contrast to the fifth-century Anglo-Saxon migration which was accompanied by the wholesale introduction of a Germanic burial rite (Dickinson, this volume), the burials of ninth- and tenth-century Scandinavian settlers have proved difficult to identify. The *Anglo-Saxon Chronicle* provides a documentary record for raids followed by settlement, and there is a rich layer of Old Norse-influenced place-names, particularly in the area which later became known as the Danelaw, as well as other changes to everyday language. Archaeological evidence, however, has been much more elusive, leading scholars to assume a rapid cultural assimilation of the settlers. Genetic evidence for ninth- and tenth-century settlers has proved problematic, although isotope analysis has begun to help us identify specific Norse individuals (Hedges, this volume). Nonetheless there are changes to personal dress accessories which show Scandinavian influence (Webster, this volume) and indicate changes in costume, and in the tenth century, stone sculpture is used to mark the founder burials of a new elite with a preference for Scandinavian iconography. In each of these cases, however, it is more appropriate to talk of a hybrid Anglo-Scandinavian identity, rather than Danish, Norse, or Viking. This chapter will examine the circumstances that led to Scandinavian invaders being assimilated into Anglo-

Saxon England and ensured that it was the Anglo-Saxons, not the Vikings, who came to be regarded as the ancestral English.

Documentary sources

The popular stereotype of the Vikings as axe-waving barbarians leaping from their dragon ships, cutting down Anglo-Saxon clerics, looting their coastal monasteries, and carrying off women and children into slavery is now generally seen to provide only a limited reflection of late eighth- and ninth-century reality. It is the aspect emphasized in contemporary ecclesiastical sources, such as the letters of Alcuin, although the label *wicing* only occurs five times in the *Anglo-Saxon Chronicle*, where it refers to small raiding parties (Fell 1986; 1987). Documentary sources often identify these war-bands as being different from other ninth-century armies because they are pagans or heathen. At other times they describe them by generic regional identifiers, such as *Dani* (Danes) and *Nordmanni* (Norsemen) although it is equally clear that such terms are unreliable guides to country of origin. More helpfully raiders may be identified as coming from a more specific region within Scandinavia, such as the men of Vestfold, Jutland, or Hordaland, or as the followers of a particular Scandinavian leader, such as the armies of Olafr, Svein, Thorkel or Cnut. But even the tenth- and eleventh-century Scandinavian armies were mixed groups of opportunist warriors keen to gain portable wealth or more permanent landholdings.

The members of both the early raiding parties and later armies expressed their identity in terms of loyalty to a leader, or a region. The Scandinavian nations were only formed in the context of overseas expansion, just as the early English state crystallized out of resistance to invasion and as an expression of the growing importance of the Kingdom of Wessex. Ideas of group solidarity on both sides may have flourished in the face of external threats but would also have been subject to political deals between rival leaders. On both sides of the North Sea these beginnings were also emphasized and romanticized during nineteenth-century nationalism, bolstering the origin myths of the industrial and trading nations of northern Europe and Scandinavia (Wawn 2000).

As a result of archaeological excavation of early urban centres in England and Scandinavia this first Viking stereotype of rampant warrior has been redressed by a second model of an entrepreneurial traveller and trader. This role is also represented in documentary sources through the account of the visit of the Scandinavian merchant Ohthere to Ælfred's court, and his account of how he travelled north to take tribute of walrus ivory and furs from hunters who lived beyond the Arctic

Circle, and then returned to the towns of southern Scandinavia to trade (Bately and Eglert 2007). However, the cultural identity of these early traders was just as fluid as that of the warriors. Excavations of the cemeteries associated with these early towns, such as the wealthy graves at Birka, near modern Stockholm, have revealed a complex cultural melting pot of costume and ornaments (Ambrosiani 2001; 2004).

A third model is that of the farmer-settler, granted a landholding in return for military service, or even purchasing an estate, and building ties with the local population through intermarriage. By the time of the later waves of Scandinavian invasion in the eleventh century, those ninth-century warriors who had shared out the lands of Mercian and Northumbrian lords had in turn become the local 'establishment' (Hadley 1997). When Æthelred II 'gave orders for all the Danish people who were in England to be slain on St Brice's Day' it is likely that this referred to no more than a minority of recent arrivals, rather than the majority of the population who would have been of mixed Danish and English descent (Innes 2000). There is evidence for Anglo-Scandinavian political interaction and accommodation in most parts of northern and eastern England (Hadley 2006: 28–71) and there are similarities between the institutions of the so-called Danelaw and other areas of England (Hadley 2000). In fact 'Dane' and 'Danelaw' were used as part of the construction of identity in eleventh-century documents (Innes 2000), and the term *Dena lagu* or 'Danelaw' was first used by Wulfstan *c.*1008 to distinguish the legal traditions of northern and eastern England from those in Mercia and Wessex. The distinction was then seized upon as part of the Victorian polarization of a Scandinavian 'them' and an Anglo-Saxon 'us'.

In fact, Scandinavian leaders adopted an indigenous style of rule, or looked to continental analogues across the English Channel. They also adopted the local trappings of lordship, taking on the title of king, issuing coins, and collaborating with the church in return for its support. In certain circumstances and prompted by the need to make statements of group identity, they chose to make reference to their Scandinavian pagan background. For example, in the context of rivalry between Northumbria and Wessex, Olaf Guthfrithson used Old Norse on his coinage (Blackburn 2004). Similarly, elaborate funerary displays in mound burials in north-west England, as at Claughton Hall (Edwards 1998) and Cumwhitton (Brennand 2006), relate to the politics of the Irish Sea region and the expression of a Hiberno-Norse identity.

In summary, therefore, the Scandinavian settlers who arrived in England did not have a common identity. Furthermore, any shared sense of ethnic identity would have been challenged by other tensions, such as those of gender, age, or status. The Scandinavian elite were quick to form local alliances which cross-cut ethnic divides and did not promote any sense of Scandinavian unity.

Many did not come to England direct from Scandinavia but from Continental Europe or the Irish Sea area, where they would have assimilated other cultures. This paved the way for the assimilation that occurred between the native Anglo-Saxons and Scandinavians and for the addition of new layers of language, material culture, and behaviour which came to comprise Anglo-Scandinavian identity. Traditional ethnic models of 'them' and 'us' are inadequate to describe the complexity of cross-cutting identities at play in England in the ninth to eleventh centuries (Trafford 2000). Furthermore, there is no reason to expect a common response to the situation. In short, there was no single hybrid Anglo-Scandinavian identity, but a range of strategies, dependent upon context.

Place-names and linguistic evidence

Language, like artefacts, could be manipulated to display ethnic or political allegiance (Hines 1991: 418). Matthew Townend has argued that there were two separate speech communities in ninth- and tenth-century England. Each maintained its own place-names: for example, Whitby and *Streoneshalh*; Derby and *Northworthig* (Townend 2000; 2002). Anglo-Scandinavian society was bilingual, but was not comprised of bilingual individuals. He concludes that the languages were mutually (but not completely) intelligible, without the need for bilingualism, or for interpreters, particularly in the context of likely spheres of interaction, such as trade and exchange. The Old Norse language in England was not used for writing, but the use of Old English to commemorate the rededication of the church at Kirkdale on a monumental sundial (Richards 2004a: 185–6) does not mean that the population had stopped speaking Old Norse.

Indeed, Townend argues for the survival of a distinct Old Norse-speaking community into the eleventh century. Norse personal names became popular all over England in the eleventh century. In the Domesday Book, 50 per cent of personal names in Cheshire are Scandinavian. Furthermore 30 per cent of the manors are held by men with Scandinavian names, with a concentration in the Wirral. In itself this might be inconclusive: Norse personal names may have worked their way into the fashionable stock of personal names by the time they were recorded in Domesday Book. The elite takeover of estates which followed the Norman Conquest also led to a domination of French personal names in the thirteenth century, without any large group of Norman French-speakers. However, the huge variety of the Norse naming stock has led Abrams and Parsons to argue that they represent communities of native Norse-speakers (Abrams and Parsons 2004).

Townend suggests that the death of Old Norse eventually occurred through the process of intermarriage over several generations. Mixed marriages would have led to children being brought up to speak English by their mothers. Old Norse therefore died out within the gradual breakdown of a distinctive Scandinavian culture and identity in mixed households. It is in this context that we can understand the development of new naming practices (Hadley 2006: 119). Many of the Scandinavian names in northern and eastern England are rather different from those personal names recorded in Scandinavia. In England new names were created out of the individual elements of compound names within Anglo-Scandinavian households.

Settlement archaeology

If one turns to the settlement archaeology of late Saxon England there is little that is diagnostically Scandinavian, in settlement location, layout, or in building form. Nonetheless it is reasonable to link tenth-century changes to the disruption caused by Viking activity and to the creation of an Anglo-Scandinavian identity.

Batey (1995) has reviewed the evidence from a handful of excavated upland settlements in northern England, comprising Ribblehead (North Yorks) (King 1978), Simy Folds (Co. Durham) (Coggins et al. Batey 1983) and Bryant's Gill (Cumbria) (Dickinson 1985). She concludes that there are various features that can be paralleled with Norse sites in Scotland, including clusters of buildings of different functions associated with yards, paved areas, and field systems; the use of stone facing and rubble interiors, clay bedding for walls, and flat stone slabs to form level surfaces; and the presence of wall benches. This writer (Richards 2000a) has argued, however, that these traits have much to do with the environmental conditions and are found on upland sites of pre-Viking date. Nonetheless, subsequent discussion of these sites (Coggins 2004; King 2004), whilst admitting that it is impossible to say that they were the homes of Norse settlers, have concluded that they must have lived in structures very much like them.

Similar problems are faced in trying to claim a Scandinavian origin for buildings in lowland England. The identification of an aisled building at Waltham Abbey (Essex) as a 'Viking hall' rests upon the supposedly Scandinavian character of the building, and an historical association with 'Tovi the Dane' who held estates at Waltham under Cnut (Huggins 1976). The absence of timber wall-posts has been claimed by the excavator to imply that the hall was turf-walled. However, the hall may well have been built quite late in the eleventh century and as James Graham-Campbell has reminded us, if it was indeed turf-walled, then it is unlikely to have been built by anyone with any pretensions to high status from Denmark (Graham-Campbell 1977: 427).

The construction of bow-sided halls is a distinctive feature of tenth-century villages in Jutland, reaching their most developed form in the Trelleborg-type ring fortresses established by Harald Bluetooth to control and manage his kingdom. It has been suggested that the presence of bow-sided buildings in England is an indication of Scandinavian settlement (Rahtz 1976), although they range widely in size and date, and are found in urban as well as rural contexts, as well as within and beyond the Danelaw. The halls at Cheddar (Somerset), North Elmham (Norfolk), Goltho (Lincs), and Sulgrave (Northants) are substantial symmetrical structures, each with a tripartite internal division, following the Danish exemplars, but they are the residences of the social elite rather than being specifically Scandinavian (Richards 2000a: 301; see also Gardiner, this volume).

Whilst we may not be able to identify Scandinavians in the settlement record, we may be able to observe their impact on tenurial and landholding arrangements, or on the artefactual assemblage associated with a site. At Goltho, the original farmstead was replaced in the tenth century by a fortified complex comprising a hall, kitchen, garderobes, and workshop, probably a weaving shed. Whilst we cannot conclude that the new hall was constructed for a Scandinavian lord, this restructuring of the settlement was accompanied by the introduction of artefacts of Scandinavian or continental origin, including a gaming piece, four bone pins, and a bridle-bit (Beresford 1987: 181–4).

At Cottam (East Yorkshire) an eighth-century Anglo-Saxon farmstead set within a sub-rectangular enclosure was abandoned in the late ninth century. The farm was relocated some 100 metres to the north, adjacent to the same prehistoric trackway that had served its predecessor. As far as we can tell there was little change in the design of the buildings, small timber-framed halls with earthfast posts (Richards 1999). However, the new settlement was entered via a monumental timber gateway designed to have maximum impact on visitors approaching from the south. Its role was symbolic rather than defensive as the other sides of the settlement were enclosed by pretty minimal ditches. Ann Williams (1992) records that in eleventh-century sources a thegn's residence was expected to have a *burh-geat* or gatehouse and was typically enclosed by hedges, fences, or ditches. The later settlement at Cottam produced examples of Scandinavian artefacts, including a Borre-style buckle and a Jelling-style brooch, as well as new forms of strap-end and disc brooches. There were also two small copper-alloy bells decorated with ring-and-dot ornament. Bells of this particular form are not found in Scandinavia but they have been recovered from a variety of sites in the parts of Britain where Scandinavians settled (Richards 2000a: 305). They may have served as decorative fittings on horse harness, or possibly as hawking bells, i.e. bells attached to the foot of a falcon or hawk so as to make it easier to find the bird if it became tangled in a bush during a hunt. In any case the artefact type emerged in the Scandinavian colonies in the context of lordly display, and like many of the other aspects of Cottam, may represent an expression of Anglo-Scandinavian lordship.

Excavation within the area of the later medieval South Manor of Wharram Percy has revealed that there was an elite settlement focus here from the eighth century onwards (Stamper and Croft 2000). A weapon smith operated here in the eighth century, in an area adjacent to a post-built hall, and since the tenth-century finds also included a decorated sword hilt it seems likely that the smith's successors continued to work for the Anglo-Scandinavian lords of Wharram. The sword hilt is closely paralleled by another from Coppergate in York, and other tenth-century finds include a belt-slide and strap-end manufactured in the Borre style, probably in Norway. It is likely that at some point in the tenth century both the manorial boundary bank and the nearby peasant tofts were laid out, marking the beginning of the nucleated planned village (Richards 2000b). In the early/mid eleventh century a two-celled stone church was constructed in the valley bottom, although there is some evidence this was preceded by a tenth-century timber church. In any case it was probably in the early eleventh century that the founder burials of the first 'lord of the manor' and his family were laid out under re-worked Roman sarcophagi lids, just to the east of the chancel (Stocker 2007: 272). The settlement re-organization and the introduction of churchyard burial at Wharram Percy was clearly accompanied by cultural change, but it is significant that aspects of Anglo-Scandinavian lordship were evoked by association with a Roman elite that had existed in the area centuries earlier.

There is a similar lack of diagnostic Scandinavian features in the growing number of towns that flourished in England from the tenth century onwards. The appearance of cellared buildings in trading towns such as Chester and York may reflect a new permanent urban population of resident craftworkers, and the need to store raw materials and finished stock, but these changes took place both in areas of Scandinavian settlement and beyond (Mason 1985; Hall 2000). The archaeology of the 'five boroughs' of Derby, Nottingham, Leicester, Stamford, and Lincoln, referred to in the *Anglo-Saxon Chronicle* entry for AD 942 as being under Scandinavian control (Hall 1989), is indistinguishable from that of Anglo-Saxon *burhs*. One imagines that it was in these urban trading centres that cultural interaction between people of different ethnic backgrounds was at its most intense. It is in the marketplace that speakers of different languages would have most needed to communicate, and where makers of costume jewellery had to appeal to a wide range of customers. Indigenous populations clearly contributed to urban developments but the economic and political climate led to the rapid emergence of a hybrid artistic culture in towns (Hall 2000). This culture preserves Scandinavian elements although undiluted Scandinavian influence is rare.

In Stamford, the occupation of the town by a Scandinavian army provided the catalyst for the development of an industrial-scale pottery industry. Stamford ware was wheel-thrown and decorated with red paint and glaze, pointing to influence from northern France and suggesting that continental potters arrived in the wake of the army, or at least that the settlers had good contacts on the continent facilitating the recruitment of craftworkers (Kilmurry 1980: 176–7). There had been no extensive tradition of wheel-thrown pottery use either amongst Scandinavian settlers or the indigenous population of England, where local handmade wares were used. With the widespread introduction of industrial-scale pottery both groups were faced with a new cultural product. The adoption of the new mass-produced wares shows widespread acculturation, achieved within the household, in the process of cooking and serving food (Hadley 2006: 179). In this case Anglo-Scandinavian material culture therefore comprised a product that was neither Anglo-Saxon nor Scandinavian in origin. Once more, however, there is no single Anglo-Scandinavian identity. Pottery forms expressed regional identities at a lower level (Symonds 2003: 30–3). In Lincolnshire, Stamford ware is largely found south of the River Witham, whilst Torksey ware and pottery made in Lincoln is found to the north. Symonds notes that the different pottery traditions mirror different sculptural traditions, suggesting that shared regional identities were expressed both by the elite and more broadly within society at large.

Costume and dress accessories

Dress fittings are often used in the display of ethnicity and other aspects of social identity (Thomas 2000). There was a significant increase in the production of base-metal dress fittings and artefacts in the tenth century, but we should be wary of equating these with large numbers of low-status Scandinavian immigrants (Thomas 2000: 239–40). Collaboration with metal detectorists has led to the recording of hundreds of dress fittings and items of costume jewellery. Considerable amounts of Anglo-Scandinavian metalwork have been recovered from Norfolk, Suffolk, Lincolnshire, and eastern Yorkshire in particular (Margeson 1996; 1997; Leahy and Paterson 2001). In some areas the concentrations of metal artefacts correspond with those places with large numbers of Scandinavian place-names, although we should be aware that these are also the regions of ploughzone agriculture and with a tradition of good cooperation between detectorists and archaeologists.

Examination of the metalwork reveals that whilst some examples were manufactured in Scandinavia, others were manufactured in England but incorporate Scandinavian and Anglo-Saxon elements. Others show Carolingian influence, providing evidence for cross-Channel contact. Scandinavian forms include trefoil brooches, small quadrangular openwork brooches, and convex disc brooches. However, the majority of forms combine Scandinavian and English forms and styles (see also Webster, this volume). In York, Anglo-Saxon disc brooches were decorated with Scandinavian animal ornament comprising backwards-looking Jelling-style beasts.

In East Anglia, a series of disc brooches were decorated with an interlace pattern derived from the Borre style. A fine example was found during excavation of the castle bailey in Norwich, and the concentration of this type in Norfolk has led to the suggestion that they were manufactured in Norwich (Leahy and Paterson 2001: 195–6; Margeson 1997: 23).

This fusion of cultural markers is characteristic of the creation of Anglo-Scandinavian identity in eastern England. Stylistic borrowings often travelled between different forms of jewellery. The Scandinavian animal ornament found on Anglo-Saxon disc brooches was not simply copied from Scandinavian disc brooches for example, but was derived from other metalwork forms, such as pendants. Such transfers also took place between Scandinavian forms. A disc brooch from South Ferriby has the typical Scandinavian convex profile but was decorated with Jelling-style backwards-looking animals; it must represent a transfer of a Scandinavian motif from one artefact type to another (Leahy and Paterson 2001: 195–6). Changes in the form of costume jewellery recovered by metal detectorists may often reflect more fundamental changes in the style of dress that remain invisible to us. For example, it appears that the Scandinavian fashion for women to wear a pair of oval brooches was replaced in England by a single trefoil brooch holding a shawl in place. The trefoil brooches from Taverham and Colton in Norfolk have the fine decoration typical of examples manufactured in Scandinavia, but the form was taken up locally and other examples were probably made in East Anglia (Margeson 1997: 18–19).

Strap-ends are another dress accessory which commonly combine Scandinavian and Anglo-Saxon or Irish features. Irish influence is found particularly in Northern England, where there are also sculptural indications of links with the Hiberno-Norse. A strap-end from St Mary Bishophill Senior, York, has Borre-style ring-knot design decoration with indigenous ring-and-dot on the reverse. A second example from Coppergate has Borre-style interlace modified into the triquetra motif familiar from Irish metalwork. Richard Hall (2000: 319–20) has suggested that, in York, factional disputes between those of Scandinavian descent and the local population meant it was unwise to display items of clear Scandinavian or English affiliation. Recent research (Ashby 2006) on bone and antler combs, an underexploited resource for social explanation, has demonstrated the importance of personal accessories in the construction and maintenance of identity, but has also highlighted the absence of combs of a pure Scandinavian form in Anglo-Saxon contexts.

It is clear that Scandinavians and Anglo-Saxons actively used material culture in the process of cultural assimilation, with rapid integration. This must also indicate that there was rapid integration of dress styles, particularly for women, given the rarity of oval brooches, which were typical of Scandinavian strap dresses but which could not be adopted into Anglo-Saxon costume. It is no coincidence that there was a high level of experimentation with female dress accessories, particularly disc brooches, as these would have been familiar in both societies. It is also significant that the ninth- and tenth-century Borre and Jelling styles are generally found on female dress accessories, whilst the tenth- and eleventh-century Urnes and Ringerike styles are found on items associated with the display of male lordship, especially horse fittings. In the first phase of Scandinavian settlement, acculturation was frequently achieved through intermarriage and the creation of a female Anglo-Scandinavian identity, whereas with Cnut's North Sea hegemony over England and Denmark in the eleventh century it was the males who came to display Anglo-Scandinavian lordship.

IDENTITY IN DEATH

Burials of a Scandinavian form are rare in England, although it must be admitted that attempts to identify Scandinavian burials have been hampered by the lack of a clear diagnostic type in Scandinavia, and by the variety of burial rites performed in ninth- to eleventh-century England (Hadley 2002; Halsall 2000). Nonetheless, in contrast to the Northern or Western Isles of Scotland and the Isle of Man, where settlers appear to have emphasized their Scandinavian lineage, the shortage of weapon burials in England has led to the conclusion that settlers quickly adopted indigenous burial practices (Graham-Campbell 2001; Richards 2002).

The failure to find Viking burials was once assumed to be a result of the first settlers having utilized pre-existing churchyards, yet despite the recent excavation of several ninth- to eleventh-century cemeteries, there are still few Scandinavian graves. There is, however, a small number of burials in which an overtly Scandinavian identity is expressed. A member of the Viking Great Army was buried in full war gear adjacent to the Mercian royal shrine at Repton (Derbyshire), during the over-wintering of AD 873–4 (Biddle and Kjølbye-Biddle 2001). On the hill at Heath Wood, Ingleby, overlooking Repton and the Trent frontier, there is a small cremation cemetery. There are some sixty mounds in four groups, some of which were built over the funeral pyre, whilst cremated offerings brought from elsewhere were placed in others. Several of the pyres also included offerings of sacrificed animals as well as fragments of cremated weaponry, including both swords and shields. I have argued elsewhere (Richards 2004b) that the cemetery commemorates the Viking Great Army, and therefore was in use for a relatively short period of time in the late ninth century. Those buried in Heath Wood can be said to have been behaving in a self-consciously Viking style. The handful of mound burials in north-west England (Edwards 1998), including the small group of inhumations recently excavated at Cumwhitton (Cumbria), can also be interpreted as signalling a clear Scandinavian identity (Griffiths 2004: 131–8).

New analytical techniques hold out the possibility of being able to define biological origins and there is genetic evidence in Cumbria and north-east Derbyshire that can plausibly be interpreted as reflecting a Scandinavian influx into a hitherto sparsely populated region (Evison 2000). Stable isotope analysis can be used to indicate the country of birth and childhood. In the case of the woman buried with a pair of Scandinavian oval brooches at Adwick-le-Street (South Yorks), isotope analysis has placed the woman's origin as probably in the Trondheim area of Norway, or possibly north-east Scotland (Speed and Walton Rogers 2004). Nonetheless it is important to remember that neither genetic nor skeletal markers can be used as direct markers of ethnic affiliation, and they are therefore of little help in defining Anglo-Scandinavian identity.

In Anglo-Scandinavian England, far from being used to maintain a memory of Scandinavian folk practices, it appears that burial was used by the newcomers as a strategy to accelerate their integration into Anglo-Saxon society. In particular, the settlers quickly adapted the Anglo-Saxon monastic habit of erecting stone crosses and turned them into high status burial markers. Dawn Hadley has described the extensive and diverse range of funerary practices in Lincolnshire. Although there are no burials which have been identified as Viking, there are many examples of stone funerary commemoration, as well as stone-lined graves, coffins, clinker-built biers, charcoal layers, and burial in a mound, as at Swinhope. Hadley suggests that 'perhaps in a region seemingly heavily settled by Scandinavians, overt displays of Scandinavian identity were less necessary' (2006: 252). The role of sculpture in our understanding of Anglo-Scandinavian England has therefore been re-assessed. It was once seen as a marker of the location of Scandinavian settlements. Stocker and Everson have examined how sculptural styles have been modified according to the political circumstances in a given region (Everson and Stocker 1999: 80–7; Stocker 2000). In towns, sculpture was used as a medium for competitive social display amongst the merchant classes (Stocker and Everson 2001). In the countryside, Stocker has identified numerous churches with only a few stone monuments, and a few churches with many monuments. These were not the mother churches of a region, but those located near what he argues were trading places—St Mark's and St Mary le Wigford in Lincoln, Marton, Bicker, St Mary Bishophill, Yarm, Kirklevington, and Lythe. These concentrations of monuments reflect sizeable numbers of newcomers in the form of merchants whose social competitiveness was played out through funerary display.

Both stone sculpture and the earlier weapon burials feature overt displays of elite male lordship and warrior status, as exemplified by the series of warrior crosses from Ryedale in North Yorkshire (Lang 2001). The role of hunting, as depicted on the reverse of one of the Middleton crosses, was clearly an important aspect of Anglo-Scandinavian lordship, and the significance of the hunting pack in signifying a rural elite has come down to the recent past. The development of a new category of funerary monument, the so-called hogback tombstone, is another symbol of Anglo-Scandinavian lordship. Lang (1984) has described it as a colonial monument. It has been suggested that most were carved in the period AD 920–70, during a period of intense Hiberno-Norse influence in the Viking Kingdom of York. The ancestry of the form lies in Anglo-Saxon recumbent stone slabs, as revealed by the excavation of the burials of the Viking rulers of York, probably placed adjacent to the Minster church, juxtaposed with the idea of an Irish house shrine and a bow-sided hall. The occurrence of gripping beasts, apparently bears, at either end of the hogback monuments has been the subject of much speculation, including the idea that they symbolize re-birth (Stocker 2000). In several of the Brompton examples a muzzle is clearly depicted, suggesting that the intention may have been to signify bear-baiting.

Hadley (2006) has argued that Anglo-Scandinavian sculpture also expresses family identity. She emphasizes the role of aristocratic women in the commemoration and preservation of dynastic memory, and their part in the transmission of cultural and artistic traditions through marriage. Marriage strategies were a means by which Scandinavian settlers secured their position and authority in England, and marriage provided context for the renegotiation of both ethnic and religious affiliation.

Sculpture also provides a window on the processes by which Scandinavian settlers were Christianized (Abrams 2000; 2001). Sculpture is a medium 'in which competing religious concepts were made mutually comprehensible' (Bailey 1980). In York the Scandinavian and Northumbrian elites were buried in the same cemetery; the grave monuments incorporate Scandinavian imagery (Lang 1991). At Gosforth a monumental cross juxtaposes a Crucifixion scene on one face with a depiction of Ragnarök on the others. This combination of Christian and Scandinavian mythic imagery reflects some of the ambiguities of Anglo-Scandinavian identity (Bailey 1980). David Stocker (2000) argues that the sculptures represent a new and self-confident identity, forged from the amalgamation of Christian and Scandinavian ideas.

Churches must have played an important part in the expression of identity in tenth-century England. Religion was a matter of group identity, not just personal belief. The foundation of private chapels adjacent to proto-manorial halls went hand-in-hand with Anglo-Scandinavian lordship. The possession of a church was an important status symbol as well as a source of status (Richards 2004a: 178–88). Many urban churches were also founded by the Anglo-Scandinavian elite. In Chester, York, Exeter, Norwich, Southwark, Chichester, Grimsby, and London there are dedications to St Olaf. These urban foundations remind us that for much of the first half of the eleventh century England and southern Scandinavia were ruled as one kingdom and shared a common cultural tradition.

In conclusion, it is clear that there was no single experience of settlement or interaction, and whilst it is helpful to talk about an 'Anglo-Scandinavian identity' this was not derived from a simple combination of Anglo-Saxon culture on the one hand and Scandinavian on the other. The impact of heterogeneous incoming groups was expressed differently in different regions, and provided a major dynamic in the written, linguistic, and archaeological record. This is not to imply a solely peaceful interaction, but rather that incoming peoples frequently responded to local circumstances by appropriating aspects of local language, culture, and behaviour. The label Anglo-Scandinavian disguises a host of interactions played out within every household and market at local level.

References

ABRAMS, L. (2000). 'Conversion and assimilation', in Hadley and Richards (eds.), *Cultures in Contact*, 135–53.
—— (2001). 'The conversion of the Danelaw', in Graham-Campbell *et al.* (eds.), *Vikings and the Danelaw*, 31–44.
—— and PARSONS, D. N. (2004). 'Place-names and the history of Scandinavian settlement in England', in Hines, Lane, and Redknap (eds.), *Land, Sea and Home*, 379–431.
AMBROSIANI, B. (ed.) (2001). *Birka Studies*, Volume 5: *Eastern Connections, Part 1*. Stockholm: Birka Project, Riksantikvarieämbetet.
—— (ed.) (2004). *Birka Studies*, Volume 6: *Eastern Connections, Part 2*. Stockholm: Birka Project, Riksantikvarieämbetet.
ASHBY, S. P. (2006). 'Trade in Viking Age Britain: identity and the production and distribution of bone and antler combs', in J. Arneborg and B. Grønnow (eds.), *Dynamics of Northern Societies*. Proceedings of the SILA/NABO Conference on Arctic and North Atlantic Archaeology, Copenhagen, May 10th–14th, 2004. Studies in Archaeology and History Volume 10. Copenhagen: Publications from the National Museum, 273–9.
BAILEY, R. (1980). *Viking Age Sculpture in Northern England*. London: Collins.
BATELY, J. and EGLERT, A. (eds.) (2007). *Ohthere's Voyages: A Late Ninth-Century Account of Voyages Along the Coasts of Norway and Denmark and its Cultural Context*. Roskilde: Viking Ship Museum.
BATEY, C. (1995). 'Aspects of rural settlement in Northern Britain', in D. Hooke and S. Burnell (eds.), *Landscape and Settlement in Britain AD 400–1066*. Exeter: University Press: 69–94.
BERESFORD, G. (1987). *Goltho: The Development of an Early Medieval Manor c.850–1150*. English Heritage Archaeological Report 4. London: English Heritage.
BIDDLE, M., and KJØLBYE-BIDDLE, B. (2001). 'Repton and the "great heathen army", 873–4', in Graham-Campbell *et al.* (eds.), *Vikings and the Danelaw*, 45–96.
BLACKBURN, M. (2004). 'The coinage of Scandinavian York', in R. A. Hall, D. W. Rollason, M. Blackburn, D. N. Parsons, G. Fellows-Jensen, A. R. Hall, H. K. Kenward, T. P. O'Connor, D. Tweddle, A. J. Mainman, and N. S. H. Rogers, *Aspects of Anglo-Scandinavian York*. The Archaeology of York 8/4. York: Council for British Archaeology, 325–49.
BRENNAND, M. (2006). 'Finding the Viking dead'. *Current Archaeology* 204: 623–9.
COGGINS, D. (2004). 'Simy Folds: twenty years on', in Hines, Lane, and Redknap (eds.), *Land, Sea and Home*, 325–34.

—— Fairless, K. J., and Batey, C. (1983). 'Simy Folds: an early medieval settlement in Upper Teesdale, Co. Durham'. *Medieval Archaeology* 27: 1–26.

Dickinson, S. (1985). 'Bryant's Gill, Kentmere: another "Viking-period" Ribblehead?', in J. R. Baldwin and I. D. Whyte (eds.), *The Scandinavians in Cumbria*. Edinburgh: Scottish Society for Northern Studies, 83–8.

Edwards, B. J. N. (1998). *Vikings in North West England: The Artifacts*. Lancaster: Centre for North-West Regional Studies, University of Lancaster.

Everson, P. and Stocker, D. (1999). *Corpus of Anglo-Saxon Stone Sculpture*, Volume 5: *Lincolnshire*. Oxford: Oxford University Press.

Evison, M. P. (2000). 'All in the genes? Evaluating the biological evidence of contact and migration', in Hadley and Richards (eds.), *Cultures in Contact*, 277–94.

Fell, C. (1986). 'Old English *wicing*: a question of semantics'. *Proceedings of the British Academy* 72: 295–316.

—— (1987). 'Modern English *Viking*', in T. Turville-Petre and M. Gelling (eds.), *Studies in Honour of Kenneth Cameron*. Special issue of *Leeds Studies in English*, New Series 18: 111–22.

Graham-Campbell, J. (1977). 'British Antiquity 1976–77: Western British, Irish and late Anglo-Saxon'. *Archaeological Journal* 134: 418–35.

—— (2001). 'Pagan Scandinavian burial in the central and southern Danelaw', in Graham-Campbell *et al*. (eds.), *Vikings and the Danelaw*, 105–23.

—— Hall, R., Jesch, J. and Parsons, D. (eds.) (2001). *Vikings and the Danelaw: Select Papers from the Proceedings of the Thirteenth Viking Congress, Nottingham and York, 21–30 August 1997*. Oxford: Oxbow Books.

Griffiths, D. (2004). 'Settlement and acculturation in the Irish Sea region', in Hines, Lane, and Redknap (eds.), *Land, Sea and Home*, 125–38.

Hadley, D. M. (1997). 'And they proceeded to plough and support themselves: the Scandinavian settlement of England', *Anglo-Norman Studies* 19: 69–96.

—— (2000). *The Northern Danelaw: Its Social Structure, c.800–1100*. London and New York: Leicester University Press.

—— (2002). 'Burial practices in Northern England in the Later Anglo-Saxon Period', in S. Lucy and A. Reynolds (eds), *Burial in Early Medieval England and Wales*. Society for Medieval Archaeology Monograph Series 17. Leeds: Maney, 209–28.

—— (2006). *The Vikings in England: Settlement, Society and Culture*. Manchester and New York: Manchester University Press.

—— and Richards, J. D. (eds.), (2000). *Cultures in Contact: Scandinavian Settlement in England in the Ninth and Tenth Centuries*. Studies in the Early Middle Ages 2. Turnhout: Brepols.

Hall, R. A. (1989). 'The Five Boroughs of the Danelaw: a review of present knowledge'. *Anglo-Saxon England* 18: 149–206.

—— (2000). 'Anglo-Scandinavian attitudes: archaeological ambiguities in late ninth- to mid-eleventh-century York', in Hadley and Richards (eds.), *Cultures in Contact*, 311–24.

Halsall, G. (2000). 'The Viking presence in England? The burial evidence reconsidered', in Hadley and Richards (eds.), *Cultures in Contact*, 259–76.

Hines, J. (1991). 'Scandinavian English: a creole in context', in P. S. Ureland and G. Broderick (eds.), *Language Contact in the British Isles*. Tübingen: Niemeyer, 403–27.

—— Lane, A. and Redknap, M. (eds.) (2004). *Land, Sea and Home*. Society for Medieval Archaeology Monograph 20. Leeds: Maney Publishing.

HUGGINS, P. J. (1976). 'The excavation of an 11th-century Viking hall and 14th-century rooms at Waltham Abbey, Essex, 1969–71'. *Medieval Archaeology* 20: 75–133.

INNES, M. (2000). 'Danelaw identities: ethnicity, regionalism and political allegiance', in Hadley and Richards (eds.), *Cultures in Contact*, 65–88.

KILMURRY, K. (1980). *The Pottery Industry of Stamford, Lincs.* BAR British Series 84. Oxford: British Archaeological Reports.

KING, A. (1978). 'Gauber High Pasture, Ribblehead: an interim report', in R. A. Hall (ed.), *Viking Age York and the North*. CBA Research Report 27. London: Council for British Archaeology, 21–5.

—— (2004). 'Post-Roman upland architecture in the Craven Dales and the dating evidence', in Hines, Lane, and Redknap (eds.), *Land, Sea and Home*, 335–44.

LANG, J. T. (1984). 'The hogback: a Viking colonial monument'. *Anglo-Saxon Studies in Archaeology and History* 3: 85–176.

—— (1991). *Corpus of Anglo-Saxon Stone Sculpture*, Volume 3: *York and Eastern Yorkshire*. Oxford: Oxford University Press.

—— (2001). *Corpus of Anglo-Saxon Stone Sculpture*, Volume 6: *Northern Yorkshire*. Oxford: Oxford University Press.

LEAHY, K. and PATERSON, C. (2001). 'New light on the Viking presence in Lincolnshire: the artefactual evidence', in Graham-Campbell *et al.* (eds.), *Vikings and the Danelaw*, 181–202.

MARGESON, S. (1996). 'Viking settlement in Norfolk: a study of new evidence', in S. Margeson, B. Ayers, and S. Heywood (eds.), *A Festival of Norfolk Archaeology*. Hunstanton: Norfolk and Norwich Archaeological Society, 47–57.

—— (1997). *The Vikings in Norfolk*. Norwich: Norfolk Museums Service.

MASON, D. J. P. (1985). *Excavations at Chester: 26–42 Lower Bridge Street 1974–6: the Dark Age and Saxon Periods*. Volume 3 of *Grosvenor Museum Archaeological Excavation and Survey Reports*. Chester: Grosvenor Museum.

RAHTZ, P. A. (1976). 'Buildings and rural settlement', in D. M. Wilson (ed.), *The Archaeology of Anglo-Saxon England*. Cambridge: Cambridge University Press, 49–99.

RICHARDS, J. D. (1999). 'Cottam: an Anglian and Anglo-Scandinavian settlement on the Yorkshire Wolds'. *Archaeological Journal* 156: 1–110.

—— (2000a). 'Identifying Anglo-Scandinavian settlements', in Hadley and Richards (eds.), *Cultures in Contact*, 295–309.

—— (2000b). 'The Anglo-Saxon and Anglo-Scandinavian evidence', in Stamper and Croft (eds.), *Wharram*, 195–200.

—— (2002). 'The case of the missing Vikings: Scandinavian burial in the Danelaw', in S. Lucy and A. Reynolds (eds.), *Burial in Early Medieval England and Wales*. Society for Medieval Archaeology Monograph 17. Leeds: Maney, 156–70.

—— (2004a). *Viking Age England*. Revised edition. Stroud: Tempus.

—— (2004b). 'Excavations at the Viking Barrow Cemetery at Heath Wood, Ingleby, Derbyshire'. *Antiquaries Journal* 84: 23–116.

SPEED, G., and WALTON ROGERS, P. (2004). 'A burial of a Viking woman at Adwick-le-Street, South Yorkshire'. *Medieval Archaeology* 48: 51–90.

STAMPER, P. and CROFT, R. (eds.) (2000). *Wharram: A Study of Settlement in the Yorkshire Wolds*, Volume 8: *The South Manor*. York University Archaeological Publications 10. York: University of York.

STOCKER, D. (2000). 'Monuments and merchants: irregularities in the distribution of stone sculpture in Lincolnshire and Yorkshire in the 10th century', in Hadley and Richards (eds.), *Cultures in Contact*, 179–212.

—— (2007). 'Pre-Conquest stonework – the early graveyard in context', in S. Mays, C. Harding, and C. Heighway (eds.), *Wharram, Volume 11: The Churchyard*. York University Archaeological Publications 13. York: University of York, 271–87.

—— and EVERSON, P. (2001). 'Five towns funerals: decoding diversity in Danelaw stone sculpture', in Graham-Campbell *et al.* (eds.), *Vikings and the Danelaw*, 223–43.

SYMONDS, L. (2003). 'Territories in transition: the construction of boundaries in Anglo-Scandinavian Lincolnshire', in D. Griffiths, A. Reynolds, and S. Semple (eds.), *Boundaries in Early Medieval Britain*. Anglo-Saxon Studies in Archaeology and History 12. Oxford: Oxford University School of Archaeology, 28–37.

THOMAS, G. (2000). 'Anglo-Scandinavian metalwork from the Danelaw: exploring social and cultural interaction', in Hadley and Richards (eds.), *Cultures in Contact*, 237–55.

TOWNEND, M. (2000). 'Viking Age England as a bilingual society', in Hadley and Richards (eds.), *Cultures in Contact*, 89–105.

—— (2002). *Language and History in Viking Age England: Linguistic Relations between Speakers of Old Norse and Old English*. Studies in the Early Middle Ages 6. Turnhout: Brepols.

TRAFFORD, S. (2000). 'Ethnicity, migration theory and the historiography of the Scandinavian settlement of England', in Hadley and Richards (eds.), *Cultures in Contact*, 17–39.

WAWN, A. (2000). *The Vikings and the Victorians: Inventing the Old North in Nineteenth-Century Britain*. Cambridge: D. S. Brewer.

WILLIAMS, A. (1992). 'A bell-house and a burh-geat: lordly residences in England before the Norman Conquest', in C. Harper-Bill and R. Harvey (eds.), *Medieval Knighthood IV: Papers from the fifth Strawberry Hill Conference 1990*. Woodbridge: Boydell, 221–40.

CHAPTER 5

THE ENDING OF ANGLO-SAXON ENGLAND

IDENTITY, ALLEGIANCE, AND NATIONALITY

DAVID GRIFFITHS

TRADITIONALLY, Anglo-Saxon England met its end on Senlac Hill near Hastings, Sussex, late in the day on 14 October 1066, when Harold (II) Godwineson, king for less than a year, was slain. As his exhausted and bloodied army lost the will to continue resisting the Norman charges, in that gathering autumnal darkness thus perished the Old English kingdom. There is no doubt that this was perceived by near-contemporary chroniclers as a great national defeat and political fracture, but the question of the 'ending' of the Anglo-Saxon way of life, language, and culture is altogether a less clear-cut affair. Such a question presumes not only that there was an 'end' to these things rather than evolutionary change prompted by new influences and political realities, but also that there was something coherent or even monolithic about Anglo-Saxon England itself which could have a single, traceable ending. The evidence of history, archaeology, place-names, and newer techniques of biological research (Hedges, Richards, this volume) suggests that complexity, nuance, and also contradiction far outweigh simple or trite explanations.

The enduring modern fascination with '1066' as the key event in the ending of Anglo-Saxon England and the onset of the Middle Ages is itself an anachronism. The 'national story' of cross-channel invasion is redolent of the concerns of the nineteenth and twentieth centuries. The clash of arms at Hastings, following the recent defeat of a Norwegian invading force at Stamford Bridge, Yorkshire, nevertheless remains perhaps the most enduring image of heroic defeat in English history, and the school of 'what might have been' (sometimes extended to 'counterfactual history') remains a favourite topic of popular debate. Yet historians have for some time sought to overcome the symbolism of this defeat as the end of Anglo-Saxon England with arguments for continuity and a more nuanced assessment of change in eleventh-century England. The traditional assumption of the defeat as presaging the alien takeover of a proud and unified nation, the rapid and complete replacement of Old English lordship with its Norman feudal counterpart, and of Germanic and Scandinavian influences with French ones, all now look in question after three or four decades of revisionism. The orthodoxy of an abrupt ending, prompted by the traditional dominance of political narrative, has given way to a search for those elements of Anglo-Saxon England which survived, and those elements of Norman England which were already prefigured before the Conquest. Archaeology has contributed a deepening awareness that for the majority of people the stuff of everyday life in England was very little different at the end of the eleventh century to what it had been in the middle. Indeed so far has the pendulum swung that first-year archaeology students are now hardly ever asked the essay question, 'Would an archaeologist recognize the Norman Conquest?', so generally negative seems the answer.

The diminution of the Norman Conquest as a significant occasion of social and economic change can however be taken too far. The unprecedented detail on a national scale provided by Domesday Book, compiled as a vast inventory of the assets of the conquered kingdom, is unambiguous in its litany of reduced values, waste, and destruction to the fabric of Edward the Confessor's England between 1066 and 1086. Coins of William and his immediate successors are rarer finds in England than those of Cnut and Edward the Confessor (Metcalf 1998), suggesting that the money supply declined, indicating a drop in trading activity. The once-thriving towns of Thetford, Ipswich, Oxford, Cambridge, Chester, York, and Durham all experienced steep declines in their prosperity and urban fabric (e.g. Oxford, Ipswich, and Chester lost up to half of their houses between 1066 and 1086), and immense new castles were imposed upon the urban streetscape of these places, as indeed in many other English towns. Shortly after these were erected, the architectural heritage of the Anglo-Saxon church in both town and countryside was overwhelmed by the construction of new edifices, some of which, such as Durham, were of extraordinary scale and ambition.

Border areas in the west, east, and north in particular were laid waste, partly because of the continuing threat after the Conquest from Welsh, Norwegian, and

Danish invaders, and the stubborn refusal of the population in many areas to submit to Norman rule. The Welsh marches were re-fortified with a rash of castles, in a direct continuation of the militarization of the border in the earlier eleventh century. The Conqueror brought with him his close associates such as Odo of Bayeux, William FitzOsbern, and Robert d'Oilly, and significant landed power was concentrated in their hands soon after the Conquest. The rights to much ecclesiastical property were transferred to Norman monasteries. Lesser but nonetheless powerful and independent figures such as Hugh d'Avranches of Chester were imposed as regional governors. The overlords of the English changed, as indeed did many of their lesser brethren in the shires. Robert of Rhuddlan and William Maldebeng 'Malbank' were two lesser Norman figures who secured extensive lands along the Welsh border and in Cheshire (Sawyer and Thacker 1987: 335–8). Recent archaeozoological research, comparing English and French animal bone data-sets from before and after the Conquest, points towards the arrival of a more ostentatious hunting and feasting culture, which left its mark in discarded food waste. This included a higher incidence of pigs, which appears to have been a Norman preference (Sykes 2007).

Many other Anglo-Saxon or Anglo-Scandinavian lords probably did what most of the middle-ranking have done in every post-conquest scenario since time immemorial: they transferred allegiance, kept their heads down, even perhaps changed their names—at least in legal and official terms—to more Norman-sounding ones, and just got on with making a living as before. However, often under-stressed in attitudes to social, economic, and political change in the eleventh century is the extent to which the country taken over by William of Normandy was itself a new and uneasy confederation. Many of the elements visible in the aftermath of the Norman Conquest—inter-regional stress, social and political re-alignment, changes to lordship, economy, and agriculture, were already happening in the century before the fateful landing of William's forces at Pevensey.

If there was a high-water mark in the 'national' fortunes of pre-Norman England it could well have been the day in 973, as described in the D and E versions of the *Anglo-Saxon Chronicle*, when the 29-year old King Edgar, newly consecrated at Bath, took his retinue to Chester and received the submission of six kings of northern and western Britain. The post-Conquest writer 'Florence' [John] of Worcester elaborated the story to include eight kings, all mentioned by name, and states that these newly-subservient allies rowed the proud young English King on the Dee from the palace to the monastery of St John before an approbatory crowd of ealdormen and nobles (Whitelock 1979: 228). Edgar had already recognized the distinctiveness of the customs and liberties of the Danelaw in return for its loyalty. This was an act which, whilst implicitly recognizing that the vast area of Anglo-Scandinavian influence in the east and north (Richards, this volume) was now a part of his kingdom on equal terms with the west and south, earned him the disapproval of less accommodating voices, and he was criticized in the *Anglo-Saxon*

Chronicle (in a panegyric written a generation or two later by Archbishop Wulfstan): 'Yet he did one ill-deed too greatly, he loved evil foreign customs and brought too firmly heathen manners within this land and attracted hither foreigners and enticed harmful people to this country' (Whitelock 1979: 225).

The year 973 was also the year in which Edgar decreed that an entirely new coinage of royal inspiration and control should replace the multifarious local issues which were being produced in the shire mints, a key step in establishing a 'national' economy, especially in the urban centres (see Britnell 2000). Coins perhaps above all symbolized the kingdom in miniature, bearing (in most cases) the bust of the ruler in a long echo of the Roman style. Their minting, which was closely controlled and limited by the royal authorities, especially after Edgar's reform of 973, was one of the most effective economic controls practised by the emerging English state. Edgar, 'Ruler of the Angles, Friend of the West Saxons and Protector of the Mercians' as the *Anglo-Saxon Chronicle* had it, died suddenly the following year. This comment in itself offers an interesting side-light on the differing perceptions of the West Saxon monarchy in various parts of the newly-united realm. He was succeeded briefly and inadequately by his eldest son Edward, who, as Sir Frank Stenton put it, 'offended many important persons by his intolerable violence of speech and behaviour' (Stenton 1971: 372), subsequent to which in 978 he was murdered and a coalition of nobles put his younger brother Æthelred II ('The Unready') on the throne.

The troubled reigns of Edward and Æthelred revealed once again the deep-seated stresses and fissures in the English kingdom and betrayed its recent and violent origins. Mercia, once the senior Anglo-Saxon kingdom under Offa, and which lost its last vestiges of independence from Wessex in 918 when Edward the Elder took it over from his deceased sister Æthelflæd, remained divided between the English influence to its south and west and the Anglo-Scandinavian influence to the north and east. English *burhs* at Chester and along the Mersey valley at Runcorn, Thelwall, and Manchester, and at Bakewell and Nottingham, extended the system of roads, beacons, defences, mints, and military obligations which had once saved Wessex under Alfred into the north midlands. Cledemutha, the last of Edward the Elder's *burhs* in the north-west, was founded in 921, almost certainly at Rhuddlan on the Clwyd in north-east Wales, and was intended to pacify and annexe the unstable Anglo-Welsh border west of the Dee (Quinnell and Blockley 1994; Griffiths 2001, 2006). Edward died at Farndon on the Cheshire/Wales border in 924 after subduing a rebellion of the Welsh, who were in league with the townspeople of his own *burh* at Chester (*Anglo-Saxon Chronicle* [ASC], Whitelock 1979: 218; William of Malmesbury, *English Historical Documents* [EHD] 8, ibid. 305).

Edward's preoccupation had a long history: Alfred, as Offa and Coenwulf of Mercia before him, had spent vital time and energy on trying to establish a satisfactory overlordship of the 'North Britons' (i.e. the Welsh). A meeting between Æthelstan and Welsh princes at Hereford brought forth a promise of a rich tribute and set the Wye as the border between Mercia and south-east Wales. For a brief period there was a sense of diplomatic consensus as Hywel 'Dda' of Dyfed in particular led the way in adopting English ways of governance with a royal law code and produced a short-lived silver coinage. An agreement to establish twelve justices in disputes between the English and Welsh in the border territories of Ergyng and Ewias on either side of the Wye possibly dates from soon after the Hereford meeting (Stenton 1965: 6–7), and is useful evidence not only of compromise, but incidentally that Englishness, Welshness, and other 'national' affiliations were thrown into more acute relief in border regions than in the hinterlands of both countries. Despite this accommodation, the Welsh border remained a flashpoint of conflicting loyalties, however, particularly in the north, which was not covered by the Hereford agreement.

Æthelstan quickly turned his attention to the 'West Welsh' of Cornwall who in the mid tenth century occupied Exeter and had eroded the territorial supremacy of Wessex on its rear flank. Cornwall and Devon were late and uneasy additions to the ambit of Wessex. The former territory of the kingdom of Dumnonia, the south-west peninsula had survived as a distinct area of Celtic influence until a series of British defeats by the West Saxons in the seventh century (Todd 1987: 272). English settlement in the eighth and ninth centuries, particularly in Devon, infiltrated the British landscape and seems to have been a patchy affair, dense in places, but which broke apart the coherence of the British landscape and further undermined the decaying territorial integrity of Dumnonia. Æthelstan's decisive actions in 936 expelled the Cornish from Exeter (Whitelock 1979: 307), and further isolated Cornwall from Devon. This *coup de grâce* against the vestiges of Dumnonia seems to have established the current shire division along the Tamar, whilst subjecting Cornwall itself to the imposition of the English hundredal system of local government. Nevertheless, significant local differences in landscape and lordship remained between Devon, Cornwall, and the counties to their east (Herring 2006; Turner 2006).

In the north, Æthelstan attacked Scotland in 934, and extended English power into Cumberland as the remnants of western Northumbria came under his control, and the Hiberno-Norse settlers of the west coast appear to have abandoned much of their overt loyalty to Dublin and York following the English victory at *Brunanburh* in 937 (Dodgson 1957; Wainwright 1975). The Britons of Cumbria and Strathclyde continued to lose ground in the middle decades of the tenth century to a new alliance between Æthelstan's successor Edmund and the Scottish king Malcolm. In the immediately subsequent generation, Edgar's ceding of Lothian (a territory of significant Anglian influence) to Kenneth of Scotland speaks of compromise and pragmatism, opening the way to the tableau on the Dee, in which Kenneth himself, according to 'Florence', was one of the oarsmen.

North of the Mersey–Humber line, however, English authority remained tenuous and partial. After Æthelstan's death there was a brief resurgence of Viking power, initially led by Olaf Cuaran, in York and the northern Danelaw (Downham 2007), but the initiative was regained by Edmund. Despite the routing of Erik Bloodaxe in 954 and the assumption of permanent authority over York and Northumbria by Eadred which lasted throughout Edgar's reign, the reign of Æthelred II saw renewed severe strain on Anglo-Saxon authority in the Danelaw in the face of sustained Viking raids and systematic extortions, beginning in earnest around 980 and rapidly increasing in scale. This created a long period of instability and friction, culminating in the invasion of Svein Forkbeard of Denmark in 1013. The presence of concerted Danish forces in England led to Æthelred's temporary exile, and ultimately to the exhausted compromise whereby Svein's son Cnut assumed the crown in 1016.

There are signs throughout the long and difficult reign of Æthelred that the quest for internal loyalty and suspicions of treachery reached the point of paranoia. This was perhaps justified: the advances of the early to mid tenth century seemed about to vanish. The renewed raids occurred as the weakness of the kingdom was exposed after Edgar's untimely death. There seemed thereafter to have been a resurgence of the horrors of a century before: Æthelred even briefly revived the policy of Alfred in founding new *burhs* in upland strongholds such as Old Sarum and South Cadbury, in these cases to replace more vulnerable lowland towns at Wilton and Ilchester. Most infamous amongst his acts was his decree of 1002 which 'ordered to be slain all the Danish men who were in England—this was done on St Brice's Day (13 November)' (ASC, Whitelock 1979: 238–9). Far from being an empty threat, this led to a public atrocity in Oxford known as the 'St Brice's Day Massacre'. This was described in Æthelred's renewal of privileges to St Frideswide's monastery (EHD 127, Whitelock 1979: 590–1) occasioned by the church having been burnt down by the townspeople, with the small Danish population of the city inside having sought sanctuary and bolted themselves within. The Danes, the renewal says, 'had sprung up in this land, sprouting like cockle amongst the wheat'.

Æthelred's 1002 decree may have brought about a pogrom by some of his subjects in the southern counties where Danes found themselves singled out as a beleaguered and feared minority, and provided an excuse for Svein to invade England, but it almost certainly had little or no effect within the Danelaw. His legal policies upheld Edgar's pragmatic recognition of the differences between English and Scandinavian areas of the kingdom—in a law code issued at Wantage in 997 (EHD 43, Whitelock 1979: 439–42) he legislated directly for the Scandinavian areas, referring exclusively to the administration of wapentakes as opposed to English hundreds; indeed the language of the code has been remarked upon by Patrick Wormald as indicative of a strong Scandinavian influence (Wormald 1999: 327–9) and its content may have been partly the work of Sigeferth, the bishop of the see of Lindsey (Lincoln) (Innes 2000: 72). Shortly after Æthelred's death his son Edmund 'Ironside' and Uhtred, Earl of Northumbria, raided north-west Mercia

(ASC, Whitelock 1979: 248) because as 'Florence' later described: '[the Mercians] would not go out to fight the army of the Danes' (ibid).

Indeed, the near-success of the revolt against Harold II by Tostig, Earl of Northumbria in 1065, and the invasion of his ally Harald Hardrada of Norway in 1066, are an indication of only the shallowest and most compromised loyalties continuing in the north through to the Norman Conquest. Tostig and Harald achieved a great victory over the earls Edwin and Morcar at Fulford and were only stopped at Stamford Bridge by the king himself hastening north with all the forces he could muster, thereby leaving the south coast fatally exposed. The north did not settle down after the Norman victory, and the distinctive influence of the Danelaw remained strong (Richards, this volume). William's violent depredations in Cheshire and Northumbria after the Conquest may be seen partly as a response to the continuing effects of these pre-Conquest upheavals, with their egregious slight against the authority of the throne to which William felt himself entitled by law as well as Conquest.

The 'end' of Anglo-Saxon England was therefore, in political terms at least, a ragged and discordant affair within which the Norman Conquest certainly represented a major upheaval, but not one which was inflicted on anything like an ethnically-unified populace. Membership of the *Gens Anglorum* was still very far indeed from being associated with the citizenship of a country, although being the subject of a monarch is a closer approximation and indeed one which survived as a terminological fossil until recent times. (The personal nationality of the king seems not to have mattered in this as much as the symbol of the monarchy—as has been shown by the succession of Danish, Norman-French, Welsh, Scottish, Dutch, and German individuals who have occupied the throne since 1016). If recognized in 'national' terms at all, Englishness was more likely to have been a construct of language and political and ecclesiastical allegiance; geographic loyalties were still small-scale and backward-looking, and language probably only came to the fore as an acute factor in notions of identity when confronted on a daily basis by speakers of another tongue, namely at this time Norse/Danish, Welsh, Irish, French, Frisian, or German.

What is undeniable, however, is that whilst a sense of membership of a 'national' race was certainly a factor in notions of identity, this was in itself a cultural and cognitive perception and far indeed from being prompted or conditioned by innate biology alone. It was quite possible to possess a non-English ancestry and a genetic inheritance of non-English character, yet by aspiration, apparel, religion, language, and social context to feel and believe oneself to be as 'English' as the next man or woman—and indeed *vice versa* where English biological ancestry was subsumed into a different cultural identity—Scandinavian perhaps, or Norman-French. Moreover, notions of identity were subject to generational change, and even alteration during an individual's lifetime. Far from being a passive reflection of changing social conditions, this often fast-paced and pragmatic form of self-redefinition takes on the guise of a deliberate choice, one which in many cases was prompted and assisted by manipulation of the symbolism of regional and national loyalties.

A change of equal significance to national conquest and attempts at unification in later Anglo-Saxon England was the development of urban life, and the drawing-in of the countryside increasingly to an urban-focused economy. By any definition there had been few towns in ninth-century England (Astill 2000), with those that existed serving mostly administrative and ecclesiastical functions. Itinerant kingship and lordship based on the great rural estates predominated, and the demands of urban markets seem to have reached a historical low-point. The tenth century saw considerable change as not only the military *burhs* imposed by Alfred and his successors, but independent, often smaller-scale, developments of urban character around other foci such as monasteries and ports, began to concentrate economic and political power in towns. By 1100, in marked contrast to the situation in 900, very few areas of England were more than a day's ride from at least a small market town, and larger towns of 1,000 or more inhabitants were becoming regionally dominant across a far larger proportion of the kingdom than previously (Holt 2000, Griffiths 2003).

There were regional variations in the density and frequency of towns and markets. The geographical extremities of England in the far north and south-west remained largely non-urbanized, as did Wales and Scotland. There was still a perceptible difference between Wessex and 'English' Mercia, and the former Danelaw. In the former, besides the major regional burghal centres such as Winchester, Oxford, and Worcester, there were more medium and smaller towns often at sub-shire level, such as Pershore, Malmesbury, Marlborough, or Frome. To the north-east of Watling Street, however, there were fewer towns, but these tended to be more comparable in size to the larger towns in the midlands and south (Griffiths 2003: Fig. 3.5). This difference is perhaps an indication that more rural market activity persisted in the Danelaw area, with the larger towns such as York, Lincoln, Stamford, and Thetford serving larger and less well-defined hinterlands than their Mercian and West Saxon counterparts. Trade and the minting of coinage were strictly controlled and limited to towns, particularly after Æthelstan's Grately Laws of *c.* 926–30 (EHD 35, Whitelock 1979: 419–21). It is possible that these royal sanctions, which given the persistence of some legal distinction may have been enforced less rigidly in the former Danelaw, led more middle-ranking places in Wessex and English Mercia to seek town status than in areas to the north and east.

The process by which England was divided into shires and their sub-unit of hundreds, based on the unit of the hide, an approximation to one household and its land (these were known as wapentakes and carucates in the Danelaw), led to more assertive rural–urban links. Shires had certainly existed in England prior to Alfred but were formalized and consolidated in the tenth century (EHD 39, Whitelock 1979: 429–30), as large estates of the mid Saxon period were divided and re-organized into smaller (and arguably more efficient) units (Hooke 1988). Hundred assemblies met at moot-mounds (known as Things in the Anglo-Scandinavian areas of the north-west) and it was to the shire towns that the rural populace looked increasingly for their commercial opportunities.

There are unambiguous signs deriving from over fifty years' concerted research into settlement formation that a substantial proportion of English villages were re-planned in the ninth to eleventh centuries. The 'champion' country associated with the stubborn clay lands of the midlands saw the greatest changes towards village nucleation, whereas dispersed settlement remained common in the western and eastern parts of the country. A wide swath, stretching from Northumberland to Dorset, of nucleated villages set within open fields had largely come about by the time of the Conquest, with considerable internal variation and permutation of nucleated and dispersed models over differing geologies and along its borders, with some nucleated clusters to be found within the ostensibly 'dispersed' areas to the east and west (Lewis et al. 2001: 191ff; Jones and Page 2006). This morphological pattern is entirely at variance with the political boundaries between Wessex, Mercia, and the Danelaw, and also spans equally the areas of predominantly Anglo-Saxon and Scandinavian place-names. Explanations for village re-organization and nucleation have included a recent and convincing case for the environmentally-driven need on the part of lordship to bring together people and resources to maximize production in areas of demanding soil conditions (Williamson 2003). However it is impossible to overlook the emerging urban populations and markets as a principal driving factor in re-defining the role of the countryside. Given that environmental and soil conditions had not suddenly altered, the timing of these changes is too close to that of the shire, burghal, and urban innovations to be anything other than contingent upon them, at least to a significant extent.

The widespread development of urban topography cannot be underestimated as a factor in cultural change and the development of notions of identity. People unrelated by ancestry and seigneurial affiliation came to live in close proximity to each other. The presence of foreigners and the resulting melange of languages, religions, and dialects were less unusual in towns than in the country districts. Commerce and administration characterized day-to-day life, both of which were more outward-looking and politically-aware professions than the main rural pursuits of agriculture, hunting, fishing, or foresting. There are signs in the emergence of guilds (EHD 136–9, Whitelock 1979: 603–7) that membership of urban-based elites had become a defining factor in social and economic life before the Norman Conquest and that a distinction between town and country in terms of social rank and class was becoming more prevalent.

Many wealthy lords possessed urban properties as well as rural ones, and the two were often interlinked to provide a means of sustaining trade and distribution of rural produce and maintaining political status (Fleming 2003). Throughout English towns from York to Chester, to Canterbury, Oxford, and Winchester (and indeed in those port-towns which developed in Ireland at Dublin, Waterford, Wexford, and Cork), apart from the public and ecclesiastical spaces, most urban land was divided into long tenements with narrow street frontages. These had the main commercial property at the front, with open space, cesspits, ancillary buildings, and occasionally higher-status halls behind. Buildings tended to be slightly less regularized than the property boundaries themselves, the positions and extents of which were increasingly defined in law.

Winchester and Westminster in particular saw ambitious royal building projects in the eleventh century, in which new and dominant ecclesiastical and secular complexes were raised, expressing the power and authority of Wessex as the head of the English Kingdom. Nevertheless, there are remarkably few characteristics in the known stock of information about pre-Norman town topography or urban architecture which can point to anything but pragmatic and functional imperatives. But with the exception of the new monumental structures and defences, which made more use of stone, urban buildings of the later tenth and eleventh century were largely constructed of timber. These included rectangular cellared or semi-basemented buildings of solid staved and planked walls with one (occasionally perhaps two) above-ground storeys, hall-type structures characterized by timber sills or parallel sets of post-holes which in some cases formed internal aisles, and smaller and simpler self-supporting sheds and workshops often without earthfast footings. These building types had often replaced flimsier structures of wattle with internal roof supports, or simple sunken-featured dwellings which were characteristic of the earlier years of the tenth century. Stone footings were as yet less common than earthfast timber walls, and only became more dominant with the advent of timber framing in the later twelfth century (Gardiner 2004: 353). Excavations of tenth- and eleventh-century cellared buildings in York (Hall 1994: 48–51), Thetford (Rogerson and Dallas 1984: 26–8), London (Horsman *et al.* 1988: 108–16; Milne 1992), Canterbury (Blockley *et al.* 1995: 357–65), Wallingford (Dodd 2003: 41), Oxford (Blair 1994: 163–5; Dodd 2003: 35–40), and Chester (Mason 1985; Ward 1994) do not easily permit strong delineation into regional types on ethnic grounds. Signs of urban re-planning around the time of the Norman Conquest have been highlighted, e.g. at Flaxengate, Lincoln Periods VII and VIII (Perring 1981: 18–21), and at Oxford (Blair 1994: 159–67; Dodd 2003: 23–5), but the acuity of these observations tends to struggle against the problems of precise dating, especially on less recent excavations lacking well-defined radiocarbon- or dendro-chronologies. Moreover many of the more common pottery types current around the time of the Conquest (McCarthy and Brooks 1988: 66–70; Hinton 2005: 160–1) are relatively stable (leading to the common appellation 'Saxo-Norman') so are generally unhelpful in dating immediate pre- and post-Conquest phases.

A significant shortcoming in the archaeological evidence for pre-Norman timber building in England, of which almost nothing survives above-ground (the eleventh-century Greensted Church, Essex (Fig. 5.1), being a possible survival), is

Figure 5.1 Greensted Church, Essex (Anthony Lambie)

the fact that we may only base our interpretations on foundations, cut features, and floor deposits, and the use of space which they imply, and hence we tend to draw very cautious conclusions about outward symbolism and identity. The superstructures of the buildings which lined urban streets, which were no doubt in many cases highly decorated both internally and externally, are largely lost to us and it is these which must have expressed the identities, beliefs, and professions of their inhabitants. Decorative display is a powerful means of carrying unwritten messages (especially useful in a semi-literate society), and one where more portable forms of material culture help to define changing beliefs and allegiances. As stated above, ethnic identity and national allegiance were not a biologically-fixed status but a complex and often transient response to social conditions involving a strong measure of individual or group choice or perhaps choice-by-compulsion. This 'instrumentalist' definition of the process (acculturation) by which a flexible and malleable construct of identity and allegiance was modified is a key aspect of recent anthropological and archaeological writing (e.g. Barth 1969; for a summary see Jones 1997: 73ff.), which has more recently been applied to situations in the early medieval period (e.g. Myhre 1998; Frazer and Tyrell 2000; Hadley and Richards 2000; Barrett 2004; Griffiths 2004, 2010). Common to these studies is an acceptance that the production, use, and discard of material culture is in itself ideologically as well as functionally driven.

Everyday domestic and working life in the tenth and eleventh centuries was characterized above all by the use of simple organic materials such as wood, flax, reed, and animal products such as leather, bone, horn, and antler. Where objects of these materials have survived, such as the extraordinary corpus of wooden objects from Viking Dublin (Lang 1988), it is clear that they were imbued with vibrant renditions of contemporary style and decoration. However, except in waterlogged anaerobic contexts such as those revealed in excavations at 16–22 Coppergate, York (Mainman and Rogers 2000; Hall *et al.* 2004), and at Fishamble Street / Wood Quay, Dublin (Lang 1988), much of this material has vanished from the archaeological record. Pottery was relatively common and spanned a spectrum from utilitarian to high-status display items, as indeed did iron objects, whereas non-ferrous metals, glass, and simply-modified natural minerals such as amber and jet were much more expressive of display than their relatively simple functions as clothes-fasteners or personal grooming items need have demanded at a functional level.

Evidence from York, Dublin, London, Lincoln, and Winchester suggests that the manufacture of small dress items was predominantly an urban pursuit. Many of these were decorated with renditions of zoomorphic and abstract art styles ranging from the apparently southern-English-centred Trewhiddle style of the ninth century to tenth- and eleventh-century styles showing more pronounced Scandinavian influences. Increasing production in cheaper alloys of copper and lead allowed the reproduction of these styles on a scale hitherto unprecedented, whereas precious metal production seems to have declined (Thomas 2000: 239). The work of the Portable Antiquities Scheme (PAS) in England since the late 1990s has resulted in the recording and collation of large numbers of metal-detected finds which were previously falling through the net of archaeological awareness. This new corpus of material shows that the small dress-items of base metal bearing Anglo-Scandinavian designs, which were probably produced in the towns of the Danelaw, are far more common in the eastern counties, and to a lesser extent elsewhere in England, than previously realized. Nevertheless, certain high-status secular and monastic sites in the eastern counties, such as Flixborough, Lincolnshire (Loveluck 2001), apparently remained free of these populist Scandinavian influences in material culture— reinforcing the point that their adoption was not universal, but a conscious choice which was not taken by some.

Three of the Anglo-Scandinavian metalwork styles in particular seem to have stimulated widespread indigenous adaptive fashions in England: the Borre style of animal masks and ring-chains, and the later more fluid and open Ringerike style of hooked vegetal fronds, pear-shaped *fleur-de-lis*, and standing quadrupeds, and the sparer Urnes style, most often with its characteristic ribbon animals with elongated snouts and lentoid eyes (see Webster, this volume). The Ringerike and Urnes styles are particularly significant in the context of changing identities and allegiances towards the end of the Anglo-Saxon period, as they spread well beyond the Danelaw to southern England, reaching a high-point during the reign of Cnut and his sons (1016–42). They are also common in Ireland, particularly the Ringerike style, not least on the wooden objects from Dublin (Lang 1988). The 'Winchester style', a term which arose from findings of objects including those in Martin Biddle's excavations there in the 1960s and early 1970s (Hinton 1990: 494–7; Hinton 2005: 134–5), is a fusion of Carolingian acanthus ornament and flourishes of the Ringerike and Urnes styles, most often expressed on openwork dress items such as strap-ends, mounts, and brooches. It is however as likely that the centre of metalwork production was in the comparatively cosmopolitan London, where a production waster bearing this style has been found in excavations at the Guildhall Yard (G. Egan, pers. comm.).

One of the most impressive public statements of the period of Cnut's rule is the St Paul's graveyard stone from London (Fig. 5.2), a limestone slab found in 1852 bearing the names of two individuals who had the stone laid, Ginna and Toki, in runes along its edge. In its central panel is a carved 'great beast' standing quadruped with a serpent in its central panel. The design is an extremely accomplished rendition of the Ringerike style (which must have been yet more visually impressive when fresh as there are still detectible traces of red, black, and white paint), yet it was found in a context of Christian burial at the centre of English rule. Stone sculpture, as a fixed and public art form, was particularly well-suited to the promotion of messages of Christian conversion, political allegiance, and ethnic transformation, and hence was a key medium of acculturation. It was a favoured means of marking the rural landscape, especially in ethnically mixed border areas (Sidebottom 2000), and was also a prominent feature in urban spaces, especially ecclesiastical ones. The adaptation, seen on the St Paul's Stone, of an originally Scandinavian style and its conversion into a statement about Christian England is redolent of the pragmatic fusion of themes of Scandinavian and English identity during Cnut's reign. By the mid eleventh century, the zenith of production of these styles seems to have passed, when the need to assert convergence in Scandinavian and Anglo-Saxon symbolism and identity had waned.

The Conquest effected a transformation of the focus of social and political aspiration on the part of lordly and ecclesiastical elites and the nascent urban classes (Thomas 2003). English survived as the language of the overwhelming majority, but acquired a significant salting of French expressions via the growing numbers of bilingual speakers in England, many of whom occupied important positions. There are signs from after the Conquest that Englishness became the butt of pejorative humour and probably outright discrimination within court circles

Figure 5.2 Limestone grave slab from St Paul's Churchyard, London (Museum of London)

(Short 1995), and it must have been clear to all who witnessed the demolition of the English urban minsters and the erection of their huge Norman successors that the visible symbols of the Anglo-Saxon kingdom were being systematically erased, as its administrative and territorial structures were being maintained and even exported back to Normandy. It is, therefore, in the successive time-lags between precipitous political fracture, changing outward fashions in dress and ornament, everyday concerns of subsistence and shelter, and lastly of all in people's inner sense of familial and group belonging, that the process of changing identity and nationality may be witnessed.

References

Astill, G. (2000). 'General Survey, 600–1300', in Palliser (ed.), *The Cambridge Urban History of Britain*, Volume 1, 27–49.

Barth, F. (ed.) (1969). *Ethnic Group and Boundaries: The Social Organisation of Culture Difference*. Boston: Little Brown.

Barrett, J. (2004). 'Beyond war or peace: the study of culture contact in Viking Age Scotland', in Hines *et al.* (eds.), *Land, Sea and Home*, 207–18.

Blair, J. (1994). *Anglo-Saxon Oxfordshire*. Stroud: Sutton.

Blockley, K., Blockley, M., Blockley, P., Frere, S. S., and Stow, S. (1995). *Excavations in the Marlowe Car Park and Adjoining Areas*. Volume 5 of *The Archaeology of Canterbury*. Canterbury: Canterbury Archaeological Trust.

Britnell, R. (2000). 'The Economy of British Towns 600–1300', in Palliser (ed.), *The Cambridge Urban History of Britain*, Volume 1, 105–26.

Dodd, A. (ed.) (2003) *Oxford Before the University: The Late Saxon and Norman Archaeology of the Thames Crossing, the Defences and the Town*. Thames Valley Landscapes Monograph 17. Oxford: Oxford Archaeology.

Dodgson, J. McN. (1957). 'The background to Brunanburh'. *Saga Book of the Viking Society* 14: 303–16.

Downham, C. 2007. *Viking Kings of Britain and Ireland*. Edinburgh: Dunedin.

Fleming, R. (2003). 'Lords and labour', in W. Davies (ed.), *From the Vikings to the Normans: Short Oxford History of the British Isles*. Oxford: Oxford University Press, 106–37.

Frazer, W. O., and Tyrell, A. (2000). *Social Identity in Early Medieval Britain*. Leicester: Leicester University Press.

Gardiner, M. (2004). 'Timber buildings without earth-fast footings in Viking-Age Britain', in Hines *et al.* (eds.), *Land, Sea and Home*, 345–58.

Griffiths, D. (2001). 'The North-West frontier', in D. Hill and N. Higham (eds.), *Edward the Elder 899–924*. Manchester: Manchester University Press, 167–87.

—— (2003). 'Exchange, trade and urbanisation', in W. Davies (ed.), *From the Vikings to the Normans, Short Oxford History of the British Isles*. Oxford: Oxford University Press, 72–104.

—— (2004). 'Settlement and acculturation in the Irish Sea region', in Hines *et al.* (eds.), *Land, Sea and Home*, 125–38.

—— (2006). 'Maen Achwyfan and the context of Viking settlement in north-east Wales'. *Archaeologia Cambrensis* 155: 143–62.

—— (2010). *Vikings of the Irish Sea*. Stroud: The History Press.

Hadley, D. M. and Richards, J. D. (eds.) (2000). *Cultures in Contact: Scandinavian Settlement in England in the Ninth and Tenth Centuries*. Turnhout: Brepols.

Hall, R. A. (1994). *Viking Age York*. London: Batsford/English Heritage.

—— *et al.* (2004). *Aspects of Anglo-Scandinavian York*. The Archaeology of York 8. York: Council for British Archaeology.

Herring, P. (2006). 'Cornish strip fields', in S. Turner (ed.), *Medieval Devon and Cornwall*. Macclesfield: Windgather Press, 44–77.

Hines, J., Lane, A., and Redknap, M. (eds.) (2004). *Land, Sea and Home*. Society for Medieval Archaeology Monograph 20. Leeds: Maney Publishing.

HINTON, D. A. (1990). 'Buckles and other clothes fittings', in M. Biddle, *Object and Economy in Medieval Winchester*. Winchester Studies 1.2. Oxford: Oxford University Press.

—— (2005). *Gold and Gilt, Pots and Pins, Possessions and People in Medieval Britain*. Oxford: Oxford University Press.

HOLT, R. (2000). 'Society and population 600–1300', in Palliser (ed.), *The Cambridge Urban History of Britain*, Volume 1, 79–104.

HOOKE, D. (1988). *Anglo-Saxon Settlements*. Oxford: Basil Blackwell.

HORSMAN, V., MILNE, C., and MILNE, G. (1988). *Building and Street Development near Billingsgate and Cheapside*. Aspects of Saxo-Norman London 1. London and Middlesex Archaeological Society Special paper 11. London.

INNES, M. (2000). 'Danelaw identities, ethnicity, regionalism, and political allegiance', in Hadley and Richards (eds.), *Cultures in Contact*, 65–88.

JONES, R. and PAGE, M. (2006). *Medieval Villages in an English Landscape*. Macclesfield: Windgather Press.

JONES, S. (1997). *The Archaeology of Ethnicity*. London: Routledge.

LANG, J. T. (1988). *Viking-Age Decorated Wood: A Study of its Ornament and Style*. Volume 1 of *Medieval Dublin Excavations 1662–81, Series B*. Dublin: National Museum of Ireland, Royal Irish Academy.

LEWIS, C., MITCHELL-FOX, P., and DYER, C. (2001). *Village, Hamlet and Field: Changing Settlements in Central England*. Macclesfield: Windgather Press.

LOVELUCK, C. P. (2001). 'Wealth, waste and conspicuous consumption. Flixborough and its importance for mid and late Saxon settlement studies', in H. Hamerow and A. MacGregor (eds.), *Image and power in the Archaeology of Early Medieval Britain: Essays in Honour of Rosemary Cramp*. Oxford: Oxbow, 78–130.

MAINMAN, A., and ROGERS, N. S. H. (2000). *Craft, Industry and Everyday Life: Finds from Anglo-Scandinavian York*. Volume 17, fasc. 14 of *The Archaeology of York: The Small Finds*. York: Council for British Archaeology.

MASON, D. J. P. (1985). *Excavations at Chester: 26–42 Lower Bridge Street 1974–76; The Dark Age and Saxon Periods*. Volume 3 of *Grosvenor Museum Archaeological Excavation and Survey Reports*. Chester: Grosvenor Museum.

McCARTHY, M., and BROOKS, C. (1988). *Medieval Pottery in Britain 900–1600*. Leicester: Leicester University Press.

METCALF, D. M. (1998). *An Atlas of Anglo-Saxon and Norman Coin Finds 973–1086*. Oxford: The Ashmolean Museum.

MILNE, G. (1992). *Timber Building Techniques In London c.900–1400: An Archaeological Study of Waterfront Installations and Related Material*. London: London and Middlesex Archaeological Society.

MYHRE, B. (1998). 'The archaeology of the Early Viking Age in Norway', in H. B. Clarke, M. Ní Mhaonaigh, and R. Ó Floinn (eds.), *Ireland and Scandinavia in the Early Viking Age*. Dublin: Four Courts Press, 3–36.

PALLISER, D. M. (ed.) (2000). *The Cambridge Urban History of Britain, Volume 1: 600–1540*. Cambridge: Cambridge University Press.

PERRING, D. (1981). *Early Medieval Occupation at Flaxengate, Lincoln*. Volumn 9–1 of *The Archaeology of Lincoln*. London: Council for British Archaeology.

QUINNELL, H. and BLOCKLEY, M. R. (1994). *Excavations at Rhuddlan, 1969–73, Mesolithic to Medieval*. CBA Research Report 95. York: Council for British Archaeology.

Rogerson, A. and Dallas, C. (1984). *Excavations in Thetford 1948–59*. East Anglian Archaeology 22. Norwich: Norfolk Museums Service.

Sawyer, P. H., and Thacker, A. T. (1987). 'Domesday Survey', in B. E. Harris and A. T. Thacker (eds.), *Victoria History of the County of Cheshire*, Volume 1. London: Institute of Historical Research.

Short, I. (1995). 'Tam Angli quam Franci: self definition in Anglo-Norman England'. *Anglo-Norman Studies* 18: 153–75.

Sidebottom, P. (2000). 'Viking Age stone monuments and social identity in Derbyshire', in Hadley and Richards (eds.), *Cultures in Contact*, 213–35.

Stenton, D. M. (1965). *English Justice between the Norman Conquest and the Great Charter 1066–1215*. London: Allen and Unwin.

Stenton, F. M. (1971). *Anglo-Saxon England*. 3rd edition. Oxford History of England. Oxford: Clarendon Press.

Sykes, N. (2007). *The Norman Conquest: A Zooarchaeological Perspective*. British Archaeological Reports International Series 1656. Oxford: Archaeopress.

Thomas, G. (2000). 'Anglo-Saxon metalwork from the Danelaw: exploring social and cultural interaction', in Hadley and Richards (eds.), *Cultures in Contact*, 237–55.

Thomas, H. M. (2003). *The English and the Normans: Ethnic Hostility, Assimilation and Identity*. Oxford: Oxford University Press.

Todd, M. (1987). *The South-West to AD 1000*. London: Longman.

Turner, S. (2006). 'The medieval landscape of Devon and Cornwall', in S. Turner (ed.), *Medieval Devon and Cornwall*. Macclesfield: Windgather Press, 1–9.

Wainwright, F. T. (1975). *Scandinavian England*. Ed. H. P. R. Finberg. Chichester: Phillimore.

Ward, S. (1994). *Excavations at Chester: Anglo-Saxon Occupation within the Legionary Fortress, Sites Excavated 1971–81*. Volume 7 of *Grosvenor Museum Archaeological Excavation and Survey Reports*. Chester: Grosvenor Museum.

Whitelock, D. (1979). *English Historical Documents*, Volume 1: *c.500–1042*. London: Eyre Methuen.

Williamson, T. (2003). *Shaping Medieval Landscapes: Settlement, Society, Environment*. Macclesfield: Windgather Press.

Wormald, P. (1999). *The Making of English Law I: King Alfred to the Twelfth Century*, Volume 1: *Legislation and its Limits*. Oxford: Blackwell.

CHAPTER 6

ANGLO-SAXON MIGRATION AND THE MOLECULAR EVIDENCE

ROBERT HEDGES

Introduction

Although much has been written about the archaeological evidence for the transition from Roman Britain to Anglo-Saxon England, the demographic perspective has remained elusive. This is particularly frustrating given that such a visible and complete change in customs, language, economy, settlement pattern, and polity took place within what is, geographically and temporally, a well-defined setting. The obvious question, however—what it took for 'continental influences' so rapidly to dominate most of a country following 400 years of Roman rule—cannot be answered without demographic evidence.

The still-developing molecular methodologies in archaeological science hold promise to provide such evidence. In their absence, much thought has been expended in bringing the conventional range of archaeological evidence to bear on this question. This will not be reviewed here (but see Hamerow 2005) although the issue remains wide open. Central to the question is the number of immigrants, their place of origin, their composition in terms of age and gender, and the period and duration of their migration. We would also like to know how the local British population changed—i.e. did it emigrate, die out, become assimilated (and if so, was it clearly differentiated?), or continue separately in a reduced and all but archaeologically invisible form? Except for the question of geographical origin, where the correspondence of cultural traits has provided relatively clear-cut answers which are pleasingly consistent with later written sources, the archaeological evidence only addresses these issues indirectly, and potentially at the expense of a theoretical framework which begs the question in the first place.

Molecular evidence has the strong advantage of avoiding cultural and social assumptions, and so circumvents this element of circular argument. It is much more directly related to the actual demographic processes. Furthermore, at least at the molecular level, interpretation of the data is, in principle, objective. However, as will emerge in the discussion to follow, there are many pitfalls in assessing the significance and reliability of molecular data, mainly due to the uncontrolled context in which past biological events took place. In practice, such methods require a large set of validated data to establish their own reliability, but this is rarely possible. The difficulty is not new—it occurs, for example, though far less severely, with dating—and the main way to deal with it has been to draw on as many different techniques as possible, and to proceed with care and humility. The point is worth emphasizing, because the methods described here owe their current interest to their potential rather than their achievements so far.

The molecular methodologies and their relation to the sample material

There are three methods to be discussed: the analysis of archaeological human bone chemistry as evidence of dietary geography; the molecular analysis of archaeological human bone for genetic information as evidence of population relatedness; and the molecular statistics of living human genomes as evidence of past geographic dispersal. Two of these methods deal directly with information that has been preserved within the archaeological material, while the third relies on the retention within the modern population of local genetic information of the ancient population in the face of subsequent history as a sort of palimpsest.

It may be helpful at this stage to consider how well the skeletal material is likely to represent post-Roman demography. Roughly 10,000 'early' Anglo-Saxon inhumations and cremations have been recovered (Lucy 2000), and they exhibit a wide range of mortuary ritual. Most are from well-defined cemeteries, which in many cases can be associated with nearby settlements, suggesting a more or less direct representation (although we are now recognizing that apparently a single settlement can have several cemeteries associated with it and that large cremation cemeteries, e.g. Spong Hill, must contain the dead of several communities). However, the cemetery assemblages lack a sufficient number of children to represent a demographically realistic population and it is therefore presumed that children were generally buried elsewhere. Inhumations recognizably within the Romano-British tradition are rare (and their dating is problematic), as are settlements.

There is thought to have been a population of 2–4 million in Britain in the third to fourth centuries AD (Millett 1990), and by the end of the fifth century one might suppose around 1 million people in the regions of east and southeast England, which were most heavily influenced by Anglo-Saxon culture. Within less than two centuries, Anglo-Saxon settlement density attained a village about every 2–5 km (Hamerow 2005: 274), at least in some regions where archaeological survey has been most active. Given that excavated settlements typically indicate small communities of about fifty people (to within a factor of two), these numbers imply a total population within southern and eastern England of around 250,000. While the uncertainties here are daunting, the result appears to be realistic. If such a population was reached in 200 years with a growth rate of 1 per cent per year (i.e. slightly less than the current world average growth rate) it would have started with a population of about 30,000. This implies that, to achieve the settlement density observed, there was either a very substantial initial population (tens of thousands) or a sustained high growth rate. However, this assumes no significant contribution to the settlement density and cemeteries from the original Romano-British population, and that assumption is likely to be a false one. Natural causes, other than virulent epidemics, are unlikely to have diminished the British population more rapidly than by 1–2 per cent per year, and while some migration or retreat westwards is likely to have occurred, the question of where the remains of the indigenous population are located is key. Short of fastidious ethnic cleansing, the Romano-British population would have greatly outnumbered the incomers for any feasible assumption of Anglo-Saxon immigration and growth throughout the first and most of the second centuries of immigration. If we focus only on Anglo-Saxon settlements and estimated populations, the total number of living people over the two centuries concerned would have been about 500,000, most of whom would have been alive during the later part, and from which about 2 per cent have been recovered as skeletal remains. This sketch is intended to provide a perspective, rather than to present specific scenarios, although a recent publication which does present such scenarios is considered below.

Molecular techniques

Geographic evidence based on bone chemistry

This evidence is based on the incorporation of certain geographically distinguishable atoms into bone from the diet. The distinction is made possible by measuring the isotopic ratio of the particular atoms, and in this context the useful elements are oxygen and strontium (lead is also sometimes considered). Oxygen (O) isotopes are found to vary geographically, mainly due to processes affecting rainfall and thereby drinking water, while strontium (Sr) isotopes are locally determined by the formation age of the underlying rock, although these processes can be complicated by subsequent geological mixing, soil development, and plant uptake. The bones of humans eating plants or drinking water become 'labelled' with the local isotopic values from these elements. There is additional isotopic alteration for the light element oxygen during metabolism in animals; this, however, is fairly well understood and accounted for. Each isotope provides independent evidence, and both have been exploited in a number of studies (e.g. Muller *et al.* 2003; Knudson and Price 2007).

Under ideal conditions isotopic approaches appear to work well, although even then it is difficult to provide independent verification. What is meant by 'working well' is that human individuals can be recognized whose bones (or, more usually and reliably, teeth) have an isotopic signature that indicates a geographic origin during childhood which is different from where they have been buried. The relevance to Anglo-Saxon immigration is that such an approach might identify individuals buried in English cemeteries whose bones or teeth were formed in, say, north-western Continental Europe. The method would thus identify actual immigrants.

There are, however, several reasons why the method may not be able to provide useful information in this particular case, and why a degree of optimism is needed to deploy isotopic methods to try and resolve the Anglo-Saxon issue. The fundamental problem is whether sufficient and consistent isotopic differences exist between English sites and the continental regions from which the immigrants originated. Such differences (the 'signal') must be much greater than the variability found in a local population (the 'noise'), especially since recognition is essentially on an individual, rather than a statistical basis. For various complicated reasons, we do not know, a priori, how much consistent difference to expect, except that it should be rather small. One way to address this is to measure bones of local animals that would not have migrated (see, for example, Bentley *et al.* 2004). There are two further difficulties. It is known that bones during burial can and do alter in their Sr isotope values, as well as in their O isotope values (at least when measured on the carbonate fraction—the phosphate fraction is more stable, but technically more difficult to measure). Therefore tooth enamel rather than bone is usually measured, so revealing the geography of early diet (that is, within the first 3–8 years or so when enamel is forming). Secondly, sampling problems can be formidable. If, say, one in ten skeletons are immigrants (and this seems a high number, though based on the earlier suggestion of 30,000 growing to 250,000), then at least forty individuals per cemetery need to be measured to obtain a very rough estimate of the scale of immigration (i.e. to within a factor of two). In practice, with a less than complete distinction in geographical isotope signal, the number would need to be greater.

Work has, however, started. Strontium seems a better bet than oxygen, both because the signal has a chance to be more definite (O isotopes in precipitation in eastern England are not very different from e.g. Denmark) and because there are fewer metabolic complications (for example, O isotopes are altered in teeth during nursing). One encouraging aspect of this is that the complexity of burial rites (such as the quantity and variety of grave goods) might enable any discovered Sr pattern to be linked to behaviour—e.g. correlating with males buried with weapons—and provided the association is unambiguous, this would help validate the approach.

So far, two papers have been published which take the first steps towards addressing this issue. In particular, Montgomery *et al.* (2005) gives a very useful account of the issues involved, with more detail than is possible here. In that work, a single Anglian cemetery (West Heslerton, in east Yorkshire) was studied for Sr and O isotopic variation as well as lead (Pb). Tooth enamel from some forty individuals was analysed for Sr, and while small but suggestive differences were observed within the Anglian population as a whole, no convincing signal of different geographic origins, either at the individual or culturally-defined group level, was found. This may have been either because there were immigrants but they were not different in their isotopic composition or because there were no immigrants in the sample, so the outcome was inconclusive. The work does nevertheless demonstrate the complications that arise, especially in the absence of relevant 'control' samples (such as known contemporary non-Anglian individuals). For example, some slight statistically discernible isotopic differences were indeed found, but it was suggested these could just as well be due to (unidentified) food supplies from different and less local sources. The finding that those who died as children were apparently more definitively 'local' than the adult population also suggests that locality might be present as a weak isotopic signal, or that the children's diet differed. An earlier study, to characterize local Sr isotope compositions for Anglo-Saxon burials (Evans and Tatham 2004), gives an indication of the data necessary to help define the problem.

In an interesting analogous study published on a Romano-British cemetery in southern England (Evans *et al.* 2006) the strengths and weaknesses of the methodology in action can be appreciated for a situation where the outcome was more useful and definite (and, significantly, where the putative geographical distinction was very much greater). Whether Sr isotopy can ever usefully address the question of Anglo-Saxon migration remains to be tested—a first step would be to characterize the compositions of Continental examples.

Population shifts from ancient DNA evidence

We turn now to the possibility of distinguishing populations on the basis of surviving information about their genetic composition. Even for modern populations with full availability of genetic information, genetic distinctions between different populations are patchy at best. There may, however, have been useful distinctions between Continental Anglo-Saxon and Romano-British populations; it is primarily a question of showing that English Anglo-Saxon cemeteries as a whole are genetically much more like Continental Anglo-Saxons than like Romano-British cemeteries (or not). Genetic distinctions can be based on DNA that is only maternally inherited (that is, DNA found not at the nucleus in chromosomes but in the numerous cell organelles known as mitochondria), or that is only paternally inherited (that is, DNA in the Y-Chromosome), or DNA in which copies from both parents can be represented (autosomal DNA). Because of recombination between parental copies, autosomal DNA does not enable genealogies to be constructed, and is mainly useful at a population rather than an individual level; most work in following populations has been done with mtDNA and Y-chromosomal DNA.

Whether ancient DNA (aDNA) can be used at all depends on whether any DNA survives, and despite nearly twenty years of work, the ability to recover human aDNA from most archaeological contexts is still extremely limited. With the exception of permafrost, most burial sites are not conducive to good preservation, and original DNA becomes both lost and damaged. Most work focuses on recovering mtDNA, which is present in far more copies than nuclear DNA and thus more likely to be recovered. To cope with the loss and damage to DNA, extremely sensitive methods have been developed—based on the 'polymerase chain reaction' (PCR) method—but these are liable to favour the detection of contaminating DNA (which is less damaged), which furthermore cannot be easily distinguished, especially when the DNA being sought is so similar to that of the investigators. (The situation is easier in recovering aDNA from Neanderthals).

Therefore ancient DNA studies, especially on humans, have a very chequered record, yielding results which are comparatively meagre for the effort involved, and furthermore are extremely difficult to corroborate. It follows that aDNA human studies have tended to focus on unusually well-preserved specimens and/or projects in which the genetic distinctions between populations can be expected to be very clear. Anglo-Saxon burials fulfil neither of these criteria. Furthermore, although mtDNA, being more abundant, is easier to detect, a Y-chromosomal difference might be more likely if the Anglo-Saxon migration was in fact a military invasion rather than a population movement. Nevertheless, there is now one recently published study on Anglo-Saxon mtDNA (Töpf *et al.* 2006) which, while not providing definitive answers, does give a sense of what is involved, and so is described in some detail below.

In this research, ancient mtDNA was successfully detected and analysed from five sites—Newark Street near Leicester (fourth century Romano-British), Buckland near Dover (fifth–sixth century), Norton near Cleveland Market (sixth century), Market Lavington near Salisbury (sixth–seventh century) and Castle Mall in Norwich (tenth century)—from teeth from a total of 48 individuals out of a starting collection of 160. The genetical types (haplotypes) were identified, verified, and compared with the geographical distribution found within modern Europe. While all the sites show haplotypes that conform generally to familiar mitochondrial lineages identified in contemporary north-west Europe, the authors found a statistically significant difference between the mitochondrial genetic make-up from the much-later Norwich site and that of the earlier sites when taken together. The authors discuss how this might have come about in terms of Mesolithic populations occupying 'Doggerland', i.e. the former land bridge between Denmark and England. It is difficult to see how this study could address the question of Anglo-Saxon immigration given the samples available. One would require adequate Romano-British samples to establish a pattern from before, and ideally a comparison with, fifth- to sixth-century Continental populations, to see what differences could then be expected, in addition to a sufficient representation of burials from early Anglo-Saxon cemeteries in England. When one bears in mind that samples selected should be teeth, that at least two in three are likely to give no results, and that any results have to be rigorously and elaborately checked (such as independent corroboration by separate collaborating research groups), the magnitude of the task is apparent. Furthermore, this, at best, addresses only the female half of the problem—the Y-chromosomal evidence will be even more challenging to procure. Nevertheless, aDNA does provide the keys to this problem, even if the effort of recognizing and then repairing the locks will be arduous and expensive.

Using genetic information from living populations

Results more relevant to Anglo-Saxon immigration have been achieved from the wealth of genetic data now technically available on contemporary populations. The research is shaped by two main issues: firstly, our knowledge of genetic variation between individuals and within 'ethnic groups', while very large in terms of current data, is still very small in terms of the total variation that exists; second, to reconstruct past population-genetics events from present genetic distributions relies on selecting scenarios and initial conditions from an overwhelming range of possible histories, inviting both subjective interpretation and the need for ever more context.

Essentially, the most variable regions identified in human DNA have been studied in samples taken from living humans, in relation to geographic, ethnic (e.g. Ashkenazi Jews) and linguistic patterning. Variability in mtDNA (which accounts for only 1/200,000th of the total genomic DNA sequence) is reasonably well understood; that for the Y-Chromosome is becoming quite well characterized. Both of these genetic systems, as mentioned, allow genealogies to be constructed and can provide historical evidence for female- or male-only mating patterns. For example, Y-chromosomal variation has been shown to correlate well with (male-inherited) surnames in England. Many other patterns of variability exist in the remaining twenty-two chromosomes, of which some represent selective effects, while many are apparently random, but if distinctive enough, they can act as 'labels' within a breeding population. Given the genealogical potential from mt- and Y-DNA data, it is natural to analyse current genetic variability in terms of historical processes including mutation within the inherited sequences as well as admixture between populations. Thus the patterns found can be interpreted as having a time depth set by known mutation rates, helping to provide a historical dimension for understanding how populations come to differ geographically. In this way, European population prehistory from the Palaeolithic to beyond the Neolithic has been reconstructed (see, for example, Semino *et al.* 2000, Simoni *et al.* 2000, and Richards *et al.* 2002). Although the present outcome remains highly provisional and somewhat controversial, it does provide specific hypotheses for further work. It also provides a framework of haplotype distributions (that is, DNA sequences inherited together) of populations in time and space, which is the background for the more recent population history in Europe (where time has been too short for mutations).

The fact that a sensible European history can be reconstructed at all shows that the deeper roots of human genetic differences have not been completely obscured by subsequent migrations. Nevertheless, the issue of how much overprinting of a geographically based genetic pattern is brought about by subsequent population movements will always be relevant, the more so where genetic differences are liable to be slight. This appears to be the case for genetic distributions in England, and several papers have addressed this. Summarizing and relating them is not straightforward because they have tended to sample different populations, with different aims in mind. Given that the present distribution is the culmination of all of history, it is not surprising that one cannot use it to address one historical event in isolation.

Our current understanding of the British background is taken from two studies (Wilson *et al.* 2001 and McEvoy *et al.* 2004) which have examined Y-, mt-, and recombining DNA variation in Britain in relation to the overall Continental variation. Their specific aim was to detect any signal showing that Celtic peoples (represented principally by samples from Ireland) have genetic affinities with those in Central Europe, on the basis of a hypothetical Iron Age immigration. No such signal was found, although a general homogeneity of Atlantic genetic composition was demonstrated. The results, rather like those discussed in Töpf *et al.* (2006) on aDNA, are discussed in terms of pre-Neolithic distributions in Europe, although the effects of Viking migration, e.g. in the Orkneys, are taken into account. No sites from eastern England were sampled, so that there is no direct connection with the specific question of Anglo-Saxon immigration. It is also worth pointing out that the studies, especially Wilson *et al.* (2001), were interested in comparing differences in male and female immigration histories, although following McEvoy *et al.* (2004), essentially none was found.

A more direct attack on the Anglo-Saxon question was published by Weale *et al.* in 2002, in which 313 people from seven English and Welsh towns in an east–west transect were analysed for Y-chromosome variants, and compared to those from the Frisian islands, Norway, etc. They showed a clear difference between England and Wales, with the current English population similar to Friesland rather than to Norway, and on this basis the author argued for a 50 per cent contribution to present day English male genes from an Anglo-Saxon introgression. This would seem to be a clear and bold claim, although the paper includes several caveats, in particular the possibility that the signal is due to Danish (rather than Norwegian) Viking immigration. In fact it is quite difficult to establish that such introgression was not substantially earlier or later, although population growth models, which have their own assumptions to consider, work best for the Anglo-Saxon period.

This work was followed by a wider geographic sampling by Capelli *et al.* in 2003, although it included only three clearly Anglo-Saxon towns out of a total of twenty-four sampled in the British Isles. The more recent paper confirms the strong east–west variation in Y-chromosome composition in the present-day British Isles, but does not help resolve the question of how this arose. Indeed, the difficulty of distinguishing Anglo-Saxon and Viking immigrations became clearer. At present, therefore, the available evidence can be used to support a hypothesis of substantial Anglo-Saxon immigration, or to support numerous alternative and rather less well formulated immigrations, from prehistoric to post-Conquest times. However, the existing data do at least establish a genetic difference across present-day Britain (in males; the situation for females is far less clear) which points to large-scale movement from the Continent.

This issue has been taken further in a recent paper (Thomas *et al.* 2006) which presents demographic models of how a realistic Anglo-Saxon immigration could give rise to the large putative contribution to Y-chromosome haplotypes observed in contemporary England. This is essentially a fleshing-out of the demographic issues raised in the introduction to this paper, however with the emphasis on genetic descent. That is, for such a high proportion of Anglo-Saxon

Y-chromosomal genes to be currently present, either the Anglo-Saxon immigration was numerically overwhelming, or a smaller number of immigrants must have reproduced faster than the local population and furthermore ensured this selective advantage applied only to their own genetic stock. Thomas *et al.* call this second possibility 'apartheid', and, to explain the data, show that the selective advantage must be strong (10–20 per cent), long lasting (200–250 years), and rather rigidly maintained for the ancestral male genotype, for this explanation to work.

The main advantage of such an explicit model is the questions it brings into focus. For example, were the initially much more numerous but selectively disadvantaged native Britons buried in Anglo-Saxon cemeteries, or elsewhere? If buried together, does the burial evidence suggest any marked difference between natives and immigrants in both social and reproductive fitness? The model, with an approximately constant population, implies that early on, the differential selection would more likely be towards rapid growth of the newcomers, rather than a catastrophic local population decline (although the bringing of new diseases to the island might have such an effect). After time, as the balance of the two separate populations changed, differential reproduction would come about mainly through the decline of the remaining British population. This suggests that influences on reproductive survival would have been altering over time, in order to establish and maintain an ascendance of Anglo-Saxon Y-haplotypes.

Actually, many feasible scenarios can be constructed, with analogues of genocide, ethnic cleansing, enslavement, social demoralization, as well as more biological ones of disease epidemics and access to adequate nutrition. None has been so far identified in the archaeological record. The paper shows that a gradual and less dramatic decline over centuries, for whatever reason, could also be effective. It should be borne in mind that this argument has been proposed to account for a particular interpretation of the current genetic distribution—as due to Anglo-Saxon genetic introgression—which is by no means universally accepted in any case (because it cannot be separated from other, especially later, genetic introgressions from the Continent). The interpretation could be tested if, or when, Y-chromosomal aDNA were recovered from Anglo-Saxon cemeteries, and this still seems the best way for a definitive solution. In contrast to aDNA studies, however, which are wholly dependent on the survival of original DNA, modern DNA studies can expect to increase in scope and power, benefiting from the extraordinary increase in molecular genetic knowledge driven by biomedical research. Genetic systems may well be discovered in future which enable much more finely resolved geographical differences to be identified, despite subsequent population turbulence.

CONCLUSION

At first sight, the techniques described here promise to provide the answers to enduring questions about Anglo-Saxon demography. Their current lack of unequivocal success is no reason to become disillusioned. The problem is harder than at first it looks; the knowledge these techniques deploy is still developing and experience of application is still quite limited. It is more a matter of time, rather than of luck, for the molecular genetic methods to reach more definitive conclusions—though given the resources and knowledge needed, this may not be very soon. In order to identify immigrants through bone isotopic chemistry, however, some luck (principally in finding isotopic differences in a well-controlled setting) will be essential.

The methods described are making a contribution by providing their own perspective and focus on enduring questions. Demographic issues need to be thought through and related to evidence such as, for example, the diet of populations and life histories of individuals. In particular, the absence of evidence concerning the demographic fate of those with indigenous traditions contrasts uneasily with the abundance of evidence for the bearers of the incoming culture, and this major archaeological challenge is highlighted when it comes to interpreting the molecular data.

REFERENCES

BENTLEY, R. A., PRICE, T. D., and STEPHAN, E. (2004). 'Determining the "local" $87Sr/86Sr$ range for archaeological skeletons: a case study from Neolithic Europe'. *Journal of Archaeological Science* 31(4): 365–75.

CAPELLI, C., REDHEAD, N., ABERNETHY, J. K., GRATRIX, F., WILSON, J. F., MOEN, T., HERVIG, T., RICHARDS, M., STUMPF, M. P. H., UNDERHILL, P. A., BRADSHAW, P., SHAHA, A., THOMAS, M. G., BRADMAN, N., and GOLDSTEIN, D. B. (2003). 'A Y chromosome census of the British Isles'. *Current Biology* 13(11): 979–84.

EVANS, J. A., and TATHAM, S. (2004). 'Defining "local signature" in terms of Sr isotope composition using a tenth- to twelfth-century Anglo-Saxon population living on a Jurassic clay-carbonate terrain, Rutland, UK.' *Geological Society Special Publication* 232: 237–48.

—— STOODLEY, N., and CHENERY, C. (2006). 'A strontium and oxygen isotope assessment of a possible fourth century immigrant population in a Hampshire cemetery, southern England'. *Journal of Archaeological Science* 33(2): 265–72.

HAMEROW, H. (2005). 'The earliest Anglo-Saxon kingdoms,' in P. Fouracre (ed.), *The New Cambridge Medieval History*, Volume 1. Cambridge: Cambridge University Press.

KNUDSON, K. J., and PRICE, T. D. (2007). 'Utility of multiple chemical techniques in archaeological residential mobility studies: case studies from Tiwanaku- and Chiribaya-affiliated sites in the Andes'. *American Journal of Physical Anthropology* 132(1): 25–39.

LUCY, S. (2000) *The Anglo-Saxon Way of Death*. Stroud: Sutton Publishing.

MCEVOY, B., RICHARDS, M., FORSTER, P., and BRADLEY, D. (2004). 'The longue duree? of genetic ancestry: multiple genetic marker systems and celtic origins on the atlantic facade of Europe'. *American Journal of Human Genetics* 75(4): 693–702.

MILLETT, M. (1990). *The Romanization of Britain: An Essay in Archaeological Interpretation*. New York: Cambridge University Press.

MONTGOMERY, J., EVANS, J. A., POWLESLAND, D., and ROBERTS, C.A. (2005). 'Continuity or colonization in Anglo-Saxon England? Isotope evidence for mobility, subsistence practice, and status at West Heslerton'. *American Journal of Physical Anthropology* 126(2): 123–38.

MULLER, W., FRICKE, H., HALLIDAY, A. N., MCCULLOCH, M. T., and WARTHO, J.-A. (2003). 'Origin and Migration of the Alpine Iceman'. *Science* 302 (5646): 862–6.

RICHARDS, M., MACAULAY, V., TORRONI, A., and BANDELT, H.-J. (2002). 'In search of geographical patterns in European mitochondrial DNA'. *American Journal of Human Genetics* 71(5): 1168–74.

SEMINO, O., PASSARINO, G., OEFNER, P. J., LIN, A. A., ARBUZOVA, S., BECKMAN, L. E., DE BENEDICTIS, G., FRANCALACCI, P., KOUVATSI, A., LIMBORSKA, S., MARCIKIAE, M., MIKA, A., MIKA, B., PRIMORAC, D., SANTACHIARA-BENERECETTI, A. S., CAVALLI-SFORZA, L. L., and UNDERHILL, P. A. (2000). 'The genetic legacy of paleolithic Homo sapiens sapiens in extant Europeans: a Y chromosome perspective'. *Science* 290 (5494): 1155–9.

SIMONI, L., CALAFELL, F., PETTENER, D., BERTRANPETIT, J., and BARBUJANI, G. (2000). 'Geographic patterns of mtDNA diversity in Europe'. *American Journal of Human Genetics* 66(1): 262–78.

THOMAS, M. G., STUMPF, M. P. H., and HÄRKE, H.(2006). 'Evidence for an apartheid-like social structure in early Anglo-Saxon England'. *Proceedings of the Royal Society – Biological Sciences (Series B)* 273(1601): 2651–7.

TÖPF, A. L., GILBERT, M. T. P., DUMBACHER, J. P., and HOELZEL, A. R. (2006). 'Tracing the phylogeography of human populations in Britain based on 4th–11th century mtDNA genotypes'. *Molecular Biology and Evolution* 23(1): 152–61.

WEALE, M. E., WEISS, D. A., JAGER, R. F., BRADMAN, N., and THOMAS, M. G. (2002). 'Y chromosome evidence for Anglo-Saxon mass migration'. *Molecular Biology and Evolution* 19(7): 1008–21.

WILSON, J. F., WEISS, D. A., RICHARDS, M., THOMAS, M. G., BRADMAN, N., GOLDSTEIN, D. B. (2001). 'Genetic evidence for different male and female roles during cultural transitions in the British Isles'. *Proceedings of the National Academy of Sciences of the United States of America* 98(9): 5078–83.

CHAPTER 7

DRESS AND IDENTITY

GALE R. OWEN-CROCKER

INTRODUCTION: NOW AND THEN

We live in a world where royalty wear denim and where artificial diamonds gleam as brightly as gemstones. The coy icons on the doors of public toilets preserve the illusion of a gender distinction in the human silhouette which is now outmoded—most women wear trousers (though few western European men would wear a skirt). Despite the unisex shapes of today's garments, there are subtle male/female distinctions in terms of appropriate fabric, cut, and colour, to contravene which is considered to be 'making a statement'. Our fashions change year by year as a result of deliberate economic intent: a market has been created to fund a profit-making industry. We are subject to advertising, media-created role models, and peer pressure—many a seasonal student dress-style would not be found in fashion magazines. We own lots of clothes and we go shopping for them, trying on different items or the same garment in different sizes until we find something that 'suits' us. We have large mirrors to consider the effect. We buy on whim, not just for necessity, and when we are tired of a garment or it has got shabby we throw it away or recycle it to a charity. Rarely in western Europe and America does anyone repair clothes, though the drudgery of patching and darning is just a couple of generations distant. Laundry, on the other hand, has become a daily necessity; many garments are only worn once before washing. We have many fabrics, natural, 'man-made', and mixed. Some garments are knitted; they have elasticity. Clothing is machine made and mass-produced. We have a choice of colours and patterns; fabrics can be printed.

Globalization means that western European dress is worn world-wide. Most countries, however, (except England) retain a national dress and regional variations of it, sometimes reserved for special occasions—a Japanese girl may wear a *kimono* for her graduation. Most European traditional costumes are relatively modern, but outside Europe, older traditions survive: the origins of the *kimono* are contemporary with Anglo-Saxon England; the Indian *dhoti* and *sari* are far older. Religious observers often wear traditional garments, sometimes one sex or the other manifesting the faith. Intriguingly, although the shape is maintained, modern materials are accepted: the *tallit*, or prayer shawl, of the orthodox Jewish man, traditionally made of wool, is now available in acrylic fibres; the Islamic woman's *niqab*, a cover for the face, may come with elastic or velcro fastenings.

Cultures where modern European dress is regularly worn may adopt archaic dress for formal and ceremonial occasions: legal procedures, coronations and investitures, parades. It may be anachronistic for a contemporary soldier to strap on a sword, but that is part of his 'dress uniform'; adopting a wig may be a seventeenth-century practice but the act carries with it the historical authority of the procedure of justice. Occupational uniforms are still worn but have lost much of the military flavour which characterized them a hundred years ago. They are regularly updated to take account of fashion and, as in the case of flight attendants, to make the wearers attractive to the customers.

The following aspects of twenty-first century clothing and identity are taken for granted:

- A choice of natural and man-made fibres; mechanization and mass-production
- Commercial distribution and customer choice
- Economically-driven fashion changes accompanied by acceptance of obsolescence and a decrease in repairing
- The ownership of a wardrobe of clothes which are regularly changed, laundered, and selected
- Global fashion, which is effectively western European
- Blurring of gender and social distinctions in dress-style
- Selective use of traditional costumes for religious, ceremonial, and festive purposes

The following discussion considers the evidence for Anglo-Saxon dress in relation to these criteria.

Raw Materials and Manufacture

In Anglo-Saxon times only 'natural' fibres were available: wool from sheep, linen from flax; and imported silk, unravelled from the cocoon of the silk moth.[1] Domesticated sheep were exploited for milk, cheese, meat, parchment, and leather as well as fleece. There was a variety of breeds—primitive brown woolly sheep, white sheep introduced by the Romans and black-faced sheep with more hairy wool, introduced by the Vikings—and a good standard of wools (Ryder 1964; 1974). Seasonal shearing was probably introduced later, so Anglo-Saxons may have relied on wool from moulting and individual plucking or shearing of animals as required. Natural wool colours ranged from white through shades of brown to black, and therefore clothing could be made in a variety of tones without dyeing. Woollen garments could be produced quickly since wool can be used straight from the fleece, with fibres pulled out of the mass and twisted with the fingers; better results are achieved, however, if the wool is first cleared of twigs and other attachments, washed to remove grease, and untangled by combing.

Linen production was a longer process, involving planting flax seed, weeding, harvesting, removal of seed pods, retting (rotting) the woody stems in water or a dewy field, drying, beating, and 'scutching' the flax stems to break them and release the fibres inside, then repeated heckling or combing of those fibres to prepare them for spinning.

Silk was not cultivated in Britain, but imported, as finished garments, lengths of cloth, or sewing/embroidery threads. It has been suggested that silk weaving was carried out in England on the basis of the supposed 'insular design' of a piece of woven silk, now in Maaseik, Belgium (Calberg 1951; Budny and Tweddle 1984; the silk bears a representation of the biblical King David) but it is limited evidence on which to build a supposed industry. 'Insular design' may have influenced workshops outside England, and in any case designer and artisan need not operate in the same place.

Wool and linen thread was made by spinning the fibres with the fingers and a drop spindle, which rotated with the aid of a whorl, a large bead of stone, glass, clay, or more rarely amber or jet, that acted as a flywheel. Spindle whorls are frequent archaeological finds. Spun fibre was woven into cloth. The traditional weaving equipment of north-west Europe was a relatively simple device, called in modern times 'the warp-weighted loom' (Hoffmann 1964), consisting of heavy

---

[1] Other fibres were potentially available, but they do not seem to have been much used: goat hair and horse tail hair are attested, and there is some recent evidence of hemp; fibre can be made from the nettle plant but has not been found in an Anglo-Saxon context. Cotton was being used in China but did not reach England at this time and was not imported from the West Indies and America until the sixteenth century.

wooden uprights leaning against a wall and supporting a horizontal beam to which warp threads are attached. The warp threads hang down and are tied in groups to annular weights (Fig. 24.2). Clay loom-weights and double-ended pin-beaters used with this loom are common finds on early and mid Saxon occupation sites and metal sword-shaped beaters appear in high-status female graves.[2] This loom type is suited to making the plain weave ('tabby'), simple twill, and more complex patterned twills which are well attested by archaeological finds (Coatsworth and Owen-Crocker 2007). It is a matter of discussion whether the relatively uncommon 2 x 1 twills, which are not ideally suited to the warp-weighted loom, were also made on this loom or if they were products of a different technique and survivals of a Celtic minority culture among the Anglo-Saxons. It was suggested in a series of publications by Elisabeth Crowfoot that a two-beam loom (which has a second horizontal strut instead of the free-hanging weights at the bottom) was used to produce this cloth. I have discussed the evidence elsewhere (Owen-Crocker 2007). Penelope Walton Rogers (2007: 110) distinguishes between 2 x 1 twills on sites with Roman ancestry and high status and Kentish sites where the textiles may be imports.

Recent debates concern the use of different textile types in early Anglo-Saxon England—relative preferences for linen or wool and the use of different spinning and weaving techniques: Z/Z and Z/S spinning, tabby, simple twill, and patterned twill. While either linen or wool could be used for the *peplos* which was the characteristic early Anglo-Saxon female garment, there has been scholarly discussion of whether a preference for one fibre over the other was a matter of chronological development or related to regional and wider geographical contexts. Recent research suggests changes began in eastern England, reflecting developments across the North Sea, passing more slowly to West Saxon areas (Walton Rogers 2007: 104–9).

A decline in the use of the warp-weighted loom from the mid ninth century is indicated by the diminution of loom-weights and double-ended pin-beaters on the archaeological scene. The appearance of single-ended pin-beaters, characteristic of the two-beam loom, suggests this device was introduced, or re-introduced, at that time. In towns the two-beam loom was rapidly replaced by the horizontal treadle loom (introduced c. AD 1000), though vertical looms survived for specialist weaving (Walton Rogers 2001). Textile production until this point had been traditionally female work (Walton Rogers 2007: 9–47), and spinning remained so until the Industrial Revolution (the introduction of the spinning wheel in c.1400 speeded up production but it was still hand- and later foot-operated and used by women); but the treadle loom, which was capable of weaving long pieces of cloth, and was more productive than vertical looms, was operated by men. The development of towns went hand-in-hand with commercial production. With the transfer to male

---

[2] Beaters were used for compacting the weft. These metal examples are probably symbolic and prestigious, the possessions of women who owned weaving workshops and weavers. The beaters used by the workers were probably bone or wood.

operatives, weaving became a professional craft which, not much later in the Middle Ages, would be formalized into guilds (Walton Rogers 2003). The increased output of weavers must have increased the demand for spun thread, attested to some extent by what appears to be an increasingly organized production of spindle whorls in the later Anglo-Saxon period (Henry 1999).

The Anglo-Saxons also made narrow bands and cords by non-loom processes, particularly tablet weaving. Tablet-woven bands, which have warp threads twined together as well as a weft thread, are strong yet flexible. They were used for edging garments, and probably for belts and straps. Knitting was not introduced until the sixteenth century, although the Scandinavian technique of *nålebinding*, which employs a single needle and the fingers of one hand, is attested by an archaeological find of a woollen sock from Anglo-Viking York (Walton 1989: 341–5, 435).

One of the differences between hand-production and today's mechanization is time. For the Anglo-Saxons, hours and weeks might pass between the conception of a garment and its completion. We can assume garments were valued accordingly. The opportunity for replacement of clothes was limited by resources, financial and material, so garments would be darned and patched. Some may not always have been made from new material in the first place, but cobbled together from recycled pieces, like an ancient tunic from Bernuthsfeld, Germany (Farke 1998). Garments such as leg-wraps were probably not always purpose-made, but contrived for warmth from worn-out items like those found with a fourteenth-century male burial excavated in Boksten, Sweden (Nockert 1982; Owen-Crocker 2004: 257, fig. 210).

Cloth could be dyed at any stage in the process. Wool may be dyed in the fleece, as spun threads, or as a finished piece of weaving. However, dye-testing of textile from Anglo-Saxon graves has proved negative apart from some tablet-woven bands which edged women's sleeves. This may mean that artificial pigment was never present, or that colour has been lost over centuries of burial. There is evidence of dyeing in an urban context, in the form of waste from a woad vat in Anglo-Viking York (Hall 1997; Walton Rogers 1997: 1766–71; 2002) and traces of the dye-plants dyer's greenweed, madder, and weld. Other potential sources of dye are lichens and barks. The remarkable survival of colours in the woollen embroidery threads of the eleventh-century Bayeux Tapestry demonstrates the competence of dyers and the durability of pigments. The Bayeux Tapestry has ten colours, shades of green, blue, red, brown, and yellow, all made from a combination of indigotin, madder, and woad (Bédat and Girault-Kurtzeman 2004). Surviving Anglo-Saxon silk embroideries also include many colours. The merchant character in Ælfric's *Colloquy* claims to import both silks and dyestuffs. Kermes, an expensive, imported insect dye which produced bright red colouring, has been attested from England, for example at Coppergate, York (Tweddle 1989). Another desirable colour was purple, which could be produced from lichen but at its most prestigious was derived from whelks.

It is probable that garments were not washed much. Washing might fade any artificial dyes that had been used, and laundering would decrease the natural weather-proof qualities of wool, the fibres of which cling to one another with tiny hooks. The weave of surviving textile fragments is usually visible; there is no felting, which frequent washing might produce.[3]

Some garments were not tailored: they were wrapped round the body and secured by a fastener. Other garments required sewing, and we should remember that every tool was handmade, from the bone or metal sewing needle, with its tiny eye through which the thread passed, to shears for cutting the cloth. It is not known if every household or family unit in the early Anglo-Saxon village produced its own clothes, or if there were specialists. By the mid Saxon period, rural estates probably supported workshops which provided clothing for their dependents. This is also true of monastic houses[4] which, in addition to clothing monks and nuns, would make and maintain mass vestments. Materials might be purchased by patrons or financed by bequests.

Garments were secured by brooches, buckles, clasps, and pins. Most surviving examples are metal: iron, copper alloy (bronze), silver, or gold, or combinations of these. The precious metals were acquired by melting down older objects, including Roman coins. Many brooches and buckles were decorated on the visible face, by techniques including casting, engraving, and inlaying. Anglo-Saxon metalwork was skilled and sophisticated (Coatsworth and Pinder 2002). Its exponents learned from and surpassed foreign craftsmen, as shown by the Sutton Hoo, Suffolk, jewellers' adaptation of Celtic millefiori glass inlays, and the Kentish development of Frankish techniques into magnificent gold and garnet cloisonné jewellery.

Although near-identical items of metalwork could be made by casting, hand-manufacture produced distinctions even between pairs of brooches intended to be matching. Dress ornaments can be categorized by shape and size, and their decoration labelled according to style, but it is the variety of metalwork which impresses. Metal jewellery, above all, informs us about the identity of early Anglo-Saxons. Some items, such as brooches and wrist clasps, are gender-related. Status is reflected in size, complexity of decoration, and use of gold, silver, and garnet. Typology may relate to ethnicity and regional affinities. If decorative motifs on metalwork, such as birds, horse-heads, interlaced snakes, and human faces, were originally significant, this jewellery may have been linked to the identity of its original owner, having personal, amuletic, or religious meaning now lost. Engraved personal names on ninth- to eleventh-century jewellery suggest intimate links between artefacts and owners. Inscriptions sometimes personify the brooch or ring: a silver disc from Cuxton, Kent, proclaims *Ælfgivv me ah*, 'Ælfgivu owns me'. Its central ornament depicts a bird of prey and its victim (Wilson 1964: no. 14, plate

---

[3] Deliberate felting of wool by teaselling and fulling, was, as part of complex finishing processes, extensively practised in the later Middle Ages, but is rarely suggested by surviving Anglo-Saxon textiles.

[4] The term 'monastic' includes both female convents and male monasteries, as well as the double houses, for men and women, which were popular in England until the Viking Age.

XVII). We do not know if this reflected the lady's enjoyment of falconry; or was simply a 'stock' jeweller's motif (the Sutton Hoo purse-lid, three centuries earlier, includes a similar motif).

Few dress fasteners of organic materials survive (Owen-Crocker 2004: 46), though sufficient other items survive from urban sites to demonstrate that the Anglo-Saxons were skilled at working bone, horn, antler, and wood. Some of the inhumations found in Anglo-Saxon cemeteries without metalwork may have been supplied with organic fasteners.

Animal skins were tanned and worked into leather. There is evidence that the skin of mature cattle, calf, deer, goat, pig, and sheep was used (Watson 1998: 234), though generally only small fragments of leather survive, attached to buckles, to items found bunched at the hips and, in some Lincolnshire cemeteries, to wrist clasps. Leather was therefore used for belts, suspension straps, and cuffs, though not by everyone and not uniformly in every area. Survival of fur is rare, though it makes sense to suppose that fleeces and furs were used as linings and as warm garments. Penelope Walton Rogers (2007: 172) has recently identified some buckled capes of animal pelt in women's graves. A simple poncho that exploits the natural shape of the animal, with the human head coming through the neck-hole, as attested from ancient times in northern Europe (Hald 1980: 347–54) could have been made from the skins of domesticated sheep or cattle, which were smaller than today's. Literary evidence confirms the use of fur garments, particularly in the late Anglo-Saxon period (Owen-Crocker 2004: 76–7, 181–2, 244–5; Walton Rogers 2007: 172). Pile-woven cloaks, which probably imitated fur in their shaggy effect, were a high-status alternative for men in the seventh century (Owen-Crocker 2004: 182–3).

Excavation in late Anglo-Saxon and Anglo-Viking London, Winchester, and York has produced many shoes: flat-soled, leather 'turn-shoes' (made inside-out, then turned), thonged (not nailed) together. The commonest type is the ankle-high shoe, but lower slippers and taller boots also survive (Owen-Crocker 2004: 160–2). Evidence of footwear from graves is limited, and known only from the seventh and eighth centuries (Owen-Crocker 2004: 190–1). Its absence from earlier graves may be an accident of survival, or may reflect differences between early and later practices, or of urban and rural life. Agricultural labourers depicted ploughing and sowing in late Anglo-Saxon manuscripts work barefoot, which may be authentic; undeniably it is easier to clean mud off feet than shoes!

Dress and chronology

The Anglo-Saxon period is usually divided into 'early' (mid fifth to seventh centuries), middle (eighth and ninth centuries) and late (tenth and eleventh centuries). The early period can itself be divided into an era of migration and settlement followed by one of political and religious change, with the consolidation of kingdoms and their conversion to Christianity occurring at the end of the sixth and the seventh centuries. The fifth to seventh centuries are characterized by the practice of providing many of the dead with grave-goods. Cemetery archaeology, particularly furnished inhumation, is the richest available source of information on Anglo-Saxon clothing (Owen-Crocker 2004, *passim*, especially pp. 35–132, 138–48, 152–7, 160, 166–7, 190, 194–6; Walton Rogers 2007: 49–247). Metal dress fasteners can be excavated from graves, where they have maintained more-or-less their original position since burial,[5] giving a framework for reconstructing the clothing. Dress accessories often cluster near the hips, suggesting suspension from a belt. Decorative jewellery, especially beads and pendants, may preserve its character and location. Fragments of textile, often but not always mineralized, may be found attached to metalwork, most commonly iron brooch-pins (Coatsworth and Owen-Crocker 2007). The fibre, spin direction, and weave of the cloth can often be identified. Scraps of leather are also preserved on metalwork, particularly on buckles and other belt fittings, but these have not been researched as systematically as the textile remains and there is untapped potential evidence in fragments on older finds of metalwork in museums, if not too deteriorated or contaminated by preservative treatment.

From the evidence of grave-goods it is possible to sketch in reconstructions of clothing. The cemetery finds can be interpreted from comparative material such as Roman sculptures of Germanic men and women, and supplemented by organic artefacts from earlier Scandinavian and later urban Anglo-Saxon/Anglo-Viking archaeological finds. A female 'folk-costume' for women can be reconstructed with some confidence, based on the incidence of brooches worn in pairs at the shoulders. These evidently secured a tubular gown, similar to the Greek *peplos*, which could be worn over a sleeved garment and under a cloak, shawl or cape. The two brooches could be arranged in slightly different positions, and it was possible to clasp the characteristic garment with a single brooch. There are, however, a number of uncertainties about this costume. The gown is generally assumed to be ankle-length (largely because women in antique art and later medieval art are usually represented in long garments), but there is no evidence to confirm it; a recent reconstruction experiments with a long undergown, with a buckled belt suspending items including a knife, then a short *peplos* over it, which could be easily hitched up to reach the tools (Fig. 7.1a; Owen-Crocker 2004: 38). Women's costume was augmented by beads, monochrome and polychrome, of glass, paste, and amber and occasionally crystal. Festoons of beads were suspended between the

---

[5] Sometimes the body appears to have been tipped during burial, displacing jewellery to one side; subsequent disturbance resulting from subsidence of the earth, decomposition of the body, and animal activity may also disturb grave-goods.

Figure 7.1 Reconstructions of early Anglo-Saxon female dress: (a) Short peplos, drawn by Rosalyn Smith; (b) Anglian dress with long peplos, drawn by Christine Wetherell; (c) Frankish coat costume from Kent (illustration by Anthony Barton)

shoulder brooches, and other bead groups were suspended from brooches, attached to girdles, and used individually. (The reconstruction of the order of beadstrings is difficult since the suspension thread is mostly rotted away, and the tiny beads drop among the bones.)

There are regional variations of the folk-costume, notably in Anglian areas where metal wrist clasps, a third, central brooch, and distinctive 'girdle hangers' were worn (Fig. 7.1b). In Kent a different costume including a front-fastening garment and a Frankish-inspired front-fastening jacket over it, involving a total of four brooches, was adopted by women in the sixth century (Fig. 7.1c; Walton Rogers 2007: 189–91). There was a change in women's dress in the seventh century, marked by the disappearance of the paired brooch fashion, apart from very small annular and penannular brooches; occasional, opulent, round brooches were worn singly. Linked pins appeared. There were fewer bead-ornaments than before, and amber largely disappeared. Instead there were simple neck ornaments of small glass beads, and festoons consisting of beads slung on, or across, metal rings, strung from shoulder to shoulder. This fashion remained until at least the late seventh century, as attested by a female grave at Lower Brook Street, Winchester, Hampshire (Hawkes 1990). Amethyst beads, perhaps re-cycled continental pendants, appeared in the seventh century, as did necklaces of gold and silver wire beads hung with metal and garnet pendants, and, a sign of the Christian faith, small jewelled crosses. These were presumably confined to the rich.

The archaeological evidence for the early period, though it exists in profusion, leaves many gaps. Although there is a great deal of evidence of women's dress, most of it comes from the shoulder and chest area, plus remains of bags and tools from the hips; neither the migration/settlement burials nor the seventh-century graves give much evidence for leg- and footwear, and the form of head covering (if any) is largely to be guessed at. We cannot know if the many graves without metal fasteners were occupied by women who wore the same costume fastened by organic pins, or stitched together; or if they wore a different, simpler, costume. The cemetery evidence for male burials is much less consistent than for female, with occasional belt buckles and other belt fittings, and a few pins. The richest male graves—notably the seventh-century barrow burials from Taplow, Buckinghamshire, and Sutton Hoo, and a chamber grave from Prittlewell, Essex—all contain evidence of costume which is unique in some way (see below).

Furnished burial after the seventh century is attested very rarely: the helmet found at Coppergate, York, was probably from a disturbed grave; and an eighth-century female grave at Boss Hall, Ipswich, Suffolk, included a brooch and pendants which had been contained in a bag. Apart from a few cases of this kind, archaeological evidence for dress from the middle and late Saxon periods comprises: stray finds of dress accessories; brooches from hoards; and discarded items from occupation sites, including textile fragments and shoes. These have no associations, skeletal or otherwise, though the latter two categories can often be dated, hoards from coins and urban finds by stratification.

This limited artefactual evidence must be set against surviving texts and representations of dress in later Anglo-Saxon art. Archaeological material augments and contradicts both to a surprising degree! The rare examples of recognizable items of clothing are dissimilar from artistic representations. There is a linen garment excavated from Llan-gors, near Brecon, Powys, Wales, which may date to the destruction of *Brecenanmere* by the forces of Æthelflæd, 'Lady of the Mercians', in 916. Its location suggests that it is Welsh rather than Anglo-Saxon, but as a unique find from the period it demands attention. It was preserved by being charred and subsequently left in waterlogged silt, events which obliterated any colour. About a third of the remaining woven surface is embroidered with birds, animals, and plants, including a border of stylized lions (Granger-Taylor and Pritchard 1991). No Anglo-Saxon art shows such motifs on garments or such extensive decoration. Both art and documentary evidence suggest ornament was mostly confined to garment borders, and as depicted, it is simple and geometric (Fig. 7.2). Artists' suggestions of more extensive decoration are faint and unsystematic; they suggest stylized floral shapes and geometric strips. Likewise, silk caps found in York and Lincoln bear no resemblance to any illustrations in Anglo-Saxon art. They may be a fashion confined to women of Viking stock. The headdresses have been recovered from Viking towns in England; similar caps, made of both wool and silk, have been found in Viking Dublin. However, similar caps were possibly worn under the veils and wimples which are the usual female headdress depicted in Anglo-Saxon manuscripts. Stray finds testify to an increased use of pins, with disc-headed examples occurring in the eighth and ninth centuries, and less decorative ones in the tenth century. Strap-ends are common finds from the late Saxon period, many of them simply made from metal sheet which was folded and riveted, others more complex and decorated. It is impossible to know what proportion of these derive from clothing; neither pins nor strap-ends are typically shown in art.

Brooches of the tenth and eleventh centuries are predominantly circular. The grandest are silver; others are base metal, suggesting that brooch-wear was becoming more widely distributed among social levels. However, there is inconsistency in the evidence about their use: the only personal name engraved on a brooch is a woman's, on the back of an example from Sutton, Isle of Ely, Cambridgeshire (Wilson 1964: 174–7 and plates XXXI–XXXII; Page 1964: 86–8) and, as has been shown, women were the users of brooches in the early Anglo-Saxon period. However, brooches do not generally feature in women's dress in late Anglo-Saxon art, whereas small, round brooches, worn as cloak fasteners, are often depicted on men. They are never decorated, however, and other brooch types which appear occasionally in late Anglo-Saxon archaeology (Owen-Crocker 2004: 206–8) are not represented at all. Although there are archaeological finds of

Figure 7.2 Three types of masculine dress (BL MS Stowe 944, fol. 6v, reproduced by permission of the British Library)

finger rings, some engraved with names, both male and female, finger rings never appear in art; and the penannular torques, arm-, or neck-rings occasionally pictured are not attested from Anglo-Saxon archaeology (Owen-Crocker 2004: 270, figs. 158, 223).

Dress and gender

Dress appears to have been strongly gendered throughout the Anglo-Saxon period. Indisputable instances of cross-dressing—where bones of one sex are accompanied by grave-goods normally associated with the opposite sex—are rare (Walton Rogers 2007: 198–9) and male/female silhouettes are very different in Anglo-Saxon art. Though clothing for both sexes was primarily functional—for warmth and decency—its extra-utilitarian use seems to have been different for men and women. In folk cemeteries, male identity was occasionally stated by belt equipment, but more often by weapons. Female identity, however, seems to have been established through costume. The surviving items are mostly metal dress accessories, which by their different raw materials, shape, size, and decoration testify to the date of the burial and potentially the tribal affiliations, belief system, and the general rank and role of the woman buried.

We cannot know if the costume in which a woman was buried was that which she wore in everyday life; wrist clasps, for example, might have been put on the body to imply that the woman was of a social status where she did not have to roll up her sleeves and work, which may or may not have been true. Brooches of different types might suggest that the woman had originated in one area and moved to another, perhaps on marriage; alternatively some of the brooches might not have belonged to that woman at all but were old trinkets which could be spared for burial. The decoration on jewellery might have been relevant to some characteristic or beliefs of its first owner; but whether that same woman was buried in it, or whether it had changed hands is unknown. Research is now suggesting that the choice of dress, especially the *peplos*, the pin, accessories such as keys and even the weave of the textile worn, may relate to a woman's age and stage of life—particularly to the child-bearing years, and to marriage (Lee 2004; Walton Rogers 2007: 178).

Women's costume changed several times during the Anglo-Saxon period, apparently in response to foreign and religious stimuli, men's hardly at all. The clasps introduced in the late fifth century were, in England, confined to women's wrists. In Scandinavia, men also wore clasps, at ankles as well as wrists, but this male fashion was not imported (Hines 1984: 35–109). The delicate pin suites and tiny

Figure 7.3 Male and female dress (Oxford, Bodleian Library, MS Junius 11, p. 45)

brooches which appeared at the neck in conversion-period cemeteries perhaps fastened light veils, a response to Christian encouragement for women to cover the head. It is possible that the voluminous head covering of women in most late Anglo-Saxon art, either in the form of a scarf wrapped round head and neck or a wimple with an aperture for the face, was itself imported from the Continent, ultimately from the Near East, via Christian art (Fig. 7.3). In the conversion period, jewellery, especially women's, expressed the new faith.

DRESS AND ETHNICITY

Initially the Anglo-Saxon migrants proclaimed their Germanic identity by their choice of dress. This is evidenced archaeologically by the typology and positioning of clothing fasteners. In the first century and a half of the Anglo-Saxon era there was a considerable amount of regional variety in terms of brooch types, use of wrist clasps in Anglian areas, and in the combination of Jutish and Frankish traditions in Kent, which by the mid sixth century was demonstrating a different style of female dress from the rest of Anglo-Saxon England.

Anglo-Saxon clothing styles were subject to influence by an influx of foreign styles and the people that brought them: returning royalty and bishops with their entourages, merchants, diplomats, new immigrants, including brides, visiting ecclesiastics, and raider-settlers. As suggested above, fashion may also have been influenced 'second hand' by the introduction of portable foreign artworks: illuminated manuscripts and ivory carvings. It is likely that any stranger to a region would have been instantly recognizable as such by appearance as well as speech. This visual effect was, however, not so much about the silhouette of the figure as about hair- and beard-styles, shape and decoration of dress accessories such as brooches, buckles, and bags, and, by the end of the Anglo-Saxon period at least, by the characteristic colour of their clothes: a Viking visitor from Dublin to the Anglo-Viking city of York, for instance, might wear purple, and a Viking from Scandinavia blue, whereas madder-dyed red was a favourite among the local population. Natural fleece colours, including black, were typical of Frisians and north Saxons, whereas dyed black identified Rhinelanders, green, Flemings and tawny-red, Swabians (Walton Rogers 1997: 1769). Some foreigners travelled far: Theodore, a seventh-century Greek, became archbishop of Canterbury; Ohthere, a Norwegian who had voyaged to the Arctic, and Wulfstan, who had visited eastern Europe via the Black Sea, visited King Alfred in the ninth century; they were, however, rarities. Frisian merchants from across the North Sea would have been more common. Anglo-Saxon England did not, as far as is known, receive visitors from outside Europe. Exotic goods like silk and lapis lazuli passed through chains of traders and the Anglo-Saxons would never have seen the Chinese or Himalayan workers who produced them.

Apart from lingering northern paganism, reintroduced by Scandinavian settlers, Christianity was the only religion. Christianity was manifested through dress, but the other world-religions which are highly visible now were not experienced by the Anglo-Saxons. There seems to have developed a common basic style of secular dress across Christian Europe which manifested itself for women as long garments worn in layers and headdresses that hooded the whole head, neck, and shoulders; and for men a tunic no longer than the knee, worn over close-fitting trousers, with the optional addition of a rectangular cloak secured by a circular brooch, usually at the right shoulder (Figs. 7.2–3). There were variations, as between open veils, wrap-around scarves, and wimples for women. Evidently there were controversies, for example about the appropriateness of luxurious dress for people in the religious life and the suitability of long gowns for upper class men (Owen-Crocker 2004: 133–7, 173–4). In brief, however, secular figures, distinctly male and female, were clearly distinguishable from ecclesiastics in mass vestments both in life and in art. Furthermore, in art, angels, Christ, and the deity wore the *pallium* and *tunica* of

Roman tradition and so were easily distinguishable from both laymen and ecclesiastics (Fig. 7.2).

Dress and belief

The early Anglo-Saxons were pagans, and they almost certainly acknowledged the northern gods and mythological tales which were recorded centuries later by the Icelander Snorri Sturlusson, familiar to us as 'Norse legends'. The names of major deities, Woden and Thunor, of Eoster, a goddess of the spring, and the winter festival of Yule have been passed down to us in the names of our landscape and seasons; a taste for heroic battles against trolls and dragons is preserved in the Old English poem *Beowulf*. The details of pagan practices and beliefs are lost to us, since the Christian writers who were the Anglo-Saxons' historians had little interest in preserving them. It is clear, however, that early Anglo-Saxons displayed their belief-system on their bodies. The Sutton Hoo purse lid has cloisonné plaques depicting linked horses (the horse was sacred in Germanic belief), a man between two beasts or monsters, which is perhaps mythological, and a bird of prey and its victim. Cruel-beaked birds, together with serpentine animals, appear repeatedly on high-class metalwork, perhaps to protect the wearer, perhaps to remind him or her of legends. The three surviving seventh-century helmets bear protective boar figures: the Benty Grange, Derbyshire, and Wollaston, Northamptonshire, helmets have boar crests and the Sutton Hoo helmet (Fig. 7.4a) has boar heads and a flying dragon on its face mask, plus a double-headed dragon crest and plaques depicting Woden-cult images. Some women's brooches bear human faces (Fig. 7.4b); many have stylized horse-heads (Fig. 7.4c). Circular gold pendants known as bracteates are decorated with images now jumbled for us, but probably representing heroes, monsters, and myth (Fig. 7.4d).

The Anglo-Saxons evidently believed in healing magic. Some of the beads worn by women, especially amber and crystal, may have been prophylactic. So too were the animals' teeth and claws worn at the neck, the trinkets carried in pouches at the hip, including a few miniature Woden's spears and Thunor's hammers, and, probably, the crystal balls in silver slings dangling from the belts of wealthy Kentish women.

Christianity was formally introduced into England by St Augustine's mission to Kent in 597 and St Paulinus' and St Aidan's to Northumbria in 627 and 633 respectively, though there may have been some remnants of Romano-British Christianity in both areas and the influx of Frankish settlers to Kent in the sixth century may have brought knowledge of it before Augustine's mission. Cruciform

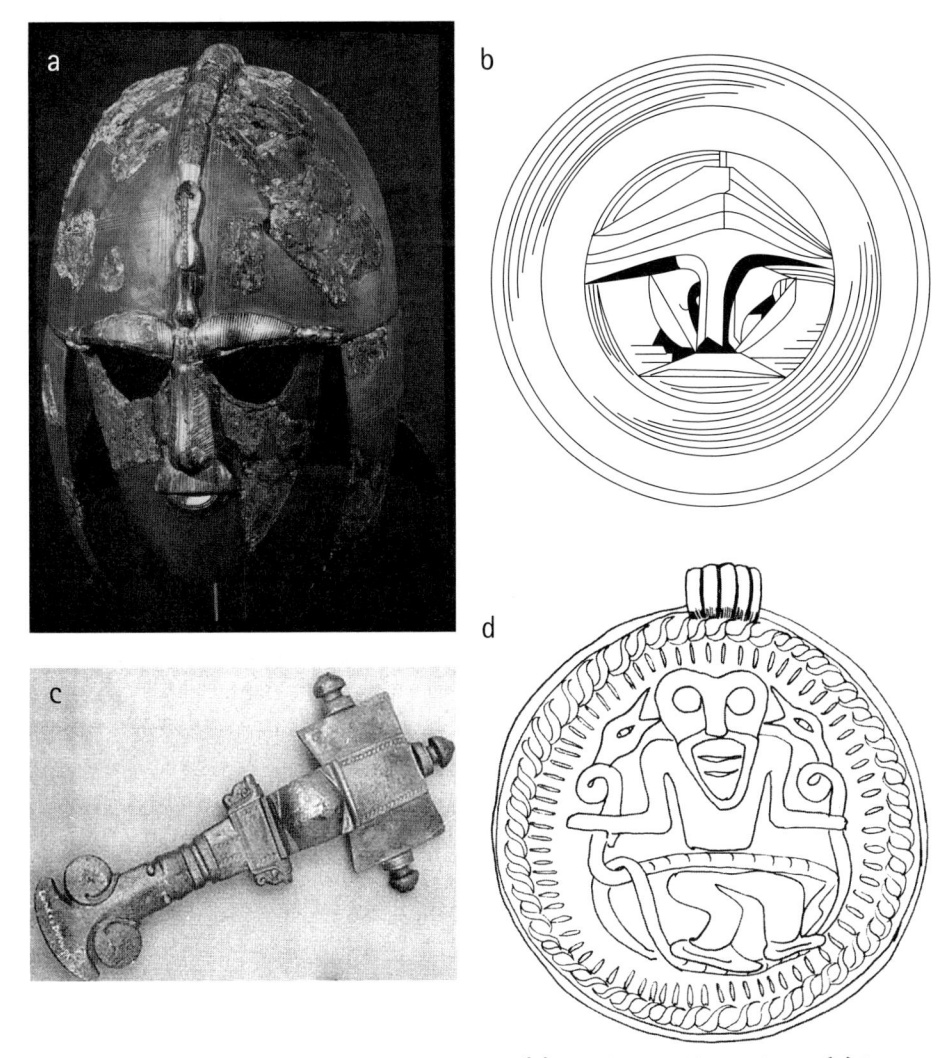

Figure 7.4 Pagan belief on dress accessories: (a) The Sutton Hoo helmet; (b) Button brooch with human face, drawn by Rosalyn Smith; (c) Cruciform brooch with stylized horse-head; (d) Necklace pendant with man and snakes, drawn by Rosalyn Smith

designs appear on Kentish disc brooches as early as the late sixth century, perhaps simply as ornament, but perhaps influenced by the Christianity already established across the Channel. Tiny crosses in millefiore glass on the Sutton Hoo shoulder clasps (Fig. 7.5a), in gold brocading on sixth-century women's headdresses (Fig. 7.5b), and in the form of perforations on Kentish buckles (Fig. 7.5c) are possibly deliberate Christian emblems. The chamber-grave at Prittlewell included two small gold-foil crosses, which had perhaps been attached to the burial garment, proclaiming that their owner, though richly provided with material possessions, had died in

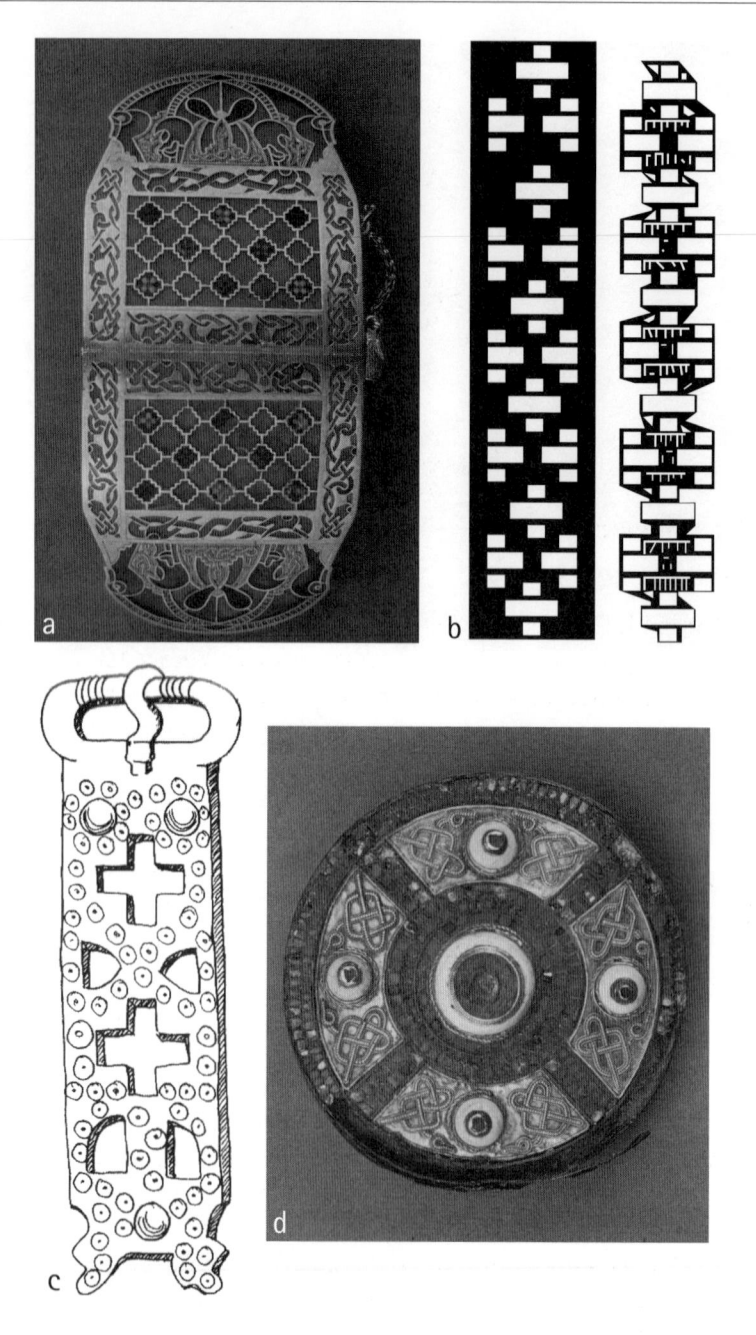

Figure 7.5 Christian belief on dress accessories: (a) (i) Millefiori glass crosses on the seventh-century Sutton Hoo shoulder clasps (ii) Detail; (b) Crosses in gold brocading on a sixth-century woman's headdress (Bifrons), surviving gold and reconstruction; (c) Cruciform perforations on a seventh-century Kentish buckle (Sibertswold), drawn by Christine Wetherell; (d) Cloisonné brooch with cross and quincunx design, seventh-century; (e) Necklace pendant with cruciform decoration, eighth-century (Boss Hall), drawn by Rosalyn Smith

e

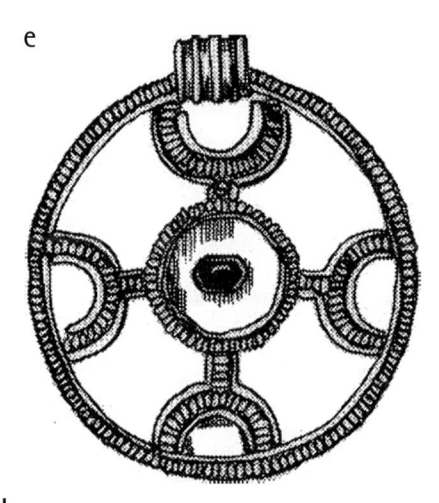

Figure 7.5 Continued

the Christian faith. The cross appears prominently on circular necklace pendants, and free-hanging gold crosses, decorated with garnets, appear in the seventh century. The magnificent polychrome disc brooches of seventh-century Kent are decorated with cloisonné garnet crosses, their arms interspersed with four circular bosses. With a large central boss in the middle, this quincunx design may represent the five wounds of Christ. As the brooch type evolves, the shapes of the cloisons become more uniform and the Christian design more prominent (Fig. 7.5d). Although this brooch type evidently went out of use by the late seventh century (Owen-Crocker 2004: 139), the fashion for Christian designs on jewellery continued, as demonstrated by cruciform pendants (Fig. 7.5e) and a cloisonné brooch decorated with a cross and five bosses, very late seventh- to eighth-century grave-goods from Boss Hall. The cross features on eighth-century flat-headed pins, and the combination of cruciform and quincunx design persists on silver brooches from the ninth to eleventh centuries.

Christian emblems appear on two ninth-century silver finger-rings which have royal names inscribed on them: the *Agnus Dei* or 'Lamb of God' is represented on Queen Æthelswith's ring (Wilson 1964: 6, 23, 117–19, plate XI.1; pp. 82–3), and creatures which are probably peacocks, emblems of resurrection and eternal life, appear together with crosses on King Æthelwulf's (Wilson 1964: 6, 23, 141–2, plate XIX.31; p. 82). A stole and maniple probably made in Winchester in the early tenth century, preserved in the tomb of St Cuthbert, depict in needlework the figures of Old Testament prophets, busts of saints, two popes with their deacons, and the *Dextra Dei* or 'Hand of God'. The figures are named in embroidered letters and the names of the patron and original owner of the embroideries are recorded on both (Freyhan 1956). The stole and maniple, first worn by Bishop Frithestan of Winchester, who died in 931, are effectively embroidered prayers.

The skilful and assured use of gold and silk in these vestments anticipates by several centuries the celebrated *opus anglicanum* ('English work'), in which chasubles, copes, and orphreys were encrusted with sumptuous embroidery that included figures.

Written records of gifts reveal that from the very early days of Anglo-Saxon Christianity, imported silks were used for ecclesiastical vestments (Dodwell 1982: ch. 5); the scraps of silk in a small amuletic container in a baby's grave at Updown, Kent, were perhaps a holy relic, cut from such a vestment (Hawkes 1982; Coatsworth and Owen-Crocker 2007: 68). If the Anglo-Saxons dressed their celebrants in silks they also 'dressed' their deceased saints, their altars, and their church crosses. Clothing relics and church furniture in expensive and exotic textiles was a token of the honour in which the saint (or altar, or cross) was held. Ironically, in adopting eastern silk textiles, the Anglo-Saxons may have associated what they held most holy with pagan belief: a Byzantine silk found in the tomb of St Cuthbert bears the image of a pagan nature goddess (Flanagan 1956); many other motifs on the silk textiles which circulated in medieval Europe had their origin in ancient non-Christian beliefs (McDowell 1993; Muthesius 1997). Precious materials were used to make small containers for relics which were worn on the person by pious people, confirming their Christian identity: a silk pouch dyed with kermes and embroidered with a cross, containing vegetable fibre, was an archaeological find from York (Tweddle 1989); a gold and jewelled reliquary cross on a chain was found in Edward the Confessor's tomb when it was opened in the seventeenth century (Cigaar 1982: esp. p. 91).

Deacons, priests, and bishops wore mass vestments according to their rank (see below). These garments, which derived from Roman tradition, covered the legs and hung loosely, ensuring that the figure of the celebrant was quite different in shape from that of the secular man in short, girdled tunic and close-fitting trousers. Outside the context of mass, priests seem to have worn secular dress, as do the tonsured figures, singing from books, who accompany King Edward's body to church in the Bayeux Tapestry (Wilson 1985: plate 30). Their tonsure, a hairstyle imitating Christ's Crown of Thorns, ensured their religion was always displayed by their bodies. Monks, nuns, and vowesses associated with the religious life covered their heads, monks with cowls, women with veils. The cowl must have appeared quite distinctive as—according to art—men in secular dress were bare-headed, and, at least by the time Archbishop Dunstan included in a manuscript a drawing of himself depicted as a humble monk, monastic habits were long (Oxford, Bodleian Library, MS Auct., F.4.32, fol. 1). As far as women were concerned, religious dress was probably not unlike the secular in style, but dark-coloured and without decoration (Owen 1979: esp. 204, 220–1).

DRESS AND STATUS

Ownership of a brand-new garment was no doubt dependent on status, and hand-me-downs would be normal. At the lower end of the social scale, dress would be inextricably linked to identity, since a person would appear in the same garments day after day, year after year. Only the wealthy would enjoy a choice of garments. The outstandingly rich male buried *c.* AD 625 in the Sutton Hoo Ship Burial (Mound 1) was supplied with two pairs of shoes, several yellow-dyed cloaks, and (probably) alternative sets of jewelled belt equipment (Carver 2005). (No skeletal remains were found in the Sutton Hoo Ship Burial but these may have dissolved in the acidic subsoils prior to excavation.) The chamber grave at Prittlewell contained a casket which had probably once held spare textiles—clothing or bedding. Tenth- and eleventh-century ladies bequeathed multiple garments in their wills (Owen 1979).

Prosperity was marked by ownership of gold: buckles, brooches, and gold embroidery or brocading on garments. Gold fragments at the heads of well-equipped female skeletons, mostly in Kent, usually interpreted as embroidered or brocaded fillets (Crowfoot and Hawkes 1967; Crowfoot 1969), but recently as gold-edged veils (Walton Rogers 2007: 96, 191), were perhaps a relic of bridal finery which their owners continued to wear on special occasions. Evidence of men wearing gold thread is rarer: an X-ray of a soil block from Prittlewell shows a gold edging (Coatsworth and Owen-Crocker 2007: 9, fig. 3), and the princely burial at Taplow included gold thread, recently interpreted as part of a 'warrior jacket' (Walton Rogers 2007: 216, fig. 5.64); surprisingly, there is no evidence of this fashion among the property of the individual buried in Mound 1 at Sutton Hoo, the richest Anglo-Saxon burial known. Very skilled and time-consuming workmanship probably distinguished the costumes of the very rich. The Llan-gors garment, which is woven in very fine linen—23 threads per centimetre—and embroidered in precisely counted stem-stitch with silk thread, is witness to the quality achievable.

When Anglo-Saxon fashion changed, as it did at the beginning of the seventh century, the old styles disappeared with surprising speed. It seems from the limited evidence that people did not continue to wear a costume which had become 'old fashioned', though they appear to have treasured as antiques individual items of metalwork, such as brooches manufactured in the continental homelands, Roman coins and brooches, and well-worn Anglo-Saxon pieces. It has been suggested, however, that the new dress style of the seventh century was a deliberate adoption of Mediterranean costume (Geake 1997: 120; Geake 1999). The Sutton Hoo king, whose grave-goods included ceremonial regalia of sceptre, standard, and 'wand', may have cultivated the self-image of a ruler in the Roman tradition: the pair of shoulder-clasps, evidently designed to fasten a protective garment of Roman style, are unique in an Anglo-Saxon context. The provision of a purse containing Frankish coins, in the context of a culture which did not yet have a money economy, suggests the king was also mimicking his influential neighbours.

Masculine authority was marked by special garments: military belt equipment; the helmet—only four survive from the seventh and eighth centuries; the mail coat—there is evidence of only one, from Sutton Hoo; the crown—insignia of kingship in art, but not attested by any Anglo-Saxon archaeological find; and the long robe, attested by some late Anglo-Saxon art but very possibly iconic, not realistic. The hierarchy of clergy was marked by the vestments appropriate to each degree which were consecrated and ritually assumed at the ordination ceremony: an *alba* girdled with a *cingulum*, for deacons; the *planeta* or *casula* for priests; the *alba* and *planeta* for bishops; and the episcopal garments with the addition of the *pallium* for archbishops. The *pallium* was entirely personal to the archbishop and he was buried in it when he died. All of these ranks wore the narrow strip of material called a *stola*, but they wore it differently: the deacon over the left shoulder, the priest and higher ranks round their shoulders to symbolize their yoke or responsibility, crossed for the priest, hanging down vertically for higher ranks (Fig. 7.2; Keefer 2007: esp. 15 and 39, figs. 2.1–2.4). Hierarchical status therefore was instantly recognizable to those with specialized knowledge, though artists may have manipulated the vestments they depicted for symbolic effect (Keefer 2007: 30–9).

Garments changed hands as gifts, which were not always given out of spontaneous generosity, but in exchange for favours, past or hoped for. The cream Byzantine silk garment with a self-coloured pattern of birds and exotic beasts in roundels in which King Edward the Confessor was buried in 1066 may have entered England as a diplomatic gift that paid for mercenaries or which was given at the new king's coronation in anticipation of future partiality (Cigaar 1982; Granger-Taylor 1994). Donations and bequests to religious establishments and gifts to and from Anglo-Saxon missionaries to the Continent were not entirely altruistic: the benefactor expected to be repaid by prayer—for him/herself, and especially for his/her soul after death, and the souls of loved ones.

Conclusions

Some of the characteristics of Anglo-Saxon dress and its manufacture would be true of any pre-industrial society, but some are peculiar to the Anglo-Saxon people as they went through rapid social change: migrations, from tribal to central rule, from rural to urban occupation, and the adoption of the literate and humanistic culture which went hand-in-hand with the pervasive new faith, Roman Christianity.

Anglo-Saxon dress was made from entirely natural fibres, the choice of which may have been to some extent regionally, chronologically, and socially determined. Domestic production was normal in Anglo-Saxon villages, but was to some extent organized by the mid Saxon period to meet the needs of estates, prosperous households, and religious communities. In the late Anglo-Saxon/Anglo-Viking period there is evidence of more commercialized activity in towns. There was some limited choice for the wealthy patron and the urban dweller, but this probably came at the commissioning, rather than the finished-product stage. Recycling of items of dress was normal practice. There was a polar difference between the rich and poor in terms of ownership of garments. The majority had few, and well-worn clothes. Social distinctions were evidently not manifested in the style of the garments so much as in the materials—silk and fine linen—and decoration, especially gold, and the ownership of a conspicuous number of clothes.

There were clear gender distinctions throughout the period and identifiable fashion changes for women, probably inspired by foreign contacts and Christianity. There is some ambiguity about men's dress but apparently few developments. Strong ethnic and regional distinctions in the early Anglo-Saxon period gave way to a more uniform style of secular dress found throughout Christian Europe. Dress and dress accessories were used to indicate spiritual belief; cowls and veils eventually became the norm for men and women committed to the religious life but uniform habits were not yet adopted. Priests, when not celebrating mass, and women associated with the religious life seem to have worn secular dress, albeit in sober colours, for women at least. Mass vestments, gifts to shrines, and church furnishings exploited luxurious textiles. The ecclesiastical hierarchy was distinguished by costume. Special dress designated kings and other authority figures.

Dress was clearly indicative of identity, though the evidence which passes down to the modern researcher is to a large extent of a constructed identity. It should be understood to have been created by those who prepared a corpse for the grave, or by the artist who portrayed a king or historical person semiotically, rather than a reflection of personal choice. Clearly, though, for leaders of society, luxury cloth, embroidery, and gold ornament proclaimed their importance; for the poor, identity was manifested in their only ragged garment.

REFERENCES

BÉDAT, I., and GIRAULT-KURTZEMAN, B. (2004). 'The technical study of the Bayeux Tapestry', in P. Bouet, B. Levy, and F. Neveux (eds.), *The Bayeux Tapestry: Embroidering the Facts of History*. Caen: Presses universitaires de Caen, 83–109.

BUDNY, M., and TWEDDLE, D. (1984). 'The Maaseik embroideries'. *Anglo-Saxon England* 13: 65–96.

CALBERG, M. (1951). 'Tissus et broderies attribués aux saintes Harlinde et Relinde'. *Bulletin de la Societé royale d'Archéologie de Bruxelles*: 1–26.
CARVER, M. (2005). *Sutton Hoo: An Anglo-Saxon Princely Burial Ground and its Context*. Reports of the Research Committees of the Society of Antiquaries of London, No. 69. London: The British Museum Press.
CIGAAR, K. (1982). 'England and Byzantium on the eve of the Norman conquest (The Reign of Edward the Confessor)'. *Anglo-Norman Studies* 5: 78–96.
COATSWORTH, E. and OWEN-CROCKER, G. R. (2007). *Medieval Textiles of the British Isles AD 450–1100: An Annotated Bibliography*. British Archaeological Reports British Series 445. Oxford: Archaeopress.
—— and PINDER, M. (2002). *The Art of the Anglo-Saxon Goldsmith: Fine Metalwork in Anglo-Saxon England; its Practice and Practitioners*. Woodbridge: Boydell.
CROWFOOT, E. (1969). 'Early Anglo-Saxon gold braids: addenda and corrigenda'. *Medieval Archaeology* 13: 209–10.
—— and HAWKES, S. C. (1967). 'Early Anglo-Saxon gold braids'. *Medieval Archaeology* 11: 42–86.
DODWELL, C. R. (1982). *Anglo-Saxon Art: A New Perspective*. Manchester: Manchester University Press.
FARKE, H. (1998). 'Der Männerkittel aus Bernuthsfeld—Beobachtungen während einer Restaurierung', in L. Bender Jørgensen and C. Rinaldo (eds.), *Textiles in European Archaeology: Report from the 6th NESAT Symposium, 7–11th May 1996 in Boras*. GOTARC Series A, Volume 1. Gothenburg: Göteborg University, Department of Archaeology, 99–106.
FLANAGAN, J. F. (1956). 'The Figured-Silks', in C. F. Battiscombe (ed.), *The Relics of St Cuthbert*. Oxford: Oxford University Press, 484–525.
FREYHAN, R. (1956). 'The place of the stole and maniple in Anglo-Saxon art of the tenth century', in C. F. Battiscombe (ed.), *The Relics of St Cuthbert*. Oxford: Oxford University Press, 409–32.
GEAKE, H. (1997). *The Use of Grave-Goods in Conversion-Period England, c.600–c. 850*. British Archaeological Reports British Series 261. Oxford: Hedges.
—— (1999). 'Invisible kingdoms: the use of grave-goods in seventh-century England'. *Anglo-Saxon Studies in Archaeology and History* 10: 203–15.
GRANGER-TAYLOR, H. (1994). '166. Silk from the tomb of Edward the Confessor', in David Buckton (ed.), *Byzantium: Treasures of Byzantine Art and Culture from British Collections*. London: British Museum Press for the Trustees of the British Museum, 151–3.
—— and PRITCHARD, F. (1991). 'A fine quality Insular embroidery from Llan-gors Crannóg, near Brecon', in M. Redknap, N. Edwards, S. Youngs, A. Lane, and J. Knight (eds.), *Pattern and Purpose in Insular Art*. Oxford: Oxbow, 91–9.
HALD, M. (1980). *Ancient Danish Textiles from Bogs and Burials*. English edition, trans. J. Olsen. Publications of the National Museum of Denmark, Archaeological-Historical Series 21. Copenhagen: National Museum of Denmark.
HALL, A. R. (1997). Untitled, in Walton Rogers, *Textile Production at 16–22 Coppergate*, 1767.
HAWKES, S. C. (1982). 'The archaeology of conversion: cemeteries', in James Campbell (ed.), *The Anglo-Saxons*. Oxford: Phaidon, 48–9.
—— (1990). 'The Anglo-Saxon necklace from Lower Brook Street', in M. Biddle (ed.), *Artefacts from Medieval Winchester, Part 2: Object and Economy in Medieval Winchester*. Winchester Studies 7.ii. Oxford: Oxford University Press, 621–7.

HENRY, P. A. (1999). 'Development and change in late Saxon textile production: an analysis of the evidence'. *Durham Archaeological Journal* 14–15: 69–76.

HINES, J. (1984). *The Scandinavian Character of Anglian England in the Pre-Viking Period.* BAR British Series 124. Oxford: British Archaeological Reports.

HOFFMANN, M. (1964). *The Warp-Weighted Loom: Studies in the History and Technology of an Ancient Implement.* Oslo: Universitetsforlaget.

KEEFER, S. L. (2007). 'A matter of style: clerical vestments in the Anglo-Saxon Church'. *Medieval Clothing and Textiles* 3: 13–39.

LEE, C. (2004). 'Grave matters: Anglo-Saxon textiles and their cultural significance'. *Bulletin of the John Rylands Library* 86(2): 203–21.

McDOWELL, J. A. (1993). 'Sassanian textiles', in J. Harris (ed.), *5000 Years of Textiles*. London: British Museum Press, 68–70.

MUTHESIUS, A. (1997). *Byzantine Silk Weaving AD 400 to AD 1200.* Vienna: Verlag Fassbaender.

NOCKERT, M. (1982). 'Some new observations about the Boksten costume', in L. Bender Jørgensen and K. Tidow (eds.), *NESAT I, Textilsymposium Neumunster: Archaeologische Textilfunde: 6.5–8.5.1981.* Neumunster: Textilmuseum Neumunster, 277–82.

OWEN, G. R. (1979). 'Wynflæd's wardrobe'. *Anglo-Saxon England* 8: 195–222.

OWEN-CROCKER, G. R. (2004). *Dress in Anglo-Saxon England: Revised and enlarged edition.* Woodbridge: Boydell.

—— (2007). 'British Wives and Slaves? Possible Romano-British techniques in "Women's Work"', in N. J. Higham (ed.), *Britons in Anglo-Saxon England.* Woodbridge: Boydell and Brewer, 80–90.

PAGE, R. I. (1964). 'The Inscriptions', Appendix A to Wilson, *Anglo-Saxon Ornamental Metalwork*, 67–90.

RYDER, M. L. (1964). 'The history of sheep breeds in Britain'. *Agricultural History Review* 12: 1–12, 65–82.

—— (1974). 'Wools from antiquity', *Textile History* 5(2): 100-110.

TWEDDLE, D. (1989). Untitled, in P. Walton, *Textiles, Cordage and Raw Fibre from 16–22 Coppergate*, 378–81.

WALTON, P. (1989). *Textiles, Cordage and Raw Fibre from 16–22 Coppergate.* Volume 17, fasc. 5 of *The Archaeology of York: The Small Finds.* London: Council for British Archaeology.

WALTON ROGERS, P. (1997). *Textile Production at 16–22 Coppergate.* Volume 17, fasc. 11 of *The Archaeology of York: The Small Finds.* Dorchester: Dorset Press.

—— (2001). 'The re-appearance of an old Roman loom in medieval England', in P. Walton Rogers, L. Bender Jørgensen, and A. Rast-Eicher (eds.), *The Roman Textile Industry and its Influence.* Oxford: Oxbow, 158–71.

—— (2002). 'Textile production', in P. Ottaway and N. Rogers (eds.), *Craft, Industry and Everyday Life: Finds from Medieval York.* Volume 17, fasc. 15 of *The Archaeology of York: The Small Finds.* York: Council for British Archaeology, 2732–5.

—— (2003). 'The Anglo-Saxons and Vikings in Britain, AD 450–1050', in D. Jenkins (ed.), *The Cambridge History of Western Textiles.* Cambridge: Cambridge University Press, 124–32.

—— (2007). *Cloth and Clothing in Early Anglo-Saxon England, AD 450–700*, York: Council for British Archaeology.

WATSON, J. (1998). 'Organic material associated with metalwork', in T. Malim, J. Hines, and C. Duhig (eds.), *The Anglo-Saxon Cemetery at Edix Hill (Barrington A), Cambridgeshire*. York: The Council of British Archaeology, 230–50.

WILSON, D. M. (1964). *Anglo-Saxon Ornamental Metalwork 700–1000 in the British Museum*. London: Trustees of the British Museum.

—— (1985). *The Bayeux Tapestry: The Complete Tapestry in Colour*. London: Thames and Hudson.

PART II

RURAL SETTLEMENT

CHAPTER 8

OVERVIEW: RURAL SETTLEMENT

HELENA HAMEROW

INTRODUCTION

No major synthesis of the evidence for rural settlements of the whole Anglo-Saxon period has been attempted since Philip Rahtz published his seminal paper on the subject (1976). Two of the main reasons for this are the relatively small number of large-scale settlement excavations, only a few of which have been fully published, and the continuing dominance of the study of fifth- to seventh-century cemeteries and grave-goods. Indeed, Rahtz described the archaeology of Anglo-Saxon settlements as 'unsatisfactory, incomplete and largely unpublished' (1976: 55). The past twenty years, however, have seen a new generation of Anglo-Saxon settlements come to light which have been investigated on an impressive scale. We now have evidence of sufficient quantity and quality to enable settlements to be considered as dynamic social arenas rather than passive agglomerations of 'features', although much important new information still awaits publication or remains largely hidden in the 'grey literature' of archaeological field units. These excavations, combined with the results of several major field surveys (e.g. Parry 2006), enable a far more detailed picture of Anglo-Saxon settlement to be drawn than was possible thirty years ago. As the contributors to this section make plain, it is a picture of far greater complexity and diversity than could have been imagined at the time that Rahtz's pioneering survey was published.

Despite the advances of recent decades, certain basic questions remain unanswered. This is in part because most Anglo-Saxon rural settlements are disappointingly 'clean' in archaeological terms, yielding few finds other than pottery and bone, and often little even of these. Middens and preserved ground surfaces, particularly those associated with buildings, remain rare. Preservation of organic materials is often poor, and we have yet to identify and excavate a single waterlogged settlement of this period, the chief exception being the mid Saxon mill at Tamworth (Staffordshire), where well-preserved, waterlogged timbers were excavated (Rahtz and Meeson 1992).

The geographical distribution of known settlements remains uneven: few have been recognized, for example, in the West Midlands, and the north-west of England. Examples of excavated settlements remain sparse even in some counties known to have been critically important in the formation of the earliest Anglo-Saxon kingdoms, such as Kent.[1] Counties such as Oxfordshire, Cambridgeshire, Suffolk, and Northamptonshire, on the other hand, have yielded relatively large numbers of settlements. Distinctive post-Roman settlements have also been identified in what became the south-western counties of Wessex, although they remain rare. Poundbury and Alington Avenue in Dorset and the re-occupied Iron Age hillforts at South Cadbury and Cadbury-Congresbury in Somerset have all produced evidence of timber buildings dating to between the fifth and seventh centuries, while excavations at Mawgan Porth on the north Cornish coast provide evidence of the distinctive building tradition manifest in Devon and Cornwall (Green and Davies 1987; Davies 1986; Alcock 1982; Rahtz et al. 1992; Gardiner, this volume). But despite the uneven spread of sites, a comparative approach is now possible and, for the first time, we can consider how and why rural settlements developed in different ways in different regions, not only within Britain, but around the North Sea zone (Hamerow 2002).

Factors affecting the recognition of settlements clearly come into play when considering their geographical distribution. While there seems to have been a genuine tendency for early Anglo-Saxon (i.e. mid fifth- to mid seventh-century) settlements to be on light soils, for example on river terraces, it is also true that settlements are easier to identify on such soils, particularly on aerial photographs, and that gravel extraction is one of the chief means by which they have come to light (Hamerow 1992; 1999). While aerial photography remains extremely important in identifying settlements (for example, on the Yorkshire Wolds; Stoertz 1997: 58–9), some sites not previously recognized on aerial photographs have been identified through field-walking (the systematic collection of artefacts from the

---

[1] Significant headway has been made in filling some of these 'blanks', however: in 1972, Addyman wrote that 'there is hardly an excavated [Anglo-Saxon] house from the whole of Yorkshire', yet one of the most extensive settlement excavations ever to be undertaken in England began only six years later in the Vale of Pickering, at West Heslerton (Powlesland 1987).

surface of ploughed fields), as was the case with Chalton, Hampshire (Addyman *et al.* 1972). Even field-walking, however, is of only limited use in identifying Anglo-Saxon settlements because of the friability of much of the pottery of this period and the use of perishable building materials. Geophysical survey (especially magnetometry) also has a role to play, notably in defining in greater detail settlements already recognized in aerial photographs. The post-built timber buildings associated with many Anglo-Saxon settlements are generally not discernible on aerial photographs nor susceptible to geophysical prospection, but both can be used to identify *Grubenhäuser* (sunken-featured buildings, discussed below) with a fair degree of reliability (David 1994: 6–7). Serendipity will, however, always have a role to play in the discovery of Anglo-Saxon settlements: the impressive, high-status settlement at Cowdery's Down, Hampshire, came to light during the investigation of a complex of cropmarks dating to the Bronze Age and Civil War era (Millett 1984).[2]

A final difficulty is presented by the dispersed nature of most early and mid Anglo-Saxon settlements and their lack of obvious focal points or clear 'edges'. This means that archaeologists cannot take the same approach to sampling settlements of this period as to a Roman villa or later medieval villages. Large-scale excavation has demonstrated that the significance of the results obtained by excavating one Anglo-Saxon settlement in its entirety, or near entirety, is on the whole not equalled by investigating small fragments of four or five settlements, which may provide little beyond a few more examples of buildings and a few more dots on a distribution map, as Philip Barker recognized over thirty years ago (Barker 1977: 16–20).

While the scale of excavation of Anglo-Saxon settlements has remained relatively small when compared to some sites on the other side of the North Sea, there are notable exceptions: the excavation at Mucking, Essex, remains one of the largest in Britain, at *c.* 140,000 m² (Hamerow 1993; Fig. 10.1) while at Yarnton, Oxfordshire, *c.* 55,000 m² of the 15 ha investigated yielded Anglo-Saxon buildings (Hey 2004). Other extensively excavated settlements whose plans have been published in detail are Catholme, Staffordshire (Losco-Bradley and Kinsley 2002), and Cottenham, Cambridgeshire (Mortimer 2000). The epic excavations at West Heslerton, Yorkshire, have uncovered over 200,000 m² since work began in 1978 (Powlesland 2003).

Written sources such as charters, law codes, and place-names have the potential to contribute enormously to our understanding of the character of, in particular, later Anglo-Saxon settlement and landscape, as work by Hooke, Gelling, and others

---

[2] There still remain whole categories of Anglo-Saxon occupation sites that elude precise definition, such as so-called 'productive sites' of mid Saxon date which have yielded significant quantities of coinage and metal finds, but little or no evidence of buildings. At least some of these are likely to have been periodic market places (see Pestell and Ulmschneider, this volume). Other mid Saxon sites, such as Lake End Road, near Dorney, Berkshire, appear to have consisted of little more than dozens of pits of uncertain function (Foreman *et al.* 2002). In his contribution, Gardiner draws attention to a whole series of impermanent sites such as shielings, which have scarcely begun to be investigated.

has shown (Hooke 1988 and this volume; Gelling 1984 and this volume), yet they shed frustratingly little light on the character of individual settlements and buildings. For understanding the character and diversity of buildings and settlements, archaeology remains our primary, and yet arguably the most under-utilized, resource.

Settlement layout and buildings

In 1976, so few Anglo-Saxon settlements had been excavated on an adequate scale that Rahtz was able to deal in detail only with buildings; the evidence for layout was too slight to be considered. It is thus in the study of the layout of settlements and in particular the recognition of the importance from the seventh century onwards of enclosures and boundaries that some of the most significant advances have been made. Although they varied in size, shape, and presumably function, these enclosures shared certain characteristics, namely relatively insubstantial ditches (albeit probably augmented with banks, fences, or hedges), evidence of repeated re-cutting, indicating maintenance over relatively long periods, and in many cases, reconfiguration to meet changing needs. What those needs were remains a matter for conjecture, although there can be little doubt that the introduction of semi-permanent enclosures marked a real social and economic watershed, as Ulmschneider and Gardiner make clear (see also the seminal paper published on this subject by Reynolds in 2003).

The appearance of ditched enclosures and droveways in settlements has been attributed to a shift towards more intensive stock-rearing practices and away from a broadly-based regime geared towards self-sufficiency, a proposition worth examining more closely (e.g. Blinkhorn 1999: 16). It would of course always have been necessary to prevent cattle and sheep from getting too close to buildings and damaging them. This was presumably achieved in the early Anglo-Saxon period by 'hefting'—that is, keeping animals outside year-round, on large tracts of unfenced grazing land well away from the settlement (Hart 2004). Gardiner's identification of possible Anglo-Saxon 'shielings' may be of relevance here. The appearance of enclosures and droveways suggests that animals were, for some reason, being kept closer to settlements than they had been previously, and that droveways and paddocks were therefore necessary to keep them safely away from buildings.

If the general principle is accepted that, unless absolutely necessary, farmers enclose crops rather than animals, then one possible explanation for why animals were being kept closer to settlements is a shortage of readily accessible pasture, perhaps as arable expanded onto heavier soils, or to make collection of manure easier (see also Oosthuizen, this volume). The concentration of settlements associated with rectilinear enclosures near the fen edge in Cambridgeshire could also reflect the need to keep stock near settlements in a landscape that was too wet for winter grazing.[3] An increase in the size of flocks and the number of plough oxen being kept may also help account for such a shortage. The development of hay meadows may have been yet another factor in the appearance of enclosures, as animals would have to be kept off these meadows until the hay was cut. Evidence for both an expansion of arable and the introduction of hay meadows in the mid and late Saxon periods has been found (for example at Yarnton; Hey 2004: 46–57).

Some enclosures define plots which may be described as 'informally regular' (as opposed to 'geometrically rigid'; Roberts 2008: 125) in mid to late Saxon settlements. At Quarrington, Lincolnshire, for example, a series of rectilinear enclosures was established in the second phase of the settlement when three earthfast timber buildings were constructed close together, two apparently abutting a fence-line (Taylor 2003: 273, fig. 7). The settlement included three evenly spaced, east-west aligned ditches defining parcels of land—possibly fields or paddocks. Occupation appears to have ceased by the ninth century, although remains of ridge-and-furrow indicate that later ploughing followed the same orientation as the mid Saxon enclosures. The size of enclosures at rectilinear settlements such as Cottenham and West Fen Road Ely, furthermore, remained remarkably consistent over time, suggesting a measure of legal control over the passing down of properties across the generations (cf. Mortimer *et al.* 2005: 129). The settlement of Catholme in Staffordshire was established as a series of enclosed farmsteads and trackways, probably in the late sixth or seventh century (Fig. 37.1). The repeated re-cutting of the enclosure ditches as well as the placement of a single human burial at the entrances to two of the enclosures strongly suggests that here too enclosures served to demarcate ancestral properties (Hamerow 2006). Around the same period, increasing efforts were devoted to prolonging the life-spans of important timber buildings both by repairing them and by the introduction of new building techniques (Hamerow, this volume). In this way, even timber buildings could have become features in the landscape much in the same way that, by the tenth century, as Morris argues, local churches had transformed the landscape by effectively becoming part of it.

The appearance of regular house-plots in late Saxon settlements presumably reflects some form of assessment and there has been a tendency to assume that earlier planned layouts and systems of enclosure were similarly reflections of lordship (see Reynolds 2003: 131). The question of the role of lordship in the organization of individual settlements is linked to a wider debate about whether

---

[3] There are interesting parallels with the appearance of stock enclosures and droveways in eastern England in the Bronze and early Iron Ages (Pryor 1996). I am greatly indebted to Ros Faith and Debby Banham, whose suggestions have contributed much to the ideas put forward here.

the creation of common fields was the result of a slow evolution or a dramatic restructuring of the landscape overseen by lords who replaced small, scattered farms with nucleated villages (see also Oosthuizen, this volume). This debate, set out most recently by Rippon, is far from resolved and we still 'do not understand the actual process whereby a landscape of dispersed settlement was transformed into one of villages and common fields' (Rippon 2008: 20). We should be cautious, therefore, about assuming that eighth- and ninth-century lords were able to exercise a high degree of control over peasant communities, or indeed that these same communities were incapable of establishing and maintaining such regular layouts themselves.

Defining status

As Gardiner notes, late Saxon society was 'strongly hierarchical and marked by considerable inequalities of wealth' and formal power appears to have been mediated through settlements (this volume). Yet Ulmschneider demonstrates how difficult establishing the status of a settlement can be in practice given the paucity of artefacts and environmental remains found at most sites, although the presence on a small number of late Saxon settlements of 'special purpose' buildings such as kitchens, barns, halls etc. is a useful indicator of status (Hamerow, this volume). This lack of artefactual evidence is one reason why excavations at Flixborough, south of the Humber estuary in Lincolnshire, have assumed particular importance (Loveluck 2007). Traces of some forty buildings dating to the mid and late Saxon periods were uncovered, but what makes the site truly exceptional is the preservation of large quantities of artefacts (some 15,000) and hundreds of thousands of animal-bone fragments contained in refuse middens sealed by blown sand. Clear and sometimes radical changes in the character and status of the settlement during the eighth to tenth centuries have prompted a renewed debate about how the status of settlements should be defined.

Despite the size of the excavation, only part of the settlement was uncovered and its core may well lie outside the excavated area. Nevertheless, the detailed stratigraphic sequences allowed changes in the configuration of the settlement to be traced in some detail. Some phases, such as the mid ninth century, saw deliberate clearance and remodelling, while in the first half of the tenth century the relatively small buildings of the preceding period were demolished and replaced by much larger ones. Marked changes in animal-husbandry practices and craft production have also been traced. The finds demonstrate that already by the seventh century Flixborough was part of a pattern of contact across the North Sea and English

Channel. Despite the fact that continental coinage had ceased to arrive by the ninth century, imports from other regions of England were reaching the settlement. The evidence for the later ninth and tenth centuries suggests that exchange was severely disrupted, presumably as a result of Viking activity.

The question of whether Flixborough represents an undocumented minster has generated considerable debate (summarized by Blair 2005: 206–12). Because historically attested monasteries have in the past been targeted for excavation, there is a danger of circularity in arguing that the finds they produce—such as styli and window glass, both of which were present at Flixborough—are *exclusively* markers of such communities. Loveluck argues that in the eighth century Flixborough was an aristocratic estate centre, becoming monastic (or part of a monastic estate) in the ninth, when the evidence for literacy is most marked and craft production reached its peak; it was then 'secularized' in the later ninth and early tenth centuries, when it appears to have been of ordinary status. Sometime later in the tenth century, the presence of large buildings and evidence for hunting and feasting suggest that the community had regained elite status. As remarkable as the evidence from Flixborough is, such changes in status are not in themselves surprising, as written sources for the period clearly indicate that royal and aristocratic residences could be converted into monasteries, and vice versa (see Blair 2005: 186–7, 279–90, and 323–9).

The 'profligate' discarding of material goods—including iron tools, widely assumed to have been of high value in early medieval society—so evident at Flixborough, may not, Loveluck suggests, have been restricted to high-status sites, at least not in the eastern, commercially-developed part of the country, and the scarcity of metal objects in most excavated settlements, generally assumed to be the result of recycling, could be largely due to post-depositional factors. In short, the number of imports, coins, and other 'high-status' finds at Flixborough could merely reflect exceptional preservation conditions rather than exceptional status. This has enormous implications for our interpretations of other, less well-preserved settlements. Should certain types of imports and 'luxuries' necessarily be regarded as indicators of high status and can the lack of such items be taken as evidence of impoverishment? Even Flixborough, despite being interpreted as of high status in the later tenth century on the basis of its large buildings, produced very little metalwork dating to that period.

Explaining the unfeasibly high proportion of excavated settlements of the mid to late Saxon periods that display at least some of the trappings of high status in terms of their layout and buildings and/or their material culture will require further research. It is entirely reasonable to question whether imported goods, certain kinds of dress items, and other artefacts should necessarily be seen as 'badges of wealth and rank' and the explanation for the large proportion of high-status settlements may, as Ulmschneider suggests below, lie in our interpretations of the archaeological record (see also Loveluck 2007: 147). Yet the alternative possibility, that the settlements of later Anglo-Saxon peasants may be all but invisible in archaeological terms, should not be discounted. This is one of many uncertainties that future excavations of the rural settlements of this formative period may resolve.

REFERENCES

ADDYMAN, P., LEIGH, D., and HUGHES, M. (1972). 'Anglo-Saxon houses at Chalton, Hampshire'. *Medieval Archaeology* 16: 13–32.

ALCOCK, L. (1982). 'Cadbury-Camelot: a fifteen-year perspective'. *Proceedings of the British Academy* 63: 355–88.

BARKER, P. (1977). *The Technique of Archaeological Excavation*. New York: Universe Books.

BLAIR, J. (2005). *The Church in Anglo-Saxon Society*. Oxford: Oxford University Press.

BLINKHORN, P. (1999). 'Of cabbages and kings: production, trade and consumption in mid Saxon England', in M. Anderton (ed.), *Anglo-Saxon Trading Centres: Beyond the Emporia*. Glasgow: Cruithne Press, 4–24.

DAVID, A. (1994). 'The role of geophysical survey in early medieval archaeology'. *Anglo-Saxon Studies in Archaeology and History* 7: 1–26.

DAVIES, S. (1986). 'Excavations at Alington Avenue, Fordington, Dorchester'. *Proceedings Dorset Natural History and Archaeology Soc.* 107: 101–10.

FOREMAN, S., HILLER, J., and PETTS, D. (2002). *Gathering the People, Settling the Land: The Archaeology of a Middle Thames Landscape*. Oxford: Oxford Archaeology.

GELLING, M. (1984). *Place-names in the Landscape*. London: Dent.

GREEN, C., and DAVIES, S. (1987). *Excavations at Poundbury, Dorchester, Dorset, 1966–1982, Volume 1: The Settlements*. Dorchester: Dorset Natural History and Archaeological Society.

HAMEROW, H. (1992). 'Settlement on the gravels in the Anglo-Saxon period', in M. Fulford and L. Nichols (eds.), *Developing Landscapes of Lowland Britain: The Archaeology of the British Gravels*. London: Society of Antiquaries, 39–46.

—— (1993). *Excavations at Mucking, Volume 2: The Anglo-Saxon Settlement*. London: English Heritage.

—— (1999). 'Anglo-Saxon timber buildings: the continental connection', in H. Sarfatij et al. (eds.), *In Discussion With the Past: Archaeological Studies Presented to W.A. van Es*. Amersfoort: ROB, 119–28.

—— (2002). *Early Medieval Settlements: The Archaeology of Rural Communities in North-West Europe 400–900*. Oxford: Oxford University Press.

—— (2006). 'Special deposits in Anglo-Saxon settlements'. *Medieval Archaeology* 50: 1–30.

HART, E. (2004). *The Practice of Hefting*. Ludlow: E. Hart.

HEY, G. (2004). *Yarnton: Saxon and Medieval Settlement and Landscape*. Oxford: Oxford Archaeological Unit.

HOOKE, D. (ed.) (1988). Anglo-Saxon Estates in the Vale of the White Horse. *Oxoniensia* 52: 129–44.

LOSCO-BRADLEY, S., and KINSLEY, G. (eds.) (2002). *Catholme: An Anglo-Saxon Settlement on the Trent Gravels in Staffordshire*. Nottingham: University of Nottingham.

LOVELUCK, C. (2007). *Rural Settlement, Lifestyles and Social Change in the Later First Millennium AD: Anglo-Saxon Flixborough in its Wider Context*. Excavations at Flixborough 4. Oxford: Oxbow.

MILLETT, M., with JAMES, S. (1984). 'Excavations at Cowdery's Down, Basingstoke, 1978–1981'. *Archaeological Journal* 140: 151–279.

MORTIMER, R. (2000). 'Village development and ceramic sequence: the Middle to Late Saxon village at Lordship Lane, Cottenham, Cambridgeshire'. *Proceedings of the Cambridgeshire Antiquarian Society* 89: 5–33.

—— REGAN, R., and LUCY, S. (2005). *The Saxon and Medieval Settlement at West Fen Road, Ely: The Ashwell Site*. East Anglian Archaeology 110. Cambridge: Cambridge Archaeological Unit.

PARRY, S. (2006). *Raunds Area Survey: An Archaeological Study of the Landscape of Raunds, Northamptonshire 1985–94*. Oxford: Oxbow.

POWLESLAND, D. (1987). 'Excavations at Heslerton, North Yorkshire 1978–82'. *Archaeological Journal* 143: 53–173.

—— (2003). *25 Years of Archaeological Research on the Sands and Gravels of Heslerton*. Colchester: The Landscape Research Centre.

PRYOR, F. (1996). 'Sheep, stockyards and field systems. Bronze Age livestock populations in the Fenlands of eastern England'. *Antiquity* 70: 313–24.

RAHTZ, P. (1976). 'Buildings and rural settlement', in D. Wilson (ed.), *The Archaeology of Anglo-Saxon England*. Cambridge: Cambridge University Press, 49–98.

—— and MEESON, R. (1992). *An Anglo-Saxon Watermill at Tamworth*. London: Council for British Archaeology.

—— WOODWARD, A., BURROW, I., EVERTON, A., WATTS, L., LEACH, P., HIRST, S., and FOWLER, P. (1992). *Cadbury Congresbury 1968–73: A Late/Post-Roman Hilltop Settlement in Somerset*. British Archaeological Reports British Series 223. Oxford: Archaeopress.

REYNOLDS, A. (2003). 'Boundaries and settlements in later sixth to eleventh-century England'. *Anglo-Saxon Studies in Archaeology and History* 12: 98–136.

RIPPON, S. (2008). *Beyond the Medieval Village: The Diversification of Landscape Character in Southern Britain*. Oxford: Oxford University Press.

ROBERTS, B. (2008). *Landscapes, Documents and Maps: Villages in Northern England and Beyond, AD 900–1250*. Oxford: Oxbow Books.

STOERTZ, C. (1997). *Ancient Landscapes of the Yorkshire Wolds*. London: RCHME.

TAYLOR, G. (2003). 'An early to middle Saxon settlement at Quarrington, Lincolnshire'. *Antiquaries Journal* 83: 231–80.

CHAPTER 9

ANGLO-SAXON TIMBER BUILDINGS AND THEIR SOCIAL CONTEXT

HELENA HAMEROW

As John Blair notes elsewhere in this volume, Anglo-Saxon England was a 'wooden world' in which timber buildings predominated in settlements of all kinds. Despite the great progress made in the fifty years since Radford described the study of these buildings as 'one of the most intractable problems in the whole range of early medieval studies' (1958: 27), key issues remain unresolved regarding their origins, construction, and function, and consideration of the relationship between buildings and the social life of Anglo-Saxon communities has scarcely begun.

EARTHFAST BUILDINGS

Whether the origins of the earthfast, rectangular timber buildings found in early Anglo-Saxon settlements (Fig. 9.1) lie in Roman Britain or, like *Grubenhäuser*, on the other side of the North Sea, was hotly debated in the 1980s (Dixon 1982).

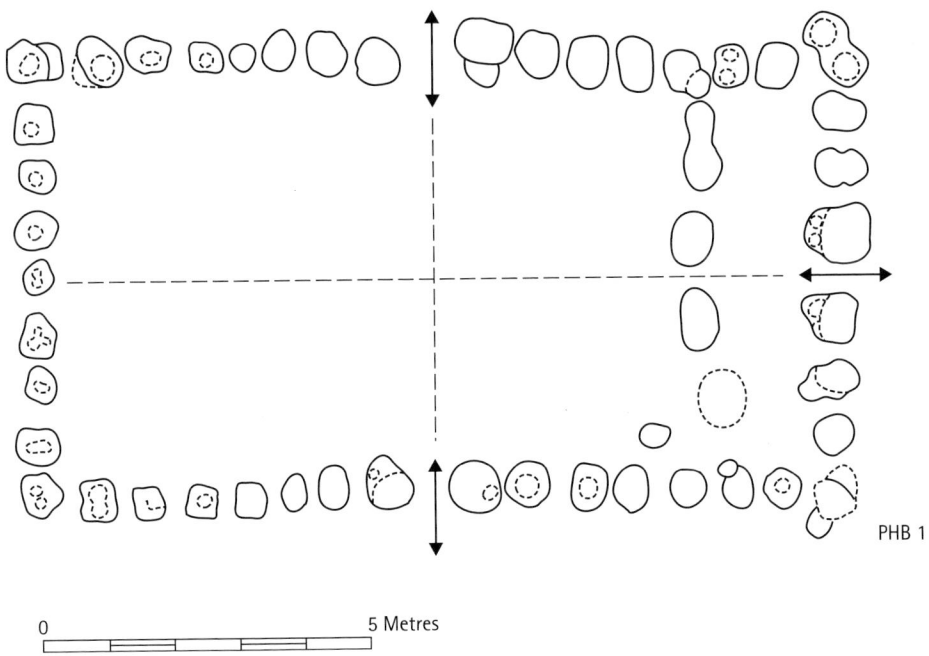

Figure 9.1 An Anglo-Saxon house with entrances and lines of symmetry indicated (after Hamerow 1993)

We now know that the layout of at least some Anglo-Saxon buildings compares closely with buildings on the Continent (Zimmermann 1988; Hamerow 1999). Yet despite widespread dimensional regularity implying a considerable degree of cultural contact, no three-aisled longhouse of the type that for centuries constituted the main type of farmhouse on the other side of the North Sea has ever been found in England. The fact that the *Grubenhaus* is found throughout early Anglo-Saxon England in a form apparently unchanged from the European mainland suggests that the reason for the absence of the longhouse has little to do with ethnic identity. Perhaps the answer lies in the fact that the construction of a longhouse and associated buildings as seen in the enclosed, ancestral farmsteads of north-west Europe required access not only to substantial quantities of material capital (i.e. timber) but also to considerable 'social capital' in the form of reciprocal labour obligations, perhaps extending across several communities. Social capital of this kind may have been difficult to accumulate during the social, economic, and political upheavals of fifth- and sixth-century Britain.

In a seminal study published in 1972, Peter Addyman felt it was too soon to classify Anglo-Saxon timber buildings, of which few examples were yet known, although he was the first to recognize the introduction of post-in-trench, and occasionally sill-beam, construction in the mid and late Saxon periods. More than three decades later, however, the number of closely dated Anglo-Saxon buildings remains too small for a clear architectural typology to be advanced, while the irregularity and incompleteness of many ground-plans make them difficult to interpret.

These difficulties notwithstanding, certain trends can be identified (Fig. 9.2). Several studies suggest that fifth-century buildings adhered most closely in layout to what has been dubbed the two-square module (Marshall and Marshall 1991 and 1993; James *et al.* 1985). They were, furthermore, uniformly small (i.e. less than 12 m in length), aligned east-west, and built using timbers set into individual post-holes. A striking degree of standardization can be observed in the ground-plans of some early Anglo-Saxon buildings (Fig. 9.3; Hamerow 1999).

The sixth century saw somewhat greater variation in the length and proportion of buildings. The use of foundation trenches was introduced towards the end of that century, as were annexes at one or both gable ends; the latter, however, were rare and had largely gone out of use by the eighth century. The first exceptionally large buildings (i.e. with floor areas greater than 100 m²) also appeared *c*.600. Very

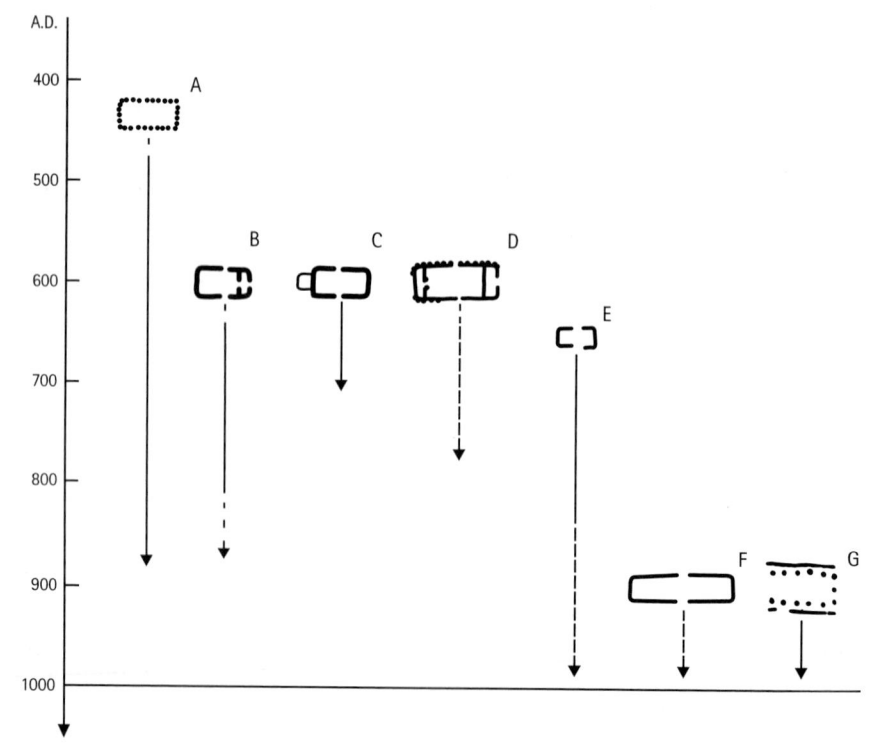

Figure 9.2 Suggested chronological development of Anglo-Saxon earthfast timber buildings

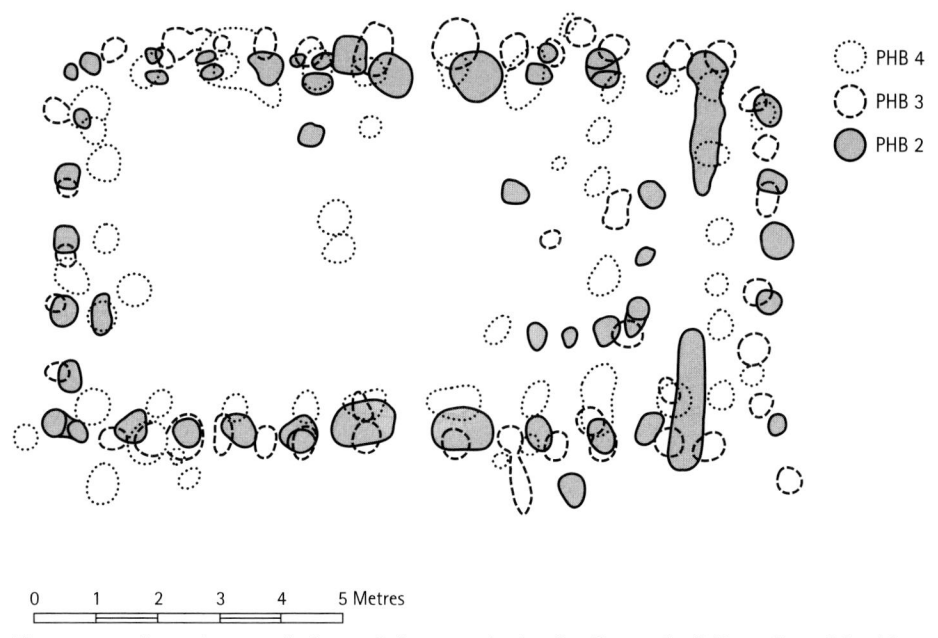

Figure 9.3 Superimposed plans of three early Anglo-Saxon buildings from Mucking (after Tummuscheit 1995)

small buildings (i.e. less than 6 m in length) also became more common in the seventh century, by which time around half of all buildings used foundation trenches. By the eighth and ninth centuries, foundation trenches were used in more than 75 per cent of buildings and the two-square module had ceased to predominate as a wider range of proportions came into use. Indeed, the late Saxon period is marked by a diversification of building forms and constructional techniques generally. By the tenth century, building with continuous foundation trenches was becoming less common and there was a trend towards buildings with load-bearing side walls, and shallower (or even non-existent) end-wall trenches (Gardiner 1990: 242). Around the beginning of the eleventh century, there appears to have been a return to the use of posts set in individual post-holes (ibid.).

Apart from churches and a handful of high-status late Saxon buildings, timber construction—mostly using oak—continued to dominate during the mid and late Saxon periods. Post-in-trench and plank-in-trench foundations enabled the construction of larger, especially wider, buildings, with a variety of wall constructions (Addyman 1972; Marshall and Marshall 1993).[1] Within these broad trends, however,

---

[1] This discussion is restricted to buildings with earthfast foundations; by definition, those without earthfast foundations are unlikely to leave any archaeological trace, although their existence by the later Saxon period is not in doubt. A building identified as a kitchen at Goltho had no earthfast foundations, but was recognized by its well-preserved clay floor (Beresford 1987: 59).

considerable variability in constructional techniques is apparent, even within the same settlement. Thus two tenth-century buildings at Steyning, Sussex—potentially contemporary and nearly identical in size—were built using quite different techniques, one with planks set end-to-end, the other with squared timbers (Gardiner 1993: 27). At the seventh- to tenth-century settlement at Flixborough, Lincolnshire, some buildings had paired posts (implying the use of tie-beams), while others had irregularly spaced posts; some made use of base plates at ground level, others below ground level; others still were built partly or entirely using post-in-trench construction (Darrah 2007). The correlation between foundation type and building dimensions is far from absolute: while post-in-trench and plank-in-trench buildings display a greater variation in width, they are not invariably wider than post-hole structures (Marshall and Marshall 1991: 36). Different types of foundations were sometimes even combined within the same building, as at Catholme (Losco-Bradley and Kinsley 2002: 86).

In short, it remains unclear why one form of foundation was chosen over another. One theory is that some constructional techniques—the use of sill-beams or stave-built walls for example—were more prestigious than others because they made more lavish use of timber and were more labour-intensive (Scull 1991: 55). It is notable in several cases that one wall of a building was more carefully built than the others. At Steyning, for example, the southern wall of Building A made 'extravagant use of planks clearly exceeding the number required purely for structural purposes' in contrast to the northern wall, which contained fewer posts, perhaps in order to 'display the status and wealth of the owner' (Fig. 9.4; Gardiner 1993: 32).

In his paper on the Anglo-Saxon house, Addyman noted that it would be surprising 'if the combined effects of environment, differing resources and varying inherited tradition had not produced wide regional variations' (1972: 304). Yet the geographical uniformity of building traditions across much of England during the fifth to seventh centuries has proved remarkable. By the late Saxon period, however, as building layouts and constructional methods began to diversify, regional variation comes more clearly into focus. Several studies have identified distinctive building types in upland Britain, although the number of buildings that have been firmly dated to this period remains small. King has recently observed, following Morris, that 'so little [is] known of the post-Roman building tradition in upland Britain, that identifying subsequent innovations [is] made more difficult' (2004: 335).[2]

---

[2] Few 'ordinary' farmsteads of the eighth to tenth centuries in north-western England have been identified and still fewer excavated. The examples we have suggest that it may be possible to detect an upland building tradition characterized by rectangular buildings with walls comprising facing stones and rubble interiors, rounded corners and internal wall benches (Coggins 2004; Richards 2000: 299–300). It would, however—as Gardiner observes (this vol.)—be unwise to regard these buildings as 'Anglo-Scandinavian' in any meaningful sense.

TIMBER BUILDINGS AND THEIR SOCIAL CONTEXT 133

Building A

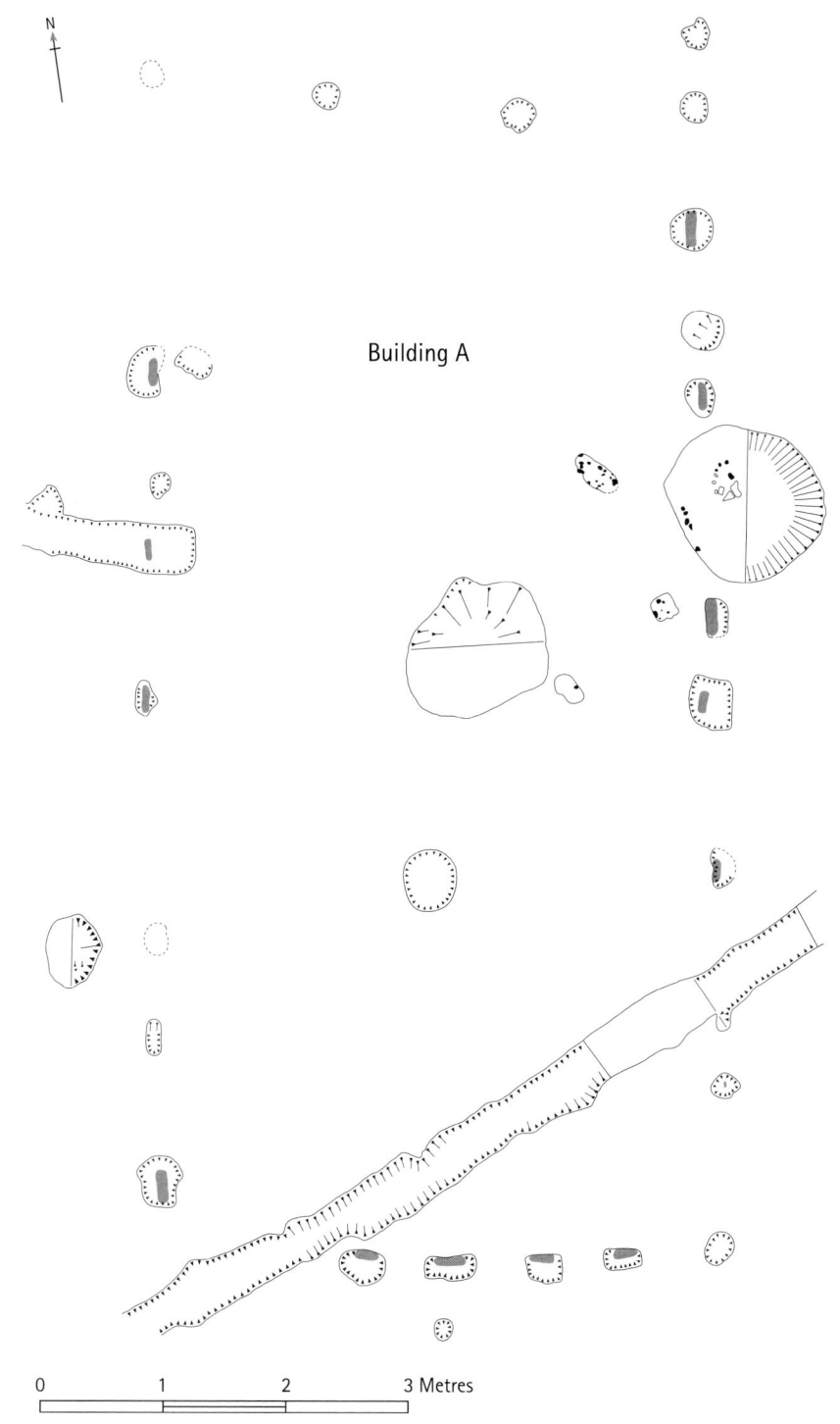

0 1 2 3 Metres

Figure 9.4 Building A from Steyning (after Gardiner 1993)

Despite the adoption of the early Saxon *Grubenhaus* at least as far north-west as Fremington, Cumbria (Oliver *et al.* 1996), building techniques thereafter generally diverge quite markedly from what is found in southern and eastern Britain. The chief difference is the apparent absence in northern England of earthfast footings after *c*.800 and the construction instead of essentially 'self-supporting' buildings. Gardiner, in his survey of these buildings, sees the use of dry-stone and gravel footings—introduced in the eighth century—as a milestone after which 'various methods were used...to try to increase the longevity of the timbers, either by raising them above the ground, or by protecting them in other ways from moisture' (Daniels 1988: 175 and fig. 26; Loveluck 2001: 85 and fig. 5.6; Gardiner 2004: 345). At the monastic site at Hartlepool, Cleveland, buildings with stone footings were in some cases direct replacements for earlier earthfast structures. This is particularly striking in the case of a building which had originally been built using post-in-trench construction: 'The posts were removed and the trench backfilled; the trench then had limestone slabs laid on the top of it. It must be concluded that the superstructure was cut off at ground level and stone footings inserted beneath [it]' (Daniels 1988: 177).

Gardiner argues that by increasing the longevity of certain buildings through the use of stone footings, their inhabitants sought to '[project] an image of the permanence of sacred or secular power' (2004: 351). The impact that the changing social requirements of buildings, in particular a new interest in establishing buildings as quasi-permanent features in the landscape, had upon the archaeological 'life-cycle' of timber buildings is worth considering more closely.

The life cycle of the Anglo-Saxon house

Evidence for the repair, rebuilding, and modification of buildings has been used to reconstruct the 'cultural biographies' of individual dwellings in later prehistory, following the work of Kopytoff (1986; see also Ingold 2000: 187–8). Archaeologists have, for example, demonstrated that bronze-age and iron-age houses in the southern Netherlands rarely show signs of repair or rebuilding and must therefore have been abandoned after only one phase of occupation (Gerritsen 1999: 79). While the recognition that farmsteads regularly shifted location is not new, it has conventionally been assumed to be the result of economic and ecological factors, above all farming methods. Gerritsen and others have argued, however, that social and cultural factors should also be considered and have noted that links exist in many pre-industrial societies between the lifecycles of houses and their occupants (ibid.: 81; cf. Brück 1999).

Early Anglo-Saxon buildings also on the whole display little evidence of substantial repair or renewal, although exceptions can of course be found. Of the nine reasonably complete ground-plans of post-hole buildings at Mucking, for example, none produced unambiguous evidence of repair or remodelling, although some double posts could arguably be interpreted in this light (Hamerow 1993). The relative scarcity of evidence for repair and rebuilding suggests that the majority of early Anglo-Saxon buildings were abandoned while still habitable and were either dismantled or left to decay *in situ*.

Some of the earliest evidence for significant rebuilding, repair, or modification of Anglo-Saxon buildings comes from Cowdery's Down and Yeavering, both of which were occupied during the first half of the seventh century. At Cowdery's Down, two of the four buildings in phase B were entirely replaced by others erected on the same 'footprint', while in the next phase Structure C10 appears to have been shortened by rebuilding the end walls (Millett 1984: 213). A similar process is apparent at Yeavering, where many of the major buildings underwent several phases of rebuilding (Hope-Taylor 1977).

Evidence for repair and complete rebuilding becomes more common in the mid and late Saxon periods. Darrah has estimated—based on evidence for the use of oak roundwood 0.20–0.25 m in diameter—that buildings at Flixborough would have needed repairs after approximately twenty years, with major rebuilding required after forty years. Detailed analysis of the buildings as well as dendrochronological evidence from Denmark suggests a life-span of between twenty-five and fifty years for most of the Flixborough buildings, several of which showed signs of repair and/or repeated rebuilding (Darrah 2007; Loveluck 2007: 50). Excavations at Renhold Water End West (Bedfordshire) revealed the ground-plans of five timber

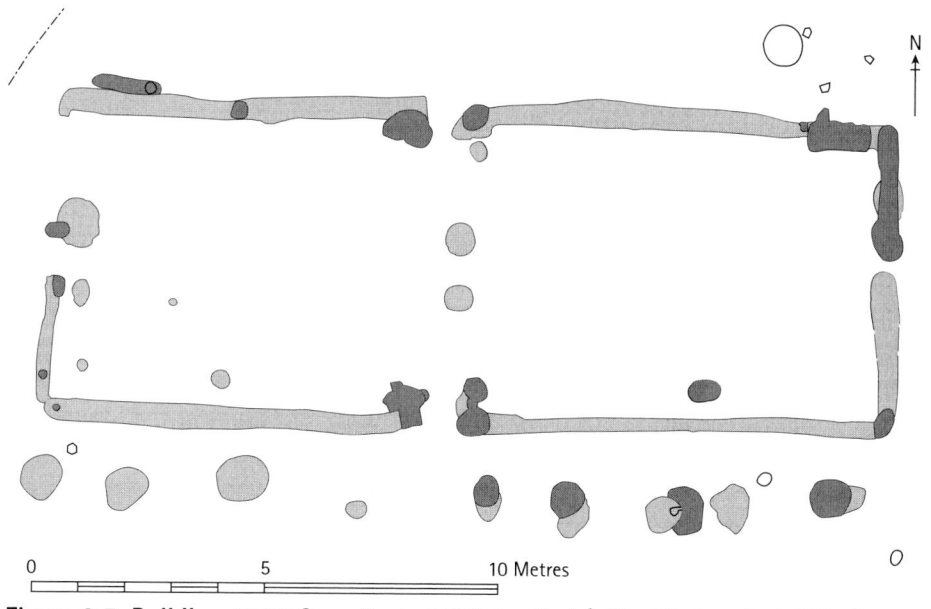

Figure 9.5 Building 9150 from Renhold Water End (after Timby *et al.* 2007)

buildings dating to between the tenth and twelfth centuries (Timby *et al.* 2007). Building 9150—a substantial structure measuring some 19 m x 7 m—had undergone a series of modifications. The eastern (gable) entrance replaced an earlier wider entrance; the beam-slots had been re-cut and posts cut into the beamslots may also indicate repairs (Fig. 9.5). Two, and possibly three, phases of rebuildings on the same plot are also evident at the probable late Saxon estate centre at Springfield Lyons, Essex (Tyler and Major 2005: 131).

As already noted, the introduction of stone and gravel footings in northern England from the eighth century may have been linked to a desire to extend the longevity of important buildings. This appears to be supported by the evidence for the repair and rebuilding of certain earthfast buildings whose life-cycles could thus span several human generations, thereby embodying and evoking links with ancestors. It is likely that there was a connection between this development and the growing importance of landholding and inheritance.

Form, function, and the configuration of internal space

Anglo-Saxon building remains are singularly uninformative where function is concerned, lacking as they usually do durable building materials, preserved floor levels, and evidence of their internal layout or of household activities; indeed it is not even possible to be sure that all buildings referred to as 'houses' were in fact dwellings. Yet an examination of the internal layout of Anglo-Saxon buildings—notably the positioning of entrances, hearths, and subdivisions—can enrich our understanding of these enigmatic structures.

The majority of timber buildings of the fifth to seventh centuries consisted, as far as can be determined, of one room. These buildings were almost invariably entered by means of opposing doorways positioned centrally within the long walls. A third doorway in one of the gable walls (and, very rarely, a fourth) is less common and mostly confined to larger than average buildings. Some buildings contained a small compartment, usually at the eastern end, which in most cases could be entered from the outside as well as from inside the building (Fig. 9.1). It is notable that most, and potentially all, of these buildings are likely to date to the late sixth or seventh century.

Another distinctive feature of the same period is a small number of buildings with an annexe at one or both gable ends (Fig. 9.6). Unlike the compartments discussed above, these annexes could only be entered from within the building (with the apparent exception of a building at Brandon, Suffolk; Carr *et al.* 1988: 374). Annexes, like compartments, were restricted to bigger than average buildings, yet their function remains obscure. Some have seen a connection with early churches with narthex, nave, and chancel and therefore regard them as a marker of high status (Dixon 2002: 96). While a strong case can be made for regarding Building B1 at Yeavering—surrounded as it is by conversion-period burials—and

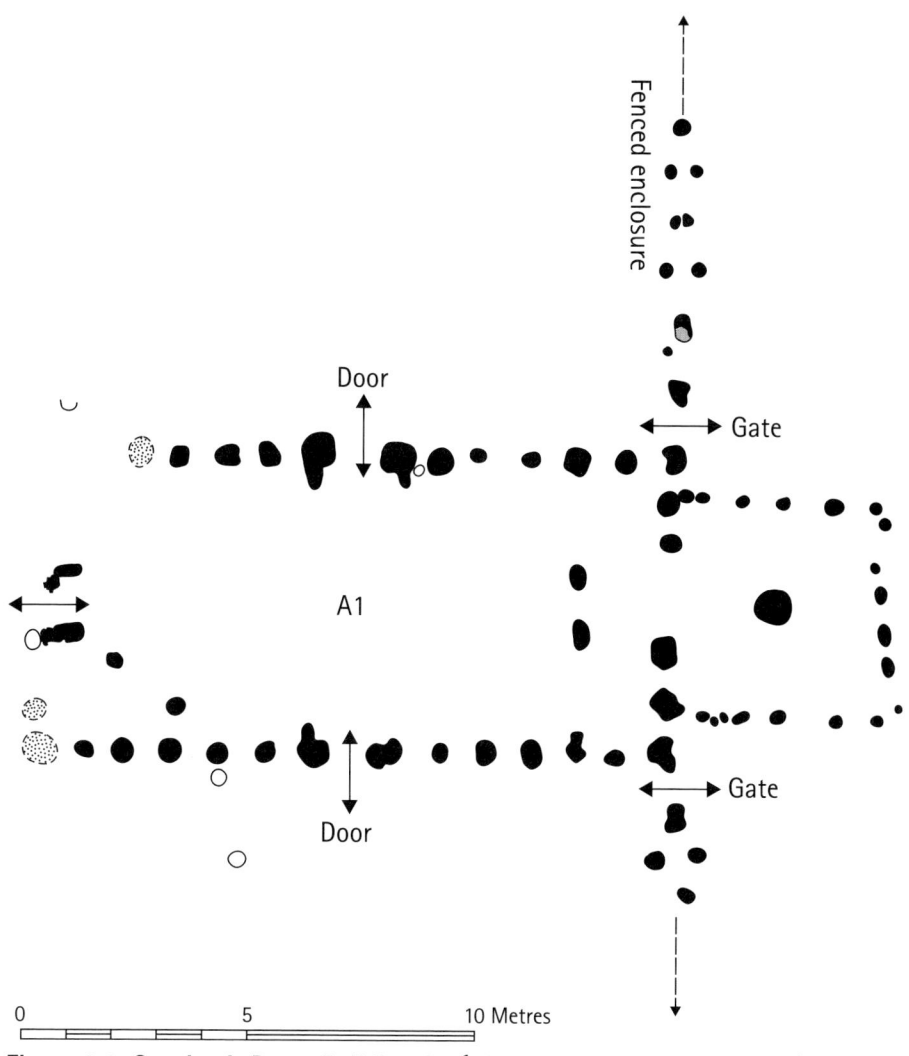

Figure 9.6 Cowdery's Down Building A1 (after Millett and James 1984)

the annexed buildings at Brandon and Northampton as having served a religious function, other examples such as those at Cowdery's Down should not be assumed to have done so (Hope-Taylor 1977; Carr *et al.* 1988; Blair 1995; James *et al.* 1985: 190). James *et al.* nevertheless have drawn attention to two buildings with square annexes—Cowdery's Down A1 and Thirlings C—which contained a central post or feature (Fig. 9.6; James *et al.* 1985; it is possible, however, that the feature inside Thirlings C predated the annexe: O'Brien and Miket 1991: 67). They draw a convincing analogy with the small square structures at Yeavering and New Wintles Farm, Oxfordshire, argued by Blair to have served a cultic function, and indeed to represent a kind of 'domestic shrine' (James *et al.* 1985: 190; Blair 1995: 19, fig. 11).

The precise function of annexes and compartments cannot be determined and doubtless varied, but in almost all cases the entranceways into compartments were aligned with the gable entrance[s] of the building. This would have facilitated both procession through the building and inter-visibility (as in the case of the axially aligned Buildings A1 and A2 at Chalton: Addyman et al. 1972: 19–20). A notable exception to this rule is found at Yeavering, where a 'purposeful asymmetry' is apparent in several buildings (Hope-Taylor 1977: 91). In Buildings C2, C3, and A3, for example, entrances in the gable ends and the partitions were deliberately staggered (Hope-Taylor 1977: figs. 17 and 38). In a few instances, buildings with compartments and annexes were articulated with enclosures. In the case of Chalton buildings A1 and AZ1, the compartments led directly into the enclosures by means of a doorway in the gable wall, providing 'private access' (Addyman and Leigh 1973: 14 and fig. 3). In contrast, the annexes of Cowdery's Down A1 and Yeavering A1(b) and A3(a) projected into enclosures, yet curiously did not provide entry into them (Fig. 9.6; Millett 1984: 201–3; Hope-Taylor 1977).

Clearly then, building traditions of the fifth to seventh centuries placed considerable emphasis on regularity, formality, and even symmetry, which was particularly marked in larger and arguably more important buildings (Fig. 9.1). Exactly how social relationships were played out within the formalized space of the early Anglo-Saxon house may be irrecoverable, but these relationships may be illuminated by ethnographic examples of houses organized 'in accordance with a set of homologous oppositions' such as front and back, light and dark, or male and female, as set out by Bourdieu in his classic study of the Kabyle house (Bourdieu 1990; Gosden, this vol.).[3]

Although Marshall and Marshall have demonstrated that there was a general increase in the mean size of Anglo-Saxon buildings over time, buildings of the eighth and ninth centuries show little evidence of increased internal partitioning (Marshall and Marshall 1991: 42; 1993: 380). Their layouts suggest, furthermore, that regularity was less important than before, with both the number and placement of entrances varying widely, with relatively few buildings following the earlier norm of two central, opposed doorways. Some buildings had only a single doorway, such as Hartlepool Buildings VIII, X, and XIV, and North Elmham Buildings Z and U (Daniels 1988; Wade-Martins 1980: figs. 84, 120);[4] others had two entrances in the same wall, as in the long hall at the royal settlement at Cheddar, Somerset, and Building 3 at Springfield Lyons (Fig. 9.7A; Rahtz 1979: fig. 30; Tyler and Major 2005: fig. 72). Evidence for partitions did survive, however, in the long hall at Goltho

---

[3] The seventh-century princely chamber grave excavated at Prittlewell, in which vessels, furniture, and other items were carefully arranged on the floor and hung on the walls of the chamber, may have been intended to evoke the formal layout of the hall (MoLAS 2004).

[4] The Hartlepool buildings are exceptionally small and there may be a relationship between the size of the building and the number of entrances. The smallest buildings at Chalton also tended to have only one doorway (Daniels 1988; Champion 1977: 364).

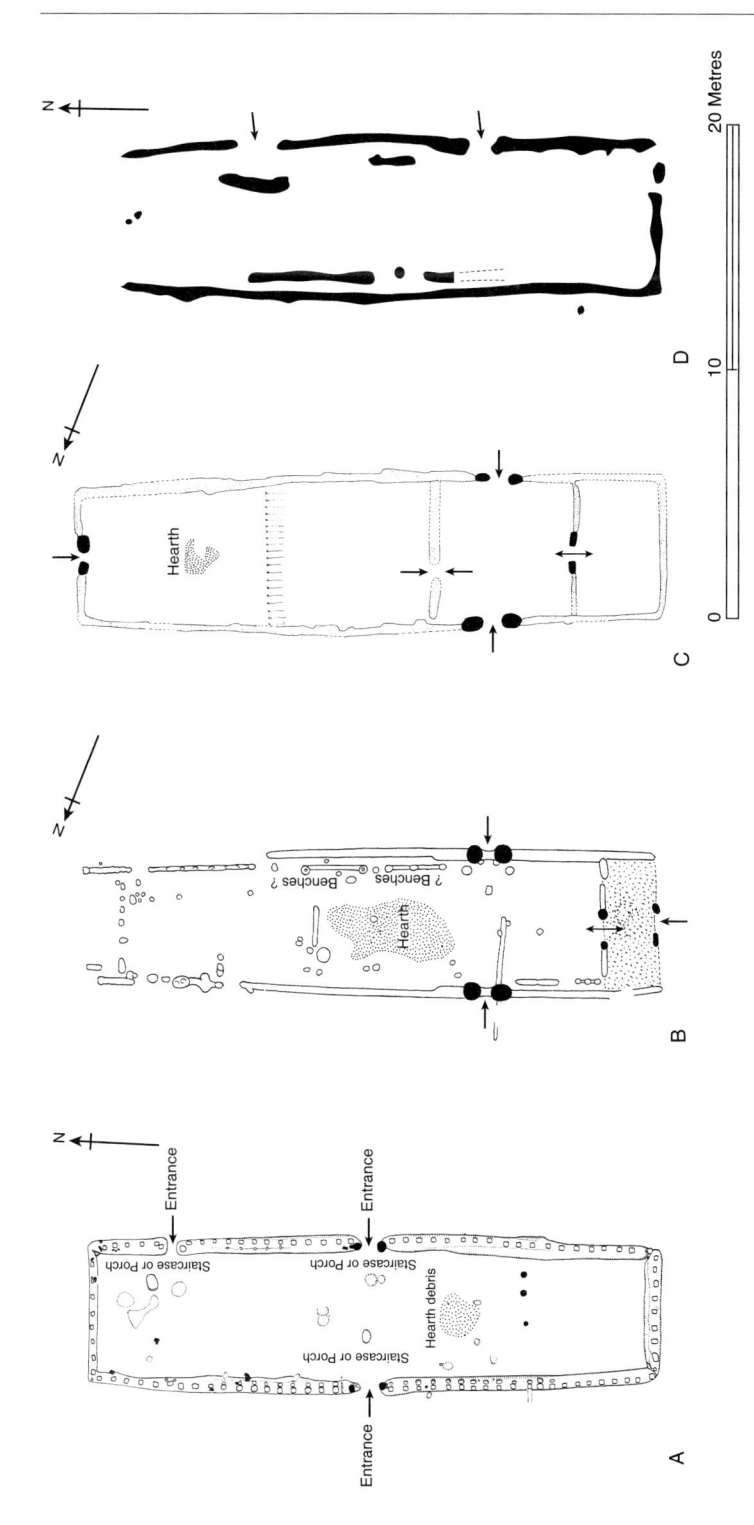

Figure 9.7 Late Saxon long halls from Cheddar (A), Sulgrave (B), Goltho (C), and Bicester (D) (after Rahtz 1979, Davison 1977, Beresford 1987, Harding and Andrews 2002)

(Fig. 9.7c). A partition divided the interior into a large, eastern room containing a hearth, a smaller western 'antechamber', and a still smaller annexe. The hearth room—the floor of which had been raised in the eastern half by about half a metre—could be entered from the outside by means of a narrow doorway in the eastern gable wall, while opposing, much wider doors in the long walls led into the 'antechamber'.

The importance of doorways is emphasized throughout the period by the use of massive doorposts and evidence for their frequent repair and replacement. At North Elmham, one of the internal doorposts marking the entranceway between the two rooms in Building S had been replaced two or three times, as had the posts in the northern and southern doorways of Building 9150 at Renhold, Water End (Fig. 9.5; Wade-Martins 1980: 61; Timby *et al.* 2007). Doorways appear to have been given ritual emphasis in Building A2 at Yeavering, which contained the horn of a sheep or goat in a doorpost in the southern wall, while the 'teeth of ox and boar were identified in the door-pits of the eastern and western partitions'; the gable-end doorways in C4(a) also displayed signs of elaboration (Hope-Taylor 1977: 53, fig. 39). The importance accorded to entrances in settlements as a whole is echoed in the careful positioning of gated entrances into late Saxon enclosed settlements of thegnly status, as described by Gardiner (this vol.).

Written sources indicate that the hearth possessed considerable symbolic importance in Anglo-Saxon England. In addition to the famous passage in Bede's *Ecclesiastical History* in which a human life is compared to the flight of a sparrow through the great hall—'Inside there is a comforting fire; outside the wintry storms of snow and rain are raging. This sparrow flies swiftly in through one door of the hall, and out through another' (*HE* II.13)—are two legal clauses in which the hearth is used to represent an entire house or property, as in the late seventh-century laws of King Ine of Wessex (Whitelock 1955: nos. 32, 61): 'Church-scot is to be paid from the haulm ['stubble', referring to fields from which the harvest had been gathered] and the hearth where one resides at midwinter'. In the eleventh-century laws of Cnut, an individual described as *heorðfæst*, or seated at a hearth, was one who owned his own property (Whitelock 1955: no. 20a; Dölling 1958: 52). Few examples of *in situ* hearths have, however, been identified in Anglo-Saxon buildings. The lack of preserved floor surfaces is undoubtedly responsible for this. At Flixborough, for example, where ground surfaces were comparatively well preserved, a relatively high proportion of buildings produced evidence for hearths (Loveluck 2007). It may be that some buildings originally had raised timber floors, which would also help account for the lack of hearths (Millett 1984: 240–1).

Four of the ground-level buildings from West Stow produced evidence of hearths, three of which were positioned in the middle of the building at almost precisely the same distance from the western gable wall (Buildings 1, 2, and 3; West 1986). The hearth in Yeavering Building D4, identified on the basis of a 'circular patch of reddened clay', also lay more or less centrally within the 'room' to the west of the central corridor formed by the opposing entrances (Hope-Taylor 1977: 117, fig. 53). Several examples of *in situ* hearths—mostly sited along the central axis of the building—are known from mid and late Saxon buildings (e.g. Springfield Lyons Building 3, Faccombe Netherton Buildings 3 and 9, North Elmham Building Z, and Portchester Building S13: Tyler and Major 2005: fig. 72; Fairbrother 1990: figs. 4.7 and 4.16; Wade-Martins 1980: fig. 84; Cunliffe 1976: fig. 22).

The variety of constructional techniques used in late Saxon buildings is paralleled by a diversification of forms. While rectangular buildings still predominated, square forms also occur. At Springfield Lyons, a square building with unusually deep foundation trenches, measuring approximately 4 m x 5.4 m (Building 1), has tentatively been identified as a free-standing tower associated with another building (Tyler and Major 2005: 193). The base of what may have been another tower of similar dimensions, but stone-built and dating to the eleventh century, was excavated at Portchester, which was by this time presumably a manorial centre (Cunliffe 1976: 60). The impact on the late Saxon landscape of these first towers—and the bells which, according to the documents, rang out from them—must have been considerable, as Morris observes (this volume). A small number of cellared buildings—long recognized in urban contexts such as York and London—have also been identified on rural sites, notably at Bishopstone, Sussex, where the remains of a cellared building probably represent the base of another tower (Thomas 2005).

Anglo-Saxon laws and other written sources suggest that, by the tenth century at least, food preparation, storage, stabling of animals, and other activities were sited in separate buildings; yet while kitchens, stables, bakehouses, etc. are all mentioned by name, their physical appearance is nowhere described (Dölling 1958: 55–8). Recent work on the eleventh-century text known as *Gerefa*, which contains instructions for a reeve on the management and tending of his lord's farm, suggests that references to, for example, a kitchen, could just as well refer to an area or room within the house, rather than a separate building (Gardiner 2006).

While it may be that the decision to build a rectangular or square building was essentially governed by its intended use, identifying the functions of excavated buildings remains highly problematic, and archaeologists have sometimes been too ready to assign specific functions to excavated buildings (Gardiner, this volume). Nevertheless, convincing examples of halls, kitchens, and latrines have all been identified.

Halls

A group of exceptionally large Anglo-Saxon buildings with a floor area measuring more than 100 m² (James *et al.* 1985) may reasonably be identified as the halls (OE *healles*) referred to in Anglo-Saxon literature, which are distinguished in written sources from ordinary houses (OE *hus*) and appear as exceptional, one-roomed structures containing the 'high seat' of the lord and benches for his followers. In these buildings, 'all public business such as the reception and feasting of visitors

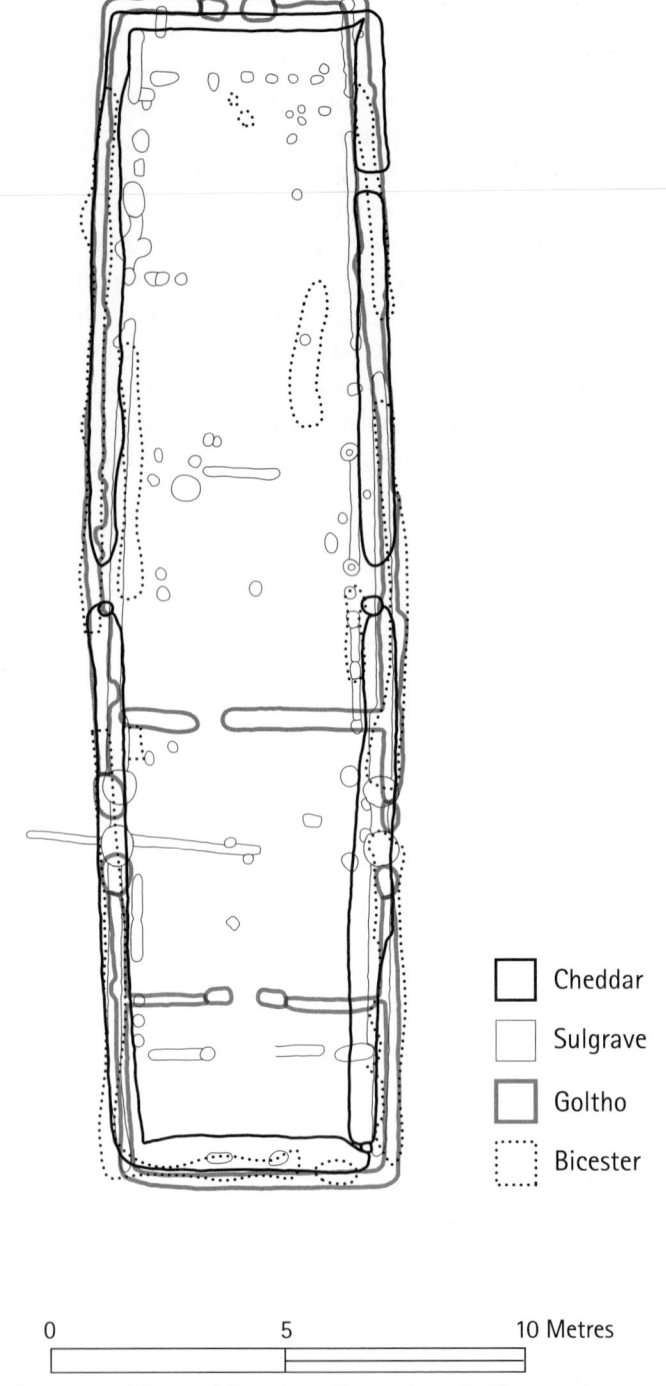

Figure 9.8 Plans of four late Saxon long halls superimposed

[took] place' (Cramp 1957: 71; Dölling 1958: 52). The highly formalized and symmetrical layouts of the largest buildings at the settlements at Yeavering and Cowdery's Down have already been noted. Four tenth-century examples of so-called 'long halls' excavated at Sulgrave, Northamptonshire; Goltho; Bicester, Oxfordshire; and Cheddar reflect a continuing interest in formalized, standardized layout, and display strikingly close similarities in plan (Figs. 9.7 and 9.8).[5] The internal arrangement and use of space would have been quite different in each of the four buildings, however, to judge from the positioning of doorways and hearths. Despite their elongated proportions and the fact that they are slightly wider in the middle than at the ends, they appear to relate to the earlier building tradition seen at Yeavering (James *et al.* 1985 and fig. 14). The tenth century also saw a break with this earlier tradition, however, with the appearance of a new kind of 'narrow aisled' hall, in which the longevity of roof-carrying posts was increased by placing them inside the building (Fig. 9.9; Gardiner 2004).

Kitchens and bakehouses

Buildings containing ovens which can reasonably be identified as detached kitchens or bakehouses are rare. Building AM at North Elmham, Norfolk, dated to the mid Saxon period, appears to have housed a series of three clay-lined ovens, although their contemporaneity with the building could not be conclusively demonstrated. The main part of the building was nearly square, measuring around 5.4 m x 6.0 m. Building S11 at Portchester, which measured *c.* 5.8 m x 8.5 m and dated to the ninth or tenth century, contained a rectangular oven constructed mainly of re-used Roman tiles and limestone lumps set in clay (Wade-Martins 1980: 69–73; Cunliffe 1976: 29–32). A series of five kitchens—not all contemporary—was identified at Goltho (Beresford 1987: 59; Fig. 12.4). Building 16 at Springfield Lyons has been tentatively identified as a kitchen based on the plant remains in the vicinity of the building, while two small, square structures—Buildings 2 and 20—were also interpreted as detached kitchens (Tyler and Major 2005: 193). Finally, Building D3 at Yeavering, which contained two hearths, was associated with a 'working hollow' immediately to the north and a pit complex immediately to the west; the fills of both the pits and the working hollow contained large quantities of bone fragments, mostly cattle long bones, which had been chopped and split (Hope-Taylor 1977: 103–6). The hearths, together with the evidence for butchery, led the excavator to describe D3 as a 'kitchen'. While it is very likely to have been connected with the

---

[5] Measurements specified in the Boldon Book, an estate record of the services of the tenants of the Bishop of Durham in the second half of the twelfth century, shed interesting light on this phenomenon. It specifies that the villeins of Bishop Auckland were to build for the Bishop a 'Great Hall in the forest, 60 feet long and 16 feet broad within the posts', dimensions which are remarkably close to those of the late Saxon 'long halls' (Rees 1963: 162). I am grateful to James Campbell for drawing this to my attention.

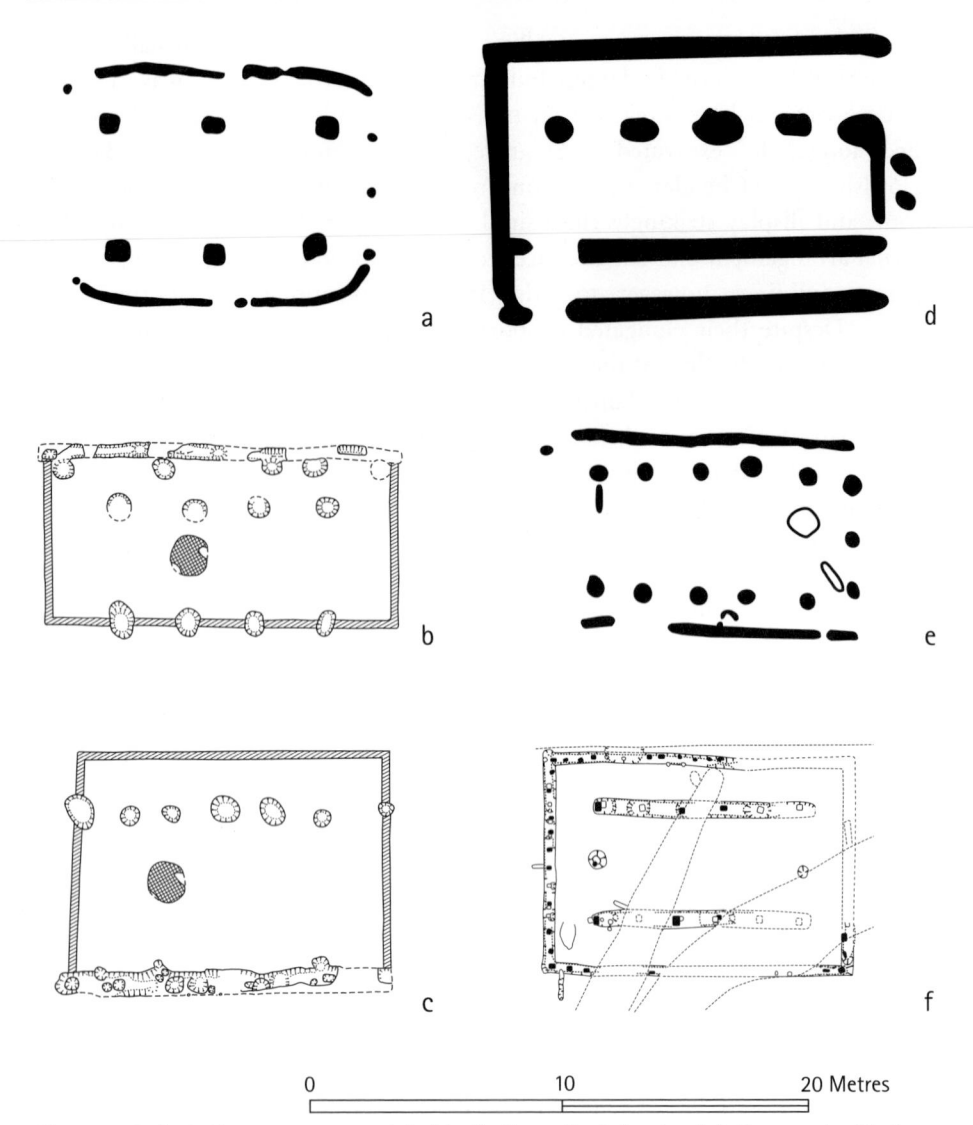

Figure 9.9 Late Saxon narrow-aisled halls from Portchester (a), Faccombe Netherton (b, c, f), Raunds (d), and Ketton (e) (after Cunliffe 1976, Fairbrother 1990, Boddington 1996, Meadows forthcoming)

preparation and ritual consumption of food, its early date and position within a cultic complex, including a 'temple' and cemetery, emphasize its uniqueness.

Barns and granaries

The scarcity of grain-storage facilities on Anglo-Saxon settlements has long puzzled archaeologists and stands in marked contrast to iron-age and Romano-British settlements. As Gardiner notes, it is likely that unthreshed grain was stored in the

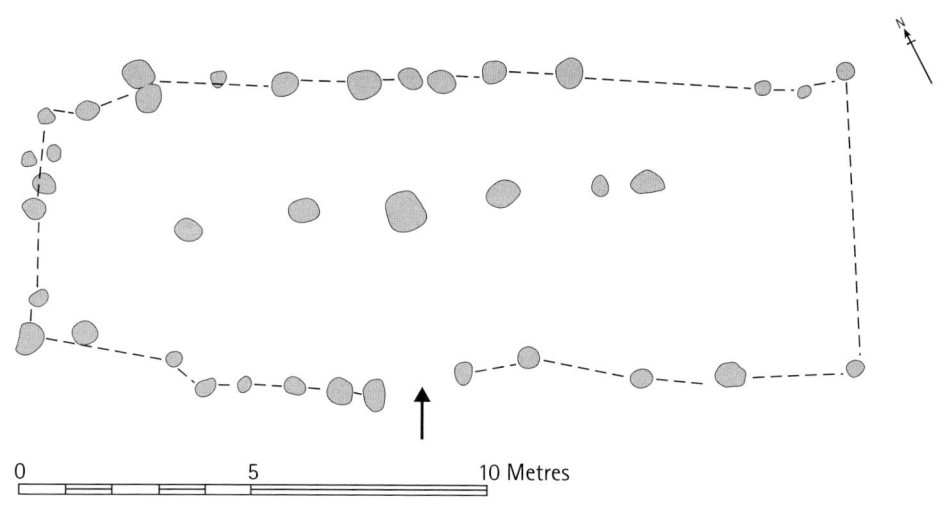

Figure 9.10 A probable barn from Higham Ferrers (Northants) (after Hardy and Charles 2007)

rafters of houses,[6] in *Grubenhäuser*, and/or in ricks (which would leave no archaeological trace) and threshed as the need arose (this volume; see also Hamerow 2002: 22–38). A few Anglo-Saxon granaries have been identified—for example at Pennyland, Buckinghamshire; Orton Hall Farm, Cambridgeshire; and Yarnton (Williams 1993: 82; MacKreth 1996: 89–90; Hey 2004: 124–5, figs. 6.22–23). Buildings which can reasonably be interpreted as barns are, however, extremely rare. Two of the most convincing examples are two elongated post-built structures with a central line of roof-supporting posts running along their length identified at the mid Saxon estate centre at Higham Ferrers, Northamptonshire (Fig. 9.10; Hardy and Charles 2007: 32–5, 40, 162–3). Similarities with early medieval barns excavated in the Netherlands, together with a concentration of cereal grains from one of the post-holes of Building 2664, support their interpretation as barns (Hamerow 2002: fig. 2.15).

Latrines

A number of latrines have also been identified in late Saxon settlements, in most cases lying adjacent to major buildings. At Bishopstone, an apsidal-ended structure enclosing a central cess-pit was interpreted as a latrine, as were rectangular

---

[6] Large deposits of cereals associated with a few Anglo-Saxon timber buildings—such as the charred oats found in the post-holes of Building 6 at Springfield Lyons and Structure 1200 at Chapel Street, Bicester—are suggestive of grain storage (Tyler and Major 2005: 195; Pelling 2002: 170).

structures at North Elmham and Faccombe Netherton, where the latrine lay adjacent to Building 9, identified as the 'hall' (Thomas 2005; Wade-Martins 1980: 142-5; Fairbrother 1990: 65 and fig. 4.18). At Goltho, a long, narrow cess-pit was housed in a structure that appears to have been attached to the corner of a large building; two other cesspits may have been housed in similar structures (Fig. 12.4; Beresford 1987: 57, 68, 79, fig. 68).

Nearly all the buildings identified as kitchens, towers, or latrines date to the mid and late Saxon period and most if not all come from settlements of high status. The curious lack of excavated 'ordinary' settlements of the late Saxon period (considered by Ulmschneider, this volume) introduces a danger of circularity into any discussion of status, yet it is not unreasonable to suggest, based on current evidence, that the construction of special-purpose buildings was itself a marker of high status in late Saxon England.

GRUBENHÄUSER (SUNKEN-FEATURED BUILDINGS)

Grubenhäuser are by far the most numerous type of Anglo-Saxon building to have been excavated, yet their reconstruction and function remain topics of debate. Despite their ubiquity, no comprehensive study of Anglo-Saxon *Grubenhäuser* had been undertaken until a recent monograph by Jess Tipper (2004) who describes them as 'typically sub-rectangular in shape, measuring c. 3 x 4 m in area x c. 0.3–0.5 m in depth with sides sloping down to a roughly flat base. There are often two post-holes along the short walls of the pit... although the number of post-holes varies from zero to six, including additional post-holes in the four corners of the pit. These post-holes presumably took the supports for the superstructure' (2004: 1).

Tipper's analysis of over 400 buildings broadly confirms that the proportion of *Grubenhäuser* to earthfast timber buildings in a settlement relates to underlying geology; settlements sited, for example, on chalk are less likely to contain large numbers of *Grubenhäuser*. Although their dimensions vary widely, Tipper identifies 'a strong central tendency for c. 4 m x 3 m' (2004: 64; Tables 18 and 19), with the seventh century seeing the appearance of larger *Grubenhäuser* (cf. Hamerow 1993: 11). Neighbouring structures can, however, have markedly different depths, from just a few centimetres to around a metre. Tipper's study demonstrates that there is no correlation between the length/width of the sunken area and the depth, and that depth is therefore likely to relate to function (2004: 65–6). A final typological conundrum is why some *Grubenhäuser* had two posts while others had four or six. Tipper's study establishes that while the number of posts is not related to chronology, there is regional patterning: while buildings with two posts are the most

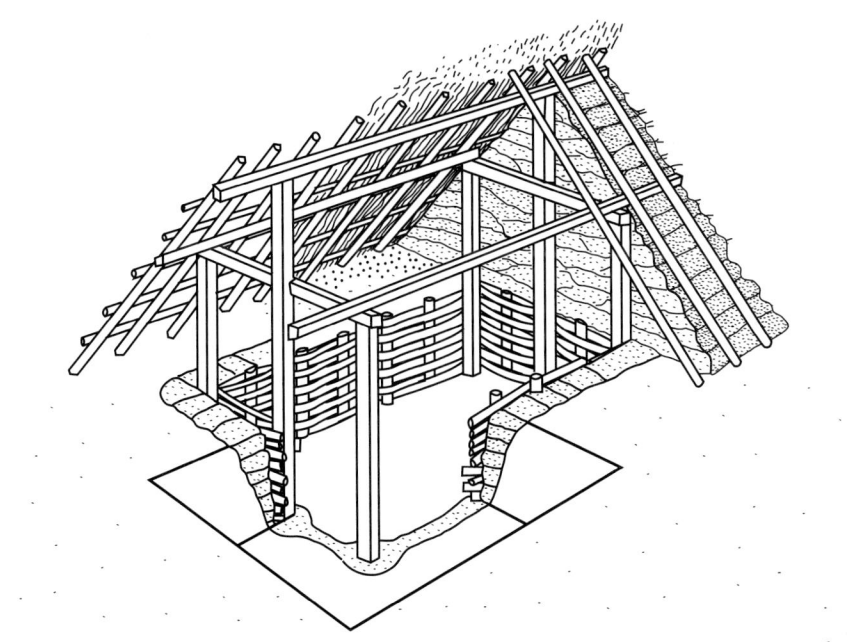

Figure 9.11 Reconstruction of a *Grubenhaus* as a sunken-floored structure (after Heidinga and Offenberg 1992)

common overall, those with six posts are largely restricted to East Anglia and the south-east of England (ibid.: 68–70).[7]

Grubenhäuser have most often been reconstructed, based on a range of historic and ethnographic analogies, with a sunken floor and a roof supported by two ridge-posts and rafters extending down to the ground, to form a tent-like structure which would have required a minimum of labour and materials and was assumed to be relatively short-lived in comparison to earthfast timber buildings (Fig. 9.11). Stanley West, based on his excavations at West Stow, was the first to argue that the sunken hollow had in fact been covered by a planked floor which rested on joists laid on the ground surface and across the pit (West 1969; West Stow Environmental Archaeology Group 1974). The evidence on which this was chiefly based is as follows (West 1986, 1: 116–21):

1. Timbers interpreted as floor planks had been preserved in two buildings that had been destroyed by fire.
2. None of the pits yielded evidence for an entrance.
3. None of the pits showed evidence of wear or erosion despite having been dug into sandy subsoil.

---

[7] This corresponds with the evidence for regional traditions elsewhere around the North Sea littoral (Hamerow 2002: 31).

4. Some pits had very restricted floor areas.
5. The fine, homogeneous nature of the lowest fill was suggestive of debris that had filtered through the cracks in floorboards.
6. Clay hearths in the upper fills of several *Grubenhäuser* overlapped the edge of the hollow suggesting that they had rested on a suspended floor, while two dog skeletons found in one of the hollows were thought to be the remains of animals that had crawled into the space under the floor.

(West 1986: 23)

West suggested that the most likely function of the sub-floor space was to improve air circulation, thus prolonging the life of the main structural timbers; storage was seen as another possible use. He acknowledged, however, that while his model resolved certain problems of interpretation, it created others, and one could not assume that all *Grubenhäuser* had suspended, planked floors (West 1986: 120).

Tipper echoes many of West's observations in pointing out that some of the evidence used to support the 'sunken-floored' model does not withstand close scrutiny (2004: 74–93). He further suggests that gable posts (which are often relatively shallow and occasionally even absent) were not essential to the stability of the building and were effectively scaffolding for a superstructure which was 'self-supporting with the main weight of the roof borne on wall-posts or load-bearing turf walls around the outside of the pit' (ibid.: 93). Evidence from a few *Grubenhäuser* for the repair and replacement of gable posts militates against this interpretation, however (ibid.: 72). Tipper also argues that virtually all of the stakeholes identified on the bases of *Grubenhäuser*, which would make little sense beneath a suspended floor, represent rodent or root disturbance 'mistaken as stakeholes by excavators with preconceptions of what a typical *Grubenhaus* should look like' (ibid.: 88). He also concludes that no unequivocal examples of hearths contemporary with the buildings' use could be identified and that the burnt clay deposits at West Stow reflect the re-use of partly back-filled hollows (ibid.: 89–92).

Tipper concludes that the suspended-floor model 'fits more easily with most of the archaeological evidence' but admits that 'aspects of this interpretation are also problematical' (ibid.: 93). While his study exposes as flawed some of the evidence used to argue for sunken floors, it has not identified any direct evidence for suspended floors. The lack of evidence for entrances, wear on the floor, occupation layers, and lining of the sides of the pit, as well as the restricted and/or uneven floors of many of the structures could in part be explained by the growing evidence, discussed below, that one of the main uses of *Grubenhäuser* was for storage.

The plausibility of the 'suspended floor' model is also open to scrutiny. While some stakeholes may have been misidentified, others clearly have not. The excavators of several *Grubenhäuser* at Riverdene, Hampshire, excavated numerous stakeholes on their bases; the area outside the structures was carefully examined to ensure that these were not the result of natural disturbance, but 'no similar features were seen outside the [*Grubenhaus*]' (Hall-Torrance and Weaver 2003: 80).[8] The marked variability in the depth of these buildings is difficult to explain if the pit served merely as an air-space. Of the few excavated *Grubenhäuser* to have burnt down, most have produced evidence of planks which could be the remains of floors, yet it should be recalled that the laying of a timber floor requires a great deal of labour and materials. Indeed, the earliest surviving vernacular buildings, which date to the late twelfth and early thirteenth centuries, do not have planked ground floors (Walker 1999), and so it would be remarkable if the majority of buildings in sixth-century England possessed them. Finally, a few *Grubenhäuser* have been found with rows of clay loom-weights resting on the base of the hollow, which have generally been interpreted as having fallen from upright, warp-weighted looms (Rahtz 1976: fig. 2.12). Such rows are unlikely to have survived intact if the loom and/or loom-weights had collapsed into the hollow along with a planked floor.

In the absence of decisive new evidence, the debate about the superstructure of *Grubenhäuser* relies heavily on issues of plausibility; there is some evidence in support of both models, although evidence for suspended floors would by its very nature be elusive. It is likely that the archaeological features which have been grouped together as *Grubenhäuser* in fact comprise more than one kind of superstructure, as West recognized (1986: 116–21). While the 'sunken-floored' model has often been uncritically adopted, 'suspended floors' have also been proposed for structures which in fact produced little evidence to support either reconstruction, sometimes to counter the traditional view of these buildings as 'unsophisticated and low-cost structures' (Tipper 2004: 78).

If most *Grubenhäuser* possessed suspended floors and could therefore have been as substantial as earthfast buildings, then this has enormous implications for our interpretations of Anglo-Saxon settlements. First, it would mean that they represent at least as great an expenditure of labour and materials as earthfast buildings. Far from regarding them as ancillary structures—the conventional interpretation adopted by both West and Tipper (West 1986; Tipper 2004: 184)—*Grubenhäuser* would need to be regarded as of equal status to, if not higher than, earthfast buildings, as Rahtz was the first to recognize (1976: 79). Evidence for the function of these structures must be considered before returning to this fundamental problem.

Tipper's re-evaluation includes a detailed study of *Grubenhaus* fills in order to establish whether the artefacts they contain reflect the date and function of the buildings—an assumption often made but rarely tested. The evidence indicates

---

[8] Other features in the bases of some *Grubenhäuser* also seem inconsistent with the use of a suspended floor, such as the evenly formed ramp at one end of a large *Grubenhaus* excavated at Hurst Park, East Molesey, Surrey (Andrews and Crockett 1996). A *Grubenhaus* excavated at Wharram Percy not only produced evidence of a hearth, stakeholes, a 'trampled chalk surface' and a wattle revetment, but had been partly dug into an earlier Roman ditch, the fill of which 'had become trampled to form a hard compacted surface' (Milne and Richards 1992: 20, 82).

that, once abandoned, *Grubenhaus* pits were usually rapidly back-filled (Tipper 2004: 104–5). This may seem encouraging to those who hope to find clues to the buildings' uses in the finds they contain, but Tipper's investigation suggests that the processes by which the pits filled up were anything but straightforward.

Based on a small number of micromorphological studies and re-evaluation of excavation records, Tipper concludes that 'occupation layers' identified in *Grubenhäuser* at West Stow and elsewhere were actually secondary. He believes, furthermore, that the discovery in some buildings of cross-joining sherds (i.e. joining pieces of the same vessel) found in lower, middle, and upper fills suggests that even *Grubenhäuser* with clearly tripartite fills must have been 'backfilled in a single phase or, at least, that the material derived from a single source' (Tipper 2004: 107). This apparently contradictory evidence notwithstanding, Tipper's analysis leads him to conclude that 'most of the material in *Grubenhaus* fills was the result of tertiary deposition[9] with no direct relationship to the function of the buildings' (2004: 160).

Not all the material found in *Grubenhaus* fills is tertiary, however. At Radley, Barrow Hills, Oxfordshire, for instance, the fill of a *Grubenhaus* that had been dug through a Neolithic burial (Bradley 1992: 132 and fig. 5) contained bone fragments from the same burial, demonstrating that it had been at least partly backfilled with material originally excavated from the pit—material that clearly had not travelled far. Furthermore, the presence of large, unabraded sherds in *Grubenhaus* fills is not uncommon and also points to secondary, rather than tertiary, deposition.[10]

There is general agreement that *Grubenhäuser* had a variety of uses (Rahtz 1976: 76; Hamerow 2002: 31–5; Tipper 2004: 160–85). One of these is for grain storage, as on some continental settlements (Hamerow 2002: 34), although some grain appears to have been stored in the rafters of houses and other structures (see above). Comparable evidence has been found at West Heslerton, where several *Grubenhäuser* were found to have contained 'large quantities of carbonized grain on the bases of their pits' (Powlesland 1997: 106). Another use was for textile production. The most numerous artefacts in them other than pottery sherds are clay loom-weights, both fired and unfired; spindle whorls, pin-beaters, and other implements are also commonly found (Rahtz 1976: 76–9; Leahy, this volume). As already noted, loom-weights are sometimes found resting on the base of the pits in neat, sometimes overlapping, rows, and Tipper accepts that some groups of loom-weights represent 'primary deposits which were destroyed *in situ*' (2004: table 55; 168). Clearly, some of these buildings were used for cloth production, although

---

[9] That is, they derive from midden deposits that could have been carried across the site to be used as backfill for abandoned buildings.

[10] The pottery from the three buildings at Botolphs (W. Sussex), for example, 'was unabraded and comprised large sized sherds, a substantial number of which were conjoining. The bone showed little sign of gnawing or erosion' (Gardiner 1990: 239).

there is no reason to assume that this was the only or even chief activity which took place inside them, nor that weaving was not also carried out in earthfast timber buildings (see Hamerow 2002: 33 for continental examples of ground-level buildings used for weaving).

THE RELATIONSHIP BETWEEN *GRUBENHÄUSER* AND EARTHFAST TIMBER BUILDINGS

As already noted, if the suspended-floor model is accepted, then *Grubenhäuser* could have had the same floor area as earthfast timber buildings with virtually indistinguishable superstructures.[11] Nevertheless, the traditional consensus, namely that *Grubenhäuser* were ancillary buildings which were shorter-lived than and served different functions to their earthfast counterparts, largely stands (e.g. West 1986: 151). At West Heslerton, for example, where *Grubenhäuser* were found mostly in the north-western part of the site and earthfast timber buildings in the east, the former is interpreted as comprising a 'craft and industry' zone and the latter a 'housing' zone (Tipper 2004: 184; Powlesland 1997: 110–13).

This raises more than a few conundrums. Why, for example, was it necessary to go to the effort and cost involved in digging a pit and constructing a suspended planked floor, if in terms of size and external appearance, the two types of building were broadly comparable? If a sub-floor space conferred significant benefits such as extending the life of the main structural timbers, why were not all buildings constructed in this way? Finally, why would greater effort and materials be expended on buildings that were used for storage and/or craftworking, than on dwellings?[12]

We do not as yet have the evidence at our disposal to resolve these apparent contradictions. It is of interest, however, to note a small number of apparently 'hybrid' buildings that display some of the attributes of both earthfast timber buildings and *Grubenhäuser*. Building D3 at Yeavering, for example, possessed a sunken floor around 1 m deep, but in almost every other respect resembled a typical earthfast timber building, measuring around 12 m x 6 m and containing two

---

[11] Indeed, on a number of sites, the floor areas of the smallest timber buildings are no greater than the sunken areas of the largest *Grubenhäuser* (e.g. at Chalton and Eye Kettleby: Champion 1977; N. Finn pers. comm.).

[12] Ever since the discovery of earthfast timber buildings, it has been widely accepted that *Grubenhäuser* are unlikely to have functioned as dwellings. Of West Heslerton, the excavator says: 'one thing we can be reasonably certain of is that [*Grubenhäuser*] did not provide housing' (Powlesland 1997: 107).

central, opposed doorways in the long walls. It was ringed by external post-holes interpreted by the excavator as representing 'buttresses' (Hope-Taylor 1977: 103–4). A building at Flixton Quarry (Suffolk) possessed a shallow, sunken area (c. 4.0 x 3.2 m and c. 0.2 m deep) with two large gable posts at either end. Just outside this sunken area, however, running along the long sides of the structure, were shallow foundation trenches into which were set a series of post-holes (Boulter 2006). The distinction between earthfast timber buildings and *Grubenhäuser* may yet prove to have been less rigid than archaeologists have tended to assume.

References

Addyman, P. (1972). 'The Anglo-Saxon house: a new review'. *Anglo-Saxon England* 1: 273–308.
—— and Leigh, D. (1973). 'The Anglo-Saxon village at Chalton, Hampshire: second interim report'. *Medieval Archaeology* 17: 1–25.
—— —— and Hughes, M. (1972). 'Anglo-Saxon houses at Chalton, Hampshire'. *Medieval Archaeology* 16: 13–32.
Andrews, P., and Crockett, A. (1996). 'Hurst Park East Molesey, Surrey: Riverside settlement and burial from the Neolithic to the early Saxon periods', in P. Andrews and A. Crockett (eds.), *Three Excavations Along the Thames and Its Tributaries, 1994: Neolithic to Saxon Settlement and Burial in the Thames, Colne, and Kennet Valleys.* Salisbury: Wessex Archaeology, 51–104.
Beresford, G. (1987). *Goltho: The Development of an Early Medieval Manor, c 850–1150.* London: Historic Buildings and Monuments Commission.
Blair, J. (1995). 'Anglo-Saxon pagan shrines and their prototypes'. *Anglo-Saxon Studies in Archaeology and History* 8: 1–28.
Boddington, A. (1996). *Raunds Furnells: The Anglo-Saxon Church and Churchyard.* London: English Heritage.
Boulter, A. (2006). *An Assessment of the Archaeology Recorded in Flixton Park Quarry.* Unpublished assessment report of the Suffolk County Council Archaeological Service.
Bourdieu, P. (1990). *The Logic of Practice.* Cambridge: Polity Press.
Bradley, R. (1992). 'The excavation of an oval barrow beside the Abingdon Causewayed Enclosures, Oxfordshire'. *Proceedings of the Prehistoric Society* 58: 127–42.
Brück, J. (1999). 'Houses, lifecycles and deposition on Middle Bronze Age settlements in southern England'. *Proceedings of the Prehistoric Society* 65: 1–22.
Carr, R., Tester, A., and Murphy, P. (1988). 'The Middle-Saxon settlement at Staunch Meadow, Brandon'. *Antiquity* 62 (235): 371–6.
Champion, T. (1977). 'Chalton'. *Current Archaeology* 59: 364–9.
Coggins, D. (2004). 'Simy Folds: twenty years on'. In Hines *et al.* (eds.), *Land, Sea and Home*, 325–34.
Cramp, R. (1957). 'Beowulf and Archaeology'. *Medieval Archeaology* 1: 57–77.
Cunliffe, B. (1976). *Excavations at Portchester Castle,* Volume 2: *Saxon.* London: Society of Antiquaries.

Daniels, R. (1988). 'The Anglo-Saxon monastery at Church Close, Hartlepool, Cleveland'. *The Archaeological Journal* 145: 158–210.

Darrah, R. (2007). 'Identifying the architectural features of the Anglo-Saxon buildings at Flixborough and understanding their structures', in C. Loveluck (ed.), *Rural Settlement, Lifestyles and Social Change in the Later First Millennium AD: Anglo-Saxon Flixborough in its Wider Context*. Oxford: Oxbow, 51–66.

Davison, B. (1977). 'Excavations at Sulgrave, Northamptonshire, 1960–76. An interim report'. *The Archaeological Journal* 134: 105–14.

Dixon, P. (1982). 'How Saxon is the Saxon house?'. In P. Drury (ed.), *Structural Reconstruction: Approaches to the Interpretation of the Excavated Remains of Buildings*. BAR British Series 110. Oxford: British Archaeological Reports, 275–86.

—— (2002). 'The reconstruction of the buildings', in Losco-Bradley and Kinsley (eds.), *Catholme*, 89–99.

Dölling, H. (1958). *Haus und Hof in Westgermanischen Volksrechten*. Münster: Aschendorffsche Verlagsbuchhandlung.

Fairbrother, J. (1990). *Faccombe Netherton: Excavations of a Saxon and Medieval Manorial Complex*. 2 vols. London: The British Museum.

Gardiner, M. (1990). 'An Anglo-Saxon and medieval settlement at Botolphs, Bramber, West Sussex'. *The Archaeological Journal* 147: 216–75.

—— (1993). 'The excavation of a Late Anglo-Saxon settlement at Market Field, Steyning, 1988–89'. *Sussex Archaeological Collections* 131: 21–67.

—— (2004). 'Timber buildings without earth-fast footings in Viking-Age Britain', in Hines et al. (eds.), *Land, Sea and Home*, 345–58.

—— (2006). 'Implements and utensils in *Gerefa* and the organization of seigneurial farmsteads in the High Middle Ages'. *Medieval Archaeology* 50: 260–7.

Gerritsen, F. (1999). 'To build and to abandon. The cultural biography of late prehistoric houses and farmsteads in the southern Netherlands'. *Archaeological Dialogues* 6(2): 76–97.

Hall-Torrance, M., and Weaver, S. (2003). 'The excavation of a Saxon settlement at Riverdene, Basingstoke, Hants. 1995'. *Proceedings Hants Field Club* 58: 63–105.

Hamerow, H. (1993). *Excavations at Mucking, Volume 2: The Anglo-Saxon Settlement*. London: English Heritage.

—— (1999). 'Anglo-Saxon timber buildings: the continental connection', in H. Sarfatij et al. (eds.), *In Discussion With the Past: Archaeological Studies Presented to W. A. van Es*. Amersfoort: ROB, 119–28.

—— (2002). *Early Medieval Settlements: The Archaeology of Rural Communities in North-West Europe 400–900*. Oxford: Oxford University Press.

Harding, P., and Andrews, P. (eds.) (2002). 'Anglo-Saxon and medieval settlement at Chapel Street, Bicester: Excavations 1999–2000'. *Oxoniensia* 67: 141–79.

Hardy, A., and Charles, B. (2007). *Death and Taxes: The Archaeology of a Middle Saxon Estate Centre at Higham Ferrers, Northamptonshire*. Oxford: Oxford Archaeology.

HE: Colgrave, B., and Mynors, R. A. B. (eds.) (1969). Bede, *Ecclesiastical History of the English People*. Oxford: Clarendon Press.

Heidinga, H. A., and Offenberg, G.A.M. (1992). *Op Zoek naar de vijfde eeuw: de Franken tussen Rijn en Maax*. Amsterdam: De Bataafsche Leeuw.

Hey, G. (2004). *Yarnton: Saxon and Medieval Settlement and Landscape*. Oxford: Oxford Archaeological Unit.

Hines, J., Lane, A., and Redknap, M. (eds.) (2004). *Land, Sea and Home*. Society for Medieval Archaeology Monograph 20. Leeds: Maney Publishing.

Hope-Taylor, B. (1977). *Yeavering: An Anglo-British Centre of Early Northumbria*. London: HMSO.

Ingold, T. (2000). *The Perception of the Environment: Essays on Livelihood, Dwelling and Skill*. London: Routledge.

James, S., Marshall, A., and Millett, M. (1985). 'An early medieval building tradition'. *Archaeological Journal* 141: 182–215.

King, A. (2004). 'Post-Roman upland architecture in the Craven Dales and the dating evidence', in Hines *et al.* (eds.), *Land, Sea and Home*, 335–44.

Kopytoff, I. (1986). 'The cultural biography of things: commoditization as process', in A. Appadurai (ed.), *The Social Life of Things: Commoditization In Cultural Perspective*. Cambridge: Cambridge University Press, 64–91.

Losco-Bradley, S., and Kinsley, G. (eds.) (2002). *Catholme: An Anglo-Saxon Settlement on the Trent Gravels in Staffordshire*. Nottingham: University of Nottingham.

Loveluck, C. (2001). 'Wealth, waste, and conspicuous consumption. Flixborough and its importance for mid and late Saxon settlement studies,' in H. Hamerow and A. MacGregor (eds.), *Image and Power in the Archaeology of Early Medieval Britain: Essays in Honour of Rosemary Cramp*. Oxford: Oxbow Books, 78–130.

—— (2007). *Rural Settlement, Lifestyles and Social Change in the Later First Millennium AD: Anglo-Saxon Flixborough in its Wider Context*. Excavations at Flixborough 4. Oxford: Oxbow.

MacKreth, D. (1996). *Orton Hall Farm: A Roman and Early Anglo-Saxon Farmstead*. Manchester: University of Manchester.

Marshall, A., and Marshall, G. (1991). 'A survey and analysis of the buildings of early and middle Anglo-Saxon England'. *Medieval Archaeology* 35: 29–43.

——(1993). 'Differentiation, change and continuity in Anglo-Saxon buildings'. *Archaeological Journal* 150: 366–402.

Meadows, I. (forthcoming). 'The excavation of a Late Saxon site at the Castle Cement Quarry, Ketton, Rutland'.

Millett, M., with James, S. (1984). 'Excavations at Cowdery's Down, Basingstoke, 1978–1981'. *Archaeological Journal* 140: 151–279.

Milne, G., and Richards, J. (1992). *Wharram: A Study of Settlement on the Yorkshire Wolds, Volume 7: Two Anglo-Saxon Buildings and Associated Finds*. York: Department of Archaeology, University of York.

MoLAS (Museum of London Archeaological Service) (2004). *The Prittlewell Prince: The Discovery of a Rich Anglo-Saxon Burial in Essex*. London: MoLAS.

O'Brien, C., and Miket, R. (1991). 'The early medieval settlement of Thirlings, Northumberland'. *Durham Archaeological Journal* 7: 57–92.

Oliver, T., Howard-Davis, C., and Newman, R. (1996). 'A post-Roman settlement at Fremington, near Brougham', in J. Lambert (ed.), *Transect Through Time*. Lancaster: University of Lancaster, 127–69.

Pelling, R. (2002). 'Charred plant remains' in Harding and Andrews (eds.), 'Anglo-Saxon and medieval settlement', 167–70.

Powlesland, D. (1997). 'Anglo-Saxon settlements, structures, form and layout', in J. Hines (ed.), *The Anglo-Saxons from the Migration Period to the Eighth century: An Ethnographic Perspective*. Woodbridge: Boydell Press, 101–16.

RADFORD, C. R. (1958). 'The Saxon house: a review and some parallels'. *Medieval Archaeology* 1: 27–38.

RAHTZ, P. (1976). 'Buildings and rural settlement', in D. Wilson (ed.), *The Archaeology of Anglo-Saxon England*. Cambridge: Cambridge University Press, 49–98.

——(1979). *The Saxon and Medieval Palaces at Cheddar*. BAR British Series 65. Oxford: British Archaeological Reports.

REES, W. (1963). 'Survivals of ancient Celtic custom in medieval England', in J. R. R. Tolkien et al., *Angles and Britons*. Cardiff: University of Wales Press 148–68.

RICHARDS, J. (2000). 'Identifying Anglo-Scandinavian settlements', in D. Hadley and J. Richards (eds.), *Cultures in Contact: Scandinavian Settlement in England in the Ninth and Tenth Centuries*. Turnhout: Brepols, 295–310.

SCULL, C. (1991). 'Post-Roman Phase I at Yeavering: a re-consideration'. *Medieval Archaeology* 35: 51–63.

THOMAS, G. (2005). 'Bishopstone, East Sussex'. <www.sussexpast.co.uk/research>. Last accessed, 2008.

TIMBY, J., BROWN, R., HARDY, A., LEECH, S., POOLE, C., and WEBLEY, L. (2007). *Settlement on the Bedfordshire Claylands: Archaeology along the A421 Great Barford Bypass*. Bedfordshire Archaeology Monograph 8. Oxford: Oxford Archaeology & Bedfordshire Archaeological Council.

TIPPER, J. (2004). *The Grubenhaus in Anglo-Saxon England*. Yedingham: Landscape Research Centre.

TUMMUSCHEIT, A. (1995). *Ländliche Siedlungen des 5–7. Jh. in England und ihre kontinentalen Vorgänger*. Unpublished MA thesis, Christian-Albrechts University, Kiel.

TYLER, S., and MAJOR, H. (2005). *The Early Saxon Cemetery and Later Settlement at Springfield Lyons, Essex*. East Anglian Archaeology 111. Chelmsford: Essex County Council.

WADE-MARTINS, P. (1980). *Excavations in North Elmham Park*. 2 vols. East Anglian Archaeology 9. Gressenhall: Norfolk Museums Service.

WALKER, J. (1999). 'Late 12th- and early 13th-century aisled buildings: a comparison'. *Vernacular Architecture* 30: 21–53.

WEST, S. (1969). 'The Anglo-Saxon village of West Stow: an interim report of the excavations'. *Medieval Archaeology* 13: 1–20.

——(1986). *West Stow: The Anglo-Saxon Village*. 2 vols. East Anglian Archaeology 24. Ipswich: Suffolk County Planning Department.

WEST STOW ENVIRONMENTAL ARCHAEOLOGY GROUP (1974). 'Experiment and the Anglo-Saxon environment', in T. Rowley (ed.), *Anglo-Saxon Settlement and Landscape*. BAR British Series 6. Oxford: British Archaeological Reports, 78–86.

WHITELOCK, D. (1955). *English Historical Documents I, c. 500–1042*. London: Eyre & Spottiswoode.

WILLIAMS, R. (1993). *Pennyland and Hartigans: Two Iron Age and Saxon Sites in Milton Keynes*. Aylesbury: Buckinghamshire Archaeological Society.

ZIMMERMANN, W. H. (1988). 'Regelhafte Innengliederung prähistorische Langhäuser in den Nordseeanrainerstaten: Ein Zeugnis enger, langandauernder kultureller Kontakte'. *Germania* 66(2): 465–89.

CHAPTER 10

SETTLEMENT HIERARCHY

KATHARINA ULMSCHNEIDER

In England, the excavation of settlement sites started badly. Early excavators, having missed the evidence for timber buildings at sites such as Sutton Courtenay in the 1930s, famously formed the picture of the Anglo-Saxons 'living in miserable huts (sunken-featured buildings commonly known as *Grubenhäuser*) in almost as primitive a condition as can be imagined' (Lethbridge and Tebbutt 1933: 149; Hamerow 2002: 7). This view of poverty and peasant hovels was to remain influential over the next forty years, and only began to be more forcefully challenged from the 1970s onwards. By then, impressive timber buildings, such as those at Yeavering (below) had been found. Still, there remained an implicit association between building types and status. To Rahtz (1976: 52) it seemed that the evidence related 'more to the extremes of society, the palaces and sunken featured buildings, than to the "middle class", the prosperous farmer'.

With settlement excavations being few in number and small in size, the focus of settlement archaeology at this time still rested heavily on buildings, in particular on the structure of halls, and implicitly on their size and status. This focus would have been reinforced by the written sources, such as *Beowulf*, which portrayed the king and his great hall as the focal point of early medieval society, and Bede, who was forever concerned with the various ranks of kings, sub-kings, and churchmen. It was therefore not astonishing to see archaeologists leaning towards a hierarchy of sites based on the social status of the occupants, with royal vills perceived to be at the top (superseded only by as-yet-unexcavated urban palace complexes), followed by episcopal/ecclesiastical sites and thegnly residences (the latter only appearing in the later Saxon period), and finally a large number of rural settlements, including farmsteads and hamlets (Rahtz 1976: 91, 68, 58). Urban sites were considered to be yet another, separate category.

In the last thirty years, this simple, monarcho-centric view of settlement hierarchy has given way to a much more differentiated and in many ways less clear-cut picture. This is based not only on the realization that there is a large variety of sites hiding under the umbrella term of 'rural settlements', but also on re-evaluations of how 'status' may be deduced from the archaeological record. Similarly, questions have also been raised about whether the traditional classification of sites into royal, ecclesiastical, rural, and urban is a useful one and has not artificially restricted our ability to recognize the full complexity of settlements in this period. Especially for the mid Saxon period, it is now becoming clear that settlements were far more diverse than previously thought. Some of these sites seem to have fulfilled a wide range of different functions, displaying elements not just of one, but potentially several of the groups mentioned above. Consequently, there have been new avenues of inquiry into the relationship and dynamics between them. This article does not claim to be a complete survey of the issues pertaining to the study of settlement hierarchy, nor can it begin to provide even a basic discussion of the most important archaeological sites and artefact studies. Background studies and further details therefore can be found in the references. The focus instead has been on identifying some of the areas of debate in the field, to chart current approaches, and to suggest which areas may warrant exploration in the future.

THE EARLY SAXON PERIOD

Common indicators that have been used to denote high status have been, among others, the size and construction techniques of a settlement's buildings, its morphology, location, functions, and organization. During the early Saxon period, most of the buildings on settlements were either *Grubenhäuser* or small post-built timber halls. While they display some variations in their constructional techniques, none of these buildings seems to be significantly different or unusual enough to warrant assignment of any particularly high status (although there may have been some focal buildings). There is also little evidence for most sites being carefully planned or laid out. Mucking (Fig. 10.1), for example, showed no clear overall design, boundaries, or many enclosure groups, such as pens or paddocks. Neither are there many signs of functional specialization. On the whole, occupation seems

A 5th Century
B 6th Century
C 7th Century

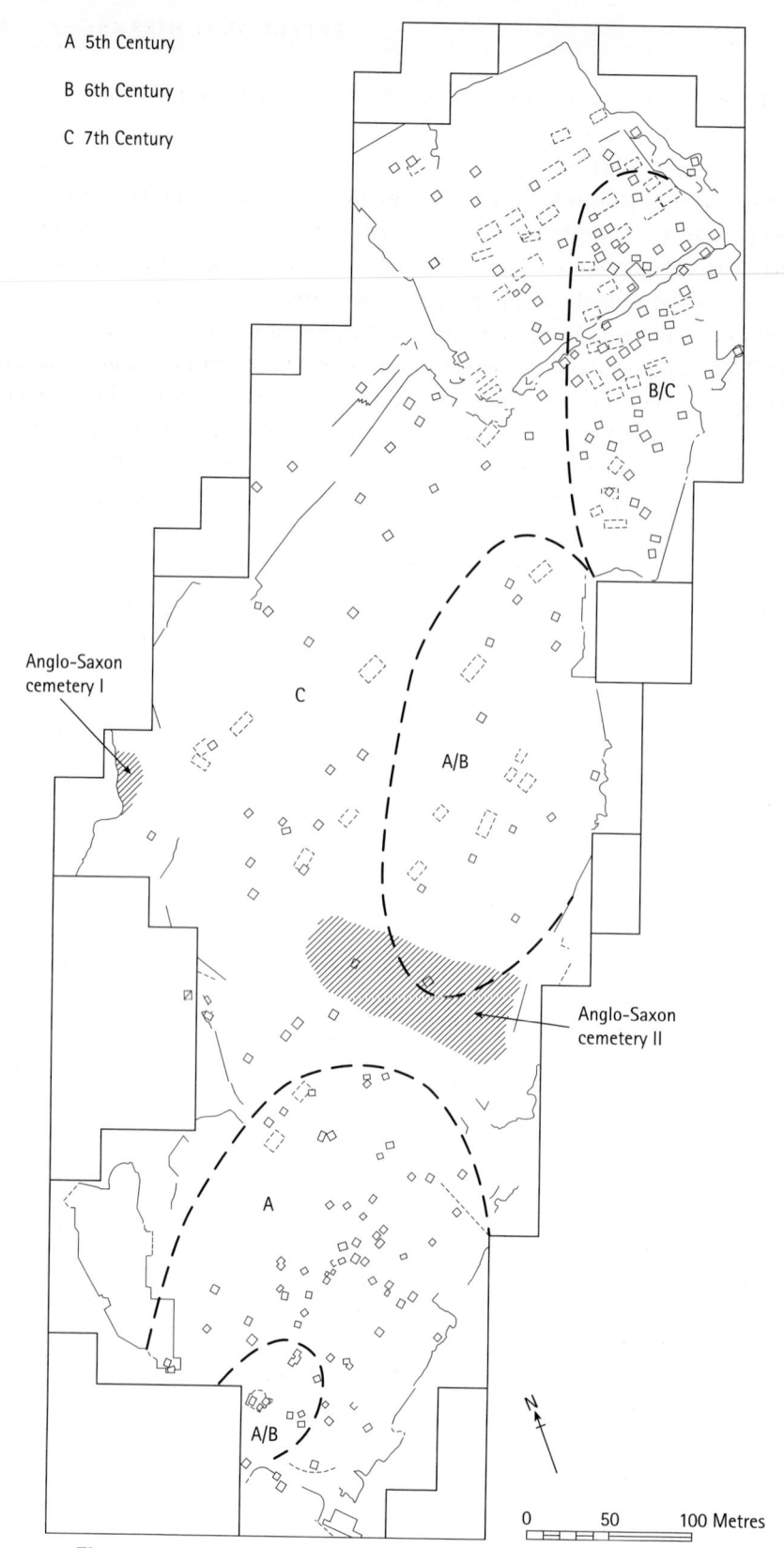

Anglo-Saxon cemetery I

Anglo-Saxon cemetery II

Figure 10.1 The settlement at Mucking (after Hamerow 2002)

to have been scattered and showed little signs of planning beyond a rough east-west alignment of houses (Hamerow 1993).

Current interpretations broadly envisage most early settlements consisting of one or a series of shifting, loosely arranged little farmsteads/households, of relatively equal size (Hamerow 2002; for an alternative view, though controversial, see Tipper 2004). Particularly during the fifth and sixth centuries, following the upheavals of the migrations, it is thought that there may have been little social differentiation between family groups, or if there was, it has not found its way into the settlement record. This evidence seems largely reflected by burial sites. While evidence from cemeteries suggests some ranking of people, this ranking seems to have been largely among individuals of families/households, rather than between households (e.g. Scull 1993; Härke 1997), perhaps suggesting, as Loseby (2000: 345) has argued, that 'power in early Anglo-Saxon England resided in persons rather than places.'

However, excavations at the settlement site of West Heslerton may now challenge this picture. Among the earliest elements of the site appear to have been boundaries, and the site is also claimed to have been structured and zoned, and perhaps to contain a high-status element (Powlesland 1997; 1998; 2000). The currently published evidence is too scant to allow any useful discussion yet, which must await full publication of the site. It may very well be, however, that the small sample of sufficiently excavated early Saxon sites may mask greater variations among these settlements (for Catholme, see Losco-Bradley and Kinsley 2002), although there seems as yet no evidence to propose any visible hierarchy among them.

From c. AD 600 onwards, however, some settlements clearly begin to witness great changes. Timber buildings start to show more complexity in their construction techniques with the introduction of foundation trenches, plank construction, and annexes, as well as the development, for the first time, of substantial halls with floor spaces of over 100m^2 (Hamerow 2004: 303 and this volume). 'Great halls', such as C12 at Cowdery's Down, were now located in a central position, and showed a highly sophisticated building technique, and lavish consumption of resources. It appears that a section of society now had begun to develop that could command access not only to labour, but also to skilled craftsmen and a wide range of natural resources. Such settlements have been interpreted as the seasonal residences of elites (Millett 1984: 249) or even the palace of a tribal leader (Marshall and Marshall 1993: 400).

The pinnacle of the development of the great hall may be seen at the seventh-century site at Yeavering (Fig. 10.2), with its meticulously planned group of central buildings, carefully aligned, actively controlling access and space through fenced enclosures, and, unlike most halls of the period, rebuilt on the same spot. Identified by Bede as a royal vill, Yeavering also differed from other settlements in its range and variety of specialist structures and buildings, including, among others, a possible temple and church, a timber grandstand for assemblies of a sizeable

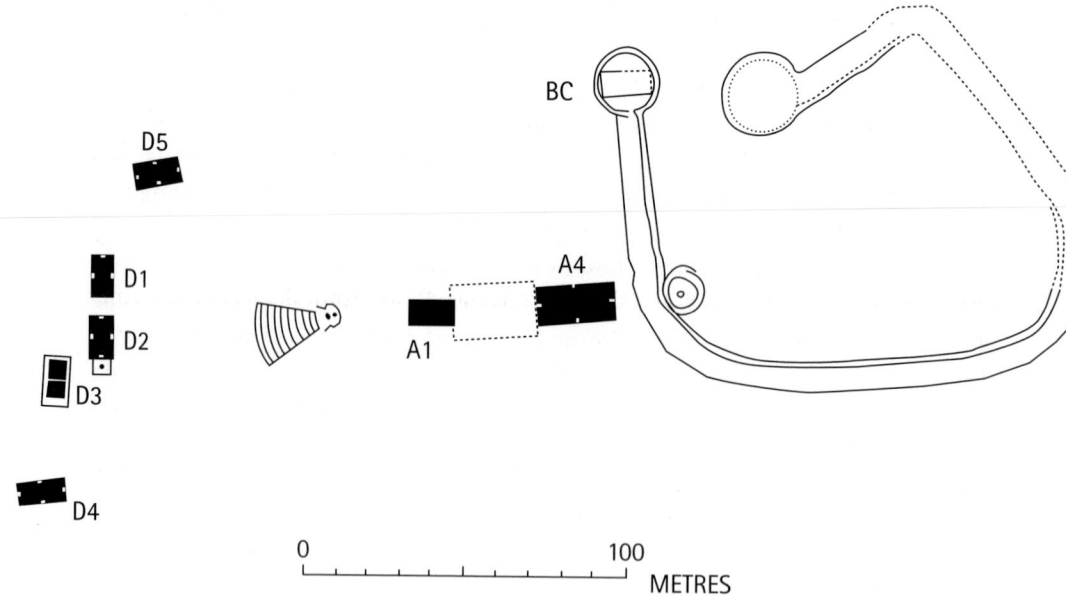

Figure 10.2 The seventh-century royal site at Yeavering (Phase IIIc) (after Hope-Taylor 1977)

number of people, and a large enclosure. Large investments were not made only in buildings, however, but also in planning and the choice of location, with the wide visibility and alignment to a number of ancient structures signalling a complex and carefully constructed meaning. Despite its grandeur, Yeavering, however, neither appears to have been a permanent residence, nor a particularly long-lived one, being abandoned within a century in favour of Milfield (Hope-Taylor 1977).

Social change and the development of an elite is also apparent in the burial record, with the rise of extremely rich barrow burials in the seventh century, either isolated or in special cemeteries (Härke 1997: 148). So far, the picture of social hierarchy being closely reflected in the archaeological record holds. However, as we move further into the mid Saxon period, the evidence seems to become much less clear.

THE MID SAXON PERIOD

One of the most important changes that has been recognized in the mid Saxon period is the great expansion in different settlement and site types. These include the emergence, among others, of 'urban' centres—the *emporia/wics*, 'ecclesiastical' sites, and also so-called 'productive' sites—i.e. places, whether excavated or metal-detected, that produce large quantities of coins and metalwork. As this listing shows, some of the places identified do not fit easily into the established categories, and similar evidence is becoming available when considering the huge variety of sites lumbered together under the 'productive sites' and 'rural' settlement headings (see below). This raises questions not only as to how useful these traditional categories are, but also how such a seemingly heterogeneous set of sites can be linked in any clear hierarchy.

These problems are apparent in studies of mid Saxon settlement hierarchies. Based on a study of Ipswich Ware, Blinkhorn (1999: 8), for example, seems to favour a ranking of *emporia*, royal vills/palaces, nucleated rural settlements with a significant ecclesiastical component ('ecclesiastical settlements'), and rural farming communities ('rural sites'). In contrast, Moreland, from an economic point of view, sees major ecclesiastical sites as of far greater importance, probably even more so than secular sites, followed by similar but less well endowed settlements, sites involved in more rural production, and finally a bottom rung of sites, servicing the above, but 'currently archaeologically invisible' (Moreland 2000: 96 for details and examples). Palmer argues for a role-related hierarchy, in this case again an economic one, which would place *emporia* at the top, followed by sites which functioned as central places and markets (many 'productive' and ecclesiastical sites), rural sites with strong evidence for specialized production (some of them with ecclesiastical connections), and ordinary rural sites trading in occasional surpluses (Palmer 2003: 2002; 53–5).

This shows that we seem to have much greater problems in clearly identifying the apex of the settlement hierarchy in the mid Saxon period. One of the reasons may be that there is a much wider range of settlements which are planned and contain large buildings, raising the question whether settlements with such buildings can automatically be regarded as being of high status (e.g. Yarnton; Hey 2004: 65, 89–90). Instead it now seems that the overall ratio of large timber buildings may be of greater importance (James *et al.* 1984: 185–6), as well as the association of other buildings with them, and, certainly by the tenth century, the presence of a 'defensive' enclosure (Faith 1997: 163–4; for an alternative view on the nature of these enclosures, see Gardiner, this volume). However, despite the increasing presence of enclosures on mid Saxon sites (Reynolds 2003), enclosed seigneurial sites at present remain a feature of the late Saxon period (see below). In general, the origins of defences and fortresses in this period are obscure, with arguably the first properly defensive sites being associated with the kings of Mercia in the eighth and ninth centuries (Blair 1999; Bassett 2007; Anglo-Saxon civil defence project, <www.ucl.ac.uk/archaeology/project/beyond-burghal/research-design.htm>).

If it has become more difficult to infer high status from single buildings and layout in the mid Saxon period, conversely, it is now also becoming increasingly clear that the absence of such sophisticated structures cannot automatically be taken to equate to low status. Blair has drawn attention to the potentially great importance of tents and other temporary structures for use by the elites (Blair 2005:

279), and they may very well have been used at sites such as Yeavering. Equally, the use of the natural landscape as a backdrop for royal, church, and other assemblies has been noted by writers such as Pantos (2001: 61–175) and Cubitt (1995: 32–9, esp. 35). A potential example of just such a meeting place may have been excavated at Lake End Road, Dorney, where multiple pits produced a wide range of high-status finds and exotic imports, but neither coins nor residential evidence (Foreman *et al.* 2002).

This is not to argue, however, that there is no validity in interpreting highly organized settlements with sophisticated buildings as being of higher status, merely that their interpretation must be considered carefully against the background of other sites. For example, assuming we had no written sources telling us about the evolution of the church in the seventh and eighth centuries, might we not have ended up with even higher-status buildings? Due to their rarity compared with other building types and novel, highly complex technique of construction, the presence of stone buildings would imply access to new technological skills, specialist labour, and significant new resources. On such a reading of the archaeological evidence would we not have to place many ecclesiastical sites with stone structures at the top of the settlement hierarchy? Many of them are highly structured, organized, and often enclosed (Blair 2005). They also often show great continuity, and, when not destroyed by Viking attacks, remained or were rebuilt on the same spot for great lengths of time. While stone buildings were probably more long-lived by the nature of their construction material, enduring use of a particular place would seem to suggest the presence of a high-status controlling authority of some considerable permanency.

Closely related to this, and clearly another reason for the confusion at the top of the mid Saxon settlement hierarchy, is the currently rather curious lack of visibly apparent royal sites. In general, our knowledge of royal sites of the mid Saxon period is scant. The only securely-excavated example, Yeavering, is early and short-lived, while the stone hall of the suggested mid Saxon palace complex at Northampton has now been re-interpreted as the refectory of a monastery (for the Northampton debate, see J. Williams 1979; 1984; Blair 1996). However, there may very well be royal palaces of stone waiting to be discovered, particularly in towns (Blair 1996: 121 with references).

That the current evidence is unlikely to reflect the real picture is suggested by Rahtz (1999), among others, who showed that a total of at least 193 royal sites are known for the Anglo-Saxon period from written sources. Given the fairly large number of known sites as well as the preoccupation in the written sources of this period with the importance of kings, it is interesting that on the present evidence royal sites neither seem to be easily identifiable nor do their locations appear to have been particularly long-lived or preserved in many other ways (this may not hold true for urban palaces, though, which have been suggested to underlie later buildings, although as yet we do lack any firm archaeological evidence for this; for a recent discussion of the archaeological and historical evidence for royal sites, see Blair 2005: 275–83).

The reasons for this lack of visibility are much debated. Some archaeologists, such as Loveluck, argue that it has to do with our inability to identify royal/high-status secular sites from the archaeological record (e.g. at Flixborough; Loveluck 1998). Conversely, Blair argues for royal sites being by their nature more ephemeral in this period than ecclesiastical ones (for the ecclesiastical versus secular site debate, see Loveluck 2001; 2007; and Blair 2005: 204–12, note 112 at 206). Others, such as Hines (1997b: 391), are left wondering whether there is much point in trying to distinguish between high-status royal and ecclesiastical sites at all (for a rebuttal of this idea, see Blair 2005: 211, although there may be a point where such distinctions become 'anachronistic', Blair 1996: 121). These debates reflect yet another conundrum of mid Saxon settlement studies, namely the difficulties archaeologists often still face in identifying the exact functions of sites (e.g. the 'productive sites' debate, see Pestell and Ulmschneider 2003). Many settlements of this period fulfilled a much wider range of functions, making it difficult to decide according to which factors sites should be ranked. Their functions also in some cases appear to overlap with other categories of site. For example, many ecclesiastical and 'rural' sites seem to perform similar economic functions, and there is also the possibility that some royal functions may have taken place at sites other than royal vills (Palmer 2002: 175, 134; this also could help explain their lack of visibility).

At present, the archaeological picture, unlike the evidence from the written sources, seems confused. This is not helped by the curious absence of stone structures so far from sites securely identified as royal. In this respect the Anglo-Saxon evidence stands in stark contrast to the highly developed and complex royal residences of the Carolingians, both in rural and town settings and later often located within defensive enclosures, which provided highly visible 'theatres of kingship' (Loveluck 2005: 238–9, for clearer settlement hierarchies on the Continent; for current debates relating to the role of kings in the emergence of the emporia, see Pestell, this volume).

It would therefore appear that, while social ranking played an important part in the settlement hierarchy, it is at present not as clearly reflected in the archaeological record as one would hope. Indeed, it may not have been the only factor influencing and shaping the mid Saxon settlement hierarchy. Interesting in this respect are the results of new studies of coins and other imports at settlement sites, which have begun to suggest that economic factors contributed much more towards the settlement hierarchy of mid Saxon England than has previously been acknowledged. (For a study of sites in receipt of traded goods in the London hinterland, see Palmer 2002; 2003. For Kent, see Brookes 2003; 2007. For Lincolnshire and East Anglia, see Ulmschneider 2000a; Newman 1999.) These ideas are based on recent re-evaluations of how 'status' may be deduced from the artefactual record.

It has generally been argued that the presence of rare, imported, or exotic goods on a site can be taken as an indicator of high status or the special role of the site. In this way 'status' has been attached to a wide variety of finds and materials, from gold, silver, and other unusual metalwork finds to non-local pottery, precious stones, coins, and glass, to mention just a few. For most of the early Saxon period, where access to imported and exotic goods seems to have been rare, and mostly restricted to a small group of people, this inference would appear to be well-justified. However, as we move into the mid Saxon period, the picture becomes more complex. With the huge expansion of trade networks and economic production, a much wider range of settlement sites can now be seen to acquire access to such imported items, be it the newly appearing *emporia*, ecclesiastical sites, and other estate centres, 'productive sites', or many of the sites lumped together under the 'rural' settlement heading (for corresponding changes in the layout and organization of 'rural' settlements, see Moreland 2000; Hamerow 2002).

As a result, archaeologists are now being forced to reconsider their notions about how high status can successfully be postulated from finds on single sites. For example, Continental pottery and other goods have usually been taken as secure evidence for the high status of a settlement. However, as the above studies show, they can also appear on some otherwise ordinary 'rural' sites, usually located in coastal regions, around major inlets, or along important transport routes, which seems to have provided them with the possibility of opportunistic access to passing trade (Palmer 2002: map 5.3). Similar observations about the importance of geography in the distribution of traded goods have also been made for Ipswich Ware. While this pottery is much rarer outside East Anglia and seems often to be linked to high-status sites, within the kingdom it appeared regularly on 'ordinary' rural sites (Blinkhorn forthcoming; Newman 1999).

Increasing awareness of these issues now calls for a much more subtle interpretation of the available finds evidence on settlement sites. Continuing regional and inter-regional studies of sites and their finds, taking into account variations in wealth, the economic roles of sites, and access to routes and goods, are therefore of the utmost importance. Such studies would also help to test Palmer's hypothesis that we may eventually find 'a rationally and economically explicable settlement hierarchy', and that the 'key factors' of this hierarchy may turn out to be 'location and economic function rather than social rank', although the latter 'was inevitably part of this equation' (Palmer 2002: 175, 154).

Challenging the notion that every site with imported goods must be of high status may also help at least in part to resolve another major conundrum of the mid Saxon period, namely the apparent lack of settlements at the bottom of the settlement pyramid. These, by rights, should be the most numerous. According to this new reading of the evidence, however, many of the sites, such as those in the Lincolnshire fenland, which have produced lava querns and Ipswich ware, but otherwise do not appear exceptional (Ulmschneider 2000a: 62–3, 91, 103), could be re-interpreted as lower-order settlements, advantaged by their geographical location which provided access to passing trade routes (for such effects at coastal sites, which may display their own hierarchy, see Loveluck and Tys 2006). Palmer has demonstrated that similar geographical advantages apply inland, when lower-order sites are found 'close to settlement clusters or major ecclesiastical sites' (Palmer 2002: 170). If an increasing number of mid Saxon settlements were eventually to be re-interpreted in this way it would remove the need to postulate the rather unsatisfactory bottom rung of 'currently archaeologically invisible' sites (above, Moreland 2000: 96).

On the whole, it is becoming clear that there is no simple equation between artefacts and/or buildings and status. This recognition is forcing archaeologists to consider new ways in which sites may be distinguished from each other in terms of status. This includes looking not only at the types and constructions of buildings and associated access to resources, labour, and building materials, and their access to large quantities of diverse and high-quality imported goods, but also at the quality and diversity of their finds assemblages; their association with nearby high-status burial grounds or cemeteries; the diversity of craft activities and specialization of certain industries; access to and use of leading technologies; settlement location, organization, layout, and intended display; and the patterns of production and consumption of plants and animals. Similarly, we must be careful not to be unduly influenced by the written evidence as to the importance of social rank in this period. Not only is archaeology revealing a much greater complexity and diversity of settlements and functions than anticipated from the literary sources, it also has revealed that the status of communities could change (Loveluck 2001). These factors in themselves must make us doubt the existence of any readily definable settlement hierarchy.

THE LATE SAXON PERIOD

By the later Anglo-Saxon period, the picture presented by the buildings and settlement record in many ways seems to become more clear-cut (for a more detailed evaluation of the late Saxon settlement evidence, see Gardiner, this volume). Both royal and noble residences beome clearly visible in the archaeological record. At Cheddar (Fig. 10.3), the royal complex scores highly in many of the categories indicative of high status, be it the careful layout and ordering of the site, the nature and range of its finds, patterns of consumption, or its enclosure, including a stormwater ditch, ditches and fences, and an elaborate gateway and marker post (Rahtz 1979; Blair 1996). Technologically complex timber halls and

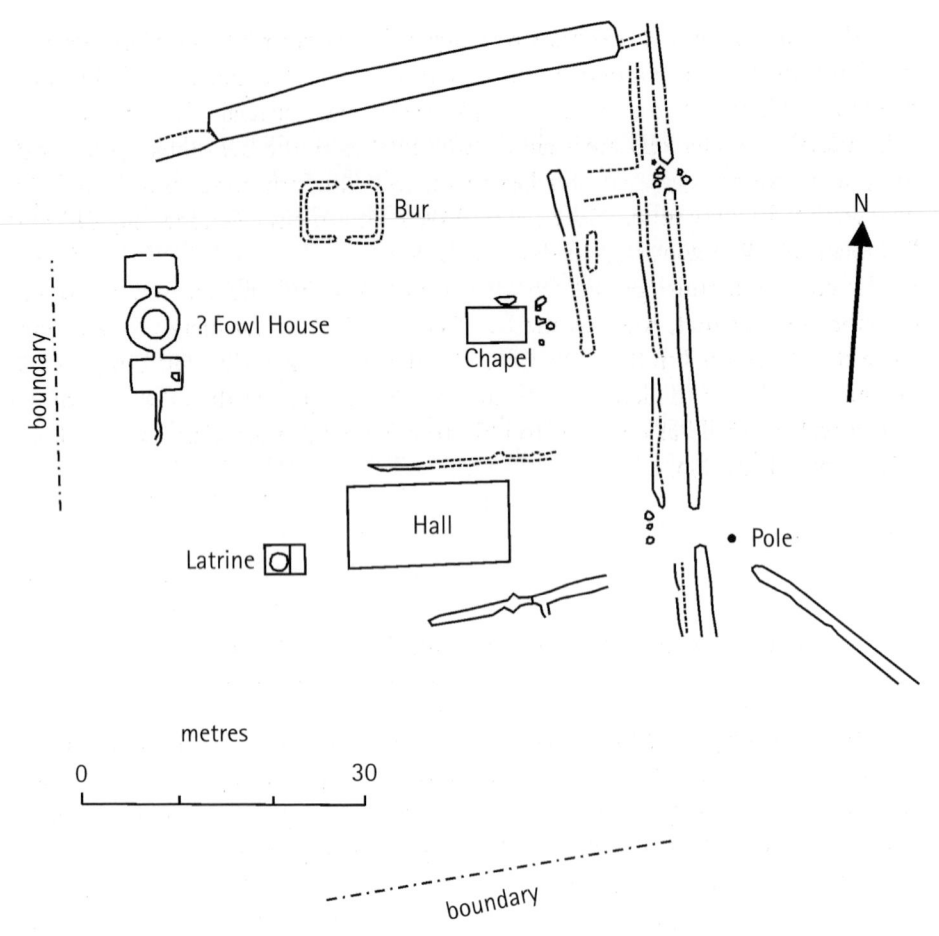

Figure 10.3 Cheddar: the early tenth-century royal complex (Period 2) (after Reynolds 1999)

smaller specialist structures are found, such as a latrine and a possible fowl-house, the latter perhaps displaying high-status Continental parallels (although see Gardiner, this volume; Hey 2004). Also, stone structures, such as the chapel, are now part of the site.

Similar developments, though perhaps not always as elaborate, are found on other royal and seigneurial sites, such as Goltho (Beresford 1987). These sites were often surrounded by enclosures, and contained a range of carefully laid out buildings, at least one elaborate hall, and stone structures, such as a church or possible belfry (see, for example Goltho, Fig. 12.4; for a discussion of these sites and related changes in the landscape, see Williams 1986; Faith 1997; Reynolds 1999). That social rank was now closely linked to the holding of land, and increasingly reflected in the possession of a range of appropriate buildings, is also suggested by an early eleventh-century text known as *Gebyncðo* ('Dignities'), one of the 'promotion laws', listing the requirements necessary to become a thegn. These included five hides of land, a bell and burh-gate, and a seat and special office in the king's hall. Added in a later text are a church and kitchen and a bell-house (Whitelock 1979, no. 51; Keynes 1999, with further references). Similarly, kings and the nobility now seem to become much more clearly linked with towns (Fleming 1993; Hill and Rumble 1996; Blair 2005: 330–41; Bassett 2007).

The current picture gained from archaeological and literary sources would therefore suggest that, towards the late Saxon period, social hierarchy was once more clearly reflected in the settlement record, with kings visibly wielding a much tighter control over the landscape, economy, and people. At the other end of the hierarchy, this would also appear to hold true for the peasant class (see Gardiner, this volume; Faith 1997).

Conclusion: future developments

At present, the picture of the Anglo-Saxon settlement hierarchy is far from definitive. Reasons for this are manifold, and ways of remedying the situation are not easy. One factor which has not been mentioned so far is the general lack of large-scale excavations. Unlike their Continental counterparts, most excavations of settlements in England are either partial or based on 'rescue' operations. This holds true for all categories of sites, from mid Saxon monasteries to royal sites, 'productive' sites, and 'rural' settlements. The pitiful evidence provided by this key-hole archaeology lies at the bottom of many of the present disputes, be it the nature of the Flixborough settlement, the lack of royal sites, or the current debates about 'productive sites' (Richards 1999; Ulmschneider 2000b; Pestell and Ulmschneider 2003), which has led to well-intentioned, but fundamentally flawed, attempts to compare sites according to their average find densities (Richards 1999: 76–9). In addition, many key sites and surveys, such as the Ipswich Ware project, West Heslerton, Brandon (Suffolk), and Wicken Bonhunt (Essex) still await publication.

Still, as shown, promising new avenues for exploring the evidence for settlement hierarchies have been forthcoming from comparative studies of site assemblages and related functions of settlements within specific geographical areas. Clearly more research must be focused on the understanding of economic processes, which ultimately would have underpinned all types of settlement. Where possible, closer studies should be conducted of the movement of utilitarian goods, and detailed analyses of faunal remains (including patterns of production and consumption), which would help work out important interdependencies and hierarchical relationships between local and perhaps even regional sites. For example, the settlement at West Fen Road, Ely, has recently been suggested to have been 'deliberately established as a food-producing site for the nearby monastery' (Mortimer et al. 2005: 148), and increasing specialization in and movements of animals and foods is also apparent from surveys of animal bone and plant remains (e.g. Rackham 1994; Crabtree 1996; Dobney et al. 2007; Part IV, this volume). Similarly, evidence for industrial production, trade, and access to technology and imported goods must be re-evaluated in the light of local and regional patterns (Part VI, this volume). More research also needs to be done on understanding other role-related hierarchies, and the functional complexities of sites over time. Clearly much more differentiated models are now needed, which must also address the possibility of hierarchies within certain settlement types, as well as the increasing evidence for clusters of economically and socially linked settlements, some of which would eventually develop into central places (Palmer 2002; Brookes 2007. For the 'multiple estate' model, see Jones 1979 and 1985; Williamson 1993).

Finally, and on an entirely speculative note, could the sudden apparent diversity in mid Saxon settlement (and burial evidence) and the related problems in defining a clear social hierarchy be a reflection of greater social fluidity, with trade, craft, and economic specialization now allowing increasing access to wealth even at the lowest level of the status hierarchy? Could we perhaps even question whether the mid Saxon hierarchy was as clear-cut as the written sources suggest? Whatever the answers, certainly from the middle of the eighth century onwards, settlement, economic, and social hierarchies became increasingly defined. In almost all aspects of life, kings and elites can now be seen to assert more power over the landscape and people. Whether this represents increased royal power alone, or also the church's belief in social differentiation (e.g. Steane 2001: 17) remains to be seen.

References

Anderton, M. (ed.) (1999). *Anglo-Saxon Trading Centres: Beyond the Emporia*. Glasgow: Cruithne Press.
Bassett, S. (2007). 'Divide and rule?: The military infrastructure of eighth and ninth century Mercia'. *Early Medieval Europe* 15(1): 53–85.
Beresford, M. (1987). *Goltho: The Development of an Early Medieval Manor c.850–1150*. London: Historic Buildings & Monuments Commission for England.
Blair, J. (1996). 'Palaces or minsters? Northampton and Cheddar reconsidered'. *Anglo-Saxon England* 25: 97–121.
——(1999). 'Forts and fortifications', in Lapidge et al. (eds.), *The Blackwell Encyclopaedia of Anglo-Saxon England*, 191-2.
——(2005). *The Church in Anglo-Saxon Society*. Oxford: Oxford University Press.
Blinkhorn, P. (1999). 'Of cabbages and kings: production, trade and consumption in Middle Saxon England', in Anderton (ed.), *Anglo-Saxon Trading Centres*, 4–23.

——(forthcoming). *The Ipswich Ware Project.*
BROOKES, S. (2003). 'The Early Anglo-Saxon framework for Middle Anglo-Saxon economics: the case of East Kent', in Pestell and Ulmschneider (eds.), *Markets in Early Medieval Europe*, 84–96.
——(2007). *Economics and Social Change in Anglo-Saxon Kent AD 400–900: Landscapes, Communities and Exchange.* British Archaeological Reports British Series 431. Oxford: Archaeopress.
CRABTREE, P. (1996). 'Production and consumption in an early complex society: animal use in Middle Saxon East Anglia'. *World Archaeology* 28(1): 58–75.
CUBITT, C. (1995). *Anglo-Saxon Church Councils c.650–c.850.* London: Leicester University Press.
DOBNEY, K., JAQUES, D., BARRETT, J., and JOHNSTONE, C. (2007). *Farmers, Monks and Aristocrats: The Environmental Archaeology of an Anglo-Saxon Estate Centre at Flixborough, North Lincolnshire.* Oxford: Oxbow.
FAITH, R. (1997). *The English Peasantry and the Growth of Lordship.* London: Leicester University Press.
FLEMING, R. (1993). 'Rural elites and urban communities in Late Saxon England'. *Past & Present*, 141(1): 3–37.
FOREMAN, S., HILLER, J., and PETTS, D. (2002). *Gathering the People, Settling the Land: The Archaeology of a Middle Thames Landscape; Anglo-Saxon to Post-Medieval.* Oxford: Oxford Archaeology.
HÄRKE, H. (1997). 'Early Anglo-Saxon social structure', in Hines (ed.), *The Anglo-Saxons from the Migration Period to the Eighth Century*, 125–70.
HAMEROW, H. (1993). *Mucking*, Volume 2: *The Anglo-Saxon Settlement.* London: English Heritage.
——(2002). *Early Medieval Settlements.* Oxford: Oxford University Press.
——(2004). 'The archaeology of Early Anglo-Saxon settlements: past, present and future', in N. Christie (ed.), *Landscapes of Change.* Aldershot: Ashgate, 301–16.
HEY, G. (2004). *Yarnton: Saxon and Medieval Settlement and Landscape; Results of Excavations 1990–96.* Oxford: Oxford University School of Archaeology.
HILL, D., and RUMBLE, A. R. (eds.) (1996). *The defence of Wessex: The Burghal Hidage and Anglo-Saxon Fortifications.* Manchester: Manchester University Press.
HINES, J. (ed.) (1997a). *The Anglo-Saxons from the Migration Period to the Eighth Century: An Ethnographic Perspective.* Woodbridge: Boydell.
——(1997b). 'Religion: The limits of knowledge', in Hines (ed.), *The Anglo-Saxons from the Migration Period to the Eighth Century*, 375–410.
HOPE-TAYLOR, B. (1977). *Yeavering: An Anglo-British Centre of early Northumbria.* London: HMSO.
JAMES, S., MARSHALL, A., and MILLETT, M. (1984). 'An early medieval building tradition'. *Archaeological Journal* 141: 182–215.
JONES, G. (1979). 'Multiple estates and settlement history', in P. H. Sawyer (ed.), *English Medieval Settlement.* London: Edward Arnold, 9–34.
——(1985). 'Multiple estates perceived', *Journal of Historical Geography*, 11(4): 352–63.
KEYNES, S. (1999). 'Thegn', in Lapidge *et al.* (eds.), *The Blackwell Encyclopaedia of Anglo-Saxon England*, 443–4.
LAPIDGE, M., BLAIR, J., KEYNES, S., and SCRAGG, D. (eds.) (1999). *The Blackwell Encyclopaedia of Anglo-Saxon England.* Oxford: Blackwell.
LETHBRIDGE, T., and TEBBUTT, C. (1933). 'Huts of the Anglo-Saxon period'. *Cambridge Antiquarian Society's Communications* 33: 133–51.

Losco-Bradley, S., and Kinsley, G. (2002). *Catholme: An Anglo-Saxon Settlement on the Trent Gravels in Staffordshire*. Nottingham: University of Nottingham.

Loseby, S. T. (2000). 'Power and towns in late Roman Britain and Early Anglo-Saxon England', in G. Ripoll and J. M. Gurt (eds.), *Sedes regiae (ann. 400–800)*. Barcelona: Reial Acadèmia de Bonas Lletres, 319–70.

Loveluck, C. P. (1998). 'A high-status Anglo-Saxon settlement at Flixborough, Lincolnshire', *Antiquity* 72: 146–61.

——(2001). 'Wealth, waste and conspicuous consumption. Flixborough and its importance for Mid and Late Saxon settlement studies', in H. Hamerow and A. MacGregor (eds.), *Image and Power in the Archaeology of Early Medieval Britain*. Oxford: Oxbow, 78–130.

——(2005). 'Rural settlement hierarchy in the age of Charlemagne', in J. Story (ed.), *Charlemagne: Empire and Society*. Manchester: Manchester University Press, 230–58.

——(2007). *The Early Medieval Settlement Remains from Flixborough, Lincolnshire*. Volume 1 of *Excavations at Flixborough*. Oxford: Oxbow/English Heritage.

——and Tys, D. (2006). 'Coastal societies, exchange and identity along the Channel and southern North Sea shores of Europe AD 600–1000'. *Journal of Marine Archaeology* 1: 140–69.

Marshall, A., and Marshall, G. (1993). 'Differentiation, change and continuity in Anglo-Saxon buildings'. *Archaeological Journal* 150: 366–402.

Millett, M., with James, S. (1984). 'Excavations at Cowdery's Down, Basingstoke, Hampshire, 1978–81'. *Archaeological Journal* 140: 151–279.

Moreland, J. (2000). 'The significance of production in eighth-century England', in I. L. Hansen and C. Wickham (eds.), *The Long Eighth Century: Production, Distribution and Demand*. Leiden: Brill, 69–104.

Mortimer, R., Regan, R., and Lucy, S. (2005). *The Saxon and Medieval Settlement at West Fen Road, Ely: The Ashwell Site*. Cambridge: Cambridge Archaeological Unit.

Newman, J. (1999). 'Wics, trade and hinterlands – the Ipswich region', in Anderton (ed.), *Anglo-Saxon Trading Centres*, 32–47.

Palmer, J. B. O. (2002). *The Emporia of Mid-Saxon England: Hinterlands, Trade and Rural Exchange*. Unpublished D.Phil Thesis, University of Oxford.

——(2003). 'The hinterlands of three southern English *emporia*: some common themes', in Pestell and Ulmschneider (eds.), *Markets in Early Medieval Europe*, 48-60.

Pantos, A. (2001). *Assembly-Places in the Anglo-Saxon Period: Aspects of Form and Location*. Unpublished DPhil thesis, University of Oxford.

Pestell, T., and Ulmschneider, K. (eds.) (2003). *Markets in Early Medieval Europe: Trading and Productive Sites*. Macclesfield: Windgather Press.

Powlesland, D. (1997). 'Anglo-Saxon settlements, structures, form and layout', in Hines (ed.), *The Anglo-Saxons from the Migration Period to the Eighth Century*, 101–16.

——(ed.) (1998). 'The West Heslerton Assessment', *Internet Archaeology*, 5. <http://intarch.ac.uk/journal/issue5/westhes/index.html>.

——(2000). 'West Heslerton settlement mobility: a case of static development', in H. Geake and J. Kenny (eds.), *Early Deira: Archaeological Studies of the East Riding in the Fourth to Ninth Centuries AD*. Oxford: Oxbow, 19–26.

Rackham, J. (ed.) (1994). *Environment and Economy in Anglo-Saxon England: A Review of Recent Work on the Environmental Archaeology of Rural and Urban Anglo-Saxon Settlements in England*. York: Council for British Archaeology.

Rahtz, P. (1976). 'Buildings and rural settlement', in D. Wilson (ed.), *The Archaeology of Anglo-Saxon England*. Cambridge: Cambridge University Press, 49–98.

——(1979). *The Saxon and medieval palaces at Cheddar: excavations, 1960–62*. Oxford: British Archaeological Reports.

——(1999). 'Royal sites', in Lapidge *et al.* (eds.), *The Blackwell Encyclopaedia of Anglo-Saxon England*, 399–401.

Reynolds, A. (1999). *Later Anglo-Saxon England: Life and Landscape*. Stroud: Tempus.

——(2003). 'Boundaries and settlements in later sixth to eleventh-century England'. *Anglo-Saxon Studies in Archaeology and History* 12: 98–136.

Richards, J. D. (1999). 'What's so special about "productive sites"? Middle Saxon settlements in Northumbria'. *Anglo-Saxon Studies in Archaeology and History* 10: 71–80.

Scull, C. (1993). 'Archaeology, Early Anglo-Saxon society and the origins of Anglo-Saxon kingdoms'. *Anglo-Saxon Studies in Archaeology and History* 6: 65–82.

Steane, J. M. (2001). *The Archaeology of Power: England and Northern Europe, AD 800–1600*. Stroud: Tempus.

Tipper, J. (2004). *The Grubenhaus in Anglo-Saxon England: An Analysis and Interpretation of the Evidence from a Most Distinctive Building Type*. Yedingham: Landscape Research Centre.

Ulmschneider, K. (2000a). *Markets, Minsters, and Metal-Detectors: The Archaeology of Middle Saxon Lincolnshire and Hampshire Compared*. British Archaeological Reports British Series 307. Oxford: Archaeopress.

——(2000b). 'Settlement, economy and the "productive" site in Anglo-Saxon Lincolnshire, A.D. 650–780'. *Medieval Archaeology* 44: 53–79.

Whitelock, D. (ed.) (1979). *English Historical Documents, c. 500–1042*. 2nd edition. London: Eyre and Spottiswoode.

Williams, A. (1986). '"A bell-house and burhgeat": lordly residence in England before the Norman Conquest', in C. Harper-Bill and R. Harvey (eds.), *The Ideals and Practice of Medieval Knighthood*. Woodbridge: Boydell, 221–40.

Williams, J. H. (1979). *St Peter's Street, Northampton: Excavations, 1973–1976*. Northampton: Northampton Development Corporation.

——(1984). 'From "palace" to "town": Northampton and urban origins'. *Anglo-Saxon England* 13: 113–36.

Williamson, T. (1993). *The Origins of Norfolk*. Manchester: Manchester University Press.

CHAPTER 11

LOCAL CHURCHES IN THE ANGLO-SAXON COUNTRYSIDE

RICHARD MORRIS

MORE than five hundred years lay between the arrival of the Augustinian mission at the end of the sixth century and the point—let us say, the middle of the twelfth century—when most of England's nine or ten thousand medieval churches had been brought into existence. A survey of relationships between Anglo-Saxon churches and their surroundings thus poses many questions, most of which can be simplified to two: what kinds of churches, when? (Figure 11.1)

For a given church we might ask when, by whom or what kind of people it was founded, how it was built, what status it held, and why it was put where it was, or in one place rather than another. We could go on to ask how those relationships evolved, and how, or if, they were remembered as time passed. Once a church existed it would undergo change, in appearance, use, or size if not in status or function, and so itself become an evolving influence on the surroundings in which it stood. Similar considerations apply to the surroundings. As others in this book explain, the 'Anglo-Saxon landscape' was a realm of co-varying regions and economies, some quite uniform, others highly differentiated, within which hierarchies of settlement changed in shape, function, and complexity as time passed (Rippon 2007; Williamson 2007; Gittos, Ulmschneider, this volume).

Figure 11.1 Kirk Hammerton, North Yorks. Once regarded as a late Saxon building with older parts, the chancel, nave, and tower built of salvaged Roman stone are probably no older than 1080

The examination of churches in their contexts rather than as disembodied entities goes back at least to the 1920s, in the work of historical topographers like H. E. Salter (1921; 1936). Archaeological study of churches and landscape together began in earnest in the 1970s, in circumstances described elsewhere (Blair and Pyrah 1996; Blair 2005: 2–3 and this volume). The subject has moved well beyond the point where it lay forty years ago, when issues of church and landscape, if considered at all, were dominated by an assumption that answers would only be found in written records, and that phenomena would be typified by 'a small number of well-documented places' (Blair 2005: 2). Given that few Anglo-Saxon churches (particularly local ones) appear in written records before the late eleventh century, one effect of that text-fixed approach was to back-project categorizations derived from later medieval sources. More recent archaeological, textual, and interdisciplinary work shows not only that this was anachronistic—the later binary of 'parochial' and 'monastic' does not work for Anglo-Saxon England (ibid.: 2–3)— but also that categories of church within the Anglo-Saxon period underwent change as time passed. More on this later.

Methodological progress made since the 1970s is reflected in a large body of published local, regional, and thematic studies. In the first, local, category are results of investigations made at key Anglo-Saxon religious sites, or at places which have come to be regarded as key on the strength of the quality or scale of the data they have provided. Among these are well-known Anglo-Saxon churches of different kinds like Earl's Barton (Audouy et al. 1995), Kirkdale (Rahtz and Watts 2003), Deerhurst (Rahtz et al. 1997) and Barton-upon-Humber (Rodwell and Rodwell 1982; Waldron and Rodwell 2007), and several religious houses which had previously been known chiefly or entirely from written sources, as in the case of Wearmouth-Jarrow (Cramp 2005–6) and St Oswald's Gloucester (Heighway 1999), or Eynsham (Hardy et al. 2003; cf. Baker 2005). The landscape contexts of Jarrow and Whitby have been re-assessed, modifying, if not disposing of, the isolationist topos (Wood 2006). We now have better understanding of mid Saxon complexes of ambiguous or protean character like Flixborough (Dobney 2007; Loveluck 2007; Loveluck and Atkinson 2007) and Brandon (Carr et al. 1988), of different kinds of burial place (Hadley 2000; Hadley and Buckberry 2005), and a number of closely-examined small churches. Among these last are Burnham (Coppack 1986), Wharram Percy (Bell and Beresford 1987), Rivenhall (Rodwell and Rodwell 1993), and perhaps most notably Raunds, Northamptonshire, where the full excavation of a late Anglo-Saxon church and its cemetery together, both in an arrested state of development and so undisturbed by later grave-digging and expansion, is an important reference point of continuing value (Boddington 1996). A cognate case at Ketton, Rutland, awaits publication (cf. Blair 2005: 381–2). Over the border in Wales, Capel Maelog offers welcome western perspective (Britnell 1990; see below). Also to the west, with a funerary background in late antiquity, is Gloucester's suburban St Mary-de-Lode (Bryant and Heighway 2004). Cumulatively such results enable us to generalize. However, so large has been the flow of information that some of the first generation of published studies are already in need of revision. This has been so for Wharram Percy (Mays et al. 2007 revisit earlier interpretations), with repercussions for dependent statements. It will arise elsewhere.

Among regional and urban studies, Turner's work on south-west England (2006), David Stocker and Paul Everson on early Romanesque towers in Lincolnshire (2006), and archaeologically-calibrated ecclesiastical geographies for several provincial cities (Jones et al. 2003; Baker and Holt 2004) contribute to a tightening of focus. Thanks to continuing progress of the Corpus of Anglo-Saxon Stone Sculpture (CASSS) we are also approaching—in some areas, have passed—the point at which generalizing hypotheses can be put forward about issues such as the cultural *milieux* of eighth-century religious houses, or entire regional episodes of lay church-founding (Everson and Stocker 1999). CASSS is two-thirds done and scheduled for completion by 2015. Its archaeological value extends far beyond sculpture and art history.

Thematic explorations include graves and burial (Geake 1997; Gittos 2002; Lucy and Reynolds 2002; Hadley and Buckberry 2005), local saints and cults (Blair 2002), churches on Roman buildings (T. Bell 1996; 2005), connotations of *spolia* (Stocker and Everson 1990), the birth and growth of local churches (Blair 2005: 368–425), the co-location of churches and ancient offering places (Stocker and Everson 2003), and the origins of urban parish boundaries (Baker and Holt 1998).

Long-standing attempts to categorize church location in relation to social structure have been put on a new footing by Stocker and Everson (2006), whose work on village plan-form analysis in Lincolnshire reveals some churches to have been founded in 'private' spaces like manorial curiae, and others in 'public' areas such as greens and commons. Application of this methodology elsewhere will in due course transform understanding of later Anglo-Saxon church-community interactions over much of England. Studies in cultural history have also begun to play into the wider picture (e.g. Lees and Overing 2006; Orton *et al.* 2008). There is

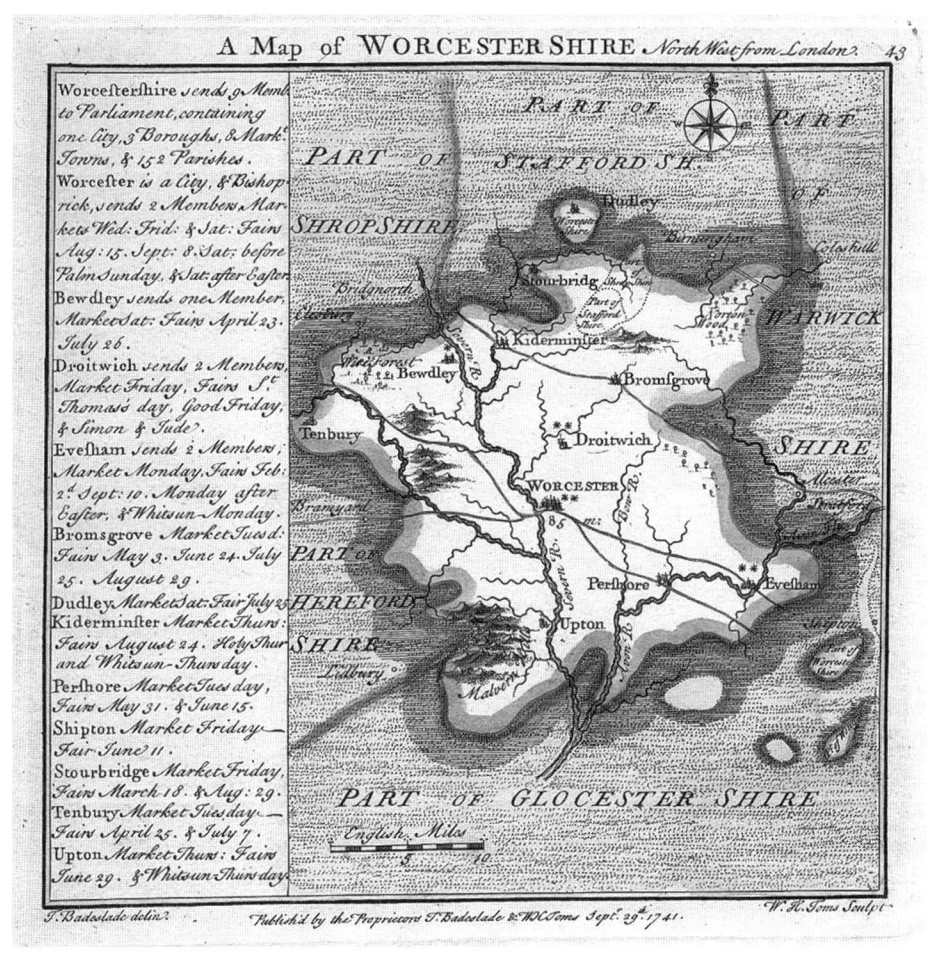

Figure 11.2 Map of Worcestershire from Thomas Badeslade's *Chorographia Britanniae* (1742). Bromsgrove lies towards the north of the county. With a border of some 40 miles, its parish extended north to Birmingham.

better international contextualization (e.g. Delaplace 2005; Zadora-Rio 2003). Above all, we have John Blair's fine, integrating, searching book *The Church in Anglo-Society* (2005), which covers all the matters that most readers would expect to arise under the present title, and more.

All these are left to speak for themselves, the aim in what follows being not to repeat what has already been said but to trace four groups of themes that merit further attention: chronology, burial arrangements between the eighth and tenth centuries, the significance of wood and stone in relation to regionality, and aspects of Anglo-Saxon archaeology that extend beyond the Anglo-Saxon age. In doing so it is worth echoing John Blair by pointing to the difficulty inherent in attempts to link local developments with an all-England framework. If, for instance, as looks possible, the character of later mid Saxon burial arrangements could be highly local, then extrapolating from a few examples may not take us far. Given the bitty nature of written and physical sources with which we must work, a search for generalizing statements thus runs the risk of producing a purported picture of everywhere that does not describe anywhere (Blair 2005: 6). At the broadest level it is a question how much more can be usefully said in the absence of a full list of known Anglo-Saxon religious sites, with accompanying mapping, from which quantitative comparisons could be made and conclusions drawn (cf. Blair 2005: 7).

Finding dates

Any study involving Anglo-Saxon churches begins with *Anglo-Saxon Architecture*, the corpus compiled by H. M. and Joan Taylor (1965; 1978). Indispensable as it remains, however, there is now wide agreement that the Taylors' scheme of dates is problematic. This is partly because the period divisions they selected (partly inherited from Baldwin Brown) were arbitrary, but also because there were too few buildings that could be securely linked to contemporary written records to anchor chronology for the rest (Taylor and Taylor 1978: xiii). The problem becomes acute in the Taylors' 'Period C' (950–1100), to which about 80 per cent of the c.400 buildings they list belong. When Blair writes that: 'The stylistic arguments do now seem to be pushing all but a small minority of our standing "Anglo-Saxon" local churches into and beyond the last eighty or so years of Anglo-Saxon history' (2005: 412), he is putting it mildly. Many of these buildings are turning out on closer study to have been built after 1080, or later. Among them are the forty or so so-called 'late-Saxon' or 'Saxo-Norman overlap' towers of Lincolnshire (Stocker and Everson 2006). Together with their kin in Yorkshire and the north-east, nearly all of these towers—and with them, where coeval, the naves to which they were attached—can now be seen as works of the first or second generation after the Norman Conquest. Thus is it is that a building like Kirk Hammerton, once imagined to be possibly as old as 800 (Taylor and Taylor 1965: 361), more recently held to epitomize the 'Great Rebuilding' that is said to have quickened through the mid eleventh century (Blair 2005: 411; Gem 1988), may be no older than the beginning of the reign of Henry I. The church stands at the end of a planned village ranged around what is now an infilled long rectangular green. The entire layout may have been blocked out in one go (Fig. 11.1).

In itself such recalibration is uncontroversial. During the 1970s Harold Taylor himself concluded that the basis for a dating framework for Anglo-Saxon architecture, akin to the independently-anchored style-critical framework that was arrived at for Romanesque and Gothic in the nineteenth century, did not yet exist (Taylor 1976; Taylor and Taylor 1978: xiii). Volume 3 of *Anglo-Saxon Architecture* took the form it did—essentially, concentrating attention on the comparative description and tabulation of architectural elements—as a step towards that goal. These things are mentioned for two reasons. One is that concepts of a great rebuilding and 'vernacular threshold' need better benchmarking. The other is that there is more to learn about the timing and process by which local churches appeared on the scene. Did they arrive gradually and cumulatively, for instance, or in strong pulses, with many foundations within a few years (cf. Stocker 2000)? And at what point did churches become landscape features, or monuments for the spectator, hinted at in place-names like Vowchurch—'multicoloured church'—or Whitchurch?

Answers to both questions, we now suspect, may vary considerably from region to region. Blair's conception of the institutional and physical transformation of local churches 'as a tide which rose in eastern and southern England around 1000, rolled slowly but steadily westwards and northwards through the eleventh century, but failed to spread far into the highland zone until after our period' (2005: 420–1) is persuasive, but awaits fuller calibration: correlation of the character and chronology of church provision with regionality in settlement is a great project that awaits the undertaking. Yet for all that has been written on the subject, our corpus of reliable, closely-dated 'birth moments' of Anglo-Saxon local churches is actually still quite small. Out of a minimum of c.4,000 local churches likely to have been standing by AD 1050 (Morris 1989), the number for which archaeology has provided *closely*-dated origins is no more than twenty-five—about 0.6 per cent. Very few have had the benefit of the volley of high precision ^{14}C determinations which have given the finer-grained chronological picture that is now available for the early stages of the graveyard at Wharram Percy, showing its genesis around the middle of the tenth century (Mays *et al.* 2007: 193–215).

Archaeologically, moreover, there is a strong evidential bias towards the east and south. This is partly because this is where the largest provincial cities of pre-Conquest England were situated. Such towns were thick with churches, and during the later twentieth century a combination of economic development and pastoral re-organization provided many opportunities to examine them. A cognate bias exists among rural churches, for which the excavated corpus shows a preponderance from the central province of settlement, 'village England', where churches of abandoned and shrunken settlements have provided archaeological opportunities, and parts of East Anglia. As a result, our picture of the early growth of local churches is sharper in areas like Lincolnshire and Norfolk than it is, say, in Cheshire or Worcestershire. While Blair is right to 'warn against the temptation to assume a developed system of local churches unless the sources actually show one' (2005: 421), in large later medieval mother-parishes like Bromsgrove, Worcestershire, or Sandbach in Cheshire, it is difficult to think that the failure of sources to show local chapels before the thirteenth century is telling the whole story. Blair's warning, indeed, can be moderated by another he has given, that a study of landscape 'has to ask "What was going on *here*?", and to recognize that *something* must have been going on there, even if no documents survive to tell us what it was' (Blair 2005: 2). For example, Bromsgrove stands for many areas outside the Central Province, where mother parishes with numerous manorial chapelries (Bromsgrove had at least five) lasted beyond the Reformation. Even in well-documented dioceses like Worcester, the fact that such chapels often escaped record until the later Middle Ages does not necessarily mean that they were all latecomers (Fig. 11.2).

Returning to the Taylors and the last years of their Period C (Harold Taylor preferred neutral to dynastic or cultural terms for periodization), there is consensus that a substantial body of local church buildings is best categorized neither as 'Anglo-Saxon' nor 'Norman' but as belonging to a distinct category of its own, receptive to continental innovation, that was gaining momentum from *c*.1050 (Blair 2005: 411–17, at 412; Fernie 1983: 171, 112–53; Gem 1988). If the archaeologically-studied examples are typical, and if more widely surviving fragments of tenth- and early eleventh-century grave markers can be regarded as proxies for an earlier generation of local one- and two-cell churches, then most of these later eleventh- and earlier twelfth-century projects were replacements. As Blair says, they 'mark a cultural horizon' (2005: 415), for it is the ghosts of their plans and the fonts with which they were provided that so often exist at the heart of the later medieval churches we see today. The fonts, significantly, form the first generation of stone and lead fonts that we can recognize.

In eastern England, then, while local churches were coming into existence from *c*.900, they are transformed to landscape features, putting down roots and pushing up towers, from the eleventh century. In the towers hung bells, their voices speaking across fields to call local people, lament the dead, glorify feasts, mourn at funerals, fight disease, suppress lightning, mark feast days, and calm the winds. Towers are meant to be seen, and their bells heard, across landscape (Christie 2004). Steeples were so numerous in late medieval England that they may by then have been perceived almost as parts of the landscape itself. When did they begin to arise, and whence came the impulse to alter the landscape by building them?

If the Bayeux Tapestry is any guide, southern England (at least) in the late eleventh century was already a well towered and turreted place. The later English fondness for crowning great churches with central towers may have continued a later Anglo-Saxon penchant—evidenced by literary and graphical sources as well as architectural survival—for crossing, axial, and lateral towers. Alongside these was a specialized type of tower serving as the nave, which Blair has suggested marked 'the beginning of the drive for architecturally imposing manorial churches' (2005: 412). The proximity of two of the best examples—Barton-on-Humber and Earls Barton—to substantial earthworks (Fig. 11.3) lends support to the suggestion that such towers usher in 'an apparent thegnly fashion for . . . combining ecclesiastical, residential, and defensive functions' (Blair 2005: 412–13). Barton-on-Humber is dated from structural timberwork to *c.*1000 (Rodwell and Rodwell 1982), Earls Barton to the first half of the eleventh century (Audouy *et al.* 1995; cf. Fernie 1983: 138–45). If these dates are right and reflect the wider picture, then it does look as

Figure 11.3 Earl's Barton, Northamptonshire: architecturally elaborate early eleventh-century tower-church (extended later) co-located with ringwork (Ashmolean Museum. Photographed by Major George Allen in 1938)

Figure 11.4 Coin of Edward the Elder (899–924) bearing image of a structure that suggests features in common with aristocratic towers of a century later (Stack Catalogue)

though the new elaborated architecture of lordship made its appearance early in the eleventh century—which would accord with the failure of archaeological excavation to find a local church provided with a tower before this date. With this said, what looks like a tower of similar character is depicted on coins of Edward the Elder (899–924) (Fig. 11.4). Unless this harks back to designs on Roman coinage, it hints at a possibility that the genre of embellished tower was introduced up to a century sooner than the examples we can still see.

LANDSCAPES OF BURIAL

A fully satisfactory continuous narrative for burial in England between c.600 and 1100 has yet to be written. The beginning and end of the story are fairly clear, with cemeteries of well-recognized and evolving character existing in the sixth and seventh centuries (Boddington 1990; Geake 1997), increasing formality attaching to ecclesiastical designation of churchyards in the tenth (Gittos 2002; Zadora-Rio 2003), leading to some thousands of local churchyards by the end of the eleventh. The problem is what happened in between. The once-fashionable idea that in the eighth century 'vernacular' or non-Christian forms of burial gave way to burial in cemeteries that became submerged beneath later churchyards is no longer accepted. A revised view centres rather on evidence for a plurality of practices and places that lasted at least until the eleventh century, and in some areas longer, involving cemeteries of different kinds, large and small, some long lasting, others ephemeral (Hadley and Buckberry 2005). The list of excavated examples resists easy summary, and again is predominantly, and problematically (from the point of view of what was going on elsewhere), eastern. On it are multiple cemeteries in the vicinity of ecclesiastical sites, sites remote from but possibly mothered by churches, burials in the vicinity of barrows and prehistoric burial enclosures (Wilson 1992: 67; Williams 1997), and a growing list of later Saxon urban and rural cemeteries that seem to have existed on their own.

A characteristic of the list is the unlooked-for way in which many sites get onto it. Taking recent cases from Yorkshire, several discoveries made in the course of routine development are found in the 'grey literature' of the planning system. One of them was at Thornton Steward, where the corridor for a water pipeline ran through an unanticipated cemetery, away from settlement and about a quarter of a mile from the church (Johnson 2003). The cemetery had been used between the mid seventh century and the early eleventh. Chance also played a part at Spofforth, where barn conversions and housing development across the road from the church exposed a large eighth- to ninth-century burial ground that included burials in iron-bound chests (Johnson 2003; for the genre of fittings, cf. Kjølbye-Biddle 1995). In some respects the Spofforth case resembles Crayke, where excavation in search of a documented seventh-century monastery met graves of the eighth to eleventh centuries, forgotten under later medieval ridge and furrow, outside the present churchyard boundary (Adams 1990). Chance of a different kind has influenced the interpretation of a cemetery at Riccall Landing. Unlike the others, this had been known for nearly half a century, but until recently had been explained by the speculation that it contained Scandinavian casualties of 1066. Reappraisal shows that the cemetery was in use from the seventh to twelfth centuries (Hall *et al.* 2008).

Burial across a wide area followed by contraction or re-adjustment of boundaries is known in a number of places (Blair 2005: 467). It is sometimes associated with long-lived places of special prestige. Spofforth (Fig. 11.5) may be a case in point, for its later status as a Percy stronghold, the church by then having gained a colossal chancel that housed Percy tombs and sheltered priests singing masses for their souls, invites the thought that the place had held particular aristocratic meaning all along. If so, it should be possible to predict the occurrence of such sites elsewhere. Small towns and elite villages with urban tendencies and dynastic

Figure 11.5 Spofforth, North Yorks. Remains of the fortified Percy residence stand at the apex of the open triangle at the far side of the settlement, beyond an infilled market street or green. The rebuilt church stands on the nearer edge of the settlement. Part of an eighth-/ninth-century cemetery occupied the area under the group of houses across the road to its south (Photo: R. Morris).

connections—the kinds of place sometimes regarded as 'new' by later medieval economic historians—are among the places one would look for them.

A more specialized but possibly linked line of enquiry concerns the district saints, typically aristocrats or royalty of the seventh and eighth centuries, who appear to have been enshrined in local minsters. Evidence for them is especially rich in the south midlands, where they have been correspondingly well studied. 'Recent research has emphasized the tenuous, sometimes accidental nature of the surviving evidence for local cults: it is quite possible that many more have been forgotten' (Blair 1994: 73). It may be that every mother church had a sub-regional guardian saint (Blair 2002), an idea which archaeology encourages to the extent that there are more bits of shrines in pre-Conquest churches than we have known saints to occupy them or written records to explain. At Hovingham (North Yorks.) is the side of a shrine carved around 800 which in its scenes evokes the incarnation and resurrection (Lang 1991: 146–8; Hawkes 1993; Morris 2008: 22). Anglo-Saxon shrine fragments at South Kyme indicate another Lincolnshire cult revolving around a lost saint. The enormous near-complete Anglo-Saxon churches at Brixworth in Northamptonshire and Wing in Buckinghamshire were provided with elaborate circulatory crypts of international type for the display of relics to visitors—yet in neither case do we know who the saint was. While it is possible that these costly structures were built to hold secondary relics, or important relics from afar which never arrived or were afterwards lost, it is simpler to see them as the lodgings of sub-regional saints whose identities had by the later Middle Ages been forgotten, transposed, or later downplayed outside their immediate localities to avoid attracting papal attention. This likelihood increases when we approach the same places through sixteenth- and early seventeenth-century sources. At the end of the Middle Ages play-making, games, and alcoholic conviviality were accompaniments to traditional religion. The place for them was churchyards. At the Reformation these pursuits were banned. Not all communities accepted this, and it is of interest to find that Wing and South Kyme were centres of resistance, holding out beyond 1600 with the support of local Catholic gentry. A list of other midland places with active convivial traditions in later sixteenth-century records reads like a roll call of Anglo-Saxon minsters.

Such responses are likely to tie back to the various unencumbered mid–later Saxon graveyards with which we began. Hitherto they have been studied simply as places of burial. Yet all the signs are that they were places where prescriptive functions ran wider, to activities which to judge by prohibitions being issued in the twelfth—thirteenth centuries included dancing, singing, gambling, wrestling, and trading (Klausner 1990: 347–8, 395; cf. Sawyer 1981; Blair 2005: 382).

WOOD AND STONE

In a real sense, Anglo-Saxon churches *were* the landscape. There is a correlation between the whereabouts of surviving Anglo-Saxon churches, architectural features like stripwork, and England's geology (Morris 1989: 302–5). Stone churches are found in the Jurassic belt that crosses the country from south-west to north-east, and on some adjacent formations, but seldom elsewhere, and in some areas, apparently, not at all. The distribution of later-Anglo-Saxon grave markers presents a similar picture. Complementary considerations apply to the use of wood, for wood, like stone, was a special resource that was not uniformly available and needed to be husbanded with care.

These points invite several thoughts. One is that churches were normally built using local materials, and that only the wealthier patrons brought materials from afar. A corollary would be that blanks on the map do not necessarily reflect an actual lack of churches but could instead be a sign of building in a less durable medium, presumably wood, or cob. Other factors may have been in play. The comparative numerousness of churches in the Jurassic belt implies not only access to stone, but also the presence of specialized skills needed to win and work it—a craft. Until the later eleventh century, when church-building in stone became common over much of the country, this craft may have been practised more in some areas than in others. Its evolution, if there was one, through the mid and late Saxon periods has not yet been traced.

There are several strands to this. One is the need to test the assumption that stone churches typically had wooden predecessors. Another is to look again at the idea that the eleventh-century rebuilding boom brought with it a rising demand for cut stone that 'stimulated the first systematic freestone quarrying since Roman times' (Blair 2005: 414; cf. Parsons 1990).

The idea that an earlier timber phase lies behind every other parish church has become one of those things that 'everyone knows'. Literary evidence for timber churches is indeed considerable, and since the 1960s has been reinforced by archaeology. John Blair writes that the excavated evidence that has accumulated 'suggests that timber churches, not necessarily unimposing but inevitably short-lived, remained the norm in many if not most regions at the Conquest and beyond'. Thus five out of six recent church excavations in Essex, and another in Oxfordshire, 'located timber phases replaced by post-Conquest rebuildings' (2005: 392). This is no less than we might expect from linguistic evidence. The Old English vocabulary of construction attests a wooden world wherein 'to build' was *timbrian*, 'buildings' were *getimbro*, and *beam* meant 'tree' or 'post'. Over most of England, moreover, the use of wood for domestic and agricultural building remained the norm until the end of the Middle Ages.

So much is agreed, but evidence for the ubiquity of timber churches is not as straightforward as has been presented. Some of the timber phases supposedly revealed by archaeology turn out on reappraisal to be the marks of construction activity like scaffolding or shuttering (Rodwell 1986), incidentally reminding us that archaeology's default mode is to find what it expects to see. Alongside examples of excavated churches which began with a first timber phase are others which did not, or cases like Wharram Percy where evidence for a first timber phase is insecure. Do place-names like Woodkirk (Yorks West Riding), Woodchurch (Kent), or Stokenchurch (Bucks.) reflect the typicality of such structures, or their singularity? Some of the documented cases are ambiguous. For instance, the agreement of *c*.1060 that records the gift of timber for building a church and buildings in the township of Studham (Beds.) does not say that the church is to be made of wood, simply that timber is being used in its construction (Crick 2007, No. 16; Blair 2005: 388 and n.80). In 1086, a timber church at Old Byland in the North Riding of Yorkshire seems to have been sufficiently curious for the

Domesday compilers to depart from their usual formula to describe it as an *ecclesia lignea* (320b).

Unless we are to suppose that church builders and sculptors before *c*.1000 invariably recycled Roman materials, then clearly *some* stone was being acquired in some areas at some times. This is in any case shown by the existence of small stone local churches like Raunds, and the existence of skills for making the stone grave-covers that marked their founders' graves. Such building and production appears initially to have been regional rather than general (more on this below), but even if—as Stocker has suggested (2007: 284–5)—Roman funerary stonework (like sarcophagi) was being symbolically linked with commemoration in the tenth and eleventh centuries, and possibly bestowed in ways with special meaning, this would still call for craftsmen who were capable of sourcing and handling the stone and doing the work. Monastic renewal and the rebuilding of religious houses in the tenth century may have expanded demand for such skills, and so increased capacity for local projects. Stone, however, had been used for building and sculpture since the seventh century; the issue here is whether its winning and working before *c*.950 was intermittent, and so presumably reliant on skills imported on each occasion, each project a self-contained episode, or whether in some areas a continuum of skills existed throughout. The presence or absence of worked stone in this period may signal issues of near and distant power.

For reasons given, then, the idea that wood preceded stone may conceal a more intricate picture, which in places may have had perceptual as well as practical dimensions. Why, given their prowess in working with wood, and the possible trouble of finding churchwrights who knew how to work with stone, did the makers of local churches build in stone at all? The simplest explanation is that the stone church was as much an imaginative statement as it was a physical structure. If wood is for life, and death, stone is time without end. The Church as a community of believers rests on Peter, *petros*, stone (Matt. 16:18). By being built of stone, a church becomes a type of the Church. Meanwhile, *cementarius*, a medieval word for mason, reminds us of the extent to which surviving churches reflect access to lime. For Bede, lime and masonry had a symbolic aspect: the fire that burnt the stone was purifying, while lime mortar bound many small, individual stones into one great entity—the Church (in biblical imagery, Israel was just one stone: Isa. 28: 16). Lime was of course easier to obtain in regions where Jurassic or Cretaceous formations lay close to the surface than in areas where other rocks predominate. Was this a further factor influencing the regional contrasts discussed above?

The idea that an age of timber church-building preceded an age of stone may oversimplify a more intricate picture. Is it significant that tree-ring dating of the one 'Anglo-Saxon' timber church that actually survives, at Greensted in Essex (Fig. 5.1), places the felling of the trees that were split to make its logs between 1063 and the end of the eleventh century (Tyers 1996)? Place-names like Felkirk

(Yorks. West Riding) or Berechurch (Essex), 'planked' and 'boarded', respectively, occur in the twelfth and thirteenth centuries. Moreover, in some parts of the country timber church-building continued until the end of the Middle Ages. A map of surviving medieval timber churches and part-churches shows a distinctive distribution that correlates with other regional characteristics, among them areas like Cheshire that retained a mother-parish structure down to the nineteenth century. We may hypothesize that stone did not everywhere displace wood; rather, there were regions where the preference for wood was longer-lasting. That preference, moreover, may in turn have been influenced by institutional differentiation. It is noticeable that the wooden churches in Cheshire tend to be parochial chapels, and that where parochial chapels were rebuilt in brick in the eighteenth century it was timber churches that were being replaced. If mother churches were built of stone and chapels of wood, then perhaps here is the starting point for a more developed answer to Blair's suggestion of a rolling threshold of rebuilding and endowment that did not arrive in parts of western England until after our period.

A corollary may be that in other areas the preference for stone existed earlier than we currently suppose, and that some churches never had wooden phases at all. Both ideas have implications for regionality, and for criteria we use for dating. There is also an implication for landscape. The quarries we see today tend to be very large excavations in a small number of places. This intensive pattern has come to dominate modern assumptions about earlier exploitation, which is generally perceived as similar in principle but smaller in scale. However, it may be that most medieval quarrying was *extensive* rather than intensive, and that it followed stone outcrops from township to township, sometimes for very long distances. Some of these 'benches' can still be seen, as along the northern edge of the Howardian Hills in North Yorkshire, where the Roman road leading west from Malton runs for miles along a distinctive shelf cut into the vale flank, and is flanked by intermittent surviving earthworks where stone extraction has taken place. Nearby, a similar bench about seven miles long runs eastwards along the north side of the Coxwold-Gilling gap from Ampleforth to East Ness.

Limestones from hereabouts have been used in buildings from the Roman period to the eighteenth century (the place-name Stonegrave on the northern bench is attested as early as the eighth century and translates roughly as 'stone quarry') (Morris 1985). Both benches are associated with runs of churches, including at least several, like Hovingham, Stonegrave (Fig. 11.6), and Appleton-le-Street (Fig. 11.7), with mid Saxon antecedents (Morris 2008; Rahtz et al. 2000). It is difficult not to suspect that these different aspects coalesce in underlying factors to do with access to, and control of, special resources. However, the one study made so far has taken its cue from the modern, industrial pattern by assuming that all the stones came from a single source (Senior 1990). An allied tendency on the part of art historians has been to link given pieces of Anglo-Saxon stone sculpture with known exposures, thereby fostering suppositions

Figure 11.6 Stonegrave, North Yorks. A quarry bench follows the limestone escarpment across country, through woodland (lower right) past the village of Stonegrave and beyond the modern quarry (upper right). Digging for stone hereabouts may have gone on at least from the Roman period; the place-name ('stone hole', 'quarry') is recorded in the eighth century as the name of a religious house (Photo: R. Morris).

which pass into the wider literature that currently-known exposures are the places whence the stone was actually taken. The issue of extensive, cross-country quarrying has implications for landscape and church-building along the length of England's Jurassic stone outcrop.

Longitudinal history

To explore some Anglo-Saxon questions, we need to go outside the Anglo-Saxon period. Studies which demonstrate this are now well known. One of them deals with Lincolnshire's Witham valley, which shows a deep-rooted association between churches, causeways, bridges, and offering places (Stocker and Everson 2003). The

Figure 11.7 Appleton-le-Street, North Yorks. The nucleus of the church is Anglo-Saxon. The eponymous 'Street' seen north of the church follows a quarry bench for some miles (Photo: R. Morris).

phenomenon invites re-assessment of Anglo-Saxon church-landscape choices at other places, like Dorchester-on-Thames, Jarrow, Ely, even Westminster. The significance of movement, journeys and crossings, indeed, can easily be underestimated in studies where mapped landscape can come to look like static space. (One of the chapels in the mother-parish of Bromsgrove that long went unnoticed in Worcester records nonetheless made it onto the Gough Map—it stood beside a long-distance route.) A history of journeys and meetings may similarly lie behind the mirroring of seventh- and eighth-century ecclesiastical centres such as Ripon, Ledsham, and Dacre by henge complexes at the entrances to trans-Pennine dales (Morris forthcoming).

Another emerging group of questions concerns how and why pieces of particular features that had landscape presence (like orthostats and high crosses), or stones that had 'micro-landscape' significance, like the carved stone monuments that marked founders' graves, have survived to the extent that they do. Functionalist explanations along the lines that such pieces of sculpture were re-used as building material, or chance discovery of haphazardly discarded pieces, while acceptable in some cases, will no longer do for all. This is evident not only from the numbers but also the ways in which such stones may survive. In the later rite of parish church consecration, the initiative at the start of the ceremony rested with the incumbent and churchwardens of the old parish whence the new parish was being cut. Hence a possible mechanism was the bestowal of sculpture from a mother church to a daughter. The sculptural relationship between Otley and Weston (West Yorks.) offers a potential example (Coatsworth 2008: 268–9), as does the eighth- or early ninth-century cross-plaque at Middleton (North Yorks.). Here the cross was set iconically in the church tower, although in morphological terms Middleton looks to be too young a settlement to have generated such a monument itself (Lang 1991: 187) (Figure 11.8).

A different kind of mechanism is suggested by the finding *in situ* of carved stones marking putative founder graves at Raunds and Wharram Percy (Stocker 2007). At Wharram the sites of these graves were respected as the church developed, the dynastic beginning still acknowledged, if not remembered, centuries later. Elsewhere such stones were sometimes sequestered at the Reformation, for instance being placed in blocked rood stairs, as at Colsterworth (Lincs.), this in turn influencing rediscovery in the nineteenth century, whence modern perceptions of pattern.

Anglo-Saxon church history was once conceptualized in two halves—pre- and post-Viking—and told as a story in three acts: a monastic flourishing in the seventh and eighth centuries, institutional decay and Viking destruction in the ninth, reform, renewal, and growing localism in the tenth and eleventh. Today, 'the evolution of institutions through the whole period' is told as 'one continuous story' (Blair 2005: 7). If one were to conceptualize in landscape terms, however, then the most dramatic and far-reaching change of all was the introduction from the ninth century of common-field systems over the east midlands and adjoining areas of northern and central-southern England (Roberts and Wrathmell 2000; 2002: 59–82; Stocker 2006: 59–64). Accepting that areas of common field existed in woodland as well as champion areas (Rippon 2007), and that the central province was itself a realm with internal differences (Williamson 2007), it remains the case that common-field England underwent a totalizing change on an enormous scale. Down to around AD 900, England was still 'plotted and pieced' in ways that went back to prehistory. By 1100, the central province had been wiped over. In some areas, like Buckinghamshire and parts of Leicestershire and Lincolnshire, open fields occupied more than 90 per cent of parish area.

Common fields were laid out over most of the Vale of Pickering in the late Saxon period. The 30 km² of contiguous geomagnetic survey—incorporating 30 ha of open area excavation—carried out in the Vale of Pickering speaks volumes (Fig. 11.10). Down to the late ninth century the entire area teemed with prehistoric sacred vernacular features, most of which were still visible and in some cases were actively curated (Powlesland 2009). While there is no reason to suggest that early-medieval people hereabouts were aware that their surroundings had been so

Figure 11.8 Middleton-by-Pickering, North Yorks. (a) Middleton in the foreground, Pickering beyond, illustrates the place-name. In (b), the church is seen in the lower right of the village plan and is integral to it (Photo: R. Morris).

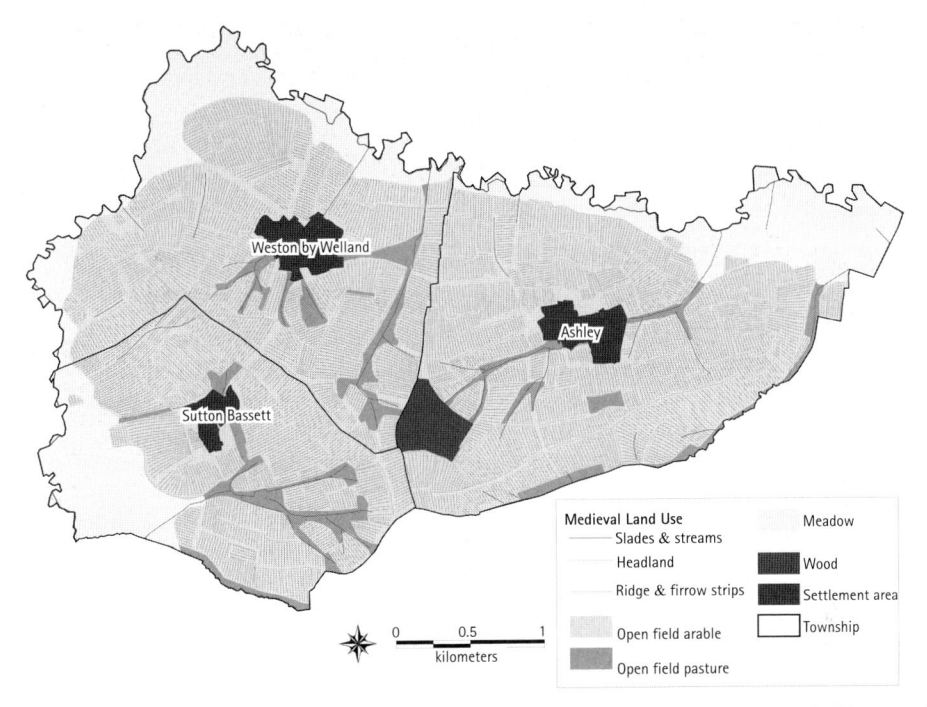

Figure 11.9 Open fields and rural resources at Weston-by-Welland, Ashley and Sutton Bassett, Northants (Foard, Hall and Partida 2009). In such landscapes, earlier features of the kind visible in Fig. 11.10 were usually overwritten.

anciently shaped, the survival of so many details of sacred vernacular landscape invited the active construction of memories and ritual pasts. It was into such landscapes, rich in ancient references, that the first minsters—and with them the occupants' conceptions of wilderness—crosses, royal prayer houses, and oratories were emplaced.

In champion areas common fields expunged these features, and with them, presumably, whatever stories, names, myths, or ideas had adhered to them (e.g. Briggs 2007). Hence, in the central province, local Anglo-Saxon churches founded after the common-field revolution—the large majority—were born into a world void of these ancient associations. Such modern landscapes and the communal settlements from which they were farmed called for new customs to define them. Some of the older protectors may have been re-personified in certain saints and angels, like Botolph, Helen, or Michael, and outside the central belt old cult sites persisted (Blair 2005: 421). From the tenth/eleventh century, however, religious geography became increasingly linked in imagination less with the local past than with landscapes far away—Rome, Jerusalem, Galilee, Sinai.

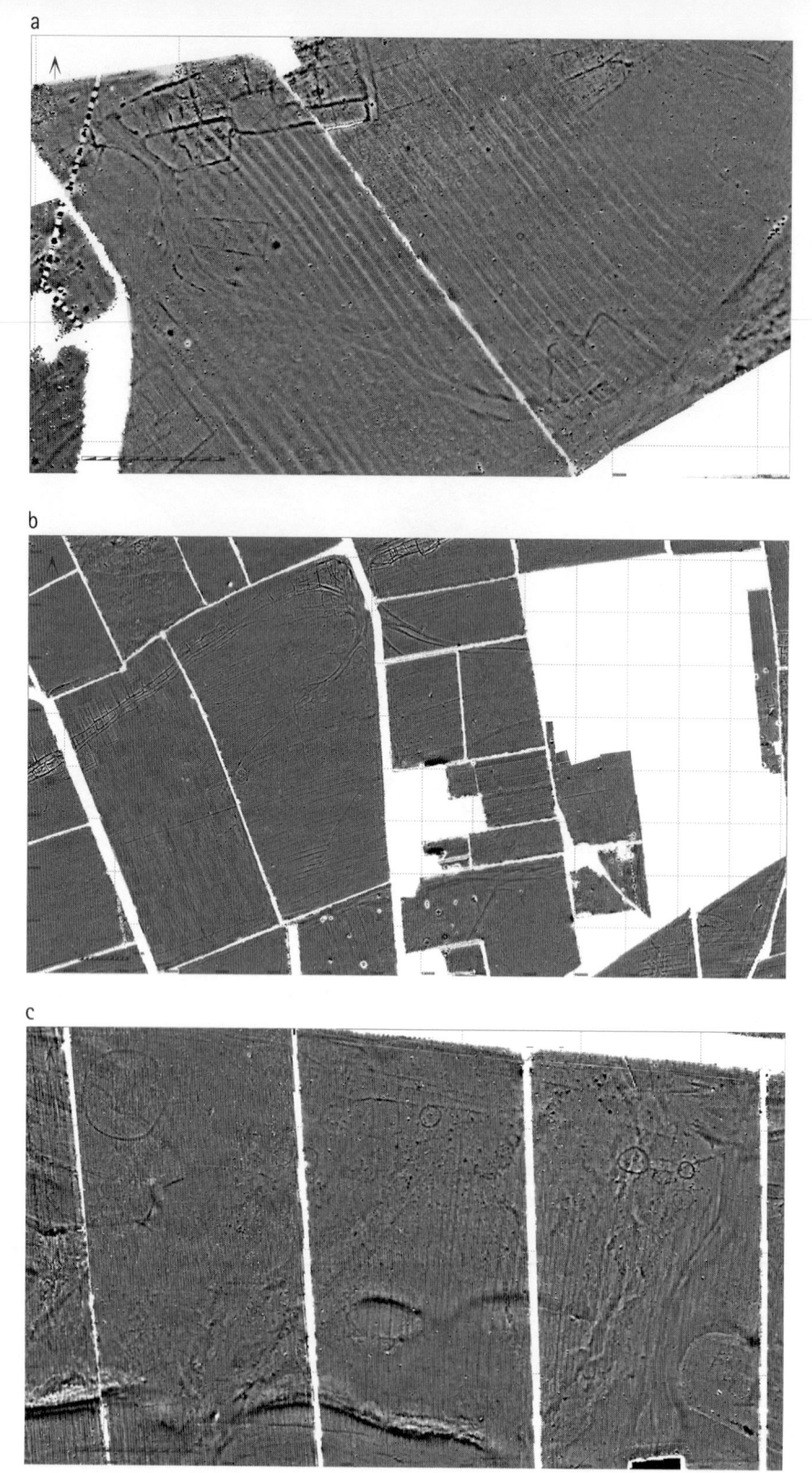

Figure 11.10 Extracts from geomagnetic survey in the Vale of Pickering, North Yorks. Extracts from 30 km² of geomagnetic survey reveal an early medieval landscape of living, burial, and devotion that in many respects was inherited from prehistory. Strips of the common fields that overwrote it from the later ninth or tenth century are also visible (reproduced with kind permission of the Landscape Research Centre).

Acknowledgements

Parts of this chapter owe much to discussion with and criticism from David Stocker, Tony Abramson, and Ian Wood, to whom I extend my best thanks. The discussion of stone sources and early quarrying on pp. 189–9 incorporates ideas and suggestions contributed by David Stocker, to whom I am indebted for permission to refer to them in advance of fuller publication.

References

ADAMS, K. A. (1990). 'Monastery and village at Crayke, North Yorkshire'. *Yorkshire Archaeological Journal* 62: 29–50.

AUDOUY, M., DIX, B., and PARSONS, D. (1995). 'The tower of All Saints' Church, Earl's Barton, Northamptonshire: its construction and context'. *Archaeological Journal* 152: 73–94.

BAKER, N. (2005). 'Urban monasteries in England'. *Antiquity* 79: 304, 461–3.

—— and HOLT, R. (1998). 'The origins of urban parish boundaries', in T. R. Slater and G. Rosser (eds.), *The Church in the Towns*. Aldershot: Ashgate, 209–35.

———— (2004). *Urban Growth and the Medieval Church: Gloucester and Worcester*. Aldershot: Ashgate.

BELL, R. D., and BERESFORD, M. W. (1987). *Wharram Percy: The Church of St Martin*. Volume 3 of *Wharram: A Study of Settlement on the Yorkshire Wolds*. Society for Medieval Archaeology Monograph 11. London: Society for Medieval Archaeology.

BELL, T. W. (1996). 'Churches on Roman buildings: Christian associations and Roman masonry in Anglo-Saxon England'. *Medieval Archaeology* 42: 1–18.

—— (2005). *The Religious Reuse of Roman Structures in Early Medieval England*. British Archaeological Reports 390. Oxford: Archaeopress.

BLAIR, J. (ed.) (1988). *Minsters and Parish Churches: The Local Church in Transition 950–1200*. Oxford: Oxford University Committee for Archaeology.

—— (1994). *Anglo-Saxon Oxfordshire*. Stroud: Alan Sutton.

—— (2002). 'A saint for every minster? Local cults in Anglo-Saxon England', in A. T. Thacker and R. Sharpe (eds.), *Local Saints and Local Churches in the Early Medieval West*. Oxford: Oxford University Press, 455–94.

—— (2005). *The Church in Anglo-Saxon Society*. Oxford: Oxford University Press.

—— and PYRAH, C. (eds.) (1996). *Church Archaeology: Research Directions for the Future*. CBA Research Report 104. York: Council for British Archaeology.

BODDINGTON, A. (1990). 'Models of burial, settlement and worship: the final phase reviewed', in E. Southworth (ed.), *Anglo-Saxon Cemeteries: A Reappraisal*. Stroud: Sutton, 177–99.

—— (1996). *Raunds Furnells: The Anglo-Saxon Church and Churchyard*. London: English Heritage.

BRIGGS, K. (2007). 'Seven Wells'. *Journal of the English Place-Name Society* 39: 7–44.

BRITNELL, W. J. (1990). 'Capel Maelog, Llandrindod Wells, Powys: excavations, 1984–1987'. *Medieval Archaeology* 34: 27–96.

BRYANT, R., and HEIGHWAY, C. (2004). 'Excavations at St. Mary de Lode Church, Gloucester, 1978–9'. *Transactions of the Bristol and Gloucestershire Archaeological Society* 121: 97–178.

CARR, R. D., TESTER, A., and MURPHY, P. (1988). 'The Middle-Saxon settlement at Staunch Meadow, Brandon'. *Antiquity* 62 (235): 371–7.

CARVER, M. (ed.) (2003). *The Cross Goes North: Processes of Conversion in Northern Europe AD 300–1300*. York: York Medieval Press.

CHRISTIE, N. (2004). 'On bells and bell-towers: origins and evolutions in Italy and Britain, AD 700–1200'. *Church Archaeology* 5/6: 13–30.

COATSWORTH, E. (2008). *Corpus of Anglo-Saxon Stone Sculpture, Volume 8: Western Yorkshire*. London: British Academy.

COPPACK, G. (1986). 'St Lawrence Church, Burnham, South Humberside: the excavation of a parochial chapel'. *Lincolnshire History and Archaeology* 21: 39–60.

CRAMP, R. (2005–6). *Wearmouth and Jarrow Monastic Sites*, Volumes 1 and 2. Swindon: English Heritage.

CRICK, J. (ed.) (2007). *Charters of St Albans*. Oxford: Oxford University Press for the British Academy.

DELAPLACE, C. (ed.) (2005). *Aux origins de la paroisse rurale en Gaule Méridionale IVe—IXe siècles*. Paris: Editions Errance.

DOBNEY, K. (2007). *Farmers, Monks and Aristocrats: The Environmental Archaeology of Anglo-Saxon Flixborough*. Volume 3 of *Excavations at Flixborough*. Oxford: Oxbow.

EVERSON, P., and STOCKER, D. A. (1999). *Lincolnshire*. Corpus of Anglo-Saxon Stone Sculpture 5. Oxford: British Academy.

FERNIE, E. (1983). *The Architecture of the Anglo-Saxons*. London: B. T. Batsford.

FOARD, G., HALL, D., and PARTIDA, T. (2009). *Rockingham Forest: An Atlas of the Medieval and Early-Modern Landscape*. Northampton: Northamptonshire Record Society.

GEAKE, H. (1997). *The Use of Grave-Goods in Conversion-Period England, c.600–c.850*. British Archaeological Reports 261. Oxford: Hedges.

GEM, R. (1988). 'The English parish church in the eleventh and early twelfth centuries: a great rebuilding?', in Blair (ed.), *Minsters and Parish Churches*, 21–30.

GITTOS, H. (2002). 'Anglo-Saxon rites for consecrating cemeteries', in Lucy and Reynolds (eds.), *Burial in Early Medieval England and Wales*, 195–208.

HADLEY, D. M. (2000). 'Burial practices in the Northern Danelaw c.650–1100', *Northern History* 36(2): 199–217.

—— and BUCKBERRY, J. L. (2005). 'Caring for the dead in later Anglo-Saxon England', in *Pastoral Care in Late Anglo-Saxon England*. Anglo-Saxon Studies 6. Woodbridge: Boydell, 121–47.

HALL, R. A., BUCKBERRY, J., STORM, R., BUDD, P., HAMILTON, W. D., and MCCORMACK, G. (2008). 'The medieval cemetery at Riccall Landing: a reappraisal'. *Yorkshire Archaeological Journal* 80: 55–92.

HARDY, A., DODD, A., and KEEVIL, G. D. (2003). *Aelfric's Abbey: Excavations at Eynsham Abbey, Oxfordshire, 1989–92*. Thames Valley Landscapes Monograph 15. Oxford: Oxford Archaeology.

HAWKES, J. (1993). 'Mary and the cycle of resurrection: the iconography of the Hovingham Panel', in R. M. Spearman and J. Higgitt (eds.), *The Age of Migrating Ideas*. National Museums of Scotland. Stroud: Sutton, 254–60.

HEIGHWAY, C. (1999). *The Golden Minster: The Anglo-Saxon Minster and Later Medieval Priory of St Oswald at Gloucester*. CBA Research Report 117. York: Council for British Archaeology.

JOHNSON, P. (2003). 'Cemetery excavations at Village Farm, Spofforth: archaeological post-excavation assessment'. Unpublished report, Northern Archaeological Associates.

JONES, M. J., STOCKER, D. A., and VINCE, A. (2003). *The City by the Pool: Assessing the Archaeology of the City of Lincoln*. Oxford: Oxbow.

KJØLBYE-BIDDLE, B. (1995). 'Iron-bound coffins and coffin-fittings from the pre-Norman cemetery', in D. Phillips and B. Heywood (eds.), *Excavations at York Minster*, Volume 1 (2 parts). London: Royal Commission on the Historical Monuments of England, 489–521.

KLAUSNER, D. N. (1990). *Records of Early English Drama: Herefordshire, Worcestershire*. Toronto: University of Toronto Press.

LANG, J. (1991). *Corpus of Anglo-Saxon Stone Sculpture*, Volume 3: *York and Eastern Yorkshire*. London: British Academy.

LEES, C. A., and OVERING, G. R. (eds.) (2006). *A Place to Believe in: Locating Medieval Landscapes*. Pennsylvania: Pennsylvania State University Press.

LOVELUCK, C. (2007). *Rural Settlement, Lifestyles and Social Change in the Later First Millennium AD: Anglo-Saxon Flixborough in its Wider Context*. Volume 4 of *Excavations at Flixborough*. Oxford: Oxbow.

—— and ATKINSON, D. (2007). *The early medieval settlement remains from Flixborough, Lincolnshire: the occupation sequence, c. AD 600–1000*. Oxford: Oxbow.

LUCY, S., and REYNOLDS, A. (eds.) (2002). *Burial in Early Medieval England and Wales*. Society for Medieval Archaeology Monograph 17. London: Society for Medieval Archaeology.

MAYS, S., HARDING, C., and HEIGHWAY, C. (2007). *Wharram: A Study of Settlement on the Yorkshire Wolds*, Volume 11: *The Churchyard*. York: York University Publications 13.

MORRIS, G. E. (1985). 'The significance of the place-name, Stonegrave'. *Journal of the English Place-Name Society* 17: 14–19.

MORRIS, R. (1989). *Churches in the Landscape*. London: J. M. Dent.

—— (2008). *Journeys from Jarrow*. Jarrow Lecture 2004. Jarrow: St Paul's Church.

—— (forthcoming). 'Looking for Loidis'.

ORTON, F., WOOD, I. N., and LEES, C. A. (2008). *Fragments of History: Rethinking the Ruthwell and Bewcastle Monuments*. Manchester: Manchester University Press.

PARSONS, D. (ed.) (1990). *Stone Quarrying and Building in England AD43–1525*. Chichester: Phillimore/Royal Archaeological Institute.

POWLESLAND, D. (2009). 'Why bother? Large scale geomagnetic survey and the quest for "Real Archaeology"', in S. Campana and S. Piro (eds.), *Seeing the Unseen: Geophysics and Landscape Archaeology*. CRC Press, 167–82.

RAHTZ, P., and WATTS, L. (2003). 'Three ages of conversion at Kirkdale, North Yorkshire', in Carver (ed.), *The Cross Goes North*, 289–309.

—— —— and BUTLER, H. T. L. (eds.) (1997). *St. Mary's Church, Deerhurst, Gloucestershire: Fieldwork, Excavations, and Structural Analysis, 1971–1984*. Society of Antiquaries of London, Research Committee Report 55. Woodbridge: Boydell.

────── and SAUNDERS, K. (2000). 'Appleton-le-Street: All Saints Church'. *Ryedale Historian* 20: 24–31.

RIPPON, S. (2007). 'Emerging regional variation in historic landscape character: the possible significance of the "long eighth century"', in M. Gardiner and S. Rippon (eds.), *Medieval Landscapes: Landscape History after Hoskins*, Volume 2. Macclesfield: Windgather, 105–21.

ROBERTS, B. K., and WRATHMELL, S. (2000). *An Atlas of Rural Settlement in England*. London: English Heritage.

────── (2002). *Region and Place: A Study of English Rural Settlement*. London: English Heritage.

RODWELL, W. J. (1986). 'Anglo-Saxon church building: aspects of design and construction', in L. A. S. Butler and R. K. Morris (eds.), *The Anglo-Saxon Church: Papers in Honour of H. M. Taylor*. CBA Research Report 60. London: Council for British Archaeology, 156–75.

────── and RODWELL, K. (1982). 'St Peter's Church, Barton-upon-Humber: excavation and structural study, 1978–81'. *Antiquaries Journal* 62(2): 283–331.

────── (1993). *Rivenhall: Investigations of a Roman Villa, Church and Village, 1950–77*. CBA Research Report 80. York: Council for British Archaeology.

SALTER, H.E. (1921). *The Historic Names of the Streets and Lanes of Oxford*. Oxford: Clarendon Press.

────── (1936). *Medieval Oxford*. Oxford Historical Society 100.

SAWYER, P. H. (1981). 'Fairs and markets in early medieval England', in N. Skyum-Neilsen and N. Lund (eds.), *Danish Medieval History: New Currents*. Copenhagen: Museum Tusculanum Press, 153–68.

SENIOR, J. B. (1990). 'Hildenley limestone: a fine quality dimensional and artifact stone from Yorkshire', in Parsons (ed.), *Stone Quarrying and Building*, 147–68.

STOCKER, D. A. (2000). 'Monuments and Merchants: irregularities in the distribution of stone sculpture in Lincolnshire and Yorkshire in the tenth century', in D. Hadley and J. Richards (eds.), *Cultures in Contact: Scandinavian Settlement in England in the Ninth and Tenth Centuries*. Turnhout: Brepols, 179–212.

────── (2006). *England's Landscape: The East Midlands*. London: English Heritage.

────── (2007). 'Pre-Conquest stonework—the early graveyard in context', in Mays et al. (eds.), *Wharram*, 271–87.

────── and EVERSON, P. (1990). 'Rubbish recycled: a study of the re-use of stone in Lincolnshire', in Parsons, *Stone Quarrying and Building*, 83–101.

────── (2003). 'The straight and narrow way: Fenland causeways and the conversion of the landscape in the Witham Valley, Lincolnshire', in Carver (ed.), *The Cross Goes North*, 271–88.

────── (2006). *Summoning St Michael: Early Romanesque Towers in Lincolnshire*. Oxford: Oxbow.

TAYLOR, H. M. (1976). 'The foundations of architectural history', in P. V. Addyman and R. K. Morris (eds.), *The Archaeological Study of Churches*. London: Council for British Archaeology, 3–9.

────── and TAYLOR, J. (1965). *Anglo-Saxon Architecture*, Volumes 1 and 2. Cambridge: Cambridge University Press.

────── (1978). *Anglo-Saxon Architecture*, Volume 3. Cambridge: Cambridge University Press.

TURNER, S. (2006). *Making a Christian Landscape: The Countryside in Early Medieval Cornwall, Devon and Wessex*. Exeter: University of Exeter Press.

TYERS, I. (1996). 'Tree-ring analysis of the timbers of the stave church of Greensted, Essex'. Unpublished report of the Ancient Monuments Laboratory.

WALDRON, A. with RODWELL, W. J. (2007). *St Peter's, Barton-upon-Humber, Lincolnshire—A Parish Church and its Community*, Volume 2: *The Human Remains*. Oxford: Oxbow.

WILLIAMS, H. (1997). 'Ancient landscapes and the dead: the re-use of prehistoric and Roman monuments as early Anglo-Saxon burial sites'. *Medieval Archaeology* 41: 1–32.

WILLIAMSON, T. (2007). 'The distribution of "woodland" and "champion" landscapes in medieval England', in M. Gardiner and S. Rippon (eds.), *Medieval Landscapes: Landscape History after Hoskins*, Volume 2. Macclesfield: Windgather, 89–104.

WILSON, D. M. (1992). *Anglo-Saxon Paganism*. London: Routledge.

WOOD, I. N. (2006). 'Bede's Jarrow', in C. A. Lees and G. R. Overing (eds.), *A Place to Believe in: Locating Medieval Landscapes*. Pennsylvania: Pennsylvania State University Press, 67–84.

ZADORA-RIO, E. (2003). 'The Making of churchyards and parish territories in the early-medieval landscape of France and England in the 7th–12th centuries: a reconsideration'. *Medieval Archaeology* 47: 1–19.

CHAPTER 12

LATE SAXON SETTLEMENTS

MARK GARDINER

Much has been written on late Saxon settlement patterns in the last couple of decades, but very little about the settlements themselves. The result is that we know a good deal more about the countryside in which people lived and farmed than about the farms they occupied. Yet the extraordinary growth in archaeological fieldwork has made it possible to discuss Anglo-Saxon settlements with greater confidence and in considerably more detail than when the subject was last reviewed by Rahtz (1976) more than thirty years ago. Perhaps this lack of scholarly interest in the settlements of those who lived and farmed in the countryside reflects our contemporary experience in which manual labour and the production of food plays very little part. However, the work of cultivating land was central for the vast majority of the 275,000 or so individuals enumerated in Domesday Book shortly after the close of the Saxon period and for their families.

The study of settlements must begin from the basis that late Saxon society was strongly hierarchical and marked by considerable inequalities of wealth. We may assume that these differences will probably be reflected in the settlements. By the thirteenth century, and very probably before, buildings were one of the most important ways by which social status was demonstrated. It is useful, therefore, to discuss settlements in two broad groups—those which might be described as 'high-status', which in historical terms means those belonging to thegns and their social superiors, and those of the peasants, which would include the *geneat* and others whose servile work duties are described in *Rectitudines Singularum Personarum* (Liebermann 1903: 444–53; Swanton 1975: 21–5). The rural settlements of these two broad groups are considered first, while the final section examines impermanent settlements associated with animal herding.

High-status settlements

A significant number of sites has been identified by archaeologists as belonging to those of 'thegnly' status, and this is probably a fair reflection of the historical reality. Those who lay at and beyond the upper margin of what might reasonably be described as peasants were comparatively numerous, though still a minority of society. This class proliferated in the tenth century as estates were parcelled up and leased out to new men, and occasionally women, and to associates of the powerful (Dyer 1996: 176-81; Faith 1997: 153–77; V. King 1996: 103–11). Archaeologists have attempted to identify manorial sites using a variety of indicators—the layout and character of buildings, the presence of manorial appurtenances, such as a mill, and proximity to a church or chapel. Analysis of the evidence suggests that although there were relatively few such sites before 900, they subsequently appear in increasing numbers (Gardiner 2007: 175).

Documentary sources give little indication of the character of high-status settlements, although it is worth considering what can be deduced before turning to the excavated evidence. We might expect that any large farmstead would have had a number of buildings—a house and perhaps a dairy, a granary, and other ancillary farm structures. Typically, accommodation on a larger farmstead would have comprised a chamber (a private room or bedroom) and a hall. King Alfred's recension of St Augustine's *Soliloquies* says that men on a royal estate slept in the chamber, the hall, on the threshing floor, and even in prison. We should not understand this as a list of typical accommodation, but as comment on the range of places where people of descending status might sleep (Carnicelli 1969: 77; Rahtz 1979: 132; Blair 1993: 2). *Gerefa*, an eleventh-century text, suggests that on the larger sites there were separate buildings or rooms for brewing, and for storing items for the table (the spence), as well as a kitchen, dairy, granary, and bakehouse (Gardiner 2006).

Archaeologists have attempted to use *Geþyncðo*, a text attributed to Archbishop Wulfstan (c.1002–1023), to recognize features specific to a thegn's residence. The text says that a thegn should possess a church and kitchen, bell-house and enclosure gate (*cirican & kycenan, bellhus & burhgeat*; Liebermann 1903: i. 456). The Old English text suggests that these were chosen not only as symbols of status, but also for their assonance, and therefore we need to be rather cautious before ascribing particular significance to them. Nevertheless, the character of the *burhgeat*, often translated as 'gatehouse', has much exercised archaeologists, who have sometimes regarded it as a predecessor to the later medieval keep (for the considerable literature on the subject, see Renn 1994: 182, n. 28). This cannot be so. The problem has arisen from a misunderstanding of the meaning of the word, *burh*, which might be used, not only for a fortification, but for any manorial enclosure (Williams 1992: 226–8). A *burhgeat*, therefore, might well be no more than the gateway to the manor site. Wulfstan might have chosen simply to write *burh*, but the rhythm of the passage required a bipartite word.

It is appropriate to begin the discussion of the archaeological evidence with a consideration of the *burh* or enclosure which surrounded many high-status settlements. The enclosures around these sites were deeper than the field ditches found on peasant farms. They were intended to give privacy and to discourage the casual intruder, but they were not effective as a defence and would not have kept out anyone more determined. The ditches were generally between 1 m and 1.5 m deep below contemporary ground surface and on some sites there is evidence for an internal bank which may have been capped with a hedge. Their inadequacy as a defence is most obvious if they are compared with the earthen banks and ditches around contemporary towns which really were intended to keep out attackers (e.g. Royal Commission on Historical Monuments 1959; Dalwood and Edwards 2004: 55). Manorial enclosures were sometimes rectilinear in plan, often with rounded corners, but rarely regular in shape. The enclosure at North Shoebury Hall (Essex) is more carefully laid out than most, but the ditch at Whitehouse Road, Ipswich (Suffolk), first dug in the eighth or ninth century and continuing in use into the eleventh century, is more typical (Fig. 12.1).

The entrances were marked by a gap in the ditch, but a few enclosures also had gates indicated by pairs of posts. The posts were set back behind the ditch and on the line of a presumed bank, though this rarely survives as an upstanding feature. The entrances at Steyning (Sussex), Little Paxton (formerly Hunts.) and Cheddar (Somers.) are particularly notable because they had two outer posts and a smaller hole between which seems to have been for a catch post for a two-leaf gate (Gardiner 1993: 27–8; Fig 12.2). The importance of the entrance at the royal site of Cheddar was further emphasized by the use of a double enclosure ditch, each presumably with an internal bank, and, just outside the gate, by a large post-hole containing a timber 0.6 m in diameter. The excavator suggested that the post may have been a flagstaff or a carved timber (Rahtz 1979: 166–7). At Cheddar, Little Paxton (Cambs.), and North Shoebury smaller ditches were used to mark the approach to the enclosure entrance (Addyman 1969: fig. 6; Rahtz 1979: fig. 12; Wymer and Brown 1995: fig. 41). The conjunction of manor house and church is a commonplace of the English countryside, and many churches were established during the eleventh century immediately outside the manor site. Certainly, visitors to Faccombe Netherton (Hants), Goltho (Lincs.), Hatch Warren (Hants), and Trowbridge (Wilts.), amongst others, could hardly have failed to notice the church as they approached the manor site (Fairbrother 1990; Fasham *et al.* 1995; Graham

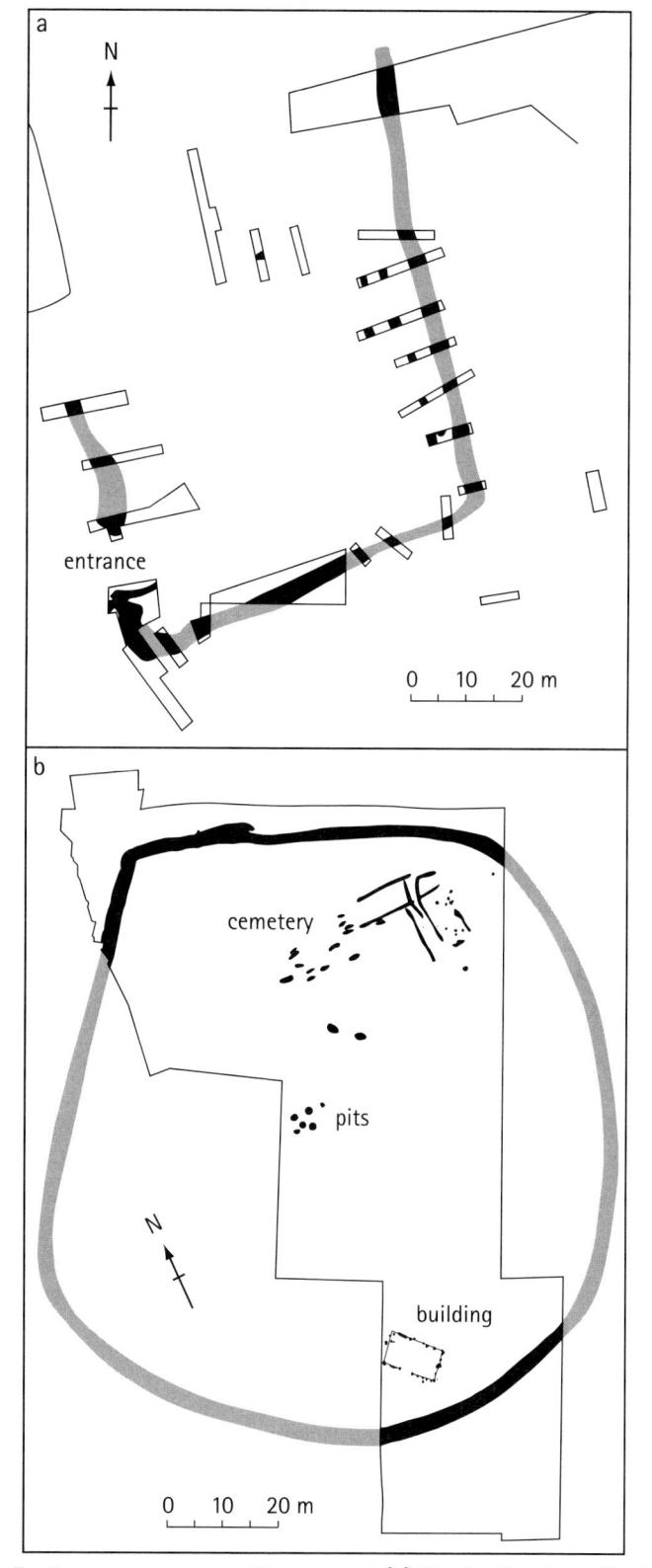

Figure 12.1 Enclosures around settlements at (a) North Shoebury Hall (Essex) and (b) Whitehouse Road, Ipswich (Suffolk) (after Wymer and Brown 1995)

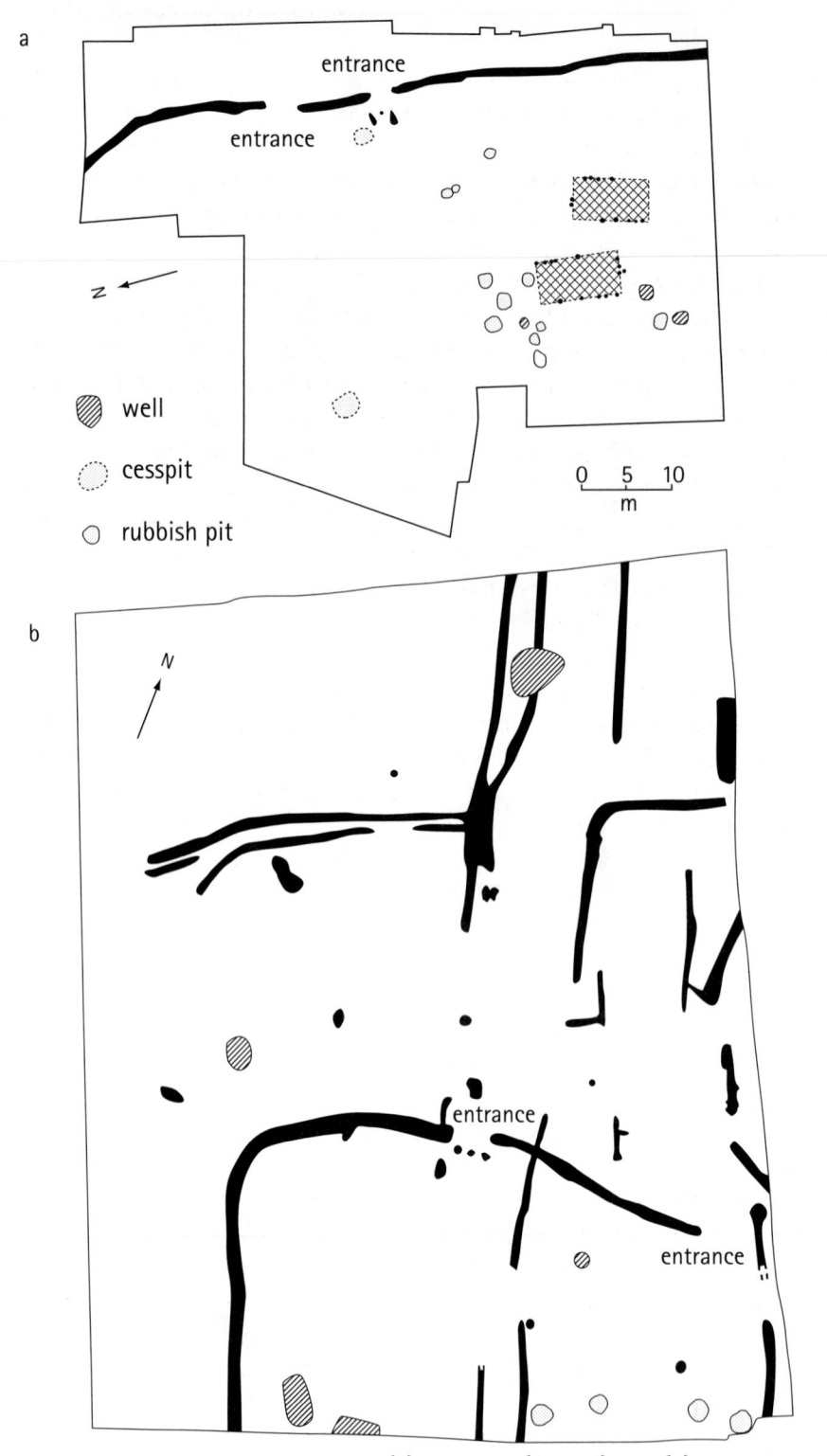

Figure 12.2 Enclosures with gates at (a) Steyning (Sussex) and (b) Little Paxton (formerly Hunts.) (after Gardiner 1993 and Addyman 1969)

and Davies 1993). If possession of a church was an indicator of a thegn, as *Geþyncðo* states, then this symbol of status might well have been placed where it would have been apparent to visitors.

The entrances to high-status settlements were intended not only to provide an approach to the farmstead and enclosures, but also to frame the buildings in a manner which was no less formal than the designed landscapes found around castles from the twelfth century onwards (Liddiard 2000). The development of the enclosure and buildings at West Cotton (Northants) exemplifies this. The complex was constructed around 950 and a broad trackway was established which gave access from the south-east to the area in front of the manorial enclosure (Fig. 12.3a). Like many such enclosures, there were two entrances. The one to the east was for work use and gave access to the mill, and the second on the west was for visitors and domestic purposes and led directly to the hall. The domestic entrance was initially very broad, but was later restricted by extending the enclosure ditch and adding a gate. Access to the chamber building which stood next to the hall was only possible through the hall building or an entrance in a palisade next to it. Between 975 and 1000 the complex was rebuilt (Fig. 12.3b). Part of the enclosure ditch was infilled and a courtyard created through the construction of a kitchen and barn. Access to the courtyard was limited by a timber fence and ditch. The changing organization of buildings and ditches at West Cotton shows how the space around the hall and the entrance to it was carefully managed. By the eleventh century a clear distinction was made between the hall approach, the domestic space of the courtyard, the agricultural space of the barn and area to the south and the more private space marked by the presence of one certain and two other possible cesspits to the rear of the chamber building (Chapman forthcoming).

The type of development seen at West Cotton can also be found at other high-status sites. There was a growing emphasis during the later tenth and early eleventh centuries on the presentation of a carefully managed approach and an increasingly formal division of space into functional areas. For example, at Goltho there is a definite contrast between the plans of the tenth- and eleventh-century phases (Periods 3, 4, and 5; for a summary of the views on the dates for Goltho, see Creighton 2002: 24). In the earliest phase there was a cesspit towards the site of the entrance, and a water pit and rubbish pit in front of the hall (Fig. 12.4a). None of these seems in keeping with the creation of an impressive approach. In the next phase, in the early eleventh century, there was a clear line of approach marked by a ditch, directing visitors to the front side of the hall. The adjoining buildings formed three sides of a courtyard and the cesspits were hidden away from view behind the chamber (Fig. 12.4b). The formality of approach was even more apparent when the buildings were slightly rearranged in the mid eleventh century and a broad, ditched trackway was created which led almost to the door of the hall (Fig. 12.4c).

The development of the planned high-status settlement is also reflected in the emergence of a very particular arrangement of buildings—the long range. This

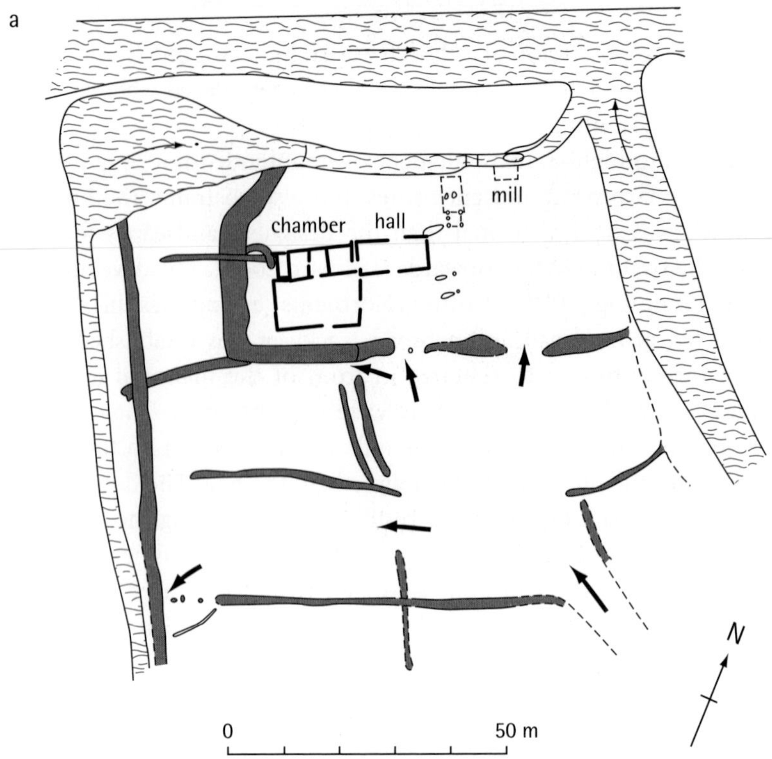

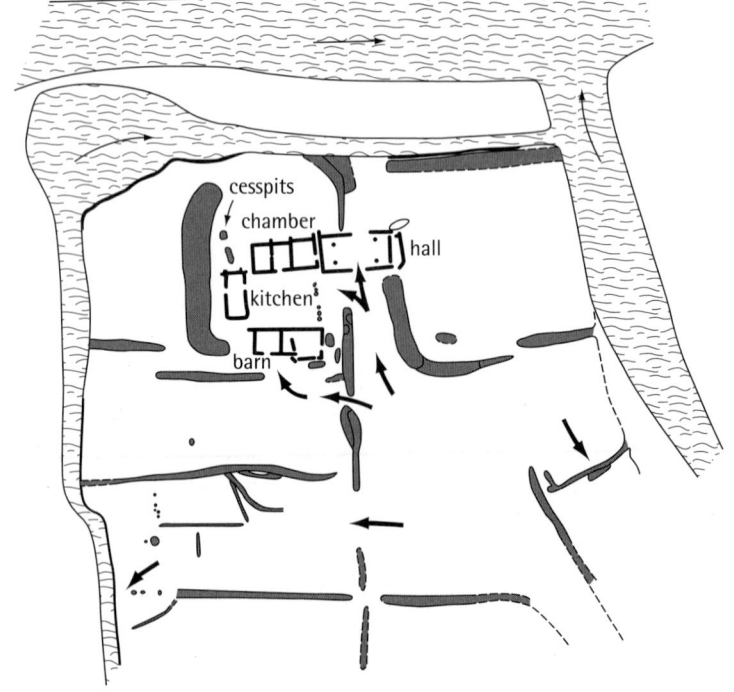

Figure 12.3 The development of the enclosures at West Cotton, Northants (after A. Chapman forthcoming)

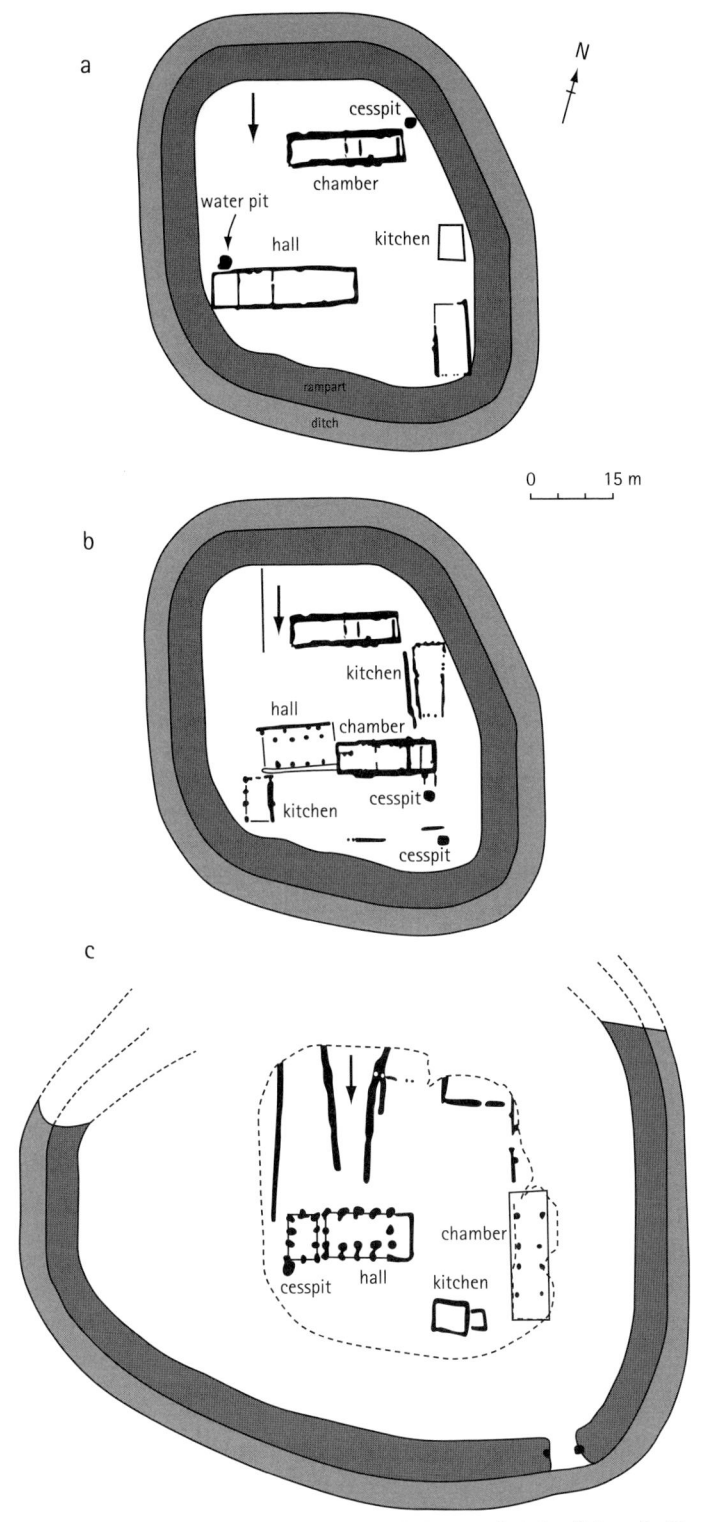

Figure 12.4 The development of the manorial site at Goltho (Lincs.), Phases 3 to 5 (adapted from Beresford 1987)

term was first applied to the buildings at Raunds Furnells and subsequently to those at West Cotton (Figs. 12.3A, B), but a similar arrangement can be seen at Goltho (Period 4: early eleventh century; Fig. 12.4B) and at Sulgrave. The particular feature of this plan was the construction of a contiguous hall and chamber to form a single range. Convenience of access from the hall to the chamber may have been one reason for this plan, but another seems to have been the presentation of an extended facade to the visitor. The ranges at the first three of these sites are strikingly similar. Each comprises a hall with narrow aisles and a slightly narrower domestic building divided into several rooms with central doorways through the internal walls. The building at Sulgrave dating to the late tenth century is more difficult to understand because of the circumstances of excavation, but it seems to have comprised a building with a hall and domestic rooms (Davison 1977; and see Hamerow, this volume).

Blair (1993: 5–8, 10) has drawn a contrast between the axial arrangement of buildings (of which the long range with its contiguous structures is one type) and the courtyard arrangement. This distinction does not seem to be borne out by more recent excavations. It was possible, as at Raunds Furnells and Goltho, to combine the two patterns, with an axial arrangement of hall and chamber forming one side of a courtyard, and completed on the other sides by farm and further domestic buildings. The courtyard plan seems to emerge from a much looser grouping of buildings during the late tenth century when, as Reynolds (2003: 128) has shown, a rectilinear arrangement became more common on manorial sites. Overall, there is an increasing interest in the arrangement of space, as if ideas about 'proper' practice had been adopted by the elite. It is not certain whether these ideas had permeated downwards from the most wealthy. The royal site of Cheddar has such a different array of buildings from the normal manorial site that it hardly stands comparison. The pre-Conquest phases of Cheddar (Periods 1 and 2 using dating from Blair 1996: 116) seem to lack domestic buildings, and the Long Hall and West Hall 1 are exceptional for the length of the former, and the width and the end entrance of the latter. The oddly-shaped Structure X at Cheddar, which had two rectangular buildings set either side of a circular one, remains without parallel. Its identification as a fowl house on a site otherwise devoid of farm buildings is not convincing (Rahtz 1979: 130–2; see Fig. 9.7).

It is rarely certain what functions were performed in the external spaces on high-status sites. At West Cotton we can make a reasonable guess because the buildings and enclosures form a clear pattern, but the pattern of usage is less evident on other sites where the only indicator of the activities in the areas between buildings may be pits and ditches. Even these are few in number as rubbish pits are rarely found on late Saxon sites; the rubbish was generally collected in surface middens for later use for manuring fields. Even cesspits are uncommon. Again, human waste was generally kept in middens for use as manure. Steyning is unusual in this respect since the rubbish was dumped in pits and large cesspits were dug. Differences in the form and the fill of rubbish pits and cesspits on that site allowed these to be distinguished from the shallow wells. There was a clear pattern, with wells mainly situated to the south side of the buildings, while the rubbish was deposited to the north. The two cesspits were set well away from the buildings; each must have had a latrine building above them, though no trace was found in excavation. One cesspit, rather curiously, stood close to the entrance to the enclosure (Fig. 12.2a). A similar pattern is found at Little Paxton where there was a separation of wells, situated both inside and outside the enclosure, and rubbish pits (Fig. 12.2b).

It is also difficult to determine the functions of agricultural buildings. These formed a smaller proportion of the total number of buildings on the late Saxon farmstead than on its modern equivalent. Barns and granaries were relatively rare on farmsteads throughout the medieval period. Crops must have been stored in ricks after harvesting and used or threshed for grain as required. Ricks generally leave no archaeological trace, though a penannular gully at Wharram Percy about 4.8 m across may have been dug to ensure that a cropstack remained dry (Stamper and Croft 2000: 46–7). The small enclosures recorded near to the manorial sites at Coton Park near Rugby (Warwicks.) and at Raunds Furnells may have been occupied by haystacks and cornricks (Maull 2001; Audouy and Chapman 2009).

Peasant settlements

Those seeking the origins of the English village have often turned to the two centuries between 850 and 1050, and closely scrutinized the evidence for signs of the formation of nucleated settlements. However, no excavation has produced anything which resembles the type of settlement familiar from the fourteenth century onwards with a series of closely set buildings facing on to a central road or green. It might be argued that such sites have not been found because they are now beneath existing settlements and consequently are not accessible for excavation. However, enough deserted medieval villages have been excavated to show that they do not overlie Saxon sites of similar form, though they may have been preceded by smaller settlements of a different character. It seems clear that the settlement pattern of late Saxon England was more dispersed than in later centuries, when buildings tended to congregate on street frontages and had nucleated into hamlets and villages. The tendency towards nucleation was particularly marked in the band of England which runs from eastern Somerset across the eastern Midlands to County Durham and Northumberland. That region, which has been termed the 'Central Province', was characterized by a large number of villages in the late medieval period, but its distinctive settlement pattern may only have started to emerge towards the end of the Saxon period (Roberts and Wrathmell 2002: 6–12; Parry 2006: 126–7).

The development of a more nucleated pattern has been traced in the very large-scale excavations at Stratton near Biggleswade (Beds.). The landscape of the tenth and eleventh centuries was divided by a series of large curvilinear enclosures, amongst which were a number of small farmsteads (Lewis et al. 1997: fig. 3.4). The farms typically consisted of one or two structures, generally with an adjacent shallow well. They were rarely situated in their own enclosures, but in the angles of ditched boundaries, or at the point at which the ditches met roads. During the twelfth century, and certainly by the thirteenth, these farmsteads were abandoned and new ones were established either side of a road. Two processes took place to produce a hamlet—the density of occupation increased and the farmsteads began to congregate more closely on the street-frontage.

It has proved very difficult to understand the plan and use of space in individual peasant farms and their relationship to the wider landscape. Unlike high-status settlements, which were surrounded by substantial ditches, the boundaries around peasant settlements were much slighter. The evidence for hedge and fences is rarely recognized in excavation, though at North Elmham it was possible to identify minor boundaries which make the arrangement of farmsteads considerably more comprehensible. North Elmham was completely re-organized at the beginning of Period 3 when a single high-status settlement was replaced by two peasant farmsteads. This change should probably be placed a little later than in the published report, and attributed to the middle of the eleventh century. (A reconsideration of the dating of the site will be presented elsewhere.) Almost all the buildings on both these farms were subsequently replaced by others, usually on the same spot, and it is useful to refer to these later structures to assist with an understanding of function. The interpretation suggested below is significantly different from that of the excavator.

The two farmsteads, constructed about 90 m apart, were very similar in character. The houses themselves were relatively small buildings, measuring only 5.3 m by 3 m in one case and 6.4 m by 4.2 m in the other, and each had only a single room with a door (marked by rectangular postholes set at right angles to the wall line) towards the end wall (Fig. 12.5). Large square structures close to each farmhouse were interpreted by the excavator as barns, though it is questionable whether they were roofed buildings or enclosures. A further building of uncertain function stood a short distance from each house. These were both set with one wall on the line of a fence. There was no identifiable yard at either farmstead and neither farmhouse had a clear relationship to the nearby roads (Wade-Martins 1980: 153–62).

Much the same pattern of houses, outbuildings, and enclosures can be seen in the tenth- and eleventh-century phases at Stratton Biggleswade, where there were three farmsteads, and at nearby Marston Moretaine (Beds.) and Westbury (Bucks.) where there was one each (information from Albion Archaeology; Edmondson and Steadman 2001: 50; Ivens et al. 1995: 136–8). The houses on these sites were considerably larger than those at North Elmham. The doorways were set centrally in the long wall of the house, in contrast to the end entrances at the Norfolk site.

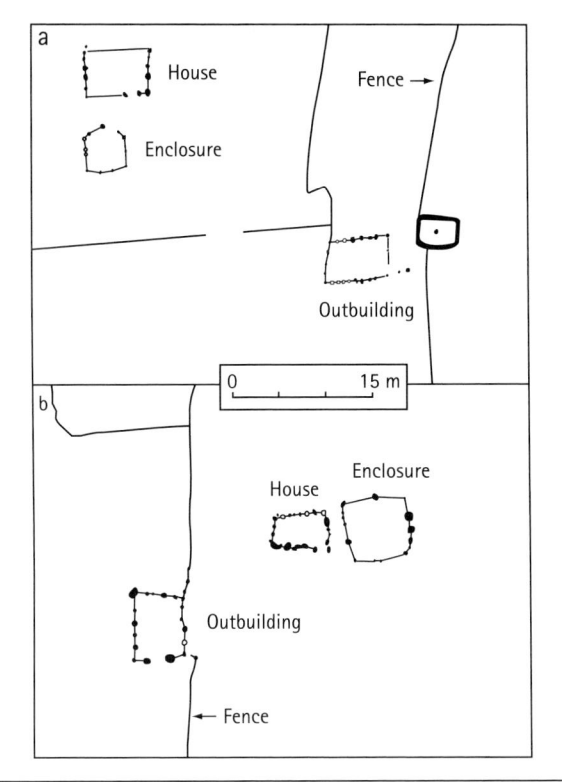

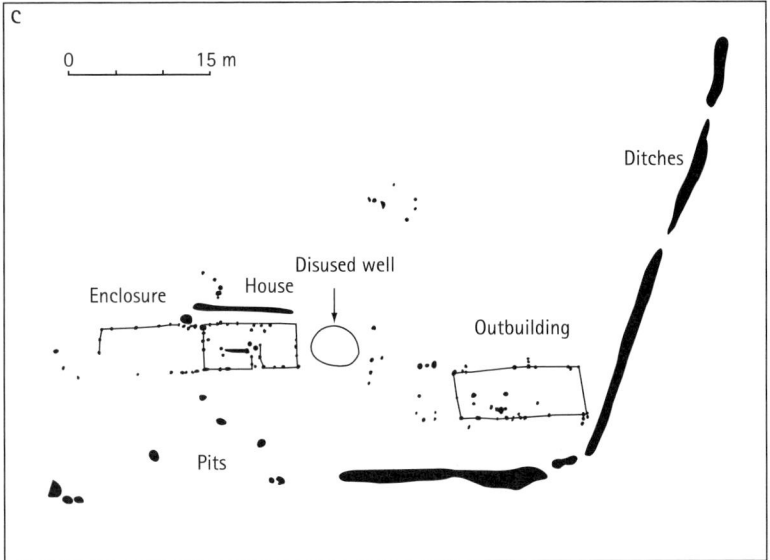

Figure 12.5 Peasant farmsteads at North Elmham and Stratton Biggleswade (after Wade-Martins 1980 and Albion Archaeology)

The hearths were placed just beyond the entrance in one half of the house, which was presumably the living end or hall. The half on the other side of the entrance may have served as the chamber or sleeping end, although equally it could have been used for storage or food preparation. The largest of the buildings at Stratton, which measured 15.2 m by 6.1 m, had an internal partition 2 m from the end providing a rather small room. The entrances of most houses faced out towards other buildings or enclosures. There was both a practical value in arranging the farm buildings in this way since it made movement between them easier, particularly in bad weather, and possibly there was also some benefit in reducing the risk of theft. However, the result was to create a plan without a clear line of approach and without a view of the facade of the house, exactly the opposite of high-status buildings.

Clear regional traditions of building were established by the late Saxon period. The farmsteads in Norfolk and east Midlands sites had many similarities, both with each other and with settlements recorded elsewhere in lowland England. Farms typically comprise a house, an outbuilding, and an enclosure. The buildings were constructed with numerous timber posts set in postholes or a continuous wall trench. In Cornwall and Devon there was a quite different form of building and pattern to the farmsteads. Some buildings were constructed with turf walls lined on the interior with stakes. The interpretation of such buildings has been disputed, but the evidence from the earlier phases at Treworld (Cornwall) when the stakes were placed in narrow trenches is particularly persuasive. The use of turf and stake construction in the supposed latest phases is less certain and the stake-holes may, in fact, be contemporary with later stone buildings constructed on the site (Dudley and Minter 1966: 38–43; Austin 1985: 71–3; Henderson and Weddell 1994). Another example of a building with stakes set within a trench was found at Tresmorn (Cornwall). The sequence of buildings on that site is particularly interesting as it suggests a development from the rectangular farmhouses, similar to those in the east Midlands, to structures with a byre or shippon (Beresford 1971). The shippon was a room at one end of the farmhouse for keeping animals; living accommodation was provided at the other. This type of building is commonly known to buildings historians as a longhouse. It is particularly unfortunate that the chronology of the Tresmorn buildings is so speculative, since the date of the emergence of the longhouse plan is important for understanding the development in farmsteads in western and northern England.

Much the same problems of dating beset the understanding of the stone-built farmsteads found at Mawgan Porth on the north coast of Cornwall (Bruce-Mitford 1997). The use of stone appears initially to represent a rather different tradition of construction, but these Cornish buildings bear a strong resemblance to thirteenth-century buildings at Hound Tor and Dean Moor on Dartmoor (Fox 1958; Beresford 1979). The arrangement of buildings around a courtyard, the use of crosswings to provide additional accommodation, and the longhouse plan are features also found at these other sites. This resemblance must raise queries about the dating of Mawgan Porth, which is attributed to the tenth and eleventh centuries on the evidence of one coin, which was not clearly stratified, and the presence of bar-lug pottery. However, excavation at Launceston Castle (Cornwall) has shown that this pottery did not continue in production after 1075 (Saunders 2006: 269–70). Mawgan Porth cannot have continued in use much after the last quarter of the eleventh century, and the site is confirmed, therefore, as a remarkably early example of the longhouse building plan which only became common in subsequent centuries in the south-west.

Another tradition of stone construction is found in northern England. Five sites have been excavated in the Pennines with stone buildings dating to around AD 850. The sites at the 'Priest's House' and Prior's Rakes on Malham Moor (Lancs.) are poorly recorded and, apart from noting that they were both small houses of probable ninth-century date with hearths set against the centre of the long wall and entrances at one end of the long wall, not a great deal more can be said (Raistrick 1962: 90; A. King 2004: 337–8). The building at Bryant's Gill in Upper Kentmere (Cumberland) was considerably larger, measuring 10 m in length (Dickinson 1985). Buildings from three farmsteads have been excavated at Simy Folds (Co. Durham) and broadly resemble those on Malham Moor, except that they each comprise groups of structures arranged around courtyards (Coggins *et al.* 1983; Coggins 2004). A further site was excavated at Ribblehead (N. Yorks.) and is significantly different, not only because of the size of the house, but also due to its design. It measured 4 m wide, but almost 19 m long internally, which is exceptional for buildings of this period anywhere in England. Furthermore, the presence of gable-end entrances also mark this building as unusual (King 1978; 2004). There were two out-buildings nearby, which were identified as a kitchen and smithy.

These sites have been identified as the farmsteads possibly of Viking settlers (Morris 1981: 241). There is no substantial evidence to support this view for most of these sites. We do not know what a 'normal' site in the Pennines should look like and whether these were typical or not. However, Ribblehead does stand out among these sites both for the size and plan of the house. The interesting comparison made by the excavator with buildings of the Norse phase at Jarlshof on Shetland will deserve further consideration when the final report is published (A. King 2004: 340).

IMPERMANENT SETTLEMENTS

The areas of 'wold' (higher land in parts of lowland England), marshland, woodland, moorland, and other poorer soils, though unattractive for agriculture, were often used for open grazing in the late Saxon period (Hooke 1989: 113–17; 1998: 139–

95; Fox 1996; 2006). Some may have been grazed throughout the year, but in other places the livestock was driven out from the lands around the settlement in the spring and returned in the autumn after the meadow had been mown and the corn cut. Huts used by the animal herders are mentioned in a few Anglo-Saxon charters, but are often known only from place-names. The Old English place-name element *scēla* used in northern England has led to the adoption of the term 'shieling' for settlements of this sort. The buildings on shielings used by animal herders either during the summer grazing season or for shorter periods during lambing or calving have largely escaped archaeological scrutiny, or have not been recognized for what they are. However, there are a small number of excavated examples of these impermanent settlements. Three shieling huts with slightly sunken floors were found beneath the later medieval buildings at Hound Tor on Dartmoor. The presence of a hearth in one and charcoal in another suggests that they were occupied (Beresford 1979: 110–12). The huts could be attributed to the period before the thirteenth century, and similar buildings have now been found elsewhere. A shepherd's hut with a similar depressed floor and hearth was found at West Hythe (Kent) and attributed to the late eleventh or early twelfth century (Gardiner *et al.* 2001: 176–8). A further building with a sunken floor was found high on the South Downs at North Marden (Sussex) close to the end of a prehistoric barrow. Subsequent topsoil stripping around the site shows that it was not part of a larger settlement, but stood in isolation (Drewett *et al.* 1986; Down and Welch 1990: 221–3). It was dated to the period between the eighth and tenth centuries and like the others may be identified as a herder's hut. These huts continued the tradition of sunken-featured buildings found in earlier centuries and this type of simple building may have continued in use for temporary settlements as late as the thirteenth century (Allen 2004: 131).

Stock kept on rough pasture may have roamed freely under the occasional oversight of their herders, but periodically the animals would have been rounded up for various purposes—to move them on, for lambing and calving, and to separate the ewes and lambs, cows and calves. A distinctive form of enclosure was constructed from the late Saxon period onwards on the downland of southern England and on the Cotswolds to help with the management of stock. These were rectangular ditched enclosures, usually situated in valley bottoms and sometimes on valley sides where they gave protection to the animals. Few examples have been excavated, and they generally have little dating evidence (Smith 2005). The enclosure at Easton Lane, Winchester (Hants) was unusual in producing pottery both from the enclosure ditch and from nearby pits, indicating that there was a settlement close by. Animal bones found in a pit 400 m to the south of the enclosure included those of ewes and the skeletons of at least four new-born lambs suggest the presence of a breeding flock. A pit within the enclosure included the bones of two young crows. These were very likely killed by the shepherd because the birds attack and prey upon new-born lambs. The enclosure was smaller than folds recorded elsewhere, measuring 40 m by 16.5 m, and was dated to the tenth or eleventh century (Fasham *et al.* 1989: 75–80, 97–9). A further sheep pen of possible Saxon date has been noted on Overton Down (Fowler 2000: 81–2).

Conclusions

The distinction which has been made here between high-status and peasant settlements is fundamental to our understanding of late Saxon settlement. The difference is not just one of scale or number of buildings, but runs through almost every aspect of the settlements. This surprising conclusion has emerged from the study of the archaeology, although the historical evidence does not suggest that there was such a sharp cleavage in society (Gillingham 1995: 140–1). It will need to be tested against the results from future excavations. There were on the one hand those who could afford a suite of buildings, and, more particularly, took the time and effort to set them within ditched enclosures in a manner calculated to impress visitors. The implication was that the occupants had not only the wealth to build and support such settlements, but also that they were aware of the conventions which governed their organization. On the other hand, there were peasants whose settlements lacked substantial boundaries, were only loosely governed by any conventions of plan, and for whom display was not a significant consideration.

This pattern is most clear in lowland England, where the significant number of excavated sites allows general patterns to be observed. Further work is required to show whether it applies equally in the north and south-west. The relations of lords to their peasants may have been quite different in Cornwall where the communal control of resources seems to have been much stronger. Herring (2006: 74) sees the Cornish hamlets, of which Mawgan Porth is an example, both as the basic unit of settlement and as a manifestation of the cooperative group which managed blocks of land.

Finally, it is useful to glance a little beyond the iconic date of AD 1066 and look briefly at subsequent development at high-status sites. The establishment during the late eleventh or earlier twelfth century of castles on the sites of pre-Conquest settlements at Goltho and Sulgrave has attracted considerable comment, for it suggests that in some places the Norman elite took over the residences of their Saxon predecessors. The persistence of manorial settlements, whether fortified or not, across the divide of the Norman Conquest is now attested on a large number of sites (Gardiner 2007). Viewed from a late Saxon perspective, we can see the establishment of ringworks and mottes as evidence for the continuation of the practice of display at high-status sites. Castles are no longer regarded as purely military structures, and indeed many were patently unsuitable for defence. Instead, they are viewed as symbolic displays of wealth and power. The addition of a motte and a bank to the perimeter of an existing high-status site was therefore only a further stage in a pattern of elite display at such sites which dates from at least the tenth century.

Acknowledgements

Much of the unpublished work cited here was collected by Dr Emily Murray with the support of a grant from the Leverhulme Trust. I am grateful to Joanna Caruth and the Suffolk County Council Archaeological Service, and to Andy Chapman and Northamptonshire Archaeology, and to Albion Archaeology for allowing me to cite their work in advance of publication. Katharina Ulmschneider kindly commented on an earlier draft. The illustrations were prepared by Libby Mulqueeny.

References

Addyman, P. V. (1969). 'Late Saxon settlements in the St Neots area: II, the Little Paxton settlement and enclosures'. *Proceedings of the Cambridge Antiquarian Society* 62: 59–93.

Allen, T. (2004). 'Swine, salt and seafood: a case study of Anglo-Saxon and early medieval settlement in north-east Kent'. *Archaeologia Cantiana* 124: 117–35.

Audouy, M., and Chapman, A. (2009). *Raunds: The Origin and Growth of a Midland Village, AD 450–1500*. Oxford: Oxbow Books.

Austin, D. (1985). 'Dartmoor and the upland village of the south-west of England', in D. Hooke (ed.), *Medieval Villages: A Review of Current Work*. Oxford: Oxford University Committee for Archaeology, 71–9.

Beresford, G. (1971). 'Tresmorn, St Gennys'. *Cornish Archaeology* 10: 55–73.

—— (1979). 'Three deserted medieval settlements on Dartmoor: a report on the late E. Marie Minter's excavations'. *Medieval Archaeology* 23: 98–158.

—— (1987). *Goltho: The Development of an Early Medieval Manor c.850–1150*. London: Historic Buildings & Monuments Commission for England.

Blair, J. (1993). 'Hall and chamber: English domestic planning 1000–1250', in G. Meirion-Jones and M. Jones (eds.), *Manorial Domestic Buildings in England and Northern France*. London: Society of Antiquaries, 1–21.

—— (1996) 'Palaces or minsters? Northampton and Cheddar reconsidered'. *Anglo-Saxon England* 25: 97–121.

Bruce-Mitford, R. (1997). *Mawgan Porth: A Settlement of the Late Saxon Period on the North Cornish Coast; Excavations 1949, 1954, and 1974*. London: English Heritage.

Carnicelli, T. A. (1969). *King Alfred's Version of St. Augustine's 'Soliloquies'*. Cambridge, MA: Harvard University Press.

CHAPMAN, A. (forthcoming). *West Cotton, Raunds: A Study of Medieval Settlement Dynamics, AD 450–1450*. Oxford: Oxbow Books.
COGGINS, D. (2004). 'Simy Folds: twenty years on', in J. Hines, A. Lane, and M. Redknap (eds.), *Land, Sea and Home*. Leeds: Maney, 325–44.
—— FAIRLESS, K. J., and BATEY, C. E. (1983). 'Simy Folds: an early medieval settlement site in Upper Teesdale, Co. Durham'. *Medieval Archaeology* 27: 1–26.
CREIGHTON, O. (2002). *Castles and Landscapes: Power, Community and Fortification in Medieval England*. London: Equinox Publishing.
DALWOOD, H., and EDWARDS, R. (2004). *Excavations at Deansway, Worcester, 1988–89: Romano-British Small Town to Late Medieval City*. York: Council for British Archaeology.
DAVISON, B. K. (1977). 'Excavations at Sulgrave, Northamptonshire 1960–76: an interim report'. *Archaeological Journal* 134: 105–14.
DICKINSON, S. (1985). 'Bryant's Gill, Kentmere: another 'Viking-period' Ribblehead?', in J. R. Baldwin and I. D. White (eds.), *The Scandinavians in Cumbria*. Edinburgh: Scottish Society for Northern Studies, 83–8.
DOWN, A., and WELCH, M. G. (1990). *Chichester Excavations VII: Apple Down and the Mardens*. Chichester: Chichester District Council.
DREWETT, P., HOLGATE, B., FOSTER, S., and ELLERBY, H. (1986). 'The excavation of a Saxon sunken building at North Marden, West Sussex, 1982'. *Sussex Archaeological Collections* 124: 109–18.
DUDLEY, D., and MINTER, E. M. (1966). 'The excavation of a medieval settlement at Treworld, Lesnewth, 1963'. *Cornish Archaeology* 5: 34–58.
DYER, C. C. (1996). 'St Oswald and 10,000 West Midland Peasants', in N. P. Brooks and C. Cubitt (eds.), *St Oswald of Worcester: Life and Influence*. London: Leicester University Press, 174–93.
EDMONDSON, G., and STEADMAN, S. (2001). 'Archaeological investigations at Church End Lower School, Marston Moretaine'. *Bedfordshire Archaeology* 24: 47–56.
FAIRBROTHER, J. R. (1990). *Faccombe Netherton: Excavations of a Saxon and Medieval Manorial Complex*. London: British Museum.
FAITH, R. J. (1997). *The English Peasantry and the Growth of Lordship*. London: Leicester University Press.
FASHAM, P. J., FARWELL, D., and WHINNEY, R. (1989). *The Archaeological Site at Easton Lane, Winchester*. Winchester: Hampshire Field Club and Archaeological Society.
—— KEEVILL, G. and COE, D. (1995). *Brighton Hill South (Hatch Warren): An Iron Age Farmstead and Deserted Medieval Village in Hampshire*. Salisbury: Trust for Wessex Archaeology.
FOWLER, P. J. (2000). *Landscape Plotted and Pieced: Landscape History and Local Archaeology in Fyfield and Overton, Wiltshire*. London: Society of Antiquaries of London.
Fox, A. (1958). 'A monastic homestead on Dean Moor, S. Devon'. *Medieval Archaeology* 2: 141–57.
Fox, H. S. A. (1996). 'Introduction: transhumance and seasonal settlement', in H. S. A. Fox (ed.), *Seasonal Settlement*. Leicester: University of Leicester, 1–23.
—— (2006). 'Fragmented manors and the customs of the Anglo-Saxons', in S. Keynes and A. P. Smyth (eds.), *Anglo-Saxons: Studies Presented to Cyril Roy Hart*. Dublin: Four Courts Press, 78–97.
GARDINER, M. F. (1993). 'The excavation of a Late Anglo-Saxon settlement at Market Field, Steyning, 1988–89'. *Sussex Archaeological Collections* 131: 21–67.

—— (2006). 'Implements and utensils in Gerefa, and the organization of seigneurial farmsteads in the High Middle Ages'. *Medieval Archaeology* 50: 260–7.
—— (2007). 'The origins and persistence of manor houses in England', in M. F. Gardiner and S. Rippon (eds.), *Medieval Landscapes in Britain*. Macclesfield: Windgather Press, 170–82.
—— Cross, R., Macpherson-Grant, N., and Riddler, I. (2001). 'Continental trade and non-urban ports in mid-Anglo-Saxon England: excavations at *Sandtun*, West Hythe, Kent'. *Archaeological Journal* 158: 161–290.
Gillingham, J. (1995). 'Thegns and knights in eleventh-century England: who was then the gentleman?'. *Transactions of the Royal Historical Society*, 6th series, 5: 129–53.
Graham, A. H., and Davies, S. M. (1993). *Excavations in Trowbridge, Wiltshire, 1977 and 1986–1988*. Salisbury: Trust for Wessex Archaeology.
Henderson, C. G., and Weddell, P. J. (1994). 'Medieval settlements on Dartmoor and in West Devon: the evidence from excavations'. *Devon Archaeological Society Proceedings* 52: 119–40.
Herring, P. (2006). 'Cornish strip fields', in S. Turner (ed.), *Medieval Devon and Cornwall: Shaping an Ancient Countryside*. Macclesfield: Windgather, 44–77.
Hooke, D. (1989). 'Pre-Conquest woodland: its distribution and usage'. *Agricultural History Review* 37: 113–29.
—— (1998). *The Landscape of Anglo-Saxon England*. London: Leicester University Press.
Ivens, R., Busby, P., and Shepherd, N. (1995). *Tattenhoe and Westbury: Two Deserted Medieval Settlements in Milton Keynes*. Aylesbury: Buckinghamshire Archaeological Society.
King, A. (1978). 'Gauber High Pasture, Ribblehead—an interim report', in R. A. Hall (ed.), *Viking Age York and the North*. London: Council for British Archaeology, 21–5.
—— (2004). 'Post-Roman upland architecture in the Craven Dales and the dating evidence', in J. Hines, A. Lane, and M. Redknap (eds.), *Land, Sea and Home*. Leeds: Maney, 335–44.
King, V. (1996). 'St Oswald's Tenants', in N. P. Brooks and C. Cubitt (eds.), *St Oswald of Worcester: Life and Influence*. London: Leicester University Press, 100–16.
Lewis, C., Mitchell-Fox, P., and Dyer, C. C. (1997). *Village, Hamlet and Field: Changing Medieval Settlements in Central England*. Manchester: Manchester University Press.
Liddiard, R. (2000). 'Castle Rising, Norfolk: A Landscape of Lordship?'. *Anglo-Norman Studies* 22: 169–86.
Liebermann, F. (1903). *Die Gesetze der Angelsachsen*, Volume 1. Halle an der Saale: Max Niemeyer.
Maull, A. (2001). 'Excavations of the deserted medieval village of Coton at Coton Park, Rugby, Warwickshire, 1998'. Unpublished report by Northamptonshire Archaeology.
Morris, C. D. (1981). 'Viking and native in northern England: a case study', in H. Bekker-Nielsen, P. Foote, and O. Olsen (eds.), *Proceedings of the Eighth Viking Congress*. Odense: Odense University Press, 223–44.
Parry, S. (2006). *Raunds Area Survey: An Archaeological Study of the Landscape of Raunds, Northamptonshire 1985–94*. Oxford: Oxbow Books.
Rahtz, P. A. (1976). 'Buildings and rural settlement', in D. M. Wilson (ed.), *The Archaeology of Anglo-Saxon England*. Cambridge: Cambridge University Press, 49–98.
—— (1979). *The Saxon and Medieval Palaces at Cheddar*. Oxford: British Archaeological Reports.

RAISTRICK, A. (1962). 'The archaeology of Malham Moor'. *Field Studies* 1: 72–100.
RENN, D. (1994). 'Burhgeat and Gonfanon: two sidelights from the Bayeux Tapestry'. *Anglo-Norman Studies* 16: 177–98.
REYNOLDS, A. J. (2003). 'Boundaries and settlement in later six to eleventh-century England'. *Anglo-Saxon Studies in Archaeology and History* 12: 98–136.
ROBERTS, B. K., and WRATHMELL, S. (2002). *Region and Place: A Study of English Rural Settlement*. London: English Heritage.
ROYAL COMMISSION ON HISTORICAL MONUMENTS (1959). 'Wareham West Walls'. *Medieval Archaeology* 3: 120–38.
SAUNDERS, A. D. (2006). *Excavations at Launceston Castle, Cornwall*. Leeds: Society for Medieval Archaeology.
SMITH, N. (2005). 'Medieval and later sheep farming on the Marlborough Downs', in G. Brown, D. Field, and D. McOmish (eds.), *The Avebury Landscape: Aspects of the Field Archaeology of the Marlborough Downs*. Oxford: Oxbow Books, 191–201.
STAMPER, P. A., and CROFT, R. A. (2000). *Wharram: A Study of Settlement on the Yorkshire Wolds*, Volume 8: *The South Manor Area*. York: University of York.
SWANTON, M. (1975). *Anglo-Saxon Prose*. London: Dent.
WADE-MARTINS, P. (1980). *Excavations in North Elmham Park 1967–1972*. Gressenhall: Norfolk Museums Service.
WILLIAMS, A. (1992). 'A bell-house and a burh-geat: lordly residences in England before the Norman Conquest'. *Medieval Knighthood* 4: 221–40.
WYMER, J. J., and BROWN, N. R. (1995). *Excavations at North Shoebury: Settlement and Economy in South-East Essex 1500BC–AD1500*. Colchester: Essex County Council.

PART III
MORTUARY RITUAL

CHAPTER 13

OVERVIEW: MORTUARY RITUAL

TANIA M. DICKINSON

Introduction

The mortuary rituals practised in Anglo-Saxon England have bequeathed a source of information that permeates almost every part of our understanding of the period. Self-evidently, burials supply the raw data for biologically-based analyses of the human population (see Parts I and VII), and burial sites are an integral component of the settled landscape (see Part II). In particular, because the inclusion of durable objects makes burials highly visible, they dominate the archaeological record of the fifth to seventh centuries: for this phase they provide the bulk of the artefacts which sustain studies of craft production and art styles (see Part V), and the construction of an archaeological chronology. Above all, however, presumptions and interpretations made about mortuary practice are intimately intertwined with those which lie at the heart of Anglo-Saxon archaeology as a whole (see Part X): that is, about the nature of social, economic, and political structures (see Parts VI and IX), religious beliefs and practices (Part VIII), and, most contentiously but also fundamentally, Anglo-Saxon cultural identity and migration (Part I). But because of this wide relevance, and in response to developments over the last forty years in archaeological mortuary theory, research has increasingly turned back on itself to ask what sort of source are Anglo-Saxon burials, and how can, or should, they be examined and explained?

The developing study of Anglo-Saxon burials

Anglo-Saxon burials have been studied for over three centuries, but only fairly recently has their historiography become of critical interest, as part of the self-conscious development of theory and method within an explicit archaeology of early medieval burial (best followed through the proceedings of three landmark conferences: Rahtz et al. 1980; Lucy and Reynolds 2002; Semple and Williams 2007; see also Lucy 1998: 5–21; Dickinson 2002; for recent book-length syntheses: Lucy 2000; Williams 2006c; and for a wider north European context: Kjeld Jensen and Høilund Nielsen 1997; Effros 2003).

Although the first documented record of Anglo-Saxon burials dates from the seventeenth century (Browne 1658), antiquarian interest really began in the eighteenth century, as finds from chance discoveries and, increasingly, deliberate investigation, came to be valued not just as treasure or art, but as material witnesses to England's perceived ancestral inhabitants. The Reverend Bryan Faussett's excavations of Kentish barrow cemeteries have always stood out for their careful recording and curation of finds, and are still of value today (Faussett 1856; Rhodes 1989; Novum Inventorium Sepulchrale 2007). Like other antiquarians, Faussett equated his finds with Britons or Romans, but his younger contemporary, James Douglas (1793), recognizing the presence of associated post-Roman coins, argued that the burials dated from the Anglo-Saxon period. The implications of this were not realized, however, until the middle decades of the nineteenth century, when a surge in field activity, generating a mass of reports to journals and material for museums, went hand-in-hand with a drive to explain the finds through knowledge derived from historical and literary sources, such as Bede, the *Anglo-Saxon Chronicle*, and *Beowulf*. John Kemble saw the parallels between English and continental cremation cemeteries as evidence of the migration of pagan Germanic peoples, whilst Thomas Wright and Charles Roach Smith identified the individual tribes of Angles, Saxons, and Jutes from basic, regional differences in grave-goods. As recent critical historiographies have emphasized, however, these readings had been construed in the light of contemporary industrial, national, and imperial experience, and of prevailing racial and evolutionary theories (including their inherently moral and qualitative judgements). In turn, they played a significant role in constructing Victorian mentalities, national and class identity, and particularly the overall notion of an *Anglo-Saxon* past, which was to endure (e.g. Lucy 1998: 9–12; Williams 2006a; 2006b; 2007; 2008; see Part I).

Whilst the mid Victorian period was formative in establishing a concentration on early Anglo-Saxon grave-goods and an interpretative framework in terms of ethnicity and religion, these were mostly prosecuted in a sketchy manner.

More systematic codification and synthesis of data that could generate historical reconstructions—artefact classification, the drawing of parallels, especially with continental and Scandinavian material, dating, and mapping—began only in the early twentieth century. E. T. Leeds, whose chronological-spatial surveys were built round Bede's tribal trilogy, and initially entirely on burial data, might be called the father of Anglo-Saxon archaeology (e.g. Leeds 1912; 1913; 1936; cf. Dickinson 1980: 11–12; and especially now MacGregor 2007), but two of his seniors were equally important: Reginald Smith for his surveys of Anglo-Saxon antiquities (viz. burials) in early volumes of the *Victoria History of the Counties of England* and in the guide to the British Museum's collection (Smith 1923); and George Baldwin Brown for the two volumes in his *The Arts in Early England* which provided comprehensive coverage of Anglo-Saxon cemeteries and grave-goods (Baldwin Brown 1915)—a feat never emulated! And it was the Swede, Nils Åberg (1926), who first and systematically presented evolutionary typologies according to the methods developed by Scandinavian and German prehistorians in order to chart the chronological development of Anglo-Saxon grave-goods.

This cultural-historical and empiricist tradition, with its ultimate goal of making burials contribute to the (re-)writing of Anglo-Saxon history, continued to develop through the middle decades of the twentieth century, and beyond, exemplified by the work of J. N. L. Myres (1969; 1977), Vera Evison (e.g. Evison 1965), and Sonia Chadwick Hawkes (e.g. Chadwick 1958; Hawkes and Pollard 1981), among many others. Audrey Meaney (1964) brought order to the mass of sites known up to 1960 in a still invaluable gazetteer and bibliography: her brief introduction considered burial practices in terms of ethnic, heathen, and social custom, but gave no tally of the number of sites included. Grave-goods were studied more comprehensively and in ever more detail for their bearing on chronology and cultural connexions. A particularly influential hypothesis, developed from continental research, was that the first Anglo-Saxon burials represented late Roman or sub-Roman employment of Germanic troops as federate war-bands prior to a mass migration, which allowed for a degree of continuity with Roman Britain (Hawkes and Dunning 1961; Myres 1969; further developed and modified by Böhme 1986; Welch 1993). Another was modelling a 'Final Phase' of burial with grave-goods in the seventh century in terms of a staged transition to a Christian mode of burial (Meaney and Hawkes 1970: 45–58; cf. Welch, this volume). Grave-goods were also being considered technologically and, in an intuitive way, as a key to social rank, especially after the spectacular discoveries of arguably royal burials at Sutton Hoo in 1938 and 1939 (Bruce-Mitford 1975). To make detailed, primary classificatory work and synthesis manageable, regional studies of burials became popular (e.g. Eagles 1979; Welch 1983; Hines 1984). Excavation standards had also improved significantly, especially since the 1950s: the recording, and retention, of finds by individual grave, and the planning of graves and their layout within cemeteries became the norm, though prompt publication often remained difficult (cf. Meaney and Hawkes 1970; Evison 1987; Hawkes and Grainger 2006).

In the mid 1970s doubts began to be expressed about existing methodologies, and some advocated instead the use of radically different paradigms derived from prehistoric theoretical archaeology. The competing discourses were consciously captured in *Anglo-Saxon Cemeteries 1979* (Rahtz et al. 1980). Chris Arnold's contribution (Arnold 1980) and John Shephard's elsewhere (Shephard 1979a; 1979b) invoked processualist arguments that burial practices were not static or innate cultural traits, but the outcomes of economic and social adaptations, from which differing systems of social organization, and their evolution, could be detected. Both authors exploited the newly introduced possibilities of computerized analysis to quantify the status or rank of Anglo-Saxon burials from the cost (or effort) invested in their grave-goods and grave structures, assuming, like the cultural historians, that there was a direct and functional equivalence between burials and a living society. Post-processualist theoreticians were already arguing, however, that burial was a matter of symbolic and ritual action which expressed ideals that might mask or subvert, as much as reflect, reality. Meaning could be read only through context and multi-dimensionally, as exemplified by Ellen-Jane Pader's paper for *Anglo-Saxon Cemeteries 1979* on the variability in both the constituents and placing of grave-goods according to the age and gender of the deceased, and their location within a cemetery (Pader 1980; see also Pader 1982).

In the last twenty years symbolic and contextual approaches have developed and diversified. Julian Richards (1987) explored how the designs of cremation urns and their associated grave-goods expressed individual (age and gender) and group (regional and national) identities—a radical departure from Myres' use of comparable diagnostics to indicate chronology—although the bewildering array of correlations left much unexplained, and in Mats Ravn's (2003) re-working of the cremations from the cemetery at Spong Hill, Norfolk, using improved data and different computer techniques, just four main groupings were recognized. Using a national sample of inhumation cemeteries, Heinrich Härke (1992) conclusively demonstrated that weapon-burial was not necessarily a sign of a warrior, but a symbolic act, even a mythic evocation of a masculine, martial ethnicity (cf. Härke 1997). Using an almost identical sample, Nicholas Stoodley (1999a) went on to show how the form and contents of graves were structured by gender and age as a strategy for negotiating status and identity within and between families, households, and communities; variation in the patterns between regions and over time gave the possibility of relating these to wider historical developments.

Nonetheless, the perception of high variability in the data, which such analyses throw up, combined with the idea that mortuary rituals and artefacts were immanent agents of social structure, effective and knowable only in the instance of their implementation, led Sam Lucy (1998), with reference to east Yorkshire, to argue that statistically valid study of burial contexts was possible only at a local level, starting with individual grave-assemblages, building up to their context within burial grounds, and thence within the landscape. The symbolic and ideological significance of a burial's place in the landscape, in relation to topography, route-ways, or pre-existing monuments, was also explored at this time by Howard Williams (summarized in Williams 2006c: 179–214). Williams (2006c; this volume) has further developed debate by highlighting how the archaeological perception of graves and cemeteries as fixed tableaux obscures their testimony to extended sequences of behaviour. Mortuary rituals, he proposes, should be understood as technologies of remembrance, which transformed the deceased bodily and meta-physically, drawing symbolically on their identity in life and at death, and thereby constituted a new identity (memory) in the minds of witnesses and potentially (e.g. through acts of commemoration) of those who come after. In some ways analogous to this model is Martin Carver's conception of grand barrow burial, as at Sutton Hoo, as a work of poetry or performative art (Carver 2005: 312).

Although most of the new theoretical approaches have focused on burials with grave-goods, their message is equally relevant to those without, which has had a liberating effect on understanding middle and late Anglo-Saxon mortuary ritual, opening it up for the first time to serious analysis (see Hadley, this volume). There has also been an impact on the format of excavation reports, which now cover far more systematically skeletal biology and cemetery organization; many now also include a social analysis, although from a variety of theoretical positions (e.g. Evison 1987; Sherlock and Welch 1992; Boyle *et al.* 1995; Malim and Hines 1998).

CURRENT RESEARCH ISSUES

Anglo-Saxon burial studies thus have at their disposal increasingly sophisticated means of interpretation and a body of data which has grown progressively in quantity and quality, but problems remain. Perhaps most fundamental is whether Anglo-Saxon burials can be studied historically or must be consigned to their own realm of discourse (cf. Dickinson 2002; Hines 2007). If burial practices are histori-cally contingent and multi-dimensional, then consideration of variation over time seems integral to assessing their context, and categorically to ignore information provided by written sources seems perverse, notwithstanding the critique of early culture-history. Equally, while the singularity of a burial, representing a specific past individual and moment in time, makes it powerfully attractive and the first unit of analysis, with the cemetery the second, study cannot remain at a local level only. The contexts of burial extend to the regional, national, and beyond, offering means to explore and test hypotheses. Otherwise there is the danger that discussion becomes an endless parade of data or play upon difference: it might appeal to modern Western relativism and prioritization of individual choice and identity, but goes against the grain of explanatory archaeology, which must find meaning through patterning in data. Of course, there is always a methodological trade-off between reducing a multiplicity of data to some meaningful pattern, on the one hand, and not suppressing or overlooking divergent data, on the other hand, and the wider the area from which samples are taken the more extreme this will become (cf. Penn and Brugmann 2007: esp. 12–16).

More to the point, but actually more intractable, is why Anglo-Saxon mortuary rituals show the patterning that they do, and why they varied and changed, questions intimately linked to why a distinctive style of burial with grave-goods appeared in the fifth century and more or less went out of use in the course of the seventh century. The understanding that social factors—gender and age especially, wealth or status, and circumstances of and at death, more variably—played a major role in structuring mortuary ritual has certainly dispelled simplistic notions that change is the consequence of new people (Anglo-Saxons) or new beliefs (Christianity), but need not rule out these factors altogether. If mortuary rituals are understood as performances or displays, then they become potent arenas for expressions of social competition and social cohesiveness, which might be expected to be more overt when circumstances were actually more fluid or uncertain (Halsall 1998). Thus the dynamics of the gendered early Anglo-Saxon ritual of inhumation with grave-goods could be symptomatic of changes in household and community statuses consequent upon the ending of Roman Britain, the immigration of some new populations, and subsequently in the late sixth and seventh centuries of the emergence of a new, premier social elite (Stoodley 1999a: 136–42). The last has long seemed evident in the appearance of lavish barrow burials.

Quite how these dynamics were given form might be further illuminated by Williams' ideas about memory, in that in principle they allow the dissection of specific instances in relation to pre-existing and expected custom (social and religious) and its subsequent transformation through practice. Whether and how personal memory can be discriminated from group memory archaeologically, however, and each from acts of commemoration and the creation of a social tradition, is problematic (Devlin 2007a; 2007b; Hines 2007). Moreover, if the focus is on individual actions, and written testimony is lacking, explanations become unverifiable speculation. And while the presence of durable grave-goods makes such behaviours more apparent, an absence of the former does not necessarily indicate an absence of the latter: gender, for example, would have been clear from clothing, with or without any accoutrements (Walton Rogers 2007: 249).

Social analyses have also been compromised by problems of methodology. Most significant is chronology, which ought to be an essential first step, but the long and complicated record within culture-history of dating grave-goods, though without assured results, has led to it either being ignored (e.g. Pader 1982; Richards 1987) or applied in a second-hand and generalized manner (e.g. Lucy 1998; Stoodley 1999a). Further, study of unaccompanied burials, notably in the middle and late Anglo-Saxon period, is necessarily dependent on carbon-14 dating, but this has been all too rare. Stratigraphic relationships are also uncommon, especially in early Anglo-Saxon cemeteries, though recently Kevin Leahy (2007) has exploited apparent superimpositions of cremation urns in correlation with their decorative designs as a basis for a site chronology, and Carver has used grave-relationships (vertical and horizontal) with carbon-14 dating to phase the late Roman and Anglo-Saxon cemetery at Wasperton, Warks. (Carver *et al.* 2009). The horizontal development through time of cemeteries has also had some specific utility, as at Spong Hill (Hills 1994: 42) or Dover Buckland (Evison 1987), but most cemeteries seem to develop polyfocally, making this technique more difficult to apply (Sayer 2007).

Recent initiatives to establish the dating of Anglo-Saxon burials systematically, and as a basis for social explanation, are therefore long overdue and very welcome (Hines *et al.* 1999; Penn and Brugman 2007; Brugmann in Parfitt and Anderson forthcoming; Hines forthcoming). These involve the use of Correspondence Analysis to seriate grave-assemblages into relative phases, and their dating in absolute terms through correlation with material on the Continent, where this methodology has been much better established and benefits from more extensive coin-associated dating and from some dendrochronological dates. In the English Heritage project (Hines, forthcoming), the chronology of the late sixth to early eighth centuries will be further refined by using Bayesian modelling to integrate seriations of assemblages with a suite of high-precision carbon-14 dates (cf. Scull and Bayliss 1999; Welch, this volume). Published results to date allow the detection of at least four phases spanning the late fifth to early seventh centuries in Kent (Brugmann 1999) and in East Anglia (Penn and Brugmann 2007), the latter enabling changes in the social manifestations of burial to be charted through time. These methods are not without difficulties, however: the possibilities for phasing male assemblages are not precisely in line with those for female assemblages, the fifth century remains problematic (cf. Brugmann, this volume), and equivalence between regional chronologies, and with it fixed absolute dates, is open to debate: the carbon-14 dating programme should be crucial here. Also, it must be accepted that these computerized methods are producing a smoothed and abstract model of variation within given samples of grave-assemblages that cannot be simply applied to date specific graves outside the sample, and even within it (the dating of the Spong Hill inhumations being a case in point: Penn and Brugmann 2007: 45–7 and 59).

Effective social analysis also needs to have available consistent and reliable skeletal data. There is a growing recognition that criteria for identifying essential biological attributes, such as sex and age, themselves need to be reviewed, and controls developed for practitioner bias, especially if debates about, for example, blurred or non-normative gendering are to be resolved (Gowland and Knüsel 2006).

Finally, the growing sophistication of theory poses questions about appropriate field techniques (cf. Rahtz *et al.* 1980). Most burial grounds are discovered by accident, which more recently includes through metal-detecting activity, and are therefore already in some way damaged or incomplete. At a broad scale this need not matter; although the density of cemeteries may be much greater than had been envisaged previously, the overall distribution has not changed significantly (Ravn 2003: 93–4). But analysis of mortuary ritual and social organization, at an intra- and inter-site level, really requires complete burial grounds, and therefore strategies to detect them and to maximize data recovery. This would also need to include methods for protecting and finely dissecting stratigraphy (cf. Carver 2005: 13–57; Martin Carver, pers. comm.) and for the preservation, retrieval, and analysis of organic materials, such as textiles (Walton Rogers 2007: 248) and especially human skeletal material, which ironically has been missing or impaired in so many recent, otherwise high-quality site investigations (e.g. Leahy 2007; Penn and Brugmann 2007; Carver *et al.* 2009).

Anglo-Saxon mortuary rituals—a brief outline

The variability and complexity of the evidence and the range of competing interpretative approaches thus make Anglo-Saxon mortuary rituals a rich field for research, but a challenge to summarize. In the three chapters which follow, their nature and significance is detailed from the authors' differing personal perspectives, and the same is true of the outline provided here.

The three chapters divide the mortuary rituals chronologically: into those of the fifth and sixth centuries, sometimes called the pagan, the Migration, or the early Anglo-Saxon period; a 'long seventh century', often called the Final Phase (that is, of early Anglo-Saxon burial), but sometimes the Conversion period (and recently just the late Phase: Walton Rogers 2007); and the eighth to eleventh centuries, generally referred to as late, later, or middle and late Anglo-Saxon, but sometimes as Christian. Although the dominant mortuary characteristics of each phase are not in doubt, they are not rigidly self-contained, and there is a degree of overlap and continuity between them; nor do they correlate neatly with the early, middle, and late Anglo-Saxon periods used elsewhere in the discipline. Further, the absolute dates at which various transitions in mortuary practice should be placed are still open to analysis, especially those encompassed by the term 'Final Phase', whilst the lack of agreement on phase names exemplifies the continuing debate about why the mortuary rituals changed, and in particular the roles of Germanic migration and Christianity.

The archetypal burial rites of the fifth and sixth centuries (Williams, this volume), which effectively define the beginning of the Anglo-Saxon period in material culture terms, are often telegraphed as 'burial with grave-goods' or 'accompanied burial'. They involved a dressed corpse, the clothing evidenced where fittings or accoutrements survive, which was either cremated or inhumed. In the former case, pyre-remains and sometimes additional small artefacts were usually placed in a receptacle, most commonly a pottery urn, and deposited in a pit; in the latter case, additional objects, such as furnishings, vessels, or weaponry, were also sometimes placed in the grave. Burials could occur in isolation, but normally belonged to cemeteries, either of one rite alone or both together, though in variable proportions: those consisting mainly or exclusively of cremations, and especially those with large numbers of cremations (up to more than 2,000), were concentrated in eastern England from Yorkshire to Essex, whereas accompanied inhumation spread, eventually, throughout England from Northumberland to Dorset. Burial grounds are generally discrete, but the dispersal of clusters of burials in or along a wider 'mortuary' zone are increasingly being recognized (e.g. Saltwood, Kent: Richardson 2005: 69–70; cf. Dickinson 2004: 42).

As indicated above, enormous energies have been expended on explaining when and why these burial rituals began, but without a sure consensus emerging. Arguments have depended on drawing typological analogies with finds from continental cemeteries, north and south of the Roman imperial frontier, which are ultimately anchored in absolute time by associations with late Roman coinage. However, the difficulties of finely dating handmade pottery and dress accoutrements like brooches, buckles, and beads (especially when burnt), and the rarity of such early material in England anyway, especially from undisturbed contexts, means that chronology is inexact: broadly speaking, the first such burials in England might date from the first half or perhaps rather the middle third of the fifth century, or even more narrowly from the second quarter of the century (Hines 1990, esp. 21–8; Welch 1999). Nonetheless, the similarities which cremation cemeteries in eastern England share with those in northern Germany and adjacent districts, not just in the material culture of their pottery and grave-goods, but in their entire mortuary process (which, correspondingly, differs from the cremating practices occasionally still observed in late Roman Britain; Philpott 1991: 50–2), strongly suggest that they were first created by migrant Germanic communities.

The contexts of the earliest accompanied inhumations in England are more complicated. Their style of dressed and weapon-accompanied burial made its first appearance in the late fourth century in northern Gaul, as a modification of established late Roman inhumation rituals, but was soon emulated in the lower Rhineland, the Netherlands, and Lower Saxony. It is hotly debated whether this militarized and gendered symbolism and display was initiated specifically by

Germanic troops serving with the late Roman army as regular soldiers or federated war-bands, in some cases accompanied by their womenfolk (Böhme 1986; 1989; Welch 1993), or merely by prominent local families, who were jostling for status and power in the break-up of the Empire (Halsall 2000). Given the uncertain dating, the relatively few English examples could encompass federates from north or south of the Roman *limes*, particular local (sub-)Romano-British families, and free Germanic settlers.

In characterizing the earliest Anglo-Saxon mortuary rituals two further factors should be borne in mind, however. First is the almost complete lack of evidence for continuity between burial grounds exhibiting archetypal late Roman and Anglo-Saxon mortuary rituals, which implies, at least among some communities, a change in ideas not only about how, but also where the dead should be interred. Where both Anglo-Saxon cremations and accompanied inhumations inaugurate a new site in the early or mid fifth century, as at Mucking II, Essex (Evison 1979: 138–41) or Abingdon, Oxon (Leeds and Harden 1936), then perhaps a common—immigrant—explanation remains the most plausible. Second, however, is the likelihood that for much of the fifth century *unaccompanied* inhumation was actually the most common burial ritual. By the fifth century this had become the normal mode of disposal within the western Roman provinces (often with west-east alignment), but it was also a pervasive minority practice within early Anglo-Saxon cemeteries in general (about 17 per cent of adult graves in a national sample: Stoodley 1999a: 24, 76, and 91). Only carbon-14 dating can define its true contexts. Pertinently, this has shown that a late Roman cemetery at Queenford Mill, Dorchester-on-Thames, Oxon, was being used from the fourth to the early sixth century, that is concurrently with cemeteries in the locality where archetypal Anglo-Saxon mortuary rituals were practised (Chambers 1987; but against this see now Hills and O'Connell 2009). Unaccompanied inhumation also seems to characterize the earlier fifth-century phase especially of the cemetery at Wasperton, Warks., which most unusually was used continuously by people practising first late Roman and, later, Anglo-Saxon styles of mortuary ritual (Carver et al. 2009; cf. Scheschkewitz 2006).

It is not until *c*. AD 470/80 that archetypal early Anglo-Saxon mortuary rituals, and especially inhumation with grave-goods, can be shown to occur on a wide scale, numerically and geographically. By this date, grave-assemblages consisted mostly of insular products, which exhibit distinctive and developing regional complexions, especially the items associated with dress (cf. Owen-Crocker, this volume; Walton Rogers 2007: 107 ff.). Regionalism is also evident in burial practices themselves, most obviously in the degree to which cremation continued to be popular, but also in a range of inhumation practices (e.g. see various analyses in Stoodley 1999a). Although the terms Anglian, Saxon, and Kentish (or Jutish) are still commonly used to describe these regional zones (with an overlapping Anglian/Saxon zone: Walton Rogers 2007: 107–8), these are convenient, short-hand labels rather than adequate descriptions or explanations of an underlying social reality. To what extent and in what ways the cemeteries reflect exclusive communities or more fluid emulation and integration is still open to debate. Certainly, the chronology of the changing composition of inhumation assemblages now suggests that the high period of early Anglo-Saxon mortuary ritual lasted for not much more than a century, during which time there were changes in the quantity, quality, and also partly in the kind of durable artefacts committed to graves (Hines *et al.* 1999; Penn and Brugmann 2007). These insights have yet to be fully integrated with those gained from analysing assemblages from the points of view of social status and identity or the deployment of technologies of remembrance, or alongside a chronology for cremation practice. By the later sixth century a polarization in the level of commitment to inhumation with grave-goods becomes detectable. At this stage, accompanied burial can be said to enter its 'Final Phase', just as Merovingian burial practice on the Continent, albeit in diverse ways, entered its later phases.

Between the late sixth and early eighth centuries the use of grave-goods remained widespread, but uneven: an overall decline in usage stands in contrast to the occurrence of the most lavish assemblages of all in the Anglo-Saxon mortuary corpus (Welch, this volume). The regionalized female burial costumes of the fifth and sixth centuries, with their strongly north European affinities, seem to have been rapidly abandoned in favour of a more universal style influenced by late Merovingian and Byzantine fashions (Geake 1997; Walton Rogers 2007). These changes were associated, on the one hand, with a general decline in the use of grave-goods to signal gender and age and, on the other hand, with a shift in the way such symbolism was deployed: symbols of masculinity became confined to adults and exclusive, whereas symbols of femininity were given to adults and children alike (Stoodley 1999b). Publication of the English Heritage chronology project (Hines, forthcoming) should make it easier to chart the relationship of changes in the types and occurrences of grave-goods with the other marked feature of this period—increasingly diverse types of mortuary practice.

Whilst some of the large communal cemeteries in use during the fifth and sixth centuries continued into the seventh century, many were abandoned; in particular, few cremation cemeteries can be positively demonstrated to date far into the seventh century. Instead, a range of new burial places came into existence. Barrow burials, found both in isolation and in clusters, are a hallmark of this phase, sometimes, but not always, accompanied by spectacularly rich assemblages (Shephard 1979a; Webster 1992). Another classic feature is the foundation of inhumation cemeteries marked by more regularly west-east oriented graves, a reduced level of depositing grave-goods, and sometimes close proximity to an abandoned Migration-period cemetery—the archetypal cemeteries of the 'Final Phase', as originally conceived (Leeds 1936: 96–114; Boddington 1989). Some new foundations entirely or almost entirely lack grave-goods; some of these are specifically associated with early ecclesiastical (minster or monastic) foundations or churches, and others represent the sites of judicial execution.

Diversification remains a significant aspect of mortuary ritual from the eighth to the eleventh centuries, so that distinctions between burials of this period and the preceding one are not as clear-cut as used to be supposed (Hadley, this volume). On the one hand, burials are much more likely to be rigorously oriented, and on occasion densely packed and inter-cut. More of them can be associated with places of Christian practice and, thanks to a greater availability of written information, some burial rituals can be interpreted in terms of theological or popular beliefs about the fate of the body and soul after death. On the other hand, although artefacts in graves had indeed become rare, they, and clothed burial, were by no means obsolete. Moreover, burial places not associated with any religious site, but generally in or adjacent to a settlement, are increasingly recognizable, and many mortuary practices (e.g. internal grave structures or furniture, stone monuments, and the location of graves within a cemetery) correlate with aspects of social identity, such as rank, gender, age, and physical appearance or health, rather than being specifically or solely expressions of religious ideology. Indeed, burial within a bounded churchyard seems to have arrived as the norm quite late in Anglo-Saxon England, resulting as much from economic and social developments in lordship as from clerical prescription.

Conclusion

Just as the communal (or ethnic) identity of the deceased cannot alone satisfactorily explain the introduction and continued practice of the archetypal early Anglo-Saxon mortuary rituals, so too the advent of Christian theological beliefs and institutions cannot alone explain their demise and the evolution of alternative burial practices. The chronological and contextual complexities of all these developments, as well as primary theoretical considerations, mean that a web of economic, social, and ideological factors must be taken into account.

Disentangling this web in the future will involve integration of theorized interpretations with a good chronology. For the period c. AD 400–725, there is now the prospect that a multiple-phase chronology can be devised from grave-assemblages, comparable in kind if not degree to those available for continental row-grave cemeteries; but if analyses of burials without grave-goods are to be in any way comparable, then a strategy for wider-scale scientific dating will have to be devised. Also, whilst the critical historiography of earlier burial studies has brought an acute awareness of our predecessors' biases and predilections, there is scope in future to research the social and political factors driving current research directions; both may be blinkered and misled in their readings of Anglo-Saxon mortuary ritual.

REFERENCES

ÅBERG, N. (1926). *The Anglo-Saxons in England during the Early Centuries after the Invasion.* Uppsala: Almqvist & Wiksells.

ARNOLD, C. J. (1980). 'Wealth and social structure: a matter of life and death', in Rahtz *et al.* (eds.), *Anglo-Saxon Cemeteries 1979*, 81–142.

BALDWIN BROWN, G. (1915). *The Arts in Early England*, Volumes 3–4: *Saxon Art and Industry in the Pagan Period*. London: John Murray.

BODDINGTON, A. (1989). 'Models of burial, settlement and worship: the Final Phase reviewed', in E. Southworth (ed.), *Anglo-Saxon Cemeteries: a Reappraisal*. Stroud: Alan Sutton Publishing, 177–99.

BÖHME, H. W. (1986). 'Das Ende der Römerherrschaft in Britannien und die angelsächsische Besiedlung Englands im 5. Jahrhundert'. *Jahrbuch d. Römisch-Germanischen Zentralmuseums Mainz* 33: 469–574.

——(1989). 'Gallien in der Spätantike: Forschungen zum Ende der Römerherrschaft in den westlichen Provinzen'. *Jahrbuch d. Römisch-Germanischen Zentralmuseums Mainz* 34: 770–3.

BOYLE, A., DODD, A., MILES, D., and MUDD, A. (1995). *Two Oxfordshire Anglo-Saxon Cemeteries: Berinsfield and Didcot*. Oxford: Oxford Archaeological Unit.

BROWNE, T. (1658). *Hydriotaphia, Urne-Buriall, or, a Discourse of the Sepulchrall Urnes lately found in Norfolk*. London: Henry Brome.

BRUCE-MITFORD, R. L. S. (1975). *The Sutton Hoo Ship-burial*, Volume 1. London: British Museum Publications Ltd.

BRUGMANN, B. (1999). 'The role of continental artefact-types in sixth-century Kentish chronology', in Hines *et al.* (eds.), *The Pace of Change*, 37–64.

CARVER, M. O. H. (2005). *A Seventh-century Princely Burial Ground and its Context*. London: The British Museum Press.

——HILLS, C. M., and SCHESCHKEWITZ, J. (2009). *A Frontier Cemetery in Early Medieval Britain: Wasperton on the Warwickshire Avon*. Woodbridge: Boydell.

CHADWICK, S. E. (1958). 'The Anglo-Saxon cemetery at Finglesham, Kent: a reconsideration'. *Medieval Archaeology* 2: 1–71.

CHAMBERS, R. A. (1987). 'The late and sub-Roman cemetery at Queenford Farm, Dorchester-on-Thames, Oxon'. *Oxoniensia* 52: 35–69.

DEVLIN, Z. L. (2007a). 'Social memory, material culture and community identity in early medieval mortuary practices', in Semple and Williams (eds.), *Early Medieval Mortuary Practices*, 38–46.

——(2007b). *Remembering the Dead in Anglo-Saxon England: Memory Theory in Archaeology and History*. British Archaeological Reports British Series 446. Oxford: Archaeopress.

DICKINSON, T. M. (1980). 'The present state of Anglo-Saxon cemetery studies', in Rahtz *et al.* (eds.), *Anglo-Saxon Cemeteries 1979*, 11–23.

——(2002). 'Review article: What's new in early medieval burial archaeology?'. *Early Medieval Europe* 11: 71–87.

——(2004). 'An Early Anglo-Saxon cemetery at Quarrington, near Sleaford, Lincolnshire: report on excavations, 2000–2001'. *Lincolnshire History and Archaeology* 39: 24–45.

DOUGLAS, J. (1793). *Nenia Britannica: or, a Sepulchral History of Great Britain*. London: John Nichols.

EAGLES, B. (1979). *The Anglo-Saxon Settlement of Humberside*. BAR British Series 68 (1–2). Oxford: British Archaeological Reports.

EFFROS, B. (2003). *Merovingian Mortuary Archaeology and the Making of the Early Middle Ages*. Berkeley/Los Angeles: University of California Press.

EVISON, V. I. (1965). *The Fifth-century Invasions South of the Thames*. London: The Athlone Press.

——(1979). 'Distribution maps and the first two phases', in V. I. Evison (ed.), *Angles, Saxons, and Jutes: Essays Presented to J. N. L. Myres*. Oxford: Clarendon Press, 126–67.

——(1987). *Dover: The Buckland Anglo-Saxon Cemetery*. London: Historic Buildings and Monuments Commission England.

FAUSSETT, B. (1856). *Inventorium Sepulchrale: An Account of Some Antiquities at Gilton, Kingston, Sibertswold, Barfriston, Beakesbourne, Chartham, and Crundale, in the County of Kent, from A.D. 1757 to A.D. 1773*. Ed. C. Roach Smith. London: printed for subscribers only.

GEAKE, H. (1997). *The Use of Grave-goods in Conversion-period England, c.600–c.850*. British Archaeological Reports British Series 261. Oxford: Hedges.

GOWLAND, R., and KNÜSEL, C. J. (2006). 'Introduction', in R. Gowland and C. J. Knüsel (eds.), *Social Archaeology of Funerary Remains*. Oxford: Oxbow Books, ix–xiv.

HALSALL, G. (1998). 'Burial, ritual and Merovingian society', in J. Hill and M. Swan (eds.), *The Community, the Family and the Saint: Patterns of Power in Early Medieval Europe*. Turnhout: Brepols, 325–38.

——(2000). 'Archaeology and the Late Roman frontier in northern Gaul: the so-called "Föderatengräber" reconsidered', in W. Pohl and H. Reimitz (eds.), *Grenze und Differenz im frühen Mittelalter*. Vienna: Österreichischen Akademie der Wissenschaften, 167–80.

HÄRKE, H. (1992). *Angelsächsische Waffengräber des 5. bis 7. Jahrhunderts*. Cologne: Dr Rudolf Habelt GmbH.

——(1997). 'Material culture as myth: weapons in Anglo-Saxon graves', in Kjeld Jensen and Høilund Nielsen (eds.), *Burial & Society*, 119–27.

HAWKES, S. C., and DUNNING, G. C. (1961). 'Soldiers and settlers in Britain, fourth to fifth century: with a catalogue of animal-ornamented buckles and related belt-fittings'. *Medieval Archaeology* 5: 1–70.

——and GRAINGER, G. (2006). *The Anglo-Saxon Cemetery at Finglesham, Kent*. Oxford: Oxford University School of Archaeology.

——and POLLARD, M. (1981). 'The gold bracteates from sixth-century Anglo-Saxon graves in Kent, in the light of a new find from Finglesham'. *Frühmittelalterliche Studien* 15: 316–70.

HILLS, C. M. (1994). 'The chronology of the Anglo-Saxon cemetery at Spong Hill, Norfolk', in B. Stjernquist (ed.), *Prehistoric Graves as a Source of Information: Symposium at Kastlösa, May 21–23, 1992*. Stockholm: Kungl. Vitterhets och Antikvitets Akademien, 41–9.

——and O'CONNELL, T. C. (2009). 'New light on the Anglo-Saxon succession: two cemeteries and their dates'. *Antiquity* 83: 1096–1108.

HINES, J. (1984). *The Scandinavian Character of Anglian England in the Pre-Viking Period*. BAR British Series 124. Oxford: British Archaeological Reports.

——(1990). 'Philology, archaeology and the *adventus Saxonum vel Anglorum*', in A. Bammesberger and A. Wollmann (eds.), *Britain 400–600: Language and History*. Heidelberg: Carl Winter, 17–35.

——(2007). 'Review of *Death and Memory in Early Medieval Britain* by Howard Williams'. *Medieval Archaeology* 51: 310–12.

——(ed.) (forthcoming). *Anglo-Saxon England c. 570–720: The Chronological Basis*. London: Society for Medieval Archaeology (Monograph Series).

——Høilund Nielsen, K., and SIEGMUND, F. (eds.) (1999). *The Pace of Change: Studies in Early-medieval Chronology*. Oxford: Oxbow Books.

KJELD JENSEN, C., and HØILUND NIELSEN, K. (eds.) (1997). *Burial & Society: The Chronological and Social Analysis of Archaeological Burial Data*. Aarhus: Aarhus University Press.

LEAHY, K. (2007). *'Interrupting the Pots': The Excavation of Cleatham Anglo-Saxon Cemetery*. CBA Research Report 155. York: Council for British Archaeology.

LEEDS, E. T. (1912). 'The distribution of the Anglo-Saxon saucer brooch in relation to the Battle of Bedford, AD 571'. *Archaeologia* 63: 159–202.

——(1913). *The Archaeology of the Anglo-Saxon Settlements*. Oxford: The Clarendon Press.

——(1936). *Early Anglo-Saxon Art and Archaeology*. Oxford: The Clarendon Press.

——and HARDEN, D. B. (1936). *The Anglo-Saxon Cemetery at Abingdon, Berkshire*. Oxford: Ashmolean Museum.

LUCY, S. (1998). *The Early Anglo-Saxon Cemeteries of East Yorkshire: An Analysis and Reinterpretation*. BAR British Series 272. Oxford: British Archaeological Reports.

——(2000). *The Anglo-Saxon Way of Death*. Stroud: Sutton Publishing.

——and REYNOLDS, A. (eds.) (2002). *Burial in Early Medieval England and Wales*. Society for Medieval Archaeology Monograph 17. London/Leeds: Maney.

MACGREGOR, A. (2007). 'E. T. Leeds and the formulation of an Anglo-Saxon archaeology of England', in M. Henig and T. J. Smith (eds.), *Collectanea Antiqua: Essays in Memory of Sonia Chadwick Hawkes*. British Archaeological Reports International Series 1673. Oxford: Archaeopress, 27–44.

MALIM, T., and HINES, J. (1998). *The Anglo-Saxon Cemetery at Edix Hill (Barrington A), Cambridgeshire*. CBA Research Report 112. York: Council for British Archaeology.

MEANEY, A. (1964). *A Gazetteer of Early Anglo-Saxon Burial Sites*. London: George Allen & Unwin.

——and HAWKES, S. C. (1970). *Two Anglo-Saxon Cemeteries at Winnall*. Society for Medieval Archaeology Monograph 4. London.

MYRES, J. N. L. (1969). *Anglo-Saxon Pottery and the Settlement of England*. Oxford: The Clarendon Press.

——(1977). *A Corpus of Anglo-Saxon Pottery of the Pagan Period*. Cambridge: Cambridge University Press.

NOVUM INVENTORIUM SEPULCHRALE (2007). *Novum Inventorium Sepulchrale: Kentish Anglo-Saxon Graves and Grave Goods in the Sonia Hawkes Archive*. July 2007, 1st edition. <http://web.arch.ox.ac.uk/archives/inventorium>, accessed 3 March 2008.

PADER, E.-J. (1980). 'Material symbolism and social relations in mortuary studies', in Rahtz et al. (eds.), *Anglo-Saxon Cemeteries 1979*, 143–59.

——(1982). *Symbolism, Social Relations and the Interpretation of Mortuary Remains*. BAR International Series 130. Oxford: British Archaeological Reports.

PARFITT, K. and ANDERSON, T. (forthcoming). *Buckland Anglo-Saxon Cemetery, Dover: Excavations 1994*. Canterbury Archaeological Trust.

PENN, K., and BRUGMANN, B. (2007). *Aspects of Anglo-Saxon Inhumation Burial: Morning Thorpe, Spong Hill, Bergh Apton and Westgarth Gardens*. East Anglian Archaeology

Report 119. Dereham: Historic Environment, Norfolk Museums and Archaeology Service.

PHILPOTT, R. A. (1991). *Burial Practices in Roman Britain: A Survey of Grave Treatment and Furnishing AD 43–410*. British Archaeological Reports British Series 219. Oxford: Archaeopress.

RAHTZ, P., DICKINSON, T., and WATTS, L. (1980). *Anglo-Saxon Cemeteries 1979*. BAR British Series 82. Oxford: British Archaeological Reports.

RAVN, M. (2003). *Death Ritual and Germanic Social Structure (c. AD 200–600)*. British Archaeological Reports International Series 1164. Oxford: Archaeopress.

RHODES, M. (1989). 'Faussett rediscovered: Charles Roach Smith, Joseph Mayer, and the publication of *Inventorium Sepulchrale*', in E. Southworth (ed.), *Anglo-Saxon Cemeteries: a Reappraisal*. Stroud: Alan Sutton Publishing, 25–64.

RICHARDS, J. D. (1987). *The Significance of Form and Decoration of Anglo-Saxon Cremation Urns*. BAR British Series 166. Oxford: British Archaeological Reports.

RICHARDSON, A. (2005). *The Anglo-Saxon Cemeteries of Kent*. BAR British Series 391 (1–2). Oxford: British Archaeological Reports.

SAYER, D. (2007). 'Drei südenglische Gräberfelder aus angelsächsischer Zeit und ihre Organisation', in C. Grünewald and T. Capelle (eds.), *Innere Strukturen von Siedlungen und Gräberfeldern als Spiegel gesellschaftlicher Wirklichkeit? Akten des 57. Internationalen Sachsensymposions vom 26. bis 30. August 2006 in Münster*. Münster: Aschendorff GmbH, 79–88.

SCHESCHKEWITZ, J. (2006). *Das spätrömische und angelsächsische Gräberfeld von Wasperton, Warwickshire*. Bonn: Dr Rudolf Habelt GmbH.

SCULL, C., and BAYLISS, A. (1999). 'Radiocarbon dating and Anglo-Saxon graves', in U. von Freeden, U. Koch, and A. Wieczorek (eds.), *Völker an Nord- und Ostsee und die Franken: Akten des 48. Sachsensymposiums in Mannheim vom 7. bis 11. September 1997*. Bonn: Dr Rudolf Habelt GmbH, 39–50.

SEMPLE, S., and WILLIAMS, H. (eds.) (2007). *Early Medieval Mortuary Practices*. Anglo-Saxon Studies in Archaeology and History 14. Oxford: Oxford University School of Archaeology.

SHEPHARD, J. (1979a). 'The social identity of the individual in isolated barrows and barrow cemeteries in Anglo-Saxon England', in B. C. Burnham and J. Kingsbury (eds.), *Space, Hierarchy and Society: Interdisciplinary Studies in Social Area Analysis*. BAR International Series 59. Oxford: British Archaeological Reports, 47–79.

——(1979b). *Anglo-Saxon Barrows of the Later Sixth and Seventh Centuries A.D.* Unpublished Ph.D. thesis, University of Cambridge.

SHERLOCK, S. J., and WELCH, M. G. (1992). *An Anglo-Saxon Cemetery at Norton, Cleveland*. CBA Research Report 82. London: Council for British Archaeology.

SMITH, R. A. (1923). *A Guide to the Anglo-Saxon and Foreign Teutonic Antiquities in the Department of British and Medieval Antiquities*. London: The British Museum.

STOODLEY, N. (1999a). *The Spindle and the Spear: A Critical Enquiry into the Construction and Meaning of Gender in the Early Anglo-Saxon Burial Rite*. British Series 288. Oxford: British Archaeological Reports.

——(1999b). 'Communities of the dead: the evidence for living populations from Early Anglo-Saxon cemeteries', in D. Mowbray, R. Purdie, and I. P. Wei (eds.), *Authority and Community in the Middle Ages*. Stroud: Sutton Publishing Ltd, 1–17.

WALTON ROGERS, P. (2007). *Cloth and Clothing in Early Anglo-Saxon England AD 450–700*. CBA Research Report 145. York: Council for British Archaeology.

WEBSTER, L. E. (1992). 'Death's diplomacy: Sutton Hoo in the light of other male princely burials', in R. Farrell and C. Neuman de Vegvar (eds.), *Sutton Hoo: Fifty Years After*. Oxford, OH: American Early Medieval Studies, 75–81.

WELCH, M. G. (1983). *Early Anglo-Saxon Sussex*. BAR British Series 112 (1–2). Oxford: British Archaeological Reports.

—— (1993). 'The archaeological evidence for federate settlement in Britain within the fifth century', in F. Vallet and M. Kazanski (eds.), *L'Armée Romaine et les Barbares du IIIe au VIIe Siècle*. Paris: Mémoires de l'Association Francaise d'Archéologie Mérovingienne 5, 269–78.

—— (1999). 'Relating Anglo-Saxon chronology to continental chronologies in the fifth century AD', in U. von Freeden, U. Koch, and A. Wieczorek (eds.), *Völker an Nord- und Ostsee und die Franken: Akten des 48. Sachsensymposiums in Mannheim vom 7. bis 11. September 1997*. Bonn: Dr Rudolf Habelt GmbH, 31–8.

WILLIAMS, H. (2006a). 'Heathen graves and Victorian Anglo-Saxonism: assessing the archaeology of John Mitchell Kemble', in S. Semple (ed.), *Anglo-Saxon Studies in Archaeology and History*, 13. Oxford: Oxford University School of Archaeology, 1–18.

—— (2006b). 'Digging Saxon graves in Victorian Britain', in R. Pearson (ed.), *The Victorians and the Ancient World*. Newcastle-upon-Tyne: Cambridge Scholars, 61–80.

—— (2006c). *Death and Memory in Early Medieval Britain*. Cambridge: Cambridge University Press.

—— (2007). 'Forgetting the Britons in Victorian Anglo-Saxon archaeology', in N. Higham (ed.), *Britons in Anglo-Saxon England*. Woodbridge: The Boydell Press, 27–41.

—— (2008). 'Anglo-Saxonism and Victorian archaeology: William Wylie's *Fairford Graves*'. *Early Medieval Europe* 16: 49–88.

CHAPTER 14

MORTUARY PRACTICES IN EARLY ANGLO-SAXON ENGLAND

HOWARD WILLIAMS

INTRODUCTION

The furnished cremation and inhumation graves of the later fifth and sixth centuries AD have been assigned to the pagan 'Anglo-Saxons' for over two centuries. Augmenting recent developments in early medieval burial archaeology, this chapter presents the argument that mortuary practices were mechanisms for the construction of memories and, in turn, the constitution of identities during the turbulent socio-economic, political, and religious transformations of the fifth and sixth centuries AD.

Memory is here defined as a social and cultural phenomenon (for a broader discussion see Williams 2001; 2006: 1–35). This follows from the widespread use of 'memory' to refer to perceived and imagined pasts shared between people and generated through social and ritual practices (e.g. Connerton 1989; Rowlands 1993; Assmann 2006). This approach has been widely applied to the study of mortuary practices by historians, sociologists, and anthropologists, as well as within the burgeoning interdisciplinary fields of death studies and memory studies (for reviews, see Williams 2006; Jones 2007; Williams and Sayer 2009). Over the last decade in particular, archaeologists have explored the 'social' and 'cultural' memories reproduced through mortuary practices for many periods of the human past (e.g. Chesson 2001; Bradley 2002; Jones 2007) including the early Middle Ages (Bradley and Williams 1998; Effros 2003; Halsall 2003; Williams 2006; 2007c; Fern 2007). These studies have included analyses of the pivotal roles of practical actions, including the deployment of material culture, the human body, monumentality, and landscapes as media for the selective remembrance of the dead and their situating in relation to histories, mythologies, and identities. Building on these approaches, mortuary practices are here defined as 'technologies of remembrance' (Jones 2003; 2007). The funeral and subsequent rituals were a *châine opératoire* of practical actions, performances, materialities, and places through which memories were forged and re-made (Jones 2003; Williams 2005a: 254–5, 260–4; 2006: 20–2; Jones 2007; see also Devlin 2007: 15–16). Three themes set the scene for this argument: the mortuary process, mortuary variability, and mortuary change.

The mortuary process

Death in the fifth and sixth centuries AD can be best considered a ritualized *transition* rather than a biological event. Mortuary practices mediated the parallel transformation of the identities of the corpse, the soul or spirit of the deceased, and the survivors (Metcalf and Huntingdon 1991: 79–108). This was a process of selective remembrance, with inhumation and cremation practices, in different ways, involving many stages and settings through which the identities of the dead were commemorated (Hirst 1985: 19; Williams 2006: 36–144). Material culture seems to have held pivotal roles in orchestrating the commemoration of the dead through mortuary practices by creating memorable scenes that incorporated multi-vocal symbolic allusions (Carver 2000), made more powerful by the brevity of their display (Halsall 2003), and enhanced by the choreographed transformation and consignment of the corpse, and the subsequent memorialization of the burial location (Williams 2006: 117–21). Through the relationship of material culture, cadaver, monuments, and place, the social memory of the dead person was constituted.

Mortuary variability

If death was a memory-making transition in early Anglo-Saxon England, the dead were not all treated or remembered equally. The archaeological record reveals complex regional and local variability as well as internal diversity within every cemetery (e.g. Hines 1999; 2002; Lucy 2002).

In addition to practical, economic, and environmental influences, three social factors may also have had a bearing on mortuary variability. First, adverse circumstances of death may have created 'bad deaths' that required the extreme measures often described by archaeologists as 'deviant' burial practices (Hirst 1985: 38–43; Williams 2006: 96–102; Williams 2007b: 117–19; Reynolds 2009). Second, the social identity of the deceased, including age and gender (Härke 1997b: 126–37; Lucy 1998; Stoodley 1999: 105–25; Stoodley 2000; Crawford 2000; Gowland 2007), kinship (Sayer 2009), social status and ethnicity (Härke 1997b: 141–51; Stoodley 1999: 91–104, 126–35), as well as the wider social network of the mourners, is likely to have directed the character of the mortuary procedures. It is frequently recognized that mortuary variability does not provide a direct 'window' onto social organization, but instead an idealized and stylized portrayal for remembrance after the funeral (Pader 1982; Härke 1997a and b; Carver 2000). Third, the commemorative nature of funerals was directed by power relationships among the mourners, including the deceased's family (e.g. Effros 2003: 173), and arguably other groups as well, such as friends, neighbours, and ritual specialists (Dickinson 1993; Williams 1999). Therefore, while mortuary practices may be considered as analogous to artistic compositions resulting from the 'intentional' outcomes of the mourners (Carver 2000; Halsall 2003), they were unlikely to have been the conscious results of a single composer's design. Mortuary variability served to reconfigure social memories and to constitute social identities through selective choices concerning how to remember the dead according to the circumstances of death and social identity, as well as the conflicting ideals and relationships among the mourners.

Mortuary change

Regarding mortuary practices as technologies of remembrance also helps us to understand continuities and changes in funerary traditions over time, as neither manifestations of a static collective consciousness, nor purely situational performances. As in most agrarian traditional societies, the pressures to appease and to fulfil the expectations of the deceased, the living audience, ancestors, and deities would serve to constrain the potential for radical changes in mortuary practice. Social memory was therefore not simply about the selective remembrance of the deceased's identity during the mortuary process and the differential remembrance of social individuals and groups (Williams 2006: ch. 1). It also concerned establishing and reproducing structures of practice that bound separate funerals into an enduring mortuary tradition (Williams 2006: 220).

Hence it is unlikely that 'early Anglo-Saxon' mortuary traditions were invented *de novo* as a Germanic 'fashion' in the fifth century. They bear evidence of multiple influences from southern Scandinavia and Continental north-west Europe (Hills 1993; 1998; 1999: 21–4) and perhaps also late Romano-British mortuary traditions (Philpott 1991; Gowland 2007; see Dickinson, this volume). Innovations were by degree rather than dramatic transformation. They were the result of the selective choices made by mourners in relation to remembered and adapted pasts negotiated at the local level.

Mortuary traditions were created and evolved through strategies of remembering and forgetting, building upon and selecting relevant traditions of practice. Even the seemingly innovative 'princely burials' at the end of the period in question contain few elements that are not drawn from existing local practices, albeit exaggerated and manipulated for their new context (Williams 2001: 65–7; Carver 2005: 496–7; see also Newman in Carver 2005: 483–7).

In combination, understanding the mortuary process, variability, and change provide the background from which a fuller exploration of later fifth- and sixth-century cremation and inhumation practices can be based.

CONTRASTING MORTUARY TECHNOLOGIES

Many communities in early Anglo-Saxon England had a choice between at least two contrasting mortuary technologies, cremation and inhumation, and in most regions the two disposal methods were used in varying proportions. Isolating a single explanation and meaning for each rite remains elusive. Cremation was certainly the older rite and became increasingly less common during the sixth century. However, regarding cremation as more Germanic, more pagan, or simply a hang-over of older traditions, is an inadequate and simplistic approach to its survival alongside inhumation for well over a century (Williams 2002).

It is also tempting to see the rites as arbitrary distinctions: both rites were concerned with the visual display of the dead (in the grave or on the pyre) and their subsequent interment, albeit leaving very different archaeological traces. Alternatively, it is possible to regard the disposal methods in terms of binary opposites involving contrasting trajectories of the dead, perhaps linked to diametrically different 'meanings', attitudes towards the social person, and world-views (Brush 1988; Williams 2005a: 265–7; Fern 2007: 102; Gibson 2007: 291–4).

The difficulty with both these approaches is that we are not comparing like with like in terms of the quantity or quality of evidence. Moreover, what appear markedly different deposits contain evidence that many of the same procedures could be followed *during* the rituals prior to deposition (such as dressing the dead and providing the deceased with vessels and animal remains).

A more satisfactory approach is to regard them as neither identical nor complete opposites, but as *relational technologies*. Rather than each disposal method having an inherent singular cultural or religious meaning, they were employed to define coherent group mnemonic traditions as well as to simultaneously create social and religious distinctions between groups, both within and between burying communities. In other words, context seems to have defined the significance of the two technologies (see Hills 1999: 21). Just as there is no single motivation to cremate or inhume in modern Britain (Davies 1997: 32, 138–41, 231–4), there were probably many factors influencing the disposal method selected in the fifth and sixth centuries AD. In some instances the disposal method offered a long-repeated shared rite that may have defined a sense of community history and identity in death (as with the communities using large cremation cemeteries). In other instances, the two methods may have been employed to visually distinguish between two families or households using the same burial rite (as when employed in 'mixed-rite' cemeteries: Williams 2002). In further instances, both cremation and inhumation could equally have served as 'deviant' rites, reserved for only certain individuals.[1]

Cremation practices

Early Anglo-Saxon cremation burials appear from sometime in the middle of the fifth century, earlier than most inhumation graves (Dickinson, this volume). Both rites persist alongside each other through the period and across most of southern and eastern England (Hills 1999: 20; Leahy 2007: 10–13), although the use of cremation varies considerably in character and frequency between cemeteries, localities, and regions. In some cemeteries and areas, cremation appears to be used briefly and then rapidly abandoned, as at Croydon, Surrey (McKinley 2003). In other cemeteries, it appears that cremation was retained as a minority rite alongside inhumation graves, as at Lechlade, Gloucestershire (Boyle et al. 1998: 38). In further cases it appears that both rites were used contemporaneously for many decades in broadly equal proportions, perhaps utilized by different status groups, families, or households within the same or neighbouring communities. Examples of 'mixed-rite' cemeteries include Portway, Andover, Hampshire (Cook and Dacre 1985) and Great Chesterford and Springfield Lyons, both in Essex (Evison 1994; Tyler and Major 2005).

In eastern England there are different relationships between the two disposal methods. Cemeteries are found where cremation is the dominant mode of disposal. Such sites persisted alongside cemeteries in which inhumation prevailed, and occasional examples of mixed-rite cemeteries are also known. 'Cremation cemeteries' can be extremely large (comprising over two thousand burials), and can

---

[1] I would like to thank Edeltraud Aspoeck for drawing my attention to this idea.

therefore be considered to be central burial places serving numerous households and communities (Faull 1976: 231). Examples of this site-type are Spong Hill, Norfolk (Hills 1977; 1999; Hills *et al.* 1994); Newark, Nottinghamshire (Kinsley 1989); Cleatham, Lincolnshire (Leahy 1998; 2007); and Sancton, East Yorkshire (Timby 1993).

Cremation practices can be reconstructed from the careful examination of the artefacts and bones left in the burial, through experimental archaeology, and by drawing analogies from ethnographic, historical, and forensic sources (McKinley 1994: 72–81; Williams 2004b). The process included the preparation of the body and the building of the pyre, the placing and posing of the body on the pyre, the sacrifice of animals, and the placing of artefacts, materials, and substances with the body. This composition of the pyre had similarities, but also important differences, when compared with the contemporary preparation of furnished inhumation graves (Fig. 14.1). Just as the inhumation tableau was short-lived prior to the filling of the grave, the pyre tableau was equally ephemeral and quickly followed by its vivid conflagration. Further divergences between the two disposal methods include the fact that while funerals involving the inhumation of the body could have involved post-burial rituals such as the raising of a memorial and visiting the grave, cremation ceremonies involved contrasting engagements with the remains of the dead. Indeed, cremation did not end with the burning of the body. Subsequent practices included the cooling and examination of the pyre debris, followed by the selection, collection, and storage of the ashes. There is evidence to suggest that not all ashes were retrieved and subject to burial, and some may have been circulated among the survivors. Moreover, an unknown but potentially substantial time-period may have elapsed between cremation and the subsequent burial of a portion of the ashes, making it possible that all urns, for some time, resided in temporary storage areas near the pyre site, in the home, or at the burial site (McKinley 1994: 82–6; McKinley in Gibson 2007: 277–80).

Therefore, rather than a medium for simply the display of the deceased's identity upon the pyre, cremation can be regarded as an 'ideology of transformation' involving a sequence of places, materials, and practices (see Williams 2001). It was a process that sequentially reconfigured the deceased's identity through the preparation and burning of the cadaver and the treatment of the ashes. It is possible that post-cremation practices may have been concerned with the rebuilding of the deceased's identity by placing the dead in a distinctive urn with selected artefacts. This 'journey' from corpse to ashes may even have been linked to shamanistic concepts of the person, and pagan afterlife beliefs (Pluskowski, this volume; Williams 2004b; 2006: 90–6).

The key mortuary artefact of the post-cremation rituals was the cinerary urn (Hills 1999: 17). Unurned cremations seem to be rare (apart from south of the Thames) suggesting that a ceramic container—even when only a humble re-used domestic pot—was an important practical and ritual component of the cremation

Figure 14.1 Artist's impression of a wealthy late sixth-century cremation ceremony (by Kelvin Wilson, reproduced with kind permission, © Kelvin Wilson)

process. Bronze containers are only occasionally used as cinerary urns, and their use appears to be common only among a small group of princely barrow-burials as at Coombe, Kent, and Sutton Hoo, Suffolk (Carver 2005: 67–106). The majority of urns in eastern England were decorated by incised lines and dots, sometimes combined with stamped and plastic decoration. At some sites, domestic vessels were used, but at many it appears that urns were made for, or at least selected especially for, the funeral. Indeed, the size, shape, and decoration of cinerary urns have been interpreted as a symbolic grammar communicating aspects of the social identity of the deceased, and intended to be seen by those gathering around the burial-pit (Richards 1987; 1992). Further acts of transformation could relate to the pot. The occasional deliberate 'holing' of the pot prior to burial could be seen as a further means of articulating the fragmentation of social ties with the living, and/or the release of the deceased's spirit (Richards 1987: 77).

The most important materials within cinerary urns were the burnt bones of humans and animals. Sometimes this bone is absent, hinting at the possibility that 'cenotaph' urn-burials may have sometimes taken place when the body was not available (McKinley 2003: 11–12). The human remains found in most urns are often heavily fragmented by the funerary fire and the subsequent burial and retrieval processes. Despite this, burnt human remains often retain invaluable information to the expert osteologist. The recoverable data can include the number of individuals present (sometimes urns contain the remains of two or more persons), their age, and sex. Pathologies can also be identified. Meanwhile the weight, degree of fragmentation, and bone-colour can allow aspects of the pyre technology and post-cremation practices to be reconstructed (McKinley 1994: 82–6). For example, Jackie McKinley argues for the ashes from urns from Spong Hill, Norfolk, that early Anglo-Saxon cremation seems to have been an efficient process with a high firing temperature, hinting that specialist knowledge may have been required to replicate this efficiency on a regular basis.

Julie Bond's work on Spong Hill and Sancton has revealed that a wide range of domestic animals were sacrificed and placed on pyres, either as joints of meat (mainly sheep/goat and pig), or as whole animals (horse, cattle, and dog: Bond 1996). Wild animals, including deer and fox, were also occasional offerings. The horse seems to have held a special role in the cremation process, placed whole, particularly with adult individuals. Adult males and females could both be accompanied by horses, contrasting with the association of adult male weapon burials with horse sacrifice in sixth- and early seventh-century inhumation graves (Bond 1996; see also Williams 2005b; Fern 2007; Pluskowski, this volume). In some cases the volume of ashes created by humans and animals in combination required the burial of the animal remains in a second, often undecorated, 'animal accessory' vessel (McKinley 1994: 93–4; see also Williams 2005b; Fern 2007).

The artefacts from cinerary urns fall into two main groups. Pyre-goods included the burned remains of artefacts placed with the dead upon the pyre, and (especially when found fused to cremated bone) indicate that the dead were dressed and adorned on the pyre in a manner comparable with the tableau created within the grave for the inhumed dead (see below). Items of this kind include dress accessories and personal possessions such as brooches and beads, but also gifts (perhaps of food and drink) added to the pyre, such as pottery and glass vessels. Although partly obscured by the destruction and fragmentation caused by the cremation process, studies suggest that the quality and quantity of items varied in relation to the social identity of the deceased (Richards 1987; Ravn 2003). The absence of certain artefact-types commonly found with the inhumed dead is also notable, including the low proportion of knives, buckles, and (in particular) weaponry. Given that fragments of sword hilts are found in rare instances, it is likely that weapons had been present on the pyre but were selectively retrieved from the ashes prior to burial as part of a ritualized practice of recycling and circulating pyre-damaged artefacts among the survivors (Williams 2005a).

The second group of materials from cinerary urns is grave-goods—artefacts either deliberately selected from the pyre debris and/or added to the ashes unburned following cremation. These artefacts include bone and antler combs, and toilet implements (including tweezers, shears, razors, and blades). It appears that these objects had a special role in post-cremation ceremonies (Williams 2003; 2007c). For example, at the cemetery of Alwalton, Cambridgeshire, the vast majority of cinerary urns contained the (deliberately) broken fragments of antler combs (Gibson 2007: 263–4, 293). Practices varied between sites, and at the mixed-rite cemetery at Worthy Park, Kingsworthy, Hampshire, a different pattern was apparent. Miniature antler combs, and in one case a full-sized comb, were found in some cinerary urns in association with small iron miniature tool-kits suspended from iron rings (Hawkes and Grainger 2003: 124–5, 130; and see Fig. 14.2).

Despite this varied application, a common theme is that grave-goods were closely connected with the presentation and management of the body's surface in life and death. They were practical objects, but may have had amuletic and symbolic significance in the cremation process through their association with hair and grooming. In different cultures, the management of hair is often utilized as a medium and metaphor for bereavement (expressing loss and affinity with the dead) as well as a means of commemoration (for discussions, see Williams 2003; 2007c). It seems that these items may have been placed by the survivors to articulate the rebuilding and reconstitution of social identity and ties between the living and the dead as an ancestor, following the dissolution and transformation of the cremation process (Williams 2007c).

The proportion of cremation burials is likely to be under-represented at many sites, since their pits tend to be smaller and shallower than inhumation graves. Indeed, details of pit-cuts and size are often limited because of the nature of soil conditions. In some instances, however, cinerary urns have been found associated with a range of internal structures, including stones and Roman tiles (at Caistor-by-Norwich; Myres and Green 1973: Plate XV) either used to line pits or cover urns. These objects are as much a part of the burial ritual as the placing of the urns themselves, and the choice of stones may have been intended to protect the dead

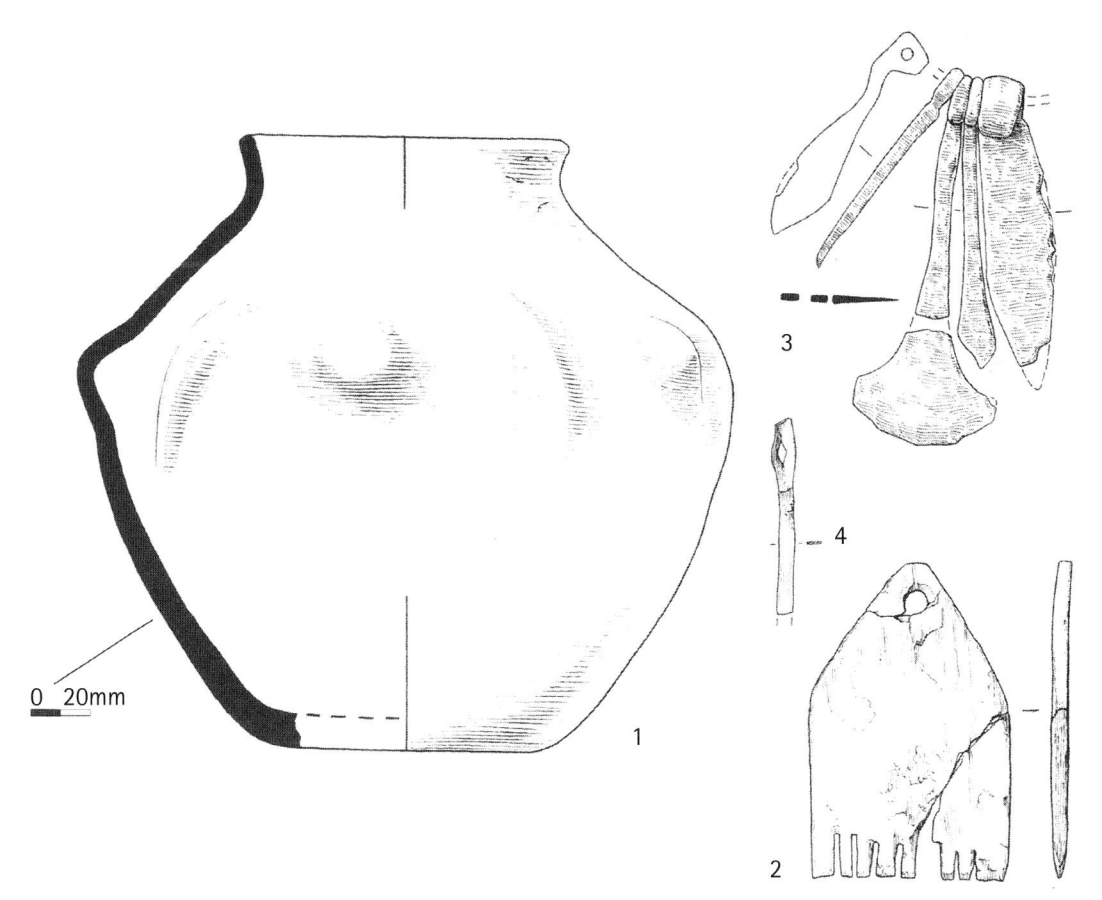

Figure 14.2 Cinerary urn with bossed decoration (1) and artefacts—an antler comb (2), miniature iron tools (3), and a copper-alloy lace tag (4)—found in grave C23 from the mixed-rite early Anglo-Saxon cemetery at Worthy Park, Kingsworthy, Hampshire (reproduced with kind permission after Hawkes and Grainger 2003)

from disturbance and/or to distance the living from the dead. In further cases, they may indicate the remains of damaged cairns raised over graves (Leahy 2007: 29).

Despite detailed analysis, the precise spatial organization of cremation cemeteries is a topic that requires further investigation (e.g. Hills 1980; Leahy 2007). In contrast to inhumation graves, cinerary urns are sometimes found in large groups, sometimes in lines or curvilinear arrangements. This suggests either that urns could be stored above ground for long periods before collective burial, or that graves received above-ground markers, and perhaps only temporary covers facilitating the precise positioning of extra urns, before their permanent back-filling and the raising of a monument (e.g. McKinley 1994: 103–5).

The monument employed for the cremation process was an ephemeral one, namely the pyre itself. More than simply a pile of wood, pyres require specialist knowledge to build correctly. There is no reason why these pyres might not have included sections of the deceased's house, wagon, store-chest, and boat. Pyres might be adorned with food offerings, textiles, and other organic coverings. They could have been covered with canopies, flags, and other furnishings that do not leave archaeological traces. There are, however, rare occasions where pyre-sites are found, sometimes close to cremation burials, and hinting at the range of ritual practices conducted at cemeteries that normally leave scant evidence (e.g. Gibson 2007: 243, 295). Despite this evidence, only ethnographic analogies can inform archaeologists as to the potential complexity and monumentality of pyres (McKinley 1994; Williams 2004b).

Monuments associated with cremation burials also rarely survive intact because they tend to be small and ephemeral. The cists and stone-coverings mentioned above suggest that the locations of urns were sometimes marked. Low mounds are likely to have surmounted many urns and urn-groups. These are sometimes indicated by surviving ring-ditches (e.g. Tyler and Major 2005: 3–4). Post-holes are occasionally uncovered, singly or in linear arrangements, associated with cremation burials (Mayes and Dean 1976: 11). At a number of southern English sites, four- and five-post structures are interpreted as 'houses of the dead', possibly used to cover and/or to contain the remains of multiple, successive cremation episodes (Evison 1988: 35–6; Down and Welch 1990: 25–35; Boyle et al. 1995: 123; Gibson 2007: 249). These structures hint at the possibility that many urns were stored above-ground, making relative estimations of cremation and inhumation burials more challenging than is usually imagined.

Only with the high-status ('princely') graves of the late sixth century and early seventh century are cremation burials located beneath sizeable mounds, as at Asthall in Oxfordshire (Dickinson and Speake 1992), and Sutton Hoo in Suffolk (Carver 2005: 67–106). This could represent the adaptation of existing cremation traditions to a new level of competitive mortuary display and symbolism associated with an emergent elite.

The provision of pyre-goods, grave-goods, and animal remains, as well as the size, form, and decoration of the cinerary urns, all varied within and between cemeteries. This variation can sometimes be associated with the social identity of the deceased as revealed by the osteological evidence for age and sex (Ravn 2003: 99–129; Richards 1987; Williams 2007c). Cremation was therefore not the great equalizer serving to destroy or down-play identities in comparison with inhumation (Brush 1988: 83; Devlin 2007: 33–5) or the 'cheap option' that it is sometimes portrayed to be in Western society (McKinley 2007). Given the investment cremation required for burning the body and the length of the ritual process, if anything, the opposite might be the case: cremation required specialist knowledge and considerable materials, and facilitated greater opportunities for articulating social differences among the dead both upon the pyre and in the grave (see Richards 1995: 58; Leahy 2007: 227). Certainly, the rite encompassed considerable variation deployed to mark important social distinctions within and between communities. Moreover, the choice to cremate may itself have been used to mark social distinctions from groups who employed other modes of disposal. Therefore, cremation in early Anglo-Saxon England was a social display in which the identities of the dead were publicly portrayed, and yet simultaneously the practice was one of transformation and reconstitution for the living and the dead: a technology of remembrance. Fire disaggregated the body, and the cremation process involved the selective deployment of substances, materials, artefacts, monuments, and places in transforming the dead. Yet the community's recollections of the person were sorted and selected, and the body was metaphorically reconstructed using tokens and unique pottery vessels, before the final act of deposition could take place.

Inhumation practices

Furnished inhumations are found in all areas of southern and eastern England, with a slightly broader distribution than cremation. As with cremation, there is considerable variety in the performance of the rite at cemetery, local, and regional levels. Our understanding of inhumation practices relies on a mixture of artefacts, materials, bone, and contextual data gained from the careful investigation of graves and related features (e.g. Duhig in Malim and Hines 1998: 154–99; Haughton and Powlesland 1999: 78–96; Cox in Haughton and Powlesland 1999: 172–88).

Cemetery arrangements were rarely formal, although some sites reveal clusters, rows, and lines of burials suggesting a degree of social organization (Sayer 2009). Grave orientations are diverse, and seem to be a response to the local topography of the cemetery, although there is an overall propensity at many sites for burial with the head either to the west or south (e.g. Down and Welch 1990: 16–17). Most graves contained just one body, although multiple interments are sometimes found, situated both side-by-side and superimposed. Some were simultaneous while others were successive additions to a remembered burial place (Stoodley 2002). A supine extended posture is common, but flexed and crouched burials were regularly employed (e.g. Boyle *et al.* 1995: 116–18; Haughton and Powlesland 1999: 89–91). Prone (face-down) burials are found in a minority of instances but at many cemeteries (Haughton and Powlesland 1999: 91–2). The treatment of the body was clearly no less the principal focus than in cremation ceremonies, providing the medium for the display and constitution of social identity.

Bodies were often dressed for death. Female costume is best known, incorporating brooches, necklaces, keys, bag collections, and other dress accessories. Mortuary costume varied between and within cemeteries, suggesting its complex and changing use as a medium for the expression of female identities at multiple levels (e.g. Hines 1999; Stoodley 1999). For example, the study of the cemetery at Edix

Hill, Barrington, Cambridgeshire, revealed multiple contemporaneous female costumes (Hines 2002).

Female mortuary costume probably consisted of more than the deceased's 'best clothes', being instead a composite costume of the deceased's possessions selected for burial by those conducting the funeral, combined with artefacts placed by the survivors with and upon the body. In the case of the rich adult female burial in grave 18 from Butler's Field, Lechlade, Gloucestershire (Boyle et al. 1998: 61–2, 154, 157), evidence was found of nine beads by the skull, interpreted as hair ornaments. Elements of clothing included three brooches, two of which were saucer brooches fixing a peplos-style dress, and the third a great square-headed brooch fixing a cloak. From the saucer brooches were suspended over 300 beads (mainly of glass and amber). Around the neck was a beaver-tooth pendant and a toilet set. At the waist were the remains of a belt-buckle, and on the hands were three spiral finger rings. To the left of the head were placed a collection of artefacts, including a scutiform pendant, a spindle whorl, an antler comb, and a wooden vessel. A bag with a rim of ivory was placed to the left of the left thigh and contained a range of items including rings of iron and bronze, iron nails, a knife, and three Roman coins (Fig. 14.3).

The detailed analysis of mineralized textiles can often allow the partial reconstruction of the costume and other soft furnishings surrounding the dead body (Harrington 2007; e.g. Walton Rogers in Haughton and Powlesland 1999: 143–71; Crowfoot in Filmer-Sankey and Pestell 2001: 207–12). Wear analysis can sometimes discern that costume-sets were made from mixtures of old and worn items combined with fresh (either rarely worn or newly-acquired) brooches (Parfitt and Brugmann 1997: 46–50). Overall the burial costume contained subtle messages conveyed by the position of brooches, beads, and other dress accessories relating not only to the dead individual but to their social position, kin-group, and community (e.g. Pader 1982; Hirst 1985: 46–8). Regional and national studies have shown that variability in clothing the dead was closely connected to gender, age, status, and perhaps also ethnicity (Stoodley 1999, 2000, and this volume).

Male burial costume is less well known, since fewer metal artefacts were employed. That adult males were clothed in death is primarily reflected in the presence of belt buckles and knives. These items cross-cut gender divisions and age groups, but even these appear to be carefully chosen to articulate the identity of the deceased (e.g. Härke 1989; Marzinzik 2003; Williams 2007c). Children tend to have poorer graves, but can receive a special assemblage of artefacts rarely found placed together in the same way in adult graves (Crawford 2000; Stoodley 2000).

A further category of artefacts might be distinguished from clothing, and defined as 'grave gifts' (though see Crawford 2004). As with the costume, these might also have been a mixture of some of the prized possessions of the deceased, and offerings by the survivors. The best studied of these 'grave gifts' are weapons, almost always found with males. Heinrich Härke has studied the multi-vocal

Figure 14.3 A wealthy sixth-century grave of an adult female aged between 25 and 30 excavated at the early Anglo-Saxon cemetery from Butler's Field, Lechlade, Gloucestershire, and reconstructed in the Corinium Museum, Cirencester (reproduced with kind permission, © Corinium Museum)

symbolism of placing weapons with the dead (Fig. 14.4). Rather than simplistic statements of warrior occupation, Härke (1990; Dickinson and Härke 1992; Härke 1997a and b) argued that the number and combination of weapons were deliberately interred to communicate the gender, age, social status, and ethnicity of the deceased. Most were interred with adults but some children could also receive weapons (see also Crawford 2000).

Food and drink were also placed in certain graves, most often revealed by the presence of their containers, including pottery vessels, buckets, glass vessels, and drinking horns. Plant and animal remains sometimes survive and also suggest that both food offerings and sacrifices were associated with burial ritual (e.g. Filmer-Sankey and Pestell 2001: 255–9; Lee 2007). These were likely to have been status symbols, but also alluded to the social exchange of food and drink in mortuary rituals and commemorative practices linked to feasting. While nowhere near as commonplace as their occurrence in cremation burials, other 'gifts' placed with the

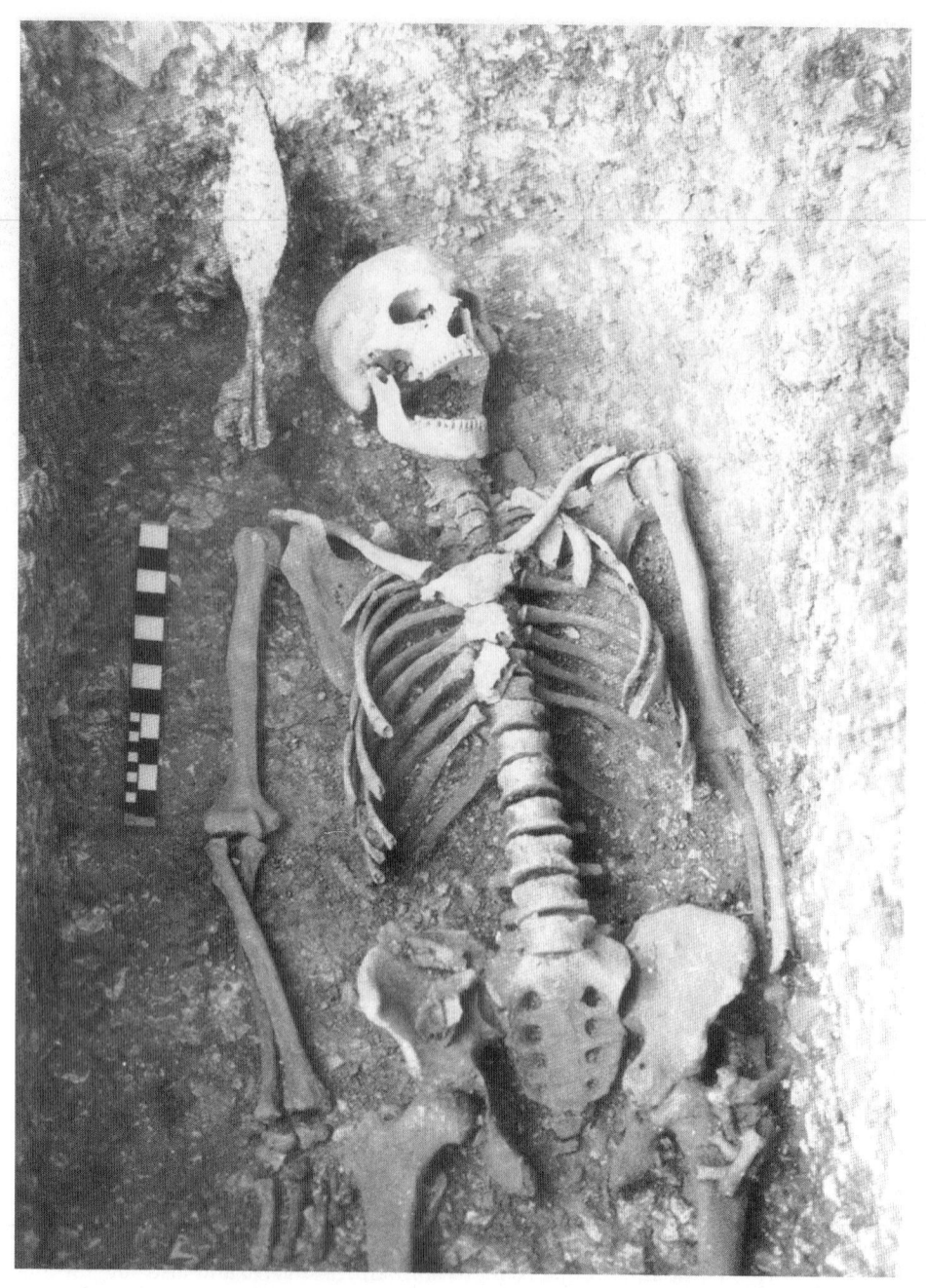

Figure 14.4 Adult male aged between 40 and 50 years of age interred with a spearhead and knife from grave 83, Worthy Park, Kingsworthy, Hants. Reproduced with kind permission after Hawkes & Grainger 2003: 139. © Oxford University School of Archaeology.

dead can include whole animals (almost always horses) placed with adult male weapon burials (Fern 2007).

Clothing and grave-gifts were only aspects of the furnished inhumation burial of the early Anglo-Saxon period. The traces of coffins are found in many burial sites, as at Spong Hill, Norfolk (e.g. Hills *et al.* 1984: 6). Some of the complexity of soft furnishings present in early Anglo-Saxon graves is revealed through the careful examination of mineralized textile remains (Harrington 2007). At Snape, Suffolk, the soil conditions revealed other forms of internal grave structures. These included organic linings and coverings, as well as biers and even whole boats used to contain the body (Filmer-Sankey and Pestell 2001: 204–14). This last phenomenon is a rare occurrence but was evidently the forerunner to the use of larger sea-going vessels beneath burial mounds at Snape and Sutton Hoo in the late sixth and early seventh century (Carver 1995).

Chamber graves are also known for wealthier burials, providing a secure space within which lavish mortuary displays were conducted. At Spong Hill, two turf-and-timber rectangular chambers were identified and dated to the sixth century. The high-status character of these graves was confirmed by the rich grave goods (including weapons), and the ring-ditches surrounding the graves (Hills *et al.* 1984: 6).

The composition of the burial deposit could be complex, yet it represented only one stage of the burial process. There are hints from fly pupae preserved by metal corrosion products that graves could have been left open, or only temporarily covered, for several days prior to the final back-filling event (Filmer-Sankey and Pestell 2001: 226). This means that the inhumation was a display that could facilitate a range of rites before, during, and after the composition of the grave.

The back-filling of the graves seems to have involved as many practices as the composing and adorning of the body. The placing of grave-gifts discussed above was as much a process of closure as it was the creation of a single composition. For example, shields were often placed outside and over the body and the coffin, obscuring much of the burial deposit beneath (Dickinson and Härke 1992). At West Heslerton, there are indications that spears were broken before being placed in the grave. This suggests that their fragmentation and consignment was as important as their display with the cadaver (Williams 2007b). At Snape, deposits of food offerings, coverings made of organic material, as well as artefacts (including parts of boats, fragments of saddle querns, burnt flints, pottery scatters, and possibly cremated bone) augmented the rituals of back-filling the grave (Filmer-Sankey and Pestell 2001: 242–6). Burnt oak timbers could be placed into the fill of inhumation graves at Snape (Filmer-Sankey and Pestell 2001; Williams 2006: 129–33), and alongside bodies in certain graves from (for example) Berinsfield, Oxfordshire (Boyle *et al.* 1995: 121–3) and Portway, Andover (Cook and Dacre 1985: 55). This evidence suggests that fire-rituals were sometimes enacted prior to, or during, back-filling, perhaps to obscure the aroma of the corpse, to purify the grave-space, and/or to protect the living from the pollution of the dead (see also Effros 2003: 165–6).

The arrangement of the grave also varied. Where grave-cuts can be identified, they often appear functional excavations, large enough simply to contain the body in an extended, flexed, or crouched posture. Sometimes natural hollows or existing ditches were exploited (Filmer-Sankey and Pestell 2001: 239). Yet on occasions archaeologists have identified a range of ledges (e.g. Cook and Dacre 1985: 55) and posts (Filmer-Sankey and Pestell 2001: 238–9) associated with the grave. Some were part of the grave-structures (coffins and chambers), while others may have been canopies over the grave (Hirst 1985: 24). Ledges may have served as steps to help mourners to access the grave and place artefacts with the cadaver, or as supports for organic structures or coverings. Posts might have assisted in the lowering of the coffin, as well as in marking the grave (see Williams 2006: 133–5).

Archaeologists know surprisingly little about the nature of post-burial commemorative practices associated with inhumation graves. Monuments raised over graves are sometimes recognized. Post-holes and slots indicate the former presence of markers above, or adjacent to, some graves (e.g. Evison 1988: 32; Hirst 1985: 25). At Sewerby, a layer of chalk blocks was found associated with at least one post-hole. This layer overlay graves 41, 42, and 49. It can be interpreted as a low platform sealing multiple graves. Therefore, this seems a rare instance of a surviving and modest mortuary monument. It could indicate that stone-settings, cairns, and mounds demarcated many more graves than is usually appreciated (Hirst 1985: 38; see also Haughton and Powlesland 1999: 88–9). Circular and rectangular ditches are sometimes located, and appear to demarcate the burial space. Perhaps they mark the outer edge of a fence or bank as often as they defined the edges of burial mounds (see also Struth and Eagles 1999). Often these ditches are interrupted by a causeway at the eastern end (for west-east orientated graves), which would have allowed mourners access to the grave, and may hint at the significance attached to the grave as a place of veneration and commemoration (e.g. Filmer-Sankey and Pestell 2001: 13; Hawkes and Grainger 2006: 157–60).

It is important to remember that mounds do not require ditches, and can be scraped up or made of turf. Therefore the absence of ring ditches around many graves is not evidence for the absence of above-ground monuments. Mounds and other grave-markers may have been a widespread occurrence in the early Anglo-Saxon inhumation practice, but it appears that sizeable burial mounds were a rare phenomenon before the later sixth century (Shephard 1979).

In combination, this evidence allows an appreciation of the complex mortuary variability within the inhumation tradition of the later fifth and sixth centuries AD in southern and eastern England. It is also possible to glean elements of the complex mortuary processes associated with inhumation. Graves would have provided a rich display, but not a single tableau, since many artefacts and materials would have successively augmented and concealed the body through its composition and consignment.

Cemeteries, monuments, and landscapes

Early Anglo-Saxon cemeteries were more than collections of graves. Cemeteries were 'places of power' in the early Anglo-Saxon landscape (Härke 2001). Whether cremation or inhumation was predominantly practised, or both rites were deployed together, burial sites and graves were locales where public ritual performances took place (Fig. 14.5). Cemeteries were also places select groups had power over, controlling where and what death rituals stated about the past, present, and future. Consequently, cemeteries may have served as places where the power of the living, dead kin, the ancestors (real or invented), and the past were articulated. Burial locations may therefore have held memories and associations actively used by the living in a variety of claims over territory and resources, and as statements of group identity (see also Arnold 1997; Williams 1997; Williams 2006: 195–7; Sayer 2009).

Understanding cemeteries as places requires some appreciation of their above-ground appearance. As we have seen with the mixed-rite cemetery of Appledown, Sussex (Down and Welch 1990), and Finglesham, Kent (Hawkes and Grainger 2006: 18, 28–32), mounds and 'mortuary houses' could surmount graves. Yet how they were elaborated when freshly raised, and whether they were maintained over time, cannot be easily ascertained. There is little surviving evidence for the management of vegetation, internal divisions, paths, and even buildings associated with burial sites. Other cemetery structures may have included 'shrines', but their functions, and their difference from 'mortuary houses', remain unclear (Hirst 1985: 24; Blair 1995). An important point is that the appearance and prominence of a burial site would not have rested on the form of a single early Anglo-Saxon monument. Many cemeteries would have held an 'accrued' prominence; the accumulation of memorials would have rendered them distinctive landscape features even if individual monuments were modest in their proportions (Sayer and Williams 2009). For example, the Cleatham cremation cemetery provides evidence that the same spot was used again and again for the interment of cinerary urns over many generations. Cinerary urns were cut through earlier burials up to seven times in succession. Clearly the significance of the place took precedence over enduring individual monuments or the preservation of and respect for earlier urns (Leahy 2007: 29).

A further appreciation of cemeteries as places comes from considering in detail their chronological and spatial development. Härke (1997b: 138) reviewed three

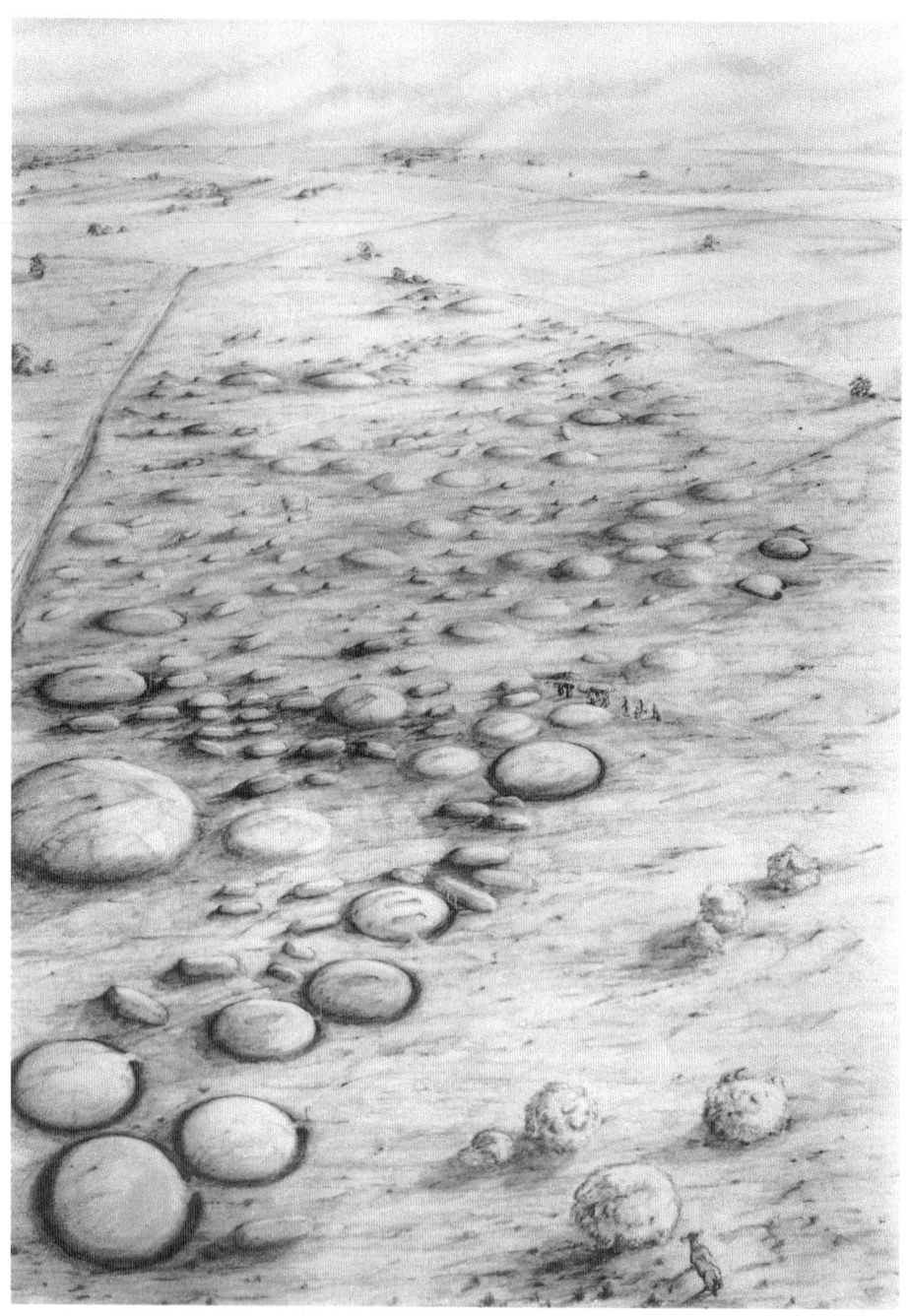

Figure 14.5 Artist's impression of the Finglesham cemetery, a long-running burial location that began life in the fifth century and persisted into the seventh century. By Edward Impey, reproduced with kind permission after Hawkes and Grainger 2006. © Oxford University School of Archaeology.

clear patterns in cemetery development: monocentric, horizontal stratigraphic, and polycentric. In some cases it is possible to show on the micro-scale how cemeteries developed, including their spread in many directions from a single focus (monocentric), or their spread in one direction from a core (horizontal stratigraphic). In other instances, it is possible to see multiple foci of development perhaps connected to families or households, sometimes demonstrably containing groups of mixed ancestry (Härke 1995; Stoodley 1999: 131–5; Tyler and Major 2005: 186–9). In some cases, the clustering of child graves and the graves of one gender suggests a supra-familial spatial organization at work (Lucy 1998; Stoodley 1999: 135; Sayer 2009). For example, at West Heslerton, North Yorkshire, there are clusters of child graves in one sector of the cemetery (Haughton and Powlesland 1999: 84–5). Likewise, there is evidence for the clustering of weapon graves at West Heslerton (Haughton and Powlesland 1999: 84). Therefore the identities of the dead were articulated and commemorated through the spatial organization and development of early Anglo-Saxon burial sites as well as through the contents of graves. Focusing on the analysis of Mill Hill, Deal, and Finglesham, both in east Kent, Duncan Sayer has recently put forward the argument that these household clusters of the sixth century gave way to family-orientated burial arrangements during the seventh century in east Kent. Hence cemetery space articulated the transformation of social arrangements through time, and ideals of group identity (Sayer 2009; Fig. 14.5).

If internal cemetery space was employed to commemorate group identities, the overall burial location could add to this message. Certain prominent landmarks appear to have been often selected as focal points for cemeteries, or parts of cemeteries, from the late fifth century AD. At Buckland, Dover (Evison 1987: 14) and Mill Hill, Deal (Parfitt and Brugmann 1997), both in Kent, circular ring-ditches of prehistoric date seem to have provided focal points for early Anglo-Saxon graves. At West Heslerton, North Yorkshire, the cemetery focused upon a series of Neolithic and early Bronze Age monuments (Haughton and Powlesland 1999: 23–80). Roman monuments might attract similar re-use, as at Great Chesterford, where the excavator postulated that the arrangement of the early Anglo-Saxon graves clustered around a series of early Romano-British mounds (Evison 1994: 39–43). This phenomenon becomes increasingly popular in the early Christian period, but has widespread roots in pre-Christian practice (Williams 1997; Semple 2003; Semple, this volume; Williams 2006: 181–5).

Boundary features may have also influenced the location of burial sites as at Appledown, Sussex (Down and Welch 1990: 15–17). At Portway, Andover, Hampshire, the presence of a linear boundary of prehistoric date defined the eastern side of the cemetery, and may have been retained as some form of territorial boundary in the fifth and sixth centuries AD (Cook and Dacre 1985; Stoodley 2007). Activities other than burial may have taken place close to graves. For example, 'burnt stone features' found at Snape, Suffolk, can be tentatively interpreted as cooking pits, perhaps associated with feasting and rituals connected to the commemoration of the dead (Filmer-Sankey and Pestell 2001: 259–61). The cemetery was a social space as well as a location for burial.

To some extent, the term 'cemetery' is not helpful in understanding the wider landscape context of early Anglo-Saxon burials. The term suggests to the modern reader a planned and clearly defined burial space. This detracts from the possibility that graves may often only be the most visible aspect of complex mortuary geographies including multiple foci consisting of isolated graves (e.g. Samuels and Russell 1999), small and short-lived burial groups serving farms and settlements (e.g. Patrick et al. 2007), and larger burial sites serving numerous communities that persisted for centuries (see McKinley 1994: 69–71; Hills 1999; Williams 2004a). The term 'cemetery' also detracts from the other locations associated with mortuary practices other than burial. These might have included settlements, mortuaries, pyre sites, shrines and temples, ancient monuments, and natural sacred sites, including springs and trees (Hamerow 2006; Williams 2006: 190–5).

Finally, the worked and inhabited landscape cannot be ignored. Archaeological evidence is showing that, rather than being situated on marginal land, early Anglo-Saxon burial sites were often incorporated into the routines of labour and living. Burial grounds seem often to have been situated in close proximity to routes (e.g. Brookes 2007). Increasingly, the evidence is pointing towards burial locations being adjacent to, or a short distance from, each other, as well as from contemporary settlements (e.g. Hamerow 1993; Dickins et al. 2005; see Williams 2006: 187–90). Therefore, for many early Anglo-Saxon communities, the graves of the dead were collectively visible and prominent aspects of their living environment, even if the funerals were temporary displays by design, and the memorials raised over individual graves were often ephemeral. The presence of the dead permeated the early Anglo-Saxon landscape.

Conclusions

Early Anglo-Saxon mortuary archaeology is a rich and vibrant arena of archaeological research. We still do not have all the answers, although new developments in the theories, methods, and data available to us promise to transform our understanding of early Anglo-Saxon graves and cemeteries, with implications for offering manifold insights into the societies in this period (see also Williams 2007a). Moreover, the critical appraisal of both current and past approaches is essential for research to develop in new and innovative ways (Williams and Sayer 2009; see also Dickinson, this volume). Yet, based on current and available approaches and data, the evidence presented here illustrates that mortuary practices of the later fifth and sixth centuries provide no single and straightforward window onto ethnic origins, religious beliefs, or social structures. Partly this is simply because there was no single 'Anglo-Saxon Way of Death' (Lucy 2000), with no single 'Anglo-Saxon' society behind it. The fifth and sixth centuries AD are defined by mortuary variability and complexity rather than by a singular coherent tradition. What the mortuary practices do indisputably show is how the detailed and contextual analysis of burial data reveals the social and commemorative importance of mortuary practices for communities at this time. Funerals were processes of economic investment, theatrical display, and ritual transition. Meanwhile, cemeteries were spaces and places in the landscape within which social memories and identities were reproduced and transformed.

Defining mortuary practices as technologies of remembrance sheds new light on the historical context of their deployment among the fragmented and fluid societies and communities that inherited the southern and eastern territories of the Roman province of *Britannia* in the fifth century, and on how they developed through the sixth and into the seventh century. In particular, mortuary performances provided contexts for creating a sense of historical depth and public affirmation for what may have often been short-lived and experimental social identities and religious systems. This approach, therefore, presents a new framework for studying early Anglo-Saxon mortuary practices, particularly in relation to the character of society, and social change, in early medieval Europe during the fifth and sixth centuries. Simultaneously, it emphasizes the role of early Anglo-Saxon mortuary studies as a case study for wider theoretical and methodological debates in the broader field of mortuary archaeology, as well as interdisciplinary studies of death and memory in the past and the present.

Acknowledgements

Thanks to the editors, Edeltraud Aspoeck, Meggen Gondek, Aleks Pluskowski, Duncan Sayer, and Elizabeth Williams, for commenting on earlier drafts of the paper.

References

Arnold, C. J. (1997). *An Archaeology of the Early Anglo-Saxon Kingdoms*. 2nd edition. London: Routledge.

Assmann, J. (2006). *Religion and Cultural Memory*. Stanford: Stanford University Press.

Blair, J. (1995). 'Anglo-Saxon pagan shrines and their prototypes', in D. Griffiths (ed.) *Anglo-Saxon Studies in Archaeology and History*, Volume 8. Oxford: Oxford Committee for Archaeology, 1–28.

Bond, J. (1996). 'Burnt offerings: animal bone in Anglo-Saxon cremations'. *World Archaeology* 28(1): 76–88.

Boyle, A., Dodd, A., Miles, D., and Mudd, A. (1995). *Two Oxfordshire Anglo-Saxon Cemeteries: Berinsfield and Didcot*. Thames Valley Landscapes Monograph No. 8. Oxford: Oxford Archaeological Unit.

——Jennings, D., Miles, D., and Palmer, S. (1998). *The Anglo-Saxon Cemetery at Butler's Field, Lechlade, Gloucestershire*. Thames Valley Landscapes Monograph No. 10. Oxford: Oxford Archaeological Unit.

Bradley, R. (2002). *The Past in Prehistoric Societies*. London: Routledge.

——and Williams, H. (eds.) (1998). *The Past in the Past: The Reuse of Ancient Monuments*. World Archaeology 30 (1). London: Routledge.

Brookes, S. (2007). 'Walking with Anglo-Saxons: landscapes of the dead in early Anglo-Saxon Kent', in Semple and Williams (eds.), *Early Medieval Mortuary Practices*, 143–53.

Brush, K. (1988). 'Gender and mortuary analysis in pagan Anglo-Saxon archaeology'. *Archaeological Review from Cambridge* 7(1): 76–89.

Carver, M. (1995). 'Boat-burial in Britain: ancient custom or political signal?', in O. Crumlin-Pedersen and B. Munch Thye (eds.) *The Ship as Symbol in Prehistoric and Medieval Scandinavia*. Studies in Archaeology and History Volume 1. Copenhagen: Publications of the National Museum, 111–24.

——(2000). 'Burial as poetry: the context of treasure in Anglo-Saxon graves', in E. Tyler (ed.), *Treasure in the Medieval West*. York: York Medieval Press, 25–48.

——(2005). *Sutton Hoo: A Seventh-Century Princely Burial Ground and its Context*. London: British Museum.

Chesson, M. S. (ed.) (2001). *Social Memory, Identity and Death: Anthropological Perspectives on Mortuary Rituals*. Archaeological Papers of the American Anthropological Association 10. Arlington, VA.

Connerton, P. (1989). *How Societies Remember*. Cambridge: Cambridge University Press.

Cook, A., and Dacre, M. (1985). *Excavations at Portway, Andover 1973–5*. Oxford University Committee for Archaeology Monograph No. 4. Oxford.

Crawford, S. (2000). 'Children, grave goods and social status in early Anglo-Saxon England', in J. Sofaer Derevenski (ed.), *Children and Material Culture*. London: Routledge, 169–79.

——(2004). 'Votive deposition, religion and the Anglo-Saxon furnished burial ritual'. *World Archaeology* 36(1): 87–102.

Davies, D. J. (1997). *Death, Ritual and Belief: The Rhetoric of Funerary Rites*. London: Cassell.

DEVLIN, Z. (2007). *Remembering the Dead in Anglo-Saxon England: Memory Theory in Archaeology and History.* British Archaeological Reports British Series 446. Oxford: Archaeopress.

DICKINS, A., MORTIMER, R., and TIPPER, J. (2005). 'The early Anglo-Saxon settlement and cemetery at Bloodmoor Hill, Carlton Colville, Suffolk: a preliminary report', in S. Semple (ed.), *Anglo-Saxon Studies in Archaeology and History*, Volume 13. Oxford: Oxford University School of Archaeology, 63–79.

DICKINSON, T. (1993). 'An Anglo-Saxon "cunning woman" from Bidford-upon-Avon', in M. Carver (ed.), *In Search of Cult: Archaeological Investigations in Honour of Philip Rahtz.* Woodbridge: Boydell, 45–54.

——and HÄRKE, H. (1992). *Early Anglo-Saxon Shields.* Archaeologia 110. London: Society of Antiquaries of London.

——and SPEAKE, G. (1992). 'The seventh-century cremation burial in Asthall Barrow, Oxfordshire: a reassessment', in M. Carver (ed.), *The Age of Sutton Hoo.* Woodbridge: Boydell, 95–130.

DOWN, A., and WELCH, M. (1990). *Chichester Excavations VII.* Chichester: Chichester District Council.

EFFROS, B. (2003). *Merovingian Mortuary Archaeology and the Making of the Early Middle Ages.* Berkeley: University of California Press.

EVISON, V. (1987). *Dover: Buckland Anglo-Saxon Cemetery.* Archaeological Report No. 3. London: Historic Buildings and Monuments Commission for England.

——(1988). *An Anglo-Saxon Cemetery at Alton, Hampshire.* Monograph 4. Stroud: Hampshire Field Club and Archaeological Society.

——(1994). *An Anglo-Saxon Cemetery at Great Chesterford, Essex.* CBA Research Report 91. London: Council for British Archaeology.

FAULL, M. (1976). 'The location and relationship of the Sancton Anglo-Saxon cemeteries'. *Antiquaries Journal* 56(2): 227–33.

FERN, C. (2007). 'Early Anglo-Saxon horse burial of the fifth to seventh centuries AD', in Semple and Williams (eds.), *Early Medieval Mortuary Practices*, 92–109.

FILMER-SANKEY, W., and PESTELL, T. (2001). *Snape Anglo-Saxon Cemetery: Excavations and Surveys 1824–1992.* East Anglian Archaeology 95. Ipswich.

GIBSON, C. (2007). 'Minerva: an early Anglo-Saxon mixed-rite cemetery in Alwalton, Cambridgeshire', in Semple and Williams (eds.), *Early Medieval Mortuary Practices*, 238–350.

GOWLAND, R. (2007). 'Beyond ethnicity: symbols of social identity from the fourth to sixth centuries in England', in Semple and Williams (eds.), *Early Medieval Mortuary Practices*, 56–65.

HALSALL, G. (2003). 'Burial writes: graves, texts and time in early Merovingian Northern Gaul', in J. Jarnut and M. Wemhoff (eds.), *Erinnerungskultur im Bestattungsritual.* Munich: Wilhelm Fink, 61–74.

HAMEROW, H. (1993). *Excavations at Mucking*, Volume 2: *The Anglo-Saxon Settlement.* London: English Heritage.

——(2006). '"Special deposits" in Anglo-Saxon settlements', *Medieval Archaeology* 50: 1–30.

HÄRKE, H. (1989). 'Knives in early Saxon burials: blade length and age at death'. *Medieval Archaeology* 33: 144–8.

——(1990). '"Warrior graves"? The background of the Anglo-Saxon weapon burial rite'. *Past and Present* 126: 22–43.

——(1995). 'Weapon burials and knives', in Boyle *et al.*, *Two Oxfordshire Anglo-Saxon Cemeteries*, 67–75.

——(1997a). 'Material culture as myth: weapons in Anglo-Saxon graves', in C. K. Jensen and K. Hoilund Nielsen (eds.), *Burial and Society*. Aarhus: University of Aarhus, 119–27.

——(1997b). 'Early Anglo-Saxon social structure', in J. Hines (ed.), *The Anglo-Saxons from the Migration Period to the Eighth Century: An Ethnographic Perspective*. Woodbridge: Boydell, 125–59.

——(2001). 'Cemeteries as places of power', in M. de Jong and F. Theuws (eds.), *Topographies of Power in the Early Middle Ages*. Leiden: Brill, 9–30.

HARRINGTON, S. (2007). 'Soft furnished burial: an assessment of the role of textiles in early Anglo-Saxon inhumations, with particular reference to east Kent', in Semple and Williams (eds.), *Early Medieval Mortuary Practices*, 110–16.

HAUGHTON, C., and POWLESLAND, D. (1999). *West Heslerton: The Anglian Cemetery*, Volume 1: *The Excavation and Discussion of the Evidence*. London: English Heritage.

HAWKES, S. C., and GRAINGER, G. (2003). *The Anglo-Saxon Cemetery at Worthy Park, Kingsworthy, near Winchester, Hampshire*. Oxford University School of Archaeology Monograph 59. Oxford.

————(2006). *The Anglo-Saxon Cemetery at Finglesham, Kent*. Monograph 64. Oxford: Oxford University School of Archaeology.

HILLS, C. (1977). *The Anglo-Saxon Cemetery at Spong Hill, North Elmham*, Part I: *Catalogue of Cremations*. East Anglian Archaeology 6. Dereham.

——(1980). 'Anglo-Saxon cremation cemeteries, with particular reference to Spong Hill, Norfolk', in P. Rahtz, T. Dickinson, and L. Watts (eds.) *Anglo-Saxon Cemeteries 1979*. BAR British Series 82. Oxford: British Archaeological Reports, 197–208.

——(1993). 'Who were the East Anglians?', in J. Gardiner (ed.), *Flatlands and Wetlands: Current Themes in East Anglian Archaeology*. East Anglian Archaeology 50. Dereham, 14–23.

——(1998). 'Did the people of Spong Hill come from Schleswig-Holstein?'. *Studien zur Sachsenforchung* 11: 145–54.

——(1999). 'Spong Hill and the Adventus Saxonum', in C. E. Karkov, K. M. Wickham-Crowley, and B. K. Young (eds.), *Spaces of the Living and the Dead: An Archaeological Dialogue*. American Early Medieval Studies 3. Oxford: Oxbow, 15–26.

——PENN, K., and RICKETT, R. (1984). *The Anglo-Saxon Cemetery at Spong Hill, North Elmham*, Part III: *Catalogue of Inhumations*. East Anglian Archaeology 21. Dereham.

————(1994). *The Anglo-Saxon Cemetery at Spong Hill, North Elmham*. Part V: *Catalogue of Cremations*. East Anglian Archaeology 67. Dereham.

HINES, J. (1999). 'The sixth-century transition in Anglian England: an analysis of female graves from Cambridgeshire', in J. Hines, K. Høilund Nielsen, and F. Siegmund (eds.), *The Pace of Change: Studies in Early-Medieval Chronology*. Oxford: Oxbow, 65–79.

——(2002). 'Lies, damned lies, and the Curriculum Vitae: reflections on statistics and the populations of early Anglo-Saxon inhumation cemeteries', in Lucy and Reynolds (eds.), *Burial in Early Medieval England and Wales*, 88–102.

HIRST, S. (1985). *An Anglo-Saxon Inhumation Cemetery at Sewerby East Yorkshire*. York University Archaeological Publications 4. York.

JONES, A. (2003). 'Technologies of remembrance. Memory, materiality and identity in Early Bronze Age Scotland'. In H. Williams (ed.), *Archaeologies of Remembrance: Death and Memory in Past Societies*. New York: Kluwer/Plenum, 65–88.

——(2007). *Memory and Material Culture*. Cambridge: Cambridge University Press.
KINSLEY, A. (1989). *The Anglo-Saxon Cemetery at Millgate, Newark-on-Trent, Nottinghamshire*. Nottingham: University of Nottingham.
LEAHY, K. (1998). 'Cleatham, North Lincolnshire, the "Kirton in Lindsey" Cemetery'. *Medieval Archaeology* 42: 94–5.
——(2007). *'Interrupting the Pots.' The Excavation of Cleatham Anglo-Saxon Cemetery*. CBA Research Report 155. York: Council for British Archaeology.
LEE, C. (2007). *Feasting the Dead: Food and Drink in Anglo-Saxon Rituals*. Woodbridge: Boydell.
LUCY, S. (1998). *The Early Anglo-Saxon Cemeteries of East Yorkshire*. BAR British Series 272. Oxford: British Archaeological Reports.
——(2000). *The Anglo-Saxon Way of Death*. Stroud: Sutton.
——(2002). 'Burial practice in early medieval eastern England: constructing local identities, deconstructing ethnicity', in Lucy and Reynolds (eds.), *Burial in Early Medieval England and Wales*, 72–87.
——and REYNOLDS, A. (eds.) (2002). *Burial in Early Medieval England and Wales*. Society for Medieval Archaeology Monograph Series 17. Leeds: Maney.
MALIM, T., and HINES, J. (1998). *The Anglo-Saxon Cemetery at Edix Hill (Barrington A), Cambridgeshire*. CBA Research Report 112. London: Council for British Archaeology.
MARZINZIK, S. (2003). *Early Anglo-Saxon Belt Buckles (Late 5th to Early 8th Centuries AD): Their Classification and Context*. British Archaeological Reports British Series 357. Oxford: Archaeopress.
MAYES, P., and DEAN, M. J. (1976). *An Anglo-Saxon Cemetery at Baston, Lincolnshire*. Sleaford: Society for Lincolnshire History and Archaeology.
MCKINLEY, J. (1994). *The Anglo-Saxon Cemetery at Spong Hill, North Elmham, Part 8: The Cremations*. East Anglian Archaeology 69. Dereham.
——(2003). 'The early Saxon cemetery at Park Lane, Croydon'. *Surrey Archaeological Collections* 90: 1–116.
——(2007). 'Cremation ... the cheap option?' in R. Gowland and C. Knüsel (eds.), *Social Archaeology of Funerary Remains*. Oxford: Oxbow, 81–9.
METCALF, D., and HUNTINGDON, R. (1991). *Celebrations of Death: The Anthropology of Mortuary Ritual*. 2nd edition. Cambridge: Cambridge University Press.
MYRES, J. N. L., and GREEN, B. (1973). *The Anglo-Saxon Cemeteries of Caistor-by-Norwich and Markshall*. London: Society of Antiquaries.
PADER, E.-J. (1982). *Symbolism, Social Relations and the Interpretation of Mortuary Remains*. BAR International Series 130. Oxford: British Archaeological Reports.
PARFITT, K., and BRUGMANN, B. (1997). *The Anglo-Saxon Cemetery on Mill Hill, Deal, Kent*. Society for Medieval Archaeology Monograph Series 14. Leeds.
PATRICK, P., FRENCH, C., and OSBORNE, C. (2007). 'Rescue excavations of an early Anglo-Saxon cemetery at Gunthorpe, Peterborough', in Semple and Williams (eds.), *Early Medieval Mortuary Practices*, 204–37.
PHILPOTT, R. (1991). *Burial Practices in Roman Britain: A Survey of Grave Treatment and Furnishing, AD 43–410*. British Archaeological Reports British Series 219. Oxford: Archaeopress.
RAVN, M. (2003). *Death Ritual and Germanic Social Structure*. British Archaeological Reports International Series 1164. Oxford: Archaeopress.

REYNOLDS, A. (2009). *Anglo-Saxon Deviant Burial Customs*. Oxford: Oxford University Press.
RICHARDS, J. D. (1987). *The Significance of Form and Decoration of Anglo-Saxon Cremation Urns*. British Archaeological Reports British Series 166. Oxford: British Archaeological Reports.
——(1992). 'Anglo-Saxon symbolism', in M. Carver (ed.), *The Age of Sutton Hoo*. Woodbridge: Boydell, 131–49.
——(1995). 'An archaeology of Anglo-Saxon England', in G. Ausenda (ed.), *After Empire: Towards an Ethnology of Europe's Barbarians*. Woodbridge: Boydell, 51–74.
ROWLANDS, M. (1993). 'The role of memory in the transmission of culture'. *World Archaeology* 25(2): 141–51.
SAMUELS, J., and RUSSELL, A. (1999). 'An Anglo-Saxon burial near Winthorpe Road, Newark, Nottinghamshire'. *Transactions of the Thoroton Society of Nottinghamshire* 103: 57–83.
SAYER, D. (2009), 'Laws, funeral and cemetery organisation: the seventh-century Kentish family', in Sayer and Williams (eds.), *Mortuary Practices and Social Identities*, 141–69.
——and WILLIAMS, H. (eds.) (2009). *Mortuary Practices and Social Identities in the Middle Ages: Essays in Burial Archaeology in Honour of Heinrich Härke*. Exeter: University of Exeter Press.
SEMPLE, S. (2003). 'Burials and political boundaries in the Avebury region, north Wiltshire', in D. Griffiths, A. Reynolds, and S. Semple (eds.), *Boundaries in Early Medieval Britain*. Volume 12 of *Anglo-Saxon Studies in Archaeology and History*. Oxford: Oxford University School of Archaeology, 72–91.
——and WILLIAMS, H. (eds.) (2007). *Early Medieval Mortuary Practices*. Volume 14 of *Anglo-Saxon Studies in Archaeology and History*. Oxford: Oxford University School of Archaeology.
SHEPHARD, J. (1979). 'The social identity of the individual in isolated barrows and barrow cemeteries in Anglo-Saxon England', in B. C. Burnham and J. Kingsbury (eds.), *Space, Hierarchy and Society: Interdisciplinary Studies in Social Area Analysis*. British Archaeological Reports International Series 59. Oxford: British Archaeological Reports, 47–79.
STOODLEY, N. (1999). *The Spindle and the Spear*. British Archaeological Reports British Series 288. Oxford: British Archaeological Reports.
——(2000). 'From the cradle to the grave: age organization and the early Anglo-Saxon burial rite'. *World Archaeology* 31(3): 456–72.
——(2002). 'Multiple burials, multiple meanings? Interpreting the early Anglo-Saxon multiple interment', in Lucy and Reynolds (eds.), *Burial in Early Medieval England and Wales*, 103–21.
——(2007). 'New perspectives on cemetery relocation in the seventh century AD: the example of Portway, Andover', in Semple and Williams (eds.), *Early Medieval Mortuary Practices*, 154–62.
STRUTH, P., and EAGLES, B. (1999). 'An Anglo-Saxon barrow cemetery in Greenwich Park', in P. Pattison, D. Field, and S. Ainsworth (eds.), *Patterns of the Past: Essays in Landscape Archaeology for Christopher Taylor*. Oxbow, Oxford, 37–52.
TIMBY, J. (1993). 'Sancton I Anglo-Saxon Cemetery. Excavations carried out between 1976 and 1980'. *Archaeological Journal* 150: 243–365.
TYLER, A., and MAJOR, H. (2005). *The Early Anglo-Saxon Cemetery and Later Saxon Settlement at Springfield Lyons, Essex*. East Anglian Archaeology 111. Chelmsford: Essex County Council.

WILLIAMS, H. (1997). 'Ancient landscapes and the dead: the reuse of prehistoric and Roman monuments as early Anglo-Saxon burial sites'. *Medieval Archaeology* 41: 1–31.

——(1999). 'Identities and cemeteries in Roman and early medieval archaeology', in. P. Baker, C. Forcey, S. Jundi, and R. Witcher (eds.), *TRAC 98 Proceedings of the Eighth Annual Theoretical Roman Archaeology Conference*. Oxford: Oxbow, 96–108.

——(2001). 'Death, memory and time: a consideration of mortuary practices at Sutton Hoo', in C. Humphrey and W. Ormrod (eds.), *Time in the Middle Ages*. Woodbridge: Boydell and Brewer, 35–71.

——(2002). '"The Remains of Pagan Saxondom"? Studying Anglo-Saxon cremation practices', in Lucy and Reynolds (eds.), *Burial in Early Medieval England and Wales*, 47–71.

——(2003). 'Material culture as memory: combs and cremation in early medieval Britain'. *Early Medieval Europe* 12(2): 89–128.

——(2004a). 'Assembling the dead', in A. Pantos and S. Semple (eds.), *Assembly Places and Practices in Medieval Europe*. Dublin: Four Courts Press, 109–34.

——(2004b). 'Death Warmed Up: the agency of bodies and bones in early Anglo-Saxon cremation rites'. *Journal of Material Culture* 9(3): 263–91.

——(2005a). 'Keeping the dead at arm's length: Memory, weaponry and early medieval mortuary technologies'. *Journal of Social Archaeology* 5(2): 253–75.

——(2005b). 'Animals, ashes and ancestors', in A. Pluskowski (ed.), *Just Skin and Bones? New Perspectives on Human-Animal Relations in the Historical Past*. British Archaeological Reports International Series 1410. Oxford: Archaeopress, 19–40.

——(2006). *Death and Memory in Early Medieval Britain*. Cambridge: Cambridge University Press.

——(2007a). 'Introduction: themes in the archaeology of early Medieval death and burial', in Semple and Williams (eds.), *Early Medieval Mortuary Practices*, 1–11.

——(2007b). 'The emotive force of early medieval mortuary practices'. *Archaeological Review from Cambridge* 22(1): 107–23.

——(2007c). 'Transforming body and soul: toilet implements in early Anglo-Saxon graves', in Semple and Williams (eds.), *Early Medieval Mortuary Practices*, 66–91.

——and Sayer, D. (2009). 'Halls of mirrors: death and identity in medieval archaeology', in Sayer and Williams (eds.), *Mortuary Practices and Social Identities*, 1–22.

CHAPTER 15

THE MID SAXON 'FINAL PHASE'

†MARTIN WELCH

INTRODUCTION

There is a continuum of burial practices between the late sixth century and the early eighth century with those described by Howard Williams for the early Saxon period in the previous contribution to this volume. Each burial records a transition from one existence to another, but with the possibility that this included a belief in a continued existence of the deceased within the grave deposit itself. The variability of funerary practices can be taken to represent expressions of social memories and identities. These invoke ancestors and assert claims to ownership over land, persons, and other resources. In all probability, burial was the responsibility of household and kin groups within a community, but was witnessed by the whole community, and additionally by neighbouring communities for more important individuals. That need not rule out special roles for persons with religious or magical powers (Old Norse *seiðr*) and other related skills (Dickinson 1993; Price 2002). More specifically, we can suggest that older women may have had the duty of preparing the corpse by washing and dressing it, combing the hair and so forth. Likewise it is conceivable that male or female heads of household in pre-Christian society exercised religious roles during the funeral process and presided over ceremonies before, during, and after the actual burial itself (Bartel 1982).

In the later fifth and sixth centuries, regional differences in costume fittings appear to be used to signal ethnic identities, but these are now replaced by dress fashions that are remarkably standardized across the Anglo-Saxon parts of England. Other significant changes also occur in this period. In particular, cremation goes out of fashion, disappearing entirely within the seventh century. Then, while the inhumation of a fully-dressed corpse continues on into the eighth century, it is increasingly accompanied by only the most basic items, such as a buckle representing a belt, or most commonly just a knife. Elaborate dress fittings, weaponry, and vessels become relatively rare over time, though they do not disappear entirely. Rather, the repertoire of objects included with burials changes between the sixth and early seventh centuries, and again around the middle of the seventh century, when new items such as lockable wooden chests and small metal workboxes make an appearance (Geake 1997; 1999). In adopting new fashions and modifying their burial practices in the last third of the sixth century, the Anglo-Saxons appear to be following the example of their Frankish Continental neighbours across the Channel and beyond the Rhine. We observe in east Kent the replacement of a female coat-based costume fastened by four brooches in two matched pair sets down the length of the coat (Walton Rogers 2007: 190–3, figs. 5.44–45) by a dress with a single showy jewelled disc brooch at the throat (Parfitt and Brugmann 1997; Brugmann 1999). Subsequently this new single-brooch fashion was to spread across much of England (Geake 1997: map 4).

As the seventh century also sees the conversion of the Anglo-Saxon kingdoms to Christianity, beginning with Augustine's arrival in Kent in 597 and ending with Sussex, Hampshire, and the Isle of Wight in the 670s and 680s, it has been tempting to describe its inhumations as Christian (Lethbridge 1931: 82–5; 1936: 27–9). This can be expressed in a more neutral fashion by assigning them to a Conversion Period (Geake 1997). Yet it is not until the eighth century that inhumations at cemeteries, other than those in monasteries, were routinely wrapped in shrouds rather than dressed in normal clothing (Blair 2005: 240). The other widely-adopted label for this period is the Final Phase. It seems that this was a term first proposed by E. T. Leeds (1936: 96–114) in a published lecture in which he described the range of items recovered from inhumations attributable to a fourth phase of burial in Kent. In earlier lectures he had labelled the first phase as Jutish, the second as Frankish, and the third as Kentish, this last being characterized by Salin Style II animal ornament on metalwork (ibid. 43–4 and 59). For his fourth phase he compared dress fittings from cemeteries across England as far north as Uncleby in Yorkshire, demonstrating that these shared a great deal in common with those from Kentish cemeteries. In his description of this final phase of furnished burial, he viewed it as a continuation of pagan practice as opposed to the creation of a new and specifically Christian burial practice.

Whether the terms Final Phase or Conversion Period should be assigned to the mid Saxon period, as implied in the present chapter heading, is open to question. By the 1960s, a simple division between the archaeologies of pagan or early Anglo-Saxon England and a Christian or late period, extending up to the Norman

Conquest and indeed beyond, no longer seemed adequate. With the development of ceramic studies and settlement archaeology between the late 1950s and 1970s, a tripartite division became the norm (Hurst 1976: 284–6 and Rahtz 1976: fig. 2.1). A mid Saxon period with notional dates of *c*.650–*c*.850 was defined using pottery forms and technology as a primary feature. In particular, Ipswich-type wares named after the excavated kiln sites in Ipswich itself were widespread across East Anglia, although more thinly distributed across the rest of England. We should note, however, that the dating of the earliest Ipswich ware pottery is now attributed to *c*.700 rather than *c*.650 (Blinkhorn forthcoming). This makes it questionable whether the mid Saxon period can really be pushed as early as *c*.600 as has been suggested (e.g. Geake 1997: 1).

Coinage, initially in gold, then in silver, and finally in a debased copper alloy, has also been linked to definitions of the mid Saxon period (e.g. Metcalf 1993). So-called *sceatta* coins minted in England from the later seventh century onwards represent the Anglo-Saxon adoption of an internationally recognized silver coinage to facilitate trade with the Franks and across northern Europe. These in turn were replaced by the flat silver pennies created in imitation of Charlemagne's coin reforms in the second half of the eighth century. So the presence of *sceattas*, *stycas*, or early pennies on a site will confirm a mid Saxon date for it. If we turn to the burials, however, coins are extremely rare in sixth-century graves and only gradually become more common as the seventh century progresses in England. The earliest coins are Continental imports, or occasionally local copies of such imports, but by the later seventh and early eighth centuries we find *sceattas* minted in southern England, for example at Finglesham, Kent, Grave 145 (Hawkes *et al.* 1966: 116; Hawkes and Grainger 2006: 103–5, fig. 2.120, pl. XVII E) and at Harford Farm, Norfolk, Grave 18 (Penn 2000: 75–6, fig. 86).

If, following Leeds, we are willing to restrict the Final Phase label to describe cemeteries founded around or after the middle of the seventh century (Hyslop 1963; Meaney and Hawkes 1970; Boddington 1990), by which date most Anglo-Saxon kingdoms were nominally Christian, then we can equate the Final Phase with the mid Saxon period. If instead we use the term Final Phase to define a broad period that followed the cessation of multiple brooch dress fashions and ornament in animal art of Salin Style I, and sees its replacement by dress and weapon fittings decorated in Salin Style II (Leeds' Kentish and Final phases combined), then the mid Saxon label seems much less appropriate. Hines (1984; 1999) attributed such a change to *c*.570, while Geake (1997) placed it somewhat later, dating it to *c*.580 in Kent and to *c*.600 for the rest of England. Pushing the beginning of the mid Saxon period to *c*.570 or 580, let alone *c*.600, and equating the early Saxon period with the previous Migration Period (as defined by Hines, borrowing from Scandinavian and German terminology) seems unreasonable, particularly as we have large numbers of cemeteries that span this transition. The present author prefers to emphasize the continuity of early Saxon furnished burial and use the term Final Phase to represent burial practices that have their origins towards the end of the sixth century and disappear early in the eighth century. Ideally, we require a new label to describe the burial practices centred on the seventh century, but for the moment no one can come up with a satisfactory alternative for Final Phase other than the Conversion Period, which is not entirely satisfactory either.

Princely and other elite burials between the late sixth and eighth centuries

Exceptionally furnished large-scale chamber graves or burials in chambers constructed in or beneath ships make their appearance in the archaeological record at the end of the sixth and the beginning of the seventh century. They are associated typically with ornament in Salin Style II, and thus fall within the broad period definition of the Final Phase. The barrow cemetery at Sutton Hoo in Suffolk with its possibly royal ship burial contained both cremations and inhumations (Carver 2005), the cremations being deposited typically in bronze vessels. There is a case for regarding the cremations in mound burials as the earliest phase of barrow construction here and noting the peripheral locations of the mounds containing inhumations. The latter include the two ship burials (Mounds 1 and 2), and a weaponed male burial accompanied by his horse under Mound 17. Further princely chamber graves at Asthall in Oxfordshire (cremation), Broomfield and Prittlewell in Essex, and Taplow in Buckinghamshire (inhumations), are also well known (Dickinson and Speake 1992; Hirst *et al.* 2004; Carver 2005: fig. 222; Fig. 15.1).

It is unlikely to be coincidental that Anglo-Saxon kingdoms emerge into the historical record around this time, and these burials have been interpreted as commemorating a ruling elite (e.g. Yorke 1990). Women are rare among these inhumations, and it is particularly unfortunate that the only high-status adult female burial at Sutton Hoo in Mound 14 had been so badly disturbed, probably in the nineteenth century, prior to its modern excavation in the 1980s. It would have been invaluable to have had sufficient evidence to reconstruct her original appearance and costume and compare her to such near-contemporary Frankish elite graves as the lady in St Denis sarcophagus 49 (James 1992: 248-50; Wieczorek *et al.* 1996: 936–9; Fleury and France-Lanord 1998: 109–10; 124–59).

Instead, these elite graves principally comprise men buried with the symbols of their social and political role as military leaders. The Sutton Hoo Mound 1 warrior can be characterized as equipped in the manner of a Roman general, or even perhaps an emperor (Filmer-Sankey 1996). His helmet is modelled ultimately on a fourth-century Roman cavalry parade helmet, his shield is similarly an oversized

Figure 15.1 Diagrammatic 3D reconstruction of Prittlewell burial (© Museum of London Archaeology Service)

decorated parade item, and the gold- and garnet-decorated shoulder clasps probably fastened a leather tunic and imitate the epaulettes of Roman body armour. He also possessed a ring mail shirt, while a showy solid gold belt buckle and the garnet and gold fittings to his sword and sword belt help to complete the picture. We can compare him to the ivory diptych portrait of the *magister militum* Stilicho, admittedly depicted without armour, dating to the beginning of the fifth century (Heather 1996: pl. 9). The decorated ornamental whetstone, with or without the stag and ring terminal, is likely to represent a symbol of authority, though whether it was a symbol of an overlord ruler (*brytenwealda*), a king, or was specific to the royal house of the person buried here cannot easily be resolved (Webster and Backhouse 1991: no. 17). The possibility that the Frankish boy 'prince' placed in a stone tomb in a mid-sixth-century mortuary chapel (later built over by Cologne Cathedral) was buried with a baton made of lathe-turned wood suggests that specific symbols of authority might be placed in royal or princely tombs (James 1992: 248; Wieczorek *et al.* 1996: 216; 438–47; 931–3). Another item from the Sutton Hoo ship burial claimed to be symbolic is the iron stand formerly identified as a royal standard. It is now re-interpreted as a tall portable lamp stand appropriate to the itinerant life of a seventh-century ruler, and a parallel exists from the near-contemporary Prittlewell princely chamber grave (Hirst *et al.* 2004).

Anthropological analysis of the *Beowulf* poem implies that kings and princes were expected to reward their followers with gold treasure, armour, and weapons, all of which are present in their own burials. The sons of noble warriors entered service around the age of six, were first awarded weapons and armour as teenagers, when they would prove themselves by undertaking challenges, and thereafter be rewarded at regular intervals for their loyal service. At a later stage of their careers they would marry and receive landed estates granted for a lifetime (Bazelmans 1999). The great halls of phase 4C at Cowderys Down in Hampshire may represent a residence associated with such a lifetime gift (Millett 1984; Welch 1992: 50–1). The entertainment of the warrior followers with feasts prepared using cauldrons suspended with a great chain from the beams of the great hall would be accompanied by alcohol consumption and the recitation of verse to the playing of a lyre. More intimate pleasures of the elite such as board games are also represented in their burials.

It has been pointed out that furnished burials in this period, of which princely burials are the most extreme examples, represent a deliberate and committed policy of taking valuable artefacts out of circulation by either burning them on a pyre, or by destroying them through burial (Crawford 2004: 97–8). In contrast to contemporary Frankish practice in northern France and elsewhere, grave robbing to recover such artefacts shortly after burial did not normally occur in England, and even in east Kent it was a minority practice (Härke 2000: 391–2, Table 5). This implies that the investment in furnished burial by rural communities was considered to be worthwhile, and that these communities produced sufficient surpluses to permit them to replace treasures and artefacts deposited with the dead.

The two gold foil crosses seemingly placed over the eyes of the man buried at Prittlewell imply that a military leader could accept Christian baptism and still be buried with this paraphernalia (Fig. 15.1). Less high-status male burials are also found with grave-goods containing specifically Christian symbols, such as the buckle decorated with a Christian fish symbol found with a male burial in a seventh-century cemetery near the Eccles Romano-British villa in Kent (Webster and Backhouse 1991: 25, fig. 7; Fig. 15.2). After the middle of the seventh century, however, kings and lesser members of royal families came to prefer burial in the side chapels (*porticus*) of monastic churches, or in cemeteries adjacent to such churches. In this they were following the example of Kentish rulers, starting with Æthelberht and his Frankish consort Bertha at a monastery just outside Canterbury (Gem 1997: 100–1, figs. 35–8, colour pl. 12; Welch 2007: 238–9). We tend to assume that such royal burials were

Figure 15.2 Eccles Grave 19 buckle, front and back views. (Photo: R. Wilkins, Institute of Archaeology, University of Oxford)

deposited in appropriate robes and accompanied by at least one vessel, as is the case with seventh-century burials in stone or plaster coffins under the church at St Denis near Paris (Fleury and France-Lanord 1989). In certain cases, however, the Anglo-Saxon royal dead may have been buried according to monastic conventions, as appropriate to their place of burial (Blair 2005: 229–30). Unfortunately we have no way of knowing, as their burials have not survived to be recorded in modern times.

There is one notable clerical furnished burial towards the end of the seventh century provided by the shrine of St Cuthbert, now housed in Durham Cathedral. Bishop Cuthbert had been buried in a priestly costume in 687 that almost certainly included a small garnet-set gold pendant cross. Subsequently exhumed in 698, his body was declared uncorrupted, leading to his immediate canonization, and was enshrined above ground in the monastic church at Lindisfarne. Near-contemporary sources make it clear that, when buried, he had been wearing a waxed shroud, a head cloth, priestly garments, and shoes, and had been accompanied by various other items including a chalice, ivory comb, scissors, a linen cloth, and paten. Only the outer garments were removed in 698 and replaced with fresh items, which probably explains why the gold pectoral cross remained undiscovered amongst his undergarments until his shrine was more thoroughly investigated in 1827 (Battiscombe 1956; Coatsworth 1988; Webster and Backhouse 1991: no. 98). The survival of much of the incised-decorated wooden coffin from the 698 shrine, together with some of the gifts added to the shrine over the centuries after 700, is extremely unusual in an English context. The translation of his shrine to the Norman cathedral of Durham in 1104 and the opening of the shrine by Henry VIII's commissioner in 1537 (Aird 1998) would normally have resulted in the loss of all such evidence. Fortunately, both the Normans and the Tudor commissioner failed in particular to observe the jewelled cross, which can be related to others recovered from furnished female graves in seventh-century cemeteries. The closest parallel is provided by the cross from a cemetery at Ixworth, Suffolk (Webster and Backhouse 1991: no. 11). Stylistically earlier is the cross setting for a Byzantine gold coin from Wilton, Norfolk, which had been eroded out of a coastal cliff. Its *cloisonné* garnet settings are related to, and contemporary with, the very fine gold jewellery from the Sutton Hoo Mound 1 ship burial (ibid. no. 12). Rather simpler and smaller gold pectoral crosses have been recorded from a seventh-century female costume set at Milton Regis, Kent (Fig. 15.3), and as the centrepiece of an elaborate jewelled gold necklet from the cemetery at Desborough, Northamptonshire (ibid. no. 13). Cuthbert's pectoral cross may well have been his own property, perhaps originally a gift from a devout admirer, and it was certainly of some age when buried with him. At least one ancient repair, and the use of small rectangular recut garnets set in pale gold, imply manufacture no later than the third quarter of the seventh century, and possibly a bit earlier.

Figure 15.3 Milton Regis gold cross pendant and other pendants. (Photo: R. Wilkins, Institute of Archaeology, University of Oxford)

The fashion for barrow burial did not end with the 'princely' graves, but rather seems to have been adopted by the landed nobility in the second half of the seventh century, continuing on into the early eighth century. Women are more visible amongst these later graves, wearing gold jewellery with linked pin sets as at Roundway Down near Avebury, or laid out on a wooden bed with an elaborate assemblage of grave finds as at Swallowcliffe Down near Salisbury (Shepherd 1979; Speake 1989; Blair 2005: 230, fig. 29), both in Wiltshire. Similarly dressed women were placed under barrows in the Peak District, again with dress pin sets, as at Cow Low, and with a gold pendant cross and other fittings at Winster Moor. The equivalent men were accompanied typically by weapon sets including shields and bronze bowls, as at Galley Hills near Banstead in Surrey, Lowbury Hill in Berkshire, and Ford near Salisbury in Wiltshire (Evison 1963). At two sites they possessed helmets as well. These occur at Benty Grange in the Peak District, and Wollaston in Northamptonshire (Bruce-Mitford and Luscombe 1974; Webster and Backhouse 1991: no. 46; Meadows 1997). The implication is that barrows provided valid alternatives to church burials within the Final Phase, and were indicators of social prestige (Burnell and James 1999). The emphasis placed on the Scandinavian and pagan overtones of the Sutton Hoo mounds by Carver (2005) may not apply to these isolated barrows. There is every reason to believe that the individuals buried in them in Wiltshire, Northamptonshire, and Derbyshire within the later seventh and early eighth centuries were baptized Christians (Blair 2005: 230).

The re-use of prehistoric barrows and the location of new Anglo-Saxon barrows in the landscape has attracted increased attention in recent years. There was a clear preference for re-using large imposing round barrows in locations that dominated routes, and isolated Anglo-Saxon primary barrows were similarly placed so that they would be visible to travellers, whether by land or water. The positioning of the Sutton Hoo barrow cemetery overlooking the River Deben is well known (Williams 2001), and similarly the Taplow barrow was clearly visible from the Thames (Webster 1992). The Wollaston barrow was very close to a Roman road, and would have been visible from the river as well (Meadows 1997). In a survey of Anglo-Saxon burials in the Avebury region of Wiltshire, Sarah Semple has emphasized their relationship to roads, and their political value in physically demonstrating hereditary claims of ownership in a period when this landscape was being disputed between the West Saxons and the Mercians (Semple 2003). The commandeering of older monuments would also symbolize both the reality and legitimacy of current landholders in the landscape. Indeed, barrows may well have functioned as landowners' charters in a pre-literate society, providing proof of the right to receive food rents and services from those who farmed the estates. A further use for former barrows from the later seventh century onwards was, on occasion, as a prominent location for public executions, as occurred for example on Mound 5 at Sutton Hoo (Carver 2005; Williams 2001: 67–70). The presence of victims buried around the gallows and thus now separated from communal cemeteries contrasts with pre-Christian treatment of criminals.

DATING BURIALS AND CEMETERIES

One of the less satisfactory aspects of the archaeology of this period has been our ability to date its burials correctly. On the few occasions when we can trace a linear development across a cemetery with a long period of use, it is possible to propose a relative sequence and phasing using horizontal stratigraphy (sometimes referred to as topochronology). This helps to confirm some assemblages as earlier than others. The phases 3–7 proposed at the Buckland cemetery near Dover (Evison 1987) represent the most successful application of this methodology, borrowed from the analysis of contemporary Continental cemeteries. The availability of artefact types such as buckle sets that can be matched in those Continental sites also means that it is easier to relate assemblages from Kentish cemeteries to Continental absolute-chronology schemes founded on coin-dated grave groups. Nevertheless, not all of Evison's attributions of graves to a particular phase have been accepted (e.g. Geake 1997: 76). Beyond Kent, archaeologists have typically been content to separate a broadly sixth-century phase (Migration Period) from a broadly seventh-century phase (Final Phase), as at Barrington (Malim and Hines 1998), Barton-on-Humber (Drinkall and Foreman 1998), and Lechlade (Boyle *et al* 1998).

Finer dating is possible for the more elaborate dress assemblages thanks to a small but important corpus of graves that also contain coins, as at Sibertswold, Kent, Grave 172 (Geake 1997: 9; Hawkes *et al.* 1966: 111–13, fig. 3; Meaney and Hawkes 1970: 47–8, pl. VI), particularly from the middle of the seventh century onwards. We are less confident now that we can utilize the devaluation of Continental gold coinage by the addition of silver during the first half of the seventh century to provide an indirect dating tool. This assumed that gold jewellery in southern England was normally manufactured from freshly melted-down imported coin, implying that gold–silver ratios of such jewellery could provide a *terminus post quem* for its production (Geake 1997: 10; Hawkes *et al.* 1966). While it does seem to be the case that gold jewellery in Kent became visibly paler over time within the seventh century, this does not provide a precise dating aid. Silver replaces gold around the middle of the century, as on the Crundale buckle (Webster and Backhouse 1991: no. 6), and copper alloy is substituted for gold to provide the cell walls of the last versions of the jewelled disc brooch (Meaney and Hawkes 1970: 39–42, pl. IV; Hawkes 1974: 254–5).

For those who have remained unconvinced by the chronologies proposed so far for the object types recovered from Final Phase graves, there is a project in progress that will provide more definitive answers. The availability of high-accuracy radiocarbon dating obtained from human bone with an organic content means that we are now able to date every burial sampled to a twenty-year or thirty-year period at one sigma (with a probability of 67% for dates that are ±10 or ±15). Doubling these figures to two sigma will give us a probability value of 95 per cent. The assemblages belonging to burials that can provide a radiocarbon date, and also others where human bone is not available, are then separately assessed using Correspondence Analysis. The results from the two methods are then matched using Bayesian statistical techniques. The end product should be a sequence of phases, each with spans of thirty years—roughly a human generation. These phases will take us from the sixth century to the end of furnished burial in the later seventh or early eighth century, and will provide a check on the dating attributions made by previous scholars. This ambitious project, funded by English Heritage, will enable us to follow the changes that take place within the Final Phase and to develop a much more refined analysis (Hines forthcoming).

Preliminary results appear to indicate that the established traditional sequence will be vindicated in broad outline, though we can expect to see some re-adjustments. We can also anticipate subtle changes taking place every generation, so that rather than worry about whether the Final Phase begins *c*.570 or *c*.600, we can accept that some changes occurred in the phase beginning *c*.570 and others *c*.600, and so on. Particularly interesting is the initial finding that women buried with 'classic' Final Phase dress fittings (dress pin(s), necklet of pendants and wire rings, workbox, chatelaine, etc.) seem to belong to a single generation centred on the third quarter of the seventh century. Of course, the final report of the project may yet produce some surprises, and it must be emphasized that the present author does not have privileged access to its data. Nevertheless, it is an exciting prospect that we will soon have a firmer foundation on which to discuss the burial practices of this period.

ARTEFACT TYPES IN ASSEMBLAGES BETWEEN C.570 AND C.650 AND AFTER 650

We can use those cemeteries in Kent that span the sixth and seventh centuries to follow the changes in dress fashion that take place over time. The adoption of the Frankish fashion for wearing a single jewelled disc brooch at the throat around 570 has already been mentioned. This leads to the more sophisticated plate brooches with *cloisonné* garnet and glass settings and then on to the elaborate composite jewelled brooches that appear to go out of fashion around the middle of the seventh century. Sometimes miniature additional brooch fittings are combined with a composite brooch such as the silver safety-pin *fibula* found in Grave 205 at Kingston Down (Faussett 1856: pl. I; Webster and Backhouse 1991: no. 32). Examples of similar safety-pin silver brooches occur at a number of sites distant from Kent, e.g. at Swallowcliffe Down in Wiltshire, and at Uncleby in Yorkshire (Geake 1997: fig. 4.13, map 20; 1999: fig. 6a). On one occasion we can show that a composite disc brooch was still in use at the very end of the seventh century. Admittedly the brooch was no longer being worn as a costume fitting in the grave, for it was located, perhaps hidden, in a bag placed under the head of a woman at Boss Hall near Ipswich. This burial was dated by coins (a Sigebert *solidus* and a B *sceat*) to some time after 690 (Webster and Backhouse 1991 no. 33; Crawford 2004: 95).

Dress pins start to occur more regularly in female dress assemblages as the seventh century progresses, though more commonly as single pins in Kent rather than in matched pairs linked by chains found outside Kent after *c*.650. Pendants become fashionable, starting with disc forms and including versions setting garnets, amethysts, or patterned glass. There are also necklets made up of silver-wire rings and single-coloured glass beads, occasional decorated glass beads, and in some cases imported amethyst beads. Chatelaine fittings are worn suspended from the waist, often consisting of linked iron bars accompanied by iron keys, and tools such as shears, while a lidded cylindrical copper-alloy box containing thread, cloth fragments, and pins features in one or more cases in each cemetery. These so-called workboxes seem likely to have functioned as amulet or reliquary cases. Wooden chests that have metal hinges and locks are another significant addition to the repertoire of inhumation grave goods in this period. Glass vessels, iron-bound buckets, and other wooden vessels are found in the better furnished graves.

In male graves, belt sets with triangular plates imitate Frankish forms and seem to be introduced in the late sixth century, and span the first half of the seventh century. Later that century, small buckles with rectangular plates become typical, and later still there are cast openwork forms, again influenced by Frankish fashions. Weapon burial occurs frequently in Kentish cemeteries, with spearheads being common finds, particularly in the first half and around the middle of the seventh century. Two-edged swords continue to be deposited in cemeteries such as Buckland up to the middle of the century (Evison 1987: text fig. 26), but single-edged *seax* weapons become acceptable substitutes, particularly in the later seventh century. Shields are also relatively numerous in the first half of the seventh, with continuation of the use of Group 3 convex-coned bosses and the Group 6 low-coned forms. The tall-cone versions that are introduced during the seventh century are relatively rare, but these do imply larger shields, and changes in fighting tactics. Imported wheel-thrown pottery features from the late sixth century onwards in Kent, but is very rare outside Kent. Bronze vessels of Frankish and Byzantine types appear to be status symbols imported through international trading networks, and an insular British version (the so-called Celtic hanging bowls) were clearly highly prized. Glass vessels also occur relatively frequently, both imports from the continent and forms that were probably manufactured in Kent.

The Kentish influence on the repertoire of finds recovered from the furnished graves in cemeteries founded around the middle of the seventh century, such as Chamberlains Barn in Bedfordshire (Hyslop 1963), or Winnall near Winchester (Meaney and Hawkes 1970), has long been noted. It is equally true of the seventh-century graves in a cemetery founded in the late fifth or early sixth century, as at Lechlade (Boyle *et al.* 1998). What is remarkable about the dress fittings in particular is the degree of uniformity found across Anglo-Saxon England, though there are a few hints at regional fashions, as with the small annular brooches with Style II bird heads that are found in Lincolnshire and Yorkshire. Helen Geake has emphasized, however, the Roman links in the dress fashions adopted across England, particularly the Byzantine parallels for combining linked pins with necklets made up of linked wire rings and beads (Geake 1997; 1999). She has seen the abandonment of traditional Germanic dress at the end of the Migration Period, and the adoption of Roman fashions in the Final Phase, as a political statement.

She argues that the Anglo-Saxons identified themselves as legitimate heirs by conquest to the Romans who had ruled Britain. Indeed, Bede, writing in the early eighth century, portrays the now Christian Anglo-Saxons as a divinely chosen people with the moral right to control the destiny of the native British. Geake believes that this is expressed in the material culture of the Anglo-Saxons. For example, the Sutton Hoo ship burial presents a warlord equipped to look as close to a Roman general or emperor as was possible (Filmer-Sankey 1996).

Returning to the regions outside Kent, we should note that the decline in weapon burial is much more marked, with fewer graves containing spears or single-edged seaxes, and with both two-edged swords and shield fittings very rare indeed. Lastly, while the repertoire of finds in the majority of graves in the later seventh century is limited to a few dress items and a domestic knife, there are on occasion much fuller assemblages that include additional items such as one or more glass vessels, wooden chests, and workboxes, marking out individuals who were given special treatment in death. Blair has suggested that in cemeteries used in the second half of the seventh century and the first two decades of the eighth century, around 45 per cent of burials were unaccompanied by visible finds, 25 per cent accompanied by just a knife, and the remaining 30 per cent by more than one object type (Blair 2005: 240). Within that 30 per cent, however, there would only be one or two elaborately furnished burials. Nevertheless he did recognize that in some cases up to 72 per cent of burials might contain finds assemblages, as at Harford Farm near Norwich (Penn 2000), whereas in others that proportion was as low as 10 per cent, as at Broomfield in Shropshire (Stanford 1995).

Other aspects of cemeteries in use during the Final Phase period in Kent are the existence of cemeteries largely consisting of barrows, and the range of graves enclosed by both penannular and annular ring-ditches, as well as other grave structures (Faussett 1856; Hogarth 1973; Struth and Eagles 1999). The inclusion of at least a few graves covered by mounds or enclosed by ring-ditches is a normal feature in many seventh-century burial grounds outside Kent. Again, although a majority of inhumations buried between the fifth and sixth centuries are aligned east-west with the head at the west end, whole cemeteries exist in which north-south orientation is the norm, and other cemeteries occur in which a variety of grave orientations ranging between east-west and north-south are normal into the early seventh century. A more regular east-west orientation, with graves tending to be grouped in neat rows, is a feature of the seventh to eighth centuries, and reflects the adoption of Continental practice within Frankish Gaul and beyond from the late fifth century onwards (Halsall 1995a: 9–13). This may be linked to closer relations with the Franks following conversion to Christianity, or even to the adoption of a specifically Christian organization of burials orientated to relate to the rising of the dead at the Last Judgement.

The 'Final Phase cemetery' phenomenon and a proposed 'Final Phase model'

Up to this point we have been looking at the Final Phase as a period that reflects changes in material culture and burial practice that took place across most of north-west Europe around the end of the sixth century. There were differences in the details with which these changes were manifested between Frankish Gaul and Anglo-Saxon England, but in broad terms we are looking at a similar phenomenon (Burnell and James 1999). So we seem to be considering social changes with an international dimension, though we should recognize that the dominance of gender-neutral grave finds noted by Halsall as typical of seventh-century Frankish burial in eastern France is not really matched in England, particularly in Kent where weapon burial continues with sub-adults (Halsall 1995b; Welch 2008).

The term 'Final Phase' is often used in a more specialized sense to refer to common features shared by cemeteries founded around the middle of the seventh century and abandoned no later than the early decades of the eighth century. Often these have been paired with an earlier cemetery which is the immediate precursor located within 100 to 500 metres, or even less. The characteristics of such burial grounds were summarized by Miranda Hyslop as part of her analysis of the pair of cemeteries revealed on Chamberlains Barn near Leighton Buzzard (Hyslop 1963: 190–1), and her list was confirmed by Sonia Hawkes in her discussion of the Winnall II cemetery near Winchester (Meaney and Hawkes 1970).

Andy Boddington questioned whether religious conversion was the primary factor behind the foundation of such cemeteries around the middle of the seventh century, and introduced the location of the associated settlements into the equation (Boddington 1990: 181, 194–6). As Boddington recognized, however, assumptions that cemeteries would normally be located on marginal agricultural land near the boundaries of territorial units (Bonney 1966; Goodier 1984) seem to be contradicted by the frequency with which cemeteries and settlements are located on adjacent sites, implying that the cemeteries are central within the territorial units, rather than marginal (Welch 1985). Settlements can shift when their infield areas lose their viability due to soil exhaustion, though the shift might be small scale or fairly major, possibly into another landscape zone. Settlement shift is a feature of the mid Saxon period and in the past has been referred to as a 'mid Saxon shuffle', but this term may make it appear to be a more uniform process than was actually the case. In a society that lived in timber buildings set in earthfast post-holes or trenches that were designed to last no more than a human generation, the obstacles to moving a settlement to meet economic, social, or political requirements were limited. Cemetery locations would move with their settlements, the old site being abandoned and a new one inaugurated. We should be careful to avoid imposing our modern ideas of the value of permanent settlement in one place as either desirable or necessary in this period (*pace* Rahtz 1976: 60 and the concept of 'failed' settlements).

Miranda Hyslop's point in the case of the two cemeteries at Chamberlains Barn was that they were so close together—about 80 yards apart (Hyslop 1963: 163)— that the shift from one cemetery to another would not have required or have been a result of a settlement relocation. Taken together with the regular orientation of graves in neat rows for Cemetery II, in contrast to Cemetery I (ibid. figs. 2 and 3), the absence of cremation, the relatively high proportion of graves with no visible finds or just a knife, the rarity of weapons, and the range of dress fittings present in the fuller grave assemblages, she argued that such a burial ground may have been founded at the insistence of the missionary priests who had converted its population. Its former cemetery was seen as polluted by pagan practices that were unacceptable to the Church. This thesis has been challenged, and it is commonplace to observe that the early Church seems uninterested in the burial of lay people unless they requested burial in or near a church, and to note that burial in a consecrated graveyard or churchyard did not become the norm before the development of parishes between the tenth and twelfth centuries (Boddington 1996; Thompson 2004). It has also been pointed out that overtly Christian artefacts such as small pendant crosses on necklets are relatively rare, but then we can equally observe that pagan iconography can appear on seventh-century artefacts. Examples are the triangular buckle from Finglesham, Kent, Grave 95 (Hawkes *et al.* 1965; Hawkes 1982; Webster and Backhouse 1991: 22, fig. 2; Hawkes and Grainger 2006), with its armed warrior figure in the first half of the century, or a gold pendant showing a man carrying two snakes from a mid-seventh-century necklet from the Riseley, Horton Kirby cemetery in west Kent (Hawkes 1982; Fig. 15.4). This brings to mind the curious fact that it was not until the reign in Kent of Æthelberht's grandson, Eorcenbert (640–64), that pagan worship was forbidden by royal decree (Bede *HE* III.8). The Church seems to take a stronger line with what it perceives as unacceptable pre-Christian practices as the seventh century progresses, and this may well have included some aspects of burial practices.

The evidence from the Apple Down cemetery in West Sussex (Down and Welch 1990) does seem to confirm that we should not assume that the attitude of missionary clergymen was static throughout the Final Phase, and that Hyslop may have had a valid point here. Interestingly, cremation was still being practised at Apple Down as late as the second half of the seventh century, evidenced by burnt or partially melted metalwork recovered from the ploughsoil, including small buckles typical of costume in the later seventh century (ibid. figs. 2.68, 2.71, 2.73; pl. 42B). There is some limited evidence for burial features associated with such late cremations, notably a small ring-ditch with a cremation pit at its centre, and two more cremation pits cut into its boundary ditch (ibid. 40, figs. 2.25, 2.61; pls. 18–19).

Figure 15.4 Riseley grave group pendants. (Photo: R. Wilkins, Institute of Archaeology, University of Oxford)

The contemporary inhumations would not have looked out of place elsewhere in England, however (ibid. fig. 2.46).

Significantly, Apple Down was located in a region that apparently was not subject to missionary activity until the 670s and 680s. It is worth noting that what is left of a small separate cemetery on the hilltop above the main burial ground contained no cremations and is organized in neat rows of east-west graves. The repertoire of grave finds is very limited in Cemetery 2, mostly consisting of knives, and a majority of graves here were unfurnished (ibid. 13–14, figs. 2.5–6, 2.50). So although the Apple Down community adopts the new dress fashions at the beginning of the Final Phase period, perhaps around the end of the sixth century, part of its community continues to cremate its dead until the whole community is converted nearly a century later. A new cemetery then seems to be founded at the top of the same hill on which the community had always buried its dead, presumably in the 680s, and the new location was unpolluted by cremation. It seems reasonable to argue that the destruction of the corpse by fire was unacceptable to a Church which anticipated the dead rising from their graves at the Last Judgement. The evidence suggests that we cannot ignore the probability that the missionary clergy started to intervene in burial practices by the middle of the seventh century, while accepting that furnished burial of both laity and clergy fully dressed was not an issue for the Church in this period.

Conclusions

The period covered by this review sees a variety of burial practices co-existing in different communities. The clergy and monks were being buried relatively simply in their robes or in shrouds in monastic cemeteries, or in the side chapels of churches in the case of their abbots and bishops. They used wooden coffins, in some cases marked by modest inscribed stones, or else enhanced with painted plaster, as was the case for the metropolitan bishops of Canterbury (Gem 1997: 100–1, fig. 38), as well as some stone sarcophagi. In this they followed Mediterranean Roman traditions. For the Anglo-Saxon political elite, a recently established norm was barrow burial accompanied by the symbols of power and of the lifestyle of the warrior caste. This applied equally whether the dead were cremated or inhumed, and whether or not specialized coffins such as ships, wood-lined chambers, or beds were used, usually following Scandinavian traditions and forms. Well before the end of the period, royalty had moved on from barrow deposition to adopt church burial, but a new landed nobility seems to have taken up barrow burial in the later seventh century, only abandoning it during the early eighth century.

Cremation was already going out of fashion during the sixth century and, where it survived, conversion to Christianity assured its disappearance. It is reasonable to conclude that cremation could never be acceptable to the Catholic Church. On the other hand, furnished inhumation continues into the early eighth century in the cemeteries of small rural farming communities. Even then the end of the Final Phase period, c.720, does not see the disappearance of all burial furnishings, for graves containing the occasional knife or glass vessel, etc. can be found in subsequent centuries. Nevertheless, grave furnishings marking status in this world and the next were no longer relevant to an afterlife where individuals will be judged by their actions in this world. Shroud burial took over in the new cemeteries, founded by rural communities in which to bury their own dead, during the remainder of the eighth century and beyond, because furnished burial had lost its rationale. There is no need to invoke supposed changes in inheritance laws, heavy taxation by power-hungry kings, or gifting to the Church, to explain the end of furnished burial. It probably ceased when people came to believe it was redundant.

Only a favoured few members of the laity could gain the privilege of being buried in a monastic or minster churchyard before the ninth century, and we believe that most people were buried in small unenclosed community cemeteries, which may have been blessed by a priest, but where it was still unusual for a priest to have administered the last rites, or to have presided over the burial itself. By contrast, sinners were deliberately separated when subject to capital punishment and buried at the site of execution. Nevertheless, the transition to shroud burials for the laity in subsequent cemeteries during the eighth century is still poorly understood. It deserves further exploration, utilizing the high-accuracy radiocarbon dating that is already beginning to provide us with independent dating evidence within the Final-Phase period itself. At the moment it is difficult to identify correctly, let alone date, such cemeteries unless the occasional distinctive artefact accompanies one or more burials.

REFERENCES

AIRD, W. M. (1998). *St Cuthbert and the Normans: the Church of Durham 1071–1153*. Woodbridge: Boydell.

BARTEL, R. (1982). 'A historical review of ethnographical and archaeological analyses of mortuary practice'. *Journal of Anthropological Archaeology* 1: 32–58.

BATTISCOMBE, C. F. (1956). *The Relics of St Cuthbert*. Oxford: Oxford University Press.

BAZELMANS, J. (1999). *By Weapons Made Worthy: Lords, Retainers and their Relationship in Beowulf*. Amsterdam: Amsterdam University Press.

BLAIR, J. (2005). *The Church in Anglo-Saxon Society*. Oxford: Oxford University Press.

BLINKHORN, P. W. (forthcoming). *The Ipswich Ware Project: Society, Ceramics and Trade in Middle-Saxon England*. London: Medieval Pottery Research Group.

BODDINGTON, A. (1990). 'Models of burial, settlement and worship: the Final Phase reviewed', in E. Southworth (ed.), *Anglo-Saxon Cemeteries: A Reappraisal*. Stroud: Sutton, 177–99.

——(1996). *Raunds Furnells: The Anglo-Saxon Church and Churchyard*. London: English Heritage.

BONNEY, D. (1966). 'Pagan Saxon burials and boundaries in Wiltshire'. *Wiltshire Archaeological Magazine* 61: 25–30.

BOYLE, A., JENNINGS, D., MILES, D., and PALMER, S. (1998). *The Anglo-Saxon Cemetery at Butler's Field, Lechlade, Gloucestershire*, Volume 1. Oxford: Oxford University Committee for Archaeology.

BRUCE-MITFORD, R., and LUSCOMBE, M. R. (1974). 'The Benty Grange Helmet and some other supposed Anglo-Saxon helmets', in R. L. S. Bruce-Mitford (ed.), *Aspects of Anglo-Saxon Archaeology*. London: British Museum Publications, 223–52.

BRUGMANN, B. (1999). 'The role of Continental artefact-types in sixth-century Kentish chronology', in Hines *et al.* (eds.), *The Pace of Change*, 37–64.

BURNELL, S., and JAMES, E. (1999). 'The archaeology of conversion on the continent in the sixth and seventh centuries: some observations and comparisons with Anglo-Saxon

England', in R. Gameson (ed.), *St Augustine and the Conversion of England*. Stroud: Sutton, 83–106.

CARVER, M. (2005). *Sutton Hoo: A Seventh-Century Princely Burial Ground and its Context*. London: British Museum Press.

COATSWORTH, E. (1988). 'The pectoral cross and portable altar from the tomb of St Cuthbert', in G. Bonner, D. Rollason, and C. Stancliffe (eds.), *St Cuthbert, his Cult and his Community to AD 1200*. Woodbridge: Boydell, 287–301.

CRAWFORD, S. (2004). 'Votive deposition, religion and the Anglo-Saxon furnished burial ritual'. *World Archaeology* 36: 87–102.

DICKINSON, T. M. (1993). 'An Anglo-Saxon "cunning woman" from Bidford-upon-Avon', in M. Carver (ed.), *In Search of Cult: Archaeological Investigations in Honour of Philip Rahtz*. Woodbridge: Boydell, 45–54.

——and SPEAKE, G. (1992). 'The seventh-century cremation burial at Asthall Barrow, Oxfordshire: a reassessment', in M. Carver (ed.), *The Age of Sutton Hoo*. Woodbridge: Boydell, 95–130.

DOWN, A., and WELCH, M. (1990). *Chichester Excavations VII: Apple Down and the Mardens*. Chichester: Chichester Civic Society.

DRINKALL, G., and FOREMAN, M. (1998). *The Anglo-Saxon Cemetery at Castledyke South, Barton-on-Humber*. Sheffield: Sheffield Academic Press.

EVISON, V. I. (1963). 'Sugar-loaf shield bosses'. *Antiquaries Journal* 63: 38–96.

——(1987). *Dover: Buckland Anglo-Saxon Cemetery*. Archaeological Report 3. London: Historic Buildings and Monuments Commission for England.

FAUSSETT, B. (1856). *Inventorium Sepulchrale*. Ed. C. R. Smith. London.

FILMER-SANKEY, W. (1996). 'The "Roman emperor" in the Sutton Hoo ship burial'. *Journal of the British Archaeological Association* 149: 1–9.

FLEURY, M. and FRANCE-LANORD, A. (1998). *Les Trésors mérovingiens de la basilique de Saint-Denis*. Woippy: Gérard Klopp S.A.

GEAKE, H. (1997). *The Use of Grave-Goods in Conversion-Period England, c.600–c.850*. British Archaeological Reports British Series 261. Oxford: Hedges.

——(1999). 'Invisible kingdoms: the use of grave-goods in seventh-century England'. *Anglo-Saxon Studies in Archaeology and History* 10: 203–15.

GEM, R. (1997). 'The Anglo-Saxon and Norman churches', in R. Gem (ed.), *The English Heritage Book of St Augustine's Abbey*. London: English Heritage, 90–122.

GOODIER, A. (1984). 'The formation of boundaries in Anglo-Saxon England: a statistical study'. *Medieval Archaeology* 28: 1–21.

HALSALL, G. (1995a). *Early Medieval Cemeteries: An Introduction to Burial Archaeology in the Post-Roman West*. Skelmorlie: Cruithne Press.

——(1995b). *Settlement and Social Organization: The Merovingian Region of Metz*. Cambridge: Cambridge University Press.

HÄRKE, H. G. H. (2000). 'The circulation of weapons in Anglo-Saxon society', in F. Theuws and J. L. Nelson (eds.), *Rituals of Power: From Late Antiquity to the Early Middle Ages*. Leiden: Brill, 377–92.

HAWKES, S. C. (1974). 'The Monkton brooch'. *Antiquaries Journal* 54: 245–56.

——(1982). 'The archaeology of conversion: cemeteries', in J. Campbell (ed.), *The Anglo-Saxons*. Oxford: Phaidon, 48–9.

——and GRAINGER, G. (2006). *The Anglo-Saxon Cemetery at Finglesham, Kent*. Oxford: Oxford University School of Archaeology.

——Davidson, H. R. E., and Hawkes, C. F. C. (1965). 'The Finglesham Man'. *Antiquity* 39: 17–32.

——Merrick, J. M. and Metcalf, D. M. (1966). 'X-ray fluorescent analysis of some Dark Age coins and jewellery'. *Archaeometry* 9: 98–138.

HE: Colgrave, B., and Mynors, R. A. B. (eds.) (1969). Bede, *Ecclesiastical History of the English People*. Oxford: Clarendon Press.

Heather, P. (1996). *The Goths*. Oxford: Blackwell.

Hines, J. (1984). *The Scandinavian Character of Anglian England in the Pre-Viking Period*. BAR British Series 124. Oxford: British Archaeological Reports.

——(1999). 'The sixth-century transition in Anglian England: an analysis of female graves from Cambridgeshire', in Hines et al. (eds.), *The Pace of Change*, 65–79.

——(ed.) (forthcoming). *Anglo-Saxon England c.570–720: The Chronological Basis*. London: Society for Medieval Archaeology Monograph Series.

——Høilund Nielsen, K., and Siegmund, F. (eds.) (1999). *The Pace of Change: Studies in Medieval Chronology*. Oxford: Oxbow.

Hirst, S., Nixon, T., Rowsome, P., and Wright, S. (2004). *The Prittlewell Prince: The Discovery of a Rich Anglo-Saxon Burial in Essex*. London: Museum of London Archaeology Service.

Hogarth, A. C. (1973). 'Structural features in Anglo-Saxon graves'. *Archaeological Journal* 130: 104–19.

Hurst, J. G. (1976). 'The pottery', in Wilson, *The Archaeology of Anglo-Saxon England*, 283–348.

Hyslop, M. (1963). 'Two Anglo-Saxon cemeteries at Chamberlains Barn, Leighton Buzzard, Bedfordshire'. *Archaeological Journal* 120: 161–200.

James, E. (1992). 'Royal burials among the Franks', in M. Carver (ed.), *The Age of Sutton Hoo*. Woodbridge: Boydell Press, 243–54.

Leeds, E. T. (1936). *Early Anglo-Saxon Art and Archaeology: being the Rhind lectures delivered in Edinburgh 1935*. Oxford: Clarendon Press.

Lethbridge, T. C. (1931). *Recent Excavations in Anglo-Saxon Cemeteries in Cambridgeshire and Suffolk: A Report*. Cambridge: Bowes and Bowes for the Cambridge Antiquarian Society.

——(1936). *A Cemetery at Shudy Camps, Cambridgeshire: Report of the Excavation of a Cemetery of the Christian Anglo-Saxon Period in 1933*. Cambridge: Bowes and Bowes for the Cambridge Antiquarian Society.

Malim, T., and Hines, J. (1998). *The Anglo-Saxon Cemetery at Edix Hill, Barrington A, Cambridgeshire*. CBA Research Report 112. York: Council for British Archaeology.

Meadows, I. (1997). 'The Pioneer Helmet'. *Northamptonshire Archaeology* 27: 191–3.

Meaney, A., and Hawkes, S. C. (1970). *Two Anglo-Saxon Cemeteries at Winnall, Winchester, Hampshire*. London: Society for Medieval Archaeology.

Metcalf, D. M. (1993). *Thrymsas and Sceattas in the Ashmolean Museum, Oxford*. London: Royal Numismatic Society and Ashmolean Museum.

Millett, M., with James, S. (1984). 'Excavations at Cowdery's Down, Basingstoke, Hampshire, 1978–81'. *Archaeological Journal* 140: 151–279.

Parfitt, K., and Brugmann, B. (1997). *The Anglo-Saxon Cemetery on Mill Hill, Deal, Kent*. London: Society for Medieval Archaeology.

PENN, K. (2000). *Excavations on the Norwich Southern Bypass, 1989–91*, Part 2: *The Anglo-Saxon Cemetery at Harford Farm, Caistor St Edmund, Norfolk*. East Anglian Archaeology 92. Dereham: Archaeology and environment division, Norfolk Museum Service.

PRICE, N. S. (2002). *The Viking Way: Religion and War in Late Iron Age Scandinavia*. Uppsala: Uppsala University, Department of Archaeology and History.

RAHTZ, P. (1976). 'Buildings and rural settlement', in Wilson, *The Archaeology of Anglo-Saxon England*, 49–98.

SEMPLE, S. (2003). 'Burials and political boundaries in the Avebury region, north Wiltshire'. *Anglo-Saxon Studies in Archaeology and History* 12: 72–91.

SHEPHERD, J. (1979). 'The social identity of the individual in isolated barrows and barrow cemeteries in Anglo-Saxon England', in B. C. Burnham and J. Kingsbury (eds.), *Space, Hierarchy and Society*. BAR International Series 59. Oxford: British Archaeological Reports, 49–79.

SPEAKE, G. (1989). *A Saxon Bed Burial on Swallowcliffe Down*. London: Historic Buildings and Monuments Commission.

STANFORD, S. C. (1995). 'A Cornovian farm and Saxon cemetery at Bromfield, Shropshire'. *Transactions of the Shropshire Archaeological and Historical Society* 70: 95–141.

STRUTH, P., and EAGLES, B. (1999). 'An Anglo-Saxon barrow cemetery in Greenwich Park', in P. Pattison, D. Field, and S. Ainsworth (eds.), *Patterns of the Past: Essays in Landscape Archaeology for Christopher Taylor*. Oxford: Oxbow, 37–52.

THOMPSON, V. (2004). *Dying and Death in Later Anglo-Saxon England*. Woodbridge: Boydell.

WALTON ROGERS, P. (2007). *Cloth and Clothing in Early Anglo-Saxon England AD 450–700*. York: Council for British Archaeology.

WEBSTER, L. (1992). 'Death's diplomacy: Sutton Hoo in the light of other male princely burials', in R. Farrell and C. Neuman de Vegvar (eds.), *Sutton Hoo: Fifty Years After*. Oxford, OH: American Early Medieval Studies, University of Miami, 75–81.

——and BACKHOUSE, J. (1991). *The Making of England: Anglo-Saxon Art and Culture AD 600–900*. London: British Museum Press.

WELCH, M. (1985). 'Rural settlement patterns in the Early and Middle Anglo-Saxon Periods'. *Landscape History* 7: 13–25.

——(1992). *The English Heritage Book of Anglo-Saxon England*. London: English Heritage.

——(2007). 'Anglo-Saxon Kent to AD 800', in J. Williams (ed.), *The Archaeology of Kent to AD800*. Woodbridge: Boydell, 187–248.

——(2008). 'Report on excavations of the Anglo-Saxon cemetery at Updown, Eastry, Kent'. *Anglo-Saxon Studies in Archaeology and History* 15: 1–146.

WIECZOREK, A., PÉRIN, P., VON WELCK, K., and MENGHIN, W. (1996). *Die Franken Wegbereiter Europas*. Mainz: P. Von Zabern.

WILLIAMS, H. (2001). 'Death, memory and time: a consideration of the mortuary processes at Sutton Hoo', in C. Humphrey and W. M. Ormrod (eds.), *Time in the Medieval World*. Woodbridge: York Medieval Press in association with Boydell Press, 35–71.

WILSON, D. M. (1976). *The Archaeology of Anglo-Saxon England*. London: Methuen.

YORKE, B. (1990). *Kings and Kingdoms of Early Anglo-Saxon England*. London: Seaby.

CHAPTER 16

LATE SAXON BURIAL PRACTICE

D. M. HADLEY

INTRODUCTION

Until very recently, research on the funerary practices of the later Anglo-Saxon period (*c*.750–1100) has been hampered by a paucity of extensively excavated and fully published cemeteries. Large-scale excavations of late Anglo-Saxon cemeteries—in which hundreds of burials were encountered—have been conducted at, for example, North Elmham (Norfolk) (Wade-Martins 1980), St Nicholas Shambles, London (White 1988), Raunds (Northamptonshire) (Boddington 1996), St Peter's, Barton-upon-Humber (Lincolnshire) (Rodwell and Rodwell 1982; Waldron 2007), Old Minster, Winchester (Kjølbye-Biddle 1975; 1992), Monkwearmouth and Jarrow (County Durham) (McNeil and Cramp 2005; Lowther 2005), and Cherry Hinton (Cambridgeshire) (Ferrante di Ruffano and Waldron n.d.). Not all of these cemeteries are, however, fully published, while several have only reached full publication in recent years. More typical of the funerary record of the period are small-scale and piecemeal excavations, often developer-funded undertakings in advance of construction, many of which are unpublished or only partially published (Parkhouse *et al.* 1983; Ayers 1985; Rodwell and Rodwell 1985; Pearson 1989; Scobie *et al.* 1991; Blair 1992; Potter and Andrews 1994; Phillips and Heywood 1995; Adams 1996; Hall and Whyman 1996; Garner 2001; Buckberry and Hadley 2001; Rudkin 2001; Wilmott forthcoming).

LATE SAXON BURIAL PRACTICE 289

Another difficulty is presented by the fact that many cemeteries of this period have been greatly disturbed by successive generations of burial, or by the encroachment of later buildings (Kjølbye-Biddle 1975; White 1988: 9–10; Phillips 1995: 75) (Fig. 16.1). Furthermore, it can be difficult to date burials that are largely unfurnished with grave goods, while stratigraphic evidence typically permits only a broad potential date range to be assigned (e.g. McNeil and Cramp 2005: 78–80; Lowther 2005: 173–5), as, often, does radiocarbon dating, which, in any case, is rarely undertaken on more than a few skeletons in a cemetery (e.g. Boddington 1996: 72; Adams 1996: 181). Unsurprisingly, perhaps, there have been few overviews of the funerary archaeology of the later Anglo-Saxon period (Hadley 2000; 2002; Thompson 2004: 117–26; Buckberry 2007). Pervading themes in discussions of the burials of this period are the influence of Christian beliefs on burial practices, and the chronology of the emergence of churchyard burial as the norm (Thompson 2002; 2004);

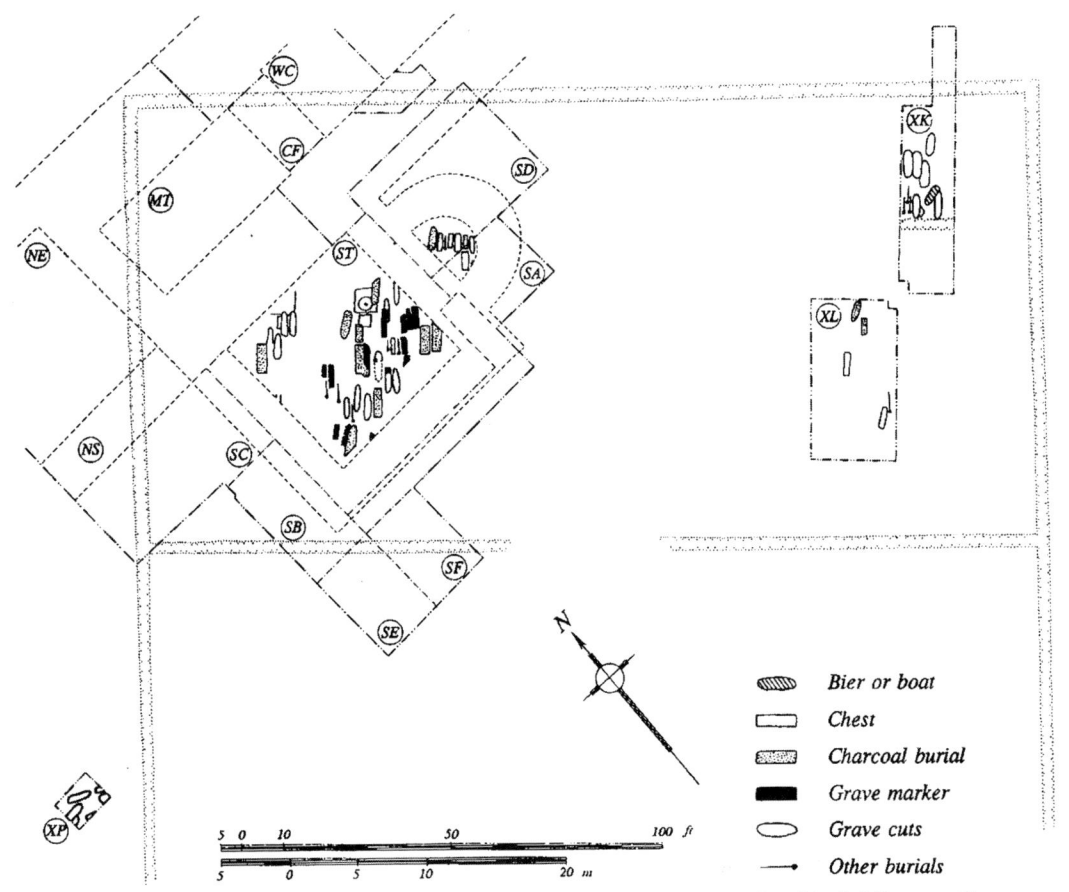

Figure 16.1 Plan of the late Anglo-Saxon cemetery excavated at York Minster. The excavations revealed that the eleventh-century cathedral had been built over part of a cemetery, which had a diverse array of burial types (see Fig. 16.3). (English Heritage)

only recently have the influences on burials of other factors, including life cycle, gender, social status, and health, been explored (Buckberry 2007; Hadley 2010; 2009b).

OUTLINE

Following the conversion of the pagan Anglo-Saxons, which gathered pace over the course of the seventh century (Blair 2005: 8–78), the writings of Bede and various saints' *Lives* suggest that burial near churches became an option for members of religious communities, kings, bishops, and probably also members of the aristocracy (Blair 2005: 228–45). However, the written record provides an imperfect picture of the emergence of churchyard burial as the norm.

First, we should not overlook the role of the church in western Britain, in providing places of Christian burial. Although the institutional workings of these churches are largely obscure, and few ecclesiastical structures can be securely dated to before the tenth century (Petts 2002), several cemeteries spanning the centuries from the Roman period into the seventh and eighth centuries or later have been excavated in western Britain, including those at Cannington, Somerset (Rahtz *et al.* 2000), Llandough, Glamorgan (Holbrook and Thomas 2005), and the Atlantic Trading Estate, Barry, Glamorgan (Petts 2002: 32–3).

Secondly, the written sources have nothing to say about those seventh- and early eighth-century cemeteries that were apparently not located near to churches but which include artefacts incorporating Christian symbolism. These have been taken as evidence that some, at least, of the first generations of Anglo-Saxon Christians continued to be interred in traditional cemeteries (Blair 2005: 230–3). Even if it is deemed dubious to infer the personal religious affiliations of individuals from burial furnishings, nonetheless, graves incorporating Christian symbols reveal the influence of Christianity on the material expression of status and identity in funerary contexts in the seventh and early eighth centuries (Geake 1999). Following the decline of the furnished burial rite, it has often been assumed that churchyard burial was swiftly adopted (Hyslop 1963: 191–2; Meaney and Hawkes 1970: 53–4; Faull 1976: 232), but it is becoming increasingly apparent that the burials of the mid eighth century and later are not all to be found beneath medieval and later churchyards, and not all were certainly associated with a church (Blair 1994: 72–3; Hadley 2000: 202–7, 209–12). Churchyard burial is now thought unlikely to have become universal until the tenth century (Blair 2005: 463–71; Hadley 2000: 209–15).

Later Anglo-Saxon cemeteries mainly consist of supine burials aligned west-east, and rows of graves can often be discerned (Rodwell and Rodwell 1982: 299;

Boddington 1996: 49–57; Gilmour and Stocker 1986: 90–1). Yet despite this regularity, the form of burial in these cemeteries was highly varied, and included diverse types of coffin, while graves were often lined with stones, crushed chalk, or charcoal (Kjølbye-Biddle 1992: 226–33; Hadley and Buckberry 2005: 132–8; Buckberry 2007: 117–21), and marked with stone covers and crosses (Bailey 1996: 77–104) (Figs. 16.1, 16.2, 16.3). Although grave goods had essentially ceased to be deposited by c.730 (Geake 1997: 134), later Anglo-Saxon graves still occasionally contain artefacts, the product of both clothed burial and deliberate deposition (Hadley and Buckberry 2005: 138–40; Hadley 2009b).

Aspects of churchyard burial are first documented in any detail from the late ninth century, when, for example, soul-scot, a burial tax paid to the appropriate minster church, is first mentioned (Tinti 2005: 32–5), while in tenth-century sources the definition of consecrated ground begins to be codified (Gittos 2002) and regulations concerning access to burial in consecrated ground emerge (Reynolds 1999: 103–4). The disappearance of the practice of depositing grave goods and the abandonment of earlier cemeteries, routinely deemed to be the burial grounds of pagans, has frequently been assigned to ecclesiastical intervention (reviewed in Boddington 1990: 179–82; Samson 1999: 120–5), yet there are surprisingly few references to burial practices in written sources before the end of the tenth century (Hadley and Buckberry 2005: 122–5). There is also little to suggest that the Church actively or consistently concerned itself with the form that the burials of the laity should take (Bullough 1983: 185–6). The diversity of burial rites confirms the silence of the written record, and it also belies assumptions periodically expressed that the Church ushered in an egalitarian burial rite (reviewed in Hadley 2004: 305–7). Indeed, if Christian burial is deemed to be a practice conducted according to specific ecclesiastical guidelines, then, as Victoria Thompson (2004: 32) has recently observed, 'there was no such thing as Christian burial'.

From the late tenth century, written sources have much to say about the liturgical arrangements for the dying and deceased, but the practical aspects of burial, including the digging of the grave, preparation of the body, and its committal to the ground, are scarcely mentioned, and it is possible that members of the laity, including friends and family, were involved (Thompson 2004: 57–88). In addition, guilds also had responsibility for arranging the burial of their deceased members (Rosser 1988; Thompson 2004: 112–15). Despite the silence of the written record, the regularity with which certain grave types occur, and evidence for plots and rows within churchyards, indicate that grave digging was a coordinated activity, undertaken, perhaps, by the Anglo-Saxon equivalent of a sexton (Gilmour and Stocker 1986: 91–2; Thompson 2004: 116–17). Nonetheless, the variety inherent in the form of graves within individual cemeteries is, perhaps, another indication of the involvement of the family and community in funerary preparations.

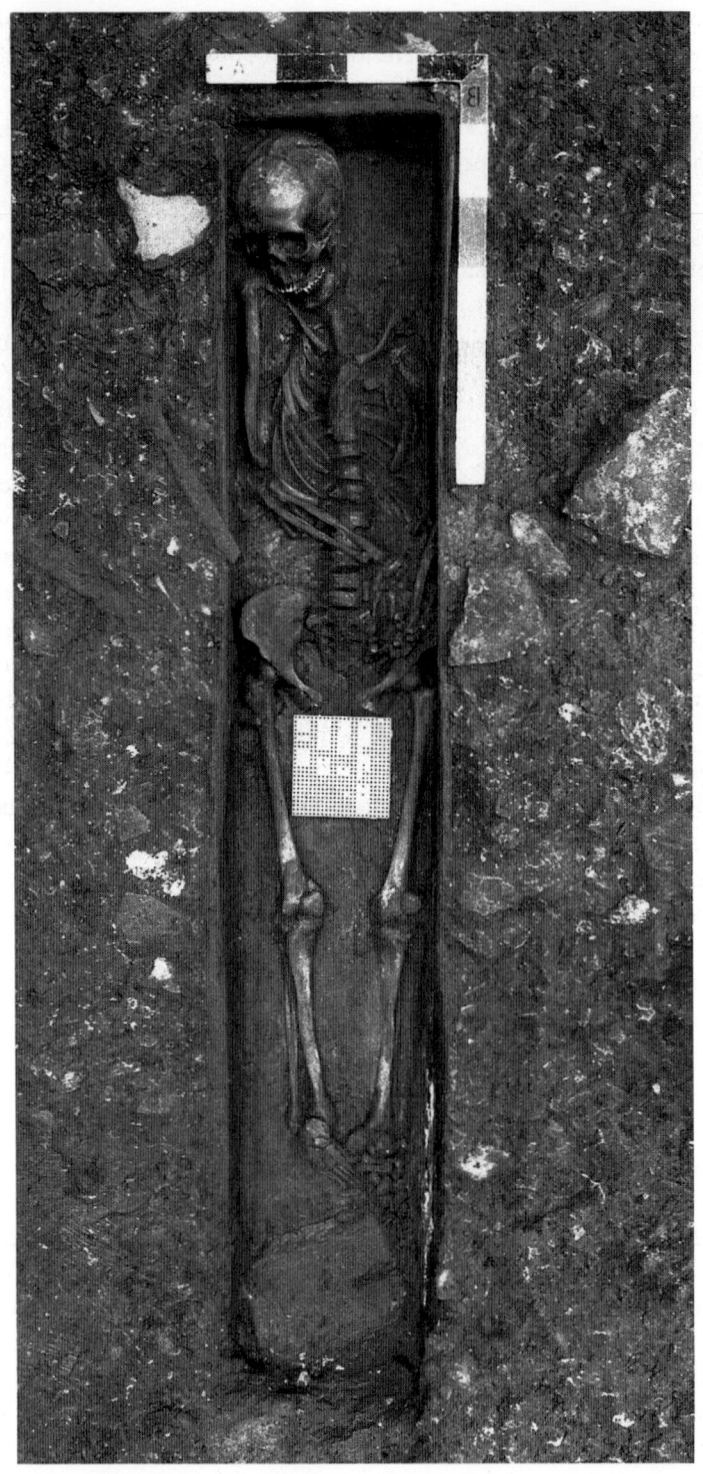

Figure 16.2 A coffined burial in a cemetery dated to the tenth/eleventh century at Swinegate in York, possibly associated with the 'lost' church of St Benet (York Archaeological Trust)

Figure 16.3 Late Anglo-Saxon burials from York Minster: (from left to right) interment beneath a stone grave cover, in a wooden coffin, and in stone-lined graves (English Heritage)

Mortuary variability

Cemeteries of the eighth to eleventh centuries exhibit a series of regularly-occurring variables (Hadley 2000: 207–8; Thompson 2004: 117–26; Buckberry 2007), which seem both to have been acceptable to the Church and to have had meaningful currency within later Anglo-Saxon society (Figs. 16.1, 16.3). However, only recently has there been any investigation of this variability, or of the factors that influenced which individuals were afforded particular funerary rites. It is becoming apparent that, in contrast to the influence of gender and stage in the life cycle on funerary provision in earlier Anglo-Saxon cemeteries (Stoodley 1999a, 1999b, and this volume), in the later Anglo-Saxon period the incidences of diverse forms of grave furniture do not normally or consistently correlate with either the age or sex of the deceased (Hadley and Buckberry 2005: 141–2; Buckberry 2007: 121–6; Hadley 2009a: 145–6). The marked contrast with practices in earlier centuries has been assigned to two factors: conversion to Christianity, and the emergence of more stable social hierarchies (Stoodley 1999a: 103–6; Hadley 2004: 303–5). Together these may have contributed to an increased tendency for similarity of display in the graves of all family members, largely irrespective of age or sex (Hadley 2009a). The clustering of distinctive grave types accorded to both adults and infants in some cemeteries is also suggestive of family strategies in funerary practices, as is the clustering of adult and infant burials around above-ground markers (Phillips 1995: 83–4; Boddington 1996: 50; Mays et al. 2007: 224–6; Hadley 2009a). Furthermore, the higher levels of both simultaneous and consecutive multiple burial than in the earlier Anglo-Saxon period (Stoodley 2002) may be another reflection of the influence of family status on funerary strategies, as successive burials referenced the graves of family members (Hadley 2010: 107).

The increased visibility of infant burials in later Anglo-Saxon cemeteries, in comparison with the cemeteries of earlier centuries (Crawford 1999: 78–9), may reflect both Christian concern for the souls of all family members and also the importance attached to infant burials as a marker of family status (Hadley 2010: 107). Infant burials are sometimes found in distinctive locations, such as within or clustered around the walls of a church (Boddington 1996: 54–5; Ferrante di Ruffano and Waldron n.d.; Wilmott forthcoming). It has been suggested that this latter practice had baptismal resonance, as the rainwater dripped onto the graves from the eaves of the church (Crawford 1993: 88; Boddington 1996: 55, 69), and this privileging of infant burials close to the fabric of the church may derive from limited access to baptism, which was an essential rite for entry into the Christian faithful (Crawford 1993; 2008). However, not all infants were buried in distinctive locations, and it is probable that family status, the sex of the child, and their position within the family were also factors determining burial location (Hadley 2010: 108).

Although the burials of males and females are rarely distinguished, a small number of adult male burials were provided with more elaborate coffins (Kipling and Scobie 1990; Kjølbye-Biddle 1995: 500–5), while disproportionate numbers of male burials sometimes occur in prominent locations, such as near to the church or churchyard monuments (Hadley 2004: 311–14; Buckberry 2007: 125–6; Hadley 2009a). Some of these males were probably members of religious communities (Kjølbye-Biddle 1992: 223, 228, 233; Heighway and Bryant 1999: 208–15), but the slight tendency to privilege male graves in prominent locations in seemingly ordinary local churchyards may reveal that male burials were sometimes employed by the laity to make claims to status (Boddington 1996: 54–6; Buckberry 2007: 125–6; Hadley 2009a). It has been argued, for example, that a number of adult males were interred at Raunds after a delay, during which time putrefaction had commenced and the skeletal remains had been dislocated in the coffin, and this has been interpreted as indicating the extended nature of funerary rituals for these men. This was probably as a result of their high status, since they were located close together in an area of the cemetery with the greatest numbers of coffins and grave markers (Boddington 1996: 36–7, 48; Williams 2006: 108). The burial of infants close to prominent male burials—such as the so-called 'founder's grave' beneath a decorated stone grave-cover at Raunds (Boddington 1996: 51)—may be further evidence for both the importance of male graves as markers of status and the influence of family ties on burial location (Hadley 2010).

Unlike in the later Middle Ages, when diseased individuals were often buried separately from the remainder of the Christian population (Gilchrist 1992: 114–16), in the later Anglo-Saxon period individuals who had experienced significant physical impairment or serious illness rarely seem to have received distinctive funerary provision (Hadley and Buckberry 2005: 146; Hadley 2010). This contrast may derive from the fact that although disease was routinely linked with sin in the later Middle Ages this association was not generally articulated in the later Anglo-Saxon period (Thompson 2004: 92–8). Although this equality of funerary provision for the physically impaired and sick does not prove that they were routinely well treated in life, or were able or permitted to aspire to all roles in society (Crawford 2010), nonetheless their treatment in death would have conveyed important messages about their social acceptance and prospects in the afterlife (Hadley 2010: 108–10).

There are, however, a few exceptions to this generalization, as physically impaired individuals have been found buried outside or at the limits of a small number of churchyards. For example, the single burial encountered beyond the limits of the churchyard at North Elmham, Norfolk, had a severely disorganized left tibial head, with bony outgrowths into the knee joint, possibly the result of a penetrating wound, and it was the only burial with the head placed to the east rather than the west (Wade-Martins 1980: 189). At Raunds there are three physically impaired adult males located at the limits of the churchyard: one exhibited signs of leprosy; one had a shortened left humerus and shortened and atrophied right femur, while destruction at the distal end of the right femur and a distorted patella suggested limited mobility of this limb; and the third individual had a shortened and atrophied left humerus, which subsequent osteoarthritis may have rendered largely immobile (Boddington 1996: 41–2, 69, 118, 120). Finally, in the tenth-century phases of the former monastic cemetery at Ailcy Hill, Ripon, Yorkshire, there were several unusual burials including that of a young adult male with a pronounced distortion of the lower vertebral column, possibly resulting from spinal tuberculosis, who was buried with the head to the east; this phase of the cemetery also included a multiple burial and other burials on diverse, non-normative alignments (Hall and Whyman 1996: 76–8, 98). This may suggest that, despite the general equality afforded physically impaired individuals, some communities had doubts about their place within the churchyard (Hadley 2010: 105–6), although it is debatable whether it was the lay community or members of the clergy who exerted such control over cemetery topography (Hadley 2004: 309–10).

A handful of other irregular burials, typically occurring in small numbers and in isolated contexts, are known from the later Anglo-Saxon centuries. For example, at the Cook Street and Upper Bugle Street sites in *Hamwic*, Southampton, Hampshire, several burials dating to between the eighth and tenth centuries were encountered cut into the fills of ditches, and the disarray of the limbs of at least one such burial suggests it may have been a hurried interment (Garner 2001: 172–5, 181). In Winchester, two burials, probably of ninth-century date, were excavated at a distance from the known churchyards in marshy ground at The Brooks (Scobie *et al.* 1991: 37, 39, 64–5), while at Yarnton, Oxfordshire, the ninth-century remains of at least seven individuals were found in pits and ditches within the settlement, separate from the adjacent cemetery (Hey 2004: 75, 163), and a number of burials have been recovered from the Saxon foreshore in London (Bradley and Gordon 1988; McCann and Orton 1989; Ayre and Wroe-Brown 1996: 20). These irregular burials are poorly understood, and may in some cases have been attempts to conceal illicit deaths, but it is possible that some represent community, or even ecclesiastical, decisions to exclude certain individuals from communal burial grounds.

It is important, however, to set ostensibly unusual rites in context. Prone burial in a ditch may betoken haste, but in the cemeteries of monasteries such as Wearmouth (McNeil and Cramp 2005: 85), Jarrow (Lowther 2005: 176), and Beckery chapel, Glastonbury (Somerset) (Rahtz and Hirst 1974: 33), prone burial may have been a mark of humility or penance (Hadley 2010: 105–6). Elsewhere, concentrations of irregular burials—multiple and careless interments, diverse burial alignments, and evidence for decapitation or bound limbs—have been interpreted as evidence of the burial grounds of those who had been judicially executed, as well as other individuals, such as excommunicates, adulterers, and those lacking legal surety, who, according to tenth-century legislation, were also excluded from burial in consecrated ground (Reynolds 1997; Hayman and Reynolds 2005; Buckberry and Hadley 2007). Such cemeteries were mainly located away from contemporary settlements, typically on hundred boundaries, but nonetheless often in visible locations, such as hilltops, near barrows, and adjacent to major routeways (Reynolds 1997: 348; Hayman and Reynolds 2005: 242–52). Although the exclusion of individuals from burial in consecrated ground is first documented in the tenth century, radiocarbon dating of skeletons from execution cemeteries such as Staines, Middlesex (Hayman and Reynolds 2005: 252), South Acre, Norfolk (Whymer 1996: 88), and Walkington Wold, Yorks. (Buckberry and Hadley 2007: 312) suggests that this practice commenced as early as the seventh century. This has been linked to the emergence of kingship and state administrative apparatus and to the growing influence of Christianity on the Anglo-Saxon kingdoms (Reynolds 1997: 37–9). In sum, there is considerable evidence from a wide array of sites to suggest that behaviour and status in life and anticipated fate in the afterlife informed burial provision in later Anglo-Saxon England.

THE INDIVIDUAL IN THE GRAVE

The Church does not appear to have offered specific guidelines about the form that burial should take (Bullough 1983: 185–6; Morris 1983: 50; Thompson 2002: 229–30). Nonetheless, churchmen did have a broadly articulated series of responses to the prospect of death, which provide an important context for understanding later Anglo-Saxon burials. In a recent survey, Victoria Thompson (2002; 2004: 122–6) revealed that later Anglo-Saxon ecclesiastical sources emphasize fear of unconfessed and sudden death, concern with the subsequent fate of the soul, and fear of the grave as a place where the body would decay and be subject to the ravages of worms, and she has suggested that the latter fears may have prompted the increasingly enclosed nature of later Anglo-Saxon graves, including the use of coffins and various types of grave lining. Such responses were perhaps also encouraged by the contemporary belief that the bodies of the most holy, that is saints, were identifiable by their incorruptibility (Thompson 2002: 235–8). It has also been suggested that ecclesiastical influences on burial can be identified in the use of coffins with locks (Phillips 1995: 83–4; Hall and Whyman 1996: 99–110; Fig. 16.4), which may reflect the literary and visual association with death of St Peter, who was symbolised by keys (Thompson 2004: 125–6, 129–31). Furthermore, the presence of charcoal in later Anglo-Saxon burials is widely regarded as reflecting ecclesiastical emphasis on the importance of humility and penance. It has been variously suggested that charcoal may have been linked with the 'sackcloth and ashes' of the monastic rites for burial (Daniell 1997: 158–9), or with the purifying penitential ashes of the Ash Wednesday ceremonies (Thompson 2004: 118–22), while the perceived indestructible qualities of charcoal may have symbolized eternity (Kjølbye-Biddle 1992: 231). The use of charcoal, and other materials such as sand and chalk, has also been identified as a means of preparing a dry grave, which would have evoked associations with cleanliness and purity (Holloway 2010).

Although ecclesiastical attitudes to death and dying may have informed the construction of the grave, such attitudes are unlikely to have been evenly disseminated, as the high degree of variability between cemeteries suggests. The capacity of individuals and families to respond to these attitudes must also have varied, and it is, perhaps, not surprising that the churchyards of major minsters and cathedrals have produced the greatest diversity of burial provision, reflecting their role in providing places of burial for the elite (Kjølbye-Biddle 1992: 226–33; Phillips 1995) (Fig. 16.1). Indeed, evidence for plating of coffin nails and fittings suggests that even if coffin use was informed by concerns to protect the corpse, it also provided an opportunity for social display (McNeil and Cramp 2005: 80–1). Moreover, excavations at Winchester Old Minster have revealed that many of the graves containing charcoal also contain coffins with elaborate iron fittings,

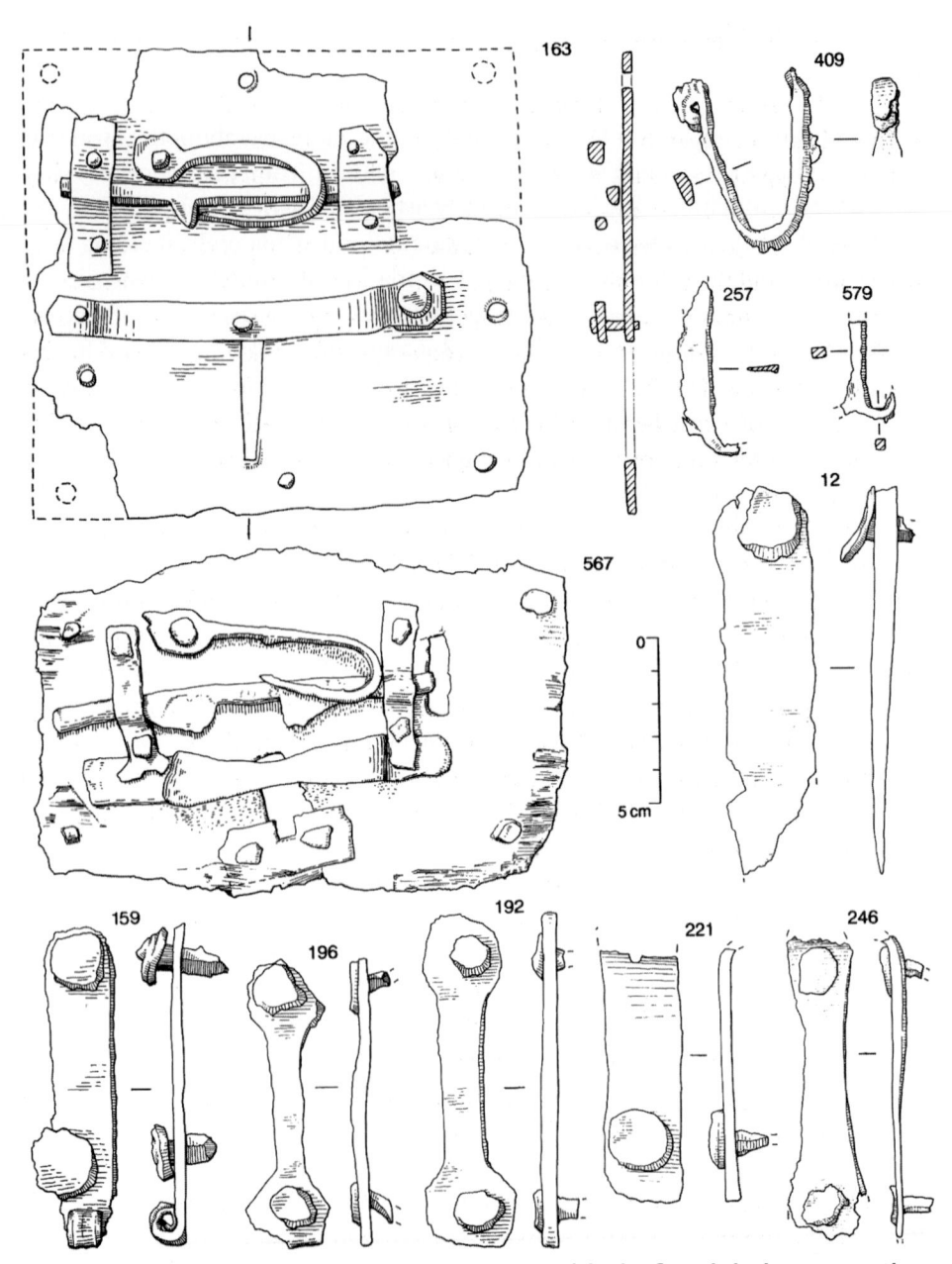

Figure 16.4 Iron hinge straps, stapled hasps, and locks found during excavations at Ailcy Hill, Ripon, Yorkshire., which suggest burial in wooden chests, possibly re-used items of domestic furniture.

reinforcing the high-status associations of such grave variations (Kjølbye-Biddle 1992: 231).

Seventh-century furnished burials are often regarded as the last generation ('Final Phase') of pagan burials (Boddington 1990), yet there is little in the written record to suggest that grave goods were regarded as un-Christian (Samson 1999: 120–5; Thompson 2004: 107–12). Indeed, many seventh-century burials include artefacts with Christian associations, including cross-shaped pendants and decorative mounts, and the gold foil crosses excavated recently in a richly furnished burial chamber at Prittlewell, Essex (Geake 1999; Blair 2005: 230–3; see Fig. 15.1). Furthermore, Cuthbert, bishop of Lindisfarne (d. 687), was apparently buried in his priestly robes and his shoes 'in readiness to meet Christ', and he was provided with an array of items befitting his status, while other artefacts and rich textiles were added to the tomb over the following centuries (Coatsworth 1989; Muthesius 1989; Welch, this volume).

St Cuthbert's tomb is a remarkable survival, but many cemeteries have produced limited evidence to suggest that clothed burial was a widespread phenomenon. Artefacts from graves indicative of clothed burial include belt-buckles, strap-ends, ear-rings, finger-rings, hair pins, beads, and items which would often have been suspended from belts, such as knives and combs (Hadley and Buckberry 2005: 140; Hadley 2009c). Gold thread from graves at York Minster (Phillips 1995: 91), Winchester Old Minster (Biddle 1990: 469, 480) and Repton (Derbyshire) (Biddle and Kjølbye-Biddle 2001: 85–6), suggests burial in elaborate costume, and serves as a tantalizing reminder of the loss of clothing in perishable materials, such as linen, silk, and wool (Thompson 2004: 35; Hadley 2009b). Provision for the afterlife is routinely regarded as a pagan phenomenon, yet in a Christian context clothed burial and the interment of the accoutrements of office were arguably a means of ensuring status after death, and of providing the deceased with what they might need in the afterlife to ease the passage to salvation (Samson 1999: 125–32). It has, accordingly, recently been argued that the readiness with which archaeologists distinguish grave goods from the attributes of Christian burial, including evidence for clothed burial and also coffins, shrouds, and shroud pins, may have created a false dichotomy that does not reflect Anglo-Saxon perceptions (Thompson 2004: 108).

Preparations for burial must have involved specific decisions about what to place on the body and in the grave. Elisabeth van Houts (1999: 93–120) has discussed the ways in which memories of individuals and events were often associated with specific artefacts by chroniclers and will-makers, describing such items as 'pegs for memory' (van Houts 1999: 109–10), and this should alert us to the likelihood that grave finds such as finger rings may have held specific mnemonic associations with the deceased (Hadley 2009b). The emphasis placed on the bestowal of textiles in later Anglo-Saxon wills may also provide a context for the faint evidence for organic items in graves, including what appear to be pillows placed under skulls at

Barton-upon-Humber (Waldron 2007: 26–7) and Raunds (Boddington 1996: 37) (Fig. 16.5). Surviving early medieval textiles often carry inscriptions and portraits (van Houts 1999: 102–6), and it is entirely possible that funerary garments would have conveyed information about the status of the deceased, through the quality and appearance of the fabric, and may also have incorporated commemorative images.

Some of the items placed in graves may have had amuletic or apotropaic qualities. For example, it has been suggested that white quartz pebbles may have symbolised purity or served as 'lucky charms' (Daniell 1997: 165; Hill 1997: 172–3; Holbrook and Thomas 2005: 37), while the practice may have been informed by a statement from the Book of Revelation (2: 17) that 'To him that overcometh ... I will give a white stone, and in the stone a new name written, which no man knoweth save that he receiveth it', serving to reinforce the protective and spiritual dimensions of the stones placed on and around the corpse. The presence of stones in the mouth or over the eyes has occasionally been noted (White 1988: 24; Boddington 1996: 42; Buckberry and Hadley 2001: 15–16), and this may have been influenced by recognition of the eyes and the mouth as conduits of sin, among the

Figure 16.5 Organic remains preserved in waterlogged conditions at Barton–upon–Humber, Lincs., including traces of a grass-filled pillow in the coffin of this grave (Warwick Rodwell)

parts of body blessed by a priest on the death bed (Daniell 1997: 165; Thompson 2004: 76–82).

Environments conducive to good organic preservation, such as those encountered at Barton-upon-Humber (Rodwell and Rodwell 1982: 312) and the Guildhall site in London (Bateman 1997: 117), have occasionally revealed the presence of rods of hazel or willow in graves. These have been variously interpreted as symbolic of pilgrim staffs or of the Resurrection (Daniell 1997: 167–8), since it has been observed that hazel and willow are both trees that 'if coppiced regularly, become effectively eternal' (Bateman 1997: 119). Attention has also been drawn to the fact that the wood used for these rods had recognised curative properties (Gilchrist 2008: 126–8). Coins also occasionally occur in graves. While some may have been residual, or the product of casual loss, coins placed in the hand, on the chest or head, or deposited beneath the skull, were certainly deliberate depositions (Blunt and Pagan 1975: 18–28; Kipling and Scobie 1990; Phillips 1995: 90–1; Hadley 2009b). It is possible that this was a provision for the afterlife: this is not a documented Anglo-Saxon custom, but such practices were certainly still being condemned in the later Middle Ages (Daniell 1997: 150). Alternately, it has recently been suggested that coins were ritual deposits, recognized for their amuletic qualities deriving from the Christian imagery they incorporate and their circular form, widely recognized for its magical properties (Gilchrist 2008: 133–5; Hadley 2009b).

Graves were undoubtedly focal points for individual commemoration. This is implied by the referencing of earlier graves in the creation of later burials (Boddington 1996: 50) and the evidence for above-ground markers, which prompted the viewer to remember and pray for the deceased, especially, but not only, in cases where individuals were depicted or named. A series of simple stones inscribed with personal names dating to the seventh to ninth centuries survive from York (Lang 1991: 60–7), Whitby, Yorkshire (Lang 2001: 141–56), and Wearmouth and Jarrow (Cramp 1984: 110–13, 123–4), and they were probably intended to commemorate members of religious communities, but this practice had clearly been extended to the laity by the later Anglo-Saxon period (Bailey 1996: 77–104). For example, an eleventh-century grave cover from Stratfield Mortimer, Berkshire, records that 'Ægelward son of Kypping was buried in this grave' (Tweddle *et al.* 1995: 336).

Commemorative inscriptions were also sometimes placed within graves. Examples include a lead plaque from Kirkdale, Yorkshire, pre-dating the mid tenth century, which appears to incorporate the word *ban-cest* (meaning 'bone-chest' or 'coffin') (Watts *et al.* 1997: 52–75), a tenth-century lead cross recovered during excavations at the Roman baths in Bath, Somerset, carrying an inscription recording the death of one Eadgyfu 'a sister of the community' (Cunliffe 1979: 90, 138–9), and a lead cross from a grave at Cumberworth, Lincolnshire, incised with a Latin text dating to *c*.1000, which seems to invoke the powers of Christ on behalf of the deceased: 'through this sign of Christ...the small foulness..., he who by the power of the cross redeemed the world from death, shattered hell or threw open heaven' (Sawyer 1999: 156–7). An unique stone (c. 20 cm x 16.5 cm) from a grave at Newent, Gloucestershire, bears the names of the Evangelists and also that of a certain Edred, presumably the deceased, and it depicts the Crucifixion and what has been interpreted as a Last Judgement scene (Zarnecki 1953). It appears to have been a skeuomorph of a book, possibly provided for use in the afterlife (Thompson 2004: 90), and it prompts us to consider whether the placing of actual books in graves was a contemporary practice that is lost to the archaeological record.

The placing of stones on and around the face may be further evidence that the grave was the focus of mourners' concern about the individual. This practice has been described as 'protective' and indicative of 'compassion and care' (Boddington 1996: 48, 69), and its frequency may reflect a widespread Christian belief in 'the vulnerability of the corpse and its equal share, with the soul, in the struggle for salvation' (Thompson 2004: 118). Study of later Anglo-Saxon homilies suggests that the corpse was perceived as retaining a degree of consciousness (Thompson 2004: 50–2), and this may explain such specific and personalized actions in the preparation of the grave as the packing of stones around the left knee of one individual at Raunds; swelling of the tibia suggests the limb could not be straightened (Boddington 1996: 42). As Howard Williams (2006: 111) has recently observed, this treatment perhaps indicates that for the mourners 'the cadaver still held elements of the deceased's personhood bound into its flesh and bones'. Moreover, the provision of stones may have reflected a belief that the resurrected body would be healed (Williams 2006: 111). Indeed, such ideas may have been informed by views such as that expressed by Ælfric of Eynsham, who wrote that at the resurrection 'even if he were formerly lame when alive, yet his limbs will be all healthy for him' (Pope 1967: 432; Thompson 2004: 123–4).

The fate of human remains in graves also seems to have been of considerable concern. When graves were cut into by subsequent burials, the earlier remains are often stacked in an orderly fashion around the edges of the grave, and this seems to be a specifically later Anglo-Saxon phenomenon, much less common at either earlier or later dates (Hadley 2001: 43; Cherryson 2007: 132). This practice may be another reflection of contemporary concerns about the fate of the body in the grave and the implications for the soul of bodily decay. The exhumation of human remains and their re-interment elsewhere is also a relatively common feature of later Anglo-Saxon cemeteries. For example, at Barton-upon-Humber at least twenty-five graves were carefully emptied to make way for the foundations of the first phase of the church (Rodwell and Rodwell 1982: 294), while a grave elsewhere in the churchyard, which was marked by post-holes at each corner, perhaps for some sort of shrine or canopy, had been emptied of its interment before a rubble foundation base for a cross or other funerary monument was laid (Rodwell and Rodwell 1982: 300). At Addingham, Yorkshire, there are at least nine graves in the western part of the excavated cemetery containing no interments, while graves further east contained the remains of more than one adult individual (Adams 1996:

161–7, 181–4), perhaps suggesting a desire to acquire burial close to some unknown focal point, which, if it were not to be achieved at the moment of interment, was acquired later by moving the remains of the deceased (Fig. 16.6). The movement of dead bodies was hardly unfamiliar in the later Anglo-Saxon centuries when the translation of saints' remains, in particular from northern England to the newly

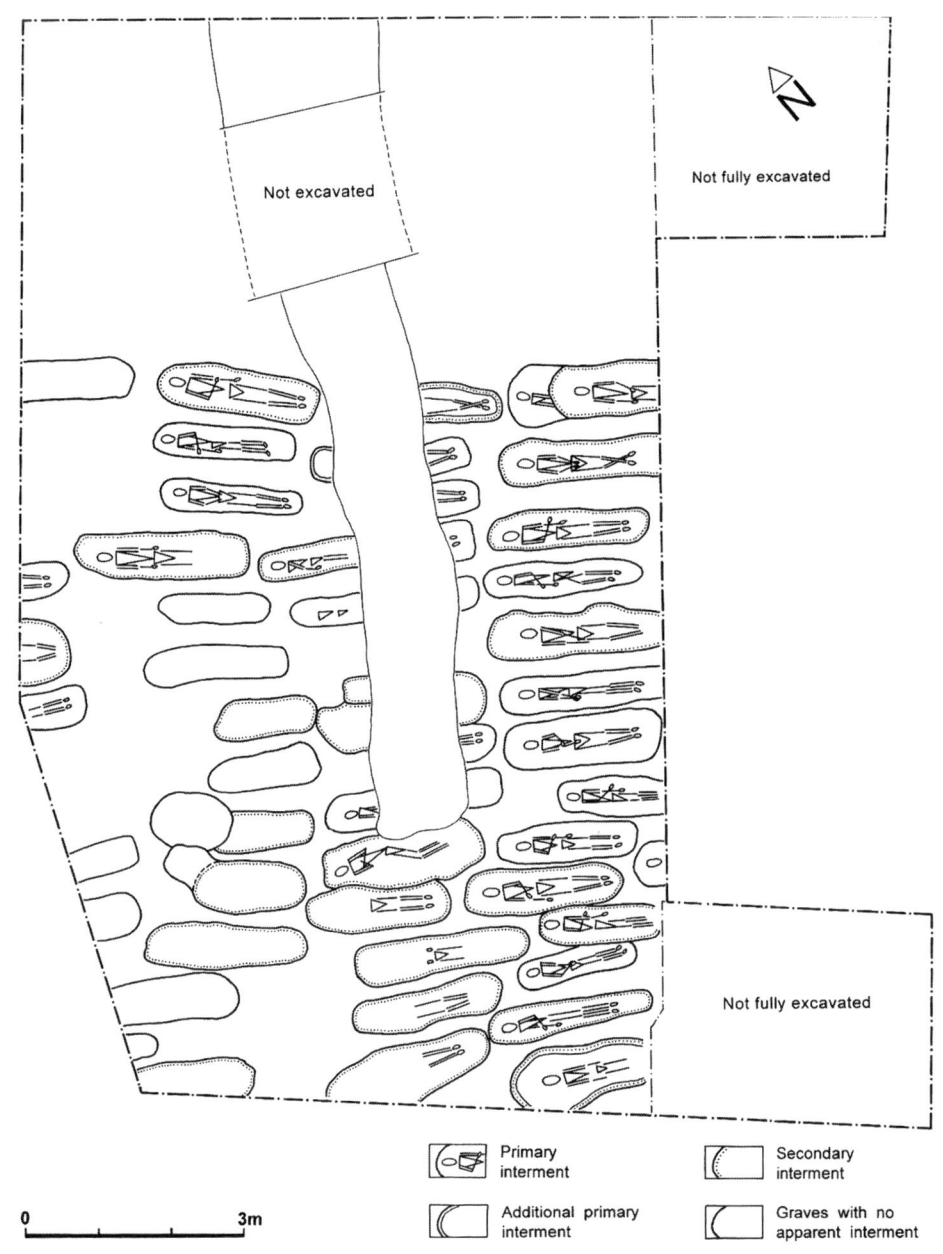

Figure 16.6 Plan of a cemetery dated to the eighth to tenth centuries excavated at Addingham, Yorks. (Adams 1996)

(re-)founded monasteries of southern England and East Anglia, was a common occurrence (Rollason 1986), and this may have served to legitimize the movement of human remains on a more localized level.

Settlements in the landscape

It was once thought that early Anglo-Saxon cemeteries were located at a distance from contemporary settlement, and that the close relationship of places of settlement and burial was a later Anglo-Saxon development. However, archaeological evidence increasingly suggests that cemeteries and settlements had long been closely related (Boddington 1990; Blair 2005: 59). Nonetheless, there was considerable relocation of both cemeteries and settlements, and the cemeteries of the later Anglo-Saxon period are generally remote from those of an earlier date (Blair 2005: 236–7). However, this does not necessarily reveal that there was a distinct break in funerary geography, since cemeteries came into and went out of use throughout the Anglo-Saxon period, and for a variety of reasons (Hadley 2000: 205–7; Hadley and Buckberry 2005: 128; Hadley 2007).

Undoubtedly, conversion to Christianity and the eventual adoption of new burial places associated with churches posed problems for individuals and communities with respect to the fate of their ancestors in the afterlife, and also for the capacity of those ancestors to continue to stake claims to territory (Blair 2005: 58). One, albeit not common, solution may have been to construct churches near to barrows which had been used in earlier generations for burial, as appears to have been the case at Taplow, Buckinghamshire (Stocker et al. 1995; Semple 1998: 120). It is also possible that some churches were built in pre-existing cemeteries. This is, however, difficult to prove, since the gradual abandonment of grave goods had largely been completed before many of the earliest churchyards came into existence (Blair 2005: 236–7), and only limited evidence for the presence of furnished early Anglo-Saxon burials has been recovered from churchyards (Morris 1983: 59–62; Blair 2005: 236–7). Nonetheless, the first known phases of many churches disturbed earlier burials (Rodwell and Rodwell 1982: 294; Geake 1997: 135), suggesting that churches were sometimes located in pre-existing burial grounds, and the continuing use of such sites for burial may have been another strategy for maintaining connections with a community's ancestors and its traditions.

Many later Anglo-Saxon cemeteries were located on, or adjacent to, land previously, and apparently relatively recently, used for domestic occupation. Only rarely, however, is the extent of the occupation pre-dating later Anglo-Saxon cemeteries extensively excavated, or its nature fully understood, and it is generally difficult to determine the interlude between occupation and burial (Hadley 2007: 194–5).

The abandonment of part or all of later Anglo-Saxon cemeteries is also relatively common. This was partly the result of the contraction of the cemeteries of minster churches, perhaps following a change of status in the church, or after other churches in the vicinity acquired the rights of burial (Blair 1994: 72–3), and the increased tendency for enclosing consecrated ground (Gittos 2002: 202–4). Other cemeteries were obliterated by the construction of castles in the decades around 1100 (Creighton 2005: 116–23). Evidence for burials beyond the confines of churchyards may also indicate the presence of one or more small, short-lived cemeteries located within and among rural settlements, not all necessarily associated with a church (Hadley 2007: 197–9). Such burial foci may have been successive, but it is possible that they relate to different social groups or families within communities, in a practice that has also been observed on the Continent (Theuws 1999; Zadora-Rio 2003). The final transition to churchyard burial, probably during the ninth and tenth centuries in many places, has been described as marking 'an important phase in the conceptualization of the parish community' (Zadora-Rio 2003: 9). The Church undoubtedly encouraged this process, although the frequent juxtaposition of local churches and manorial complexes suggests that there was also seigneurial influence (Hadley 2007: 199).

Given the financial, spiritual, and emotional investment made in graves, the growing evidence for abandoned and disturbed later Anglo-Saxon cemeteries is striking. Evidently, alongside the emphasis placed in recent studies on the importance of social memory in the context of funerary display (Williams 2006), we need to recognize that the abandonment, and perhaps even strategic 'forgetting', of the dead was also a dimension of early medieval burial rites. The not infrequent evidence for re-use of funerary monuments is a related phenomenon: for example, at York Minster some grave slabs were re-cut to make head and foot stones for later graves (Lang 1991: 67–70), while many tenth-century monuments were incorporated into the tenth- or eleventh-century phases of churches (Everson and Stocker 1999: 111, 152). Nonetheless, the dead were not necessarily abandoned lightly or without a struggle. This is suggested by the archaeological evidence for the careful exhumation of bodies prior to the building of churches and castles (Rodwell and Rodwell 1982: 294; Miles 1986; Hadley 2007: 199–200). Moreover, although recycled funerary monuments were sometimes used as rubble in church-building campaigns, elsewhere they were set with the decorative scheme still visible, suggesting an on-going commemorative role for the monument.

Conclusion

Archaeologists of the early Anglo-Saxon centuries have long since demonstrated the potential of incorporating burial evidence into our histories of early medieval society, and have, for example, elucidated the ways in which social, ethnic, and gendered identities were both reflected in, and constructed through, mortuary ritual. Only recently, however, have the cemeteries of the later Anglo-Saxon period been afforded the same level of scrutiny. While discussion of ecclesiastical influences predominates, some studies have begun to elucidate the ways in which burial reflected and constituted social status, and articulated concerns about the needs of the family in the present and anticipation of the future in the afterlife.

Acknowledgements

I am grateful to Sally Crawford for feedback on a draft version of this chapter. I would also like to thank Warwick Rodwell, English Heritage, Maney Publishers, and York Archaeological Trust for permission to reproduce photographs and plans.

References

ADAMS, M. (1996). 'Excavation of a pre-Conquest cemetery at Addingham, West Yorkshire'. *Medieval Archaeology* 40: 151–91.
AYERS, B. (1985). *Excavations Within the North-East Bailey of Norwich Castle*. East Anglian Archaeology 28. Gressenhall: East Anglian Archaeology.
AYRE, J., and WROE-BROWN, R. (1996). 'Æthelred's Hythe to Queenhithe: the origin of a London dock'. *Medieval Life* 5: 14–25.
BAILEY, R. N. (1996). *England's Earliest Sculptors*. Toronto: Pontifical Institute of Medieval Studies.
BATEMAN, N. (1997). 'The early 11th to mid 12th-century graveyard at Guildhall, City of London', in G. de Boe and F. Verhaeghe (eds.), *Death and Burial in Medieval Europe*. Zellik, Belgium: Instituut voor het Archeologisch Patrimonium, 115–20.
BIDDLE, M. (1990). *Object and Economy in Medieval Winchester*, Volume 2. Oxford: Clarendon Press.
BLAIR, J. (1992). 'The origins of the Minster Church at Shipton under Wychwood: human burials from Prebendal House'. *Wychwood's History* 7: 4–9.
——(1994). *Anglo-Saxon Oxfordshire*. Stroud: Sutton.
——(2005). *The Church in Anglo-Saxon England*. Oxford: Oxford University Press.
BLUNT, C. E., and PAGAN, H. E. (1975). 'Three tenth-century hoards: Bath (1755), Kintbury (1761), Threadneedle Street (before 1924)'. *British Numismatic Journal* 45: 19–32.
BODDINGTON, A. (1990). 'Models of burial, settlement and worship: the final phase reviewed', in E. Southworth (ed.), *Anglo-Saxon Cemeteries: A Reappraisal*. Stroud: Sutton, 177–99.
——(1996). *Raunds Furnells: The Anglo-Saxon Church and Churchyard*. London: English Heritage.

BRADLEY, R., and GORDON, K. (1988). 'Human skulls from the River Thames, their dating and significance'. *Antiquity* 62: 503–9.

BUCKBERRY, J. L. (2007). 'On sacred ground: social identity and churchyard burial in Lincolnshire and Yorkshire, c.700–1100', in Semple and Williams (eds.), *Early Medieval Mortuary Practices*, 117–29.

——and HADLEY, D. M. (2001). 'Fieldwork at Chapel Lane, Fillingham'. *Lincolnshire History and Archaeology* 36: 11–18.

————(2007). 'An Anglo-Saxon execution cemetery at Walkington Wold, Yorkshire'. *Oxford Journal of Archaeology* 26(3): 309–29.

BULLOUGH, D. (1983). 'Burial, community and belief in the early medieval West', in P. Wormald (ed.), *Ideal and Reality in Frankish and Anglo-Saxon Society*. Oxford: Blackwell, 177–201.

CHERRYSON, A. K. (2007). 'Disturbing the dead: urbanisation, the Church and the post-burial treatment of human remains in early medieval Wessex, c.600–1100 AD', in Semple and Williams (eds.), *Early Medieval Mortuary Practices*, 130–42.

COATSWORTH, E. (1989). 'The pectoral cross and portable altar from the tomb of St Cuthbert', in G. Bonner, D. Rollason, and C. Stanicliffe (eds.), *St Cuthbert, his Cult and his Community*. Boydell: Woodbridge, 287–301.

CRAMP, R. (1984). *Corpus of Anglo-Saxon Stone Sculpture*, Volume 1: *County Durham and Northumberland*. Oxford: Oxford University Press.

CRAWFORD, S. (1993). 'Children, death and the afterlife', *Anglo-Saxon Studies in Archaeology and History* 6: 81–91.

——(1999). *Childhood in Anglo-Saxon England*. Stroud: Sutton.

——(2008). 'Special burials, special buildings? An Anglo-Saxon perspective on the interpretation of infant burials in association with rural settlement structures', in K. Bacvarov (ed.), *Babies Reborn: Infant/Child Burials in Pre- and Protohistory*. British Archaeological Research Reports International Series 1832. Oxford: Archaeopress, 197–204.

—— (2010). 'Differentiation in the later Anglo-Saxon burial ritual on the basis of mental or physical impairment: a documentary perspective', in J. L. Buckberry and A. K. Cherryson (eds.), *Later Anglo-Saxon Burial, c.650 to 1100AD*. Oxford: Oxbow, 91–100.

CREIGHTON, O. H. (2005). *Castles and Landscapes: Power, Community and Fortification in Medieval England*. London: Equinox.

CUNLIFFE, B. (1979). *Excavations in Bath 1950–1975*. Bath: Committee for Rescue Archaeology in Avon, Gloucestershire and Somerset.

DANIELL, C. (1997). *Death and Burial in Medieval England, 1066–1550*. Routledge: London.

EVERSON, P., and STOCKER, D. (1999). *Corpus of Anglo-Saxon Stone Sculpture*, Volume 5: *Lincolnshire*. Oxford: Oxford University Press.

FAULL, M. (1976). 'The location and relationship of the Sancton Anglo-Saxon cemeteries'. *Antiquaries Journal* 56: 227–33.

FERRANTE DI RUFFANO, L., and WALDRON, T. (n.d.). 'The skeletal analysis of an Anglo-Saxon population from Cherry Hinton'. Unpublished report on behalf of Archaeological Solutions Ltd.

GARNER, M. F. (2001). 'A middle Saxon cemetery at Cook Street, Southampton (SOU823)'. *Proceedings of the Hampshire Field Club and Archaeological Society* 56: 170–91.

GEAKE, H. (1997). *The Use of Grave-Goods in Conversion-Period England, c.600–c.850*. British Archaeological Reports British Series 261. Oxford: Hedges.

——(1999). 'Invisible Kingdoms: the use of grave-goods in seventh-century England', in T. Dickinson and D. Griffiths (eds.), *The Making of Kingdoms.* Anglo-Saxon Studies in Archaeology and History 12. Oxford: Oxford University School of Archaeology, 203–15.
GILCHRIST, R. (1992). 'Christian bodies and souls: the archaeology of life and death in later medieval hospitals', in S. Bassett (ed.), *Death in Towns: Urban Responses to the Dying and the Dead.* Leicester: Leicester University Press, 101–18.
——(2008). 'Magic for the dead? The archaeology of magic in later medieval burials'. *Medieval Archaeology* 52: 119–59.
GILMOUR, B. J. J., and STOCKER, D. A. (1986). *St Mark's Church and Cemetery.* The Archaeology of Lincoln 13 (1). London: Council for British Archaeology.
GITTOS, H. (2002). 'Creating the sacred: Anglo-Saxon rites for consecrating cemeteries', in Lucy and Reynolds (eds.), *Burial in Early Medieval England and Wales,* 195–208.
HADLEY, D. M. (2000). 'Burial practices in the Northern Danelaw, c.650–1100'. *Northern History* 36: 199–216.
——(2001). *Death in Medieval England: An Archaeology.* Stroud: Tempus.
——(2002). 'Burial practices in Northern England in the later Anglo-Saxon period', in Lucy and Reynolds (eds.), *Burial in Early Medieval England and Wales,* 209–28.
——(2004). 'Gender and burial practices in England, c.650–900', in L. Brubaker and J. M. H. Smith (eds.), *Gender in the Early Medieval World: East and West, 300–900.* Cambridge: Cambridge University Press, 301–23.
——(2007). 'The garden gives up its secret: the developing relationship between rural settlements and cemeteries c. 800–1100', in Semple and Williams (eds.), *Early Medieval Mortuary Practices,* 194–203.
——(2009a). 'Engendering the grave in later Anglo-Saxon England', in G. McCafferty, S. Terendy, and M. Smekal (eds.), *Proceedings of the 2004 Chacmool Conference.* Calgary: University of Calgary Press, 145–54.
——(2009b). 'Burial, belief and identity in later Anglo-Saxon England', in R. Gilchrist and A. Reynolds (eds.), *Fifty Years of Medieval Archaeology.* Society for Medieval Archaeology Monograph 30. London: Society for Medieval Archaeology, 465–88.
——(2010). 'Burying the socially and physically distinctive in later Anglo-Saxon England', in J. L. Buckberry and A. K. Cherryson (eds.), *Later Anglo-Saxon Burial, c.650 to 1100AD.* Oxford: Oxbow, 101–13.
——and BUCKBERRY, J. L. (2005). 'Caring for the dead in later Anglo-Saxon England', in F. Tinti (ed.), *Pastoral Care in Late Anglo-Saxon England.* Woodbridge: Boydell, 121–47.
HALL, R. A., and WHYMAN, M. (1996). 'Settlement and monasticism at Ripon, North Yorkshire, from the 7th to 11th centuries A.D.'. *Medieval Archaeology* 40: 62–150.
HAYMAN, G., and REYNOLDS, A. (2005). 'A Saxon and Saxon-Norman execution cemetery at 42–54 London Road, Staines'. *Archaeological Journal* 162: 215–55.
HEIGHWAY, C., and BRYANT, R. (1999). *The Golden Minster: The Anglo-Saxon Minster and Later Medieval Priory of St Oswald at Gloucester.* CBA Research Report 117. York: Council for British Archaeology.
HEY, G. (2004). *Yarnton: Saxon and Medieval Settlement and Landscape.* Thames Valley Landscapes Monograph 20. Oxford: Oxford Archaeological Unit.
HILL, P. (1997). *Whithorn and St Ninian: The Excavation of a Monastic Town.* Stroud: Sutton.
HOLBROOK, N., and THOMAS, A. (2005). 'An early-medieval monastic cemetery at Llandough, Glamorgan: excavations in 1994'. *Medieval Archaeology* 49: 1–92.

HOLLOWAY, J. (2010). 'Material symbolism and death: charcoal burial in later Anglo-Saxon England', in J. L. Buckberry and A. K. Cherryson (eds.), *Later Anglo-Saxon Burial, c.650 to 1100AD*. Oxford: Oxbow, 81–90.

HYSLOP, M. (1963). 'Two Anglo-Saxon cemeteries at Chamberlains Barn, Leighton Buzzard, Bedfordshire'. *Archaeological Journal* 110: 161–200.

KIPLING, R., and SCOBIE, G. (1990). 'Staple Gardens 1989'. *Winchester Museums Service Newsletter* 6: 8–9.

KJØLBYE-BIDDLE, B. (1975). 'A Cathedral Cemetery: problems in excavation and interpretation'. *World Archaeology* 7: 87–108.

——(1992). 'The disposal of the Winchester dead over 2000 years', in S. Bassett (ed.), *Death in Towns: Urban Responses to the Dying and the Dead*. Leicester: Leicester University Press, 210–47.

——(1995). 'Iron-bound coffins and coffin-fittings from the pre-Norman cemetery', in Phillips and Heywood (eds.), *Excavations at York Minster*, Volume 1, 489–521.

LANG, J. T. (1991). *Corpus of Anglo-Saxon Stone Sculpture*, Volume 3: *York and Eastern Yorkshire*. Oxford: Oxford University Press.

——(2001). *Corpus of Anglo-Saxon Stone Sculpture*, Volume 6: *Northern Yorkshire*. Oxford: Oxford University Press.

LOWTHER, P. (2005). 'The Jarrow pre-Norman burial ground', in R. Cramp (ed.), *Wearmouth and Jarrow Monastic Sites*, Volume 1. Swindon: English Heritage, 173–86.

LUCY, S. and REYNOLDS, A. (eds.) (2002). *Burial in Early Medieval England and Wales*. Society for Medieval Archaeology Monograph 17. London: Society for Medieval Archaeology.

MAYS, S., HARDING, C., and HEIGHWAY, C. (2007). *Wharram: A Study of Settlement on the Yorkshire Wolds*, Volume 11: *The Churchyard*. York: University of York.

MCCANN, B., and ORTON, F. (1989). 'The Fleet Valley Project'. *London Archaeology* 6: 102–5.

MCNEIL, S., and CRAMP, R. (2005). 'The Wearmouth Anglo-Saxon Cemetery', in R. Cramp (ed.), *Wearmouth and Jarrow Monastic Sites*, Volume 1. Swindon: English Heritage, 77–90.

MEANEY, A. L., and HAWKES, S. C. (1970). *Two Anglo-Saxon Cemeteries at Winnall, Winchester, Hampshire*. Society for Medieval Archaeology Monograph 4. London: Society for Medieval Archaeology.

MILES, T. J. (1986). 'The excavation of a Saxon cemetery and part of the Norman castle at North Walk, Barnstaple'. *Proceedings of the Devon Archaeological Society* 44: 59–84.

MORRIS, R. K. (1983). *The Church in British Archaeology*. CBA Research Report 47. London: Council for British Archaeology.

MUTHESIUS, A. (1989). 'Silks and saints: the rider and peacock silks from the relics of St Cuthbert', in G. Bonner, D. Rollason, and C. Stanicliffe (eds.), *St Cuthbert, his Cult and his Community*. Woodbridge: Boydell, 343–66.

PARKHOUSE, J., ROSEFF, R., and SHORT, J. (1993). 'A late Saxon cemetery at Milton Keynes village'. *Records of Buckinghamshire* 38: 199–221.

PEARSON, N. (1989). 'Swinegate excavation'. *York Archaeological Trust Interim Report* 14 (4): 2–9.

PETTS, D. (2002). 'Cemeteries and boundaries in western Britain', in Lucy and Reynolds (eds.), *Burial in Early Medieval England and Wales*, 24–46.

PHILLIPS, D. (1995). 'The pre-Norman cemetery', in Phillips and Heywood (eds.), *Excavations at York Minster*, Volume 1, 75–92.

——and HEYWOOD, B. (eds.) (1995). *Excavations at York Minster*, Volume 1: *From Roman Fortress to Norman Cathedral*. London: HMSO.

POPE, J. C. (ed.) (1967). *Homilies of Ælfric, A Supplementary Series*, Volume 1. Early English Text Society 259. Oxford: Oxford University Press.

POTTER, T. W., and ANDREWS, R. D. (1994). 'Excavation and survey at St Patrick's Chapel and St Peter's Church, Heysham, Lancs'. *Antiquaries Journal* 74: 55–134.

RAHTZ, P., and HIRST, S. (1974). *Beckery Chapel Glastonbury*. Glastonbury: Glastonbury Antiquarian Society.

——— and WRIGHT, S. (2000). *Cannington Cemetery*. Britannia Monograph Series 17. London: Society for the Promotion of Roman Studies.

REYNOLDS, A. (1997). 'The definition and ideology of Anglo-Saxon execution sites and cemeteries', in G. de Boe and F. Verhaeghe (eds.), *Death and Burial in Medieval Europe*. Zellick, Belgium: Instituut voor het Archeologisch Patrimonium, 33–41.

——(1999). *Late Anglo-Saxon England: Life and Landscape*. Stroud: Tempus.

RODWELL, W., and RODWELL, K. (1982). 'St Peter's Church, Barton-upon-Humber: excavation and structural study, 1978–81'. *Antiquaries Journal* 62: 283–315.

———(1985). *Rivenhall: Investigations of a Villa, Church, and Village, 50–1977*. CBA Research Report 55. London: Council for British Archaeology.

ROLLASON, D. (1986). 'The shrines of saints in later Anglo-Saxon England: distribution and significance', in L. A. S. Butler and R. K. Morris (eds.), *The Anglo-Saxon Church*. CBA Research Report 60. London: Council for British Archaeology, 32–43.

ROSSER, G. (1988). 'The Anglo-Saxon gilds', in J. Blair (ed.), *Minsters and Parish Churches: the Local Church in Transition 950–1200*. Oxford University Committee for Archaeology Monograph 17. Oxford: Oxford University Committee for Archaeology.

RUDKIN, D. J. (2001). 'Excavations at Bevis's Grave, Camp Down, Bedhampton, Hants'. Unpublished report. Fishbourne Roman Palace Museum.

SAMSON, R. (1999). 'The Church lends a hand', in J. Downes and T. Pollard (eds.), *The Loved Body's Corruption*. Glasgow: Cruithne, 120–44.

SAWYER, P. H. (1999). *Anglo-Saxon Lincolnshire*. Lincoln: History of Lincolnshire Committee for the Society for Lincolnshire History and Archaeology.

SCOBIE, G., ZANT, J. M., and WHINNEY, R. (1991). *The Brooks, Winchester: A Preliminary Report on the Excavations, 1987–88*. Winchester Museums Service Archaeology Report, 1. Winchester: Winchester Museums Service.

SEMPLE, S. J. (1998). 'A fear of the past: the place of the prehistoric burial mound in the ideology of middle and later Anglo-Saxon England'. *World Archaeology* 30(1): 109–126.

SEMPLE, S., and WILLIAMS, H. (eds.) (2007). *Early Medieval Mortuary Practices*. Anglo-Saxon Studies in Archaeology and History 14. Oxford: Oxford University Committee for Archaeology.

STOCKER, D., WENT, D., and FARLEY, M. (1995). 'The evidence for a pre-Viking church adjacent to the Anglo-Saxon barrow at Taplow, Buckinghamshire'. *Archaeological Journal* 152: 441–51.

STOODLEY, N. (1999a). *The Spindle and the Spear: a Critical Enquiry into the Construction and Meaning of Gender in the early Anglo-Saxon Burial Rite*. BAR British Series 288. Oxford: British Archaeological Reports.

——(1999b). 'Burial rites, gender and the creation of kingdoms: the evidence from seventh-century Wessex', in T. Dickinson and D. Griffiths (eds.), *The Making of Kingdoms*. Anglo-

Saxon Studies in Archaeology and History 12. Oxford: Oxford University School of Archaeology, 99–107.

——(2002). 'Multiple burials, multiple meanings? Interpreting the early Anglo-Saxon multiple interment', in Lucy and Reynolds (eds.), *Burial in Early Medieval England and Wales*, 103–21.

THEUWS, F. (1999). 'Changing settlement patterns, burial grounds and the symbolic construction of ancestors and communities in the late Merovingian southern Netherlands', in C. Fabech and J. Ringtved (eds.), *Settlement and Landscape: Proceedings of a Conference in Århus, Denmark*. Moesgård, Denmark: Jutland Archaeological Society, 337–49.

THOMPSON, V. (2002). 'Constructing Salvation: a homiletic and penitential context for late Anglo-Saxon burial practice', in Lucy and Reynolds (eds.), *Burial in Early Medieval England and Wales*, 229–40.

——(2004). *Dying and Death in Later Anglo-Saxon England*. Woodbridge: Boydell.

TINTI, F. (2005). 'The "costs" of pastoral care: church dues in late Anglo-Saxon England', in F. Tinti (ed.), *Pastoral Care in Late Anglo-Saxon England*. Woodbridge: Boydell, 27–51.

TWEDDLE, D., BIDDLE, M., and KJØLBYE-BIDDLE, B. (1995). *Corpus of Anglo-Saxon Stone Sculpture*, Volume 4: *South-East England*. Oxford: Oxford University Press.

VAN HOUTS, E. (1999). *Memory and Gender in Medieval Europe, 900–1200*. Basingstoke: Macmillan.

WADE-MARTINS, P. (1980). *Excavations in North Elmham Park 1967–72*. East Anglian Archaeology 9 (2 volumes). Gressenhall: East Anglian Archaeology.

WALDRON, T. (2007). *St Peter's, Barton-upon-Humber, Lincolnshire*, Volume 2: *The Human Remains*. Oxford: Oxbow.

WATTS, L., RAHTZ, P., OKASHA, E., BRADLEY, S. A. J., and HIGGITT, J. (1997). 'Kirkdale—the Inscriptions'. *Medieval Archaeology* 40: 51–99.

WHITE, W. (1988). *Skeletal Remains from the Cemetery of St Nicholas Shambles, City of London*. London: MOLAS.

WHYMER, J. J. (1996). 'The excavation of a ring ditch at South Acre', in J. J. Wymer (ed.), *Barrow Excavations in Norfolk, 1984–88*. East Anglian Archaeology 77. Dereham: East Anglian Archaeology, 58–89.

WILLIAMS, H. (2006). *Death and Memory in Early Medieval Britain*. Cambridge: Cambridge University Press.

WILMOTT, T. (forthcoming). 'An Anglo-Saxon church and its cemetery: excavation in The Booths, 1985–86'. West Yorkshire Archaeology Service.

ZADORA-RIO, E. (2003). 'The making of churchyards and parish territories in the early-medieval landscape of France and England in the 7th–12th centuries: a reconsideration'. *Medieval Archaeology* 47: 1–19.

ZARNECKI, G. (1953). 'The Newent funerary tablet'. *Transactions of the Bristol and Gloucester Archaeological Society* 72: 49–55.

PART IV

FOOD PRODUCTION

PART IV

FOOD PRODUCTION

CHAPTER 17

OVERVIEW: RURAL PRODUCTION

DELLA HOOKE

OVER the last few decades, an increasingly clear picture has begun to emerge of the rural landscape of Anglo-Saxon England and how it was exploited. Much of the new evidence has come from archaeology, as the following chapters show, resulting not only from the excavation of new sites but from the refinement of techniques such as analyses of pollen and bones. But these offer only pinhole views through a dark mantle covering the remainder of the landscape. While aerial photography transformed our knowledge of the distribution of prehistoric sites across England, it was arguably less useful in deciphering the settlement patterns of the early medieval period. The new technique of LiDAR (Light Detection and Ranging) survey can now penetrate beneath woodland and is likely to produce equally impressive results—in this case it may help to cast light upon the age of much of what we think of as 'ancient' woodland by indicating islands of early or medieval settlement and cultivation that were subsequently lost to woodland regeneration.

CHANGES IN TIME AND PLACE

Climatic fluctuations must have affected farming throughout the early medieval period (Dark 2000: 19–28). Climatic deterioration in the fifth century challenged farmers who were already trying to cope with an impoverished economic situation following the Roman withdrawal, especially with the loss of urban and military markets. A return to more traditional systems based more upon pastoralism is suggested by the retraction of arable land, although outside northern England there seems to have been only limited reversion to woodland at this time. On the downlands of southern England extensive areas of grazing are suggested by the later charter evidence, leaving earlier 'Celtic' fields as relict systems beneath grassland until relatively recent times. A possible period of warming with increased sunspot activity around the eighth century AD, however, may have given rise to more favourable conditions for agriculture, now able to flourish in a more settled political situation. New high-yielding crops such as bread wheat (Moffett, below) could be grown, and technologically more advanced methods were put into use.

Developments in Britain need to be seen within a wider European framework, as early medieval communities were not economically isolated or undifferentiated: modern archaeological investigations have shown that 'their economies and cultural interaction were complex and diverse' (Hamerow 2002: 4). Settlement types found on the continent were not always replicated in Anglo-Saxon England—the great timber longhouses such as those excavated at Ezinge in the Frisian marshes or Feddersen Wierde in Lower Saxony may not have been needed in a climate in which cattle could remain out of doors in the winter; nor might the economic conditions existing in fifth- and sixth-century Britain have encouraged such an outlay. Sunken-featured buildings, on the other hand, were adopted, if mostly as buildings for carrying out rural crafts such as textile production (Part II, and Leahy, this volume).

Stabilization of settlement appears to have taken place during the later seventh and eighth centuries, reflecting an intensification of production in the rural countryside that was taking place across much of north-west Europe. Goods were also being distributed more readily and new foci of activity were developing as new administrative structures replaced old tribal loyalties. Hamerow rejected the break-up of multiple estates, something that was obviously occurring at about this time, as a prime factor in effecting change, but recognized the demands of the new *emporia* in stimulating production as well as the need for the secular and Church landlords of the new estates to produce a surplus. Agricultural changes proceeded at different rates in different regions, but often involved the intensification of crop production and crop specialization. Crucially, the chapters in this Part identify changes in crop cultivation in this phase, with less emphasis on pastoralism, as in other parts of the North Sea zone, incidentally affecting farmstead and village layout.

Settlements not only became more stable but a rural hierarchy evolved, especially as monasteries and towns became growing 'consumer' communities. Expansion of agriculture into new regions might take place, such as in the Kempen region of the southern Netherlands; in England this might be reflected by a move onto heavier, previously neglected, soils. New agricultural systems might be put into place with the emphasis upon the role of the demesne, greater specialization in certain crops or animals, and, perhaps, diminished self-sufficiency. In northern Europe sandy soils could be manured by the addition of turf; in England, 'Celtic' fields might give way to infield/outfield systems or strip fields (Oosthuizen, below). It is important to note that the latter were found from the seventh century in parts of Europe but were still spreading in the eighth and ninth centuries. Crop rotation was almost certainly leading to the re-organization of field systems and the greater use of the mouldboard plough in cereal production. More intensive farming methods required a bigger labour force or a pooling of labour and capital (oxen and ploughs) within villages, with collective rights over certain resources such as pasture and pannage.

In Scandinavia, Callmer (1991) has argued that there was little scope for the expansion of farmland, and instead higher yields had to be achieved to feed the larger communities that were replacing the earlier kin-based settlement groups. This perhaps gave rise to subdivided field systems and the need to use the same arable land for longer periods, and, together with crop rotation, produced a system that was usually based upon an infield/outfield type of open-field farming (see, too, Engelmark 1989). Communities also included growing numbers who were agriculturally non-productive. This process he ascribes to the Early Viking Age (beginning c.800), corresponding with the situation in late Anglo-Saxon England.

Callmer also argues that crop rotation may have been introduced into Scandinavia from the Baltic. Once again, the spotlight appears to focus upon Germanic territories, where Tacitus, in his *Germania* (26), refers to the sharing out of land by allotment among some Germanic plain-dwelling tribes in Roman times, prior to AD 98. The late Professor Hans-Jürgen Nitz long argued for the early establishment of a common-field system in a relatively sophisticated form in Germany, seeing it being carried into newly colonized regions by Frankish overlords as early as the mid eighth century (Nitz 1988). The evidence for this is largely derived from later sources, however, and the situation across such a large area as western and central Europe was far more complex than may at first appear. Hildebrandt (1988) more cautiously envisages a greater need for crop rotation in German regions after the ninth century and sees this as the driving force in the spread of open-field farming at a later date. He notes that a three-field system appears to have been operating in the northern Rhine area by AD 793, with three-field crop rotation confirmed by the ninth and tenth centuries, and with far more widespread evidence of such a practice by this date coming from north-eastern France and the western Eifel.

By the tenth century, three-field systems involving winter crop, summer grain, and fallow can be traced across central Europe, a change in cereal cultivation confirmed by the palaeobotanical evidence in the 'old-settled areas' (Hildebrandt 1988: 279–80, fig. 13.1). Hildebrandt argues that winter crops, including bread grains, replaced summer grains to a varying degree from region to region, but that this was not necessarily combined with the subdivision of the arable; he was loth to accept 'a fully developed common-field system' before 'the beginning of the High Middle Ages [AD 1050]' (ibid.: 284), suggesting instead that crop rotation could have been earlier than common-field arrangements with the crops grown on single parcels of land, the change to common fields occurring as more land was taken into cultivation. This was not entirely based upon geography, for in the valleys of the Rhine and Main the cultivation of vines preserved a system of two-field cultivation. Nor did this three-field system spread to more mountainous regions; summer-grown oats remained the staple crop on many Corvey Abbey estates as late as the eleventh century.

While the old idea of the first Anglo-Saxon migrants bringing with them villages and open fields, therefore, is not substantiated by the archaeological evidence, the apparent spread of ideas throughout Europe in successive centuries, responding to changing social and administrative conditions, still has to be taken into account. It does not appear to have been environmental challenges alone that necessitated change—while Myhre (1999) has placed the emphasis upon 'ideological, cultural, social and political factors', the role of lordship remains disputed; but the presence of a relatively servile and easily manoeuvred workforce would certainly have aided re-organization in England, either upon the multiple estates of the Crown or the Church, or on the newly emerging 'proto-manors' of the eighth century (see below). The cultural component (if made possible by climatic factors) may be illustrated by the choice of bread wheat over other grains in later Anglo-Saxon England as one of dietary preference, perhaps encouraged as white bread became a status symbol on royal or ecclesiastical estates (Banham forthcoming).

The changes that occurred at this time (i.e. from the eighth century onwards) were not confined to agricultural systems but also involved estate fragmentation and changing settlement patterns, all of which are likely to have been closely interlinked. It remains difficult to decide which may have taken precedence, and the intensity of change certainly varied across the country. It has been argued, on the basis of pottery dating, that the nucleation of settlement began within royal or ecclesiastical multiple estate units before estate fragmentation (Hall 1981; Taylor 1983; Brown and Foard 1998: 91). Open-field farming on an extended scale must have been associated with this. If true, it would suggest that the change in settlement patterns and the adaptation of farming systems were being deliberately encouraged by the governing elite rather than emerging as a result of the new tenant-lords of the eighth century onwards attempting to increase yields to meet their individual financial commitments and taxes (Fox 1981). In such a scenario, agriculture was rendered more efficient and the peasantry suffered a decline in status, while the open fields may have developed on the land 'occupied by bond cultivators on the inland of great estates' (Williamson 2003: 70). Certainly in tenth-century west Wales strip systems appear to have been virtually confined to the bond lands of the royal *maerdref* and ecclesiastical centres in which a particularly servile kind of tenure was maintained (Jones 1972). The development of the full open-field system may, however, have taken several centuries to achieve (see below).

Indeed, while the chronology of change has certainly to be considered, the spatial context of change is equally important. Regions of intense cultivation tended to remain centred where they had first emerged in prehistoric and Roman times (although actual field systems might differ), while beyond lay marginal zones of woodland, heath, and moorland, the degree of development of which is likely to have varied over time. Depending upon the underlying geology and topography, and affected by several thousand years of exploitation of the natural environment, linkages between different zones developed as a way of utilizing complementary resources (Hooke 1985: 75–88). Seasonal transhumance of this kind may have been in place by the Iron Age (Ford 1976), but is clearly identifiable in the early Anglo-Saxon period in regions such as the midland Hwiccan territory or the Weald of south-eastern England, 'folk regions' identifiable as the earliest English administrative groupings (Hooke 1986). Estate linkages are still much in evidence in later Anglo-Saxon England, sometimes expressed purely in later administrative arrangements—surviving in the form of dependent berewicks or ecclesiastical chapelries (Fig. 17.1).

Neither the marginal nor the intensively cultivated regions were experiencing the intensity of use that would be reached in medieval times. In the west midlands, the open fields had still not spread as far as township boundaries: enclosed fields and minor settlements are recorded that were later to be subsumed into the open fields; many woodland areas were still frequented by shepherds and herdsmen taking stock to seasonal pastures. Documentary evidence in the form of charters and charter boundary clauses from about the eighth century onwards for the first time provides much fine detail of land use although this is not available for all regions; place-names offer a much better coverage but supply only a framework for the tapestry that is rural England.

Field and landscape patterns in some areas indicate more regional links persisting from earlier periods but still based upon resource management related to a more local topography. One of these was a regular pattern of linear alignments—field boundaries and parallel routeways—linking upland watershed areas with river valleys, a facet of seasonal transhumance (see 'Marginal landscapes' below). Relict patterns of this kind can be identified most clearly in parts of eastern England, especially on the Norfolk/Suffolk border and in Essex, although similar patterns have been observed elsewhere, as in the Bourn valley of Cambridgeshire, well within the open-field zone (Williamson 2000: 147; Oosthuizen 2005), on higher ground in Hertfordshire, or in an area of Herefordshire around Pembridge (here the pattern appears to have preceded a dyke system probably constructed in the early Anglo-Saxon period: White 2003: 43–51; Ray and White 2004). In other, more marginal, regions, however, like the northern Peak District, oval enclosures can be identified that may have occurred in pairs, as at Roystone Grange in

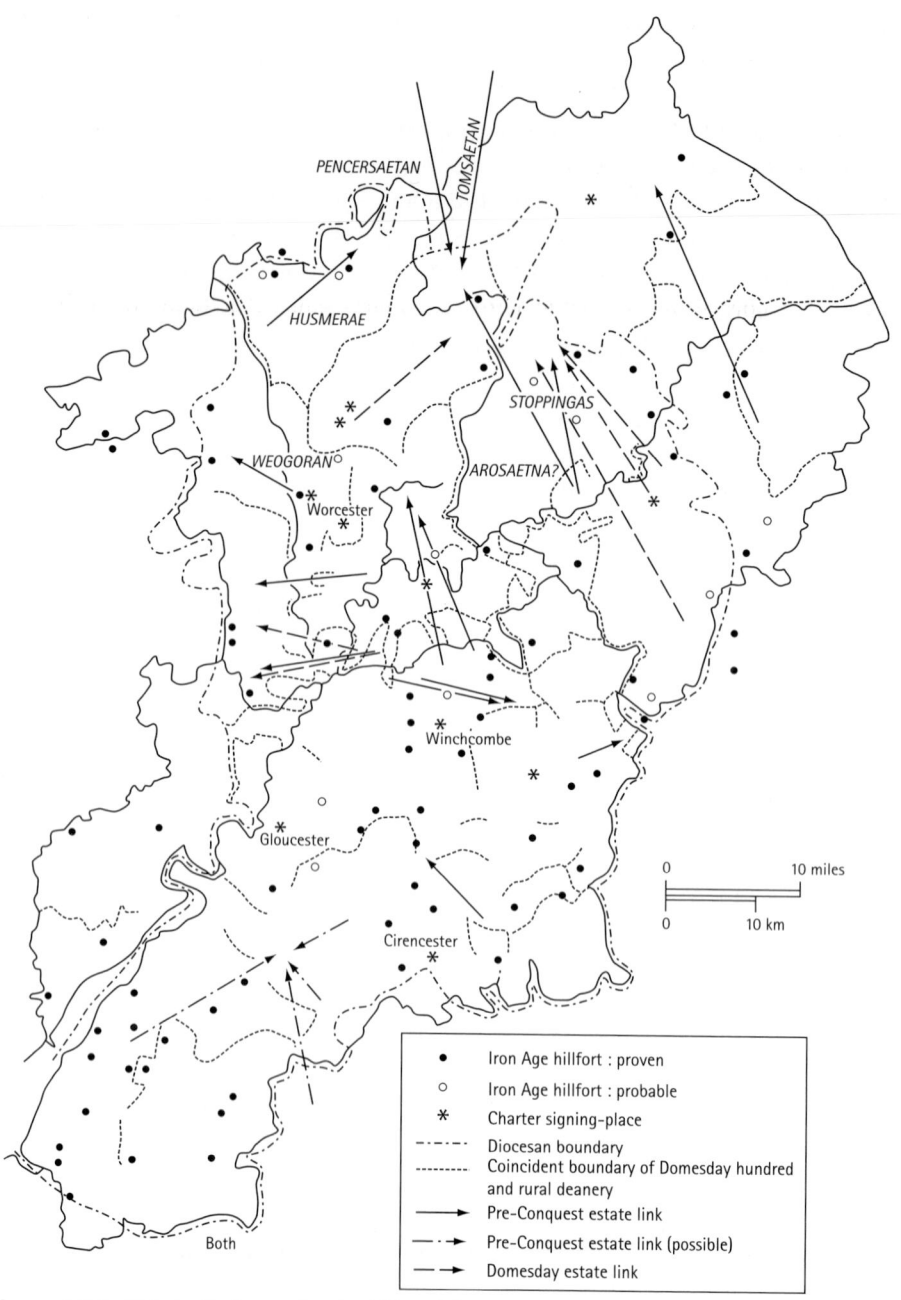

Figure 17.1 Estate linkages in the West Midlands. Reproduced by kind permission from Hooke 1985

Derbyshire, and may have had their origins in Roman field systems (Hodges 1991), with crop-growing 'ovals' linked to 'pasture ovals' (ibid.; also Atkin 1985). In eastern England Taylor (2002) has shown settlement around oval-shaped patches of common or meadow, probably initially developing in the Iron Age or Roman period. Oosthuizen discusses (below) the chronological uncertainties involved in deciphering common patterns that can be identified over many periods, as such patterns might arise at any time, especially with the shift of settlement to newly developing areas. In Suffolk, Warner (1987) has identified oval-shaped patterns which he argues were associated with secondary 'hall' settlements in regions of wood-pasture in late Anglo-Saxon times.

REGIONS PREDOMINANTLY OF CROP CULTIVATION

One of the most important developments in Anglo-Saxon times was the spread of open-field farming, a subject treated in this Part by Oosthuizen. Changes seem to have been most influential in the areas already under intensive agriculture, for here open-field systems were to be established which were to persist for almost 1,000 years as an effective way of exploiting the land (Hooke 1981). This kind of development, however, occurred in different ways across the country, and both spatial factors and chronological change have to be considered.

The region most affected by the development of open-field agriculture seems to have been a broad swath across England stretching from Dorset north-eastwards to Yorkshire (Roberts and Wrathmell 2002: esp. 61, fig. 3.2). Here, open field was to dominate, although not necessarily at first in a fully evolved form. Where the full 'midland system' developed, settlement patterns were also drastically altered—scattered settlements were abandoned as village nuclei replaced them.

It was, however, only in the regions of intensive crop production that the open-field system was to fully develop. In the east midlands an organized pattern of long, regularly laid out strips, extending from village nuclei as far as estate margins, can eventually be identified. While some initially argued that this was the pattern from the start, with the open fields laid out over earlier Saxon settlement sites, other researchers now see this as the result of later periods of expansion and re-organization in the ninth or tenth centuries. While Oosthuizen has suggested that Mercian expansion may have been a contributory factor (although the system is not found within the Mercian heartland), others have suggested the involvement of Danish investment (Brown and Foard 1998: 91). In the west midlands the charter evidence indicates less evidence of such re-planning, for here the open fields only gradually subsumed the enclosed fields and minor settlements that lay beyond the open-field nucleus, many persisting up to at least the eleventh century. Indeed, it has been argued (see Thirsk 1964; Fox 1981: 100–1; Jones and Page 2006: 82–3) that it was growing populations, combined with the loss of distant pastures through estate fragmentation, that necessitated the introduction of the fallow field and the intricacies of the open-field system over a period between the ninth and the mid thirteenth century (see, too, Oosthuizen below).

Moreover, the situation in this country, especially as one moves westwards, shows that open fields were not necessarily directly related to population pressure, for they also developed around tiny hamlet nuclei in regions such as the Welsh Borderland, and many wood-pasture regions within the main open-field belt that were relatively lightly settled. Either this was a first step towards open-field farming through the utilization of early infields, or the open-field system revealed its potential quite rapidly and became the preferred model for new manorial lords wherever they were establishing their demesnes. In the Welsh borderland the agricultural land seems to have been associated with scattered hamlet nuclei, most of which failed to become large village nucleations (Sheppard 1979). The resultant pattern was a plethora of relatively small townships within a single parish area, each with its restricted area of open field. It was only in the more heavily populated areas such as the central Wye valley that increasing pressure was to lead to (?re-organized) three-field systems more akin to the 'midland system'. Does this suggest that an 'in-field' type of open field was at first practised in such marginal zones before this became adapted into a multi-field system in some areas through later re-organization? Even then, the date of the introduction of such elements as the subdivision of holdings might not be restricted to a specific short period—at Whittlesford in Northamptonshire it seems to have occurred in the tenth century (Jones and Page 2006: 92–5), and it may well have been a similarly late introduction in other wood-pasture regions.

An infield-outfield system certainly seems to have characterized much of the rest of western England, with limited patches of open field again developing around hamlet nuclei set amidst more pastoral or marginal landscapes. It is likely that the pastoral element of farming played a greater role in these regions and was less suited to the restrictions of open-field farming. In general, population densities were lower, high stock numbers provided manure for the infield, and the occasional cultivation of the outfield could supply any crop deficit. What was to unite these systems was the recognition of community, rather than individual, rights: fields were farmed 'in common' and crops were usually grown in strips held by an individual only for the growing season; these could be scattered across the field system which might be literally 'open', i.e. without internal enclosing boundaries between parcels; animals were cared for as a single herd or flock by the community's shepherd or herdsman. The community was usually that of the township or tithing, often based upon the Anglo-Saxon estate. In eastern England, the situation appears to have been more complex and is still incompletely understood.

Williamson (2003), working in this region, has adopted a more environmental approach in arguing that it was difficult stagnogley soils, subject to excessive moisture followed by rapid drying out, that demanded an intensive short period of ploughing necessitating the type of cooperation offered by the open-field system.

Agricultural techniques and field systems obviously varied across the country, and Oosthuizen shows how much still remains to be understood, but what is clear is that although the chronological aspect of change needs to be examined, it is important to remember that a spatial framework has also to be considered.

Marginal landscapes

In the 'linked estate model', domestic stock seem to have been taken considerable distances to their seasonal pastures and patterns of what appear to have been droveways can still be clearly seen within the present-day road pattern. The distant pastures were sometimes referred to as *dænbære* or *swinbære*—the source of the numerous 'den' place-names found in the Weald. Indeed, the importance of taking pigs to forage in the woodlands for acorns or beech-mast in the early autumn led to much of the woodland recorded in the eastern and south-eastern circuits of Domesday Book being assessed by the numbers of pigs it might support. Although sites yielding good bone evidence are few, the exceptional abundance of pig bones from Wicken Bonhunt (O'Connor, below), on the boulder-clay-covered plateau of north-west Essex, may be reflecting such a regional pattern. This traditional form of land use must have greatly influenced the nature of Anglo-Saxon woodland, for grazed woodland remains relatively open, with denser stands only in more inaccessible places. It is, however, a sustainable resource. And certain species of tree, like the ash and oak, are well able to resist grazing pressure in such wood-pasture regions. Many species of trees could also be pollarded to yield not only timber, grown out of the reach of animals, but valuable leaf fodder (Hooke forthcoming). Transhumance links can also be reconstructed in the moorlands regions of the south-west and in the Pennines and Cumbria, and in some regions where coastal marshes or low-lying fenlands offered valuable summer pasture, as in eastern England (Silvester 1988).

As Sykes' chapter illustrates, hunting was a favourite pastime of the aristocracy in Anglo-Saxon England. The concept of forests had been introduced in the Frankish kingdoms in Europe by the seventh century and, although there was no legal concept of protection such as the Forest Law which was to be introduced by the Normans, already certain areas can be identified in which hunting was regularly carried out. *Haga* enclosures, documented in charter boundary clauses and place-names, either offered protection to deer or (or as well) might be used in the drive, the normal kind of hunting practised in England in later Anglo-Saxon times (Hooke 1989). Hunting may indeed have led to woodland regeneration in the later part of the period in some regions.

In areas of limited open-field development, the landscape was to develop quite differently to that of the main crop-growing regions. Waste was slowly settled or remained available for assarting in medieval times and such areas were to be characterized by individual farms; some bore names incorporating Old English terms which suggests that they may have been early features of the landscape—such as the various 'herdwicks' or the 'worths'. Such a landscape can be seen evolving in some regions in the charters of later Anglo-Saxon England—as in central Worcestershire, for instance. Here a scatter of small woods or patches of wood-pasture were very much in evidence, with hedges bounding many of the fields—the kind of landscape that was later to be called a 'bocage' (as opposed to a 'champion') landscape. Sites with regions well supplied with open pasture, on the other hand, such as the Yorkshire Wolds, have produced animal-bone assemblages dominated by sheep, important both for their meat and their wool. Here, however, stock, including cattle, may have been managed as part of a mixed farming tradition, whereas on the poor soils of the Norfolk Breckland specialized sheep rearing was a more feasible practice (O'Connor, below).

Conclusions

Any discussion of rural production in Anglo-Saxon England must therefore consider both the chronological and spatial aspects of the evidence. If anything like a true picture of the environment at this time is to be obtained, more environmental studies are urgently required—whether of pollen series, or snails, beetles, and the like.

References

ATKIN, M. (1985). 'Some settlement patterns in Lancashire', in D. Hooke (ed.), *Medieval Villages: A Review of Current Work*. Oxford University Committee for Archaeology Monograph 5. Oxford: Oxford University Committee for Archaeology, 171–86.

BANHAM, D. (forthcoming). '"In the sweat of thy brow shalt thou eat bread": cereals and cereal products in the Anglo-Saxon landscape', in N. Higham and M. Ryan (eds.), *Anglo-Saxon Landscape*. Woodbridge: Boydell and Brewer Ltd.

BROWN, T., and FOARD, G. (1998). 'The Saxon landscape: a regional perspective', in P. Everson and T. Williamson (eds.), *The Archaeology of Landscape: Studies Presented to Christopher Taylor*. Manchester: Manchester University Press, 67–94.

CALLMER, J. (1991). 'The process of village formation', in B. E. Berglund (ed.), *The Cultural Landscape during 600 years in Southern Sweden—the Ystad Project*. Copenhagen: Ecological Bulletins, 337–49.

DARK, P. (2000). *The Environment of Britain in the First Millennium AD*. London: Duckworth.

ENGELMARK, R. (1989). 'Makrofossilanalys från L. Tvären och Baldrindetorp', in *By, huvudgård och kyrka: Studier i Ystadsområdets medeltid*. Lund Studies in Medieval Archaeology 5. Stockholm: Almqvist & Wiksell, 49–50.

FORD, W. J. (1976). 'Some settlement patterns in the central region of the Warwickshire Avon', in P. H. Sawyer (ed.), *Medieval Settlement: Continuity and Change*. London: Edward Arnold, 274–94.

FOX, H. (1981). 'Approaches to the adoption of the Midland system', in Rowley (ed.), *The Origins of Open-Field Agriculture*, 64–111.

HALL, D. (1981). 'The origins of open-field agriculture—the archaeological fieldwork evidence', in Rowley (ed.), *The Origins of Open-Field Agriculture*, 22–38.

HAMEROW, H. (2002). *Early Medieval Settlements: The Archaeology of Rural Communities in North-West Europe 400–900*. Oxford: Oxford University Press.

HILDEBRANDT, H. (1988). 'Systems of agriculture in Central Europe up to the tenth and eleventh centuries', in Hooke (ed.), *Anglo-Saxon Settlements*, 275–90.

HODGES, R. (1991). *Wall-to-Wall History: The Story of Roystone Grange*. London: Duckworth.

HOOKE, D. (1981). 'Open-field agriculture—the evidence from the pre-Conquest charters of the West Midlands', in Rowley (ed.), *The Origins of Open-Field Agriculture*, 39–63.

——(1985). *The Anglo-Saxon Landscape: The Kingdom of the Hwicce*. Manchester: Manchester University Press.

——(1986). 'Territorial organisation in the Anglo-Saxon West Midlands; central places, central areas', in E. Grant (ed.), *Central Places, Archaeology and History*. Sheffield: J. R. Collis, 79–93.

——(ed.) (1988). *Anglo-Saxon Settlements*. Oxford: Basil Blackwell.

——(1989). 'Pre-Conquest woodland: its distribution and usage'. *Agricultural History Review* 37: 113–29.

——(forthcoming). *Trees in Anglo-Saxon England*. Woodbridge: Boydell and Brewer.

JONES, G. R. J. (1972). 'Post-Roman Wales', in H. P. R. Finberg (ed.), *The Agrarian History of England and Wales*. Cambridge: Cambridge University Press, 283–382.

JONES, R., and PAGE, M. (2006). *Medieval Villages in an English Landscape: Beginnings and Ends*. Macclesfield: Windgather Press.

MYHRE, B. (1999). 'Together or apart—the problem of nucleation and dispersal of settlements', in C. Fabech and J. Ringved (eds.), *Settlement and Landscape: Proceedings of a Conference in Arhus, Denmark, May 4–7 1998*. Copenhagen: Jutland Archaeological Society, 125–9.

NITZ, H-J. (1988). 'Settlement structures and settlement systems of the Frankish Central State in Carolingian and Ottonian times', in Hooke (ed.), *Anglo-Saxon Settlements*, 249–73.

Oosthuizen, S. (2005). 'New light on the origins of open-field farming?'. *Medieval Archaeology* 49: 165–94.

Ray, K., and White, P. (2004). *Herefordshire's Historic Landscape: a Characterisation.* Herefordshire Studies in Archaeology Series 1. Hereford: Herefordshire Archaeology.

Roberts, B. K., and Wrathmell, S. (2002). *Region and Place: A Study of English Rural Settlement.* London: English Heritage.

Rowley, T. (ed.) (1981). *The Origins of Open-Field Agriculture.* London: Croom Helm.

Silvester, R. (1988). *The Fenland Project, 3: Marshland and the Nar Valley, Norfolk.* East Anglian Archaeology 45. Norwich.

Sheppard, J. A. (1979). *The Origins and Evolution of Field and Settlement Patterns in the Herefordshire Manor of Marden.* Department of Geography Occasional Paper 15. London: Queen Mary College, University of London.

Taylor, C. C. (1983). *Village and Farmstead: A History of Rural Settlement in England.* London: Book Club Associates.

——(2002). 'Nucleated settlement: a view from the frontier', *Landscape History* 24: 53–72.

Thirsk, J. (1964). 'The common fields'. *Past and Present* 29: 3–25.

Warner, P. (1987). *Greens, Commons and Clayland Colonization: the Origins and Development of Green-side Settlement in East Suffolk.* Department of English Local History Occasional Paper 2. Leicester: University of Leicester Press.

White, P. (2003). *The Arrow Valley, Herefordshire: Archaeology, Landscape Change and Conservation.* Hereford: Herefordshire Archaeology.

Williamson, T. (2000). *The Origins of Hertfordshire.* Manchester: Manchester University Press.

——(2003). *Shaping Medieval Landscapes: Settlement, Society, Environment.* Macclesfield: Windgather Press.

CHAPTER 18

WOODS AND THE WILD

NAOMI SYKES

Introduction

In his *History of the English People* (McClure and Collins 1994: 9), Bede eulogized the wild animals available in Britain, and it is clear from other sources of evidence that the Anglo-Saxon landscape was populated with a wider variety of species than exist in today's: wolves (*Canis lupus*), bears (*Ursus arctos*), lynx (*Lynx lynx*), wild boar (*Sus scrofa*), beavers (*Castor fiber*), and cranes (*Gus grus*). Despite this faunal richness, little consideration has been given to how these wild animals were perceived and engaged with by the people who lived alongside them. Admittedly, evidence for Anglo-Saxon attitudes to wild animals is sketchy by comparison to the amount of information for the post-Conquest period, and the attention placed on later medieval hunting, fowling, and fishing is understandable (e.g. Cummins 1988; Rooney 1993; Almond 2003). Lack of research has, however, fostered a belief that wild animals were of little importance to the Anglo-Saxon population, an assumption that is both unfounded and unrealistic. Farming societies are seldom ambivalent to wild animals—they may be viewed as threats, pests, totems, sources of food, or raw materials, but even where they are not exploited they always carry social meaning. It has been demonstrated repeatedly that the relationship between humans and wild animals, particularly hunted species, reflects a society's structure and ideology: different animals have different meanings to different societies (e.g. Cartmill 1993). Investigation of wild animal exploitation in Anglo-Saxon England has, therefore, the potential to reveal much about the social development which occurred between AD 410 and 1066.

Recently, Anglo-Saxon scholars have begun to recognize the contribution that the study of wild animal exploitation can make to their field. Historical and zooarchaeological analyses of hunting (Sykes 2005; Marvin 2006), hawking (Dobney and Jacques 2002; Oggins 2004), and fishing (Barrett *et al.* 2004; Tsurushima 2007) have provided important information about both the socio-economic and religious changes of the period. Through landscape and place-name studies, Hooke (1989; 1998), Mew (2001), Liddiard (2003), and Gautier (2007) have even been able to argue that forests and parks—traditionally viewed as Norman introductions—are a legacy of the pre-Conquest period. This chapter integrates all these strands of information with evidence from iconography and material culture to examine how and why the relationship between humans and wild animals changed through the course of the Anglo-Saxon period. Sources of information for the period are uneven. For the early part, grave-goods provide a valuable source of information but texts are scarce. Documentary sources become increasingly abundant through the middle and late parts and these, together with evidence from place-names, balance the absence of grave-goods. Animal-bone data are available for the whole Anglo-Saxon period (see Fig. 18.1), but this source of information is not without problems. For instance, the recovery of bird and fish bones is dependent upon sieving, a practice that excavators have not always adopted as standard. Identification may be equally problematic, especially between closely related species such as wolves and dogs, and wild boar and domestic pigs. For these reasons the zooarchaeological record as reported by specialists is unlikely to be a true reflection of wild animal exploitation and should be considered in conjunction with other strands of information. Nevertheless, examination of the evidence for the exploitation of land and sea mammals, birds, and fish makes it possible to understand the changing ways people interacted with the world around them.

EARLY ANGLO-SAXON PERIOD: EARLY FIFTH TO LATE SEVENTH CENTURIES

The withdrawal of the Roman Empire took with it the hunting, fowling, and fish-eating culture that had developed over the four centuries of occupation. Few zooarchaeological assemblages dating between the fifth and seventh centuries contain high frequencies of wild animals, their remains typically comprising less than 1 per cent of the total assemblage (Figs. 18.1 and 18.2). Where present, roe deer (*Capreolus capreolus*) and red deer (*Cervus elaphus*) usually predominate, although

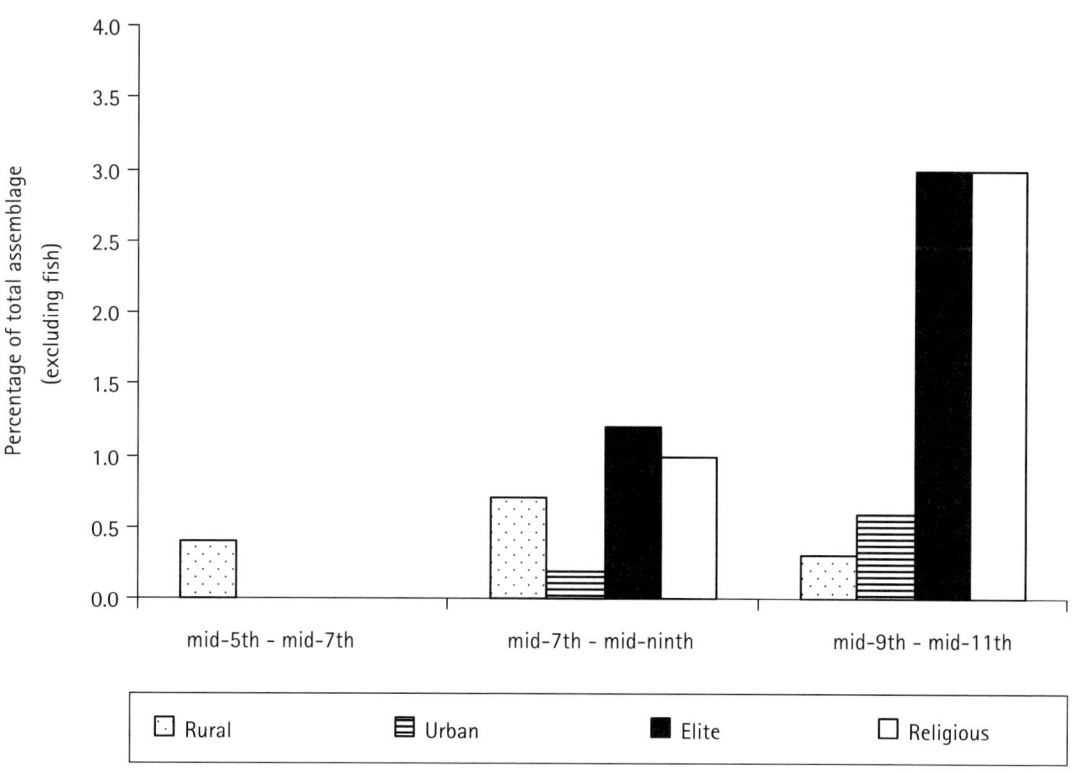

Figure 18.1 Variation in representation of wild mammals on Anglo-Saxon sites of different type, shown as a percentage of the total bone assemblage (excluding fish). The chart is based on ninety-six assemblages, the raw data for which are presented in Sykes 2007b.

the latter is generally represented by shed antler rather than meat-bearing bones, suggesting that the species was valued more as a supplier of raw materials for artefact manufacture than as quarry or food source.

West Stow in Suffolk has produced the best set of wild fauna for any early Anglo-Saxon settlement but this is a reflection of the exceptional size of the assemblage rather than evidence of intensive exploitation: over 100,000 fragments were identified but wild animals still total less than 1 per cent. Given the size of the assemblage it is interesting that no wild boar remains were identified, but eight other species of wild mammal were noted, including red and roe deer, hare (*Lepus* sp.), badger (*Meles meles*), fox (*Vulpes vulpes*), and bear (Crabtree 1990). The bear, represented by a single metacarpal (paw bone), has been interpreted as an imported skin, rather than a hunted animal. That some hunting did take place at this site is testified by the post-cranial deer bones and the presence of four iron arrowheads, hunting weapons that are particularly rare before the mid eleventh century (Jessop 1996).

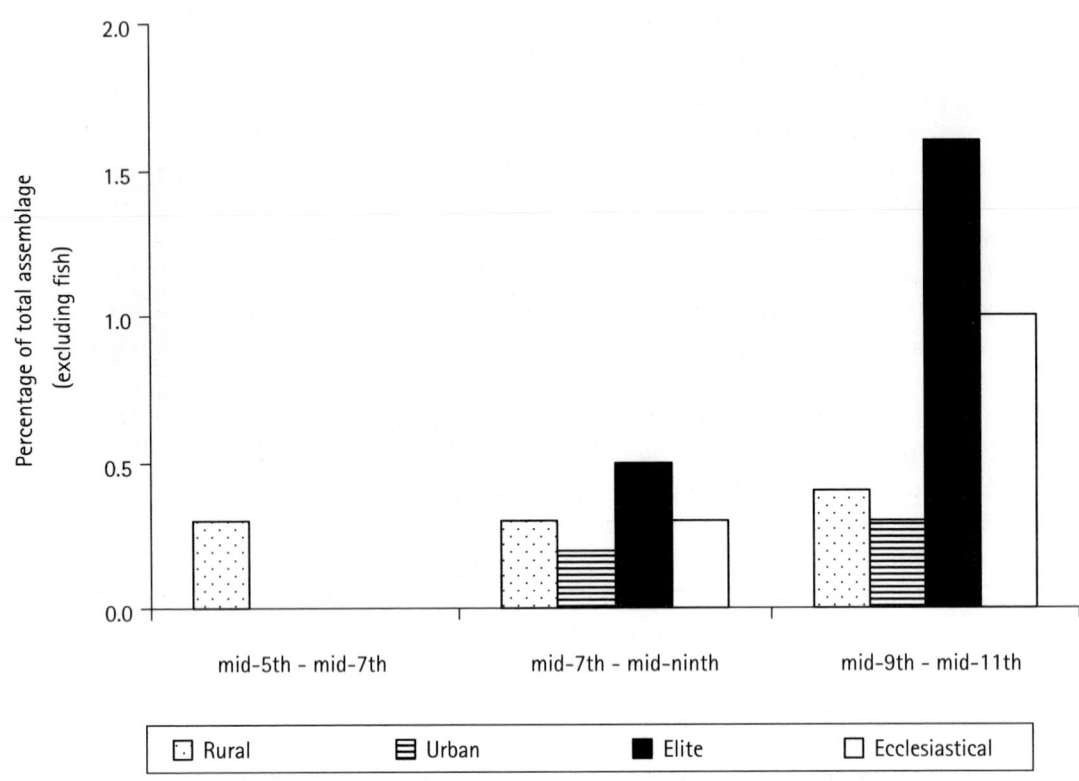

Figure 18.2 Variation in representation of wild birds on Anglo-Saxon sites of different type, shown as a percentage of the total bone assemblage (excluding fish). The chart is based on ninety-six assemblages, the raw data for which are presented in Sykes 2007b.

Wildfowling appears to have been a more common activity at West Stow. Seventeen species of wild bird are recorded and, of these, cranes are the most numerous (Crabtree 1990). West Stow produced very few fish bones, just fifteen identifiable specimens belonging to pike (*Esox lucius*), perch (*Perca fluviatilis*), and flatfish (*Pleuronectes/Platichthys* sp.). The frequency of fish would probably have been greater had the site been sieved but it is noteworthy that fish are equally scarce on other early sites even where sieving was undertaken, as at Lechlade in Gloucestershire (Maltby 2003).

Two sites have provided good evidence for the early exploitation of fish and marine resources. Despite lack of sieving, excavations at Bishopstone in Sussex yielded the remains of conger eel (*Conger conger*) and whiting (*Merlangius merlangus*), together with thousands of shells belonging to mussels (*Mytilus edulis*), periwinkles (*Littorina littorea*), oysters (*Ostrea edulis*), and limpets (*Patella vulgate*) (Gebbles 1977). Limpets were also abundant at Bantham in Devon, a British site which also produced a range of marine fish including sea bream (*Sparidae*), horse mackerel (*Trachurus trachurus*), bass (*Dicentrarchus labrax*), and cod (*Gadus morhua*). According to Coy (1981) these fish were fairly small, suggesting that they had been caught from the shore rather than through deep-sea fishing. With the exception of Bishopstone and Bantham, the general dearth of fish bones in early Anglo-Saxon deposits seems to add credence to Bede's claim that St Wilfrid arrived among the South Saxons to find them starving because they did not know how to fish (McClure and Collins 1994: 193). Isotopic analyses of human remains from Berinsfield, Oxfordshire, provided no indication that the population was consuming marine fish, although freshwater species were possibly being eaten (Privat *et al.* 2002).

Poor representation of wild animals in fifth- to seventh-century domestic assemblages promotes an impression of a landscape devoid of wildlife; however, the evidence from non-anthropogenic deposits paints a different picture. Radiocarbon dating of the animal remains from Kinsley Cave in Yorkshire demonstrated that both brown bear and lynx were living in early Anglo-Saxon England: a lynx femur from this site returned a calibrated date of AD 425 to AD 600 (Hetherington *et al.* 2006) and a bear vertebra was dated to the fifth/early sixth century (Hammon in press). If, then, large carnivores and other wild animals co-existed with the communities, the decision not to exploit them reveals something about early Anglo-Saxon attitudes to the natural world: did farmers view wild animals as irrelevant to their pastoral lifestyle, or were they perceived as having greater significance?

One needs only to look at early Anglo-Saxon material culture to realize that wild animals carried a symbolism far beyond the realm of economics and diet; whilst these creatures figure small in domestic assemblages, wild animals, particularly predatory birds and fish, figure more prominently in iconography and as artefacts (see Hawkes 1997; Dickinson 2005; Webster, this volume). This is exemplified by the early-seventh-century grave-goods from Sutton Hoo in Suffolk, Mound 1, purportedly the final resting-place of the East Anglian King Raedwald (Carver 1998). Animal motifs include non-naturalistic Style 2 creatures, as on the shoulder clasps and the great gold buckle; the former also has intricate boar representations and the latter has raptors' heads on the sides, recognizable from the curved beaks which occur again on the hanging-bowl patch, and with winged bodies on the shields and the purse-lid. Wild boar features again on the helmet, the whetstone was topped by a red deer stag figurine, and a three-dimensional fish was in the hanging-bowl. Physical remains of several wild animals were also present. Drinking-horns, represented only by their metal mounts, were recovered from both Mounds 1 and 2, the size of the pair in the former showing that they derived from aurochsen (*Bos primagenius*), the wild progenitor of domestic cattle. This species was extinct in Britain by the end of the Bronze Age, so the Sutton Hoo drinking-horns, and similar examples from Taplow, Buckinghamshire, must have been imported from the continent (van Vuure 2005: 56). Other exceptional finds from Sutton Hoo include the remains of an otter-skin cap, and fragments of beaver fur found preserved on the wooden lyre, perhaps representing the instrument's case (Stoves 1983).

These last examples indicate that animal pelts were more frequently used than is suggested by the archaeological record with its poor organic preservation. Occasionally it is possible to infer the presence of fur and pelts from skeletal patterning, notably the over-representation of paw bones, which were usually left attached to skins. In addition to the West Stow bear metacarpal, bear phalanges (toes) have been recovered from cremation urns at Spong Hill in Norfolk and Sancton in Yorkshire, leading Bond (1994) to conclude that furs played a role in early Anglo-Saxon funerary rites. Elsewhere, bear claws appear to have been used as amulets, and it is as amulets that wild animals are perhaps best represented in this period: individual bear claws, eagle talons, and boar, wolf, and even beaver teeth have been recovered from funerary contexts (see Meaney 1981; Crabtree 1995; Lucy 2000). Where it is possible to age and sex the human skeletons, these amulets are often found with women and children, perhaps suggesting an association with fertility or protection (Meaney 1981: 134). Adult male burials are more usually accompanied by weapons and sometimes helmets. As at Sutton Hoo, these grave-goods often carry animal motifs, demonstrating that these creatures were valued for the strength that even their image could impart (Lucy 2000: 51; Dickinson 2005). Pagan cosmologies are often zoocentric, with animals seen as having power equal to, or in excess of, humans. Christian paradigms, however, place humans far above animals in the Chain of Being, resulting in a different world view (see Pluskowski 2006).

Mid Saxon period: from the late seventh to the mid ninth century

Whether or not the Christian conversion changed attitudes towards wild animals, it certainly affected the range of evidence available for archaeologists to reconstruct them. With the end of grave-good deposition and the wearing of anything but Christian amulets, we lack the sources of information that were so useful for the preceding period (Meaney 1992: 116). Whilst the claws and teeth of wild animals no longer adorned people's bodies, these creatures continued to inhabit their minds. Place-names provide direct evidence that the landscape was visualized, demarcated, and understood in terms of the wildlife it contained. In addition to demonstrating the importance of wild animals to Anglo-Saxon society, place-names also hint that the demise of some of the country's native species should be attributed to the mid Saxon period.

Based on the scarcity of place-name and zooarchaeological evidence for bears, several authors have suggested that this species became extinct in England between the eighth and the tenth century (Dent 1974; Yalden 1999: 11; Hammon in press). Similarly, Aybes and Yalden (1995) argued that the restriction of wolf place-names to the northern counties reflected its increasing rarity across southern England. Wolves are also poorly represented in the archaeological record: only one specimen, from Ramsbury in Wiltshire, has been identified for the whole of Anglo-Saxon England (Pluskowski 2006: 23). Ramsbury, a site of high status, also produced the remains of at least two beavers, including the skull of a juvenile animal. The skull exhibited skinning marks, perhaps suggesting that beaver fur was prized earlier and more widely than the historical evidence indicates: the tenth-century Laws of the Welsh King Hywell Dda are the first to mention the high value placed upon beaver furs. Archaeological finds of beaver remains are otherwise rare for the mid Saxon period and, on the basis of place-name evidence, it has been argued that beavers were scarce by this point, although it was not until the eighteenth century that the species finally succumbed to the pressures of habitat change and human predation (Aybes and Yalden 1995; Yalden 1999: 134; Coles 2006).

If human predation contributed to the eventual extinction of the English beaver, this is certainly the case for the crane, which became a target for exploitation in the mid Saxon period. The species is highly visible in both Anglo-Saxon place-names (Boisseau and Yalden 1998) and in mid-seventh- to mid-ninth-century animal-bone assemblages: their remains are present in about 43 per cent of wild bird assemblages of this period and are well represented on sites of both high and low status (Sykes 2005; 2007a). Over-utilization, however, appears to have impacted upon crane populations, and their remains are markedly less abundant in assemblages dating to later periods: 30 per cent in mid-ninth- to mid-eleventh-century assemblages and just 16 per cent for the eleventh and twelfth centuries. It is noteworthy that the mid Saxon focus on cranes is coincident with the first historical evidence for hawking in England: in 748 x 52 King Æthelberht II of Kent asked Boniface to send from Germany two falcons specifically for catching cranes (Kylie 1911: 157). It is also in this period that hunting birds begin to appear in zooarchaeological assemblages, albeit only those from elite sites. A near-complete skeleton of a sparrow hawk (*Accipiter nisus*) was recovered from the eighth-century levels at Hartlepool monastery (Allison 1988) and peregrine falcon (*Falco peregrinus*) remains were recovered from both Ramsbury (Coy 1980) and the seventh- to tenth-century site of Brandon, Suffolk (Crabtree 1996). At Flixborough in Lincolnshire most of the raptorial bird remains belonged to buzzard (*Buteo buteo*) and red kite (*Milvus milvus*). Neither of these species is traditionally employed in falconry but the exceptional frequency of wildfowl on this site—thousands of bones from wild geese, ducks, and waders were recovered—led Dobney and Jacques (2002) to conclude that some falconry was taking place. Perhaps the most remarkable avian find from Flixborough was a mid-eighth- to early-ninth-century pit containing the bones of at least eight cranes, surely the remains of a feast (Dobney et al. 2007: 73). That the mid Saxon elite were beginning to appreciate the capture and consumption of wildfowl is shown graphically in Fig. 18.2, which demonstrates that wild birds are slightly better represented on high-status settlements than on those of lower status.

The emergence of status-based variation in wild animal exploitation is even clearer when the mammal remains are considered (Fig. 18.1). As in the preceding period, few assemblages contain large quantities of wild mammal bone but there is a clear trend towards increased abundance of butchered and burnt deer bones amongst foods remains, evidence that these animals were being eaten rather than simply transformed into material culture. Marvin (2006) has suggested that the hunting of deer and the cutting up and sharing of venison bound together the arms-bearing men of the mid Saxon period, the symbolism of these acts perhaps explaining why, in *Beowulf*, Hrothgar saw it appropriate to name his great hall 'Heorot', the hart. Evidence for the breaking and redistribution of venison can be found in the zooarchaeological record. Deer assemblages from elite sites demonstrate an over-representation of jaw bones by comparison to post-cranial elements, indicating that the meat-bearing bones were consumed and discarded elsewhere (Fig. 18.3). This pattern is all the more interesting when it is recognized that, where present, deer assemblages from lower-status settlements tend to contain a higher proportion of meat-bearing elements: this was the case at Collinbourne Ducis, Wiltshire (Hamilton-Dyer 2001a), Eynesbury, Cambridgeshire (Sykes 2004), and Wolverton Turn, Buckinghamshire (Sykes 2007b). It seems possible that these patterns reflect communal hunting and venison redistribution: a peacetime equivalent of warfare and the distribution of the spoils.

Whilst some sections of mid Saxon society were beginning to consume wild mammals and birds, there is no evidence that the inhabitants of *wics* and *emporia* followed suit (Figs. 18.1 and 18.2). Scarcity of game animals on these sites has been taken as evidence that *wic* populations had no control over their provisions, being reliant on beef and mutton redistributed from elite sources (O'Connor 1994; 2001). Trading settlements do stand out, however, for the quantities of fish they yield. At Sandtun in Kent, for instance, over 4,000 fish remains were recovered (Hamilton-Dyer 2001b). Cod and whiting were the dominant species and the presence of fish-hooks suggests that both were caught by hand-lining from small boats. Herring (*Clupea harengus*) and mackerel (*Scomber scombrus*) were also well represented and were probably caught with driftnets, whilst the flatfish and eels (*Anguilla anguilla*) were taken by trapping and netting. Similar ranges of species, presumably caught through similar methods, have also been noted at mid Saxon Southampton (*Hamwic*), York, Ispwich, and London. Work by Barrett *et al.* (2004) suggests that these trading settlements are the exception rather than the rule. Other site-types seldom have large quantities of fish bones. Where present, freshwater and migratory species predominate, suggesting localized exploitation based on the

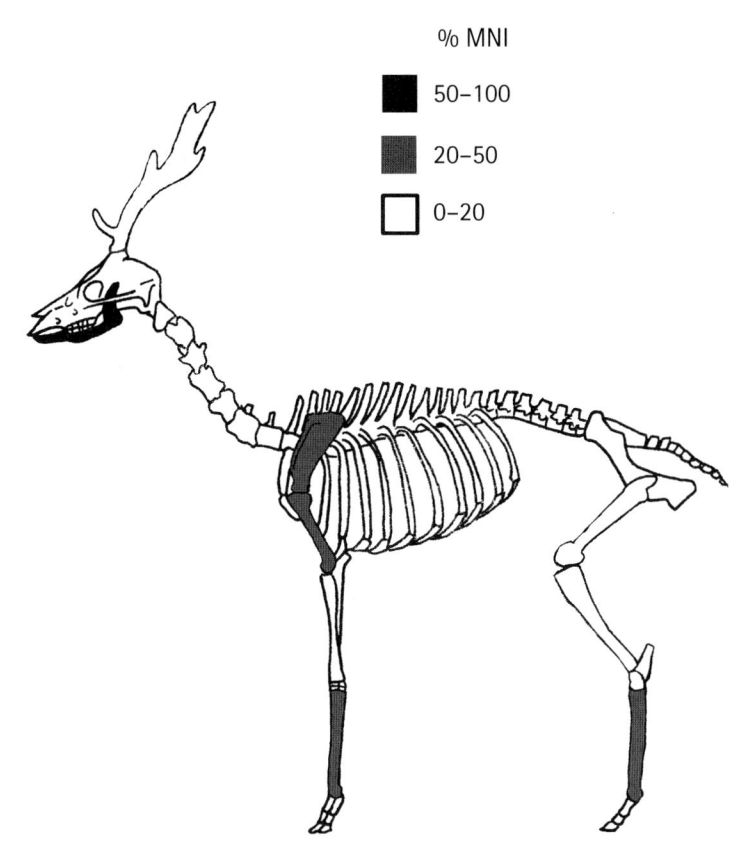

Figure 18.3 Anatomical representation of red and roe deer remains from elite sites dating to the mid Saxon period. Calculated as a percentage of the Minimum Number of Individuals (MNI), MNI = 34

many estuarine fish-traps that were being laid out in this period (O'Sullivan 2003). The possibility that these traps were elite enterprises is supported by finds of eel, salmon, perch, trout, and pike at sites such as Eynsham Abbey (Mulville 2003), Lake End Road (Powell 2002) and Flixborough, although it is equally plausible that these species were acquired via food rents: the Laws of Ine (688 x 94) specify that 5 salmon and 100 eels would be expected from 10 hides of land (Whitelock 1968).

Whilst marine fish are rare on elite sites, marine mammals are occasionally noted. Flixborough is again a key example: hundreds of cetacean bones were recovered, including the remains of bottlenose dolphins (*Tursiops truncates*) and minke whales (*Balaenoptera acutorostrata*). The sheer quantity of cetacean bones at Flixborough suggests a scenario whereby schools of sea mammals were herded into the nearby estuary and slaughtered en masse, although the possibility that the remains derive from strandings cannot be ruled out. That stranded whales were occasionally butchered and their remains utilized is indicated by the Franks Casket, carved from whalebone in Northumberland and carrying the message that it 'swam on to the shingle' (Gardiner 1997: 174).

The Franks Casket, and other examples of worked whale bone dating from the eighth century—the Gandersheim casket and the Blythburgh tablet (Gardiner 1997: 181)—demonstrate that the remains of wild animals were still being modified into new objects, but the mid Saxon period marked a fundamental shift from the preceding phase, with wild animals being used increasingly for food, especially by elite groups: a trend that was set to continue into the later Saxon period.

Late Saxon period: the mid ninth to the mid eleventh centuries

The late Saxon period witnessed dynamic social and economic change: the establishment of *burhs* in the late ninth century fundamentally changed urban development (see Hall, this volume); at the same time the break-up of the multiple estates enabled the emergence of a newly-landed thegnly class (Fleming 2001). These transformations are directly reflected in patterns of wild animal exploitation.

Increased representation of wild fauna in urban assemblages (Fig. 18.1) is, in part, related to the development of craft industries, notably bone/antler working (MacGregor 1991) and the fur trade (Fairnell 2003), which were established in many towns by 1050. But wild mammals, birds, and fish were also beginning to play a greater role in the urban diet. O'Connor (1994; 2004; and this volume) linked this growing dietary diversification to townsfolk taking a greater role in food procurement but also to the advent of consumer choice. Evidence that suppliers were becoming specialized to meet consumer demands is provided by Aelfric's *Colloquy* (c. 987 x 1001), which refers to professional huntsmen, fowlers, and fishers (Garmonsway 1939). Whilst most professionals were in the service of a lord, it seems probable that any surpluses they caught were sold on the open market. Aelfric's fisherman, for instance, sold his catch to the urban population, adding that 'I cannot catch as many as I can sell' (Garmonsway 1939: 26–30). His statement betrays the extensive fish trade that must have existed by the early eleventh century, evidence for which is also apparent in the zooarchaeological record. Barrett *et al.* (2004) have shown that patterns of fish consumption changed dramatically in the decades around AD 1000: not only do fish remains begin to appear in considerable quantities on urban sites but there is also a marked shift away from the exploitation of freshwater fish towards marine species, notably herring and cod. Aelfric's fisher does not mention cod, indeed the Anglo-Saxons had no word for the species (Sayers 2002, cited in Barrett *et al.* 2004: 623), and it seems possible that many of the *G. morhua* bones in late Anglo-Saxon deposits derive from imported individuals. Herring, on the other hand, were well known: they are mentioned by Aelfric's fisher, in several eleventh-century charters, and *c*.1086 the Domesday Book was able to record herring tolls and fisheries along the east coast of England (Tsurushima 2007: 196–200).

Motivation for the rise of the fishing industry is unclear and different scholars have proposed various hypotheses to account for the change: the introduction of new fishing technologies (driftnets or long line and hooks), climate change, Viking influence, widespread adoption of Christian fasting practices, and commercial revolution have all been suggested (Hagen 2002: 160; Barrett *et al.* 2004; Serjeantson and Woolgar 2006; Tsurushima 2007). In all probability, the impetus was complex and multi-causal but the association between marine fish and urban settlement does suggest that the movement began in towns long before it spread to the countryside. On rural settlements, in particular secular and religious elite sites, fish consumption also increased but continued to focus on freshwater and migratory species, perhaps suggesting that they were more prized than marine fish (Sykes 2007a). Tsurushima (2007: 196) has argued that the status attached to fish was dependent on region: herring may have been commonplace in the east but were apparently rare and sought after in the West Country, where salmon fisheries predominated. This is clear from the *c*.1050 charter for Tidenham in Gloucestershire, a manor which possessed 101 *cytweras* or basket weirs, devices specifically for catching salmon. The charter states that 'every rare fish which is of value—sturgeon, porpoise, herring' belonged to the lord and insists that, in return for a lease of land, the Archbishop of Canterbury was to deliver an annual rent of 30,000 herring and six porpoises, the former presumably obtained from Kentish waters (Robertson 1939: 204–19). The late Saxon elite were, therefore, going to some lengths to secure their supplies of freshwater and 'rare' fish, and it may even be that feudal claims to species such as sturgeon, porpoise, and whale were first established in this period. Certainly Gardiner's (1997) historical and archaeological work on cetacean exploitation concluded that whales and porpoises were viewed as elite property from the early eleventh century, their ownership and consumption becoming an element of competitive display amongst the late Saxon aristocracy.

Senecal (2001: 252) coined the term 'thegnly culture' to describe the composite habits and activities that emerged as the new aristocratic class sought to jockey for social position. If, as Senecal argues, conspicuous displays of wealth were key to securing power, it seems likely that hunting, falconry, and the consumption of game were important components of the package. Figure 18.2 indicates a marked mid-to-late Saxon increase in wildfowl exploitation by the elite, and several high-status settlements of this date have yielded complete skeletons of hunting birds (Cherryson 2002). Excavations at Faccombe Netherton in Hampshire, for instance, produced a complete skeleton of a female goshawk that exhibited leg bone injuries which Sadler (1990: 506) suggested may have been inflicted by jesses. Historical references for falconry are also more common for the late Saxon period: Oggins (2004) provides many examples demonstrating that by the late tenth century falconry had become an accepted part of the aristocratic lifestyle. This is supported by iconographic evidence: both the Bayeux Tapesty and the Cotton Tiberius calendar depict the elite engaged in falconry, the latter suggesting this was an activity for the month of October. For September, the calendar depicts a hunting scene, men with dogs and spears setting off to stick wild boar. Hunting too, it seems, had become an activity linked directly with the elite. Animal-bone data indicate that wild mammals are approximately three times better represented on high-status sites of late Saxon date compared with those from the preceding period (Fig. 18.1).

The status associations attached to hunting are also clear from documentary sources. Ælfric Bata's colloquies, written at the start of the eleventh century, referred to hunting as an activity of 'kings and great men' and Asser's *Vita Aelfredi* (*c*.893) mentioned hunting, alongside reading and warfare, as part of princely education (Marvin 2006). Even where hunting was undertaken by professional huntsmen, rather than kings or lords themselves, these hunt servants ranked socially higher than other labourers: Aelfric's huntsman held the first seat in the king's hall and was well rewarded for his service (Garmonsway 1939: 83).

Aelfric's hunter provides a considerable amount of information about his favoured quarry and the methods he uses to catch them. He makes no mention of bows and arrows, which is perhaps unsurprising given that there is little historical, iconographic, or archaeological evidence for their use in late Saxon England (e.g. Jessop 1996; Bradbury 1997; Lewis 2007: 113). Instead, he states that, using dogs, he drove wild animals—wild boar, stags, roe deer, and hare—into nets and killed them once they became ensnared (Garmonsway 1939: 56–60). When asked if he uses any other method for taking wild animals, Aelfric's hunter replies that he occasionally chased beasts with swift hounds. Other evidence for the chasing of game is also provided by the Life of St Dunstan (*c*.1000), which describes how King Edmund, while staying at his residence in Cheddar in the 940s, used dogs to flush out and pursue a deer, following on horseback to the very edge of the Gorge (Rahtz 1979: 17). It is interesting to note that excavation at the Cheddar palace yielded an uncommonly high percentage of red deer, a species suited to being chased over long distances (Higgs and Greenwood 1979). In general, however, the 'drive' rather than the chase is believed to have been the standard pre-Conquest hunting technique, employed by both professionals and elite alike (Gilbert 1979; Cummins 1988). It would have been a highly effective technique for obtaining large quantities of game in a single event, although to be successful it would have required the participation of many people. The Domesday Book mentions that citizens of Hereford, Shrewsbury, and Berkshire were obliged legally to act as drivers (Loyn 1970: 366), and it seems likely that this ability to muster manpower was used as a conspicuous display of royal or thegnly resources (Cummins 1988: 51).

Most late Saxon hunting apparently took place in wooded areas, such as the *siluis uenationibus*, 'woods for hunting', mentioned in the charter for Grimley, Worcestershire (Sawyer 1968: no. 1370). The Domesday account for Worcestershire refers to a *haia in qua capiebant ferae*, 'enclosure in which they used to capture wild animals' (Hagen 1998: 135), and Hooke (1989) has shown that place-names including the elements *haie* (hedge) or *haga* (enclosure) tend to be associated with woodland. Some refer specifically to deer, such as the *haiae capreolis*, 'hays for taking roe deer', recorded for both Cheshire and Shropshire (Thorn and Thorn 1986: 6.14) and the *derhage* at Ongar in Essex (Rackham 1997: 125). The fact that Ongar's *derhage* later became Ongar Great Park has led several researchers to suggest that *haie*, *haga* and *deor-fald* were little different in role and physical form to post-Conquest parks (Hooke 1989; Liddiard 2003). In his study of Sussex, Gautier (2007) reached the same conclusion, arguing that the ownership of hunting parks was a trait common to the pre-Conquest elite on both sides of the channel, and that, like fisheries and mills, they were key elements supporting its luxury lifestyle, their value demonstrated by the *Rectitudines Singularum Personarum* which required that *geneats* and cottagers maintained them on behalf of the lord or king (Lemanski 2005: 32–3).

The association between *haga*, hunting, and the elite is demonstrated well by Faccombe Netherton in Hampshire, a late Saxon manor for which a 'white haga' was recorded in 961 (Hooke 1989: 128). During excavation of this settlement a substantial wild mammal assemblage was recovered, and of the species represented roe deer was the most numerous. Other assemblages from late Saxon elite sites— Goltho in Lincolnshire (Jones and Ruben 1987) and Bishopstone, Sussex (Ingrem n.d.)—are also dominated by roe deer remains. However, if roe deer were the main quarry in these wooded landscapes, the interpretation of *haiae* and *hagan* as parks is problematic because they are notoriously unsuitable as park animals, the males in particular becoming dangerously territorial when confined. Perhaps the *haie* and *haga* were intermittent boundary structures rather than continuous enclosures, allowing nets to be erected in the gaps (Sykes 2007c). This would explain why the Domesday Book often records *haiae* in the plural whereas parks are referred to in the singular (Liddiard 2003: 12).

However deer were caught, animal-bone assemblages from late Saxon sites suggest a change in the treatment and consumption of venison. By contrast to mid Saxon assemblages (Fig. 18.3), deer skeletal patterning for elite sites shows that all parts of the body are represented, with meat-bearing elements from the forelimb being particularly abundant (Fig. 18.4). This suggests that venison was no longer being redistributed as symbol of community but rather that the elite were privatizing venison and consuming it as a marker of social difference. It is often suggested that hunting and venison consumption became linked to the aristocracy only after 1066 but the evidence presented above makes it clear that

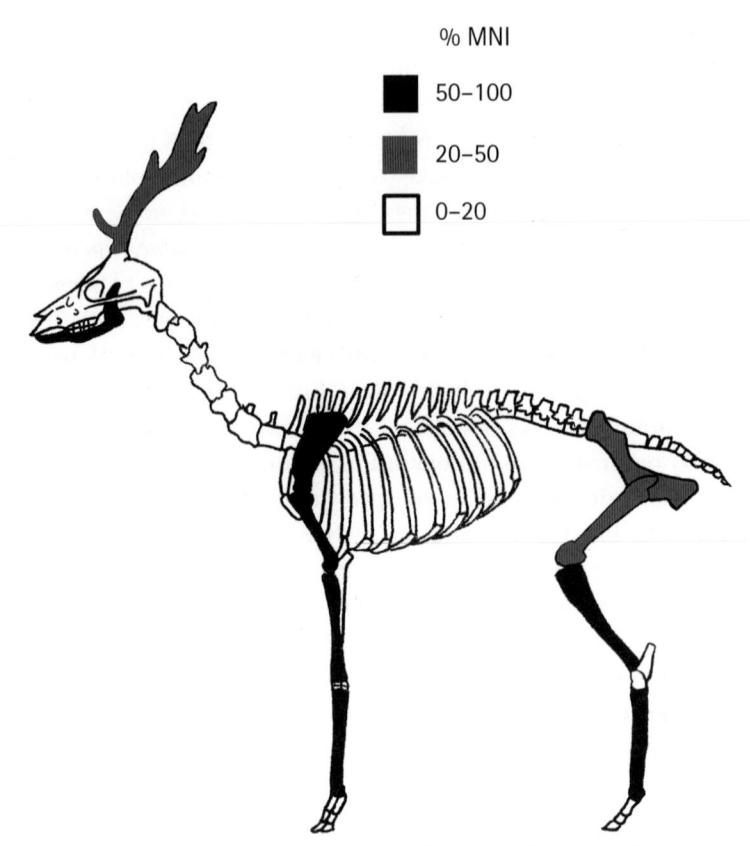

Figure 18.4 Anatomical representation of red and roe deer remains from elite sites dating to the late Saxon period. Calculated as a percentage of the Minimum Number of Individuals (MNI), MNI = 50

the Normans would have been very familiar with the hunting institutions already in place in late Saxon England.

Conclusion

During the six centuries encompassed by the Anglo-Saxon period the relationship between humans and wild animals changed dramatically. The move from paganism to Christianity, commercial development, and the emergence of rigid social hierarchies all played a role, influencing not only the desire to engage in hunting, fishing, and fowling but also the species deemed suitable for exploitation.

Evidence for early Anglo-Saxon England is dichotomous. In a period when wild fauna were probably more varied and abundant than at any subsequent point, people seemingly avoided wild resource exploitation and certainly derived little sustenance from hunting, fowling, and fishing. In many respects, it seems that wild animals were valued more alive than dead. Even when wild animals were killed, their remains were carefully transformed into objects—amulets, drinking-horns, bone artefacts, and furs—that appear to have derived their significance from the character of the living animal. Indeed, it seems possible that the remains of fierce creatures—bears, wolves, aurochsen, and raptorial birds—were chosen specifically in the hope that the traits of these animals would be transferred to whoever possessed their body parts. A belief that even images carried the essence of the living animal may equally explain the association between wild animal motifs and weapons, such as shields and boar-crested helmets. Evidence from funerary deposits demonstrates that wild animal images and body parts are perhaps most closely associated with elite individuals; however, no social group appears to have had a monopoly over wild animals.

A facade of egalitarianism was maintained into the mid Saxon period when, it seems, wild mammals were hunted communally and the meat redistributed accordingly. For the first time, wild animals were beginning to make a contribution to the diet and game animals, especially cranes, are found on all site-types, perhaps with the exception of *wics* and *emporia*, where fish represent the main wild animals consumed. However, it is clear that the elite were beginning to employ hunting and fowling as symbols of power. This new association with the elite seems to mark a change in Anglo-Saxon attitudes to wild animals: rather than being admired and avoided, wild creatures were coming to be viewed as resources that could be captured and eaten by those who had the ability to do so.

By the late Saxon period, attitudes to wild animals had shifted further still. Historical, iconographic, and archaeological evidence all indicate a new emphasis on 'property': that the ability to consume animals derived from hunting, fowling, and fishing had become something of a metaphor for ownership of land, water, and shore. This transformation in the perception of animals must be linked to the emergence of the newly-landed thegnly class, for whom property equalled power. At the lower end of the social scale, peasants were now required to maintain deer fences and act as drivers during hunting, but there is little evidence to suggest that they were rewarded through the redistribution of venison or game. Instead, hunting and fowling had become overt symbols of social hierarchy with restrictions being placed on access to particular species, notably cetaceans and some fish species. Whilst the rural population appear to have been following these new codes of conduct, wild animal exploitation in the urban environment was seemingly governed by a different agenda, that of commercialization. The development of the fishing trade saw large numbers of marine fish being landed in urban ports and consumed by the town's inhabitants. Other wild animals are also better represented in urban assemblages, suggesting that town populations had greater control over their provisions. It seems unlikely that townsfolk were directly involved in the hunting or fowling process—these activities now being undertaken by professionals—so the relationship between humans and wild animals had become increasingly remote, a situation far from that experienced by the early Saxon population.

REFERENCES

ALLISON, E. (1988). 'The bird bones', in R. Daniels (ed.), 'The Anglo-Saxon monastery at Church Close, Hartlepool, Cleveland'. *Archaeological Journal* 145: 158–210, at 199–201.

ALMOND, R. (2003). *Medieval Hunting*. Stroud: Sutton.

AYBES, C., and YALDEN, D. W. (1995). 'Place-name evidence for the former distribution and status of wolves and beavers in Britain'. *Mammal Review* 25: 201–27.

BARRETT, J., LOCKER, A. M., and ROBERTS, C. M. (2004). '"Dark Age Economics" revisited: the English fishbone evidence AD 600–1600'. *Antiquity* 78: 618–36.

BOISSEAU, S., and YALDEN, D. W. (1998). 'The former status of the crane *grus grus* in Britain'. *Ibis* 140: 482–500.

BOND, J. (1994). 'The cremated animal bone', in J. McKinley (ed.), *The Anglo-Saxon Cemetery at Spong Hill, North Elmham, Part 8: The Cremations*. Norwich: East Anglian Archaeology Report 69, 121–35.

BRADBURY, J. (1997). *The Medieval Archer*. Woodbridge: Boydell.

CARTMILL, M. (1993). *A View to a Death in the Morning: Hunting and Nature Through History*. Cambridge, MA: Harvard University Press.

CARVER, M. (1998). *Sutton Hoo: Burial Ground of Kings?* London: British Museum Press.

CHERRYSON, A. (2002). 'The identification of archaeological evidence for hawking in medieval England'. *Acta Zoologica Cracoviensia* 45: 307–14.

COLES, B. (2006). *Beavers in Britain's Past*. Oxford: Oxbow Books.

COY, J. (1980). 'The animal bones', in J. Haslam (ed.) 'A middle Saxon iron smelting site at Ramsbury, Wiltshire'. *Medieval Archaeology* 24: 1–68, at 41–51.

—— (1981). 'The animal bones', in R. J. Silvester (ed.), 'An excavation on the post-Roman site of Bantham, South Devon'. *Devon Archaeological Society Proceedings* 39: 89–118, at 106–10.

CRABTREE, P. (1990). *West Stow: Early Anglo-Saxon Animal Husbandry*. East Anglian Archaeology 47. Bury St Edmunds.

—— (1995). 'The symbolic role of animals in Anglo-Saxon England: evidence from burials and cremations', in K. Ryan and P. J. Crabtree (eds.), *The Symbolic Role of Animals in Archaeology*. MASCA Research Papers in Science and Archaeology 12. Philadelphia: University of Pennsylania Press, 20–6.

—— (1996). 'Production and consumption in an early complex society: animal use in middle Saxon East Anglia'. *World Archaeology* 28(1): 58–75.

CUMMINS, J. (1988). *The Hound and the Hawk: the Art of Medieval Hunting*. London: Weidenfield and Nicholson.

DENT, A. (1974). *Lost Beasts of Britain*. London: Harrap.

DICKINSON, T. M. (2005). 'Symbols of Protection: the significance of animal-ornamented shields in early Anglo-Saxon England'. *Medieval Archaeology* 49: 109–63.

DOBNEY, K., and JACQUES, D. (2002). 'Avian signatures for identity and status in Anglo-Saxon England'. *Acta Zoologica Cracoviensia* 45: 7–21.

————— BARRETT, J., and JOHNSTONE, C. (2007). *Farmer, Monks and Aristocrats: The Environmental Archaeology of Anglo-Saxon Flixborough.* Volume 3 of *Excavations at Flixborough.* Oxford: Oxbow Books.

FAIRNELL, E. (2003). *The Utilisation of Fur-bearing Animals in the British Isles: A Zooarchaeological Hunt for Data.* Unpublished MSc dissertation, University of York.

FLEMING, R. (2001). 'The new wealth, the new rich and the new political style in late Anglo-Saxon England'. *Anglo-Norman Studies* 23: 1–22.

GARDINER, M. (1997). 'The exploitation of sea-mammals in medieval England: bones and their social context'. *Archaeological Journal* 154: 173–95.

GARMONSWAY, G. N. (1939). *Aelfric's Colloquy.* London: Methuen.

GAUTIER, A. (2007). 'Game parks in Sussex and the Godwinesons'. *Anglo-Norman Studies* 29: 51–64.

GEBBLES, A. (1977). 'The animal bones', in M. Bell (ed.), 'Excavations at Bishopstone'. *Sussex Archaeological Collections* 115: 1–299, at 277–84.

GILBERT, J. (1979). *Hunting and Hunting Reserves in Medieval Scotland.* Edinburgh: John Donald.

HAGEN, A. (1998). *A Handbook of Anglo-Saxon Food: Processing and Consumption.* Frithgarth: Anglo-Saxon Books.

——— (2002). *A Second Handbook of Anglo-Saxon Food and Drink: Production and Distribution.* Frithgarth: Anglo-Saxon Books.

HAMILTON-DYER, S. (2001a). 'Animal bone', in J. Pine (ed.), 'The excavation of a Saxon settlement at Cadley Road, Collingbourne Ducis, Wiltshire'. *Wiltshire Archaeological and Natural History Magazine* 94: 88–117, at 102–9.

——— (2001b). 'Bird and fish remains', in M. Gardiner, R. Cross, N. Macpherson-Grant, and I. Riddler, 'Continental trade and non-urban ports in mid-Saxon England. Excavations at Sandtun, West Hythe, Kent'. *Archaeological Journal* 158: 161–290, at 255–61.

HAMMON, A. (in press). 'Bears', in T. O'Connor and and N. J. Sykes (eds.), *Extinctions and Invasions: a Social History of British Fauna.* Oxford: Windgather Press, 95–103.

HAWKES, J. (1997). 'Symbolic lives: the visual evidence', in J. Hines (ed.), *The Anglo-Saxons from the Migration Period to the Eighth Century: An Ethnographic Perspective.* Woodbridge: Boydell, 311–44.

HETHERINGTON, D. A., LORD, T. C., and JACOBI, R. M. (2006). 'New evidence for the occurrence of Eurasian lynx (*Lynx lynx*) in medieval Britain'. *Journal of Quaternary Science* 21: 3–8.

HIGGS, E., and GREENWOOD, W. (1979). 'Faunal report', in Rahtz (ed.), *The Saxon and Medieval Palaces at Cheddar,* 354–62.

HOOKE, D. (1989). 'Pre-conquest Woodland: its distribution and usage'. *Agricultural History Review* 37(2): 113–29.

——— (1998). *The Landscape of Anglo-Saxon England.* Leicester: Leicester University Press.

Ingrem, C. (n.d.) 'Assessment of the Animal Remains from Bishopstone, Sussex', unpublished report to the Sussex Archaeological Society, 2005.

JESSOP, O. (1996). 'A new artifact typology for the study of medieval arrowheads'. *Medieval Archaeology* 40: 192–205.

Jones, R. T., and Ruben, I. (1987). 'Animal bones, with some notes on the effects of differential sampling', in G. Beresford (ed.), *Goltho: The Development of an Early Medieval Manor c.850–1150*. English Heritage Archaeological Report 4. London: English Heritage, 197–206.

Kylie, E. (1911). *The English Correspondence of St Boniface*. London: Chatto and Windus.

Lemanski, S. J. (2005). *The 'Rectitudines Singularum Personarum': Anglo-Saxon Landscapes in Transition*. Unpublished MA thesis, University of Akron.

Lewis, M. J. (2007). 'Identity and status in the Bayeux Tapestry: the iconographic and artefactual evidence'. *Anglo-Norman Studies* 29: 100–20.

Liddiard, R. (2003). 'The deer parks of Domesday Book'. *Landscape* 4(1): 4–23.

Loyn, H. R. (1970). *Anglo-Saxon England and the Norman Conquest*. London: Longman.

Lucy, S. (2000). *The Anglo-Saxon Way of Death: Burial Rites in Early England*. Gloucester: Sutton.

Macgregor, A. (1991). 'Antler, bone and horn', in J. Blair and N. Ramsay (eds.), *English Medieval Industries: Craftsmen, Techniques, Products*. London: Hambledon Press, 355–78.

Maltby, M. (2003). 'Animal bone', in C. Bateman, D. Enright and N. Oakey (eds.), 'Prehistoric and Anglo-Saxon settlements to the rear of Sherbourne House, Lechlade: excavations in 1997'. *Transactions of the Bristol and Gloucestershire Archaeological Society* 121: 23–96, at 71–6.

Marvin, W. P. (2006). *Hunting Law and Ritual in Medieval English Literature*. Cambridge: Brewer.

McClure, J., and Collins, R. (eds.) (1994). *Bede: The Ecclesiastical History of the English People*. Oxford: Oxford University Press.

Meaney, A. L. (1981). *Anglo-Saxon Amulets and Curing Stones*. BAR British Series 96. Oxford: British Archaeological Reports.

——(1992). 'Anglo-Saxon idolators and ecclesiasts from Theodore to Alcuin; a source study'. *Anglo-Saxon Studies in Archaeology and History* 5: 103–25.

Mew, K. (2001). 'The dynamics of lordship and landscape as revealed in a Domesday study of the Nova Foresta'. *Anglo-Norman Studies* 23: 155–66.

Mulville, J. (2003). 'Phases 2a–2e: Anglo-Saxon occupation', in A. Hardy, A. Dodd, and G. Keevil (eds.), *Aelfric's Abbey: Excavations at Eynsham Abbey, Oxfordshire 1989–92*. Volume 16 of *Thames Valley Landscapes*. Oxford: Oxford University School of Archaeology, 343–60.

O'Connor, T. P. (1994). '8th–11th Century economy and environment in York', in J. Rackham (ed.), *Environment and Economy in Anglo-Saxon England*. CBA Research Report 89. London: Council for British Archaeology, 136–47.

—— (2001). 'On the interpretation of animal bone assemblages from *wics*', in D. Hill and R. Cowie (eds.), *Wics: The Early Medieval Trading Centres of Northern Europe*. Sheffield: Sheffield Academic Press, 54–60.

Oggins, R. (2004). *The Kings and Their Hawks: Falconry in Medieval England*. London: Yale.

O'Sullivan, A. (2003). 'Place, memory and identity among estuarine fishing communities: interpreting the archaeology of early medieval fish weirs'. *World Archaeology* 35(3): 449–68.

Pluskowski, A. (2006). *Wolves and the Wilderness in the Middle Ages*. Woodbridge: Boydell.

Powell, A. (2002). 'Animal bone', in S. Foreman, J. Hiller, and D. Petts (eds.), *Gathering the People, Settling the Lands: The Archaeology of a Middle Thames Landscape*, Volume 3:

Anglo-Saxon to Post-Medieval. Volume 14 of *Thames Valley Landscape Monographs.* Oxford: Oxford Archaeology, 44–9.

PRIVAT, K. L., O'CONNELL, T. C., and RICHARDS, M. P. (2002). 'Stable isotope analysis of human and faunal remains from the Anglo-Saxon cemetery at Berinsfield, Oxfordshire: dietary and social implications'. *Journal of Archaeological Science* 29(7): 779–90.

RACKHAM, O. (1997). *The History of the Countryside: The Classic History of Britain's Landscape, Flora and Fauna.* London: Phoenix.

RAHTZ, P. (1979). *The Saxon and Medieval Palaces at Cheddar: Excavations 1960–62.* BAR British Series 65. Oxford: British Archaeological Reports.

ROBERTSON, A. J. (1939). *Anglo-Saxon Charters.* Cambridge: Cambridge University Press.

ROONEY, A. (1993). *Hunting in Middle English Literature.* Woodbridge: Boydell and Brewer.

SADLER, P. (1990). 'The faunal remains', in J. R. Fairbrother (ed.), *Faccombe Netherton: Excavations of a Saxon and Medieval Manorial Complex II.* British Museum Occasional Paper 74. London: British Museum, 462–508.

SAWYER, P. H. (1968). *Anglo-Saxon Charters: An Annotated List and Bibliography.* London: Offices of the Royal Historical Society.

SAYERS, W. (2002). 'Some fishy etymologies: Eng. *Cod,* Norse ¿*orskr,* Du. *Kabeljauw,* Sp. *Bacalao'. NOWELE: North-Western European Language Evolution* 41: 17–30.

SENECAL, C. (2001). 'Keeping up with the Godwinesons: in pursuit of aristocratic status in late Anglo-Saxon England'. *Anglo-Norman Studies* 23: 251–66.

SERJEANTSON, D., and WOOLGAR, C. M. (2006). 'Fish consumption in medieval England', in C. M. Woolgar, D. Serjeantson, and T. Waldron (eds.), *Food in Medieval England: History and Archaeology.* Oxford: Oxford University Press, 102–30.

STOVES, J. L. (1983). 'Examination of hairs from the Sutton Hoo musical instrument', in R. Bruce-Mitford (ed.), The *Sutton Hoo Ship Burial,* Volume 3. London: British Museum, 723–5.

SYKES, N. J. (2004). 'Neolithic and Saxon animal bone', in C. J. Ellis (ed.), *A Prehistoric Ritual Complex at Eynesbury, Cambridgeshire: Excavation of a Multi-Period Site in the Great Ouse Valley, 2000–2001.* East Anglian Archaeology Occasional Paper 17. Salisbury: Trust for Wessex Archaeology, 187–9.

——(2005). 'The dynamics of status symbols: wildfowl exploitation in England AD 410–1550'. *Archaeological Journal* 161: 82–105.

——(2007a). 'Animal bones and animal parks', in R. Liddiard (ed.), *The Medieval Deer Park: New Perspectives.* Macclesfield: Windgather Press, 49–62.

——(2007b). 'The animal bone', in S. Preston (ed.), 'Bronze Age occupation and Saxon feature at the Wolverton Turn enclosure, near Stony Stratford, Milton Keynes'. *Records of Buckinghamshire* 47: 81–117, at 103–9.

—— (2007c). *The Norman Conquest: a Zooarchaeological Perspective.* British Archaeological Reports International Series 1656. Oxford: Archaeopress.

THORN, F., and THORN, C. (eds.) (1986). *Domesday Book, 25, Shropshire.* Chichester: Phillimore.

TSURUSHIMA, H. (2007). 'The eleventh century in England through fish-eyes: salmon, herring, oysters, and 1066'. *Anglo-Norman Studies* 29: 193–213.

VAN VUURE, C. (2005). *Retracing the Aurochs: History, Morphology and Ecology of an Extinct Wild Ox.* Sofia/Moscow: Pensoft Publishers.

WHITELOCK, D. (1968). *English Historical Documents,* Volume 1: *c. 500–1042.* London: Eyre and Spottiswoode.

YALDEN, D. (1999). *A History of British Mammals.* London: T. and A. Poyser.

CHAPTER 19

FOOD PLANTS ON ARCHAEOLOGICAL SITES

THE NATURE OF THE ARCHAEOBOTANICAL RECORD

LISA MOFFETT

THIS paper aims to give a summary of the current state of archaeobotanical knowledge of food plants from English archaeological sites from the fifth to the eleventh century. It looks at the species that have been recovered and at the biases introduced by different types of preservation, and briefly considers whether the archaeobotanical evidence can be used to look beyond the basic 'shopping list' of plants to activities related to production and consumption. Processing plants—and animals—into food has been the subject of excellent reviews by Banham (2004) and Hagen (2006), using both archaeological and historical evidence, and addressing the cultural and economic context of food. This paper will be confined to a more strictly archaeological approach and will consider some of the strengths and limitations of the archaeobotanical evidence, but is neither an in-depth study of any particular aspect, nor a comprehensive review. Sites mentioned in the text are given only as indicative examples.

Preservation bias and dating

It is important to understand the processes of preservation of plant remains on archaeological sites because this directly determines what kinds of plant remains may be found, or whether there are any preserved at all. What survives of the organic material brought to and produced on a site will be biased by human activity and preservation conditions; even apparently well-preserved archaeobotanical evidence is in fact undergoing a process of slow deterioration.

The commonest way in which plant remains are preserved on archaeological sites in Britain is by charring. Charring requires exposure to fire under reducing (anaerobic) conditions, which burns away most of the organic material leaving a carbon skeleton with approximately the same gross morphology as the original item, though this is often partial or distorted. The carbon skeleton is not subject to bacterial decay, but it is very delicate and prone to mechanical damage from various processes such as freezing and thawing, wetting and drying, or biological disturbance, not to mention being trodden on by humans and animals before it is ever buried. Reducing conditions generally occur in the lower portions of a fire that is not hot enough to cause the material to simply vaporize. Delicate material tends to be destroyed regardless and generally only the more robust items survive. Being burned under reducing conditions is clearly a result of particular human activities and would generally preserve only materials that were deliberately exposed to fire in some way, even if the intention was not actually to burn them. Cereals and their associated weeds are some of the most common materials (apart from wood charcoal) preserved by charring. Accidents must also have happened, of course, and the evidence from minor accidents may not always be distinguishable from deliberate burning. Considering the large amount of highly combustible material that must have been present on Anglo-Saxon sites the available evidence seems to suggest that major accidents with fire were few.

Plant remains are also preserved by permanent waterlogging in anoxic conditions. Most decay organisms require oxygen, and when this is depleted decay is greatly slowed. Some bacteria can survive in anoxic conditions but the process of decay is much slower and plant remains in highly anoxic conditions can survive for a long time. Soil chemistry is highly complex and the factors that account for whether waterlogged organic material is preserved, and how well or how poorly, are not yet fully understood. Waterlogging can preserve a much wider range of materials than charring usually does, but there is still a tendency for more robust items to be better preserved. Anoxic waterlogged conditions on archaeological sites are most frequent in wells, latrines, and the bottoms of deeper pits and ditches—deposits in the fills of sunken-featured buildings are rarely conducive to plant survival. Since people tend to avoid living on wet ground, waterlogged features are not common near human occupation. Even wells and latrines are rare except in towns, in which waterfront sites also often preserve organic remains.

Mineral replacement can occur when calcium phosphate and/or calcium carbonate are present in abundant amounts, and where there is sufficient soil moisture to dissolve and transport them into the plant tissues. Sometimes the plant tissues themselves are not replaced, but the minerals form a cast of the internal parts of woody structures such as fruit stones. Conditions for mineral replacement are most likely in latrines and other pits where human or animal waste is present. Such situations are relatively rare. Mineralized remains are generally difficult to identify although occasionally woody seeds such as fruit stones and fig pips can be very well preserved.

Metal corrosion products such as iron, copper, and lead oxides are toxic to decay-causing micro-organisms. Pollen and plant tissue can be preserved in or near these corrosion products, though obviously the amounts are usually small, as with the fabric from flax or hemp on the back of brooches (Walton Rogers 2007: 59–60).

Anglo-Saxon plant remains are often very poorly dated: ceramics vary considerably in how well they can be dated; some sites are aceramic, and many are poor in other finds. The calibration curve for radiocarbon dating for much of the late Saxon period is very broad and can provide only very imprecise dates, making it difficult or impossible to distinguish pre- and post-Conquest periods even when plant material is dated directly. The calibration curve also affects the dating of some ceramic series so that some late Saxon sites can only be dated as tenth to twelfth centuries. Bayesian modelling may have some potential to improve these results if a sequence is reliable but this kind of extensive dating programme is not often done. The earlier part of the period can potentially produce very good radiocarbon dates, but unfortunately, fifth- and sixth-century sites have produced little in the way of plant remains in secure contexts, because few wells or rubbish-pits were dug. Much of the rubbish was presumably spread on fields as manure.

Cereals

It was once thought that emmer (*Triticum dicoccum* Schübl) and spelt (*Triticum spelta* L.), the glume wheats of earlier periods, fell out of use with the arrival of Anglo-Saxon agriculture, but it now seems that their use persisted, although possibly not everywhere. Emmer from two sites in the Thames valley has been radiocarbon-dated to the early part of the period (Pelling and Robinson 2000). Emmer was the main wheat of most of prehistoric Britain but appears to have been a very minor and local crop during the Roman period, at least in southern Britain.

Pelling and Robinson suggest that the early Anglo-Saxon settlers of the Thames valley may have brought their emmer with them from their homeland in the north German coastal area, where emmer had continued in cultivation. Spelt, the main wheat of the Roman period, may also have continued in use at least in some areas. Spelt has been found in both early and late contexts in East Anglia (Murphy 1994a; van der Veen 1993) and from ninth-century contexts in Gloucester (Green 1979). In those examples residuality is considered unlikely, though is always a factor to consider, especially as no Anglo-Saxon spelt remains have been directly radiocarbon-dated.

Spelt and emmer are different species of wheat. Spelt is closely related to bread wheat and emmer to the rivet and durum wheats. Despite their biological differences they have some characteristics in common that distinguish them from their free-threshing relatives. Glume wheats hold the grains tightly enclosed in the chaff and cannot be threshed in the same way as free-threshing wheats such as bread wheat. Some form of processing has to be undertaken to remove the grain from the chaff, such as pounding in a mortar with a pestle, or loose milling. Although this appears to be more labour-intensive there is an advantage in that glume wheats stored unprocessed in the spikelet are less susceptible to pests in storage.

Emmer and spelt are also both more suitable for making ale. There is evidence for malting spelt from a number of sites in Roman Britain (van der Veen 1989) and spelt is brewed for beer even today. It is not necessary to remove the grain from the spikelets in order to make malt as the chaff can be sieved out later. There is currently no evidence for malting emmer or spelt in the Anglo-Saxon period in Britain, although there is evidence for malting barley (e.g. Moffett 2007a), so the possible use of glume wheats for making ale remains speculative. Emmer and spelt can also be ground to flour for bread but neither will make a leavened loaf that will rise as well as one made from bread wheat due to the difference in their glutins. Grains of any cereal can also be roasted for extra flavour and cooked either cracked or whole as groats, as in pottage, or crushed for a porridge.

The very sparse nature of the evidence in the early part of the Anglo-Saxon period makes it extremely difficult to discern how widespread the glume wheats may have been and whether they were re-introduced or persisted from earlier periods. Emmer and spelt may have been cultivated only very locally, and perhaps on a small scale, though further research is needed to test this. It is possible that choice of these crops varied between individual households, with some families preferring certain foods or drinks made with these cereals and keeping them for their own consumption or exchanging them within a limited market. Use of these cereals may also mark wider cultural differences between groups of people, perhaps reflecting their origins.

Bread wheat (*Triticum aestivum* L.) is much more commonly found and is assumed to have been used for bread. It occurs in Britain from the Neolithic onwards, but appears to have become a widespread staple only in the Anglo-Saxon period. It is sometimes seen as being less labour-intensive because it is free-threshing, though indeed the labour of threshing and winnowing it is not light (Hillman 1984). The use of a free-threshing wheat could be seen as an agricultural 'improvement' but the fact is that many generations of farmers in Britain knew about bread wheat, did grow it on occasion, and yet appear mostly to have preferred the glume wheats, suggesting that labour may not have been the deciding factor. There is also little reason at present to think that biological differences were a factor. Spelt and bread wheat in any case differ very little biologically. Both belong to a single biological species (*T. aestivum*) and are fully interfertile. Hardiness and productivity vary with variety and environmental conditions. The local varieties of spelt, and before spelt, emmer, had probably become well adapted to local conditions.

As we have just seen, the changeover from glume wheats to free-threshing bread wheat was not total, yet nevertheless there was a great change in emphasis which must be the result of differences from the previous period that may relate to food preferences as well as to agricultural technique. Incoming settlers may have brought their own crops with them, and the knowledge of how to grow those crops, and what foods to make from them. Traditions such as these are not lightly changed as subsistence farmers cannot afford to take too many risks with unfamiliar crops and methods, though they may experiment on a small scale. Generally, too, people are conservative in their approach to food and tend to prefer the foods they have grown up with. The extent to which incoming farmers may have influenced the indigenous farmers, and vice versa, is an important facet of the wider cultural exchange of influences as well as of such outright displacement as took place.

Late in the Anglo-Saxon period a fourth wheat was probably introduced—a free-threshing member of the group of wheats (also a single biological species) which includes rivet wheat, durum (or macaroni) wheat, and emmer. This wheat is considered most likely to be rivet wheat (*Triticum turgidum* L.) on the grounds that durum wheat, which is also free-threshing, is less suited to the British climate as it needs plenty of sun to ripen well. It is not possible to distinguish rivet from durum wheat without whole ears or spikelets, however, and these have not been found so far. Rivet wheat has mostly been found in post-Conquest contexts (Moffett 1991)—and in post-medieval thatch (Letts 1999). At Higham Ferrers in the Nene valley in Northamptonshire, a small amount of rivet wheat was radiocarbon-dated by accelerator mass spectrometry to cal. AD 770–1000 (1150 ± 45 BP) (OxA-10126), so seems to be pre-Conquest (Moffett 2007a). It was also found in the Nene valley, only a few miles from Higham Ferrers at West Cotton, but unfortunately there are no radiocarbon dates for it there, and as the ceramics can only be attributed to the tenth to twelfth centuries a pre-Conquest date is not certain (Campbell 1994).

Rivet wheat flour is better suited to biscuit- than to bread-making, though this does not mean that Saxon bakers did not use it for the latter. Especially in good summers rivet wheat can be very productive (Percival 1921), and it may be that bread made of mixed bread and rivet wheat flours was perfectly acceptable. It is even possible that they were grown together, as so far rivet wheat remains have only been found with those of bread wheat. Identifications of rivet wheat (and bread wheat) have to be made on the chaff, especially the rachis remains (fragments of stem from the ear), as the grains are not reliably distinguishable. It is quite possible, therefore, that the chaff of the two wheats became mixed after threshing and that what appears to be a mixed crop (or maslin) is in fact two separately grown crops.

Rivet wheat straw is a tall crop, although old varieties of bread wheat are also tall compared with modern varieties. The straw of rivet wheat, however, is particularly strong and this would make it especially suitable for thatching. Its awns (the 'beard' on bearded wheats) are also very stiff and strong and thus discouraging to birds, and it is resistant to rust (Percival 1921). As a crop, therefore, it may have had a number of merits that made up for its poorer bread-making qualities. Rivet wheat is, however, less hardy in the cold and wet than bread wheat. Even in the medieval and post-medieval periods it has so far not been found north of Cheshire (Moffett 1991).

Rye (*Secale cereale* L.) also has a long, strong straw suitable for thatch, and is a hardy cereal. It can grow a deep root system which allows it to thrive on droughty soils. Rye is occasionally found on Roman sites (Clapham 2008), but is not common until the Anglo-Saxon period, when it appears to have been much more widely grown. Rye straw was found in abundance in ovens at late Saxon Stafford where it may have been used for fuel (Moffett 1994), and it may have had a similar use at West Cotton (Campbell 1994). Rye's tolerance for droughty, sandy soils could mean that it was grown more in areas too dry for wheats, but no such relationship has been firmly established so far. The growing of rye could represent food preferences possibly associated with incoming Germanic peoples. Rye by itself makes a very dense but moist bread, but can be mixed with bread wheat to produce a lighter loaf.

Barley (*Hordeum vulgare* L.) is also widely found on Saxon sites throughout the period. Probably most of this is six-row hulled barley, although with poorly preserved material it can be difficult to distinguish the asymmetric grains which are characteristic of the lateral florets of six-row barley. It is often not possible to tell whether an assemblage of barley is six-row, two-row, or mixed. The rachis fragments are diagnostic when well preserved, but these seldom survive. Clear evidence for two-row barley appears to be mostly late Saxon, as at London (Jones *et al.* 1991) and Stafford (Moffett 1994).

Two species of oat have been found, the common oat (*Avena sativa* L.) and the bristle oat (*Avena strigosa* Schreb.). They are difficult to distinguish from each other and from the wild species of oats (*A. fatua* L. and *A. sterilis* L.) which commonly infest cereal fields. The basal grains of common oat are generally larger than bristle oat and the wild species, but its upper grains overlap so much in size with other oat species that this is only a rough indication at best. Only the chaff fragments (the spikelet forks) are diagnostic and these are fragile and rarely survive. Oat is found widely on Anglo-Saxon sites, sometimes in such abundance and with such large grains that it is clearly a crop. Bristle oat was found at Stafford (Moffett 1994) and possibly at Norwich (Murphy 1994b).

Legumes

Legumes are less commonly found than cereals, probably because their seeds were less commonly exposed to fire. At *Hamwic*, comparison of charred and mineralized material from the same mid Saxon pits produced far more mineralized remains of peas (*Pisum sativum* L.) and beans (*Vicia faba* L.) than charred, suggesting that the mineralized material was a better reflection of what people were actually eating (Carruthers 2005). Peas and beans are found widely in sites throughout the period. The peas are generally round, smooth, and fairly small, characteristics typical of field peas. The field beans are also round and small, resembling the 'Celtic bean'. When poorly preserved it can be surprisingly difficult to distinguish beans from peas.

Large seeded legumes resembling cultivated vetch (*Vicia sativa* subsp. *sativa*) have been found at several sites such as Wraysbury (Astill and Lobb 1989), and Higham Ferrers (Moffett 2007a), but it has not been possible to make a definite identification due to the lack of the diagnostic hilum. At West Cotton, however, cultivated vetch was definitely identified (Campbell 1994). Cultivated vetch is a fodder crop which would have been eaten by humans only in times of starvation as the seeds contain toxins (Ressler 1962). Lentils (*Lens culinaris* Medik) are also occasionally found, as at Yarnton (Stevens 2004), London (Jones *et al*. 1991), and *Hamwic* (Clapham 2005). In Britain, lentil is not a very productive food crop for humans as the plants need warm summers to produce well-filled pods. Plot (1705) records lentil being grown as a post-medieval green fodder crop, so perhaps there was a long history of lentil being grown for that purpose. Both lentil and vetch would have made useful rotation crops with cereals.

Fruits and nuts

Evidence for fruit is rarely abundant, but nevertheless widespread, occurring mostly in pits and waterlogged contexts of various kinds. Fruit stones are frequently preserved by mineral replacement, and where this is the case are likely to indicate the former presence of faecal material. For most fruits cultivation and domestication have had little effect on the shape or size of the seeds and therefore it is usually not possible to distinguish wild from cultivated fruit on this basis. The same is generally true of nutshell remains. Plumstones are an exception, but in the Anglo-Saxon period the types of plums grown were still primitive and the plumstones are mostly of a morphologically wild type.

Whether wild, or cultivated in gardens and orchards, there is evidence that the Saxons utilized a considerable range of fruit. Apple (*Malus sylvestris* (L.) Mill), elderberry (*Sambucus nigra* L.), hawthorn (*Crataegus monogyna* Jacq), sloe (*Prunus spinosa* L.), bramble (*Rubus* sect. Glandulosus Wimm & Grab), grape (*Vitis vinifera* L.), possibly gooseberry (cf. *Ribes uva-crispa*), plum (*Prunus domestica* L.), and possibly quince or pear (cf. *Cydonia oblonga/Pyrus communis*) identified from the stone cells—the gritty bits in the flesh of these fruits—were found from a combination of mineralized, charred, and waterlogged material at *Hamwic* (Carruthers 2005; Hunter 2005; Clapham 2005), and walnut (*Juglans regia* L.) was also found there in a different excavation (Green 1994). A pit deposit with faecal material from Beverley produced walnut, hazel (*Corylus avellana* L.), plum, strawberry (*Fragaria vesca* L.), raspberry (*Rubus idaeus* L.), elderberry, and bilberry (*Vaccineum myrtillus* L.) (Hall and Huntley 2007)—evidence for a diversity of fruit and nuts in the diet even from a much less complex site. Combined charred, waterlogged, and mineralized deposits in *Lundenwic* produced evidence for grape, fig (*Ficus carica* L.), strawberry, blackberry, elder, apple/pear, sloe/plum, and hazel nuts (Davis in prep).[1]

Hazel, walnut, raspberry, blackberry, dewberry (*Rubus caesius* L.), rose (*Rosa* sp(p).), strawberry, rowan (*Sorbus aucuparia* L.), hawthorn, apple, sloes, plums (wild types *P. domestica* s.l. and *P. domestic* subsp. *insititia* (L.) Bonnier & Layens), cherry (*Prunus* sect. Cerasus), bilberry, elderberry, fig (possibly residual from an earlier period), and grape were found in a range of waterlogged Anglian (mid ninth- to later eleventh-century) contexts at 16–22 Coppergate, York (Kenward and Hall 1995), and other ninth- to eleventh-century York sites have produced a smaller, but similar, range (Hall and Huntley 2007). *Lundenwic*, *Hamwic*, and York were important urban centres and the recovery of this range of plant materials is due both to the amount and type of human activity and to the extensive sampling to recover biological remains undertaken at these sites.

A smaller range of fruit was found at the late Saxon rural settlement at Springfield Lyons, including bramble, possibly raspberry, rose, sloe, bullace/damson, hawthorn, apple, elder, and hazel (Murphy 1994a), which probably represents a more rural assemblage of locally grown and collected fruit. These remains came from a variety of contexts, mainly post-holes, slots, and ditches relating to buildings. The plant remains were preserved by charring and mineral replacement, so it

---

[1] I am grateful to the author for permission to use her unpublished work.

is possible that the circumstances of preservation have under-represented fruit remains on this site compared to the sites with waterlogged preservation. Compared to Springfield Lyons, however, the charred pear (*Pyrus* sp.), hawthorn, and sloe seeds from West Cotton (Campbell 1994), and the fragments of apple pip and hazel nutshell from Chester (Hall and Huntley 2007) seem minor, but these are more typical of the sparse evidence found on the majority of Saxon sites.

Walnuts may have been imported (Dickson 1991), and it is true that they seem to be present more often in urban contexts. Waterlogged conditions tend to be more frequent in port towns and this may bias the apparent occurrence of the species. Walnut trees are thought to have been grown by the Romans, and since it is a fairly long-lived tree, some may have survived the changes of the post-Roman era, protected because they were valued. Fig and grape are also possible imports, but the same argument applies. It is not known whether fig trees were cultivated or whether the finds are all of dried imported fruit. Much depends on how unsettled the countryside really was after the Romans left and whether there was sufficient stability at least in a few areas for treasured vines and trees to be protected and propagated. Knowledge and propagules may also have arrived with incoming settlers, if not in the first wave, then soon after. The absence of evidence may only be reflecting the general scarcity of evidence for the early Anglo-Saxon period.

Many fruits such as crab apple, hawthorn, rose, sloe, bullace/damson, elder, and bramble may have been mainly collected from hedgerows and woodland edges, and bilberry from moors and bogs. Other fruits such as strawberry, raspberry, pear, and gooseberry are less widely found and would have been more convenient to obtain by cultivating them. Wild apples, pears, and plums (such as bullace and damson) can vary from tree to tree in their size, flavour, and productivity. Favoured trees could be given special protection. Reproducing favoured trees, as with domestic apples, pears, and plums, would have required knowledge of grafting, as they do not come true from seed.

VEGETABLES AND FLAVOURINGS

The rich urban deposits have also produced a substantial range of plants whose seeds could have been used as flavourings, although in the case of native species it is not always possible to say that they actually were. Vegetables are more elusive, as the seeds of some are indistinguishable from their wild relatives, and the vegetative parts that are the part eaten seldom survive. As Banham (2004) points out, the Anglo-Saxons probably made no distinction between herbs for flavouring and vegetables. Records of many of these plants appear in medical texts, so they may have been used both for curing ills and for enhancing the flavour of food (Banham 2004).

The seeds of mustard, cabbage, and their close wild relatives (*Brassica* spp. and *Sinapis* spp.) are difficult or impossible to distinguish from each other. This is particularly unfortunate since these were likely to have been important vegetables, but the seeds often encountered on archaeological sites are just as likely to have come from wild plants since many of this group are common weeds of crops and disturbed ground. Seeds of many *Brassica* species (including wild species) can be used as flavouring in their own right and may on occasion have been collected for this purpose, though no large caches of *Brassica* seeds have so far been found to suggest this.

Plants used for their vegetative parts (leaves, stems, roots) are not generally allowed to go to seed except to provide seed for next year's crop (or for sale). With the exception of leaf epidermis of leek, noted below, all the plants discussed here which might have been used for vegetables or flavourings are represented archaeologically by their seeds. Plants such as carrot (*Daucus carota* L.), parsnip (*Pastinaca sativa* L.), and celery (*Apium graveolens* L.) are native species that could have been growing in many common habitats such as road- and path-side verges, waste ground, the edges of ditches, rough pasture, and crop fields. The presence of a few seeds (or in some cases a single seed) of such species tells us little about whether they were really cultivated. In such cases the archaeological context is important, as is the rest of the archaeobotanical assemblage, for interpreting the possible origin of the seeds.

Local habitat may also be an important factor. Carrot and parsnip, for example, are more likely to be found on chalky soils. They might be considered to be less likely as a weed in areas far from such soils, though this can be deceptive if fields have been limed, or in urban areas where building materials and human disturbance may create habitats where plants can thrive far from their natural environs. Beet (*Beta vulgaris* L.) is primarily a coastal plant and is probably a cultivated plant when found far inland.

Other plants such as dill (*Anethum graveolens* L.), coriander (*Coriandrum sativum* L.), caraway (*Carum carvi* L.), fennel (*Foeniculum vulgare* Mill), leek (*Allium porrum* L.), summer savory (*Satureja hortensis*), and pot marigold (*Calendula officinalis*) are not native and need human care in order to survive for long in Britain.

Flax (*Linum usitatissimum* L.), hemp (*Cannabis sativa* L.), and opium poppy (*Papaver somniferum* L.) all have oily seeds, but there is no evidence as yet that the seeds were used in this way. There may have been little need for vegetable oil where animal fats were readily available, though the extra richness of oily seeds in cooking may still have been appreciated. Flax and opium poppy can be used as flavourings for bread and other food. Opium poppy would also have been used medicinally. Flax and hemp were probably mainly fibre crops, and there are many examples of waterlogged flax, sometimes with the stems indicative of flax retting for fibres. The presence of flax and hemp seeds in association with other food plants, however, suggests that they may sometimes have been used in food.

The mid Saxon deposits at *Hamwic* had seeds of charlock/mustard, possibly cress (cf. *Lepidium sativum* L.), dill, coriander, fennel, caraway, lovage (*Levisticum officinale* WDJ Koch), carrot, leek, opium poppy, celery, catmint (*Nepeta cataria* L.), thyme (*Thymus* sp.), sweet cicely (*Myrrhis odorata* (L.) Scop.), flax, hemp, oregano (*Oreganum* sp.), sage (*Salvia* sp.), and hop (*Humulus lupulus* L.) (Green 1994; Carruthers 2005; Clapham 2005). Many of these plants were also found in Anglian York, as well as summer savory, pot marigold, bog myrtle (*Myrica gale* L.), black mustard (*Brassica* cf. *nigra*), other *Brassica* species, beet, fragments of leek leaf epidermis, and a number of 'greens' such as cornsalads (*Valerianella* spp.), and fat hen/goosefoot species (*Chenopodium* spp.) which may have been collected from various disturbed habitats. Flax seeds found at York were frequently found in association with bran, suggesting that they may have been used to flavour bread (Kenward and Hall 1995: 754). Waterlogged ninth- to eleventh-century contexts at Whitefriars Street and Fishergate, Norwich, between them produced seeds of flax, hemp, hop, celery, parsnip, pot marigold, opium poppy, possibly dill, beet, and mustard/cabbage (Murphy 1983; 1994b). *Lundenwic* sites produced beet, opium poppy, flax, hemp, carrot, celery, and possibly (less certainly identified) dill, fennel, and mustard (Davis in prep.; Jones *et al.* 1991).

Flax and opium poppy were found at Higham Ferrers. West Cotton produced hardly any evidence for vegetables or flavourings apart from some seeds of Brassica spp. which could also represent weeds. As with the fruit remains, these usually non-waterlogged rural sites have much less evidence, but it is far from clear how much this is a difference between the economy of urban and rural sites, and how much is due to different types of preservation.

Conclusions

Cereals are the commonest food plant remains on Anglo-Saxon sites, but despite their ubiquity have been little studied beyond the level of site reports. Despite being common, they are not necessarily abundant, nor does every site produce the same range: they are sparse, for example, in many of the mid Saxon *Lundenwic* samples, but there are exceptions such as the charred barley deposit at 28–31 James Street (Hunter 2004). They are also sparse in the sunken-featured buildings at Radley Barrow Hills (Moffett 2007b) and in the early phases at Yarnton (Greig *et al.* 2004), West Cotton (Campbell in press), Springfield Lyons (Murphy 1994a), and Higham

Ferrers (Moffett 2007a). Later phases at some of these sites, however, have abundant cereal remains.

Rye is both common and abundant at Stafford (Moffett 1994), is the commonest crop found at Staunch Meadow (Murphy 1994a), and is also very abundant at Wolvesey, Winchester, in Wessex (Green 1994), but is relatively scarce at Higham Ferrers (Moffett 2007a) and hardly present at all at *Hamwic* (Hunter 2005). Glume wheats are found on a limited number of Anglo-Saxon sites, especially early ones, although this number is increasing as more are investigated. Chaff remains are generally rare but can be abundant in particular deposits as at West Cotton (Campbell 1994) and *Hamwic* (Hunter 2005). These are only examples of variations in cereal remains between sites, and as yet we have very little understanding of what any of these variations mean.

Even from this brief summary of archaeobotanical evidence it is clear that the taphonomy of botanical assemblages produces an apparent dichotomy between the waterlogged urban deposits which have produced most of the evidence for fruit, nuts, vegetables, and herbs, and the non-waterlogged rural sites where the evidence is mainly charred, and biased towards cereals. Waterlogging preserves some items that do not survive charring very well, but many of the waterlogged seeds discussed above are sometimes also found charred. It is probably more significant that most seeds of fruit, vegetables, and herbs are unlikely to end on a fire unless there is a reason for disposing of them in that way. Rubbish in towns, however, appears often to have been disposed of in pits or simply dumped outside without burning. Organic layers generally appear to contain material of very mixed origin that includes food plants, but also weed seeds, and often insect remains which are also of mixed origin. Even where organic remains do not survive because the deposits are not waterlogged, urban rubbish deposits are more likely to contain mineralized remains of food plants, which is consistent with a more intensive disposal of faecal material than is generally met with on rural sites. Urban sites almost by definition are a more intensive catchment for rubbish, with larger numbers of people living closer together and engaging in a greater variety of activities. Does this concentration of evidence, however, actually reflect a difference in access to food plants?

Very few of the food plants discussed here are likely to have been imported. Most are easily cultivated in England, and some of the fruits, nuts, and vegetable or flavouring plants may have been collected wild rather than cultivated. Given this, it could be argued that people in the countryside, even those without wealth, could have had access to many of these plants even though there is only a small amount of archaeobotanical evidence so far that they did.

The archaeobotany of Anglo-Saxon food plants has received less attention than it deserves, partly because it is perceived to be poor in evidence, especially compared with the Roman and later medieval periods. It is clear, however, even within the limited scope of this study, that the evidence, though limited in certain respects, is far from poor and constitutes an undervalued resource for research. Among the issues needing closer study are how local occurrences may reflect differences in local foods/cultural origins in the early part of the Anglo-Saxon period, and how this does or does not change with time. Regional studies looking at the wider distributions of cereal crops may also reveal differences within and between regions. Changes in time need to be correlated with better dating. Mixed urban deposits and sparse samples from both urban and rural sites often discourage sampling, or analysis of samples taken, and yet when viewed with evidence from other sites such evidence can show us much about the use of food plants. There is a need for more data to allow patterns to be seen, and the scarceness of evidence for non-cereal food plants on rural sites will only be addressed by more extensive sampling and recovery on appropriate sites. A strategic approach is very much needed, but this will only be possible when we have some more synthetic research available to point the way.

REFERENCES

ASTILL, G.G., and LOBB, S. J. (1989). 'Excavation of prehistoric, Roman, and Saxon deposits at Wraysbury, Berkshire'. *Archaeological Journal* 146: 68–134.

BANHAM, D. (2004). *Food and Drink in Anglo-Saxon England*. Stroud: Tempus.

BIRBECK, V. (ed.) (2005). *The Origins of Mid-Saxon Southampton: Excavations at the Friends Provident St Mary's Stadium 1998–2000*. Salisbury: Wessex Archaeology.

CAMPBELL, G. (1994). 'The preliminary archaeobotanical results from Anglo-Saxon West Cotton and Raunds', in Rackham (ed.), *Environment and Economy in Anglo-Saxon England*, 65–82.

—— (in press). 'The charred plant remains', in A. Chapman, *West Cotton, Raunds: A Study of Medieval Settlement Dynamics, AD 450–1450; Excavation of a Deserted Medieval Hamlet in Northamptonshire, 1985–89*. Oxford: Oxbow Books.

CARRUTHERS, W. J. (2005). 'Mineralised plant remains', in Birbeck, *The Origins of Mid-Saxon Southampton*, 157–63.

CLAPHAM, A. J. (2005). 'Waterlogged plant remains', in Birbeck, *The Origins of Mid-Saxon Southampton*, 173–81.

—— (2008). 'Charred plant remains', in A. B. Powell, P. Booth, A. P. Fitzpatrick, and A. D. Crockett, *The Archaeology of the M6 Toll 2000–2003*. Oxford/Salisbury: Oxford Wessex Archaeology, 275–85.

DAVIS, A. (2004). 'Plant remains from mid Saxon London'. Unpublished Museum of London Archaeological Services report.

—— (in prep.). 'Plant remains from four mid-Saxon sites (Sites SGA89, BOB91, DRY90 and BRU92)', in *Saxon Lundunwic*. Publication in preparation. Museum of London.

DICKSON, C. (1991). 'Macroscopic fossils of garden plants from British Roman and medieval deposits', in D. Moe, J. H. Dickinson, and P. M. Jorgensen (eds.), *Garden History: Garden Plants, Species, Forms and Varieties from Pompeii to 1800*. Rixensart: PACT 42, 47–71.

GREEN, F. J. (1979). 'Plant remains', in C. M. Heighway, A. P. Garrod, and A. G. Vince, 'Excavations at 1 Westgate Street, Gloucester, 1975'. *Medieval Archaeology* 23: 159–213.

—— (1994). 'Cereals and plant foods: a re-assessment of the Saxon economic evidence', in Rackham (ed.), *Environment and Economy in Anglo-Saxon England*, 83–8.

GREIG, J., PELLING, R., ROBINSON, M., and STEVENS, C. (2004). 'Environmental evidence', in G. Hey, *Yarnton: Saxon and Medieval Settlement and Landscape, Results of Excavations 1990–96*. Oxford: Oxford Archaeology, 351–64.

HAGEN, A. (2006). *Anglo-Saxon Food and Drink: Production, Distribution and Consumption*. Hockwold cum Wilton: Anglo-Saxon Books.

HALL, A. R., and HUNTLEY, J. P. (2007). *A Review of the Evidence for Macrofossil Plant Remains from Archaeological Deposits in Northern England*. English Heritage Research Department Series 87. London: English Heritage.

HILLMAN, G. C. (1984). 'Interpretation of archaeological plant remains: the application of ethnographic models from Turkey', in W. van Zeist and W. A. Casparie (eds.), *Plants and Ancient Man*. Rotterdam: A. A. Balkema, 1–41.

HUNTER, K. (2004). 'The plant remains', in J. Leary, *Tatberht's Lundenwic*. London: Pre-Construct Archaeology, 35–58.

—— (2005). 'Charred plant remains', in Birbeck, *The Origins of Mid-Saxon Southampton*, 163–73.

JONES, G., STRAKER, V., and DAVIS, A. (1991). 'Early medieval plant use and ecology', in A. Vince, *Anglo-Saxon and Norman London 2: Finds and Environmental Evidence*. London and Middlesex Archaeological Society Special Paper 12, 347–88.

KENWARD, H. K., and HALL, A. R. (1995). *Biological Evidence from 16–22 Coppergate*. Volume 14, fasc. 7 of *The Archaeology of York*. York: Council for British Archaeology.

LETTS, J. (1999). *Smoke-Blackened Thatch, a Unique Source of Plant Remains from Southern England*. London/Reading: English Heritage/University of Reading.

MOFFETT, L. (1991). 'The archaeobotanical evidence for free-threshing tetraploid wheat in Britain.' *Palaeoethnobotany and Archaeology*, International Workgroup for Palaeoethnobotany, 8th Symposium at Nitra-Nové Vozokany 1989. Acta Interdisciplinaria Archaeologica 7. Nitra: Slovak Academy of Sciences, 233–43.

—— (1994). 'Charred cereals from some ovens/kilns in late Saxon Stafford and the botanical evidence for the pre-*burh* economy', in Rackham (ed.), *Environment and Economy in Anglo-Saxon England*, 55–64.

—— (2007a). 'Crop economy and other plant remains', in A. Hardy, B. M. Charles, and R. J. Williams, *Death and Taxes: The Archaeology of a Middle Saxon Estate Centre at Higham Ferrers, Northamptonshire*. Oxford: Oxford Archaeology, 158–78.

—— (2007b). 'Charred cereals and other plant remains', in R. Chambers and E. McAdam, *Excavations at Barrow Hills, Radley, Oxfordshire, 1983–5, Volume 2: The Romano-British Cemetery and Anglo-Saxon Settlement*. Thames Valley Landscapes Monograph 25. Oxford: Oxford Archaeology, 290–5.

MURPHY, P. (1983). 'Plant macrofossils', in B. Ayers. and P. Murphy, *A Waterfront Excavation at Whitefriars Street Car Park, Norwich, 1979*. East Anglian Archaeology Report 17. Norwich: Norfolk Archaeological Unit, 40–4.

—— (1994a). 'The Anglo-Saxon landscape and rural economy: some results from sites in East Anglia and Essex', in Rackham (ed.), *Environment and Economy in Anglo-Saxon England*, 23–39.

—— (1994b). 'Plant macrofossils (excluding wood and mosses)', in B. S. Ayers, *Excavations at Fishergate, Norwich, 1985*. East Anglian Archaeology 68. Gressenhall: East Anglian Archaeology, 54–8.

Pelling, R., and Robinson, M. (2000). 'Saxon emmer wheat from the upper and middle Thames valley, England'. *Environmental Archaeology* 5: 117–19.

Percival, J. (1921). *The Wheat Plant*. London: Duckworth.

Plot, R. (1705). *The Natural History of Oxford-shire*, second edition. Oxford/London: Charles Brome/John Nicholson.

Rackham, J. (ed.) (1994). *Environment and Economy in Anglo-Saxon England*. CBA Research Report 89. York: Council for British Archaeology.

Ressler, C. (1962). 'Isolation and identification from common vetch of the neurotoxin β-cyanoalanine, a possible factor in neurolathryism'. *Journal of Biological Chemistry* 237 (3): 27–38.

Stevens, C. (2004). 'Charred plant remains', in G. Hey, *Yarnton: Saxon and Medieval Settlement and Landscape*. Thames Valley Landscapes Monograph 20. Oxford: Oxford Archaeological Unit, 351–64.

van der Veen, M. (1989). 'Charred grain assemblages from Roman-period corn driers in Britain'. *Archaeological Journal* 146: 302–19.

——(1993). 'Grain impressions in early Anglo-Saxon pottery from Mucking', in H. Hamerow, *Excavations at Mucking*, Volume 2: *The Anglo-Saxon Settlement*. London: English Heritage, 80–1.

Walton Rogers, P. (2007). *Cloth and Clothing in Early Anglo-Saxon England, AD 450–700*. CBA Research Report 145. York: Council for British Archaeology.

CHAPTER 20

....

ANIMAL HUSBANDRY

....

TERRY O'CONNOR

It is a useful cliché to observe that crops and livestock were the 'engine' of Anglo-Saxon society, providing a wide range of food and craft resources, acting as currency and stored wealth, and integrating with soil husbandry both to ensure the production of essential resources and to mould the landscapes in which Anglo-Saxon peoples lived. Apart from their economic role, animals were a significant part of the Anglo-Saxon ideational realm (Crabtree 1995; Bond 1996; Magennis 2003; Bond and Worley 2006; Sykes, this volume), and probably carriers of zoonotic diseases such as tuberculosis (Roberts *et al.* 1998). Although livestock may not embody the creative and symbolic dimension of Anglo-Saxon lives in quite the same way as, for example, brooches or poetry, animal bones are nonetheless a significant aspect of the archaeology of this period, and of far greater importance than simple inferences of diet or meat yield.

This chapter reviews the source material for an archaeological study of Anglo-Saxon animal husbandry, namely the excavated remains of the livestock themselves. Appreciably more excavated evidence is available now than the five assemblages called upon by Clutton-Brock (1976), but any synthesis is only as good as the material on which it is based.

Source Material

The first issue to consider is that different assemblages have been described and reported by different researchers, often with different objectives, making their comparability open to question. However, it is simply not practicable to revisit each assemblage to ensure absolute continuity of methods and comparability of results, and we have to take into account the working methods and objectives involved in each project. The second issue is that any one assemblage is only a sample of certain aspects of the Anglo-Saxon world, defined and limited by geographical region and date, but more subtly so by our understanding of the range of production, consumption, and deposition processes that might have contributed to the excavated assemblages. We must take care to avoid circular arguments by understanding the larger context of the bones before deciding which research questions are the most pressing, which can be addressed at our present state of knowledge, and which must be shelved for the future.

The earliest, and possibly best known, of Anglo-Saxon animal-bone assemblages is that from the fifth- to seventh-century settlement at West Stow, Suffolk (Crabtree 1989a; 1989b; 1990; 1994). The site was variously excavated in 1957–61 and 1965–72, collecting in excess of 175,000 bone fragments seen during excavation of pits, ditches, post-holes, and *Grubenhäuser* (SFBs), with no sieving (screening) explicitly for bones. West Stow introduces the difficulty of equating quantities of bones with numbers of livestock, to say nothing of economic 'importance'. Fragments attributable to caprines (sheep and/or goat, see below) outnumbered those of cattle, yet estimated minimum numbers of cattle outnumbered caprines, and meat-weight estimates would indicate that cattle provided much the majority of the red meat consumed at West Stow *if* we take the bone debris as a proxy measure of diet (Crabtree 1989b: 106–7). The same caveat applies to all of the assemblages discussed here. West Stow has tended to dominate discussions of early Anglo-Saxon settlement and economy. However, the extensive West Heslerton site in Yorkshire has now yielded a substantial assemblage from Anglian contexts (Richardson in prep.), as has a much smaller nearby site at Kilham (Archer 2003). Material from both sites was unpublished at the time of writing, but data were made available for inclusion in this survey.

Turning to the mid Saxon period, the ambiguous nature of some sites becomes apparent. Two in East Anglia—Brandon and Wicken Bonhunt—make a striking contrast. Brandon was a substantial settlement, with industrial activity and at least two churches (Carr *et al.* 1988; Crabtree 1996). Caprines outnumbered cattle in the substantial assemblage from Brandon, whilst the Wicken Bonhunt assemblage is dominated by pig bones, which make up nearly three-quarters of the identifiable mammal bones (Crabtree 1996). Ipswich ware dominates the ceramic assemblages from both sites (Wade 1980), so they can be regarded as broadly contemporaneous, despite the quite different inferences that might be drawn from their respective bone assemblages. Another East Anglian site, North Elmham Park, has yielded a useful late Saxon assemblage (Noddle 1980), though the socio-economic context is again quite distinctive (Wade-Martins 1980).

A number of questions attend the bone assemblage from Flixborough, North Lincolnshire (Loveluck 1998; Dobney *et al.* 2007). The settlement sequence at this site extends from the late seventh to the tenth century, and consists of a number of buildings with metalled pathways, areas with evidence of industrial activity, and phases of refuse dumping, giving rise to substantial excavated assemblages of bone and artefacts, published when this chapter was in a late stage of preparation. Loveluck (1998: 147) describes the stratified dump deposits as 'unprecedented' in mid to late Saxon archaeology, though the 'middens' at Wharram South Manor could be a less extensive and differently-preserved representation of the same range of depositional activities (Stamper and Croft 2000).

Elsewhere, Portchester Castle, Hampshire, gave a large assemblage from mostly mid Saxon contexts within the *litus saxonicum* fort (Grant 1976). There is a small late Saxon component at West Cotton, Northamptonshire (Albarella and Davis 1994), and recent work in East Yorkshire has produced useful mid Saxon assemblages from Burdale (excavated 2006–7 and currently unrecorded), and from the South Manor site at Wharram Percy (Pinter-Bellows 2000). A little to the north of these Wolds sites lies West Heslerton, from which there is also a substantial mid Saxon assemblage. Wharram yielded a 'special' deposit of cattle and dog bones (Stamper and Croft 2000: 36–7), a reminder that not all Anglo-Saxon bone deposits had their origins in economic activity. 'Special' deposits have been discussed recently by Hamerow (2006).

Assemblages from 'urban' contexts have come from a number of towns. Southampton (Bourdillon and Coy 1980; Bourdillon 1988; 1994), Ipswich (Jones and Serjeantson 1983), Thetford (Jones 1984), Lincoln (O'Connor 1982; Dobney *et al.* n.d.), York (O'Connor 1989; 1991), and Beverley (Scott 1991) have all yielded assemblages of mid or late Saxon date. There is an ongoing debate regarding the interpretation of these assemblages as the consumption part of a market economy, or provisioning under a command economy (O'Connor 2001a; Roskams and Saunders 2001). Whatever the case, they tell us *something* about Anglo-Saxon husbandry, even though we should be cautious about drawing simplistic inferences. The London region has also yielded a number of assemblages relevant to this study, notably from the mid Saxon sites at Maiden Lane and Jubilee Hall, summarized by West (1993a). Assemblages from northern England are problematic, as the question of 'Viking' influence in late Saxon times becomes an issue. York has been argued to show strong Scandinavian influences (O'Connor 2004).

This overview is not comprehensive, but draws on a number of well-excavated assemblages distributed through the length of eastern England. Simple categorization into 'urban' (= consumers) and 'rural' (=producers) assemblages would be unwise. Although these labels undoubtedly apply to some sites, there are others (Flixborough, Portchester, North Elmham Park) for which a more nuanced interpretation will be required.

THE LIVESTOCK

This section summarizes regional and diachronic variation in relative abundance, then reviews what we know regarding the morphology and appearance of Anglo-Saxon livestock.

To start with relative abundance, the three main livestock taxa (cattle, sheep, pigs) dominate the zooarchaeological assemblages. Horses were present in small numbers at most of the sites, generally as a few per cent of all mammal bones, and goats occur frequently but in very small numbers, even in assemblages recorded by researchers familiar with sheep/goat differentiation. This is an almost legendary problem, and the source of copious literature (e.g. Boessneck et al. 1964; Rowley-Conwy 1998), and there is appreciable inter-observer variation in the confidence and regularity with which the species are distinguished in published material (O'Connor 2003a: 114–15). It is likely that the great majority of specimens reported as 'sheep', as 'sheep/goat' or as 'caprine' (or 'ovicaprid' or 'caprovine') are sheep *sensu stricto*. Accordingly, this chapter includes under the taxon 'sheep' all caprine identifications not specifically referred to goat. That compromise can only be justified because goat appears to be genuinely scarce in these assemblages.

Consistent quantification of relative abundance is also problematic (see Grayson 1984; O'Connor 2001b, among many others). In this review, relative abundance data are treated with caution, avoiding over-sophisticated analyses. The form of quantification most frequently used in the published studies is a simple count of identified fragments (NISP). A high proportion of the data are derived from hand-collected material. The vulnerability of NISP data to differential recovery of large and small taxa is well known. For this review, a selection 'for' cattle and 'against' sheep should be assumed for all assemblages.

Table 20.1 summarizes the NISP data collated for this study. Absolute abundance has been converted to relative abundance by calculating two indices. Expressing the NISP for each taxon as a percentage of the total allows the three percentages to be plotted on a tripolar graph (e.g. King 1978; 1996; Dobney et al. 2007), but there are two objections to this approach. The first is simply that some people find tripolar graphs very difficult to read. The second is that the three percentages obtained for each sample are fully interdependent: a high percentage for one taxon must necessarily depress the percentages for the other two. The degree of interdependence

Table 20.1. Comparandum NISP data from Anglo-Saxon sites, with sources.

Site	Source	Cattle	Sheep	Pig	Total	C/P	S/P
Beverley Lurk Lane phase 4	Scott 1991	2162	882	614	3658	3.52	1.44
Beverley Lurk Lane phase 5	Scott 1991	1921	651	649	3221	2.96	1.00
Brandon, Suffolk; Period 1	Crabtree & Campana unpub.; Crabtree 1996	337	1063	670	2070	0.50	1.59
Brandon; Period 2	Crabtree & Campana unpub.; Crabtree 1996	401	1148	336	1885	1.19	3.42
Brandon; Period 3	Crabtree & Campana unpub.	491	563	240	1294	2.05	2.35
Flixborough Phase 3b	Dobney et al 2007	2939	2166	1582	6687	1.86	1.37
Flixborough Phase 4-5b	Dobney et al 2007	2557	3440	2559	8556	1.00	1.34
Flixborough Phase 6	Dobney et al 2007	2567	2277	1702	6546	1.51	1.34
Flixborough Phase 6iii	Dobney et al 2007	1042	950	574	2566	1.82	1.66
Flixborough Phase 2-3a	Dobney et al 2007	1104	872	716	2692	1.54	1.22
Ipswich, Vernon Street	Jones & Serjeantson 1983	3408	1934	1973	7315	1.73	0.98
Kilham, Early Saxon	Archer 2003	1199	1253	126	2578	9.52	9.94
Lincoln Flaxengate Timber Phase 1	O'Connor 1982	791	425	145	1361	5.46	2.93
Lincoln Flaxengate Timber Phase 2	O'Connor 1982	2856	1338	528	4722	5.41	2.53
Lincoln Flaxengate Timber Phase 3	O'Connor 1982	1094	489	229	1812	4.78	2.14
London, Jubilee Line	West 1993a	843	329	365	1537	2.31	0.90
London, Maiden Lane	West 1993a	2898	850	1547	5295	1.87	0.55
London, National Gallery Extension	West 1993b	475	661	470	1606	1.01	1.41
London, Peabody Buildings	West 1993b	2292	1118	1466	4876	1.56	0.76
North Elmham Park; Period 1	Noddle 1980	2424	2808	2182	7414	1.11	1.29
North Elmham Park; Period 2	Noddle 1980	1046	1503	827	3376	1.26	1.82
Portchester Castle	Grant 1976	5074	2695	1719	9488	2.95	1.57
Southampton, Melbourne St	Bourdillon & Coy 1980	23888	14477	6949	45314	3.44	2.08
Thetford	Jones 1984	919	650	394	1963	2.33	1.65
West Heslerton, Anglian	Richardson in prep	10455	11187	2112	23754	4.95	5.30
West Heslerton Mid Saxon	Richardson in prep	3155	4216	658	8029	4.79	6.41
Wicken Bonhunt	Crabtree 1996	5138	3853	20954	29945	0.25	0.18
Wharram South Manor Phases 2+3	Pinter-Bellows 2000	1170	1863	295	3328	3.97	6.32
Wharram South Manor Phase 4	Pinter-Bellows 2000	646	911	158	1715	4.09	5.77
West Stow Phase 1	Crabtree 1990	2539	3479	1638	7656	1.55	2.12
West Stow Phase 2	Crabtree 1990	4811	6944	1912	13667	2.52	3.63
West Stow Phase 3	Crabtree 1990	523	725	308	1556	1.70	2.35
York, Fishergate Period 3	O'Connor 1991	8296	3421	1295	13012	6.41	2.64

Anglo–Saxon assemblages

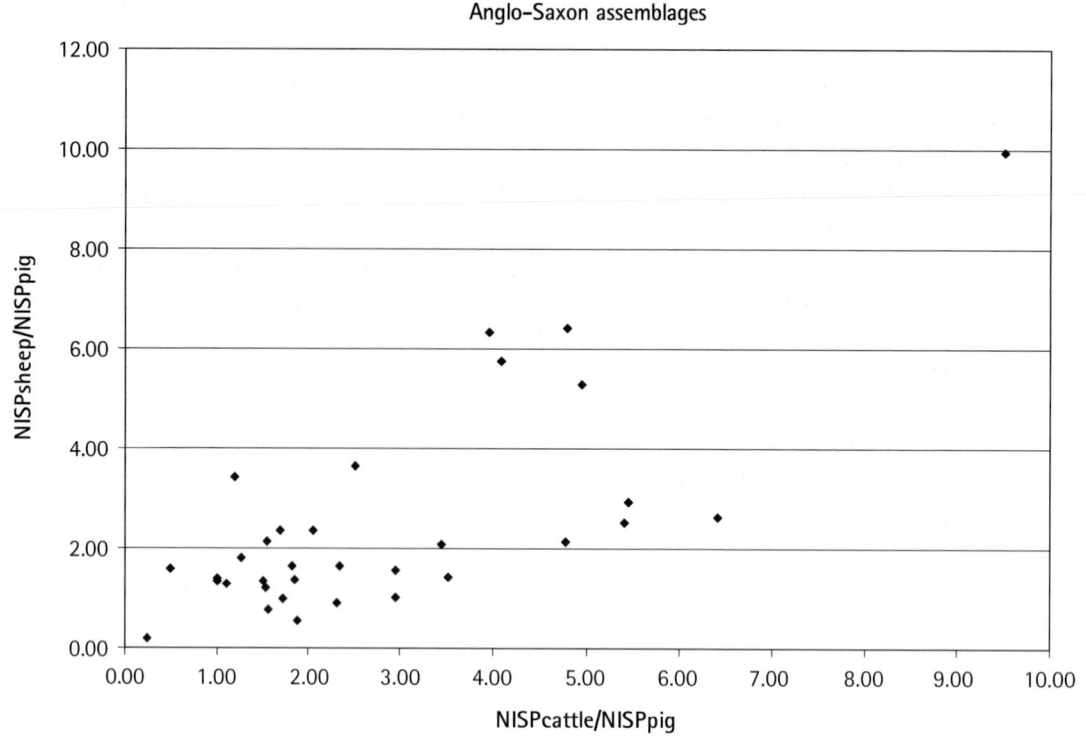

Figure 20.1 Relative abundance of the three main domesticates in the Anglo-Saxon assemblages discussed in this chapter

can be reduced by expressing the abundance of each of two of the taxa as a ratio relative to the abundance of the third. The ratios NISPcattle/NISPpig (abbreviated to C/P) and NISPsheep/NISPpig (S/P) are used here, allowing the data to be plotted on a conventional graph (Fig. 20.1). This procedure does not fully mitigate interdependence, which is inherent in any relative abundance quantification, but the resulting ratios and graphs are comparatively simple to comprehend. In addition, by using the 'medium-sized' taxon as the denominator in both ratios, differential recovery acting for or against the larger and smaller taxa ought to displace samples to 'top left' or 'bottom right', where the possible effects of differential recovery or identification can be considered individually.

The main axis of variation in Fig. 20.1 extends from the graph origin towards the top-right corner, and represents the variation between 'high pig' and 'low pig' assemblages. Nearest the origin is Wicken Bonhunt, with an exceptionally high relative abundance of pig. At the other extreme lies the early Anglo-Saxon assemblage from Kilham, East Yorkshire, distinguished by a very low proportion of pig bones, hence high values for both indices. Closer to the main cluster are four 'low pig, high cattle' outliers (three late ninth- and tenth-century assemblages from

Lincoln, and an eighth-century assemblage from York), and four 'low pig, high sheep' outliers (West Heslerton and Wharram Percy). These are amongst the most northerly assemblages in the dataset. However, all phases at Flixborough, just south of the Humber, fall into the same cluster as Ipswich and London sites, so we should beware of reading a simple regional trend.

The second axis of variation is orthogonal to the first, and separates 'high sheep, low cattle' assemblages from 'low sheep, some cattle'. The several assemblages from West Stow and Brandon tend to the former group, suggesting that the 'high sheep' attribute has more to do with geographical region (i.e. East Anglia) than with date (late fifth to eighth century). Again, these assemblages were recorded by the same person, and an observer bias towards sheep must be considered. However, the highest S/P ratios of all were recorded at Wharram Percy and West Heslerton, recorded by different researchers to West Stow and Brandon. In all, it seems unlikely that observer bias or differential recovery accounts for all the variation along this axis, and therefore likely that sheep were particularly abundant in early to mid Saxon central East Anglia.

The pattern is one of an integrated livestock economy in which all three of the major domesticates played their part, with some regional variation, and notable exceptions at sites such as Wicken Bonhunt. Cattle are a major component of all assemblages, regardless of region, rural or urban status, or presumed soil type, and are most abundant in mid Saxon York. There are some indications of a preference for sheep at rural sites in East Anglia and East Yorkshire. Horse and goat are generally present but never abundant.

Turning to the animals themselves, biometric studies have generally been undertaken in order to make site-to-site comparisons of the size and conformation of livestock. Given the early date of West Stow, Crabtree (1989b) made comparisons with pre-Roman livestock from the same region, concluding that there was little evidence of any significant change, and little evidence has emerged to indicate that the Anglo-Saxon settlement of England was accompanied by any substantial change in livestock. One time-trend that has shown up is a decrease in size of sheep from the mid Saxon period to post-Conquest times (Pinter-Bellows 2000: 178–82; O'Connor 1991; Dobney *et al.* n.d.; Dobney *et al.* 2007: 169). It would be condescending simply to assume that late Saxon farmers could not breed and feed larger sheep had there been a reason for doing so. More likely, this size decline reflects the role of sheep as negotiable 'small change', important to the pastoral economy in terms of numbers rather than individual productivity. Even before the size decrease, these livestock were small by modern standards. Archer's (2003) shoulder height estimates for Kilham are typical: cattle 113 cm, sheep 56 cm. There was clearly no pressure to select the largest bulls and cows to breed; possibly quite the reverse. Larger plough oxen would have been less manoeuvrable and tractable, and even a small ox carcass would yield a quantity of meat requiring well-organized and prompt redistribution, salting, and smoking. Beasts that yielded, say, 50 per cent more meat per carcass could have been a significant logistical problem. The simplest description of Anglo-Saxon livestock would seem to be that they were fit for Anglo-Saxon, not modern, purpose.

Husbandry

Evidence for husbandry strategies is derived in the main from age at death estimation and consequent mortality profiles. Mortality profiles derived by different researchers from epiphyseal fusion and from dental eruption and attrition can be difficult to reconcile. However, some useful comparisons can be made, either by quantifying maturation 'landmarks' that all authors will have recorded, or by recalibrating age-at-death data into broad calendar-age groups.

To start with cattle, they were the tractors of pre-industrial Europe, and no doubt valued for milk, hide, and horn as well. We might expect, therefore, to find mostly adult cattle in death assemblages unless there were over-riding local pressures for earlier slaughter. Dental eruption and epiphyseal fusion data generally indicate the majority of animals in most Anglo-Saxon assemblages to have been skeletally adult at the time of death, and therefore probably at least 4 years old. Wharram is a little unusual in that at least one quarter of the cattle represented in both mid and late Saxon assemblages had heavily worn third molars, consistent with an age at death exceeding 7–8 years. As the chalk soils around Wharram are unlikely to have caused accelerated dental attrition, the evidence probably genuinely reflects the mortality profile. Something similar is seen in mid to late Saxon assemblages from Flixborough, in which fully adult to elderly cattle predominate in all phases (Dobney et al. 2007: 125–48). At York and Ipswich, and in late Saxon phases at Lincoln, minor proportions of cattle seem to have been killed around 24 to 30 months old, with their second molars in wear but the third molar just forming or beginning to erupt. In seasonal terms, that age category would span roughly through summer to autumn. A slightly older group of mandibles, from animals around 3 years old, features in the age distributions from Portchester (Grant 1976: 276) and *Hamwic* (Bourdillon and Coy 1980: 105–8). What is notable is the scarcity of remains of young calves at Anglo-Saxon sites. Only at West Stow, the earliest site in this survey and arguably a largely self-sustaining 'village', Crabtree (1989b: 69–96) noted a distinct peak, possibly divisible into perinatal deaths and deaths of calves in their first autumn, with another possible cluster of cattle culled in their second autumn. At West Heslerton, there is a minor peak of perinatal calves in the Anglian assemblage, but not in the mid Saxon material, perhaps indicating less on-site breeding of cattle in the later phases. Anglian West

Heslerton also has a minor peak indicating some culling of cattle during their first winter. This is not reflected in the similarly early and nearby Kilham site, where the cattle were predominantly adults, with just a few 2- to 3-year-olds.

Turning to sheep, again the majority in most assemblages are adults aged between about 3 and 6 years at death, but a few sites show minor peaks of younger animals. At Ipswich, there is a distinct peak of 6- to 12-month-old individuals, culled or otherwise dying during their first autumn to winter period. Something similar is seen in some London sites (National Gallery Extension, Jubilee Lane: West 1993a; 1993b). At Portchester, the peak of young animals is a little later, typically as the second molar is forming and just breaking through the alveolar bone. At York, the peak is later still, as the second molar is just beginning to wear. This stage, arguably of sheep coming into their second summer (Jones 2005), is distinctly *under*-represented at Portchester. What we have, therefore, at these mid Saxon sites is a diversity of husbandry strategies under which most sheep have been kept to adulthood, though not necessarily to old age, with varying patterns of culling taking out animals ranging from 6 to 18 months of age. The results from mid Saxon Wharram are interesting in this respect, including sheep of a full range of ages from a few months to about 4 years, but few older animals. By Phase 4 (late Saxon), the age at death profile is much more focused on 2- to 4-year-olds.

The retention of adults is consistent with a balanced strategy of sustaining breeding stock whilst taking at least two clips of wool from each. The culling of younger animals is probably not amenable to a single interpretation, as the timing ranges from autumn through to the following early summer. The late Saxon assemblages from Beverley and Lincoln lack any discernible 'young peak', with the great majority of sheep mandibles from dentally mature animals. There is some evidence from Lincoln that an increased proportion of younger sheep—second-year animals—came into the city from the mid eleventh century onwards (O'Connor 1982: 23–4). The early Saxon assemblage from West Stow is intriguing in that there are young sheep, probably culled in the autumn of their first year, but not perinatal lambs. It may be that stillborn lambs and others that died very shortly after birth were disposed of away from the settlement. Something similar is seen in the Anglian material at West Heslerton, with a minor peak around MWS7–9 (so around 6–7 months old) but few obviously perinatal individuals, and there are few very young individuals in the Kilham assemblage.

Pigs might be expected to show evidence of the serial culling of animals for meat, there being little else to be done with a pig. That is the pattern seen at most mid Saxon sites: a progressive mortality profile with only a minority of pigs attaining skeletal maturity. We should beware of interpreting pig mortality in terms of seasonal culling. Pigs, unlike sheep and cattle, have the capacity to breed at almost any time of year, given appropriate feeding and a willing mate. Thus at Brandon, Crabtree (1996) noted a minor mortality peak around MWS 6–10 (*sensu* Grant 1982), which she interpreted as a first-year cull, but this cull should not be assumed to indicate a cull undertaken in a specific season. A similar cull is seen in Flixborough phases 3b and 6, i.e. mid eighth to early ninth century, and tenth century, respectively (Dobney et al. 2007: 125–48). An interesting exception to the pattern of pig mortality is that seen at Wicken Bonhunt, where a high proportion of the pig mandibles came from animals at least in their third year, and some appreciably older (Crabtree 1996). That distribution alone would be consistent with the culling of a breeding herd. However, the epiphyseal fusion evidence indicates that maybe one third of the pigs were killed in their first year. In other words, there are young pigs represented by limb elements but not represented by mandibles. The same anomaly is seen at some London sites, notably National Gallery Extension (West 1993b), and at York (O'Connor 1991). In the latter case, the dental evidence showed a remarkable distribution attributable to pigs killed at just over 1 year old and just over 2 years old, whilst epiphyseal evidence indicated a higher proportion of first-year pigs. The site may have been supplied with young pig carcasses without their heads, thus bringing unfused humeri and radii on to it without their corresponding mandibles. The mid Saxon material from West Heslerton almost complements this distribution, with an appreciable proportion of pigs in exactly the age gap missing at York. At nearby Wharram, the mid Saxon assemblages have pigs spanning a range of ages, with a concentration on third- and fourth-year pigs, i.e. adults. By the late Saxon phase, this concentration has shifted to second-year pigs, more like the West Heslerton distribution.

Role and value

Mortality profiles are proxy evidence of husbandry regimes, reflecting the need for, and value placed upon, the diverse resources yielded by farm livestock.

In general, cattle mostly seem to have been killed and butchered as adults. The general paucity of really old cattle, other than at Wharram, and of weanling calves argues against the keeping of specialized dairy herds, and suggests, too, that the balance between productivity and demand was such that cows and steers could be slaughtered after just a couple of years' yield of secondary products. At 4 to 5 years old, it is reasonable to suppose that even relatively slowly-maturing cattle would have yielded perhaps two cycles of calving and lactation, and a couple of years pulling the plough. Cattle seem to have been a multi-purpose resource, with little indication either that there was an appreciable demand for cattle as beef carcasses or that replacement was problematic. If ploughing as a form of obligation or rent largely drove the husbanding of cattle, the evidence shows beasts being drafted into the plough team perhaps in their second year, to be replaced after three or four years. The need to maintain plough teams would have put a premium on the provision of fit adult cattle, young enough to be in their physical prime and to be trained to the yoke, and hence justifying slaughter for beef only when beyond that time of their lives. The occasional cull of third-year (i.e. 24- to 36-month-old) cattle seen at some sites (York, Lincoln, Ipswich, *Hamwic*) may represent the culling of stock not needed for breeding or for the plough team. Speculating just a little, the third-year beasts could be mostly surplus males, as males tend to be the surplus sex in breeding herds, plus females that failed to get in calf at the first or second attempt or were otherwise undesirable. This interpretation gains support from the fact that we find the third-year beasts most commonly in assemblages from towns (=consumers?), which would seem the obvious means of disposal of fit but surplus stock.

Apart from traction power, meat, and milk, cattle yielded horn, bone, and hide, all of them significant raw materials in Anglo-Saxon England (Driver 1984; Foreman 1991; Hinton, Leahy, this volume). Horn is rarely preserved in archaeological deposits, so direct evidence of its use is sparse. Missing from most Anglo-Saxon sites are the accumulations of cattle horn-cores often found on medieval urban sites, and generally interpreted as representing slaughterers' and/or horn-workers' premises (Bond and O'Connor 1999: 380; Dobney *et al.* n.d.: 29 and 84). This may indicate that horn-working was more of a household craft in Anglo-Saxon England than in later centuries. Bone was certainly utilized as a resource (e.g. Armstrong *et al.* 1991; Stamper and Croft 2000). Although an appreciable proportion of Anglo-Saxon bone artefacts can only be attributed to 'mammalian compact bone', the size and shape leave little doubt that most are derived from cattle or horse limb bones, and it follows that cattle bone was widely used for artefacts. The use of hide is more difficult to infer from zooarchaeological evidence, as the material itself only survives in exceptional burial conditions. The predominance of adult cattle in bone assemblages need not indicate that cattle-derived leather was necessarily thick and coarse. A comparison of mortality data with the raw material of an unusually extensive corpus of Viking Age leather artefacts at Coppergate, York, showed far more frequent use of calf leather than the bone assemblages would have indicated (O'Connor 2003b).

Difficult though it is to generalize about sheep mortality, the relatively low proportion of old adults at most sites suggests that the production of wool was not the highest and exclusive priority. A sheep slaughtered before 3 years of age will probably only have yielded two clips of wool. Although these two fleeces are likely to be the best quality that the sheep will produce, it should go on to produce several more years' worth of wool before quality and quantity seriously decline, giving a cull of, perhaps, 5- to 7-year-olds. A high proportion of first- and second-year sheep would seem to indicate culling for meat, perhaps as a means of adjusting flock size in relation to autumn grazing and fodder, or 'cashing in' wealth stored on the hoof. It would be rational to reduce numbers around mid to late summer, when the culled sheep would have benefited from spring grazing, keeping only breeding stock and reserving the great majority of autumn grazing and fodder for the cattle. Such a cull would take out animals aged about 5–6 months and 17–18 months. The mortality profiles from a number of mid Saxon sites resemble some such strategy, though with the timing of the cull varying from first autumn to second summer at different sites. That variation may reflect differences in the provision of winter grazing, or in the local value of wool. Where wool had an appreciable value, there would have been some advantage to keeping hogg lambs into their second year so as to 'crop' the first full fleece. A younger, first-year cull, of animals aged around 3 to 4 months, would indicate some use of sheep for dairying, those lambs being the culled surplus males (e.g. O'Connor 1998). However, none of the sites reviewed for this paper showed such a cull. That does not mean that sheep were not used as dairy animals, only that specialized dairy flocks were not maintained (or were not sampled by any of these sites). If a few ewes in any and every flock were regularly milked, little recoverable trace would survive in the archaeological record.

A further role for sheep, and one that is too often neglected, is that of muck-spreader. A flock of sheep can convert the stubble and aftermath of an arable harvest into meat, wool, and milk, meanwhile distributing nitrogen- and phosphate-rich liquid and solid fertiliser around the field. Cattle probably found their primary role pulling the plough. Sheep, too, would have found their place in an arable-dominated economy. A further merit of sheep, perhaps more so than cattle, is their capacity to thrive on land that would otherwise be unproductive, hence the abundance of sheep in upland Britain even today. The indication that central East Anglia may have been especially favourable to sheep would be consistent with the relatively poor soils of Breckland (see, for example, Crabtree's discussion of West Stow, 1989b: 106–8). In contrast, mid Saxon York is distinctly dominated by cattle, consistent with the heavy but potentially fertile soils of the surrounding clay vale. On the lighter chalk soils of the Wolds only two days' drove to the east, the bones from Kilham, West Heslerton, and Wharram indicate that sheep also played a significant economic role, indicating largely arable or mixed farming rather than largely pastoral.

Only at Wicken Bonhunt do the pig remains indicate some special status, in this case for the site rather than for the species. Pigs probably featured as converters of refuse into meat, although a case for associating pigs with woodland forage can still be made. The rather low abundance of pigs at the East Yorkshire sites may reflect the open nature of the Wolds landscape by Anglo-Saxon times.

The impression that we get of animal husbandry through the Anglo-Saxon centuries is that mixed farming was carried on throughout eastern England, generally quite successfully, with minor local adaptations. In some instances, those may have been adaptations to local environmental conditions (sheep on light soil in Breckland and East Yorkshire, abundant draft cattle in the claggy Vale of York), and in others adaptations to social or political pressures (specific demands of rent or labour). What is not apparent is any evidence that the supply of meat or other animal carcass products was under intense pressure, of the sort that could lead to widespread culling of sub-adult animals, or that autumn culling was necessitated by difficulties in keeping stock through the winter. Throughout the Anglo-Saxon period, most cattle and sheep at most sites lived to maturity. Either that shows some success in maintaining animals through the winter, or the archaeological record is failing to represent considerable numbers of sub-adult animals. As more assemblages are studied, many of them well-preserved and of exemplary recovery, the latter possibility becomes increasingly untenable.

Conclusion

This is no more than a brief overview of the current state of our knowledge relating to Anglo-Saxon animal husbandry based on the zooarchaeological record. What emerges is a picture of husbandry systems that were broadly similar throughout eastern and southern England, with local adaptations to environmental conditions and, perhaps, to local needs and demands. There is little indication that pastoral systems were under particular stress, and clear evidence that cattle and sheep, though certainly slaughtered for meat, were not primarily raised for that purpose. Many questions remain for the future. Biometric evidence shows little phenotypic variation between assemblages, but does that reflect genotypic variation? New biomolecular techniques may enable us to ask whether cattle herds were very 'local' and inbred, or whether there was appreciable exchange of genes between regions. It may also become possible to correlate age and sex information more precisely, allowing inferences about culling patterns to be refined and tested. It is likely that biomolecular techniques will drive the next few years of research into Anglo-Saxon livestock, and therefore essential that all scholars of this period engage with the potential and shortcomings of these new methods to ensure that we ask the useful questions, not just the obvious ones.

Acknowledgements

I am most grateful to Jane Richardson (WYAS) and Dominic Powlesland for generously making the results from West Heslerton available ahead of publication, and to Sue Archer for the Kilham data from her MSc dissertation.

References

Albarella, U., and Davis, S. J. M. (1994). 'The Saxon and medieval animal bones excavated 1985–1989 from West Cotton, Northamptonshire'. Ancient Monuments Laboratory Report 17/94.

Archer, S. A. (2003). *The Zooarchaeology of an early Anglo-Saxon Village: The Faunal Assemblage from Kilham, East Yorkshire*. MSc dissertation, University of York.

Armstrong, P., Tomlinson, D., and Evans, D. H. (eds.) (1991). *Excavations at Lurk Lane Beverley 1979–82*. Sheffield Excavation Reports 1. Sheffield: Collis.

Boessneck, J., Müller, H.-H., and Teichert, M. (1964). 'Osteologische Unterscheidungsmerkmale zwischen Schaf (*Ovis aries* L.) und Ziege (*Capra hircus* L.)'. *Kühn-Archiv* 78: 5–129.

Bond, J. M. (1996). 'Burnt offerings. Animal bone in Anglo-Saxon cremations'. *World Archaeology* 28(1): 76–88.

—— and O'Connor, T. P. (1999). *Bones from Medieval Deposits at 16–22 Coppergate and Other Sites in York*. Volume 15, fasc. 5 of *The Archaeology of York*. York: Council for British Archaeology.

—— and Worley, F. (2006). 'Companions in death: the roles of animals in Anglo-Saxon and Viking cremation rituals in Britain', in R. Gowland and C. Knüsel (eds.), *Social Archaeology of Funerary Remains*. Oxford: Oxbow Books, 89–98.

Bourdillon, J. (1988). 'Countryside and town: the animal resources of Saxon Southampton', in D. Hooke (ed.), *Anglo-Saxon Settlements*. Oxford: Blackwell, 177–95.

—— (1994). 'The animal provisioning of Saxon Southampton', in D. J. Rackham (ed.), *Environment and Economy in Anglo-Saxon England*. CBA Research Report 89. York: Council for British Archaeology, 120–5.

—— and Coy, J. P. (1980). 'The animal bones', in P. Holdsworth, *Excavations at Melbourne Street, Southampton, 1971–76*. CBA Research Report 33. London: Council for British Archaeology, 79–121.

Carr, R. D., Tester, A., and Murphy, P. (1988). 'The Middle-Saxon settlement at Staunch Meadow, Brandon'. *Antiquity* 62: 371–7.

Clutton-Brock, J. (1976). 'The animal resources', in D. M. Wilson (ed.), *The Archaeology of Anglo-Saxon England*. London: Methuen, 373–92.

Crabtree, P. (1989a). 'Sheep, horses, swine and kine: a zooarchaeological perspective on the Anglo-Saxon settlement of England'. *Journal of Field Archaeology* 16(2): 205–13.

—— (1989b). *West Stow: Early Anglo-Saxon Animal Husbandry*. East Anglian Archaeology 47. Gressenhall.

—— (1990). 'Zooarchaeology and complex societies', in M. B. Schiffer (ed.), *Advances in Archaeological Method and Theory*, Volume 2. New York: Academic, 155–204.

—— (1994). 'Animal exploitation in East Anglian villages', in D. J. Rackham (ed.), *Environment and Economy in Anglo-Saxon England*. CBA Research Report 89. York: Council for British Archaeology, 40–54.

—— (1995). 'The symbolic role of animals in Anglo-Saxon England: evidence from burials and cremations', in K. Ryan and P. Crabtree (eds.), *The Symbolic Role of Animals in Archaeology*, Volume 8. MASCA Research Papers in Science and Archaeology 12. Philadelphia: MASCA, 21–6.

—— (1996). 'Production and consumption in an early complex society: animal use in Middle Saxon East Anglia'. *World Archaeology* 28(1): 58–75.

—— and CAMPANA, D. V. (1991). 'The faunal remains from Brandon'. Unpublished MS.
DOBNEY, K. D., JAQUES, S. D., and IRVING, B. G. (n.d., *c.* 1996). *Of Butchers and Breeds: Report on Vertebrate Remains from Various Sites in the City of Lincoln*. Lincoln Archaeological Studies 5. Lincoln: City of Lincoln Archaeological Unit.
—— —— JOHNSTONE, C. J., and BARRETT, J. H. (2007). *Farmers, Monks and Aristocrats: The Environmental Evidence of Anglo-Saxon Flixborough*. Volume 3 of *Excavations at Flixborough*. Oxford: Oxbow Books.
DRIVER, J. (1984). 'Zooarchaeological analysis of raw-material selection by a Saxon artisan'. *Journal of Field Archaeology* 11: 397–403.
FOREMAN, M. (1991). 'The bone and antler', in Armstrong *et al.* (eds.), *Excavations at Lurk Lane Beverley 1979–82*, 183–96.
GRANT, A. (1976). 'The animal bones', in B. Cunliffe, *Excavations at Portchester Castle*. Reports of the Research Committee 32. London: Society of Antiquaries, 262–87.
—— (1982). 'The use of tooth wear as a guide to the age of domestic ungulates', in B. Wilson, C. Grigson, and S. Payne (eds.), *Ageing and Sexing Animal Bones from Archaeological Sites*. BAR British Series 109. Oxford: British Archaeological Reports, 91–108.
GRAYSON, D. (1984). *Quantitative Zooarchaeology*. London: Academic Press.
HAMEROW, H. (2006). '"Special Deposits" in Anglo-Saxon Settlements'. *Medieval Archaeology* 50: 1–30.
JONES, G. (1984). 'Animal bones', in A. Rogerson and C. Dallas, *Excavations in Thetford 1948–59 and 1973–80*. East Anglian Archaeology Report 22. Norwich, 187–92.
—— (2005). 'Tooth eruption and wear observed in live sheep from Butser Hill, the Cotswold Farm Park and five farms in the Pentland Hills', in D. Ruscillo (ed.), *Recent Advances in Ageing and Sexing Animal Bones*. Oxford: Oxbow Books, 155–78.
JONES, R. T., and SERJEANTSON, D. (1983). 'The animal bones from five sites at Ipswich'. Ancient Monuments Laboratory Report 3951. London: English Heritage.
KING, A. (1978). 'A comparative survey of bone assemblages from Roman sites in Britain'. *Bulletin of the Institute of Archaeology* 15: 207–32.
—— (1999). 'Diet in the Roman world: a regional inter-site comparison of the mammal bones'. *Journal of Roman Archaeology* 12: 168–202.
LOVELUCK, C. P. (1998). 'A high-status Anglo-Saxon settlement at Flixborough, Lincolnshire'. *Antiquity* 72: 146–61.
MAGENNIS, H. (2003). *Anglo-Saxon Appetites: Food and Drink and their Consumption in Old English and Related Literature*. Dublin: Four Courts Press.
NODDLE, B. A. (1980). 'Identification and interpretation of the mammal bones', in Wade-Martins (ed.), *Excavations in North Elmham Park*, 377–409.
O'CONNOR, T. P. (1982). *Animal Bones from Flaxengate, Lincoln c. 870–1500*. Archaeology of Lincoln 18/1. London: Council for British Archaeology.
—— (1989). *Bones from Anglo-Scandinavian Levels at 16–22 Coppergate*. Volume 15, fasc. 3 of *The Archaeology of York*. London: Council for British Archaeology.
—— (1991). *Bones from 46–54 Fishergate*. Volume 15, fasc. 4 of *The Archaeology of York*. London: Council for British Archaeology.
—— (1998). 'On the difficulty of detecting seasonal slaughter of sheep'. *Environmental Archaeology* 3: 5–11.
—— (2001a). 'On the interpretation of animal bones from *wics*', in D. Hill and R. Cowie (eds.), *Wics: The Early Medieval Trading Places of Northern Europe*. Sheffield: Sheffield Academic Press, 54–60.

—— (2001b). 'Animal bone quantification', in D. R. Brothwell and A. M. Pollard (eds.), *Handbook of Archaeological Sciences.* Chichester: John Wiley, 703–10.

—— (2003a). *The Analysis of Urban Animal Bone Assemblages.* Volume 19, fasc. 2 of *The Archaeology of York.* York: Council for British Archaeology.

—— (2003b). 'The osteological evidence', in Q. Mould, I. Carlisle, and E. Cameron, *Leather and Leatherworking in Anglo-Scandinavian and Medieval York.* Volume 17, fasc. 6 of *The Archaeology of York.* York: Council for British Archaeology, 3231–4.

—— (2004). 'Animal bones from Anglo-Scandinavian York', in R. A. Hall *et al., Aspects of Anglo-Scandinavian York.* Volume 8, fasc. 4 of *The Archaeology of York.* York: Council for British Archaeology, 427–45.

PINTER-BELLOWS, S. (2000). 'The animal remains', in Stamper and Croft (eds.), *Wharram,* 167–84.

RICHARDSON, J. (in prep.). Animal bones from West Heslerton, Yorkshire.

ROBERTS, C. A., BOYLSTON, A., BUCKLEY, L., CHAMBERLAIN, A. C., and MURPHY, E. (1998). 'Rib lesions and tuberculosis: the palaeopathological evidence'. *Tubercle and Lung Disease* 79(1): 55–60.

ROSKAMS, S. P., and SAUNDERS, T. (2001). 'The poverty of empiricism and the tyranny of theory', in U. Albarella (ed.), *Environmental Archaeology: Meaning and Purpose.* London: Kluwer Scientific, 61–74.

ROWLEY-CONWY, P. (1998). 'Improved separation of Neolithic metapodials of sheep (*Ovis*) and goats (*Capra*) from Arene Candide cave, Liguria, Italy'. *Journal of Archaeological Science* 25: 251–8.

SCOTT, S. (1991). 'The Animal bones', in Armstrong *et al.* (eds.), *Excavations at Lurk Lane Beverley 1979–82,* 216–33.

STAMPER, P., and CROFT, R. (eds.) (2000). *Wharram: A Study of Settlement in the Yorkshire Wolds,* Volume 8: *The South Manor.* York University Archaeological Publications 10. York: University of York.

WADE, K. (1980). 'A settlement site at Bonhunt Farm, Wicken Bonhunt, Essex', in D. G. Buckley (ed.), *Archaeology in Essex to AD 1500.* CBA Research Report 34. London: Council for British Archaeology, 96–102.

WADE-MARTINS, P. (1980). *Excavations in North Elmham Park.* East Anglian Archaeology Report 9. Norwich.

WEST, B. (1993a). 'Birds and mammals', in R. Cowie and R. Whytehead, 'Two Middle Saxon occupation sites: excavations at Jubilee Hall and 21–22 Maiden Lane'. *Transactions of the London and Middlesex Archaeological Society* 39: 150–4.

—— (1993b). 'Birds and mammals from the Peabody site and National Gallery', in R. L. Whytehead and R. Cowie, 'Excavations at the Peabody site, Chandos Place, and the National Gallery'. *Transactions of the London and Middlesex Archaeological Society* 40: 150–68.

CHAPTER 21

ANGLO-SAXON FIELDS

SUSAN OOSTHUIZEN

THE problem that lies at the heart of this chapter is how and when the small, rectilinear or irregular fields of Roman Britain were transformed into the open and common fields of medieval England.[1] Open fields were found throughout the country (Fig. 21.1), characterized by irregularity of layout, arable management, and the patterns of tenure within them; they were subdivided so that internal divisions were not sufficient to hamper access across them, and were internally organized into strips that were usually grouped into bundles called furlongs (e.g. Thirsk 1964: 3). By 1300, a specialized form of open field, here called 'common fields', had evolved across central England from Wiltshire to Yorkshire, in a region recently termed the 'Central Province' (Roberts and Wrathmell 2002: 124 and 144; see also Fig. 21.2). Common field systems were more regular in all aspects: the entire arable of each vill tended to lie in just two or three equal-sized fields, which were managed on a regular rotation, and between which holdings were evenly distributed; perhaps more importantly, fallowing was communally regulated across the whole system—unlike open fields where fallowing tended to be ordered by individual field or furlong (e.g. Fox 1981).

---

[1] The reasons for the introduction of open and common fields are equally obscure, and little is known about why they originated, or the processes which led to their formation. There is a complex historiography behind these questions, recently well summarized by Williamson (2003: 1–21; see also Oosthuizen 2007).

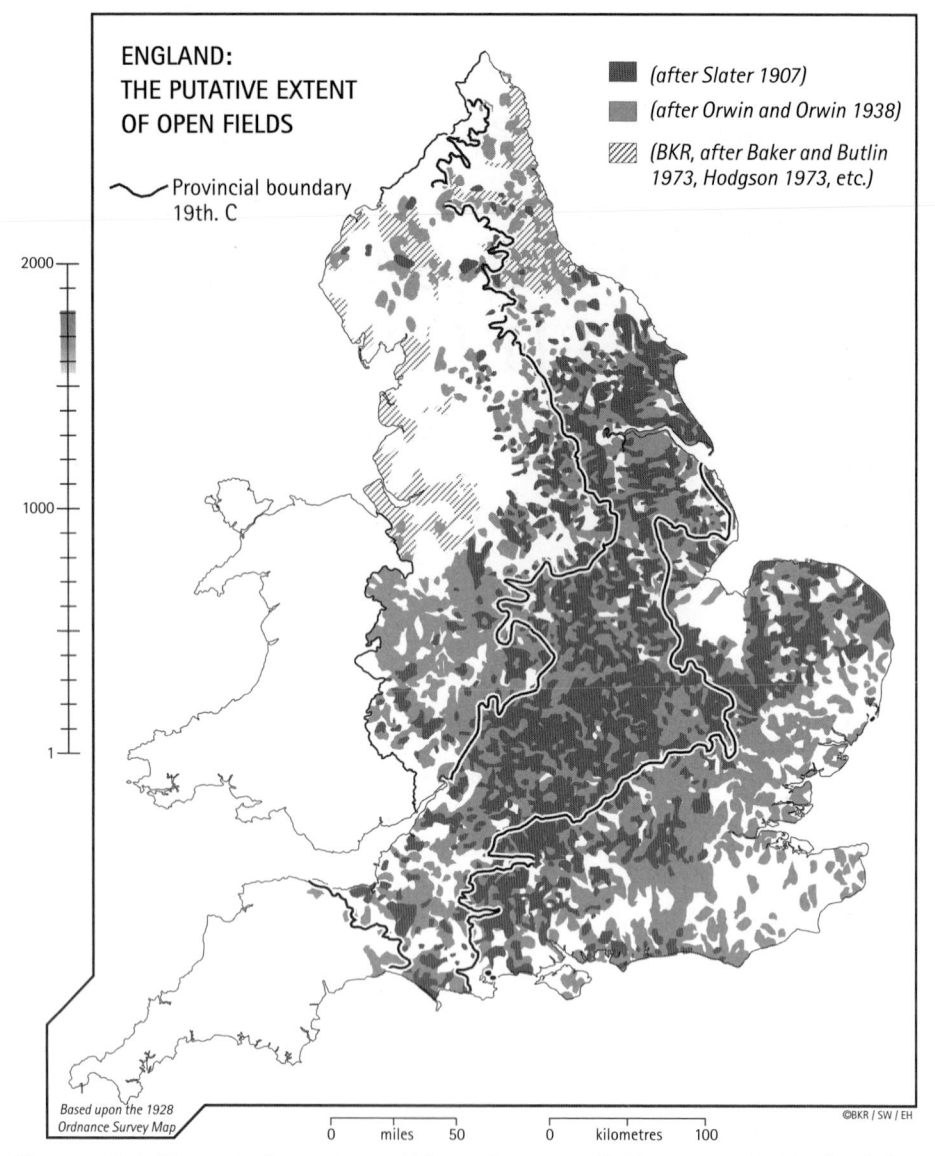

Figure 21.1 The putative extent of irregular open-field systems in England (reproduced by kind permission from Roberts and Wrathmell 2002: fig. 5.10, q.v. for references in the key)

For much of the twentieth century it was generally accepted that open and common fields were an introduction that followed, directly or indirectly, the Anglo-Saxon migrations of the fifth and sixth centuries (e.g. Hoskins 1988: 45–7; Stenton 1971: 280). This interpretation assumed that Anglo-Saxon migrants, who (it was believed) had supplanted Romano-Britons over much of England by the

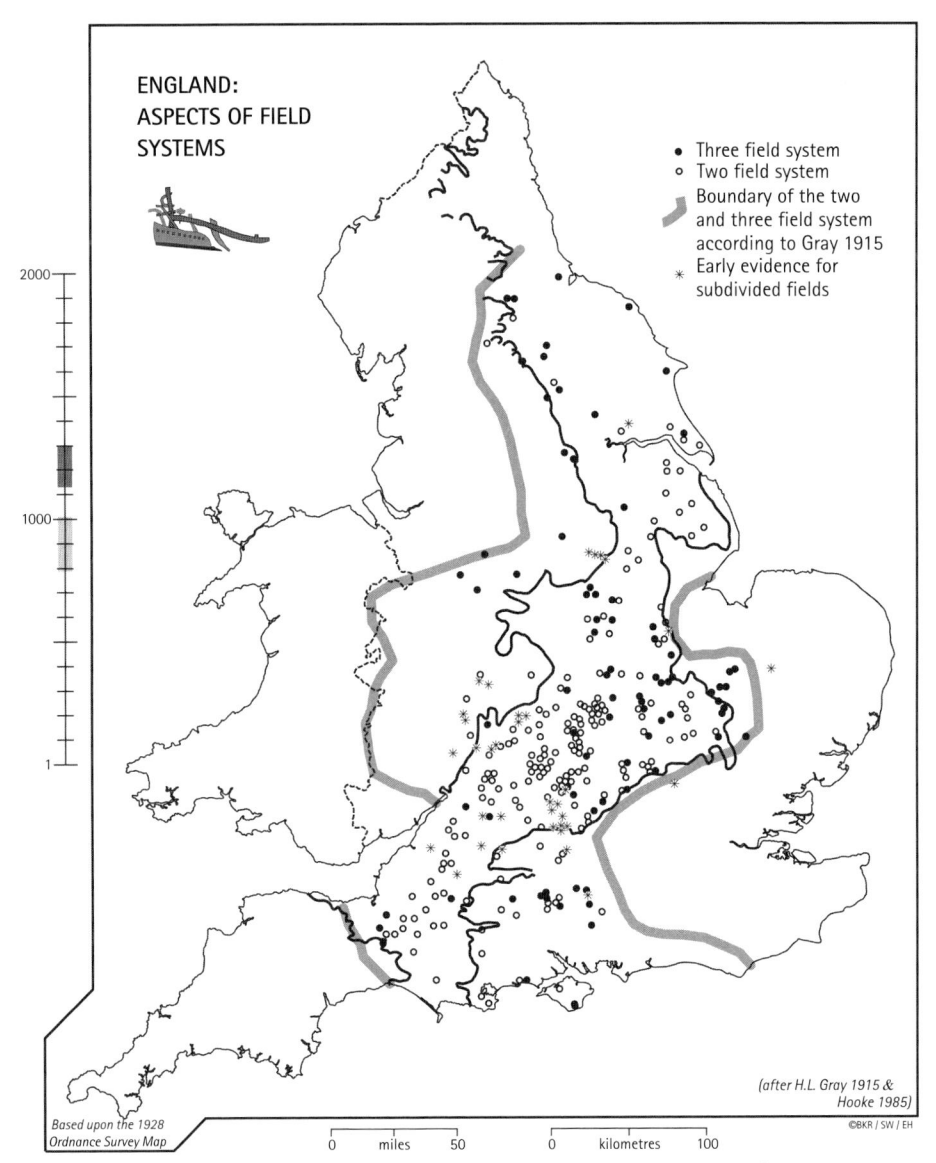

Figure 21.2 The distribution of common-field systems in England (reproduced by kind permission from Roberts and Wrathmell 2002: fig. 5.4)

early seventh century, imposed new cultural forms—of which field systems were just one—on all aspects of southern British life and thereby erased all evidence of the past, just as the English language all but obliterated Brittonic.

The past thirty years have seen the emergence of new archaeological evidence which indicates that Anglo-Saxon England demonstrated significant continuities with its Roman and prehistoric predecessors in the patterns of settlement, population, material culture, local administration, and landscape that characterized prehistoric and Roman Britain (Taylor 1983; Williamson 1987; Bassett 1989; Härke 1997; Henig 2002; Loveluck and Laing, this volume). There were, however, also important discontinuities, especially in political and economic structures (Esmonde Cleary 2000 and this volume). As a result, the problem of the transformation of field systems between about 400 and 1100 should be re-assessed to explore the extent to which Romano-British traditions of land division and arable management disappeared under, or were adapted to, new patterns of cultivation. The method adopted here follows that of Finberg: 'to clear our mind of preconceptions, to work forwards from the beginning, and to examine the admittedly inadequate evidence as it comes' (1972: 401).

This chapter examines the sparse and often unsatisfactory physical indicators of continuities and discontinuities in the layout and management of arable fields during the Anglo-Saxon centuries. Questions of tenure and organization are difficult to determine as they rely on documents which are usually inexplicit in their references to fields and therefore susceptible to a range of interpretations. Nonetheless, Taylor's reminder remains pertinent that archaeologists should never 'forget...that without historical evidence ridge-and-furrow, for example, would be totally meaningless beyond the certainty that it was formed from a technique of ploughing. [Archaeologists] would never realize the complex pattern of landholding, communal cultivation and social organization just from the physical remains themselves' (1981: 16).

Early Anglo-Saxon fields and farming

By the late fourth century AD the English rural landscape was largely cleared, generally occupied by dispersed farms and hamlets, each surrounded by its own fields but often sharing other resources in common (e.g. Taylor 1983: 83–106). Such fields, whether of prehistoric or Roman origin, fall into two very general types, found both separately and together: irregular layouts, in which one field after another had been added to an arable hub over many centuries; and regular rectilinear layouts, often roughly following the local topography, that had resulted from the large-scale division of considerable areas of land. Evidence of differential manuring probably indicates an infield-outfield basis, the core arable (the infield) being cultivated continuously without a fallow period, and therefore needing annual manuring (e.g. Williamson 1984). Fields and grassland lying further away (the outfield) were cultivated for just a few years at a time, before returning to grass, often for long periods.

Such stability was reversed within a few decades of 400 as early Anglo-Saxon farmers, affected both by the collapse of Roman Britain and a climatic deterioration which reached its nadir around 500, concentrated on subsistence, converting to pasture large areas of previously ploughed land (Payne 2007). At Yarnton, Oxfordshire, for example, fields on the heavy clays were converted to grass in the fifth and sixth centuries, and only the low-lying lighter soils in the flood-plain of the Thames were cultivated (Hey 2004: 40–1). Similar evidence for a reduction in the area of ploughed land has been found at places like Haddon and other sites near Peterborough, Cambridgeshire; Mucking and Springfield Lyons, both Essex; Barton Bendish, Witton, and Hales and Loddon, all Norfolk; and West Stow, Suffolk (Lawson 1983: 75; Davison 1990: 18–19; P. Murphy 1994: 37; Rogerson *et al.* 1997: 20 and 23; Upex 2002: 89).

Only rarely, however, were arable fields completely abandoned, as in Rockingham Forest or the more marginal uplands of Exmoor, where Romano-British fields have been found under regenerated woodland (Foard 2001; Rippon *et al.* 2006: 49; see also Rackham 1986: 74). There is a growing consensus that few 'large tracts of countryside reverted to woodland... in the post-Roman period, though on a local level some regeneration no doubt occurred' (P. Murphy 1994: 37). Pollen records from Devon and west Somerset show little change in ground cover between the fourth and sixth centuries, indicating 'continuity in an essentially pastoral landscape' (Rippon *et al.* 2006: 49). The landscapes at Yarnton and Barton Court, both Oxfordshire, Micklemere and Pakenham, both Suffolk, and Colchester and Springfield Lyons, both Essex, all remained open perhaps because much former arable continued to be grazed (Hey 2004: 40–1; Miles 1984: 25; P. Murphy 1994: 25–7 and 37). The timescales of such changes might, furthermore, be attenuated—arable land at Biddlesden in Whittlewood was abandoned to mixed woodland during the fourth century AD, well before the end of Roman administration in Britain, while in parts of Northamptonshire, woodland regeneration did not even begin until the sixth century (Jones and Page 2006: 56; Taylor 1983: 121).

Open landscapes might not, however, necessarily preserve earlier field boundaries. On Salisbury Plain in Wiltshire, for example, at least some prehistoric and Roman hedges, ditches, or earthworks had already sufficiently disappeared by the seventh century to be ignored by tithing boundaries of that date (McOmish *et al.* 2002: 111). Prehistoric and Roman field systems in parishes ranging from Berkshire to Northamptonshire, Nottinghamshire, and Derbyshire are similarly ignored by medieval parish boundaries established from the eighth century onwards (Hooke 1988a: 130; Hooke 1998: 64; Hall 1982: 54–5; Unwin 1983: 344). At Faxton, Northamptonshire; Maxey, Cambridgeshire; and in west Cambridge and south-east Essex, medieval open fields were laid out on completely new alignments across the abandoned remains of earlier settlements and fields (Brown and Foard 1998: 74; Addyman 1964: 24; Hall and Ravensdale 1974; Rippon 1991).

On the other hand, evidence across southern and central England increasingly shows the persistence of prehistoric and Roman field layouts into and, in some cases, throughout the Anglo-Saxon period, whether or not such fields were continuously ploughed. Landscapes at Yarnton, Oxfordshire, and Mucking, Essex, remained unchanged throughout the fifth century, while at Barton Court, Oxfordshire, the 'grid of ditched paddocks or closes' of a Roman villa estate formed a general framework for the Anglo-Saxon settlement there (Hey 2004: 37–9; Hamerow 1993: 94; Miles 1984: 14, 16). Similar evidence has been found at Sutton Courtenay, Berkshire (Hamerow et al. 2007: 115). The Romano-British fields at Church Down in Chalton and Catherington, both in Hampshire, Bow Brickhill, Buckinghamshire, and Havering, Essex, were all ploughed into the seventh century (Cunliffe 1973: 183–8; Lewis et al. 1997: 92; Bradley et al. 1999: 251; Gaimster and Bradley 2003: 242). The mid Saxon settlement at Catholme, Staffordshire, was built on the northern part of Romano-British farmland which may either have 'passed entire into Anglo-Saxon hands' or simply have continued to be held by 'a local British population which had never gone away' (Losco-Bradley and Wheeler 1984: 105; Hamerow 2002a: 128). 'Part of a system older than the common fields, into which the furlongs were fitted and from which the layout of the common fields emerged' may have survived in some parts of Northamptonshire, such as Castle Ashby and Walgrave (RCHME 1979: lxii). Topographical evidence suggests that a pre-Roman field system at Caxton, Cambridgeshire, was simply absorbed into a later common-field layout, and earlier ditches consistently underlie medieval headlands or strip boundaries at Wharram Percy, Yorkshire, and Caldecote, Hardwick, Teversham, and Duxford, all Cambridgeshire (Oosthuizen 1998; Beresford and Hurst 1979: 82; Taylor and Fowler 1978: 159; Oosthuizen 2006: 81–3).

Physical continuity could be extensive. In Wiltshire, the ridges of medieval cultivation at West Chisenbury and Fyfield Down fit into 'the framework of much older lynchets that had fossilized patterns of Roman fields modifying prehistoric ones', while Romano-British field boundaries at Wylye survived in medieval parish boundaries (McOmish et al. 2002: 111; Fowler 2000: 235–7; Hooke 1988b: 131). A rectilinear field layout at Strettington, Sussex, follows the alignments of a prehistoric dyke on one side and of a Roman road on the other; its fields are respected by, and probably pre-date, parish boundaries, some of which were almost certainly in place by the seventh century (Nash 1982: 42). At Wylye, Wiltshire; Sutton Walls, Herefordshire; Compton Beauchamp, Oxfordshire; Burton Lazars, Leicestershire; Lichfield, Staffordshire; and Goltho, Lincolnshire, medieval field layouts appear to have been created simply by the adaptation and modification of existing prehistoric or Roman fields (Hooke 1988a: 123–5; Sheppard 1979: 33; Brown 1996: 43; Bassett 1980–1: 93-121; Bassett 1985). At Haddon, Orton Longueville, Elton, and Warmington near Peterborough, all in Cambridgeshire, and Grantham, Lincolnshire, earlier field systems continued to be cultivated throughout the Anglo-Saxon period, simply being incorporated into medieval field layouts (Upex 2002: 87–94; Gaimster and Bradley 2001: 294–5). Rectilinear—probably Iron Age—field systems survive in many medieval fields in Buckinghamshire, in central, western, and southern Hertfordshire, Cambridgeshire, and the Elmhams and Ilketshalls in Suffolk, while the Royal Commission on Historic Monuments suggested that 'an early date can be inferred' for a rectilinear field layout at Tadlow, Cambridgeshire (Bull 1993: 16; Williamson 2000: 144–52; Taylor and Fowler 1978: 159; Warner 1996: 44–53; Rackham 1986: 158; RCHME 1968: xxx). Continuous post-Roman agricultural usage is believed to explain the persistence of large-scale landscapes like the 'system of sinuous and roughly parallel lands and boundaries' at Scole and Dickleborough, both Norfolk, and in prehistoric alignments fossilized in medieval furlong boundaries in the Bourn Valley, Cambridgeshire (Williamson 1987; Oosthuizen 2006: 68–90).

Continuity in the early Anglo-Saxon period of infield-outfield agriculture is implied by increased densities of pottery scattered during manuring that appear to favour some arable areas over others at, for example, Barnsley Park, Gloucestershire; Raunds, Northamptonshire; Barton Bendish, Witton, and Hales and Loddon, Norfolk (Webster 1967; Fowler 1975; Parry 2006: 93; Rogerson et al. 1997: 20; Lawson 1983: 73-5; Davison 1990: 18–19). An early or mid Saxon infield has been proposed for Higham Ferrers, Northamptonshire (Brown and Foard 1998: 78). Early Anglo-Saxon outfields have been identified at Chalton, Hampshire; Raunds, Northamptonshire; and Eton Rowing Lake and Dorney, both in Berkshire, even though they make their first documentary appearance only in the tenth-century 'Heath Fields' recorded at places like Chieveley and Donnington, Berkshire (Cunliffe 1973: 185; Parry 2006: 93; Hiller et al. 2002: 65; Hooke 1981a: 206–10).

In conclusion, where arable cultivation continued in early Anglo-Saxon England, there seems to have been considerable continuity with the Roman period in both field layout and arable practices, although we do not know whether there were also changes to patterns of tenure or the regulation of cultivation (see also Hamerow 2002b: 152). The greatest perceptible alterations in land usage between about 400 and 600 are therefore in the proportions of the land of each community that lay under grass or the plough, rather than in changes to the layout or management of arable fields.

Mid Saxon arable agriculture: overview

The period between the mid seventh century and the end of the ninth appears to have been one of considerable innovation. The area of land under the plough expanded rapidly: at Witton, Norfolk, for example, its extent doubled from about

100 to 200 acres—and doubled again by the eleventh century (Lawson 1983: 74–5). Pollen evidence from lowland Devon and from Yarnton, Oxfordshire, shows a marked extension and intensification of cereal growing in the seventh and eighth centuries (Rippon *et al.* 2006: 49–53; Hey 2004: 48–9). The area under arable cultivation was extended at Chellington, Bedfordshire, in the same period (Brown and Taylor 1993: 109). On the other hand, the onset of alluviation resulting from more intensive ploughing came later at Yarnton, Oxfordshire, and in Whittlewood and other places in Northamptonshire, beginning only in the mid ninth century (Brown and Foard 1998: 82; Hey 2004: 54 and 265; Jones and Page 2006: 93).

Although the expansion of arable cultivation sometimes occurred within the framework of earlier prehistoric and Romano-British field boundaries, this was not the only way: the creation of mid Saxon arable layouts by substantial modification of existing fields has been suggested at Dorchester and Sherborne, both Dorset, and in the Bourn Valley, Cambridgeshire, while at Chalton, Hampshire, older field systems were abandoned in favour of an entirely new arrangement (Keen 1984; Oosthuizen 2005; Cunliffe 1973: 183–8). It is difficult to evaluate the significance of such shifts in cultivation, which have been a persistent characteristic of the English landscape for millennia (Taylor 1983). Were they just part of the long-term ebb and flow of human activity across the landscape, or were they something entirely new? If so, how might that change be characterized?

Whether field layouts were unchanged, converted, or new, infield-outfield cultivation seems to have remained the dominant form of arable management in the mid Saxon centuries. Raunds, Northamptonshire, for example, lay divided between a number of small settlements, each with its own infield ranging from about 100 to 200 acres set within a wider area of apparently uncultivated land (Parry 2006: 93 and 96). Differential manuring supporting more intensive cultivation of the infield is a common feature of mid Saxon landscapes, like those at Shapwick, Somerset; Chellington, Bedfordshire; Peterborough, Cambridgeshire; or in Norfolk at Barton Bendish, Witton, and Hales and Loddon (Aston 1999: 27; Brown and Taylor 1993: 106; Upex 2002: 84 and 90–4; Rogerson *et al.* 1997: 19–20; Lawson 1983: 75–7; Davison 1990: 18–19).

Relatively new research indicates that the expansion of ploughed land was linked to specialization in and intensification of crop production between about 600 and 900 (e.g. Hamerow 2002b: 152–5). It is highly significant that this process was contemporary with the emergence of kingdom-states: Mercian kings oversaw the rapid expansion of regional and international trade in central southern England, undertook economic management that included the issue and standardization of coinage, and granted very large estates to monasteries and minsters, to whose abbots and abbesses they were often closely related (Moreland 2000; Oosthuizen 2007).

The connection between arable cultivation, the emergence of large estates, and burgeoning regional and international trade is nicely illustrated in the proliferation of watermills in this period, some with more than one wheel (Meeson and Rahtz 1992: 156; *British Archaeology* 1995: 5). They appear to have been constructed for the large-scale processing of far more grain than was required for subsistence, perhaps with the aim of trading surpluses to generate capital for investment or for luxury goods (Moreland 2000: 103; Fowler 2002: 176; Blair 2005: 253 and 256). Archaeological evidence for specialized production of grain has been found at Yarnton, Oxfordshire, where crops were threshed, winnowed, and probably fine-sieved before they were stored (Hey 2004: 361). Centres of such directed arable production may also be identified in place-names like Barley ('barley clearing'), Lincolnshire; Reydon ('rye hill'), Suffolk; or Waddington ('wheat hill'), London (Gelling 1984: 260, 306, and 319; Faith 1997: 47–8).

Demands for increased arable productivity could not be met solely by extending the area under the plough: the introduction of new, higher-yielding crops, innovations in ploughing technology, and a managed approach to manuring, may each have contributed both to improving and maintaining increased arable outputs. Bread wheat (*triticum aestivum*) and barley (*hordeum* sp.) became dominant in the mid Saxon period over spelt (*triticum spelta*) and emmer (*triticum dicoccon*), the lower-yielding wheats of prehistoric and Roman Britain (see Moffatt, this volume). Rye was cultivated separately for the first time (rather than mixed with other grains), and legumes were also more widely planted, perhaps as a 'green manure'. Flax and hemp were grown on a scale that could support the industrialized production of linen at places like Barton Court and Yarnton, both Oxfordshire; Flixborough, Lincolnshire; and Brandon, Suffolk (Miles 1984: 25; Hamerow 2002b: 153; Hey 2004: 48; Bradley and Gaimster 2000: 299; Carr *et al*. 1988: 375; P. Murphy 1994: 34–5).

Such improvements were supported by technological investment. The mouldboard plough, last generally in use in the Roman centuries, appears to have become widespread once more, and made possible the cultivation of heavy clay soils, more difficult to till, but also more fertile than the lighter soils of the valleys and river floors. Its benefits were that it both cut *and* turned the soil, replacing the ard or scratch-plough which, as its name suggests, simply scored the land. Jones has suggested that new crops are a 'direct record of the ecological impact of the transition from ard cultivation to deep ploughing' (quoted in Fowler 2002: 213–14). At Yarnton, Oxfordshire, for example, the use of the mouldboard plough enabled the return of arable cultivation to the claylands on higher ground, in a process which was at its most intense in the eighth and ninth centuries (Hey 2004: 48–9 and 362–4). It has been suggested that the heavy plough was also responsible for the aratral curve of some of the trackways around the mid Saxon settlement at Catholme, Staffordshire (Losco-Bradley and Kinsley 2002: 29).

The third agricultural innovation of the period seems to have been the development of more structured methods for fertilizing the infields, often on a considerable scale. The maintenance of soil fertility through intensive manuring had been an integral part of the farming regime since before the Roman period, but the extension of arable fields over a greater area, coupled with demands for increased yields, meant that the production of manure now required more formal management in order to produce predictable, and sufficient, quantities of grain. In addition to the 'green manures' mentioned above, three other strategies for fertilizing arable fields may also have been adopted.

First, it has been argued that the introduction of managed hay meadows at Yarnton, Oxfordshire, between about 650 and 850 was as much for the production of manure by stalled animals as for overwintering stock. The manure was stored in middens until it was spread on the fields before ploughing, and explains a substantial increase in the pollen of henbane, a weed specific to middens (Hey 2004: 49). Evidence for such meadows is still unusual, but another has been identified at Dorney and Eton Rowing Lake, Berkshire, while a late Anglo-Saxon example has been recognized at West Cotton, Northamptonshire (Hiller *et al.* 2002: 57; Campbell 1994: 76).

A second potential innovation for improving soil fertility is suggested by the structure of a mid Saxon field system across the lower northern slopes of the Bourn Valley, Cambridgeshire. There, parallel furlongs were separated by long strips of common pasture up to 54 yards wide. The integration of these grassy commons into the arable layout, it has been argued, meant that sheep which grazed on them by day added fresh nutrients to the soil when they were folded on the stubbles at night, rather than simply recycling the remnants of the previous crop (Oosthuizen 2006: 108).

A third possible innovation is the introduction of regular fallowing into crop rotations on the infield, suggested by the replacement in the pollen record of perennial by annual weeds at Yarnton, Oxfordshire, in the mid Saxon period, and at West Cotton and Raunds, both Northamptonshire, in the late (Hey 2004: 48 and 362; Campbell 1994: 77–81; Parry 2006: 35–6). The interpretation of this evidence as fallowing depends, however, on the assumption that previously the whole of each infield had been cultivated each year, and that fallowing was a technique used only on the outfields. This is difficult to prove either way, although it should be noted that, in medieval Breckland for example, parts of the infield were allowed to lie fallow on a flexible basis (Postgate 1962: 88–96; Postgate 1973: 300–3).

Mid Saxon agricultural innovation therefore seems to have included an increase in the area under cultivation, and the introduction of new crops, new technologies, and new approaches to maintaining the fertility of the soil, within the familiar structures of infield-outfield cultivation which remained the basis of arable management (e.g. Aston 1988: 97; Rippon *et al.* 2006: 58-64). To what extent did field layouts in this period reflect a similar process of agricultural innovation within existing frameworks?

Mid Saxon field layouts

Mid Saxon field layouts appear to be divided into two very general types: enclosed and unenclosed (as settlements also appear to have been: Reynolds 2003).

Enclosed field layouts

There is consistent evidence throughout the Anglo-Saxon period for the introduction of enclosed arable fields laid out in an irregular circle, oval, or rounded rectangle, and enclosed by a substantial hedge, bank, and/or ditch. Such fields were frequently subdivided, but their internal divisions did not provide physical barriers to movement from one subdivision to another, and the fields therefore lay 'open' (Atkin 1985; Roberts and Wrathmell 2002: 96–115; Rippon et al. 2006: 66–7). They have been identified within and outside the Central Province as far apart as Brent, Cutcombe, and Withy, all Somerset; Higham Ferrers, Northamptonshire; Walpole St Andrew and West Walton, both Norfolk; Crosby Ravensworth, Cumberland; and Cockfield, County Durham, as well as at other sites discussed below (Rippon 1994: 243-5; Shaw 1991: 16–17; Silvester 1988: 69 and 95; Roberts 1996: 26; Roberts 1981: 145–61). Pollen evidence indicating the expansion of cereal cultivation in Somerset in the seventh and eighth centuries coincides closely with an early grant of existing arable land at Brent to Glastonbury Abbey in 693, where one of these irregular ovals still exists (Rippon 1994: 243–5; ASCP: Sawyer 238).

Enclosed fields ranged in area from about thirty acres in Somerset to as many as 200 acres in Suffolk, and appear to fall into two groups—those shared between a (generally small) number of cultivators, and those containing the demesne land of an estate centre (Rippon 1994: 244; Warner 1987: 30 and 33).

Surviving oval fields divided between a relatively small number of men have been identified across England, especially but not exclusively outside the Central Province. Historical research demonstrates that, in the medieval period and after, a single open field bounded by enormous banks at Cutcombe, Somerset, for example, was divided between the five farms of the parish, and at Tunley, Lancashire, an arable oval was shared by four cultivators (Aston 1988: 94–5; Atkin 1985; Roberts and Wrathmell 2002: 96–116). In other places, although such fields appear to have been partitioned, there is little or no evidence to show whether their divisions were related to tenure and, if so, how.

Examples of arable demesne also laid out in rough oval or rounded rectangular shapes have been found across England, including the Central Province. At Aston Magna, Gloucestershire, for example, 'all the demesne land is surrounded by a dyke outside' by 904, and has been identified on topographical grounds with a small oval enclosure of between twenty and thirty acres (Faith 1997: 171–2). The mid Saxon demesnes at Kislingbury, Hardingstone Hall, Raunds, Higham Ferrers, and Wollaston, all in Northamptonshire, each consisted of a compact block, that at Wollaston including the sites of a Roman villa and an early Anglo-Saxon settlement (Hall 1984: 51–2; Hall 1988: 114–15; Hall 1983: 117–19). Similar examples have been identified at Daventry in Northamptonshire; Whaddon, Litlington, and Balsham, all Cambridgeshire; Grewelthorpe, Yorkshire; and at Wenhaston Old Hall and Hinton Hall, both Suffolk, where a 'long, curving ring-fence boundary...which forms the nucleus of the manorial demesne' enclosed areas of 200 acres or more (Brown 1991: 78; Oosthuizen 1993: 95–7; Oosthuizen 2002; Oosthuizen 1996: 28; Roberts 1985: 25; Warner 1987: 30 and 33). Such landscapes might offer a physical context for the demesne at Tredington, Warwickshire, which in the tenth century lay 'in addition' to the rest of the estate (Hooke 1981a: 207). Costen and Faith have suggested that place-names including the element 'worthy', found from Devon to Lancashire, might record a subset of such oval enclosures (Costen 1992; Faith 2006: 9; see also Faith 1998). The possibility of an earlier origin for such demesnes is suggested by provision in the late seventh-century laws of King Ine of Wessex for the enclosure of the arable land of single farmsteads (possibly demesne, and sometimes identified as 'inland') (Finberg 1972: 416; Faith 1997: 170–4; Yorke 1995: 268).

Although large curvilinear fields may appear to be original in a mid Saxon context, they had a prehistoric and Roman ancestry. Examples—apparently for arable—have been identified at Iron Age sites like Park Brow, Sussex; Grateley South, Hampshire; and Alrewas, Staffordshire; and at the Roman farmstead at Royston Grange, Derbyshire; and High Knowes, Northumberland (Drewett *et al.* 1988: 135; Cunliffe 1993: 221; Smith 1978-9: 12; Hodges 1991: 84; Topping 2008: 343-8). It has been suggested that the large ovals at Tunley and Wrightington, Lancashire, which survive in the modern landscape, may also have had prehistoric origins (Atkin 1985: 179).[2] Such forms were used not only for arable fields, but also for settlements, pastures, defended sites, and places of ritual (e.g. Drewett *et al.* 1988: 135, 149–51; Cunliffe 1993: 93–5, 141–4, and 168–82; see also Stoertz 1997: 57). They seem more likely to represent continuity of a traditional vocabulary of landscape layout than an Anglo-Saxon innovation.

---

[2] Oval enclosures for arable continued to be laid out in and outside central, southern England throughout the late Anglo-Saxon period and into the later Middle Ages, with well-known examples at South Radworthy (Devon), Tetsworth (Oxon), Hathersage (Derbys.), Hunsterson in Wybunbury (Cheshire), Wheldrake (Yorks.), Cockfield (Co. Durham), Waitby (Westmoreland), and Puxton (Somerset) (Riley and Wilson-North 2001: 97; Bond 1985: 115; Roberts and Wrathmell 2002: 98–9; Atkin 1985; Sheppard 1966; Roberts 1981: 149; Roberts 1993: Rippon 2007).

Unenclosed fields

Other new mid Saxon field layouts took the form of unenclosed fields created on a roughly geometric layout heavily influenced by the local topography. Examples can be found as far apart as Berkshire, Oxfordshire, and Yorkshire (Harvey 1980; 1983; 1984; 1985; Hooke 1988a; Pocock 1968; Powlesland 1986: 165). At Dorchester, Dorset, a large, open-field system, possibly created in the eighth century, was so 'extensive and regular that it is clear that it results from a deliberate act of planning' (Keen 1984: 236). It was made up of long, slightly wany, parallel field divisions running from east to west, that pre-date the medieval open fields. A mid Saxon, perhaps eighth-century, date is proposed for a similar, and equally large, field system at Sherborne (ibid.: 210, 221, and 230). Those at Dorchester and Sherborne are very like an enormous open field set out south-west of Cambridge perhaps between about 700 and 850, modifying and adapting earlier field layouts. It extended over seven square miles across four parishes, and was subdivided into long, parallel furlongs running from west to east along the valley contours (Oosthuizen 2006: 91–113). Seminal work in Northamptonshire suggested that many common-field layouts there, with a regular or sub-regular structure, were laid out from the eighth century onwards, and a similar date has been suggested for the boundaries and ditches that formed the framework of a regular field system at Kempston, Bedfordshire (Hall 1982: 46; Gaimster and Bradley 2003: 221).

Such field systems sometimes incorporated and/or adapted earlier rectilinear layouts like those already noted at Wylye, Wiltshire; Compton Beauchamp, Oxfordshire; Burton Lazars, Leicestershire; Lichfield, Staffordshire; and Goltho, Lincolnshire (Hooke 1988a: 123–5; Brown 1996: 43; Bassett 1983: 93–121; Bassett 1985: 32–4). What they fossilized was the underlying framework of the fields, rather than every hedge and ditch, as existing fields were adapted to changing patterns of arable management. Such large-scale preservation of prehistoric and Roman field systems has been found across England where, as Williamson has commented of Norfolk, 'centuries of piecemeal alteration have preserved the essential orientation of field layout but not in every case the original boundaries' (1987: 425).

Landscape division on an approximately rectilinear basis was not new in England in the Anglo-Saxon period. Considerable areas had been divided into long, narrow units often about 200 metres wide in successive phases of landscape planning in the prehistoric and Roman centuries (it was internal subdivisions of these units which resulted in the network of small rectangular fields that are now so familiar to landscape historians), often influenced by local topography and drainage. Early Anglo-Saxon cultivators had ploughed such ancestral fields each year. As with ovals and circles, new rectilinear layouts in the mid Saxon period and later may represent continued use of a familiar form rather than an introduction. One way to address this issue is to consider in turn each of the components making up the internal structure of open fields.

Evidence for open fields, block demesnes, furlongs, and strips in mid Saxon England

The irregular open-field layouts of later medieval England were characterized by three distinctive features: their open aspect across internal subdivisions; the tendency for demesne land to lie in one or more blocks outside the open fields; and their internal subdivision into furlongs and strips. Do such features occur in mid Saxon field layouts and, if so, to what extent might they be regarded as innovative?

The earliest known documentary reference to open fields seems to be those described in the well-known clause in the laws of Ine of Wessex:

If husbandmen have a common meadow or other share-land to enclose, and some have enclosed their share and others have not, and if cattle eat up their common crops or grass, then let those to whom the gap is due go and make amends to the others who have enclosed their share

(trans. Finberg 1972: 416)

The 'common... share-land' of the clause was interpreted by both Finberg and, later, Fox as a field in shared ownership which was bounded by a single hedge, perhaps like the enclosed ovals described above (Finberg 1972: 416–17; Fox 1981: 87–8). Fox argued convincingly that the field described in the clause was open. Only this, he suggested, would explain the damage that a stray cow might make to common crops of corn or grass (Fox 1981: 87). The same kind of landscape may have been described in charters like that for Ardington, Berkshire, where 'the arable is common' in the tenth century, or that for Tidenham, Gloucestershire, in 956, whose tenants contributed to the 'acre fencing' which separated open arable from pasture (Fox 1981: 84; Roberts and Wrathmell 2002: 131). (There is an early reference to common land at Cofton Hackett, Worcestershire, in 849, but it might describe either arable or uncultivated ground: Hooke 1981b: 58.)

It seems very probable that open fields were present in mid Saxon contexts. There are no other early references to common land with which to compare Ine's clause, nor does archaeological evidence at present elucidate whether he was addressing the problems of compensation and culpability within such layouts because they were perennial, or because they were new.

Block demesnes have already been discussed, with examples cited from Gloucestershire, Warwickshire, Northamptonshire, Yorkshire, Cambridgeshire, and Suffolk (Faith 1997: 171–2; Hooke 1981a: 207; Hall 1984: 51–2; Hall 1988: 114–15; Hall 1983: 117–19; Roberts 1985: 25; Oosthuizen 1993; Oosthuizen 2002; Oosthuizen 1996: 28; Warner 1987: 29–33). They were present all across England, including the Central Province (Roberts and Wrathmell 2000), in the mid Saxon period, only to disappear from the Central Province by about 1300 while persisting elsewhere. Given the evidence for the antiquity of this type of enclosure, there must at least be some doubt about whether it can be claimed as an Anglo-Saxon innovation.

Furlongs appear frequently in documents by the mid tenth century. The earliest known are those at Hordwell, Hampshire, and Water Eaton, Oxfordshire, recorded in charters of 903 and 904 respectively, and therefore established features by those dates (Seebohm 1883: 107–8; Hooke 1988a: 126; Hooke 1981a: 190–1). However, furlongs at Dorchester and Sherborne, both Dorset, and in the Bourn Valley, Cambridgeshire, appear to have been an integral part of the structure of the field layouts for which an eighth-century date is proposed (above: Keen 1984; Oosthuizen 2005). Furlongs certainly appear to have existed by the late ninth century and may have been present in at least some new unenclosed mid Saxon fields from the outset. In other places, they appear to have been derived from modifications of existing rectilinear field patterns—creating larger units by retaining those earlier field boundaries that were useful and grubbing up those that were not: the common-field furlongs at Lichfield, Staffordshire; Burton Lazars, Leicestershire; Goltho, Lincolnshire; and Orton Longueville and Caxton, both Cambridgeshire, are not obviously different in layout from any other medieval field patterns, yet each of these field systems is structured, to a greater or lesser extent, on prehistoric or Roman fields (Bassett 1980–1; Brown 1996; Bassett 1985; Upex 2002; Oosthuizen 1998; see for comparison, for example, Hartley 1983; 1984; 1989). The layout of furlongs appears to be derived from the modification or adaptation of existing landscapes to (possibly new) systems of cropping or tenure, about which we know almost nothing in this period.

Like furlongs, strips are well represented in tenth-century documents (e.g. Hooke 1981a: 206–7; Hooke 1981b: 58; Hooke 1988a: 123; Hooke 1998: 206; Dr C. R. Hart, pers. comm.), but they may have been widespread much earlier: Hall suggested that they were the earliest form of mid Saxon field division in Northamptonshire, pre-dating furlongs (Hall 1982: 48–9), and the same has been argued on topographical grounds for Holderness, Yorkshire (Harvey 1980: 185). Small rectilinear fields in Somerset, probably dating from the seventh and eighth centuries, appear to have been subdivided by low banks into 'long, narrow, curving, strip-like subdivisions', as were eighth- or ninth-century fields at West Walton and Walpole St Andrew, Norfolk (Rippon *et al.* 2006: 59 and 66; Silvester 1988: 95 and 69). There are indications that strips were an intrinsic part of the structure of the large mid Saxon field system in the Bourn Valley, Cambridgeshire, since they were respected by a parish and hundred boundary which was in place by the early tenth century (Oosthuizen 2006: 99–107). The most enigmatic evidence of all comes from Milfield, Northumberland, where evidence for eighth- or ninth-century arable cultivation has been found in close association with traces of undated ridge and furrow (Bradley and Gaimster 2000: 299).

The division of arable land into strips had, however, even earlier antecedents: prehistoric examples have been identified on St David's Head, Pembrokeshire, and in Northumberland (K. Murphy 2001: 94; Topping 1989; 2008). Iron Age examples have been excavated at Sawtry, Cambridgeshire (Richard Newman, pers. comm.). The Roman arable field at Roystone Grange, Derbyshire, was divided into strips about 40 metres wide, and Roman strip fields have also been identified at King's Worthy, Hampshire; Great Wymondley, Hertfordshire; in Somerset, Dorset, Nottinghamshire, and Lincolnshire, and perhaps at Burnham Market, Norfolk (Hodges 1991: 79; Applebaum 1972: 90–5; Arnold 1984: 57; Williamson 2003: 81). At Frocester, Gloucestershire, excavation revealed early post-Roman strip cultivation on a different alignment from the ridge and furrow of later medieval fields (Price 2000: 242).

The evidence surveyed so far seems therefore to suggest that large, open, arable fields subdivided into strips were present in, if not before, the mid Saxon period; there were some significant continuities with prehistoric and Roman systems of field layout and of infield-outfield cultivation; block demesnes and furlongs may each have evolved from traditional forms of dividing and managing land. About the management of cropping (was it communal?) and tenure (how was it distributed?), almost nothing is known (cf. Oosthuizen 2007). None of the mid Saxon fields considered above could be described as an open- or common-field *system*, yet it is clear that some of the *characteristics* of such field systems were already visible in that period even if they had not yet coalesced into open- or common-field arrangements (cf. Oosthuizen 2007).

It is possible that at some point between about 600 and 950, familiar forms of layout and arable cultivation may have been combined with new, more communal systems of tenure to form irregular open fields. Yet this revolution is only inferred from later evidence, and the question of its relationship with the fission of the large estates of the mid Saxon period into the townships and parishes of the later Middle Ages is virtually unresearched. Still to be investigated is how and when further changes were introduced in the Central Province in the development of regular common fields.

Later Anglo-Saxon field layout

The overall layouts and arable management that seem to have characterized early and mid Saxon fields appear in many cases to have persisted through the period after 900, suggesting that the transformation of irregular open fields into regular common fields across the English Midlands may not have occurred until after the Anglo-Saxon period.

Only one detailed, large-scale archaeological investigation of the origins of a late Anglo-Saxon open- or common-field layout has taken place: at Raunds,

Northamptonshire, where pottery scatters from late Anglo-Saxon manuring (perhaps of the late ninth or early tenth centuries) lie contained within the boundaries of medieval common-field furlongs (Hall 1982; Parry 2006: 133). Nor were such scatters evenly distributed across the arable fields; instead, they indicate that intensive manuring of selected areas continued to be practised in the late Anglo-Saxon period. What is particularly interesting is that the late Anglo-Saxon furlongs which were most intensively manured were frequently laid out across mid Saxon infields (Parry 2006: 93, 133, and 276). If the same areas were being continuously manured in the middle and in the late Anglo-Saxon periods, was this activity undertaken within the same field boundaries in both periods, or were new fields established over existing arable from about 900 onwards?

An important conclusion from Raunds is that the patterns of manuring show the variation in intensity which indicates that infield-outfield cultivation was still being undertaken there in the later Anglo-Saxon period—that is, the fields and furlongs of Raunds were still being cultivated as an open field at that time, and not as a common field (Parry 2006: 133 and 276). Evidence for late Anglo-Saxon differential manuring has also been observed at Whittlewood, Northamptonshire, and Whittlesford, Cambridgeshire (Jones and Page 2006: 93; Taylor and Arbon 2007: 38). Perhaps most significantly, Raunds, Whittlewood, and Whittlesford all lie within the Central Province in which common, not open, fields were characteristic by 1300; the Vale of Pickering is another example (Allerston 1970: 104).

The conclusion that common fields had not yet emerged in the later Anglo-Saxon landscape is supported by two observations, both drawn from documentary evidence and analysis. First, as Thirsk pointed out as long ago as 1964, in a point elaborated upon by Fox in 1981, there is no evidence before the Norman Conquest for the *communal regulation* of fallowing, which both regarded as the key indicator of common-field cultivation (Thirsk 1964: 5–7; Fox 1981). And second, recent analysis of arable land recorded in Domesday Book suggests that the proportion of land in each vill that lay under the plough had by no means yet reached its maximum by the eleventh century. As late as 1086, only between 30 and 40 per cent of the available land seems to have been cultivated in most Midland and East Anglian parishes (Hesse 2000; Roberts and Wrathmell 2002: 187; Oosthuizen 2006: 44). Both points are important because, if there were sufficient pasture for the community livestock outside the open fields, then there would be no requirement for half or a third of the arable to lie fallow each year, and no requirement for the communal regulation of fallowing. While open fields may have been unexceptional between about 900 and 1100, it seems that fully-developed common-field cultivation had yet to develop.

Conclusion

The old view that completely new forms of field system came with the Anglo-Saxon migrants has been revised in the light of evidence for the adaptation and modification of existing layouts. Infield-outfield agriculture, practised in Britain for centuries before the Anglo-Saxon period, continued in many places to form the basis of cultivation into the Middle Ages and later (cf. Winchester 1987: 74–6), and the open fields which emerged by the seventh century may also have evolved from traditional forms of arable layout and cultivation in England. Most Anglo-Saxons seem either to have cultivated existing fields, or to have created new open arable enclosures, long rectilinear land divisions, and strips, the former directly taken over, the latter adapted, from the practices of their Roman (or prehistoric) predecessors. Whether such apparently inherited similarities in form reflected similarities in patterns of tenure and communality of land management also passed down across the centuries is still unknown. The fact that mature common fields, those specialized regular forms of irregular open-field systems, were restricted to the Central Province and are not visible before about 1100 at the earliest does not help to answer this question. One of the central questions which this raises is the extent to which some or all of the tenurial and managerial features of both open and common fields may be identifiable in the early and mid Saxon periods, before or at the same time as the physical field systems began to form.

The chronology outlined above, bedevilled by sparsity of evidence, suggests that the process of the transformation of ancient into medieval fields may have been more attenuated than previously supposed. If open fields were already a feature of the mid Saxon period, and if common fields are only visible from around 1100, then the period of arable transformation in which open and common fields successively appeared may have spanned at the very least five or six hundred years and been comprised of at least two phases.

What is known about common-field systems is still vastly outweighed by what is unknown, despite over a century of scholarship. Collaborative research between archaeologists, both by excavation and by topographical surveys, and historians, for the reasons outlined by Christopher Taylor and quoted at the beginning of this chapter, is required. The origins of evenly distributed and intermingled tenure and of community regulation of fallowing and cropping are issues that still resonate because common-field systems formed a framework for agricultural management, landholding, and social relations that persisted in many places across the Central Province until modern times, creating political, social, and economic structures and attitudes that endure into the twenty-first century.

Acknowledgements

The work reported here was undertaken during a period of sabbatical leave granted by my Department, the University of Cambridge Institute of Continuing Education, for which I am grateful. Professor Brian Roberts and Mr Stuart Wrathmell generously allowed me to use illustrative material they had published elsewhere. I am grateful to colleagues for discussing my work with me, especially Mr Christopher Taylor and Professor Mary Hesse. Mr Julian Munby kindly corresponded with me.

References

ADDYMAN, P. (1964). 'A Dark Age settlement at Maxey, Northants.'. *Medieval Archaeology* 8: 20–73.

ALLERSTON, P. (1970). 'English village development'. *Transactions of the Institute of British Geographers* 51: 95–109.

APPLEBAUM, S. (1972). 'Roman Britain', in H. P. R. Finberg (ed.), *The Agrarian History of England and Wales*, Volume 1.2: *AD 43–1042*. Cambridge: Cambridge University Press, 5–267.

ARNOLD, C. J. (1984). *Roman Britain to Saxon England*. London: Croom Helm.

ASCP: ANGLO-SAXON CHARTERS PROJECT. Sawyer Charter 238. <http://www.aschart.kcl.ac.uk/content/charters/text/s0238.html>, accessed August 2007.

ASTON, M. (1988). 'Land use and field systems', in M. Aston (ed.), *Aspects of the Medieval Landscape of Somerset*. Taunton: Somerset County Council, 83–99.

—— (1999). '"Unique, traditional and charming". The Shapwick Project, Somerset'. *Antiquaries Journal* 79: 1–58.

ATKIN, M. A. (1985). 'Some settlement patterns in Lancashire', in D. Hooke (ed.), *Medieval Villages: A Review of Current Work*. Oxford: Oxford University Committee for Archaeology, 170–85.

BAKER, A. R. H., and BUTLIN, R. (1973). *Studies of Field Systems in the British Isles*. Cambridge: Cambridge University Press.

BASSETT, S. (1980–1). 'Medieval Lichfield: a topographical review'. *Transactions of the Staffordshire Archaeological and Historical Society* 22: 93–121.

——(1985). 'Beyond the edge of excavation: the topographical context of Goltho', in H. Mayr-Harting and R. I. Moore (eds.), *Studies in Medieval History Presented to R. H. C. Davis*. London: Hambledon, 32–4.

——(ed.) (1989). *The Origins of the Anglo-Saxon Kingdoms*. Leicester: Leicester University Press.

BERESFORD, M., and HURST, J. G. (1979). 'Wharram Percy: a case study in microtopography', in P. Sawyer (ed.), *English Medieval Settlement*. London: Arnold, 52–85.

BLAIR, J. (2005). *The Church in Anglo-Saxon Society*. Oxford: Oxford University Press.

Bond, C. J. (1985). 'Medieval Oxfordshire villages and their topography: a preliminary discussion', in D. Hooke (ed.), *Medieval Villages: A Review of Current Work*. Oxford: Oxford University Committee for Archaeology, 101–23.

Bradley, J., and Gaimster, M. (2000). 'Medieval Britain and Ireland, 1999'. *Medieval Archaeology* 44: 235–354.

——Gaimster, N., and Haith, C. (1999). 'Medieval Britain and Ireland, 1998'. *Medieval Archaeology* 43: 226–302.

British Archaeology (1995). 'Anglo-Saxon watermill found on Tyne'. *British Archaeology* 11: 5.

Brown, A. E. (1991). *Early Daventry: An Essay in Early Landscape Planning*. Leicester: University of Leicester and Daventry District Council.

——(1996). 'Burton Lazars, Leicestershire: a planned medieval landscape?'. *Landscape History* 18: 31–45.

——and Foard, G. (1998). 'The Saxon landscape: a regional perspective', in P. Everson and T. Williamson (eds.), *The Archaeology of Landscape*. Manchester: Manchester University Press, 67–94.

——and Taylor, C. C. (1993). 'Chellington field survey'. *Bedfordshire Archaeological Journal* 23: 98–110.

Bull, E. J. (1993). 'The bi-axial landscape of prehistoric Buckinghamshire'. *Records of Buckinghamshire* 35: 11–27.

Campbell, G. (1994). 'The preliminary archaeobotanical results from Anglo-Saxon West Cotton and Raunds', in J. Rackham (ed.), *Environment and Economy in Anglo-Saxon England*. York: Council for British Archaeology, 65–82.

Carr, R., Tester, A., and Murphy, P. (1988). 'The Middle Saxon settlement at Staunch Meadow, Brandon'. *Antiquity* 62: 371–7.

Costen, M. (1992). '*Huish* and *Worth*: Old English survivals in a later landscape'. *Anglo-Saxon Studies in Archaeology and History* 5: 65–83.

Cunliffe, B. (1973). 'Chalton, Hants: the evolution of a landscape'. *Antiquaries Journal* 53(2): 173–90.

——(1993). *Wessex to A.D. 1000*. London: Longman.

Davison, A. (1990). *The Evolution of Settlement in Three Parishes in South-East Norfolk*. East Anglian Archaeology 49. Gressenhall.

Drewett, P., Rudling, D., and Gardiner, M. (1988). *The South-East to A.D. 1000*. London: Longman.

Esmonde Cleary, A. S. (2000). *The Ending of Roman Britain*. London: Routledge.

Faith, R. (1997). *The English Peasantry and the Growth of Lordship*. Leicester: Leicester University Press.

——(1998). 'Hides and Hyde Farms in central and southern England: a preliminary report'. *Medieval Settlement Research Group Annual Report* 13: 33–8.

——(2006). 'Worthys and enclosures'. *Medieval Settlement Research Group Annual Report* 21: 9–14.

Finberg, H. P. R. (1972). 'Anglo-Saxon England to 1042', in H. P. R. Finberg (ed.), *The Agrarian History of England and Wales*, Volume 1.2: *AD 43–1042*. Cambridge: Cambridge University Press, 385–525.

Foard, G. (2001). 'Medieval woodland, agriculture and industry in Rockingham Forest, Northamptonshire'. *Medieval Archaeology* 45: 41–95.

FOWLER, P. J. (1975). 'Continuity in the landscape', in P. J. Fowler (ed.), *Recent Work in Rural Archaeology*. Bath: Adams and Dart, 123–32.

——(2000). *Landscape Plotted and Pieced: Landscape History and Local Archaeology in Fyfield and Overton, Wiltshire*. London: Society of Antiquaries.

——(2002). *Farming in the First Millennium*. Cambridge: Cambridge University Press.

FOX, H. S. A. (1981). 'Approaches to the adoption of the Midland system', in Rowley (ed.), *Origins of Open Field Agriculture*, 64–111.

GAIMSTER, M., and BRADLEY, J. (2001). 'Medieval Britain and Ireland, 2000'. *Medieval Archaeology* 45: 233–379.

———— (2003). 'Medieval Britain and Ireland, 2002'. *Medieval Archaeology* 47: 199–340.

GELLING, M. (1984). *Place-Names in the Landscape*. London: Dent.

HALL, C., and RAVENSDALE, J. R. (1974). *The West Fields of Cambridge*. Cambridge: Cambridge Record Society.

HALL, D. (1982). *Medieval Fields*. Aylesbury: Shire Publications.

——(1983). 'Fieldwork and field books: studies in early layout', in B. K. Roberts and R. E. Glasscock (eds.), *Villages, Fields and Frontiers*. BAR International Series 185. Oxford: British Archaeological Reports, 115–31.

——(1984). 'Fieldwork and documentary evidence for the layout and organization of early medieval estates in the English Midlands', in K. Biddick (ed.), *Archaeological Approaches to Medieval Europe*. Kalamazoo, IL: University of Michigan Press, 43–68.

——(1988). 'The late Saxon countryside: villages and their fields', in D. Hooke (ed.), *Anglo-Saxon Settlements*. Oxford: Blackwell, 99–122.

HAMEROW, H. (1993). *Excavations at Mucking*, Volume 2: *The Anglo-Saxon Settlement*. Swindon and London: English Heritage and British Museum Press.

——(2002a). 'Catholme: the development and context of the settlement', in Losco-Bradley and Kinsley, *Catholme*, 123–9.

——(2002b). *Early Medieval Settlements: The Archaeology of Rural Communities in North-West Europe, 400–900*. Oxford: Oxford University Press.

——HAYDEN, C., and HEY, G. (2007). 'Anglo-Saxon settlement near Drayton Road, Sutton Courtenay, Berkshire'. *Archaeological Journal* 164: 109–96.

HÄRKE, H. (1997). 'Early Anglo-Saxon social structure', in J. Hines (ed.), *The Anglo-Saxons from the Migration Period to the Eighth Century: An Ethnographic Perspective*. Woodbridge: Boydell and Brewer, 125–60.

HARTLEY, R. (1983). *The Medieval Earthworks of Rutland*. Archaeological Report 7. Leicester: Leicester Museums.

——(1984). *The Medieval Earthworks of North West Leicestershire*. Archaeological Report 9. Leicester: Leicester Museums.

——(1989). *The Medieval Earthworks of Central Leicestershire*. Leicester: Leicester Museums.

HARVEY, M. (1980). 'Regular field and tenurial arrangements in Holderness, Yorkshire'. *Journal of Historical Geography* 6(1): 3–16.

——(1983). 'Planned field systems in eastern Yorkshire: some thoughts on their origin'. *Agricultural History Review* 31(2): 91–103.

——(1984). 'Open field structure and landholding arrangements in eastern Yorkshire'. *Transactions of the Institute of British Geographers* (New Series) 9: 60–74.

——(1985). 'The development of open fields in the central Vale of York: a reconsideration'. *Geografiska Annaler* 76B: 35–44.

HENIG, M. (2002). 'Roman Britain after 410'. *British Archaeology* 68: 8–11.
HESSE, M. (2000). 'Domesday land measures in Suffolk'. *Landscape History* 22: 21–36.
HEY, G. (2004). *Yarnton: Saxon and Medieval Settlement and Landscape*. Oxford: Oxbow Books.
HILLER, J., PETTS, D., and ALLEN, T. (2002). 'Chapter 5: Discussion of the Anglo-Saxon archaeology', in S. Foreman, J. Hiller, and D. Petts (eds.), *Gathering the People, Settling the Land*. Oxford: Oxford Archaeology, 57–72.
HODGES, R. (1991). *Wall-To-Wall History*. London: Duckworth.
HOOKE, D. (1981a). *Anglo-Saxon Landscapes of the West Midlands: The Charter Evidence*. BAR British Series 95. Oxford: British Archaeological Reports.
——(1981b). 'Open-field agriculture—the evidence from the pre-Conquest charters of the West Midlands', in Rowley (ed.), *Origins of Open Field Agriculture*, 39–63.
——(1988a). 'Early forms of open field agriculture in England'. *Geografiska Annaler* 70B: 121–31.
——(1988b). 'Regional variation in southern and central England in the Anglo-Saxon period and its relationship to land units and settlement', in D. Hooke (ed.), *Anglo-Saxon Settlements*. Oxford: Blackwell, 123–51.
——(1998). *The Landscape of Anglo-Saxon England*. Leicester: Leicester University Press.
HOSKINS, W. G. (ed.) (1988). *The Making of the English Landscape*. London: Guild.
JONES, R., and PAGE, M. (2006). *Medieval Villages in an English Landscape: Beginnings and Ends*. Macclesfield: Windgather.
KEEN, L. (1984). 'The towns of Dorset', in J. Haslam (ed.), *Anglo-Saxon Towns in Southern England*. Chichester: Phillimore, 203–48.
LAWSON, A. (1983). *The Archaeology of Witton, near North Walsham, Norfolk*. East Anglian Archaeology 18. Gressenhall.
LEWIS, C., MITCHELL-FOX, P., and DYER, C. (1997). *Village, Hamlet and Field*. Manchester: Manchester University Press.
LOSCO-BRADLEY, S., and KINSLEY, G. (2002). *Catholme: An Anglo-Saxon Settlement on the Trent Gravels in Staffordshire*. Nottingham: Nottingham University Press.
——and WHEELER, H. M. (1984). 'Anglo-Saxon settlement in the Trent valley: some aspects', in M. Faull (ed.), *Studies in Late Anglo-Saxon Settlement*. Oxford: Oxford Department for External Studies, 103–14.
MCOMISH, D., FIELD, D., and BROWN, G. (2002). *The Field Archaeology of Salisbury Plain*. Swindon: English Heritage.
MEESON, R., and RAHTZ, P. (1992). *An Anglo-Saxon Watermill at Tamworth*. CBA Research Report 83. York: Council for British Archaeology.
MILES, D. (ed.) (1984). *Archaeology at Barton Court Farm, Abingdon, Oxon*. Oxford and York: Oxford Archaeological Unit and Council for British Archaeology.
MORELAND, J. (2000). 'The significance of production in eighth-century England', in I. L. Hansen and C. Wickham (eds.), *The 'Long' Eighth Century*. Leiden: Brill, 69–104.
MURPHY, K. (2001). 'A prehistoric field system and related monuments on St David's Head and Carn Llidi, Pembrokeshire'. *Proceedings of the Prehistoric Society* 67: 85–99.
MURPHY, P. (1994). 'The Anglo-Saxon landscape and rural economy: some results from sites in East Anglia and Essex', in J. Rackham (ed.), *Environment and Economy in Anglo-Saxon England*. CBA Research Report 89. York: Council for British Archaeology, 25–37.
NASH, A. (1982). 'The medieval fields of Strettington, West Sussex, and the evolution of land division'. *Geografiska Annaler* 64B(1): 41–9.

OOSTHUIZEN, S. (1993). 'Saxon commons in South Cambridgeshire'. *Proceedings of the Cambridge Antiquarian Society*, 82: 93–100.
——(1996). *Cambridgeshire From the Air*. Stroud: Sutton.
——(1998). 'Prehistoric fields into medieval furlongs? Evidence from Caxton, South Cambridgeshire'. *Proceedings of the Cambridge Antiquarian Society* 86: 145–52.
——(2002). 'Unravelling the morphology of Litlington, South Cambridgeshire'. *Proceedings of the Cambridge Antiquarian Society* 91: 55–61.
——(2005). 'New light on the origins of open field farming?'. *Medieval Archaeology* 49: 165–93.
——(2006). *Landscapes Decoded: The Origins and Development of Cambridgeshire's Medieval Fields*. Hatfield: University of Hertfordshire Press.
——(2007). 'The Anglo-Saxon kingdom of Mercia and the origins and distribution of common fields'. *Agricultural History Review* 55(2): 153–80.
PARRY, S. (2006). *Raunds Area Survey*. Oxford: Oxbow Books.
PAYNE, S. (2007). 'New insights into climate history'. *British Archaeology* 92: 54.
POCOCK, E. A. (1968). 'The first fields in an Oxfordshire parish'. *Agricultural History Review* 16(2): 85–100.
POSTGATE, M. R. (1962). 'The field systems of Breckland'. *Agricultural History Review* 10(2): 80–101.
——(1973). 'Field systems of East Anglia', in A. R. H. Baker and R. A. Butlin (eds.), *Studies of Field Systems in the British Isles*. Cambridge: Cambridge University Press: 281–324.
POWLESLAND, D. (1986). 'Excavations at Heslerton, North Yorkshire 1978–82'. *Archaeological Journal* 143: 53–173.
PRICE, E. (2000). *Frocester: A Romano-British Settlement, its Antecedents and Successors*. Gloucester: Gloucester and District Archaeological Research Group.
RACKHAM, O. (1986). *The History of the Countryside*. London: Dent.
RCHME (1968). *West Cambridgeshire*. London: HMSO.
——(1979). *Archaeological Sites in Central Northamptonshire*. London: HMSO.
REYNOLDS, A. (2003). 'Boundaries and settlements in later sixth- to eleventh-century England'. *Anglo-Saxon Studies in Archaeology and History* 12: 98–136.
RILEY, H., and WILSON-NORTH, R. (2001). *The Field Archaeology of Exmoor*. Swindon: English Heritage.
RIPPON, S. (1991). 'Early planned landscapes in South-East Essex'. *Essex Archaeology and History* 22: 46–60.
——(1994). 'Medieval wetland reclamation in Somerset', in M. Aston and C. Lewis (eds.), *The Medieval Landscape of Wessex*. Oxford: Oxbow Books, 239–53.
——(2006). *Landscape, Community and Colonisation: The North Somerset Levels during the 1st to 2nd Millennia AD*. CBA Research Report 152. York: Council for British Archaeology.
——FIFE, R. M., and BROWN, A. G. (2006). 'Beyond villages and open fields: the origins and development of a historic landscape characterized by dispersed settlement in South-West England'. *Medieval Archaeology* 50: 31–70.
ROBERTS, B. K. (1981). 'Townfield origins: the case of Cockfield, County Durham', in T. Rowley (ed.), *The Origins of Open Field Agriculture*. London: Croom Helm, 145–61.
——(1985). 'Village patterns and forms: some models for discussion', in D. Hooke (ed.), *Medieval Villages: A Review of Current Work*. Oxford: Oxford University Committee for Archaeology, 7–25.

——(1993). 'Five Westmoreland settlements: a comparative study'. *Transactions of the Westmoreland and Cumberland Antiquarian and Archaeological Society* 93: 131–43.
——(1996). 'The Great Plough: A hypothesis concerning village genesis and land reclamation in Cumberland and Westmoreland'. *Landscape History* 18: 17–30.
——and WRATHMELL, S. (2000). *Atlas of Rural Settlement in England.* Swindon: English Heritage.
——(2002). *Region and Place.* Swindon: English Heritage.
ROGERSON, A., DAVISON, A., PRITCHARD, D., and SILVESTER, R. (1997). *Barton Bendish and Caldecote: Fieldwork in South-West Norfolk.* East Anglian Archaeology 80. Gressenhall.
ROWLEY, T. (ed.) (1981). *The Origins of Open Field Agriculture.* London: Croom Helm.
SEEBOHM, F. (1883). *The English Village Community.* London: Longmans.
SHAW, M. (1991). 'Saxon and earlier settlement at Higham Ferrers, Northamptonshire'. *Medieval Settlement Research Group Annual Report* 6: 15–19.
SHEPPARD, J. (1966). 'Pre-enclosure field and settlement patterns in an English township'. *Geografiska Annaler* 48B: 59–77.
——(1979). *The Origins and Evolution of Field and Settlement Patterns in the Herefordshire Manor of Marden.* Occasional Paper 15. London: Queen Mary College Department of Geography.
SILVESTER, R. J. (1988). *The Fenland Project, Number 3: Norfolk Survey, Marshland and Nar Valley.* East Anglian Archaeology 45. Gressenhall.
SMITH, C. (1978–9). 'The historical development of the landscape in the parishes of Alrewas, Fisherwick and Whittington: a retrogressive analysis'. *Transactions of the South Staffordshire Archaeological and Historical Society* 20: 1–14.
STENTON, F. M. (1971). *Anglo-Saxon England.* Oxford: Oxford University Press.
STOERTZ, C. (1997). *Ancient Landscapes of the Yorkshire Wolds.* Swindon: RCHME.
TAYLOR, C. C. (1981). 'Archaeology and the origins of open-field agriculture', in Rowley (ed.), *Origins of Open Field Agriculture*, 13–21.
——(1983). *Village and Farmstead.* London: George Phillip.
——and ARBON, A. (2007). 'The Chronicle Hills, Whittlesford, Cambridgeshire'. *Proceedings of the Cambridge Antiquarian Society* 96: 21–40.
——and FOWLER, P. J. (1978). 'Roman fields into medieval furlongs?', in H. C. Bowen and P. J. Fowler (eds.), *Early Land Allotment in the British Isles.* BAR British Series 48. Oxford: British Archaeological Reports, 159–62.
THIRSK, J. (1964). 'The common fields'. *Past and Present* 29: 3–25.
TOPPING, P. (1989). 'Early cultivation in Northumberland and the Borders.' *Proceedings of the Prehistoric Society,* 55: 161–79.
——(2008). 'Landscape narratives: the South East Cheviots Project'. *Proceedings of the Prehistoric Society* 74: 323–64.
UNWIN, P. T. H. (1983). 'Townships and early fields in North Nottinghamshire'. *Journal of Historical Geography* 9(4): 341–46.
UPEX, S. (2002). 'Landscape continuity and fossilisation of Roman fields'. *Archaeological Journal* 159: 77–108.
WARNER, P. (1987). *Greens, Commons and Clayland Colonization.* Leicester: Leicester University Press.
——(1996). *The Origins of Suffolk.* Manchester: Manchester University Press.
WEBSTER, G. (1967). 'Excavations at the Romano-British Villa in Barnsley Park, Cirencester, 1961–1966'. *Transactions of the Bristol and Gloucestershire Archaeology Society* 86: 74–83.

WILLIAMSON, T. (1984). 'The Roman countryside: settlement and agriculture in NW Essex'. *Britannia* 15: 225–30.
——(1987). 'Early co-Axial field systems on the East Anglian Boulder Clays'. *Proceedings of the Prehistoric Society* 53: 419–31.
——(2000). *The Origins of Hertfordshire.* Manchester: Manchester University Press.
——(2003). *Shaping Medieval Landscapes.* Macclesfield: Windgather.
WINCHESTER, A. (1987). *Landscape and Society in Medieval Cumbria.* Edinburgh: John Donald.
YORKE, B. 1995. *Wessex in the Early Middle Ages.* Leicester: Leicester University Press.

PART V

CRAFT PRODUCTION AND TECHNOLOGY

CHAPTER 22

OVERVIEW: CRAFT PRODUCTION AND TECHNOLOGY

GABOR THOMAS

SOURCES AND LIMITATIONS OF EVIDENCE

MATERIAL encounters with the past frequently generate speculation on craft techniques and processes. But as long as the popular view prevailed that the Anglo-Saxon artist was far inferior in skill and artistry to his Romano-British predecessor and his continental counterpart—a perception still widely held as late as the interwar years of the twentieth century (see, for example, Kendrick 1938: 61)—enquiry of this kind received little impetus or encouragement. The watershed came in 1939 with the discovery of the Sutton Hoo treasure, a dazzling witness to the virtuoso craftsmanship and technical brilliance of Anglo-Saxon art of the Conversion period. The comprehensive and meticulous programme of conservation, analysis, and reconstruction which ensued presented a clear demonstration of how 'technology' as a complementary perspective to traditional art-historical studies can bring new meaning to encounters with the Anglo-Saxon material world and how ill-placed we are without it to judge the generations of able hands which brought this world into being (Bruce-Mitford 1975–1983).

Some of the greatest advances of recent generations have been won by harnessing science to probe beneath the surface of objects. A growing battery of analytical techniques now exists for determining the chemical or elemental composition of an object to source its raw materials. Thanks to such analysis we now know that the coloured window glass from the Northumbrian monastery of Monkwearmouth/Jarrow was most probably re-melted from cullet originating from glass furnaces in the Levant and adjacent regions (Freestone and Hughes 2006). Rather closer to home, we can also now prove that mid Saxon Ipswich held a monopoly over the production of the eponymous pottery discovered over a broad spread of eastern England (Blinkhorn 2004). Yet the visual examination of manufactured objects, the traditional preserve of art history, still holds an important place in modern scholarship. Stylistic analysis, as Webster shows below, long directed at developing chronological frameworks for the Anglo-Saxon period, is increasingly being turned towards the symbolic and cognitive realms of craftwork production, providing new insights into the cultural and cosmological climate which shaped different forms of artistic expression (Webster 2003).

Of course, as Leahy explores below, our knowledge base has also been expanded by a steady rise in the corpus of excavated settlements responsible for bringing to light a complementary spectrum of workshop evidence in the form of tools, production detritus, and infrastructure such as kilns and furnaces (e.g. Bayley 1991). With standardized sampling strategies used on modern excavations the range of evidence may also include less visually-arresting clues such as minute fragments of hammerscale that can be used to precisely locate the otherwise silent footprint of a smithy (e.g. Salter 2004). As we shall presently see, such evidence is of more than purely technical interest, for it constitutes a material basis for examining the scale and organization of craftwork production across a range of media and in a range of settlement contexts spanning the Anglo-Saxon era, and thus a corrective to the internal biases of the historical sources (Dodwell 1982). Combined, the results of object-based analyses and excavation have borne fruit in an impressive and growing body of literature ranging from microscopic dissections of individual objects (taking in aspects of construction, composition, and style), whether found in isolation such as the Coppergate helmet (Tweddle 1992), or in assemblages such as the Sutton Hoo treasure, through to wider surveys of individual crafts exemplified by relevant fascicules emanating from Anglo-Scandinavian sites excavated in York.

In spite of this progress it is important that we do not lose sight of the fact that our source material is but a minuscule and inherently-biased proportion of the total productive output of the Anglo-Saxon age. Beyond the interaction of a wide range of post-depositional factors, we must take into account the cultural attitudes of the Anglo-Saxons themselves, two aspects of which are highly influential. The first is that many of the materials discussed below by Hinton—chiefly glass and metals, but also wood—were recycled according to the changing dictates of fashion and availability (Wilson 1984: 9–10). The second is a pivotal change in depositional practices consequent upon the cessation of furnished burial as a general rite during the second half of the seventh century; with the notable exception of hoards and lingering votive practices, the archaeology of the post-Conversion period is thus largely made up of stray losses and rubbish divorced from primary contexts of use. These and other factors combine to create a massive influence on the representativeness and condition of different classes of material evidence. Further, we must be aware that only certain craft processes—those leaving behind durable traces of part-made objects, equipment, and workshop detritus—will breach the threshold of archaeological visibility. Finally, and casting a shadow over the interpretation of all relevant classes of the material record, is the issue of dating. It is a salutary reminder that in most cases it is simply impossible to date a physical remnant of Anglo-Saxon craftworking, whether a tool, by-product, or finished article, to within the working lifetime of a single craftsman.

Fortunately other sources can be called upon both as a means to fill gaps in understanding and to construct a contextual framework around material-derived observations. Whereas historical, literary, and epigraphic evidence can help to shed light on the identity and social context of Anglo-Saxon artisans, experimental archaeology can aid in reconstructing the practice of individual crafts; comparative ethnography meanwhile can inform our notions of how artisans were regarded by contemporary society, whether practising in the domestic sphere or beyond as peripatetic guardians of 'reserved knowledge'. Arguably, some of the most successful studies to date, exemplified by Coatsworth and Pinder's recent examination of the Anglo-Saxon goldsmith (2002), are those which have taken up the challenge of integrating archaeological evidence with these comparative strands. Yet as these authors would agree, this holistic approach is only possible for the best documented of contemporary crafts—those held in the highest esteem by the Anglo-Saxons themselves (Dodwell 1982: 44–8).

CHRONOLOGICAL OVERVIEW

Fifth–seventh centuries

Somewhat paradoxically given the wealth of object-derived information yielded by furnished graves, our knowledge of craftworking between the fifth and seventh centuries is riddled with gaps and ambiguities. This stems partly from a lack of supporting literary and epigraphic sources, but also from a dearth of workshop evidence associated with such media as glass and non-ferrous metals. We know correspondingly little of the identity and careers of contemporary artisans, although it is possible to gain some impression of their social role from burials interpreted with reference to a wider understanding of the evolving social and political structures of early Anglo-Saxon England (Hinton 2003; Fig. 22.1—the back of the brooch is inscribed with the first metalworker's name to be recorded). Amongst the domestic crafts, textile manufacture is best attested by the persistent discovery of spinning and weaving implements on settlements (though not without its own problems of interpretation) complementing the picture provided by fragments of clothing preserved by mineral replacement in graves (Walton Rogers 2007); the almost total absence of wet sites from this period means that we are very ill-informed on the most ubiquitous crafts of all: wood- and leather-working.

Nevertheless, the generalization can be made that most craft production at this early period proceeded at a domestic level within the sphere of self-sufficient rural communities, leaving the production of non-utilitarian goods (ideological apparatus used in expressions of personal and group identity within early Anglo-Saxon

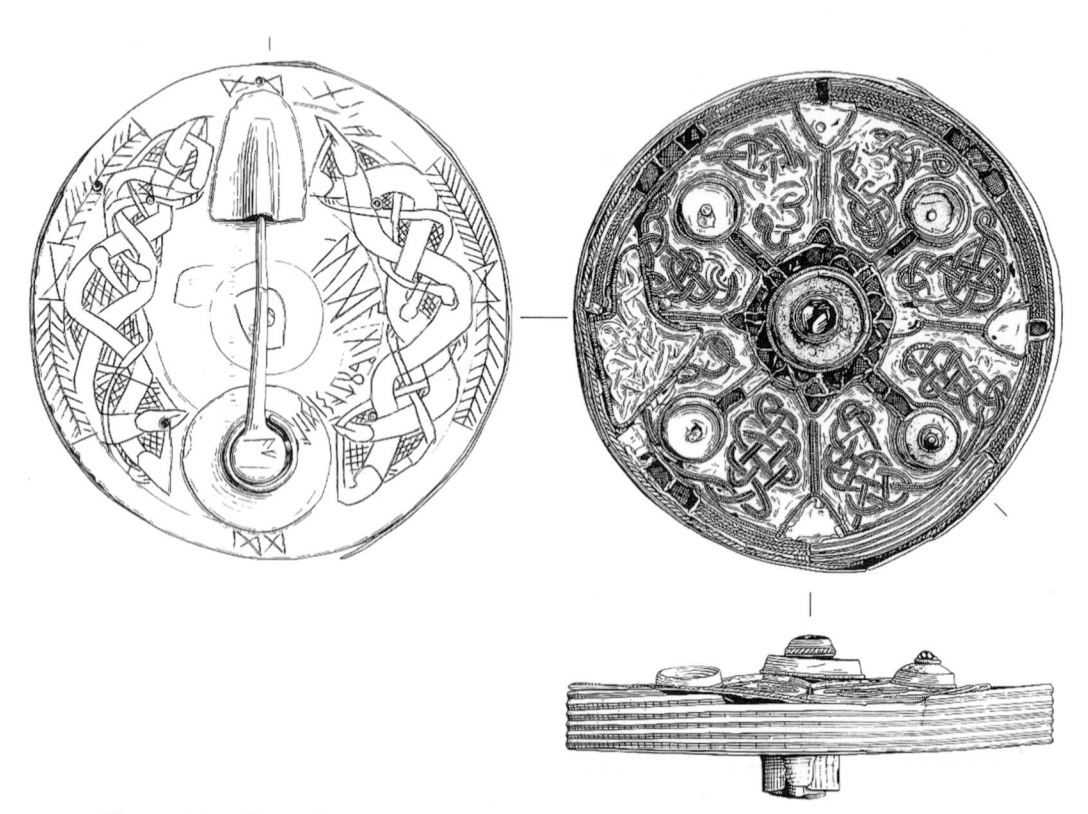

Figure 22.1 Seventh-century composite disc brooch from Harford Farm, Caistor St Edmund, Norfolk. Front: gold, garnets, and ivory boss, with repair patch (cf. Pestell, this volume Fig. 29.5); back: silver, with incised Style 2 animal decoration and runic inscription 'Luda [possibly Tuda] repaired [the] brooch' (drawing by Steven Ashley reproduced by kind permission of Norwich Castle Museum and Art Gallery from Penn 2000: 45–9). Diameter 71 mm.

society) in the hands of a relatively small contingent of itinerant specialists. Various sources of evidence support the view that production at the more specialized end of the craft spectrum was low output, not least the impermanent nature of smithies attested at Mucking and other contemporary settlements (McDonnell 1993), and the fact that recycled as opposed to freshly smelted sources of copper alloy were used for casting jewellery (Bayley 1992: 809; Brownsword and Hines 1993). Although we must be wary of basing conclusions on negative evidence, it is perhaps significant that Anglo-Saxon England has nothing to compare in scale or intensity to the migration-period jewellery workshop site at Helgö, Sweden (Holmqvist 1972) nor, for that matter, the concentrations of fine metalworking forming a persistent theme on elite residences in the Celtic west (Hinton 2005: 39–49; Loveluck and Laing, this volume). The academic consensus emerging from detailed study of migration-period brooches also favours a scenario involving periodic activity by itinerant jewellers who left their mark in localized clusters of brooches displaying family tendencies in style and design, rather than distribution from a few centralized workshops (Hines 1997a, 211ff.; Hinton 2003: 263–4). Less certain is the precise casting technology employed, more particularly whether or not the regular tool-kit of the itinerant jeweller might include a selection of durable models allowing him to replicate his chosen design while on the move (Coatsworth and Pinder 2002: 69–86).

The theme of itinerancy, central to our conception of the smith in Germanic society, has received fresh impetus in the form of the recent discovery of an extensively equipped grave at Tattershall Thorpe, Lincolnshire, dating to the second half of the seventh century (Hinton 2000). Aspects of this unique find, not least its liminal landscape context, support the view otherwise hinted at in contemporary cultural expressions of the Wayland legend, that smiths in early Anglo-Saxon society could be regarded as outsiders, as much feared as they were revered for their magical skills and 'reserved' knowledge. The contents of the burial invite a closer consideration of two themes of wider relevance. The first is the extent to which the smith of Conversion-period England was, as expressed in the early laws, of bond social status (Hinton 2003: 267–8). Such need not preclude a level of itinerancy given the mobile character of kingship at this period. But the fact that the Tattershall Thorpe smith was evidently in possession of a range of costly and imported luxuries destined for embellishing jewellery suggests that he was able to obtain raw materials independently of a patron (Hinton 2000: 112–15). Second is the smith's eclectic tool-kit showing him to be capable of crafting both wrought-iron objects and fine jewellery (Figs. 22.2, 3; and see Leahy, this volume); in this sense he evokes an age, as yet untouched by the product-based specialization of later centuries, when generalists might be individually capable of creating such complex composite items as a pattern-welded sword or, collectively, the splendour of the Sutton Hoo regalia.

Figure 22.2 Slotted iron tool with holes of uneven diameter; probably a draw-plate for reducing the diameter of iron wire, or a nail-making bar, from Tattershall Thorpe, Lincolnshire. Length 114 mm (photograph by Robert White reproduced by kind permission of Lincolnshire County Council)

Recent research focused on this period is also helping to identify early tendencies towards the more organized productive and redistributive networks of the mid Saxon economy. One notable example concerns so-called Charnwood pottery, made in the sixth and seventh centuries from clay attributable on compositional grounds to a single source in modern-day Leicestershire (Williams and Vince 1997). Enjoying a wide distribution across eastern and midland England, the market for this ware far surpassed the localized orbit characterizing most handmade pottery of the same period. It would thus appear that Charnwood prepared the ground for the emergence of Maxey- and Ipswich-type wares as dominant traditions within the same region, the most ceramically developed in all of mid Saxon England.

If it is the case that craft specialization occurs 'in response to different circumstances and opportunities related to supply and demand and the social context of the artisan' (Brown 1999: 309–10), the one place where we might expect to find increased levels of craft specialization at this early period is politically ascendant Kent. As is well documented, the Kentish royal dynasty exploited its close dynastic and commercial links with Francia during the later sixth and seventh centuries to

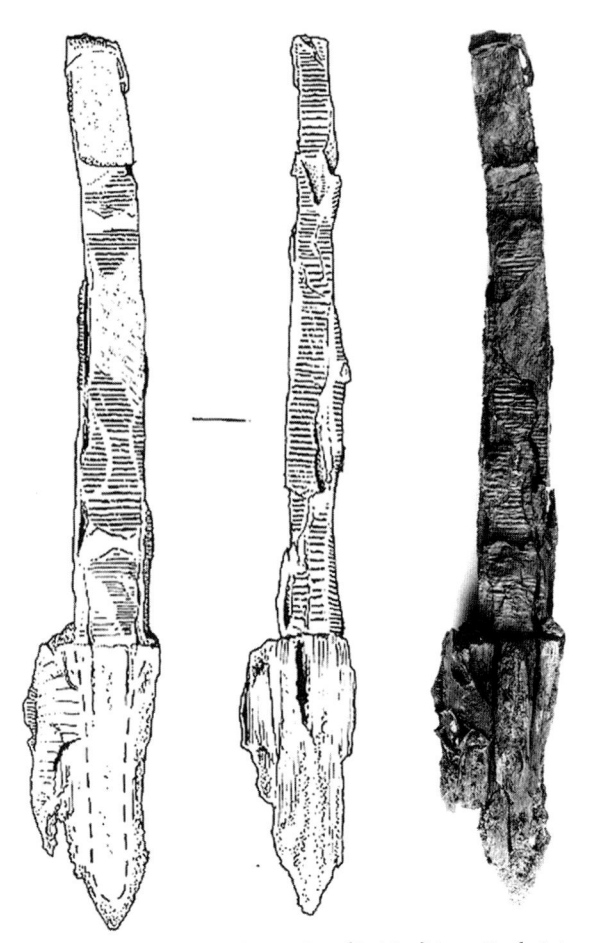

Figure 22.3 Iron file, with remains of wooden (?alder) handle (cf. Leahy, this volume Fig. 24.4). Length 161 mm (photograph by Robert White reproduced by kind permission of Lincolnshire County Council)

obtain gold, garnets, and other imported luxuries which, along with Style II animal ornament, formed the ingredients for a distinctive polychrome style synonymous with Kentish aristocratic identity (Huggett 1988; Høilund Nielsen 1999; Welch 2007: 191–3). The workshops engaged in the production of this style and other characteristically Kentish media such as glass vessels remain to be found, but must surely have existed given the strong implication of a significant and sustained pooling of apparatus, and technical expertise passed down through successive generations (Hinton 2003: 266–7). Nonetheless, we can look to strong circumstantial evidence in the form of the place-name Faversham (OE='the village of the smith'), an important early royal estate centre expressed archaeologically in the 'King's Field' Anglo-Saxon cemetery with its exceptionally rich array of glass and gold-and-garnet jewellery (Coatsworth and Pinder 2002: 219). It is perhaps in places such as Faversham and its other Kentish counterparts that we see some of the earliest signs of kingship playing a direct hand in the conversion of estate surpluses into status-enhancing goods (Peregrine 1991; Campbell 2003).

The eighth and ninth centuries

The developing relationship between craft specialization and political centralization can be traced with some clarity during the mid Saxon period thanks to a growing corpus of excavated complexes forming integrated components of royal vills and monastic estates—places where emerging state authority was invested in the landscape. Coinciding with an eighth-century boom in the economy of north-west Europe, these archaeological phenomena bear witness to a step-change in the productivity of agricultural estates (whether under secular or ecclesiastical lordship) evident *inter alia* in new types of infrastructure and technology for extracting raw materials and converting agricultural surpluses: watermills at Tamworth and Old Windsor; grain-drying facilities at Hereford, Hoddom, and Higham Ferrers; salt-working at Droitwich; and iron-smelting at Ramsbury (Hinton 1990: 44; Lowe 2006; Hardy *et al.* 2007; Haslam 1980). This ramping-up in the productive capacity of agricultural estates finds its corollary in the domain of craft production in a dramatic upturn in the manufacture of standard types of dress accessory—pins, strap-ends, and hooked tags—found in greatest numbers in the eastern half of England (Blair 2005: 133, note 256; Pestell and Ulmschneider 2003). Metallurgical analysis would appear to indicate that this explosion was fuelled by new sources of freshly smelted brass used also to debase contemporary silver coinages (Bayley 1992: 808–10; Metcalf and Northover 1989).

The centralization of resources and infrastructure at estate complexes made them natural havens for craft activity as reflected in a consistent range spanning the working of textiles, bone, wood, leather, iron, and non-ferrous metals. Whilst much of the industry found at these sites was no doubt geared towards meeting the domestic and agricultural needs of the wider estate, in a few notable cases we are presented with more concrete evidence for elite-focused production. One such example is the smithy attached to the excavated portion of a mid Saxon settlement at Wharram Percy, North Yorkshire, if, as seems likely, hilt-guards and pommels found there attest to the temporary presence of a weapon-smith, a class of specialist whose skills were intimately bound up with the martial ideal and expressions of elite identity (Richards 2000: 196).

With the exception of stone-carving and glass-working found amongst the wealthiest tier of monastic institutions such as Glastonbury, Barking, and Monkwearmouth/Jarrow, there is surprisingly little to differentiate contemporary settlements in terms of their craft profiles, a factor which feeds into the widely acknowledged problems of site characterization during this relatively poorly documented period (Hines 1997b; Loveluck 2001; Hamerow, this volume). The recent claim that coins may have been minted at monasteries serves to further blur perceived economic distinctions between secular settlements on the one hand and ecclesiastical ones on the other (Gannon 2003: 188–92). One specialization that does have distinctly monastic overtones, however, is fine metalworking, particularly when combined with millefiori and reticella glass rods consumed in the production of shrines, book-covers, and other liturgical finery.

Despite the accrual of valuable workshop evidence from excavated settlements, important questions still remain a long way from elucidation. One essential to building an informed appreciation of the economic role of contemporary settlements is the extent to which the products of craftworking were intended for external sale or redistribution. For example, does the intensified production of fine textiles witnessed at Flixborough during the late eighth to mid ninth centuries (as suggested by the comparative delicacy of weaving implements deposited in phase 3) reflect the material requirements of an upwardly-mobile—perhaps monastic—household, or rather a pragmatic attempt by its occupants to gain a lucrative foothold in the supply of regional markets (Loveluck and Walton Rogers 2007: 102–12)?

Although by no means unique to this period, these questions are particularly intractable in the eighth and ninth centuries when, as a result of the growth of universal artefact styles, many standard categories of dress accessory defy localization. Metalwork displaying high levels of standardization combined with a focused geographical distribution can sometimes point towards a probable source of manufacture, for example York in the case of a group of Trewhiddle-style strap-ends bearing nearly identical versions of a coiled beast (Thomas 2001). But without diagnostic workshop evidence in the form of identifiable moulds or models, it is impossible to make definitive statements. Inasmuch as stylistic distinctions can be defined at this period, more often than not these reveal themselves not at a local but at a regional or supra-regional scale. Thus one can speak of a distinctly 'Mercian' school of late-eighth-century art characterized by a lively zoomorphic style seen on sculpture and portable items of chip-carved metalwork, or, into the ninth century, a 'Northumbrian' version of the Trewhiddle style (Webster 2001; Thomas 2006). As these names imply, one cannot ignore the influence of political boundaries on style, but by linking distant centres within common networks of communication and interaction, the Church and coastal trade also played their part, particularly in the economically precocious zone of eastern England (Plunkett 1998; Blair 2005: 210–12).

One remaining arena where craftwork production was concentrated at this period was in the coastal *emporia* or *wics*, settlements which flourished as international trade expanded (Scull 1997; Hill and Cowie 2001; Pestell, this volume). With their prodigious assemblages of craftworking debris in organic materials, metals, and glass, there has been a tendency in the past to equate the craft profile of these sprawling settlements with full-time specialization. In fact, amongst the English *wics* it is only iron-working and potting that display evidence for production in fixed locales for sustained periods of time (Andrews 1997: 205); and even in such cases the consensus of academic opinion favours seasonal or intermittent production (Scull 1997: 288, 300). A closer examination of the spatial context of craftworking in *wics* gives a similar impression that the time of the full-time professional had yet to come. Not only are the buildings associated with craft activity barely distinguishable from domestic units on rural settlements but there is also a tendency for more than one craft to be practised within the same spatial setting, a pattern seen in the continental *emporia* such as Ribe, Denmark (Andrews 1997: 205; Malcolm and Bowsher 2003: 168; Jensen 1993: 7). On the other hand, assessments must also take into account growing evidence for the zoning of certain crafts, most recently proposed in relation to the identification of a boneworking enclave in the Six Dials area of *Hamwic* (Riddler 2001). Whether such zoning relates to the collective impetus of interdependent artisans, the controlling hand of a higher authority, or perhaps the cultural and ethnic affiliations of the artisans involved is open to question, but it bespeaks a level of organization that can only have been equalled (if at all) at larger monastic complexes.

The tenth and eleventh centuries

Over this period we encounter the beginnings of a radical shift in the location of craft production from the countryside into the urban sphere, culminating (at least in the case of the larger towns) in the formation of specialized craft guilds which were to become a standard ingredient in medieval town life from at least the twelfth century, when they were first attested historically (Ramsay 1991: xvi). Yet this transition, one which was to effectively signal the end of the itinerant smith of old, was a gradual process synchronous with the economic development of centres which were not to reach their full productive capacity as towns until the second half of the tenth century at the earliest (Astill 2000: 37–42; 2006).

Accordingly, rural power bases, now also including a new tier of thegnly residences built on the estates of a burgeoning local aristocracy, continued to provide a setting for skilled artisans well into the tenth century (Hinton 2005: 165). Excavation has confirmed the periodic presence of goldsmiths at the royal residence of Cheddar (Rahtz 1979) and the manorial complex attached to the estate of Faccombe Netherton, Hampshire (Fairbrother 1990), bequeathed (*c.* AD 950) in the will of Wynflæd, who made explicit reference to the employment of a goldsmith in another one of her bequests (Coatsworth and Pinder 2002: 22 and 208–9). As this last example attests, the growth of an active land market, backed up by new forms of literate bureaucracy (charters and wills), provides new terrain for exploring the social identity of late Anglo-Saxon artisans. Collectively, these sources demonstrate that craftsmen could occupy a wide spectrum of social niches reflecting the reality of social mobility in late Anglo-Saxon England (Dodwell 1982: 75–9). Whereas some were clearly tied to patrons as part of movable households, bequests by and to smiths indicate that others could attain considerable wealth and social standing within free society, sufficient in some cases for them to enter the ranks of thegnhood, as is demonstrated by a number of multiple-manor-holding goldsmiths named in Domesday Book (Coatsworth and Pinder 2002: 210–26; Dodwell 1982: 78).

Another insight into the growing status of master craftsmen is provided by makers' inscriptions. Whilst this tradition is attested as early as the late seventh century in an English context, it is only during the late Saxon period that the practice becomes more commonplace, suggesting that an increasing number of craftsmen could claim membership of the literate minority and exploit the medium of writing to bolster their reputations (Coatsworth and Pinder 2002: 220–5). Perhaps most evocative of this trend are sword-blades of standardized manufacture and wide northern European distribution bearing the makers' names 'ULFBERHT' and 'INGELRI' which can be regarded as brand-names reflecting truly international reputations (Peirce 2002: 7–9; Hinton 2005: 125).

Further insight into the changing domain of the skilled artisan at this period can be obtained by returning to the estate complex of Flixborough. Thanks to a tightly-phased stratigraphic sequence covering four centuries of continuous occupation, this is one of the few sites offering a diachronic perspective on craft production in a rural setting. In terms of its craft production, Flixborough in the tenth century presents a very different picture to the ninth. The manufacture of fine cloth and of cast objects in lead and non-ferrous metals (a proportion of which may have been destined for the export market) disappears, to be replaced by the more workaday pairing of smithing and textile production in coarser fabrics (Loveluck 2007: 105). Generalizing from the Flixborough evidence, one could argue that production on late Saxon rural estates had become more streamlined and internally focused, echoing similar concerns for efficient management documented in contemporary estate memoranda such as *Gerefa* (Gardiner 2006).

The move to urban-based craft production and the gains in efficiency and productive output brought in its wake has been likened to England's first industrial revolution (Hodges 1989: 150–86). For the freelance specialist the attractions of an urban base were considerable: the security of regulated trading conditions, royal protection, a wide consumer market, and the opportunity for establishing partnerships and cooperatives with fellow artisans. Those of bond status on the other hand were no doubt forcibly installed, as lords acquired new urban holdings. Technological developments soon followed. The adoption of the flue-kiln and kick-wheel in pottery production and the horizontal loom in textile manufacture both belong to this phase of urban expansion (Hodges 1989: 155–62; Henry 1999; Owen-Crocker 2004: 267–82). So too do technical improvements in the smith's art—the use of purer, low-phosphorus ores and of scarf and butt-welded steel cutting edges on knives and other blades (Tylecote and Gilmour 1986: ch. 2; Pleiner 2008: 222–3). Fine metalworking witnessed its own developments, including the mass production of pewter jewellery using solid re-usable moulds such as those found in Southampton and Ipswich (Hinton 2005: 158). However, the products of these new urban workshops do not only bear the stamp of technological innovation and mass production. Garments and footwear embody a greater diversity of styles best explained as the rise of urban fashions (Hinton 2005: 162–3), whilst finds of jewellery are sometimes imbued with the eclecticism that defined late Anglo-Saxon towns as cultural environments, as reflected in the hybridized 'Anglo-Scandinavian' ornament found on brooches made in York, or several pewter disc-brooches from London closely mimicking those mass-produced in Carolingian workshops on the Rhine (Hall 2000; Wamers 1986; Fig. 22.4).

Whilst most of the larger towns of late Anglo-Saxon England have yielded workshop evidence spanning a consistent range of urban crafts (Clarke and Ambrosiani 1995: 158–72), arguably the greatest contribution to understanding has been made by excavations at Coppergate in York which uncovered four tenements, each witnessing intense and sustained craft activity over the Anglo-Scandinavian period (Mainman and Rogers 2004). This work has provided one of the best opportunities yet for interrogating the working conditions of a sub-section of the artisan community of a late Anglo-Saxon town, although invariably some of

Figure 22.4 Lead–alloy brooch from London. Diameter 39mm (photograph by G. Thomas reproduced with kind permission of Museum of London Archaeological Services)

the questions inspired by the wealth of data have stretched the archaeological evidence to its interpretative limits.

One of the themes to emerge from the Coppergate evidence is that of interdependence, for several crafts are represented across and indeed within each of the four tenements, both within the workshops and in the yards behind. Thus over a forty-five-year period (Period 4B) four major crafts were practised on Tenements C and D: ferrous and non-ferrous metalworking, leather-working, and wood-turning, supplemented by the minor crafts of antler- and amber-working. Clear concentrations of activity are also apparent during the same period: with wood-turning, leather-working, and the manufacture of lead alloy focusing on Tenement B, the manufacture of leather sheaths and scabbards, and smithing, on C, and the working of silver and copper alloy on D. The problem comes in ascertaining whether this multiplicity represents a series of sequential bursts too short to be recognized archaeologically (such as might be expected if each of the tenements were leased to itinerant craftsmen practising seasonally), or alternatively, the operation of several crafts within a single tenement concurrently (Mainman and Rogers 2004: 482). Whatever the case, the archaeological evidence suggests that the product-based zoning implied by occupational street-names coined at this period (Dodwell 1982: 76–7; Fellows-Jensen 2004) belies a rather more complex and diverse situation with definite echoes of the interdependence characterizing production within mid Saxon *wics*.

Under the revitalizing programme of the Benedictine Reform Movement, the monastic crafts were also to receive a significant boost at this period. The historical sources leave us in little doubt that the major reformed houses were centres of the highest cultural achievement and their output, particularly in manuscript illumination, goldwork, and embroidery, gained England an esteemed artistic reputation on the international stage (Dodwell 1982: 44). This activity was personified by monk-abbots at the apex of the ecclesiastical hierarchy—St Dunstan of Glastonbury, Spearhafoc of Abingdon and Mannig of Evesham—renowned as patrons and expert goldworkers, painters, and calligraphers, a versatility borne out by the close relationship cultivated between different fields of artistic expression serving the Church (Gameson 1995). From the same sources, we also gain snippets of information on the organization of monastic crafts: the fact that abbot-artists such as Spearhafoc were engaged in completing major commissions for both royalty and the Church, in the latter case visiting several Benedictine houses to supervise teams of lay goldsmiths (Dodwell 1982: 48–52; Coatsworth and Pinder 2002: 208–10).

Workshops in the service of the late Anglo-Saxon Church were no less innovative than urban ones supplying the lay market. They can probably claim the investment-mould technology used to cast complex three-dimensional items such as the openwork censer covers from Canterbury and Pershore, more sophisticated in design than anything previously to emerge from an Anglo-Saxon milieu, ecclesiastical or secular (Backhouse *et al.* 1984: cat. nos. 73 and 74; Coatsworth and Pinder

2002: 72–3). New technology, later described by the twelfth-century writer Theophilus, was also deployed in the casting of church bells, as attested archaeologically in the form of moulds and pits excavated at St Oswald's, Gloucester, and the Old Minster, Winchester (Backhouse et al. 1984: cat. nos. 145 and 146; Davies and Ovenden 1990); and the same range of sites witnesses parallel developments in other categories of church furnishing including window glass and floor tiles (Backhouse et al. 1984: cat. nos. 141–4; Biddle and Hunter 1990).

In comparison to their pre-Viking forebears, reformed houses have yielded surprisingly little in the way of direct archaeological evidence for workshop activity—Glastonbury Abbey, with its glass-working kilns, and Beverley Minster, Yorkshire, with its debris from glass-working, lead-casting, textile manufacture, leather- and antler-working, being notable exceptions (Bayley 2000; Armstrong et al. 1991: 19–22). Whilst this situation partly reflects the fact that the later establishments have received less systematic excavation (Cramp 1972: 203), it is also worth considering whether such evidence might simply be more difficult to pinpoint archaeologically. The ninth-century plan of the Carolingian monastery of St Gall, with its circumscribed quarters for goldsmiths, blacksmiths, and fullers, suggests that the more formalized layout of reformed institutions may have had a constraining effect on the spatial setting of craftwork activity, in contrast to the more generalized spread seen on mid Saxon sites (Coatsworth and Pinder 2002: 24–6). This factor might explain why recent excavations sampling a sizeable portion of the late Anglo-Saxon claustral complex of Eynsham Abbey, Oxfordshire, yielded only minimal evidence for production beyond that directly concerned with the construction of the monastic buildings themselves (Dodd and Hardy 2003: 487–92).

REFERENCES

ANDREWS, P. (1997). *Excavations at Hamwic*, Volume 2: *Excavations at Six Dials*. York: Council for British Archaeology.

ARMSTRONG, P., TOMLINSON, D., and EVANS, D. H. (1991). *Excavations at Lurk Lane Beverley, 1979–82*. Sheffield: Collis.

ASTILL, G. (2000). 'General Survey 600–1300', in D. Palliser (ed.), *The Cambridge Urban History of Britain*, Volume 1: *600–1540*. Cambridge: Cambridge University Press, 27–50.

——(2006). 'Community, identity and the later Anglo-Saxon town: the case of Southern England', in W. Davies, G. Halsall, and A. Reynolds (eds.), *People and Space in the Middle Ages, 300–1300*. Turnhout: Brepols, 233–54.

BACKHOUSE, J., TURNER, D. H., and WEBSTER, L. E. (eds.) (1984). *The Golden Age of Anglo-Saxon Art 966–1066*. London: British Museum Press.

BAYLEY, J. (1991). 'Anglo-Saxon non-ferrous metalworking: a survey'. *World Archaeology* 23(1): 115–30.

—— (1992). *Anglo-Scandinavian Non-Ferrous Metalworking from 16–22 Coppergate*. Volume 17, fasc. 7 of *The Archaeology of York*. London: Council for British Archaeology.

—— (2000). 'Saxon glass-working at Glastonbury Abbey', in J. Price (ed.), *Glass in Britain and Ireland AD 350–1100*. British Museum Occasional Paper 127. London: British Museum, 161–88.

BIDDLE, M., and HUNTER, J. (1990). 'Window glass', in M. Biddle (ed.), *Object and Economy in Medieval Winchester*. Winchester Studies 7.2. Oxford: Clarendon Press, 350–85.

BLAIR, J. (2005). *The Church in Anglo-Saxon Society*. Oxford: Oxford University Press.

BLINKHORN, P. (2004). 'Pottery', in G. Hey, *Yarnton: Saxon and Medieval Settlement and Landscape*. Oxford: Oxford Archaeology, 267–73.

BROWN, K. (1999). 'Metalworking', in M. Lapidge, J. Blair, S. Keynes, and D. Scragg (eds.), *The Blackwell Encyclopaedia of Anglo-Saxon England*. Oxford: Blackwell, 308–10.

BROWNSWORD, R., and HINES, J. (1993). 'The alloys of a sample of Anglo-Saxon great square-headed brooches'. *Antiquaries Journal* 73: 1–10.

BRUCE-MITFORD, R. L. S. (1975–83). *The Sutton Hoo Ship Burial*, 3 volumes. London: British Museum Press.

CAMPBELL, J. (2003). 'Production and distribution in early and middle Saxon England', in T. Pestell and K. Ulmschneider (eds.), *Markets in Early Medieval Europe: Trading and 'Productive' Sites, 650–850*. Macclesfield: Windgather Press, 12–19.

CLARKE, H., and AMBROSIANI, B. (1995). *Towns in the Viking Age*. Leicester: Leicester University Press.

COATSWORTH, E., and PINDER, M. (2002). *The Art of the Anglo-Saxon Goldsmith*. Woodbridge: Boydell.

CRAMP, R. (1976). 'Monastic sites', in D. M. Wilson (ed.), *The Archaeology of Anglo-Saxon England*. Cambridge: Methuen, 201–52.

DAVIES, R. M., and OVENDEN, P. J. (1990). 'Bell-founding in Winchester in the tenth to thirteenth centuries', in M. Biddle (ed.), *Object and Economy in Medieval Winchester*. Winchester Studies 7.2. Oxford: Clarendon Press, 100–23.

DODD, A., and HARDY, A. (2003). 'The Anglo-Saxon Sequence', in A. Hardy, A. Dodd, and G. D. Keevill (eds.), *Aelfric's Abbey: Excavations at Eynsham Abbey, Oxfordshire, 1989–1992*. Thames Valley Landscapes Monograph 16. Oxford: Oxford Archaeology, 463–92.

DODWELL, C. R. (1982). *Anglo-Saxon Art: A New Perspective*. Ithaca, NY: Cornell University Press.

FAIRBROTHER, J. R. (1990). *Faccombe Netherton: Excavations of a Saxon and Medieval Manorial Complex*. 2 volumes. Occasional Paper 76. London: British Museum.

FELLOWS-JENSEN, G. (2004). 'The Anglo-Scandinavian street-names of York', in R. Hall et al. (eds.), *Aspects of Anglo-Scandinavian York*. Volume 8, fasc. 4 of *The Archaeology of York*. York: Council of British Archaeology, 357–71.

FREESTONE, I. C., and HUGHES, M. J. (2006). 'The origins of the Jarrow glass', in R. Cramp, *Wearmouth and Jarrow Monastic Sites*. Swindon: English Heritage, 147–54.

GAMESON, R. (1995). *The Role of Art in the Late Anglo-Saxon Church*. Oxford: Clarendon Press.

GANNON, A. (2003). *The Iconography of Early Anglo-Saxon Coinage: Sixth to Eighth Centuries*. Oxford: Oxford University Press.

GARDINER, M. (2006). 'Implements and utensils in *Gerefa* and the organisation of seigneurial farmsteads in the High Middle Ages'. *Medieval Archaeology* 50: 260–7.

HALL, R. A. (2000). 'Anglo-Scandinavian attitudes', in D. M. Hadley and J. D. Richards (eds.), *Cultures in Contact: Scandinavian Settlement in England in the Ninth and Tenth Centuries.* Turnhout: Brepols, 311–24.

HARDY, A., CHARLES, B. M., and WILLIAMS, R. J. (2007). *Death & Taxes: The Archaeology of a Middle Saxon Estate Centre at Higham Ferrers, Northamptonshire.* Oxford: Oxford Archaeology.

HASLAM, J. (1980). 'A middle Saxon iron smelting site at Ramsbury, Wiltshire'. *Medieval Archaeology* 24: 1–68.

HENRY, P. A. (1999). 'Development and change in late Saxon textile production: an analysis of the evidence'. *Durham Archaeological Journal* 14–15: 69–76.

HILL, D., and COWIE, R. (eds.) (2001). *Wics: The Early Medieval Trading Centres of Northern Europe.* Sheffield: Sheffield Academic Press.

HINES, J. (1997a). *A New Corpus of Anglo-Saxon Great Square-Headed Brooches.* Woodbridge: Boydell.

——(1997b). 'Religion: the limits of knowledge', in J. Hines (ed.), *The Anglo-Saxons from the Migration Period to the Eighth Century: An Ethnographic Perspective.* Woodbridge: Boydell, 375–410.

HINTON, D. A. (1990). *Archaeology, Economy and Society: England from the Fifth to the Fifteenth Century.* London: Routledge.

——(2000). *A Smith in Lindsey: The Anglo-Saxon Grave at Tattershall Thorpe, Lincolnshire.* Society for Medieval Archaeology Monograph Series 16. London: Society for Medieval Archaeology.

——(2003). 'Anglo-Saxon smiths and myths', in D. Scragg (ed.), *Textual and Material Culture in Anglo-Saxon England.* Cambridge: D. S. Brewer, 261–82.

——(2005). *Gold and Gilt, Pots and Pins: Possessions and People in Medieval Britain.* Oxford: Oxford University Press.

HODGES, R. (1989). *The Anglo-Saxon Achievement.* London: Duckworth.

HØILUND NIELSEN, K. (1999). 'Style II and the Anglo-Saxon elite'. *Anglo-Saxon Studies in Archaeology and History* 10: 185–201.

HOLMQVIST, W. (ed.) (1972). *Excavations at Helgö IV: Workshop Part I.* Stockholm: Historie och Antikvitets Akademien.

HUGGETT, J. W. (1988). 'Imported grave goods and the early Anglo-Saxon economy'. *Medieval Archaeology* 32: 63–96.

JENSEN, S. (1993). 'Early towns', in S. Hvass and B. Storgaard (eds.), *Digging into the Past: 25 Years of Archaeology in Denmark.* Copenhagen: Royal Society of Northern Antiquaries/Højburg: Jutland Archaeological Society, 202–5.

KENDRICK, T. D. (1938). *Anglo-Saxon Art to A. D. 900.* London: Methuen.

LOVELUCK, C. (2001). 'Wealth, waste and conspicuous consumption: Flixborough and its importance for middle and late rural settlement studies', in H. Hamerow and A. MacGregor (eds.), *Image and Power in the Archaeology of Early Medieval Britain: Essays in Honour of Rosemary Cramp.* Oxford: Oxbow Books, 79–130.

——(2007). *Rural Settlement, Lifestyles and Social Change in the Later First Millennium AD: Anglo-Saxon Flixborough in its Wider Context.* Excavations at Flixborough 4. Oxford: Oxbow Books.

——and WALTON ROGERS, P. (2007). 'Craft and technology—non-agrarian activities underpinning everyday life', in C. Loveluck, *Rural Settlement, Lifestyles and Social Change in the Later First Millennium AD: Anglo-Saxon Flixborough in its Wider Context*. Excavations at Flixborough 4. Oxford: Oxbow Books, 99–112.

Lowe, C. (2006). *Excavations at Hoddom Dumfriesshire: An Early Ecclesiastical Site in South-West Scotland*. Edinburgh: Society of Antiquaries of Scotland.

Mainman, A., and Rogers, N. (2004). 'Craft and economy in Anglo-Scandinavian York', in R. Hall *et al.* (eds.), *Aspects of Anglo-Scandinavian York*. Volume 8, fasc. 4 of *The Archaeology of York*. York: Council of British Archaeology, 459–87.

Malcolm, G., and Bowsher, D., with Cowie, R. (2003). *Middle Saxon London: Excavations at the Royal Opera House 1989–99*. Museum of London Archaeological Services Monograph 15. London: Museum of London.

McDonnell, G. (1993). 'Slags and ironworking residues', in H. Hamerow (ed.), *Excavations at Mucking*, Volume 2: *The Anglo-Saxon Settlement: Excavations by M. U. Jones and W. T. Jones*. London: English Heritage, 82–3.

Metcalf, D. M., and Northover, J. P. (1989). 'Coinage alloys from the time of Offa and Charlemagne to *c*. 864'. *Numismatic Chronicle* 149: 101–20.

Owen-Crocker, G. R. (2004). *Dress in Anglo-Saxon England*. 2nd edition. Woodbridge: Boydell.

Peirce, I. (2002). *Swords of the Viking Age*. Woodbridge: Boydell Press.

Peregrine, P. (1991). 'Some political aspects of craft specialization'. *World Archaeology* 23(1): 1–11.

Pestell, T., and Ulmschneider, K. (2003). 'Introduction: early medieval markets and "productive sites"', in T. Pestell and K. Ulmschneider (eds.), *Markets in Early Medieval Europe: Trading and 'Productive' Sites, 650–850*. Macclesfield: Windgather Press, 1–10.

Pleiner, R. (2008). 'Iron and ironworking', in J. Graham-Campbell and M. Valor (eds.), *The Archaeology of Medieval Europe*, Volume 1: *Eighth to Twelfth Centuries AD*. Aarhus: Aarhus University Press, 220–3.

Plunkett, S. J. (1998). 'The Mercian perspective', in S. Foster (ed.), The St Andrews Sarcophagus: A Pictish Masterpiece and Its International Connection. Edinburgh: Society Antiquaries of Scotland, 202–25.

Rahtz, P. A. (1979). *The Saxon and Medieval Palaces at Cheddar*. BAR British Series 65. Oxford: British Archaeological Reports.

Ramsay, N. (1991). 'Introduction', in J. Blair and N. Ramsay (eds.), *English Medieval Industries*. London: Continuum.

Richards, J. D. (2000). 'The Anglo-Saxon and Anglo-Scandinavian evidence', in P. A. Stamper and R. A. Croft (eds.), *Wharram: A Study of Settlement in the Yorkshire Wolds*, Volume 8: *The South Manor*. York University Archaeological Publications 10. York: University of York, 195–200.

Riddler, I. (2001). 'The spatial organisation of bone-working at *Hamwic*', in D. Hill and R. Cowie (eds.), *Wics: The Early Medieval Trading Centres of Northern Europe*. Sheffield: Sheffield Academic Press, 75–84.

Salter, C. (2004). 'Ferrous metalworking debris', in G. Hey, *Yarnton: Saxon and Medieval Settlement and Landscape*. Oxford: Oxford Archaeology, 307–11.

Scull, C. (1997). 'Urban centres in pre-Viking England?', in J. Hines (ed.), *The Anglo-Saxons from the Migration Period to the Eighth Century: An Ethnographic Perspective*. Woodbridge: Boydell, 269–310.

Thomas, G. (2001). 'Strap-ends and the identification of regional patterns in the production and circulation of ornamental metalwork in late Anglo-Saxon and Viking-age

Britain', in M. Redknap, N. Edwards, S. Youngs, A. Lane, and J. Knight (eds.), *Pattern and Purpose in Insular Art: Proceedings of the Fourth International Conference on Insular Art*. Oxford: Oxbow Books, 39–49.

——(2006). 'Reflections on a "9th-century" Northumbrian metalworking tradition: a silver hoard from Poppleton, North Yorkshire'. *Medieval Archaeology* 50: 143–64.

TWEDDLE, D. (1992). *The Anglian Helmet from Coppergate*. Volume 17, fasc. 8 of *The Archaeology of York*. London: Council for British Archaeology.

TYLECOTE, R. F., and GILMOUR, B. J. J. (1986). *The Metallography of Early Ferrous Edge Tools and Edged Weapons*. BAR British Series 155. Oxford: British Archaeological Reports.

WALTON ROGERS, P. (2007). *Cloth and Clothing in Early Anglo-Saxon England, A.D. 450–700*. CBA Research Report 145. York: Council for British Archaeology.

WAMERS, E. (1986). 'Frühmittelalterliche Funde aus Mainz. Zum Karolingisch-Ottonischen Metallschmuck und seinen Verbindungen zum Angelsächsischen Kunsthandwerk', in *Frankfurter Beitrage zur Mittelalter Archäologie I*. Bonn: Schr. Frankfurter Mus. Vor- u. Frühgesch. 9, 11–56.

WEBSTER, L. E. (2001). 'Metalwork of the Mercian Supremacy', in M. P. Brown and C. A. Farr (eds.), *Mercia: An Anglo-Saxon Kingdom in Europe*. London: Leicester University Press, 263–77.

—— (2003). 'Encrypted visions: style and sense in the Anglo-Saxon minor arts, A.D. 400–900', in C. E. Karkov and G. H. Brown (eds.), *Anglo-Saxon Styles*. Albany: State University of New York, 11–30.

WELCH, M. (2007). 'Anglo-Saxon Kent to A. D. 800', in J. Williams (ed.), *The Archaeology of Kent to A. D. 800*. Woodbridge: Boydell, 187–248.

WILLIAMS, D., and VINCE, A. (1997). 'The characterization and interpretation of early to middle Saxon granitic tempered pottery in England'. *Medieval Archaeology* 41: 214–20.

WILSON, D. M. (1984). *Anglo-Saxon Art*. London: Thames & Hudson.

CHAPTER 23

RAW MATERIALS: SOURCES AND DEMAND

DAVID A. HINTON

SETTING the scene for his *Ecclesiastical History* in the early eighth century, Bede described Britain's organic wealth, its crops, trees, pasture, birds, fish, dye-producing shell-fish, and even vines. Inorganics included its salt springs, the wonder of its black jet, and its rich veins of copper, lead, iron, and silver—south-western tin and Welsh gold did not get a mention. Nor did Bede refer to what are now called the 'secondary products' of animals, the wool, leather, horn, and bone that were essential for many crafts; and, despite being someone who had the rare distinction amongst his contemporaries of spending much of his life in masonry buildings, he made no mention of stone.

TIMBER AND TREES

Anglo-Saxon England was indeed favourably placed for both arable and pastoral farming, with woodland, moor, and marsh providing uncultivated resources (see Part IV above). Timber for buildings, and for ships such as those at Sutton Hoo and Graveney, had to come from trees left to grow to good lengths in woods, forests, or hedges, often coppiced to encourage straight and prolific growth as well as to obtain poles and fuel from the loppings. The close-set, often large post-holes of many ground-level buildings imply that there were no shortages of suitable timber, and part of a late tenth-century oak arcade-post re-used in a City of London waterfront shows that the townspeople had access to mature trees derived from woodland that was not yet as intensively managed as it was to be later in the Middle Ages (Goodburn 1993: 81; Hamerow, this volume). The plank-lined cellar buildings that appear in many towns at much the same time also show unrestrained use of timber, as do bridges and causeways (Harrison 2004: 101–4 for summary), so new carpentry developments such as the aisled construction from which the arcade-post must have derived were not introduced to counter any lack of supply. Mid Saxon London, *Lundenwic*, already had some buildings with wooden shingles on their roofs, though most were reed-thatched (Malcolm and Bowsher 2003, 152-3); presumably nearly all rural structures were thatched, with straw, reeds, or heather.

Waterlogged sites like those along London's Thames frontage are producing evidence of the full range of things for which wood was used or, like the barrels lining some wells, re-used. Those were usually oak, but other stave-built vessels were of yew, willow, and pine, with bindings of hazel, ash, and willow, though the small pails found in many graves, and larger buckets such as those in Mound 1 at Sutton Hoo, were metal-bound, the former usually in copper alloy, the latter in iron. Turners making cups and bowls in York, Winchester, and other towns had access to a range of woods such as ash, alder, maple, and yew, but surprisingly do not seem to have used beech (Morris 2000). The natural patterns of burr-wood were appreciated, as the maple cups in Mound 1 at Sutton Hoo show. Improved conservation and analytical techniques mean that more residues of mineralized remains, usually trapped on metal surfaces, can be identified to species; only about half the wooden shields were made from willow or poplar, for instance, despite the invariable 'linden' of the poetry, and alder, maple, birch, ash, oak, beech, and lime were all used—apparently with no preference for a particular species in any particular region (Watson 2000). Handles for iron tools also varied, though shock-absorbent ash was preferred for hammers.

METALS

Wood also provided charcoal, needed by metalworkers and others for its more intense heat and carbon input. Charcoal-burning normally involves above-ground clamps and does not leave archaeological traces, but 'charcoal pits' have been recorded at sites close to where iron ores were smelted, such as Bestwall, Dorset, and West Runton, Norfolk (Ladle 2004; Tylecote 1967), as the furnaces swallowed up very large amounts. The ores at Bestwall were derived from iron-rich heathstone, at Runton from locally abundant ferruginous conglomerate stone, and from naturally occurring iron nodules. These were either surface deposits or easily dug from shallow pits; the reference to *mina ferri* in a late-seventh-century Kent charter should not be taken to imply a shaft-mine. Bog ores were also widespread. Ore quality varied, usually containing other minerals such as phosphorus and manganese that were difficult to remove, and could cause problems both in the working and in the quality of the subsequent products.

Most ore-containing nodules needed to be dried in roasting hearths; if those were at ground level, traces of them may not survive. The nodules were then hammered into smaller pieces, before going into furnaces. These might only be shallow bowls in the ground, which were usually clay-lined and show intense burning. The final fills may contain the residues of their clay superstructures, and the heavily vitrified clay nozzles, or *tuyères*, to which leather bellows were attached. This basic technology did not even allow for slag to be tapped off; it merely sank to the bottom of the furnace, and might subsequently be removed as a solid 'hearth bottom'. The iron that is left is called 'bloomery'. Early furnaces have been reported from Rook Hall, Essex, with a thermoluminescence date for one centring around AD 530, and there the quantity of evidence suggests that a wide area was being supplied; an adjacent site, Slough House Farm, has produced slag and hearth bottoms, though not definite smelting furnaces, and takes production on into the seventh century (Wallis and Waughman 1998: 125–9, 223–7, 233). Radiocarbon dates indicate production in Rockingham Forest, Northamptonshire, from the fifth century onwards, though furnaces investigated are notably smaller than some of the Roman period (Bellamy *et al.* 2000–1). Bestwall has a sixth-century radiocarbon date (Ladle 2004: 13), so operations there began before the Wessex kings took political control of south-east Dorset.

Analysed slags are different from Roman specimens (McDonnell 1988; Salter 1988), so production was not simply a revival of older methods maintained by a few workers through the fifth and sixth centuries. Roman techniques had included shaft furnaces with provision for tapping out molten slag. 'Flow lines' have been reported in the structure of some Anglo-Saxon iron objects, but they can be accidental rather than a result of tapping; tap-slags identified at Quarrington, Lincolnshire, and in Rockingham Forest do seem to be later sixth-century, however, from contexts into which little Roman residual material intruded (Taylor 2003: 235–7, 256; Mudd 2006: 92–3). Otherwise, smelting slag found at settlements like Mucking, Essex, is thought to be from bowl furnaces (McDonnell 1993). Excavations at Ramsbury, Wiltshire, revealed several eighth-/ninth-century furnaces, clay-lined and mostly with stone side-walls—the stone providing a useful flux. Some were re-lined for further use, in some cases several times, so that they became more like shaft furnaces, though not necessarily producing a different ore or saving fuel.

One, however, had an outlet for slag to flow through, and this tapping would have allowed for a longer firing of a larger load (Haslam 1980).

Scale of production seems to have increased in the mid Saxon period. As well as Ramsbury, smelting sites that have produced mid Saxon radiocarbon dates since the discussion by Crossley (1981) include Rockingham Forest and Northampton, Northamptonshire; Exmoor, Devon; the Blackdown Hills and Carhampton, Somerset; Gillingham, Dorset; Romsey, Hampshire; Millbrook, Sussex; and Billingford and Burrow Hill, in Norfolk. A mill at Worgret, near Wareham, Dorset, had so much slag around it that it may have been used to work a heavy hammer—no furnaces were observed at the site, so it was probably not also powering bellows. One of its timbers has been dated by dendrochronology to the end of the seventh century (Maynard 1988; Hinton 1992). It may have been part of an integrated operation that included Bestwall a mile away, where the sixth-century date is the earliest of several, others running on to the ninth century. Some of the ore used at Ramsbury had been taken there from 30 kilometres away, testimony to the scale of operation. Ramsbury, Wareham, Northampton, and probably Romsey were on estates that had royal or church connections, or both. They are evidence of the intensification process that seems linked to the growth of kingdoms, and to royal and church estates.

The temperature reached inside even a shaft furnace was probably too low to melt out enough phosphorus to enable most wrought iron to absorb sufficient carbon during further working to produce a steel-like iron, needed for sharpness. Smithing as well as smelting took place at Ramsbury, the range of products including tools such as tongs, household equipment, and small decorative items, some of which do seem to have become steel (Haslam 1980: 33–41). Knives and swords with a separate edge of high-carbon iron welded to the wrought iron of the rest of the blade show how the best smiths eked out what they could get, perhaps from Sweden, or even Spain. Analysis of steel bars and a tool found at *Hamwic* have indicated production from decarburization of molten cast iron (Mack *et al.* 2000), but such an advanced technology seems unlikely to have been known in northern Europe, let alone England, and the metal could possibly have been a rare import, perhaps from Italy.

Many more mid than late Saxon smelting sites have been found. The West Runton site is dated by pottery to the tenth/eleventh centuries, with production evidence spread across a wide area. The only furnace located was not a pit, but the remains of a hard red clay surface, on to which tiles or stones would have been placed. A low shaft furnace was then built above this floor; slag could have been tapped from it. A furnace excavated in the new town at Stamford, Lincolnshire, probably also had a shaft (Mahany *et al.* 1982: 105–44). Such urban production may also have taken place in York (Ottaway 1992: 478), and certainly continued in Northampton as it developed into a town (Cleere 1979). The first and last of those places have good ironstone below or close to them, and production may increasingly have concentrated where ores were readily available in quantities to sustain production on a larger scale than in the mid Saxon period, as at West Runton. There, the industry was not maintained beyond the eleventh century. The Millbrook site in Sussex only operated in the ninth, despite being close to East Grinstead, the only Wealden site where Domesday Book recorded a *ferraria* in the late eleventh century. Domesday entries for Alvington and Gloucester are evidence for extensive Forest of Dean production (Meredith 2006), but most physical remains were presumably eradicated by later working. Longer-distance transport must have become more viable, a reflection of changing patterns of demand. The Gloucester smiths had to supply bars of iron, but also rods specified to be 'ductile' for ships' nails, implying differences of steel content.

Of the more valuable metals, gold had to be imported, mostly in the form of coins. The flow of Byzantine and other subsidies to the Franks, who passed some of it on to Kent and perhaps to other client-kings, made it relatively plentiful in the later sixth and first part of the seventh centuries, although the recently discovered hoard at Patching, Sussex, shows that occasionally gold arrived earlier, as the latest coin there dates to 461–5 (Abdy 2006; Blackburn, this volume, for coinage generally). Patching also contained two crude gold rings, suggesting that some of the metal arrived in bullion form. One of the Patching rings is of such a pure alloy that direct supply from the Visigothic kingdom of Spain is likely. Exchange sometimes involved ingots, like the two in the Sutton Hoo purse, and one recently found in Norwich (Ayers 2004: 8).

Although Bede knew of the existence of silver in parts of England—usually in veins adjacent to lead—there is no direct evidence of its extraction in the Anglo-Saxon period despite records of royal interest in the Mendips and of payments in silver from Derbyshire (Maddicott 1989: 45–7; Hill 1981: 107–11 for maps). Once existing Romano-British stocks were exhausted, silver was imported, either as coins like the *siliquae* that were also in the Patching hoard, or as plate like the eastern Mediterranean set at Sutton Hoo. The increasing numbers of silver coins of the late seventh and eighth centuries surely required more substantial supplies, however, and imports from the Harz mountains, as also more certainly from the later tenth century, or from the mines at Melle, near Poitiers (Grierson and Blackburn 1986: 236), are likely. In the ninth and tenth centuries, bullion ingots, rings, and coins, usually from the Near East by way of the Baltic and the Vikings, were the main source. Cupellation, to separate silver from baser metals, was practised in *Hamwic* (Bayley 1996), though apparently not in *Lundenwic*.

As with silver, so also extraction of copper is not known in England before the twelfth century. Supplies of the materials for copper-alloy brooches and such-like probably derived from the recycling of scrap from Roman sites and occasional discoveries of hoards of small base-metal coins (Mortimer 1991). Gilding was much practised on fifth- and sixth-century copper-alloy jewellery—for which smiths needed not only a small amount of gold but also mercury, from Spain or elsewhere, though the only actual survival is from Anglo-Scandinavian York (Bayley 1992: 789,

795). Gilding was also practised at *Hamwic*, where one site produced a small mortar in which gold and mercury would have been ground (Oddy 1996; Bayley and Russel 2008). Fire-gilding is easier on the bronzes of the early period than on later gunmetals and brasses, which contain more zinc; their increase from the eighth century suggests new metal supplies and imports, so that *Hamwic* makes a contrast to Anglo-Scandinavian York (Hinton 1996: 6, 60; Bayley 1992: 803–10).

Like copper, much lead may have come from Roman ruins, but a late-seventh-century charter shows that by then the metal was sought after in greater quantity by churches, not only in England, and the wealth of the Derbyshire Peak District's seventh-century graves is likely to have derived from the local elite's control of the source (Loveluck and Laing, this volume)—Domesday Book recorded *plumbariae* in Derbyshire. Extraction from sources exploited in the Roman period such as the Pennines, Cumbria, and Weardale may not have re-started until the twelfth century, but royal interest in the Mendips could be significant, as with silver (Maddicott 1989: 45–7). Surprisingly, lead tanks containing tools have been found at several sites, including recently Flixborough (Leahy, this volume) and York (Mainman and Rogers 2004: 466), though lead vats for salt-boiling would have been a source of greater demand.

Lead is a constituent of pewter, which also needs tin. For the Britons of Cornwall and Devon, tin may have been an export in the fifth to seventh centuries as ingots at Praa Sands show (Turner 2006: 74–5), and later may help to account for the late-ninth-century Trewhiddle hoard and for the size and value of Exeter (Maddicott 1989: 19–32; Hatcher 1973). It was needed for bells, so again the references are to church use, but white-metal coating of iron objects such as spurs is an example of the skill with which metalworkers used their materials. Small trinkets like brooches have been increasingly found, particularly in the later period, though not, as used to be thought, exclusively (Thomas, Leahy, this volume; Hatcher and Barker 1974: 19–24 for documentary records). Lead was used on some pottery for glazing, but probably only at tenth- and eleventh-century Stamford in such quantity that recycling of scrap would not have been sufficient. Stamford potters had other contacts with metalworkers, as their refractory clays were particularly suitable for making heat-resistant crucibles (Kilmurry 1980: 168).

Glass, colourants, earth materials, and salt

Glass beads are widespread in early Anglo-Saxon graves. For these, recycled Roman scrap is the likeliest raw material. Great skill was not needed to make the simplest, only a few crucibles and a hearth, but inlaying trails of contrasting colours required more knowledge, and workshops in Kent and East Anglia have been postulated, though on the basis of distribution, not of direct evidence (Guido 1999: 118).

Considerably more difficult was the making of glass vessels. Analyses suggest that in the fifth century at least small amounts of raw glass were still reaching England; during the sixth, supplies were usually eked out by the addition of potash, derived from plants. Cullet, obtained by melting old or broken vessels, may have been avoided at first (Freestone *et al.* 2008: 33–40). Faversham, Kent, has been advanced as a possible manufacturing site where sufficient skill could be accumulated; again the evidence is not direct, but is suggested by the large proportion of vessels found in the King's Field cemetery there, and the likelihood is that it was a royal centre where metalsmiths also worked (Evison 2000a: 68; Perkins 2000). The large numbers of sherds in *Hamwic* allow the possibility of glass-making in the mid Saxon *wic*, but even trace-element analyses were not conclusive; they showed that different production centres can be recognized though not thereby definitively located (Hunter and Heyworth 1998: 61). Those analyses revealed some of the minerals then being included, almost certainly deliberately, which gave a wider range of colours: deep blue from cobalt, red from copper, white from tin, or yellow from various blends of lead, tin, and antimony, with iron and manganese in the original sands and alkalis adding variation (ibid.: 34–41; cf. colours in books and churches, below). Although very few whole glass vessels survive after grave-good deposition had ceased, different forms can nevertheless be identified and suggest some regionalization, with production in Northumbria/East Anglia as well as in *Hamwic* argued on that basis (Stiff 2003: 246–7). In the late period, glass-making became an urban craft using both potash and high-lead mixtures, as in Winchester, Lincoln, York, and London (Bayley and Doonan 2000), for rings, beads, and textile smoothers; potash glass unfortunately does not survive well and is under-represented.

At Jarrow, Bede had the experience of marvelling at coloured windows made from small pieces of glass (Cramp 2006: 56–79). Excavation has shown that window glass was less uncommon than used to be thought, and is likely to have been made in furnaces found at Glastonbury and Barking Abbeys, or later in towns like Winchester or York which had several churches to supply (Bayley 2000). The makers were presumably itinerants, travelling to each commission, though whether they were expected to bring with them their own stocks of the materials that they needed, or could rely on patrons to supply them, is not known. The seventh-century smith's grave at Tattershall Thorpe included the base of a blue glass beaker that was probably being carried either to slice and fit into cloisonné work, or to melt down and remake into domed studs or beads (Evison 2000b). Small tesserae excavated at Whitby, Flixborough, and other mid Saxon sites were probably imported from the Mediterranean deliberately for recycling, not for re-use in mounts (Evison 1991).

If cloth were to have colours beyond those that occurred naturally in a sheep's fleece, dyes were needed. Before dyeing, the yarn or cloth usually had to be prepared with a mordant, so club-moss had to be gathered or imported, and mixed with ash. Blue came from woad; it had to be soaked in alkali—urine, lime, and potash—so to modern noses at least was very smelly and may have been kept on the margins of settlements where it was prepared; the plant grows well in East Anglia. Browns could be obtained from tannins. The weld plant, or greenweed, can be grown in England, but madderwort is less tolerant and more likely to have been imported, so red was more prestigious; stained pots in which it was stored occur in the mid and late Anglo-Saxon periods. Although Bede knew of shell-fish, actually dog-whelks, from which a crimson red can be had, only lichens and madder have been detected on cloths; the brighter red of kermes beetles' eggs was even more valuable and may already have been imported before the Norman Conquest (Owen-Crocker 2004: 305-7; Biggam 2006; Walton Rogers 2007: 37–8). Modern scientific techniques have detected Bede's shell-fish dye on some very special manuscript pages (Budny 1999: 243–4); other colours were derived from metals including arsenic, lead, and copper, mixed in various ways (Brown 2003: 280–4). For wall-paintings in churches, iron oxides provided red and yellow, calcium carbonate—sometimes with lead—white, and carbon black, all very recently identified (by Emily Howe and Brian Singer: Gem and Howe 2008, 126–9, 143–4; Rodwell *et al.* 2008: 85–92; for inks, see Gameson, this volume).

More prosaic amongst raw materials, but vital, was salt. Domesday evidence for coastal production is considerable (Keen 1988), though the sites themselves have not survived erosion and re-working. As boiling demands large quantities of fuel, peat as well as wood was probably consumed in quantity; as both were readily available it would not have been worth shipping coal even down the east coast— there was little other demand for that fuel, which is too sulphurous for iron smelting and smithing, and is not suitable for domestic open hearths. Recent work at Droitwich has shown that the brine springs there were in use in the fifth and sixth centuries, as well as in the seventh and later when they appear in documentary records. Brine from wells was guided into lead vats in stone-lined rectangular boiling hearths, using timber as fuel. Significantly, both kings and bishops had interests in the profits (Hurst 1997).

Even more basic earth materials were exploited. Clay mixed with sand provided daub for walling, floors, hearths, and ovens (Hughes 2004). Extraction pits in *Lundenwic* and *Hamwic* for clay, and for gravel for yards and street surfaces, came to be filled with the rubbish that contains the debris of so much of the processing evidence (explored by Leahy, this volume). Some buildings were whitewashed. The 'brickearth' on which those *wics* sit (see chapters by Pestell and Hall) could be used too for making loom-weights, more often fire-hardened in the mid than in the late Anglo-Saxon period (Walton Rogers 2007: 30). Spindle whorls were also sometimes made of clay, though were more usually made of stone or bone (ibid.: 25–6).

Hardly requiring higher temperatures than fired loom-weights was much of the early Anglo-Saxon pottery, particularly fabrics in which chaff, perhaps from animal dung, was mixed to give the clay a little more strength. This organic-tempered pottery is found from at least the sixth century through to the eighth and ninth, in both British and Anglo-Saxon areas. Presumably it represents an easily obtained material that needed no great effort to collect and to fire, a typical everyday household product (Peacock 1982: 8–11 for classification terminology). Perhaps more specialized were those potters who used quartz sands, crushed flints and other stones, and shell fragments, as tempers. Most controversial of all recent identifications has been of pottery containing granodiorite, which occurs in England only around Charnwood Forest in Leicestershire—collection of the mineral from now-exhausted surface drift deposits would result in much more mixed tempers—which has been found in pots up to 100 miles from its source, a much wider distribution in the sixth and seventh centuries than mere unglazed pottery would have been expected to travel, whether by trade, or kin contact and gift exchange (Williams and Vince 1997).

A few pots were imported, perhaps only the distinctive burnished and tin-foil-decorated eighth-/ninth-century Tating ware from the Rhineland because they were sought after, though earlier wheel-thrown bottles might have been valued for more than just their contents. The adoption at the Ipswich *wic* for the first time in the post-Roman period of at least a slow wheel and updraught kilns was a technological advance reflecting a market demand rather than a uniquely suitable clay source. Unless there was more production at Northampton than has yet been discovered, the Stamford potters mentioned above were probably the only ones able to exploit a natural advantage, for their white clays could not only be thrown very thinly and glazed attractively, but were also heat-resistant (Kilmurry 1980). They can be classified as operating within a nucleated workshop industry, probably with artisans employed to supplement family labour. The three groups of potters recorded in Domesday Book were rurally based, probably with lower costs but less immediately responsive to market demand, though urban kilns that must still have existed in Stamford and elsewhere were not included in the record.

Textiles and Animal Products

Cloth from wool and linen from flax or hemp could be made from native products (see Leahy, this volume; Coatsworth and Owen-Crocker 2007; Walton Rogers 2007 for craft production). Silk was very rare until the eighth century, but by the eleventh had become a marketed product, even used as decorative additions to shoes. York and Lincoln have produced fragments which have been shown by a fault in their weaves to have come from the same bale, presumably being touted round the towns (Pritchard 1984: 59–64; Pritchard 1991: 230–2; Henry 2004: 454; Owen-Crocker 2004: 298–302, and this volume).

Animal skins could provide both furs and leather. The former might be imported luxuries like the marten skins recorded as one of Chester's eleventh-century trades, and those presumably brought to King Alfred by the Norwegian Ohthere (Howard-Johnston 1998), though evidence of sheep- or lambskins is hard to come by except in the particular circumstances of mineralization, such as on sword scabbards (Cameron 2000: 37). Leather was clearly important, for boots, shoes, belts, gloves, caps, and just possibly some trousers and other clothing (Owen-Crocker 2004: 187–99). Tanning involves various stages of which some leave no trace, such as the pegging out of skins for dogs to lick clean of blood and flesh. Dogs also helped to provide dung and urine, necessary with wood-ash, oak bark, and quicklime to soak into the skins. This needed pits, as well as a regular flow of water: rows of rectangular pits in *Lundenwic* relied on wells, not flowing streams, as did tanners in *Hamwic* if they were responsible for the deposits of burnt chalk excavated there; alternatively, they may have been smoking their hides in pits (Malcolm and Bowsher 2003: 183–4; Andrews 1997: 231–6). Winchester's Tanner Street had a watercourse running through it (Cherry 1991: 295–7). Pits in York originally interpreted as for tanning are now interpreted as cellars, but waste shows that the craft was practised somewhere in or close to the town (Hall and Kenward 2004: 407). Finer leather, for supple gloves and for books, required tawing, a dry process involving alum and egg yolks. Vegetable tanning was also practised. The number of calf skins needed to produce a single high-quality vellum manuscript was prodigious—over 500 for one book—and may account for the high ratio of young cattle slaughtered at Green Shiel on Lindisfarne (Bruce-Mitford 1969: 2; O'Sullivan 2001: 42).

Animals also supplied bone for glue and oil—flax seeds may also have provided the latter—as well as for making into a variety of tools, ornaments, handles, and the like (MacGregor 1985 for an overall summary). Combs were the most specialized product, as some skill was needed to saw the teeth into bone plates, and to fit metal rivets to hold them together; antler was usual for the backs or centre strips, as it is harder. Antler was used for other items too, such as prickers, stamps, dies, and moulds, so had to be collected. Horn for drinking-horns, lantern windows, an occasional helmet like the one at Benty Grange, and other things requiring a thin but durable sheet is unfortunately a rare archaeological survival, but the imported aurochs horns at Sutton Hoo show the lengths to which the wealthy would go to obtain a rare material. Waste horn cores are evidence of urban horners in *Hamwic* and *Lundenwic*—goat horns being particularly in demand in the former, presumably because they were straighter (Bourdillon and Coy 1980: 97; Malcolm and Bowsher 2003: 182). Elephant ivory was available for a few purse-rings and the like in the early period, probably replaced in the ninth century by walrus ivory. Whalebone was an occasional beach find that could be used for a very special purpose such as making the Franks Casket, or for weaving-battens, important symbolically, or for a mundane chopping-board (Hills 2001; and see Sykes, Webster, this volume).

Animal fat was probably much used for tallow candles, though beeswax may have been preferred for its more delicate smell, as it was later in the Middle Ages. Wax was also needed for mould-making (Leahy, below). Charred fragments of honey bees in *Lundenwic* and York may have been from skeps that allowed their owners to make their own mead, but the wax would have been useful too (Leary 2004: 10–11: Hall and Kenward 2004: 397–8).

Stone and stones

For most mid Saxon stone buildings, Roman ruins supplied enough both for rubble walls and squared dressings (Eaton 2000), but the stone for the church at Jarrow in which Bede worshipped, and for the hall in which he ate, may have included some that was freshly quarried for the use of the Gaulish masons recorded there (Cramp 2006: 162). The many tall cross-shafts and large rectangular sculptured panels suggest at least knowledge of where appropriate stones could be levered out. The Lichfield panel is of Ancaster stone and had travelled 95 kilometres to get from its Lincolnshire source; as it would be hard to have carved it when the quarry sap had dried out, it is unlikely to be a Roman slab re-used (Rodwell *et al.* 2008: 58). Quarrying became more systematic after the mid tenth century: Barnack stone from Northamptonshire was among the first to be widely distributed (Parsons 1991: 4–9; Jope 1964 remains useful). The early-eleventh-century chapel at Bradford-on-Avon, Wiltshire, was built in very fine dressed stone from immediately local limestone; lesser churches used what they could get without incurring huge costs, but Combe Down/Box 'Bath' stone was going to Winchester in quantities suggesting that it was not Roman rubble being re-used (Worssam 1995; also Alexander 2007: 72–3). Other limestones coming into use included Quarr from the Isle of Wight, and Taynton, Oxfordshire. By the 1050s Upper Greensand from around Reigate on the North Downs was being carried to Westminster (Tatton-Brown 2001: 189–92). Just as Domesday Book recorded some but not all clay potters, so for stone quarries it included Taynton's, but not others.

Partly no doubt because they could be used as ballast, some stones travelled over long distances. Honestones are often difficult to tie down geologically, but Norway is a likely source for the increasingly widespread and therefore probably regularly traded metamorphic types (Crosby and Mitchell 1987; also Goffin 2003: 202). Schist was also used for ingot moulds in Anglo-Scandinavian York. Greywackes thought to be from Scotland are also found, as well as more local stones such as Kentish Rag. Volcanic lava for quernstones and millstones, imported from deposits around Mainz, used to be thought rare, but has now been found in so many different contexts and in all centuries except possibly the fifth that it must have been a traded product at least from the eighth century, after which it was certainly brought in as rough-outs and completed in England (Goffin 2003: 204–9). Sandstones were also used for grinding. A specialist usage was of fine-grained black touchstones by goldsmiths; one found in Winchester has gold streaks still clearly showing. It could have come from a Cumbrian source, but the Bristol Coalfield is geographically more likely (Oddy and Tylecote 1990: 77). As this area was also the source of the *Hamwic* sandstone mortar, metalworkers may have known of specialist sources there.

A few spindle whorls were made of soft stones like chalk, requiring little effort in their working. Another calcite, magnesite, is now only found around Faversham, and was occasionally used in jewellery. Crystal beads are not uncommon, and the smaller ones could have been English, but not the larger. Cristobalite, another quartz, was occasionally used. The rare crystal balls could only have been imported (Huggett 1988: 70–2); the large crystal in the Alfred Jewel may have been a diplomatic gift from the Vatican (Kornbluth 1989).

Despite Bede's knowledge of it, Whitby jet is not commonly found in early Anglo-Saxon graves; Anglo-Scandinavian York has more of it. A few spindle whorls were made from shale, as were some rings found in London; in both cases, the source is more likely to have been Roman waste than material newly arrived from Dorset. Amber, by contrast, was freshly obtained, probably imported from the Baltic rather than taken from the North Sea; it was much used for early necklaces, was worked in *Lundenwic* though not so far as is known in *Hamwic*, and again in later York, where steatite (soapstone) is a clear sign of Scandinavian taste in bowls for cooking, though is thought to have been brought from the Shetlands rather than from Norway (Huggett 1988: 64–8; Parker 2000; Mainman and Rogers 2000: 2541–4); it was also used in small pieces for ingot moulds (Bayley 1992: 772–6). In *Lundenwic*, a limestone lamp may have re-used a piece of Roman masonry, and a carved bowl looks so out of place as to suggest an import (Goffin 2003: 204).

Whether semi-precious garnets (see Pestell, this volume) were all imported ready-cut into plates or still in their raw state is not certain, though at least their cutting to shape must have been done in England in association with goldworking. Their supply may have depended on good relations with the Franks, like the gold coins; certainly the flat ones fade from the record at much the same time as English thrymsas ended, and a vogue in the late seventh century for large domed garnets and other stones and glass mounts could imply new trade routes that also brought cowrie shells from the Near East into *Lundenwic* and *Hamwic*, continuing a small earlier supply. Emeralds and sapphires also occasionally reached England, or at least late seventh-century Kent (Bimson and Freestone 2000: 131).

Conclusion

The raw materials used in the Anglo-Saxon period were varied, but generally indicate the nature of the economy: dependent primarily upon agricultural production; recycling whenever possible; importing little but luxuries from overseas, but with lava querns showing capacity for more basic commodities to travel by boat; and with pottery showing that networks in the early period may have been underestimated, even if gift exchange was the main impetus. The later period was developing a market-based commercialized system. This is explored further below by Leahy in his study of the crafts which used the materials, and in the contributions on trade and the economy (Part VI).

References

Abdy, R. (2006). 'After Patching: imported and recycled coinage in fifth- and sixth-century Britain', in B. Cook and G. Williams (eds.), *Coinage and History in the North Sea World, c. A.D. 500–1250: Essays in Honour of Marion Archibald*. Leiden: Brill, 75–98.

Alexander, J. S. (2007). 'The introduction and use of masons' marks in Romanesque buildings in England'. *Medieval Archaeology* 51: 63–82.

Andrews, P. (1997). *Excavations at Hamwic*, Volume 2: *Excavations at Six Dials*. CBA Research Report 109. York: Council for British Archaeology.

Ayers, B. (2004). 'The urban landscape', in C. Rawcliffe and R. Wilson (eds.), *Medieval Norwich*. London/New York: Hambledon and London, 1–28.

Bayley, J. (1992). *Anglo-Scandinavian Non-Ferrous Metalworking from 16–22 Coppergate*. Volume 17, fasc. 7 of *The Archaeology of York*. London: Council for British Archaeology.

——(1996). 'Crucibles and cupels', in D. A. Hinton, *The Gold, Silver and Other Non-Ferrous Alloy Objects from Hamwic*. Southampton Archaeology Monographs 6. Stroud: Tempus.

——(2000). 'Saxon glassworking at Glastonbury Abbey', in Price (ed.), *Glass in Britain and Ireland*, 161–88.

——and Doonan, R. (2000). 'Glass manufacturing evidence', in A. J. Mainman and N. S. H. Rogers, *Finds from Anglo-Scandinavian York*. Volume 17, fasc. 14 of *The Archaeology of York*. York: Council for British Archaeology, 2519–28.

——and Russel, A. (2008). 'Making gold-mercury amalgam: the evidence for gilding from Southampton'. *Antiquaries Journal* 88: 37–42.

Bellamy, B., Jackson, D., and Johnston, G. (2000–1). 'Early iron smelting in the Rockingham Forest area: a survey of the evidence'. *Northamptonshire Archaeology* 29: 303–28.

BIGGAM, C. P. 2006. 'Knowledge of whelk dyes and pigments in Anglo-Saxon England'. *Anglo-Saxon England* 25: 23–56.

BIMSON, M., and FREESTONE, I. C. (2000). 'Analysis of some glass from Anglo-Saxon jewellery', in Price (ed.), *Glass in Britain and Ireland*, 131–5.

BOURDILLON, J., and COY, J. (1980). 'The animal bones', in P. Holdsworth, *Excavations at Melbourne Street, 1971–76*. Southampton Archaeological Research Committee 1. CBA Research Report 33. London: Council for British Archaeology, 79–120.

BROWN, M. P. (2003). *The Lindisfarne Gospels: Society, Spirituality and the Scribe*. London: British Library.

BRUCE-MITFORD, R. L. S. (1969). 'The art of the *Codex Amiatinus*'. *Journal of the British Archaeological Association* 32: 1–25.

BUDNY, M. (1999). 'The *Biblia Gregoriana*', in R. Gameson (ed.), *St Augustine and the Conversion of England*. Stroud: Sutton, 237–84.

CAMERON, E. A. (2000). *Sheaths and Scabbards in England AD 400–1100*. British Archaeological Reports British Series 301. Oxford: Archaeopress.

CHERRY, J. (1991). 'Leather', in J. Blair and N. Ramsay (eds.), *English Medieval Industries*. London: Hambledon Press, 295–318.

CLEERE, H. F. (1979). 'The metallurgical remains', in J. H. Williams, *St Peter's Street, Northampton: Excavations 1973–1976*. Archaeological Monograph 2. Northampton: Northampton Development Corporation, 278–9.

COATSWORTH, E., and OWEN-CROCKER, G. R. (2007). *Medieval Textiles of the British Isles AD 450–1100: An Annotated Bibliography*. British Archaeological Reports British Series 445. Oxford: Archaeopress.

CRAMP, R. (2006). *Wearmouth and Jarrow Monastic Sites*, Volume 2. Swindon: English Heritage.

CROSBY, D. D. B., and MITCHELL, J. G. (1987). 'A survey of British Metamorphic hone stones of the 9th to 15th centuries A.D. in the light of Potassium-Argon and Natural Remanent Magnetization studies'. *Journal of Archaeological Science* 14: 483–506.

CROSSLEY, D. W. (1981). 'Medieval iron smelting', in D. W. Crossley (ed.), *Medieval Industries*. CBA Research Report 40. London: Council for British Archaeology, 29–41.

EATON, T. (2000). *Plundering the Past: Roman Stonework in Medieval Britain*. Stroud: Tempus.

EVISON, V. I. (1991). 'Two tesserae fragments', in L. Webster and J. Backhouse (eds.), *The Making of England: Anglo-Saxon Art and Culture AD 600–900*. London: British Museum Press, 145.

——(2000a). 'Glass vessels in England A.D. 400–1100', in Price (ed.), *Glass in Britain and Ireland*, 47–104.

——(2000b). 'Bag beaker fragments', in D. A. Hinton, *A Smith in Lindsey: The Anglo-Saxon Grave at Tattershall Thorpe, Lincolnshire*. Leeds: Society for Medieval Archaeology Monograph 16, 76–83.

FREESTONE, I. C., HUGHES, M. J., and STAPLETON, C. P. (2008). 'The composition and production of Anglo-Saxon glass', in V. I. Evison, *Catalogue of Anglo-Saxon Glass in the British Museum*, ed. S. Marzinzik. London: British Museum, 29–46.

GEM, R., and HOWE, E. (2008). 'The ninth-century polychrome decoration at St Mary's Church, Deerhurst'. *Antiquaries Journal* 88: 109–64.

GOFFIN, R. (2003). 'The stone objects', in Malcolm and Bowsher (eds.), *Middle Saxon London*, 197–209.

GOODBURN, D. (1993). 'Fragments of a 10th-century timber arcade from Vintner's Place on the London waterfront'. *Medieval Archaeology* 37: 78–92.
GRIERSON, P., and BLACKBURN, M. (1986). *Medieval European Coinage*, Volume 1: *The Early Middle Ages (5th–10th Centuries)*. Cambridge: Cambridge University Press.
GUIDO, M. (1999). *The Glass Beads of Anglo-Saxon England c. AD 400–700*. Ed. M. Welch. London: Boydell Press for Society of Antiquaries of London.
HALL, A. R., and KENWARD, H. (2004). 'Setting people in their environment: plant and animal remains from Anglo-Scandinavian York', in R. A. Hall (ed.), *Aspects of Anglo-Scandinavian York*. Volume 8, fasc. 4 of *The Archaeology of York*. York: Council for British Archaeology, 327–426.
HARRISON, D. (2004). *The Bridges of Medieval England*. Oxford: Clarendon Press.
HASLAM, J. (1980). 'A middle Saxon iron smelting site at Ramsbury, Wiltshire'. *Medieval Archaeology* 24: 1–68.
HATCHER, J. (1973). *English Tin Production and Trade before 1550*. Oxford: Clarendon Press.
——and BARKER, T. C. (1974). *A History of British Pewter*. London: Longman.
HENRY, P. A. (2004). 'Changing weaving styles and fabric types: the Scandinavian influence', in J. Hines, A. Lane, and M. Redknap (eds.), *Land, Sea and Home*. Society for Medieval Archaeology Monograph 20. Leeds: Maney.
HILL, D. (1981). *An Atlas of Anglo-Saxon England*. Oxford: Basil Blackwell.
HILLS, C. (2001). 'From Isidore to isotopes: ivory rings in early medieval graves', in H. Hamerow and A. MacGregor (eds.), *Image and Power in the Archaeology of Early Medieval Britain: Essays in Honour of Rosemary Cramp*. Oxford: Oxbow Books, 131–46.
HINTON, D. A. (1992). 'Revised dating of the Worgret structure'. *Proceedings of the Dorset Natural History and Archaeological Society* 114: 258–9.
——(1996). *The Gold, Silver and Other Non-Ferrous Alloy Objects from Hamwic*. Southampton Archaeology Monographs 6. Stroud: Alan Sutton.
HOWARD-JOHNSTON, J. (1998). 'Trading in fur from Classical Antiquity to the early Middle Ages', in E. Cameron (ed.), *Leather and Fur: Aspects of Early Medieval Trade and Technology*. London: Archetype Publications, 65–79.
HUGGETT, J. W. (1998). 'Imported grave-goods and the Anglo-Saxon economy'. *Medieval Archaeology* 32: 63–96.
HUGHES, R. (2004). 'Wattle and daub', in Leary, *Tatberht's Lundenwic*, 115–40.
HUNTER, J. R., and HEYWORTH, M. P. (1998). *The Hamwic Glass*. CBA Research Report 116. York: Council for British Archaeology.
HURST, J. D. (ed.) (1997). *A Multi-Period Salt Production Site at Droitwich: Excavations at Upwich*. CBA Research Report 107. York: Council for British Archaeology.
JOPE, E. M. (1964). 'The Saxon building-stone industry in southern and midland England'. *Medieval Archaeology* 8: 91–118.
KEEN, L. (1988). 'Coastal salt production in Norman England'. *Anglo-Norman Studies* 11: 133–79.
KILMURRY, K. (1980). *The Pottery Industry of Stamford, Lincolnshire, c. AD 850–1100*. BAR British Series 84. Oxford: British Archaeological Reports.
KORNBLUTH, G. A. (1989). 'The Alfred Jewel: reuse of Roman *spolia*'. *Medieval Archaeology* 33: 32–7.
LADLE, L. (2004). *Pits, Pots and People: The Archaeology of Bestwall Quarry, Wareham, Dorset*. Wareham: Bestwall Archaeology Project.

LEARY, J. (2004). *Tatberht's Lundenwic: Archaeological Excavations in Middle Saxon London*. Pre-Construct Archaeology Monograph 2. London.
MACGREGOR, A. (1985). *Bone, Antler, Ivory and Horn: The Technology of Skeletal Materials Since the Roman Period*. Beckenham: Croom Helm.
MACK, J., MCDONNELL, G., MURPHY, S., ANDREWS, P., and WARDLEY, K. (2000). 'Liquid steel in Anglo-Saxon England'. *Historical Metallurgy* 34(2): 87–96.
MADDICOTT, J. (1989). 'Trade, industry and the wealth of King Alfred'. *Past and Present* 123: 3–51.
MAHANY, C., BURCHARD, A., and SIMPSON, G. (1982). *Excavations in Stamford, Lincolnshire, 1963–1969*. Society for Medieval Archaeology Monograph Series 9.
MAINMAN, A. J., and ROGERS, N. S. H. (2000). *Finds from Anglo-Scandinavian York*. Volume 17, fasc. 14 of *The Archaeology of York*. York: Council for British Archaeology.
——— (2004). 'Craft and economy in Anglo-Scandinavian York', in R. A. Hall (ed.), *Aspects of Anglo-Scandinavian York*. Volume 8, fasc. 4 of *The Archaeology of York*. York: Council for British Archaeology, 459–87.
MALCOLM, G., and BOWSHER, D. (2003). *Middle Saxon London: Excavations at the Royal Opera House 1989–99*. Museum of London Archaeological Service Monograph 15. London: Museum of London.
MAYNARD, D. (1988). 'Excavations on a pipeline near the River Frome, Worgret, Dorset'. *Proceedings of the Dorset Natural History and Archaeological Society* 110: 77–98.
MCDONNELL, G. (1988). 'Ore to artefact—a study of early ironworking technology', in E. A. Slater and W. O. Tate (eds.), *Science and Archaeology, Glasgow 1987*. BAR British Series 196. Oxford: British Archaeological Reports, 283–93.
——— (1993). 'Slags and ironworking residues', in H. Hamerow, *Excavations at Mucking*. English Heritage Archaeological Report 21. London: English Heritage, 82–3.
MEREDITH, J. (2006). *The Iron Industry of the Forest of Dean*. Stroud: Tempus.
MORRIS, C. A. (2000). *Wood and Woodworking in Anglo-Scandinavian and Medieval York*. Volume 17, fasc. 13 of *The Archaeology of York*. York: Council for British Archaeology.
MORTIMER, C. (1991). 'A descriptive classification of early medieval copper alloys'. *Medieval Archaeology* 35: 104–7.
MUDD, A. (2006). 'Early to middle Saxon iron smelting furnaces at the kitchen garden, Fineshade Abbey, Northamptonshire'. *Northamptonshire Archaeology* 34: 81–95.
ODDY, W. A. (1996). 'Fire-gilding in early medieval Europe', in D. A. Hinton, *The Gold, Silver and Other Non-Ferrous Alloy Objects from Hamwic*. Stroud: Alan Sutton, 81–3.
——— and TYLECOTE, R. F. (1990). 'Objects associated with gold working', in M. Biddle (ed.), *Object and Economy in Medieval Winchester*. Winchester Studies 7.2. Oxford: Oxford University Press, 76–81.
O'SULLIVAN, D. (2001). 'Space, silence and shortage on Lindisfarne: the archaeology of asceticism', in H. Hamerow and A. MacGregor (eds.), *Image and Power in the Archaeology of Early Medieval Britain: Essays in Honour of Rosemary Cramp*. Oxford: Oxbow Books.
OTTAWAY, P. (1992). *Anglo-Scandinavian Ironwork from Coppergate*. Volume 17, fasc. 6 of *The Archaeology of York*. London: Council for British Archaeology.
OWEN-CROCKER, G. R. (2004). *Dress in Anglo-Saxon England*. Woodbridge: Boydell Press.
PARKER, I. (2000). 'Jet and amber identification and provenancing', in A. J. Mainman and N. S. H. Rogers, *Finds from Anglo-Scandinavian York*. Volume 17, fasc. 14 of *The Archaeology of York*. York: Council for British Archaeology, 2470 and 2501–8.

Parsons, D. (1991). 'Stone', in J. Blair and N. Ramsay (eds.), *English Medieval Industries*. London: Hambledon Press, 1–28.

Peacock, D. (1982). *Pottery in the Roman World: An Ethnographic Approach*. London/New York: Longman.

Perkins, D. J. (2000). 'Jutish glass production in Kent and the problem of the base cups'. *Archaeologia Cantiana* 120: 297–310.

Price, J. (ed.) (2000). *Glass in Britain and Ireland A.D. 350–1100*. British Museum Occasional Paper 127. London: British Museum.

Pritchard, F. A. (1984). 'Late Saxon textiles from the City of London'. *Medieval Archaeology* 28: 46–76.

——(1991). 'Small finds', in A. Vince (ed.), *Aspects of Saxo-Norman London*, Volume 2: *Finds and Environmental Evidence*. London and Middlesex Archaeological Society Special Paper 12, 120–278.

Rodwell, W., Hawkes, J., Howe, E., and Cramp, R. (2008). 'The Lichfield angel: a spectacular Anglo-Saxon painted sculpture'. *Antiquaries Journal* 88: 48–108.

Salter, C. (1988). 'The ironworking slag from the River Frome site', in D. Maynard, 'Excavations on a pipeline near the River Frome, Worgret, Dorset'. *Proceedings of the Dorset Natural History and Archaeological Society* 110: 77–98, at 82–5.

Stiff, M. (2003). 'The glass finds', in Malcolm and Bowsher (eds.), *Middle Saxon London*, 241–50.

Tatton-Brown, T. (2001). 'The quarrying and distribution of Reigate stone in the Middle Ages'. *Medieval Archaeology* 45: 189–201.

Taylor, G. (2003). 'An early to middle Saxon settlement at Quarrington, Lincolnshire'. *Antiquaries Journal* 83: 231–80.

Turner, S. (2006). *Making a Christian Landscape: The Countryside in Early Medieval Cornwall, Devon and Wessex*. Exeter: University of Exeter Press.

Tylecote, R. F. (1967). 'The bloomery site at West Runton'. *Norfolk Archaeology* 34: 187–214.

Wallis, S., and Waughman, M. (1998). *Archaeology and Landscape in the Lower Blackwater Valley*. East Anglian Archaeology 82. Gressenhall.

Walton Rogers, P. (2007). *Cloth and Clothing in Early Anglo-Saxon England AD 450–700*. CBA Research Report 145. York: Council for British Archaeology.

Watson, J. (2000). 'Wood', in D. A. Hinton, *A Smith in Lindsey: The Anglo-Saxon Grave at Tattershall Thorpe, Lincolnshire*. Society for Medieval Archaeology Monograph 16, 86–93.

Williams, D., and Vince, A. (1997). 'The characterisation and interpretation of early to middle Saxon granitic tempered pottery in England'. *Medieval Archaeology* 41: 214–20.

Worssam, B. C. (1995). 'Regional geology', in D. Tweddle, M. Biddle, and B. Kjølbye-Biddle, *Corpus of Anglo-Saxon Sculpture*, Volume 4: *South-East England*. Oxford: Oxford University Press, 10–21.

CHAPTER 24

ANGLO-SAXON CRAFTS

KEVIN LEAHY

INTRODUCTION AND SOURCES OF EVIDENCE

'Anglo-Saxon crafts' covers the manufacture of everything made over a period of more than 600 years, from everyday pots to the finest goldwork. Recent years have seen a massive increase in our knowledge of Anglo-Saxon crafts, with the publication of a number of important works dealing with particular trades: goldsmiths (Coatsworth and Pinder 2002); cloth and clothing (Walton Rogers 2007); and the reports published by the York Archaeological Trust on wood and woodworking (Morris 2000), bone, antler, ivory, and horn (MacGregor et al. 1999), leather and leatherworking (Mould et al. 2003), the iron from Coppergate (Ottaway 1992), and non-ferrous metalworking (Bayley 1992). Some attempts have been made to summarize what is known: Wilson contributed a useful chapter in his edited book (Wilson 1976) and I have tried to review the current state of knowledge (Leahy 2003). This chapter can only give an overview of Anglo-Saxon crafts and refer to some of the issues involved.

What then are our sources of evidence? The dream of any student of early crafts is a well-preserved workshop, with tools, manufacturing debris, and examples of objects that have failed at various stages of production (Fig. 24.4 nos. 1–2). Workshops have been found: York's Anglo-Scandinavian Coppergate provides an outstanding example and demonstrates the multiplicity of crafts being carried out in a relatively small area, but there is less evidence for earlier periods and we lack anything like Dunadd, Argyll, with its casting debris (Lane and Campbell 2000) or the Scandinavian production sites like Ribe, Denmark (Jensen 1991), and Helgö, Sweden (Lamm 1980). Non-ferrous objects (copper-alloy, gold, and silver) may retain marks left by the files and tools used to cut the metal, and some objects bear evidence of use, re-use, and repair. Early technical treatises can be informative; the best of them, Theophilus *On Diverse Arts*, dates to shortly after our period, but is still of great value (Hawthorne and Smith 1979). The techniques employed by craftworkers in the developing world provide insights, as can evidence from our own recent past; craft tools did not change much and sources like Salaman's *Dictionary of Woodworking Tools* (1992) and *Dictionary of Leatherworking Tools* (1986) can be useful. Experimental work carried out by living history re-enactment groups may also add to our understanding and, finally, we have the evidence of the materials themselves: laws of chemistry and physics were as unchangeable and unforgiving in the Anglo-Saxon period as they are now. These gave the materials their properties and imposed the constraints under which objects were fashioned.

WOOD AND TIMBER

It would be hard to over-emphasize the importance of wood in the Anglo-Saxon world, but although it was used everywhere, and for everything, little is found except on water-logged sites like the mill at Tamworth, Staffordshire (Fig. 24.1 no. 1). Usually all that survives are metal fittings, or rows of post-holes showing where a timber building once stood. Perhaps our best evidence for Anglo-Saxon woodworking comes from the tools used, particularly six hoards of mid and later Saxon carpenters' tools, but evidence for the early part of the period is poor, as there are no hoards, and tools were rarely placed in graves. The hoard from Flixborough, North Lincolnshire, appears the most comprehensive and contains what may be a full tool kit: 'T'-shaped axes and adzes, spoon bits for drilling holes, drawing knives for making rounded objects such as pegs, and a bill used for clearing light wood - everything that would be needed to build a house or a boat (Fig. 24.1 nos. 2–3, 6–9, 11). Most iron tools changed little over the centuries and can only be dated by their context or associations, although the distinctive 'T'-shaped axe does seem to have been a mid and later Saxon type. The only tool hoard for which we have a direct date is from Stidriggs, Dumfries, where associated wood yielded a radiocarbon date of AD 775–892 at one standard deviation. At Stidriggs; Westley Waterless, Cambridgeshire; and Flixborough, hoards of tools were found in lead vats of a type that occurs in mid Saxon contexts, or bearing motifs of that period. The larger of two tanks at

442   K. LEAHY

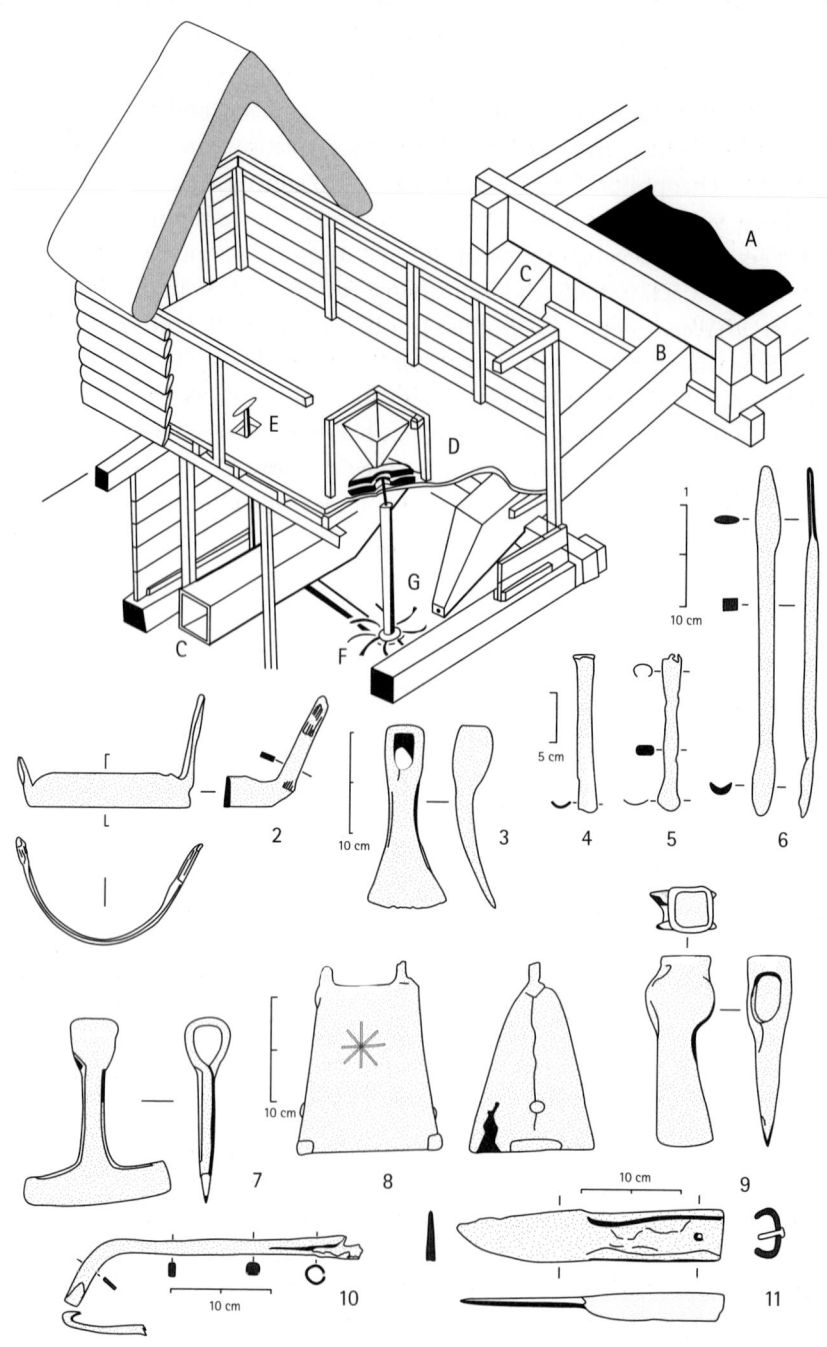

Figure 24.1 (1) Reconstruction of the ninth-century water mill at Tamworth, Staffordshire. The water from the river was retained in the pond by a revetment (A). From here it could either go down chute B to emerge from jet G and drive the

Flixborough had been inverted over the smaller to form a container, but the tanks' function, and the reason for their association with tools, remains a mystery.

Most of the Anglo-Saxon tools so far found were designed for heavy carpentry and there are few examples of lighter tools like the chisels, gouges, and planes suitable for fine work, two exceptions being shown in Fig. 24.1 nos. 4 and 5. While the lack of small tools might be due to accidents of survival (an axe being more robust than a chisel), the few surviving small Anglo-Saxon wooden objects do not suggest a tradition of sophisticated joinery. The coffin/reliquary in which the body of St Cuthberht was placed in AD 698 was a high-status object, but is more remarkable for its incised decoration than the quality of the joinery (Leahy 2003: fig. 13). Its base was housed in slots cut into the ends and in steps cut into the sides, but elsewhere simple butt-joints were used. On a larger scale, mortise and tenon joints were used in the construction of the mid Saxon mill at Tamworth (Fig. 24.1 no.1). These were secured by driving wedges through the extended ends of the tenons (Rahtz and Meeson 1992). Musical instruments represent the apex of the woodworker's art as they must be thin, light, and stand the tension of the strings.

horizontal water wheel (F); or if the wheel was not in use, the water was diverted down the relief chute (C). The power from the water wheel was transmitted to the mill stones (D) by a vertical shaft. The gap between the mill stones was adjusted by raising and lowering the 'lightening bar' through lever E. This sophisticated structure survived through being partly burnt down and then waterlogged. Reconstruction by the author after F. W. B. Charles in Rahtz and Meeson 1992.

Below: Anglo-Saxon wood-working tools (all drawings by the author): (2) Drawing knife for making rounded wooden objects such as dowels. The asymmetry of the handles is an original feature and it is likely that there was a handle on one side of the blade and a knob on the other. Flixborough hoard, ninth century. (3) Adze, a transverse axe used for shaping timber objects. Flixborough hoard, ninth century. (4–5) Gouges (spoon-like wood chisels): Item 4, one-piece gouge from the Nazeing, Essex; hoard, eleventh century (drawing after Morris 1983). This object was made in one piece with a solid iron handle. Item 5, socketed gouge from Crayke, Yorks., ninth century (drawing after Wilson 1976). (6) Spoon-bit: the flat tang was fitted into a wooden cross-bar, which was turned, the sharpened spoon drilling the hole. Flixborough hoard, ninth century. (7) 'T'-shaped axe, the characteristic axe of the early medieval period. Flixborough hoard, ninth century. (8) Copper-coated iron bell of the type found in early medieval tool hoards. Flixborough hoard, ninth century. (9) Axe-hammer, Flixborough hoard, ninth century. (10) Wood-turning tool from York (drawing after Morris 2000). (11) Bill or slasher used for clearing light wood. Flixborough hoard, ninth century

When forming the sound-box for the Sutton Hoo lyre, the makers carved it from solid maple: they seem to have known their limitations.

Intelligent use was made of the properties of different woods. Oak is excellent for building as it resists rot and large timbers could be made by splitting tree trunks which, in the absence of large saws, was important (Darrah 1982). Shield boards were usually made from light woods like lime, poplar, alder, or willow (Dickinson and Härke 1992). The base of the seventh-century bed from Swallowcliffe Down, Wiltshire, was sprung using a lattice of ash laths (Speake 1989). Alder was the preferred wood used in the manufacture of lathe-turned wooden cups and bowls at Coppergate (Morris 2000). These were made on a pole-lathe with the work-piece fixed on to a mandrel around which a cord was wound, fixed at one end to a treadle, the other to a springy pole. The cord was pulled by pushing down on the treadle, and, once the stroke was complete, the pole straightened, pulling the cord back, raising the treadle ready for the next stroke. As a pole-lathe had a reciprocating action, the tool (Figure 24.1 no. 10) was disengaged after each stroke, allowing the work-piece to turn back to its starting-point. This reciprocating principle was used on a smaller scale on the bow-lathe, where turning was done by a manually operated bow-string.

Knowledge of other minor, but still important, aspects of woodworking is limited. Evidence for coopering comes, in the main, not from barrels, but from buckets and vats, the metal fittings of which survive in early Anglo-Saxon graves. An eighth-century oak cask bound with hazel or willow hoops was found at Southampton, and by the tenth and eleventh century we have evidence for casks from Durham, York, and Winchester. There is no evidence for the use of heated iron hoops being fitted to barrels during the Anglo-Saxon period, the staves being bound with withies. Basketry is represented by a few finds but these seem to span the whole Anglo-Saxon period; baskets found at Odell, Bedfordshire, gave a radiocarbon date of AD 520 ± 40. These were made on solid wooden bases drilled for the vertical withies; bases have also been excavated in Anglo-Scandinavian York. To date, no Anglo-Saxon wheel has been found, but manuscript illustrations suggest that shrink-fitted iron tyres were not being used.

Amongst the largest and finest products of the Anglo-Saxon woodworker were ships such as the 27-metre-long vessel in Mound 1 at Sutton Hoo (Bruce-Mitford 1975). This dated from the later sixth or early seventh century and, like the tenth-century Graveney ship, was clinker-built with over-lapping planks (strakes) joined together by rows of iron rivets. These rivets were short lengths of iron rod with a mushroom-shaped head on one end. The rivets were inserted through holes drilled through the overlapping planks, and diamond-shaped washers were placed over their protruding ends, which were then hammered, expanding the metal to secure the two planks together. Lacking the screw thread, the Anglo-Saxon craftsmen would have made extensive use of wedges to secure clamps and vices while working (McGrail 1980 for the building sequence).

POTTERY

In many crafts there was little in the way of fundamental changes in technology during the Anglo-Saxon period; changes took place in what was being made, and in the organization of production, rather than in the methods or tools used. Changes did, however, occur in pottery manufacture. During the fifth century the highly competent Roman tradition of wheel-thrown pottery collapsed, to be replaced by hand-formed pots which, in the case of cinerary urns, seem to have been made with more enthusiasm than expertise. However, it can no longer be assumed that this pottery was home-made, as closely linked vessels, like those made by the 'Sancton-Baston' and 'Illington-Lackford' potters, were widely distributed, and pottery containing acid igneous rock from the Charnwood area of Leicestershire is found throughout the east Midlands and beyond (Williams and Vince 1997). Production sites are known for mid Saxon Ipswich ware, which occurs throughout East Anglia and on important sites outside the region. Ipswich ware was hard-fired and made using a slow turntable rather than being thrown on a potter's wheel. The wheel was re-introduced into England during the ninth century, a time when production in much of England became based in, and around, the nascent towns. Both the wheel and the use of lead glaze on pottery made at Stamford, Lincolnshire, were probably introduced from northern France. An important and widely traded product of the Stamford kilns were crucibles (Fig. 24.4 no. 5) made of clean, white-firing clay that was heat-resistant (Kilmurry 1980).

TEXTILES

The craft for which we have the best evidence is the manufacture of textiles, spinning and weaving equipment being commonly found. Traces of textiles survive in water-logged conditions or when buried against a metal object as often occurred in early Anglo-Saxon graves. Many early and mid Saxon settlement sites produce clay loom-weights (Fig. 24.2 no. 2), which, in the early period, were often not fired, merely being dried. Loom-weights have been found in rows, leading to the suggestion that they had fallen from a loom, although as it seems unlikely that a fully-rigged loom would have been abandoned, the weights may have been stored on rods; some were perhaps deliberately deposited (Hamerow 2006: 18–19).

Annular clay weights represent the warp-weighted loom, a piece of equipment that was in common use in England from the fifth century until around AD 900 but which remained in use in northern Scandinavia into the twentieth century,

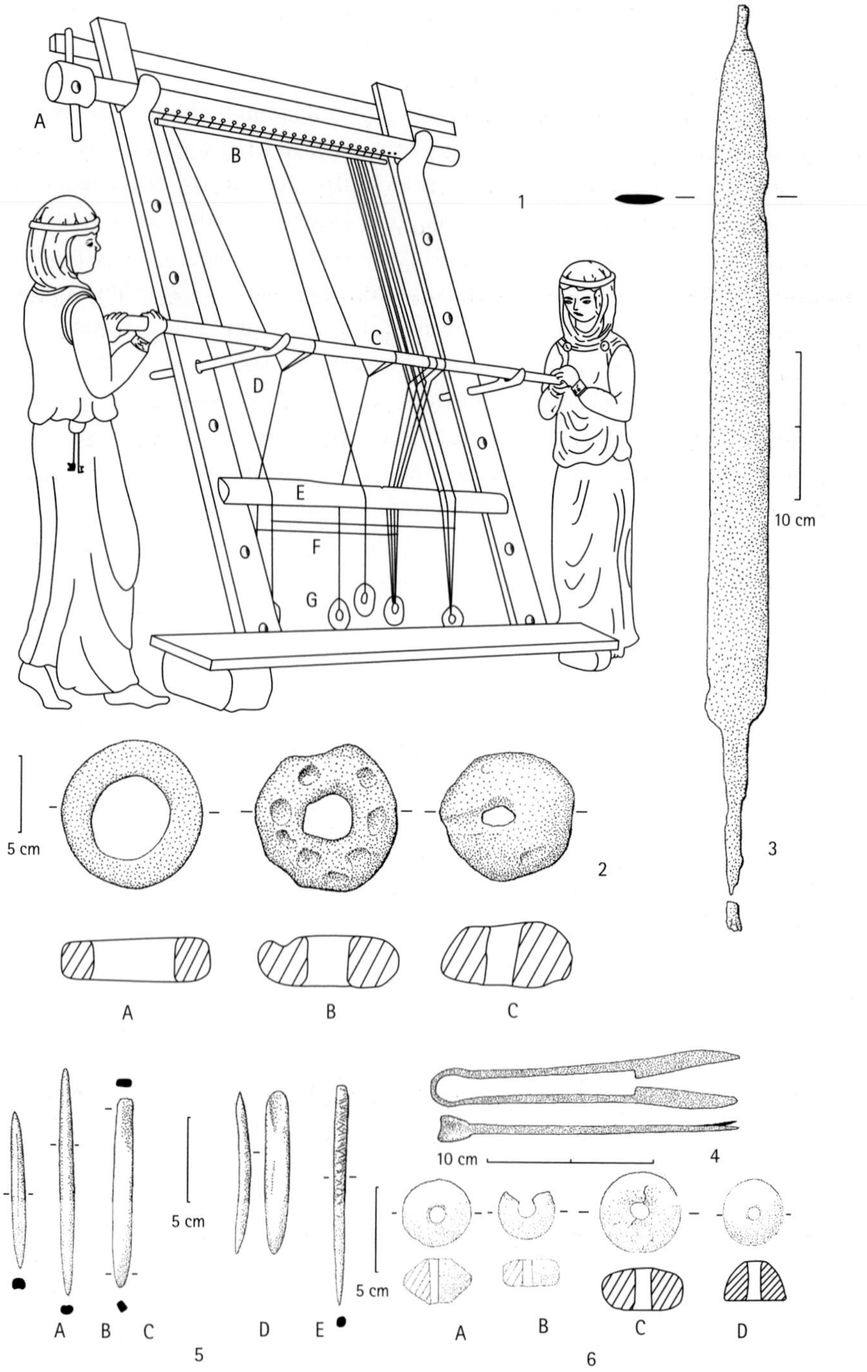
A
B
C
D
E
F
G
1
10 cm
3
5 cm
2
A
B
C
10 cm
4
5 cm
A
B
C
D
E
5
5 cm
A
B
C
D
6

showing how they were used (Fig. 24.2 no. 1). At the start of weaving the warp threads were attached to a strip of braid fixed to the top roller (Fig. 24.2 no. 1 B). The weights kept the 'vertical' warp threads under gentle tension while the horizontal 'weft' threads were woven between them. The loom was not vertical as it had to lean back at a slight angle in order to be worked. Alternate warp threads were passed behind and in front of a bar across the lower part of the loom (Fig. 24.2 no. 1 E), allowing the weft thread to be passed between them. Other warp threads were attached by threads to rods, 'heddles', and, by raising them, it was possible to offer the weft a different route between the warp threads (Fig. 24.2 no. 1 C). As weaving progressed, the weft threads were pushed up on the warps using a bone pin-beater (Fig. 24.2 no. 6 ABC) or an iron weaving sword (Fig. 24.2 no. 3). Pin-beaters often show a very high degree of polish through constant handling and have fine grooves worn around their tips. Weaving swords resemble and were even sometimes made from weapons, but have what appears to be a tang at both ends (a socketed version is also known). Some examples had pattern-welded blades. When weaving had progressed down to a level at which it was no longer easy to pass the weft between the warps, the newly woven cloth was taken up on a roller at the top of the loom (Fig. 24.2 no. 1 A). It was possible to make cloths 2 metres wide using a warp-weighted loom. The women (in the Anglo-Saxon period the making of textiles is assumed to have been almost exclusively a female pursuit) worked in pairs or as a team of three; there would need to be one at each side of the loom to raise the

Figure 24.2 Textile production (drawings by the author except no. 1)
(1) Reconstruction by Dianne Leahy of a warp-weighted loom in use (N. B. for clarity most of the warp threads have been omitted): (A) Top roller with spokes for taking up the cloth as it is woven; (B) Starting braid stitched to top roller; (C) Heddle bar connected to alternate warp threads by leashes. By raising this, a second shed is formed through which the weft is passed; (D) The shed, through which the weft thread is passed; (E) The shed bar which forms the natural shed though which the weft is passed; (F) The warp threads are linked together to keep them in line; (G) The clay loom-weights which keep the vertical warp threads under tension. (2) A Early Anglo-Saxon, doughnut-shaped loom-weight from Sutton Courtenay (after Dunning et al. 1959); B Later 'intermediate' weight from Nettleton Top, Lincs.; C Typical mid Saxon loom-weight, bun-shaped with a small hole (drawing after Mainman and Rogers 2000). (3) Iron weaving sword from the Buckland, Dover cemetery (drawing after Evison 1987). (4) Iron shears from Flixborough. (5) ABC bone-pin beaters from West Stow, Suffolk (after West 1985). These are of the type used on the warp-weighted loom. DE bone pin-beaters from Winchester (after Biddle 1990). These beaters are of the sort used on the two-beam, vertical loom introduced in the tenth century. (6) AB pottery spindle whorls, C antler whorl, all from West Stow (drawings after West 1985). D later type bone spindle whorl from York (after MacGregor et al. 1999).

heddle bars and perhaps a third to pass the skein of thread through the shed to form the weft.

Using the warp-weighted loom, Anglo-Saxon women were able to produce a variety of weaves with different effects. By attaching a number of heddles to different sets of warp threads it was possible to make more elaborate weaves. The basic weave was the simple 'tabby', where alternate warp and weft threads passed under and over each other, but much use was made of 'twill' weaves, where the weft passed over two warp threads and then under two threads, a 2/2 twill. By moving the heddles in sequence it was possible to give the effect of a diagonal grain moving across the fabric. Other, more complicated, weaves were produced using different combinations of warp and weft threads to give broken diamond twills, and decorative effects were obtained by combining 'Z' (clockwise) and 'S' (anti-clockwise) spun threads.

Not all Anglo-Saxon textiles were made on the warp-weighted loom; much use was made of tablet-weaving to make braids for edging garments. Tablet-weaving involves the use of a set of small square or triangular tablets with holes through their corners. The warp threads pass through these holes with the threads in the two upper and two lower holes forming the alternating 'under' and 'over' threads. After each pass of the weft, tablets are given a half, or quarter, turn to produce a patterned weave. Although vegetable dyes were often used, it appears that most cloth was not dyed but that naturally coloured fleeces were used for effect.

Once clipped from the sheep, wool only needed to be cleaned and combed to align the fibres, but the preparation of vegetable fibres, mainly flax, is much more complicated and would have involved a long process of breaking down the stems by hammering, rotting, and pulling through iron combs. Once the fibres had been extracted they were spun into thread using a drop-spindle—the bone, ceramic, or stone 'whorls', which acted as flywheels during spinning, being common finds (Fig. 24.2 no.5 ABCD). While spindle whorls are widespread throughout settlement sites, the distribution of loom-weights seems to have been concentrated in particular zones, suggesting that spinning was carried out everywhere, but that weaving concentrated around particular buildings.

During the course of the Anglo-Saxon period the form of the clay loom-weights changed: early weights are shaped like ring doughnuts, on intermediate loom-weights the central hole is proportionally smaller, and later examples look like bun doughnuts with a small hole through them (Fig. 24.2 no. 2 ABC). Towards the end of the ninth century loom-weights vanish from the archaeological record, the warp-weighted loom being replaced by the two-beam, or tapestry, loom, which had been used during the Roman period and was re-introduced from the continent. A two-beam loom has no weights but has rollers at both top and bottom. Its presence can be recognized archaeologically by the distinctive form of bone pin-beaters used, one long, like a pencil, the other with a point at one end and a flat chisel-like end at the other (Fig. 24.2 no. 6 DE). Particular weaves are believed to be typical of the two-beam loom. (For dress and costume, see Owen-Crocker, this volume.)

Antler, Bone, and Animal Products

In the early medieval period, many of the objects that are now made out of plastic (combs, handles, etc.) were made from bone or antler. These skeletal materials are similar in nature but the thick, solid sections of antlers are more useful for making objects. Comb fragments are found on most Anglo-Saxon sites where conditions allow bone to survive. Combs were assembled from separate pieces and designed to take advantage of the directional properties of antler, which is stronger in some directions than others, the thin tooth-plates being cut at 90 degrees to the side pieces that held the plates into position (MacGregor and Currey 1983).

Other animal products were used, leather being much more important than the meagre survivals suggest. Leather shoes were found at Sutton Hoo and in later contexts in London and Anglo-Scandinavian York. At Sheffield's Hill, Lincolnshire, traces of the leather facing of a sixth-century wooden shield board were preserved and some of the knives were in decorated sheaths. Traces of sword scabbards are also known (Cameron 2003). The tangs of many Anglo-Saxon knives retain traces left by the horn handles with which they were once fitted. Horn is plastic when heated, a characteristic employed to make the horn plates used on the helmet from Benty Grange, Derbyshire. It was used to make drinking-horns, as found at Sutton Hoo and Taplow.

Ironworking

In addition to providing evidence for Anglo-Saxon woodworking, the tools discussed above are, in themselves, the sophisticated products of another craftsman, the smith. Iron ores are widespread in England (see Hinton, this volume). After smelting, the iron was turned into objects entirely by use of the hammer, thus 'wrought iron'. Heated to between 700°C and 1,250°C, iron becomes malleable and easily shaped. At these temperatures it is prone to oxidation and, to reduce this, it is sprinkled with sand. This sand, combined with iron, forms the ubiquitous hammerscale found on Anglo-Saxon sites; smithing slag also indicates how widely iron was worked. Its properties are unlike those of other metals: two pieces of white-hot iron put together and hammered will fuse, forming a strong weld. Iron is a poor conductor of heat, making it possible to locally heat and work one part of an object while leaving the rest cold, and a small area could be heated and bent while the rest of the object was unaffected and retained its strength. Hammer-welding was used to great effect (if little advantage) in making pattern-welded blades for which strips of iron were twisted, flattened, and fused together to produce blades marked with

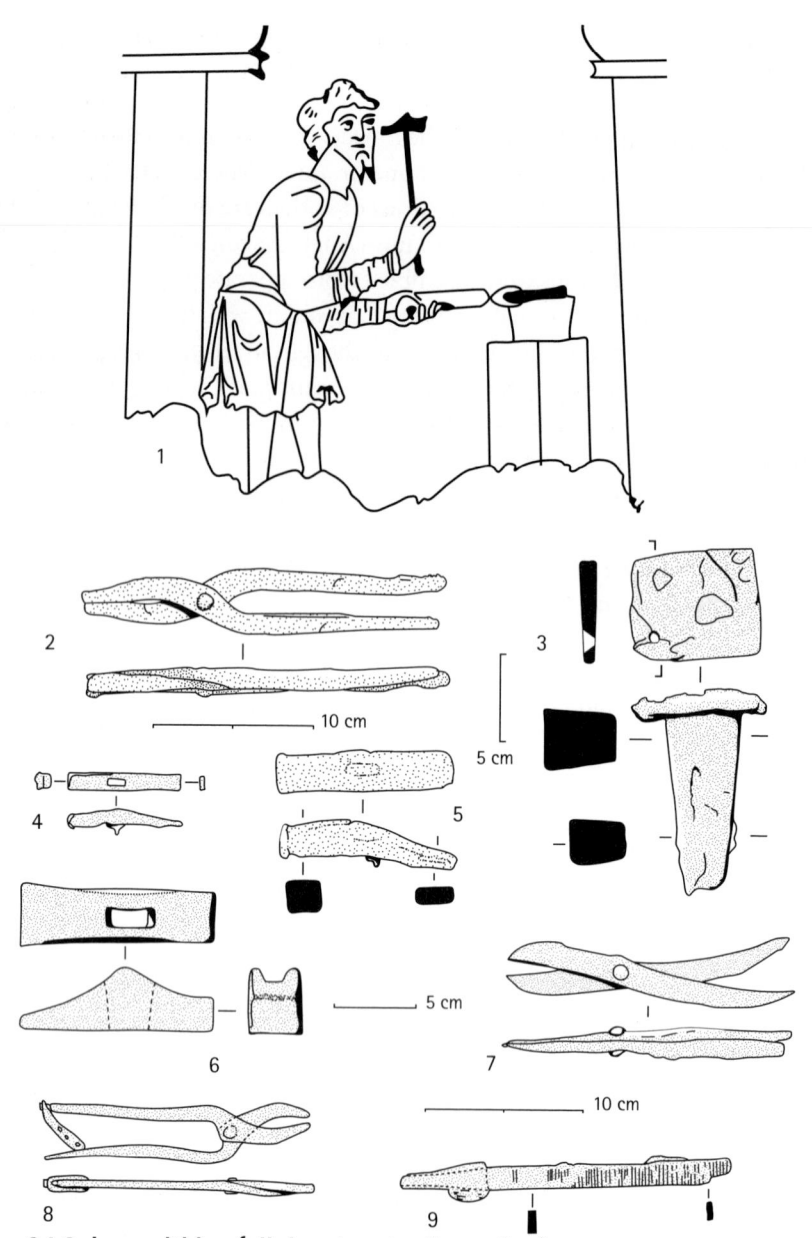

Figure 24.3 Ironsmithing (all drawings by the author)
(1) Drawing of an Anglo-Saxon smith, (drawing based on the eleventh-century Caedmon manuscript, Bodleian Library, Junius II). The hammer is of the type found at Tattershall Thorpe and Thetford (below) and the anvil is set in a wooden block which is the way in which the Tattershall anvil would have been used. (2) Seventh-century smith's tongs, from the Tattershall Thorpe grave (drawing after Hinton 2000). (3) Iron stake anvil from Tattershall Thorpe (drawing after Hinton 2000). (4–5) Iron hammers from Tattershall Thorpe (drawing after Hinton 2000). (6) Iron

zigzag patterns. Complex, thin iron objects like shield bosses were made in one piece to overcome the difficulties involved in hammer-welding the sections together.

Wrought iron is soft and weak but its properties can be massively improved by holding iron bars at high temperature in a hearth heated by charcoal. Carbon from the charcoal is absorbed into the surface of the iron to form steel, a tough, hard alloy that can be heat-treated to give a sharp cutting edge. Carburization was a slow and difficult process and steel was used economically, a band of steel being added to the edge of a tool, or a thin strip of steel being sandwiched between two layers of iron where it formed the cutting edge. Many of the iron ores found in Britain contain phosphorus and, while this is a problem to modern iron makers, it does give a wrought iron that can be work-hardened to some extent. Unfortunately, the presence of phosphorus prevents the take-up of carbon, so phosphoric irons cannot be converted to steel.

NON-FERROUS METALWORKING

Unlike the ironworker, early Anglo-Saxon craftsmen working non-ferrous metals had to rely on salvaged scrap or materials imported from elsewhere. The metals were usually combined to form alloys: copper + tin = bronze, copper + zinc = brass. Alloys are stronger and harder than pure metals and easier to cast, having lower melting-points and being less prone to porosity caused by gas bubbles.

The basic methods used to work non-ferrous metals differ from those used to work iron. Much shaping was carried out by casting molten metal into moulds and, while hammer-working was used, non-ferrous metals, with the exception of gold, cannot be welded. Other methods, such as brazing and riveting, were used to fix non-ferrous objects together. In the casting process the metal was placed in a crucible (Fig. 24.4 nos. 4–5) and heated above its melting point to give the 'super-heat' that allowed it to flow into the mould before solidifying. The moulds were usually made from clay, but stone moulds were used for casting ingots and antler moulds for lead alloys. Most moulds were of the two-part type, the pattern being embedded between two layers of clay (Fig. 24.4 no. 3 A–D). These were then separated to allow the removal of the pattern, after which they were joined together

hammer from Thetford (drawing after Rogerson and Dallas 1984). The form can be paralleled on the Caedmon drawing shown above. (7) Shears for cutting sheet metal, Tattershall Thorpe (drawing after Hinton 2000). (8) Hand-vice/tongs from Flixborough, eighth–ninth century. (9) Iron file, Tattershall Thorpe, seventh century (drawing after Hinton 2000)

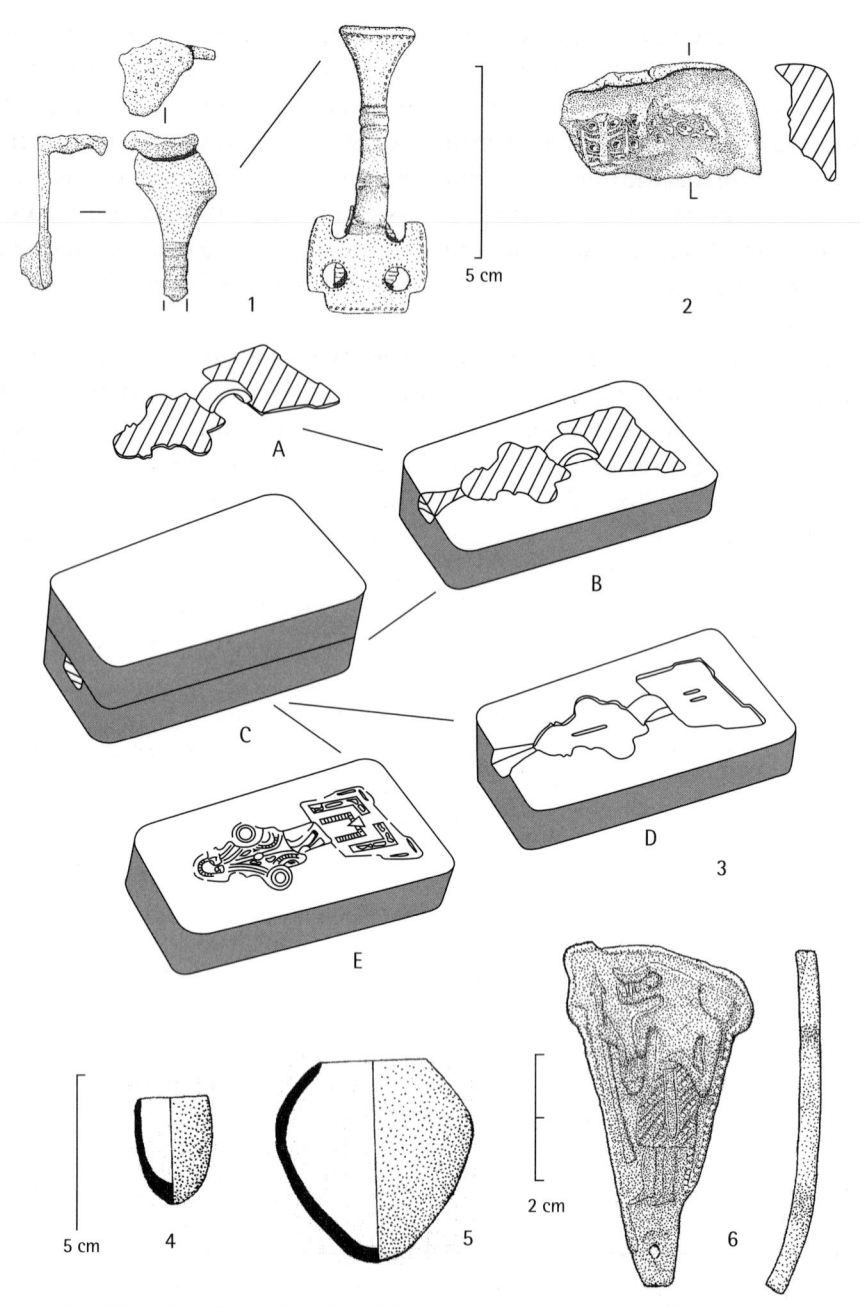

Figure 24.4 Metalwork production (all drawings by the author)
(1) Foot of a mis-cast early Anglo-Saxon small-long brooch with the casting gate and pouring basin still attached, Winterton, Lincs. Also shown is a comparable small-long brooch from the Cleatham, Lincs. cemetery. (2) Fragment of a clay mould for casting square-headed brooches from Mucking, Essex, sixth century AD (drawing after Jones 1980). This fragment represents one half of a two-part mould

and heated to dry and harden the clay before the molten metal was poured into the resultant mould. It is likely that much of the decorative detail was added directly to the clay mould. While pairs of brooches are common they are never identical in detail, suggesting that they were not being made from the same original pattern. It has been found that the elaborate animal art seen on early Anglo-Saxon metalwork is actually easier to cut as a negative impression into the mould than as a positive pattern from which the mould could be made (Axboe 1984). As they are very hard-fired and often contain traces of slag, crucible fragments are more common finds than moulds.

The evidence for early Anglo-Saxon metalworking is sparse. In 1991 Bayley was able to list over ninety excavations in England that had produced evidence for early medieval metal working, but half of these were in just six urban centres and were late in date. Fragments of a clay mould for casting great square-headed brooches were found in the fill of a sixth-century *Grubenhaus* at Mucking, Essex (Fig. 24.4 no. 2; Jones 1980), and mould fragments for making decorated objects were found in the fill of an eighth-century *Grubenhaus* at Wharram Percy, Yorkshire (Bayley and Lang 1992). Clay moulds for making eighth-century objects were found in a ditch associated with the monastery at Hartlepool, Cleveland (Bayley 1988), and part of a mould for casting a ninth-century strap-end was found at Carlisle (Taylor and Webster 1984). A workshop of tenth-century date was found at Faccombe (Netherton), Hampshire (Fairbrother 1990). Seven hearths were excavated inside a timber building, three measuring 2 m x 3 m which had been burnt red, and four smaller ones each around 500 mm in diameter. One contained crucible fragments and another a crucible bearing traces of gold, found standing on a bed of charcoal. The small furnaces were thought to have been used for melting the metal, with

of the sort shown below (no. 3). (3) Suggested process by which the mould for a square-headed brooch was made: (A) Undecorated model or pattern; (B) Model embedded in clay with a channel for the molten metal added; (C) A second slab of clay used to make the other side of the mould; (D–E) The two halves are separated and the pattern removed. A negative version of the decoration is cut into the soft clay forming one side of the mould and the catch plate and spring fitting cut in the other side. The two halves are then put back together and dried before the molten metal is poured into the mould. (4–5) Clay crucibles from York (drawing after Bayley 1992). While the smaller crucible was probably locally made, the larger example was made at Stamford in Lincs. Crucibles from Stamford were widely distributed and used for precious metals. (6) Pressblech die for making foil mounts from Fen Drayton, Cambs. A sheet of foil would have been placed on top of the die and covered with a lead or leather pad. This was struck with a mallet transferring the design onto the foil. The Fen Drayton die is interesting as the figure of the wolf-warrior also appears on dies from Torslunda in Sweden which can, in turn, be linked to the foils used on the Sutton Hoo helmet (Bruce–Mitford 1978)

moulds being heated in the larger pits. It is interesting that the hearths were within a building allowing the craftsmen to assess the temperature of the molten metal in low light.

During the later Saxon period it is likely that the 'lost wax' process was used to make complex objects. This involves making a wax model of the object to be cast, to which are added all the details, together with the channels through which the metal will enter the mould. The wax model is covered in fine clay, perhaps by dipping it in a clay slurry. Once the required thickness has been built up the mould is inverted and heated, melting out the wax and firing the clay. The mould is then turned upright and molten metal poured in to produce a metal replica of the wax model.

The low survival rate of clay moulds on early Anglo-Saxon sites may relate to their friability after use, but they are common on sites outside Anglo-Saxon England like Dunadd and the Mote of Mark. This paucity of early Anglo-Saxon non-ferrous metalworking sites is puzzling, particularly as Heald (forthcoming) has been able to argue that in Scotland the manufacture of fine metal objects was not restricted to the aristocratic sites. Was there something about the organization of early Anglo-Saxon metalworking that has led to this apparent lacuna or have we just been unlucky?

Something of a mystery surrounds fragments of lead cruciform brooches that have been recorded by the Portable Antiquities Scheme and it has been suggested that they were patterns or models used in the process of making moulds. I am not convinced by this interpretation, as the inclusion of a stage involving the manufacture of a lead 'model' in the process of making a mould is an unnecessary complication. While accepting that no lead cruciform brooch has been found in a grave, they have been found on cemetery sites and lead examples of other forms of brooch occur in graves. In the late Saxon period lead brooches were fitted with iron pins and must have been used and worn.

Unlike copper alloy and silver that were usually cast to shape, gold objects were generally 'fabricated', that is, assembled from sheet metal. What would have been solid on a copper-alloy object was made up as a box in gold. This was necessary because of the high value of gold but was made possible by the ease with which gold can be soldered or welded. A method of joining known as 'eutectic soldering' was employed, which involves the use of a copper salt mixed with an adhesive and possibly a flux. When heated, the carbon in the adhesive burns, reducing the copper salt to copper. This is absorbed by the gold or silver to produce an alloy with a lower melting-point than the parts to be joined (a eutectic) and it firmly bonds them together. Eutectic soldering was used to attach filigree and granulation to surfaces and, while it sounds a straightforward process, it calls for considerable skill as the work-piece has to be heated to near its melting-point. Too low a temperature and it will not work; too high and work must start again.

Metalworking tools

We have only one Anglo-Saxon set of metalworker's tools—the objects found in the seventh-century smith's grave at Tattershall Thorpe, Lincolnshire (Figure 24.3 nos. 2–5, 7, 9; Hinton 2000), although metalworking tools have been found on excavations elsewhere. It is unusual to get tools in a grave, with the exception of objects related to textile working. The Tattershall Thorpe grave is unusual in other respects, being isolated and not part of a cemetery, and some of the objects from the burial are of Continental type, suggesting that the metalworker may have been a foreigner. In the grave was what appears to be a full tool-kit for the working of non-ferrous metals: tongs, shears, files, hammers, an anvil, a possible engraving tool, and an iron bell. These bells are interesting as they have also been found in tool hoards at Flixborough (Fig. 24.1 no. 8) and in the Swedish Mästermyr hoard, and it is possible that they formed part of a tradesman's equipment, allowing him to announce his presence while travelling, or his arrival in a community.

The decoration of metal objects

Once the object was fashioned there was often a need to decorate it. During the sixth to eighth centuries the surfaces of many copper-alloy and silver objects were gilded using a fire-gilding process in which gold was dissolved in mercury, the resultant 'amalgam' then being applied to the surface of the metal. This was heated, boiling off the mercury to leave a very thin layer of gold on the surface of the object. In the ninth century, silver and silvering replaced gilding as the main finish applied to metal objects and was often used in combination with 'niello', a black silver/copper sulphide which, applied to the surface, gave the pleasing black-and-white effect characteristic of the 'Trewhiddle' style.

Amongst the finds from Tattershall Thorpe was a mass of copper-alloy off-cuts, probably intended for the melting pot, and six garnets: two cut to shape, three irregular, and a chip. Garnet inlay was one of the glories of early Anglo-Saxon metalwork. Garnets can be found all over Europe but few of these locations contain stones that are suitable for use in jewellery and sources as far away as Bohemia and even Sri Lanka have been suggested. Garnet has no natural cleavage, making it impossible to simply split off the thin, flat plates used in cloisonné work, so this has to be done by sawing the stones, using an abrasive such as sand applied with a soft iron or copper blade. The blade would be moved back and forth between two pairs of pegs and the sand grains, becoming embedded in the soft metal, would cut the garnets. When cut, groups of stones were stuck, using resin, on to the face of a flat stone and successively fine abrasives were applied to a second stone which was worked across it. In this way large numbers of stones could be polished and cut to thickness at once. Garnets were cut to the complex shapes used in cloisonné work by mounting the thin garnet plates on to the end of a stick and holding it against an abrasive-covered metal wheel, revolved with a bow (Bimson 1985). The shaped stones were set in cells on the face of the object being decorated, these cells often containing a sheet of corrugated gold foil to scatter the light and animate the stones. Not all garnets were set in gold; we are seeing increasing numbers of base-metal objects decorated with cloisonné work.

Enamel was also inlaid into metal, particularly on the mounts on hanging-bowls. These objects are usually found in Anglo-Saxon contexts, particularly graves, but their decorative style shows them to have been made by craftsmen working in a Celtic tradition. Enamelling consists of a glass inlay fused to the surface of the metal. It was commonly used in Roman Britain but was not employed in the Germanic homelands and its use is likely to have been a survival from Roman Britain. We are now seeing enamel inlay on purely Anglo-Saxon objects like cruciform brooches, ninth-century strap-ends, and a series of tenth- and eleventh-century brooches and mounts.

A further form of decoration which may have been more common than finds suggest is the use of appliqué. In recent years a number of Pressblech dies have been found, so they were less uncommon than used to be thought. The dies consist of relatively thick (generally 3–4 mm) copper-alloy plate, one face of which bears, in low relief, a positive version of a design. The other faces of the dies are unfinished and rough. Pressblech dies were used to make thin foil mounts which were then applied to larger objects like brooches, drinking-horns, and the Sutton Hoo helmet. In use the dies were covered with a layer of thin sheet metal which in turn was covered with either a lead or a leather pad which was struck with a mallet and the design transferred from the die to the sheet metal. I am puzzled by the survival of so many dies when the multiple foils produced from them are so rare. It is possible that the thickness of the dies has ensured their survival while the thin foils, many possibly made out of tinned bronze as on the Sutton Hoo helmet, have been lost to corrosion.

Glass

It appears that glass was being worked in Anglo-Saxon England as there are some forms of glass vessel that are most commonly found here (Evison 2008). Beads were also being manufactured and there is evidence for glass-working in tenth-century urban contexts. Even though glass objects were being made in England, the glass itself was probably not being produced here. The making of glass from the raw materials, suitable sand, lime, and soda or potash, requires a lot of heat and it is necessary to reach a temperature of around 1,700° C. Once fusion has taken place the effect of the alkali brings the melting point down to a more reasonable 1,100–1,400° C, making the glass much easier to work. In antiquity, glass from the eastern Mediterranean was redistributed from Italy in the form of small cubes (see also Hinton, this volume).

Conclusion

Many changes occurred during the six centuries of the Anglo-Saxon period, society moving from fractured tribal groups to a unified kingdom. The collapse of centralized government with the end of Roman Britain brought changes: the end of a coin economy would have made it difficult to market goods, and large government contracts would have been a thing of the past. Was this accompanied by a technological collapse? The pottery industry does not seem to have benefited from the Anglo-Saxon take-over, but there does not seem to have been any fall in the quality of metalwork; indeed the ironwork appears to have improved. The re-appearance of the widespread use of coins and the growth of *wics* in the mid Saxon period may have led to an increased demand for goods, and the growth of towns in the late Saxon period brought changes, with production becoming centralized and probably more specialized (see Blackburn, Hall, and Pestell, this volume). We can gain some appreciation of the economic power of these later Saxon/Anglo-Scandinavian towns by looking at the range of materials being worked, and of objects made, at Coppergate: it was a production power-house. Much less is known about the organization of crafts in the earlier part of the Anglo-Saxon period. Therein lies the challenge.

References

AXBOE, M. (1984). 'Positive and negative versions in the making of chip-carved ornament'. *Universitets Oldsaksammlings Skrifter, ny rekke* 5: 31–42.
BAYLEY, J. (1988). 'Crucibles and Moulds', in R. Daniels, 'The Anglo-Saxon monastery at Church Close, Hartlepool'. *Archaeological Journal* 145: 158–210, at 184–7.
—— (1991). 'Anglo-Saxon non-ferrous metalworking: a survey'. *World Archaeology* 23: 115–30.
—— (1992). *Anglo-Scandinavian Non-Ferrous Metalworking 16–22 Coppergate*. Volume 17, fasc. 7 of *The Archaeology of York*. York: Council for British Archaeology.
—— and LANG, J. (1992). 'The metalworking evidence, with a note on the stylistic evidence of the moulds', in G. Milne and J. D. Richards, *Two Anglo-Saxon Buildings and Associated*

Finds. Volume 7 of *Wharram: A Study of Settlement on the Yorkshire Wolds*. York University Archaeological Publications 9. York: York University: 59–66.
BIDDLE, M. (1990). *Object and Economy in Medieval Winchester*. Winchester Studies 7.2. Oxford: Clarendon Press.
BIMSON, M. (1985). 'Dark-Age garnet cutting'. *Anglo-Saxon Studies in Archaeology and History* 4: 125–8.
BRUCE-MITFORD, R. (1975). *The Sutton Hoo Ship Burial*, Volume 1: *Excavations, Background, the Ship, Dating and Inventory*. London: British Museum.
—— (1978). *The Sutton Hoo Ship Burial*, Volume 2: *Arms, Armour and Regalia*. London: British Museum.
CAMERON, E. A. (2003). *Sheaths and Scabbards in England A.D. 400–1100*. British Archaeological Reports British Series 301. Oxford: Archaeopress.
COATSWORTH, E., and PINDER, M. (2002). *The Art of the Anglo-Saxon Goldsmith*. Woodbridge: Boydell and Brewer.
DARRAH, R. (1982). 'Working unseasoned oak', in S. McGrail (ed.), *Woodworking Techniques before AD 1500*. BAR International Series 129. Oxford: British Archaeological Reports, 219–29.
DICKINSON, T., and HÄRKE, H. (1992). 'Early Anglo-Saxon Shields'. *Archaeologia* 110. London: Society of Antiquaries of London.
DUNNING, G. C., HURST, J. G., MYRES, J. N. L., and TISCHLER, F. (1959). 'Anglo-Saxon pottery: a symposium'. *Medieval Archaeology* 3: 1–78.
EVISON, V. I. (1987). *Dover: Buckland Anglo-Saxon Cemetery*. London: English Heritage.
—— (2008). *Catalogue of Anglo-Saxon Glass in the British Museum*. Ed. S. Marzinzik. British Museum Research Publication 167. London: Trustees of the British Museum.
FAIRBROTHER, J. R. (1990). *Faccombe Netherton: Excavations of a Saxon and Medieval Manorial Complex*. British Museum Occasional Paper 74. London: British Museum.
HAMEROW, H. (2006). '"Special deposits" in Anglo-Saxon settlements', *Medieval Archaeology* 50: 1–30.
HAWTHORNE, J. G., and SMITH, C. S. (1979). *Theophilus, on Divers Arts*. New York: Dover.
HEALD, A. (forthcoming). 'Rethinking the Early Historic non-ferrous metalworking products, messages and politics' in S. T. Driscoll, J. Geddes, and M. A. Hall (eds.), *'We Know Considerably More about the Picts': Studies of an Early Medieval European Society for the 21st Century*. Northern World Series. Turnhout: Brill.
HINTON, D. A. (2000). *A Smith in Lindsey: The Anglo-Saxon Grave at Tattershall Thorpe, Lincolnshire*. Society for Medieval Archaeology Monograph 16.
JENSEN, S. (1991). *The Vikings of Ribe*. Ribe: Antikvariske Samling.
JONES, M. U. (1980), 'Metallurgical finds from a multi-period settlement at Mucking, Essex', in W. A. Oddy (ed.), *Aspects of Early Metallurgy*. British Museum Occasional Paper 17. London: British Museum, 117–20.
KILMURRY, K. (1980). *The Pottery Industry of Stamford, Lincolnshire, c. A.D. 850–1100*. BAR International Series 84. Oxford: British Archaeological Reports.
LAMM, C. (1980). 'Early medieval metalworking on Helgö in central Sweden', in W. A. Oddy (ed.), *Aspects of Early Metallurgy*. British Museum Occasional Paper 17. London: British Museum, 97–116.
LANE, A., and CAMPBELL, E. (2000). *Dunadd: An Early Dalriadic Capital*. Oxford: Oxbow Books.
LEAHY, K. A. (2003). *Anglo-Saxon Crafts*. Stroud: Tempus.

MACGREGOR, A., and CURREY, J. (1983). 'Mechanical properties as conditioning factors in the bone and antler industry of the 3rd to the 13th century AD'. *Journal of Archaeological Science* 10: 71–7.

—— MAINMAN, A. J., and ROGERS, N. S. H. (1999). *Bone, Antler, Ivory and Horn from Anglo-Scandinavian and Medieval York*. Volume 17, fasc. 12 of *The Archaeology of York*. York: Council for British Archaeology.

MAINMAN, A. J., and ROGERS, N. S. H. (2000). Volume 17, fasc. 14 of *The Archaeology of York*. York: Council for British Archaeology.

MCGRAIL, S. (1980). 'Ships, shipwrights and seamen', in J. Graham-Campbell, *The Viking World*. London: Frances Lincoln, 36–63.

MORRIS, C. A. (1983). 'A late Saxon hoard of iron and copper-alloy artefacts from Nazeing, Essex'. *Medieval Archaeology* 27: 27–39.

—— (2000). *Wood and Woodworking in Anglo-Scandinavian and Medieval York*. Volume 17, fasc. 13 of *The Archaeology of York*. York: Council for British Archaeology.

MOULD, Q., CARLISLE, I., and CAMERON, E. (2003). *Leather and leatherworking in Anglo-Scandinavian and Medieval York*. Volume 17, fasc. 16 of *The Archaeology of York*. York: Council for British Archaeology.

OTTAWAY, P. (1992). *Anglo-Scandinavian Ironwork from Coppergate*. Volume 17, fasc. 6 of *The Archaeology of York*. London: Council for British Archaeology.

RAHTZ, P. A., and MEESON, R. (1992). *An Anglo-Saxon Watermill at Tamworth*. CBA Research Report 83. London: Council for British Archaeology.

ROGERSON, A., and DALLAS, C. (1984). *Excavations in Thetford, 1948–59 and 1973–80*. East Anglian Archaeology 22. Gressenhall.

SALAMAN, R. A. (1986). *Dictionary of Leatherworking Tools, c. 1700–1950*. Revised edition. Mendham, NJ: Astragal Press.

—— (1992). *Dictionary of Woodworking Tools*. Revised edition. Mendham, NJ: Astragal Press.

SPEAKE, G. (1989). *A Saxon Bed Burial on Swallowcliffe Down*. English Heritage Archaeological Report 10. London: English Heritage.

TAYLOR, J., and WEBSTER, L. (1984). 'A late Saxon strap-end mould from Carlisle'. *Medieval Archaeology* 28: 178–81.

WALTON ROGERS, P. (2007). *Cloth and Clothing in Anglo-Saxon England*. CBA Research Report 145. York: Council for British Archaeology.

WEST, S. (1985). *West Stow, the Anglo-Saxon Village*. 2 volumes. Ipswich: Suffolk County Planning Department.

WILLIAMS, D., and VINCE, A. (1997). 'The characterisation and interpretation of early to middle Saxon granitic tempered pottery in England'. *Medieval Archaeology* 41: 214–20.

WILSON, D. M. (1976). 'Craft and industry', in D. M. Wilson (ed.), *The Archaeology of Anglo-Saxon England*. London: Methuen, 253–82.

CHAPTER 25

STYLE: INFLUENCES, CHRONOLOGY, AND MEANING

LESLIE WEBSTER

INTRODUCTION

This chapter examines Anglo-Saxon style from several angles: as part of a complex artistic tradition, and—despite limitations—as a tool in securing the chronological framework for material culture.[1] But as a cultural signifier, style also gives insights into belief systems, into expressions of status and cultural identity, even into religious, political, and economic process. The influences which fuelled the emergence of new styles illuminate the range and complexity of Anglo-Saxon contacts with other peoples and cultures; while analysis of style evolution and usage contributes to our understanding of societal changes over 700 years. In short, style study provides an unexpectedly revealing window onto the Anglo-Saxon world.

---

[1] Throughout the Anglo-Saxon period, the lack of securely dated artefacts means that the dating of Anglo-Saxon style is, to say the least, an inexact science, particularly for the early period, up to *c.* AD 600. With few independently dated artefacts on which to secure the framework, the chronology for this period has relied upon stylistic and morphological comparisons based on independently dated Continental material, which are not universally easy to apply, given the regional complexity seen in the early Anglo-Saxon material (Brugmann 1999; Hines 1999a; 1999b; Welch 1999).

The subject is not without practical difficulties. Closely dated objects are scarce, and surviving evidence is partial: up to the mid seventh century, it consists largely of grave-goods, mainly metalwork, but also funerary pottery, which followed essentially different stylistic traditions (Richards 1987); for the later period there are even greater lacunae. Embroidered textiles, for example, are recorded in wills and other documents from the later Anglo-Saxon period, but only a tiny number survive. Wall paintings are even scarcer (Park 1999); but the most serious gap in the evidence is represented by the paucity of decorated woodwork. It is clear from the prevalence of 'chip-carved' metalwork, and from the rapid flourishing of stone sculpture, that wood-carving was central to the making of an Anglo-Saxon stylistic tradition; yet almost nothing survives, apart from St Cuthbert's coffin and the Cleveland casket (Battiscombe 1956; Backhouse *et al.* 1984: no. 129). Waterlogged deposits containing secular material in Anglo-Scandinavian York hint at what is generally lacking (Webster and Backhouse 1991: no. 253; Morris 2000).

Despite gaps in the evidence, and the great cultural and political transformations which took place, certain recurring themes can be seen, defining a broader 'Anglo-Saxon Style', traceable from the early metalwork to the manuscripts and sculpture of the Christian period. The interplay of word and image seen in later church art, where the text itself can be an image, and an image can carry a complex narrative, draws deeply on a tradition of reading images with embedded meanings, fully familiar to the pagan wearers of decorated jewellery (Magnus 1999: 161–2; Brown 2000: 3; Webster 2005). Ordering perception of the world was central to Anglo-Saxon visual culture, manifested in highly stylized, formulaic vocabularies, in the construction of elaborate frameworks, and in an abiding fondness for tricks and puzzles—visual counterparts to kennings and other riddling structures in the oral traditions of Old English poetry. Motifs drawn from the natural world, especially the animal world, are prominent, often expressing lively, sometimes turbulent, animation. A fascination with busy surfaces, with restless movement and gesture, is an abiding theme, and rich colour forms an important interface between the arts of the fine metalsmith and the manuscript painter (Dodwell 1982: 33–7). And in a post-Roman world, the influence of Roman stylistic tradition is never far away.

This is a complex story, with a correspondingly enormous literature, so a brief survey can only address the main trends. For further (and rewarding!) exploration the reader is referred to the accompanying bibliography.

Beginnings

The earliest Anglo-Saxon settlers, arriving from north Germany and southern Scandinavia in the first half of the fifth century, were well acquainted with the

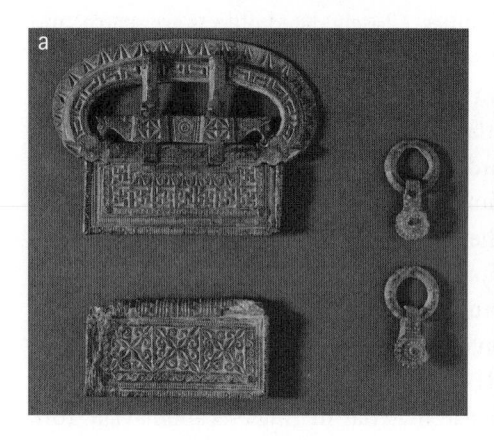

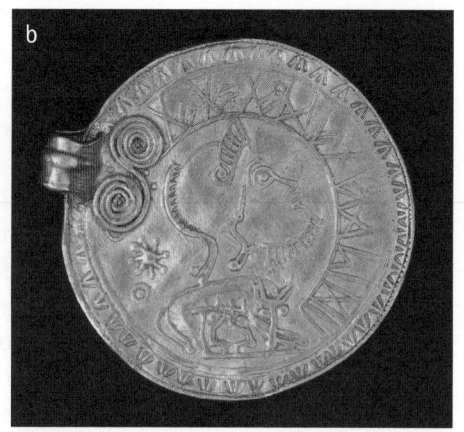

Figure 25.1 Beginnings: (a) Late Roman chip-carved military belt set, Kent: late fourth/early fifth century (reproduced by kind permission of the Trustees of the British Museum); (b) Gold bracteate based on a Roman fourth-century *Urbs Roma* coin, Undley, Suffolk: fifth century (reproduced by kind permission of the Trustees of the British Museum); (c) Roman buckle with deity between monsters: fourth century (After G. Haseloff); (d) Square-headed brooch fragment with deity between monsters, Galsted, Jutland: early fifth century (reproduced by kind permission of the Trustees of the British Museum)

stylistic vocabulary of the late Roman Empire—especially its military metalwork. Some had perhaps served in the Roman army and had received military belt sets decorated in provincial Roman style, marking their status (Hawkes and Dunning 1961; Schön 1999: 94–5) (Fig. 25.1a). Others may have acquired it as booty, or through exchange; some may even have been made by Germanic craftsmen (Inker 2006). Settlers from northern Germany and southern Scandinavia were probably also familiar with Roman prestige gold coinage, *solidi*, and the rarer imperial gold medals, *multipla*. All these had a powerful influence on the imagination of Germanic smiths (Axboe and Kromann 1992; Axboe 2007: 151), who created distinctive regional styles, such as the Scandinavian Sösdala and Nydam Styles, and the Saxon Relief Style which appears on north German brooches (Salin 1904; Haseloff 1981; Inker 2006). Prestige weapons and brooches derived from Roman forms were decorated with transformed versions of imperial images on gold coins and medallions, and of the god-masks, sea-monsters, and geometric ornament on the military buckles (Haseloff 1981: 132–41). On the die-impressed gold disc pendants known as bracteates (Fig. 25.1b), the emperor and his horse were transformed into images of Odin and his attributes (e.g. Axboe 2007: 67–70, 109–11); while apotropaic animal and mask decoration from the belt sets was also adapted to Germanic myth, altering form as well as meaning in the new context (Fig. 25.1c, d). Geometric motifs, such as stars, egg and dart borders, key patterns, and scrollwork, also entered the new repertoire (e.g. Jørgensen *et al.* 2003: 292, 408).

The fifth century: Quoit-Brooch Style

Meanwhile, in Britain in the first half of the fifth century, another style, also derived from late Roman provincial metalwork, had developed in parallel with those of the continental incomers, taking its name from the distinctive quoit brooches on which it occurs. It was inspired not only by the ornament of military buckles, such as the speckled animals on a set from Fallward, north Germany (Schön 1999: 95), but by that on some early-fifth-century prestige jewellery as on a decorated bangle from the Hoxne hoard (Whitfield 1995: 98, fig. 12) (Fig. 25.2a, b). The light engraving and stamping of its simpler manifestations also recall that on some of the fifth-century Roman-style buckles perhaps issued by Romano-British civil authorities, after the Roman garrisons were recalled in *c*.410 (Hawkes and Dunning 1961). The style is characterized by lightly engraved, sometimes partly gilded, geometric decoration, by processional animals, and by human masks (Fig. 25.2c). The animals are coherent individuals, frisky quadrupeds or sea-beasts, often with speckled bodies suggesting fur. Some, as in the paired doves on the finest quoit brooches, are even modelled in three dimensions (Fig. 25.2d). Though

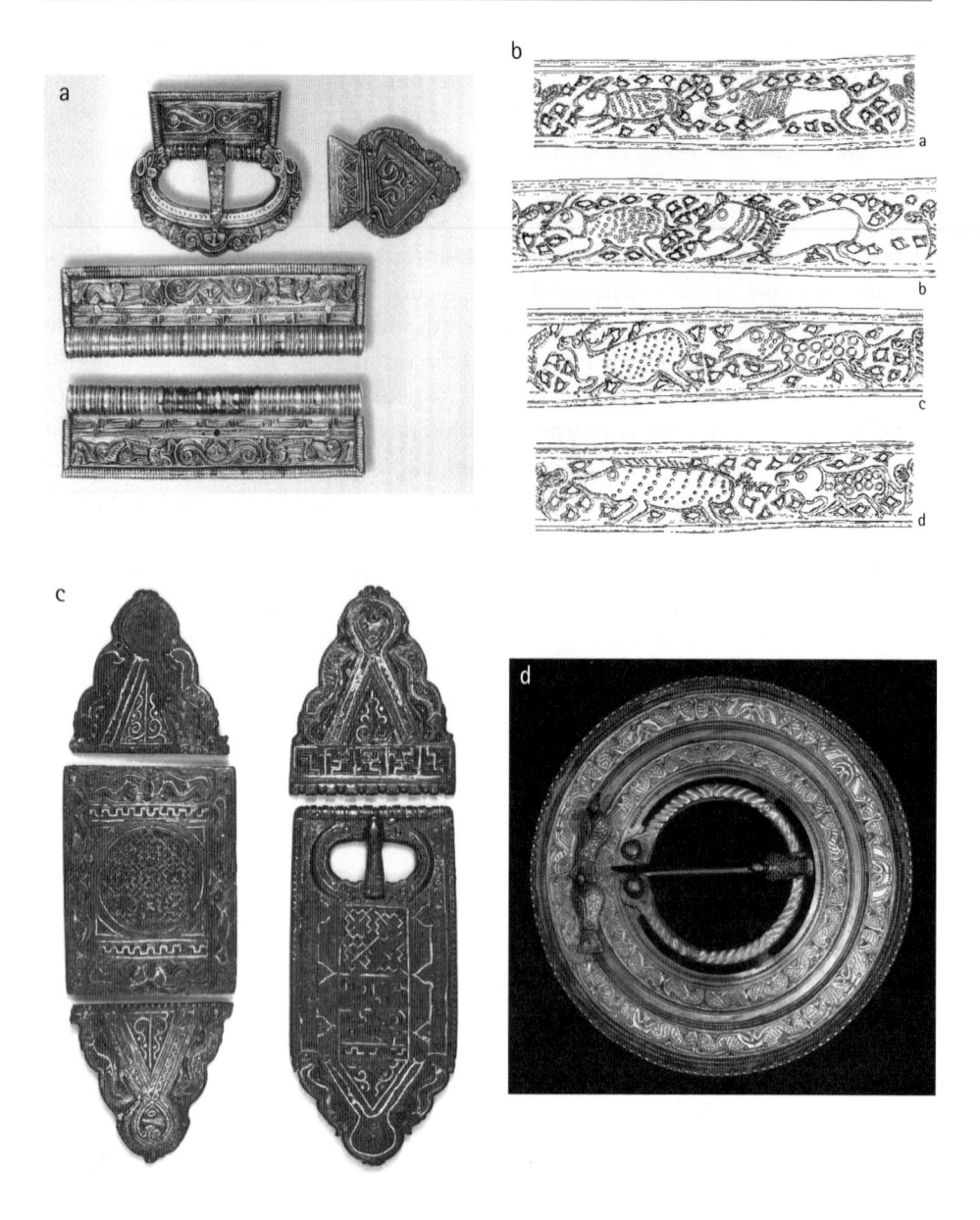

Figure 25.2 The fifth-century Quoit-Brooch style: (a) Roman-style military belt set, Fallward, N. Germany: late fourth/early fifth century (reproduced by kind permission of the Museum Burg Bederkesa, Bad Bederkesa, Germany); (b) Roman gold bracelet with hunt scene, Hoxne, Suffolk: early fifth century (drawing by S. Crummy reproduced by kind permission of the Trustees of the British Museum); (c) Roman-style military belt set, Mucking, Essex, grave 117: early fifth century (reproduced by kind permission of the Trustees of the British Museum); (d) Silver quoit brooch, Sarre, Kent: early fifth century (reproduced by kind permission of the Trustees of the British Museum)

they draw upon a similar Roman vocabulary, the effect is very different from the high-relief chip-carved surfaces and creatures of Germanic metalwork. The forms are different too. None of the objects decorated in this style are of Germanic type; instead, they consist of quoit brooches and other brooch types of non-Germanic form, military-style buckles and belt fittings of late Roman type, as well as tear-shaped pendants and occasional decorative mounts from weapons (Evison 1965; Suzuki 2000).

For whom and by whom this fine metalwork was produced in the early part of the fifth century has been much discussed. The style itself has in the past been argued to have Gallo-Roman, Jutish, or Frankish origins (Leeds 1936: 3–7; Hawkes 1961; Evison 1965), but consensus now favours production within its predominantly south-eastern distribution zone, in a British milieu creating indigenous versions of late Roman metalwork (Ager 1985). Its social significance, however, remains debatable. That the items bearing it occur with Anglo-Saxon objects in burials does not mean that all were worn by, and/or buried with, Anglo-Saxons, merely that furnished inhumation had been adopted by their high-status owners in the mid to later fifth century; they may have wished to articulate a particular identity, perhaps British, or possibly a relationship between incomers and surviving British elites—through marriage, for example, or as Germanic mercenaries (Hills 2003: 95–9; Loveluck and Laing, this volume). It remains of course possible that objects in this style were simply produced by local craftsmen for the elite of both populations.

THE FIFTH CENTURY: SAXON RELIEF STYLE

The first unquestionably Germanic style to appear in England, overlapping with the relatively short lifespan of the Quoit-Brooch Style, is the Saxon Relief Style, recently discussed by Inker (2006). This emerged amongst the Saxons of North Germany in the early fifth century, appearing on brooches of the region, notably *Stutzarmfibeln*, and equal-armed and saucer brooches; examples of all these occur in Anglo-Saxon graves, though decorated examples of the first are uncommon. Angled cutting, or 'chip-carving', of the models from which the moulds were made is central to this style, in which geometric motifs and semi-naturalistic animals drawn from Roman metalwork form the principal elements. Chip-carving is in origin a wood-carving technique, seen most spectacularly in richly decorated wooden artefacts preserved in early-fifth-century burials at Fallward, Lower Saxony, where Roman-derived geometric motifs decorate elaborate containers and furniture, including a remarkable ceremonial chair (Schön 1999) (Fig. 25.3a). In gilded metalwork, its many facets distract the eye with reflective, glittering surfaces.

Figure 25.3 The fifth-century Saxon Relief Style: (a) Wooden ceremonial chair, Fallward, N. Germany: late fourth/early fifth century (reproduced by kind permission of the Museum Burg Bederkesa, Bad Bederkesa, Germany); (b) Equal-armed brooch, Haslingfield, Cambs.: fifth century (after V. I. Evison); (c) Saucer brooch with spiral ornament, Mucking, Essex, grave 639: late fifth century (reproduced by kind permission of the Trustees of the British Museum)

Inker associates this style, through its relationship to military metalwork, with warrior culture, and has argued that the brooches worn by women may have represented shields, complementing the men's Roman-style belt sets, and reflecting their military rank (Inker 2006: 77, 81). The various forms of equal-armed brooch which occur in England, the most elaborate with scroll ornament and crouching animals, did not outlast the fifth century, and none is decorated with Style 1 animal ornament (Fig. 25.3b). The Saxon Relief Style continued on the long-lived saucer brooches, especially in their cast form, with some geometric motifs continuing into the sixth century, when they were progressively superseded by Style 1 zoomorphic ornament (Fig. 25.3c).

THE LATER FIFTH AND SIXTH CENTURIES: STYLE 1

Eclipsing both the Quoit-Brooch Style and the Saxon Relief Style towards the end of the fifth century, the style most closely identified with a developing Anglo-Saxon cultural identity in the sixth century is Style 1, first identified and discussed by Scandinavian archaeologists (e.g. Salin 1904; Åberg 1922; 1924; Holmqvist 1955). A complete account of Anglo-Saxon Style 1 has yet to be written. Haseloff's magisterial analysis (1981) demonstrated its continental origins and development, while recent studies by Leigh (1980; 1984) and Dickinson (1999; 2002; 2005; 2007; 2009) have transformed our understanding of its construction and meaning.

Style 1 grew out of the Nydam Style in southern Scandinavia during the mid fifth century, and seems to have reached south-east England shortly after, probably via square-headed brooches of south Scandinavian type and gold foil bracteates rather than directly through Nydam Style imports such as bow brooches, only two possible examples of which have been found in England (Welch 1999: 36, fig. 1; Richardson 2008). Like its Scandinavian models, the Anglo-Saxon version is centred on animal motifs, though scroll work and other geometric patterns also contribute to the repertoire. Haseloff identified four main phases of Style 1, all overlapping to some degree (1981: 174–216). Naturalistic images drawn from late Roman human and zoomorphic ornament are progressively deconstructed into formulaic assemblages of individual body parts, whose nature may only be understood through knowledge and careful interrogation. The effect is often chaotic, but under even the apparently most random assemblage of heads and limbs, there usually lies an embedded grammar enabling decipherment (Dickinson 1999; 2002; 2005; 2007; 2009)

(Fig. 25.4a). Disordered images conceal a deeper order. This is a cosmological arena where beasts and animal-men tangle in iconic oppositions, and ambiguous shape-shifters morph from animal into human in one and the same image, read differently according to their orientation (Leigh 1984; Haseloff 1981: 452–4; Webster 2003a: figs. 3, 5). Semi-naturalistic animal images are rare in the repertoire, complete human figures even more so; this could reflect the lack of wood-carving, however, as birds of prey and other predatory creatures from sixth-century shield decoration (Dickinson 2005), and the unique three-dimensional figure enthroned on a cremation urn from Norfolk (Hills 1987: fig. 53), suggest that more realistic images may in fact have played a significant part in the stylistic vocabulary. Defining the elaborate ornament of prestige brooches and other high-status metalwork, frameworks are used to contain and control design fields, drawing the eye, and giving structure to the whole (Webster 2003a: 14–15).

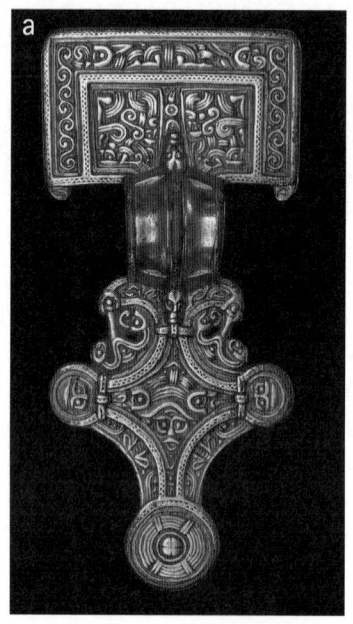

Figure 25.4 The later fifth and sixth centuries: Style 1. (a) Silver square-headed brooch, Chessel Down, Isle of Wight: early sixth century; (b) Gilded bronze buckle with garnet inlay, Howletts, Kent: early sixth century; (c) Gilded bronze cruciform brooch, Sleaford, Lincs.: later sixth century; (d) Silver rim-mount from a drinking horn (detail): Taplow, Bucks., early sixth century (all reproduced by kind permission of the Trustees of the British Museum)

Figure 25.4 Continued

Anglo-Saxon Style 1 first appears in Kent, which had strong early links with Jutland; Haseloff's Phase A zoomorphic vocabulary of Jutlandic square-headed brooches and the man/beast dynamic of C-type bracteates shaped its local development in the late fifth and early sixth centuries (Haseloff 1981; Dickinson 2007). The style quickly spread beyond Kent, initially through high-level gift-giving and exchange, as may be suggested by the early-sixth-century Kentish drinking-horn mounts from the princely burial of c.600–610 at Taplow, Buckinghamshire (Webster 2007), and similar vessel mounts from a coin-dated burial at Carisbrooke Castle, Isle of Wight (Webster 1999, 2008; Dickinson 1999). At the same time, a distinctive Kentish Style 1 developed: more elliptical and more fluid than other regional versions, and making bold use of the polychrome contrasts of silver, garnets, and niello (a black silver/copper sulphide) in the Frankish manner, it defines Kentish female and male dress accessories towards the middle of the sixth century (Brugmann 1999) (Fig. 25.4b). The polychrome style identified with this rich and increasingly powerful kingdom, and its satellite, the Isle of Wight, is quite different from, for example, the restrained, largely geometric, decoration of great square-headed brooches from East Anglia (Hines 1997), from the zoned Style 1 of the Thames valley saucer brooches (Dickinson 1993), and from the chaotic zoomorphs of the 'florid' cruciform brooches of late sixth-century Anglian England (Leeds and Pocock 1971) (Fig. 25.4c). Clearly, Style 1 played a part in expressing local cultural identity, in which the emergence of regional polities in the course of the sixth century may be reflected.

It could also carry other ideological meaning, as recent approaches to Scandinavian and Anglo-Saxon material have suggested. Hauck and others (e.g. Hauck 1970; 1978; 1986; Axboe 2007) have convincingly argued for a mythic interpretation of the iconography of the gold bracteates, which are closely linked to other forms of Style 1: here human and man-beast images represent not mortal men, but gods; and these, with the attendant animals which both protect and threaten, also symbolize man's relationship with the supernatural world, a source of protection, but also of danger. This has been extended into discussion of the ornament on high-status brooches and elite male gear, such as buckles, weapons, shield-mounts, horse-trappings, and drinking vessels (Magnus 1997; 1999; Hedeager 1999a; 1999b; Dickinson 2002; 2005; 2007) (Fig. 25.4d). Such artefacts are texts; their apotropaic images may also represent origin myths, signalling not just social identity, but where power came from. At elite levels, it has been argued, such objects, decorated in the most extended and complex versions of Style 1, may have been worn or used in cultic and ceremonial contexts, reinforcing authority and its social structures (Magnus 1999; Dickinson 2007).

THE LATER SIXTH AND SEVENTH CENTURIES: STYLE 2

In some areas, Style 1 continued up to and beyond 600, but already in the later sixth century—perhaps as early as the 570s—its lineal descendant, Style 2, had arrived in

Kent. Its detailed chronology in England lacks refinement, but will be more firmly grounded by the current modelling programme based on high-precision radiocarbon dating of furnished burials, which promises a more secure chronology for the late sixth to eighth centuries (Scull and Bayliss 1999). Like Style 1, it appears to have originated in southern Scandinavia some time after the mid sixth century, spreading subsequently to other Germanic peoples, including the Anglo-Saxons (Speake 1980; Høilund Nielsen 1999a; 1999b). In England, it continued to develop throughout the seventh century, eventually feeding into the art of the Christian church.

Høilund Nielsen (1999a) argued for two main streams within the English material, basing her conclusions on computer seriations of selected individual motifs—an Anglian stream developing directly from Scandinavian Style 2, and a Kentish stream which derives from Frankish versions, themselves ultimately dependent on Scandinavian models. As she emphasized, this was a preliminary survey, likely to need adjustments as the growing volume of new finds alters the quantity, distribution, and range of Style 2 artefacts;[2] nevertheless, it currently provides a useful basis for understanding the origins and development of this influential style in England.

Common to both streams is a new emphasis on symmetrical, regularly interlacing decoration, based on animals which are articulated in a more immediately coherent and legible manner than their Style 1 ancestors. Whether the decoration is executed in gold wire, in die-impressed foils, in cast metalwork, or most spectacularly in garnet-inlaid cloisonné work, there is a consistent grammar and vocabulary of long-jawed snake-bodied creatures, some backward-turning, and interlacing pairs or processions (Haseloff 1981: 647–50). The beaked heads of birds of prey are more prominent than in Style 1, but man-beasts are absent. Gold seems to have played a significant part in the genesis and development of the style. Prominent among sixth-century Scandinavian precursors of Style 2 are gold beaded-wire scabbard fittings with symmetrically interlacing animals (e.g. Speake 1980: 53; Haseloff 1981: 246–59); while the augmented availability of gold coins in the later sixth and early seventh centuries, particularly in Kent (Blackburn, this volume; and for their use in jewellery, S. C. Hawkes *et al.* 1966; Brown and Schweizer 1973), seems linked to the rapid success of the style in England. Gold's ductility lends itself very readily to the construction of sinuous interlace designs in beaded wire, and the primacy of this technique is demonstrated by the fact that Style 2 on metal foils and cast artefacts often copies the appearance of beaded-wire decoration.

---

[2] Høilund-Nielsen's seriations have produced some anomalies, particularly with the 'Anglian' material, the statistical significance of which may be clarified as more data become available for analysis. Some of these high-quality 'Anglian' artefacts have Kentish or southern English provenances; does this mean that such things were widely exported, or is a more complex production scenario indicated? And at the heartland of Anglian Style 2, Sutton Hoo, a very clear Frankish connection is visible in the ornament of the great gold buckle.

As this suggests, Style 2, at least initially, is also a style made for elites, appearing on Frankish-derived buckles and disc brooches, at first in Kent. The gold buckle and clasps from the princely burial of c.600–10 at Taplow, overlooking the Thames on the Chiltern edge, show how Kentish Style 2 soon spread (Fig. 25.5a). The awkward beaded-wire animal on the buckle lacks the fluency of the interlacing filigree creatures on the clasps, arguably the latest objects in the burial. The buckle's Frankish form, with its kidney-shaped loop and coarse cloisonné work, the jerky animal ornament, and evident wear, suggest a manufacture date as early as the 570s. The presence of these princely Kentish artefacts, along with several other Kentish-style prestige objects in the burial, suggests a powerful Kentish political interest extending west of London (Webster 1999).

Power politics, and the linked spread of Christianity from Kentish-based missions, assisted the wider diffusion of Kentish-type Style 2 via prestige metalwork. The Anglian version (Speake 1980; Høilund Nielsen 1999a), seen particularly in Suffolk, Norfolk, and Lincolnshire, probably emerged c.600. It is inevitably dominated by the stupendous jewellery from Sutton Hoo Mound 1, with its virtuoso displays of polychrome garnet and millefiori cloisonné work, its elaborate riddles of interlacing creatures, and its mythical emblems of men and monsters (Fig. 25.5b). This unquestionably royal jewellery is clearly in a league of its own, compared with most Anglian Style 2 metalwork and even with surviving high-class jewellery from Kent. Nevertheless, there is a clear kinship between the style of this metalwork, probably produced by internationally peripatetic goldsmiths, and lesser versions, such as the wreathed snakes on the garnet-inlaid pendant from Bacton, interlacing creatures on dies from Icklingham, and processional animals on mounts from Bamburgh, Caenby, and a number of cast harness fittings from the Anglian regions (Speake 1980: fig. 15b; Webster and Backhouse 1991: nos. 39, 40, 45). Filigree ornament is less prominent here, and complex garnet inlays more common, than in Kentish Style 2. The interlocked, long-jawed, labyrinthine creatures, often with distinctive lentoid eyes and marked contouring, and with 'heads and limbs . . . so far apart that it may be some time before one discovers how they connect' (Nordenfalk 1977:17), were to have a particularly visible influence on the decoration of the earliest Northumbrian manuscripts, discussed below.

The social dynamics of Style 2 are similar to those of its precursor (Høilund Nielsen 1999b; Hedeager 1999a). Like Style 1, it can clearly carry meaning which signals both identity and protection, whether religious—as in an extraordinary garnet-inlaid sword pommel from Ludlow (Webster 2005: 32, fig. 7, a, b)—or political, as in the Sutton Hoo Mound 1 burial, where the style articulates a new iconography of *Romanitas* and Scandinavian origin myth—a particularly potent mixture for a competitive seventh-century Anglo-Saxon king (Webster 1992; Filmer-Sankey 1996). Humbler items, such as the gold pendants which replaced the bracteates in Kent, also suggest that the protective power of zoomorphic motifs had not yet died (Speake 1980: 85–92; Webster and Backhouse 1991: no. 8) (Fig. 25.5c);

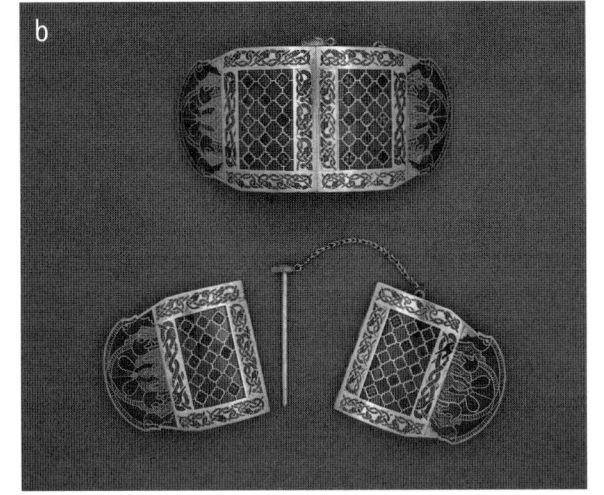

Figure 25.5 The later sixth and seventh centuries: Style 2. (a) Gold buckle with garnet and glass inlays, Taplow, Bucks.: later sixth century; (b) Gold clasps with garnet and millefiori glass inlay, Sutton Hoo, Suffolk, Mound 1: first quarter of seventh century; (c) Gold pendant with birds of prey motif, Dover, Kent, grave 29: first quarter of seventh century; (d) Gilded silver male figure, Carlton Colville, Suffolk: first half of seventh century (all reproduced by kind permission of the Trustees of the British Museum)

indeed, there is sometimes a degree of assimilation with Christian iconography, as the long-jawed intertwining creatures which guard the seventh-century sculptured entrance to Benedict Biscop's monastery church at Wearmouth seem to suggest. Liminal depictions of intertwining beasts are seen elsewhere in early medieval Christian contexts—e.g. on the steps of the remarkable sixth-century hypogeum at Poitiers—but the Wearmouth beasts clearly reveal a Style 2 ancestry (Bailey 1996: fig. 38, pl. 16; Flammin 2004).

Perhaps in reaction to the new Christian religion, it is at this period that semi-naturalistic depiction of the human figure, in what appear to be specifically pagan mythic contexts, resurfaces (Fig. 25.5d). The semi-naked dancer in a horned headdress on a seventh-century buckle from Finglesham, the uncanny miniature deities from Carlton Colville, Suffolk, and elsewhere, and of course the extended figural narrative of the Sutton Hoo helmet, all suggest another stylistic dimension to Anglo-Saxon art which may have been prominent in perishable media such as wood; only a very few survivals, such as a bone plaque from Southampton, carved with Anglian Style 2 animals, hint at this lost body of art (Hawkes and Grainger 2006: fig. 2.102; Webster 2002; Geake 2007: 224–7; Webster and Backhouse 1991: no. 44).

The later seventh and eighth centuries: Christian art, new influences and directions

The progress of Christianity throughout England in the seventh century brought about radical cultural transformations. The new church needed scholars to instruct its monks and clergy, along with bibles and other religious books; making manuscripts was a paramount task (see Gameson, this volume). The churchmen and scholars who came from Italy, and even further afield, brought new influences from Gaul, Rome, and Byzantium into the Anglo-Saxon stylistic repertoire. The new stone-built monasteries at Wearmouth/Jarrow were furnished with sculptures directly inspired by Mediterranean models, and skilled glaziers from Gaul made coloured window glass (Cramp 1986); painted narrative icons from Italy, as well as manuscripts such as the St Augustine Gospels and other models from the Mediterranean world of late antiquity, were to provide a transforming inspiration to Anglo-Saxon craftsmen (Webster and Backhouse 1991: no. 1).

The Mediterranean was not the only direction from which new ideas came: the influence of Christian missions from Ireland and their outpost on Iona was equally strong, particularly in Northumbria, but also in East Anglia and Mercia. Through missionary activity and monastic foundations in Gaul and Italy itself, Irish Christianity also had its own particular relationship with classicizing traditions of manuscript making, and of decoration. The distinctive style that characterizes some of the finest surviving late-seventh- and eighth-century manuscripts shows a bold assimilation of Anglo-Saxon, Mediterranean, and Celtic models (Nordenfalk 1977), very different from the overtly classicizing style of manuscripts and sculpture produced in centres of Roman Christianity, such as Jarrow and Wearmouth. After the Synod of Whitby in 664, the activity of the Celtic church was checked; but Irish cultural influences remained very powerful.

The resulting style is usually called Hiberno-Saxon, but the more neutral term 'Insular' is also used, since attribution to a particular centre, or even a country, is sometimes contentious. The oldest surviving Insular gospel book, the Book of Durrow, has been variously ascribed to Ireland, Northumbria, and Iona, and dated over an equally broad range, though most scholars now date it to between 650 and 700 (Nordenfalk 1977: 34–47; Alexander 1978: no.6; Backhouse 1981: 36; Brown 2003: 47–8) (Fig. 25.6a). It displays many of the stylistic conventions which characterize the more elaborate manuscripts of this type: decorated initials, and densely patterned 'carpet' pages, derived from eastern Early Christian models, with outer frames mostly of broad interlace, surrounding elaborate inner panels, all but one of which contain elements in the shape of the Cross. Ribbon interlace of late-antique derivation is accompanied by grid and geometric patterns based on Anglo-Saxon cloisonné cellwork, by Celtic curvilinear trumpet and hair-spring spiral motifs, and most strikingly on one page by processions of interlacing long-jawed creatures which in their carefully framed body parts, as well as in their overall design, proclaim close kinship to Anglian Style 2 metalwork models. The influence of inlaid metalwork is also prominent in the Eagle and Man evangelist symbols, contained in cell-like frames and with chequer patterns reminiscent of millefiori inlays like those on the Sutton Hoo clasps.

The later Insular manuscripts, with their larger, more elaborate illuminated pages, build upon and extend this programme, and add to it elaborately decorated canon tables. The developed style comprises a tumultuous menagerie of birds, dogs, and other creatures, minutely detailed Celtic spiral ornament, cellwork grids, and meticulous interlace, all carefully framed. But this exquisite ornament is more than aesthetically pleasing; it carries a profound spiritual message. The harmonious complexity of the carpet pages, canon tables, and great decorated initials presents subtle and structured images of a divinely ordered world, emphasized by repeated cross motifs, and the great Chi-Rho initials which mark the account of Christ's incarnation (Fig. 25.6b). These were images designed for close contemplation and interpretation, alongside the texts they accompany.

The most magnificent of this series is the Lindisfarne Gospels, probably made in commemoration of the translation of the relics of St Cuthbert at Lindisfarne in 698 (Alexander 1978: no. 9; Backhouse 1981; Brown 2003). It introduces evangelist portraits derived from early Christian models, but the flattened rhythmical patterns of the drapery and hair are far from the naturalistic conventions of late antiquity (Fig. 25.6c, left). No physical bodies underlie these flat brightly-coloured garments; the elaborately framed and patterned figures are, like the carpet pages and the great decorated initials, images of a spiritual truth. Similar figures appear on the Genoels Elderen, Belgium, ivory diptych, sometimes regarded as Northumbrian; and even more stylized versions occur in other Insular manuscripts, such as a Durham gospel-book and the Lichfield Gospels (Alexander 1978: nos. 10, 21; Webster and Backhouse 1991: no. 141).

However, late antique models were followed to very different effect elsewhere. The *Codex Amiatinus* is one of three complete bibles written under Abbot Ceolfrith's direction at Wearmouth/Jarrow, and was taken by him to Rome in 716 (Bruce-Mitford 1969; Alexander 1978: no. 7). So faithful is it to its sixth-century Italian model, Cassiodorus' *Codex Grandior*, that it was not recognized as Anglo-Saxon until the late nineteenth century (Meyvaert 1996; O'Reilly 2001). The manuscript has almost no hint of Insular style in it, and stands quite apart from the Hiberno-Saxon tradition, as a comparison of the *Amiatinus* image of the prophet Ezra with that of the St Matthew portrait in the Lindisfarne Gospels clearly shows (Fig. 25.6c). Though they had similar exemplars, the two are stylistically quite different: the naturalistically modelled Ezra figure writes in a spatially visualized library, quite unlike Lindisfarne's flattened Matthew image, pasted into a void (Backhouse 1981: 40, 83–4).

Because relatively few decorated manuscripts survive from this period, our understanding of stylistic variation is inevitably partial; but in the much more plentiful surviving sculpture we see a different aspect of the powerful stylistic influence of early Christian models.[3] From such sources came naturalistic figural and animal images, and the dominant motif of the fruiting vine, often inhabited by men, birds, and other creatures, which are typical of much pre-Viking sculpture in the North—whether architectural, or in the form of free-standing crosses, such as those at Bewcastle, Cumbria, and Ruthwell, Dumfriesshire (J. Hawkes 2003). The vine motif refers to Christ's words in John 15: 1–8, 'I am the true vine'; in this image, the creatures which inhabit it represent the faithful dwelling in Christ. Though very different in style, the profusely scrolling foliage and its symbiotic life-forms reflect the same focus on the interaction of natural and supernatural worlds seen in the carpet pages of Northumbrian manuscripts—something deeply ingrained in Anglo-Saxon visual culture, back even to the interplay of gods, animals, and men that is Style 1.

The naturalistic presentation of the human image is seen most spectacularly in the eighth-century Ruthwell Cross (Fig. 25.6d). This remarkable monument also deploys script and text in specific ways: its vinescroll decoration is framed by a poetic meditation on the Crucifixion, written in Old English and in runes; while

---

[3] The volume and variety of Anglo-Saxon sculpture is such that this chapter can only discuss a few key examples. The reader is referred to the excellent regional survey volumes published by the *Corpus of Anglo-Saxon Stone Sculpture*, overseen by Professor Rosemary Cramp. Amongst many valuable recent publications, her own insightful contributions to the subject are essential reading, as are also those of Richard Bailey and Jane Hawkes, who have particularly illuminated our understanding of the iconography of this large and complex body of material; see individual entries in the bibliography.

Figure 25.6 The later seventh and eighth centuries: Christian art, new influences and directions. (a) The Book of Durrow, carpet page with animal processions: mid/late seventh century (reproduced by kind permission of Trinity College Library, Dublin); (b) The Lindisfarne Gospels, Chi-Rho initial: early eighth century (reproduced by kind permission of the British Library, London); (c) Lindisfarne Gospels, St Matthew, and *Codex Amiatinus*, Ezra: early eighth century (after R. L. S. Bruce-Mitford); (d) The Ruthwell Cross; Christ adored by beasts: first half of the eighth century (photograph by D. Wright)

Figure 25.6 Continued

the sides with Christological figural narratives carry scriptural texts in Latin and the Roman alphabet (Bailey 1996: 61–9).

Subtle interplay of word and image, derived from early Christian art, also appears in the elaborate display scripts of Insular gospel-books, and in the eighth-century Northumbrian whale-bone box known as the Franks Casket, with its unique combination of scenes from Christian, classical, and Germanic tradition (Webster 1999; Neuman de Vegvar 2008). The crowded images are framed by carefully arranged texts, mostly in runes, some of them riddling or encrypted; images and texts are evidently intended to be read in more than one way. Though far from classical in its simplified figural style, the decorative programme of the box is closely modelled on an early Christian reliquary casket similar to the fourth-century Brescia *lipsanothek* with its juxtaposition of Old and New Testament scenes, an object type which might have entered England in the later seventh or early eighth century. Its message is a Christian one, probably intended for a royal owner, in which stories of a Germanic mythic past, the fall of Jerusalem, and the foundation of Rome, tell a greater Christian message about good and bad rule in a divinely ordered world, where salvation comes through Christ. In this ambitious and complex object, the creative interaction of northern pagan tradition and Roman Christianity, which fuelled the art and culture of the seventh and eighth centuries, comes graphically alive.

The eighth century: the emergence of a Mercian Style

The influence of the Hiberno-Saxon Style continues not only in Northumbria—for example, in the zoomorphic decoration of the later-eighth-century York helmet (Tweddle 1992)—but further afield, in sculpture from Lincolnshire, south-western Mercia, and Wessex, lasting into the early ninth century (Bailey 2002: 20; Cramp 2006: 41–58). But as the fortunes of Northumbria declined in the eighth century, the ascendant kingdom of Mercia became a new focus of artistic innovation, as it came to dominate much of England south of the Humber. Manuscripts such as the Vespasian Psalter and the Stockholm *Codex Aureus*, both probably made in Canterbury around the mid eighth century, show a new, confident use of Italo-Byzantine models in their figural scenes, and in the use of gold to embellish the page (Alexander 1978: nos. 29, 30; Webster and Backhouse 1991: nos. 153, 154). A new kind of animal style also begins to appear in these manuscripts, finding its mature expression in the engagingly quirky creatures seen in the later-eighth-century Barberini Gospels (Alexander 1978: no. 36; Farr 2000) (Fig. 25.7a). This manuscript, with its skilfully modelled naturalistic evangelist portraits, was probably made at *Medeshamstede* (Peterborough), a major ecclesiastical foundation. Its sprightly animal ornament has close stylistic links with manuscripts of the slightly later Tiberius group (Brown 2001), and with metalwork, sculpture, and bone carving of the period.

At much the same time, a new figural style emerges in the church sculpture of the Mercian supremacy, again influenced by Italo-Byzantine exemplars, including textiles and ivories as well as manuscripts. Elegant, light-footed holy figures with floating draperies, framed in slender arcading, appear in architectural sculpture, particularly in the east Midlands, e.g. at Breedon, Castor, and Fletton, while centaurs, chimeras, and other classical motifs invade the inhabited vinescroll friezes (Cramp 1977; Jewell 1986; 2001; Plunkett 1998). A recent discovery shows how crisply carved and colourful such sculpture once was: a painted archangel from an annunciation scene was found during excavations in Lichfield Cathedral, Staffordshire, a Mercian royal and ecclesiastical centre (Fig. 25.7b). The sculpture probably came from the shrine of St Chad, Lichfield's first bishop, and dates to c.800 (Rodwell et al. 2008). Exceptionally well-preserved, its subtly modulated palette of red, yellow, black, and white gives a rare insight into the colourful appearance of church interiors in this period, also seen in Deerhurst church, Gloucestershire (Gem and Howe 2008).

Closely related to manuscript ornament, a distinctive style of animal decoration characterizes sculpture and metalwork from the Mercian area, typified by the vigorously confronted beasts, tongues lolling from their sharply toothed jaws, wings pricked up, and tails twirling into knots, on the cross shaft from Elstow, Bedfordshire (Cramp 1977; Jewell 2001). The style has many variants, but a common theme is that of sprightly speckled animals, splayed or rampant, enmeshed in fine looping interlace (Bakka 1963; Webster 2001a; 2001b). It is the dominant ornament of the secular metalwork of the Mercian supremacy, such as the brooches and pins from high-status sites at Brandon, Suffolk, and Flixborough, Lincolnshire, and on the paired large disc brooches from a jeweller's hoard at Pentney, Norfolk (Webster and Backhouse 1991: nos. 66, 69, 187). Recent work by Gannon (2003) has also drawn attention to its significant role on royal and ecclesiastical eighth-century coinage. However, the most extraordinary versions are associated with elite weapons, such as the sword fittings from Fetter Lane, London (Fig. 25.7c), and from near Beckley, Oxfordshire, or the scabbard chapes and pommel from St. Ninian's Isle (Webster and Backhouse 1991: nos. 173, 177, 178; Webster 2001b: 272–3). In their repertory of artfully constructed, gaping-jawed creatures, some reduced to mere ellipses, or engulfed in thickets of foliage and interlace, there is an esoteric flamboyance which suggests the confidence and authority of those who knew how to read, as well as to wear, such strikingly hermeneutic decoration.

The decoration of this secular metalwork clearly owes something to the Anglo-Saxon riddling zoomorphic tradition. But that of the surviving ecclesiastical metalwork from this period—and a rare survival of embroidered church textile, now in Maaseik, Belgium (Budny and Tweddle 1985)—follows its Mediterranean

Figure 25.7 The eighth century: the emergence of a Mercian style. (a) The Barberini Gospels, opening of St John's Gospel: later eighth century (reproduced by kind permission of the Biblioteca Apostolica Vaticana, Rome); (b) Angel of the Annunciation, from a shrine, Lichfield Cathedral: late eighth century (reproduced by kind permission of the Dean and Chapter, Lichfield Cathedral); (c) Silver sword hilt, Fetter Lane, London: late eighth century (reproduced by kind permission of the Trustees of the British Museum); (d) Gilded copper chrismatory: later eighth century (in private possession); (e) The Gandersheim (Braunschweig) Casket: late eighth century (reproduced by kind permission of the Herzog Anton Ulrichsmuseum, Braunschweig, Germany)

Figure 25.7 Continued

models more closely. It shares many stylistic traits with the manuscripts and sculpture; in particular a springy, open version of the vine-scroll, inhabited by quirky quadrupeds and birds, is characteristic of a number of fine pieces of ecclesiastical metalwork taken or made abroad by eighth-century Anglo-Saxon missionaries. The ornament on the great altar cross from Bischofshofen, Salzburg, and a recently recognized Anglo-Saxon house-shaped chrismatory with Christological images (Fig. 25.7d) is paralleled in the liturgical bowl from a Viking grave at Ormside, Cumbria (Webster and Backhouse 1991: nos. 133, 134; Fogg 2007: 16). Their lively and subtle decoration, sometimes with vine shrubs springing up from chalices, incorporates Eucharistic and baptismal symbols; the iconographic complexity of some of this ornament is exemplified by the Gandersheim Casket, a whale-bone chrismatory which probably reached Germany during the tenth century (Marth 2000) (Fig. 25.7e). This delicately carved container, closely related in style to the Barberini Gospels, was probably made at Peterborough, where it has close sculptural parallels; its form and decoration evoke a remarkable cosmological geometry (Bailey 2000; Pape 2000, especially 20–1). Its gallery of sprightly winged and crawling creatures includes birds, quadrupeds, and lizards, symbolizing the three orders of living things created by God, while its mathematically proportioned construction and decorative programme, based on grids of twelve, allude to the perfection of Creation, in which the numbers 6 and 12 carry cosmological significance. Alongside this, the inhabited vine decoration and the subtly concealed crosses on the lid refer to Christ's sacrifice; the whole a symbol of divine creation redeemed in Christ (Elbern 2000; Webster 2000). This is Mercian Style at its most elegant and subtle.

The ninth century: the rise of Wessex and the innovations of Alfred's reign

The end of the eighth century witnessed the first recorded Viking raids on England's coasts; these rapidly escalated into the grinding wars which dominated the following century, with devastating effect (e.g. Dodwell 1982: 8–10). The manuscripts, ecclesiastical metalwork, and sculpture which survive from this period are few indeed, placing a disproportionate emphasis on secular metalwork as an indicator of stylistic developments. Nevertheless, metalwork is plentiful, and more widespread than in the previous century, and not just because more hoards were buried—despite the disruptions, coin and 'prolific site' finds indicate an active economy and thriving market for secular metalwork (Pestell and Ulmschneider 2003; Pestell, this volume).

The ubiquitous Trewhiddle Style, which decorates so much personal metalwork from this time, is named after a mixed hoard of secular and religious metalwork and coins buried c.868 in a remote part of Cornwall, perhaps in reaction to Viking attacks in the south-west. The style's origins, however, lie in the Mercian animal style, as the freshly manufactured silver brooches from the Pentney hoard, dating to the first third of the ninth century, suggest; the largest brooch is a fine example of early Trewhiddle Style, deposited alongside paired brooches decorated in late Mercian Style (Webster and Backhouse 1991: no. 187) (Fig. 25.8a). Metalwork in this style occurs throughout England, and regional variations in both form and decoration are increasingly recognized (Webster and Backhouse 1991: 268–83; Thomas 2006). Simple monochromatic contrast is used to good effect: animal, foliage, or geometric ornament is carved in the metal base, and its background filled with a contrasting inlay of niello. Usually, the ornament is divided by beaded frames into many small panels or fields, to emphasize individual motifs—typically, animated creatures with notched and speckled bodies. Similar beasts occur in manuscripts of the Tiberius group, such as the Tiberius Bede, and the Royal Bible, dated to c.820–40 (Fig. 25.8b); in their initials and canon table arcading, panels of tiny pale creatures cavort against black backgrounds in direct imitation of metalwork (Alexander 1978: nos. 33, 32; Wilson 1984: 94-6; Webster and Backhouse 1991: nos. 170, 171).

The Wessex kings who eclipsed those of Mercia in the ninth century had, like them, close contacts with Carolingian Francia, and with Rome (Keynes 1997). In 856 King Æthelwulf, a generous donor to the favoured royal shrine at St Denis outside Paris, as well as to Rome, sealed his close relationship with the emperor by his marriage in 856 to Judith, daughter of Charles the Bald; it is thus no surprise that the influence of Carolingian culture, and especially court art, became important during the middle years of the ninth century, even if little beyond metalwork survives to illustrate this. A few pieces of high-quality Carolingian metalwork found in England, with characteristic acanthus leaf or figural ornament, reflect these contacts, such as the panels on one side of the Winchester reliquary and the fine silver belt-fitting found outside the Alfredian burh at Wareham, Dorset, to which might be added the newly discovered bowl from the Vale of York hoard and its close parallel from Halton Moor (Hinton et al. 1981; Webster and Backhouse 1991: no. 256; Wamers and Brandt 2005; Cooper 2007). The direct influence of Carolingian iconography is also seen in a Trewhiddle Style gold ring with King Æthelwulf's name, bearing an unusual motif of peacocks drinking at the Fountain of Life, directly related to images in Carolingian royal manuscripts (Webster 2003b: 91–3).

Carolingian influences increased under Alfred, who turned to continental scholars and churchmen for help in his programme of religious and educational renewal, and brought skilled craftsmen to his court, from whom he commissioned many wonderful gold and silver treasures (according to his biographer Asser; Keynes and Lapidge 1983: chs. 91, 101). Amongst the little of this that survives are some six gold fittings, probably the handles of manuscript pointers, such as Alfred sent out to each of his bishops with a translation of Gregory the Great's *Regula*

Pastoralis. The Alfred Jewel is the most elaborate of these, a substantial polished crystal overlying an enamelled plate with a figure with emphatic eyes, the whole set in a filigree-encrusted frame terminating in a socket for the pointer in the shape of a beast's head, and inscribed 'Alfred had me made' (Hinton 2008) (Fig. 25.8c). The innovative use of crystal and enamel is very probably influenced by Carolingian metalwork such as Alfred might himself have seen in Francia, or had brought to this country (Webster 2003b: 99–101). The other five are less complex, though all are gold and most have differing combinations of crystal, enamel, animal heads, and blue glass.

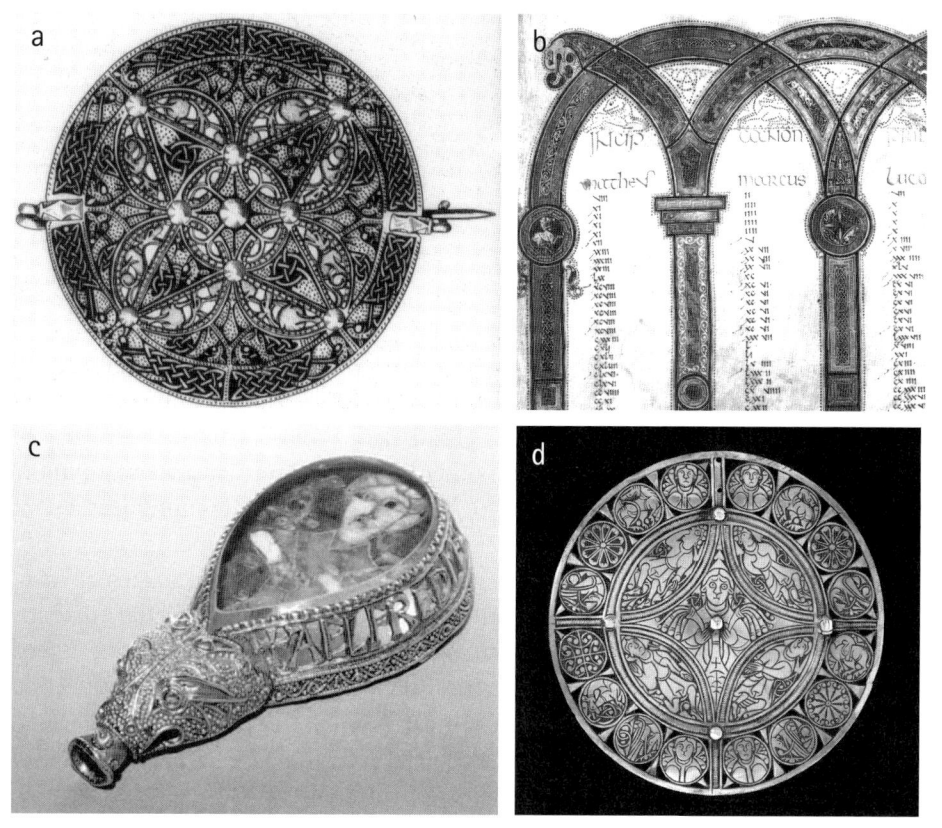

Figure 25.8 The ninth century: the rise of Wessex, and innovations of King Alfred's reign. (a) Silver disc brooch from the Pentney, Norfolk, hoard: first quarter of the ninth century (reproduced by kind permission of the Trustees of the British Museum); (b) The Royal Bible, detail from canon tables: c.820–840 (reproduced by kind permission of the British Library, London); (c) The Alfred Jewel: late ninth century (reproduced by kind permission of the Visitors of the Ashmolean Museum, Oxford); (d) The Fuller Brooch: late ninth century (reproduced by kind permission of the Trustees of the British Museum); (e) Part of a cross-shaft, East Stour, Dorset: late ninth/tenth century (reproduced by kind permission of the Trustees of the British Museum)

Figure 25.8 Continued

The figure on the Alfred Jewel has been identified as an image of spiritual and temporal Wisdom, reflecting Alfred's emphasis on spiritual education and Christian rule in his programme of renewal (Pratt 2003; Webster 2003b). This use of symbolic iconography is seen in certain other high-status secular metalwork of the late ninth century, reflecting Alfredian preoccupations. The supremely fluent decoration of the Fuller Brooch depicts the five senses as human figures, with Sight at its centre; encircling the senses are roundels containing images of men, birds, and animals in late Trewhiddle Style, interspersed with rosettes, perhaps signifying sensate creation (Fig. 25.8d). Like the image of Wisdom on the Alfred Jewel, the figure of Sight on the brooch has very prominent eyes, reflecting references in Alfred's writings to the mind's eyes, the conduit through which spiritual and temporal wisdom is obtained (Pratt 2003). Other artefacts—the Abingdon sword, with its evangelist symbols, emphasizing the Christian warrior, and the grape-harvesting youth on a late ninth-century strap-end from Cranborne, recalling the Eucharistic sacrifice—are equally subtle visual sermons (Webster 2003b). The cross-shaft from Codford St Peter, Wiltshire, with a light-footed harvester of grapes, may also reflect a related iconography; it is certainly from Wessex, and probably belongs to the Alfredian period (Webster 2003b: 89; for an alternative view, see Cramp 2006: 210–11).

By the end of the ninth century, the influence of Carolingian models becomes ever more visible. Although the modest manuscripts that survive from this period contain initials with animal ornament that clearly descends from the Trewhiddle menagerie (e.g. Temple 1976: nos. 1 and 2), new elements appear. The solemn figures of the

Fuller Brooch suggest acquaintance with the paintings and ivories of Carolingian court schools, as does a fragment of wall-painting with crowded figures, from a Winchester excavation context dating to before 903 (Backhouse *et al.* 1984: no. 25; Park 1999: 464); and the brooch's leonine quadrupeds, backward-turning birds, and fleshy lobed leaves look forward to the Carolingian-inspired acanthus decoration and more naturalistic creatures of tenth-century ornament (e.g. Backhouse *et al.* 1984: nos. 17–18; Temple 1976: nos. 3, 6, 7, and 9). So too does the lush, lobed vegetation with peltate leaves on the back of the Alfred Jewel, and similar lobed and peltate flower elements in some slightly later Wessex sculpture, as on the cross-shafts from East Stour, Dorset, and Colyton, Devon (Backhouse *et al.* 1984: no.23, pl. 11; Cramp 2006: 101–2, 80–2) (Fig. 25.8e). These new kinds of figural, foliage, and animal styles become increasingly important in the tenth century.

THE TENTH AND ELEVENTH CENTURIES: THE WINCHESTER STYLE AND ANGLO-SCANDINAVIAN INFLUENCES

The definitive style of the tenth and eleventh centuries is named after the royal and ecclesiastical centre at Winchester, which was a great focus of patronage and production in the arts of this period, as many manuscripts and other artefacts directly associated with it attest. But there were other important regional artistic centres such as Worcester, Ramsey, and Canterbury—not to mention workshops producing secular artefacts, of which many more survive than of fine ecclesiastical pieces. Sculptures such as the great rood at Romsey, Hampshire (Fig. 25.9a), and the flying angels that were probably part of a similar composition at Bradford-on-Avon, Wiltshire, and wall-paintings as at Nether Wallop, Hampshire, reflect reformed liturgical practice and show the Winchester Style's proliferation (Wormald 1971; Gem and Tudor Craig 1981; Wilson 1984; Tweddle *et al.* 1995; Gameson 1999; Cramp 2006). It subsumed several variants within its repertoire, and developed over time. But its chief elements remained constant: a gesturing figural style with fluttering draperies,[4] derived from Carolingian models drawing on Byzantine

---

[4] The inspiration for Lewis Carroll's famous 'Anglo-Saxon attitudes' (*Through the Looking Glass, and what Alice found there* (1872), ch. 7):

'What curious attitudes he goes into!' [Alice exclaimed] (For the Messenger kept skipping up and down, and wriggling like an eel . . . with his great hands spread out like fans on each side.) 'Not at all', said the King. 'He's an Anglo-Saxon Messenger—and those are Anglo-Saxon attitudes. He only does them when he's happy.'

Figure 25.9 The tenth and eleventh centuries: the 'Winchester' Style. (a) Christ on the Cross, Romsey Abbey, Hampshire: late tenth century (reproduced by kind permission of the Trustees of the British Museum); (b) Figure of Philosophy from a Boethius manuscript: late tenth century (reproduced by kind permission of Trinity College, Cambridge); (c) Ivory figures of St John the Evangelist and the Virgin Mary, from a crucifixion group: late tenth century (reproduced by kind permission of the Trustees of the British Museum); (d) Frontispiece showing King Edgar offering the New Minster Charter: after 966 (reproduced by kind permission of the British Library, London)

Figure 25.9 Continued

styles; lush acanthine ornament influenced by eastern French manuscripts and ivories (West 1993; Cramp 2006: 51–5); and animal motifs which mix elements from the earlier Anglo-Saxon tradition with continental Franco-Saxon versions (Wormald 1945). Dynamic line drawing, the lavish use of gold, and richly modelled figure painting, are prominent in manuscripts, and ivory carving became increasingly important, as supplies of walrus ivory from arctic waters became available (Beckwith 1972; Fell and Lund 1984: 58–62; Roesdahl 1995). The finest reflect the expressive energy and dynamic line of the manuscripts; and they were often painted or inlaid with gold (e.g. Backhouse et al. 1984: no. 120; Williamson and Webster 1990). The losses inflicted by the renewed Viking attacks of the later tenth century, and the exaction of harsh Danegeld payments, mean that very little significant church metalwork survives from this period—or indeed earlier—though later accounts of some of the major churches describe magnificent golden statues and elaborately decorated shrines and altars (Dodwell 1982: 195–201).

The roles of court and church were central in promoting the new styles. Alfred's successors, especially Æthelstan (924–39) and Edgar (959–75), built on the important links with the Continental church and courts which he had fostered (Gameson 1995). Æthelstan was an avid collector and donor of relics, presenting many rich gifts to the shrine of St Cuthbert at Chester-le-Street (Co. Durham). Among these were the richly embroidered stole and maniple made for Bishop Frithestan of Winchester (909–16); here, elongated Byzantine-style figures of ecclesiastics and prophets with delicately fluttering garments, and acanthus with lobed and peltate leaves, already mark the beginnings of the Winchester Style (Battiscombe 1956: pls. 24, 25, 31, and 32; Wilson 1984: 205–7, fig. 190). Another gift to the shrine was a manuscript of the *Lives of St Cuthbert*, made c.937; its frontispiece shows Æthelstan presenting the book to the saint (Temple 1976: no. 6; Wilson 1984: fig. 203). The design, with its richly painted naturalistic figures framed by delicate acanthine vegetation with feeding creatures, is a foretaste of later Winchester Style manuscripts. The development of the new style became intimately associated with the Benedictine monastic reform movement, which was introduced from the Continent in the 940s.

The figure-drawing of the Winchester Style takes two principal forms (Wormald 1952). The earlier is typified by the images of the three persons of the Trinity in the Sherborne Pontifical, and of Philosophy from a Boethius manuscript, their firmly drawn cascades of drapery emphasizing their *gravitas* (Temple 1976: nos. 35, 20) (Fig. 25.9b); the second, influenced by ninth-century Reims manuscripts, is characterized by a delicate shivering line, landscapes and figures alike imbued with a dynamic quality. Typical are the emotive figures of Mary and St John in the later tenth-century Ramsey Psalter crucifixion, and the ivories from St Omer (Temple 1976: no. 41; Backhouse et al. 1984: no. 119) (Fig. 25.9c); and above all, the early-eleventh-century Harley Psalter, its Carolingian model transformed into a shimmering theatre of animated movement (Temple 1976: no. 64; Backhouse *et al.* 1984: no. 59). To the figural styles, the grandest manuscripts add a rich palette, lavish use of gold, and frames of exuberant acanthine leafwork. Two such manuscripts, both made at and for Winchester, represent the heights of this style: the New Minster Charter of 966, in which a full-page miniature depicts King Edgar offering the charter to Christ, and the Benedictional made for Bishop Æthelwold *c*.971 (Temple 1976: nos. 16, 23; Backhouse *et al.* 1984: nos. 26, 37; Deshman 1995) (Fig. 25.9d). The richly coloured, intensely glittering appearance of these grand manuscripts, honouring God's power and glory, also evokes the dramatic liturgical settings in which they were displayed.

It is notable that many manuscripts, ivories, and stone sculptures of the period emphasize contemplation on the Crucifixion and the Last Days, themes increasingly important as Viking attacks intensified around the year 1000, and with them, the possibility that the End Times were at hand (Cramp 2006: 58–9; Keynes 2008; Webster 2008). Throughout the tenth century, Scandinavian styles had been influential on metalwork and sculpture in areas of Viking settlement in the north; under Cnut (1016–35), they entered the repertoire of southern England (Kendrick 1949; Bailey 1980; 1996: chs. 5 and 6). Like Anglo-Saxon animal ornament, these styles grew out of earlier Germanic tradition, transformed by external influences (Wilson and Klindt-Jensen 1966). The earliest to take root in England, in the later ninth and tenth centuries, was the Borre Style, named, like others, after the Scandinavian find-place of objects in the style. The main features of its Anglo-Scandinavian variant are a distinctive 'ring-chain' interlace and, more rarely, triangular-headed gripping beasts, often with notched contours suggestive of filigree, which show a Carolingian influence (Fig. 25.10a). Roughly contemporary with this was the Jelling Style, typified by creatures with long ribbon bodies, sometimes ribbed and with small offshoots; this was mainly current in sculpture (Fig. 25.10b). The later tenth-century Mammen Style, rarer in England, is characterized by creatures with larger, beaded or spotted bodies, shell-spiral joints, and the addition of foliate tendrils, the latter influenced by Ottonian acanthus (Fig. 25.10c). The Ringerike Style, which developed from this in the early eleventh century, was mainly confined to southern England, and even appears in manuscripts (e.g. Kendrick 1949: pls. 72–3; Backhouse *et al.* 1984: no. 129); here, elongated acanthine tendrils shoot out from and enmesh the great beast which is the central element, its spiral articulations also greatly emphasized (Fig. 25.10d). With a mean lentoid eye, and sharp tendrilled snout, it is often engaged in combat with a snake. In the middle years of the eleventh century, the last Anglo-Scandinavian style, the Urnes Style, develops this combat motif into an elegant extreme, in which smoothly modelled long-bodied animals and slender snakes grapple in interlacing coils (Fig. 25.10e).

Figure 25.10 The tenth and eleventh centuries: Anglo-Scandinavian influences. (a) Silver pendant with gripping beasts, Little Snoring, Norfolk: late ninth century (reproduced by kind permission of the Trustees of the British Museum); (b) Silver mounts from a small shrine, with Jelling-style decoration: mid tenth century (reproduced by kind permission of the Trustees of the British Museum); (c) Bone disc, London, with Mammen style decoration: late tenth century (reproduced by kind permission of the Trustees of the British Museum); (d) Gravestone from St Paul's churchyard, London, in the Ringerike style: early eleventh century (after E. Wilson); (e) Gilded bronze brooch in the Urnes style: mid eleventh century (reproduced by kind permission of the Trustees of the British Museum)

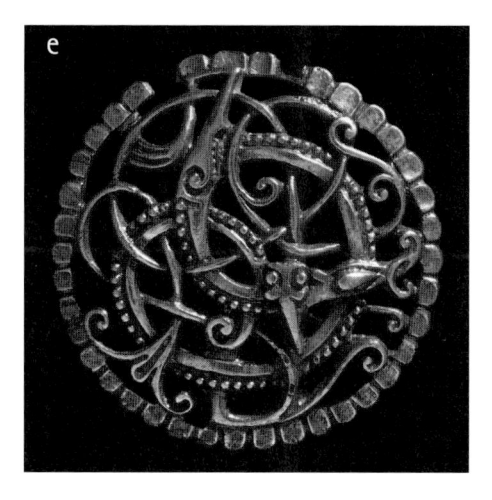

Figure 25.10 Continued

AFTERLIFE

The English version of the Urnes Style endured into the early twelfth century and, like the more hard-edged figure style which begins to appear in Anglo-Saxon art of the eleventh century, was an important indigenous element in shaping an English Romanesque style, as in the Hereford Gospels and Troper, the Tiberius Psalter, and a rare wooden survival, the Cleveland casket (Gameson 1991: 79–81; Zarnecki 1983: 17–18; Temple 1976: nos. 96–8; Backhouse *et al.* 1984: no. 129). Much indeed lived on. The Bayeux Tapestry, though a model of Norman propaganda, is Anglo-Saxon in style and workmanship (Wilson 1985; Gameson 1997: 157–211). As an embroidered celebration of heroic action, perhaps even backdrop to *chansons de geste*, it certainly sits in an Anglo-Saxon tradition implied by the record of an embroidered textile celebrating the deeds of Byrhtnoth, the defeated hero of the Battle of Maldon, 991, presented by his widow to St Etheldreda's monastery at Ely (Budny 1991), and by the fragment of sculptured frieze possibly showing the Sigurd legend, excavated in Winchester (Bailey 1996: 95–6). In its carefully framed construction, where word and image form complementary narratives, in which the borders occasionally offer a riddling commentary on the events they enclose, in its glowing colours, and in its busy sense of activity which imbues all living things, trees and flowers as well as beasts and humans, the Bayeux Tapestry is also true to the Anglo-Saxon stylistic tradition. In celebrating an end to Anglo-Saxon England, it also reflects the contribution that English style made to the new art of Anglo-Norman England, and even beyond. Here then is both an end, and a beginning.

References

Åberg, N. (1922). *Die Franken und Westgoten in der Volkerwanderungszeit*. Stockholm: Almqvist and Wiksell.
—— (1924). *Den Nordisk Folkvandringstidens Kronologi*. Stockholm: Almqvist and Wiksell.
Ager, B. (1985). 'The smaller variants of the Anglo-Saxon quoit brooch'. *Anglo-Saxon Studies in History and Archaeology* 4: 1–38.
Alexander, J. J. G. (1978). *Insular Manuscripts, Sixth to the Ninth Century*. Volume 1 of *A Survey of Manuscripts Illuminated in the British Isles*. London: Harvey-Miller.
Axboe, M. (2007). *Brakteatenstudier*. Copenhagen: Det Kongelige Nordiske Oldskriftselskab.
—— and Kromann, A. (1992). 'DN ODINN P F AUC? Germanic imperial portraits on Scandinavian gold bracteates'. *Ancient Portraiture, Image, and Message, Acta Hyperborea* 4: 271–305.
Backhouse, J. (1981). *The Lindisfarne Gospels*. Oxford: Oxford University Press.
—— Turner, D. H., and Webster, L. (eds.) (1984). *The Golden Age of Anglo-Saxon Art 966–1066*. London: British Museum.
Bailey, R. N. (1980). *Viking Age Sculpture in Northern England*. London: Collins.
—— (1996). *England's Earliest Sculptures*. Publications of the Dictionary of Old English 5. Toronto: Pontifical Institute of Mediaeval Studies.
—— (2000). 'The Gandersheim Casket and Anglo-Saxon sculpture', in R. Marth (ed.), *Das Gandersheimer Runenkästchen*. Braunschweig: Herzog Anton Ulrich's-Museum, 43–52.
—— (2002). *Anglo-Saxon Sculptures at Deerhurst*. Deerhurst Lecture 2002. Bristol: Friends of Deerhurst Church.
Bakka, E. (1963). 'Some English decorated metal objects found in Norwegian Viking graves. Contribution to the art history of the 8th century A.D.'. *Årbok for Universitetet i Bergen, Humanistik Serie*, 1: 4–66.
Battiscombe, C. F. (ed.) (1956). *The Relics of St Cuthbert*. Oxford: Clarendon Press.
Beckwith, J. (1972). *Ivory Carving in Early Medieval England*. London: Harvey-Miller.
Brown, M. P. (2000). *In the Beginning was the Word: Books and Faith in the Age of Bede*. Jarrow Lecture 2000. Jarrow: St Paul's Church.
—— (2001). 'Mercian manuscripts?: the Tiberius group and its historical context' in M. P. Brown and C. A. Farr (eds.), *Mercia, an Anglo-Saxon Kingdom in Europe*. London: Leicester University Press, 278–93.
—— (2003). *The Lindisfarne Gospels: Society, Spirituality and the Scribe*. British Library Studies in Medieval Culture. London: British Library.
Brown, P. D. C., and Schweitzer, F. (1973). 'X-ray fluorescent analysis of Anglo-Saxon jewellery'. *Archaeometry* 15: 175–92.
Bruce-Mitford, R. L. S. (1969). 'The art of the Codex Amiatinus'. *Journal of the British Archaeological Association* 32: 1–26.
Brugmann, B. (1999). 'The role of continental artefact types in sixth-century Kentish chronology', in J. Hines, K. Høilund-Nielsen, and F. Siegmund (eds.) (1999), *The Pace of Change*. Oxford: Oxbow Books, 37–64.
Budny, M. (1991). 'The Byrhtnoth tapestry or embroidery', in D. Scragg (ed.), *The Battle of Maldon A.D. 991*. Oxford: Basil Blackwell, 263–78.
—— and Tweddle, D. (1985). 'The early medieval textiles at Maaseik, Belgium', *Antiquaries Journal* 65: 353–89.

COOPER, A. (2007). 'The Harrogate hoard'. *Current Archaeology* 212: 26–30.
CRAMP, R. J. (1977). 'Schools of Mercian sculpture', in A. Dornier (ed.), *Mercian Studies*. Leicester: Leicester University Press, 191–233.
—— (1986). 'The furnishing and sculptural decoration of Anglo-Saxon churches', in L. A. S. Butler and R. K. Morris (eds.), *The Anglo-Saxon Church: Papers on History, Architecture and Archaeology in Honour of Dr. H. M. Taylor*. CBA Research Report 60. London: Council for British Archaeology, 101–4.
—— (2006). *The South-West of England*. Corpus of Anglo-Saxon Stone Sculpture 7. Oxford: Oxford University Press.
DESHMAN, R. (1995). *The Benedictional of Æthelwold*. Princeton, NJ: Princeton University Press.
DICKINSON, T. M. (1993). 'Early Anglo-Saxon saucer brooches: a preliminary overview'. *Anglo-Saxon Studies in Archaeology and History* 6: 11–44.
—— (1999). 'Early Anglo-Saxon graves and grave goods', in C. J. Young, *Excavations at Carisbrooke Castle, Isle of Wight, 1921–1996*. Salisbury: Wessex Archaeology, 87–97.
—— (2002). 'Translating animal art: Salin's Style 1 and Anglo-Saxon cast saucer brooches'. *Hikuin* 29: 163–86.
—— (2005). 'Symbols of protection: the significance of animal-ornamented shields in early Anglo-Saxon England'. *Medieval Archaeology* 49: 109–63.
—— (2007). 'The Anglo-Saxon cemetery at Old Park, near Dover, revisited', in M. Henig and J. Tyler Smith (eds.) (2007), *Collectanea Antiqua: Essays in Memory of Sonia Chadwick Hawkes*. British Archaeological Reports International Series 1673, Oxford: Archaeopress, 111–26.
—— (2009). 'Medium and message in early Anglo-Saxon art: some observations on the contexts of Salin's style I in England'. *Anglo-Saxon Studies in Archaeology and History* 16: 1–12.
DODWELL, C. R. (1982). *Anglo-Saxon Art: A New Perspective*. Manchester: Manchester University Press.
ELBERN, V. H. (2000). 'Das Gandersheimer Runenkästchen: Versuch einer Ikonographische Synthese', in R. Marth (ed.), *Das Gandersheimer Runenkästchen*. Braunschweig: Anton Ulrich's-Museum, 83–90.
EVISON, V. I. (1965). *The Frankish Settlements South of the Thames*. London: Athlone Press.
FARR, C. A. (2000). 'The Gandersheim Casket compared with Anglo-Saxon manuscripts', in R. Marth (ed.), *Das Gandersheimer Runenkästchen*. Braunschweig: Anton Ulrich's-Museum, 53–62.
FELL, C., and LUND, N. (1984). *Ohthere and Wulfstan: Two Voyagers at the Court of King Alfred*. York: Sessions.
FILMER-SANKEY, W. (1996). 'The Roman Empire in the Sutton Hoo ship-burial'. *Journal of the British Archaeological Association* 149: 1–9.
FLAMMIN, A. (2004). 'Trois marches', in C. Sapin (ed.), *Le Stuc: Visage Oublié de l'Art Medieval*. Paris: Musée Ste.-Croix de Poitiers, 47–8.
FOGG, S. (2007). *Art of the Middle Ages*. London: Paul Holberton Publishing.
GAMESON, R. (1991). 'English manuscript art in the mid-eleventh century'. *Antiquaries Journal* 71: 64–122.
—— (1995). *The Role of Art in the Late Anglo-Saxon Church*. Oxford: Clarendon Press.
—— (1997). 'The origin, art and message of the Bayeux Tapestry', in R. Gameson (ed.), *The Study of the Bayeux Tapestry*. Woodbridge: Boydell, 157–211.

—— (1999). 'The Winchester School', in M. Lapidge, J. Blair, S. D. Keynes, and D. Scragg (eds.), *The Blackwell Encyclopaedia of Anglo-Saxon England*. Oxford: Blackwell, 482–4.

GANNON, A. (2003). *The Iconography of Early Anglo-Saxon Coinage, Sixth to Eighth Centuries*. Oxford: Oxford University Press.

GEAKE, H. (ed.) (2007). 'Medieval Britain and Ireland, 2006: Portable Antiquities Scheme'. *Medieval Archaeology* 50: 211–32.

GEM, R., and HOWE, E. (2008). 'The ninth-century polychrome decoration at St Mary's Church, Deerhurst'. *Antiquaries Journal* 88: 109–64.

—— and TUDOR-CRAIG, P. (1981). 'A "Winchester School" wall-painting at Nether Wallop, Hampshire'. *Anglo-Saxon England* 9: 115–36.

HASELOFF, G. (1981). *Die Germanische Tierornamentik der Völkerwanderungszeit 1–3*. Berlin: de Gruyter.

HAUCK, K. (1970). *Goldbrakteaten aus Sievern: Spätantike Amulett-Bilder der 'Dania Saxonica' und die Sachsen-'Origo' bei Widukind von Corvey*. Munich: Münstersche Mittelalter-Schriften 1.

—— (1978). 'Brakteaten-Ikonologie'. *Johannes Hoops: Reallexikon der Germanischen Altertumskunde* 3: 361–401.

—— (1986). 'Methodfragen der Brakteatendeutung. Erprobung eines Interpretationsmusters für die Bildzeugnisse aus einer oraler Kultur. Zur Ikonologie Goldbrakteaten XXVI'. *Münstersche Mittelalter-Schriften* 24: 273–96.

HAWKES, J. (2003). 'The plant life of early Christian Anglo-Saxon art', in C. P. Biggam (ed.), *From Earth to Art: the Many Aspects of the Plant-World in Anglo-Saxon England*. Amsterdam/New York: Rodopi, 263–86.

HAWKES, S. C. (1961). 'The Jutish Style A. A study of Germanic animal ornament in southern England in the fifth century AD'. *Archaeologia* 98: 29–74.

—— and DUNNING, G. M. (1961). 'Soldiers and settlers in Britain'. *Medieval Archaeology* 5: 1–70.

—— and GRAINGER, G. (2006). *The Anglo-Saxon Cemetery at Finglesham, Kent*. Oxford: Oxford University School of Archaeology.

—— MERRICK, J. M., and METCALF, D. M. (1966). 'X-ray fluorescent analysis of some Dark Age coins and jewellery'. *Archaeometry* 9: 98–138.

HEDEAGER, L. (1999a). 'Myth and art: a passport to political authority in Scandinavia during the Migration Period'. *Anglo-Saxon Studies in Archaeology and History* 10: 151–6.

—— (1999b). 'Skandinavisk dyreornamentik. Symbolisk repræsentation af en førkristen kosmologi', in S. Fuglestvedt et al. (eds.) (1999), *Et hus med mange rom: Vennebok til Bjørn Myhre på 60 årsdagen*. Stavanger: Arkeologisk Museum i Stavanger, 219–37.

HILLS, C. (1987). *The Anglo-Saxon Cemetery at Spong Hill, North Elmham*, Part IV. East Anglian Archaeology 34. Gressenhall.

—— (2003). *Origins of the English*. London: Duckworth.

HINES, J. (1997). *A New Corpus of Anglo-Saxon Great Square-Headed Brooches*. Reports of the Research Committee 51. London: Society of Antiquaries.

—— (1999a). 'Angelsächsische Chronologie: Probleme und Aussichten', in U. von Freeden, U. Koch, and A. Wieczorek (eds.), *Völker an Nord- und Ostsee und die Franken*, 19–30.

—— (1999b). 'The sixth-century transition in Anglian England: an analysis of female graves in Cambridgeshire', in J. Hines, K. Høilund-Nielsen, and F. Siegmund (eds.), *The Pace of Change*. Oxford: Oxbow Books, 65–79.

HINTON, D. A. (2008). *The Alfred Jewel*. Oxford: Ashmolean Museum.

—— Keene, D., and Qualmann, K. (1981). 'The Winchester reliquary'. *Medieval Archaeology* 25: 45–77.

Høilund Nielsen, K. (1999a). 'Style II and the Anglo-Saxon elite'. *Anglo-Saxon Studies in Archaeology and History* 10: 185–202.

—— (1999b). 'Animal style, a symbol of might and myth: Salin's Style II in a European context'. *Acta Archaeologica* 69: 1–52.

Holmqvist, W. (1955). *Germanic Art during the First Millennium AD.* Stockholm: Almqvist and Wiksell.

Inker, P. (2006). *The Saxon Relief Style.* BAR British Series 410. Oxford: British Archaeological Reports.

Jewell, R. H. I. (1986). 'The Anglo-Saxon friezes at Breedon-on-the-Hill, Leicestershire'. *Archaeologia* 108: 95–115.

—— (2001). 'Classicism of Southumbrian sculpture', in M. P. Brown and C. A. Farr (eds.), *Mercia, an Anglo-Saxon Kingdom in Europe.* London: Leicester University Press, 246–62.

Jørgensen, L., Storgaard, B., and Thomsen, L. G. (2003). *The Spoils of Victory: The North in the Shadow of the Roman Empire.* Copenhagen: Nationalmuseet.

Kendrick, T. D. (1949). *Late Saxon and Viking Art.* London: Methuen.

Keynes, S. D. (1997). 'Anglo-Saxon entries in the *Liber Vitae* of Brescia', in J. Roberts and J. Nelson (eds.), *Alfred the Wise: Studies in Honour of Janet Bateley on the Occasion of her Sixty-Fifth Birthday.* Woodbridge: D. S. Brewer, 99–120.

—— (2008). 'An abbot, an archbishop, and the viking raids of 1006–7 and 1009–12'. *Anglo-Saxon England* 36: 151–220.

—— and Lapidge, M. (eds. and trans.) (1983). *Alfred the Great: Asser's Life of King Alfred and Other Contemporary Sources.* Harmondsworth: Penguin Books.

Leeds, E. T. (1936). *Early Anglo-Saxon Art and Archaeology.* Oxford: Clarendon Press.

—— and Pocock, M. (1971). 'A survey of the Anglo-Saxon cruciform brooches of florid type'. *Medieval Archaeology* 15: 13–36.

Leigh, D. (1980). *The Square-Headed Brooches of Sixth-Century Kent.* Unpublished Ph.D thesis, University of Cardiff.

—— (1984). 'Ambiguity in Anglo-Saxon Style 1'. *Antiquaries Journal* 64: 34–42.

Magnus, B. (1997). 'The Firebed of the Serpent: myth and religion in the Migration period mirrored through some golden objects', in L. Webster and M. Brown (eds.), *The Transformation of the Roman World AD 400–900.* London: British Museum Press, 194–207.

—— (1999). 'Monsters and birds of prey: some reflexions on form and style in the Migration Period'. *Anglo-Saxon Studies in Archaeology and History* 10: 161–72.

Meyvaert, P. (1979). 'Bede and the church paintings at Wearmouth-Jarrow', *Anglo-Saxon England* 8: 63–77.

—— Bede, Cassiodorus and the *Codex Amiatinus*. *Speculum* 71: 827–83.

Morris, C. (2000). *Wood and Woodworking in Anglo-Scandinavian and Medieval York.* Volume 17, fasc. 13 of *The Archaeology of York.* York: Council for British Archaeology.

Neuman De Vagvar, C. (2008). 'Reading the Franks Casket: contexts and audiences', in V. Blanton and H. Scheck (eds.), *Intertexts: Studies in Anglo-Saxon Culture Presented to Paul E. Szarmach.* Medieval and renaissance Texts and Studies 334/Arizona Studies in the Middle Ages and Renaissance 24. Tempe, AZ: ACMRS/Turnhout: Brepols, 141–60.

Nordenfalk, C. (1977). *Celtic and Anglo-Saxon Painting.* London: Chatto and Windus.

O'Reilly, J. (2001). 'The library of Scripture: views from the Vivarium and Wearmouth-Jarrow', in P. Binski and W. Noel (eds.), *New Offerings, Ancient Treasures: Essays in Medieval Art for George Henderson*. Stroud: Alan Sutton, 3–39.

Pape, H.-W. (2000). 'Das Gandersheimer Runenkästchen—technische Analyse, Material und Montage', in R. Marth (ed.), *Das Gandersheimer Runenkästchen*. Braunschweig: Herzog Antou Ulrich's-Museum, 19–34.

Park, D. (1999). 'Wall-paintings', in M. Lapidge, J. Blair, S. D. Keynes, and D. Scragg (eds.), *The Blackwell Encyclopaedia of Anglo-Saxon England*. Oxford: Blackwell, 464–6.

Pestell, T., and Ulmschneider, K. (eds.) (2003). *Markets in Early Medieval Europe: Trading and Productive Sites*. Macclesfield: Windgather Press.

Plunkett, S. (1998). 'The Mercian perspective', in S. Foster (ed.), *The St Andrews Sarcophagus*. Dubin: Four Courts Press, 202–26.

Pratt, D. (2003). 'Persuasion and innovation at the court of Alfred the Great', in C. Cubitt (ed.), *Court Culture in the Early Middle Ages: the Proceedings of the First Alcuin Conference*. Turnhout: Brepols, 189–221.

Richards, J. (1987). *The Significance of Form and Decoration of Anglo-Saxon Cremation Urns*. BAR British Series 166. Oxford: British Archaeological Reports.

Richardson, A. (2008). '197. Gillingham, Kent: early Anglo-Saxon gilt relief brooch (2006 T78)'. *Treasure Annual Report 2005/6*. London: British Museum and DCMS.

Rodwell, W., Hawkes, J., Howe, E., and Cramp, R. J. (2008). 'The Lichfield angel: a spectacular Anglo-Saxon painted sculpture'. *Antiquaries Journal* 88: 48–108.

Roesdahl, E. (1995). *Hvalrostand, elfenben og nordboerne I Grønland*. Odense: Odense Universitetsforlag.

Salin, B. (1904). *Die Altgermanische Thierornamentik*. Stockholm: Almqvist and Wiksell.

Scull, C., and Bayliss, A. (1999). 'Radiocarbon dating and Anglo-Saxon graves', in U. von Freeden, U. Koch, and C. Wieczorek (eds.), *Völker an Nord- und Ostsee und die Franken*, Bonn: Habelt, 39–50.

Schön, M. (1999). *Feddersen Wierde, Fallward, Flögeln*. Bremerhaven: Museum Burg Bederkesa.

Speake, G. (1980). *Anglo-Saxon Animal Art and its Germanic Background*. Oxford: Clarendon Press.

Suzuki, S. (2000). *The Quoit Brooch Style and Anglo-Saxon Settlement: a Casting and Re-casting of Cultural Identity Symbols*. Woodbridge: Boydell.

Temple, E. (1976). *Anglo-Saxon Manuscripts 900–1066*. Volume 2 of *A Survey of Manuscripts Illuminated in the British Isles*. London: Harvey-Miller.

Thomas, G. (2006). 'Reflexions on a ninth-century Northumbrian metalworking tradition: a silver hoard from Poppleton, North Yorkshire'. *Medieval Archaeology* 50: 143–64.

Tweddle, D. (1992). *The Anglian Helmet from Coppergate*. Volume 17, fasc. 8 of *The Archaeology of York*. London: Council for British Archaeology.

—— Biddle, M., and Kjølbye-Biddle, B. (1995). *Corpus of Anglo-Saxon Stone Sculpture*, Volume 4: *South-East England*. Oxford: Oxford University Press.

von Freeden, U., Koch, U., and Wieczorek, A. (eds.) (1999). *Völker an Nord- und Ostsee und die Franken*. Kolloquien zur Vor-und Frühgeschichte 3. Frankfurt: Römisch-Germanisch Kommission; Bonn: Mannheim Römisch-Museum.

Wamers, E., and Brandt, M. (eds.) (2005). *Die Macht des Silbers: Karolingische Schätze im Norden*. Regensburg: Katalog zur Ausstellung im Archäologische Museum Frankfurt und im Dom-Museum Hildesheim, in Zusammenfassung mit dem Dänischen Nationalmuseum, Copenhagen.

WEBSTER, L. (1992). 'Death's diplomacy: Sutton Hoo in the light of other male princely burials', in R. Farrell and C. Neuman de Vegvar (eds.), *Sutton Hoo: Fifty Years After*. American Early Medieval Studies 2. Oxford, OH: Miami University, 75–82.

—— (1999). 'The iconographic programme of the Franks Casket', in J. Hawkes and S. Mills (eds.), *Northumbria's Golden Age*. Stroud: Sutton, 227–46.

—— (2000). 'Style and function of the Gandersheim Casket', in R. Marth (ed.), *Das Gandersheimer Runenkästchen*. Braunschweig: Herzog Anton Ulrich's-Museum, 63–72.

—— (2001a). 'The Anglo-Saxon Hinterland: animal style in Southumbrian eighth-century England, with particular reference to metalwork', in M. Müller-Wille and L. O. Larsson (eds.), *Tiere: Menschen: Götter. Wikingerzeitliche Kunststile und ihre neuzeitliche Rezeption*. Hamburg: Veröffentlichen joachim-jungius-Gessellschaft des Wissenschaften Hamburg 90, 39–62.

—— (2001b). 'Metalwork of the Mercian supremacy', in M. P. Brown and C. A. Farr (eds.), *Mercia, an Anglo-Saxon Kingdom in Europe*. London: Leicester University Press, 263–77.

—— (2002). 'Face to face with an Anglo-Saxon deity?'. *Minerva* 13(2): 15.

—— (2003a). 'Encrypted visions: style and sense in the Anglo-Saxon minor arts', in C. E. Karkov and G. H. Brown (eds.), *Anglo-Saxon Styles*. Albany: State University of New York, 11–30.

—— (2003b). '*Ædificia nova*; treasures of Alfred's reign', in T. Reuter (ed.), *Alfred the Great*. Aldershot: Ashgate, 79–103.

—— (2005). 'Visual literacy in a protoliterate age', in P. Hermann (ed.), *Literacy in Medieval and Early Modern Scandinavian Culture*. Studies in Northern Civilization 16. Viborg: The Viking Collection, 21–46.

—— (2007). 'Taplow'. *Johannes Hoops: Reallexikon der Germanischen Altertumskunde* Band 35: 69–72.

—— (2008). 'Apocalypse Then: Anglo-Saxon ivory carving in the tenth and eleventh centuries', in C. E. Karkov and H. Damico (eds.), *Ædificia Nova: Studies in Honor of Professor Rosemary Cramp*. Kalamazoo: Western Michigan University, 226–53.

—— and BACKHOUSE, J. (eds.) (1991). *The Making of England: Anglo-Saxon Art and Culture AD 600–900*. London: British Museum Press.

WELCH, M.G. (1999). 'Relating Anglo-Saxon chronology to continental chronologies in the fifth century AD', in U. von Freeden, U. Koch, and A. Wieczorek (eds.), *Völker an Nord- und Ostsee und die Franken*, 31–8.

WEST, J. (1993). 'Acanthus ornament in late Anglo-Saxon and Romanesque England'. *L'acanthe dans la sculpture monumentale de l'Antiquité à la Renaissance*. Mémoires de la section d'archéologie et de l'histoire de l'art 4, Histoire de l'Art 6. Paris: Éditions du Comité des Travaux historiques et scientifiques, 247–68.

WHITFIELD, N. (1995). 'Formal conventions in the depiction of animals on Celtic metalwork', in C. Bourke (ed.), *From the Isles of the North: Early Medieval Art in Ireland and Britain*. Belfast: Her Majesty's Stationery Office, 89–104.

WILLIAMSON, P., and WEBSTER, L. (1990). 'The coloured decoration of Anglo-Saxon ivory carvings', in S. Cather, D. Parks, and P. Williamson (eds.), *Early Medieval Wall Painting and Painted Sculpture*. BAR British Series 216. Oxford: British Archaeological Reports, 177–94.

WILSON, D. M. (1984). *Anglo-Saxon Art*. London: Thames and Hudson.

—— (1985). *The Bayeux Tapestry*. London: Thames and Hudson.

—— and KLINDT-JENSEN, O. (1966). *Viking Art*. London: Allen and Unwin.

WORMALD, F. (1945). 'Decorated initials in English manuscripts from AD 900 to 1100'. *Archaeologia* 91: 107–35.
—— (1952). *English Drawings of the Tenth and Eleventh Centuries*. London: Faber and Faber.
—— (1971). 'The Winchester School before St Æthelwold', in P. Clemoes and K. Hughes (eds.), *England before the Conquest: Studies in Primary Sources Presented to Dorothy Whitelock*. Cambridge: Cambridge University Press, 305–14.
ZARNECKI, G. (1983). 'General Introduction', in G. Zarnecki, J. Holt, and T. Holland (eds.), *English Romanesque Art 1066–1200*. London: Arts Council of Great Britain with Weidenfield and Nicolson, 15–26.

PART VI

TRADE, EXCHANGE, AND URBANIZATION

CHAPTER 26

OVERVIEW: TRADE, EXCHANGE, AND URBANIZATION

GRENVILLE ASTILL

THIS overview seeks to draw out some connections between the contributions in this Part, and to develop some of the general points from the individual chapters, focusing on three topics: exchange and trade; the pace and character of urbanization; and the inter-relationship between urban centres.

All contributors, quite rightly, comment on the quality and quantity of the available data, and the extent to which that affects interpretation. Blackburn's chapter is timely in that it provides a critique of numismatic methodologies at a point when archaeologists are increasingly trying to reintegrate coinage into the study of the economy and of material culture. It is also noteworthy that most contributors try to exploit the potential of place-names, in some cases to emphasize continuity or continued interaction of the British populations in later Roman towns, *civitates*, and the different regions of Britain. Elsewhere we are reminded of the variety of meanings of particular words (*wics*, *burhs*) which nevertheless have acquired a preferred interpretation which has served to oversimplify and even distort understanding of the process of urbanization. Similarly, the chronological indicators or range for some of the major type sites and material culture remain surprisingly uncertain, with the possibility that some of the materials' currency could be considerably longer than usually thought (Loveluck and Laing; Henig). Such factors serve to argue that a simple evolutionary scheme for both exchange and urbanization that involved steady growth throughout the pre-Conquest period is now not necessarily appropriate to account for many of the changes noted by the contributors (including a greater variety of exchange places), and instead we may have to allow for periods of both rapid growth and stasis, and even contraction.

Exchange and trade

It is important to remember that the development of exchange and urbanization are separate processes. Indeed it has been argued that the extent of exchange was at least as great in the early Anglo-Saxon period as in the subsequent centuries (Campbell 2000a). We thus have the prospect of there being an inverse relationship between the scale of exchange and the existence of specialized sites where exchange took place. If exchange is defined as the transfer of wealth, it was a process related to the socio-economic character of Anglo-Saxon society. The extent to which this was the case is, after over thirty years, still debated, with little sign of a resolution between formalists and substantivists. The differences between the two interpretations are too often overdrawn, and the scale of exchange is generally accepted to have been related to the degree of consumption, and increasingly to that of production too (Astill 1999; Moreland 2000a; 2000b). The contrast is clearest over the function of the coinage, particularly during the eighth and ninth centuries: whether it demonstrates a highly monetized and market-based economy where such modern terms as 'balance of payments deficit' or 'trade surplus' are used; or whether it can be presented as the basis of socially-embedded transactions which had little separate economic significance (Metcalf 1993–4; Moreland 2000b; Maddicott 2002).

Often the volume of the currency is assumed to relate to a particular type of exchange: some would argue that the prolific secondary sceattas, for example, indicate a highly monetized economy which became quickly established (Pestell, below). Numismatists, however, tend to relate prolific periods of coin use to an increased availability of silver without necessarily implying that it was accompanied by a major change in the exchange system (Blackburn 1991, and below). That this may have been the case is perhaps indicated by periods of 'virtual collapse' of the coinage in the later eighth century and again in the late ninth to early tenth centuries, times when there is little independent evidence for a change in the nature of exchange. That the size of the secondary sceatta coinage was 'unsurpassed' until the 1180s (Pestell, below)—despite the intervening period being one of significant development in both state formation and towns—should cause us to consider the relationship between coinage and the dominant exchange system and indeed the developing early medieval state.

The evidence may suggest a more complicated situation where there was a continuous shift between different methods of exchange with no one method predominating until perhaps as late as c.1300. Some indeed argue that a fully developed money economy only existed in the late thirteenth century—a time which is not usually recognized as one of major urban growth, and suggests that the trajectories of exchange and urbanization were different (Bolton 2004).

Interpreting the early medieval economy as highly monetized presupposes that trading had penetrated most of society, but there is little independent evidence for this. Pestell (below) raises the possibility that the economy could be more socially specific and refers to a 'command economy' where exchange could have been essentially concerned with the collection and redistribution of tribute and surpluses from aristocratic estates. The king was engaged in this process as a member of that social group rather than in his role as monarch. The king was thus not an initiator of early medieval exchange, but rather he sought to exploit exchange by levying tolls. Equally, the use of coinage until the mid ninth century does not appear to have been an essential element in the development of the machinery of state. Wickham (2005: 344–51) has noted that the prolific use of eighth-century coinage in East Anglia was not related to the development of a state, whereas the best evidence for the latter is Mercia, where few coins or productive sites occur. A close association between the development of the currency and the state is most evident after Edgar's reform of the coinage, but we need to know how and when this association started. Indeed, it is difficult at present to characterize the nature and extent of exchange, including international contacts for the south, between the mid ninth century and the later tenth (Astill 1991: 110–11).

The extent to which the level of exchange was restricted by the difficulties and operational costs of transporting goods, particularly overland, remains an issue, but new work on pottery (Leahy, this volume) suggests that even in the early part of the period, cheap and bulky goods were being distributed by some means from inland Leicestershire, just as Stamford ware later shows a bias to waterway usage but with some means of getting pots to Oxford and beyond, presumably by carts or packhorses like those recorded as used for Droitwich salt (Hooke 1981: 133–4; Blair 2007a: 17–18). Bridge maintenance was one of the three duties routinely placed upon estates granted by charter, which must imply a road network, though little is known about their upkeep (Campbell 2000b: 182–4). Detailed information about the bridge at Rochester shows various neighbouring estates having responsibility for individual piers and lengths of decking, a construction method that probably allowed for many fords to be replaced in the late Saxon period (Harrison 2004: esp. 99–109). Improvements to waterways and to landing-places, such as 'hards' in London and Lincoln, are also mainly attributable to the later part of the period

(Blair 2007b), and the Graveney boat, sunk early in the tenth century, is evidence of coastal as well as overseas trade (Fenwick 1978).

The pace and character of urbanization

Most discussions about urbanization have assumed, first, an inexorable growth in the number of towns and, second, that each town becomes increasingly complex, as if in a steady evolutionary sequence. As Hall notes, discussion of town origins often includes a 'proto-urban' phase as if the inevitable outcome would be a town. There is also a tendency in the literature to assume that the town is a natural 'climax' in the development of early medieval settlement and that all discussions about towns should be predicated on this assumption.

The Roman legacy to medieval urban developments is, and should continue to be, debated, but perhaps the strands of past hypotheses need separate consideration. The coincidence between some Roman and medieval town centres forms the background to the discussion, but what this coincidence means needs further exploration, otherwise we are in danger (as Hall warns) of using a Whig interpretation, or more crudely hindsight, without qualifying the observation by considering the fate of the entire Romano-British urban network, or indeed the significance of those Roman towns which became important in the Middle Ages. In the absence of these considerations, recourse is often made to the better-evidenced sequences for northern Gaul and Germania, often on the assumption that there was a commonality of experience over the northern empire.

Henig takes a maximal view of the Roman inheritance: he points to the similarities of function that Roman and medieval towns might have as centres of trade, administration, religion, and political power, one or a combination of which could cause 'continuity'. If towns were founded in the Roman Empire for political and military reasons, and were more concerned with consumption than production (Palliser 2000: 21–4), then both their intended purpose and subsequent focus were different from those in medieval kingdom-states. Furthermore, the character and function of urban centres changed through time, in the third and fourth centuries as well as in the post-Roman period. We should also allow for the possibility that the Roman legacy was re-invented, re-introduced, or appropriated to suit the needs of an emerging society that sometimes had little or no direct experience of Romanization (Loveluck and Laing, below). A change of emphasis in urban functions between the fourth and the eleventh centuries could be because there was a considerable time when a minority of Roman towns retained sufficient significance to the successor society that they survived as important political, religious, and socio-economic nodes. Henig emphasizes the variety of religious purpose that some Roman towns retained—ranging from their survival as centres of British Christianity to shrines that attracted pilgrimage. On this view, they were 'centres of authority' as bishops' seats rather than as royal power bases, of which peripatetic kingship had less need. But, the question remains about the extent to which they were qualitatively different from the more numerous newly founded religious centres located in places that were rural and had no claim to an urban past.

'Centres of authority' represent an important element in the urbanization process in two ways. They may have been one of the site-types which articulated the redistribution of agricultural surpluses, particularly during and after the second half of the seventh century, when there is growing evidence for increasing production. They also indicate the high-status character of much of this exchange and the important role elites play in exchange and town formation. The contributors argue for an elite origin and a continued high-status presence at *emporia*, and also at a high proportion of the productive sites.

The relative importance of ecclesiastical as opposed to secular centres in urbanization is still debated. The continuous presence of a body of clerics would create a long-standing demand for, and the consumption of, commodities, and so would become embedded in the exchange system. This is in contrast to royal or other high-status sites which did not have the same longevity and which were only periodically occupied and so had a more transitory effect on the region (Blair 2000). It is, however, important to acknowledge that there is often an evidential gap between the foundation period of most minsters in the seventh or eighth centuries up until the eleventh, or more commonly the twelfth or thirteenth centuries, when the places are recorded as boroughs. Archaeological evidence from minsters is rare, but the few published excavations have produced small amounts of material, with a potential break in the sequences between the ninth and eleventh centuries (Astill 2006: 238–40). There is then a possibility of significant periods of change for long-established minsters as much as for secular sites; and both will influence the urban trajectory.

Similar considerations also apply to the productive sites: as Pestell shows below, the term covers a great variety of places, ranging from periodic fairs to more permanently occupied places, some (others argue the majority) of which were associated with minsters, while others may have been tax-collection points—and there is also the possibility that some functioned outside such an institutional framework (Leahy 2003). A change from an ecclesiastical to a secular purpose which has been claimed from the excavation of some high-status sites may reflect similar change in the local exchange system, and Naylor has emphasized how some productive sites could change function as a consequence of economic shifts in the area they served (Loveluck 2001; Naylor 2007).

From the mid ninth century our attention moves to the evidence for the development of defensive measures, which were part of the growing state mechanisms in Mercia and Wessex. As Hall states (below), the primary purpose of the *burhs* was as 'defensive refuges' and the creation of this infrastructure sometimes faltered. But, how and when do *burhs* become towns? Those who advocate a short chronology of urbanization argue that the *burhs* were intended to be both forts and towns at the same time as or very soon after their creation in the late ninth century (Biddle 1976: 120–34; Russo 1998: 193–231). Others want to separate the urban and military functions and argue that there is little archaeological evidence for urban settlement until the later tenth or eleventh century—and Hall cites Worcester as an example (Astill 1991; Hinton 2000: 230–5). Both interpretations adopt a primarily economic explanation of why some *burhs* became important centres—their success was essentially dependent on an intensification of both agricultural production and trade. But it is also necessary to think about the effect of imposing the *burhs* on the regions. The military advantage would have been all too obvious and indeed the *burhs* fulfilled their strategic purpose relatively quickly. Once the military need had been met, there is a tendency to assume that the value of *burhs* as a new, particular kind of settlement would have been sufficiently appreciated in the localities for them to become an important part of the exchange network. However, there remains the possibility that the pre-*burh* exchange systems may have continued to determine the economic relationships of the population, with the result that it took a considerable time for the *burhs* to be accommodated into the exchange network (Astill 2006: 235–6, 243–50, 254).

A related issue is: who had recourse to such centres as *emporia*, productive sites, and *burhs*? On the one hand there are those who argue that the aristocracy was merely one of the many groups who used such settlements from the eighth century, and this mixed demand, articulated by the market, was present throughout the Middle Ages (Russo 1998). Another view, reviving late-nineteenth-/early-twentieth-century work, sees the aristocracy (including the king) as being the essential prime mover in town creation and the sustaining influence for a considerable time, until the majority of the population had a need for centres of exchange and production, perhaps as late as the twelfth century (Astill 2000: 34–42). Some towns' impact on the countryside between the later ninth and eleventh centuries may have been minimal. The aristocracy, with their scattered estates, could have used non-market exchange systems which potentially supported early medieval towns. The *emporia* and the subsidiary collection centres of *villae regales* and minsters, may, for example, have been supported by the surplus generated from estates and tribute. Similarly, the *burhs* with their garrisons could have been manned and victualled from the aristocracy's estates (Astill 2006: 240–3). That the aristocracy had a clear interest in the *burhs* is reflected in the grants of holdings—the 'urban manors'—and they also became royal agents—moneyers and borough reeves (Fleming 1993; Campbell 2000b: 191–2). The similarity of coin loss between 'thegnly' rural residences and the *burhs*, and that these two types of site were also the location for metalworking, particularly whitesmithing, suggests that the scale of such industry was more appropriate to a patron rather than to the wider clientele that would be expected in fully-developed towns (Hinton 1986: 18). It is also possible that constituent groups within the aristocracy had differential effects on urbanization. In some towns, for example Worcester, thegnly interest in the city was waning by the later eleventh century, also the time when some thegns were pursuing their own urban initiative by founding small boroughs (Baker and Holt 1996: 140; Fleming 1993: 16–17).

Hall also makes us aware that the royal initiative in fortress/town creation was not continuous: Edward the Elder's campaign, for example, did not start until the second decade of his reign and this may be related to a relatively long period of royally-enforced land acquisition as a prelude to the *burh*-building in the east Midlands (Fleming 1985).

Many of the considerations above mainly relate to the southern half of the country; the urban experience further north cannot be accommodated within a long chronology of town growth. Intense activity is evident in the archaeological record from the later ninth century, and is also reflected in the increased outputs of the Danelaw mints and Chester in particular. The excavated evidence also emphasizes the developed and varied economic character of these towns (for example iron-smelting and pottery-making) and especially those industries which were based on the by-products of the countryside, indicating the integration of such towns with their surroundings (Astill 1991: 111–12).

The dominance of the minsters in the religious provision within later Saxon towns has received much attention, but the conditions under which subsidiary churches were created and their chronology need further investigation. In some cases church creation was regarded as an integral part of the royal commissioning of towns, in others it was not. Æthelflæd's *burh*-building, for example, was accompanied by the multiplication of churches at Shrewsbury, Chester, and Gloucester. St Oswald's in Gloucester was to become an important statement of royal power, as it was intended to be a royal mausoleum; but the translation of St Oswald's relics from Bardsey also served to enhance an identity for the town. By contrast, both Alfred and Edward the Elder excluded all foundations except nunneries (saving Winchester), and none of the new early-tenth-century bishoprics in Wessex had their seats in *burhs* (Barrow 2000: 130–1).

The creation of small churches in towns is often associated with the development of high-status urban manors, sometimes confirmed by their location in the backs of properties and the restricted access. The chronological range seems to be from the mid–later tenth to eleventh centuries. The association between churches and major thoroughfares and sometimes gates and defences may also suggest that some churches were originally intended to serve a wider congregation (Morris 1989: 168–226; Barrow 2000: 130–9). In some cases the churches had been built on sites which had previously been used for residential or industrial purposes. The proliferation of small churches, a characteristic of the later Saxon town, is usually interpreted as an index of the economic growth of these settlements. The greater number of churches in the towns of the south and east is thought to indicate those settlements' greater involvement with trade, and the dedications sometimes suggest that some churches could have served communities of foreign traders (Morris 1989: 175–8, 190–2). However, some argue that the real increase in church provision occurred in the eleventh century (Rosser 1992).

THE INTER-RELATIONSHIP BETWEEN TOWNS

Central-place theory has become the most influential way of conceptualizing the relations between different towns and also between town and country, and it is most often evident in reconstructions of 'hierarchies' of settlement. Using the information about moneyers and mints from the 973–1066 coinage, for example, it has been possible to propose a later Saxon urban hierarchy of three parts, of local, county, and provincial centres (e.g. Metcalf 1978). The theory is important in outlining the economic relationships that sustained the core of the urban system. However, we also need to take into account the peripheral elements that performed important short-term functions throughout the early Middle Ages, such as the beach-markets and possibly some productive sites during the eighth and ninth centuries. Perhaps it might be time to consider if it were possible for a 'core' urban system to survive without additional, peripheral trading-places, let alone the 'informal' trading that took place at a sub-institutional or group level?

An excessive attachment to the idea of a hierarchical system of exchange may mean we risk underestimating the importance of small-scale exchange systems for particular localities, systems which did not articulate with the higher-order centres, as in the Fens and in the coastal areas of the south-east (e.g. Spoerry 2005; Gardiner 2007). These 'dendritic' networks offer an alternative to a hierarchical system: such alternative trading arrangements and the existence of informal trade blur the distinction between town and country, and we also need to investigate chronological change in these systems.

In the eighth and ninth centuries the urban character of the country was determined by the *emporia*, which were served by high-status sites, both secular and religious, which acted as collection centres for the onward transport of agricultural surpluses, giving a basic two-part core exchange structure. To these we should now add the intermediate, arguably peripheral productive sites (which, as Pestell says, we cannot fully understand without setting them in the context of the contemporary settlement pattern) and beach-market sites. This exchange structure is different from that in contemporary Francia, one of the most commercially developed parts of Europe, where a three-level core exchange network has been proposed. The most basic and longest-established were the estate centres, followed by the *portus*, that is the regional centres such as St Denis and Verdun which were mints, fairs, and toll stations set in the major, north French, river valleys. At the estuaries of the rivers were the *emporia*, the least numerous element, but the most engaged with long-distance trade, and yet the shortest lived. As yet, we do not seem to have evidence of *portus*-type settlements in England. The other main difference is that the Frankish structure continued, with the exception of the *emporia*, to determine the urban pattern for most of the Middle Ages (Verhulst 2000). The simpler structure in England seems to have been partially dismantled after the mid ninth century with the demise of the *emporia* and most of the productive sites and perhaps some of the minsters. Without the inland urban infrastructure that survived the *emporia* in Francia, it is possible that England had to do more to develop an exchange and urban framework after the mid ninth century. That this was achieved by royal initiative is normally assumed from the *burh*-building obligations developed in the Mercia of Offa and later in Wessex.

The dating of some Mercian fortifications is debated (e.g. Hereford), while many Wessex *burhs* remain undated, except for the *terminus ante quem* of the 'Burghal Hidage'. The places listed in this document, most of which have been identified, were strategically sited and often on royal land. In some cases, Somerset for example, *burhs* were located at a distance from the estate centres/central places, perhaps because they were strategically unsuitable (Aston 1984: 173–4, 188). This reminds us that the 'Burghal Hidage' is only a record of the defensive system at *c*.914–18 (878–924?: Hall, below); elements of that system could be abandoned according to changing military need. The recommissioning of the South Cadbury and Old Sarum hillforts, or the Carisbrooke enclosure in the early eleventh century, should emphasize that the relocation of garrisons was more common than previously thought and, given the evidence of mints at some of these places, may argue that these changes had urban as well as military implications (Astill 2006: 242). Hall prefers to categorize the 'Burghal Hidage' places according to origin rather than the normal division between towns (or future towns) and forts (Biddle 1976: 126–7); by doing this he avoids emphasizing the rigidity rather than the flexibility of the system and allows for the possibility (as with South Cadbury) that some of the forts may be embryonic towns.

The urban network of the north-west illustrates this flexibility. The importance of Chester for the region is clear, but the sites newly fortified by Æthelflæd, such as Eddisbury and Runcorn, seem to have been short-lived and replaced by others created by Edward the Elder—Thelwall, Manchester, and Rhuddlan. While such changes might indicate the economically undeveloped state of the north-west and the failure of some *burhs* to integrate into the local economy (and similar, but unevidenced, changes are claimed for the Devon *burhs*), it also points to the strategic flexibility that was necessary throughout the country at this time, which is difficult to disentangle because we have no successors to the 'Burghal Hidage'. It nevertheless gives the impression that by the later tenth century (and perhaps considerably later) the urban network was still fluid (Higham 2007).

This fluidity may also be partly explained by the delay in the process by which urban functions became concentrated in one place. In some European countries, for example, a distinction has been made between the process of town growth and that of urbanization. The town is seen as part of a developing power structure and it was therefore one means by which political control was exercised. It follows that in such circumstances towns have to be seen in the context of how other central places that have an importance in that power structure develop (Andersson 2003). We cannot understand the genesis of towns without taking into account how the political—or indeed the economic—network was articulated in order to achieve this urbanization.

In the later Saxon period, what we could call urban functions (when using bundle criteria) may well have been distributed among several settlements in the same region, none of which could be regarded as a fully-fledged town. In some areas, north Wiltshire or Somerset for example, the religious and secular sites were in separate places at a distance from the economic centre (Astill 1991: 113). In some parts of the country these elements of an urban identity did not come together until after the Norman Conquest, as a result of political rather than economic fiat. But was this process irreversible? In times of political or economic stress should we consider the possibility of urban functions fragmenting? This is certainly the case if we consider the changing patterns of the trading network. It also means that it is important to investigate discontinuities in the urbanization process, and not always assume that the urban network came into being relatively early and remained fixed for most of the Middle Ages.

REFERENCES

ANDERSSON, H. (2003). 'Urbanisation', in K. Helle (ed.), *The Cambridge History of Scandinavia*, Volume 1. Cambridge: Cambridge University Press, 312–42.

ASTILL, G. (1991). 'Towns and town hierarchies in Saxon England'. *Oxford Journal of Archaeology* 10: 95–117.

—— (1999). 'Trade', in M. Lapidge, J. Blair, S. Keynes, and D. Scragg (eds.), *The Blackwell Encyclopaedia of Anglo-Saxon England*. Oxford: Blackwell Publishers, 453–4.

—— (2000). 'General survey 600–1300', in Palliser (ed.), *The Cambridge Urban History of Britain*, 27–49.

—— (2006). 'Community, identity and the later Anglo-Saxon town: the case of southern England', in W. Davies, G. Halsall, and A. Reynolds (eds.), *People and Space in the Middle Ages 300–1300.* Turnhout: Brepols, 233–54.
ASTON, M. (1984). 'The towns of Somerset', in J. Haslam (ed.), *Anglo-Saxon Towns in Southern England.* Chichester: Phillimore, 167–201.
BAKER, N., and HOLT, R. (1996). 'The city of Worcester in the tenth century', in N. Brooks and C. Cubitt (eds.), *St Oswald of Worcester: Life and Influence.* Leicester: Leicester University Press, 129–46.
BARROW, J. (2000). 'Churches, education and literacy in towns', in Palliser (ed.), *The Cambridge Urban History of Britain,* 127–52.
BIDDLE, M. (1976). 'Towns', in D. Wilson (ed.), *The Archaeology of Anglo-Saxon England.* London: Methuen, 91–150.
BLACKBURN, M. (1991). 'Money and coinage', in R. McKitterick (ed.), *The New Cambridge Medieval History,* Volume 2: *c.700–c.900.* Cambridge: Cambridge University Press, 538–59.
BLAIR, J. (2000). 'Small towns 600–1270', in Palliser (ed.), *The Cambridge Urban History of Britain,* 245–72.
—— (2007a). 'Introduction', in Blair (ed.), *Waterways and Canal-Building in Medieval England,* 1–18.
—— (ed.) (2007b). *Waterways and Canal-Building in Medieval England.* Oxford: Oxford University Press.
BOLTON, J. (2004). 'What is money? What is a money economy? When did a money economy emerge in medieval England?', in D. Wood (ed.), *Medieval Money Matters.* Oxford: Oxbow, 1–15.
CAMPBELL, J. (2000a). 'The sale of land and the economics of power in early England: problems and possibilities', in J. Campbell, *The Anglo-Saxon State.* London: Hambledon and London, 227–46.
—— (2000b). 'Was it infancy in England? Some questions of comparison', in J. Campbell, *The Anglo-Saxon State.* London: Hambledon and London, 179–99.
FENWICK, V. (1978). *The Graveney Boat.* BAR British Series 53. Oxford: British Archaeological Reports.
FLEMING, R. (1985). 'Monastic lands and England's defence in the Viking age'. *English Historical Review* 100: 247–65.
—— (1993). 'Rural elites and urban communities in late-Saxon England'. *Past and Present* 141: 3–37.
GARDINER, M. (2007). 'Hythes, small ports and other landing places in later medieval England', in Blair (ed.), *Waterways and Canal-building in Medieval England,* 85–109.
HANSEN, I. and WICKHAM, C. (eds.) (2000). *The Long Eighth Century.* Leiden: Brill.
HARRISON, D. (2004). *The Bridges of Medieval England: Transport and Society 400–1800.* Oxford: Clarendon Press.
HIGHAM, N. (2007). 'Changing spaces: towns and their hinterlands in the north west, AD 900–1500', in M. Gardiner and S. Rippon (eds.), *Medieval Landscapes.* Macclesfield: Windgather, 57–72.
HINTON, D. A. (1986). 'Coins and commercial centres in Anglo-Saxon England', in M. Blackburn (ed.), *Anglo-Saxon Monetary History.* Leicester: Leicester University Press, 11–26.

—— (2000). 'The large towns 600–1300', in Palliser (ed.), *The Cambridge Urban History of Britain*, 217–44.
Hooke, D. (1981). 'The Droitwich salt industry: an examination of the West Midland charter evidence'. *Anglo-Saxon Studies in Archaeology and History* 2: 123–69.
Leahy, K. (2003). 'Middle Anglo-Saxon Lincolnshire: an emerging picture', in T. Pestell and K. Ulmschneider (eds.), *Markets in Early Medieval Europe: Trading and 'Productive' Sites, 650–850*. Macclesfield: Windgather Press, 138–54.
Loveluck, C. (2001). 'Wealth, status and conspicuous consumption and its implications for middle and late Saxon settlements', in H. Hamerow and A. MacGregor (eds.), *Image and Power in the Archaeology of Early Medieval Europe: Essays in Honour of Rosemary Cramp*. Oxford: Oxbow Books, 78–130.
Maddicott, J. (2002). 'Prosperity and power in the age of Bede and Beowulf'. *Proceedings of the British Academy* 117: 49–71.
Metcalf, D. (1978). 'The ranking of boroughs: numismatic evidence from the reign of Ethelred II', in D. Hill (ed.), *Ethelred the Unready*. Oxford: British Archaeological Reports British Series, 159–212.
—— (1993–4). *Thrymsas and Sceattas in the Ashmolean Museum, Oxford*. 3 volumes. Oxford: Asmolean Museum.
Moreland, J. (2000a). 'Concepts of the early medieval economy', in Hansen and Wickham (eds.), *The Long Eighth Century*, 1–34.
—— (2000b). 'The significance of production in eighth-century England', in Hansen and Wickham (eds.), *The Long Eighth Century*, 69–104.
Morris, R. (1989). *Churches in the Landscape*. London: Dent.
Naylor, J. (2007). 'The circulation of early-medieval European coinage: a case study from Yorkshire, c.650–c.867', *Medieval Archaeology* 51: 41–62.
Palliser, D. (2000a). 'The origins of British towns', in Palliser (ed.), *The Cambridge Urban History of Britain*, 17–26.
—— (2000b). *The Cambridge Urban History of Britain*, Volume 1. Cambridge: Cambridge University Press.
Rosser, G. (1992). 'The cure of souls in English towns before 1000', in J. Blair and R. Sharpe (eds.), *Pastoral Care before the Parish*. Leicester: Leicester University Press, 267–84.
Russo, D. (1998). *Town Origins and Development in Early England, c .400–900AD*. Westport, CT: Greenwood Press.
Spoerry, P. (2005). 'Town and country in the medieval Fenland', in K. Giles and C. Dyer (eds.), *Town and Country in the Middle Ages: Contrasts, Contacts and Interconnections, 1100–1500*. Society for Medieval Archaeology Monograph 22. Leeds: Maney, 85–110.
Verhulst, A. (2000). 'Roman cities, *emporia* and new towns (sixth-ninth centuries)', in Hansen and Wickham (eds.), *The Long Eighth Century*, 105–20.
Wickham, C. (2005). *Framing the Early Middle Ages: Europe and the Mediterranean, 400–800*. Oxford: Oxford University Press.

CHAPTER 27

THE FATE OF LATE ROMAN TOWNS

MARTIN HENIG

Roman towns and the towns of middle and late Anglo-Saxon England, which in many instances were sited on, or adjoining, their Roman predecessors, served many similar needs: they were both foci for trade and population centres; they symbolized authority, and frequently served administrative purposes; and—often linked to the last—they were religious centres.[1] The function of towns in the period between the later fourth and the later sixth century has been seen as problematic, and approaches to them have ranged from seeing most as virtually deserted before their total re-foundation after the early Anglo-Saxon period (Brooks 1986; Esmonde Cleary 1989; Wacher 1995: 408–21) to more or less total continuity of settlement, even though this was accompanied by very considerable changes in material and cultural life (Dark 2000; Thacker and Sharpe 2002; Henig 2002: 125–44; Henig 2004a; Fulford *et al.* 2006: especially 278–80). For the most part even those who believe that Roman towns were abandoned and largely deserted have not seen their fate as the consequence of Anglo-Saxon conquest but rather as a combination of other factors, economic, climatic, famine, and epidemic disease (see especially Wacher 1995: 411–14). Those who believe in the essential continuity of these settlements would not dismiss such influences but feel that where the evidence can be examined carefully much more positive conclusions can be drawn. Although there is not space to mention every town, and indeed evidence for their post-Roman history

---

[1] I am very grateful to Dr Brian Gilmour for his encouragement, sympathy, and many useful comments and suggestions.

varies, in the opinion of the writer not a single one of them died; all of them retained a real presence and vitality in the landscape until the seventh century at least, and most, including the greatest, dominate their regions to this day.

There were undoubted changes here, as in many late-antique cities throughout Europe: in London, the throngs of merchants (*negotiatores*) upon which Tacitus (for the first century) commented, just as Bede (for the seventh) stressed the city's role as a market (*emporium*),[2] were largely absent from the fifth and sixth centuries, as elsewhere in Britain. Populations were greatly reduced and widespread layers of 'dark earth' in London and elsewhere suggest at least a major change in land use or even local desertion. Some have seen large swathes of urban landscape, even entire cities, as resembling the weed-choked ruin-fields of London and other large European cities after the bombardment of the Second World War. Nevertheless, it needs to be pointed out that very few towns have seen careful exploration of late-fourth- and fifth-century occupation layers, which are both difficult to spot and vulnerable to later disturbance, as well as to over-enthusiastic and careless excavation. Moreover, a very small proportion of the area of most former Roman town sites has been excavated. Only at Wroxeter (Barker *et al.* 1997) has there been excavation of sufficient scale and thoroughness to attest large-scale 'Dark Age' activity. New buildings, water supply, and drainage are attested in a number of towns in the fifth century and probably on into the sixth, at *Verulamium*, Silchester, Carlisle, and Dorchester, Oxfordshire, for example, sometimes—as at Wroxeter—on a massive scale, though in all cases employing timber rather than stone. That these places were something more than rural farmsteads sheltering behind decaying city walls is further suggested by inscribed stones from Silchester (in Ogham script) and Wroxeter (in Latin capitals).

Continuity in civic organization is harder to prove, but Constantius' Life of St Germanus implies that *Verulamium* was still a functioning urban community in the early fifth century, while if the entry in the *Anglo-Saxon Chronicle* about a battle at *Deorham* can be believed, Bath, Gloucester, and Cirencester were British centres of power into the second half of the sixth century. In any case the survival of a majority of the names of the main cities in both the 'Celtic' west and the 'Anglo-Saxon' east is highly suggestive. These include Canterbury (preserving the old tribal name of the *Cantii*), Winchester (*Venta*), Caerwent (*Venta*), Wroxeter (*Viroconium*), Carlisle (*Luguvalium*), London (*Londinium*), Lincoln (*Lindum Colonia*), Gloucester (*Glevum*), Cirencester (*Corinium*), Colchester (*Colonia*), and the ports of Richborough (*Rutupiae*) and Dover (*Dubris*) (see Rivet and Smith 1979: *passim*).

The Church, too, offers a basis for understanding this continuity even where evidence is tenuous (Sharpe 2001; Henig 2007). In other parts of the former north-western

---

[2] Tacitus, *Ann.* XIV, 33 (*Londinium... cognomento quidem coloniae non insigne, sed copia negotiatorum maxime celebre*); Bede, *HE* I.3 (*ipsa multorum emporium populorum terra marique venientium*).

provinces, including the nearby region of north-west Gaul, we find examples of churches with a Roman origin at the centres of walled late Roman towns and thus associated with the ruling authorities of these places, while other churches lay outside the walls in the cemeteries built on the burial places of the 'very special dead', often martyrs (Thomas 1981: 155–64; Pearce 2003; and see P. Brown 1981: 69–85). Some sort of continuity is implied by the existence of both types of church in Britain, though only a few examples can be recognized. Both Constantius in his *Vita S. Germani* (§14) describing the saint being greeted, almost certainly at *Verulamium*, in 429 by (presumably) *curiales*, '*conspicui diuites ueste fulgentes*', and Gildas (490 x 570, De Excidio 10.2) attest the existence of a *martyrium* for its famous Roman martyr Alban, presumably outside the walls on the site of the later abbey (Thacker and Sharpe 2002: 79–83 and 112–18). The *Passio Sancti Albani*, probably written in Gaul in the fifth or sixth century, was widely disseminated (Sharpe 2001) and certainly would have encouraged pilgrimage both from within and outside Britain; Bede claimed that the church on the site was still frequented in his day and this suggests religious continuity there, which ultimately conditioned a shift in urban focus as at Xanten (*ad sanctos*) where the church lies outside the (now deserted) Roman colonia (Fig. 27. 1). *Verulamium* was not, however, quickly or even entirely deserted and the site of the late Saxon church of St Michael, beside the remains of the forum and basilica, deserves further consideration. There is a reference to another martyr, a St Sixtus, whose name is preserved in the *Libellus Responsionum* of Pope Gregory the Great in correspondence with St Augustine in 601 (see Thacker and Sharpe 2002: 123–5), and most plausibly centred at Silchester, a city which seems to have been deliberately suppressed (see below) not many decades later.

Canterbury too may well have retained an important Christian status from Roman times; Bede informs us that the Augustinian mission restored an internal church (Christ Church) on the site of the later cathedral and that Christianity was practised at the cemetery church of St Martin on one of the approach roads to the south. An interesting sequence is suggested by the preservation of a Jupiter column in the crypt of the Holy Innocents Chapel of the Cathedral, which may have been re-used in the Roman church known to Bede (*HE* I.26, 33; Henig 2007: 190–1, fig. 10.1). Although the intra-mural Roman cathedral has yet to be identified, London too has yielded suggestive evidence, at least of a cemetery church, with the discovery of a fifth-century Christian-orientated coffined burial at St Martin's in the Fields a mile west of London, succeeded in the seventh century by rich Conversion-period graves. A martyr-cult could have been centred here (below).

Other cases of Christian centres being established in towns are intriguing but less straightforward. The early intra-mural church excavated in Lincoln on the site of St Paul-in-the-Bail may date from the early post-Roman period, possibly the sixth century (Gilmour 2007); its site in the forum of the colonia is suggestive, although the existence of burials has important negative implications, revealing that the old Roman civic prohibitions on urban burial had broken down. We know that Caerwent became an important Christian focus in the post-Roman period and

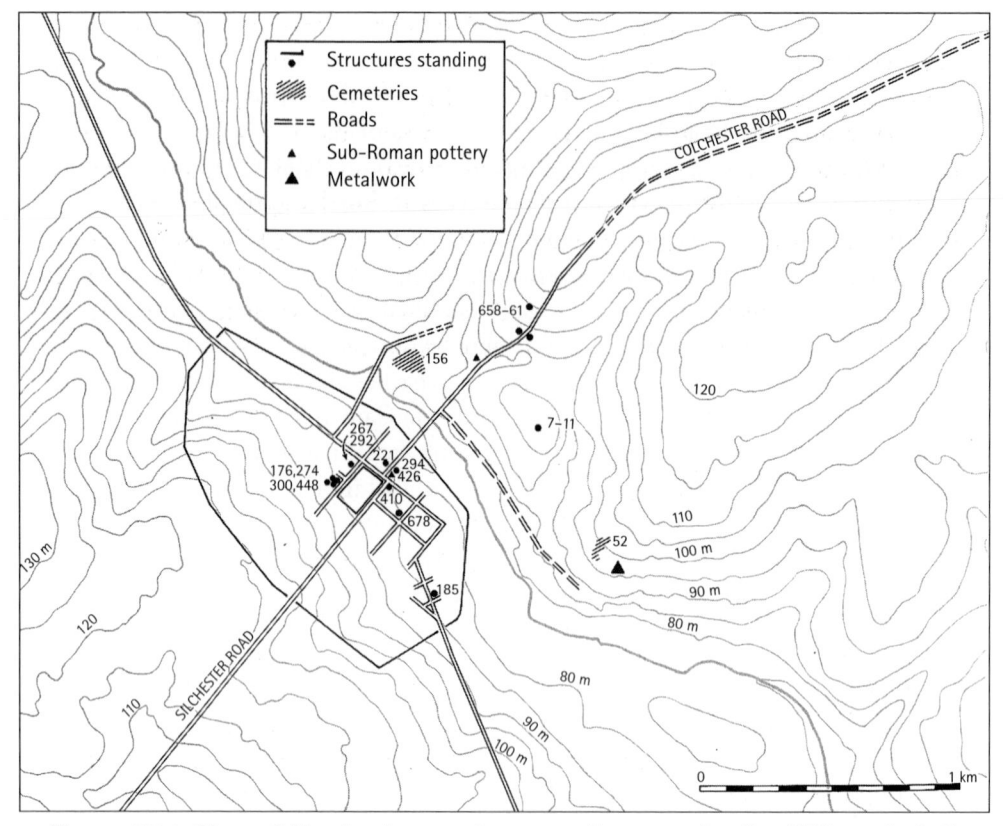

Figure 27.1 Plan of Verulamium and surrounding area in the fifth and sixth centuries. Occupation within the intra-mural *civitas* had shrunk, and structures and objects on the north bank of the River Ver presage the foundation of the medieval abbey and town (reproduced from Niblett 2005: 174 by kind permission of R. Niblett)

there is evidence both of occupation and cemeteries, but here, well beyond any notional pressure from pagan Saxons, the place may have come to serve more as a monastic enclosure for St Tathan and his monks than as a vibrant city. Nevertheless, the people of the *civitas*, probably at Caerleon as much as Caerwent, kept the memory of the martyr Julius alive at St Julian's on the east bank of the Usk south of Caerleon (Knight 2003: 120–2). A large fourth-fifth-century, probably Christian cemetery at Queenford Farm outside Dorchester, Oxfordshire, though without an associated church, is suggestive evidence; perhaps there was a church on the site of the later abbey (outside the Roman East Gate) but this has not been proved.

It is only in the past fifty years that most of the evidence apart from onomastic and very slight literary evidence has emerged and even now the conditions for recovering the fugitive layers between the remains of the fourth and eighth centuries are often not present. The almost complete absence of coins, and hence of dated pottery, renders such deposits very hard to date, and unless large areas are uncovered and as classically excavated as at Wroxeter it is hard to understand the nature of the occupation. While pagan Anglo-Saxons normally possessed a distinctive material culture, Christian graves in cemeteries outside towns are not furnished. We can point to late Roman British metalwork of the fifth century and even more distinctive British metalwork such as 'late Celtic' hanging-bowls no earlier than the late sixth century from Conversion-period graves (see Loveluck and Laing, this volume). Is the gap between the latest Roman and the earliest Anglo-Saxon a real one or a consequence of our incomplete recovery of the evidence and inadequate dating or misunderstanding of the material remains?

THE MAJOR TOWNS

The problem of deciding what happened to the towns lies in the variability of the archaeological evidence, so often truncated by later activity including excavation. The potential for investigating the possibility of continued life within Roman cities has been best demonstrated at Wroxeter. From the East Rampart of the town came a sandstone tombstone inscribed in Latin letters, possibly that of an Irish settler: *CVNORIX MACVS MA-QVI COLINE* (Barker *et al.* 1997: 237–8, fig. 326; White and Barker 1998: 106, col. pl. 13).[3] It was not in its original position and had evidently been re-used. On the Baths Basilica site Philip Barker conducted a careful excavation on a considerable scale which revealed urban life continuing into the sixth century. The basilica continued in use for most of the fifth century, but the most remarkable feature of the site was its large-scale clearance in the sixth century and a 'great rebuilding [Phase Z]' with a planned layout *in more Romanorum*, though the most substantial building, in the style of a late Roman villa, would suggest that what had once been public space had been privatized. Substantial timbers are suggestive of an ordered society, albeit different from that of the preceding conventional Roman town (Barker *et al.* 1997: 138–91 and 232–8; White and Barker 1998: 118–30). Perhaps it may best be seen as the residence of a 'tyrant' (in the non-pejorative sense of a lord), together with his retainers. Unfortunately, although many finds were recorded, most appear to be residual, apart from some pins which are best dated to the fifth century. Thereafter it may be suggested that Wroxeter did

---

[3] Peter Schrijver in his O'Donnell Lecture to the University of Oxford 2006–7, 'How Roman Britain made Ireland Celtic', sees Q-Celtic as well as P-Celtic as both originating within Roman Britain and the Irish language as only really emerging after AD 400. If he is right, in the first place the inscription needs to be placed in the later fifth or the sixth century and in the second it might be better not to make too much of the ethnicity of the deceased.

not totally die but progressively contracted to the area around St Andrew's Church, and the main focus of later medieval settlement shifted to Shrewsbury.

Such a sequence was not confined to the far west. Silchester too continued to be a vibrant city. Evidence includes a hoard of gold and silver rings, and silver coins, many of them clipped, and thus not buried until the fifth century (Fulford *et al.* 1989). Excavation in insula IX has proved especially fruitful, with plentiful evidence of flourishing urban life in late Roman times including a wholesale re-planning and rebuilding of the town in the fourth century, and further evidence for the likelihood of urban life continuing well beyond 400. As at Wroxeter, there is epigraphic evidence, here in the form of an Ogham stone (from well 1170; Fig. 27.2), inscribed TEBICATO[S] / [MAQ] I MUCO[I..]. It might be a tombstone but more plausibly has been seen as a property marker (Fulford *et al.* 2000: 18–19; Fulford *et al.* 2006: 279). The stone has been associated with an Irish settler; possibly as early as the fourth century, though once again a late-fifth-century date for the inscription seems more plausible and, in any case, the stone was re-deposited in a pit. It attests continued activity in the town probably into the sixth century or even later, and again there are hints of continued occupation, and of industrial activities, notably iron-working and the processing of bone perhaps to extract grease for tallow (Fulford *et al.* 2006: 256). A series of dykes, ditches, and banks demarcating an area around Silchester, and in one case blocking and cutting off a Roman road, emphasize continued vitality, and it has been plausibly suggested that Silchester was only abandoned in the seventh century, maybe as a consequence of the incorporation then of the Atrebatic *civitas* into Wessex; the finding of red-streaked window glass in the forum-basilica area and a palm-cup (Boon 1959: 81, fig. 41, and 83 no. C3) may point to the presence of a church or even a monastery at this late date.

In the same part of Britain, Winchester has provided valuable evidence of re-planning in the fourth century, very much on utilitarian lines and possibly serving as a fortified base for the administration of the tax in kind known as the *annona militaris* (Biddle and Kjølbye-Biddle 2007). It was possibly also the site of the *Gynaeceum* (Imperial weaving mill) situated at '*Venta*' listed in the *Notitia Dignitatum* (XI.60). Many of the inhabitants of Winchester at this time were buried at the Lankhills cemetery and amongst these graves was an element from the Danube perhaps suggestive of a 'plantation'. While the breakdown of central Roman administration in the early fifth century would have spelt an end to such official functions, the continued use of two major through-routes, testified by the continued use and wear of the axial east-west and north-south streets, shows that Winchester was not avoided and in some sense must have maintained its place as a centre of authority until the clear re-emergence of an 'Anglo-Saxon' city.

Winchester certainly has a 'Dark Age' history, encapsulated by the partial survival of its name, *Venta*, in *Uintancaestir*. Excavation suggests that in the centre, on the Cathedral Green site, there were late Roman timber buildings, and a functioning water supply. By then pottery evidence reveals a probable 'Anglo-

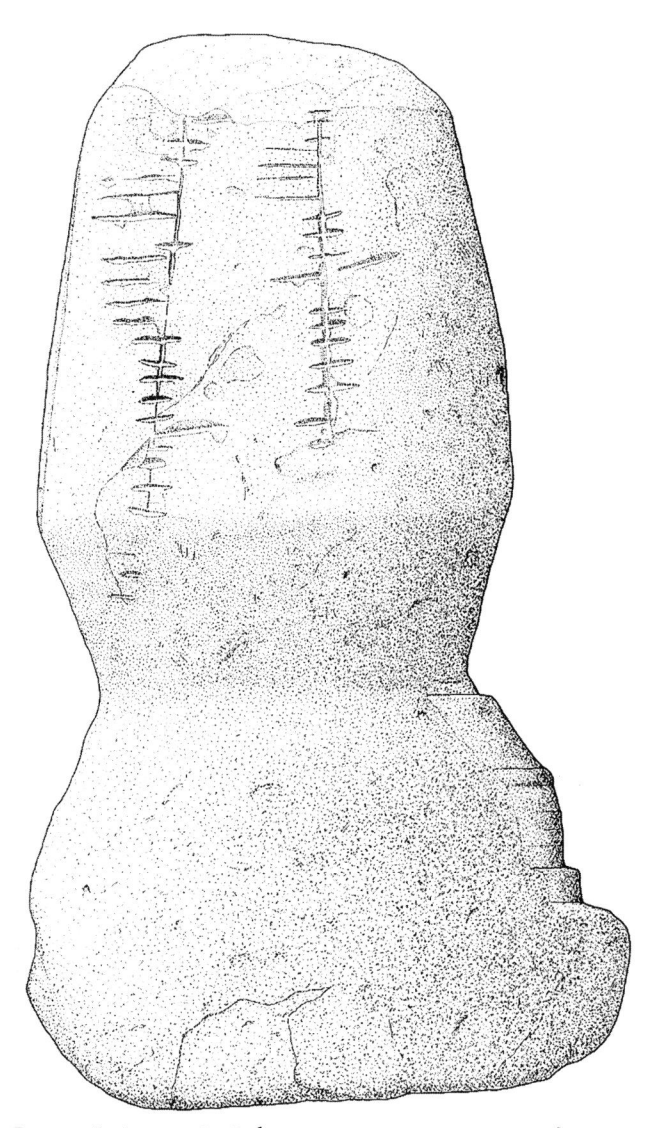

Figure 27.2 Roman baluster shaft (note mouldings at the base) with incised Ogham inscription, found in a well in Silchester. Height c.0.6 m (reproduced from Fulford et al. 2000: 11 by kind permission of the authors and the Society for Medieval Archaeology)

Saxon' presence (whatever that meant), and, although most of the Roman streets fell out of use in the fifth century, that and the axial routes show that the walled area was not deserted. Moreover, the clustering of cemeteries around Winchester is suggestive, as is the continuation of the decapitated-burial rite (familiar from Lankhills) at the Winnall cemetery. The continued importance of the walled enclosure implies that it served as a centre of authority. Ultimately that authority became that of the West Saxon royal house, whose relation to earlier powerful men on the site cannot be known, or at least cannot be known until we can resolve exactly who the *Gewissae* (the 'West Saxons') were, ethnically and politically. South of Winchester on the east bank of the River Itchen at Bitterne is a late Roman walled enclosure (often identified as *Clausentum* though the station so-called in the *Antonine Itinerary* is more probably Wickham). It may have guarded a deep-water anchorage, and was perhaps the predecessor of mid Saxon *Hamwic*, though this lay on the west bank of the river.

Verulamium has already been noted as a special case of continuity. Here excavation within and outside the walls has allowed us to understand more about the place both as a town and centre of the *Catuvellauni* and as a sanctuary, with one focus on a mausoleum/temple at Folly Lane. In the fourth/fifth century the latter was effectively replaced by the shrine of Alban, founded on the neighbouring hill, which later became known as St Alban's. *Verulamium* was sufficiently resilient to see its water-supply still being maintained in the fifth century, and in Constantius' Life of St Germanus written c.480 we seem to have an authentic glimpse of the splendidly arrayed town council of this time (above). Area excavations of the style of those at Wroxeter have not been conducted but there do seem to be ephemeral remains of wooden structures very like those in that town. Excavations beside the Abbey have found important late Roman graves, a fifth- or sixth-century silver handpin, and two items of seventh-century metalwork, a disc analogous to those attached to some hanging-bowls, and a spiral-headed pin, all suggestive of a still functioning Christian holy place (Biddle and Kjølbye-Biddle 2001: especially 65–6, fig. 14; see Fig. 27.1). Moreover, the 'British' nature of two of these finds is indicative of political control by an elite still with leanings towards a recognizable 'Roman' material culture, as is confirmed by Bede as late as the eighth century in that he still referred to *Verlamacaestir*.

Londinium, too, kept its name, and it is plausible to see it as a continuing centre of authority, although the latest intra-mural occupation deposit so far recovered is from a bath-house near Billingsgate in Thames Street, which included a 'Saxon' fifth-century disc brooch (Vince 1990: 7 and 51, fig. 27; Perring 1991: 127–31). Like other towns, London has produced deep layers of 'dark earth' which start in the third century and continue perhaps to the sixth or seventh. Various explanations have been given and it is possible that rubbish, decayed thatch, and timber might comprise some of these rich humic deposits, but the consensus is that they reflect abandonment or changing land-use, possibly for horticulture or agriculture. The recent fifth-century coffined burial discovered at St Martin's in the Fields (above) is from a site with rich seventh-century burials containing palm-cups like that from Silchester, and in one case a hanging-bowl (Swain 2007), but the distance from the walls of the city allows us to see the church as existing in a quasi-urban context and indeed later providing a new focus for *Lundenwic*. A late sixth-century text from Gaul apparently preserves the name of a martyr Augul(i)us who suffered at

Augusta, the late Roman name or title for London (Thacker and Sharpe 2002: 122–3) and it is very possible that this or another extra-mural site was his place of burial. There was probably also a Roman burial-ground at Westminster a further mile up-river from the City. A probably Christian fourth-century sarcophagus re-used in the Middle Ages preserves the name of the deceased Valerius Amandinus and his sons who buried him, Valerius Superventor and Valerius Marcellus (*RIB* no. 16). A somewhat earlier burial is represented by the funerary figure of a child found at Westminster School just outside the precincts of the Abbey (Toynbee 1964: 115–16). Despite the distance of these cemeteries from the City, they must represent at least satellite communities to *Londinium*.

Canterbury, with a name derived from that of the pre-Roman and Roman tribe of the *Cantii*, presents the same problem as London. The extra-mural church of St Martin, like St Martin's in the Fields, is a plausible Roman cemetery church and as we have seen Bede also attributed the intra-mural church on the site of the later cathedral (Christ Church) to the Romans. Other evidence is sparse: excavators record large expanses of 'dark earth', with little sign of material culture apart from a few, mainly Anglo-Saxon, finds, although a Visigothic gold tremissis struck in the name of Libius Severus or Zeno is potentially of interest (Kent 1995; Fig. 27.3) because such coins seem to have entered Britain in small numbers in the late fifth century. In all likelihood, however, this coin was bullion rather than currency, possibly used by a goldsmith as late as the seventh century. A solidus of Valentinian III is recorded in the St Pancras area of Chichester (Down 1974: 33, no. 77) and there is a hoard of gold and silver coins down to the later fifth century from Patching,

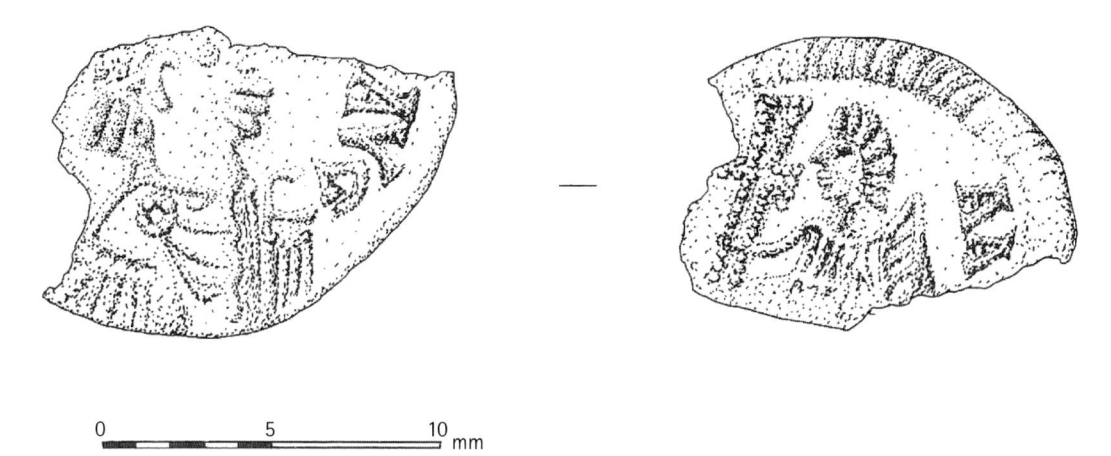

Figure 27.3 Fragment of a gold tremissis, struck in the late fifth century, found in Canterbury. Its broken condition indicates that it was valued as a source of gold rather than as currency; jeweller's rouge adhering to it, and a piece of gold sheet found in a related and contemporary layer, show that it had probably been mislaid by a goldsmith (reproduced from Kent 1995 by kind permission of the Canterbury Archaeological Trust)

near Worthing, a few miles to the east (White *et al.* 1999). These finds suggest the continuing presence of wealth in southern Britain and of continental links even though, on a minimalist view, such coins may attest no more than the presence of the odd wealthy visitor like St Germanus and not in any way the continuing vibrancy of urban life.

Lincoln (*Lindum Colonia*) was founded as a colony for retired legionary veterans and later became a regional urban centre and the seat of a bishop by the early fourth century, as attested by the *Acta* of the Council of Arles. Like Canterbury it retains its name in more or less Roman form. Although not numerous, the sub-Roman burials at the intra-mural church in the forum (above) suggest that that part of the Roman city had changed totally in character and use. There was no problem in the case of St Albans or indeed with London (St Martin's in the Fields) or Canterbury (St Martin's) as they were extra-mural, but one of the most firmly established practices in Roman culture was to keep the habitations of the living separate from the dead. Christian desire to be buried near the 'Very Special Dead' (P. Brown 1981: 69–85), the 'Saints', was a profound break with classical practice. The fact that St Paul-in-the-Bail was sited in the forum, and was used as a cemetery church, supposes a different focus, perhaps, rather than discontinuity, even though those who perpetrated it were most likely former Roman (Christian) citizens of *Lindum*, very probably descendants of those long established there. During the fourth century we must presume that there was an important (not necessarily large) church serving as the seat of the bishopric, but this has not been found and so we do not know whether it survived into the subsequent period.

York (*Eburacum*) was another bishopric attested in the Council of Arles and, with both a legionary fortress and a colonia, a site of considerable importance, though excavation down to Roman levels has only been sporadic on both banks of the Ouse. The site of the principia of the fortress below the Minster has proved to be particularly interesting; the building seems to have remained standing well into the post-Roman period and may have come to serve an ecclesiastical purpose. Study of what appear to be deposits of post-Roman animal bones, however, where sucking pig predominates, indicate secular aristocratic feasting (Gerrard 2007a) and thus a principal focus of elite secular life. At a centre of this importance one might expect a major Roman church, perhaps the cathedral, to have been designed for this purpose and, as at Trier, near the palace, in York the seat of the Dux Britanniarum. If so this was more probably in the former fortress than in the civilian colonia, but as at Lincoln the site awaits discovery.

Considerable credence is given to the hypothesis that the majority of towns served as seats of political authority from the entry in the *Anglo-Saxon Chronicle* for AD 577, in which rulers of the *Gewissae*, Cuthwine and Ceawlin, are said to have defeated a British army at *Deorham* (Dyrham), killing three of their leaders and capturing Gloucester, Cirencester, and Bath. It certainly suggests that it was plausible to think of these three 'cities' as centres of power in the second half of the sixth century. Gloucester (*Glevum*) was of course an ancient colonia and nearby

Cirencester (*Corinium*) was not only the chief city of the *Dobunni* but had most probably served as the provincial capital of the late Roman province of *Britannia Prima*. Both have yielded evidence of city life continuing into the fifth century and it almost certainly continued later. At Gloucester Bii amphora sherds possibly of fifth- or sixth-century date (but see Campbell 2007: 125 and 126 for a caveat), and the continued use of buildings after the fourth century are suggestive, and at Cirencester, which is less encumbered by later buildings, the forum paving continued to receive wear and there is evidence for timber building replacing buildings in stone (Dark 2000: 105–6).

As for the people of these cities, in a recent important thesis Yeates (2006) has established the case for the *Dobunni* tribe being essentially the same as the Hwicce, who appear in Anglo-Saxon sources. Bath will be considered more fully below. However, positive evidence for the continued existence of towns as towns as generally understood is only acceptable if one thinks in terms of shrunken populations living for the most part, at least from the second half of the fifth century, in wooden houses or huts within the walled areas of formerly vibrant cities, though it should be noted that timber-framing was an important building medium right through the Roman period. The shrinkage of the towns had little or nothing to do with the arrival of foreign settlers; it had in many instances begun in the fourth century if not before and further economic decline in the fifth century, possibly exacerbated by epidemic disease, continued the process.

SOME SMALLER TOWNS

Four towns, three of them fairly small former cantonal capitals, serve to put a more positive gloss on what happened. First Dorchester, Oxfordshire, whose 'Anglo-Saxon' name *Dorcic* preserves a 'Celtic' root. This rather small, sprawling settlement within modest earthwork fortifications was intensively occupied in the fourth century and in contrast to many towns coins of the House of Theodosius are common. There are timber buildings, some of them sunken-floored, and there are virtually contiguous late Roman (Queenford Farm, fourth–fifth century) and early Anglo-Saxon (Wally Corner, Berinsfield, fifth–sixth century) cemeteries (Hills and O'Connell 2009) which hint at a continuity of occupation and probably of population, larger than those of some of the larger towns. The probability is that the town remained a centre for Christianity, and the medieval abbey outside the East Gate might mark the site of a late Roman church or possibly even an early *martyrium*. Was the Roman aristocrat, St Birinus (Virinus), granted the town as the seat of his bishopric for this very reason (see Henig and Booth 2000: 187–92)?

Caerwent, *Castra Venta*, was the cantonal capital of the *Silures*. It could, as could *Venta Icenorum* (Caistor by Norwich), have been the location of the imperial weaving mill situated at *Venta* in the *Notitia* (though Winchester is more likely, see above); more plausibly, as it lies near the Severn and open to Irish piracy, it could have been the *Bannaventa*, home town of St Patrick (though the saint's career in Northern Ireland would favour an origin in Carlisle or the nearby fort of Birdoswald, *Banna*, for his parental estate). What is certain is that there is good evidence for continuing late occupation; indeed the forum was actually repaired in the very late fourth century, sealing a Theodosian coin. Late objects from here include a fifth- or sixth-century penannular brooch from the Eastgate cemetery, but by this time Caerwent had become as much as anything a walled monastic site associated with St Tatheus (Howell 2006: 100–1).

In East Anglia, Caistor by Norwich (*Venta Icenorum*) seems to have flourished very late, with a coin series going down to Honorius. Moreover, as at Dorchester, there is evidence for early 'Anglo-Saxon' settlement and contiguous cemeteries here (Myres and Green 1973; Pestell, this volume). In northern Britain, Carlisle, whose name is a corruption of *Luguvallium*, also flourished. As at Wroxeter there were timber buildings, but much of its infrastructure survived, such as impressive walls and the wonderful fountain admired by St Cuthbert in 685 (see Henig 2004b: 12–13). In the fifth century, freed from the restraints of the Roman state, Carlisle would appear to have expanded its territory to include the important Christian monastic centre founded by St Ninian at the end of the fourth century at Whithorn in Galloway; in course of time Carlisle probably became a focus for the British state of Rheged (McCarthy 2002: 140–54; Henig 2004b), ultimately devolving into the western centre for the Northumbrian kingdom.

The fourth 'town' was Bath (*Aquae Sulis*), mentioned above in connection with the 577 annal. Founded in the first century as a shrine for *Sulis Minerva* rather than as a town in the normal sense, its late Roman wall demarcated the limits of the sanctuary. Deposits continued to build up in the temple courtyard through the fifth century (Gerrard 2007b). The very fine enamelled penannular brooch recovered from the spring was at first conservatively dated to the fourth century (Cunliffe 1988: 23 no.48, pl. xvii) but Youngs has re-assigned it to the second half of the fifth (1995), and it should be noted that a somewhat similar late penannular brooch, albeit without such spectacular terminals, has been found at Verulamium (Niblett 2005). Cow bones possibly attest continuing pagan sacrifices to a goddess to whom, preferentially, female animals would have been offered. At some point, the gilded bronze cult statue of *Sulis Minerva* was destroyed and its head buried within the temple cella, and at the same time there may have been deliberate demolition of parts of the sanctuary (Cunliffe and Davenport 1985: 66–75 and 164–71; Gerrard 2007b). It is possible, indeed probable, that this was a stage in the thorough Christianization of the site. A further suggestion of the expansion of the church in this part of south-west Britain during the fifth and sixth centuries is provided in the construction of what must have been a baptismal font of considerable size in a nearby villa excavated at Bradford-on-Avon (Corney 2004). The hot springs of *Aquaemann* would appear to have remained in use, as a place of pilgrimage and now of Christian worship well before the ecclesiastical foundation, assigned to Osric of the Hwicce, *c*.675 (Manco 1998: 31–6).[4]

FORTS—OR TOWNS?

How was a Roman town defined in late antiquity? Those accustomed to the classic Roman city would distinguish between a *civitas*, a fortress, and a fort. That such distinctions no longer held is demonstrated by the fact that that the British and Saxon epithet associated with so many of the towns surveyed here is *castrum* (Caer,-cester). A fortress like Caerleon, or forts such as Portchester and Richborough, or, in the north of England, Birdoswald would have been regarded in the fifth century as no less urban and no less as centres of power.

Richborough (*Rutupiae*) now presents itself as a walled enclosure, a 'Saxon Shore' fort, in what had once been (and long continued to be) a substantial port-town, the main entry into Britain (Millett and Wilmott 2003); Dover (*Dubris*) further down the coast was little different in character. Although Caerleon appears to have been abandoned by Legio II Augusta late in the third century, there was certainly plentiful evidence of late Roman occupation, now evidently of a civilian nature, at the Castle Gates site down into the fifth century and perhaps beyond (Evans and Metcalf 1992: 72–5) and the strategic importance of the site on the lower River Usk is not likely to have gone unappreciated between the Roman and Norman periods. Portchester has been excavated; in all probability it was full of regimented timber buildings like Winchester and was no more and no less urban. There were certainly women present in late Roman Portchester, as hairpins and other items of female apparel attest, and a fairly dense occupation continues on through the 'Anglo-Saxon' period (Cunliffe 1976: 301–2). The *Anglo-Saxon Chronicle* records a Briton of high rank as having been killed here or nearby. Pevensey

---

[4] In this regard the name Akeman Street running from *Verulamium* (St Albans) via Alchester and Cirencester to Bath may be significant. The road, most likely established soon after AD 43 as an early limes delimiting friendly pro-Roman territory to the south from the north, continued to be of importance.

Alchester, beside the village of Wendlebury, Oxon., is a well-fortified small town which calls out for further study. It would be interesting to know how late it was occupied, as there is suggestive evidence of late-Roman-style burials cutting the infilled boundary ditch, which contained Anglo-Saxon potsherds, as well as continuity of 'Romano-British' agricultural practice in the vicinity (Henig and Booth 2000: 194–5). The eventual successor of Roman Alchester was presumably Bicester.

(*Anderitum*) is likewise mentioned in the *Anglo-Saxon Chronicle*, in this case as having fallen to an Anglo-Saxon attack in AD 491, its inhabitants being said to have fled to London (see Rivet and Smith 1979: 250–2). Whether any credence can be given to these stories is unknown, but at least they suggest the blurring of distinctions between forts and towns by the later fifth century.

No early church has yet been excavated either at Portchester or Pevensey; however, the recognition of a stone and tile baptistery together with the outlines of a church in one corner of the Richborough enclosure (P. D. C. Brown 1971) provides a close parallel to the intra-mural churches of the towns with reduced enceintes which were the norm in late Roman Gaul. The date of the baptismal tank is not certain; it has always been assumed to be fourth-century but it could be fifth. Although the seventh-century church associated with the Augustinian mission was set on a different location, more central to the enclosure, that does not rule out the continuity of a Christian presence at a site which has yielded distinctive items of late Roman metalwork, including signet-rings (Henig 1976; 1988), one with a *chi-rho* and another bearing a monogram in Merovingian style composed of letters (perhaps reading *Basia*, 'kisses'). Migration-period occupation as early as the sixth century has been noted within the walls of the Saxon Shore fort at Dover and the archaeological evidence for the church of St Martin, significantly named after the premier Gallo-Roman saint, takes it back to the seventh century (Philp 2003) although that does not rule out a still earlier date: as in the case of Richborough it is hard to believe that there was a break in occupation at the key gateway into south-east England from Francia. In northern Britain, Birdoswald is a classic case of continuity, because of its careful excavation. Here a fort was turned into a village, probably with a church (Wilmott 2001: 111–26); such a small settlement would scarcely be regarded as a town on our modern reckoning, but if it was indeed Bede's *Bannaventa* (Henig 2004b: 12), it must have been in his view!

Conclusions

Highly plausible evidence for the continued existence of the church in eastern as well as western Britain both from archaeology and also in the pages of Gildas and Bede must suggest the large-scale continuance of the native populations. However, as we have seen, this does not necessarily also suppose that the context in which Christianity flourished was any longer urban in the early Roman sense. The same problem of ecclesiastical continuity associated with what could be looked at as a case of urban decline can be observed at Caerwent, which, in the sixth century, may best be seen as little more than a monastic enclosure. There is good epigraphic testimony for people speaking Q-Celtic at Wroxeter and Silchester, but their status there is uncertain, and we should not assume that they were invaders and not local until we are more certain of the linguistic make-up of Roman Britain. Of course there are undoubted 'Anglo-Saxon' finds in many towns, revealing another element in the population, and not necessarily evidence for squatter occupation amidst the ruins. In the small town of Dorchester, Oxfordshire, the clustering of sunken-floored dwellings of Anglo-Saxon type suggests a sizeable 'Germanic' urban population. At Wroxeter and Silchester more major buildings in timber dating to the fifth and sixth centuries replacing stone buildings suggest an even more impressive attempt at asserting *romanitas*.

Cemeteries associated with (former) towns can be instructive. At Dorchester, the late Roman burials at Queenford Farm near the early Anglo-Saxon cemetery at Wally Corner, Berinsfield, suggest continuous occupation (see above). That the Winchester Lankhills cemetery (Clarke 1979), whose graves suggest the presence of a foreign, Danubian element, appears to end in the fifth century, need not suggest a hiatus in the use of the whole town, as reviewed above. Maybe a new cemetery was established. In the seventh century the decapitated burials at Winnall II may show survival of population into the Conversion period.

Most convincing of all is the fact that most Roman towns lie under their modern successors and generally, as we have seen, retain a version of their name. The old city administration might often have become in effect the fief of a chieftain and in course of time even a *villa regalis* or royal estate. Where Roman public buildings survived they might take on a new life as the abode of 'Dark Age' rulers or the sites of churches. The difficulty of this theme lies in the problem of deciding what we mean by continuity or discontinuity, as this will depend on the interests of those writing about the subject. The structure of town life was undoubtedly different from that of the period of Roman control but in virtually no case was there a total hiatus in occupation. A partial exception might be made for Chichester, despite its surviving Roman walls which later made it a *-ceaster* and the Valentinian III coin, discussed above; however, the name *Noviomagus* seems to have been lost and so far there is little evidence for even a mid Saxon presence, perhaps simply because the centre of civil and ecclesiastical power moved a few miles south to the Selsey peninsula (Munby 1984: 317–23), where a cathedral see was later established. Is this but a more extreme shift in location than those out of the walls of London and *Verulamium* to new sites in the near vicinity? Wroxeter exhibited continuing life around the important early Saxon church of St Andrew, but by the ninth century the main focus of settlement had shifted to Shrewsbury (White and Barker 1998: 138–46). Silchester was deliberately abandoned after the Conversion period for other sites within Wessex; the site of Norwich was eventually preferred to that of Caistor, and Richborough's fate was sealed, certainly not by 'barbarians' but by the relentless silting of the Wensum channel. Dover, with a similar history as town and military base, has continued to be one of the premier ports of England. In all these cases the establishment of the new replacement settlements took place well beyond the period covered by this chapter.

In the fifth and sixth centuries, towns seem to have lost their former economic role but retained something of their earlier importance as administrative and perhaps ecclesiastical centres, though admittedly not to the degree of towns in Gaul, many of which were bishoprics with cathedral churches and also extra-mural *martyria* (Knight 1999: 63–111; Pearce 2003). There is a suggestive parallel to the Continental model in Canterbury and perhaps London, and maybe also with Richborough and Dover, which were close to, if not clients of, the ruling power in Francia across the channel. The towns of Roman Britain survived as symbols of power and so most of them proudly retained their names. They often attest the continuity of Christianity, and even sometimes suggest the survival of ecclesiastical organization. The persistence of towns does not appear to give credence to any relapse into heathenism (an invention of the politically motivated Augustinian Mission, determined to re-impose 'Roman' authority on the insular, 'Celtic', church). Indeed that Mission may have been concerned in some instances, as in the case of St Sixtus, to obliterate local historical memory, though the Roman church would have honoured Alban, whose relics were, after all, venerated at Auxerre in Gaul. That there were cults left to manipulate and a Christian populace, many of them associated with towns, to provide an audience for the new Romans shows that these central places, and sometimes their suburbs and cemeteries, provided invaluable foci both for ecclesiastical re-organization and for the burgeoning, economically vibrant 'Anglo-Saxon' towns of later centuries.

REFERENCES

BARKER, P., WHITE, R., PRETTY, K., BIRD, H., and CORBISHLEY, M. (1997). *The Baths Basilica Wroxeter: Excavations 1966–9*. English Heritage Archaeological Report 8. London: English Heritage.

BIDDLE, M., and KJØLBYE-BIDDLE, B. (2001). 'The origins of St Albans Abbey: Romano-British Cemetery and Anglo-Saxon Monastery', in M. Henig and P. Lindley (eds.), *Alban and St Albans: Roman and Medieval Architecture, Art and Archaeology*. Leeds: British Archaeological Association Conference Transactions 25, 45–77.

────── (2007). 'Winchester: from *Venta* to *Wintancaestir*', in L. Gilmour (ed.), *Pagans and Christians: From Antiquity to the Middle Ages; Papers in Honour of Martin Henig, Presented on the Occasion of his 65th Birthday*. British Archaeological Reports International Series 1610. Oxford: Archaeopress, 189–214.

BOON, G. C. (1959). 'The latest objects from Silchester, Hants.'. *Medieval Archaeology* 3: 79–88.

BOYLE, A., DODD, A., MILES, D., and MUDD, A. (1995). *Two Anglo-Saxon Cemeteries: Berinsfield and Didcot*. Thames Valley Landscapes Monograph 8. Oxford: Oxford Archaeology.

BROOKS, D. A. (1986). 'A review of the evidence for continuity in British towns in the 5th and 6th centuries'. *Oxford Journal of Archaeology* 5: 77–102.
BROWN, P. (1981). *The Cult of the Saints*. Chicago and London: University of Chicago Press.
BROWN, P. D. C. (1971). 'The Church at Richborough'. *Britannia* 2: 225–31.
CAMPBELL, E. (2007). *Continental and Mediterranean Imports to Atlantic Britain and Ireland, AD 400–800*. CBA Research Report 157. York: Council for British Archaeology.
CLARKE, G. (1979). *Pre-Roman and Roman Winchester*, Part 2: *The Roman Cemetery at Lankhills*. Winchester Studies 3. Oxford: Clarendon Press.
CORNEY, M. (2004). 'The Roman villa at Bradford-on-Avon. Investigations at St Laurence School'. *ARA: The Bulletin of the Association for Roman Archaeology* 16: 1–15.
CUNLIFFE, B. (1976). *Excavations at Portchester Castle*, Volume 2: *Saxon*.Report of the Research Committee 33. London: Society of Antiquaries.
—— (ed.) (1988). *The Temple of Sulis Minerva at Bath*, Volume 2: *The Finds from the Sacred Spring*. Oxford University Committee for Archaeology Monograph 16. Oxford.
—— and DAVENPORT, P. (1985). *The Temple of Sulis Minerva at Bath*, Volume 1: *The Site*. Oxford University Committee for Archaeology Monograph 7. Oxford.
DARK, K. (2000). *Britain and the End of the Roman Empire*. Stroud: Tempus.
DOWN, A. (1974). *Chichester Excavations 2*. Chichester: Chichester District Council.
ESMONDE CLEARY, A. S. (1989). *The Ending of Roman Britain*. London: Batsford.
EVANS, D. R., and METCALF, V. M. (1992). *Roman Gates Caerleon*. Oxbow Monograph 15. Oxford: Oxbow.
FULFORD, M., BURNETT, A., HENIG, M., and JOHNS, C. (1989). 'A hoard of late Roman rings and silver coins from Silchester, Hampshire'. *Britannia* 20: 219–28.
—— HANDLEY, M., and CLARKE, A. (2000). 'An early date for Ogham: The Silchester Ogham stone rehabilitated'. *Medieval Archaeology* 44: 1–23.
—— CLARKE, A., and ECKARDT, H. (2006). *Life and Labour in Late Roman Silchester: Excavations in Insula IX since 1997*. London: Britannia Monograph 22.
GERRARD, J. (2007a). 'Rethinking the small pig horizon at York Minster'. *Oxford Journal of Archaeology* 26: 303–7.
—— (2007b). 'The temple of Sulis Minerva at Bath and the end of Roman Britain'. *Antiquaries Journal* 87: 148–64.
GILMOUR, B. (2007). 'Sub-Roman or Saxon, pagan or Christian: who was buried in the early cemetery at St Paul-in-the-Bail, Lincoln?', in L. Gilmour (ed.), *Pagans and Christians: From Antiquity to the Middle Ages; Papers in honour of Martin Henig, presented on the occasion of his 65th birthday*. British Archaeological Reports International Series 1610. Oxford: Archaeopress, 229–56.
HENIG, M. (1976). 'A monogram ring from Richborough'. *Antiquaries Journal* 56: 242–3.
—— (1988). 'A late Roman gold ring and other objects from Richborough'. *Antiquaries Journal* 68: 315–16.
—— (2002). *The Heirs of King Verica: Culture and Politics in Roman Britain*. Stroud: Tempus.
—— (2004a). 'Remaining Roman in Britain AD 300–700. The Evidence of portable art', in R. Collins and J. Gerrard (eds.), *Debating Late Antiquity in Britain AD 300–700*. British Archaeological Reports British Series 365. Oxford: Archaeopress, 13–23.
—— (2004b). '*Murum civitatis, et fontem in ea a Romanis mire olim constructum*: The arts of Rome in Carlisle and in the civitas of the Carvetii and their influence', in M. McCarthy and D. Weston, *Carlisle and Cumbria: Roman and Medieval Architecture, Art and Archaeology*. Leeds: British Archaeological Association Conference Transactions 27, 11–28.

—— (2007). '"And did those feet in ancient times?": Christian churches and pagan shrines in south-east Britain', in D. Rudling (ed.), *Ritual Landscapes of Roman South-East England*. Kings Lynn: Heritage Marketing, 189–204.

—— and BOOTH, P. (2000). *Roman Oxfordshire*. Stroud: Tempus.

HILLS, C. and O'CONNELL, T. (2009). 'New Light on the Anglo-Saxon succession: two cemeteries and their dates', *Antiquity* 83 (322): 1096–1108.

HOWELL, R. (2006). *Searching for the Silures: An Iron Age tribe in South-East Wales*. Stroud: Tempus.

KENT, J. P. C. (1995). 'The tremissis', in K. Blockley, M. Blockley, P. Blockley, S. S. Frere, and S. Stow, *Excavations in the Marlowe Car Park and Surrounding Areas*. Canterbury: Canterbury Archaeological Trust, 947–8.

KNIGHT, J. (1999). *The End of Antiquity: Archaeology, Society and Religion AD 235–700*. Stroud: Tempus.

—— (2003). 'Basilicas and barrows: Christian origins in Wales and Western Britain', in M. Carver (ed.), *The Cross goes North: Processes of Conversion in Northern Europe AD 300–1300*. York: York Medieval Press, 119–26.

MANCO, J. (1998). 'Saxon Bath: the legacy of Rome and the Saxon rebirth'. *Bath History* 7: 27–54.

MCCARTHY, M. (2002). *Roman Carlisle and the Lands of the Solway*. Stroud: Tempus.

MILLETT, M., and WILMOTT, T. (2003). 'Rethinking Richborough', in P. Wilson (ed.), *The Archaeology of Roman Towns: Studies in Honour of John S. Wacher*. Oxford: Oxbow Books, 184–94.

MUNBY, J. (1984). 'Saxon Chichester and its predecessors', in J. Haslam (ed.), *Anglo-Saxon Towns in Southern England*. Chichester: Philimore, 315–30.

MYRES, J. N. L., and GREEN, B. (1973). *The Anglo-Saxon Cemeteries of Caistor-by-Norwich and Markshall, Norfolk*. Reports of the Research Committee 30. London: Society of Antiquaries.

NIBLETT, R. (2005). 'Verulamium in the post-Roman period', in R. Niblett and I. Thompson, *Alban's Buried Towns: An Assessment of St Albans' Archaeology up to AD 1600*. Oxford: Oxbow Books, 166–77.

PEARCE, S. M. (2003). 'Processes of conversion in north-west Gaul', in M. Carver (ed.), *The Cross goes North: Processes of Conversion in Northern Europe AD 300–1300*. York: York Medieval Press, 61–78.

PERRING, D. (1991). *Roman London*. London: Seaby.

PHILP, B. (2003). *The Discovery and Excavation of Anglo-Saxon Dover*. Kent Monograph Series 9. Dover: Kent Archaeological Rescue Unit.

RIB: COLLINGWOOD, R. G., and WRIGHT, R. P. (1965). *The Roman Inscriptions of Britain, Volume 1: Inscriptions on Stone*. Oxford: Clarendon Press.

RIVET, A. L. F., and SMITH, C. (1979). *The Place-Names of Roman Britain*. London: Batsford.

SHARPE, R. (2001). 'The Late Antique Passion of St Alban', in M. Henig and P. Lindley (eds.), *Alban and St Albans: Roman and Medieval Architecture, Art and Archaeology*. British Archaeological Association Conference Transactions 25. Leeds: British Archaeological Association, 30–7.

SWAIN, H. (2007). 'London's last Roman?'. *Current Archaeology* 213: 35–9.

THACKER, A. T., and SHARPE, R. (2002). *Local Saints and Local Churches in the Early Medieval West*. Oxford: Oxbow Books.

THOMAS, C. (1981). *Christianity in Roman Britain to A.D.500*. London: Batsford.

TOYNBEE, J. C. M. (1964). *Art in Britain under the Romans*. Oxford: Clarendon Press.

VINCE, A. (1990). *Saxon London: An Archaeological Investigation*. London: Seaby.

WACHER, J. (1995). *The Towns of Roman Britain*. 2nd edition. London: Batsford.
WHITE, R., and BARKER, P. (1998). *Wroxeter: The Life and Death of a Roman City*. Stroud: Tempus.
WHITE, S., MANLEY, J., JONES, R., ORNA-ORNSTEIN, J., JOHNS, C., and WEBSTER, L. (1989). 'A mid-fifth century hoard of Roman and pseudo-Roman material from Patching, West Sussex'. *Britannia* 30: 301–15.
WILMOTT, T. (2001). *Birdoswald Roman Fort: 1800 years on Hadrian's Wall*. Stroud: Tempus.
YEATES, S. J. (2006). *Religion, Community and Territory: Defining Religion in the Severn Valley and Adjacent Hills from the Iron Age to the Early Medieval Period* BAR British Series 411. Oxford: British Archaeological Reports.
YOUNGS, S. M. (1995). 'A penannular brooch from near Calne, Wiltshire'. *Wiltshire Natural History and Archaeological Society Magazine* 88: 127–81.

CHAPTER 28

BRITONS AND ANGLO-SAXONS

CHRISTOPHER LOVELUCK
LLOYD LAING

CHANGING PARADIGMS OF INTERACTION

Within the context of the study of Britain between AD 400 and 600, the role of trade and the nature of exchange are part of the broader question, 'what happened to the indigenous population of those parts of Britain that exhibited new material and linguistic expressions of identity during the fifth and sixth centuries, known today under the label "Anglo-Saxon"?' This chapter perforce looks at the whole range of evidence for contacts between different areas and population groups, as 'trade' is only one mode of achieving 'exchange', and cannot always be singled out from the rest.

In the past fifty years, attempts to understand what happened to the native populations have mirrored theories behind the expression of ethnic and group affiliation, and the personal and collective experience of scholars and their contemporary societies. Hence, the approaches of pioneers of Anglo-Saxon archaeology, such as Leeds, Myres, Evison, and others, were led by culture-history, where material-culture assemblages were associated with 'Germanic' groups of 'Angles', 'Saxons', and 'Jutes', who according to the Venerable Bede had invaded eastern and southern Britain (Collingwood and Myres 1941; Leeds 1945; Evison 1965). Thus, the principal method of interaction between 'Britons' and 'Anglo-Saxons' proposed by the generations who had experienced the World Wars was invasion and armed conflict.

The paradigm of 'violent' relations between the indigenous population and Germanic newcomers between the fifth and seventh centuries remained paramount, especially for eastern England south of the Humber estuary, until more research began on the nature of the native contribution to, and co-existence with, Anglo-Saxon societies in northern and western England, notably in the work of Faull in Yorkshire (1977; 1981), and Miket (1980) and Cramp (1988) on Durham, Northumberland, and Cumbria. Greater awareness of a more demonstrable native British impact on the formation of Anglo-Saxon societies resulted from this work, suggested primarily by the differences in the material signatures of what we would now call 'Anglo-Saxon identity', between northern and western regions on the one hand, and eastern and southern-central England on the other. A British, in fact 'Romano-British' and late antique, legacy on aspects of 'Anglo-Saxon' material culture has been recognized in certain metalwork and decorative traditions: for example, in motifs (Dickinson 1993; Laing 2006) and in techniques such as enamelling (Laing 1999: 139–41). Perceived differences of some house types between England and the supposed Germanic 'ancestral homelands' where, for instance, animals and humans often shared the same building, led to greater emphasis being placed on Romano-British inheritance lying behind Anglo-Saxon building tradition (James *et al.* 1984; Hamerow, this volume). Furthermore, work on Anglo-Saxon burial modes and dress accessories associated with furnished inhumation demonstrated that, unlike cremations, the different Anglo-Saxon traditions were products of development in England, despite having affinities with those in northern Germany and southern Scandinavia (Hines 1984; Dickinson, this volume).

Appreciation of the active participation of both native British and incoming Germanic population elements in the creation of what we think of as 'Anglo-Saxon' was a legacy from the 1980s that was expanded in two directions in the 1990s: first, through the application of new sociological and historical research on the nature of ethnic affiliation and its expression in archaeology (Amory 1993; Jenkins 1997; S. Jones 1997; Pohl 1997; Lucy 2000a and b); and secondly, through the application of migration theories and detailed regional analyses of acculturation in western and northern England (Higham 1992; Loveluck 1995; Chapman and Hamerow 1997; Loveluck 2002; 2003).

Applications of new sociological and anthropological theories to the construction of ethnic identities stressed the error of the necessary association of physical (material culture) expressions of group membership with a group of people of a distinct biological or linguistic heritage (S. Jones 1997; Lucy 2000b). They also stressed that means of indicating group affiliation were not necessarily of long standing but could be, and were, created in the short term, re-working signs of past affiliations to create new material expressions of identity (Halsall 1995). Creation of Anglo-Saxon material culture and linguistic identity was seen as suggesting a desire of former provincial Roman populations to reflect their new 'non-Roman-ness', in apparent contrast both to other parts of the western Roman Empire, where groups with Germanic leading elements were very concerned to demonstrate affiliation to and inheritance from Rome, and to the west and north of the island of Britain. Despite being the least Romanized parts of the province, or lying beyond it, the adoption of Christianity, commemorative monuments using Latin script, and trade routes with Gaul and the Mediterranean world emphasized natives' affiliation with the late antique Roman world, in the northern and western peripheries of Britain. Studies based on migration theory and elite replacement as a means of changing methods of group expression indicated a mechanism that could have promoted the creation of 'Anglo-Saxon' identity: namely, the replacement of leading elements of British society by a new immigrant elite of mixed origins from northern Germany and southern Scandinavia (Hodges 1989; Higham 1992; Hines 1994; Scull 1995; Hines 1996). This 'take-over at the top' model, however, did not explain why the majority archaic Brittonic (P-Celtic)-speaking, or Latin-literate, populations chose to adopt a new linguistic identity for everyday communication (Coates 2007; Schrijver 2007; Tristram 2007).

In the first decade of the twenty-first century, new analytical technologies have also been applied to the question of the relationship between indigenous British and incoming 'Germanic' population elements in the creation of Anglo-Saxon societies. The approach given the greatest attention has been the application of genetic analysis to the question of migration of people from continental Europe to Britain, between the fifth and seventh centuries, but interpretation is problematic, as is the use of stable isotope, particularly strontium, analysis (see Hedges, this volume).

Insufficient attention has been paid to, or a lack of chronological or spatial resolution in analytical techniques has not allowed for, appreciation of different regional dynamics on the relationship of the indigenous and incoming population groups, who together produced Anglo-Saxon societies. Conceiving of their formation in the plural, rather than society in the singular, is critical in any attempt to examine the different levels of the British contribution. Examination of regional and chronological context is also essential in understanding ongoing relationships with the eighth- to eleventh-century societies and polities in Wales, Cornwall, Cumbria, and Scotland.

Eastern and Southern England, AD 400–600: Towns, Exchange, and the British Contribution

Life for the Britons in the mid to later fifth century may not have been life as it had been known by their predecessors in the fourth, but there is growing evidence that British authorities, some possibly *civitates* based on their late Roman predecessors, still survived as distinct entities during the period when northern Germanic and Scandinavian settlers arrived (Dark 1994; 2000; and see Henig, this volume). Continued occupation of former Romano-British townscapes as central places at Canterbury and Lincoln during the fifth and sixth centuries, and the near absence of diagnostically 'Anglo-Saxon' material culture at the latter, certainly suggest maintenance of territorial structures derived from Romano-British forebears, if not continued existence of British-controlled territories in the case of Lincoln (Esmonde Cleary 1993; M. Jones 1993). Other centres, such as *Verulamium*-St Albans and the area of the Chilterns, were also almost totally devoid of users of Anglo-Saxon traditions until the early seventh century (Rutherford Davies 1982). That the territory named Kent reflects the Brittonic tribal name of the Roman period—the *Cantii*—suggests that this territory, an Anglo-Saxon kingdom from the sixth century, remained a discrete territorial and social unit during the creation of its Anglo-Saxon society. The territory associated with the former *colonia* town at Lincoln (*Lindum*) was, likewise, not labelled with reference to an Anglo-Saxon ethnic group. Instead, it was named with reference to Lincoln as 'Lindsey' when the first Old English written sources mention it during the seventh century (Eagles 1989). Similarly, the people living in the Chiltern Hills were also labelled with reference to their geographic home, rather than any ethnic affiliation, when they became visible in the seventh-century *Tribal Hidage* document (W. Davies and Vierck 1974; Brooks 1989). Late Roman belt fittings, worn by members of the military and civil service, may suggest Germanic warriors and their families deliberately settled within a federate context by the last Roman or their succeeding British authorities.

It is clear that the British and immigrant communities in south-eastern England did not live apart without any contact, and there is evidence that some Romano-British metalworking traditions, techniques, and products persisted, to be assimilated in the creation of 'Anglo-Saxon' identity by those whose principal mode of material, and presumably linguistic, expression, derived from across the North Sea (Laing 1999: 139–41; Inker 2000: 48; Laing 2007). Similar contact and acculturation may be suggested by the presence of Romano-British objects in fifth- and sixth-century Anglo-Saxon graves, which White has argued were used as substitutes for approximately similar Anglo-Saxon objects (White 1988; 1990). The presence of intact Roman glass vessels in Anglo-Saxon graves can surely not be explained by the accident of survival on abandoned Roman sites, but rather as the heirlooms of people of Romano-British stock adopting Anglo-Saxon burial modes, or as acquisitions from them by immigrants. In contrast, however, a distinct British burial practice of unfurnished inhumation is clearly seen at the cemetery of Queenford Farm, just east of the small late Roman town at Dorchester-on-Thames, in Oxfordshire, separate from others nearby with Anglo-Saxon customs, including Dyke Hills with its military overtones (Chambers 1988; Loveluck 1994; Dickinson, Henig, this volume).

Occupation of another 'small town', at Heybridge, Essex, seems to have continued without a break from the fourth into the fifth and sixth centuries, albeit in an Anglo-Saxon form (Drury and Wickenden 1982), but this remains exceptional. Settlement location generally seems to reflect both rupture and continuity, which could reflect different relationships between different groups. Although some Romano-British villas in the south and east, either standing or in process of decay, were used as burial places and in very rare instances as sites of peripheral settlement activity, as at Barton Court Farm, near Radley, Oxfordshire (Miles 1984), their wide-scale abandonment in the early decades of the fifth century suggests the replacement of the Romano-British aristocracy by a new and numerically small immigrant elite. Support could have come from elements of an alienated, British 'colonate' peasantry in search of greater social freedoms, and ready to actively associate with that new elite through adoption of its ways of dress and verbal communication (Loveluck 1999; 2003). The only villa sites where occupation continued seem to have been sited in areas still controlled by British groups, as at Frocester Court, in the Cotswolds (Price 2003). There are, however, signs that fifth- to seventh-century Anglo-Saxon settlements were often located at sites of large fourth-century nucleated settlements, often along roads, as at Heybridge. Close association between fifth- to seventh-century (and later) Anglo-Saxon settlement location and late Roman nucleated settlements is an even more recurrent feature of areas north of the Humber, especially eastern Yorkshire (see below).

In the south-west, the evidence for British cultural survival to the end of the sixth century is fairly strong—an undiluted surviving tradition of metalworking, producing among other items hanging-bowls and penannular brooches, seems to have persisted this late (Youngs 1995; 1998), and there is evidence for the re-use of hill forts in the area into the sixth century. Early Anglo-Saxon material is generally absent except for a few stray finds, including a button brooch of probably late-fifth-/early-sixth-century date from Cadbury Castle, Somerset (Alcock 1995: 70). Some of the re-occupied hill forts (Hod Hill and Badbury Rings, Dorset, and Cadbury Congresbury, Dolebury, Worlebury, Cadbury Castle, and Ham Hill, all Somerset), have produced Anglo-Saxon material, some scholars favouring the view that they arrived there with Anglo-Saxon mercenaries employed by British leaders (Pearce 2004: 229). Beyond, *Dumnonia* remained essentially British, under a succession of local kings and sub-kings, until the gradual expansion of Anglo-Saxon control assimilated Devon, in the late seventh and eighth centuries. Cornwall lasted longer—a Cornish bishop was under Canterbury by 870, and the last king of Cornwall died in 875. Archaeology has little to contribute to the processes of Anglo-Saxon extension of influence, apart from some finds such as the Trewhiddle hoard deposited in c.869, but place-names are more helpful. Those of Anglo-Saxon origin stop fairly abruptly at the Tamar—further west the names are mostly British. This suggests that the boundary of Wessex in the ninth century lay along this line, with no Anglicization further west even after Æthelstan formalized the boundary in the early tenth century (Padel 2007; Probert 2007).

FORMATION OF THE ANGLO-SAXON SOCIETIES OF MERCIA AND NORTHUMBRIA, AD 500–700

North of the Humber estuary, and especially north of the River Tees and west of the Vale of York, the material and linguistic signatures of Anglo-Saxon identities were not taken up on any scale before the first half of the seventh century, and sometimes considerably later. The interaction between the British and Anglo-Saxon populations of northern and western Britain between AD 500 and 700 can be summarized in two forms. Firstly, interaction in the form of political alliance and warfare between polities, sometimes with British and Anglo-Saxon elites allied together against opponents comprising other allied Anglo-Saxon and British warbands: there is no sign of any perception of a collective sense of 'us' on the part of Anglo-Saxon polities, and 'them' in relation to British counterparts within seventh- and early eighth-century textual sources, especially in relation to northern Britain, whether viewed through the filter of Bede's *Ecclesiastical History* (Colgrave and Mynors 1969), the *Gododdin* of Aneirin (Koch 1997), or the *Tribal Hidage* (Brooks 1989). Secondly, interaction took the form of acculturation, producing Anglo-Saxon societies of quite different material reflections, based on different levels of British and Anglo-Saxon heritage expressed in different regions, between 500 and 700.

The kingdom of Mercia seems to have been the result of the coalescence of a conglomerate of British and Anglo-Saxon groups whose chosen means of expression became Anglo-Saxon, seemingly following the choices of the ruling lineages. Their material signatures varied, however, reflecting different extents of affiliation with long-standing British identities. Perhaps the best example can be found in the Peak District, known to have been a regionally distinct polity for purposes of tribute assessment in the *Tribal Hidage*, described as the *Pecsaetne* (W. Davies and Vierck 1974; Brooks 1989; Dumville 1989). During the early 1990s, analysis of the original Bateman archives and collections showed that barrow burial there was not an intrusive practice brought by a colonist Anglo-Saxon elite (Loveluck 1995). Primary burial in new barrows and secondary burial, re-using prehistoric barrows, had been a regional burial practice in the Roman period, for example, at Kenslow Knoll. Rituals practised in those barrows included placing quartz pebbles in the hands of the dead, and red deer antler tines in the graves. These same ritual inclusions were found in a significant proportion of the Anglo-Saxon barrow burials. They were also found as ritual inclusions in stone cist 'flat' inhumation graves of the seventh century in the Peak, a British burial tradition in which Anglo-Saxon material culture was added to the existing funerary ritual (Loveluck 1995), so not all of the rich graves need have reflected an Anglo-Saxon colonist elite. Equally likely is that British ruling lineages found it desirable to express their identity in the new high-status medium of the confederated kingdom of Mercia, principally but not exclusively through Anglo-Saxon means of display. Such a strategy could have promoted the preservation of an elite of British ancestry *in situ*, perhaps in competition with new Anglo-Saxon groups from the Trent valley, an interesting challenge for identification by ancient DNA analysis.

A British ancestry for the Peak elites and their wider population is perhaps suggested by the unusual concentration of wealth seen in the barrows. How could this have been procured? In the Roman period, the Peak District is known to have produced two specialist commodities, silver and lead, derived from silver-bearing galena ore. Small-scale extraction overseen by a native elite may have maintained a technology that it could exploit when in the seventh century lead again became socially and economically useful, as a key material used in the Roman Church tradition of Christian buildings, built for display, in mortared stone, and with lead roofing. By the early eighth century, much of the lead-bearing Peak District had been given by the Mercian kings to royal abbeys such as Wirksworth, a daughter house of Repton. When the people involved in lead production and export become visible in an Anglo-Saxon charter of AD 835, they are the local Peak population, administered by an *ealdorman*, Humberht, seemingly a local notary who rented an estate from Wirksworth (Hart 1975). He had to pay his rent as a set weight of lead.

This suggested acculturation within the context of the development of Mercia is also abundantly evident in the development of Anglo-Saxon societies in Northumbria. From the early seventh century, two territories with their own royal lineages formed the confederated kingdom, the northern called Bernicia and the southern Deira, with additional territories added as the kingdom grew. Both territorial names are of British, P-Celtic origin (Koch 1997). In terms of social inheritance, the seventh-century Anglo-Saxon societies of these Northumbrian sub-kingdoms were very different. Bernicia comprised regions formerly situated both within and beyond the Roman provinces of Britain (Loveluck 2002). The area north of Hadrian's Wall to the River Tweed comprised much of the territory labelled by the Romans as having belonged to the tribal confederacy of the *Votadini*, a name transformed in Old Welsh to *Gododdin*, and the subject of the heroic poem attributed to the seventh century (Koch 1997). The southern Bernician region, between the Rivers Tyne and Tees, had been the northern frontier zone of Roman Britain.

To the south of the River Tees, extending to the Humber estuary and encompassing all of eastern Yorkshire, lay the territory of Deira. Here, the situation seems to have been very similar to that observed in the south-east, with the creation of Anglo-Saxon identity in burial practice almost removing signs of British input. There are, however, signs of a British legacy in the active choice of including the diagnostically fifth- to sixth-century British dress accessory, the penannular brooch (especially type G), within certain wealthy, female graves: for example, Driffield-Kelleythorpe and Londesborough, East Yorkshire (Mortimer 1905; Loveluck 2003); and Norton-on-Tees, Teesside/Cleveland (Sherlock and Welch 1992; Loveluck 2002). In a British context, the penannular brooch was seemingly a dress accessory for both men and women of some social standing. In the Anglo-Saxon graves, however, the brooches are only in female contexts. It is possible that these brooches reflect heirlooms from the female side of lineages that may have been of British ancestry, representing intermarriage of native lineages with immigrant men.

In the archaeology of settlements, there also seems to have been a similar situation to eastern England south of the Humber, with a consistent relationship between the locations of fifth- to seventh-century Anglo-Saxon settlements in relation to the sites of existing Romano-British nucleated settlements, with gradual but very limited shifts as the settlements developed organically over time. Examples can be cited from Hayton, Shiptonthorpe, and Elmswell, East Yorkshire (Loveluck 1999; 2003); and Sherburn, North Yorkshire (Powlesland 2000). There is also demonstrable continuity in the use of some smaller farmstead sites, as at Staxton-Newham's Pit in North Yorkshire (Loveluck 2003). The most demonstrable influence of the existing Romano-British landscape on Anglo-Saxon settlement location in Deira, however, comes from the large-scale landscape study achieved at West Heslerton, in the Vale of Pickering, North Yorkshire, led by Dominic Powlesland, where the fifth- to seventh-century Anglo-Saxon settlement's location was conditioned by adjacent Romano-British, pagan shrines (Powlesland 2003).

North of Hadrian's Wall, diagnostic Anglo-Saxon material culture was very rare during the fifth and sixth centuries. Only a few burials exhibit an Anglo-Saxon ethnic affiliation analogous to that south of the River Tees, and most of those currently seem isolated, with the exception of the cemeteries at Milfield 'North' and 'South', in the Till valley, Northumberland (Scull and Harding 1990). Diagnostic Anglo-Saxon graves are also comparatively rare between the Rivers Tyne and Tees. Their distribution concentrates in eastern coastal locations, close to river mouths and their immediate hinterlands (Loveluck 2002). The largest concentration of

Anglo-Saxon cemeteries lay at the extreme south of Bernicia along the Tees valley, between Norton, Darlington, and Piercebridge (Pocock 1971; Miket and Pocock 1976; Sherlock and Welch 1992), with an outlier at Easington (Hamerow and Picken 1995). Isolated burials have also been found within the bounds of former Roman forts at Binchester, Co. Durham, and Corbridge, Northumberland (Miket 1980; Ferris and Jones 2000).

Away from the east coast and river valleys of Bernicia, influences from native traditions are demonstrable in burial practices. In the counties of Durham, Northumberland, the North and West Ridings of Yorkshire, and the Peak District discussed above, items of Anglo-Saxon material culture started to be used within the native British tradition of inhumation burial in stone-lined cists, between the fifth and seventh centuries (Loveluck 2002). In most cases, the items in the graves were luxury artefacts that could have acted as badges of high social rank. The incorporation of exotic 'Anglo-Saxon' items within native cist graves probably reflects the adoption of new fashions in expression of group identity and status by leading families among the British population, in a process of coalescence with Anglo-Saxon elites (Loveluck 2002). Three such cist graves have been found: Castle Eden, East Boldon, and Cornforth, Co. Durham (Cramp 1995a; 1995b). The Castle Eden burial was accompanied by a glass 'claw' beaker; the Cornforth grave by weapons; and the East Boldon individual by a late sixth- to seventh-century, garnet-inlaid buckle (Baldwin Brown 1915: 810). A cist-grave cemetery has also been excavated recently in the dunes beyond Bamburgh Castle, Northumberland. At least one grave contained a knife and buckle, and that had a radiocarbon date range of AD 560–670 at 98 per cent confidence (Young in Ziegler 2001; Young 2003). This suggests the Anglicization of the existing British, fortified centre sometime in the later sixth century.

The settlement hierarchy of Anglo-Saxon Bernicia, especially north of Hadrian's Wall, also reflects a huge legacy from the existing Roman Iron Age society of the region. Indeed, the existing settlement pattern seems to have been taken over in its entirety in the creation of the Bernician, Anglo-Saxon settlement hierarchy (Loveluck 2002). This consisted of royal fortified centres on the North Sea coast at Bamburgh, Northumberland (Bailey 1991), and Dunbar, East Lothian (Perry 2000), in modern-day Scotland (see below); royal estate centres further inland at Yeavering (Hope-Taylor 1977) and Milfield (Gates and O'Brien 1988), both Northumberland; and Sprouston, Roxburghshire (Smith 1984); and lowland hamlets and farmsteads, such as Thirlings and New Bewick (O'Brien and Miket 1991; Gates and O'Brien 1988). Typical Anglo-Saxon earthfast timber buildings and *Grubenhäuser* were used among the lowland rural settlements of the Milfield basin, although the aerial photographic evidence from Milfield and Sprouston also indicates that significant native farmsteads already existed at these settlements prior to their Anglicization, as does the excavated evidence from Yeavering.

South of Hadrian's Wall, to the Tees, a strong influence from the British population is also suggested by known Anglo-Saxon settlement location, particularly by the discovery of Anglo-Saxon remains from within former Roman forts. For example, early and mid Anglo-Saxon graves have been excavated within Binchester, Co. Durham (Ferris and Jones 2000). Sixth- to seventh-century Anglo-Saxon graves have also been excavated at Corbridge, as well as remains of a mid to late Anglo-Saxon watermill (Bidwell and Snape 1996). There is also a mid to late Anglo-Saxon church outside the fort, in the medieval and modern town centre, reflecting limited settlement drift through the Anglo-Saxon period (Loveluck 2002). Occupation of former Roman forts between the fifth and seventh centuries also seems to have been a recurrent feature in both British and Anglo-Saxon areas north of the Lune, Eden, and Tees valleys, in the former military frontier zone. Continued occupation has been demonstrated archaeologically at the forts of Birdoswald, Cumberland (Wilmott 1997; 2000), and Chesterholm, Northumberland (Casey 1994).

By the later sixth to early seventh century, the Bernician social elite probably consisted of immigrant Anglo-Saxon and native British elements by ancestry, with their chosen means of physical expression in material culture becoming that of the Anglo-Saxon component. What constituted 'Anglo-Saxon' in a Bernician context, however, owed much to a British social inheritance (Loveluck 2002). The extent of the British inheritance in Bernicia also forces us to question whether Christianity was an alien belief system prior to the foundation of the first Anglo-Saxon monasteries in the area. Northern British and Pictish societies had certainly been Christianized during the fifth and sixth centuries. The Christianity of the regions surrounding Bernicia and the demonstrable British legacy in burial and settlement traditions makes it likely that a significant proportion of the British component of Bernician society was Christian, prior to the creation of Bernician 'Anglo-Saxon' society between the mid sixth and seventh centuries. Against this background, the adoption of the Irish/British traditions of the 'Scottic' Ionan brand of Christianity by King Oswald of Northumbria, from the Bernician royal line, in 634, can be viewed as an extra layer in the creation of Bernician social and political identity, as much as religious conversion (Loveluck 2007). This use of Christianity as a force for cohesion in Bernician society seems to be expressed in the cemeteries associated with the early monastic foundation at Hartlepool, founded c.640. The graves at the Gladstone Street cemetery were all unfurnished and buried within the context of the long-standing British, stone-cist tradition. Furthermore, the graves of a family group in the otherwise male (monks?) cemetery at Church Walk were lined with stones, harking back to the native tradition (Daniels 2007). It is possible that the Gladstone Street cemetery represents a local Christian population of British descent and that the family group at Church Walk represents a local aristocratic lineage of native ancestry, stone-lining their graves in a British manner (Loveluck 2007).

Within the context of the development of Northumbrian Christianity, much has been written of its borrowing from insular traditions, particularly in the realm of ecclesiastical art. Recent analysis, however, suggests that British and Irish influence on Anglo-Saxon art has been overstressed, to the detriment of influences from the 'pagan' Anglo-Saxon legacy, and a strong admixture of other ideas from continental Europe, both Francia and Rome. Decorative devices, such as confronted trumpets, peltae, yin-yangs, and scrolls, have been viewed as alien to Anglo-Saxon work, and as a consequence of British/Irish inspiration. These design elements, however, are of Romano-British origin, and their assimilation into Insular metalwork and manuscript art is most likely to be part of a lingering tradition of Roman ornamental devices in use in fifth- and sixth- century Britain, particularly apparent in the decoration of hanging-bowls (Laing 2006; and see Webster, this volume). There is nothing exclusively 'Northumbrian' about the phenomenon: similar motifs are apparent in the Kentish Stockholm *Codex Aureus* and Vespasian Psalter. If artistic influence is to be sought, the flow is the other way, with Anglo-Saxon metalworking techniques and ornamental devices being assimilated by British and Irish societies. It is almost certainly from the Anglo-Saxons that the Picts and Irish derived their ideas about producing stone carvings in relief: the flow of ideas seems to have been from Northumbria to Iona and thence subsequently to Ireland, and probably Pictland.

The Anglo-Saxons and relations with Scotland and Wales, AD 700 to 1066

The relationship between British and Anglo-Saxon polities between the eighth and eleventh centuries can be summed up as two alternative forms of interaction: namely, periodically peaceful or warlike relations between independent British and Anglo-Saxon kingdoms, or direct conquest and periodic hegemony of Anglo-Saxon kingdoms over British polities in Cornwall, Wales, Cumbria, and southern Scotland. The modern tacit perception, however, of an almost inevitable and inexorable spread of Anglo-Saxon hegemony over western Britain, and periodic power over Scotland, between the seventh and eleventh century is not appropriate. In the early to mid seventh century, the army of the King of Gwynedd, Cadwallon, had invaded and defeated the Northumbrians in Bernicia, with the Mercians as 'junior' allies (Colgrave and Mynors 1969). Texts indicate that the Picts wielded power in northern Bernicia, after their defeat of King Ecgfrith in 685 (Colgrave and Mynors 1969; Farmer 1983; Loveluck 2007). The British (Old Welsh-speaking) kingdom of Strathclyde, with its principal centre at Glasgow, actually expanded at the expense of West Saxon and then Anglo-Danish hegemony during the tenth and eleventh centuries, to incorporate Cumbria within its dominion (Newman 1984; O'Sullivan 1984; Driscoll 2000).

Extension of Bernician influence into Scotland can be seen from the later sixth century, and resulted in the establishment of Northumbrian overlordship south of the River Forth (Duncan 1975: 65; Smyth 1984: 23–4). The presence of an Anglo-Saxon population is shown by the occurrence of Old English place-names, especially in the Lothians (Brooke 1991; Proudfoot and Aliaga-Kelly 1996: 7), as well as archaeological finds. A scatter of finds in south-east Scotland suggests that contacts with users of Anglo-Saxon material culture may have begun earlier—spearheads found at Traprain Law in East Lothian are of fifth- to sixth-century Anglo-Saxon type, and stray finds of Anglo-Saxon gold and garnet sword fittings from Wester Craigie (Dalmeny), Midlothian, and Markle, West Lothian, along with a fragment of what may have been a gold and garnet pectoral cross similar to that from Cuthbert's coffin, found near Dunbar, a buckle plate with a human figure from Ayton in the Borders, and glass beads from an inhumation burial at Dalmeny, point to the presence of an elite expressing itself in the Anglo-Saxon manner during the seventh century (Proudfoot and Aliaga-Kelly 1996: 2 and 5; Lowe 1999: 22; Blackwell 2007; Baldwin Brown 1914–15).

Growing settlement evidence in south-east Scotland attests this Anglo-Saxon overlordship and affiliation, and its incorporation into Bernicia: high-status sites include an Anglo-Saxon 'hall' which replaced a British predecessor at Doon Hill, Dunbar, East Lothian (Hope-Taylor 1980). Other rectangular wooden buildings of Anglo-Saxon type have been detected by aerial photography, including examples from the settlements at Sprouston (Smith 1991), and Hogbridge and Tyninghame, East Lothian (Lowe 1999: 32). More extensive evidence for the Anglo-Saxon presence is afforded by the sites in Dunbar itself, where discoveries include a Saxon mortar mixer and where there is evidence for timber buildings followed by timber on stone footings, and a mortared stone building, possibly a royal hall (Lowe 1999: 22; Perry 2000; Moloney 2001). Humbler structures, notably *Grubenhaüser*, are represented at Sprouston, Dunbar, and Ratho (Smith 1983; 1984). Within the Anglo-Saxon sphere of influence there is also evidence for ecclesiastical take-over, attested by the presence of sculpture in Northumbrian style notably at Abercorn, Aberlady, and Tynninghame in the Lothians, and Jedburgh in Roxburghshire. Abercorn and Old Melrose were both Anglo-Saxon monasteries which succeeded British precursors, and Aberlady has yielded some fine Anglo-Saxon ornamental metalwork of the eighth and ninth centuries (Lowe 1999: 55).

In south-west Scotland Northumbrian overlordship is also apparent. Again some stray finds point to contacts before the main Bernician advance in the late sixth century under Æthelfrith: a sixth-century brooch was found at Botel, Dumfries and Galloway, in a ditch surrounding a later medieval castle (Penman 1998: 475). The clearest evidence, however, comes from the British metalworking site at the Mote of Mark, Kirkcudbright, where Anglo-Saxon influence is apparent in the decorative schemes used in metalworking and in the form of buckles produced there. More tangible Anglo-Saxon interaction is also represented by a rock-crystal bead and runic inscriptions (Laing and Longley 2006). That this was not merely a one-way flow is perhaps suggested by a gilt interlace-decorated disc from Cumbria, which was very probably made at the Mote of Mark (O'Sullivan 1990). Again a strong Northumbrian ecclesiastical presence is apparent, both in the form of sculpture (the Ruthwell Cross, one of the finest Northumbrian monuments, is in Dumfriesshire) and in the monastic complexes that replaced the British foundation at Whithorn (P. Hill 1997), and possibly Hoddom (Lowe 1991: 1999). There are also putative Anglo-Saxon 'halls' at Kirkconnel (Clough and Laing 1969) and Cruggleton, Dumfries and Galloway (Ewart 1985). Continuing influence and interaction are attested by the occurrence in south-west Scotland of Northumbrian stycas of the late eighth/early ninth century, such as those from Luce Sands (Cormack 1965), and ornamental metalwork: strap-ends, and two swords of the ninth century (Whitfield and Graham-Campbell 1992).

North of the Firth of Forth there is little evidence for adoption of Anglo-Saxon forms of expression, communication, or display, despite the probability that Fife was briefly under Northumbrian domination, though a Style I bridle fitting from South Leckaway, Angus, lends support to some form of cultural and possibly political connection between Southern Pictland and the Anglo-Saxon communities in the sixth or early seventh centuries (Dickinson et al. 2006). Further north, finds from Scalloway Broch, Shetland, point to Anglo-Saxon contact in the same period, as well as the local imitation of an Anglian safety-pin brooch of the later seventh century (Campbell 1998: 166–7). In Scottish Dál Riata there is little evidence for contact before the Northumbrian expansion. The main evidence for influence is to be found at Dunadd, Argyll, where the metalworking assemblage again shows the influence of Anglo-Saxon types on buckle design, as well as the assimilation of Anglo-Saxon animal ornament on a mount. More tangible evidence for contact takes the form here of a gold and filigree stud, probably from a southern English composite disc brooch (Lane and Campbell 2000). In the context of metalworking, the Hunterston Brooch, although probably produced in Dál Riata, exhibits techniques and ornamental designs adopted from southern English workshops (Stevenson 1974).

In Pictland Anglo-Saxon influence is less apparent. A few early finds have been made up the east coast, including the possible discovery of an Anglo-Saxon cremation urn at 'Buchan' in Aberdeenshire (Myres 1977, Vol. 1: 222, no. 1037) and a spearhead from a burial at Watten, Caithness (Proudfoot and Aliaga-Kelly 1996: 2). Aerial photographs have revealed some evidence of *Grubenhäuser* from Fife to Moray, but most of the evidence of contact with England comes after the formation of Alba in the ninth century. Apart from the Trewhiddle-style drinking-horn mount from the Pictish fort of Burghead, Moray (Graham-Campbell 1973), there is a scatter of ninth-century strap-ends and a few pins probably of Anglo-Saxon manufacture in eastern Scotland, but Anglo-Saxon influence is more apparent in sculpture, for example on the Aberlemno Roadside and the Nigg cross-slabs, and in the St Andrews sarcophagus, though probably not in the erection of relief-decorated cross-slabs. The opposite flow of ideas (or people) is less apparent, though there is a knife handle with a Pictish ogham inscription from Weeting, Norfolk, a Pictish penannular brooch from York, and a putative Pictish sword pommel from Beckley, Oxfordshire (Henderson and Henderson 2004: 211).

There is little evidence for extensive contact between the British kingdoms of Wales and the Anglo-Saxon kingdoms in the fifth or sixth centuries, though there is epigraphic evidence showing travel, at least at the level of the British social elite, between Wales and British territories in eastern Britain. The fifth- to early-sixth-century tombstone of Aliortus of Elmet, inscribed in Latin—*Aliortus Elmetiaco Hic Iacet*—in the church of Llanelhairn in Gwynedd, demonstrates movement across the Pennines (Loveluck 2003). Anglo-Saxon artefacts from the defended settlement at Dinas Powys, Glamorgan, include a chip-carved disc and a group of bucket mounts which may have arrived as scrap metal (Alcock 1963), and glass that probably arrived as intact vessels (Campbell 2007: 92–6); another native fort, Dinorben, Clwyd, yielded a single buckle fragment (Gardner and Savory 1964: 162–3; Redknap 1991: 78). More recently, excavations at Llanbedrgoch, on Anglesey, Gwynedd, have recovered a small collection of sixth- and seventh-century Anglo-Saxon dress accessories (Redknap 2000; Redknap pers. comm.), and other objects are being reported to the National Museum of Wales by metal-detector users, under the Portable Antiquities Scheme.

With the growth of the Anglo-Saxon kingdoms on the Welsh border the evidence for direct interaction becomes more tangible. Welsh raids on Mercia in 705 and 709 may have been catalysts for the construction of Wat's Dyke, perhaps by Æthelbald (716–57); Offa's Dyke, an even longer linear boundary which partly follows the line of Wat's, was traditionally the work of the Mercian king, built probably between 784 and 796 (D. Hill and Worthington 2003). Even if a demarcatory rather than a military boundary, its psychological effect as a deterrent for communication was certainly significant, defining Wales as a physical entity for the first time.

Rhodri Mawr of Gwynedd expanded his territory to include much of Wales, and in his expansionist activities he seems to have come into conflict with the Anglo-Saxons, who besieged and sacked Degannwy, Clwyd, in 822; he and his successors were markedly more successful than the English kings in defeating Viking raiders (W. Davies 1982: 110; Redknap 2000). Subsequent pressure on Wales from the Anglo-Saxons did not result in extensive adoption of Anglo-Saxon cultural traits amongst the bulk of the population, though there is growing evidence of late Anglo-Saxon metalwork, particularly in the eastern areas of Powys, Gwent, and Glamorgan (Redknap 1995: 69). Also from Powys, possibly a gift from an English king, is the linen with silk embroidery found at Llan-gors crannog, a site subsequently destroyed by an English raid in 916 (Coatsworth and Owen-Crocker 2007: 6–7).

The most notable evidence for Anglo-Saxon advance into Welsh territory was the foundation by Edward the Elder in 921 of the Anglo-Saxon *burh* at Rhuddlan, Clwyd. Excavation has shown that the burghal settlement enclosed Anglo-Saxon-style buildings with evidence of industrial activity and a motif-piece decorated with Anglo-Saxon animal ornament (Quinnell *et al.* 1994: 169). The limited success of the settlement reflects the limited degree of West Saxon control over Welsh affairs. It would take Norman castle boroughs to re-implant the urban settlement into Wales. At the level of the tenth- and eleventh-century Welsh elites, however, particularly in the south of Wales, there was a closer relationship with the West Saxon kings of England, reflecting internal rivalries with Gwynedd. Hywel Dda, King of Deheubarth (south-west Wales), became ruler of virtually all of Wales from 942, with the support of the English kings. Coins were struck at Chester in his name, probably on the authority of the West Saxon King of England, and intended as a gift from the Anglo-Saxon monarch, emphasizing Hywel's status as allied king (W. Davies 1982: 54; Redknap 2000). His northern Welsh successors, the kings of Gwynedd, however, were to raid England and burn Hereford in the time of Edward the Confessor, principally in the reign of Gruffudd ap Llywelyn, between 1052 and 1056 (R. R. Davies 1986). Despite the successes of the Gwynedd dynasty, the names of some Welsh aristocrats in south Wales during the early to mid eleventh century also reflect increasing Anglo-Saxon influence and acculturation of the Welsh elite prior to the Norman Conquest—the famous eleventh-century cross at Carew, Pembrokeshire, is the monumental and inscribed epitaph for a Deheubarth aristocrat, with the name of 'Edwin' within his immediate genealogy, a portent of a wider acculturation that would take place from the 1090s in southern Wales (R. R. Davies 2000).

REFERENCES

ALCOCK, L. (1963). *Dinas Powys: An Iron Age, Dark Age and Medieval Settlement in Glamorgan*. Cardiff: University of Wales Press.

—— (1995). *Cadbury Castle, Somerset: The Early Medieval Archaeology*. Cardiff: University of Wales Press.

AMORY, P. (1993). 'The meaning and purpose of ethnic terminology in the Burgundian laws'. *Early Medieval Europe* 2(1): 1–28.

BAILEY, R. N. (1991). 'Gold Plaque, Bamburgh, Northumberland', in L. Webster and J. Backhouse (eds.), *The Making of England: Anglo-Saxon Art and Culture AD 600–900*. London: British Museum Press, 58–9.

BALDWIN BROWN, G. (1914–15). 'Notes on a necklace of glass beads found in a cist at Dalmeny Park, South Queensferry'. *Proceedings of the Society of Antiquaries of Scotland* 49: 332–8.

—— (1915). *The Arts in Early England: Saxon Art and Industry in the Pagan Period*, Volume 4. London: J. Murray.

BASSETT, S. (ed.) (1989). *The Origins of Anglo-Saxon Kingdoms*. London: Leicester University Press.

BIDWELL, P. T., and SNAPE, M. E. (1996). *Evaluation of Archaeological Sites Threatened by River Erosion at Corbridge, Northumberland: Post-Excavation Assessment*. Newcastle: Tyne and Wear Museums.

BINTLIFF, J., and HAMEROW, H. F. (eds.) (1995). *Europe Between Late Antiquity and the Middle Ages: Recent Archaeological and Historical Research in Western and Southern Europe*. British Archaeological Reports International Series 617. Oxford: Archaeopress.

BLACKWELL, A. (2007). 'An Anglo-Saxon figure-decorated plaque from Ayton (Scottish Borders), its parallels and implications'. *Medieval Archaeology* 51: 165–72.

BROOKE, D. (1991). 'The Northumbrian settlements in Galloway and Carrick: an historical assesment'. *Proceedings of the Society of Antiquaries of Scotland* 121: 295–327.

BROOKS, N. (1989). 'The formation of the Mercian kingdom', in Bassett (ed.), *The Origins of Anglo-Saxon Kingdoms*, 159–70.

CAMPBELL, E. (1998). 'Brooches', in N. Sharples, *Scalloway: A Broch, Late Iron Age Settlement and Medieval Cemetery in Shetland*. Oxford: Oxbow Books, 166–8.

—— (2007). *Continental and Mediterranean Imports to Atlantic Britain and Ireland, AD 400–800*. CBA Research Report 157. York: Council for British Archaeology.

CASEY, P. J. (1994). 'The end of fort garrisons on Hadrian's Wall: A hypothetical model', in F. Vallet and M. Kazanski (eds.), *L'Armée Romaine et les Barbares du IIIe au VIIe siècle*. Paris: Maison des Sciences de l'Homme, 259–67.

CHAMBERS, C. (1988). 'The late and sub-Roman cemetery at Queenford Farm, Dorchester-on-Thames'. *Oxoniensia* 52: 36–69.

CHAPMAN, J., and HAMEROW, H. (eds.) (1997). *Migrations and Invasion in Archaeological Explanation*. British Archaeological Reports International Series 664. Oxford: Archaeopress.

CLOUGH, T. H. McK., and LAING, L. (1969). 'Excavations at Kirkconnel, Waterbeck, Dumfriesshire, 1968'. *Transactions of the Dumfriesshire and Galloway Natural History and Antiquarian Society* 46: 128–39.

COATES, R. (2007). 'Invisible Britons: the view from linguistics', in Higham (ed.), *Britons in Anglo-Saxon England*, 172–91.

COATSWORTH, E., and OWEN-CROCKER, G. R. (2007). *Medieval Textiles of the British Isles AD 450–1100: An Annotated Bibliography*. British Archaeological Reports British Series 445. Oxford: Archaeopress.

COLGRAVE, B., and MYNORS, R. A. B. (eds. and trans.) (1969). *Bede's Ecclesiastical History of the English People*. Oxford: Oxford University Press.

COLLINGWOOD, R. G., and MYRES, J. N. L. (1941). *Roman Britain and the English Settlements*. Oxford: Oxford University Press.

CORMACK, W. F. (1965). 'Northumbrian coins from Luce Sands'. *Transactions of the Dumfriesshire and Galloway Natural History and Antiquarian Society* 42: 149–50.

CRAMP, R. J. (1988). 'Northumbria: the archaeological evidence', in S. Driscoll and M. Nieke (eds.), *Power and Politics in Early Medieval Britain and Ireland*. Edinburgh: Edinburgh University Press, 69–78.

—— (1995a). 'The making of Oswald's Northumbria', in C. Stancliffe and E. Cambridge (eds.), *Oswald: Northumbrian King to European Saint*. Stamford: Paul Watkins, 17–32.

—— (1995b). *Whithorn and the Northumbrian Expansion Westwards*. Third Whithorn Lecture, Whithorn.

DANIELS, R. (2007). 'The early medieval cemeteries', in R. Daniels and C. P. Loveluck (eds.), *Anglo-Saxon Hartlepool and the Foundations of English Christianity: An Archaeology of the Anglo-Saxon Monastery*. Tees Archaeology Monograph Series 3. Hartlepool: Tees Archaeology, 74–96.

DARK, K. (1994). *Civitas to Kingdom: British Political Continuity 300–800*. Leicester: Leicester University Press.

—— (2000). *Britain and the End of the Roman Empire*. Stroud: Sutton.

DAVIES, R. R. (1986). *The Age of Conquest: Wales 1063–1415*. Oxford: Oxford University Press.

—— (2000). *The First English Empire: Power and Identities in the British Isles, 1093–1343*. Oxford: Oxford University Press.

DAVIES, W. (1982). *Wales in the Early Middle Ages*. London: Leicester University Press.

—— and VIERCK, H. (1974). 'The contexts of the Tribal Hidage: social aggregates and settlement patterns'. *Frühmittelalterliche Studien* 8: 223–93.

DICKINSON, T. M. (1993). 'Early Anglo-Saxon saucer brooches: a preliminary overview'. *Anglo-Saxon Studies in Archaeology and History* 6: 11–44.

—— FERN, A., and HALL, M. A. (2006). 'An early Anglo-Saxon bridle-fitting from South Leckaway, Forfar, Angus, Scotland'. *Medieval Archaeology* 50: 249–60.

DRISCOLL, S. T. (2002). *Alba: The Gaelic Kingdom of Scotland, AD 800–1124*. The Making of Scotland Series. Edinburgh: Historic Scotland.

DRURY, P. J., and WICKENDEN, N. P. (1982). 'An early Anglo-Saxon settlement within the Romano-British Small Town at Heybridge, Essex'. *Medieval Archaeology* 26: 1–40.

DUMVILLE, D. (1989). 'The Tribal Hidage: an introduction to the texts and their history', in Bassett (ed.), *The Origins of Anglo-Saxon Kingdoms*, 225–30.

DUNCAN, A. (1975). *Scotland: The Making of a Kingdom*. Edinburgh: Oliver and Boyd.

EAGLES, B. N. (1989). 'Lindsey', in Bassett (ed.), *The Origins of Anglo-Saxon Kingdoms*, 201–12.

ESMONDE CLEARY, S. (1993). 'Late Roman towns in Britain and their fate', in Vince (ed.), *Pre-Viking Lindsey*, 6–13.

EVISON, V. I. (1965). *The Fifth-Century Invasions South of the Thames*. London: Athlone Press.

EWART, G. (1985). *Cruggleton Castle: Report on the Excavations 1976–81*. Dumfries: Dumfriesshire and Galloway Natural History and Antiquarian Society.

FARMER, D. H. (trans.) (1983). 'Bede: Lives of the Abbots of Wearmouth and Jarrow', in D. H. Farmer (ed.), *The Age of Bede*. Harmondsworth: Penguin Books, 183–208.

FAULL, M. L. (1977). 'British survival in Anglo-Saxon Northumbria', in L. Laing (ed.), *Studies in Celtic Survival*. BAR British Series 37. Oxford: British Archaeological Reports, 1–56.

—— (1981). 'The Post-Roman period', in M. L. Faull and S. Moorhouse (eds.), *West Yorkshire: An Archaeological Survey to AD 1500*. Wakefield: West Yorkshire County Council, 171–227.

—— (ed.) (1984). *Studies in Late Anglo-Saxon Settlement*. Oxford: Department of External Studies.

FERRIS, I., and JONES, R. (2000). 'Transforming an elite: reinterpreting late Roman Binchester', in T. Wilmott and P. Wilson (eds.), *The Late Roman Transition in the North*. British Archaeological Reports British Series 299. Oxford: Archaeopress, 1–11.

GARDNER, W., and SAVORY, H. N. (1964). *Dinorben: A Hillfort Occupied in Early Iron Age and Roman Times*. Cardiff: University of Wales Press.

GATES, T., and O'BRIEN, C. (1988). 'Cropmarks at Milfield and New Bewick and the recognition of *Grubenhäuser* in Northumberland'. *Archaeol Aeliana*, 5th series, 16: 1–9.

GRAHAM-CAMPBELL, J. (1973). 'The ninth-century Anglo-Saxon horn-mount from Burghead, Morayshire, Scotland'. *Medieval Archaeology* 17: 43–51.

HALSALL, G. (1995). 'The Merovingian period in NE Gaul: transition or change?', in Bintliff and Hamerow (eds.), *Europe Between Late Antiquity and the Middle Ages*, 38–57.

HAMEROW, H. F., and PICKEN, J. (1995). 'An Early Anglo-Saxon cemetery at Andrew's Hill, Easington, County Durham'. *Durham Archaeological Journal* 11: 35–66.

HART, C. E. (1975). *The Early Charters of Northern England and the North Midlands*. London: Leicester University Press.

HENDERSON, G., and HENDERSON, I. (2004). *Art of the Picts: Sculpture and Metalwork in Early Medieval Scotland*. New York: Thames and Hudson.

HIGHAM, N. (1992). *Rome, Britain and the Anglo-Saxons*. London: Seaby.

—— (ed.) (2007). *Britons in Anglo-Saxon England*. Woodbridge: Boydell.

HILL, D., and WORTHINGTON, M. (2003). *Offa's Dyke*. Stroud: Alan Sutton.

HILL, P. (1997). *Whithorn and St Ninian: The Excavation of a Monastic Town 1984–91*. Stroud: The Whithorn Trust/Sutton.

HINES, J. (1984). *The Scandinavian Character of Anglian England in the Pre-Viking Period*. BAR British Series 124. Oxford: British Archaeological Reports.

—— (1994). 'The becoming of the English: identity, material culture and language in Anglo-Saxon England'. *Anglo-Saxon Studies in History and Archaeology* 7: 49–59.

—— (1996). 'Cultural change and social organization in early Anglo-Saxon England', in G. Ausenda (ed.), *After Empire: Towards an Ethnology of Europe's Barbarians*. San Marino: Institute for Social Stress, 75–88.

HODGES, R. (1989). *The Anglo-Saxon Achievement*. London: Duckworth.

HOPE-TAYLOR, B. (1977). *Yeavering: An Anglo-British Centre of Early Northumbria*. London: Her Majesty's Stationery Office.

—— (1980). 'Balbridie and Doon Hill'. *Current Archaeology* 72: 18–19.

INKER, P. (2000). 'Technology as active material culture: the Quoit Brooch Style'. *Medieval Archaeology* 44: 22–52.

JAMES, S., MARSHALL, A., and MILLETT, M. (1984). 'An early medieval building tradition'. *Archaeological Journal* 141: 182–215.

JENKINS, R. (1997). *Rethinking Ethnicity: Arguments and Explorations*. London: Sage.

JONES, M. (1993). 'The latter days of Roman Lincoln', in Vince (ed.), *Pre-Viking Lindsey*, 14–28.

JONES, S. (1997). *The Archaeology of Ethnicity: Constructing Identities in the Past and Present*. London: Routledge.

KOCH, J. T. (1997). *The Gododdin of Aneirin: Text and Context from Dark Age North Britain*. Cardiff: University of Wales Press.

LAING, L. (1999). 'The Bradwell Mount and the use of millefiori in post-Roman Britain'. *Studia Celtica* 33: 137–53.
—— (2006). *The Archaeology of Celtic Britain and Ireland, c. AD 400–1200*. Cambridge: Cambridge University Press.
—— (2007). 'Romano-British metalworking and the Anglo-Saxons', in Higham (ed.), *Britons in Anglo-Saxon England*, 42–56.
—— and LONGLEY, D. (2006). *The Mote of Mark: A Dark Age Hillfort in South-West Scotland*. Oxford: Oxbow Books.
LANE, A., and CAMPBELL, E. (2000). *Dunadd: An Early Dalriadic Capital*. Cardiff Studies in Archaeology Series. Oxford: Oxbow Books.
LEEDS, E. T. (1945). 'The Angles, Saxons and Jutes archaeologically considered'. *Archaeologia* 91: 1–106.
LOVELUCK, C. P. (1994). *Exchange and Society in Early Medieval England, 400–700 AD*. 2 volumes. Unpublished PhD Thesis, University of Durham.
—— (1995). 'Acculturation, migration and exchange: the formation of an Anglo-Saxon society in the English Peak District, AD 400–700', in Bintliff and Hamerow (eds.), *Europe Between Late Antiquity and the Middle Ages*, 84–98.
—— (1999). 'Archaeological expressions of the transition from the Late Roman to Early Anglo-Saxon period in lowland East Yorkshire', in P. Halkon and M. Millett (eds.), *Rural Settlement and Industry: Studies in the Iron Age and Roman Archaeology of Lowland East Yorkshire*. Yorkshire Archaeological Report 4. Otley: Yorkshire Archaeological Society and East Riding Archaeology Society, 228–36.
—— (2002). 'The Romano-British to Anglo-Saxon transition—social transformations from the late Roman to early medieval period in northern England, AD 400–700', in C. Brooks, R. Daniels, and A. Harding (eds.), *Past, Present and Future: The Archaeology of Northern England*. Durham: Architectural and Archaeological Society of Durham and Northumberland Research Report 5, 127–48.
—— (2003). 'The archaeology of post-Roman Yorkshire, A.D. 400–700, overview and future research directions', in T. Manby, S. Moorhouse, and P. Ottaway (eds.), *The Archaeology of Yorkshire: An Assessment at the Beginning of the 21st Century*. Yorkshire Archaeological Society Occasional Paper 3. Leeds: Council for British Archaeology/ English Heritage, 151–70.
—— (2007). 'Anglo-Saxon Hartlepool and the foundations of English Christian identity: the wider context and importance of the monastery', in R. Daniels and C. P. Loveluck (eds.), *Anglo-Saxon Hartlepool and the Foundations of English Christianity: An Archaeology of the Anglo-Saxon Monastery*. Tees Archaeology Monograph Series 3. Hartlepool: Tees Archaeology, 186–208.
LOWE, C. E. (1991). 'New light on the Anglian "minster" at Hoddom'. *Transactions of the Dumfriesshire and Galloway Natural History and Antiquarian Society* 66: 11–35.
—— (1999). *Angels, Fools and Tyrants: Britons and Anglo-Saxons in Southern Scotland, AD 450–750*. Edinburgh: Historic Scotland.
LUCY, S. J. (2000a). 'Early medieval burials in East Yorkshire: reconsidering the evidence', in H. Geake and J. Kenny (eds.), *Early Deira: Archaeological Studies of the East Riding in the Fourth to Ninth Centuries AD*. Oxford: Oxbow Books, 11–18.
—— (2000b). *The Anglo-Saxon Way of Death*. London: Alan Sutton.

MIKET, R. (1980). 'A re-statement of evidence for Bernician Anglo-Saxon burials', in P. Rahtz, T. M. Dickinson, and L. Watts (eds.), *Anglo-Saxon Cemeteries 1979*. BAR British Series 82. Oxford: British Archaeological Reports, 289–305.

—— and POCOCK, M. (1976). 'An Anglo-Saxon cemetery at Greenbank, Darlington'. *Medieval Archaeology* 20: 62–74.

MILES, D. (ed.) (1984). *Archaeology at Barton Court Farm, Abingdon, Oxon*. CBA Research Report 50. Oxford: Council for British Archaeology.

MOLONEY, C. (2001). 'New evidence for the origins and evolution of Dunbar: excavations at the Captain's Table, Castle Park, Dunbar, East Lothian'. *Proceedings of the Society of Antiquaries of Scotland* 131: 283–317.

MORTIMER, J. R. (1905). *Forty Years' Researches in British and Saxon Burial Mounds of East Yorkshire*. London: A. Brown and Sons.

MYRES, J. N. L. (1977). *A Corpus of Anglo-Saxon Pottery of the Pagan Period*. Cambridge: Cambridge University Press.

NEWMAN, R. (1984). 'The problems of rural settlement in Cumbria in the pre-Conquest Period', in Faull (ed.), *Studies in Late Anglo-Saxon Settlement*, 155–76.

O'BRIEN, C., and MIKET, R. (1991). 'The early medieval settlement of Thirlings, Northumberland'. *Durham Archaeolaegical Journal* 7: 57–91.

O'SULLIVAN, D. (1984). 'Pre-Conquest settlement patterns in Cumbria', in Faull (ed.), *Studies in Late Anglo-Saxon Settlement*, 143–54.

—— (1990). 'Two medieval mounts in the Crossthwaite Museum'. *Medieval Archaeology* 34: 145–7.

PADEL, O. (2007). 'Placenames and the Saxon Conquest of Devon and Cornwall', in Higham (ed.), *Britons in Anglo-Saxon England*, 215–30.

PEARCE, S. (2004). *South-Western Britain in the Early Middle Ages*. Leicester: Leicester University Press.

PENMAN, A. (1998). 'Botel Bailey'. *Current Archaeology* 156: 473–5.

PERRY, D. R. (2000). *Castle Park, Dunbar: Two Thousand Years on a Fortified Headland*. Society of Antiquaries of Scotland Monograph Series 16. Edinburgh: Society of Antiquaries of Scotland.

POCOCK, M. (1971). 'A note on two Anglo-Saxon brooches'. *Yorkshire Archaeological Journal* 42: 407–9.

POHL, W. (1997). 'Ethnic names and identities in the British Isles: a comparative perspective', in J. Hines (ed.), *The Anglo-Saxons from the Migration Period to the Eighth Century*. Woodbridge: Boydell Press, 7–40.

POWLESLAND, D. (2000). 'West Heslerton settlement mobility: a case of static development', in H. Geake and J. Kenny (eds.), *Early Deira: Archaeological Studies of the East Riding in the Fourth to Ninth Centuries AD*. Oxford: Oxbow Books, 19–26.

—— (2003). 'The Heslerton Parish Project: 20 years of archaeological research in the Vale of Pickering', in T. Manby, S. Moorhouse, and P. Ottaway (eds.), *The Archaeology of Yorkshire: An Assessment at the Beginning of the 21st Century*. Yorkshire Archaeological Society Occasional Paper 3. Leeds: Council for British Archaeology/English Heritage, 275–91.

PRICE, E. (2003). *Frocester: A Romano-British Settlement, its Antecedents and Successors*. Stonehouse: Gloucester and District Archaeological Research Group.

PROBERT, D. (2007). 'Mapping early medieval language change in South-West England', in Higham (ed.), *Britons in Anglo-Saxon England*, 231–44.

Proudfoot, E., and Aliaga-Kelly, C. (1996). 'Towards an interpretation of anomalous finds and place-names of Anglo-Saxon origin in Scotland'. *Anglo-Saxon Studies in Archaeology and History* 9: 1–13.

Quinnell, H., Blockley, M., and Berridge, P. (1994). *Excavations at Rhuddlan, Clwyd, 1969–73, Mesolithic to Medieval*. CBA Research Report 95. London: Council for British Archaeology.

Redknap, M. (1991). *The Christian Celts: Treasures of Late Celtic Wales*. Cardiff: National Museum of Wales.

—— (1995). 'Insular non-ferrous metalworking from Wales of the 8th to 10th centuries', in C. Bourke (ed.), *From the Isles of the North: Early Medieval Art in Ireland and Britain*. Belfast: Her Majesty's Stationery Office, 69–73.

—— (2000). *The Vikings in Wales: An Archaeological Quest*. Cardiff: National Museums and Galleries of Wales.

Rutherford Davies, K. (1982). *Britons and Saxons: The Chiltern Region 400–700*. Chichester: Phillimore.

Schrijver, P. (2007). 'What Britons spoke around 400 AD', in Higham (ed.), *Britons in Anglo-Saxon England*, 165–71.

Scull, C. J. (1995). 'Approaches to material culture and social dynamics of the Migration Period of Eastern England', in Bintliff and Hamerow (eds.), *Europe Between Late Antiquity and the Middle Ages*, 71–83.

—— and Harding, A. F. (1990). 'Two early medieval cemeteries at Milfield, Northumberland'. *Durham Archaeological Journal* 6: 1–29.

Sherlock, S. J., and Welch, M. G. (1992). *An Anglo-Saxon Cemetery at Norton, Cleveland*. CBA Research Report 82. York: Council for British Archaeology.

Smith, I. M. (1983). 'Brito-Roman and Anglo-Saxon: the unification of the Borders', in P. Clack and J. Ivy (eds.), *The Borders*. Durham: Council for British Archaeology Regional Group 3, 9–48.

—— (1984). 'Patterns of settlement and land use of the late Anglian period in the Tweed basin', in Faull (ed.), *Studies in Late Anglo-Saxon Settlement*, 177–96.

—— (1991). 'Sprouston, Roxburghshire: an early Anglian centre of the eastern Tweed basin'. *Proceedings of the Society of Antiquaries of Scotland* 121: 261–94.

Smyth, A. (1984). *Warlords and Holy Men*. Edinburgh: Edinburgh University Press.

Stevenson, R. B. K. (1974). 'The Hunterston Brooch and its significance'. *Medieval Archaeology* 18: 16–42.

Tristram, H. (2007). 'Why don't the English speak Welsh?', in Higham (ed.), *Britons in Anglo-Saxon England*, 192–214.

Vince, A. (ed.) (1993). *Pre-Viking Lindsey*. Lincoln Archaeology Studies 1. Lincoln: City of Lincoln Archaeology Unit.

White, R. (1988). *Roman and Celtic Objects from Anglo-Saxon Graves*. BAR British Series 191. Oxford: British Archaeological Reports.

—— (1990). 'Scrap or substitute: Roman material in Anglo-Saxon Graves', in E. Southworth (ed.), *Anglo-Saxon Cemeteries: A Reappraisal*. Stroud: Sutton, 125–52.

Whitfield, N., and Graham-Campbell, J. (1992). 'A mount with Hiberno-Saxon animal ornament'. *Transactions of the Dumfriesshire and Galloway Naural History and Antiquarian Society* 67: 9–27.

WILMOTT, T. (1997). *Birdoswald: Excavations on a Roman Fort on Hadrian's Wall and its Successor Settlements, 1987–1992*. English Heritage Archaeological Report 14. London: English Heritage.

—— (2000). 'The Late Roman transition at Birdoswald on Hadrian's Wall', in T. Wilmott and P. Wilson (eds.), *The Late Roman Transition in the North*. British Archaeological Reports British Series 299. Oxford: Archaeopress, 12–23.

YOUNG, G. (2003). *Bamburgh Castle: The Archaeology of the Fortress of Bamburgh, AD 500 to AD 1500*. Newcastle-upon-Tyne: The Bamburgh Research Project.

YOUNGS, S. (1995). 'A penannular brooch from near Calne, Wiltshire'. *Wiltshire Archaelogical and Natural History Magazine* 88: 127–31.

—— (1998). 'Medieval hanging bowls from Wiltshire'. *Wiltshire Archaeological and Natural History Magazine* 91: 35–41.

ZIEGLER, M. (2001). 'The Anglo-British cemetery at Bamburgh: an e-interview with Graeme Young of the Bamburgh Castle Research Project'. *The Heroic Age* 4: 1–12.

CHAPTER 29

MARKETS, *EMPORIA*, *WICS*, AND 'PRODUCTIVE' SITES: PRE-VIKING TRADE CENTRES IN ANGLO-SAXON ENGLAND

TIM PESTELL

UNDERSTANDING of the ways in which economic activity operated in pre-Viking England continues to develop at a rapid rate. An explosion in data from excavations and metal-detecting has resulted in a voluminous and diverse literature, as well as a mass of unpublished information held in various on-line or public databases.[1] This paper summarizes the workings of those places that acted as arenas for trade and exchange in mid Saxon England, by exploring the terms that have been applied to

---

[1] Of particular importance are the online resources of the Portable Antiquities Scheme <http://www.finds.org.uk/< and of the Early Medieval Coin Corpus (EMC) <http://www.cm.fitzwilliam.cam.ac.uk/coins/emc>. Beyond the annual round-ups of excavations or finds presented in *Medieval Archaeology* and *British Numismatic Journal*, many sites or finds (notably from Norfolk) are detailed in county Historic Environment Records (HERs), administered by local council planning authorities or archaeology services.

them, how modern scholars have interpreted them, and how recent discoveries may point to future research directions.

WHAT'S IN A NAME?

While we understand a town or city in the modern world to have a variety of functions—economic, social, religious, and perhaps cultural, or intellectual—it is often more difficult to provide precise definitions that are universally acceptable. Much the same is true of mid Saxon England, when a range of places, with a variety of functions, was becoming established. Attempting to define such sites by using particular names, or applying specific terms to models generated from archaeological evidence, is inevitably problematic, as in use of the term *wic*, taken from the place-name element found in some of the earliest and (apparently) most important early trading centres: *Hamwic* (Southampton), *Lundenwic* (London), *Eoforwic* (York), and *Gippeswic* (Ipswich). An early Germanic borrowing of the Latin *vicus*, *wic* has a variety of meanings ranging from a collection of dwellings to a city district (Rumble 2001: 1). Like *vicus*, *wic* became applied to a variety of places of wide-ranging size, importance, and function, and its long-lived usage means that it need not always represent pre-Viking settlements. For instance, Ipswich and Norwich first appear as *Gip(e)s-wic* and *Norðwic* on coins of c.975 and c.930 respectively, yet it is Ipswich that has the unequivocal mid Saxon importance. A more direct witness to the term's early use comes from the legend +DE VICO LVNDONIAE on the remarkable gold *mancus* of Coenwulf of Mercia, minted c. 805–810, discovered at Biggleswade in 2001 (Blackburn 2007: 62–4). Thus far, this is uniquely early in referring to the *vicus* or *wic* in London.

No less problematic is to create an archaeological definition for *emporium*, a Latin loan-word from the Greek *emporion*, meaning 'trading place'. Bede used the term of London, while describing the province of the East Saxons: 'Its chief city is London, which is on the banks of that river and is an *emporium* for many nations who come to it by land and sea' (*HE* II.3: Colgrave and Mynors 1969: 142–3). Other terms such as *portus* were also used, a charter of 733 from Æthelbald of Mercia to Bishop Eadwulf of Rochester granting remission of toll 'in the port of London' (*in portu Lundoniae*) (Campbell 1973: no. 2; Whitelock 1979: no. 66).

Bede's choice of words is perhaps particularly significant given his alternative description of London as a city (*civitas*), the term he more frequently used of important places and particularly those of the Roman world (Campbell 1986). The discovery of a mid Saxon trading community outside the Roman walls of London suggests that distinctions between trading communities and centres based around other functions may once have existed in the minds of contemporaries. This duality is reminiscent of the eighth-century description by Huneberc of Heidenheim, an Anglo-Saxon nun describing how St Willibald arrived 'next to the city

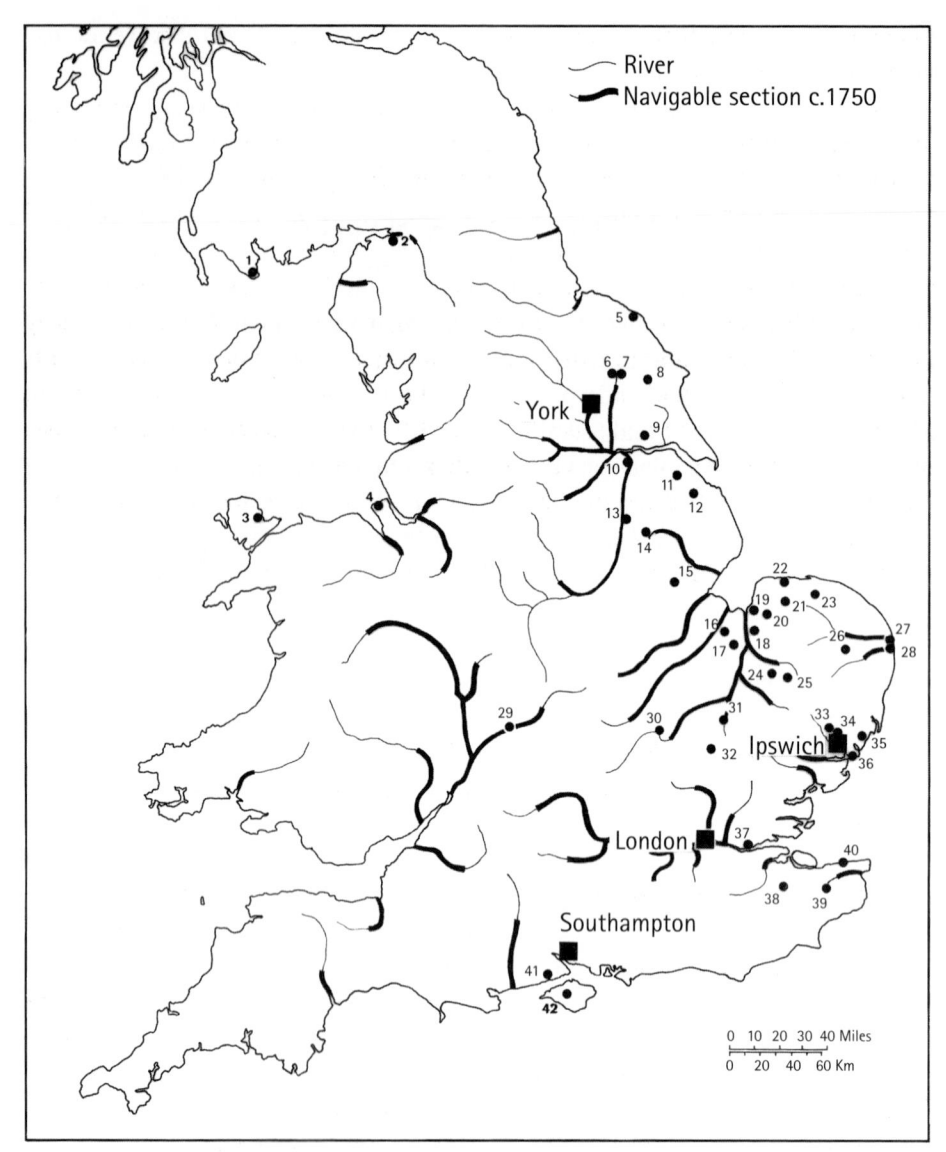

Figure 29.1 The location of the principal *emporia, wics*, 'productive', and other sites, plotted against the navigable extent of rivers c.1750 (after Sherratt 1996). Numbered sites: 1, Whithorn; 2, Carlisle; 3, Llanbedrgoch; 4, Meols; 5, Whitby; 6 & 7, Malton I and II; 8, Cottam; 9, South Newbald; 10, Flixborough; 11, Riby; 12, West Ravendale; 13, Torksey; 14, Lincoln; 15, Heckington; 16, West Walton; 17, Outwell; 18, Wormegay; 19, Bawsey; 20, Congham; 21, Rudham; 22, Burnham; 23, Hindringham; 24, Brandon; 25, Thetford; 26, Caistor St Edmund; 27, Caister by Yarmouth; 28, Burgh Castle; 29, Bidford on Avon; 30, Bedford; 31, 'near Cambridge'; 32, 'near Royston'; 33, Coddenham; 34, Barham; 35, Burrow Hill; 36, Walton Castle; 37, Tilbury; 38, Hollingbourne; 39, 'near Canterbury'; 40, Reculver; 41, 'South Hampshire'; 42, 'near Carisbrooke'

called Rouen, where there was a market' (*iuxta urbe que vocatur Rotum. Ibi fuit mercimonia*) (Morton 1999: 60; Hill 2001a: 114).

These documentary sources illustrate the diversity of terminology for trading settlements; similar problems are faced elsewhere, as Schmidt's review of the Scandinavian evidence shows, for instance (2000). Biddle's proposed twelve criteria for defining places with urban status emphasized many institutional and morphological concepts probably less important to contemporaries (Biddle 1976; Scull 1997: 271); as Hodges pointed out, despite Cogitosus' eighth- or ninth-century description of the monastic settlement of Kildare, Ireland, being a 'great metropolitan city', it is unlikely to have matched the density of many contemporary English or Frankish settlements (1982: 47). In such a context, it is questionable how useful it is to create precise definitions for *wics* or *emporia*, and how and where they can be applied to those sites that we see archaeologically. It can also conflate two possibly different types of site— early 'urban' centres, and sites used to conduct trade. As Clarke and Ambrosiani said, 'perhaps there were a number of different types of English trading site or *emporia* during the Early Middle Ages, not a single basic form' (1991: 36) (Fig. 29.1).

Explanatory models for early medieval trade

Probably the most influential early attempt to understand early medieval economics was made by Henri Pirenne, the Belgian historian, in his *Mohammed and Charlemagne*, published posthumously in 1937. In Pirenne's view, an economic continuity existed from the classical world until the seventh century, when the unity of Mediterranean society was destroyed by Arab conquests, 'the Western Mediterranean having become a Musulman lake' (Pirenne 1954: 284—the first English translation). North-west Europe's connections with the Mediterranean were severed, and the supply of gold from Africa ceased, leading to a silver currency in a smaller, inward-looking, agrarian-based economy without towns, merchants, or large-scale trade. The impact of Pirenne's work on stimulating discussion about the nature of trade contacts and of Carolingian social structures has ensured an extensive historiography (e.g. Lyon 1974; Havighurst 1976; Bachrach 1998; Delogu 1998). Of more importance is how Pirenne's ideas have been tested and challenged by a new generation of scholars using datasets unimaginable to him, drawn principally from archaeological discoveries made in the last forty years. Of these, the most influential work is arguably Richard Hodges' *Dark Age Economics* (1982, revised 1989). This continues to hold a spell over archaeologists' interpretations of early trade despite much new information found since its publication.

Hodges, investigating the origins of towns and trade in north-west Europe in the spirit of the New Archaeology, used anthropological models to examine how society began to engage in larger-scale and more wide-reaching trade. He saw emergent seventh- and eighth-century kingdoms as based upon systems of gift-giving and reciprocity in which 'kings figure most prominently in the directional down-the-line exchange... and in the sixth-century west-European long-distance trading system' (Hodges 1982: 197). The economy was thus embedded in social structures and politically orientated towards the acquisition of 'prestige goods', to enable these emergent aristocracies to build alliances with other rulers through gift exchange. Control of such goods had to be regulated as a monopoly to retain their high status, otherwise 'the initial purpose of the exchange system will be defeated' (Hodges and Whitehouse 1989: 92). This was achieved by concentrating exchanges of imported and exported goods within specialized settlements, which Hodges called *emporia* rather than *wics*. A prime example of such international contacts was seen in the presence of large quantities of Continental pottery in *emporia*, apparently indicating the import of prestige goods held within the pots, as well as the containers themselves (Hodges 1981; Blackmore 2001).

A crucial aspect of Hodges' model concerns his view of how these exchange centres evolved. He broke their development down into a series of stages in which he defined *emporia* as types A–C (1982: 50–2):

- Type 'A' trading sites or 'gateway communities' were held on boundaries, mostly on the coast, and were visited by traders either seasonally or for short periods annually.
- Type 'B' *emporia* saw 'this hitherto periodic long-distance trade' maximized by developing sites with planned streets and dwellings. These might overlie the clusters of earlier structures left by the preceding type 'A' *emporia*, the buildings being provided for large numbers of alien traders and for a native workforce. Hodges' model was influenced by surviving documentary sources, but principally by the results of archaeological excavations at Southampton and Ipswich (but not in London as the *wic* site west of the City had yet to be identified; 1982: 69–70), and on the Continent at Quentovic, Dorestad, Birka, and Hedeby.
- Type 'C' *emporia* represented those trading settlements that survived the decline of 'B' type predecessors. These regional nodes in a long-distance mercantile system mutated into sites involved in more local, dendritic, trade networks, which evolved as regional central places with political significance, for instance as local seats of government.

A number of important critiques of the approach taken by Hodges have emerged. For instance, the underlying basis of the way in which transactions were conducted has been challenged, Moreland questioning the more expressly anthropological models of gift exchange and instead emphasizing the need to consider production equally with distribution and consumption (2000a). Hodges saw kings exerting a high degree of control over trade, long-distance contact being utilized politically for reciprocal exchanges of prestige goods; *emporia* were thus developed as a means of controlling the expansion in trade seen in the seventh and eighth centuries. Saunders (1991; 2001) suggested that as secular lords became increasingly good at exploiting their own estates for profit, there was less need for *emporia*; they became, effectively, closed settlements 'reliant on the powers of the tributary king for their very existence' rather than as Hodges thought constituting 'a dynamic force in developing a market economy in Anglo-Saxon society' (Saunders 2001: 11–12). Increasingly, archaeological data from sites like Ipswich, Southampton, and London suggested that *emporia* also had an important role in the production of goods, not simply the reception of prestige items (Wade 1988; Brisbane 1988; Hobley 1988). A prime example of this is Ipswich ware pottery, produced only in Ipswich but traded widely throughout East Anglia and England more generally (Blinkhorn 1999). The extent to which rulers were able or would have wished to control all aspects of such products has become increasingly questioned; instead, tolls may have been of greater interest to them (Kelly 1992; Middleton 2005).

Another serious critique has been the general lack of contextualizing *emporia* within their hinterlands. While *emporia* were initially characterized as stimulating developments in the surrounding countryside, Moreland (2000a; 2000b) has argued the opposite, that increased agricultural productivity was an important element allowing the creation of large *emporia* like *Lundenwic* and *Hamwic*. Based on the evidence of excavated animal-bone assemblages, increased production saw the provisioning of *emporia* from the countryside (Bourdillon 1988; 1994; Crabtree 1994). Interestingly, faunal assemblages have suggested the occupants of *emporia* like *Lundenwic* and *Hamwic* to have been tied to some form of command economy, 'provisioned by a maintaining institution' (O'Connor 2001: 60; see also this volume). More generally, work by landscape archaeologists over the last twenty years has highlighted the complexity of rural organization. Developing the multiple-estate model advanced by Glanville Jones (1979; 1985), regional surveys have tried to reconstruct the 'great estates' that once covered the landscape (Williamson 1993: 83–104; Foard 1985). Much work, notably by and influenced by Blair, has also emphasized the role of the Church as a major landowner, creating 'central places' important for economic growth, often more important than royal vills in the subsequent origins of small towns (Blair 1988; 1996; and most recently restated in 2005: 246–90). This emergence of other, smaller, centres in the hinterlands has provided a further challenge to the view of *emporia* acting as lone centres in a regional trade network.

A major critique of Hodges' work has emerged through an increased understanding of mid Saxon coinage. Following the work of scholars such as Dalton and Grierson, Hodges saw coin use in an anthropological framework, with a social rather than economic importance (Hodges 1982: 106–10): the early 'sceatta' coins found in *emporia* like Southampton and Ipswich were considered 'primitive money', used 'as a medium in peripheral market exchange' and 'early cash', 'used for the payment of taxes or fines as well as in ordinary market-exchange' (ibid.: 108). Even at the time some numismatists saw a more monetized economy existing, with concentrations of coin finds elsewhere interpreted as possible market sites (Metcalf 1977). It is this aspect that has become one of the most serious challenges to Hodges' concept of the *emporia*: the number of sceatta coins found in the English countryside has risen hugely, largely through the recording of metal-detected finds, latterly through the Portable Antiquities Scheme (see Blackburn, this volume). The recognition that a small number of sites were yielding exceptional quantities of sceattas suggested that new trading sites, contemporary with the 'classic' *emporia* like *Hamwic*, were being identified. Indeed, the number of coins recovered from some sites makes it clear that they had a regional rather than just local economic importance. For instance, the 129 coins recovered at *Hamwic* compares to 146 found at Tilbury, Essex, and 124 from Bawsey in Norfolk (Blackburn 2003: figs. 3.3 and 3.4). Such discoveries linked the arguments for an increased role of other sites as central places, seeing trade conducted in a wider hinterland, with that for silver coinage being used in a more highly developed, monetized, economy than had been previously accepted. Recognition of these so-called 'productive' sites has, however, yet to lead to a true paradigm shift, perhaps partly because vague terminology has impeded development of a single explanatory model.

'Productive' sites: nomenclature and interpretations

The term 'productive' site stems from its initial use in the 1980s by numismatists to indicate sites that had been 'productive' or 'prolific' in the numbers of eighth- and ninth-century coins recovered from them. Archaeologists have long been unhappy with such a 'shorthand' term (Leahy 2000: 51), but given the difficulties in interpreting the many sites concerned, nothing better has yet been suggested. A simple approach is to use the definition proposed by Ulmschneider, that 'productive' sites are 'places, whether excavated or metal-detected, that produce large quantities of coin and metalwork finds' (2000a: 62–3). If nothing else, the term has enabled a grouping of sites that are distinctive while yet requiring closer categorization.

Interpretation is problematic not least because of the secrecy surrounding the provenance of key sites, for example that called 'near Royston', Hertfordshire, from which ninety-five coins have been recorded, through fear of 'nighthawking' (illegal metal-detecting). Others have only very recently been identified; the site known for over ten years as 'South Lincolnshire' (with 141 coins) is now disclosed as Heckington (Blackburn 2003: 26–9; Daubney 2007: 221–2). Many 'productive' sites have limited scope for archaeological analysis as they remain fundamentally unexplored except through metal-detecting; even ferrous metalwork is mostly screened out by detectorists. Only a few sites have been systematically fieldwalked to gain some idea of the size and densities of any associated pottery spreads and, typically under arable, the sites are usually plain, open, fields.

An objection to the distinction of 'productive' sites has come from Richards, based largely upon his work at Cottam in Yorkshire (1999), a site that had yielded large quantities of eighth- and ninth-century coinage and metalwork. His excavations revealed structural features, but little to suggest that the settlement had been a periodic market site or trading community. Instead it appeared more representative of 'normal' mid Saxon settlements in the area, but where deep ploughing had released coins and metalwork from sealed archaeological deposits into the ploughsoil—which had subsequently been detected. Richards also examined the relative density of metalwork found on other sites in the north of England, from which he argued that Wharram Percy, a site he regarded as another typical mid Saxon settlement, would statistically also need to be considered 'productive'. Thus, he saw 'nothing special about "productive sites"' (Richards 1999: 77–9). By 2003 Richards had slightly modified his stance to conclude that Cottam B was 'possibly part of a royal estate' where 'trading may have taken place, and this must explain the context of the metal finds', not least the coins (Richards 2003: 166). While Wharram Percy may actually display evidence of high-status occupation (Moreland 2000b: 93; Hinton 2005: 93), recent detailed investigation of early coinage in Yorkshire has shown a boom in the use of styca coins in the ninth century, exactly the period Cottam is numismatically richest. This suggests 'we should expect a large proportion of ninth-century "productive sites" in Deira to be ordinary settlements' (Naylor 2007: 52). The interpretative difficulties raised by Cottam underline the need to enhance the recovery of metal small finds on archaeological excavations using metal-detectors to bring a closer parity of data with unexcavated 'productive' sites.

This latter point perhaps emphasizes a divide in the interpretation of 'productive' sites between those that are most notable for their coinage (and implicitly important for trade or exchange), and those whose overall assemblages of metalwork seem particularly rich or atypical. While Cottam may or may not have been unusual in the area for its number of styca coins and strap-ends, metal-detected sites like Bawsey in Norfolk stand out through their prestige metalwork assemblages. These include objects not seen in normal Anglo-Saxon domestic assemblages, for instance decorative hanging-bowl fragments, styli, and precious-metal items like the silver and niello hooked tag found there (Fig. 29.2; Webster and Backhouse 1991: no. 188). Geographically, there also seem to be differences, the distribution of 'productive' sites being heavily skewed to the east of England

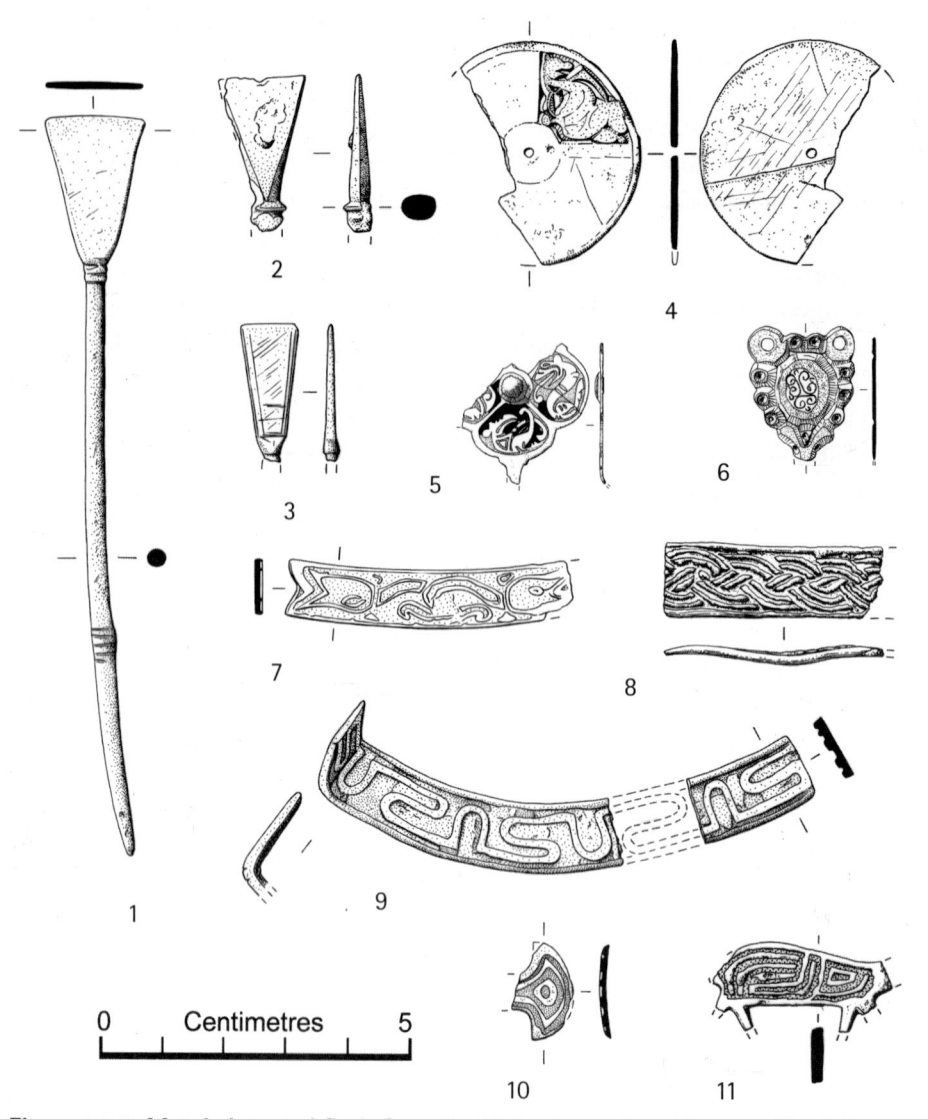

Figure 29.2 Metal-detected finds from the high-status site at Bawsey, Norfolk: 1–3, styli (1–2, copper-alloy; 3, silver); 4, copper-alloy trial-piece disc with variant Trewhiddle-style beast; 5–6, hooked tags (5 is made from silver with Trewhiddle-style animals in niello inlays); 7–11, enamelled copper-alloy mounts from hanging bowls (11 is a deer, similar to one on the Lullingstone bowl) (drawn by Steven Ashley)

(Fig. 29.1). Some caution is necessary. These are the areas which are most intensively farmed, creating a deep ploughsoil likely to contain objects; it also includes many of the counties most progressive in liaising with metal-detectorists. Nevertheless, the distribution of sites that is emerging appears to reflect an economic reality (see below). Likewise, while some 'ordinary' sites may be more vulnerable to discovery through metal-detection, most archaeologists accept that 'productive' sites are distinctive places of special activity in the seventh to ninth centuries.

Interpreting such sites has been notoriously problematic. Taking sites known through their metalwork samples, Ulmschneider has argued that the majority of 'productive' sites indicate central places involved in some form of trading activity, 'whether local, inter-regional or international' (2000b: 104). Following Blair, she emphasizes that 'it was the Church which gave a strong new impetus to the local economy', identifying many (but not all) medium and lesser 'productive sites' as minsters (ibid.: 105; 2005: 527). The presence of medieval churches on or near many 'productive' sites has certainly often contributed to the popularity of such an interpretation.

An alternative approach has been made more recently for Norfolk by Hutcheson (2006). Focusing on analysis of coinage, he takes a substantivist viewpoint, like Hodges, seeing trade as socially embedded, and analyses not individual sites but wider land-units (here modern parishes) as '"productive" land-units' (Hutcheson 2006: 79–84). This approach demonstrates the way in which coinage can be seen to have percolated across the Norfolk landscape, including areas well inland and thus away from the coast or rivers, which are the normal corridors associated with trade. He sees this as principally related to payment of taxation, which was collected throughout the landscape (ibid.: 91). Problematically, many of those parishes forming his top-ranking 'productive' land-units depend for this categorization upon individual 'productive' sites contained within them; Norwich, Thetford, and Ipswich, as towns, may be similarly excluded. Much like Ulmschneider's pioneering work, this reflects the complexity of examining the 'productivity' of finds or coins in the landscape, but, like Naylor's work in Yorkshire, provides a balance to the argument that many coin-rich sites should be directly identified with the operations of the Church.

Critiques developing this latter theme have emerged in recent years. In examining the high-status settlement at Flixborough (an excavated site with a metalwork assemblage mirroring those of 'productive' sites), Loveluck has favoured a mixed interpretation suggesting that the site, while producing huge quantities of metalwork like dress-pins and twenty-one styli, need not specifically have been a monastery (nor a manor or vill centre). Instead, he argues that the site reflects 'a complex sequence of settlement change', reflecting fluctuations in the types of elite present, and the ways they chose to display this status (Loveluck 2001: 120–1; 2007: 144–63). He has noted that were it not for the excellent surviving stratigraphy, chronological changes in character would have been unrecognized, and if ploughed out and metal-detected, the site would simply have appeared to have had an eighth- and ninth-century *floruit* before appearing to fall off in the tenth and eleventh centuries. Similar arguments appear valid for the high-status settlement at Staunch Meadow, Brandon (Carr *et al.* 1988), also often uncritically interpreted as a minster. More widely, the entire question of defining archaeological sites as 'minsters' has been the subject of some debate (Pestell 2004: 18–64), Naylor recently concluding that 'the attribution of many "productive sites" to minsters is all too often based on flimsy documentary evidence from the late Saxon period' (2004: 133).

THE LANDSCAPE OF TRADE AND EXCHANGE

While the terminology applied to trading centres in mid Saxon England has engendered considerable debate and discussion, perhaps the principal difficulty is the diversity of sites now recognized archaeologically. This has led some to see *emporia* as 'a figment of our scholarly imagination' for labelling anything as long as it has some exotic imports; 'in short, we are in danger of calling anything and everything *emporia* and then standing back amazed at their diversity' (Samson 1999: 79). Others have attempted stricter definitions, for instance Hill, suggesting that 'the size of a *wic* might be expressed as a lower limit' to distinguish such places from, for example, a farm or estate centre. Additional criteria could include, among others, the lack of defensive works before the middle of the ninth century; the presence of a craft centre; and providing evidence of long-distance trade (Hill 2001b: 75–6).

It is increasingly questionable how useful such distinctions are. It seems that in Southampton, Ipswich, and London we have three sites that look very different from any other known English trading or settlement site of this date (Figs. 29.3 and 29.4; for York, see Hall, this volume). Certainly places such as *Sandtun*, Heckington, or Tilbury may share some similarities with aspects of the 'classic' *emporia* in craftworking or coin-loss (Gardiner *et al.* 2001; Daubney 2007), but none look like them in terms of sheer size, density of occupation, or the extent of controlled infrastructural development (Scull 1997: 289). Whilst York is numismatically important in its regional context, this element reiterates the importance of other 'productive' sites in the English economic landscape. With thirty-two and eighty-nine coins of *c.*640–870 from Fishergate and the rest of York respectively, even both totals combined are less than the comparable coinage totals recovered from Whitby Abbey (157) and the 'productive' site at South Newbald (182) (Naylor 2007: 56–7). Although caution is required when comparing sites only partly excavated with greenfield sites available for metal-detection, this emphasizes the need for 'productive' sites to be better melded into site hierarchies and economic frameworks.

While much work remains to be done on the pre-sceatta phase of trade contacts, archaeological data are increasingly revealing a locational rationale for later

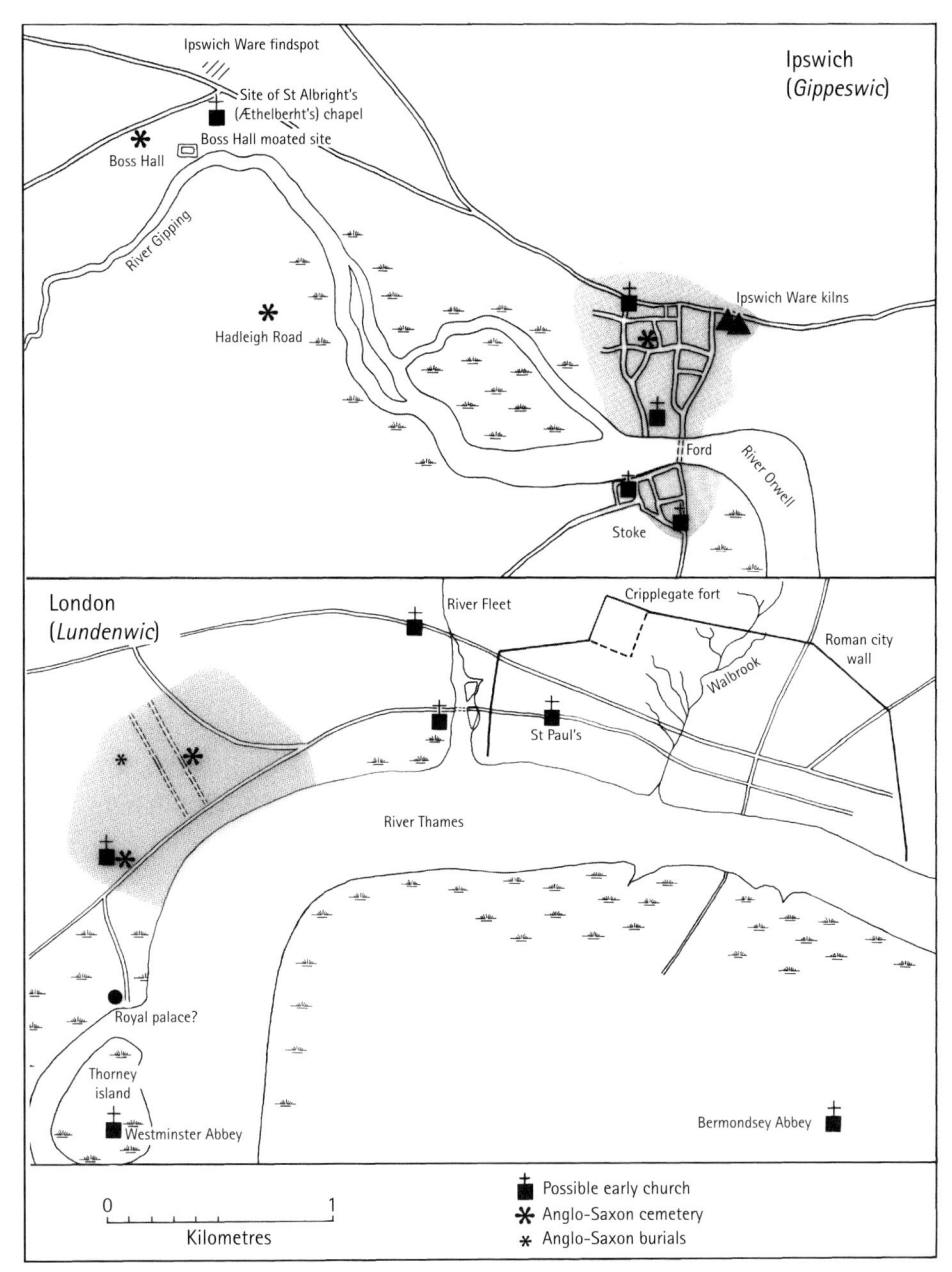

Figure 29.3 *Lundenwic* and *Gippeswic* in their wider landscape settings (to same scale as Fig. 29.4)

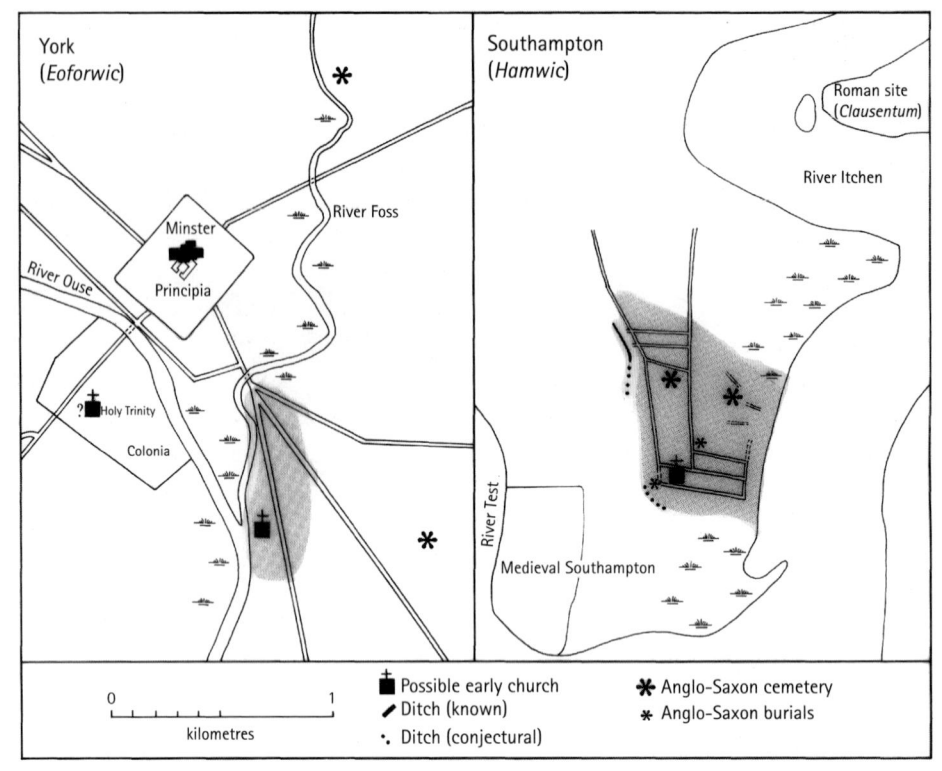

Figure 29.4 *Hamwic* and *Eoforwic* in their wider landscape settings (to same scale as Fig. 29.3)

economic foci. Study of Kent by Brookes has shown how many mid Saxon estate centres correlate with earlier patterns of wealth consumption (2003). Likewise, the appearance of four gold bracteates from Norfolk all within a six-mile radius may point to an early focus for gift exchange via the medium of a 'gateway community' that Hodges might have called a 'Type A' *emporium*. This same area later seems to have been served by a 'productive' site at Hindringham (Pestell 2003: 129–30). Yet the idea that such temporary fairs made way for permanent 'Type B' *emporia* as kings sought to control trade is now appearing too rigid a distinction. Not all 'productive' sites have associated evidence for settlement and some might best be interpreted as temporary markets or fairs, unrelated to gift exchange. An intriguing new site that may have such an interpretation was found in 2006 near Outwell on the Norfolk fen-edge, and in barely eighteen months has yielded eleven sceattas, including seven of Continental type, but only two strap-ends and a tenth-century coin. Of the limited pottery recovered, two sherds are of Ipswich ware, while a third is an import (A. Rogerson, pers. comm.). Heckington also seemingly has little other associated material culture such as pottery, and both sites may be best interpreted as temporary fairs.

Hodges has recently conceded that his 'Type C' *emporia*—those surviving as regional central places after the trading rationale for 'Type B' *emporia* declined— now appear 'a more contentious category' (2006: 67). Much of this has become clearer as an increasing number of 'productive' sites (described by Hodges as 'wiclets': ibid.: 67–8) already appear to have been central places by the start of the eighth century. Thus, Coddenham in Suffolk has yielded not only fifty early sceattas but three tremisses and twelve English thrymsas; follow-up excavations have demonstrated settlement on the site, including a hall-type building and evidence for metalworking; and to one side a seventh-century inhumation cemetery with a number of high-status graves that included a bed-burial (Everett *et al.* 2003; Newman 2003 and pers. comm.). The fact that Coddenham has good evidence for a subsequent minster church (Pestell 2003: 132–3) should not blind us to its origins as a secular centre that maintained itself within the landscape. Bawsey in Norfolk likewise begins with seventh-century gold coinage and primary sceattas and, despite a characteristically large increase of secondary sceattas *c.*700– 750, lived on into the twelfth century and was almost certainly the economic focus subsequently transferred by the East Anglian bishop to found Kings Lynn (Pestell 2001: 214–15; 2003: 125–6; Hutcheson 2006). These two examples stand for many other sites and demonstrate that, not only in their long-term stability within the landscape, but in the quantity of coinage recovered, they must have acted as significant economic drivers within the regional economy and thus had an influence on a par with *emporia* like *Hamwic* or, in an East Anglian context, *Gippeswic*.

In what sense, therefore, is it possible to view *emporia* like *Hamwic* as different or distinct from such sites? Two aspects are perhaps most clear. First, the size, and second the indications emerging for planned layouts. Excavations in *Hamwic* have revealed evidence for occupation extending over 47 hectares, with an arrangement of metalled roads on a grid pattern, established *c.*700, that appear to have been well-maintained, suggesting a central authority (Birbeck *et al.* 2005: 86–9 and 196–7; this authority is also suggested by a seventh-century cemetery with well-furnished graves: see below). Similar evidence is emerging from *Lundenwic*, now suggested as having covered an area of about 55–60 hectares, with roads pointing to an organized grid: a main north-south road discovered on the site of the Royal Opera House now has a companion running parallel to its west at St James's Street. Dating to *c.*675–700, both had been well maintained, kept clean, and had associated drains running alongside, again suggesting the hand of a central authority (Malcolm *et al.* 2003: 145–6; Leary 2004: 8 and 142–3). Ipswich's equally intensive excavations, albeit largely unpublished, have less direct evidence for a planned grid of streets: only one actual mid Saxon roadway, at St Stephen's Lane, has been excavated. The explanation seems to be that the street pattern is preserved beneath the modern roads, as excavated buildings appear to be fronting on to existing streets. Again, Ipswich occupied a large area, spilling south across the River Orwell into Stoke, to create a town of about 50 hectares (Wade 1988; 2007). York, by contrast, is still imperfectly understood, with no roads yet found and even its area uncertain, estimates ranging from 25–65 hectares down to no larger than 10 hectares (Kemp 1996: 75–7; Naylor 2004: 28; Spall and Toop 2008; Hall, this volume).

Such concentrations of occupation into large, planned, areas constitutes perhaps the most significant distinguishing aspect of the 'classic' *emporium* model. Despite their material wealth, the rural sites of Brandon and Flixborough, for instance, occupy approximately 4.75 and perhaps 2.5 hectares respectively. Bawsey's ditched hilltop enclosure of some 6 hectares is likewise clearly different from *Hamwic*, despite having yielded nearly as many coins. Much of this seems to reflect the use of these larger *emporia* as industrialized zones of craftworking, rather than specifically for the production and receipt of prestige goods. As Hinton has expressed it of *Hamwic*: 'the metalworking and the metal objects both suggest no great level of accomplishment' (1999: 27). The scale of craft production is difficult to assess. Riddler has pointed out that combs have been recovered from most sites in *Lundenwic*, while comb-working appears to have been focused on particular building complexes, a similar situation to *Hamwic* and *Gippeswic* (Riddler 2001: 61; 2004: 145–6). Sites such as Brandon or Flixborough, by contrast, reflect agricultural processing of crops, textile production rather than other craftworking, and more diverse faunal assemblages (Loveluck 2001: 94–9; O'Connor 2001).

Despite these apparent differences, excavation is increasingly highlighting earlier elite origins to such designed settlements as London, Southampton, and probably Ipswich. Once seen as *de novo* foundations, the discovery of seventh-century 'Final Phase' cemeteries at all three now indicates an active interest in them by ruling families: the rich seventh-century burial ground at St Mary's Stadium within *Hamwic* (Fig. 29.5a) has no rationale unless those buried were involved in the place's emergence as a commercial centre (Hinton 2005: 75). A context for this is Southampton's putative origin as a royal estate, the boundaries of which may relate to the medieval town's liberties, which covered about 900 hectares (3 square miles); potentially it was far larger, perhaps roughly equivalent to the late Anglo-Saxon hundred of Mansbridge, which may also have been Southampton's original minster *parochia* (Morton 1999: 57–8; Hase 1975: 124–80).

In Ipswich, the Buttermarket cemetery (ending perhaps as early as *c*.680) also yielded graves containing continental material, raising the possibility that the dead included foreigners or individuals expressing their continental connections (Scull 2009). Perhaps equally important to Ipswich is the cemetery from Boss Hall, in which a late, particularly rich, female inhumation, Grave 93, had jewellery including a composite disc brooch (Fig. 29.5b), a mounted gold *solidus* of 639–656, and a primary sceatta of *c*.700 (ibid. 16–18; Newman 1991; Webster and Backhouse 1991: no. 33). Boss Hall is probably associated with the wider political geography of *Gippeswic*,

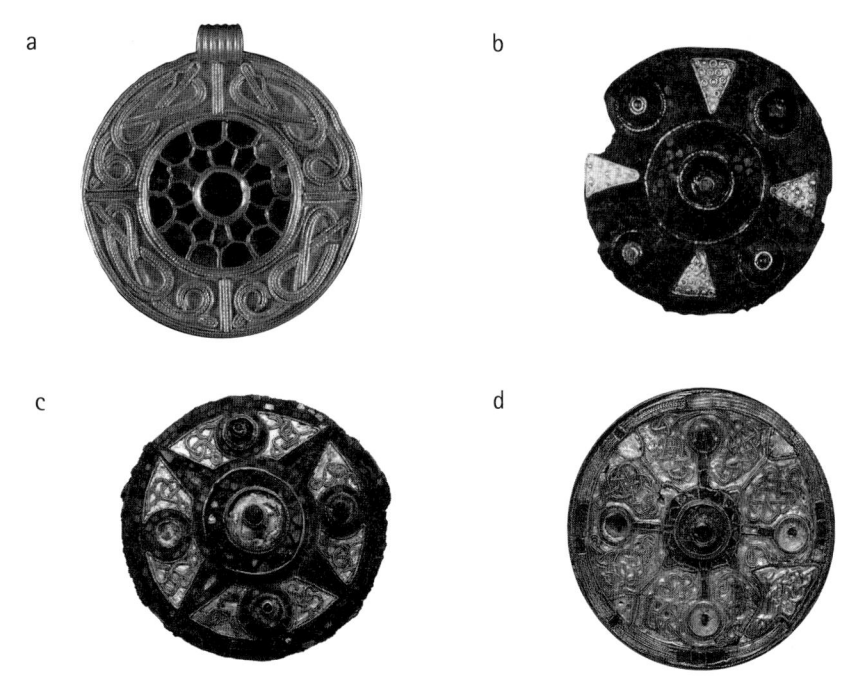

Figure 29.5 The rewards for an emergent elite: (a) gold and garnet pendant from *Hamwic* at St Mary's Stadium; composite disc brooches from (b) Boss Hall, Bramford, Ipswich; (c) Floral Street, London; and (d) Harford Farm, Caistor by Norwich. Various scales (reproduced with the kind permission of (a) Wessex Archaeology; (b) Suffolk County Council; (c) AOC Archaeology; (d) Norwich Castle Museum and Art Gallery)

being an outlying part of Bramford parish. Bramford was a royal manor in 1066, 100 acres being attached to St Peter's Church in Ipswich; this Anglo-Saxon minster had a massive six-carucate holding at the Conquest, suggestive of an early church associated with the East Anglian royal family (Pestell 2004: 127 and n. 194). Overlooking the Gipping and mid-way between the royal vill and the *emporium*, Boss Hall may have marked the ruling family's control of their wider estate (Fig. 29.3).

A similar expression of elite presence may be signalled by the series of cemeteries that is emerging to the north of *Lundenwic*'s trading area. Particularly significant among these are burials of the mid seventh century at St Martin-in-the-Fields, including grave-goods such as a blue glass cup, a hanging-bowl with enamelled escutcheons, and a gold pendant (Burton 2007; Henig, this volume). These join a gold and garnet composite disc-brooch excavated nearby in Floral Street (Fig. 29.5c).

An elite presence is explicit at many high-status sites, such as Coddenham, with its rich burials, and Caistor St Edmund near Norwich, Norfolk, where a rich 'Final Phase' cemetery at Harford Farm yielded, amongst other graves, a female burial with another gold composite disc-brooch (Fig. 29.5d). The cemetery overlooks the old Roman walled *civitas* capital of *Venta Icenorum* across the River Tas, outside which a 'productive' site has been located. Contemporaneity of sites is demonstrated, with Grave 18 yielding Series B sceattas, and the intervisibility of the two sites must have constituted an important visible reminder of the ruling family to all those trading by the river (Fig. 29.6). Sarre in Kent may provide another example. Although the cemetery there has its origins in the sixth century, its extensive size and a number of rich late graves imply a wealthy community associated with this naturally important location at a major Roman crossing point of the Wantsum channel (Brookes 2003: 88–9). It is probably not by chance that Sarre is named as a port on which remission of toll was granted to the community of Minster-in-Thanet by Eadberht II of Kent in 763–4 (Kelly 1992: 6).

Other points of similarity may bridge the apparent divide between the larger *emporia* and several 'productive' sites. A spread of twenty-three sceattas from

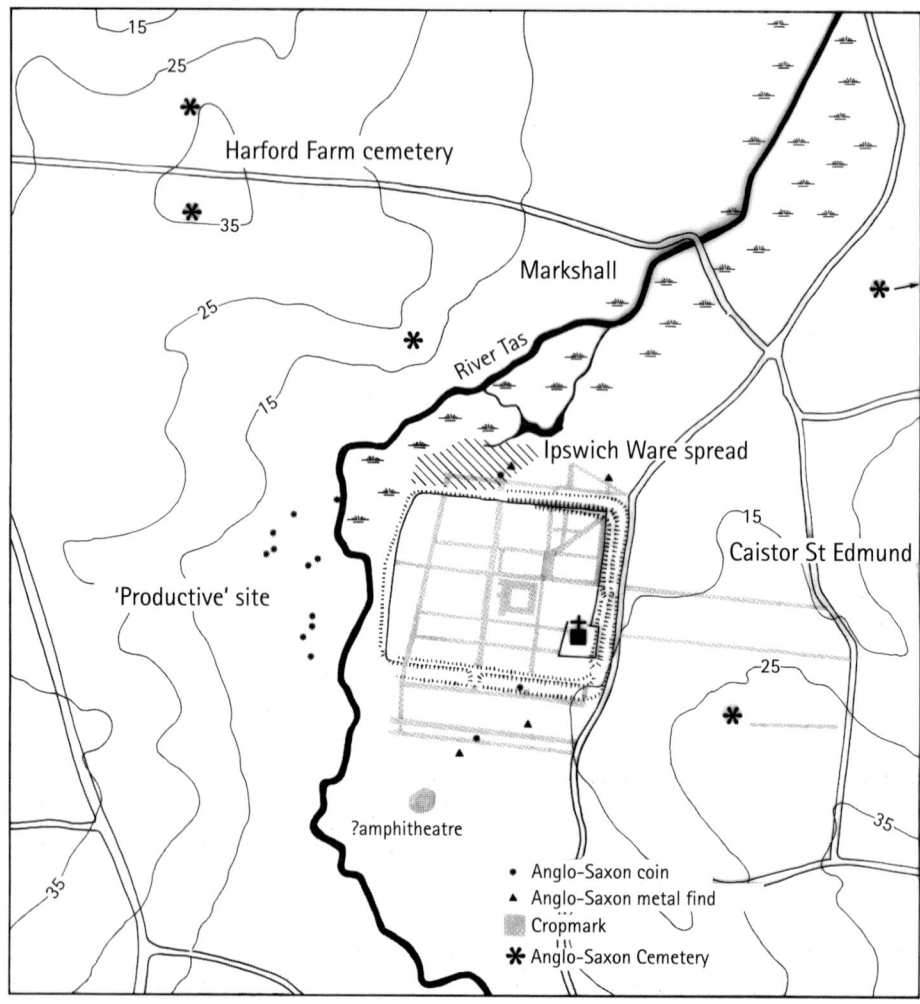

Figure 29.6 The environs of *Venta Icenorum*, Caistor St Edmund, Norfolk, showing the relationship between the 'productive' site, settlement area, and the surrounding cemeteries, notably that at Harford Farm.

outside the Roman walls of Caistor St Edmund can be compared to the situation obtaining at Burgh Castle, a Roman Saxon Shore fort, where twelve sceattas have been found outside the walls. Those sceattas known or suggested to have been found at the Roman forts of Reculver in Kent and Walton Castle in Suffolk are unfortunately unlocated, having been uncovered through erosion of the coastline, but the parallel with trading sites placed outside the walls of London, York, or Rouen may be quite deliberate.

Conclusions

Work in the last forty years has revolutionized our understanding of pre-Viking Anglo-Saxon economics. Not only has Pirenne's view of an unurbanized, introverted, agrarian economy been superseded, so too has the notion that the earliest trading centres were built upon a monopolistic system of gift exchange. Instead, we now see a mid Saxon society widely connected through a nexus of trading centres, engaged with the Continent and using a coinage which, at the height of its volume in circulation in the early eighth century, was to be unsurpassed for another five hundred years (Blackburn 2003: 31, and this volume).

Inevitably, this picture is a partial one. Much trade was focused on the North Sea littoral, stretching round to Hampshire and along the south coast. While there are contemporary trading or market sites along the south-west and western coasts of Britain, and evidence for the intensification of production at some sites, such as of salt (Maddicott 2006), the material culture away from the east is dissimilar and markedly poorer (Griffiths 2003: 71–2; Moreland 2000b: 98–101). Indeed, the 'economically precocious regions of East Anglia and Lindsey' (Blair 2005: 212) were arguably foremost in a zone of North Sea coastal communities, whose position gave them greater opportunities for the acquisition of goods considered 'high status' in more restricted inland areas (Loveluck and Tys 2006: 161–2).

If we are no longer to see the traditional *emporia* of *Gippeswic* or *Hamwic* as giant funnels through which emergent elites controlled all trade and imports, we can now propose alternative models based on the emergence of a more diverse series of sites. Unifying these is the increasingly favoured view that such places acted as toll-collection centres (Loveluck and Tys 2006: 146). Not only does this form of taxation have clear documentary evidence to support it, tolls were highly lucrative for rulers, Continental evidence suggesting that the proceeds might be worth as much as 10 per cent of the value of merchandise passing through ports or fairs (Kelly 1992: 18; McCormick 2001: 640–7; Middleton 2005).

According to Hodges' model, each major Anglo-Saxon kingdom created its own large *emporium* to control trade (except, apparently, Kent: Moreland 2000b: 72). As Scull has pointed out, London, Ipswich, and Southampton certainly appear to have been 'special-purpose settlements' (1997: 284–9), but the wealth of many newly-discovered sites allows us the prospect of gaining further insights into the political character and struggles of the heptarchy. For instance, the emergence of sites around the Fens makes political sense of the power struggle between the East Anglian and Mercian kingdoms, presumably over access to the resources and tolls that could be levied on trade that was entering through the Wash basin (Fig. 29.1).

Perhaps inevitably, the recurring question of coinage provides one final issue. Quite clearly a barter-exchange economy existed for much of the Anglo-Saxon period, extensive coin-use not precluding this. However, the sheer quantity of sceattas now known suggests an insistent link between coinage and trade that now needs to be rigorously investigated. Metcalf's work on regression analysis (2001; 2003) has illustrated the frustrations of not having any mints certainly located and it seems remarkable that despite the categorization of sceatta series, we still lack adequate research on the dies used to produce them. The ground-breaking work of Talbot in establishing a chronological sequence for all Iron Age Icenean coins based on die-linkages (2006) is instructive and points the way for early medieval numismatists. Coin analysis may also help us to understand better the rhythms of English economic life. It may be no coincidence that the short-lived phenomenon of English toll exemptions, 'an aberration in the Anglo-Saxon context' (Kelly 1992: 25), lasted between the 730s and 760s, and declined at much the same time as the volume of sceatta coins in circulation.

The processes *Dark Age Economics* strove to disentangle have undoubtedly become more complex and nuanced, but so too have the questions we have the potential to answer. Our challenge is now to integrate the range of data drawn from rural and urban sites into a tighter, single, economic framework that recognizes diversity and the particular, as well as general trends in issues of trade and exchange.

Acknowledgements

I would like to thank Keith Wade for kindly providing me with a copy of his unpublished lecture on Ipswich, delivered to the Ipswich Archaeological Trust's 'Ipswich Unearthed' conference held shortly before this paper was completed. I am grateful to Mark Blackburn and Chris Loveluck for providing me with copies of their recently published papers that I had originally read while 'forthcoming'; to Chris Scull for comments in advance of his publication of the Ipswich Boss Hall and Buttermarket cemeteries, and as ever to Kat Ulmschneider for a number of constructive observations. Finally, I acknowledge the kindness of my East Anglian colleagues Andy Hutcheson, John Newman, and Andrew Rogerson for their knowledgeable observations, discussion, and information about new sites and finds in our singularly 'productive' area of England.

REFERENCES

ANDERTON, M. (ed.) (1999). *Anglo-Saxon Trading Centres: Beyond the Emporia*. Glasgow: Cruithne Press.

BACHRACH, B. S. (1998). 'Pirenne and Charlemagne', in A. C. Murray (ed.), *After Rome's Fall: Narrators and Sources of Early Medieval History; Essays Presented to Walter Goffart*. Toronto: University of Toronto Press, 214–31.

BIDDLE, M. (1976). 'Towns', in D. M. Wilson (ed.), *The Archaeology of Anglo-Saxon England*. London: Methuen, 99–150.

BIRBECK, V., with SMITH, R. J. C., ANDREWS, P., and STOODLEY, N. (2005). *The Origins of Mid-Saxon Southampton: Excavations at the Friends Provident St Mary's Stadium 1998–2000*. Salisbury: Wessex Archaeology.

BLACKBURN, M. A. (2003). '"Productive" sites and the pattern of coin loss in England, 600–1180', in Pestell and Ulmschneider (eds.), *Markets in Early Medieval Europe*, 20–36.

—— (2007). 'Gold in England during the Age of Silver (eighth–eleventh centuries)', in J. Graham-Campbell and G. Williams (eds.), *The Silver Economy in the Viking Age*. Walnut Creek, CA: Left Coast Press, 55–98.

BLACKMORE, L. (2001). 'Pottery: trade and tradition', in Hill and Cowie (eds.), *Wics*, 22–42.

BLAIR, J. (1988). 'Minster churches in the landscape', in D. Hooke (ed.), *Anglo-Saxon Settlements*. Oxford: Basil Blackwell, 35–58.

—— (1996). 'The minsters of the Thames', in J. Blair and B. Golding (eds.), *The Cloister and the World: Essays in Medieval History in Honour of Barbara Harvey*. Oxford: Clarendon Press, 5–28.

—— (2005). *The Church in Anglo-Saxon Society*. Oxford: Oxford University Press.

BLINKHORN, P. (1999). 'Of cabbages and kings: production, trade, and consumption in Middle-Saxon England', in Anderton (ed.), *Anglo-Saxon Trading Centres*, 4–23.

BOURDILLON, J. (1988). 'Countryside and town: the animal resources of Saxon Southampton', in D. Hooke (ed.), *Anglo-Saxon Settlements*. Oxford: Basil Blackwell, 177–95.

—— (1994) 'The animal provisioning of Saxon Southampton', in J. Rackham (ed.), *Environment and Economy in Anglo-Saxon England*. CBA Research Report 89. York: Council for British Archaeology, 120–5.

BRISBANE, M. (1988). '*Hamwic* (Saxon Southampton): an 8th century port and production centre', in Hodges and Hobley (eds.), *The Rebirth of Towns in the West*, 101–8.

BROOKES, S. (2003). 'The early Anglo-Saxon framework for middle Anglo-Saxon economics: the case of east Kent', in Pestell and Ulmschneider (eds.), *Markets in Early Medieval Europe*, 84–96.

Burton, E. (2007). 'From Roman to Saxon London: Saxon burials at St Martin-in-the-Fields', in N. Christie (ed.), 'Medieval Britain and Ireland in 2006'. *Medieval Archaeology* 51: 207–302.

Campbell, A. (ed.) (1973). *The Charters of Rochester.* Anglo-Saxon Charters 1. London: British Academy.

Campbell, J. (1986). 'Bede's words for places', in J. Campbell (ed.), *Essays in Anglo-Saxon History.* London: Hambledon Press, 99–119.

Carr, R. D., Tester, A., and Murphy, P. (1988). 'The Middle-Saxon settlement at Staunch Meadow, Brandon'. *Antiquity* 62: 371–7.

Clarke, H., and Ambrosiani, B. (1991). *Towns in the Viking Age.* Leicester: Leicester University Press.

Colgrave, B., and Mynors, R. A. B. (eds.) (1969). *Bede's Ecclesiastical History of the English People.* Oxford Medieval Texts. Oxford: Oxford University Press.

Crabtree, P. (1994). 'Animal exploitation in East Anglian villages' in J. Rackham (ed.), *Environment and Economy in Anglo-Saxon England.* CBA Research Report 89. York: Council for British Archaeology, 40–54.

Daubney, A. (2007). 'Heckington', in N. Christie (ed.), 'Medieval Britain and Ireland in 2006'. *Medieval Archaeology* 51: 207–302.

Delogu, P. (1998). 'Reading Pirenne again', in R. Hodges and W. Bowden (eds.), *The Sixth Century: Production, Distribution and Demand.* Leiden: Brill, 15–40.

Everett, L., Anderson, S., Powell, K., and Riddler, I. (2003). 'Vicarage Farm, Coddenham CDD022', Archaeological Evaluation Report 2003/66. Bury St Edmunds: Suffolk County Council Archaeological Service (Unpublished).

Foard, G. (1985). 'The administrative organization of Northamptonshire in the Saxon period'. *Anglo-Saxon Studies in Archaeology and History* 4: 185–222.

Gardiner, M., Cross, R., Macpherson-Grant, N., and Riddler, I. (2001). 'Continental trade and non-urban ports in mid-Saxon England. Excavations at Sandtun, West Hythe, Kent'. *Archaeological Journal* 158: 161–290.

Griffiths, D. (2003). 'Markets and "productive" sites: a view from western Britain', in Pestell and Ulmschneider (eds.), *Markets in Early Medieval Europe*, 62–72.

Hase, P. H. (1975). *The Development of the Parish in Hampshire Particularly in the Eleventh and Twelfth Centuries.* Unpublished PhD thesis, University of Cambridge.

Havighurst, A. F. (ed.) (1976). *The Pirenne Thesis: Analysis, Criticism and Revision.* 3rd edition. Lexington: Heath.

Hill, D. (2001a). 'A short selection of contemporary sources for the wic sites', in Hill and Cowie (eds.), *Wics*, 111–18.

—— (2001b). 'End piece: definitions and superficial analysis', in Hill and Cowie (eds.), *Wics*, 75–84.

—— and Cowie, R. (eds.) (2001). *Wics: The Early Mediaeval Trading Centres of Northern Europe.* Sheffield: Sheffield Academic Press.

Hinton, D. A. (1999). 'Metalwork and the emporia', in Anderton (ed.), *Anglo-Saxon Trading Centres*, 24–31.

—— (2005). *Gold and Gilt, Pots and Pins: Possessions and People in Medieval Britain.* Oxford: Oxford University Press.

Hobley, B. (1988). 'Saxon London: *Lundenwic* and *Lundenburh*: two cities rediscovered', in Hodges and Hobley (eds.), *The Rebirth of Towns in the West*, 69–82.

HODGES, R. (1981). *The Hamwih Pottery: The Local and Imported Wares From 30 Years' Excavations at Middle Saxon Southampton and their European Context.* CBA Research Report 37. London: Council for British Archaeology.

—— (1982). *Dark Age Economics: The Origins of Towns and Trade AD 600–1000.* London: Duckworth.

—— (2006). '*Dark Age Economics* revisited', in R. Hodges (ed.), *Goodbye to the Vikings?* London: Duckworth, 63–71.

—— and HOBLEY, B. (eds.) (1988). *The Rebirth of Towns in the West AD 700–1050.* CBA Research Report 68. London: Council for British Archaeology.

—— and WHITEHOUSE, D. (1989). *Mohammed, Charlemagne and the Origins of Europe.* 2nd edition. London: Duckworth.

HUTCHESON, A. (2006). 'The origins of Kings Lynn? Control of wealth on the Wash prior to the Norman Conquest'. *Medieval Archaeology* 50: 71–104.

JONES, G. R. J. (1979). 'Multiple estates and early settlement', in P. Sawyer (ed.), *English Medieval Settlement.* London: Edward Arnold, 9–34.

—— (1985). 'Multiple estates perceived'. *Journal of Historical Geography* 11(4): 352–63.

KELLY, S. (1992). 'Trading privileges from eighth-century England'. *Early Medieval Europe* 1(1): 3–28.

KEMP, R. (1996). *Anglian Settlement at 46–54 Fishergate.* Volume 7, fasc. 1 of *The Archaeology of York.* York: York Archaeological Trust.

LEAHY, K. (2000). 'Middle Anglo-Saxon metalwork from South Newbald and the "productive site" phenomenon in Yorkshire', in H. Geake and J. Kenny (eds.), *Early Deira: Archaeological Studies of the East Riding in the Fourth To Ninth Centuries AD.* Oxford: Oxbow Books, 51–82.

LEARY, J. (2004). *Tatberht's Lundenwic: Archaeological Excavations in Middle Saxon London.* Pre-Construct Archaeology Monograph 2. London: Pre-Construct Archaeology.

LOVELUCK, C. (2001). 'Wealth, waste and conspicuous consumption. Flixborough and its importance for middle and late Saxon rural settlement studies', in H. Hamerow and A. MacGregor (eds.), *Image and Power in the Archaeology of Early Medieval Britain: Essays in Honour of Rosemary Cramp.* Oxford: Oxbow Books, 78–130.

—— (2007). *Rural Settlement, Lifestyles and Social Change in the Later First Millennium A.D.: Anglo-Saxon Flixborough in its Wider Context.* Excavations at Flixborough 4. Oxford: Oxbow Books.

—— and TYS, D. (2006). 'Coastal societies, exchange and identity along the Channel and southern North Sea shores of Europe, AD 600–1000'. *Journal of Maritime Archaeology* 1: 140–69.

LYON, B. D. (1974). *Henri Pirenne: A Biographical and Intellectual History.* Ghent: E. Story-Scientia.

MADDICOTT, J. R. (2006). 'London and Droitwich, c.650–750: trade, industry and the rise of Mercia'. *Anglo-Saxon England* 34: 7–58.

MALCOLM, G., BOWSHER, D., and COWIE, R. (2003). *Middle Saxon London: Excavations at the Royal Opera House 1989–99.* Museum of London Archaeology Service Monograph 15. London: Museum of London.

MCCORMICK, M. (2001). *Origins of the European Economy: Communications and Commerce AD 300–900.* Cambridge: Cambridge University Press.

METCALF, D. M. (1977). 'Monetary affairs in Mercia in the time of Æthelbald', in A. Dornier (ed.), *Mercian Studies.* Leicester: Leicester University Press, 87–106.

—— (2001). 'Determining the mint-attribution of East Anglian sceattas through regression analysis'. *British Numismatic Journal* 70: 1–11.

—— (2003). 'Variations in the composition of the currency at different places in England', in Pestell and Ulmschneider (eds.), *Markets in Early Medieval Europe*, 37–47.

MIDDLETON, N. (2005). 'Early medieval port customs, tolls and controls on foreign trade'. *Early Medieval Europe* 13(4): 313–58.

MORELAND, J. (2000a). 'Concepts of the early medieval economy', in I. L. Hansen and C. Wickham (eds.), *The Long Eighth Century*. Leiden: Brill, 1–34.

—— (2000b). 'The significance of production in eighth-century England', in I. L. Hansen and C. Wickham (eds.), *The Long Eighth Century*. Leiden: Brill, 69–104.

MORTON, A. (1999). 'Hamwic in its context', in Anderton (ed.), *Anglo-Saxon Trading Centres*, 48–62.

NAYLOR, J. (2004). *An Archaeology of Trade in Middle Saxon England*. British Archaeological Reports British Series 376. Oxford: Archaeopress.

—— (2007). 'The circulation of early-medieval European coinage: a case study from Yorkshire, c. 650–c. 867. *Medieval Archaeology* 51: 41–61.

NEWMAN, J. (1991). 'The Boss Hall Anglo-Saxon cemetery, Ipswich'. *Saxon: The Newsletter of the Sutton Hoo Society* 14: 4–5.

—— (2003). 'Exceptional finds, exceptional sites? Barham and Coddenham, Suffolk', in Pestell and Ulmschneider (eds.), *Markets in Early Medieval Europe*, 97–109.

O'CONNOR, T. (2001). 'On the interpretation of animal bone assemblages from wics', in Hill and Cowie (eds.), *Wics*, 54–60.

PESTELL, T. (2001). 'Monastic foundation strategies in the early Norman diocese of Norwich'. *Anglo-Norman Studies* 23: 199–229.

—— (2003). 'The afterlife of 'productive' sites in East Anglia', in Pestell and Ulmschneider (eds.), *Markets in Early Medieval Europe*, 122–37.

—— (2004). *Landscapes of Monastic Foundation: The Establishment of Religious Houses in East Anglia, c. 650–1200*. Anglo-Saxon Studies 5. Woodbridge: Boydell Press.

—— and ULMSCHNEIDER, K. (eds.) (2003). *Markets in Early Medieval Europe: Trading and 'Productive' Sites, 650–850*. Macclesfield: Windgather Press.

PIRENNE, H. (1954). *Mohammed and Charlemagne*. London: George Allen and Unwin.

RICHARDS, J. D. (1999). 'What's so special about "productive" sites? Middle Saxon settlements in Northumbria'. *Anglo-Saxon Studies in Archaeology and History* 10: 71–80.

—— (2003). 'The Anglian and Anglo-Scandinavian sites at Cottam, east Yorkshire', in Pestell and Ulmschneider (eds.), *Markets in Early Medieval Europe*, 155–66.

RIDDLER, I. (2001). 'The spatial organisation of bone-working at Hamwic', in Hill and Cowie (eds.), *Wics*, 61–6.

—— (2004). 'Production in *Lundenwic*: antler, bone and horn working', in Leary, *Tatberht's Lundenwic*, 145–8.

RUMBLE, A. (2001). 'Notes on the linguistic and onomastic characteristics of Old English *wic*', in Hill and Cowie (eds.), *Wics*, 1–2.

SAMSON, R. (1999). 'Illusory emporia and mad economic theories', in Anderton (ed.), *Anglo-Saxon Trading Centres*, 76–90.

SAUNDERS, T. (1991). 'Markets and individuals: the idealism of Richard Hodges'. *Scottish Archaeological Review* 8: 140–5.

—— (2001). 'Early mediaeval emporia and the tributary social function', in Hill and Cowie (eds.), *Wics*, 7–13.

SCHMIDT, T. (2000). 'Marked, torg og kaupang—språklige vitnemål om handle i middelalderen'. *Collegium Medievale* 13: 79–102.

SCULL, C. (1997). 'Urban centres in pre-Viking England', in J. Hines (ed.), *The Anglo-Saxons From the Migration Period to the Eighth Century: An Ethnographic Perspective*. Woodbridge: Boydell Press, 269–98.

—— (2009). *Early Medieval Cemeteries at Boss Hall and Buttermarket, Ipswich, Suffolk*. Society for Medieval Archaeology Monograph, 27.

SHERRATT, A. (1996). 'Why Wessex? The Avon River route and river transport in later British prehistory'. *Oxford Journal of Archaeology* 15(2): 211–34.

SPALL, C. A., and TOOP, N. J. (2008). 'Before *Eoforwic*: new light on York in the 6th–7th centuries'. *Medieval Archaeology* 52: 1–25.

TALBOT, J. (2006). 'The Iceni early face/horse series', in P. de Jersey (ed.), *Celtic Coinage: New Discoveries, New Discussion*. British Archaeological Reports International Series 1532. Oxford: Archaeopress, 213–41.

ULMSCHNEIDER, K. (2000a). 'Settlement, economy and the "productive" site in Anglo-Saxon Lincolnshire, AD 650–85'. *Medieval Archaeology* 44: 53–79.

—— (2000b). *Markets, Minsters and Metal-Detectors: The Archaeology of Middle Saxon Lincolnshire and Hampshire Compared*. British Archaeological Reports British Series 307. Oxford: Archaeopress.

—— (2005). 'The study of early medieval markets: are we rewriting the economic history of middle Anglo-Saxon England?', *Studien zur Sachsenforschung* 15: 517–31.

WADE, K. (1988). 'Ipswich' in Hodges and Hobley (eds.), *The Rebirth of Towns in the West*, 93–100.

—— (2007). 'The development of Anglo-Saxon Ipswich'. Unpublished lecture to 'Ipswich Unearthed' conference, 27 October 2007.

WEBSTER, L., and BACKHOUSE, J. (1991). *The Making of England: Anglo-Saxon Art and Culture AD 600–900*. London: British Museum Press.

WHITELOCK, D. (ed.) (1979). *English Historical Documents c. 500–1042*. London: Routledge.

WILLIAMSON, T. (1993). *The Origins of Norfolk*. Manchester: Manchester University Press.

CHAPTER 30

COINAGE IN ITS ARCHAEOLOGICAL CONTEXT

MARK BLACKBURN

COINS are among the most enduring and closely dated Anglo-Saxon artefacts, ones which archaeologists are often keen to find in excavations. Individually they may provide valuable dating evidence for the layers in which they occur, but set in the context of other finds from the region their contribution can be much more substantial, shedding light on the economic, social, and political circumstances of the time. Their interpretation at this level is often seen as a specialist pursuit which archaeologists may be wary to undertake. On the other hand, with the proliferation of new finds and the availability of data online, it is now much easier to study comparative material and more people have been encouraged to use the find distributions in their work. The purpose of this chapter is to discuss some uses and limitations of numismatic evidence and the specialist methodology, while illustrating the directions in which current research is developing.

Anglo-Saxon coins were produced in their millions and survive in some hundreds of thousands, yet their production and survival rates vary substantially from period to period and issue to issue, so that some coin types are quite common while others are extremely rare. An understanding of the factors influencing survival is important when interpreting the coinage and monetary economy of the period. The coins which are extant today come from two different sources—from hoards, many of which were found in the eighteenth and nineteenth centuries, and from single finds, which have increased dramatically since the 1970s through the hobby of metal-detecting. Some 300 coin hoards of the Anglo-Saxon period are recorded from the British Isles, containing perhaps 80,000 coins, and some 8,000 single finds are now on record. From Scandinavia and eastern Europe about 950 documented hoards have yielded *c*.60,000 Anglo-Saxon coins, mainly of the period 900–1050 (Blackburn and Jonsson 1981; Kluge 1981), while they are rarely found in other parts of Europe.

Most of the coins in museum and private collections must derive from hoards, although often information about where and when they were found has been lost. There are several major museums with large systematic collections of Anglo-Saxon coins, but there are many others with much smaller holdings which when considered together are very significant. Fortunately, they have been well published in the British Academy's *Sylloge of Coins of the British Isles* ('SCBI') series, which now runs to some sixty volumes and includes 32,000 Anglo-Saxon coins from 200 British and foreign museums. These records have been digitized and can be consulted from the project's online database (see www.medievalcoins.org).

There is no general survey covering the coinage of the whole Anglo-Saxon period, but Grierson and Blackburn (1986: chs. 8 and 10) take it down to the early tenth century, while Stewart (1992) considers the whole period, but mainly from the perspective of mint administration. Specialized monographs include Metcalf (1993–4) on the earliest coinages to the mid eighth century, Blunt *et al.* (1989) on tenth-century coinages, and Metcalf (1998) on aspects of the later tenth- and eleventh-century coinage and coin circulation. However, most of the literature is in the form of articles in periodicals and books, conveniently traced through the annual bibliographies in *Anglo-Saxon England*. North (1994) is a practical catalogue listing most Anglo-Saxon coin types, with attributions and chronology summarized from other publications.

COINS AS HISTORICAL DOCUMENTS

Coins are at the same time both archaeological artefacts and historical documents. Coins were one of the earliest mass-produced items to penetrate society widely. As officially sanctioned issues of the state they carry particular authority, so it might be reasonable to suppose that their inscriptions and iconography were deliberately chosen, and that their manufacture and distribution were controlled by the state. Yet, one of the challenges for the numismatist is to determine at what level decisions were taken and whether particular features do indeed represent official policy or merely result from personal preference or human error. Assessment of this requires understanding of the administration that underlay the monetary system, the role of the king and his advisors, the die-cutters, the moneyers, and those enforcing the circulation of good coinage. The names of the moneyers and, in the later Anglo-Saxon period at least, the towns in which they operated appear on the coins, so that one can track the careers of thousands of individuals. From this and occasional documentary references it is evident that moneyers were men of quite high status, responsible for financing, managing, and guaranteeing the production of coins bearing their names. In the eighth century and first half of the ninth they appear to have enjoyed a degree of autonomy in the choice of design, but increasing standardization in coin type among moneyers and latterly between mints reflects the activity of policy-makers in or close to the court, a trend also suggested by the coinage reforms of Æthelwulf of Wessex (839–58) and his sons (Blackburn 2003b).

The ruler is rarely named on the earliest Anglo-Saxon coins: the gold shillings (OE *scilling*, pl. *scillingas*) and early silver pennies (OE *pening*, pl. *peningas*; often erroneously called 'sceattas') of the seventh and first half of the eighth centuries. However, with the introduction of larger, thinner pennies early in the reign of Offa of Mercia (757–96), it became standard practice for the name and title of the king or bishop to be given. These inscriptions can be an important source of historical evidence, for they are a contemporary statement of who was reigning where and when. For pre-Viking East Anglia they identify several otherwise unrecorded kings: Eadwald (*c.*796–800), who evidently rebelled against Mercian domination after Offa's death, Æthelweard (*c.*835–45), who led his kingdom through a period of apparent stability and prosperity, and Æthelred and Oswald, who seem to have been short-lived successors to Eadmund (845–69). Coins also corroborate the account in the *Anglo-Saxon Chronicle* of the end of Mercian rule over Kent and East Anglia, and the brief West Saxon occupation of London in 829 (Fig. 30.1c).

The designs on a coin should also be regarded as complementing the inscriptions and from time to time as conveying a message, whether intentionally or unintentionally. In the first detailed study of the iconography of the earlier Anglo-Saxon coinages, Gannon (2003) has demonstrated that many of the early pennies from the first half of the eighth century have designs that carry quite sophisticated theological imagery (Fig. 30.1a), but whether this indicates a widespread general interest in religion during this age of Conversion, or direct influence of the Church on royal policy, or participation by monasteries in coin production, is a matter for debate (Naismith forthcoming). In the following generation of coinage, it is Classical influence that is most striking. Offa is often portrayed as a Roman emperor (Fig. 30.1b), sharing by inference the qualities of leadership and greatness, and perhaps implying some parallels between Mercia's domination among the English kingdoms and the former supremacy of Rome. Subsequently, instances of coin designs being used overtly as propaganda are rare, but good examples are the London-signed issues of Egbert (802–39) and Alfred (871–99), which celebrate

Figure 30.1 (a) Early penny, Series Q, East Anglia c.725–40, depicting the bust of Christ and a bird (good or Christ) fighting a snake (evil or death); (b) Offa of Mercia, penny, London, c.780–92; (c) Egbert of Wessex as king of Mercia, penny, London, 829–30 (*Sources*: (a) Lord Stewartby; (b) Fitzwilliam Museum; (c) British Museum. Images enlarged)

the West Saxons taking control of the principal Mercian *emporium* (Fig. 30.1c). Yet at the very least the image of the king was always intended to convey a sense of his authority, while the ornamental designs would have reflected contemporary taste, also paralleled in metalwork and sculpture. The Scandinavian rulers of the Danelaw knew how to harness the symbolic power of coinage to enhance their status among their Anglo-Saxon and Carolingian neighbours. The overtly Christian nature of many designs and some inscriptions on their coinages seems to be building a case for the admission of their kingdoms to the group of Western Christian states (Blackburn 2001: 135–6; 2004: 329–32).

COINS AS ARTEFACTS

Coins can be studied simply as artefacts, irrespective of whether their find provenances are known or not. We can look at their inscriptions, designs, weights, and finenesses to understand how the coinage was produced and the organization underlying it. The steel dies used to strike the coins were hand-engraved, and had sufficiently distinctive features to enable us to recognize coins that were produced from a particular die. This kind of die study is one of the numismatist's most powerful analytical tools. If photographs of a sufficiently large sample of a coinage is available, we can determine how many different obverse and reverse dies are represented in it, and from such data we can estimate statistically how many dies were originally used to strike that coinage (Esty 2006). Studies have been made of some individual mints, compiling a corpus of all its known coins, arranged according to the dies from which they were struck (e.g. Lincoln: Mossop 1970; Huntingdon: Eaglen 1999; Winchester: Harvey forthcoming). From such data estimates of the number of dies used at all mints in that type can, with some reservations, be extrapolated (e.g. Metcalf 1980: 33–4). By comparing the estimates for different types, we can get a sense of the relative size of different issues. The Scandinavian coinage of York in the 940s, for example, although today quite rare, was apparently struck on a large scale, comparable with York's output in the eleventh century when it was the second or third most productive mint in England (Blackburn 2004: 342–4).

Some scholars have gone a step further and sought to estimate the total number of coins struck by applying an average number of coins per die derived from later medieval mint accounts. Such an approach, though attractive, is fraught with difficulty because of the considerable margins of error inherent in the statistics, and in the assumption that die-life in the small private workshops of moneyers in the Anglo-Saxon period was at all comparable to that in the major factory mints of the thirteenth and fourteenth centuries. Recent studies have therefore taken a more cautious approach in quoting quite wide ranges of possible mint outputs, rather than central point estimates quoted earlier (Allen 2006; cf. Metcalf 1981). These studies have gone on to consider the volume of coinage in circulation in England, as opposed to the amount produced by the mints over a given period, but by common consent the figures produced can only be taken as indicating an order of magnitude rather than actual estimates, and they are not adequate to provide decisive evidence as to the reliability of statements on the size of tribute payments made to the Vikings in the *Anglo-Saxon Chronicle* (Gillingham 1989; Lawson 1989; Gillingham 1990).

The distinctive appearance of individual dies also opens the way to a stylistic analysis. By studying details of the design, letter forms, and spelling of the inscriptions, the work of different die-cutters can often be distinguished. Moneyers did not normally engrave their own dies, but they obtained them from die-cutters who often served several or all the moneyers at a mint or a number of mints in a region. In the late Anglo-Saxon period, when up to sixty named mints were operating simultaneously, the arrangements for die-cutting changed from time to time (Jonsson 1987: 86–95). In some types all the dies seem to have been made centrally, while in others there was delegation to a limited number of regional workshops. The most fragmented production occurred during Cnut's *Quatrefoil* types, in which some nineteen die-cutting centres have been identified (Blackburn and Lyon 1986). By the mid eleventh century, die production was mainly concentrated in London, and in the hands of foreign goldsmiths, Theoderic and Otto (Stewart 1992: 78).

INTERPRETING COIN FINDS

There is a fundamental difference between the evidence of coin hoards—groups of coins assembled and concealed or lost together on one occasion—and of single finds: coins lost individually and often accidentally. In theory a coin hoard represents a sample of the coinage circulating at the time the hoard was assembled, thus providing a 'snapshot' of the currency at that moment and place. Unfortunately, most hoards are not so straightforward, and their contents will have been influenced by many factors which have to be taken into account when trying to interpret them. Each hoard has its own particular history of the way in which it was assembled, deposited, and recovered, and when interpreting the composition of a hoard it is necessary to distinguish features that arise from the special nature of the hoard from those that reflect the currency from which it was derived. A single hoard is therefore difficult to interpret in isolation, but where there are several from the same period common patterns may emerge that shed light on the monetary circulation of the time. By way of example, the hoard found in 2003 at Brantham, Suffolk, contained ninety coins from mints in the east Midlands late in the reign of Edward the Elder (899–924), but none of the Scandinavian issues in the name of St Edmund that had dominated the currency of East Anglia until Edward's re-conquest of 917 (Blackburn 2006a: 205–8). If the Brantham hoard is representative of the coinage circulating there in the early 920s, it suggests that Edward swiftly instituted and effected a total recoinage of the Scandinavian coins, replacing them with his own coinage from eastern Mercia, but until we have some further hoards of this nature, that proposal will remain uncertain.

Hoards can be classified according to the circumstances surrounding their deposit, e.g. accidental losses, emergency hoards, savings hoards, or abandoned hoards (Grierson 1975: 130–6), but it is often impossible to determine this and so a classification that takes account of how the coins in a hoard were brought together may be more useful, e.g. a random sample of currency, a group selected on one occasion as savings, a multi-part hoard with two or more elements, or an accumulation that had been built up progressively (Blackburn 2005: 12–15, 27). Theoretically there need be no lower limit to the number of coins that can constitute a hoard (technically two coins could be a hoard), but since the evidential value of small groups is less secure, numismatists sometimes exclude these from their analyses. The number of coins surviving from a particular coinage will be strongly influenced by the number and size of hoards from that period that have been discovered. Just one single large hoard can transform our knowledge of a coinage. Thus the earlier Scandinavian coinages of the Danelaw would be rare today if it were not for the 1840 Cuerdale hoard containing some 5,000 specimens, together with 2,000 Anglo-Saxon and Carolingian coins. From some periods there are very few hoards known—from the second half of the eighth century there are merely two relatively small hoards—while from other periods the number of coin hoards rises dramatically. In some cases this clearly related to periods of unrest; the activities of the Viking army in the decade *c.*865–75 and the Norman Conquest in 1066 both prompted a substantial increase in the rate of hoards, though interestingly Cnut's conquest of England in 1015–16 had no such effect.

Until the advent of amateur metal-detecting as a hobby in the early 1970s, single finds of Anglo-Saxon coins were too few to form a coherent body of evidence suitable for analysis. Since the 1980s new finds have been recorded systematically in a special 'Coin Register' section of the *British Numismatic Journal*, and more recently in an online database, the *Corpus of Early Medieval Coin Finds from the British Isles* (www.medievalcoins.org). The new finds have opened new avenues of interpretation and have transformed our understanding of monetary circulation in the Anglo-Saxon period. They provide a much more detailed and reliable statistical basis from which to judge the volume of the currency and circulation patterns.

By charting the 8,000 single finds now on record, the rate of loss can be seen to have varied significantly over the period and in ways that hitherto would not have been expected (Blackburn 2003a). From small beginnings in the sixth and seventh centuries, when Continental gold tremisses and Anglo-Saxon shillings were the basic coinages, the rate of loss rose dramatically in the first half of the eighth century, driven in part by an influx of silver pennies from Frisia. A monetary crisis in the mid eighth century led to a virtual collapse of the currency, which appears only to have been restored by King Offa in the 780s. Thereafter a more gradual decline in the rate of coin loss suggests that the volume of coinage in active circulation hit another low at the end of the ninth and early tenth centuries. Although the rate of coin loss rose again and maintained strong levels during the later tenth and eleventh centuries, the rates of the earlier eighth century would not be equalled again until the end of the twelfth. This pattern, which perhaps reflects changes in the availability of gold and silver, is repeated in various different samples of single finds, looking at individual sites, types of sites, or regions. Some sites, such as *Hamwic*, declined or moved in the later ninth century and their finds therefore reflect only the earlier parts of this cycle (Fig. 30.2a), while others, such as Lincoln, only start then and lack the earlier coin losses (Fig. 30.2b). London, on the other hand, has coin losses from the whole period (Fig. 30.2c). The difficulty is how to determine which elements of the find profile reflect changes in activity specific to that site and which reflect changes in money supply and monetary use more generally. In order to avoid the undue influence of specific sites that are prolific with finds, a sample of isolated finds from the whole of England south of the Humber has been taken as a control, indicating the underlying variations in monetary loss. It is only by comparing the more specific samples with this that one can say something meaningful about the local monetary or commercial activity.

An alternative approach to the interpretation of single finds, championed by Metcalf in various publications (e.g. 1981; 1998), has mapped the distribution of specific coin types or the coins of particular mints in order to identify their areas of use and follow their directions of circulation. In order to mitigate the bias of concentrations at particular prolific sites or regions rich in finds generally, a form of regression analysis is used, so that it is the proportion of the local finds represented by the specific type or mint that is compared. This has been highly effective, not only in identifying probable mint places for the early anonymous pennies, but also for tracing specific patterns of coin movement between particular regions.

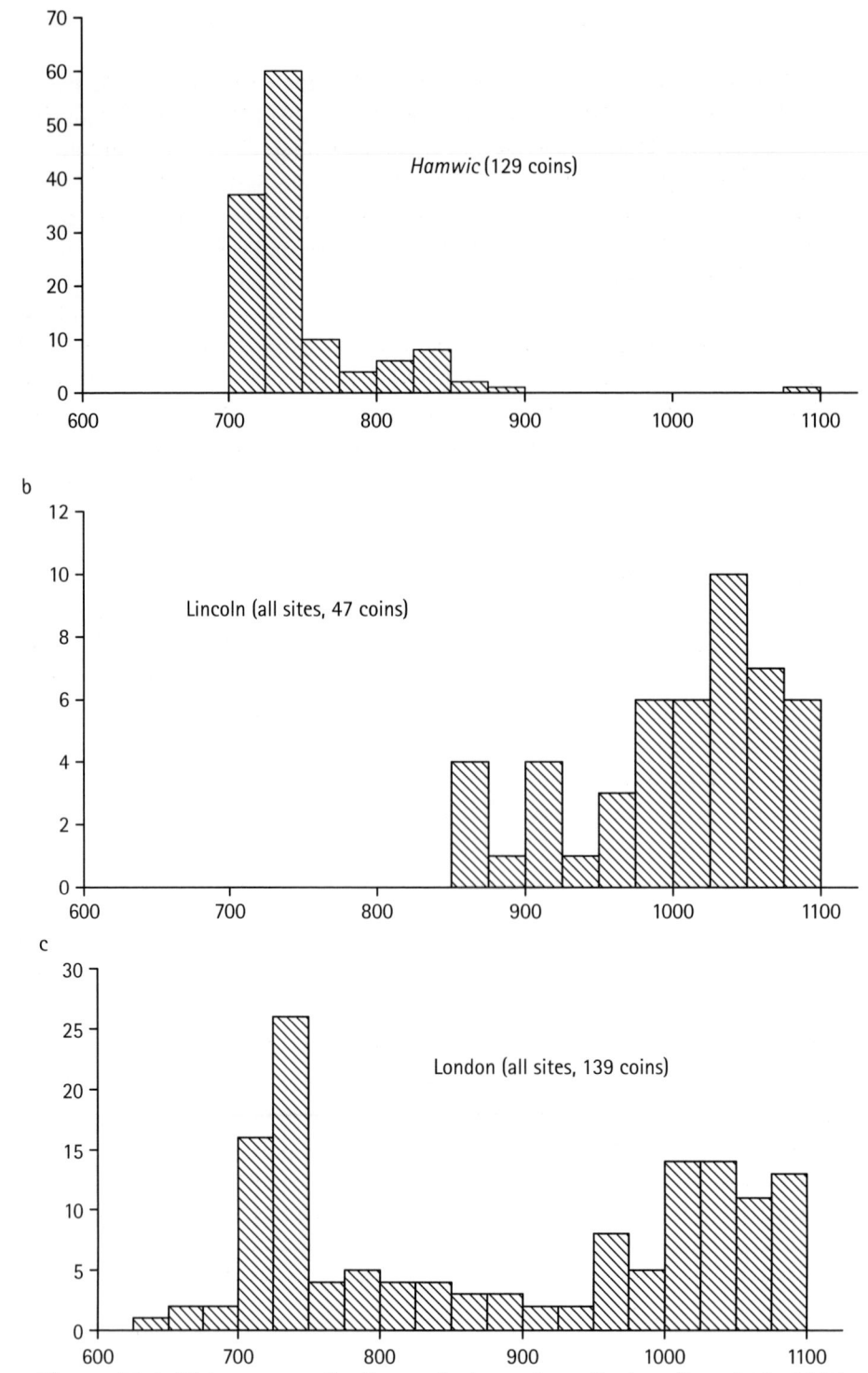

Figure 30.2 Histograms reflecting coin loss at particular sites, 600–1100 (a) Hamwic; (b) Lincoln; (c) London

COINS AS DATING EVIDENCE

Coins are often seen as particularly valuable for dating archaeological contexts, but the limitations of this evidence must be understood (Archibald 1988). It is important to distinguish between the date of production of a coin, which can often be determined fairly precisely, and the date of its loss, which is much more difficult to decide. When we speak of the date of a coin, it is usually the former that is intended, but for the purpose of dating an archaeological context, it would be more useful to know the latter.

For most Anglo-Saxon coins the date of production can be given confidently to within ten years, sometimes less. As we have seen, after the mid eighth century virtually all coins carry the name of a ruler, whose dates are usually known from historical sources. Within one reign a number of distinct coin types may have been issued, and the numismatist can often say in what order these were produced. Hoards provide the best evidence for determining the sequence of types, for if certain types are absent from a particular hoard they may have been produced after the hoard was assembled. Where we have a series of hoards that corroborate each other, they enable us to reconstruct the sequence of issues with some confidence. This has been particularly helpful in the late Anglo-Saxon period when there was a succession of coin types, each of very limited duration. Translating a fairly secure relative chronology for such a sequence into an absolute chronology for each type can be quite subjective. The classic dating for late Anglo-Saxon issues is that proposed by Dolley in the 1960s assuming that a regular cycle was intended with periods of equal duration, and while this is now seen as hypothetical, nonetheless his dates for the changes of type are likely to be accurate to within five years. This still means that the manufacture of such coins is more precisely dated than that of all other archaeological artefacts except timbers with surviving sapwood.

The dating of earlier coins without any ruler's name is also based on hoard evidence, where that is available, or on the fineness of their metal, and how this fits in with the cycles of debasement that took place. The Anglo-Saxon gold shillings of the seventh century followed Merovingian coinage in having their gold content reduced from c.90 per cent at the beginning of the century to c.20 per cent or less by c.670. This gold coinage was then replaced by a new one of fine silver pennies, and these in turn suffered a debasement over the course of the next eighty years. The broad course of these cycles of debasement can be charted by comparing the fineness of coins in different hoards, but one should not assume that that there was a simple progression which was followed in parallel at all mints (Metcalf 1993–4, vol. 3: 611–79). Fineness is therefore a valuable tool in dating but one to be used in conjunction with other forms of evidence.

A coin found in a sealed archaeological context or as a stray find from a field might in principle have been lost at any time after its manufacture. Strictly speaking the coin only provides a *terminus post quem* for the layer in which it occurred, i.e. the layer must be later than the production date of the coin. Anglo-Saxon coins had a quite limited period in circulation, generally no more than twenty to thirty years, before they were removed either as part of an official recoinage or because they were driven out by economic pressures as changes to the weight or fineness of newer coins made their circulation unviable. By studying the composition of hoards of different periods we can estimate the typical circulation period for various coin types.

Comprehensive recoinages, in which the currency was withdrawn and replaced with a new coin type, were very sporadic before the later tenth century; they occurred in *c*.675, *c*.760, *c*.792, *c*.855, *c*.863?, *c*.866, *c*.875, and *c*.880 (Blackburn 2003b). Following Edgar's major reform of the coinage in *c*.973, a new system of periodic recoinages developed in which the type was changed initially every five or six years, accelerating to every two or three years after 1035 (Dolley and Metcalf 1961: 152–4; Stewart 1992: 54–5). This rather elaborate system of taxation continued until late in the reign of Henry I (1100–35), was revived by Stephen (1135–54), and only finally abolished by Henry II (1154–89). Such short periods of circulation should provide us with a very accurate means of dating the loss of a coin struck after *c*.973. However, while the initial recoinages seem to have been pretty thorough, by the mid eleventh century they had become so frequent that it seems to have been common for some people to save their older coins and exchange them for the current type only when they were needed to make a payment. Thus the smaller (currency) hoards from this period have very short time-spans while the larger (savings) hoards often have an age profile of up to twenty or thirty years. When dating the loss of coins from an archaeological site this introduces an element of uncertainty, for although such a coin is most likely to have been lost from currency in circulation and thus close to its date of issue, it is always possible that it was somewhat older, and taken from savings.

The degree of wear on an Anglo-Saxon coin is not particularly useful as a measure of how long it had remained in circulation, as Anglo-Saxon coins are rarely seriously worn; the intensity of use was probably less than it would be in the later Middle Ages, and the periods of circulation were much shorter. The poor state of an Anglo-Saxon coin is usually down to corrosion it has suffered in the ground or more recent damage, for example being broken in the ploughsoil or during recovery.

What should a report on a coin from an archaeological site contain beyond the normal description and identification? First and foremost it should indicate the date of production, since this defines the *terminus post quem* of the layer in which it was found. It should go on to discuss the typical circulation period for that type of coinage, as that is when the coin is most likely to have been lost from general circulation. However, this provides only a degree of probability, for some older coins may have remained longer in people's possession, perhaps accidentally or in savings, and then been lost or discarded. Coins can also have been disturbed from earlier contexts and been re-deposited at any time later.

COINS IN GRAVES

The practice of placing coins in graves follows that of furnished burials generally. They fall into two broad groups: one with earlier Roman bronze coins, and the other with post-Roman gold and silver coins, which were broadly contemporary issues imported from the Continent.

Roman bronze coins, mostly of the third or fourth centuries, are quite often found in inhumations of the fifth to seventh centuries (King 1988; White 1988: 62–101; Moorhead 2006).[1] Outside Kent, about 60 per cent of the coins have been pierced once, twice, or even three times for use as ornamental pendants; in Kent the proportion is as low as 11 per cent. The Romans themselves rarely pierced coins, and thus casual finds of pierced Roman coins are likely to have been used in the early Anglo-Saxon period; they may indicate the presence of disturbed graves in a cemetery, but can also be casual losses. Even where the coins in a grave have not been pierced they may still have been sewn on to clothing. In Grave 32 at Bifrons, Kent, one of the two coins found on the chest preserved traces of the textile on which it had lain. The decorative function of many of the coins is also indicated by the proportions of female to male graves: 61 per cent of the coin graves in King's sample (1987) could be identified as female and only 14 per cent as male.

Another function of Roman bronze coins found in graves was as weights for use with balances. Complete sets of a balance and weights have been found in at least six graves of the sixth century. Among the weights were several Roman coins, some of which had been filed or had notches cut to adjust their weight. At Watchfield,

---

[1] Of 186 well-documented graves 14% were fifth-century, 60% were sixth-century, 14% were seventh-century, and 12% were undated (King 1988: 224).

Oxfordshire, a high-status male grave (F.67) found in 1983 contained a balance in a leather case together with twelve weights, seven of which were coins (Scull 1986; 1990). Other sets of weights include those from graves in Kent at Sarre, Ozingell, and two at Gilton. Significantly, both Gilton graves included touchstones for testing the purity of gold, indicating that the function of the balances was to weigh precious metal in what was essentially a non-monetary economy.

The Roman coins that were put into early Saxon graves were not ones that had remained above ground since the end of the Roman period; the circulation of Roman bronze and silver coins seems effectively to have collapsed by the mid fifth century (Reece 2002: 63–6; Abdy 2006: 83–95; Moorhead 2006: 102–9; though Williams 2006: 159–63, keeps open the possibility that some bronze remained in circulation). The coins in graves are not dominated by issues of the late fourth or early fifth centuries, but rather they contain 'a random assortment of all the commonest pieces of the Roman coinage' (Kent 1961: 18). These coins must largely have been collected in Anglo-Saxon times from the surface of Roman sites, or from the occasional hoard that had been found. Grave 22 at Brighthampton provides a good example of a rediscovered hoard, exceptionally in silver—ten early third-century *denarii* and *antoniniani* had been pierced and included with beads in the grave.

The second and much scarcer category of coins in early Anglo-Saxon graves is the gold and silver issues which are broadly contemporary coinages imported from the Continent or of local Anglo-Saxon types. Their focus is somewhat later than the bronze coins, starting in the sixth century with just a few recorded graves, even though the Patching, Sussex, hoard has shown that such coins occasionally reached Britain in the later fifth century (Abdy 2006). The grave finds built up steadily through the seventh century and into the early eighth, before ceasing quite abruptly c.730. Only twenty-three individual coins and ten 'hoards' are securely recorded as having come from graves in the phase of gold currency, down to c.675 (listing in Abdy and Williams 2006), though other unstratified coin finds, particularly ones from known cemeteries, may well be from disturbed graves. The majority (73 per cent) of the twenty-three individual coins have been adapted for use as ornaments (Williams 2006: 163), usually by the addition of a strip of precious metal to form a suspension loop; simple piercings may have been a rivet-hole for such a loop (Blackburn 2006b: 183–91, for a classification of loops). Most of the so-called 'grave hoards' are groups of looped coins that form part of necklaces placed in the grave, and only one of the ten 'hoards' from the gold phase would have represented an offering of money: that from the Sutton Hoo (Mound 1) burial comprising thirty-seven Merovingian tremisses with three gold blanks, evidently to make the sum up to forty shillings, plus two gold ingots.

As the number of furnished burials generally declined towards the end of the seventh century, so the proportion with plain coins rather than mounted ones rose significantly, as if money was being offered as a substitute for other artefacts. Rigold

(1988: 221) observed that these grave hoards from the early phase of silver pennies seem often to occur in multiples of two, eight, or twenty. The practice was widespread, from Yorkshire to Lechlade in Gloucestershire and Southampton in Hampshire, but it was concentrated mostly in Kent. At least nine graves in Kent include early silver pennies, while from other counties there are only one or two at most (Blackburn 2000). Interestingly, recent excavations at Carlton Colville, Suffolk, have revealed a grave containing a silver blank with the dimensions of an early penny attached to a silver bar, both with a metallic content similar to coins of the Primary and Intermediate phases of early pennies (*c*.675–720), and it would seem that these were another form of money substitute (Blackburn and Scull 2009). The practice of including coins in graves died out early in the eighth century, the latest example known being at Garton-on-the-Wolds, Yorkshire, which contained eight Intermediate and early Secondary pennies deposited *c*.720–5 (Rigold and Metcalf 1984: 252).

By way of a tailpiece one should mention a brief revival of the practice among Scandinavian settlers in the later ninth to mid tenth centuries. Eight graves of this period containing groups of coins have been reviewed by Biddle, in the context of two from Repton, Derbyshire, associated with the battle and wintering of the Viking Army in 873–4 (Biddle *et al.* 1986: 25–31).

Archaeological evidence for minting

Although the coins themselves record the names of more than eighty towns in which minting took place and several thousand individuals who acted as moneyers, there is scant evidence for the nature and exact locations of the mints. A late-tenth-century law code indicates that the moneyers employed others to produce the coins (IV Æthelred II, cap. 9.1), and this is supported by indications that moneyers were men of wealth and some social standing. At Winchester, the Winton Domesday entries show that in the later eleventh century minting was not carried out in a central building, but moneyers operated from their own separate tenements containing forges and clustered around the High Street (Biddle 1976: 397–400). This is likely to have been the pattern elsewhere until the monetary reform of 1180, when Henry II radically re-organized the mint administration (Allen 2007: 270–1).

Until the 1970s there were no surviving minting tools from the Anglo-Saxon period in England, and indeed very few from early medieval Europe generally, a Carolingian reverse die from the mint of Melle being a notable exception (Blunt 1986). There are now five English coin dies known from four different sites, all of them with some archaeological context. The first to be discovered were two from excavations in York at 16–22 Coppergate: an obverse of the Viking Sword St Peter type dating from 921–7 (Fig. 30.3), and an obverse die cap of Athelstan (924–39) (Pirie 1986: 33–7; Ottaway 1992: 525–7). In the same excavations there were three pieces of lead with the impressions of coin dies of the mid tenth century, which have been variously interpreted as being for testing or recording the dies. A reverse die of the *Crux* type of Æthelred II (978–1016) was found at Flaxengate in Lincoln (Blackburn and Mann 1995). One of the Short Cross type of Cnut (1016–35) came from the Thames Exchange site in the city of London (Archibald *et al.* 1995), a site which also yielded three Norman coin dies, indicating a connection with the minting process spanning a century or so, although the material could have been brought there in the eleventh century from some other location in London, dumped to consolidate the river bank. Finally, excavations at Mill Lane, Thetford, produced another reverse die, and although this was too corroded to enable it to be identified, the context in which it was found points to a late-tenth- or eleventh-century date (Blackburn and Davies 2004).

At three of these four sites there was substantial evidence for metalworking, both ferrous and non-ferrous, the latter mainly in copper alloy but with some silver and even gold, raising the possibility that these were associated with moneyers' workshops where coins were struck. In York, Coppergate tenements C and D, where the dies were found, yielded litharge cakes, cupels, parting vessels, crucibles, ingot

Figure 30.3 Iron obverse die for Sword St Peter penny from 16–22 Coppergate, York: length 91 mm (©York Archaeological Trust)

moulds, smithing slag, and scrap metals, showing that metal refining and metal-working in gold, silver, copper alloy, and iron were carried on there, silver and iron smithing being the dominant activities (Bayley 1992: 794–814; Ottaway 1992: 471–506). At Flaxengate, the spit in which the die was found also yielded crucible fragments with traces of silver and brass, smithing slag, and hammerscale. It lay in a pit behind a structure in which small-scale metalworking, including the production of copper-alloy ornaments, had taken place over a long period (Blackburn and Mann 1995: 201–2). Likewise at Mill Lane, Thetford, although the die was found in a rubbish pit without metalworking associations, in the surrounding area there is ample evidence of small-scale craft production and metalworking, in particular silver refining, brass working, and iron smithing and smelting, including finds of crucibles and litharge cakes (Starley and Doonan 2004).

We cannot be sure of the relationship between the five Anglo-Saxon coin dies and the sites on which they were found—had they been used there to strike coins, were they being recycled for their iron, or were they brought in as rubbish from another location? At least two of them—London and York—have strong associations with some aspect of the minting process through other dies and, at York, also lead trial-strikings being found. Initially, it was suggested that these were both die-cutters' workshops, but there would have been few of those in the country compared to hundreds of moneyers' workshops. The similarity between the associated finds on the York, Lincoln, and Thetford sites, with small-scale general metalwork production, in base and precious metals, suggests that they could well have been moneyers' workshops, and if so it would indicate that the production of coins was only part of a general business of craft metalwork production. This would reinforce our impression from other evidence that minting was often an occasional occupation, and moneyers were part of the mercantile community.

DIRECTIONS OF FUTURE RESEARCH

In the period after the Second World War renewed interest in Anglo-Saxon coinage was focused on classification and chronology, gathering information about extant coins and seeking to attribute them correctly to rulers and mints. During the last quarter of the twentieth century, through die-studies of individual mints or coin types, estimates of the number of dies and from these projections of the size of coinages began to be explored. Latterly, the wealth of new finds discovered with metal-detectors not only provided new material which enabled mint attributions, chronologies, and die-studies to be refined, but prompted consideration of coin circulation patterns and fluctuations in the volume of the currency. Work on all these fronts needs to continue. Without sound identifications and chronologies, all other research based on numismatic evidence is compromised. The earliest gold shillings and silver pennies remain the least well understood Anglo-Saxon coinages, despite a dramatic increase in the number of extant specimens and great progress in their study, made, in particular, by Metcalf. Fundamental questions about who issued these coins, their status, chronology, and mints have still to be answered satisfactorily.

The new finds make numismatics a dynamic subject, but they also impose a fundamental duty on numismatists and archaeologists to record them as they are made and to communicate them to other scholars, and that in itself is a considerable challenge for a small discipline such as this. Any research project that includes an element of recording or collating information about finds will make a lasting contribution to the subject and should be credited with having done so.

In the coming decades, greater emphasis will probably be placed on the wider economic and social implications to be drawn from the use of coinage. To contribute to these debates further work should be done on interpreting the pattern of single-finds, comparing them with other artefact distributions and historical data. Variations in mint output should be studied through targeted die-studies, and changes in the volume of currency in circulation need to be investigated with a range of approaches. Ideally, the results should be considered in the context of similar data for Continental coinages in order to identify trends with an international dimension, but this may not be easy since presently the study of Anglo-Saxon coinage is more highly developed than that of most of its counterparts abroad. To understand economic policy underlying the coinage at various periods, further investigation of the metallic compositions and weights of the coins ought to be carried out, and these in turn could increase our knowledge of the technology of coin production. Ultimately, it is only through combining the numismatic evidence with that drawn from archaeological, historical, and other sources that its full potential will be revealed, reinforcing the need for collaboration between early medievalists of all disciplines.

References

Abdy, R. (2006). 'After Patching: imported and recycled coinage in fifth- and sixth-century Britain', in Cook and Williams (eds.), *Coinage and History in the North Sea World*, 75–98.

—— and Williams, G. (2006). 'A catalogue of hoards and single finds from the British Isles, *c.* AD 410–675', in Cook and Williams (eds.), *Coinage and History in the North Sea World*, 11–73.

Allen, M. (2006). 'The volume of the English currency, *c.* 973–1158', in Cook and Williams (eds.), *Coinage and History in the North Sea World*, 487–523.

—— (2007). 'Henry II and the English coinage', in C. Harper-Bill and N. Vincent (eds.), *Henry II: New Interpretations*. Woodbridge: Boydell Press, 257–77.

ARCHIBALD, M. M. (1988). 'English medieval coins as dating evidence', in Casey and Reece (eds.), *Coins and the Archaeologist*, 264–301.

—— LANG, J. R. S., and MILNE, G. (1995). 'Four early medieval coin dies from the London waterfront'. *Numismatic Chronicle* 155: 163–200.

BAYLEY, J. (1992). *Anglo-Scandinavian Non-Ferrous Metalworking from 16-22 Coppergate*. Volume 17, fasc. 7 of *The Archaeology of York*. London: Council for British Archaeology.

BIDDLE, M. (ed.) (1976). *Winchester in the Early Middle Ages*. Winchester Studies 1. Oxford: Oxford University Press.

—— BLUNT, C., KJØLBYE-BIDDLE, B., METCALF, M., and PAGAN, H. (1986). 'Coins from the Anglo-Saxon period from Repton, Derbyshire: II'. *British Numismatic Journal* 86: 16–34.

BLACKBURN, M. (2000). 'The two sceattas of Series B from Grave 18', in K. Penn, *Norwich Southern Bypass, Part 2: Anglo-Saxon Cemetery at Harford Farm, Caistor St Edmund*. Gressenhall: East Anglian Archaeology 92: 75–6.

—— (2001). 'Expansion and control: aspects of Anglo-Scandinavian minting south of the Humber', in J. Graham-Campbell *et al.* (eds.), *Vikings and the Danelaw: Select Papers from the Proceedings of the Thirteenth Viking Congress*. Oxford: Oxbow Books, 125–42.

—— (2003a). 'Productive sites and the pattern of coin loss in England, 600–1180', in T. Pestell and K. Ulmschneider (eds.), *Markets in Early Medieval Europe: Trading and 'Productive' Sites, 650–850*. Macclesfield: Windgather Press, 20–36.

—— (2003b). 'Alfred's coinage reforms in context', in T. Reuter (ed.), *Alfred the Great*. Aldershot: Ashgate, 199–217.

—— (2004). 'The coinage of Scandinavian York', in R. A. Hall *et al.*, *Aspects of Anglo-Scandinavian York*. Volume 8, fasc. 4 of *The Archaeology of York*. York: Council for British Archaeology, 325–49.

—— (2005). 'Coin finds as primary historical evidence for medieval Europe', in S. Sakuraki (ed.), *Kaheinimiru Dynamism: Ou Chu Nichi Hikakuno Shitenkara (Dynamism in Coinage: Europe, China and Japan, Comparative Viewpoints), Dai 12 kai Shutsudosenkakenkyukai Houkokuyoushi in Fukuoka 2005 (Proceedings of the 12th Conference of the Coin Finds Research Group held in Fukuoka 2005)*. Fukuoka: Coin Finds Research Group, 7–50.

—— (2006a). 'Currency under the Vikings. Part 2. The two Scandinavian kingdoms of the Danelaw, c.895–954'. *British Numismatic Journal* 76: 204–26.

—— (2006b). 'The loops as a guide to how and when the coins were acquired', in S. H. Fuglesang and D. M. Wilson (eds.), *The Hoen Hoard: A Viking Gold Treasure of the Ninth Century*. Acta ad archaeologiam et artium historiam pertinentia 14 and Norske Oldfunn 20. Rome: Bardi Editore, and Oslo: Kulturhistorisk Museum, Universitetet i Oslo, 181–99.

—— and DAVIES, J. (2004). 'An iron coin die', in H. Wallis, *Excavations at Mill Lane, Thetford, 1995*. Gressenhall: East Anglian Archaeology 108: 45–7.

—— and JONSSON, K. (1981). 'The Anglo-Saxon and Norman element of north European coin finds', in M. A. S. Blackburn and D. M. Metcalf (eds.), *Viking-Age Coinage in the Northern Lands*. BAR International Series 122, Volume 1. Oxford: British Archaeological Reports, 147–255.

—— and LYON, S. (1986). 'Regional die-production in Cnut's *Quatrefoil* issue', in M. A. S. Blackburn (ed.), *Anglo-Saxon Monetary History*. Leicester: Leicester University Press, 223–72.

—— and MANN, J. (1995). 'A late Anglo-Saxon coin die from Flaxengate, Lincoln'. *Numismatic Chronicle* 155: 201–8.

—— and SCULL, C. (2009). 'Silver bar and disc: grave 11', in S. Lucy, J. Tipper, and A. Dickens, *The Anglo-Saxon Cemetery and Settlement at Bloodmoor Hill, Carlton Colville, Suffolk*. Gressenhall: East Anglian Archaeology 131: 410, 392–3.

BLUNT, C. E. (1986). 'The Carolingian die from Melle', in E. J. E. Pirie, *Post-Roman Coins from York Excavations 1971–81*. Volume 18, fasc. 1 of *The Archaeology of York*. London: Council for British Archaeology, 44–5.

—— STEWART, B. H. I. H., and LYON, C. S. S. (1989). *Coinage in Tenth-Century England*. Oxford: Oxford University Press for the British Academy.

CASEY, J. and REECE, R. (eds.) (1988). *Coins and the Archaeologist*. 2nd edition. London: Seaby.

COOK, B., and WILLIAMS, G. (eds.) (2006). *Coinage and History in the North Sea World c. 500–1250*. Leiden and Boston: Brill.

DOLLEY, R. H. M., and METCALF, D. M. (1961). 'The reform of the English currency under Eadgar', in R. H. M. Dolley (ed.), *Anglo-Saxon Coins: Studies Presented to F. M. Stenton on the Occasion of his 80th Birthday 17 May 1960*. London: Methuen, 136–68.

EAGLEN, R. (1999). 'The mint of Huntingdon'. *British Numismatic Journal* 69: 47–145.

ESTY, W. W. (2006). 'How to estimate the original number of dies and the coverage of a sample'. *Numismatic Chronicle* 166: 359–64.

GANNON, A. (2003). *The Iconography of Early Anglo-Saxon Coinage: Sixth to Eighth Centuries*. Oxford: Oxford University Press.

GILLINGHAM, J. (1989). '"The most precious jewel in the English crown": levels of danegeld and heregeld in the early eleventh century'. *English Historical Review* 104: 373–84.

—— (1990). 'Chronicles and coins as evidence for levels of tribute and taxation in late tenth- and early eleventh-century England'. *English Historical Review* 105: 939–50.

GRIERSON, P. (1975). *Numismatics*. Oxford: Oxford University Press.

—— and Blackburn, M. (1986). *Medieval European Coinage*, Volume 1: *The Early Middle Ages (5th–10th Centuries)*. Cambridge: Cambridge University Press.

HARVEY, Y. (forthcoming). 'The Winchester Mint', in M. Biddle (ed.), *The Winchester Mint and Coins and Related Finds from the Winchester Excavations of 1961–71*. Winchester Studies 8. Oxford: Clarendon Press.

JONSSON, K. (1987). *The New Era: The Reformation of the Late Anglo-Saxon Coinage*. Commentationes de nummis saeculorum IX–XI in Suecia repertis, nova series 1. Stockholm: Kungl. Myntkabinettet and Kungl. Vitterhets Historie och Antikvitets Akademien.

KENT, J. P. C. (1961). 'From Roman Britain to Saxon England', in R. H. M. Dolley (ed.), *Anglo-Saxon Coins: Studies Presented to F. M. Stenton on the Occasion of his 80th Birthday 17 May 1960*. London: Methuen, 1–22.

KING, M. D. (1987). *The Distribution and Chronology of Roman Bronze Coin-Finds on Early Anglo-Saxon Cemetery and Settlement Sites and their Significance for the Pagan Period of Anglo-Saxon History*. Unpublished BA thesis, Dept. of Archaeology, University of Cambridge.

—— (1988). 'Roman coins from Early Anglo-Saxon contexts', in Casey and Reece (eds.), *Coins and the Archaeologist*, 224–9.

KLUGE, B. (1981). 'Das angelsächsische Element in den slawischen Münzfunden des 10. bis 12. Jahrhunderts. Aspekte einer Analyse', in M. A. S. Blackburn and D. M. Metcalf (eds.), *Viking-Age Coinage in the Northern Lands*. BAR International Series 122, Volume 1. Oxford: British Archaeological Reports, 257–327.

LAWSON, M. K. (1989). '"Those stories look true": levels of taxation in the reigns of Æthelred II and Cnut'. *English Historical Review* 104: 385–406.

METCALF, D. M. (1980). 'Continuity and change in English monetary history *c.* 973–1086. Part 1'. *British Numismatic Journal* 50: 20–49.

—— (1981). 'Continuity and change in English monetary history *c.* 973–1086. Part 2'. *British Numismatic Journal* 51: 52–90.

—— (1993–4). *Thrymsas and Sceattas in the Ashmolean Museum Oxford*. Royal Numismatic Society Special Publication 27. 3 volumes. London: Royal Numismatic Society and Ashmolean Museum.

—— (1998). *An Atlas of Anglo-Saxon and Norman Coin Finds, c. 973–1086*. Royal Numismatic Society Special Publication 32. London: Royal Numismatic Society and Ashmolean Museum.

MOORHEAD, S. (2006). 'Roman bronze coinage in sub-Roman and early Anglo-Saxon England', in Cook and Williams (eds.), *Coinage and History in the North Sea World*, 99–109.

MOSSOP, H. R. (1970). *The Lincoln Mint c. 890–1279*. Newcastle upon Tyne: Corbitt and Hunter.

NAISMITH, R. (forthcoming). 'Money of the saints. Church and coinage in early Anglo-Saxon England'. *Anglo-Saxon* 2.

NORTH, J. J. (1994). *English Hammered Coinage*, Volume 1: *Early Anglo-Saxon to Henry III c. 600–1272*. 3rd edition. London: Spink.

OTTAWAY, P. (1992). *Anglo-Scandinavian Ironwork from 16–22 Coppergate*. Volume 7, fasc. 6 of *The Archaeology of York*. London: Council for British Archaeology.

PIRIE, E. J. E. (1986). *Post-Roman Coins from York Excavations 1971–81*. Volume 18, fasc. 1 of *The Archaeology of York*. London: Council for British Archaeology.

REECE, R. (2002). *The Coinage of Roman Britain*. Stroud: Tempus Publishing.

RIGOLD, S. E. (1988). 'Coins found in Anglo-Saxon burials', in Casey and Reece (eds.), *Coins and the Archaeologist*, 218–23.

—— and METCALF, D. M. (1984). 'A revised check-list of English finds of sceattas', in D. Hill and D. M. Metcalf, *Sceattas in England and on the Continent: The Seventh Oxford Symposium on Coinage and Monetary History*. BAR British Series 128. Oxford: British Archaeological Reports, 245–68.

SCULL, C. (1986). 'A sixth-century grave containing a balance and weights from Watchfield, Oxfordshire, England'. *Germania* 64: 105–38.

—— (1990). 'Scales and weights in early Anglo-Saxon England'. *Archaeological Journal* 147: 183–215.

STARLEY, D., and DOONAN, R. (2004). 'Metalworking debris', in H. Wallis, *Excavations at Mill Lane, Thetford, 1995*. East Anglian Archaeology 108: 52–6.

STEWART, I. (1992). 'The English and Norman mints, *c.* 600–1158', in C. E. Challis (ed.), *A New History of the Royal Mint*. Cambridge: Cambridge University Press, 1–82.

WHITE, R. H. (1988). *Roman and Celtic Objects from Anglo-Saxon Graves: a Catalogue and an Interpretation of their Use*. BAR British Series 191. Oxford: British Archaeological Reports.

WILLIAMS, G. (2006). 'The circulation and function of coinage in conversion-period England, *c.* AD 580–675', in Cook and Williams (eds.), *Coinage and History in the North Sea World*, 145–92.

CHAPTER 31

BURHS AND BOROUGHS: DEFENDED PLACES, TRADE, AND TOWNS. PLANS, DEFENCES, AND CIVIC FEATURES

R. A. HALL

At the end of the Romano-British period, the network of towns created during the preceding few centuries was in a decline which apparently ended with their depopulation, dereliction, and near-abandonment within the fifth century (Biddle and Kjølbye-Biddle 2007; Henig, this volume). At just a few sites, such as Wroxeter, there is evidence for occupation of some sort continuing into the sixth or even, perhaps, the seventh century (White and Barker 1998: 118ff.), but for a period there was nothing urban in the settlement pattern of England. By 1066, however, a new network had been established: over one hundred places were recorded by the compilers of Domesday Book in 1086 as having some urban characteristics (Darby

1977: 364–8; cf. Palliser 2000, *passim*). The consensus among historians and archaeologists is now that some of these places, although small by modern standards, were true towns. They were permanent settlements in which a significant proportion of the residents earned the bulk of their living not from agriculture but from crafts (on a quasi-industrial scale in a few places), services, and trade; and where livings could be won in administrative and ecclesiastical capacities (cf. Reynolds 1977: 295).

Since Biddle's (1976) synthesis of the evidence for Anglo-Saxon urbanism, one of the major advances of Anglo-Saxon archaeology has been the identification of some craft and commercial functions in a greater variety of locations. But not all of these places were towns, and neither did they all subsequently become towns. These discoveries illuminate the diversity of settlements among which a few places were developed to become the urban centres acknowledged in Domesday Book.

Understanding the function and appearance of all these settlements requires engagement with both archaeological and historical evidence. Most of the Domesday towns were categorized by the Latin terms *civitas*, *burgus*, and *villa* (Darby 1977: 289ff.); after the Norman Conquest the term 'borough' was applied to urban sites with a particular legal or constitutional status, and their occupants came to be known as burgesses. 'Borough' is derived from the Old English word *burh/byrig*, the basic meaning of which is 'defended site' (Parsons and Styles 2000: 2429f; Draper 2008). Its literary contexts indicate that it could denote various categories and sizes of defended site, including those which can fairly be described as towns. Other Old English words—*ceaster*, *geweorc*, and *fasten* among them—were also used, either interchangeably or with a specific connotation, in relation to fortified locations. When, however, a place-name incorporates or is associated with one of these words, without descriptive qualification, the precise form and function of that place in the pre-Norman period is often unclear: as in the case, for example, of settlements with the name Burton (cf. Gelling 1989: 119–22).

FROM THE FIFTH TO THE EIGHTH CENTURY

Even descriptions that seem to indicate a specific use of the term *burh* may be questionable. Some are associated with events which allegedly took place many centuries before the compilation of the source in which they are reported. Although the ninth-century *Chronicle* records under the year 547 that King Ida of Bernicia built Bamburgh, political epicentre of the Bernician kingdom, which was first enclosed with a hedge and afterwards with a wall, there is as yet no trace of these features in the archaeological record. That this description may be a late fiction (Whitelock 1965: 12, n. 6; cf. xxxi) is supported by archaeological evidence from sites ranging chronologically and geographically from sixth-/seventh-century Yeavering, Northumberland, to ninth-century and later Cheddar, Somerset, all of which suggest that Anglo-Saxon royal and aristocratic residences were not strongly fortified structures (e.g. Hope-Taylor 1977; Frodsham and O'Brien 2005; Rahtz 1979).

Another interpretative difficulty arises because some Old English scribes may have confused *burh* with another OE word, *bur*, 'chamber' or 'dwelling'. When, for example, the *Anglo-Saxon Chronicle* for 757 reports that a would-be usurper attacked King Cynewulf of Wessex during a visit to his mistress at *Meretun*, some versions claim the king was killed in a *bur*/chamber while others state that he was in a *burh*/fortress. The passage continues by referring to a fight around gates which the usurper had locked. The rather imprecise impression created is of something akin to a medieval manor-house, perhaps with a gate-house and a palisade around it, like that which Ægili is shown defending on the Franks Casket (Neuman de Vegvar 1987: 263–4).

The *Chronicle* reports other sorts of *burhs* in the late fifth and mid sixth centuries; battles were fought between Anglo-Saxons and Britons at several prehistoric or Roman defended sites which have the *burh* element incorporated in their names. It seems that although earthworks and Roman fortifications were places where their enemies took refuge, contemporary Anglo-Saxons did not themselves build defended sites. It is not therefore totally surprising that the earliest urban sites in Anglo-Saxon England also seem to have been undefended.

By *c.*700 there is place-name, documentary, and archaeological evidence that a handful of sites throughout England were distinctly different from other settlements. These are *Lundenwic* (London), *Gipeswic* (Ipswich), *Hamwic* (Southampton), and *Eoforwic* (York). At London, Southampton, and York the key areas were outside the Roman walls, while Ipswich seems to have had no Roman forerunner. Their archaeological signatures at present appear rather diverse, but their unique combination of attributes includes their relatively large size (50 hectares or more), relatively dense layout, and a role both in manufacturing and in long-distance trade (Pestell, this volume). Blackburn (2007: 63), discussing the discovery of an early-ninth-century gold coin minted DE VICO LVNDONIAE, notes this royal endorsement of London's *wic* settlement. He speculates that London's contemporary mints were there rather than within the Roman walls, and that other royal officials and functions may also have been based in the *wic*.

Although York's extent at this time has been doubted, there is archaeological evidence that a zone approximately 700m or more in length along the east bank of the River Foss was used by traders (Kemp 1996: 75–7; McComish 2007); and there are hints of an equivalent strip along the river's west bank (Fig. 31.1). Stratified finds of imported pottery suggest that both banks of the Ouse were also frequented by merchants dealing with the Continent (Mainman 1993: 561–2, 649–51), and excavations by York Archaeological Trust in 1993 between North Street and the River Ouse revealed a sequence of waterfront management that seemed to include seventh- to ninth-century phases. Set back from the rivers was the ecclesiastical focus within the former Roman fortress, although evidence for occupation there is sparse, and

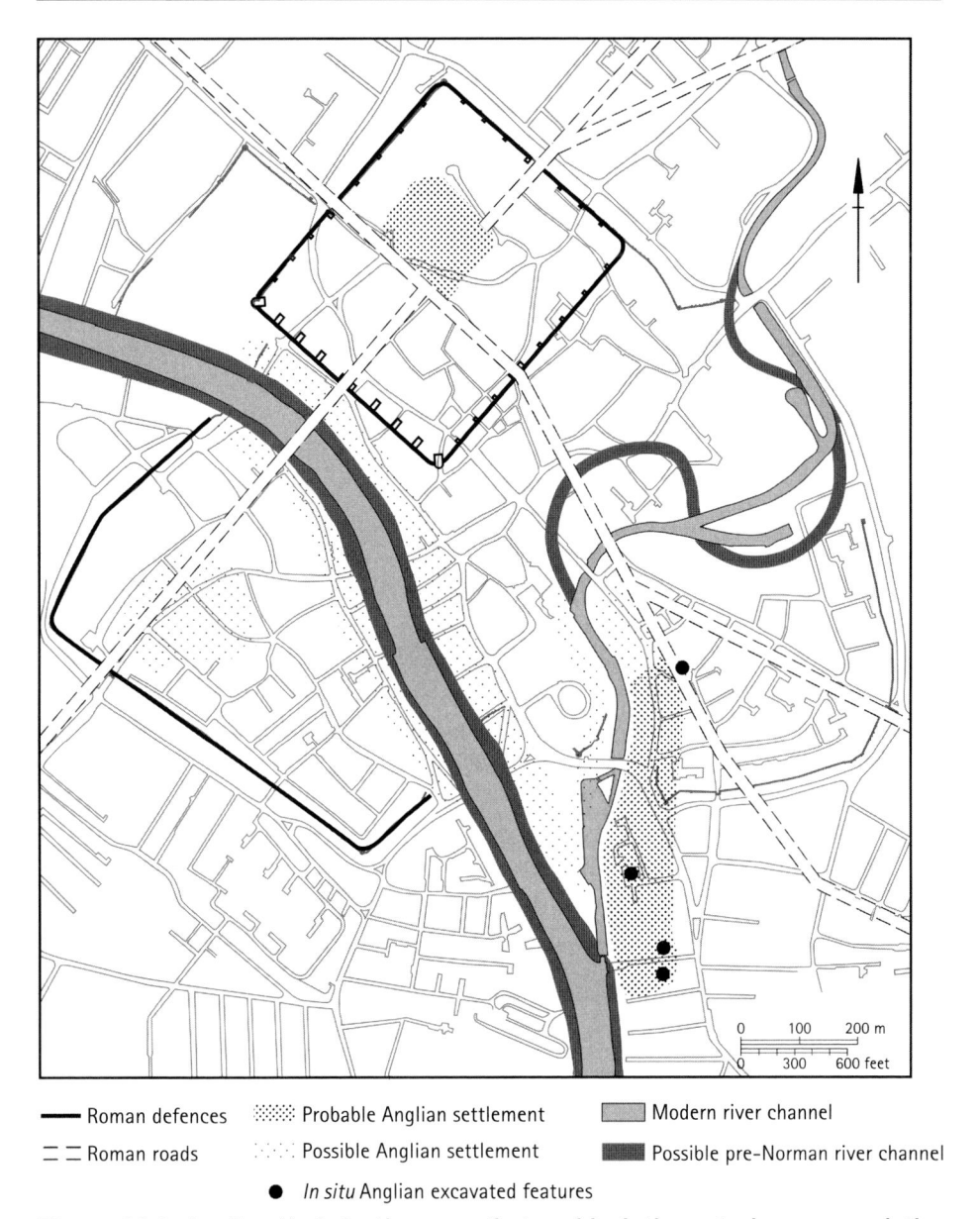

BURHS AND BOROUGHS: DEFENDED PLACES, TRADE, AND TOWNS   603

—— Roman defences   ░░░ Probable Anglian settlement   ▓ Modern river channel
= = Roman roads   ░ Possible Anglian settlement   ▓ Possible pre-Norman river channel
● *In situ* Anglian excavated features

Figure 31.1 Anglian York in the seventh to mid ninth centuries; a speculative interpretation, superimposed on the modern plan. By 1066 much of the area within the later medieval walls was occupied. (Drawing: Lesley Collett. © York Archaeological Trust)

the so-called 'Anglian Tower', added to the fortress defences and initially thought to be seventh-century, is now attributed to the late Roman era (Ottaway 2004: 142–3; R. A. Hall in preparation).

As Pestell points out (this volume), *wic* sites were not the only economic foci in mid Saxon England. Documentary evidence for regulating closely-spaced buildings hints that by the mid ninth century parts of Canterbury were also urban in nature (Brooks 1984: 27ff.), but corroborative archaeological evidence is lacking.

More generically, so-called 'productive sites' (Pestell and Ulmschneider 2003: *passim*), characterized by apparent concentrations of coin finds, include some which are at places otherwise unknown in the archaeological and documentary record. Among them are not only 'a typical rural site' such as Cottam, east Yorkshire (Richards 1999a; 1999b: 9, 90f.), but also putative beach-markets (cf. Vince 2006: 527; Griffiths *et al.* 2007: 432–3). Others were ecclesiastical sites or royal or elite residences; the latter do not appear often in the documentary record before or even after the Viking Age, except as places where charters were signed, and, in those contexts, written descriptions of them and their use were not needed.

Sometimes distinguishing one of these types of site from another on the basis of archaeological evidence is difficult; whether large buildings at Northampton were part of a secular or ecclesiastical complex has been much discussed (J. H. Williams *et al.* 1985; Blair 2005: 205). A site at Flixborough, Lincolnshire, demonstrates the possibility of dynamic changes in the period *c.*700–1000, oscillating between various secular functions and an ecclesiastical or quasi-ecclesiastical status (Loveluck 2007: 144ff.).

Early monasteries such as Glastonbury and Malmesbury, both seventh-century foundations, also had names containing the element *burh*. Importing consumables and raw materials, and stimulating production through their ownership of resources and their patronage of craftsmen, such monasteries were focal points within their locale or region. With their complement of craftsmen and their contacts with a wide, sometimes international, hinterland, they may have been the locations of fairs, markets, or other mechanisms for exchange. Within the imprecise and developing terminology of the time, biblical allusion inspired ecclesiastics to think of these relatively populous religious foci as cities of god, and thus to describe them utilizing Latin words such as *urbs* or *civitas*, and *burh* in Old English. Indeed, *burh* became a vernacular equivalent of *mynster*, meaning monastery or minster church (Blair 2005: 246ff.). The well-defined boundaries of ecclesiastical precincts, discussed by Petts (2008), presumably also contributed to this name-giving. However, all such places, whether developed under ecclesiastical or secular patronage, are best described as 'pre-urban', for they exhibit some, but only some, of the characteristics of a true town; the term 'proto-urban', with its connotations of an inevitable transition to urban status, is best avoided.

The earliest documentary reference to the building of defensive works by the Anglo-Saxons comes in the record of the Synod of Gumley in 749, when King

Æthelbald of Mercia excluded the obligations to take part in the building of fortresses and bridges from the immunities that accompanied some land grants (Sawyer 1968, no. 92; G. Williams 2005: 103). Towards the end of the century, at the Synod of Clofesho, his successor Offa (757–96) imposed on the people of Kent similar obligations of bridgework and fortress work 'against the pagans', i.e. the Vikings. This led Haslam (1987) to speculate that Offa established a network of *burhs* within his kingdom; Bassett (2007; 2008), reviewing the archaeological evidence from Tamworth (Staffordshire), Hereford, Winchcombe (Gloucestershire), and Worcester, has suggested that their earliest medieval defences can be assigned to the period of Mercian overlordship in the eighth and early ninth centuries. Evidence for the nature of contemporary activity or occupation within the substantial areas enclosed by these defences—e.g. approximately 12.2 ha at Hereford, 21.3 ha at Tamworth—is virtually absent. Hereford's evolution from an earlier estate centre where agricultural processing took place on a large scale is suggested by grain-driers sealed beneath the earliest rampart (Shoesmith 1982: 74ff.); Tamworth's significance is indicated archaeologically by the discovery of watermills dated to the ninth century (Rahtz and Meeson 1992). Nonetheless, the motivation for these large enclosures, their original purpose and function, are unclear.

NINTH-CENTURY AND LATER DEFENDED SITES

It was only in the period *c*.825–50 that defence became a priority at any of the *wic* sites: excavation at Covent Garden, London, revealed a defensive ditch some 3.1 m wide x 1.75 m deep, with stakes in the base forming a further obstruction. This ditch may have extended all around an attenuated settlement of perhaps 30–40 hectares; and may have been prompted by Viking raids on London in 842 and 851 (Malcolm and Bowsher 2003: 118ff.).

The use of strongholds became more common during the campaigns in which King Alfred of Wessex (871–99) fought the Vikings. They are documented in the *Chronicle*'s outline account of events and in Asser's contemporary biography of the king. In 873/4, for example, the Vikings took up winter quarters at Repton, Derbyshire, where excavations have shown that they constructed a D-shaped enclosure with the straight side against the former course of the River Trent. A V-shaped ditch about 8.75 m wide and 4 m deep and an internal bank defended an area of 1.46 hectares; a stone-built church in the centre of the curved side was turned into a strongpoint (Biddle and Kjølbye-Biddle 2001: 56–60). On other occasions Vikings occupied earlier defences: when over-wintering at Exeter, Devon, in 876–7 the *Chronicle* reports that 'they were in the fortress where they could not be reached', presumably a reference to an encampment within the surviving Roman walls.

The Anglo-Saxons, too, utilized defended sites in these campaigns. Asser (§54) describes an incident in 878 at *Cynuit* [Countisbury], Devon, where many Anglo-Saxons had sought refuge in a stronghold 'unprepared and altogether unfortified except for ramparts thrown up in our (i.e. Welsh) fashion' (Keynes and Lapidge 1983: 84). In the same year Alfred made 'something of a stronghold' at Athelney (Somerset). This island in the marshes does not have traces of surviving earthworks, unlike Lyng, to which it was joined by a causeway, and where, according to Asser (§92), Alfred built 'a formidable fortress of elegant workmanship'. Asser (§91) also proclaims of Alfred, 'what of the cities and towns to be rebuilt and of others to be constructed where previously there were none?' (Keynes and Lapidge 1983: 101–3).

It is a document named (in 1897) 'Burghal Hidage' which most clearly indicates the importance of a network of defended sites in the counter-offensive against the Vikings (Hill and Rumble 1996). It lists thirty-three *burhs* by name; virtually all of these places have been identified. They include Iron Age hill forts such as Chisbury, Wiltshire; Romano-British forts such as Portchester and perhaps Bitterne, both Hampshire; Romano-British walled towns such as Chichester, Sussex; Exeter, Devon; and Winchester, Hampshire; rectilinear earthworks such as those at Cricklade, Wiltshire, and Wallingford, Oxfordshire; and promontories and spurs such as Lydford, Devon, and Shaftesbury, Dorset. They are listed in correct order for a circuit around Wessex, and were apparently positioned so that no-one lived more than a day's journey from a *burh*. Most were in the kingdom of Wessex, although a few were in Mercia.

A former consensus, arrived at by correlating the tactical and strategic value of these sites in relation to events documented in other approximately contemporary sources, dated the Burghal Hidage to the reign of Edward the Elder (899–924), although perhaps with a basis in the reign of Alfred; a precise strategic context for it in 878–9 has, however, been suggested (Haslam 2006). Overall there is little doubt that their prime initial purpose was as defensive refuges for the surrounding population, and a relatively short-lived period of emptiness when large numbers of temporary refugees could find room to shelter may have been recognized archaeologically at Portchester (Cunliffe 1975: 303).

Although an accompanying formula allows the length of each *burh*'s manned defences to be calculated, their precise position is not always recognizable. Correlation of length and position is complicated on peninsular or waterfront sites, where this manned length may not equate with the total perimeter.

When *burh* defences were built anew in Wessex, and not incorporating Roman walls, they typically consisted of an earthen rampart with a ditch in front of it. Sometimes the rampart was faced with turf and was further stabilized and consolidated with horizontal lacing timbers (cf. Dodd 2003: fig 4.10). Its front was revetted with horizontal planks, held in place by vertical uprights which continued upwards to form a breastwork or palisade. The form of late-ninth-/early-tenth-century defences at West Mercian *burhs* such as Hereford, Tamworth, and Winchcombe is similar (Bassett 2008). Subsequently, the timber revetment might be replaced with a stone wall (drystone or mortared), built either on the ground surface or, as at Wallingford and Wareham, on the rampart's crest.

The form of gateways is little known. Gould (1968; 1969) presented evidence from Tamworth for what he interpreted as a massive timber gate with a bridge across it, and which he associated with the historically attested building campaign of 913. In the eleventh century a substantial stone tower, part of St Michael's church, formed one side of the north gate at Oxford (Dodd 2003: 25).

THE DEVELOPMENT OF TOWNS

The means by which some of these Burghal Hidage fortifications could acquire attributes that would sustain their existence beyond the short-term exigencies of the Viking troubles is preserved in a document of c.889–99, witnessed by King Alfred, in which his daughter Æthelflæd and her husband Ealdorman Ethelred of Mercia record their foundation of a *burh* at Worcester. They granted to the bishop part of their rights in the market and the street, with the exception of taxes on salt which were reserved to the king; they also surrendered half their rights in land rent, in fines for fighting, theft, dishonest trading, and damage to the *burh* wall, and all fines for offences which had mixed compensation (Whitelock 1979: 540–1). Encouraging commerce to win fiscal benefits was clearly the royal rationale.

Worcester has complementary archaeological evidence for topographical change in the Anglo-Saxon period. The Roman defences by the River Severn may have attracted magnate and ecclesiastical settlement before the foundation of the cathedral see for the kingdom of the Hwicce by c.680, but there is little evidence for associated commercial and craft-centred activity. When the burh was founded in c.889–99, a new and larger defensive circuit was created, and within it the waterfront was dominated by the bishop's single large *haga* [land holding]. Only at some later date, when the eastern defences were dismantled, is there evidence in the northern part of High Street for the establishment of large, primary plots of land which later still were subdivided into tenement plots (Baker and Holt 2004: 172ff., 349ff.). So it may have taken as much as a century before Worcester was developed into a truly urban centre.

Earlier, in 857, a bishop of Worcester had acquired 'a profitable little estate' (*haga*) with commercial privileges near the west gates of London (Sawyer 1968, no. 208; Whitelock 1979: 529), to facilitate trade in salt and other commodities from Worcester. His acquisition indicates that London's economic significance continued between the

Viking raid of 851 and the overwintering of the Viking army in 872. This *haga* was probably within the *wic* rather than within the Roman defences (Keene 2003: 239ff.); but archaeological, documentary, and toponymic evidence demonstrates that thenceforth the focus of redevelopment was inside the Roman walls and along the corresponding waterfront.

Numismatic evidence suggests that Alfred had gained control over London by *c*.880 (Blackburn 1998: 119); but redevelopment of the city seems to have been a lengthy process. Asser (§83) records that in 886 Alfred 'restored the city of London splendidly... and made it habitable again' (Keynes and Lapidge 1983: 97–8), and there is a further reference to Alfred discussing the *instauratio* (restoration or laying out) of London at Chelsea in 898/9 (Dyson 1978). Alfred and Æthelred of Mercia granted a Thames waterfront property within the walls to the bishop of Worcester in 889 (Sawyer 1968, no. 346), and the grant of land, with landing facilities at Æthelred's hithe, was confirmed at the Chelsea meeting of 898/9, with an adjacent property granted to the archbishop of Canterbury (Sawyer 1968, no. 1628). Excavation there has unearthed late-ninth-century timber features on the waterfront designed to facilitate ship-borne trade, and evidence for the continuation of this commerce over the next century (Wroe-Brown 1999: 13–14). Although it seems that the survival of *in situ* late Saxon deposits within the walled town is very limited, the market function in *Lundenburh* has been elucidated by excavations at 1 Poultry. A large open space at the east end of Cheapside, the market street that was the east–west axis of the town from the late ninth/early tenth century, was re-occupied at that time, when a handful of sunken-featured buildings was strung along the street frontage (Treveil and Burch 1999: 55).

Archaeologically, the best attested example of Alfred's creation of a *burh* is Winchester, where excavations revealed the creation of a new pattern of streets throughout the entire 58.2 hectares within the Roman walls. There was a spinal main street, streets leading off from it at right angles, and an internal perimeter street, which had a coin from the later part of the reign of Edward the Elder (899–924) in its first re-metalling. If all Winchester's streets were laid out in a single operation, 8,000 tonnes of flint cobbles would have been required. These streets defined large blocks of land which, as in Worcester, were later subdivided into tenements. By the late tenth century street-names indicate the location of a variety of crafts, and complementary archaeological evidence becomes more prolific (Biddle 1976: 449ff.).

Further examples of new gridded street plans have been identified within other former Roman towns (Biddle and Hill 1971). At Gloucester only half the area (7.1 hectares) of the Roman walled town was laid out in a rectilinear grid of streets, with minor lanes, perhaps not metalled, at intervals based on a multiple of a four-perch module (4, 8, or 16 perches); but no properties or plots laid out in the early years of the *burh's* existence have yet been identified (Baker and Holt 2004: 347–9). Street grids have also been recognized within new rectilinear fortifications at Wareham, Wallingford, and Cricklade (Biddle and Hill 1971).

Providing a burghal infrastructure clearly required careful planning and execution, and the deployment of very considerable resources; it did not always succeed. Asser (§91) decried laziness and other reasons why fortifications ordered by Alfred had either not been begun or completed in time, and the *Chronicle* records an example of such failure in 892. Even when fortifications had been erected, with all the marshalling of manpower and the provision of timber which that implied, there were still major tasks to be undertaken in at least some of the *burhs*. After surveying the blocks into which the interior was to be subdivided, using standard measurements (cf. Crummy 1979), stone was quarried or foraged to provide good street surfaces for Winchester and for other *burhs* including, for example, at Botolph's Lane, London (Horsman *et al.* 1988: 16; Dyson 1990: 108 n. 7), and at Castle Street and elsewhere in Oxford, where the primary phase, not certainly contemporary with the foundation of the *burh*, is dated before *c*.925 (Dodd 2003: 26–9). Metalled streets are also known from Danelaw towns such as Lincoln where, at Flaxengate, limestone rubble formed the first surface, laid down *c*.900. This was soon covered by a wider, cambered surface which incorporated a stone-lined drain (Perring 1981: 44; Jones *et al.* 2003: 260). More demanding still of specialist skills was the erection of bridges, which have been found or inferred at London and Oxford, as well as at Lincoln, Norwich, and Nottingham; Winchester's was attributed to Bishop Swithun (855–65).

There is no documentary evidence that Edward the Elder (899–924) built new *burhs* in the first decade or so of his reign, but in 909 he launched a series of campaigns against the Vikings, pursuing an offensive policy which, from 912 onwards, involved the building of fortresses in strategic locations in the southern Danelaw, Essex and, ultimately, eastern Mercia. Meanwhile his now-widowed sister Æthelflæd pursued a parallel strategy in western and then north-western Mercia. Their purpose was to dominate the surroundings and to encourage the submission of the local people. According to the *Chronicle*, this happened after Witham, Essex, was built in 912, and in 914 when the men of Bedford and many allied to Northampton submitted after fortresses were built at Buckingham. Edward's *burhs* were certainly perceived by the Vikings as a threat, and their defensive capabilities remained important. In 917, for example, when the Vikings attacked Towcester, it was defended successfully for a day, and the Vikings were beaten off; later that year it was strengthened by the addition of a stone wall thought worthy of a mention by the chronicler, perhaps because it was an innovation. Vikings from Tempsford, Bedfordshire, attacked Bedford unsuccessfully in the same year, and they failed too in attacks on *Wigingamere*, and on Maldon, Essex.

Meanwhile, the Vikings also continued to build strongholds; but their fortifications were not impregnable. In 917 the English took Tempsford by storm, and also attacked Colchester, a Roman walled town, killing all except those who escaped over the wall. Indeed, 917 was the year of *burh* battles, with both sides attacking the other's fortifications; but by its end Edward and Æthelflæd were in control of most of the former Mercia. After Æthelflæd's death in 919, Edward consolidated his position by building further *burhs* in both north-west and eastern Mercia.

Precisely what long-term aspirations Edward had for each individual site is unknown, but the increasing sophistication of Anglo-Saxon England's economic infrastructure, and thus the potential for new towns to develop, is shown in the gradual increase in the numbers of minting places successively under the control of Alfred, Edward, and Æthelstan (924–39). In 871 only London and Canterbury had named mints; by 875 they had been joined by Winchester, another Wessex mint, and one in north-west Mercia (Chester?); c.880 Gloucester was added to the list, and in the 890s there was minting at Oxford, Exeter, at another Wessex mint, and, possibly, at Shrewsbury. By c.900 there were at least nine established mints and probably a few more; when Edward died in 924 there were at least twelve mints in the south and five in West Mercia (Blackburn 1996: 162–5, and this volume). Of these seventeen named places, twelve became the most important economic and administrative centre in their county; they were shire towns in name or status. However, nineteen of the thirty-three Burghal Hidage sites did not have a mint in the first half of the tenth century, a reminder that these sites were established in the face of a relatively short-term emergency beyond which there was no automatic reason for them all to flourish. Sites such as Burpham, Sussex, had their fleeting moment of importance, but were quickly abandoned to obscurity.

Mints, then, were established by the Anglo-Saxon kings for the most part at locations which hindsight demonstrates had the geographical/topographical potential for long-term development and growth. Æthelstan's Grateley law code of c.926–30 repeated an ordinance of his father that all buying should take place within a town, and decreed that every *burh* was to be repaired annually by a set date. It also required all minting to take place in towns, and specified the number of moneyers at each (Whitelock 1979: 419–20; Blackburn 1996). Here again we see the king attempting to manipulate the law to the advantage of the new towns, and thereby to augment his revenue from taxation.

Viking / Scandinavian / Anglo-Scandinavian towns in the late ninth and tenth centuries

The areas conquered and settled by the Viking 'great army' and its followers in 876–9—East Anglia, the 'south-eastern Danelaw' (Bedfordshire, Cambridgeshire, Huntingdonshire, and Northamptonshire), eastern Mercia, and large tracts of Northumbria—were under their control for at least thirty years; in Northumbria, Viking power was still a key factor until 954. From the 880s onwards Viking rulers issued coins at various mints, including such nodal sites as York, Lincoln, Leicester, and Norwich (Blackburn 2001); but the full extent and weight of the influences which Scandinavians or Anglo-Scandinavians may have exerted on the rise of urban life in these areas has been much debated (cf. R. A. Hall 2001a).

Within East Anglia, there is 'no trace of the Danish presence in the town' at Colchester, although at some later time or times in the tenth century, when Colchester was back in English hands, it seems that new streets were laid out (Crummy 1997: 137–41). At Norwich, in contrast, it is suggested that a defended *burh* north of the river may have been established in the late ninth or early tenth century, when it was in Viking hands, with major growth in the tenth; there is also increasing evidence for contemporary activity south of the river at the foundation period (Ayers 2003: 27ff.). The early street plan at Norwich undeniably exhibits a broad regularity suggestive of some degree of planning during the late Saxon or early Norman period; it is possible that a pre-conquest 'planned town' existed at least as far south as Rose Lane. However, such regularity could alternatively have resulted from organic development extending out from the primary roads; unplanned settlements (those not deliberately laid out as an entity) 'could also appear regular owing to constraints imposed by natural or relict features acting as morphological frames' (Biddle 1975: 31; Emery 2007: 38–9).

Within the eastern part of the former kingdom of Mercia, mid-tenth-/early-eleventh-century *Chronicle* entries group together Derby, Leicester, Lincoln, Nottingham, and Stamford as 'five *burhs*' (R. A. Hall 1989; 2001b). Bastions of Viking control after 866, all but Lincoln had been taken by Edward and Æthelflæd in 917–18. All were in naturally favourable locations, on navigable rivers and with important prehistoric or Roman routeways passing through or close to them; Leicester, Lincoln, and Little Chester near Derby were fortified Roman sites. Lincoln apart (and, perhaps, questionably in the face of uncertainties over the dating of the church of St Paul in the Bail; see Henig, this volume), there is some evidence that each was an important secular and ecclesiastical focus for its hinterland in the pre-Viking period. Their development during the four decades when they were under direct Scandinavian control is generally elusive, although it is clear that the pottery industry at Stamford, which later became nationally significant, began at this time.

Lincoln's development is, however, better attested archaeologically. Study of data accumulated in four decades of excavation has revealed that this Roman fortified town was re-founded in the late ninth century, after the Vikings took control of eastern Mercia. There may have been minting at Lincoln in the late ninth century, imitating coins of Alfred; by the 920s coins were certainly struck there. In the early tenth century a metalled roadway (Flaxengate) was laid down to the east of High Street (the line of the main Roman axial road), perhaps giving access to the waterfront on the River Witham via a Roman postern gate; Hungate may represent a similar development to the west of High Street. The riverfront was reclaimed and consolidated, and a new southern suburb of Wigford developed; from the later tenth century the settlement

Figure 31.2 Composite picture of a sunken-floored building constructed at Hungate, York, c.970, incorporating timbers from a boat built in southern England ten to fifteen years earlier. The 'steps' across the building's centre result from differential excavation; the original entrance is marked by stone revetments at the rear. Scale unit: 500 mm (photographs and manipulation by Michael Andrews. © York Archaeological Trust)

both became more intensive and also expanded further into eastern and western suburbs (Stocker 2003: 141ff.; Steane 2006: 280–1; Vince 2006).

In Northumbria, York was the pre-eminent settlement of the period, continuing its pre-Viking role as an archbishop's seat. By c.1000 it was described as 'enriched with the treasures of merchants who came from all quarters' (Raine 1879: 454; Rollason 1998: 171–2), and in Domesday Book is represented as one of England's largest towns. Most of the archaeological evidence for its evolution in the early medieval period comes from sites outside the two former Roman defended settlements of fortress and civilian town, with the area between the fortress and the River Foss being redeveloped at this time. Excavations at Coppergate have revealed a sequence of Roman activity followed by an apparent hiatus in occupation or activity until the mid ninth century, when occupation resumed hereabouts. It was c.900–25 that the site was divided up into four long narrow tenement plots, apparently fronting onto the street and running back down a slope to the River Foss. At the front of each plot, gable end to the street, was a single rectangular post and wattle building, averaging at least 6.8 m long x 4.4 m wide. Erected close together to make optimum use of the available space on the street frontage, this is the earliest case of high-density urban layout yet known in early medieval England.

The Coppergate buildings seem to have been repaired or replaced at intervals of a decade or two. The preservation of palaeo-environmental evidence, such as plant macrofossils, beetles, bones of fish, birds, and animals, parasite eggs, etc., reveal that conditions inside them could be described, by comparison with modern standards, as foul and damp; but they could also be described as cosy and well-sheltered (Kenward and Hall 1995: 731; A. Hall and Kenward 2004: 384). Debris embedded in their earth floors and in the layers and features around them show that these buildings functioned as both domestic dwellings and as workshops. Raw materials, such as timber, metal ores, bone and antler, wool, jet, stone, and leather, were brought in from York's hinterland, and fashioned into necessities and luxuries for the local and regional population. The quantity of debris from metalworking, lathe-turning of wooden domestic vessels, and leatherworking suggests production on a professional scale by specialist artisans. Other craftworking in bone and antler, jet and amber, glass, and textile-making and dyeing, were apparently on less intensive, occasional or domestic, scales (Walton 1989; Bayley 1992; Ottaway 1992; Kenward and Hall 1995: 727; Rogers 1997; MacGregor *et al.* 1999; Mainman and Rogers 2000; Morris 2000; Mould *et al.* 2003).

Long-distance trade was another component in York's economy. Although some of the foreign items found within the city, such as costume accessories and jewellery, may have belonged to visitors to York rather than being objects imported for sale, soapstone bowls from Shetland, or, perhaps, Norway (Mainman and Rogers 2000: 2541) were in use, Norwegian schist hones were ubiquitous (ibid.: 2484f.), and silk, probably Byzantine in origin, was sometimes available for making up into head-scarves and other items (Walton 1989: 419–20). Raw amber, probably of Baltic origin, was cut or turned into beads, pendants, and other small items (Mainman and Rogers 2000: 2500f.). A cowrie shell from the Red Sea (Kenward and Hall 1995: 781) and a contemporary forgery of a dirham minted in the early tenth century in Samarkand (Pirie 1986: 55) expand still further the range of York's international contacts.

THE LATER TENTH AND ELEVENTH CENTURIES

From the mid tenth century onwards, as noted above in relation to Worcester, Norwich, and Lincoln, there are signs in several major towns that occupation became more intense. In London, at the site near Æthelred's hithe, there is evidence for an acceleration in the pace of development of the river frontage from the late tenth century onwards (Wroe-Brown 1999: 13–14); and a concentration of artefacts from waterfront sites indicates something of the range and extent of London's continental and further-flung trade, particularly from *c*.970 onwards (Egan 1999: 30; Blackmore 1999: 42). At Number 1 Poultry, in redevelopment approximately contemporary with the greater exploitation of the Thames waterfront, a denser row of narrow timber buildings lined the frontage in the early eleventh century (Treveil and Burch 1999: 55). Settlement to the north of the main east-west cross-town route, Cheapside, began in the tenth century, but the Guildhall area was not reached until the late tenth or early eleventh century when, it is suggested, a sunken-floored building represents 'peri-urban' agricultural activity. It was only in the 1060s–1080s that denser, urban activity began there (Bowsher *et al.* 2007: 11f., 412–13).

In York, the Coppergate site provides precisely dated evidence for when expansive redevelopment took place. In the 960s and 970s two-storey, semi-basement buildings typically measuring 7.5 m x 3.5 m internally x up to 1.8 m deep, and constructed of substantial oak timbers, replaced the earlier structures. These new and more durable buildings provided living accommodation above what was probably a storage cellar; the need for extra space was also met by erecting two closely adjacent ranks of these buildings on some of the plots. Abundant evidence suggests that by this time the street was already a focus for the cupmakers after whom it was named. And Coppergate was not the only street seeing investment, for at least the lower-lying part of Hungate, some 300 m to the north-east, was also redeveloped at almost exactly the same time (Fig. 31.2). The later tenth century, the generation or two after the final incorporation of Northumbria into the new state of England in 954, seems to have been boom-time in York.

After a period of relative peace and, perhaps, concomitant prosperity through the middle decades of the tenth century, Scandinavian attacks on England resumed in 980. Among the ravages and burnings that fill the entries of the *Chronicle* until Cnut's succession to the entire kingdom in 1016, *burhs* were particularly subject to attack, presumably because they were centres of wealth. London, Exeter, Canterbury, Norwich, Winchester, and Oxford were all targeted, as well as such *burhs* as Lydford, Wilton, Watchet, Thetford, and Maldon, which later lost importance in the wake of political and economic change.

The fortifications at Winchester in 1006 and at London in 1009 and 1013 were sufficiently strong to withstand Viking attack. In 1016 the Vikings dug a ditch so that they could drag their ships upstream of London Bridge, and encircled the *burh* with a ditch to enforce their siege, attacking by both land and water; but all to no avail. Their efforts demonstrate clearly the political and economic importance of London, as does its own Danegeld of 10,500 pounds paid in 1018.

In the face of such resistance, softer targets assumed an importance for the gathering of both booty and supplies, as they had done in the earlier round of Viking attacks (Brooks and Graham-Campbell 1986). For example, the *Chronicle* refers to the sacking of the Northumbrian royal site of Bamburgh in 993, where 'much booty was captured'. At about this time, in a document defining symbols of status, Archbishop Wulfstan of York (1002–23) recorded that if a ceorl prospered to the extent that he possessed, *inter alia*, five hides of land, a bell [house], and a gatehouse (*burh-geat*), then he was entitled to the rights of a thegn (Whitelock 1979: 468; A. Williams 1992). This sounds like the sort of manorial layout referred to above in relation to Ægili and the Franks Casket; the passage highlights that *burh* retained a wide range of connotations in the early eleventh century (cf. Gardiner, this volume).

The English response to the new round of Viking campaigns included the fortification of a series of new *burhs* in more impregnable locations. One of these has been excavated at Cadbury Castle, near South Cadbury, Somerset, an Iron Age hill fort (Alcock 1995). Sited close to both a Roman road to London and the Fosse Way route north-eastwards, it was highly defensible but also accessible, and was used as a minting place in the brief but critical period *c*.1009–19. It was fortified anew with a mortared stone wall on the crest of the slightly heightened earth rampart, enclosing about 7.3 hectares, and entered via a stone-arched gateway 2.4 m wide. Although hearths and pits of late Saxon date were found, there is no archaeological evidence for streets or plots within these defences; the only possible internal structure attributed to this period is what is interpreted as the foundations for a cruciform church that was never built. Cadbury seems to have been abandoned when the emergency need for added security for the local mint had passed, unlike Old Sarum, Wiltshire, which was retained even though the temporarily abandoned Wilton mint re-opened.

Reform of the coinage in 973 had made it obligatory for every coin to bear the name of its minting place. Thus, for the first time, it is possible to compile a complete gazetteer of mint sites and to gauge their comparative output. In the reign of Æthelred II (978–1016) at least seventy-five mints operated (Metcalf 1978: 160), and in the first half of the eleventh century some ninety minting places are attested (Metcalf 1980: 32; Fig. 31.3). At first sight, this suggests an impressive burgeoning in town life. Yet over half of all coins were struck at only a handful of mints, with London, York, and Lincoln predominant. In contrast, many of the mints, particularly in the south-west, have exiguous and intermittent outputs, for which a variety of explanations has been proposed (cf. Astill 1991: 99–100). These new mints were not necessarily in places thought of as towns; while some were considered urban by the Domesday Book compilers, who, for example, positioned Torksey at the start of the Lincolnshire text along with Lincoln and Stamford, others did not meet the compilers' criteria of urbanism and were relegated to the body of the county text, even though some of these places did later develop into towns. Nevertheless, it seems clear that right up to the Norman Conquest, kings, together with leading secular and ecclesiastical lords, attempted to foster further urban growth for the economic rewards which towns could generate. The urban infrastructure which William the Conqueror took over was one which was still developing, but which was recognizably a framework for later medieval urban growth.

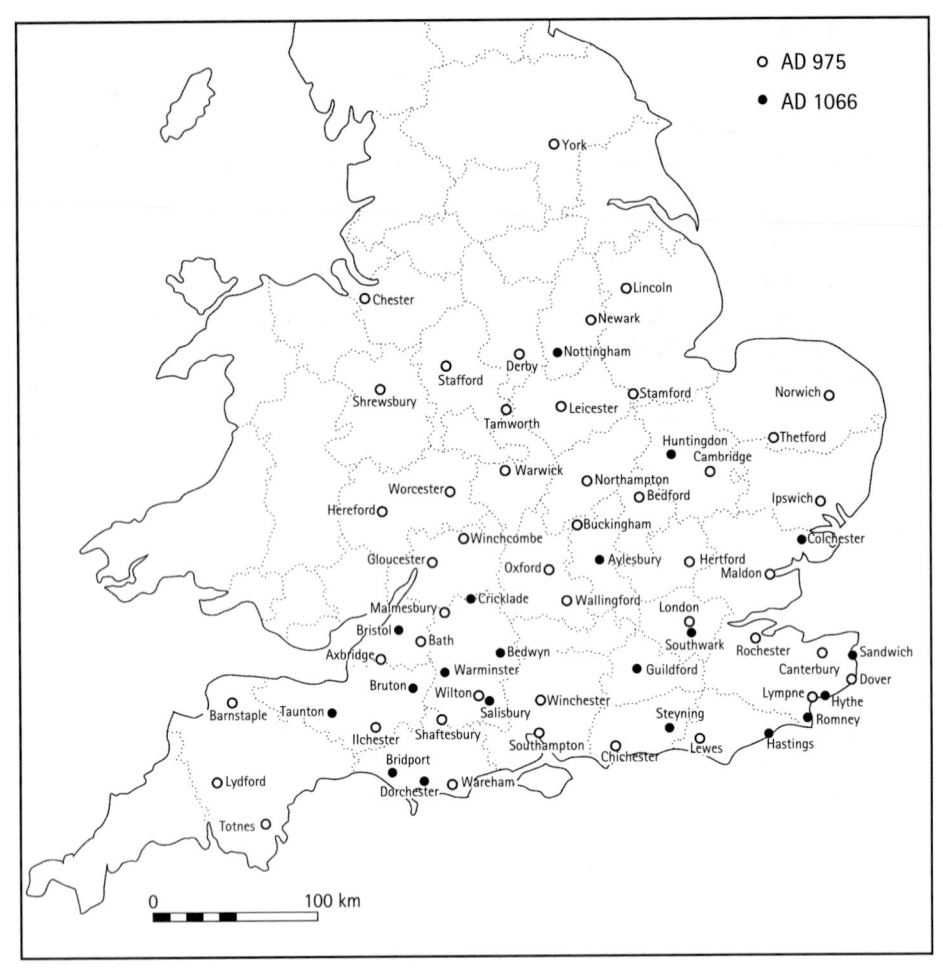

Figure 31.3 Minting-places in 975 and the additional ones operating in 1066 are the most reliable guide to urban places at those dates (based on information kindly supplied by Martin Allen; drawing by Lesely Collett. © York Archaeological Trust)

Acknowledgements

I am grateful to Judith Jesch and David N. Parsons for facilitating access to information on place-names, and to the many archaeologists and historians who have discussed their discoveries and interpretations with me.

REFERENCES

ALCOCK, L. (1995). *Cadbury Castle Somerset: The Early Medieval Archaeology.* Cardiff: University of Wales Press.

ASTILL, G. (1991). 'Towns and town hierarchies in Saxon England'. *Oxford Journal of Archaeology* 10(1): 95–117.

AYERS, B. (2003). *Norwich 'A Fine City'.* Stroud: Tempus.

BAKER, N., and HOLT, R. (2004). *Urban Growth and the Medieval Church: Gloucester and Worcester.* Aldershot: Ashgate.

BASSETT, S. (2007). 'Divide and rule? The military infrastructure of eighth- and ninth-century Mercia'. *Early Medieval Europe* 15(1): 53–85.

—— (2008). 'The middle and late Anglo-Saxon defences of western Mercian towns'. *Anglo-Saxon Studies in Archaeology and History* 15: 180–239.

BAYLEY, J. (1992). *Non-Ferrous Metalworking from Coppergate.* Volume 17, fasc. 7 of *The Archaeology of York.* London: Council for British Archaeology.

BIDDLE, M. (1975). 'The evolution of towns: planned towns before 1066', in M. W. Barley (ed.), *The Plans and Topography of Medieval Towns in England and Wales.* CBA Research Report 14. London: Council for British Archaeology, 19–32.

—— (ed.) (1976). *Winchester in the Early Middle Ages.* Winchester Studies 1. Oxford: Clarendon Press.

—— and HILL, D. (1971). 'Late Saxon planned towns'. *Antiquaries Journal* 51: 70–85.

—— and KJØLBYE-BIDDLE, B. (2001). 'Repton and the "great heathen army", 873–4', in Graham-Campbell et al. (eds.), *Vikings and the Danelaw*, 45–96.

—— —— (2007). 'Winchester: from *Venta* to *Wintancæstir*', in L. Gilmour (ed.), *Pagans and Christians: From Antiquity to the Middle Ages.* British Archaeological Reports International Series 1610. Oxford: Archaeopress, 189–214.

BLACKBURN, M. (1996). 'Mints, burhs, and the Grately code, cap. 14.2', in Hill and Rumble (eds.), *The Defence of Wessex*, 160–75.

—— (1998). 'The London Mint in the reign of Alfred', in M. A. S. Blackburn and D. N. Dumville (eds.), *Kings, Currency and Alliances.* Woodbridge: Boydell Press, 105–23.

—— (2001). 'Expansion and control: aspects of Anglo-Scandinavian minting south of the Humber', in Graham-Campbell et al. (eds.), *Vikings and the Danelaw*, 125–42.

—— (2007). 'Gold in England During the "Age of Silver"', in J. Graham-Campbell and G. Williams (eds.), *Silver Economy in the Viking Age.* London: Institute of Archaeology, University College London, 55–98.

BLACKMORE, L. (1999). 'Aspects of trade and exchange evidenced by recent work on Saxon and medieval pottery from London'. *Transactions of the London and Middlesex Archaeological Society* 50: 38–54.

BLAIR, J. (2005). *The Church in Anglo-Saxon Society.* Oxford: Oxford University Press.

BOWSHER, D., DYSON, T., HOLDER, N., and HOWELL, I. (2007). *The London Guildhall.* Museum of London Archaeological Services Monograph 36. London: Museum of London.

BROOKS, N. (1984). *The Early History of the Church of Canterbury.* Leicester: Leicester University Press.

—— and GRAHAM-CAMPBELL, J. A. (1986). 'Reflections on the Viking-Age silver hoard from Croydon, Surrey', in M. A. S. Blackburn (ed.), *Anglo-Saxon Monetary History.* Leicester: Leicester University Press, 91–110.

CRUMMY, P. (1979). 'The system of measurement used in town planning from the ninth to the thirteenth centuries'. *Anglo-Saxon Studies in Archaeology and History* 1: 149–64.

—— (1997). *City of Victory: The Story of Colchester – Britain's First Roman Town*. Colchester: Colchester Archaeological Trust.

CUNLIFFE, B. (1975). *Excavations at Portchester Castle*, Volume 2: *Saxon*. Reports of the Research Committee No. 33. London: Society of Antiquaries of London.

DARBY, H. C. (1977). *Domesday England*. Cambridge: Cambridge University Press.

DODD, A. (ed.) (2003). *Oxford Before The University*. Oxford Archaeology Thames Valley Landscapes Monograph 17. Oxford: Oxford Archaeology.

DRAPER, S. (2008). 'The Significance of Old English *Burh* in Anglo-Saxon England'. *Anglo-Saxon Studies in Archaeology and History* 15: 240–53.

DYSON, T. (1978). 'Two Saxon land grants for Queenhithe', in *Collectanea Londiniensia: Studies Presented to Ralph Merrifield*. London and Middlesex Archaeological Society Special Paper 2, 200–15.

—— (1990). 'King Alfred and the restoration of London'. *London Journal* 15(2): 99–110.

EGAN, G. (1999). 'Material from a millennium: detritus from a developing city'. *Transactions of the London and Middlesex Archaeological Society* 50: 29–37.

EMERY, P. A. (2007). *Norwich Greyfriars: Pre-Conquest Town and Medieval Friary*. East Anglian Archaeology 120. Dereham.

FRODSHAM, P., and O'BRIEN, C. (eds.) (2005). *Yeavering: People, Power and Place*. Stroud: Tempus.

GELLING, M. (1989). *The West Midlands in the Early Middle Ages*. Leicester: Leicester University Press.

GOULD, J. (1968). 'First report of the excavations at Tamworth, Staffs., 1967 – the Saxon defences'. *Transactions of the Lichfield and South Staffordshire Archaeological and Historical Society* 9: 17–29.

—— (1969). 'Third report on excavations at Tamworth, Staffs., 1968 – the western entrance to the Saxon borough'. *Transactions of the Lichfield and South Staffordshire Archaeological and Historical Society* 10: 32–42.

GRAHAM-CAMPBELL, J., HALL, R., JESCH, J., and PARSONS, D. N. (eds.) (2001). *Vikings and the Danelaw: Select Papers from the Proceedings of the Thirteenth Viking Congress*. Oxford: Oxbow Books.

GRIFFITHS, D., PHILPOTT, R. A., and EGAN, G. (2007). *Meols: The Archaeology of the North Wirral Coast*. Oxford University School of Archaeology Monograph 68. Oxford: Oxbow Books.

HALL, A., and KENWARD, H. (2004). 'Setting people in their environment: plant and animal remains from Anglo-Scandinavian York'. *Aspects of Anglo-Scandinavian York*. Volume 8, fasc. 4 of *The Archaeology of York*. York: Council for British Archaeology.

HALL, R. A. (1989). 'The Five Boroughs of the Danelaw: a review of present knowledge'. *Anglo-Saxon England* 18: 149–208.

—— (2001a). 'Anglo-Scandinavian attitudes: archaeological ambiguities in late ninth- to mid eleventh-century York', in D. M. Hadley and J. D. Richards (eds.), *Cultures in Contact: Scandinavian Settlement in England in the Ninth and Tenth Centuries*. Studies in the Early Middle Ages 2. Turnhout: Brepols, 311–24.

—— (2001b). 'Anglo-Scandinavian urban development in the East Midlands', in Graham-Campbell *et al.* (eds.), *Vikings and the Danelaw*, 143–56.

—— (in preparation). '*Eoforwic* and *Jorvik*; York in the early medieval period *c.* 400–1069', in P. V. Addyman (ed.), *Historic Towns Atlas: York*.

HASLAM, J. (1987). 'Market and fortress in England in the reign of Offa'. *World Archaeology* 19(1): 76–93.

—— (2006). 'King Alfred and the Vikings: strategies and tactics 876–886 A. D.'. *Anglo-Saxon Studies in Archaeology and History* 13: 112–54.

HILL, D., and RUMBLE, A. R. (eds.) (1996). *The Defence of Wessex: The Burghal Hidage and Anglo-Saxon Fortifications*. Manchester: Manchester University Press.

HOPE-TAYLOR, B. (1977). *Yeavering: An Anglo-British Centre of Early Northumbria*. London: Her Majesty's Stationery Office.

HORSMAN, V., MILNE, C., and MILNE, G. (1988). *Aspects of Saxo-Norman London*, Volume 1: *Building and Street Development*. London and Middlesex Archaeological Society Special Paper 11.

JONES, M. J., STOCKER, D., and VINCE, A. (2003). *The City by the Pool*. Lincoln Archaeological Studies 10. Oxford: Oxbow Books.

KEENE, D. (2003). 'Alfred and London', in T. Reuter (ed.), *Alfred the Great*. Aldershot: Ashgate, 235–49.

KEMP, R. L. (1996). *Anglian Settlement at 46–54 Fishergate*. Volume 7, fasc. 1 of *The Archaeology of York*. York: Council for British Archaeology.

KENWARD, H. K., and HALL, A. R. (1995). *Biological Evidence from Anglo-Scandinavian Deposits at 16–22 Coppergate*. Volume 14, fasc. 7 of *The Archaeology of York*. London: Council for British Archaeology.

KEYNES, S., and LAPIDGE, M. (1983). *Alfred the Great: Asser's Life of King Alfred and Other Contemporary Sources*. Harmondsworth: Penguin Books.

LOVELUCK, C. (2007). *Rural Settlement, Lifestyles and Social Change in the Later First Millennium A. D.: Anglo-Saxon Flixborough in its Wider Context*. Excavations at Flixborough 4. Oxford: Oxbow Books.

MACGREGOR, A., MAINMAN, A. J., and ROGERS, N. S. H. (1999). *Bone, Antler, Ivory and Horn from Anglo-Scandinavian and Medieval York*. Volume 17, fasc. 12 of *The Archaeology of York*. York: Council for British Archaeology.

MAINMAN, A. J. (1993). *Pottery from 46–54 Fishergate*. Volume 16, fasc. 6 of *The Archaeology of York*. London: Council for British Archaeology.

—— and ROGERS, N. S. H. (2000). *Finds from Anglo-Scandinavian York*. Volume 17, fasc. 14 of *The Archaeology of York*. York: Council for British Archaeology.

MALCOLM, G., and BOWSHER, D. (2003). *Middle Saxon London: Excavations at the Royal Opera House 1989–99*. Museum of London Monograph 15. London: Museum of London.

MCCOMISH, J. (2007). *Roman, Anglian and Anglo-Scandinavian Activity and a Medieval Cemetery on Land at the Junction of Dixon Lane and George Street, York*. Archaeology of York Web Series AYW9. <http://www.iadb.co.uk/resource>.

METCALF, D. M. (1978). 'The ranking of boroughs: numismatic evidence from the reign of Æthelred II', in D. Hill (ed.), *Ethelred the Unready*. BAR British Series 59. Oxford: British Archaeological Reports, 159–212.

—— (1980). 'Continuity and change in English monetary history *c.*973–1086, part I'. *British Numismatic Journal* 50: 20–49.

MORRIS, C. A. (2000). *Wood and Woodworking in Anglo-Scandinavian and Medieval York*. Volume 17, fasc. 13 of *The Archaeology of York*. York: Council for British Archaeology.

Mould, Q., Carlisle, I., and Cameron, E. (2003). *Leather and Leatherworking in Anglo-Scandinavian and Medieval York*. Volume 17, fasc. 16 of *The Archaeology of York*. York: Council for British Archaeology.

Neuman De Vegvar, C. L. (1987). *The Northumbrian Renaissance: A Study in the Transmission of Style*. Cranbury, NJ: Associated University Presses.

Ottaway, P. (1992). *Anglo-Scandinavian Ironwork from Coppergate*. Volume 17, fasc. 6 of *The Archaeology of York*. London: Council for British Archaeology.

—— (2004). *Roman York*. 2nd edition. Stroud: Tempus.

Palliser, D. M. (ed.) (2000). *The Cambridge Urban History of Britain*, Volume 1: 600–1540. Cambridge: Cambridge University Press.

Parsons, D. N., and Styles, T. (2000). *The Vocabulary of English Pace-Names*, Volume 2: Brace – Cæster. Nottingham: Centre for English Place-Name Studies.

Perring, D. (1981). *Early Medieval Occupation at Flaxengate*. Volume 9, fasc. 1 of *The Archaeology of Lincoln*. London: Council for British Archaeology.

Pestell, T., and Ulmschneider, K. (2003). *Markets in Early Medieval Europe*. Macclesfield: Windgather Press.

Petts, D. (2008). 'Discussion and conclusions', in J. McComish and D. Petts (principal authors), *Fey Field, Whithorn: Excavations by David Pollock and Amanda Clarke*, section 14. Archaeology of York Web Series YAT10. <www.yorkarchaeology.co.uk/resources/ayw.htm>.

Pirie, E. J. E. (1986). *Post-Roman Coins from York Excavations 1971–81*. Volume 18, fasc. 1 of *The Archaeology of York*. London: Council for British Archaeology.

Rahtz, P. (1979). *The Saxon and Medieval Palaces at Cheddar*. BAR British Series 65. Oxford: British Archaeological Reports.

—— and Meeson, R. (1992). *An Anglo-Saxon Watermill at Tamworth*. CBA Research Report 83. London: Council for British Archaeology.

Raine, J. (1879). *The Historians of the Church of York and its Archbishops*, Volume 1. London: Rolls Series.

Reynolds, S. (1977). *An Introduction to the History of English Medieval Towns*. Oxford: Clarendon Press.

Richards, J. D. (1999a). 'What's so special about "productive sites"? – middle Saxon settlements in Northumbria'. *Anglo-Saxon Studies in Archaeology and History* 10: 71–80.

—— (1999b). 'Cottam: an Anglian and Anglo-Scandinavian settlement on the Yorkshire Wolds'. *Archaeological Journal* 156: 1–110.

Rogers, P. W. (1997). *Textile Production at 16–22 Coppergate*. Volume 17, fasc. 11 of *The Archaeology of York*. York: Council for British Archaeology.

Rollason, D. W. (1998). *Sources for York History to A. D. 1100*. Volume 1 of *The Archaeology of York*. York: York Archaeological Trust.

Sawyer, P. H. (1968). *Anglo-Saxon Charters: An Annotated List and Bibliography*. London: Offices of the Royal Historical Society.

Shoesmith, R. (1982). *Excavations on and Close to the Defences*. Hereford City Excavations Volume 2. CBA Research Report 46. London: Council for British Archaeology.

Steane, K. (2006). *The Archaeology of the Upper City and Adjacent Suburbs*. Lincoln Archaeological Studies 3. Oxford: Oxbow Books.

Stocker, D. (ed.) (2003). *The City by the Pool*. Lincoln Archaeological Studies 10. Oxford: Oxbow Books.

TREVEIL, P., and BURCH, M. (1999). 'Number 1 Poultry and the development of medieval Cheapside'. *Transactions of the London and Middlesex Archaeological Society* 50: 55–60.

VINCE, A. (2006). 'Coinage and urban development: integrating the archaeological and numismatic history of Lincoln', in B. Cook and G. Williams (eds.), *Coinage and History in the North Sea World, c .A. D. 500–1250*. Leiden/Boston: Brill, 525–43.

WALTON, P. (1989). *Textiles, Cordage and Raw Fibre from 16–22 Coppergate*. Volume 17, fasc. 5 of *The Archaeology of York*. London: Council for British Archaeology.

WHITE, R., and BARKER, P. (1998). *Wroxeter: Life and Death of a Roman City*. Stroud: Tempus.

WHITELOCK, D. (ed) (1930). *Anglo-Saxon Wills*. Cambridge: Cambridge University Press.

—— (ed.) (1965). *The Anglo-Saxon Chronicle: A Revised Translation*. 2nd impression. London: Eyre and Spottiswoode.

—— (ed.) (1979). *English Historic Documents*, Volume 1: *c.500–1042*. 2nd edition. London: Eyre Methuen.

WILLIAMS, A. (1992). 'A bell-house and a *burh-geat*: Lordly residences in England before the Norman Conquest', in C. Harper-Bill and R. Harvey (eds.) *Medieval Knighthood IV: Papers from the Fifth Strawberry Hill Conference 1990*. Woodbridge: Boydell Press, 221–40.

WILLIAMS, G. (2005). 'Military obligations and Mercian supremacy in the eighth century', in D. Hill and M. Worthington (eds.) *Æthelbald and Offa: Two Eighth-Century Kings of Mercia*. British Archaeological Reports British Series 383. Oxford: Archaeopress, 103–9.

WILLIAMS, J. H., SHAW, M., and DENHAM, V. (1985). *Middle Saxon Palaces at Northampton*. Northampton: Northamptonshire County Council.

WROE-BROWN, R. (1999). 'The Saxon origins of Queenhithe'. *Transactions of the London and Middlesex Archaeological Society* 50: 12–16.

PART VII

THE BODY AND LIFE COURSE

CHAPTER 32

OVERVIEW: THE BODY AND LIFE COURSE

SALLY CRAWFORD

Introduction

The focus of this Part is the relationship between the lived experience of the individual explored through the study of the biological body, and the material culture framework within which the body exists. David Wilson's 1976 volume on Anglo-Saxon archaeology contained no sections focusing on the individual, on life course, or on what an understanding of the relationship between personal identity, community identity, and material culture can contribute to the study of Anglo-Saxon England. Though the study of the social body in the context of material culture is relatively new to Anglo-Saxon archaeology, it has long been recognized in other disciplines that a study of the life course and social life of the individual is the study of society as a whole: 'the individual, the nuclear family, the extended family, and the community—is both whole and a part, and each part contains the "program" that the whole imposes' (Minuchin and Fishman 1981: 13): by approaching the past at the individual level, archaeologists are also accessing the broader structures and social constraints which shape the individual (and to some extent, the individual's body) and which are expressed in the use and manipulation of material culture in the construction of personal/social identity. This section of the volume explores the links between the scientific analysis of skeletal material, how that analysis provides readings for social interpretation, and the tensions inherent in drawing together scientific and social approaches to the body.

The body may be studied from an osteo-archaeological approach, which focuses on the skeleton, taking measurements and comparing the physical structure of the skeleton within a scientific framework which shows presence or absence of measurable physical attributes, such as chronological age, biological gender, height, evidence for disease, and wear. The body may also be looked at within the framework of social theory, which argues that bodies are a cultural construct (Sofaer 2004). The contributors to this Part engage in lively discussions on the tension between the theoretical and methodological approaches of these two disciplines, and on the need to bring them together to form a relationship between study of the biological body and the social life of people: a bio-archaeological approach.

It may be argued that, on the one hand, evidence from individual life stories is anecdotal, and is hardly a useful starting point for understanding broader social frameworks, and, on the other, that there is nothing period-specific about human biology. The state of the body—its sex, age, and health—may be of importance to an individual, but all people can expect to experience a similar range of universal physical changes. Personal physical histories have little relevance to the events of history, or, to put it another way, questions about major political, religious, or economic events are not obviously answered by considering the place of the elderly in society, dietary practices, or the prevalence of illness and the treatment of the sick. Ill people are ill, women are women, children are children, poor people are poor—these are constants within societies, so their study provides no narrative of change: an argument which no longer has currency (Metzler 2006).

In fact, bodies are not static—they change and develop over lifetimes, and social perceptions of the body, which are closely bound to issues of personal and community identity, do change. Several forces are at work on the body. The body carries its own blueprint for development from conception to maturity, which is broadly universal across humanity, though there are genetic variations operating at racial and familial levels. The way a body changes over a lifetime may also be determined by environmental and cultural factors. The body carries with it a record of the life lived by the individual—disease, physical activity, and diet may all leave traces in the skeleton, and the body may also be subject to deliberate manipulation and distortion, which may have the intention of changing the physical appearance, or which may produce changes to the body accidentally—tattooing, trepanation, mutilation, and removal of teeth, for example. In trying to access this private life of the individual body, it quickly becomes evident that it is not a story of rigid boundaries and demarcations, but of the constant negotiations of individuals over their private and public roles, coupled with constant readings and re-readings of their changing bodies—the physical actuality of the body is negotiated, manipulated, and interpreted in an evolving interaction with other bodies, other lives, other boundaries for categorizing, limiting, or empowering the individual within their life course.

A further strand in this Part is the relationship between body and object, most often, in the context of these chapters, between the dead body and the objects interred with it. The negotiated identity of the individual within the social group may be expressed through the appearance of the body, and is also expressed through materiality, which gives meaning to the human life cycle (Gosden and Marshall 1999; Gilchrist 2000). Objects, as the following chapters illustrate, function as an extension of person: 'materiality is the frame through which people communicate identities; without these material expressions, social relations have little substantive reality because objects do not just provide the stage setting to human action, they are integral to it' (Sánchez Romero 2008: 21). A phenomenological approach to archaeology, which draws together the experience of the world, and the ways in which people interact with the surrounding world, artefacts, and other humans, allows us to see that bodies, actions, and objects are intimately and indistinguishably interwoven in the process of negotiating socialization in the life course: the body and objects cannot be disaggregated (Hurcombe 2007: 536). The training of an elite male for physical fighting will have an impact on the size of the muscle attachments visible on the skeleton; commensuality practices will have a direct impact on the growth of the body; bodily ornament, whether permanent (tattoos) or temporary (hair styles, jewellery) may assert or submerge actual biological gender, age, or physical ability.

LIFE COURSE AND MUTE GROUPS

'Life course' and 'life cycle' are both used within this section to describe the whole-life experience, but in this, as in other areas relating to the life experience, modern words impose particular readings on the past (cf. the introductory discussion in Harlow and Laurence 2002). 'Life course' implies a view of existence similar to modern Western interpretations of biology and chronology: there is a beginning at conception (or birth, or some other point before or after, dependent on cultural interpretation), and an end at death (or burial, or the decomposition of the body, or some other related point). Life has a linear, forward-looking trajectory. This view of human existence imposes a particular idea of the narrative of human life—childhood, for example, will always be an experience to leave behind, not to look forward to. 'Life cycle', by contrast, implies a return to the beginning: death is not an end, but part of a continual sequence of events, perhaps involving further post-mortem transitions before rebirth. 'Life cycle' and 'life course', therefore, argue for very different attitudes towards significant events in the individual's experience. As this Part of the volume, and also Parts III (mortuary ritual) and VIII (the archaeology of religion) indicate, while 'life course' would be the most appropriate term to apply to the Anglo-Saxon perception of human existence after the introduction of Christianity, early Anglo-Saxon ideas about personal narratives and perceptions of time remain obscure.

Life courses are diverse, and our access to understanding life courses of individuals through archaeological evidence is contingent on the extent to which our own cultural preconceptions will determine the kind of evidence retrieved, and the way in which that evidence is interpreted. Contributors to this section are particularly attempting to retrieve evidence for what anthropologists have long identified as 'mute groups': women, children, the disabled, the old. Mute-group theory, originally applied to women, and published in 1975, argued that 'those trained in ethnography evidently have a bias towards the kinds of model that men are ready to provide (or concur in)' (Ardener 1975: 2), and the assessment of inherent bias in ethnography is relevant to archaeology, too.

There are certainly invisible groups in the archaeological record (Moore and Scott 1997). At Mucking, Essex, the cemeteries associated with the settlement contained the remains of over 800 bodies. Not all those who were buried in the cemeteries reached adulthood, but all of them died at some point during or after their childhood. To put it another way, if the number of burials in the cemetery is similar to the number of people who lived in the adjacent village, then early Anglo-Saxon Mucking was the place where hundreds of children were born, lived, and played. Yet, of all the many artefacts found in the course of the excavations at Mucking, not a single one has been directly linked to the activities of children. This dearth can be extended: in the whole corpus of Anglo-Saxon material culture, the number of artefacts that have been identified as having been used by, or deposited by, children is vanishingly small. By contrast, anthropological evidence, and the long-standing findings of experimental archaeology, show that children do have a considerable agency in material culture deposition and creation (Bonnichsen 1973; Wilkie 2000a). The question is whether the invisibility of children's agency in the Anglo-Saxon material culture record is due to their real invisibility in the archaeological record, or due to an inability of archaeologists to recognize the evidence, even though the processes by which adult-world artefacts enter the archaeological record do include child agency (Fig. 32.1) (Crawford 2009).

Mute-group theory also argues that the activities of mute groups will be seen as less valid or less important than those of the dominant group. Within Anglo-Saxon archaeology, the underlying default position is to assume an adult centre of

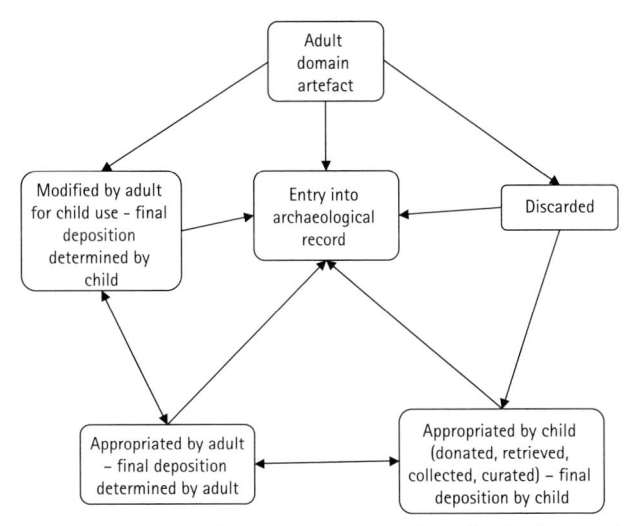

Figure 32.1 Adult-artefact pathways into the archaeological record through child agency

interest: adults are privileged in the use of inadvertently loaded vocabulary and discussion. For example, there are two areas where bodies were deposited at Yarnton, Oxfordshire (Hey 2004). One area contained a small group of six adult burials at a distance from the mid Saxon settlement. This group was identified as the community field cemetery, of the sort that seem to have been relatively common at this period, before the proliferation of parish churches in the tenth and eleventh centuries. The second area contained at least five burials, and was within the boundaries of the settlement. The bodies consisted of the remains of a woman aged between 13 and 19 years, and the fragmentary remains of at least four sub-adults, one aged 6–8 years, one aged 6–7 years, and the rest juvenile, but of unidentifiable biological age: 'it is difficult to resist the conclusion that, regardless of the Christian context of the burials, children were not considered to merit burial within the small cemetery' (Boyle 2004: 75). There were certainly two separate burial areas at this site, though only the six burials in the adult area have been designated a 'cemetery' in the site report, and it was assumed that burial in this extra-settlement area was privileged over burial within the settlement. Similarly, West Stow, Suffolk, is a site normally referenced in terms of its settlement archaeology, though in fact there were fourteen separate incidents of infant bones recovered from settlement ditches, sunken-featured building areas, and pits: analysis and discussion of these infant bones form a small paragraph in the site report (Grainger in West 1985: 59).

There appear to be two assumptions underpinning the apparent irrelevance of infant and other burials to the interpretation of the settlements at West Stow and Yarnton: first, that the settlements were unquestionably secular and domestic in nature, and second, that deposits of dead infants within the settlement area were therefore made in an essentially non-meaningful way.

Settlement site reports routinely discuss functionality of artefacts: in the site report on the early Anglo-Saxon settlement at Mucking, Essex, for example, artefacts are categorized largely according to the (implicit adult) function for which it is presumed they were made—'spinning and weaving equipment'; 'articles of dress'; 'weapons'; 'vessels'—and this approach is replicated in the discussion of the 'diverse activities' taking place on the site, including baking, quarrying, lead- and antler-working, and weaving (Hamerow 1993: 15). Explanations for the distribution and nature of the material recovered from the site are provided in terms of *in situ* work, refuse, abandonment, dumping, and accidental loss, but are not related to play at all. The actual size of the group 'children', larger than any other age group present during the lifetime of the site, is not reflected in the report, which focuses on the dominant (adult) culture, and in this, the report at Mucking does not differ from any of the many other site reports for this and other periods (Chamberlain 1997). Yet, unless the extent to which children were responsible for the creation of material culture is taken into account (children's caches, special play deposits, post-holes, and structures which form part of play spaces), discussions of, for example, special deposits, and use of space, will be problematic.

The place of children, like that of other non-dominant groups, is under-represented in archaeological analysis (as evidenced in the articles gathered in Moore and Scott 1997, for example). Furthermore, the archaeology and cultural systems of children are seen as not only less relevant to the modern archaeologist than those of the dominant, adult group, regardless of which group might have been more important in the deposition of the material which survives as an archaeological record (Schwartzman 1976; Wilkie 2000b; Crawford 2009), but also as a 'distortion' of the archaeological record (Hammond and Hammond 1981). As Mary Lewis (2007: 9) has argued, 'child activity ... has been seen as detracting from the real issues of adult behaviour', not least because children's play is not perceived as relevant to the broader study of society (Sofaer Derevenski 2000: 4). The interaction of children's play activities—'a repertoire of behaviours in which they are the only or primary actors', as Jane Eva Baxter (2005: 62) puts it—with the archaeological record is not of primary interest and importance in most archaeological reports.

Even where attention is drawn to the existence of mute groups, it may only have the effect of reinforcing the extent to which they are elsewhere not included in the dominant norm. A chapter on 'the people: social scales and social relationships' in a useful survey of later Anglo-Saxon England emphasizes, in the opening paragraph of its section on 'the ranks of men and women', that noble Anglo-Saxon women had power and property in their own right, but the rest of the entire chapter, bar one paragraph on women slaves and slave-owning, is about male people, male social scales, and male social relationships (though Sarah Semple's illustrations reconstructing Anglo-Saxon daily life in the volume are a model of social inclusiveness) (A. Reynolds 1999).

One area where the problem of identifying both vertical (status-related) and horizontal (gender, age) social groupings can be explored in a way that may retrieve potentially 'mute' groups is in the study of cemeteries (e.g. Stoodley 1999a and b; Brush 1988; Crawford 1991). This is particularly true of the early furnished inhumation burials, where the study of large data sets has enabled sophisticated analysis of the material, though important work has also been carried out on the study of later Anglo-Saxon mortuary ritual from a bio-archaeological perspective (Hadley 2004; Buckberry 2007; Hadley 2010; Hadley 2009). In this Part, burial practices, bodies, and associated objects are linked to the lived experience of people within society, and the relationship between the physical and social body as it is manifested both in the physical body itself (through diet, exercise, trauma, wear, manipulation, and modification), and in the objects which mediate the constantly negotiated social identity of the individual.

Bridging the Gap: Osteo-archaeology and Social Archaeology

The development of osteo-archaeology and the scientific analysis of the body has helped to improve our understanding of the physical condition of people in Anglo-Saxon England. Cemetery site reports routinely provide information, not just on the age, biological gender, and physical height of the dead person at the time of death, but also on any signs of genetic traits, wear, deformity, or trauma present in the skeletal record.

The transformation of these data into cultural interpretation remains, however, problematic. The fundamental importance of accurate skeletal analysis to any interpretations of the social identity of the Anglo-Saxon body is made absolutely clear in this Part, combined with a keen awareness that there exists a need to ensure that biological terminology is not mapped directly onto social interpretation, and that old osteo-archaeological reports may not reflect current practices. Recent years have seen careful reviewing of skeletal evidence from excavated cemetery sites, and discussions of skeletal evidence on the basis of published site reports have to be carried out with an awareness that some current published diagnoses of trauma have been, or may be, revised. The surviving skeletal material at Raunds, Northamptonshire, for example, has been reviewed by Jo Buckberry and Dawn Hadley, who have concluded that the 'cleft palate' identified on an adult male was caused by post-mortem changes to the bone (Buckberry and Hadley, pers. comm.).

Consistent and properly-communicated use of terminology is also essential. In 1991, I published an article in which I demonstrated that the casual and inconsistent use of terms such as 'child', 'infant', 'subadult', and 'adult' to describe skeletons in site reports was not only complicating our ability to interpret the archaeological record, but, worse, was tending to promote misunderstandings and misreadings of the evidence (Crawford 1991). Not only were the Anglo-Saxon dead being categorized in ways that may have had no relevance to their own ideas of age groups, but terminology was being applied inconsistently. One site report's 'child' was another's 'younger adult'. One site's 'infant' was another's 'child'. The ways in which the categories were being constructed were not always explained within site reports, which confused the issue when the evidence from one site was compared with another. Anglo-Saxon archaeologists were struggling to identify any child/adult age thresholds signalled in the burial ritual in part because their 'children' were culturally Anglo-Saxon adults. Still today, site reports on excavations appear where, even if a limited biological age-range in years is given for the skeleton, an additional qualifying term—'adult' or 'child'—is also given (for example, Welch 2008).

It is important that consistent terminology, which is identifiably not carrying a cultural loading, is used, and that non-archaeologists recognize that osteologists are using language to describe the body in a particular and specific way, not related to social meaning. Even using biological maturity as a standard way of categorizing the bodies causes confusion if the adult/child age threshold for Anglo-Saxons did not respect biological maturity. If a child, at 10, was entitled to inherit its parents' property, as the earliest law codes suggest, and to be held culpable for their own crimes, then that children of 10 or over were buried with adult-related grave goods is not surprising, but it does not mean that 'children were buried with adult grave goods'.

There are also problems in mapping scientific terminology onto lived experience: as Christina Lee's contribution explains, visible skeletal characteristics may have been unnoticed by their bearers, while socially—and physically—debilitating problems may leave no trace on the skeleton. 'Health' is further problematized by interpretation. The example of the males with *spina bifida occulta* who may well have lived their lives oblivious to their interesting genetic anomaly are a case in point (Härke 1990, corrected in Boyle *et al.* 1995), as is the notorious example of the woman whose pathology was interpreted as evidence of rape (Hawkes and Wells 1975), but subsequently re-interpreted as evidence for vigorous horse-riding (N. Reynolds 1988). Several initiatives to provide a database of skeletal collections and associated pathologies have been proposed, and the development of such a resource is a project for the future (R. Gowland, pers. comm.).

Biological versus cultural categories: the social context of biology

The assumption that arbitrary 'child' age ranges could be mapped directly onto Anglo-Saxon age boundaries, and that biological immaturity represented cultural immaturity, is not tenable. The interpretation that 'children' were buried with adult grave goods, and therefore childhood was not acknowledged by the Anglo-Saxons, is wrong. This is not mere quibbling over semantics. A nuanced understanding that childhood and other life experiences are a cultural, not an unvarying universal, concept has a profound impact on the way the past is interpreted. 'Adult' and 'child' are terms which carry social, as well as biological, meaning; a more obviously non-cultural way of dividing age groups where only a broad age category for the skeleton can be assigned would be better practice: the interface between osteo-archaeology and social archaeology requires a deliberate search for neutral language.

Recognizing the limitations and 'narrativium' inherent in the words used to describe the past is crucial (McKeown 2007b: 162). Nick Stoodley (below) begins his chapter by following normal distinctions between 'child' and 'adult' in the grave, but both he and Sam Lucy in her assessment of gender are aware that this simple opposition of states of being obscures the gendered and social-status-linked complexities of age-related roles in Anglo-Saxon society. The issue of what it was to be a 'child' has been much explored, and, since Grete Lillehammer's groundbreaking work in 1989, it is absolutely clear that childhood is a cultural state of being. 'Adulthood', however, has received less attention. Just as the recognition that there is a story of 'masculinity' to be told in early medieval England (Hadley 2008), as well as a feminist agenda to the interpretation of the archaeological record, so too adulthood tends to be taken as a given—a construct that, at heart, is based on the assumption that childhood is merely a temporary state on a trajectory that leads to adulthood.

Adulthood is a social construct too, and mere achievement of chronological age does not appear to have been the whole story to gaining it in early medieval England. Other factors—gender, family relationships, wealth, and social status—also had a part to play. So 11–12 is a threshold age for some children, some of whom start to gain 'adult' attributes in their grave (Crawford 1993), but, as Stoodley recognizes in his contribution, there is a second threshold in the later teens at 18 to 20. This threshold may be linked to achieving of independence for males, assoicated with the ability to start a new family (Crawford 1999). Comparative evidence from early medieval Irish law codes implies that this intermediate stage between 'childhood' and 'adulthood' was a recognized period in the lives of young men too old (and troublesome) to live at home with their parents, but not having acquired the means to establish their own homes. They were the *fer midboth*: the 'men of the middle houses', with license to behave as such young men were culturally supposed to behave—in a violent, aggressive, and risk-taking manner (McCone 1986). The case has been made that a spatial location for this adolescent group is visible in the hierarchical layout, size, and distribution of early medieval ring forts (Stout 2000: 95–97).

'Childhood' and 'Adulthood', then, do not cover the full trajectory of the life course, and even offer a misleading picture when used as binary terms to divide the whole of early Saxon life-course. 'Adulthood' was not an automatic achievement, nor was it simply defined as being 'not child', and different attributes were assigned to phases within adulthood: inlaid spears, longer than the average spear, were only associated with old males at Great Chesterford, Essex, for example (Crawford 2007).

The same issues, as Christina Lee discusses in her contribution below, pertain to health. What is 'health' anyway? The evidence we need to establish the health of an individual is both physical and cultural (Gowland 2004; King 2005). A record of physical problems does not necessarily tell us anything about how the person—or their society—lived their lives (Roberts 2000): 'medicine and the pursuit of good health could become issues of religious, cultural and political significance, going far beyond the concerns of the individual afflicted body' (Montserrat 2005: 231).

For example, a theory that children or disabled people buried with weapons represent proof that burial with weapons represented an ideal warrior status, rather than reflecting actual use of weapons by the weaponed population, on the basis that neither children nor disabled people could have actually wielded in an aggressive or war-like way the weapons with which they were buried, assumes that the Anglo-Saxons recognized the same boundaries between ability and disability as we do today. It may seem to be 'common sense' that children cannot fight, yet anthropological evidence indicates that a person below the biological age of 15, when armed with a sharp machete, can and will fight. Similarly, old age or disability does not automatically represent physical or mental weakness in every society. Ill health, mental or physical, if recognized as such by the community, will make the body 'other', outside the boundaries of the 'healthy' norm, but, as Christina Lee's contribution shows, the social impact of this 'otherness' is only just beginning to be explored in Anglo-Saxon archaeology.

Bradley Hull and Tamsin O'Connell's contribution reflects science at its cutting edge. On the one hand, there is stable isotope evidence, and on the other, there is trying to work out how that evidence reflects social or cultural practice. Hull and O'Connell's contribution teases out the potential for stable isotope analysis to offer new insights into commensuality structures, but also recognizes that there is much more to do to fully map the data onto social life.

Biology informs, but does not completely determine, the social creation of age, gender, health, and other interpretations of the individual's body. There is a difference between the physical body—the scientific 'fact' of the body, its size, shape, molecular structure—and how that body was categorized in society. The feminist and gender-based movement in archaeology and history has long insisted that biology does not determine gender. The distinction between a modern scientific categorization of the maleness or femaleness of a skeleton and the gender role given to or adopted by the individual in life, and indeed after death, are not synonymous. In the same way that gender is a cultural concept contingent on a number of factors, of which the shape and attributes of the physical body is only one, so there is equally a contrast between a physically impaired body and being recognized as unwell or physically different within society. There is also a very significant difference between biological age and social age. Perceptions of sickness and wellness, or childhood and adulthood, or maleness and femaleness, are subject to cultural interpretation and negotiation, and so are also subject to change. One person's illness is another person's claim to divine privilege. Biologically immature adults cannot be mapped directly onto social 'children', and 'childhood' is a social construct, not biologically determined. Skeletal sex is not the same as 'gender', nor can a physical impairment be mapped onto a social disability.

As the chapters in this Part show, biological information is not, in itself, beyond being manipulated and determined by cultural factors. Perceptions of race and class have a bearing on assertions of health, gender, and age, and perceptions of class may also determine something as elementary as nutrition. As Bradley Hull and Tamsin O'Connell demonstrate in their paper, we are what we eat. Access to, and availability of, food may be determined by social status, perceived ethnicity, social role (clerical or lay, for example) and other factors. A mother with poor nutritional health will have more peri- and post-natal problems; a child of a low-status mother may have little access to food, leading to poorer health and growth prospects than other children. Puberty may be delayed, and the child grow to be appreciably shorter and weaker than its socially-advantaged peers. This in turn may diminish the adult's chance of negotiating a strong position for itself in terms of age- or gender-related social status. Physical weight, height, well-being, and ability to produce heirs may all be influenced by socially-controlled access to food and resources.

BODY AND OBJECT

What was not buried with bodies may be as relevant to concepts of age, health, and sex as what was. In this context, it is worth considering that, given the relevance of grave goods in signalling what Stoodley has termed 'age grades', childhood is signalled by a lack of 'adult' grave goods—there are no specifically child-related objects. In these terms, mortuary 'childhood' is defined by an absence of adult attributes. What are the implications, then, for the social and life-course status of those adults whose grave goods are as absent, or as limited, as in the graves of children? Are these biologically mature bodies being signalled as social children? Again, the achievement of 'age' in

Anglo-Saxon life may be closely linked to status. Anthropological and historical parallels emphasize that status may be prioritized over biological age. As Niall McKeown observed for Roman slave children (2007a), their immaturity was completely subordinate: they were treated as slaves, not as children. The evidence of the Anglo-Saxon grave goods indicates that in early medieval England, too, status may have determined access to the attributes of 'adulthood' for some biologically mature members of the early Anglo-Saxon community.

These chapters focus on evidence derived from skeletal data and its relationship to mortuary ritual to build a picture of social roles and social identities in the past. Other settings need to be explored, as Sam Lucy discusses in her contribution. Women, for example, are gendered in the grave through their dress accessories first, and other items second. It has been noted that female-gendered grave accessories include items relating to what is accepted as 'women's' work—the spindle whorls, needles, and weaving battens associated with textile production (Brush 1988). It is striking, however, that the archetypal weaving object—the loom-weight—is entirely missing in the mortuary record. By contrast, the presence of loom-weights in huts in early Saxon settlements is the single object that has allowed archaeologists to begin to discuss, in a limited way, 'gendered' space with any degree of confidence. What has yet to be explored is why loom-weights, so gendered in settlement terms, are so comprehensively absent as signifiers of female gender or gendered work in the grave. There would have been no difficulty in placing loom-weights in the grave. Archaeological literature does not indicate that they should be treated as in any way valuable or special—they would have been relatively easy to manufacture, and excavated examples do not show routine evidence for personalization or decoration. Yet they cannot be written off as 'valueless', either in terms of the effort to produce them, or in terms of their symbolic potential. The collecting, working, and firing of the clay required to produce loom-weights all took effort and cost resources. Why, then, were loom-weights not retrieved from huts and re-used to weight fresh looms? Why are rows of loom-weights found in Anglo-Saxon settlements, often in the context of burnt huts? It has been suggested that there may be an element of 'special' deposition or ritual abandonment in the cessation of the use of sets of weights and the effective loss of the resource they represented to the community (Hamerow 2006; Gibson and Murray 2001).

It may be that weights had a particular ritual association, either with settlements or with the living embodiment of the women who used them, which made them inappropriate or taboo as grave goods. In this context, it may be worth considering whether all women participated in weaving, or whether the apparently 'special' nature of loom-weight sets found in the archaeological record indicates that weaving-houses, and access to weaving looms, was a socially-controlled and exclusive performance of female identity, restricted to specific groups of women.

Just as landscape and archaeological theory pervade all aspects of Anglo-Saxon archaeology (see the editors' preface, this volume), so, too, does the life course: why then should it need a separate section? In practice, though the experience of the individual is implicit in much of the discussions elsewhere in this volume, archaeology tends to discuss only those social groups who are perceived to have been dominant in material culture—in its creation, use, and deposition. The seventeenth impression of *The Anglo-Saxon Activity Book*, published in 2006 and designed to inform primary school children about the Anglo-Saxons, offers an interesting reflection of the range of beings who inhabited this version of the Anglo-Saxon world (Reeve and Chattington 2006). The copious drawings and illustrations show fifty-five separate images of men, four of women (one of whom is Mary illustrated on the Franks Casket), and four 'children', all male, of whom three are adolescents—David slaying Goliath, and two possible adolescents serving at table, though they may be older—and one is an infant, Jesus, again from the Franks Casket. There are no illustrations at all of children between infancy and puberty. Two oxen, one dog, and a range of biting beasts are also present in the book.

In terms of the types of people illustrated, it might further be added that only one person is clearly elderly—an artist's reconstruction of a feasting scene, showing a balding man with a lined face. His hand is firmly grasping the wrist of a woman with downcast eyes over whom he leans as she sits next to him. There are no illustrations of diseased or disabled people at all. In terms of activities, men are shown carrying out agricultural work, feasting, building, reading, ruling, fighting, carrying out judicial functions, and lying in state in the grave in a reconstruction of the Sutton Hoo Mound 1 burial. Of the four women, Mary is sitting with Jesus on her lap, two appear to be chatting (their function in the book is to illustrate Anglo-Saxon women's costume), and the fourth has been mentioned above, sitting at the table. The activities of the group at whom the book is aimed—children of school age—are not represented at all. 'Life course' is absent in this little book for children: social life is predominantly masculine, and only males are shown taking part in a repertoire of activities. This validation of dominant-group culture in this general book for children does no more that reflect the social representation of the Anglo-Saxon world in general archaeology books, distilled from the specialist literature, at the time the British Museum first published the book in 1984.

As the chapters in this Part demonstrate, our understanding of the body and social life, and the relationship between the physical body and materiality, not just for the dominant adult male cultural group, but for the culturally non-dominant, too, is developing: 'the description of inert (often literally dead) bodies is being replaced by analyses of the production and experience of lived bodies, in which surface and interior are no longer separated' (Joyce 2005: 152). This Part is intended to highlight these developments in Anglo-Saxon archaeology, and bring them more firmly into the mainstream of archaeological ways of thinking about the evidence. Future writers of books for children should have no difficulty in accessing and presenting an Anglo-Saxon life course which encompasses a wider social range than one dominant group.

References

Ardener, E. (1975). 'Belief and the problem of women', in S. Ardener (ed.), *Perceiving Women*. London: Malaby Press, 1–17.

Baxter, J. E. (2005). *The Archaeology of Childhood: Children, Gender, and Material Culture*. Maryland: Alta Mira Press.

Bonnichsen, R. (1973). 'Millie's camp: an experiment in archaeology'. *World Archaeology* 4: 277–91.

Boyle, A. (2004). 'Burial rite and status on the Yarnton middle Saxon settlement', in Hey (ed.), *Yarnton*, 75–6.

—— Dodd, A., Miles, D. and Mudd, A. (1995). *Two Oxfordshire Anglo-Saxon Cemeteries: Berinsfield and Didcot*. Thames Valley Landscapes Monograph No. 8. Oxford: Oxford Archaeological Unit.

Brush, K. (1988). 'Gender and mortuary analysis in pagan Anglo-Saxon archaeology'. *Archaeological Review from Cambridge* 7(1): 76–89.

Buckberry, J. L. (2007). 'On sacred ground: social identity and churchyard burial in Lincolnshire and Yorkshire, c.700–1100 AD'. *Anglo-Saxon Studies in Archaeology and History* 14: 120–32.

Chamberlain, A. T. (1997). 'Commentary: missing stages of life—towards the perception of children in archaeology', in Moore and Scott (eds.), *Invisible People and Processes*, 248–50.

Crawford, S. E. E. (1991). 'When do Anglo-Saxon children count?' *Journal for Theoretical Archaeology* 2: 17–24.

—— (1999). *Childhood in Anglo-Saxon England*. Stroud: Sutton.

—— (2007). '*Gomol is snotorest*: growing old in Anglo-Saxon England', in M. Henig and T. J. Smith (eds.), *Collectanea Antiqua: Essays in Memory of Sonia Chadwick Hawkes*. British Archaeological Reports International Series 1673. Oxford: Archaeopress, 53–60.

—— (2009). 'The archaeology of play things: theorising a toy stage in the 'biography' of objects'. *Childhood in the Past* 2: 55–70.

Gibson, C., and Murray, J. (2001). 'An Anglo-Saxon settlement at Godmanchester, Cambridgeshire'. *Anglo-Saxon Studies in Archaeology and History* 12: 137–217.

Gilchrist, R. (2000). 'Archaeological biographies: realizing human lifecycles, courses and histories'. *World Archaeology* 31: 325–8.

Gosden, C., and Marshall, I. (1999). 'The cultural biography of objects'. *World Archaeology* 31: 169–78.

Gowland, R. (2004). 'The social identity of health in late roman Britain', in B. Croxford, H. Eckardt, J. Meade, and J. Weekes (eds.), *TRAC 2003: Thirteenth Annual Theoretical Roman Archaeology Conference, Leicester*. Oxford: Oxbow, 135–46.

Hadley, D. M. (2004). 'Gender and burial practices in England, c.650–900', in L. Brubaker and J. M. H. Smith (eds.), *Gender in the Early Medieval World: East and West, 300–900*. Cambridge: Cambridge University Press, 301–23.

Hadley, D. M. (2008). 'Warriors, heroes and companions: negotiating masculinity in Viking-Age England'. *Anglo-Saxon Studies in Archaeology and History* 15: 270–84.

—— (2010). 'Burying the socially and physically distinctive in later Anglo-Saxon England', in J. Buckberry and A. Cherryson (eds.), *Burial in Later Anglo-Saxon England*. Oxford: Oxbow, 101–13.

—— (2009). 'Engendering the grave in later Anglo-Saxon England', in G. McCafferty, S. Terendy, and M. Smekal (eds.), *Proceedings of the 2004 Chacmool Conference*. Calgary: University of Calgary Press, 145–54.

HAMEROW, H. (1993). *Excavations at Mucking*, Volume 2: *The Anglo-Saxon Settlement*. London: English Heritage and British Museum Press.

—— (2006). '"Special deposits" in Anglo-Saxon settlements'. *Medieval Archaeology* 50: 1–30.

HAMMOND, G., and HAMMOND, N. (1981). 'Child's play: a distorting factor in archaeological discourse'. *Society for American Archaeology* 46: 634–6.

HÄRKE, H. (1990). '"Warrior graves"? The background of the Anglo-Saxon weapon burial rite'. *Past and Present* 126: 22–43.

HARLOW, M., and LAURENCE, R. (2002). *Growing Up and Growing Old in Ancient Rome: A Life Course Approach*. London: Routledge.

HAWKES, S. C., and WELLS, C. (1975). 'Crime and punishment in an Anglo-Saxon cemetery'. *Antiquity* 49: 118–22.

HEY, G. (ed.) (2004). *Yarnton: Saxon and Medieval Settlement and Landscape*. Thames Valley Landscapes Monograph 20. Oxford: Oxford Archaeological Unit.

HURCOMBE, L. (2007). 'A sense of materials and sensory perception in concepts of materiality'. *World Archaeology* 39: 532–45.

JOYCE, R.A. (2005). 'Archaeology of the body'. *Annual Review of Anthropology* 34: 139–58.

KING, H. (2005). 'Introduction—what is health?', in H. King (ed.). *Health in Antiquity*. London: Routledge, 1–11.

LEWIS, M. E. (2007). *The Bioarchaeology of Children: Current Perspectives in Biological and Forensic Anthropology*. Cambridge: Cambridge University Press.

LILLEHAMMER, G. (1989). 'A child is born. The child's world in archaeological perspective'. *Norwegian Archaeological Review* 22: 91–105.

McCONE, K. (1986). 'Werwolves, Cyclops, Díberga and Fíanna: juvenile delinquency in early Ireland'. *Cambridge Medieval Celtic Studies* 12: 1–22.

McKeown, N. (2007a). 'Had they no shame? Martial, Statius and Roman sexual attitudes towards slave children', in S. Crawford and G. Shepherd (eds.), *Children, Childhood and Society*. IAA interdisciplinary series, Volume 1: *Studies in archaeology, history, literature and art*. BAR International Series 1696. Oxford: Archaeopress, 52–7.

—— (2007b). *The Invention of Ancient Slavery?* London: Duckworth.

METZLER, I. (2006). *Disability in Medieval Europe: Thinking about Physical Impairment in the High Middle Ages, c.1100—c.1400*. London: Routledge.

MINUCHIN, S. and FISHMAN, H. (1981). *Family Therapy Techniques*. Cambridge, MA: Harvard University Press.

MONTSERRAT, D. 2005 'Carrying on the work of the earlier firm: doctors, medicine and Christianity in the *Thaumata* of Sophronius of Jerusalem', in H. King (ed.), *Health in Antiquity*. London: Routledge, 230–42.

MOORE, J., and SCOTT, E. (eds.) (1997). *Invisible People and Processes: Writing Gender and Childhood into European Archaeology*. London: Leicester University Press.

REEVE, J., and CHATTINGTON, J. (2006). *The Anglo-Saxons Activity Book*. 17th impression. (First printed 1984.) London: The British Museum Press.

REYNOLDS, A. (1999). *Later Anglo-Saxon England: Life and Landscape*. Stroud: Tempus.

REYNOLDS, N. (1988). 'The rape of the Anglo-Saxon women'. *Antiquity* 62(237): 715–18.

ROBERTS, C. (2000). 'Did they take sugar? The use of skeletal evidence in the study of disability in past populations', in J. Hubert (ed.), *Madness, Disability and Social Exclusion:*

The Archaeology and Anthropology of 'Difference'. World Archaeology 40. London and New York: Routledge, 46–59.

SÁNCHEZ ROMERO, M. (2008). 'Childhood and the construction of gender identities through material culture'. *Childhood in the Past* 2: 17–37.

SCHWARTZMAN, H. (1976). 'The anthropological study of children's play'. *Annual Review of Anthropology* 5: 289–328.

SOFAER, J. (2004). *The Body as Material Culture: A Theoretical Osteoarchaeology.* Cambridge: Cambridge University Press.

SOFAER DEREVENSKI, J. (ed.) (2000). *Children and Material Culture.* London: Routledge.

Stoodley, N. (1999a). *The Spindle and the Spear: a Critical Enquiry into the Construction and Meaning of Gender in the early Anglo-Saxon Burial Rite.* BAR British Series, 288. Oxford: British Archaeological Reports.

—— (1999b). 'Burial rites, gender and the creation of kingdoms: the evidence from seventh-century Wessex', *Anglo-Saxon Studies in Archaeology and History*, 10: 99-107.

STOUT, M. (2000). 'Early Christian Ireland: settlement and environment', in T. Barry (ed.), *A History of Settlement in Ireland.* London: Routledge, 81–109.

WELCH, M. (2008). 'Report on excavations of the Anglo-Saxon cemetery at Updown, Eastry, Kent'. *Anglo-Saxon Studies in Archaeology and History* 15: 1–146.

WEST, S. (1985). *West Stow: The Anglo-Saxon Village*, Volume 1: *Text.* East Anglian Archaeology 24.

WILKIE, L. (2000a). 'Not merely child's play: creating a historical archaeology of children and childhood', in Sofaer Derevenski (ed.), *Children and Material Culture*, 100–14.

—— (2000b). *Creating Freedom: Material Culture and African American Identity at Oakley Plantation, Louisiana, 1840–1950.* Baton Rouge: Louisiana State University Press.

WILSON, D. M. (ed.) (1976). *The Archaeology of Anglo-Saxon England.* London: Methuen.

CHAPTER 33

CHILDHOOD TO OLD AGE

NICK STOODLEY

INTRODUCTION

Age and the process of ageing are widely understood to be important characteristics of a person's social identity, and age is often a key determinant of social structure. It influences how people think of themselves and about each other. An individual's roles, both on a personal level and within the wider society, change during life, and the life cycle can consist of several stages, each comprising specific responsibilities and forms of behaviour. The cultural responses to different ages provide the archaeologist with a plethora of information, and scholars seeking to unravel the complexities of any given society should recognize age as a significant topic along with the other identities of gender, status, ethnicity, and religion. This chapter will review current approaches to age in early Anglo-Saxon archaeology, before presenting several case studies that demonstrate the complexity of this identity, and the value of it to our understanding of social organization during the later fifth and sixth centuries.

DEFINITIONS AND APPROACHES TO AN ARCHAEOLOGY OF AGE

Ageing is a physical process that no one can escape, but the ways in which biological age relate to life experience are not universal, because individuals grow up and develop in specific social and cultural contexts. The process of ageing is often closely related to other social identities, and in particular gender and social rank often exert a significant bearing on the way age is structured (Goldberg 2006; Sofaer Derevenski 1997). At different times, and in different places, what it means to be a child, adult, or elder, can be very different according to the social and cultural context in which age-related categories are defined. And although physiological developments are often linked to social changes, what may be considered a major landmark in one society may be absent in another (Gowland 2006: 144). Moreover, the terms that are used to define the stages in the life cycle are also context-specific and are permeated with the values and traits of the culture in which they were generated. For example, it is very difficult to study and write about children without recourse to schemas derived from the modern Western world.

The main source of archaeological evidence is the burial record, and early approaches attempted to identify age-related patterning in grave goods which, it was theorized, reflected the presence of age grades. Archaeologists had taken their lead from several important anthropological studies that had demonstrated the significance of grades in structuring tribal societies (Falkenberg 1962; Van Gennep 1960). The main limitation with this method is that it is very difficult to trace individuals over the course of their lives through burial evidence (Sofaer 2006: 118), and it also has the debilitating consequence of dividing society into a series of separate, stand-alone, immobile categories. What is missing is the human process of ageing. As Jo Sofaer (2006: 120) points out: 'the process of becoming human as we enter the world or becoming adult as we grow often seems to be missing'. Moreover, the emphasis is generally on the differences between age grades, with certain groups, such as childhood, attracting most of the attention. It also encourages a view in which the groups are perceived as largely uniform, peopled by individuals of similar social make-up, and thus overlooks the differences in gender, rank, and ethnicity which might cross-cut these categories (Gowland 2006: 145); the inter-relatedness of these identities is also being ignored.

More recently, archaeologists have taken a 'life course' approach. This does not compartmentalize age, but concentrates on the complete life cycle, arguing that individual stages can only be fully understood in relation to the whole. Close attention is paid to age-determined thresholds, because it is at these points that the interaction between age and other identities may be particularly highlighted (Gowland 2006: 145). The actual *process* of ageing can be investigated: when did significant age-related events occur, how did they impact on other social identities, and how were they expressed through material culture?

Growing up and growing old in early Anglo-Saxon England

Early Anglo-Saxon scholarship has closely mirrored developments in archaeology generally and has been successful in identifying how the early Anglo-Saxon life cycle was organized and how different ages were conceptualized. The following aims to be a brief review of the major work undertaken on this topic. Ellen-Jane Pader's (1980) research into the symbolic functions of material culture was an early attempt at examining social relations, especially sex and age, in several East Anglian cemeteries. It was shown how sex and age exerted a constraining effect on the deposition of certain artefacts and also on the position of the deceased within the grave. Suggestions about the cultural status of being a child or adult were made, and because the burials of women and children had certain features in common they were interpreted as having had a similar status (Pader 1980: 152, 155–6).

Unlike Pader's contextual analysis of assemblages, the next example focuses on a single object—the ubiquitous knife, which again demonstrates how material culture can be active in the creation and maintenance of culturally determined age groups. Heinrich Härke's (1989) examination of the length of knife blade against age of death revealed a correlation between the length of blade, age, and sex, with large knives interpreted as a symbol of adult male status.

The 1990s saw scholars of the Anglo-Saxon period studying so-called marginal groups in society, i.e. women and children. Sam Lucy (1994) studied the treatment of children in Yorkshire's early medieval cemeteries. Interesting chronological differences were found in the way adults and children were differentiated, and it was concluded that Christianity brought about more rigid ideas about what constituted a child and where the boundaries between childhood and adulthood lay. The problem of the infants, or more correctly the lack of them, was also tackled and this was a topic considered in some detail by Sally Crawford, who has also explored the influence of Christianity on concepts of childhood (1993). Both scholars demonstrated that, as a group, infants were perceived very differently to the rest of society: the majority lacked grave goods, and many were treated in other unusual ways. It was argued that high infant mortality led to heightened anxiety over the manner of their deaths, which in turn induced superstitious practices aimed at alleviating such fears (Crawford 1993). The question of what happened to their remains is still largely unanswered, however.

Both archaeological and documentary evidence was used by Crawford (1991; 1993; 1999) to investigate childhood during the Anglo-Saxon period. She successfully identified age-related patterning in the burial data: the presence of objects that apparently operated as signifiers of childhood, in addition to a general trend for younger individuals to have fewer grave goods and objects consisting of precious materials (Crawford 1999: 26–30). In combination with the written records, she was able to suggest where the boundaries of childhood lay, and concluded that, in the early Anglo-Saxon period, the majority of children buried in the early Anglo-Saxon cemeteries occupied a marginal place within the burial ritual, with a low social status. Only when they reached an age of around 11–12 years had they come, in symbolic terms, to be considered part of the adult world (Crawford 1999: 32).

During the later 1990s, some important developments took place which saw archaeological analysis and interpretations becoming increasingly sophisticated. In an overview of early Anglo-Saxon social structure, Härke (1997) focused on both written and material evidence for age groups and the thresholds bracketing these groups. A major threshold, identified from an increase in grave goods and other changes to burial practice, occurred at around 18–20 years and was interpreted as marking passage into adulthood (Härke 1997: 126–30).

Age was also attracting a modest degree of attention by research students. The present writer (1999a: 105–18) undertook a detailed examination from a large national sample of burials that was also broken down by space and time to illustrate the context-specific nature of age. Several important thresholds were identified, and these were found to be strongly determined by an individual's gender. Lucy (1998: 43–7), on the other hand, concentrated her efforts on the region of east Yorkshire, finding that certain types of object were constrained by the age of the deceased, while also demonstrating a significant degree of local variation.

Earlier work on specific age categories had now made it possible to work towards the goal of understanding the whole life course, rather than specific categories within it, but interpretations were still preoccupied with categorizing the evidence and treating age, as Sofaer noted, 'in terms of fixed points in time that can be defined on a scale' (Sofaer 2006: 127). The present writer built on his previous research (2000) by analysing the role of gender in the construction of the life cycle, but went a stage further by trying to explain what each stage in the life cycle held in terms of experiences for its respective individuals. The emphasis was placed on adulthood and what it meant to have attained this status in early Anglo-Saxon society, in order to redress the previous emphasis on younger age groups, and an attempt was made to integrate skeletal evidence to assist interpretation (Stoodley 2000: 465–68). It was concluded that the life cycle was a cultural device to bring order to the early Anglo-Saxon household by signalling the age identity of key family members as determined by their gender and status, rather than a mechanism to divide up society along the lines of age per se.

In the last couple of years exciting developments have taken place that are beginning to show the potential of combining archaeological and skeletal evidence. Becky Gowland (2006) has studied a sample of cemeteries from the south of the country, taking a life course perspective focusing on '"life pathways" and the entry/exit transitions that occur throughout the trajectory of life in a more holistic manner' (Moen 1996: 180 quoted in Gowland 2006: 145). One of the strengths of the study is Gowland's re-analysis of the skeletal data, which ensures a level of consistency in the age determinations. The analysis of the grave goods against the age of the deceased revealed the presence of several thresholds demarcating age groups: especially notable was the one recognized for both males and females in the late teens to early twenties. She also examined how age was closely bound up with an individual's gender and status, and how these identities fluctuated over the life course (Gowland 2006: 145).

THE LIFE CYCLE IN ACTION

It is clear that research has provided much valuable information about age structure during the early Anglo-Saxon period, especially the presence of a major transformation at about the 18–20 year mark that probably signifies where the transition to full adulthood was placed. Research has tended to focus on national and regional overviews, but given the context-specific nature of age, detailed local case studies that examine how it was structured at the community level are essential. The following section attempts this, and involves an analysis of three cemeteries, one from each of the major regions of early Anglo-Saxon England (Saxon, Anglian, and Kentish), to test whether a community's cultural identity had a bearing on age structure. One problem with a contextual analysis is that the size of the sample is often small, thus casting doubt on the validity of the results. In order to reduce this uncertainty, only cemeteries which have been investigated under modern conditions, and at which the majority has been recovered, were chosen. This will avoid the problems regarding the representativeness and quality of data that are often present with older and incompletely excavated sites. The data is provided by inhumation burials because the determination of age and the reconstruction of ritual practices from cremated remains can be problematic, though it should be noted that age seems to have played a role in structuring the type of pyre and grave goods deposited at cremation sites (Richards 1987: 130–4; McKinley 1994; Ravn 1998). A better understanding of age will only follow from further research into the cremation rite and from a full comparison of the evidence from the two practices.

A wide-ranging survey of the evidence will be conducted. In addition to analysing grave goods, the wider aspects of the burial rite will be examined, and a spatial analysis of each cemetery will also be undertaken. Sites were selected where the graves are organized into discrete clusters, the arrangement probably reflecting individual households (Härke 1997: 137–41; Stoodley 1999a: 126–35), and allowing an examination of how age was structured *within* local communities.

Table 33.1 Age groups	
Infant	0–1 years
Child	1–15 years
Youth	15–20 years
Adult	>20 years

Note: based on the terminology used by Stoodley (2000) and Lewis (2007).

Following Gowland (2006), a life-course approach has been taken: culturally determined age groups are identified and traced from birth to death, and the placing of transitions bracketing each are located. The relationship between age and other social identities will also be closely examined, because this will provide a clearer understanding of the differences between each age group. The study, however, relies on the age determinations provided in the excavation reports, and because these are by separate specialists, the analysis cannot claim consistent age identifications (Crawford 1991). Although the direct comparison of individuals is not possible, the material is comparable in more general terms, and to facilitate analysis, the burials were banded into categories (Table 33.1) placing individuals of similar age together. These are in no way meant to reflect early Anglo-Saxon notions of what constituted age groups: they are merely an analytical device to structure the analysis. Age-related patterning identified within these categories will then be evaluated across the age spectrum to suggest a tentative life course model.

Mill Hill, Deal

The first cemetery to be examined is from Kent: Mill Hill, Deal (Parfitt and Brugmann 1997) (Fig. 33.1). It was investigated during a rescue excavation in the 1980s, and produced a wide range of features stretching from the medieval period as far back as the Neolithic. The Anglo-Saxon cemetery focused on a prehistoric barrow, and was completely excavated, although several interments might have been lost to the plough (Parfitt and Brugmann 1997: 13). In all, seventy-six burials have been allocated to the sixth century, with the graves split between two plots. Each plot has several rows of early-sixth-century graves, forming a core around which later graves were arranged. Both plots display a mix of different ages and sexes, indicating that the household was the principle on which the cemetery was organized, although it is notable that no infants were recovered.

Located on the north-east side of the monument is Plot A, consisting of a relatively neatly laid-out group of graves. The youngest burial belongs to a child

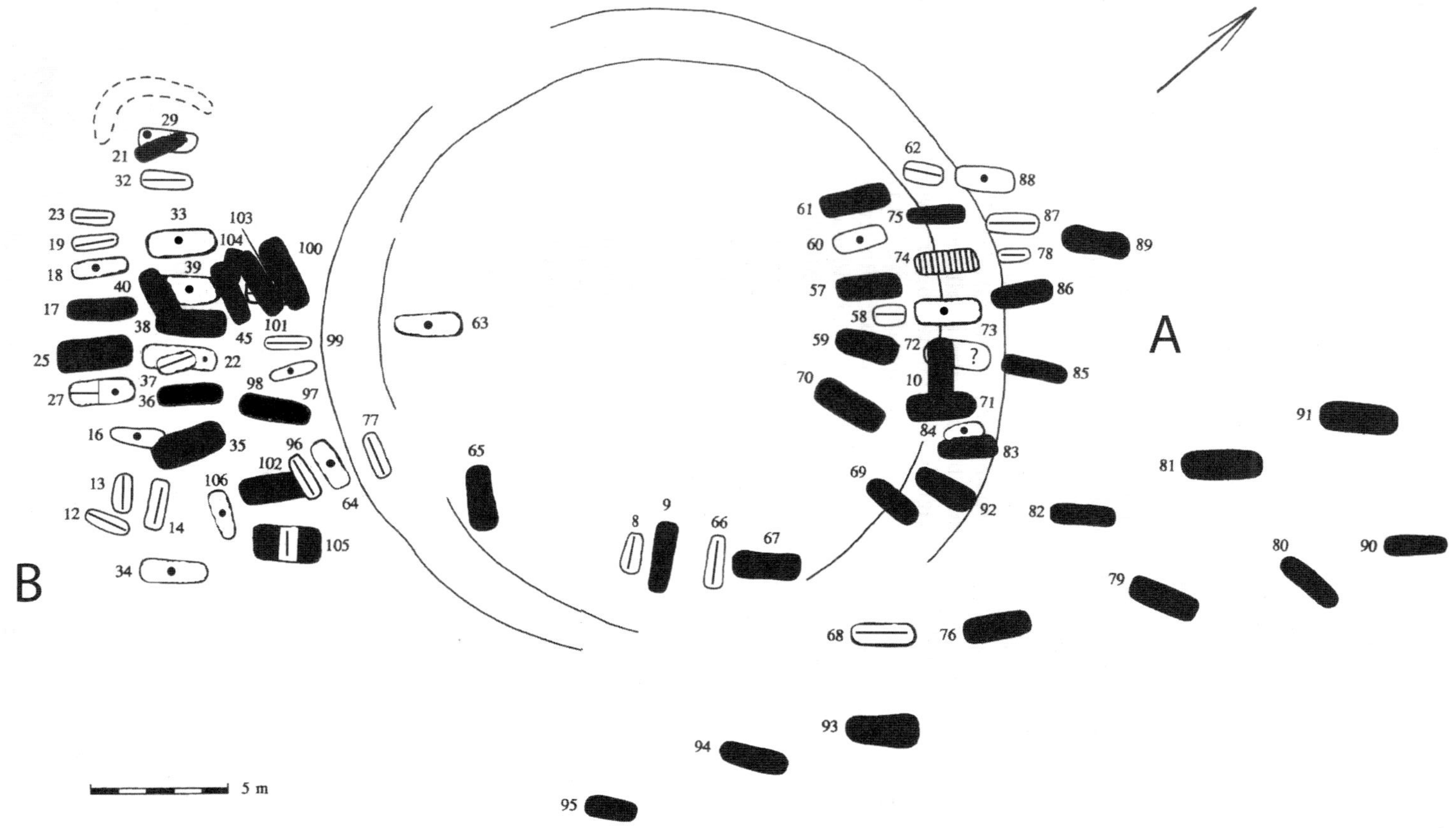

Figure 33.1 Mill Hill, Deal: Distribution of age categories (redrawn from fig. 7, Parfitt and Brugmann 1997)

Table 33.2 Children at Mill Hill, Deal: details of graves

Grave	Age	Grave Goods	Other details
Plot A			
78	2–3	wire bracelet	
66	9–10	knife	
68	12–14	knife, tweezers, necklace, spindle whorl, others	
87	12–16	knife	
Plot B			
32	2–3	knife, pin, vessel	
103	2–3		
21	1–6		
19	3–5		
96	6–8		
27	7–9	necklace, rods, iron object	multiple burial
23	7–9		
77	7–9		
99	8–9	2 beads	
37	6–12	7 beads	
105	12–14		multiple burial, head NE
14	12–16	knife	
98	14–15	knife	

of 2–3 years (grave 78), although there are several which cannot be aged (Tables 33.2–4). The burials of children are characterized by little or no grave wealth, but as age increases, individuals were eligible for a few objects, such as grave 68 containing a 12–14 year old, with some beads amongst other objects, but lacking the brooches and other items deposited with older women. Children and members of the 'youth group' are concentrated in the north of the plot, and are not distinguished spatially from the interments of older individuals. Neither are individuals in either age group differentiated by other aspects of burial practice. Members of the youth group, particularly those in the later teens, exhibit a notable increase in grave goods; for example, burial 73, with four brooches, a large necklace of 420 beads, bracelet, pins, and more besides. The nature of this assemblage is very similar to that found with the majority of adult females, especially those in their twenties, and this signals a clear change in the way females were adorned. With older age it seems that a change takes place, and although this does not apply to all women, it is notable that the majority of assemblages with women over 30 years have lost their strong feminine character: single brooches and shorter necklaces define this stage, while additional elements to the girdle, such as keys and objects in the form of iron rods, are more common.

Table 33.3 Youth at Mill Hill, Deal: details of graves

Grave	Age	Grave Goods	Other details
Plot A			
84	14–17		
60	15–17	knife	
88	17–20	knife, buckle	
73	18–21	knife, buckle, 4 brooches, lge necklace, 2 pins, bracelet, rings, chain	
Plot B			
18	14–18	buckle, brooch, necklace, 2 spindle whorls, chisel, others	
16	15–18	knife	head NE, in ditch
106	16–19	knife, buckle, rings	
29	15–20	2 pins	
39	15–20	knife, buckle, 2 x brooch, necklace, others	
33	17–19	knife, buckle, brooch, necklace, vessel, toilet item, others	
34	18–20	knife, ring, bead	
64	18–20	knife, buckle, brooch, necklace, rods	
27	18–20		
22	18–20	knife, buckle, spear	

Weapons were only placed from the age of 20, but complex assemblages involving swords, shields, and spears are restricted to individuals over 40 years of age. The wealth of these individuals is underlined by the presence of rare items such as vessels. It is intriguing that the males with weapons dating to the later sixth century are all found in a group to the south. It appears that, during the sixth century, Plot A demonstrates an important spatial development marked by the interment of adult males away from women and younger individuals.

Plot B displays a more complex arrangement of graves: three phases of thirty-eight closely placed graves dug over a variety of earlier features. Three rows of early graves, orientated with heads to south-west, are cut by later burials on a different alignment. Different ages and sexes are intermingled, and the youngest individuals are materially impoverished 2-to-3-year-olds, although grave 32 did produce a glass vessel, plus knife and pin. From roughly 7 years, jewellery is found, and takes the form of small collections of beads. During youth, other dress-related items, and many of the objects typically found with older individuals, occur, and the wealth of these is in contrast to their more frugal counterparts in Plot A. Early adulthood sees elaborate jewellery assemblages and longer festoons of beads, with the wealthiest female (burial 25B) in her early twenties.

Table 33.4 Adults at Mill Hill, Deal: details of graves

	Grave	Age	Grave Goods	Other details
Plot A				
MALE	57	20–25	knife, buckle, pursemount	
	89	20–25	knife, spear, shield	
	80	20–27	knife, spear	
	85	20–30	knife, spear, shield, other	
	79	25–25	spear, shield, chisel	
	76	30	knife, buckle, spear	
	75	30–40	knife, buckle	
	82	30–40	knife, spear	
	90	40–50	knife, buckle, spear	
	93	40–50	knife, buckle, vessel, tweezers, spear, shield, sword, others	
	81	45–55	knife, buckle, vessel, tweezers, shears, spear, shield, sword, others	
FEMALE	61	20–25	knife, buckle, vessel, 4 brooches, necklace	
	71	20–25	buckle, 3 brooches, necklace finger ring	
	59	30–40	knife, buckle, tweezers, rods, others	
	69	40+	knife, buckle, hone, beads	
	92	40–50	knife, buckle, vessel, 4 brooches, necklace, rods	coffin
	86	40–50	knife, pursemount, toilet set, needle, 5 brooches, necklace, pin, rods	
	83	40–50	knife	
	94	40–50	knife, 1 brooch, necklace, pin, ring, girdle items	
	10	45–55	knife, buckle, rod, beads	
	95	45–55	knife, necklace, 1 brooch, key, ring	
Plot B				
MALE	40	30–40	knife, 1 brooch, spear, shield, sword	
	17	35–45	knife, buckle, spear, shield	
	98	35–45	knife	
	105	35–45	knife, spear, pin	
	36	40–50	knife, tweezers, spear	
	45	40–50		
	35	50–60	knife, spear, shield	
FEMALE	25B	20–25	knife, buckle, spindle whorl, spoon, crystal ball, 5 brooches, necklace, rods, others	multiple
	65	20–25	knife, buckle, necklace, key, others	
	38	22–29	knife, buckle, ring, other	coffin, disturbed
	104	30–35	buckle, pursemount	disturbed
	25A	35–45	knife, buckle, 1 brooch, necklace	multiple
	102	35–45	knife, buckle, 2 brooches, necklace, rods, others	

If we turn to the males, it is noted that a spear was placed with a male of 18–20 years, thus on the cusp of the youth/adult group. While it is possible that shields and swords were restricted to males of over 30 years, the lack of males in their twenties makes this impossible to prove. Overall, they do not display the wealth of their counterparts in Plot A, and neither were the males of the later sixth century distinguished spatially from other household members.

Blacknall Field, Pewsey

The second cemetery is from Saxon Wiltshire: Blacknall Field, Pewsey (Annable and Eagles 2010) (Fig. 33.2). The majority of this later-fifth- to mid-sixth-century, mainly inhumation, cemetery was recovered and the graves are clustered into several groups, although two are relatively small and may represent short-lived households or appendages to the main groups. Because of this uncertainty, the analysis will concentrate on the two large plots located to the north and south of the burial ground. Each conforms to the household model, and it is significant that both produced the remains of infants. They were without grave goods, although grave 36 had a small knife and several iron fragments (Table 33.5). After the first year of life, young children throughout the cemetery were permitted grave goods, and an unusual and rare piece of child-linked jewellery is the neck ring (four examples were deposited with children ranging from 18 months to 3.5 years). Thus very young individuals were eligible for a weak feminine symbolism, but overall the majority of the youngest did not have any gender-signalling artefacts.

At about 2–3 years, a small but significant increase in burial wealth occurs with the appearance of, amongst other objects, knives and buckles. Moreover, the signalling of the feminine gender becomes stronger, and indicates a shift in the way some young children were symbolized. Several individuals throughout the cemetery were eligible for jewellery, although the assemblages are quite simple. Grave 63 (south plot) with its pair of applied disc brooches, necklace, and bracelet, is an exception, however. There is slight evidence that individuals below the age of about 14 years were more likely to attract unusual practices, such as burial in a crouched position, but this is not an exclusive trend, and neither are these practices particularly common.

It is not until the early twenties that complex jewellery assemblages become common. This marks an important change, and is further distinguished by certain brooch types and items of jewellery and personal equipment that are not found with younger individuals, e.g. finger rings, and girdle items such as keys and chatelaines. Longer bead necklaces also serve to underline the strong gender identity of women of this age. Elaborate assemblages are much more a feature of the south plot with almost all the adult women having two or in some cases three brooches, while in the north plot it is interesting that brooches are only found with females who are over 30 years of age, for example the wealthy assemblage found in grave 21 of a woman over 40 years.

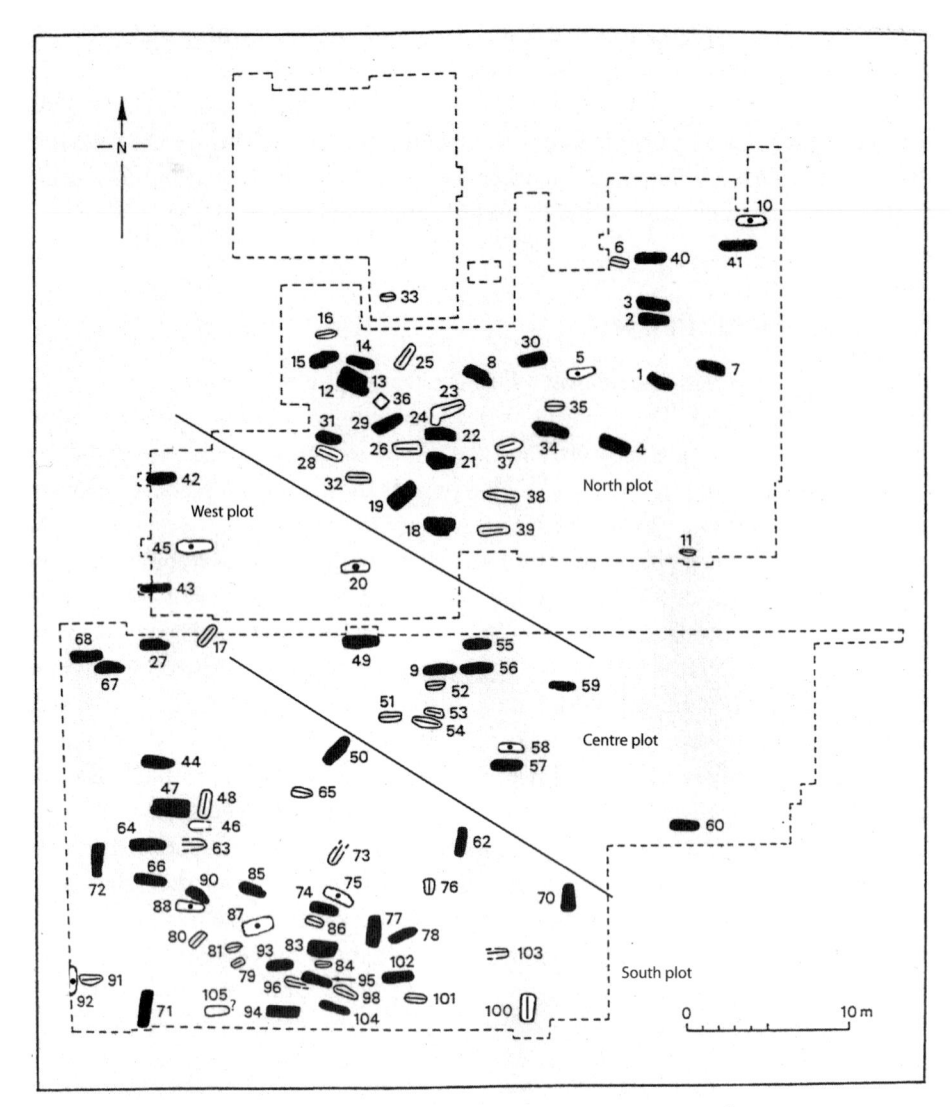

Figure 33.2 Blacknall Field, Pewsey: Distribution of age categories (lines = approximate extent of burial plots; redrawn from Stoodley 1999a, 134)

Weapons were placed from the age of 3 years: grave 100 (south plot) of a 3-to-3.5-year-old with a spear, and grave 16 (north plot) of a 7-year-old with a spear. However, these are exceptions, and in the case of the latter, it was a miniature spearhead which may even have been an arrowhead. Weapons occur in greater frequency from later youth, and different types could now be combined. This marks a major change to how individuals of this age were symbolized. Each major plot displays subtle age-related patterns however: in the northern plot rarer

Table 33.5 Infants/Children at Pewsey: details of graves

Grave	Age	Grave Goods	Other details
N Plot			
24	6m		
36	<1	small knife, iron fragments	crouched
33	1.5	neck ring, strip	right side
39	1.5		
35	2–2.5	beads, toilet set, clasp	
38	5	knife, 1 brooch, necklace, pin	
6	6		
16	7	small spear	
32	8–9		
23	8–9	buckle, 1 brooch, bead, other	
25	9		
11	9		
37	13–15	knife, buckle	
26	14–15	buckle, 2 brooches	
28	15	spear	
C Plot			
51	1.5	bronze frag.	
53	2–2.5	knife, necklace, neck ring, pin, bag collection, others	
52	2–3	knife, neck ring	
54	6–10	knife, beads, bracelet, ring	
W Plot			
17	6–8	pin	
S Plot			
46	<1		
86	2	bead, 2 perforated coins	
96	2	neck ring	
73	2–2.5	bead	crouched, orientation
79	2–3		
84	2–3	iron fragment	left side
100	3–3.5	knife, buckle, spear, other	
101	5–6	2 buckles	
91	6–7		
63	6–7	2 brooches, necklace, bracelet, toilet set	
103	6–7	knife	crouched
80	8		right side, orientation
65	8–12	beads	flexed
98	10–12		
48	14–15	2 brooches, beads	orientation

Table 33.6 Youths at Pewsey: details of graves

	Grave	Age	Grave Goods	Other details
N Plot				
	10	18	pot	
	5	19–20	knife, spear, shield	
C Plot				
	20	16–17	knife, necklace, ring, coin	
	58	16–18		
W Plot				
	45	17–18	knife, buckle, spear, shield, bead	
S Plot				
	92	15–18	beads, other	
	88	17	knife, ring, coin, other	
	87	18–19	knife, buckle	
	75	19–20	bead	

weapon types were restricted to older males. Is this a situation comparable to the restriction of brooches to older women in this plot?

Norton

The final example comes from Anglian Northumbria—Norton in Cleveland (Sherlock and Welch 1992) (Fig. 33.3). It is believed to be almost completely excavated, and displays an interesting arrangement: four separate burial plots in use at any one time during the sixth century, although Plot B with a small number of graves may be a small/short-lived group, or a subsidiary of Plot A or C. In each of the main plots the burials of children, but also youths, are on the outer edges, with the adult burials making up a core. This arrangement is clearest along the north-western edge of plot C, where several clusters of child burials can be identified. This is a cemetery that has produced a relatively large number of prone and crouched burials, but neither demonstrates a connection with a specific age.

With the exception of one infant interred in a multiple burial, infants were not present. Burial commenced from about 1 year and the two individuals (graves 62 and 101) of this age were found with single beads. Throughout the cemetery, children's burials are generally characterized by small collections of beads, single knives, and pots until about the age of 10 is reached (Table 33.8). There are no weapons, and unlike in the other case studies, other types of jewellery seldom figure. From the age of 12, other objects are encountered, but it is not really until later youth that jewellery assemblages were permitted, and pairs of annular brooches, necklaces, and other accoutrements become typical, indicating an

Table 33.7 Adults at Pewsey: details of graves

	Grave	Age	Grave Goods	Other details
N Plot				
MALE	1	22–25	sword, pin, horn	disturbed
	12	22–25	spear	left side
	34	20–25	knife, spear, shield	
	8	25–30	2 spear, shield, toe ring	
	14	25–30	knife, shield	
	3	30	fragments	
	7	35–40	knife, buckle, axe, tweezers, bead	
	22	45+	knife, buckle, spear, shield, sword	
	29	45–50	knife, buckle	orientation
	4	50	pot	
FEMALE	2	20–25	necklace, purse ring	disturbed
	41	25+		
	18	25–35	necklace, pin, comb, pot, tweezers	
	13	30	knife, beads, buckle, girdle	
	31	30–35	knife, 2 brooches, necklace, purse, toilet item	
	40	35–40		
	15	40+	3 brooches, necklace, pot	
	19	40+	knife, 2 brooches	orientation
	21	40+	knife, buckle, 3 brooches, bucket, other	
	30	45	2 brooches, pin, others	
C Plot				
MALE	9	35	spear, shield	
	49	50+	buckle	
FEMALE	60	21	2 brooches, pin, necklace	
	57	23	2 buckles, necklace, pin, purse	
	56	30	knife, 2 brooches, beads, finger ring, purse, bucket, toilet set	
	55	35+	knife, 2 brooches, toilet set	
	59	35–40	knife, others	
W Plot				
MALE	68	28–30	knife, spear, shield, bucket, tweezers, ring, others	
FEMALE	27	35–40	2 knives, 2 brooches, beads	
S Plot				
MALE	94	22–25	knife, buckle, spear, shield	
	70	23–25	knife, shield, sword, other	
	83	23–25		
	64	28–30	knife, buckle, spear	
	71	35–40		prone
	62	35–40	spear, shield	

(Continued)

Table 33.7 Continued

	Grave	Age	Grave Goods	Other details
	72	40	knife	
	47	40–45	spear, shield, sword, tweezers, ?vessel	
FEMALE	85	20	2 brooches, necklace	
	93	20	3 brooches, beads, pin	
	44	21	knife, 2 brooches, necklace, pin	
	95	25–30	knife, 2 brooches, beads, pin, other	
	50	25–30	knife, 2 brooches, necklace, bucket, purse, other	
	66	30	2 brooches	
	78	30	knife, buckle, 2 brooches, pin, other	
	104	30	buckle, 3 brooches, pin, finger ring	
	74	30–35	knife, buckle, 2 brooches, beads, other	
	90	40+	other	
	102	45+	buckle, 2 brooches, necklace, pin, ?vessel	

important shift in the marking of these individuals (Table 33.9). A steady increase in the size of the bead necklaces within the child and youth groups is also notable.

From early adulthood greater quantities of grave goods were placed, in particular elaborate feminine assemblages involving the longest festoons of beads, multiple brooches, and brooch types not found with younger individuals (for example cruciform brooches), plus pins and sleeve-clasps occur (Table 33.10). It is notable that throughout the adult group, age has little bearing on the character of the assemblage. Weapon burial follows a similar age-related pattern: grave 60 (15–21 years) with a shield and spear is the youngest, while the bulk of weapons are restricted to the adult category. On the whole the weapon assemblages are more modest than in the other two cemeteries and there is little appreciable age-related variation during the adult category.

The analysis did identify some differences between the different plots. Plot A has produced individuals with the wealthiest jewellery both in terms of quantity and quality of object. A higher number of adult weapon burials also occur in this plot. In Plot B there are no weapon burials, and in Plot D, grave 120 is the only example, but is separate from the main group by a distance of about 7 metres. Moreover, the females in Plot C generally have fewer brooches.

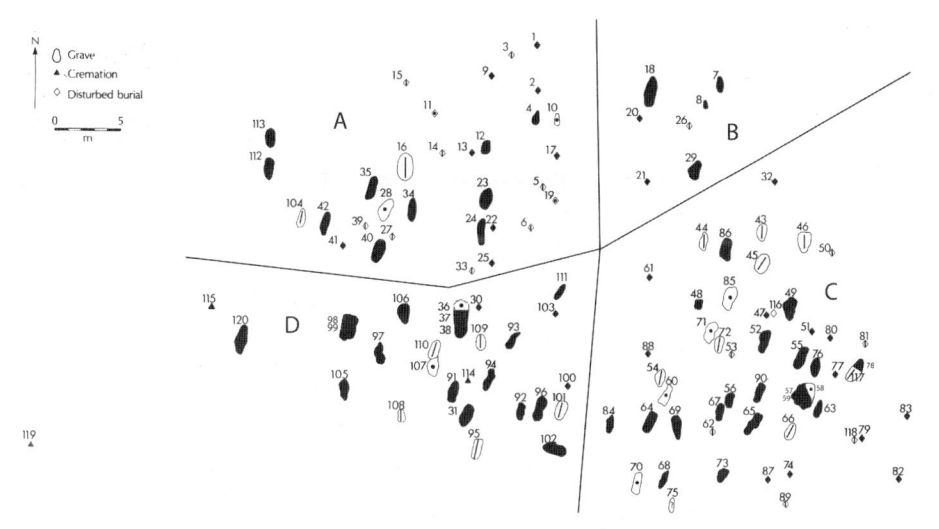

Figure 33.3 Norton: Distribution of age categories (lines = approximate extent of burial plots; redrawn from Sherlock and Welch 1992)

Discussion

The analysis has shown that the burial rite is related to an individual's age and that grave goods are the most visible aspect in the articulation of this social identity. No other aspects of the burial rite are positively age-linked, either within a cemetery, or even within an individual burial plot. Mill Hill and Norton both produced evidence to suggest that the laying out of graves may have been determined by an individual's age, showing that further methods were occasionally used to underline the differentiation expressed through the symbolism of the grave goods. Overall, there existed a strong link between the biological age of the body and objects (Sofaer 2006), and similarities were noted throughout the sample, supporting the idea of a standard set of age-related practices operating in each community, irrespective of region. The findings broadly concur with other national and regional analyses (Crawford 1999; Stoodley 1999a: 105–18; 2000; Gowland 2006), but interesting local differences in how the life cycle was organized were also found.

We shall now assess the evidence from birth to older age, while also examining how age was intertwined with other social identities to suggest how the life course was organized and the various stages of it experienced. It is clear that for the very youngest members of the community burial involved little investment. If a considerable number of infants died before their first birthday (Crawford 1991; 1993: 85; Härke 1997: 127) this may have affected the extent to which parents became emotionally involved with their newborn (Crawford 1993; Lucy 2005: 50), while

Table 33.8 Infants/Children at Norton: details of graves

	Grave	Age	Grave Goods	Other details
Plot A				
	39	2–3	pot, bone ring	
	27	5–9	buckle, pendant	
	3	7–11		
	14	10		crouched
	6	10–14		
	5	12–18	1 brooch, bead	crouched
	15	12–18		
	16	12–18	knife	
	104	12–18	1 brooch, pin	
Plot B				
	26	6–12	knife	crouched
Plot C				
	116	<1		multiple burial, reversed orientation, prone
	62	1	bead	
	72	2	1 brooch, bead	
	81	2	bead	
	117	4–8		multiple burial
	53	5–9	pot	
	43	6–10	knife	crouched
	66	10	2 brooches, beads, ring	
	118	7–11		multiple burial
	50	7–11		crouched
	45	12	knife, brooch, beads, pot, clasp	crouched
	54	12	knife, ring, key, other	
	46	12–18		
	89	12–18	knife	
Plot D				
	101	1	bead	
	108	3–5	bead	
	95	4–8		
	109	5–9	beads	
	110	5–9	knife	

their total dependency on their physical and social environment (Lewis 2007: 5) may have resulted in a marginal status and identity (Crawford 1993: 85; Stoodley 2000: 458–9). At Pewsey and Norton, their actual presence seems to suggest that the life cycle began at birth, whereas at Mill Hill, because the youngest were of 2–3 years, it suggests that children below this age were not acknowledged within the burial ritual as community members (Crawford 1993).

Table 33.9 Youth at Norton: details of graves

Grave	Age	Grave Goods	Other details
Plot A			
11	15–18	knife, buckle, 2 brooches, bead, vessel, comb, amulet, key, other	
10	15–21	beads	
19	15–21	knife, 2 brooches, necklace, purse, key, ring	crouched
28	15–21	knife, 2 brooches, necklace, pin, amulet, key	prone
Plot C			
85	16–20	buckle, 1 brooch, necklace, purse, key, ring, other	
58	15–21	bead	multiple burial, crouched
71	15–21	necklace	
60	15–21	spear, shield	crouched
70	15–21	knife, buckle, 1 brooch, necklace, toilet item, rings, clasps, key	
Plot D			
36	15–21	ring, sherds	
107	15–21	2 brooches, necklace, pin, pot	multiple burial

In fact children up to about the age of 3 are characterized by little burial wealth, marking them out as separate from older children, and also occupying a marginal position in society. From three years we can recognize a gradual change in the treatment of the youngest, however: a small but appreciable rise in both the quantity and types of grave goods. This shift in ritual treatment can be interpreted as representing a threshold demarcating the two youngest age groups. Is this change linked to their growth and the development of key skills, such as walking and talking? Their presence was gradually becoming more permanent, and in the event of death they were eligible to be interred with objects symbolizing this—the burial rite is reflecting the process by which individuals were gradually becoming cultural.

In each cemetery gender now becomes a feature of the life course for certain individuals, especially the expression of a feminine identity. It is admittedly rather weakly signalled but nevertheless it is an age-related change in status, probably linked to the attainment of feminine-related activities. By the age of 5, children are able to provide the household with help in minor chores (Lewis 2007: 6) and the fact that young (apparently female) children and older females are linked materially could be interpreted as a way in which feminine behaviour, roles, and skills were learnt. Jewellery can be viewed as integral to the way the body was moulded and understood—how a feminine identity was inscribed upon the body. As symbols, objects are especially important to the process of development, being

Table 33.10 Adults at Norton: details of graves

	Grave	Age	Grave Goods	Other details
Plot A				
MALE	12	21–25	buckle, spear	
	25	25–30	spear, sherds	crouched
	24	25–30	knife, spear	
	42	20–30	spear shield	
	34	25–35	knife, buckle, spear, shield, sherds	
	13	35–45	knife, buckle	
FEMALE	112	17–25	3 brooches	crouched
	4	21–25	2 brooches, necklace, pin, clasps, toilet items	crouched
	41	20–30	knife, 2 brooches, necklace, pin, toilet item, ring	crouched
	40	20–30	knife, 3 brooches, necklace, bracelet, ×2, clasps, key, sherds, ring, other	
	35	25–35	knife, buckle, 2 brooches, pin, necklace, clasps, key, other	crouched
	22	25–35	knife, buckle, 2 brooches, bead, clasps, key	crouched
	1	25–35	brooch, beads, pin, clasps, key	
	9	25–35	knife, 4 brooches, beads, clasps	crouched
	23	28–35	knife, buckle, 2 brooches, vessel	crouched
	113	32–38	knife, buckle, 1 brooch, necklace, sherds	crouched
Plot B				
MALE	18	25–35		
	20	25–35	bead	
FEMALE	21	25–25	buckle, 1 brooch, necklace, clasps	
	29	25–35	knife, 2 brooches, necklace, 2 pins, vessel, clasps, comb, key, ring, toilet item, others	
	7	45–61	2 brooches, necklace, pin, clasps	
Plot C				
MALE	69	17–25	buckle, spear, bead	
	67	17–25		crouched
	79	25–25	knife	multiple burial
	55	25–35	spear, shield, seax	
	64	35–45	knife, spear, shield, ring, bead	
	78	45–61	knife, buckle, toilet item	multiple burial
FEMALE	57	17–25	1 brooch, clasp, toilet item	multiple burial, crouched
	73	17–25		crouched
	87	17–25	knife, beads, 2 rings, other	crouched

	48	17–25	buckle, beads, pendant	
	40	20–30	knife, 3 brooches, necklace, clasps, 2 bracelets, key, ring, sherds, other	
	49	20–30	knife, buckle, 1 brooch, pin	
	52	25–35	knife, buckle, 1 brooch, necklace, pin, clasp, key, purse, 2 rings	
	80	25–35	1 brooch	
	63	25–35	knife, 2 brooches, necklace, clasps, key, ring	
	56	30–40	knife, 1 brooch, beads, pin, ring, clasp	crouched
	65	30–40	knife, 1 brooch, bead	
	59	35–45	knife, bead, clasp, bead	multiple burial
	68	35–45	knife, necklace, clasps, key	
	84	35–45	Bead, ring, knife, 2 brooches, 2 clasps	prone
Plot D				
MALE	31	17–25	flint blade	crouched
	91	17–25		prone
	98	20–30	1 brooch	multiple burial
	93	25–35		
	120	25–35	knife, spear, bucket	
	100	35–45	buckle, pot, amber	
FEMALE	99	17–25	comb, sherd	Multiple, prone
	38	20–30	knife, buckle	crouched
	30	25–35	3 brooches, pin, necklace	crouched
	94	25–35	knife, 3 brooches, necklace, amulet, bracelet, other	
	106	25–45	pin, sherd	crouched
	96	45–61	3 brooches, clasps, knife, sherd	
	105	45–61	2 brooches, necklace, pin, 3 rings	crouched

particularly instrumental in the transmission of ideas and concepts (Sofaer 2006: 135). Childhood is a time of socializing and education, where social norms and gender roles are learnt (Lewis 2007: 4). Is one of the main features of this age group learning, i.e. can we understand it as a 'childhood'? Through learning, such individuals may have been active participants within their own households and communities. For this age group, weapons are especially rare, implying that masculinity and the acquisition of masculine-related skills played much less of a role during the early years of the life course.

The picture is clouded by the fact that the burial rite does not rigidly follow chronological age: some children have assemblages that look out of place for their age. As the body develops, it is changed by cultural and social factors (Gowland 2006: 144). Some children develop more quickly than others, and admittance into a group may be dependent on the attainment of, for example, a certain stature, or other form of physical development, allowing participation in tasks associated with that stage. The categorization of individuals into age groups in the early Anglo-Saxon burial ritual may have been based on physiological ageing, rather than chronological age. The implication is that actual age may have been of little importance; it was the age group itself that defined this identity. At Norton, children were generally more impoverished. Does this indicate that the child group at Norton had less importance and status compared to the other two case-studies?

The upper bracket of this group appears to have been placed somewhere between 10 and 14 years depending on the cemetery, and from now a marked increase in grave goods, especially of a feminine character, is found. This indicates a threshold and a concomitant change in status and identity. The jewellery assemblages closely follow those of older women: pairs of brooches and longer bead necklaces are the defining symbols for this group. This change coincides with puberty, and the status that it reflected may also have been associated with the ability to bear children (Stoodley 2000: 465). Yet although it seems that menarche was acknowledged, it is questionable whether this threshold marked the transition to cultural adulthood, because there is another important change to the female assemblage late in the youth group (see below). The change at 12 to 14 years may have signalled a stage bound up with caring for their own young children and other individuals generally. As such it can be considered separate and distinct—neither childhood nor adulthood—and without the responsibilities of full adult status it may have given the individual a degree of autonomy. This is especially marked in Plot B at Mill Hill, and may indicate that particular importance was attached to this age by the group interring in this location.

The much higher number of individuals with gender-signalling paraphernalia, and the wealthier nature of these assemblages occurring around 18–21 years, indicate that a significant change has taken place in the identity and status of individuals of either gender. This is a major feature of all the case studies, and it is clear that an important transformation has taken place, possibly associated with a move to a key position in the community, and the acquisition of responsibilities of importance and social worth. In fact, the attainment of adulthood is often the most important of all age-related transitions, and the significant changes identified at this age are interpreted as symbolizing this identity.

From this point, an individual's gender was strongly signified, and it is clear that this identity was a defining feature of adulthood. For women this is defined by larger bead necklaces, certain brooch types that were not permitted before (Stoodley 2000: 463), plus a greater quantity of objects generally. It is abundantly clear that the women in their twenties and thirties were interred with the most elaborate sets of dress accessories and jewellery. A similar situation seems to relate to males, with the majority of weapons being found from late teens/early twenties. It is difficult to know how to interpret the male evidence, however. The fact that there is only one clear threshold contrasts with the female situation, indicating that males did not progress through a set of age-determined grades where masculine skills and behaviour were learnt. Was there just one main age-related group centring on adulthood—was masculinity very much a function of individuals who had achieved cultural maturity? Many of the children and youths without grave goods, or with objects without gender associations, must therefore have been males, but this dearth of cultural information means that it is very difficult to understand anything about young male identity and the status of such individuals within the community. There are exceptions which probably result from age being based on physiological change, as opposed to chronological age. This is, however, unlikely for young boys, and a different situation may be applicable here. Perhaps exposure to weapons from a young age was intended to familiarize them with the objects in preparation for later life.

Interestingly, the presence of an age group defined around seniority may be glimpsed by the restriction of more complex weapon sets to older males (also found by Gowland 2006: 151–2), and the presence of other objects usually considered symbols of social status, such as vessels. Are we witnessing a change in status related to skills or responsibilities? Can we envisage a particular position occupied by older males in their communities resulting from a lifetime's knowledge and experience? It is interesting that, in Pewsey's northern plot, older males *and* females had certain objects restricted to them, which might indicate that a status associated with seniority cut across gender. In contrast, the analysis also found that at Mill Hill (Plot A), older women had reduced feminine symbolism. Studies have identified a slight change to the type of assemblage granted to older women, as witnessed by a reduction in the number and variety of items of jewellery (Stoodley 2000: 461–5; Gowland 2006: 150–1), but this does not indicate a wholesale decline in gender-related responsibilities during the later stages of the life course. Rather, it may reflect a subtle change in status, as responsibilities and duties were devolved to younger household members, and could, once the older women were released from these, have resulted in greater autonomy (Gowland 2006: 151).

Conclusion

We have examined the age composition of several early Anglo-Saxon communities, and have demonstrated that age difference between individuals was by reference to specific age grades, as opposed to chronological age. Progression through the life course was undertaken in groups, with each one having important cultural meaning—each defined and reinforced through reference to a particular set of grave goods. They were firmly gender-based, but also expressed an individual's social rank, and how this fluctuated during life. The groups do not represent directly the roles and responsibilities undertaken during life; rather it is the status derived from the fulfilment of each group's activities that is symbolized. This is why the major age-related changes are marked by increases in the quantity/size of specific objects, such as necklaces, brooches, weapons, etc., and not by the appearance of completely different types of object. For women, the life course was complex, and consisted of a set of incremental stages leading to, and in preparation for, full adult status. The life-course approach has also shown how female children were linked materially to older women, and by implication made an active contribution to society. For men, one key threshold marked the passage into adulthood, but it is hard to say how they were conceptualized before this age. For both men and women, the transition to adulthood took place at a similar time, and the dramatic increase in their wealth reflects the importance and status of this transition.

The system of age groups should not be applied too rigidly, however: the analysis has shown that the evidence varies across and also within cemeteries, with certain age groups figuring more prominently than others. The relative importance of different age groups implies that age was interpreted and organized in subtly different ways. Neither should we expect this ritualized set of practices to accurately reflect the life course. It may primarily have been an ideological device intended to enhance and bring order to a society in which age-related customs were difficult to enforce. This can be expected in agriculturally-based communities, where all individuals irrespective of age and also gender were expected to pitch in and lend a hand. It could have been an oversimplification of the actual system, focusing on the key stages, and ignoring relatively less important ones such as learning to crawl, or male puberty.

Overall, the study has shown that we should always be aware of the context-specific nature of age organization. The system of age grades and what is says about the life course may have been specific to the circumstances of the fifth and sixth centuries and the more community-orientated society at that time (Stoodley 1999b), and we should not expect it to apply to later Anglo-Saxon England. Future work will need to ask how the system was altered during the seventh and eighth centuries by the major social, cultural, and economic changes accompanying the emergence of major Anglo-Saxon kingdoms, and the conversion to Christianity.

REFERENCES

ANNABLE, F. K., and EAGLES, B. N. (2010). *The Anglo-Saxon Cemetery at Blacknall Field, Pewsey, Wiltshire*. Wiltshire Archaeological and Natural History Society Monograph.

CRAWFORD, S. (1991). 'When do Anglo-Saxon children count?' *Journal of Theoretical Archaeology* 2: 17–24.

—— (1993). 'Children, death and the afterlife in Anglo-Saxon England'. *Anglo-Saxon Studies in Archaeology and History* 6: 83–91.

—— (1999). *Childhood in Anglo-Saxon England*. Stroud: Sutton.

FALKENBERG, J. (1962). *Kin and Totem: Group Relations of Australian Aborigines in the Port Keats District*. London: Oslo University Press.

GOLDBERG, P. J. P. (2006). 'Life and death: the ages of man', in R. Horrox and W. M. Ormrod (eds.), *A Social History of England 1200–1500*. Cambridge: Cambridge University Press, 413–34.

GOWLAND, R. (2006). 'Ageing the past: examining age identity from funerary evidence', in R. Gowland and C. Knüsel (eds.), *Social Archaeology of Funerary Remains*. Oxford: Oxbow Books, 143–54.

HÄRKE, H. (1989). 'Knives in early Saxon burials: blade length and age at death'. *Medieval Archaeology* 33: 144–8.

—— (1997). 'Early Anglo-Saxon social structure', in J. Hines (ed.), *The Anglo Saxons: Towards an Ethnography*. Woodbridge: Boydell, 125–70.

LEWIS, M. E. (2007). *The Bioarchaeology of Children: Perspectives from Biological and Forensic Anthropology*. Cambridge: Cambridge University Press.

LUCY, S. (1994). 'Children in early medieval cemeteries'. *Archaeological Review from Cambridge* 13(2): 21–34.

—— (1998). *The Early Anglo-Saxon Cemeteries of East Yorkshire*. BAR British Series 272. Oxford: British Archaeological Reports.

—— (2005). 'The archaeology of age,' in M. Diaz-Andreu, S. Lucy, S. Babić, and D. N. Edwards (eds.), *The Archaeology of Identity*. Abingdon: Routledge, 43–66.

MCKINLEY, J. (1994). *The Anglo-Saxon Cemetery at Spong Hill, North Elmham, Part 8: The Cremations*. East Anglian Archaeology 69. Gressenhall.

MOEN, P. (1996). 'Gender, age, and the life course', in R. H. Binstock, L. K. George, V. W. Marshall, G. C. Myers, and J. H. Schulz (eds.), *Handbook of Aging and the Social Sciences*. 4th edition. San Diego, CA: Academic Press, 171–87.

PADER, E. J. (1980). 'Material symbolism and social relations in mortuary studies', in P. Rahtz, T. Dickinson, and L. Watts (eds.), *Anglo-Saxon Cemeteries 1979: The Fourth Anglo-Saxon Symposium at Oxford*. BAR British Series 82. Oxford: British Archaeological Reports, 143–59.

PARFITT, K., and BRUGMANN, B. (1997). *The Anglo-Saxon Cemetery on Mill Hill, Deal, Kent*. Society for Medieval Archaeology Monograph Series 14. Leeds: The Society for Medieval Archaeology.

RAVN, M. (1998). *Germanic Social Structure (c. AD200–600): A Methodological Study in the Use of Archaeological and Historical Evidence in Migration Age Europe*. Unpublished PhD dissertation, University of Cambridge.

RICHARDS, J. D. (1987). *The Significance of Form and Decoration of Anglo-Saxon Cremation Urns*. BAR British Series 166. Oxford: British Archaeological Reports.

SHERLOCK, J. S., and WELCH, M. (1992). *An Anglo-Saxon Cemetery at Norton, Cleveland.* CBA Research Reports 82. York: Council for British Archaeology.

SOFAER, J. R. (2006). *The Body as Material Culture.* Cambridge: Cambridge University Press.

SOFAER DEREVENSKI, J. (1997). 'Age and gender at the site of Tiszapolgár-Basatanya, Hungary'. *Antiquity* 71: 875–89.

STOODLEY, N. (1999a). *The Spindle and the Spear: A Critical Enquiry into the Construction and the Meaning of Gender in the Early Anglo-Saxon Burial Rite.* BAR British Series 288. Oxford: British Archaeological Reports.

—— (1999b). 'Burial Rites, gender and the creation of kingdoms: the evidence from seventh century Wessex', *Anglo-Saxon Studies in Archaeology and History,* 10: 101–109.

—— (2000). 'From the cradle to the grave: age organisation and the early Anglo-Saxon burial rite'. *World Archaeology* 31(3): 456–72.

VAN GENNEP, A. (1960). *The Rites of Passage.* London: Routledge and Kegan Paul.

CHAPTER 34

DIET: RECENT EVIDENCE FROM ANALYTICAL CHEMICAL TECHNIQUES

BRADLEY D. HULL
TAMSIN C. O'CONNELL

Introduction

The scientific analysis of archaeological material has the potential to inform us about the diet of Anglo-Saxons. Recently, developments in analytical techniques have allowed researchers new insights into the daily practice of food consumption and the relationship of diet to individual, familial, and cultural organization. Eating, like breathing, is something that as humans we all must do regularly. But unlike the air we breathe, an element of choice exists in the food we consume. This choice might be personal, or informed by social constructs which limit access to some resources. Differences in diet between individuals and populations are culturally constructed. By studying diet we are able to discuss how Anglo-Saxons 'ate' their culture on a daily basis. The differences and similarities can be used to inform archaeology about how an individual was placed within the culture in which they lived.

The evidence for Anglo-Saxon diet presented here is derived from stable isotope analysis (carbon and nitrogen), ceramic residue analysis, cess pit analyses, and other archaeological features.

Floral and faunal evidence: a summary

The Anglo-Saxons had access to many of the same foods as we do in modern society, but also several natural resources which we no longer exploit. A number of wild and domesticated plants were used by the Anglo-Saxons for food, including various cereals, legumes, nuts, fruits, and vegetables (Green 1981; Hagen 1992, 1995; this volume, Part IV). From late Saxon written records such as Ælfric's *Colloquy* we learn that bread represented the staple of the daily meal. Anglo-Saxons did not live on bread alone, as texts such as the tenth century *Leechdoms* indicate that meat and dairy products were often salted and accompanied many meals (Hagen 1992: 41). Meat sources included domesticated cattle, pigs, sheep and/or goats, and fowl, as well as wild boar, birds, and deer (Haslam *et al.* 1980; Arnold 1988; Crabtree 1990; 1991; Hagen 1992; 1995; this volume, Part IV; see also The *Laws* of Ine 49.3, 55, 70.1: Attenborough 1922: 53, 55, 59). Other sources of food include secondary products—milk, cheese, and eggs—which leave almost no archaeological evidence, but could have played a major role in Anglo-Saxon diet. Seasonality was one of the major limitations in the Anglo-Saxon diet, and certain foods were regularly preserved. Fish, bacon, and beef could all be salted and last many months (Allen 2004: 125). Grains could be dried and stored. But most of the food was available for a short time only. Access to food becomes a real consideration in a seasonal context, particularly when discussing issues of disease and the general health of the population. There is debate as to whether or not pork was a high-status food in Anglo-Saxon times (Arnold 1988: 19; Crabtree 1991; Albarella 2006). Although a differential access to food could have caused a significant gap between the diets of the privileged classes and the peasantry (especially in times of drought and economic stress) (Härke 1990), Hagen (1992) suggests that such differences in diet were primarily a matter of quality, rather than access versus complete deprivation.

Archaeological floral and faunal records, where preserved in Anglo-Saxon settlement contexts, present us with some evidence for the types of food available for human consumption (Arnold 1988). From pits and abandoned structures there is evidence for a range of domestic and non-domestic animals: cattle, sheep, and pigs, but also chickens, goose, and fowl as domesticates; far less common are wild animals—deer, hare, wild birds, eels, and fish. There is also evidence for domestic flora such as rye, wheat, barley, and oats for cereals. Many other likely domesticates do not preserve regularly, which is why ceramic residue studies are informative. Although most archaeobotanical remains represent what was available, rather than what was actually consumed, fruit and plant remains from cess pits show evidence for the direct consumption of food material. The diet at the urban site at Coppergate in York contains evidence for several different food groups that are not often described in the archaeological literature, including field beans, plum, crab apple, sloe, blackberry, hawthorn, as well as oats, wheat, and rye (McCobb and Briggs 2001). Evidence of similar foods was found at the site of Abbot's Worthy, Hampshire, where, in addition to cereals, there was evidence for apples, blackberries, elderberries, sloe, hazelnuts, peas, beans, carrots, celery, and cabbage (Carruthers 1991: 74). Some of these foods, such as carrots, were grown by Anglo-Saxons, but the degree of cultivation of others is unknown.

POTTERY ANALYSIS

As well as analysing the macro-remains of foods in archaeological contexts, recent developments in analytical techniques permit the analysis of amorphous organic remains in ceramics. Pottery residues (and other materials) can be informative about the preparing, cooking, and storing of food, providing an insight into specific foodstuffs consumed in the Anglo-Saxon period.

Chromatographic and mass spectrometric techniques enable individual chemical compounds, generally lipids, to be chemically characterized from amorphous and often degraded residues left on artefacts by human activities. From such 'biomarker' molecules, the original material can then be identified. Lipids have been shown to be well preserved when adsorbed on an unglazed porous ceramic matrix, and less well-preserved but still recoverable from charred residues on the surface of potsherds. A variety of different compounds can be measured, including fatty acids, waxes, and sterols of both animal and plant origin (Evershed *et al.* 1999). So far, only a few examples are available for later Anglo-Saxon material, but the results provide specific insights into cooking and consumption.

Ceramics have been sampled at West Cotton/Raunds, Northamptonshire (Evershed *et al.* 1991; Charters *et al.* 1993; Evershed *et al.* 1994; Charters *et al.* 1997) and show evidence for epicuticular leaf waxes identifiable to the brassica family (cauliflower, Brussels sprouts, kale, broccoli, and cabbage). The presence and patterning of this residue within the pots indicates that the pots were used for boiling brassicas. In addition to providing dietary information, this represents evidence for a type of cooking method that could have been applied to other foods.

The types of fats and their distribution within pots of different shapes and sizes from West Cotton/Raunds showed that form was correlated with function: large shallow dishes had high densities of animal fats on their bases, suggesting they were placed under roasting meats to collect the dripping fat, whereas taller 'top hat' jars had the distinctive leaf waxes derived from cabbage leaves adsorbed around their rims, with no fat adsorbed on the body of the jars, suggesting that they were vegetable-boiling pots (Charters et al. 1993).

Stable isotope analysis

Most sources (literary and archaeological) cannot give more than a circumstantial view of diet, in particular the availability of specific foods, rather than a general dietary average. Stable isotope analysis of consumer tissues represents the only direct evidence for overall long-term human diet.

Background

Palaeodietary reconstruction using light stable isotopes is based on the principle that 'you are what you eat'—that molecules consumed as food are incorporated into the consumer's body tissues, and therefore that a chemical signal, passed either unchanged or altered in a quantifiable fashion from food into the body, can provide dietary information. The natural variation in the distribution of stable isotopes of carbon and nitrogen throughout different ecosystems makes it possible to use them as natural dietary tracers. When interpreted in relation to the isotopic signatures of available food sources, the combination of carbon and nitrogen isotope ratios[1] of archaeological bone, usually of the protein collagen, provides an objective and direct measure of the diet of an individual over a long time period (years) (Ambrose 1993). Due to the way that bone collagen is formed, only a long-term average is indicated, with no possibility of detecting seasonal variation (Hedges et al. 2007).

---

[1] Carbon and nitrogen isotopic values are reported as the ratio of the heavier isotope to the lighter isotope relative to an internationally defined scale, VPDB for carbon, and AIR for nitrogen (Hoefs 1997). Isotopic results are reported as δ values ($\delta^{13}C$ and $\delta^{15}N$) in parts per 1000 or 'permil' (‰) values, where $\delta^{15}N_{AIR} = [(^{15/14}N_{sample}/ ^{15/14}N_{AIR}) - 1] \times 1000$. The more positive the δ value, the more enriched the sample is with the heavier isotope.

An individual's carbon isotope signal can be used to indicate the plant types at the base of their ecosystem, due to isotopic changes during different types of plant photosynthesis (C_3 or C_4). However, in north-west Europe, where C_4 plants (such as millet) are of little importance, carbon isotopic values are most useful in distinguishing the intake of marine versus terrestrial foods, since marine environments are enriched in ^{13}C relative to temperate terrestrial ecosystems. This marine/terrestrial carbon isotopic difference is passed up the food chain, and allows us to distinguish whether humans were eating marine or terrestrial foods.

Nitrogen isotopic values show the 'trophic level effect', whereby at every step in the food chain (plant to herbivore, herbivore to carnivore, etc.) there is an approximate 3–5‰ increase in $δ^{15}N$. Measurement of $δ^{15}N$ thereby allows an assessment of an individual's position in the terrestrial food chain (herbivore, omnivore, carnivore), which for humans can be used as an indication of the relative importance of plant or animal protein in the diet. The type of animal protein, however, cannot be distinguished, i.e. the difference between meat and secondary products such as milk, cheese, or eggs, nor its quality (Katzenberg and Krouse 1989; Privat *et al.* 2005). Nitrogen isotopic values can also distinguish marine/freshwater versus terrestrial food intake, since aquatic food chains have many more 'steps' in them than terrestrial ones, resulting in marine/freshwater foods having much higher nitrogen isotopic values.

Stable isotope evidence for diet has traditionally been utilized to identify large shifts in diet (Richards 2002). Small isotopic variations are now recognized as significant, resulting from different environmental conditions such as water availability, floristic composition, and soil nitrogen chemistry (Heaton 1999).

As well as answering questions such as what past peoples ate, and how subsistence changed through time, isotopic analyses can help to investigate differences within populations, related to age, gender, and status.

Anglo-Saxon isotopic analysis

Unlike many culture groups, a large and well-documented data set of stable isotope evidence is now available for early Anglo-Saxons. The analysis of 650 humans, representing more than twenty-two sites across southern England, presents archaeology with a rare opportunity to look at diet within a culture group across space during a single period. Comparison of Anglo-Saxon diet with earlier and later archaeological groups in Britain permits an exploration of cultural and chronological trends in the use of resources. Contrasts with continental sites can indicate if a relationship existed between the dietary practice in England and other contemporary populations.

Despite the large extant archaeological human stable isotope data-set, we are only able to consider the inhumation part of the population. Cremations cannot be included as they contain no bone collagen for stable isotope analysis. The duality of

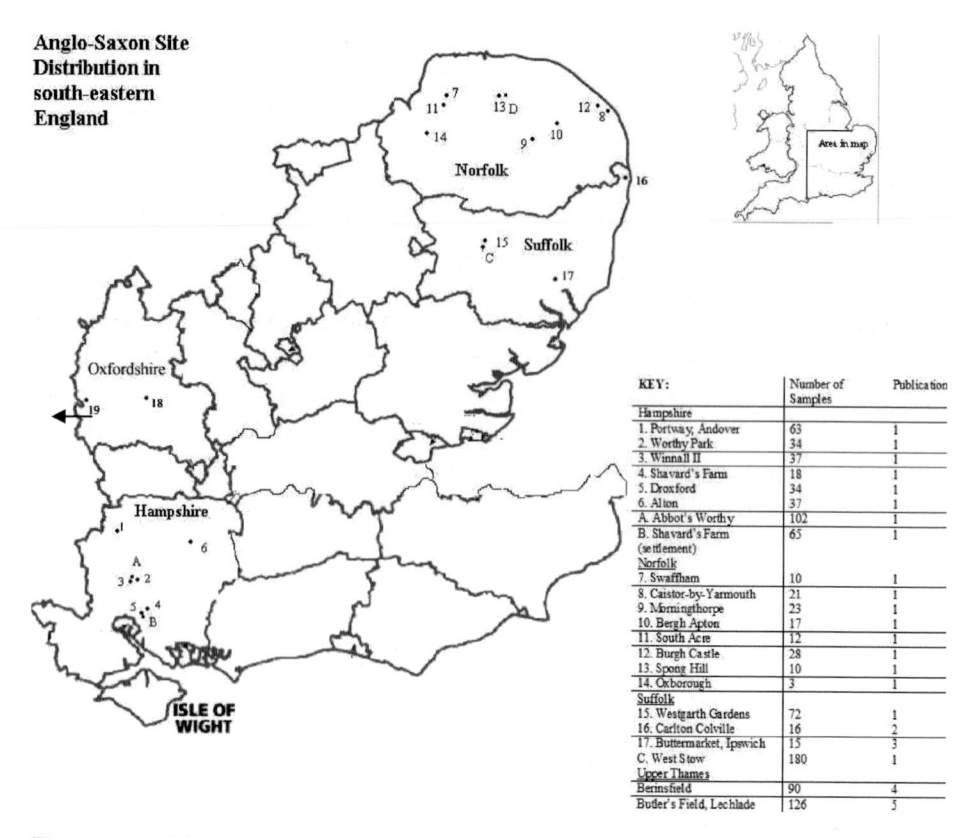

Figure 34.1 Map indicating the available stable isotope evidence for Anglo-Saxons (data taken from Hull 2008; O'Connell and Lawler 2008; Scull and Bayliss 1999; Privat et al. 2002; O'Connell and Wilson 2008)

burial methods, and our inability to analyse all burials, represent a source of bias which must be acknowledged. Based on isotopic analyses, we may never know if individuals buried in inhumations and cremations followed different daily life practices.

Here, we examine isotopic evidence for Anglo-Saxon diet at a large scale, and then explore isotopic variation in conjunction with other factors. Three themes of variation—social, geographic, and chronological—will be highlighted.

Overall results

Overall, the Anglo-Saxon stable isotope results indicate a mainly terrestrial diet, with medium to high amounts of animal protein intake depending on period/cemetery. We have almost 500 animal results from this period, including a large number of cattle, sheep, and pigs (the most common preserved food material at Anglo-Saxon settlements), as well as horse, chickens, fowl, and geese, and wild animals such as hare and deer. A comparison of animal and human stable isotope values suggests that cattle, sheep, and pig were being exploited for food, but that domestic birds such as chickens and geese also played a significant role in the protein intake. Fish is also a possible food resource later in the period.

Considering the larger species, cattle and sheep appear, on the evidence provided by bone ratios, to be the main source of animal protein, with pigs consumed in smaller quantities than other domestic species.[2] However, based on the isotopes, we cannot rule out a substantial input of pig into the diet. Cattle are generally acknowledged as an important source of protein for some Anglo-Saxons (Hagen 1992), and cattle and sheep remains, like the pigs, show evidence for processing and consumption. In previous discussions of Anglo-Saxon diet (Hagen 1992; 1995; Banham 2004) the importance of pigs as a dietary source for protein was shown as likely to vary, and isotopic results indicate that pigs were not the major animal resource. This is in line with the faunal evidence that pig remains are the least common among the three big domesticates as located in the archaeological record at many Anglo-Saxon sites (Crabtree 1990; 1991; Fasham and Whinney 1991; Hamerow 1993). Relatively low numbers of recovered pig remains were found at some of the sampled sites (Abbot's Worthy, Shavard's Farm, West Stow, and Spong Hill). The isotopic data show that the degree of omnivory among the analysed pigs was not high (as seen by similar $\delta^{15}N$ to sheep/cattle), consistent with pigs being raised in free-ranging environs (pannage, etc.) (Privat et al. 2007; Hull 2008). However, this isotopic similarity to sheep and cattle makes it difficult to identify them as a specific protein resource.

Whilst there is not much evidence for fish consumption at any of these sites (few bones have been recovered and none as yet have been successfully isotopically analysed), the extremely high nitrogen isotopic values of some of the human samples suggest that fish needs to be considered. Consumption of either freshwater or marine fish would elevate nitrogen isotopic values (Privat et al. 2007).

Our ability to identify which plants were most heavily utilized is limited, since plants do not leave a special isotopic marker for identification. Whilst we know from literary sources and archaeobotanical evidence that plant foods were consumed, the high nitrogen isotopic values in human collagen indicates that plants did not provide a high proportion of dietary protein.

Individual human nitrogen isotopic values range from 6‰ to 14‰, which equates to a large variation in individual dietary habits, most probably as a result of differing quantities of animal protein intake. The main theme from the animal evidence is one of variation (see Fig. 34.2): single species at a site could vary by as much as 4‰ in $\delta^{15}N$ and 2.5‰ in $\delta^{13}C$. The large isotopic range of Anglo-Saxon animal food resources is likely to have played a role in the human variation we observe.

---

[2] Human–animal offsets: for sheep and cattle, $\Delta^{15}N$ of ∼4‰, $\Delta^{13}C$ of ∼1.2‰; for pigs, $\Delta^{15}N$ of ∼3‰, $\Delta^{13}C$ of ∼1.0‰ (Hedges and Reynard 2007).

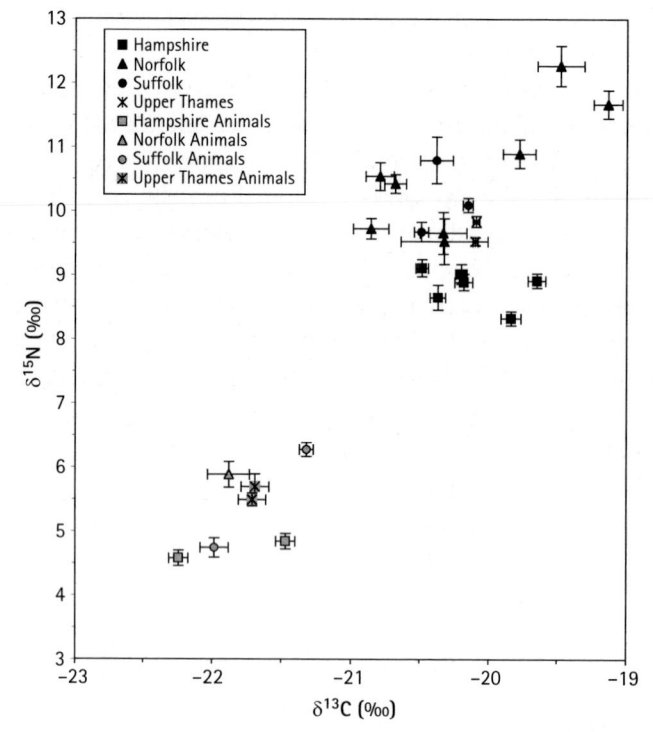

Figure 34.2 Average animal and human isotope values for the sampled sites: the sites are grouped/displayed by region

Social differences in diet

Social control of diet represents a regular mechanism for placing individuals into their cultural position actively/repetitively. We can consider gender, age, status, height, grave orientation, and burial position as physical characteristics or expressions of social organization which may be represented in diet.

Gender

Dietary differences between males and females represent social differences and can be tested through stable isotope analysis. Our ability to discuss sex difference and stable isotopes is limited by issues of preservation, since at several cemeteries in East Anglia, insufficient quantities of bone survive for an osteological sex determination (such as Ipswich: Scull and Bayliss 1999a). However, gender-based comparisons of isotopic values have been possible at fifteen sites. No isotopic difference between males and females was found at Berinsfield and Lechlade, Oxfordshire; at Carlton Colville, Suffolk; at Alton, Droxford, Portway, and Worthy Park in Hampshire; or at Bergh Apton, Burgh Castle, and South Acre in Norfolk (Privat *et al.* 2002;

Hull 2008; O'Connell and Lawler 2009). Several sites did register a sex-based diet difference. Males from Caistor-by-Yarmouth, Swaffham, and Morningthorpe in Norfolk, as well as Winnall II in Hampshire, have higher nitrogen isotopic values than females (Hull 2008). These sites partially confirm a sex-based difference for some Saxon communities. However, Shavard's Farm, Hampshire, and Westgarth Gardens, Suffolk, indicated that women had higher $\delta^{15}N$ than men.

When all of the isotope results are compared by region, we see that, generally, males have higher nitrogen isotopic values than females in Hampshire, while in Suffolk the opposite situation occurs. In Norfolk and Oxfordshire, both sexes present near identical ranges when viewed at a regional scale. So, based on isotopic indication of diet, we conclude that there is no consistent social differentiation of diet between the sexes across the majority of Saxon society. In all populations, there was a range of isotopic values within the two sexes, particularly in $\delta^{15}N$ (a proxy for animal protein consumption), which may reflect archaeologically invisible social divisions.

Wealth

Social control of diet between those of higher wealth than others can also be analysed. The classification of 'wealth' is difficult within Anglo-Saxon studies, particularly with the aim of comparison with stable isotope evidence. Many different patterns have been suggested for organizing grave material in a meaningful way (Shepard 1979; Welch 1989; Pader 1980; 1982; Härke 1989; 1990; Lucy 1998; Stoodley 1999; King 2004). The simplest seems to be the presence/absence of grave weapons, and assigning a wealth 'score' based on the presence and quantity of gendered and non-gendered grave goods.

When considering grave weapons, we find that males buried with weapons had significantly higher $\delta^{15}N$ than those buried without at three cemeteries in Hampshire and one in Norfolk: Portway, Shavard's Farm, Winnall II, and Swaffham. Yet at seven cemeteries (Alton, Droxford, Worthy Park in Hampshire; Bergh Apton, Morningthorpe in Norfolk; Westgarth Gardens in Suffolk; and Berinsfield in Oxfordshire), males buried without weapons had higher $\delta^{15}N$ than male warrior inhumations (Privat et al. 2002; Hull 2008). This indicates a long-term dietary difference between members of the same populations, but that it is not consistent across all sites.

We can also assess wealth/diet variation based on the presence and quantity of gendered and non-gendered grave goods (Privat et al. 2002; Hull 2008; O'Connell and Wilson 2008). As with the weapon/non-weapon dichotomy, the results of the analysis varied from site to site. Results from the site of Berinsfield indicate a clear dietary difference between those individuals identified as 'wealthy' and 'poor' based on burial goods (Privat et al. 2002: 786), with similar results of higher nitrogen isotopic values of grave-good-poor inhumations compared to wealthy being identified at Alton and Portway, Hampshire; Bergh Apton, Norfolk; and Westgarth Gardens, Suffolk (Hull 2008). This pattern is not universal, as at Bergh

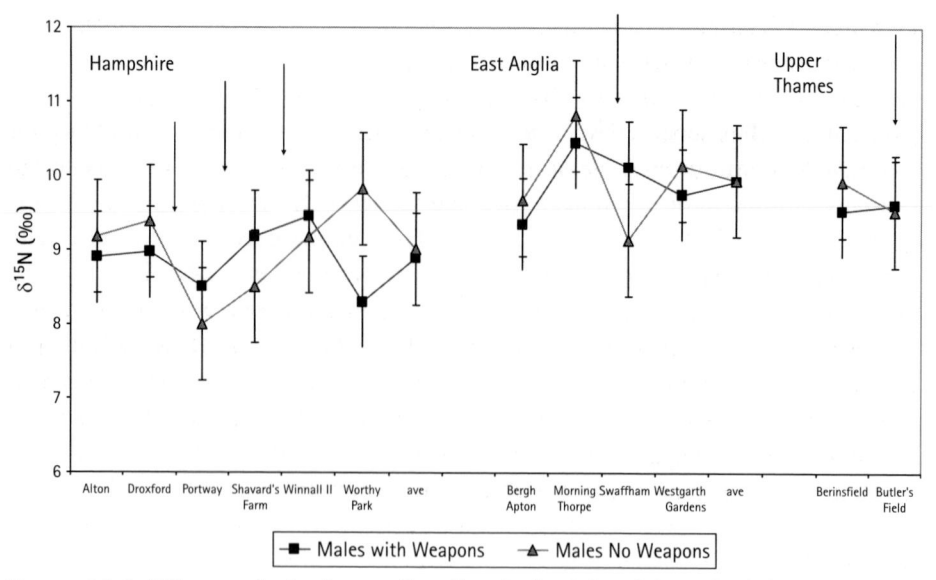

Figure 34.3 Nitrogen isotopic results of male burials with and without weapons from Hampshire; East Anglia; Berinsfield, Oxon.; and Butler's Field, Glos. (*Sources*: Hull 2008; Privat *et al*. 2002; O'Connell and Wilson 2008)

Castle, Norfolk, and Worthy Park, Hampshire, we see the reverse, with wealthy burials having higher nitrogen isotopic values. No rich/poor dichotomy was found at Caistor-by-Yarmouth, Norfolk; Carlton Colville, Suffolk; or at Droxford and Winnall II in Hampshire (Hull 2008; O'Connell and Lawler 2009). At Morningthorpe, Norfolk, wealthy and poor burials were isotopically similar, but the middle ranking graves had much higher nitrogen isotopic values. The opposite case is seen at Shavard's Farm, Hampshire, where middle ranking burials are more depleted in $\delta^{15}N$ compared to wealthy and poor (Hull 2008).

Umberto Albarella's discussion of animal consumption draws a distinction between the type and quantity of animals (particularly pig) consumed at sites of different social levels (2006). From the faunal analyses, he concludes that beef and pork were common table items in the homes of wealthy groups, while poorer Anglo-Saxons had a diet that was predominantly vegetarian, with limited access to pork only (Albarella 2006: 73). From a stable isotope perspective, we should therefore see that wealthy individuals, eating more animal protein, have higher nitrogen isotopic values than the vegetarian poor. We see this at only two sites (Bergh Castle and Worthy Park), but the reverse isotopic pattern is more commonly observed. So, whilst increased animal protein consumption is a simple explanation for higher nitrogen isotopic values in the wealthy relative to the poor, it is less easy to explain the reverse. Higher $\delta^{15}N$ among poor individuals at Berinsfield was attributed to increased utilization of freshwater resources (fish), or consumption of pig (*pace* Albarella 2006), but with an omnivorous diet (Privat *et al.* 2002: 786). This argument for pig consumption by the poor is now difficult to accept, since first, Anglo-Saxon pigs were not very omnivorous (see above), and second, the poor represented a large percentage of the living population, and there are not enough pig bones in the archaeological record for them to be consuming pigs in any quantity.

So if not pig, was fish the dominant protein source for some poor Anglo-Saxons? Fish remains are extremely rare on early Saxon sites (Barrett *et al.* 2004), which suggests that fish were not being consumed in any real quantity, or were not preserved archaeologically, or have not been recovered by excavators. Increased use of sieving in recent excavations has recovered low but significant numbers of fish bones, which suggests that fish remains are present, and may have been underestimated in the past. However, poor preservation remains a problem.

Two other potential explanations for high nitrogen isotopic values among poor individuals deal with protein intake from other sources. Recently, the impact of manuring cereal crops as a mechanism for increasing soil/plant nitrogen isotopic values has been presented (Bogaard *et al.* 2007). If Anglo-Saxon peasant farmers were actively manuring their arable fields in order to increase crop yields, they were inadvertently increasing the $\delta^{15}N$ values of the soil, and thus increasing the values of the cereals grown and of those who ate the cereals. If poor individuals had a vegetarian-based diet, as suggested by Albarella (2006), then higher nitrogen isotopic values could be attributed, at least in part, to the application of manure to their fields. Difficulties with accepting such an explanation for observed high human nitrogen isotopic values lie in the source of the manure. Manure from a large number of animals is required to raise soil nitrogen isotopic values sufficiently to increase plant isotope values. If Anglo-Saxon farmers had sufficient quantities of manure to cause this isotopic effect, it is hard to believe that they would not also have consumed a significant amount of animal protein, either as meat or as secondary products.

The second possible explanation for elevated $\delta^{15}N$ among the poor comes from a little discussed protein resource—domestic birds (chickens, geese, fowl). Chickens and geese from Abbot's Worthy, Hampshire, domestic fowl and geese at West Stow, Suffolk, and chicken from Carlton Colville, have elevated $\delta^{15}N$ compared to other domestic species (O'Connell and Lawler 2009; Hull 2008). The eggs from these birds also represent potential food resources with high nitrogen isotopic values (although yet to be tested archaeologically). If poorer elements in Anglo-Saxon society maintained household animals such as chickens, which feed cheaply on house/kitchen scraps and browse naturally, as their main protein source, they would have higher $\delta^{15}N$ than the wealthy, whose main protein input came from cattle and pigs with lower nitrogen isotopic distributions.

Age

Isotopic variation is also evident between adults and children. For those infants aged 0–4 years, a difference in nitrogen isotopic values is expected, as a result of the breast-feeding signal. When infants are being suckled, they are effectively 'eating' their mother, and as such are one step higher in the food chain, which results in elevated nitrogen isotopic values (Fogel et al. 1989; Katzenberg and Pfeiffer 1995; Fuller et al. 2005; 2006). Nitrogen isotopic values in breastfeeding infants were consistently 2–3‰ higher than the adult population, at the four sites where appropriate infant identifications were possible: Shavard's Farm, Worthy Park, Westgarth Gardens, and Portway (Hull 2008). By 3 years of age, nitrogen isotopic values had declined by 2–3‰, indicating complete cessation of the breast-feeding signal. Many youths/juveniles had lower nitrogen and carbon isotopic values than adults.

Other sources of variation

None of the other traits that could be compared to isotopic data showed consistent distinctions (i.e. height, body position, grave orientation). The non-conformity to a cultural pattern, at least in reference to diet, highlights the actual variability of practice of individuals in an apparently homogeneous culture. While not all variants showed consistent patterning, a few examples proved to be informative. Burial position was categorized by the orientation and layout of the burial. There was no simple pattern evident in the isotopic values of extended, supine individuals. However, all individuals who had been buried in a crouched or flexed position on their right side (twenty-two cases) had almost identical $\delta^{13}C$ values (−20.5‰), and similar $\delta^{15}N$ ranges, irrespective of geographic location, and had a different distribution to the rest of the local inhumed population (Hull 2008). It has been suggested that burial in a crouched position may represent a surviving 'British', population not completely acculturated to Anglo-Saxon lifeways (Higham 1992). If this interpretation is accurate, then these individuals maintained their cultural difference in relying on other dietary resources.

Unusual burials also proved to be isotopically distinct. Individuals interred in the prone position or decapitated were often isotopically distinct from those buried around them (e.g. Grave 78 at Worthy Park: Hawkes and Wells 1975; Hull 2008). This indicates that their unusual treatment in death reflected differing dietary practice during life. Any explanation as to cause would be speculative.

Geographic variation

By the start of the sixth century AD, when the majority of the sampled burials were still living, Anglo-Saxon 'culture' can be recognized as dominant in East Anglia, Kent, Hampshire, the Upper Thames Valley, and the East Midlands. Since diet represents one of the most regular sources of application of and adherence to that culture, being practised several times a day, we can consider the extent to which diet/consumption was regularized among these different regions.

When the isotope distributions of each region are compared, we find a pattern of both similarity and difference. The $\delta^{13}C$ means are all very similar ($\sim -20.1‰$) as is expected for a population living in a C_3 terrestrial environment (see Fig. 34.2). There are individual values which fall outside the cluster, but not enough to indicate any C_4-based plant material or migrating individuals (the extreme values are -18.4 and $-22.1‰$). The nitrogen isotopic values (reflecting dietary animal protein intake) show more variation between regions, with significant differences in the average $\delta^{15}N$ of each region, although with a higher degree of variability than in carbon (see Table 34.1).

The variation between human nitrogen isotopic values from the sites in Hampshire and East Anglia might at first glance suggest large diet difference, which could be interpreted as representing different cultural practice. However, when the animal isotopic evidence is introduced it becomes apparent that, in place of a cultural difference, we find a shift apparent in nitrogen isotope values of both humans and animals (see Fig. 34.2). This inter-regional variation must be caused by other mechanisms, such as differences in geology, climate/rainfall, and vegetation, as well as cultural choice in human/animal diet between the two regions. This highlights the importance of considering animal isotopic values as a baseline from which to interpret the human values—without animal data, a false conclusion could have been drawn.

The non-uniformity of the isotopic patterns across the regions is mirrored by regional differences in Anglo-Saxon burial patterns, such as the size of the

Table 34.1 Stable isotope results plotted by region (mean) for humans and animals

Region	Human $\delta^{13}C$ ‰ (1σ)	Human $\delta^{15}N$ ‰ (1σ)	Animal $\delta^{13}C$ ‰ (1σ)	Animal $\delta^{15}N$ ‰ (1σ)
Norfolk	−20.2 (0.5)	10.9 (0.9)	−21.9 (0.7)	5.9 (1.1)
Suffolk	−20.2 (0.8)	10.1 (1.3)	−21.3 (0.5)	6.3 (1.5)
Hampshire	−20.1 (1.0)	8.7 (2.7)	−21.9 (0.7)	4.7 (0.7)
Oxfordshire	−20.1 (0.7)	9.8 (1.4)	−21.7 (0.6)	6.0 (1.6)

cemetery, the type of burial, and the position in the landscape. Cremations are the most common burial type in Norfolk. The large cremation cemetery at Spong Hill, for example, contained more than 2,000 cremations and only 58 inhumations (Hills et al. 1984). Further south, the inhumation rite is dominant in Suffolk cemeteries, although cremations do occur. The tradition in Hampshire and the Upper Thames valley is represented by inhumations with some cremations (Higham 1992).

Intra-regional variation in diet may also exist. In Hampshire, a site on one side of the Meon River (Shavard's Farm) is isotopically distinct in $\delta^{13}C$ from sites on the other side of the Meon River, including Droxford, which lies only 2–3 kilometres from Shavard's Farm (Hull 2008). One explanation is that the river is a physical and social 'boundary', where populations living on either side consumed different foods from one another. It has been suggested that juxtaposed cemetery groups with larger numbers of males with weapon burials marked social boundaries between nascent Anglo-Saxon chiefdoms/kingdoms (Härke 1990). Such a cultural boundary may therefore also be a dietary one.

Another useful indicator of the overall consistency of Anglo-Saxon diet lies in the comparison with contemporaneous continental sites (Fig. 34.4). The population of the early medieval settlement of Weingarten in south-western Germany has isotopic

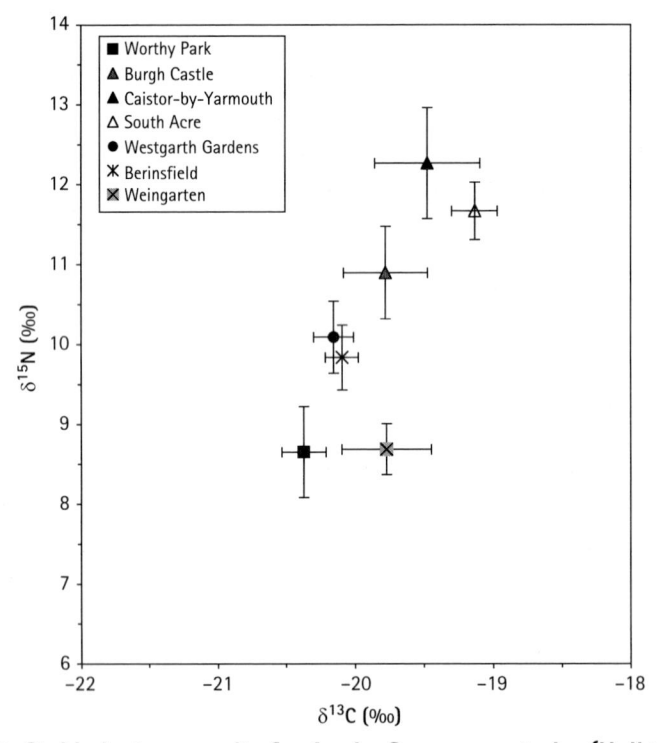

Figure 34.4 Stable isotope results for Anglo-Saxon cemeteries (Hull 2008), and the cemetery at Weingarten, Germany (Schutkowski et al. 1999) showing site averages and ± one standard deviation

values similar to those of Anglo-Saxon inhumations, despite a significant difference in both location and cultural practice (Schutkowski *et al.* 1999). The slight enrichment in German human $\delta^{13}C$ may indicate geographic or environmental differences or dietary differences, but we cannot say more, since no corresponding animal data were analysed for stable isotope evidence from Weingarten. Importantly, this comparison shows that an undisputedly different culture group does not necessarily have a different dietary pattern. So when Anglo-Saxon groups are different to each other, perhaps we need to more fully consider their difference from a 'cultural norm'.

Chronological variation

Dietary variation over time mirrors changes in daily cultural practice, and some changes/similarities can be identified by stable isotope distributions. Some diet shifts may take generations to become common enough to be identified, while others can develop in a matter of decades: as Naomi Sykes noted, 'between the fifth and sixteenth centuries England witnessed considerable economic change which surely changed dietary practices' (2006: 56). We know from the archaeological and contemporary literary records that the seventh to ninth centuries AD were a time of considerable growth/change in Anglo-Saxon society (Higham 1992).

In East Anglia, the isotopic data also suggest that a dietary shift took place between Anglo-Saxons living in the fifth to early seventh centuries AD and those living in the mid Saxon period (seventh to ninth centuries AD). There is an increase in both carbon and nitrogen isotopic values over time, comparing six early period sites (Bergh Apton, Morning Thorpe, Oxborough, Spong Hill, Swaffham, and Westgarth Gardens), and three sites from the middle period (Caistor-by-Yarmouth, Burgh Castle, and South Acre) (Fig. 34.5).

The isotopic enrichment in both nitrogen and carbon suggests that the change is most likely a result of the exploitation of fish as a food source (probably marine, but perhaps also freshwater). A general increase in fish exploitation has been noted at many locations around the North Sea from the ninth century AD, and may—in part—be attributed to the development of a market economy (Barret *et al.* 2004). As the mid Saxon sites presented in Fig. 34.5 represent early monastic communities, their religious observation may have increased the amount of fish in their diet, compared to earlier groups who had none.

Turning to the broader temporal picture, comparisons of Anglo-Saxon and late Roman isotopic values suggest that there is no continuous link between later imperial diets in Britain and those 150–200 years later. While there is some isotopic overlap, particularly in nitrogen, late Romano-British sites have higher carbon

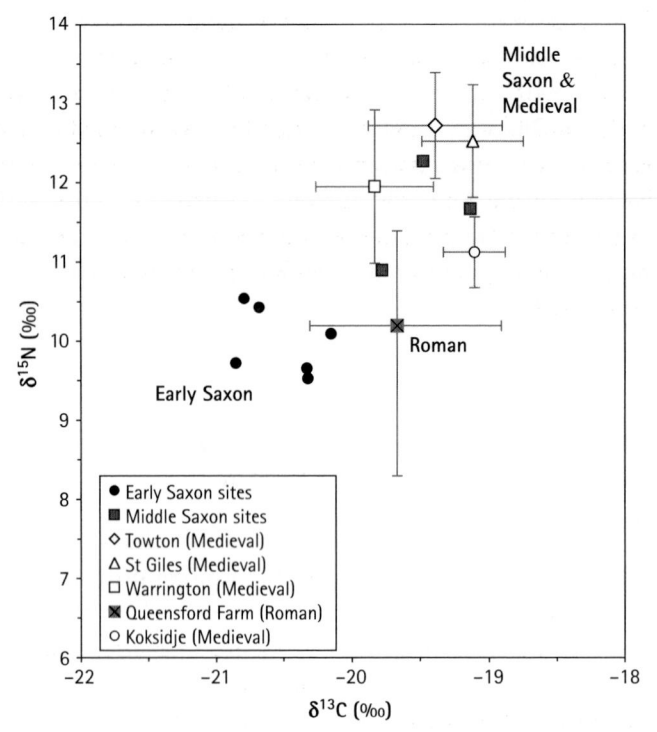

Figure 34.5 Stable isotope results for East Anglia categorized by phase, with comparative data from medieval sites in England and Belgium: Towton, St. Giles, and Warrington from Müldner and Richards (2005: Table 1, 43); Queenford Farm from Fuller et al. (2006: Table 1, 48)

isotope values than early Saxon sites, indicating that more, or different, food commodities may have been available in the Roman period (Richards et al. 1998; Fuller et al. 2006). The late Romano-British site of Poundbury shows strong correlation of carbon isotopic values with burial rite, with richer individuals having higher $\delta^{13}C$ than poorer individuals buried in wooden coffins (Richards et al. 1998). Individuals from the contemporary rural sites of Queenford Farm, Oxfordshire, and Babraham, Cambridgeshire, cluster with the poorer burials from Poundbury (Fuller et al. 2006; Friedman and O'Connell in press), and these are isotopically most similar to Anglo-Saxons, yet still higher in carbon isotopic values.

Looking at later evidence, the medieval sites of Towton, Warrington, and St Giles have similar isotopic distributions to those mid Saxon sites presented in Fig. 34.4 (Müldner and Richards 2005), as do the occupants of an early medieval monastery at Koksijde, Belgium (Polet and Katzenberg 2003). Müldner and Richards argue for a dietary shift during the medieval period, based on a nitrogen isotopic shift from 9‰ to 14‰ between Wharram Percy and later sites (Mays 1997; Müldner and Richards 2005; 2006). Based on the aforementioned dietary shift at the nine sites across the early/mid Saxon transition, together with the mid Saxon/medieval isotopic similarity, it seems more likely that a dietary tradition beginning in the mid Saxon phase (*c.* AD 750) is still common in the medieval period (*c.* AD 1200). We suggest that the overall picture is one of increasing marine resource usage beginning in the mid Saxon phase and extending to the medieval period, with marine resources playing a regular, but not dominant, role in a terrestrial-based diet, potentially in continental Europe as well as Britain. But more work is required on mid Saxon secular sites, to explore whether the increasing marine usage is common amongst the population as a whole, and not limited to monastic communities, as discussed earlier.

Discussion

Biochemical studies of diet are relevant to the rest of Anglo-Saxon archaeology because those people living in the sixth and seventh centuries did not acquire a knife, bury a loved one, or even go to war every day, but they did eat every day. Ritual, or the repetition of an act, is a mechanism by which we confirm our position in the society in which we live.

The presented picture of Anglo-Saxon diet and its relationship to culture is one of complexity. We have seen that diet—and also culture—was not practised identically at each site. Instead of a consistent pattern of diet amongst a 'culture' group identified by material remains, we find a mosaic of patterns representative of each individual group. Those patterns varied over time periods as influences changed.

While this chapter represents only a brief review of the available evidence for diet from biochemical analysis, it has highlighted the importance of multiple sites. One site is not sufficient to gain reasonable understanding of how diet functions in a culture group, much as a material seriation from one site is unacceptable. When more sites are compared, we find that each followed its own pattern. Regional variation, akin to material cultural variation, can also be drawn out more clearly through the analysis of further cemeteries.

How can we relate biochemical studies of diet to other 'scientific' studies of Anglo-Saxon populations? Recently, Capelli *et al.* (2003), Thomas *et al.* (2006), and Weale *et al.* (2002) have all examined modern population for genetic markers as proxy for the discussion of migration of Angles, Saxons, and Jutes from the continent into Britain. Stable isotopes have only a minor role to play in these types of studies, and then only after considerably more diet-based work is undertaken both in England and across areas of north Europe. Other isotopic analyses, such as those of strontium and oxygen isotopes, more appropriate to the identification of migrating populations, would need to be applied to appropriately early Anglo-Saxon cemeteries in the hopes of sampling that primary migrant group or groups (see Hedges, this volume; Budd *et al.* 2004 for discussion of this topic).

Future directions for stable isotope analysis of Anglo-Saxon material lie along two paths: first, testing the diet from the supposed Anglo-Saxon 'homelands' on the continent to discuss migration and diet, and whether a diaspora of thousands ever occurred; second, it will also be important to continue to add to the database of Anglo-Saxon cemeteries and settlements to increase our understanding of how diet functioned in those societies.

References

Albarella, U. (2006). 'Pig husbandry and pork consumption in Medieval England', in C. M. Woolgar, D. Serjeantson, and T. Waldron (eds.), *Food in Medieval England: Diet and Nutrition*. Oxford: Oxford University Press, 72–87.

Allen, T. (2004). 'Swine, salt and seafood: a case study of Anglo-Saxon and early medieval settlement in north-east Kent'. *Archaeologia Cantiana* 124: 117–34.

Ambrose, S. H. (1993). 'Isotopic analysis of palaeodiets: methodological and interpretive considerations', in M. K. Sandford (ed.), *Investigations of Ancient Human Tissue*. Langhorne, PA: Gordon and Breach Science Publishers, 59–130.

Arnold, C. J. (1988). *An Archaeology of the Early Anglo-Saxon Kingdoms*. London: Routledge.

Attenborough, F. L. (trans. and ed.) (1922). *The Laws of the Earliest English Kings*. Cambridge: Cambridge University Press.

Banham, D. (2004). *Food and Drink in Anglo-Saxon England*. Stroud: Tempus.

Barret, J. H., Locker, A. M., and Roberts, C. M. (2004). '"Dark Age economics" revisited: the English fish bone evidence AD 600–1600'. *Antiquity* 78(301): 618–36.

Bogaard, A., Heaton, T. H. E., Poulton, P., and Merbach, I. (2007). 'The impact of manuring on nitrogen isotope ratios in cereals: archaeological implications for reconstruction of diet and crop management practices'. *Journal of Archaeological Science* 34: 335–43.

Budd, P., Millard, A., Chenery, C., Lucy, S. J., and Roberts, C. (2004). 'Investigating population movement by stable isotope analysis: a report from Britain'. *Antiquity* 78: 127–41.

Capelli, C., Redhead, N., Abernethy, J. K., and Gratix, F. (2003). 'A Y chromosome census of the British Isles'. *Current Biology* 13 (May 27): 979–84.

Carruthers, W. J. (1991). 'The mineralised plant remains', in P. J. Fasham and R. J. B. Whinney (eds.), *Archaeology and the M3: The Watching Brief, the Anglo-Saxon Settlement at Abbots Worthy and Retrospective Sections*. Stroud: Hampshire Field Club/Trust for Wessex Archaeology, 67–75.

Charters, S., Evershed, R. P., Goad, L. J., Leyden, A., Blinkhorn, P. W., and Denham, V. (1993). 'Quantification and distribution of lipid in archaeological ceramics: implications for sampling potsherds for organic residue analysis'. *Archaeometry* 35: 211–23.

—————— Quye, A., Blinkhorn, P. W., and Reeves, V. (1997). 'Simulation experiments for determining the use of ancient pottery vessels: the behaviour of epicuticular leaf wax during boiling of a leafy vegetable'. *Journal of Archaeological Science* 24: 1–7.

CRABTREE, P. J. (1990). *West Stow, Suffolk: Early Anglo-Saxon Animal Husbandry.* Ipswich: Suffolk County Planning Department.

—— (1991). 'Roman Britain to Anglo-Saxon England: the zooarchaeological evidence', in P. J. Crabtree and K. Ryan (eds.), *Animal Use and Culture Change.* MASCA Research Papers in Science and Archaeology 8. Philadelphia: University of Pennsylvania, 32–9.

EVERSHED, R. P., HERON, C., and GOAD, L. J. (1991). 'Epicuticular wax components preserved in potsherds as chemical indicators of leafy vegetables in ancient diets'. *Antiquity* 65: 540–4.

—— ARNOT, K. I., COLLISTER, J., EGLINTON, G., and CHARTERS, S. (1994). 'Application of isotope ratio monitoring gas chromatography-mass spectrometry to the analysis of organic residues of archaeological origin'. *Analyst* 119(5): 909–14.

—— DUDD, S. N., CHARTERS, S., MOTTRAM, H., STOTT, A. W., RAVEN, A., VAN BERGEN, P. F., and BLAND, H. A. (1999). 'Lipids as carriers of anthropogenic signals from prehistory'. *Philosophical Transactions of the Royal Society, London,* Series B 354: 19–31.

FASHAM, P. J., and WHINNEY, R. J. B. (1991). *Archaeology and the M3: The Watching Brief, the Anglo-Saxon Settlement at Abbots Worthy and Retrospective Sections.* Stroud: Hampshire Field Club/Trust for Wessex Archaeology.

FOGEL, M. L., TUROSS, N., and OWSLEY, D. (1989). *Nitrogen Isotope Tracers of Human Lactation in Modern and Archaeological Populations.* Annual Report of the Director, Geophysical Laboratory 1988–89. Washington, DC: Carnegie Institution of Washington.

FRIEDMAN, L. G. and O'CONNELL, T. C. (in press). 'The isotopic data', in S. Timberlake (with N. Armour, N. Dodwell, and K. Anderson), *A Romano-British Cemetery and its Associated Settlement at Babraham Research Campus, Cambridgeshire.* East Anglian Archaeology. Oxford: Oxbow Books.

FULLER, B. T., FULLER, J. L., SAGE, N. E., HARRIS, D. A., O'CONNELL, T. C., and HEDGES, R. E. M. (2005). 'Nitrogen balance and d15N: why you're not what you eat during nutritional stress'. *Rapid Communications in Mass Spectrometry* 19: 2497–2506.

—— MOLLESON, T. L., HARRIS, D. A., GILMOUR, L. T., and HEDGES, R. E. M. (2006). 'Isotopic evidence for breastfeeding and possible adult dietary differences from late/sub-Roman Britain'. *American Journal of Physical Anthropology* 129: 45–54.

GREEN, F. J. (1981). 'Iron Age, Roman and Saxon crops: the archaeological evidence from Wessex', in M. Jones and G. Dimbleby (eds.), *The Environment of Man: the Iron Age to the Anglo-Saxon Period.* BAR British Series 87. Oxford: British Archaeological Reports, 129–53.

HAGEN, A. (1992). *A Handbook of Anglo-Saxon Food: Processing and Consumption.* Norfolk: Anglo-Saxon Books Ltd.

—— (1995). *A Second Handbook of Anglo-Saxon Food and Drink: Production and Distribution.* Norfolk: Anglo-Saxon Books Ltd.

HAMEROW, H. (1993). *Mucking: The Anglo-Saxon Settlement.* London: English Heritage.

HÄRKE, H. (1989). 'Early Saxon weapon burials: frequencies, distributions, and weapon combinations', in S. C. Hawkes (ed.), *Weapons and Warfare in Anglo-Saxon England.* Monograph No. 21. Oxford: Oxford University Committee for Archaeology, 49–62.

—— (1990). '"Warrior graves"? The background of the Anglo-Saxon weapon burial rite'. *Past and Present* 126 (Feb.): 22–43.

HASLAM, J., BIEK, L., and TYLECOTE, R. F. (1980). 'A Middle Saxon iron smelting site at Ramsbury, Wiltshire'. *Medieval Archaeology* 24: 1–68.

HAWKES, S. C., and WELLS, C. (1975). 'Crime and punishment in an Anglo-Saxon cemetery'. *Antiquity* 49: 118–22.

HEATON, T. H. E. (1999). 'Spatial, species, and temporal variations in the 13C/12C Ratios of C3 plants: implications for palaeodiet studies'. *Journal of Archaeological Science* 26: 637–49.

HEDGES, R. E. M., and REYNARD, L. M. (2007). 'Nitrogen isotopes and the trophic level of humans in archaeology'. *Journal of Archaeological Science* 34: 1240–51.

—— CLEMENT, J. G., THOMAS, C. D. L., and O'CONNELL, T. C. (2007). 'Collagen turnover in the adult femoral mid-shaft: modeled from anthropogenic radiocarbon tracer measurements'. *American Journal of Physical Anthropology* 133: 808–16.

HIGHAM, N. (1992). *Rome, Britain and the Anglo-Saxons.* London: Seaby.

HILLS, C., PENN, K., and RICKETT, R. (1984). *The Anglo-Saxon Cemetery at Spong Hill, North Elmham,* Part III: *Catalogue of Inhumations.* Norfolk: Norfolk Museum Service.

HOEFS, J. (1997). *Stable Isotope Geochemistry.* Berlin: Springer.

HULL, B. (2008). *Diet and Social Differentiation in Early Anglo-Saxon England: Stable Isotope Analysis of Archaeological Human and Animal Remains.* Unpublished DPhil, University of Oxford.

KATZENBERG, M. A. and PFEIFFER, S., (1995), 'Nitrogen isotope evidence for weaning age in a nineteenth century Canadian skeletal sample', in A. L. Grauer (ed.), *Bodies of Evidence: Reconstructing History through Skeletal Analysis.* New York: Wiley-Liss, 221–35.

—— and KROUSE, H. R. (1989). 'Application of stable isotope variation in human tissue to problems in identification'. *Canadian Society of Forensic Science Journal* 22: 7–19.

KING, J. M. (2004). 'Grave goods as gifts in Early Saxon burials (ca. AD 450–600)'. *Journal of Social Archaeology* 4(2): 214–38.

LUCY, S. (1998). *The Early Anglo-Saxon Cemeteries of East Yorkshire: An Analysis and Reinterpretation.* BAR British Series 272. Oxford: British Archaeological Reports.

MAYS, S. A. (1997). 'Carbon stable isotope ratios in mediaeval and later human skeletons from northern England'. *Journal of Archaeological Science* 24: 561–7.

McCOBB, L. M. E.. and BRIGGS, D. E. G. (2001). 'Preservation of fossil seeds from a 10th Century AD cess pit at Coppergate, York'. *Journal of Archaeological Science* 28: 929–40.

MÜLDNER, G., and RICHARDS, M. P. (2005). 'Fast or feast: reconstructing diet in later medieval England by stable isotope analysis'. *Journal of Archaeological Science* 32: 39–48.

—— —— (2006). 'Diet in medieval England: the evidence from stable isotopes', in C. M. Woolgar, D. Serjeantson, and T. Waldron (eds.), *Food in Medieval England: Diet and Nutrition.* Oxford: Oxford University Press, 228–38.

O'CONNELL, T. C., and LAWLER, A. (2009). 'Stable isotope analysis of human and faunal remains', in S. Lucy, J. Tipper, and A. Dickens (eds.), *The Anglo-Saxon Settlement and Cemetery at Bloodmoor Hill, Carlton Colville, Suffolk.* East Anglian Archaeology 131. Cambridge: Cambridge Archaeological Unit, 317–21.

—— and WILSON, E. J. (2008). 'Stable isotope analysis of human remains from the Anglo-Saxon cemetery at Butler's Field, Lechlade, Gloucestershire: dietary and social implications', in A. Boyle, D. Jennings, D. Miles, and S. Palmer (eds.), *The Anglo-Saxon Cemetery at Butler's Field, Lechlade, Gloucestershire,* Volume 2. Thames Valley Landscapes Monograph 10. Oxford: Oxford Archaeological Unit.

PADER, E.-J. (1980). 'Material symbolism and social relations in mortuary studies', in P. Rahtz, T. Dickinson, and L. Watts (eds.), *Anglo-Saxon Cemeteries 1979: The Fourth Anglo-Saxon Symposium at Oxford.* BAR British Series 82. Oxford: British Archaeological Reports, 143–59.

—— (1982). *Symbolism, Social Relations and the Interpretation of Mortuary Remains.* BAR International Series 130. Oxford: British Archaeological Reports.

POLET, C., and KATZENBERG, M. A. (2003). 'Reconstruction of the diet in a mediaeval monastic community from the coast of Belgium'. *Journal of Archaeological Science* 30: 525–33.

PRIVAT, K. L., O'CONNELL, T. C., and RICHARDS, M. P. (2002). 'Stable isotope analysis of human and faunal remains from the Anglo-Saxon cemetery at Berinsfield, Oxfordshire: dietary and social implications'. *Journal of Archaeological Science* 29: 779–90.

—————— NEAL, K., and HEDGES, R. E. M. (2005). 'Fermented dairy product analysis and palaeodietary repercussions: is stable isotope analysis not cheesy enough?', in J. Mulville and A. Outram (eds.), *The Archaeology of Animal Fats, Oils and Dairying*. Oxford: Oxbow Books, 60–6.

—————— and HEDGES, R. E. M. (2007). 'The distinction between freshwater- and terrestrial-based diets: methodological concerns and archaeological applications of sulphur stable isotope analysis'. *Journal of Archaeological Science* 34: 1197–1204.

RICHARDS, M. P. (2002). 'Human consumption of plant foods in the British Neolithic: Direct evidence from bone stable isotopes', in A. S. Fairbairn (ed.), *Plants in Neolithic Britain and Beyond*. Neolithic Studies Group Seminar Paper 5. Oxford: Oxbow Books, 123–35.

——HEDGES, R. E. M., MOLLESON, T. I., and VOGEL, J. C. (1998). 'Stable isotope analysis reveals variations in human diet at the Poundbury Camp cemetery site'. *Journal of Archaeological Science* 25: 1247–52.

SCHUTKOWSKI, H., HERRMANN, B., WIEDEMANN, F., BOCHERONS, H., and GRUPE, G. (1999). 'Diet, status and decomposition at Weingarten: trace element and isotope analysis on early medieval skeletal material'. *Journal of Archaeological Science* 26: 675–85.

SCULL, C., and BAYLIS, A. (1999a). 'Dating burials of the seventh and eighth centuries: a case study from Ipswich', in J. Hines, K. H. Nielsen, and F. Siegmund (eds.), *The Pace of Change: Studies in Early-Medieval Chronology*. Oxford: Oxbow Books, 80–8.

—————— (1999b). 'Radiocarbon dating and Saxon graves', in U. von Freeden, U. Koch, and A. Wieczorek (eds). *Völker an Nord- und Ostee und die Franken*. Bonn: Dr. Rudopl Habelt GmbH, 39-50.

SHEPARD, J. F. (1979). 'The social identity of the individual in isolated barrows and barrow cemeteries in Anglo-Saxon England', in B. C. Burnham and J. Kingsbury (eds.), *Space, Hierarchy and Society: Interdisciplinary Studies in Social Area Analysis*. BAR International Series 59. Oxford: British Archaeology Reports, 90–105.

STOODLEY, N. (1999). *The Spindle and the Spear: A Critical Enquiry into the Construction and Meaning of Gender in the Early Anglo-Saxon Burial Rite*. BAR British Series 288. Oxford: British Archaeological Reports.

SYKES, N. (2006). 'From *cu* and *sceap* to *beffe* and *motton*: the management, distribution and consumption of cattle and sheep AD 410–1550', in C. Woolgar, D. Serjeantson, and T. Waldron (eds.), *Food in Medieval England: Diet and Nutrition*. Oxford, Oxford University Press, pp. 56–71.

THOMAS, M. G., STUMP, M. P. H., and HÄRKE, H. (2006). 'Evidence for an apartheid-like social structure in early Anglo-Saxon England'. *Proceedings of the Royal Society B* 273: 2651–7.

WEALE, M. E., WEISS, D. A., JAGER, R. F., and THOMAS, M. G. (2002). 'Y chromosome evidence for Anglo-Saxon mass migration'. *Molecule, Biology and Evolution* 19(7): 1008–21.

WELCH, M. (1989). 'The kingdom of the South Saxons: the origins', in S. Bassett (ed.), *The Origins of the Anglo-Saxon Kingdoms*. Norwich: Anglo-Saxon Books, 75–83.

CHAPTER 35

GENDER AND GENDER ROLES

SAM LUCY

INTRODUCTION

Late in 2006, the Cambridge Archaeological Unit excavated a small later-seventh-century cemetery on the outskirts of Ely in Cambridgeshire. At the centre of the cemetery lay an elaborately furnished grave, probably under a barrow (no longer visible): grave goods included two complete blue glass palm cups; a single-sided bone comb that had been placed in a decorated padlocked box; an elaborate necklace (*in situ* around the neck), comprising a central gold cruciform pendant, a gold and garnet cabachon pendant, plus one gold and six silver bullae pendants; a silver pin on the chest; an iron knife; a firesteel; and a padlock key at the waist (Lucy *et al.* 2009; Fig. 35.1). This is one of the highest-status graves yet to be found in Cambridgeshire, and, informally, the possibility was discussed by the excavators that this may have been a 'Saxon princess': the grave-goods were immediately understood to imply a high-status female identity for the buried individual. When the bones were examined by the osteologist, it was not possible to assign a sex, because the individual buried had only been ten to twelve years old at death (biological sexing through bone identification is only possible after the skeleton has gone through the sex-related changes associated with puberty). For some reason, this surprised me—I had been expecting (again on the basis of the grave goods) the burial to be of an adult. With further thought, I recollected that, in the second half of the seventh century, there was a new trend for younger individuals to be buried with grave assemblages that would once have been considered appropriate only for adults (Geake 1997: 128–9; Stoodley 2002: 113): the gendered identity as interpreted through grave furnishing had taken on a new meaning.

I find several things interesting about this burial and its interpretation: first, that in early Anglo-Saxon mortuary archaeology, biological sex and cultural gender are generally understood as being very closely linked, at least for older children and adults; second, that age, status, and cultural identity are so closely involved in the expression of gendered identities that they are virtually impossible to tease apart; third, that these identities were changing over the course of the early Anglo-Saxon period. My final point of interest is that gender in Anglo-Saxon archaeology is an issue largely discussed in the context of cemeteries (because such identities are apparently being clearly expressed), but not when discussing evidence from settlements and other types of site. In this paper, I will first address how our current understandings of gender and gender roles have arisen, before moving on to explore possibilities for how we might interpret and understand them through the archaeological evidence available today.

PREVIOUS PERSPECTIVES ON GENDER

One point, which is made surprisingly infrequently, is that gendered dress accessories (especially brooches) have for decades been taken as ethnic signifiers. Since the time of Nils Åberg and E. T. Leeds, certain (largely female-associated) brooches have been used to identify different cultural groupings—the distribution of small-long brooches and wrist-clasps as the physical expression of 'Anglian' identity, for example. That the identification of ethnic groups in the Anglo-Saxon period relied almost entirely on female-associated items does not appear to have struck many early practitioners as odd (cf. Leeds 1913; Åberg 1926; Leeds 1936; Myres 1937); their interest was in mapping cultural/ethnic movement, rather than investigating social relations (contrasting with an early interest in gender relations by historians: cf. Turner 1799–1805; Stenton 1957; Fell 1984).

Up until the 1980s then, gender perspectives in Anglo-Saxon archaeology are best characterized by their 'common sense' approach. Few settlements had been excavated or published, so interpretation rested largely on cemetery data, and this appeared to portray a clearly gendered society (no distinction was drawn at this time between biological sex and cultural gender: such a distinction only came to be appreciated in archaeology in the 1980s through the pioneering work of Meg Conkey and Janet Spector, 1984). While this is not the place for an in-depth treatment of the development of gender theory in archaeology in general (this

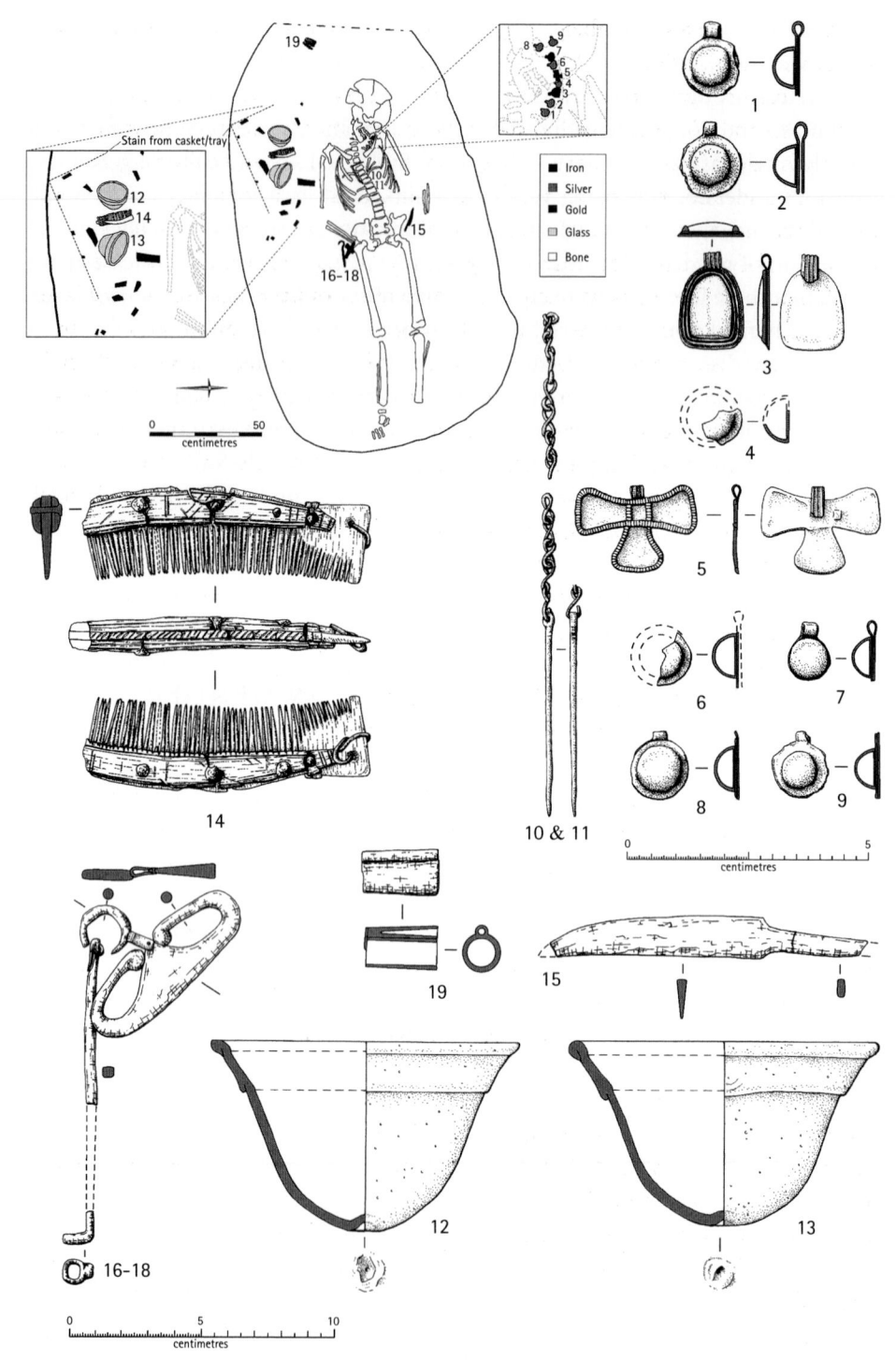

Figure 35.1 Grave 1 from Westfield Farm, Ely

has detailed coverage in, for example, Sørensen 2000 and Díaz-Andreu 2005), changing understandings within Anglo-Saxon archaeology are worth exploring.

The apparent gender division within early Anglo-Saxon burial archaeology arises from the inclusion of distinct grave-good assemblages: one that is based around the deposition of one or more weapons (spears being the most common, but shields, swords, axes, and arrowheads also form a part), and one that is based around the inclusion of decorative items such as dress accessories (mainly brooches and wrist-clasps), and other items of jewellery (strings of beads, other forms of necklaces, etc.). The 'common sense' interpretation of these distinct assemblages was naturally that males were buried with weapons and females buried with dress accessories and jewellery (cf. Hjørungdal 1994); this was a belief that was so strongly held that it was common practice for the grave-goods to be used as a proxy for sex (i.e. a burial could be sexed as female on the basis of its grave-goods) (Henderson 1989). Osteologists working on Anglo-Saxon material have even been known to request information about accompanying grave-goods to assist in the (biological) sexing of burials. On those occasions where information from the grave-goods did not coincide with that from osteological identification, some excavators would choose to rely on the grave-goods in their interpretation, as it was felt more likely to be correct (cf. Evison 1987: 123).

The rise of osteology within archaeology has been a useful corrective to such approaches, although it should be emphasized that this in itself is not a purely objective process (see, for example Donlon 1993 and Geller 2005, who have demonstrated both cultural bias in sexing individuals, and that there can be population- and age-related variations in the degree of sexual dimorphism observed on the skeleton). In 1997 I published a paper (Lucy 1997) which (drawing on Henderson 1989) tried to 'problematize' the ideas held about Anglo-Saxon sex and gender. Using two well-recorded cemeteries from East Yorkshire where independent osteological sexing of the bones had been undertaken, I analysed assemblage composition and the proportions of burials where female and male biological sex and cultural gender (as indicated by the grave-goods) coincided. While the jewellery and weapon assemblages were indeed exclusive at both sites, around half of all burials—those with no existing grave-goods, and those where the grave-goods included neither weapons nor jewellery (though items such as knives, buckles, and vessels were present)—fell outside of these categories. These new categories I termed (perhaps misguidedly) 'no goods' and 'neutral'. While the low proportions of burials whose sex and gender identifications coincided were, of course, mainly a result of the poor bone preservation encountered at the two sites, it did still make an important point. At West Heslerton, there were males with brooches, albeit older males with iron annular brooches (Lucy 2000: 89). Not all forms of jewellery and decorative dress accessories are necessarily exclusively associated with female individuals, and females can, in perhaps exceptional circumstances, be associated with weapons (Stoodley 1999: 76; see also Lucy 2000: 89 and Walton

Rogers 2007: 198–9). The main point here is to emphasize that, in Anglo-Saxon archaeology, although patterning may appear clear-cut, it cannot, in fact, be assumed: sex (biological) and expressions of gender (cultural) should be analysed as independent variables, and not treated as interchangeable. Treating them independently also has the advantage of allowing age and other social data to be incorporated into analyses. In the last twenty-five years, a number of major studies has been undertaken of Anglo-Saxon burials with this perspective and their results have proved illuminating. Studies dealing with inhumations will be looked at first, before turning to the smaller number that have looked at the cremation burial rite.

Most pioneering was the work of Ellen-Jane Pader, who in 1982 published her thesis on East Anglian cemeteries, which used a symbolic and structural approach. She concluded (albeit on the basis of three cemeteries with poor skeletal preservation) that sex-based relations were articulated by constraints placed on the use of different types of artefacts and skeletal positioning; she also recognized that these constraints differed between cemeteries.

Building on Pader's work, Karen Brush (1993) conducted a study of burial costumes using a range of fifth- and sixth-century cemeteries, finding that burial assemblages became more diverse with the age of the person buried. She argued that children's costume was a simplified version of adult dress, and that certain artefacts were age-restricted, with, for example, keys, girdle-hangers, sleeve-clasps, and shields being found with older children and adults. My own PhD (Lucy 1998) came to similar conclusions using a number of East Yorkshire cemeteries: provisioning there was highly structured by sex and age, with certain goods (square-headed brooches, swords, shields, tweezers, and tools) restricted to those over 25 years, and others restricted to those over 12 years. Moreover, I found that the burial rite itself (grave size, shape, orientation, and location within a cemetery) was structured by sex and age, but that differences between sexes and people of different age groups were marked in different ways at each cemetery (something which was also identified in East Anglia by Fisher 1995).

Using a larger sample, Nick Stoodley (1999) conducted a national survey of gender identities in early Anglo-Saxon graves, based on the analysis of 3,401 inhumations of the fifth to eighth centuries. His comparison of biological sex with gender-associated grave assemblages found strong (but not exclusive) sex-associations for most items; exclusive associations tended to be with rare items such as chisels, sharpening steels, adzes, and weaving battens. He also identified regional differences in adult gender signalling, and greater variety in female-gendered graves as to how this was done. He, too, established strong age-related patterning with regard to gender symbolism: the only weapons generally found with individuals under 15 years, for example, were small spearheads and arrowheads (something also recognized by Heinrich Härke in 1989). Different brooch types had varying age associations, while pairs of sleeve-clasps, indicating the wearing of a long-sleeved garment, were restricted to those over 10–12 years of age. Indeed, the full complement of 'feminine-type' accessories was limited to those in their late teens and older, though, as noted in the introduction, this changes in the later seventh century, as does the age association of weapon burials, with these now found mainly with older adults.

Others have looked at different aspects of the inhumation burial rite. Härke (1992) conducted an extensive analysis of the weapon burial rite, using a sample of forty-seven cemeteries. He found changing patterns in how the weapon assemblages were composed over time, and age-related differences, and concluded that the rite was largely symbolic. Helen Geake looked at the later inhumations of the seventh and eighth centuries. While her primary aim was the establishment of a secure chronological understanding of these burials, she also analysed the data for age and gender signalling, concluding that in this period male-gendered graves are more often found in the prestigious barrow-graves, while female-gendered graves are more common in the communal cemeteries. Overall there was a shift of emphasis within rich burial from male graves to female graves (Geake 1997: 128). The fact that, after AD 650, small children could be buried with grave-goods that would have formerly been considered adult indicates changing social practice, the meaning of which is unclear (*ibid.*: 129).

With greater understanding of the broad patterns, more detailed analysis has become possible. For example, Fisher (2004) analysed 106 undisturbed female burials in fifth- to sixth-century East Anglia, and established the existence of localized dress styles. Her analysis revealed that both annular brooches and small-long brooches, and square-headed and cruciform brooches were 'functional equivalents', coinciding in just one grave apiece. She thus identified a grammar of costume elements employed in alternative dress styles, and children's graves also followed this grammar. However, within this broad patterning, there was considerable individual autonomy, especially in the graves of adults, as to how the brooches were combined: 'the vocabulary and the grammar of costume voiced different social identities' (ibid.: 51). Thus, even under the wide umbrella of 'female gender identity', a large amount of variation is seen, which presumably relates to other aspects of social identity: cultural associations may play a part in this, but so also do age, position in the social hierarchy, and perhaps marital status.

In his study of the cremation burial rite Julian Richards (1987) looked both at the form and decoration of the urns themselves, and at associated grave-goods. He found, to a certain extent, that the pots had been selected as appropriate for the person(s) interred within: there were close correlations between the age and sex of the cremated remains and the size of the vessel, from infants in the shortest vessels to old adults in the tallest. Females tended to have vessels with wider rims, leading to a conclusion that pottery attributes were being used to mark different aspects of the social role, with the level of visibility of the attribute reflecting the size of audience being broadcast to. In contrast, he found very few associations between types of grave-goods and such social data: only ivory, possibly representing the inclusion of bag handles, was positively associated with females (ibid.: 126–9), but variation between practices at different cemeteries was also seen (ibid.: 201).

Mads Ravn (1998) conducted a more detailed study of the Spong Hill cremations, numbering over 2,000 burials, using multivariate correspondence analysis to study the patterning of gender, power, and status. Through this more sophisticated analytical technique, he was able to distinguish a single female assemblage, characterized by coins, glass beads, ivory, spindle whorls, silver pendants, crystal, and amber, along with three distinct male assemblages. The first consisted solely of miniature objects; the second comprised shears, playing pieces, glass vessels, horse and sheep bones, and was associated with adult males; while the third was characterized by honestones, bronze tweezers, bone beads, and weapons. Ravn thus concluded that, while the cremation rite destroyed the body, this was compensated for by the provisioning of symbolically-loaded grave-gifts (ibid.: 251–2). There may, however, have been different practices at other cremation cemeteries (see Lucy 2000: 108–13 for an overview).

Gender possibilities: burial archaeology

The studies outlined above have helped to delineate the major patterning present in early Anglo-Saxon gendered grave furnishing: use of restricted sets of grave-goods, mainly limited to certain adult males and females, but with some adaptations for those aged 12 and over, and sometimes a concomitant decline in gender signalling in older age groups. It should be emphasized that not all adult individuals are 'gendered' through their grave-goods. In the past, such individuals have been seen as of different status, or perhaps different ethnic origin, but further interpretation has been somewhat limited. They have therefore been discussed as 'gender-neutral' or 'ungendered' (Lucy 1997), a terminology which can now be considered inadequate, due to advances both in theoretical understandings of gender and bone chemistry, and also in light of increased knowledge about gendered costume, with or without other grave-goods.

In terms of how gender is now understood, age is fundamental. An important proponent of this viewpoint is Joanna Sofaer, who has shown in a series of papers the close inter-relationship of age, sex, and gendered identities (Sofaer Derevenski 1997a, b, c; 2000) and has stressed the important role that material culture plays in the cultural construction and maintenance of both age and gender identities: this can be especially potent when the material culture in question becomes part of bodily appearance (Sofaer Derevenski 2000: 398; see also Gowland 2006 and

Stoodley, this volume). When we see the creation, maintenance, and change in gender identities and inter-gender relations as being a fundamental part of the structuring of society (cf. Barrett 1988; Sørensen 1991; Conkey 1992; 1993), a wealth of interpretative possibilities present themselves. By seeing early Anglo-Saxon gendered identities not as a biological given, but as something which was dynamic and actively constructed (albeit often unconsciously, and within culturally-defined limits), local and regional differences and chronological change all become something to be identified and analysed, rather than something to be surprised by.

How then should we embark on our cemetery analyses? As stated above, independent analysis of biological sex is essential. This is now standard practice on material from modern excavations, along with determination of skeletal age, and identification of any palaeopathological changes. Solely from the human skeleton is therefore derived a physical description of the person buried: sex, age, robusticity, any diseases suffered which were associated with changes to the skeleton, occurrence and nature of any trauma, height, and some indication of nutritional status. These may in themselves contribute to our understandings of gender roles. A recent national survey, for example, revealed sex-based differences in the incidence of trauma in early medieval cemetery populations (Roberts and Cox 2003: 168–9, table 4.2): weapon injuries and cut-marks were overwhelmingly associated with males, while more females had suffered decapitation. Tuberculosis showed a greater male incidence, perhaps indicating greater contact with infected animals (ibid.: table 4.10), while the incidence of dental caries, dental abscesses, pre-mortem tooth loss, and dental calculus all showed site-specific sex differences, suggesting perhaps localized differences in access to certain foodstuffs (ibid.: tables 4.14–17). More males than females were affected by osteoarthritis (ibid.: 195), and bone fractures (ibid.: 202–3, table 4.27), pointing to another source of information for differential participation in farming and other more hazardous activities. Similarly, Nick Stoodley (1999: 119–25) has identified some tentative evidence that gendered grave-goods might be correlated with better lifestyles, as indicated by increased stature and numbers of carious teeth, and by a lower incidence of arthritis. Correlating such physical and palaeopathological information with other aspects of social identity as revealed by the burial rite should lead to more nuanced understandings of the physical and social possibilities and constraints under which these societies were organized.

Further information can now also be extracted from inhumations, using stable isotopic analyses (see Hull and O'Connell, this volume, and references therein). These can give information about diet (using nitrogen- and carbon-isotopic ratios) and place of childhood origin (using oxygen and strontium), as well as, potentially, levels of industrial pollution (using lead). While these techniques are still very much in their infancy, and their use has yet to become standard practice in field archaeology, some interesting patterns are starting to emerge. As Hull and O'Connell (this volume) state, social control of diet is a way of emphasizing the cultural position of individuals, and differences in their bone chemistry can reflect these social distinctions. Overall, the patterning is not clear-cut, but shows significant local and regional differences. Similar variability is seen when gendered assemblages are compared (see their discussion, this volume). The few analyses of oxygen and strontium isotopes that have yet been conducted suggest regional and local patterning here, too. At some sites, virtually all the population (males and females) appear to be of local origin, while probable migrants have been identified at others. At Eastbourne in Sussex, for example, in the earliest phase of the cemetery, a group of males and unsexed burials were identified as having a continental origin (unpublished data). Other 'outliers' in isotopic terms were unfurnished females, often in unusual burial positions. A similar study of material from West Heslerton in Yorkshire revealed an unexpected picture of a small number of unfurnished or very poorly furnished female continental immigrants (Budd *et al.* 2004). This type of data also therefore has considerable analytical potential, as it is able to identify male and female incomers to a population; when compared with their burial rite, this can offer useful social information.

Cremations also provide social data. As Julian Richards (1987) and Mads Ravn (1998) have already shown, the cremation rite is also a structured one, albeit on a different basis from the inhumation rite. Bone analysis can go some way to revealing sex, age, and some palaeopathological information (McKinley 1994); cremated bone also has the advantage of surviving in acidic soils, unlike inhumed bone, while analysis of variation in cremation urns and associated grave-goods reveals likewise a highly symbolic and structured practice. An additional variable to be analysed here is the amount of cremated bone included within the cremation urn: Anglo-Saxon cremation pyres have only rarely been located, and the bones seem to have been picked out from the pyre debris and removed for inclusion within the urn: the time and care taken to do this are another indicator of the effort invested by others in the burial rite (see McKinley 1994: 11, 72, 82, 85; Lucy 2000: 105–19; Williams 2002). Unfortunately, stable isotope and DNA techniques cannot be applied, due to lack of bone collagen.

When dealing with burial data, one issue that must be tackled is whether the burial treatment can give an indication of lived social roles and identities. While the burial rites show considerable variation, which often coincides with differences in age, sex, and other aspects of the physical body as inferred from the skeleton, what does that variation represent in social terms? Can burial costume, or associated grave goods, for example, be used to directly infer the deceased's role in society (warrior, head of the household), or is a more sophisticated interpretation needed? One point to make here is that objects do not have inherent meanings (though they may have obvious uses): through their use in specific contexts, they become imbued with significance in the eyes of those who use them and those who watch them being used (Sørensen 1991: 121). There may, of course, be limits on what can be used in terms of physical availability and value, and social mores may also inhibit what can be used, and in what circumstances. Cemetery evidence is further complicated by the fact that it is not unconscious, everyday practice, but intermittent and deliberate. A person's identity cannot be 'read off' from the way in which he or she was buried, but the way in which the burial was made can indicate those aspects of the deceased that the mourners thought important to emphasize (Lucy 1998: 107). Penelope Walton Rogers (2007: 247) rather poignantly expresses this as 'an act of witness to who the dead had been when alive', arguing that it is hard not to see these burials as presenting something realistic about those people's lives and relationships, given the small communities involved, and the degree of variation expressed through the burial rite.

One useful way into this debate, at least in terms of early Anglo-Saxon archaeology, is through burial costume, rather than through the general provision of grave goods. A recent study by Walton Rogers offers a valuable perspective for looking at the expression of gendered identities in burial practices, as she has analysed the fragments of preserved textiles that can assist with the reconstruction of what costumes were worn to the grave. As she so rightly points out, of a 'gender-neutral' or 'no goods' burial (as I and others have defined them): 'a body clothed in a full-length dress, with covered hair, would have instantly declared its female identity, with or without brooches, and a knee-length tunic over trousers would have been immediately identifiable as male, even without a spear or shield' (Walton Rogers 2007: 249). She thus offers a useful corrective to the overwhelming emphasis seen until now on metal dress accessories: many brooches would, at the time of burial and when worn during life, have been obscured by an outer layer such as a cloak or mantle, or by the commonly-worn head-veil (ibid.: 246). Our questions should therefore not start with the presence of jewellery or weaponry: we should first ask who, in physical terms, the person was—male or female, young or old—then whether they were buried in a male (tunic) or female (full-length dress) costume (Fig. 35.2), and only then what additional information is provided by the artefacts fastening that costume together, or placed alongside in the grave. Various studies (Fisher 1995; Lucy 1998; Parfitt and Brugmann 1997; and particularly Walton Rogers 2007) have demonstrated considerable, and sometimes unorthodox, patterning in how (particularly the female) costume was elaborated, and this can then be investigated for social meaning, with broader understandings built up from this fuller appreciation of the data.

Broader patterns may also have wider implications. Walton Rogers (2007: 234–5) draws an interesting contrast between the distribution of certain styles of metal artefacts, and of types of textile: simpler cloth-manufacturing techniques spread relatively quickly from the east of the country to the west, while brooch types remained regionalized. She puts forward the persuasive argument that this represents the frequent movement of women some distance, probably through marriage, who were then able to pass on their textile knowledge (this only achieved through sustained demonstration), perhaps as a way of gaining acceptance into

Figure 35.2 Male and female Anglo-Saxon costumes (after Walton Rogers 2007)

their new community. She also reveals a longer-term shift in gender relations, with her evidence of more valuable textiles moving from women's to men's graves in the seventh century, coinciding with greater stratification of society (ibid.: 240–1). That this occurs at the same time that the age-related distinctions in women's costumes were disappearing, but when metal-based wealth was being found increasingly in women's graves, all combines to suggest a fundamental shift in the pattern of social organization.

Gender possibilities: settlement archaeology

Investigating gender in Anglo-Saxon settlement archaeology has been a rather neglected area. The lack of direct sexing evidence in the form of skeletons appears to have made archaeologists far more wary of entering this area of debate in all but the most general terms. In fact, the interpretative possibilities are high, given the number of sites now excavated and the data available for analysis, although at this stage any discussion is rather speculative. Various types of site are included under the umbrella term of settlement: in the fifth and sixth centuries small hamlets and villages were the norm; these were often occupied for a few generations, shifting within or across a limited area. From the seventh century, more variation is seen, with the foundation of the first trading sites, or 'wics', some of which became more permanent production and distribution centres; true urban and defensive sites were an even later development. Conversion to Christianity from the very end of the sixth century also entailed the foundation of monastic houses; in the seventh and eighth centuries these could be 'joint' houses, of both men and women, as well as exclusively male and female. All of these sites have the potential to inform on gender relations and gender structures in Anglo-Saxon society.

Within villages, artefacts associated with particular types of craft production can give some indications as to the location of gendered activity. Walton Rogers (2007) has argued for textile manufacture being a predominantly female activity, and the location of its various stages can offer a more detailed understanding of how these settlements operated. The gathering of its raw products (wool, flax, hemp, dye-stuffs); their preparation (retting, combing, spinning) and the creation of the textiles themselves (weaving) leave increasingly distinct archaeological signatures, whose distribution may be discerned. At West Stow, for example, Walton Rogers (2007: 44) argues that the concentration of loom-weights in a small number of structures (as opposed to a wider distribution of spindle whorls) might represent a single household taking responsibility for the weaving needs of the whole community. Recent excavations of the Anglo-Saxon settlement at Bloodmoor Hill, Suffolk (Lucy et al. 2009) have revealed similar concentrations of loom-weights and pin-beaters, again suggesting focused activity (Fig. 35.3). Activities such as spinning are solitary ones, whereas others such as flax-retting and weaving are more often done communally, and would have taken place at different times of the day, and at different times of the year (Walton Rogers 2007: 46–7).

Other craft activities that may have been carried out by males rather than females include metalworking, woodworking (where weapons and tools are found in graves, they are almost always found with biological males), and heavier agricultural tasks (to judge from the available skeletal data). Again, examination of associated archaeological material (metalworking deposits, butchered animal bone etc.) can help paint a picture of a gendered community engaged in its daily,

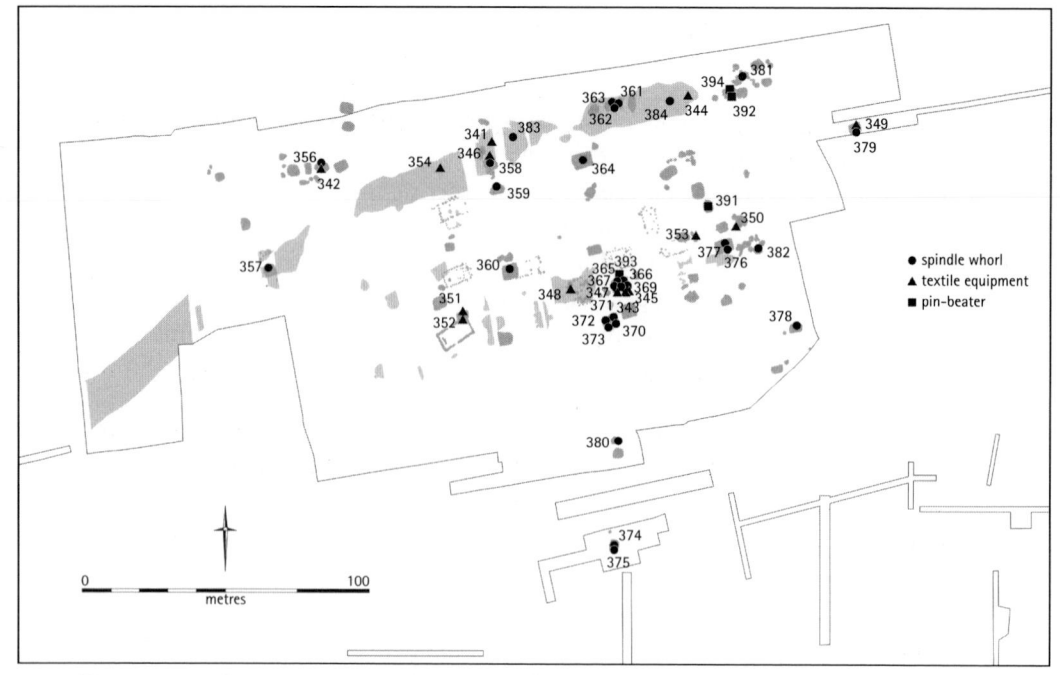

Figure 35.3 Concentrations of textile equipment at Bloodmoor Hill, Suffolk (after Lucy *et al*. 2009: fig. 4.53)

intermittent, and seasonal tasks (though see Sørensen 1996 for a nuanced discussion of the implications of activities such as metalworking for all members of a community, not just the metalworkers themselves). In particular, we can enquire about the process of producing decorative metalwork: who was driving the immense amount of variation we see in fifth- and sixth-century brooches? Were bronze-workers independently creating the various designs on the different types of brooches, or were they being commissioned to do so? Were, perhaps, the moulds even being made for them, in order that a brooch's recipient got the desired end result? If women were making metal moulds, were they also creating other things from clay? Were they indeed (as has sometimes been assumed) responsible for pottery production, as well as the creation of textile-related equipment such as spindle whorls and loom-weights? Were they also responsible for building ovens? What about the application of daub to buildings? And who did food preparation and cooking?

There is a whole realm of questions that relate to gender in Anglo-Saxon settlements that have never even been asked, and many of our assumptions about Anglo-Saxon gender roles remain untested. As our knowledge of these sites grows with increasing publication, perhaps some of the issues might start to be addressed. Similar questions can be posed of the other types of site: were '*wic*' sites comprised of balanced communities, or did they see a gender imbalance? What evidence is there for the raising of children within such settlements? Within monastic settlements, were otherwise cross-gendered activities undertaken by the men or the women within that community, or were tasks so firmly gendered that lay members had to undertake these?

CONCLUSIONS

Historical and legal sources for the Anglo-Saxon period can also contribute to the picture derived from archaeological evidence. The overarching theme of Christine Fell's (1984) *Women in Anglo-Saxon England* is of a largely equitable society (in stark contrast to the situation following the Norman Conquest), where women could, and did, wield power and influence in the upper levels of society, but also in less privileged circles: women could independently own (and bequeath) land, and could be granted charters. Marriage payment (*morgengifu*) was payment from the groom to the woman herself on marriage, and was a way of guaranteeing her financial independence and security within that marriage. One future task for Anglo-Saxon archaeology is to examine evidence, particularly from settlements, but also continuing the work started on cemetery material, in pursuit of a more detailed understanding of gender identities, gender roles, and also the construction of gendered activities within Anglo-Saxon society.

REFERENCES

ÅBERG, N. (1926). *The Anglo-Saxons in England*. Uppsala: Almqvist och Wiksell.
BARRETT, J. (1988). 'Fields of discourse: reconstituting a social archaeology'. *Critique of Anthropology* 7(3): 9–42.
BRUSH, K. (1993). *Adorning the Dead: The Social Significance of Early Anglo-Saxon Funerary Dress in England (Fifth to Seventh Centuries AD)*. Unpublished PhD dissertation, University of Cambridge.
BUDD, P., MILLARD, A., et al. (2004). 'Investigating population movement by stable isotope analysis: a report from Britain'. *Antiquity* 78(299): 127–41.
CONKEY, M. (1992). 'Does it make a difference? Feminist thinking and archaeologies of gender', in D. Walde and N. D. Willows (eds.), *The Archaeology of Gender: Proceedings of the 22nd Chacmool Conference*. Calgary: The University of Calgary, 24–33.
—— (1993). 'Making the connections: feminist theory and archaeologies of gender', in H. duCros and L. Smith (eds.), *Women in Archaeology: a Feminist Critique*. Occasional Papers in Prehistory 23. Camberra: The Australian National University.

—— and Spector, J. (1984). 'Archaeology and the study of gender', in M. B. Schiffer (ed.), *Advances in Archaeological Method and Theory 7*. New York: Academic Press, 1–38.

Díaz-Andreu, M. (2005). 'Gender identity', in M. Díaz-Andreu, S. Lucy, S. Babic, and D. Edwards, *The Archaeology of Identity: Approaches to Gender, Age, Status, Ethnicity and Religion*. Abingdon: Routledge, 13–42.

Donlon, D. (1993). 'Imbalance in the sex ratio in collections of Australian Aboriginal skeletal remains', in H. DuCros and L. Smith (eds.), *Women in Archaeology: a Feminist Critique*. Canberra: The Australian National University, 221–6.

Evison, V. I. (1987). *Dover: The Buckland Anglo-Saxon Cemetery*. HBMC Report 3. London: Historic Buildings and Monuments Commission England.

Fell, C. (1984). *Women in Anglo-Saxon England*. London: British Museum.

Fisher, G. (1995). 'Kingdoms and community in early Anglo-Saxon eastern England', in L. Anderson Beck (ed.), *Regional Approaches to Mortuary Analysis*. New York: Plenum Press, 147–66.

—— (2004). 'Faces in a crowd or a crowd of faces? Archaeological evidence for individual and group identity in Early Anglo-Saxon England', in J. R. Mathieu and R. E. Scott (eds.), *Exploring the Role of Analytical Scale in Archaeological Interpretation*. BAR International Series 1261. Oxford: Archaeopress, 49–58.

Geake, H. (1997). *The Use of Grave Goods in Conversion-Period England, c. 600–850*. BAR British Series 261. Oxford: Archaeopress.

Geller, P. (2005). 'Skeletal analysis and theoretical complications'. *World Archaeology* 37(4): 597–609.

Gowland, R. (2006). 'Ageing the past: examining age identity from funerary evidence', in R. Gowland and C. Knüsel (eds.), *Social Archaeology of Funerary Remains*. Oxford: Oxbow Books, 143–54.

Härke, H. (1989). 'Early Saxon weapon burials: frequencies, distributions and weapon combinations', in S. C. Hawkes (ed.), *Weapons and Warfare in Anglo-Saxon England*. Monograph 21. Oxford: Oxford University Committee for Archaeology, 49–61.

—— (1992). *Angelsächsische Waffengräber des 5. bis 7. Jahrhunderts*. Cologne and Bonn: Zeitschrift für Archäologie des Mittelalters, Beiheft 6.

Henderson, J. (1989). 'Pagan cemeteries: a study of the problems of sexing by grave goods and bones', in C. A. Roberts, F. Lee, and J. Bintliff (eds.), *Burial Archaeology: Current Research, Methods and Developments*. BAR British Series 211. Oxford: British Archaeological Reports, 77–83.

Hjørungdal, T. (1994). 'Have there been any male and female graves?'. *Current Swedish Archaeology* 2: 141–8.

Leeds, E. T. (1913). *The Archaeology of the Anglo-Saxon Settlements*. Oxford: Clarendon Press.

—— (1936). *Early Anglo-Saxon Art and Archaeology*. Oxford: Clarendon Press.

Lucy, S. (1997). 'Housewives, warriors and slaves? Sex and gender in Anglo-Saxon burials', in J. Moore and E. Scott (eds.), *Invisible People and Processes*. Leicester: Leicester University Press, 150–68.

—— (1998). *The Early Anglo-Saxon Cemeteries of East Yorkshire: An Analysis and Reinterpretation*. BAR British Series 272. Oxford: British Archaeological Reports.

—— (2000). *The Anglo-Saxon Way of Death*. Stroud: Sutton Publishing.

—— Tipper, J., and Dickens, A. (2009). *The Anglo-Saxon Settlement and Cemetery at Bloodmoor Hill, Carlton Colville, Suffolk*. East Anglian Archaeology 131. Cambridge: Cambridge Archaeological Unit.

McKinley, J. (1994). *The Anglo-Saxon Cemetery at Spong Hill, North Elmham, Part 8: The Cremations*. East Anglian Archaeology 69. Dereham: Norfolk Museums Service.

Myres, J. N. L. (1937). 'The present state of the archaeological evidence for the Anglo-Saxon conquest'. *History* n.s. 21: 317–30.

Pader, E.-J. (1982) *Symbolism, Social Relations and the Interpretation of Mortuary Remains*. BAR British Series 130. Oxford: British Archaeological Reports.

Parfitt, K., and Brugmann, B. (1997). *The Anglo-Saxon Cemetery on Mill Hill, Deal*. Society for Medieval Archaeology Monograph 14. Leeds: The Society for Medieval Archaeology.

Ravn, M. (1998). *Germanic Social Structure (c. AD 200–600): A Methodological Study in the Use of Archaeological and Historical Evidence in Migration Age Europe*. Unpublished PhD thesis, University of Cambridge.

Richards, J. D. (1987). *The Significance of Form and Decoration of Anglo-Saxon Cremation Urns*. BAR British Series 166. Oxford: British Archaeological Reports.

Roberts, C., and Cox, M. (2003). *Health and Disease in Britain: From Prehistory to the Present Day*. Stroud: Sutton Publishing.

Sofaer Derevenski, J. (1997a). 'Age and gender at the site of Tiszapolgár-Basatanya, Hungary'. *Antiquity* 71: 875–89.

—— (1997b). 'Engendering children, engendering archaeology', in J. Moore and E. Scott (eds.), *Invisible People and Processes*. Leicester: Leicester University Press, 192–202.

—— (1997c). 'Linking age and gender as social variables', *Ethnographisch-Archäologischen Zeitschrift* 38: 485–93.

—— (2000). 'Rings of life: the role of early metalwork in mediating the gendered life course'. *World Archaeology* 31(3): 389–406.

Sørensen, M.L.S. (1991). 'The construction of gender through appearance', in D. Walde and N. D. Willows (eds.), *The Archaeology of Gender: Proceedings of the 22nd Chacmool Conference*. Calgary: The University of Calgary, 121–8.

—— (1996). 'Women as/and metalworkers', in A. Devonshire and B. Wood (eds.), *Women in Industry and Technology: From Prehistory to the Present; Current Research and the Museum Experience*. London: Museum of London, 45–52.

—— (2000). *Gender Archaeology*. Cambridge: Polity Press.

Stenton, D. M. (1957). *The English Woman in History*. London and New York: Allen and Unwin.

Stoodley, N. (1999). *The Spindle and the Spear: A Critical Enquiry into the Construction and Meaning of Gender in the Early Anglo-Saxon Burial Rite*. BAR British Series 288. Oxford: Archaeopress.

—— (2002). 'Multiple burials, multiple meanings? Interpreting the early Anglo-Saxon multiple interment', in S. Lucy and A. Reynolds (eds.), *Burial in Early Medieval England and Wales*. Society for Medieval Archaeology Monograph 17. Leeds: Maney, 103–21.

Turner, S. (1799–1805). *History of the Anglo-Saxons*. London.

Walton Rogers, P. (2007). *Cloth and Clothing in Early Anglo-Saxon England*. CBA Research Report 145. London: Council for British Archeology.

Williams, H. (2002). 'The remains of pagan Saxondom? The study of Anglo-Saxon cremation rites', in S. Lucy and A. Reynolds (eds.), *Burial in Early Medieval England and Wales*. Society for Medieval Archaeology Monograph 17. Leeds: Maney, 47–71.

CHAPTER 36

DISEASE

CHRISTINA LEE

DETECTION AND EXAMINATION

Interest in the health and disease of Anglo-Saxon populations has grown from a preoccupation with medical texts (Cockayne 1864–66; Grattan and Singer 1952) to the study of evidence from skeletal remains (palaeopathology). Additionally, there is a relative newcomer in the field: the study of pathogens (palaeoepidemiology), which was difficult, if not impossible, to do before the arrival of forensic methods such as DNA analysis (Dutour *et al.* 1998: 242). It is important to remember that the way in which disease and impairment are studied may be reflected in the results. There is a difference between looking at disease as an imbalance in the body and regarding it as a social or cultural discontinuity (Dingwall 2001). Equally, results from clinical approaches, which rely on biological remains mainly from inhumation or cremated contexts, may not necessarily concur with perceptions of disease in Anglo-Saxon society.

The study of disease and disability in Anglo-Saxon England remains difficult. This is partly due to a lack of contemporary information, but also because the majority of known diseases leave no traces on the bone. Most of the primary information on what kinds of illnesses were suffered by the Anglo-Saxons comes either from lists of cures in medical textbooks, or from the burial record. In the latter, there is a considerable discrepancy between actual living populations and the surviving number of dead bodies. It is commonly assumed that the population profile of Anglo-Saxon England is similar to those of modern pre-developing and developing countries, where the highest number of mortalities is represented by children and the elderly. However, few neonate and new-born skeletons have been discovered among the Anglo-Saxon burials excavated so far. Many assumptions about the fecundity and health of early medieval populations are speculative, and are rooted in perceptions that life in this period was brief and brutal, assumptions which are, as will be discussed below, not necessarily borne out by the often healthy (and elderly) populations buried in Anglo-Saxon cemeteries.

Nevertheless, it should be considered that not every body was necessarily included within the community cemetery, and that not all of the cemetery may still be extant for archaeological investigation. Bodies may have decayed, and post-excavation methods may have further damaged the remains (Waldron 1994: 13). The study of the events leading to the disruption and loss of skeletal material (taphonomy) tries to calculate the ratio between the total number of dead which were once interred and the number recovered (Waldron 1994: 14). Usually, small bones, such as the phalanges and cartilaginous material, decay first, whereas long bones and the upper skull are more durable. This causes problems in the detection of some diseases, such as milder forms of leprosy or tuberculosis, which in skeletal remains are most easily detected in changes to the extremities and mandible (Anderson 1969).

Human remains do not decay at the same rate. Soil conditions can determine the survival of bone material, but even in the same conditions children's bones decay at a much faster pace than those of adults (Saunders 2000). Olivier Dutour has also observed that there are gender-specific differences in the decay of bone material, with a better rate of survival for male bones (Dutour *et al.* 1998: 248). At sites with poor preservation, such gender discrepancies may make the difference between detecting and failing to detect disease.

Any examination of human remains is dependent on the skill of the person who analyses the bones. In many early excavations, the primary interest was to detect 'treasure', and scant interest was given to the bone assemblage. The development of the discipline of palaeopathology was largely due to the efforts of medical doctors who had an interest in archaeology, such as Calvin Wells, in the second half of the twentieth century. The pioneers of the discipline, of course, had only modern samples for comparison, and some original assumptions on diet and ageing have had to be adjusted over time. It is not only the skill of the osteologist who examines the bones which determines whether disease is identified, but also the conditions of the excavation and the subsequent handling of the fragile material on its way to the laboratory.

There is also a problem when only selective samples are submitted for palaeopathological examination, since whole-scale assessments can be costly, which may mean that diseases which are not immediately visible to the untrained eye may not be picked up. More importantly, often not all of the burials can be excavated, either because some have already been disturbed, or the site has been built over in places. The majority of Anglo-Saxon cemeteries excavated are incomplete, and this is problematic for the study of populations. For example, it has been observed that very young children are under-represented in pre-Christian sites, which has led to all kinds of theories about what may have happened to the bodies of dead infants (Crawford 1993). Yet some cemeteries, such as Great Chesterford, Essex (Evison 1994), do contain clusters of infants and neonates, which may suggest not only that other areas were reserved for the burial of specific social groups, but that burial may also be differentiated by age group. It has been observed that many Anglo-Saxon cemeteries show a high degree of internal organization (Stoodley 1999), and there is a possibility that a spatial separation of the old and young, as well as the infirm and hale, has taken place. The majority of the adult populations in Anglo-Saxon sites were relatively healthy during life (until their final illness or fatal event), tall, and appear to have been well-nourished. The popular assumption that Anglo-Saxons suffered brief and brutal lives is simply not tenable from the burial record as it presents itself.

Changes in burial ritual, such as the move from cremation to inhumation, or the setting up of churchyard cemeteries in the later Saxon period, may therefore reveal more or fewer afflicted bodies simply because there is a change in the location of the dead. Some Christian sites show a tendency to group burials by gender (Hadley 2004), and in some places there are also clusters of children and people who had suffered disease or impairment (Lee 2008: 25). Christian burial is commonly associated with churchyards, but there had been no compulsion for burial in consecrated ground until the reign of King Cnut (Gittos 2002). It seems that churchyard burial remains an exception until the late Saxon period, and it is therefore interesting to note that persons with disease or congenital deformity are included in many churchyards, such as Raunds Furnells (Boddington 1996), or Hartlepool (Daniel and Loveluck 2007).

Burial in consecrated ground, close to relics and the celebration of Christian ritual, had been an ecclesiastical privilege since the advent of monasticism in Anglo-Saxon England. During the eighth and ninth centuries, such privilege may have been requested by the founders and supporters of churches (Hadley 2004: 306; Blair 2005: 463–73) and burial in consecrated ground may have been regarded as special. Of course, those buried at these sites may have been members of families with personal connections. However, the frequency with which the sick and impaired are now included suggests that there are other reasons as well. One of them may be connected to changing views of salvation and the body in late Anglo-Saxon England. Victoria Thompson has observed a growing concern about the status of the dead body in late Anglo-Saxon literary texts (Thompson 2004: esp. 102–3). Some later literary texts, which were based on patristic perceptions of disease, characterized bodily afflictions as a visible sign of sin. Such views may have led to new forms of care for the dead body and soul, such as burial in special places and physical markers of memory that could admonish the living to prayer and acts of remembrance.

Recent approaches have looked at the burial of the diseased in comparison to the non-afflicted. Dawn Hadley has shown that men and children especially receive prestigious or special treatment in churchyard burial, but that adult males are more likely to be excluded from features such as central places (Hadley 2010).

SPECIFIC DISEASES

The most frequent forms of physical change in the human skeleton are not caused by disease, but by old age. Arthritis and the general decay of health may be as 'disabling' as any other form of disease, and they are the most frequently observed condition in early medieval populations. However, bodies do not age at the same rate. A person who was living in relative comfort will age less quickly than a body which is exposed to hard labour. Modern osteologists have looked for signs of wear and tear on the bones and these provide useful data which can be studied in comparison to the wealth of grave-goods and burial options. While we should not infer status from the condition of the skeleton, it can be observed that in the period of furnished inhumation burial, there seems to be a connection between the relative wealth of burials, and arthropathies (joint diseases). While rheumatoid arthritis is virtually unknown, osteoarthritis and osteophytosis (new bone growth) are the most commonly recorded conditions. Margaret Cox and Charlotte Roberts, in their study of published material from British skeletal remains, record a slight fall of osteoarthritis since the Roman period, and note that, during the Anglo-Saxon period, osteoarthritis is more frequently observed in men than women (Roberts and Cox 2003: 195). In many cases these will have caused only some pain in life, but conditions such as ankylosing spondylitis (a gradual fusing and stiffening of the spine) could be debilitating. DISH (diffuse idiopathic skeletal hyperostosis) results in another ankylosing (calcification) of the spine. It has been connected to Forestier's Disease, and there has been a discussion about whether these conditions can be linked to prolonged periods of obesity, since most cases have been observed from men who lived in monastic communities (Rogers and Waldron 2001: 362).

Second to joint disease in the list of observable conditions are dental diseases. Most of them are caused by eating and drinking (such as the loss of tooth enamel through acid erosion, and the abrasions caused by coarsely-milled bread), as well as poor dental hygiene. Caries, tartar, and abscesses will have been commonplace. Not all of them occur at the same rate. A diet rich in carbohydrates will increase the risk of tartar (calculus) and caries (Mays 1998: 149). Roberts and Cox observe that Anglo-Saxon populations show a higher rate of calculus than the Romano-British populations (Roberts and Cox 2003: 193). Untreated caries may lead to infections of the maxillary cavity and lead to conditions such as meningitis. Abscesses may become infected, and may lead to septicaemia. It seems that, for most of the Anglo-Saxon period, dental hygiene was poor, and dental care was even less advanced. An elderly lady in grave 105 at Apple Down, Sussex, suffered part of her mandible breaking when her tooth was extracted, and seems to have suffered chronic infection (Down and Welch 1990). Teeth can also mirror periods of nutritional deficiency and severe infection. Enamel hypoplasia (visible as lines or depressions in the tooth enamel) can indicate that the person suffered a period of ill-health during the period of enamel formation.

Whereas many diseases are caused by genetic defects or changes, it is clear that diet and living conditions play a major role in the health of populations. A recent detailed study of disease of three Anglo-Saxon cemeteries (Norton, Apple Down, Castledyke) in comparison with three contemporary Alamannic (southern Germany) sites has shown that there are subtle differences in the health profiles of medieval people (Jakob 2004). The study showed that the Anglo-Saxon populations were slightly healthier, which may be linked to lifestyle.

Metabolic diseases

Metabolic diseases may be firstly identified as diseases caused by a genetic disposition which makes the afflicted predisposed to certain conditions, as, for example, the fact that women are more likely to suffer from anaemia, since menstruation, childbirth, and lactation require women to have higher levels of iron intake. Iron depletion may also be caused by parasite infection. Severe chronic anaemia manifests itself as pitting and porous lesions on the skull, especially around the eye sockets (*cribra orbitalia*). Other indicators of malnutrition are Harris Lines (transverse lines on the long bones), which indicate periods of arrested growth due to disease or childhood malnutrition (Roberts and Manchester 2005: 240).

It has been observed that early medieval people of Northern Europe were much taller than their counterparts from the seventeenth century onwards. The male Anglo-Saxons examined by Rogers were on average 3 cm taller than their Romano-British equivalents; the difference between women was 2 cm (Roberts and Cox 2003: 195). Nutrition and height have been linked in a number of modern studies, as well as genetic disposition. However, there may be a further link by looking at the diet of the earliest stages of life. Research by Mary Lewis (2002) on infant mortality in medieval to industrial populations has suggested that there was also a much lower rate of infant mortality than previously expected. She suggests that it is not urbanization, as often assumed, which is responsible for the increased rate of mortality, but a change in neonatal feeding practices. In the seventeenth and eighteenth century, colostrum, the first breast milk, was thought to be harmful, and newborn children were fed on liquids made with butter, sugar, or wine on a spoon for the first days before being breastfed (Lewis 2002: 221). Additionally, the period of breastfeeding had fallen from eighteen to seven months. Breast milk is not only highly nutritious, but also contains antibodies which protect children against diseases.

Nutrition plays an important part in maintaining a healthy immunity. Many diseases are brought on, or are exacerbated by, a poor diet. The body's response to disease depends on the immunity of a person. A healthy person is less likely to become infected. Nutrition is, of course, just one aspect of health, which also depends on environmental conditions, such as pollution and sanitation. The living conditions of a population may be reconstructed from the study of houses or middens, as well as palaeobotany. Records from the Anglo-Saxon period tell of widespread famines and cattle murrain, but the impact of such outbreaks has not been studied yet. Advances in dating skeletal remains more precisely might help to understand the severity of such recorded events, as well as to show whether there was any long-term impact on the population.

The body's natural reaction to infection is inflammation, which is only visible on the skeleton if the bone is affected (which means that the infection has not been lethal in the first impact, and perhaps even that the person survived), or if there is mummified tissue. Outbreaks of infectious diseases, such as plague and smallpox, which are highly lethal, are therefore hard to detect. Our understanding of other potential pieces of evidence, such as multiple burials, is yet too limited (Stoodley 2002; Crawford 2007), but perhaps it should be considered that some multiple burials may be 'plague' graves.

While infection is not always easy to detect, occasionally we get glimpses of other conditions affecting organs. For example, a massive bladder stone may have been the cause of death of a middle-aged male at Melbourn, Cambridgeshire (Duncan et al. 2003).

Trauma

Broken bones occur in all kinds of contexts, but the way in which they heal may be an indicator of whether a leech (doctor) was present or not. A skilled doctor must have been involved in the amputation of a left arm at School Street, Ipswich, Suffolk, since this operation was successful and the patient survived the event (Roberts and Cox 2003: 216). Roberts and Cox record 395 cases of trauma in their study, which is a total of 5.9 per cent of the overall recorded cases. Broken long bones are the most frequently recorded fracture (111 cases), followed by broken ribs (53 instances), and injuries to the collarbone (48 cases). Men had more recorded fractures than women, and a total of 73 instances of skull fractures were recorded (Roberts and Cox 2003: 202). Some of these fractures may have been associated with work-related accidents, others with warfare.

Infectious disease

In a recent study of 7,122 burials from published Anglo-Saxon cemeteries, Charlotte Roberts found evidence for infectious disease in 460 cases, a figure similar to that collected from the Roman period (Roberts and Cox 2003: 172). Infectious diseases were spread not just through close and unhygienic living conditions, but were also exacerbated through malnutrition.

A frequently observed condition in Anglo-Saxon skeletons is periostitis, an inflammation of the thin membrane on the bones. It can be caused by Staphylococcus aureus (90 per cent of modern infections are caused by this pathogen), but can also develop in response to trauma, or even as a result of metabolic diseases, such as scurvy. Staphylococcus is a group of bacteria living on skin and in mucus, and approximately 15–40 per cent of people are carriers. Unhygienic conditions will increase the chances of becoming infected. Spread of Staphylococci to the bones can lead to periostitis and osteitis, which can be seen as primary and secondary stages of the onset of osteomyelitis, inflammation of the bone with subsequent pus formation and simultaneous new bone growth (Roberts and Manchester 2005: 168–72). Osteomyelitis was observed in 22 of 1,637 examined bodies (Roberts and Cox 2003: table 4.3).[1] The majority of afflicted people were male. It is assumed that the bacteria will have been carried in the blood stream from other infected organs or soft tissue to the place of infection on the bone. The new bone growth indicates that the person survived a severe infection.

Proximity to open fire and smoke may be the reason behind the rise of maxillary sinusitis during the Anglo-Saxon period. Both the cemeteries of Raunds Furnells, Northamptonshire, and St Helen-on-the-Wall, York, have very high numbers of people with sinusitis (Roberts and Cox 2003: table 4.4; Roberts and Manchester 2005: 174). The cemeteries are very different, Raunds serving a mainly rural community, and St Helens functioning as a burial ground for the urban poor of York. Sinusitis is an inflammation of the mucous membranes of one or more sinuses (Roberts 2007: 795). The inflammation could be caused by smoke from domestic fires, but certain occupations, such as tanning and potting, had a higher exposure to harmful chemicals (Roberts 2007: 804). Occupational diseases are still an under-researched area in the study of the health of early medieval populations, and the study of bone deformation may be used to assess the exposure of certain population groups.

Polio (poliomyelitis) has been observed at several sites, including grave 5218 at Raunds Furnells (a male aged 17–18), where the afflicted person had been buried at the outermost boundary of the cemetery (Boddington 1996), and at Worthy Park, Hampshire (Hawkes and Grainger 2003). The polio virus is spread by faecal-oral

---

[1] It should be observed that Roberts and Cox's data is collected from archaeological reports and the primary examination was conducted by several paleopathologists between the late 1970s and 2003.

transmission. Unhygienic conditions, such as not washing hands after defecating, will increase the risk of transmission. Given the picture of filth that has emerged from Anglo-Saxon settlements it is surprising not to find a higher incidence of the disease.

Tuberculosis is a multifaceted disease which is hard to detect in a palaeopathological environment (Roberts 2002a: 31). The disease is caused by the mycobacterium tuberculosis, and appears in bovine as well as in human form. Like its first cousin leprosy, it can vary in severity and appearance. It is contracted via pulmonary infection or via gastrointestinal infection from milk or meat. Today it kills around three million people each year, and almost half of the world's population is infected (Roberts 2002a: 31). While the bacterium can lie dormant in persons with good immunity, poverty, a deficient diet, as well as poor living conditions, are contributing factors to the outbreak of the disease, which also requires a high population density. Tuberculosis may have developed in the transition from hunter-gatherer to agricultural societies, when humans began to live in close proximity to their animals. Tuberculosis can manifest itself in characteristic deformations of the spine, but the majority of affected people will die before such visible bone formations can develop (only about 2 per cent of the diseased will develop bone changes—Roberts 2002a: 36). Thus skeletons with changes caused by tuberculosis are most likely the survivors of the disease.

Leprosy (Hansen's Disease) is often linked with the Middle Ages since it was used as a staple in textual descriptions. The disease is caused by infection by the mycobacterium leprae, and can be latent for a period of up to twenty years. Leprosy develops in two major forms (with intermediate stages): the lepromatous or tuberculoid form. Genetic disposition and immunity determine the severity of symptoms, which can involve bone changes (especially to the maxilla and phalanges) which are archaeologically detectable, and soft tissue changes, blindness, and paralysis of the face, which are not. The examination of bone material is made more difficult since the small bones which are first affected by the disease often decay first, and since some of the 'characteristic changes' of leprosy are very similar to those caused by tuberculosis (the pathogens of both diseases are related). The examination of leprosy on skeletal remains goes back to the strict criteria of Vilhelm Møller-Christensen (1961, 1967), who was the first to systematically examine the remains of a leper cemetery. Leprosy is mentioned in medieval texts, but it is doubtful whether medieval leeches understood the full aetiology of this complex disease.

Based on text sources, there has been a wide-spread assumption that lepers were 'cast out', which is largely fictitious (Rawcliffe 2006: 5). Early burials suggest an inclusion of lepers, as for example at Beckford, Hereford and Worcester, or Edix Hill, Cambridgeshire, which may mean that their status may not have been negatively affected by their illness (Crawford 2007: 88; Lee 2006). However, we can observe that by the end of the Anglo-Saxon period, lepers seem to have been buried collectively at some sites, as for example at Norwich, St John the Baptist (Popescu 2009) or at the margins, such as at Raunds Furnells, Northamptonshire (Boddington 1996). It remains to be seen whether the location of such burials is indicative of a loss of status, or may be based on different factors. There are no known leprosaria from pre-Conquest England, despite the fact that there are several well-known contemporary houses on the continent. The proximity of a number of lepers at Norwich may suggest that this may have been affiliated with a leper colony, but so far there is no evidence for such a building. The absence of leprosaria also suggests that the care of lepers was mainly undertaken in the home. It may also indicate that the disease was not known very well, since so far there are only few cases in the pre-Christian cemeteries, but the evidence from Norwich suggests that there may be larger numbers towards the Norman Conquest.

It has been claimed that the clearance of land led to the development of marshlands in the south and east of England, which may have been endemic for malaria (Roberts and Cox 2003: 170). Malaria may be indicated in the disease named *lencten adl*, 'spring disease', in leechbooks, but the parasite infection does not leave any evidence on the bone. However, parasite infection has been linked to chronic anaemia, which can be indicated in the pitting of eye sockets (*cribra orbitalia*). The presence of such bony changes has a number of causes, but recently, the isolation of ancient DNA from the protozoan parasite has been successful (Roberts and Cox 2003: 170) and further studies may examine the connection between *cribra orbitalia* and parasite infestation.

Other diseases, such as Paget's Disease (*osteitis deformans*) are less common, but are occasionally found. Paget's is a chronic bone disorder, which manifests itself in a thickening of the bone and can affect the hearing as the bone growth is in the skull, though 60–80 per cent of people with the disease in the UK today, where the disease is more common than anywhere else in the world, have no symptoms at all. It is more common in people of European descent (Roberts and Cox 2003: 127). The causes of this disease are as yet unknown, but it is commonly assumed to be the result of a slow viral infection. However, genetic preponderance may also be a factor. Examples have been found at late Anglo-Saxon sites, including the monastery at Jarrow, Tyne and Wear, where skeletons show the characteristic thickening of the bone, as well as kyphosis (Wells and Woodhouse 1975), and Portchester (Hooper 1976).

Physical impairment

Some of the most severe disorders suffered by the Anglo-Saxon population will have been difficult to ameliorate due to the available medical knowledge base in Anglo-Saxon communities. It is however, striking to observe the range of conditions that have been detected, all of which point to the inclusion of the afflicted in social and community life.

Deafness is well recorded in textual sources, but is difficult to prove in skeletal remains. However, the skeleton of a young woman at Castledyke showed a congenital malformation of the ear-bone (Drinkall and Foreman 1998: 235). Like all delicate bones, the bones in the ear are more prone to decay in archaeological deposits, and only one side of the head could be examined for this condition.

The earliest British examples of cleft palates have been recorded for this period, for example at Burwell, Cambridgeshire (Brothwell 1981). Cleft palates are more frequent in males, and they occur if the tissue which forms the roof of the mouth on either side of the tongue, and which usually grows together in the sixth week of the baby's development in the womb, fails to join. Among human populations, cleft palates are less frequent in people whose genetic background is African, and most common in people of Asian descent. Breastfeeding babies who have a cleft palate is very difficult (usually children have to be laboriously spoon-fed) and a mammiform vessel found at Castledyke, Barton-on-Humber (Lincolnshire) has been discussed as a possible help to feed a baby with this condition (Drinkall and Foreman 1998: 309–10).

Down's Syndrome (trisomy 21), which occurs in a range of severity, and is based on a chromosomal abnormality, is also first recorded in Britain during the Anglo-Saxon period (Roberts and Cox 2003: 179). Dwarfism, a condition which is relatively rare, has also been detected in one case (ibid.).

Other conditions, which are relatively frequent in modern populations, such as congenital dislocation of the hips, are recorded less frequently. Roberts and Cox, in their collection of data, only show evidence for two cases, both of them from the post-Conversion period at Nazeingbury, Essex, and St Oswald's Minster, Gloucester (Roberts and Cox 2003: 180, table 4.5)

Other diseases

Cancer is a ubiquitous disease today and there is evidence in Anglo-Saxon England as well. Roberts and Cox list several occurrences from the Anglo-Saxon period: a malignant tumour (osteosarcoma) from the pagan cemetery at Standlake Down, Oxfordshire, on a middle-aged man, and multiple myeloma on an elderly woman from Abingdon, Oxfordshire. At Melbourn, an elderly male showed neoplasms on his neck, which indicate the development of a malignant condition in the spinal cord (Duncan *et al.* 2003). Further examples come from the seventh-century sites at Edix Hill, Cambridgeshire, and Eccles, Kent, as well as the post-conversion cemetery at Ailcy Hill, Yorkshire (Roberts and Cox 2003: 182). Roberts and Cox note that the frequency and variety of the condition increases during the Anglo-Saxon period, which may reflect changes in diet and lifestyle (ibid.: 183). Amongst them, the most severe conditions that have been excavated must be a hydrocephalus from Eccles, Kent, in an adolescent of 14–16 years of age (Manchester 1980). The condition may have been caused by an intra-cranial tumour.

If anything, the list of diseases and resulting conditions shown above underlines that the sick and impaired were reared and cared for. For some of the afflicted to live into adult age there must have been a will, as well as a method of caring for them. Additionally, those who had the misfortune to suffer from disease were cared for, as indicated, for example, in the skeleton of a woman at West Heslerton (G 114), who was severely impaired after suffering a stroke that paralysed her from the chest down (Haughton and Powlesland 1999; Roberts and Cox 2003: 217). This burial clearly demonstrates how much our interpretation of such evidence depends on our understanding of burial rites in general, since the care that the woman received (who clearly had to be helped in her daily ablutions, as well as being carried) may be contrasted with her burial position, which was being laid out prone in a ditch with her feet bound (Houghton and Powlesland 1999). The binding of the feet is interpreted as a 'ritual' in the cemetery report; however, it may be argued that a person with a severe impairment may have had her feet bound to keep her legs together as part of her care.

Healing and Health Care

Questions of healing and attitudes towards the diseased may be culturally complex and they are intrinsically linked to the position of the sick in society. Evidence for disease should be contrasted with the impact that such afflictions had for the sufferer. There is a fundamental question of whether disease, disability, or deformity were seen as problematic at all. This question is closely linked to the issue of a framework of help, if not cure, that the afflicted could utilize. Recent studies into disability in the medieval period (Metzler 2006) have queried the assumption that physical impairment equals disability.

The question of who is worthy of treatment may be examined by looking at how well injuries were cared for. The relative paucity of weapon wounds stands in contrast to the high number of weapons buried with skeletons in cemeteries, and may underline the largely peaceful nature of life in Anglo-Saxon England, and the symbolic value of weapons. However, wounds caused by weapons were found on several skulls. An examination of the pre-mortem cranial wounds has shown that some of these may have been battle injuries (Anderson 1996: 13), but that in only a small number of cases is there evidence for healing, which is indicated by a vascularization of the internal surface and remodelling of the bone. It is uncertain whether these few survivors received superior medical intervention, or whether they were just lucky enough to survive their injuries. It is also unclear whether the other group died due to a lack of medical expertise, or because of deliberate neglect. Perhaps their injuries were deemed too serious for treatment, but it is also possible that the relatively small number of people with weapon injuries received their wounds as a form of punishment. Forensic studies of injuries (Patrick 2006) do not always point to a combat situation for the injured. Mutilation was a form of punishment, especially in the late Saxon period. The cutting-off of hands for thieves was stipulated by the Laws of Cnut, and repeat offenders risked having their eyes poked out or their noses cut off (Crawford 2009).

The most finite form of punishment was, of course, execution, and the growing number of execution cemeteries excavated show that it was widely practised, especially in the post-Conversion period. However, occasionally the damage to the skeleton was post mortem, as for example at the late pre-Christian cemetery at West Heslerton, North Yorkshire, and the Christian burial ground at Raunds Furnells. The question of why the skeletons have been deliberately mutilated remains unanswered, but it is possible that this may have been a rite of defacing a criminal or enemy.

The question of who is given medical attention is hard to answer, but in another form of drilling through the skull (trepanning) a different picture emerges. Trepanning was practised by the Anglo-Saxons (Parker 1989: 74) and in the majority of cases the wounds healed neatly. The reason behind trepanning is still not clear, with explanations from a cure for migraines to medico-magical rituals being offered. However, what should be observed is that this method is with all likelihood a medical procedure (Roberts and McKinley 2002: 69), not a mutilation, and care is given to the persons treated in this way. Later sources, such as the laws of King Cnut, do not allow medical intervention for three days for a person sentenced to mutilation (Crawford 2009), which would have increased the likelihood of infection, which is not evident in the cases of trepanation from the Anglo-Saxon archaeological record.

The 'magical' items which were included in the burial rite have been interpreted as evidence for early physicians. Amulets, and especially so-called 'relic boxes', have been identified as items of healing (Meaney 1981: 9–10; Dickinson 1993), and most of these were found with female burials. Evidence for female healers and woman-specific medicine is hard to come by. Among the four leeches named in later text sources there is not a single female doctor. There are texts within the Anglo-Saxon *Prognostics* which are concerned with the development of the foetus (Chardonnes 2007: 229), but they may concern the legal status of the unborn child, rather than being evidence for gynaecological training (ibid.: 225).

Textual evidence seems to suggest the continuation of 'folk medicine' into the later Anglo-Saxon period, such as charms and rituals. In a number of cases these are only visible from clerical texts and it may be debatable how widespread such practices were. For example, the *Penitential* of Theodore refers to the penance for a woman trying to heal her child by dragging it through a clod of earth, as well as that for a woman placing her daughter in an oven (Wasserschleben 1954: 200). The *Lacnunga*, a collection of manuscripts from the turn of the first millennium, contains charms against mysterious diseases such as 'elf-shot', as well as 'flying poison' (which may be a bacterial infection, as Meaney has suggested; Meaney 1992: 16).

While we see evidence for healing in the pagan period, Christianity brought a new framework of ideas on disease to converted areas. The success of Christianity in its early days was partly based on the fact that the adherents seem to have specifically given care to the sick and needy (Porterfield 2005: 44–51). From the third century, influential writers such as Origen used medical analogies to show that, unlike their pagan deities, Christ was a physician of the soul as well as of the body (Amundsen 1996: 133). Christ is described as the 'Great Physician', and those who are in his ministry were also endowed with powers of healing (Porterfield 2005: 51). In the writings of the Church Fathers, medicine is a beneficial and God-given gift. However, there is also a notion as early as Jerome that sickness is an outward sign of sin, and a means of adjusting priorities. The sick body acts as a warning sign, and allows the sufferer to turn around and atone for his sin. Sickness is at the same time a token of sinfulness as well as a pre-mortem form of purgatory. Narratives of the uncorrupted bodies of saints thus are regarded as a token of spiritual haleness. There is little evidence that the sick were stigmatized in the Anglo-Saxon period, although they may have utilized a new form of healing which was administered at the shrines of saints. Saints were thought to be endowed with healing powers and the emergence of shrines and sepulchres also attracted a number of the sick.

The connection between religious buildings and health care may have been anticipated in special temples that were associated with the cure of disease in ancient Greece. However, there is no evidence for a deliberate provision of care before Christianity became the official religion of the Roman Empire. One of the first hospitals was founded under the directive of Basil of Caesarea around 370, who was also an important canonical influence on the study of healing and disease in Christianity. The primary aim of these early hospitals was not cure, but caring for people who could otherwise not look after themselves, which included the old, the poor, as well as the sick and impaired. Medieval monasteries had infirmaries which were under the supervision of the cellarer. The earliest record for a hospital in Anglo-Saxon England is St Peter at York, which was founded by King Athelstan in 937 and was situated roughly beneath the modern Theatre Royal (Bonser 1963: 95); others have been attributed to Flixton in Holderness, and Worcester, founded by

St Oswald. While there is not much documentary evidence for the founding of hospitals, there are plenty of monastic sites which contain graveyards with a high proportion of women or children, which are supposedly drawn from the lay population (good examples are Whithorn, Dumfries and Galloway, where the associated Life of St Ninian tells of miracle curing; and the recently recovered Hartlepool). At Ailcy Hill (Ripon, North Yorkshire), the former monastic cemetery was used in the second phase for a series of distinct burials, one of which was a young person with tuberculosis which had affected the spine (Hadley and Buckberry 2005).

The extant medical textbooks are all from a late Saxon context. Apart from the *Lacnunga*, there is the mid-tenth-century Bald's *Leechbook* (named after the person who owned the book), as well as an Old English translation of the *Peri didaxeion*. All of these treatises assume some prior form of training or knowledge, since there are no measures given for the list of ingredients. Some of these ingredients are costly and had to be imported, especially in the case of Bald's *Leechbook*, and there has so far been no consideration whether faunal remains found in graves may have come from possible potions or salves or a special diet for the sick. Examinations of monastic sites should also consider whether there is any evidence for herbs grown as part of an apothecary.

FUTURE RESEARCH

One of the most strident problems of comparing data is that there is no standard system of recording (Roberts and Cox 2003: 402). For example, there is no coherent recording of osteology (some reports note every piece of bone growth, others just note the most outstanding pathology), and there is so far no coherent system of presenting disease and impairment in reports. Future research needs to find a unified system so that data can be compared between sites.

Recent research has made much use of the scientific and forensic methods now available to archaeologists, such as isotope analysis and DNA analysis. Future examinations may include microbiological examinations which may corroborate archaeological and historical evidence. Stable isotope analysis as well as research in ancient DNA have already shown some interesting conclusions on the genetic background of the Anglo-Saxons (Montgomery *et al.* 2005), as well as their diet, and further research will show a more detailed picture of life in Anglo-Saxon England. In the light of such advancements, older research may have to be revisited. Some modern geneticists have drawn parallels between migration and genomes, methods which have been used to calculate the number of settlers in the Anglo-Saxon period (Thomas et al. 2008) and the later Viking migrants (Goodacre et al. 2005; Bowden et al. 2008). Genetic disposition, as well as lifestyle, plays an important part in the prevalence and development of diseases, and future research may examine correlations between population groups and disease.

Some diseases that may not be detectable in the bone material and information may be recovered from other sources. Pandemic outbreaks often have significant demographic, as well as economic, consequences, and changes in the economy, agriculture, or even settlements may have their origins in a decimation of resources or labour after an outbreak of epidemic disease. It has been suggested, for example, that some form of epidemic disease ravaged seventh-century Anglo-Saxon England (Bonser 1963; Maddicot 1997). While this outbreak, according to textual sources, led to a whole-scale destruction of monastic communities, as for example described in the Anonymous Life of St Cuthbert (composed between 698 and 705), the social, demographic, and economic fallout has not yet been studied. Two phases of plague were documented (the first between 664 and 666, the second from 684 to 689; Maddicot 1997: 11) and the absence of rat remains in the early burial record has led to suggestions that this is pneumonic plague, rather than the less lethal bubonic plague (Maddicot 1997). John Maddicot suggests that evidence comes from the excavated settlements from early Anglo-Saxon England (West Stow, Charlton, Mucking, Yeavering, Puddlehill), which were all given up around the turn of the eighth century, and that some contemporary cemeteries have indications for plague burial, such as the seventh-century site at Camerton (Somerset) where 115 bodies, including 40 children, appear to have been hastily buried (ibid.: 44). However, Maddicot assumes that the surviving population recovered quickly after the outbreak, contrary to evidence from later pandemics which show a very slow regeneration of populations (Benedictow 1992). The reason for this speedy recovery may be sought elsewhere. During the ninth century we see a migration of Scandinavian settlers to areas in the north and midlands of England. Contrary to assumptions largely based on texts from their West Saxon opponents, these may not have had to disperse the original population, as often claimed, but may have been able to move into largely empty lands.

Research in the efficacy of Anglo-Saxon medicine (Cameron 1993; Brennessel et al. 2005), let alone the vocabulary of some of the more obscure terms in the medical texts, may be studied complementarily to the results from osteological and scientific examinations. In addition, the data from palaeopathology should be compared to other information we have for the afflicted, which may include the burial space, structures above ground, as well as furnishing of the grave. Most importantly, a more holistic approach, which is better funded and based on a more coherent form of data collection, is required to take our understanding of Anglo-Saxon disease and healing from case studies to a more complete picture of health.

Conclusions

Just as in the twenty-first century, disease was a common companion in life. In many instances, we can see a desire to cure the afflicted, or at least to make them comfortable in Anglo-Saxon society. The popular image of the diseased and disabled as outcast or poor needs some serious challenging, in the same way as the assumption that most people lived their short lives in squalor and disease. It is debatable whether observations from modern populations can be transferred to the past. There is a need to get better acquainted with Anglo-Saxon attitudes towards the diseased and impaired, rather than making assumptions drawn from texts written for a particular audience, steeped in the exegesis of patristic sources, or which use the language of sickness to create literary images. Neither should there be an assumption that any form of pathology observed on the bone would have automatically required adjustment or medical attention. Conditions that may be observed by the modern osteologist may not have been an impediment in life at all. Depending on the space that a bone report may command within a publication, an osteologist may record minute changes (which were not felt by the person at all, such as for example the ample occurrence of spina bifida occulta, which, unlike its more sinister cousin, only affects parts of the lower spine and has very few symptoms apart from possible back pain). Even if the condition is more severe we need to consider whether this would have affected the status of the sufferer. It is feasible that Anglo-Saxon society had spaces for all kinds of people: the sick and the hale, the old and the young. It is therefore conceivable that adjustments were made on a regular basis.

References

AMUNDSEN, D. W. (1996). *Medicine, Society, and Faith in the Ancient and Medieval Worlds*. Baltimore, MD: Johns Hopkins University Press.

ANDERSON, J. G. (1969). *Studies in the Mediaeval Diagnosis of Leprosy in Denmark*. Copenhagen: Costers Bogtrykkeri.

ANDERSON, T. (1996). 'Cranial weapon injuries from Anglo-Saxon Dover'. *International Journal of International Osteoarchaeology* 6: 10–14.

BENEDICTOW, O. (1992). *Plague in the Late Medieval Nordic countries: Epidemiological Studies*. Oslo: Middelalterforlaget.

BLAIR, J. (2005). *The Church in Anglo-Saxon Society*. Oxford: Oxford University Press.

BODDINGTON, A. (ed.) (1996). *Raunds Furnells: The Anglo-Saxon Church and Churchyard*. London: English Heritage.

BONSER, W. (1963). *The Medical Background of Anglo-Saxon England: A Study in the History, Psychology and Folklore*. London: Wellcome Historical Library.

Bowden, G., Balaresque, P., King, T., Hansen, Z., Lee, A., Pergi-Wilson, G., Hurley, E., Roberts, S., Waite, P., Jesch, J., Jones, A., Thomas, M., Harding, S., and Jobling, M. (2008). 'Excavating past population structures by surname-based sampling: the genetic legacy of the Vikings in northwest England'. *Molecular Biology and Evolution* 25: 301–9.

Brennessel, B., Drout, M., and Gravel, R. (2005). 'A reassessment of the efficacy of Anglo-Saxon medicine'. *Anglo-Saxon England* 34: 183–95.

Brothwell, D. (1981). *Digging up Bones: The Excavation, Treatment and Study of Human Skeletal Remains.* 3rd edition. Oxford: Oxford University Press.

Buckberry, J. (2007). 'On sacred ground: Social identity and churchyard burial in Lincolnshire and Yorkshire, c. 700–1100'. *Anglo-Saxon Studies in Archaeology and History* 14: 117–24.

Cameron, M. (1993). *Anglo-Saxon Medicine.* Cambridge: Cambridge University Press.

Chardonnes, L. (2007). *Anglo-Saxon Prognostics: 900–1100; Study And Texts.* Leiden: Brill.

Cockayne, O. (ed.) (1864–66). *Leechdoms, Wortcunning and Starcraft of Early England.* Rolls Series, 3 volumes. London: Longman.

Crawford, S. (1993). 'Children, death and the afterlife in Anglo-Saxon England'. *Anglo-Saxon Studies in Archaeology and History* 6: 83–91.

—— (2007). 'Companions, co-incidences or chattels? Children and their role in early Anglo-Saxon multiple burials', in S. Crawford and G. Shepherd (eds.), *Children, Childhood and Society.* IAA Interdisciplinary Series, Volume 1: Studies in Archaeology, History, Literature and Art. British Archaeological Reports International Series 1696. Oxford: Archaeopress, 83–92.

—— (2009). 'Differentiation in the Later Anglo-Saxon burial ritual on the basis of mental or physical impairment: a documentary perspective', in J. L. Buckberry and A. K. Cherryson (eds.), *Later Anglo-Saxon Burial, c.650 to 1100AD.* Oxford: Oxbow.

—— Crawford, S, and Randall, T. (2002). 'Bald's Leechbook and archaeology: two approaches to Anglo-Saxon health and healthcare', in R. Arnott (ed.), *The Archaeology of Medicine: Papers given at a session of the annual conference of the Theoretical Archaeology Group held at the University of Birmingham on 20th December 1998.* BAR International Series. Oxford, 101–4.

Daniel, R., and Loveluck, C. (eds.) (2007). *Anglo-Saxon Hartlepool and the Foundations of English Christianity.* Tees Archaeology Monograph Series 3. Hartlepool: Tees Archaeology.

Dickinson, T. (1993). 'An Anglo-Saxon "cunning woman" from Bidford-on Avon', in M. Carver (ed.), *In Search of Cult: Archaeological Investigations in Honour of Philip Rahtz.* Woodbridge: Boydell, 45–54.

Dingwall, R. (2001). *Aspects of Illness.* 2nd edition. Aldershot: Ashgate.

Down, A., and Welch, M. (1990). *Chichester Excavations VII: Apple Down and the Mardens.* Chichester: Chichester District Council.

Drinkall, G., and Foreman, M. (eds.) (1998). *The Anglo-Saxon Cemetery at Castledyke South, Barton-on-Humber.* Sheffield Excavation Report 6. Sheffield: Sheffield Academic Press.

Duncan, H., Duhig, C., and Phillips, M. (eds.) (2003). 'A late Migration phase/ Final Phase cemetery at Water Lane, Melbourn'. *Proceedings of the Cambridge Antiquarian Society* 42: 57–134.

Dutour, O., Signoli, M., and Pálfi, G. (1998). 'How can we reconstruct the epidemiology of infectious disease in the past?', in C. Greenblatt (ed.), *Digging for Pathogens.* Philadelphia, PA: Balaban, 241–63.

EVISON, V. (1994). *An Anglo-Saxon Cemetery at Great Chesterford, Essex.* York: Council for British Archaeology.

GITTOS, H. (2002). 'Creating the Sacred: Anglo-Saxon rites for consecrating cemeteries', in Lucy and Reynolds (eds.), *Burial in Early Medieval England and Wales,* 195–208.

GOODACRE, S., HELGASSON, A., NICHOLSON, J., SOUTHAM, L., FERGUSON, L., HICKEY, E., VEGA, E., STÉFANSSON, K., WARD R., and SYKES, B. (2005). 'Genetic evidence for family-based Scandinavian settlement of Shetland and Orkney during the Viking period'. *Heredity* 95: 129–35.

GRATTAN, J. G., and SINGER, C. (eds.) (1952). *Anglo-Saxon Magic and Medicine.* London: Oxford University Press.

HADLEY, D. (2004), 'Negotiating family and status and gender in Anglo-Saxon burial practices, c. 600–950', in L. Brubaker and J. Smith (eds.), *Gender in the Early Medieval World.* Cambridge: Cambridge University Press, 301–23.

—— (2010). 'Burying the socially and physically distinctive in later Anglo-Saxon England', in J. L. Buckberry and A. K. Cherryson (eds.), *Later Anglo-Saxon Burial, c.650 to 1100AD.* Oxford: Oxbow, 101–13.

—— and BUCKBERRY, J. (2005). 'Caring for the dead in Late Anglo-Saxon England', in F. Tinti (ed.), *Pastoral Care in Late Anglo-Saxon England.* Woodbridge: Boydell, 121–47.

HAUGHTON, C., and POWLESLAND, D. et al. (1999). *West Heslerton: The Anglian Cemetery.* 2 volumes. Yedingham: Landscape Research Centre.

HAWKES, S., and GRAINGER, G. (eds.) (2003). *The Anglo-Saxon Cemetery at Worthy Park, Kingsworthy, near Winchester, Hampshire.* Oxford: University of Oxford, School of Archaeology.

HOOPER, B. (1976). 'The Saxon burials', in B. Cunliffe (ed.), *Excavations at Portchester Castle,* Volume 2: *Saxon.* London: Society of Antiquaries, 235–61.

JAKOB, B. (2004) *Prevalence and Patterns of Disease in Early Medieval Populations: A Comparison of Skeletal Samples from Fifth to Eighth Century Germany.* Unpublished PhD thesis, University of Durham.

LEE, C. (2006). 'Changing faces: leprosy in Anglo-Saxon England', in C. Karkov and N. Howe (eds.), *Conversion and Colonization.* Tempe: ACMRS, 59–81.

—— (2008). 'Forever young: child burial in Anglo-Saxon England', in S. Lewis-Simpson (ed.), *Youth and Age in the Medieval North.* Leiden: Brill, 17–36.

LEWIS, M. (2002). 'Impact of industrialization: comparative study of child health in four sites from medieval to postmedieval England (A.D. 850–1859)'. *American Journal of Physical Anthropology* 119: 211–23.

LUCY, S., and REYNOLDS, A. (eds.) (2002). *Burial in Early Medieval England and Wales.* Society for Medieval Archaeology Monograph 17. London: Society for Medieval Archaeology.

MADDICOT, J. R. (1997). 'Plague in seventh-century England'. *Past and Present* 156: 7–54.

MANCHESTER, K. (1980). 'Hydrocephalus in an Anglo-Saxon child from Eccles'. *Archaeologia Cantiana* 96: 77–83.

MAYS, S. (1998). *The Archaeology of Human Bones.* London: Routledge.

MEANEY, A. (1981). *Anglo-Saxon Amulets and Curing Stones.* BAR British Series 96. Oxford: British Archaeological Reports.

—— (1992). 'The Anglo-Saxon view of illness', in S. Campbell, B. Hall, and D. Klausner (eds.), *Health, Disease and Healing in Medieval Culture.* London: Macmillan, 12–33.

Metzler, I. (2006). *Disability in Medieval Europe: Thinking about Physical Impairment in the High Middle Ages c. 1100–1400*. London: Routledge.

Møller-Christensen, V. (1961). *Bone Changes in Leprosy*. Copenhagen: Munksgaard.

—— (1967). 'Evidence for leprosy in early peoples', in D. Brothwell and A. Sanderson (eds.), *Diseases in Antiquity*. Springfield: Charles Thomas, 295–306.

Montgomery, J., Evans, J., Powlesland, D., and Roberts, C. (2005). 'Continuity or colonization in Anglo-Saxon England? Isotope evidence for mobility, subsistence practice and status at West Heslerton'. *American Journal of Physical Anthropology* 126: 123–38.

Parker, S. J. (1989). 'Skulls, symbols and surgery: a review of evidence for trepanation in Anglo-Saxon England and a consideration of motives behind the practice', in D. Scragg (ed.), *Superstition and Popular Medicine in Anglo-Saxon England*. Manchester: MANCASS, 73–84.

Patrick, P. (2006). 'Approaches to violent death: a case study from early medieval Cambridge'. *International Journal of Osteoarchaeology* 16: 347–54.

Popescu, E. (ed.) (2009). *Norwich Castle: Excavations and Historical Survey 1987–98*. Dereham: Historic Environment, Norfolk Museums and Archaeology Service.

Porterfield, A. (2005). *Healing in the History of Christianity*. Oxford: Oxford University Press.

Powell, F. (1996). 'Paleopathology', in A. Bodington (ed.), *Raunds Furnells: The Anglo-Saxon Church and Churchyard*. London: English Heritage.

Rawcliffe, C. (2006). *Leprosy in Medieval England*. Woodbridge: Boydell Press.

Roberts, C. (2000). 'Did they take sugar? The use of skeletal evidence in past populations', in J. Hubert (ed.) *Madness, Disability and Exclusion: the archaeology and anthropology of 'difference'*. London: Routledge, 46-59.

—— (2002a). 'Tuberculosis: a multidisciplinary approach to past and current concepts, causes and treatments of this infectious disease', in P. Baker and G. Carr (eds.), *Practitioners, Practices and Patients: New Approaches to Medical Archaeology and Anthropology; The Proceedings of a Conference held at Magdalene College, 2000*. Oxford: Oxbow, 30–46.

—— (2002b). 'Paleopathology and archaeology: the current state of play', in R. Arnott (ed.) *The Archaeology of Medicine: papers given at a session of the annual conference of the Theoretical Archaeology Group held at the University of Birmingham on 20th December 1998*. BAR International Series. Oxford, 1–20.

—— (2007). 'A bioarchaeological study of maxillary sinusitis'. *American Journal of Physical Anthropology* 133: 792–807.

—— and M. Cox (2003). *Health and Disease in Medieval Britain: From Pre-History to the Present Day*. Stroud: Sutton.

—— and Manchester, K. (2005). *The Archaeology of Disease*. Revised edition. Stroud: Sutton.

—— and McKinley, J. (2002). 'Review of trepanations in British Antiquity focusing on funerary contexts to explain their occurrence', in R. Arnott, S. Finger, and C. Smith (eds.), *Trepanning: History—Discovery—Theory*. London: Taylor and Francis, 55–78.

Rogers, J., and Waldron, T. (2001). 'DISH and the monastic way of life'. *International Journal of Osteoarchaeology* 11: 357–65.

Saunders, S. (2000). 'Subadult skeletons and growth-related studies', in M. Katzenberg and S. R. Saunders (eds.), *Biological Anthropology of the Human Skeleton*. New York: Wiley, 1–20.

STOODLEY, N. (1999). *The Spindle and the Spear: A Critical Inquiry into the Construction and Meaning of Gender in the Early Anglo-Saxon Burial Rite*. BAR British Series 288. Oxford: British Archaeological Reports.

—— (2002). 'Multiple burials, multiple meanings? Interpreting the early Anglo-Saxon multiple interment', in Lucy and Reynolds (eds.), *Burial in Early Medieval England and Wales*, 103–21.

THOMAS, M., STUMPF, M., and HÄRKE, H. (2008). 'Integration versus apartheid in Post-Roman Britain: a response to Pattison'. *Proc. Roy. Soc. London.* B 275: 2419–21.

THOMPSON, V. (2004). *Death and Dying in Later Anglo-Saxon England*. Woodbridge: Boydell.

WALDRON, T. (1994). *Counting the Dead: The Epidemiology of Skeletal Populations*. New York: Wiley.

—— (1996). 'What was the prevalence of malignant disease in the past?'. *International Journal of International Osteoarchaeology* 6, 463-70.

WASSERSCHLEBEN, F. H. (1954). *Die Bussordnungen der Abendländischen Kirche*. Graz: Akademische Verlagsanstalt.

WELLS, C., and WOODHOUSE, N. (1975). 'Paget's disease in an Anglo-Saxon'. *Medical History* 19: 396–400.

PART VIII

THE ARCHAEOLOGY OF RELIGION

CHAPTER 37

OVERVIEW: THE ARCHAEOLOGY OF RELIGION

JOHN BLAIR

We once thought that we knew quite a lot about Anglo-Saxon Christianity, at least in comparison with most other areas of Anglo-Saxon life. Slowly, realization has grown that the narrative from written sources is—when not actually wrong—partial, distorted, and neglectful of large areas of religious organization and experience that were central to people at large. On the other hand some quite unexpected avenues, entered both through new evidence and through comparative perspectives, have been opening. Also, the archaeology of both pagan and Christian ritual and religious topography has, over the last twenty years, attracted a notably talented cohort of young Anglo-Saxonists, some of them among the present contributors. Perhaps we can now say that we know quite a lot after all, even if it is not what we once thought we knew.

An important conceptual advance has been the dismantling of two barriers that used to be taken for granted: between the religious and secular worlds, and between Christianity and paganism. We would all now recognize that the step from a pre-literate to a literate society is not by definition a step from inchoate barbarism to ordered civilization. Almost all these chapters touch, either explicitly or implicitly, on ritual continuities across the sixth to eighth centuries, and it is clear that even as late as the eleventh century, important aspects of lay Christianity were still influenced by traditional indigenous practices. The chapters also explore ways in which the worlds of secular life and of religious belief and organization influenced each other: perhaps most of all in the seventh and eighth centuries, when a Continental religious culture became so enmeshed in the priorities and strategies of the warrior aristocracy which it was simultaneously transforming. Here, then, I shall stress contacts and continuities, while also drawing attention to some parallels with other pre-industrial societies that may help us to understand our enigmatic scraps of evidence.

One important new direction (inspired by prehistory, notably Richard Bradley's *An Archaeology of Natural Places*) is awareness of the natural world, and its manipulation, as the foundation of religious cult in the landscape. Sarah Semple shows how regular human activity at places considered sacred, perhaps even including the cultivation of special plants, would have given them a character and atmosphere marking them out as distinctive, even without any built structures. Some locations, such as peaks, prominent trees or stones, fissures, pools, and pits would have looked special already, notably the latter with their suggestions of entry-points to an underworld. Long-term continuities in the choosing and preparation of sacred places probably crossed the pagan/Christian divide: when the mentor of the early-eighth-century nobleman Eanmund saw in a vision a small hill facing the sun with a cover of thorn-scrub, and told him to clear it to build his church (Blair 2005: 191–3), the geomantic undertones may have been as much indigenous as scholarly.

An especially interesting development has been the realization that one ritual recorded already in prehistory, the deposition of weapons and other objects in water, continued right through the Christian Anglo-Saxon period and beyond. Rivers, lakes, and bogs seem to have retained their other-worldly and liminal character as safe-deposits for the sacred and the dangerous: when English people of the tenth and eleventh centuries believed themselves confronted by the malevolent returning dead who refused to stay in their graves, the most common response was to deposit them in pools and mires in the manner of Iron Age bog-bodies (Blair 2009: 550–2)—a documented practice that should surely be reflected in archaeology. The world-view of ecclesiastical writers privileged classical and urban models and enclosed sacred space, but most English Christians may have been closer to those who, as Alcuin complained in the 790s, 'leave the churches and seek hilly places' (Blair 2005: 177): the landscape was the natural setting for ritual practice, and was loaded with significance.

Some of this significance derived from its previous occupants, real or imagined. The re-use of prehistoric and Roman structures for Anglo-Saxon cult, both pagan and Christian, has been another rich line of enquiry, notably in the work of Tyler Bell, Sarah Semple, and Howard Williams. Again there is a continuum. The use of Bronze Age barrows for rich burials developed during the sixth century but especially in the years after 600, when we also start to find these landmarks adopted as the foci of formal building complexes, for instance—and most spectacularly—

Yeavering. When seventh-century missionaries, following what had been Mediterranean practice from Constantine onwards, wanted to site their new churches in visibly Romano-British towns, forts, and villas, newly-converted English kings would have understood their concern, however different the theological backgrounds. The missionaries would of course have recognized the Roman ruins for what they were, whereas in English minds there may have been less clear a distinction between, say, a natural hill and a barrow which were both associated with folk-heroes. This then is another continuum, from the adoption of natural foci to the re-adoption of man-made ones.

Ritual was not confined to reserved sacred places: it is almost certain that settlements and dwellings in this culture, as in many others, were arenas for ceremonies that may have been articulated to the life cycles of peoples and of buildings. Evidence is hard to recover and interpret, and may be skewed (the building initiation rituals in some recent societies would leave no archaeological trace), but a surprising number of cases have been collected and analysed (Hamerow 2006). Whereas Anglo-Saxon dwellings provide less evidence for foundation deposits than those in some other north-west European cultures, closure deposits—made on the building's abandonment—seem common: a rite of passage and separation like a funeral? Where human burials occur in settlements or structural shrines (Hamerow 2006: 9–14; Blair 1995: 19) they tend to be in liminal locations, at entrances or on boundaries (Fig. 37.1), and of abnormal character: there may be a link between special individuals and the articulation or protection of reserved space.

Who were the 'special individuals' in pre-Christian ritual practice? One of the few things that we do seem to know about Anglo-Saxon paganism, as comes out strongly from Aleks Pluskowski's chapter, is that animals had a prominent place in it. Partly because of this, and partly because searches for analogies with the Anglo-Saxon settlers tend naturally to look northwards, recent explanatory models have placed a heavy emphasis on the shamanism of Lapland and Siberia. Seeking viewpoints outside later western European ones is certainly healthy, and it is hard to doubt that something like shamanism lies ultimately in the background. But care may be needed: it seems very doubtful if the religions of sixth-century England were shamanistic as an anthropologist of Siberia would understand the term, if only because the society was already a long way removed from that of circumpolar hunter-gatherers relying largely on animal protein. Among indigenous north Americans, for instance, the cosmology looks less purely shamanistic, the religious practitioners less like shamans and more like priests, as one moves southwards from the arctic circle (my inference drawn from data in Hunt 2002). In a society already open to such mixed influences we should surely expect mixed—and evolving—religious practices, the evolution accelerating in step with the other complex changes in the decades around 600. It is salutary to note a historian's recent perception of the late-pagan English priesthood which is as far from the

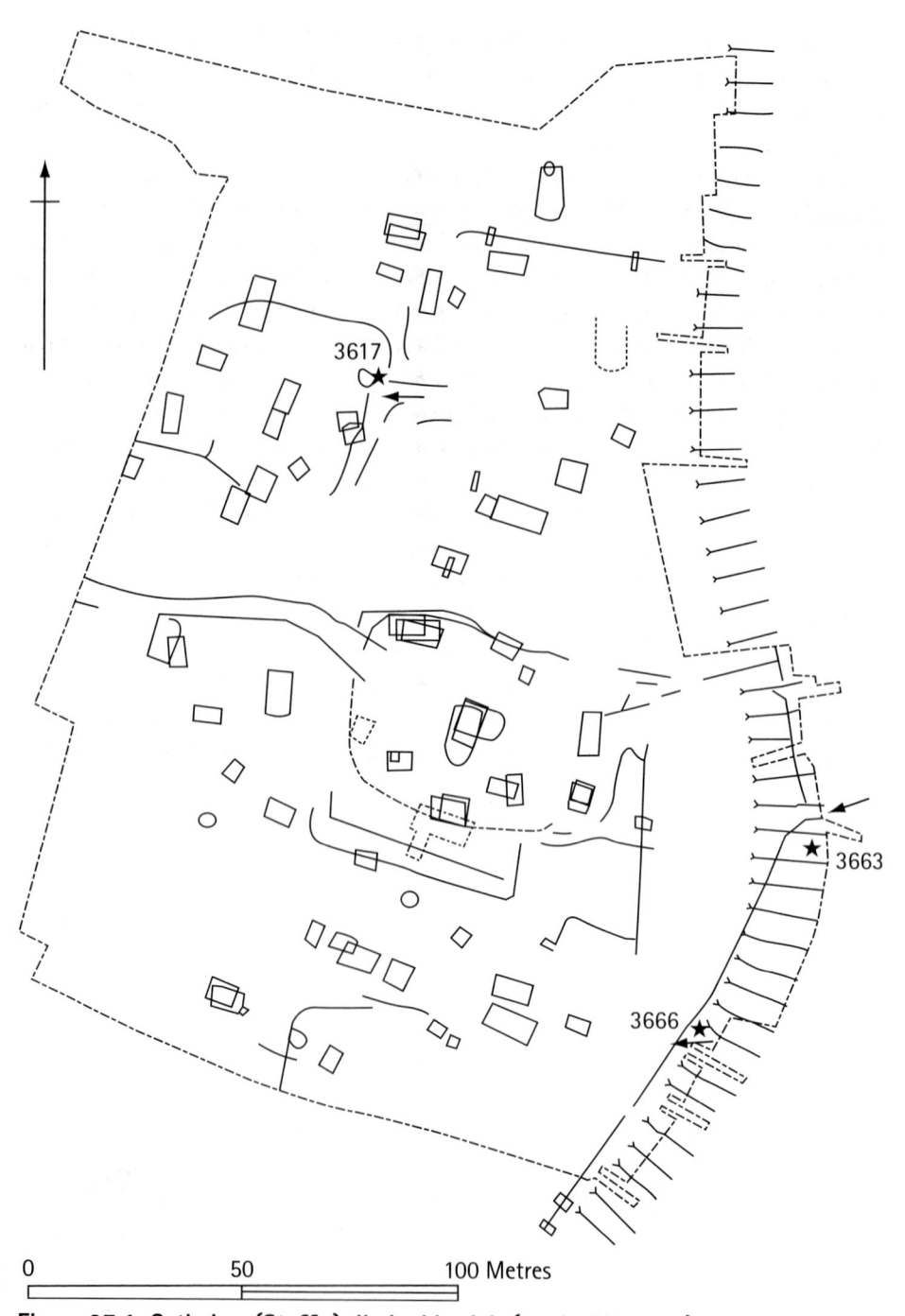

Figure 37.1 Catholme (Staffs.): liminal burials (marked by stars) in relation to the boundaries and enclosures of the Anglo-Saxon settlement. Arrows indicate the entrances to ditched enclosures (Hamerow 2006: fig. 4)

shamanic paradigm as could possibly be: organized, hierarchical, land-owning, and with powers of capital justice (Campbell 2007). If reality lies somewhere between the two extremes, it may well be that during c.550–620 it moved further away from the one and towards the other.

Here the graves of ritual specialists provide opportunities that could still be taken further. Audrey L. Meaney has very convincingly emphasized the prominence of certain women, whose amuletic 'tool-kit' changed significantly after 600 (e.g. Meaney 1989). Tania Dickinson's classic study of the Bidford-on-Avon 'cunning woman', with her shaman-like, jangling pendants (Dickinson 1993), can now be revisited in the light of several new cases of women buried with unusual equipment in unusual ways, and of Neil Price's remarkable study of these phenomena in Viking-age Scandinavia (Price 2002). One could not ask for a clearer ritual specialist than the occupant of grave AX at early-seventh-century Yeavering (Fig. 37.2), laid out on exactly the axis of the great hall with a goat-head under the feet, and what has been interpreted as a surveying-staff across the body (Hope-Taylor 1977: 67–9, 200–3). Did this person, whose gender is unknown, foreshadow the staff-bearing wise-women of later Scandinavia, two of whom are pictured in literary sources as buried at doors of the underworld (Price 2002: 112–16, 175–204; Hamerow 2006: 11)? At all events, the precise axial location of the grave encourages us to associate this individual, and the expert class to which she or he could have belonged, with the new interest in planning and alignment so apparent at both pagan and Christian sites in seventh-century England (cf. Blair 2005: 53–6, 191,

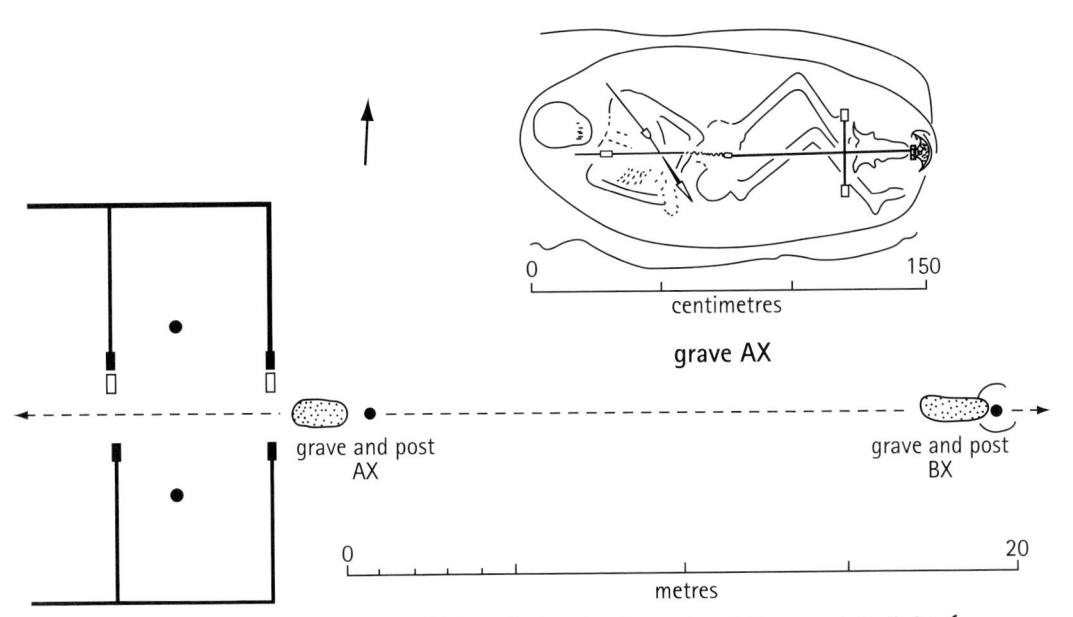

Figure 37.2 Yeavering: grave AX in relation to the axis of the great hall A4 (redrawn from Hope-Taylor 1977: figs. 25, 61)

200). Arcane and specialist knowledge is one of the characteristic signs of priestly castes: it seems possible here to glimpse change over time, and change that may have been decisive just before conversion rather than coinciding with it.

Over time, sacred places did of course acquire a man-made aspect with the building of more-or-less monumental and permanent cult structures. As discussed by Semple and Pluskowski, our scant but gradually growing knowledge of cult structures suggests that pillars or posts in the manner of a totem-pole—caricatured by Aldhelm as the 'crude little herms' of the snake and stag—were prominent, and that from around 600 these were starting to acquire more physical settings, often ditched or fenced square enclosures re-using prehistoric monuments (Blair 1995). These moves towards some kind of architectural display may reflect a dawning awareness of the Continental Church, with its much more monumental and impressive buildings. In England it was the lavish endowment of monasteries after 650 that brought the big transformation, with formal groups and lines of stone churches surrounded by complexes of buildings within enclosures: the 'herms', as Aldhelm delightedly reported, giving way to 'holy houses of prayer constructed skilfully by the talents of the architect'.

It is misleading, however, to put too strong an emphasis on stone. Right through until at least 1000, this was a wooden world in which embellishment of buildings—as of people—was largely done with textiles. Even in minsters the churches were not always of stone, and even when they were they were usually the *only* stone buildings. In ecclesiastical as in domestic life, buildings, furniture, and equipment were largely made of materials that do not survive for us to see: the real watershed here is not conversion but the eleventh century, when a combination of new ecclesiastical attitudes and newly-opened quarries generated a specialist and distinctively ecclesiastical masonry technology, seen for instance in the mass production of stone fonts. Visits to open-air folk museums in Nordic and eastern European countries bring home to us the essential transience of the settings in which people lived and worshipped through the Anglo-Saxon centuries.

Before the 1990s, Anglo-Saxon monastic sites were sunk at about the same level of obscurity as Anglo-Saxon towns before the 1960s. This comment obviously excludes the programmes of research on major churches, such as Monkwearmouth, Jarrow, Deerhurst, and Repton; but it must be recognized that those projects were essentially directed at the core buildings. We now know that we cannot understand an important minster just by looking at '*the* church': there were probably two or three churches, as well as domestic offices, living-quarters, workshops, and industrial areas up to several hundred metres apart. The challenges are increased by uncertainties about knowing a minster when we see one. Various eighth- to ninth-century sites now excavated, of which Flixborough (Lincs.) and Brandon (Suffolk) are the type cases, display what looks like a strongly ecclesiastical culture, including chapels, burials, writing-styli, and objects with Christian symbolism, combined with seemingly ordinary domestic occupation and a rich lifestyle. Are these monastic sites—in which case there seem to be a disconcertingly large number of them—or aristocratic residences strongly imbued with the monastic culture? In the past I have argued for a monastic interpretation, and would still do so, but the matter remains controversial, as the very fair assessment in Helen Gittos' chapter makes clear. The ambiguities are essentially those inherent in Bede's Letter to Ecgberht (AD 734), where he rails at aristocrats who found monasteries, obtain charters to exempt them from taxes, and then live a secular lifestyle in them. With these sites, as with so much else in eighth-century England, knowledge is increasing rapidly, but the more we know, the harder to interpret it all seems.

That should not be an excuse for failing to gather more evidence, and on an altogether larger scale. It is absurd that our archaeological knowledge of all but a few minsters is still restricted to tiny keyholes at most, and even the occasional extensive excavations on small and compact sites (Brandon is the best case) have recovered less than a third of the probable occupied area. Both to understand how minsters really functioned, and to get the ambiguous cases more in perspective, we need a series of large-scale and carefully targeted projects, equivalent to a Mucking for early Anglo-Saxon settlements or a Winchester for towns. Recently Gabor Thomas has made efforts in this direction, with his remarkable discoveries at Bishopstone (Fig. 37.3) and his current projects on the east Kent minsters. It is perhaps in this area that future editions of this *Handbook* are most likely to report real advances.

The present chapters reflect an increased knowledge of the material culture associated with Anglo-Saxon religion, and a greater awareness of its range. Thanks to metal-detecting and the Portable Antiquities Scheme, we can now debate such previously closed topics as the monetarization of monastic centres, the function of writing-styli, and the extent of book-owning as apparent from binding-mounts. So far this is largely another facet of the Flixborough debate: were these things the province of an elite monastic culture, or were styli, for instance, used by the laity for keeping accounts or as prestige ornaments? The problem is compounded by the possible handing-on of discarded monastic luxuries, which is (at least in my view) a plausible explanation for apparently liturgical objects in some rich late-seventh-century graves (Blair 2005: 259n.). We may in any case be misled by the tendency for very small—and usually trivial—things to survive: the recovery of so many pins, styli, tweezers, and so on from East Anglian sites is surely not a measure of their wealth in relation to the major minsters of the West Midlands where these things are not found, but rather the mark of an east-coast culture and economy that fostered a precocious consumerism. Similarly, it must be true that the most prized and prominent items are the ones we cannot see. The strong emphasis on textiles in Elizabeth Coatsworth's present chapter is a valuable corrective, for it would have been these above all that gave the interiors of high-status buildings, both religious and secular, their atmosphere. The tasselled pall, richly embellished with interlace, imitated on an eighth-century grave-slab at Kirkdale (Yorks.), would have been laden with significance (perhaps because it marked the tomb of a saint?) as well as intrinsically a precious object (Lang 1991: 162–3 and ills.

Figure 37.3 Bishopstone (East Sussex), late Anglo-Saxon occupation next to the minster church: excavations in progress, 2003 (photograph by Alan Rawson, © Gabor Thomas)

563–7). In asserting the profound interpenetration of secular and ecclesiastical aesthetics and modes of display, we are left with the challenge of delineating the more subtle differences in preference and register that surely did exist between them.

As this culture of consumer luxuries illustrates, religion throughout the period was intimately connected with economic organization. Given that the big pre-Christian cult sites were probably places of assembly (see Semple's chapter), it seems highly likely that—as in many societies both before and afterwards—they were also places of exchange. This was certainly so with the minsters, which quickly established themselves as sites of regular resort by the laity, and which, by the late ninth century and probably earlier, were starting to attract markets. As Helen Gittos describes, minsters were among the prime foci for late Anglo-Saxon urbanization: one Alfred-period translator rendered Bede's 'through urban places', *per urbana loca*, as *þru mynsterstowe*. The question remains how far, beyond being among the prime foci around which economic activity grouped itself, minsters contributed to its development and expansion? As consumers they must have done so, but it is also very likely that their specialized craft production, as described here by Coatsworth, was not purely for internal use: there would surely have been a wider economic spin-off from what must have been, for the time, exceptionally stable groups of expert craftspeople. Richard Gameson's chapter describes the range of different skills and techniques needed to produce books. These, of course, were distinctively ecclesiastical artefacts, but the existence of such 'production-lines' would have facilitated other kinds of output aimed at lay markets.

This overview has emphasized continuities, but the afterlife of early Anglo-Saxon belief patterns includes some striking areas of *non*-survival. One is the prominence of animals in interactions with the supernatural. Shamanistic or not, there can be no doubt that this was a major component in the fifth and sixth centuries. One might well expect it to infuse lay Christianity for centuries to come, but did it? There are late Anglo-Saxon hints, but surprisingly faint ones: the 'wild hunt' motif, and the shape-shifting of some of the malevolent returning dead; the magical eel from St Nechtan's well that prevented the guildsmen of Hartland from boiling their pot; the raven that carried the slain St Oswald's arm (Blair 2009: 547; Blair 2005: 454, 477). It is tempting to wonder whether animal ornament did continue to be more than purely decorative. Ernst Kitzinger has argued persuasively that panels of animal interlace were used apotropaically in the late seventh and eighth centuries, even in such overtly Christian contexts as the church porch at Monkwearmouth and the nasal of the Coppergate helmet (Kitzinger 1993: 4–5). That such decoration was used on textiles, and that purists perceived undesirable undertones, is suggested by Boniface's tirade in the 740s against the 'broad stripes of serpents' on the edges of garments, which he regarded as prefigurations of Antichrist (Haddan and Stubbs 1871: 382). This is of course a very long way from animal spirit-helpers, or even putting animal remains in graves, and if there are resonances they are very muted. That this should be so suggests that the institutional Church found these beliefs too indigestible to assimilate (in the way that for instance it did assimilate calendar customs and some holy sites), and succeeded in squeezing them to the margins.

Largely to emphasize how much must have been going on that we cannot see, I shall end with four ethnographic comparisons that may guide us in interpreting some of our more fragmentary data. This is emphatically not to say that Anglo-Saxon England was, in any precise sense, like these cases, but rather to illustrate how the values and practices of recorded societies, different from our own, can help the inexplicable to make some kind of sense.

The first enigma is the invisibility of physical structures housing pre-Christian ritual, until their apparent appearance a generation or two before conversion and in the context of monument re-use. But possibly it is misconceived to envisage 'temples' in anything like the usual sense. We may consider the Mansi of the Uralic region, a semi-sedentary group on the fringes of Orthodox Christianity, who have retained a rich polytheistic culture. The diverse pantheon of deities includes protector-spirits of villages, regions, or rivers, equipped with their own shrines, such as that of 'old man-gull':

> The sacral place situated 5 km from the mouth of the Prosol brook... is devoted to him. On the northern end of a rectangular meadow stands an old post darkened by time and foul weather. A four metre long pole is tied to it with seven white cloths; its pointed upper end is covered with a birchbark cap. Below the cap a 'belt' is cut out depicting the neck. The 'head' made in this way creates an anthropomorphic figure in the pole.... A small table for entertaining ['old man-gull'] stands near the pole. On the opposite side of the meadow the path comes in, and across the meadow, at a range of 2.5–3 metres from each other, lie debarked trunks. Faces of spirits are carved on their ends. Approximately 2 metres from the last... trunk is the open fireplace. The ropes, with which the sacrificed animals were brought here, are tied on the trees near it. At both sides of the fireplace lie trunks on which the participants of the rituals sit. The construction of a sacral storehouse is typical for Mansi sanctuaries. Only the end of the top roofbeam is carved like a capercaillie-head. The wooden figure of the hero *naj-oter*, wrapped in cloth and covered with a piece of birchbark, is kept inside the storehouse.
>
> (Gemuev et al. 2008: 53)

Sacred places like this have been observed widely across Nordic regions remote enough for them to have survived, for example in seventeenth-century Lapland (Fig. 37.4). Nothing is inherently incompatible with the little we know about early Anglo-Saxon religion, so the description is worth pondering. First, this shrine, like others, is not in the village protected by 'old-man gull' but on its own near the river. Secondly, the most substantial structure is not the site of ritual action, but a storehouse (sometimes several storehouses) for images and other paraphernalia. Thirdly, much of what is described would leave no archaeological trace beyond single post-holes and natural tree-roots. Fourthly, what marks it out as special is not architecture but portable equipment: the logs, the ropes, the white cloths, the images. Essentially, this is an open-air theatre for doing recognized things with recognized objects. The chances of finding its archaeological remains, let alone identifying them correctly, would be tiny, though if it were in England one could well imagine it leaving a place-name in *-bēam* or *-stapol*.

My second example reverts to the possible magical functions of animal ornament on textiles, and of the women who wove them, via a comment that does not come from Anglo-Saxon England but is relatively close in time and space. In his 'Corrector' of *c*.1010, Burchard of Worms tells a confessor to ask his penitent:

> Have you been present... at the vanities which women practise in their woollen work, in their weaving, who when they begin their weaving hope to be able to bring it about, with their incantations and with their actions, that the threads of the warp and the woof become so intertwined that unless [someone] makes use of these other diabolical counter-incantations, he will perish totally?
>
> (Migne 1880: col. 961)

Figure 37.4 A Saami shrine, pictured by the early ethnographer Johann Schefferus in his *Lapponia* (English edition, 1674: 41)

If this conception of magical power incorporated into cloth through the action of weaving and the intermeshing of the fibres was part of the early Anglo-Saxons' cultural inheritance, its implications for weaving-equipment both in female graves and in settlements are interesting. The Wixárika of Mexico, studied by the anthropologist Stacy B. Schaefer, illustrate the workings of this sort of belief-system (Schaefer 2002). In this Christian-influenced but polytheistic society, women's progression through the life cycle is linked to their growing skill in weaving, and in depicting in textiles the other-worldly forms that have been revealed to them under the influence of the hallucinogenic peyote-cactus. There is a close link between shamanic power and skill in weaving:

Women who are shamans, or who seek other means to have direct communication with the gods... can become master weavers. The apprenticeship takes at least five years to complete and closely parallels the path followed by shaman-initiates. Women learning to become master weavers are also encouraged to seek guidance from the gods, especially when they sleep at night. As Yolanda explained it, when one sleeps, the gods will help teach the sleeper through her dreams. The following day she must again try to weave.

(Schaeffer 2002: 91)

Perceptions of this general kind might constitute a background to, among other things, the very high prestige of expert women in early English monastic culture, and the prominence of elaborate and formulaic decoration in Anglo-Saxon culture generally. Sally Crawford (this volume) has suggested that the lines and stacks of loom-weights often found in sunken-featured buildings were left in place because the sacral nature of the loom, and the operations performed on it, invested them with a special status (cf. Hamerow 2006: 18–19).

Turning to Christianity, an ethnographic perspective may throw an interesting sidelight on Bede's well-known description of St Chad's original grave at Lichfield: 'the place of that burial is covered by a wooden tomb in the form of a little house, having a hole in one wall, through which those who come there out of devotion have the habit of putting a hand in and taking out some of the earth' (*HE* IV.3).

Figure 37.5 A modern example of a 'wooden tomb in the form of a little house having a hole in one wall': the grave of Klaudia Fomin (d.1990) at Nilsiä, eastern Finland (photograph by John Blair)

While this structure could have been specifically designed as a saint's shrine, little wooden houses were the standard type of grave-monument in north-eastern Scandinavia and Karelia into modern times (Fig. 37.5): if they were equally common in seventh-century England, we would have no means of knowing. It is intriguing to note that these 'houses for the dead' had, and still have, a hole in one end-wall: not for pilgrims to take out earth, but for the dead person to pass through, observe the world outside, or be fed by the living (Storå 1971: 152–6). If the early English held beliefs of this kind—as, given their very corporeal conception of the grave as residence, they could very well have done—we would certainly not be told about it by Bede; but is he describing a sanitized version of something that was rooted in lay culture?

My final example bears on an intractable problem in English Church organization during c.650–900: the near-invisibility of the small churches, founded by local lords and serving village communities, that are familiar throughout the Frankish world. Yet 'village oratories' do just occasionally get mentioned, for instance by Bede (Blair 2005: 220). Could these references offer glimpses of an informal, and therefore unrecorded, category of churches that were maintained through local religious initiative? Possibly: to the extent that such a network of 'do-it-yourself' chapels existed in a more recent landscape of peasant communities dispersed within large and rather rudimentary parishes, that of pre-revolutionary northern Russia (Milner-Gulland 2000). Official ecclesiastical involvement was remote, so the chapels and their devotional fittings were maintained by committed if uneducated laity. The fact that they could, in these circumstances, function at all is noteworthy, and one wonders whether the following evocative vignette from Karelia may give a taste of Anglo-Saxon lay devotion:

There was nonetheless not a single literate person in the village and on Sunday when visiting the village chapel, people mumbled to themselves the prayers learned from priests and monks and brought offerings of butter and wool. This was so that they would have good cattle-luck in the summer and that the cattle would thrive in other ways as well. After the people had said their prayers for a while and burned the tapers in front of the holy icons, the chapel elder (*starosta*) told them: 'Go, everyone, and eat supper'.

(Stark 2002: 36.)

An especially intriguing aspect of this Karelian society is that the peasants acknowledged the supernatural power not only of the chapels, holy sites, and icons in their own villages, but also of the great monasteries to which they sometimes made pilgrimage: but in sharply different ways. Whereas the local sites and powers were agents—sometimes malevolent ones, including even the icons—in negotiation between human communities and the other-worldly presences on their margins, the monasteries and their high culture had a more universal, moral, and theologically coherent role (Stark 2002). That the same people could, with no sense of inconsistency, hold these contrasting attitudes to Christian authority has obvious interest for our understanding of the mid Saxon devotional world: it illustrates how laity with deeply-entrenched traditional beliefs and practices need have had no great problem in accommodating to the minsters with their learning, exotic liturgy, and cosmopolitan European culture.

These exercises in exploring the almost unexplorable illustrate how frustrating it can be to push at the boundaries. As Gittos says, 'we are still a very long way from answering key questions about, for example, the extent of popular participation in the church before c.1050, whether certain areas of the landscape were considered sacred over a very long time span, or even what a minster precinct actually looked like'. Considerable progress has nonetheless been made in the last two decades, even if a large part of that progress consists in acknowledging the big holes that earlier generations of scholars were content to paper over. We only have a few pieces of the jigsaw, but we have a better sense of the scale of the picture to which they belong, and perhaps even of where to place them on the board. In some important ways archaeological opportunities are expanding, and they may help us to obtain more answers if we can learn to ask the right questions.

References

BLAIR, J. (1995). 'Anglo-Saxon pagan shrines and their prototypes'. *Anglo-Saxon Studies in Archaeology and History* 8: 1–28.
—— (2005). *The Church in Anglo-Saxon Society*. Oxford: Oxford University Press.
—— (2009). 'The dangerous dead in early medieval England', in S. Baxter *et al.* (eds.), *Early Medieval Studies in Memory of Patrick Wormald*. Farnham: Ashgate, 539–59.
CAMPBELL, J. (2007). 'Some considerations on religion in early England', in M. Henig and T. J. Smith (eds.), *Collectanea Antiqua: Essays in Memory of Sonia Chadwick Hawkes*. British Archaeological Reports International Series 1673. Oxford: Archaeopress, 67–73.
DICKINSON, T. M. (1993). 'An Anglo-Saxon "Cunning Woman" from Bidford-on-Avon', in M. Carver (ed.), *In Search of Cult: Archaeological Investigations in Honour of Philip Rahtz*. Woodbridge: Boydell Press, 45–54.
GEMUEV, I. N. *et al.* (2008). *Encyclopaedia of Uralic Mythologies*, Volume 3: *Mansi Mythology*. Helsinki: Finnish Literature Society.
HADDAN, A. W., and STUBBS, W. (1871). *Councils and Ecclesiastical Documents*, Volume 3. Oxford: Clarendon Press.
HAMEROW, H. (2006). '"Special Deposits" in Anglo-Saxon Settlements'. *Medieval Archaeology* 50: 1–30.
HOPE-TAYLOR, B. (1977). *Yeavering: an Anglo-British Centre of Early Northumbria*. London: H.M.S.O.
HUNT, N. B. (2002). *Shamanism in North America*. New York: Firefly.
KITZINGER, E. (1993). 'Interlace and icons', in R. M. Spearman and J. Higgitt (eds.), *The Age of Migrating Ideas*. Edinburgh: National Museum of Scotland, 3–15.

LANG, J. (1991). *Corpus of Anglo-Saxon Stone Sculpture*, Volume 3: *York and Eastern Yorkshire*. Oxford: Oxford University Press.

MEANEY, A. (1989). 'Women, witchcraft and magic in Anglo-Saxon England', in D. G. Scragg, (ed.), *Superstition and Popular Medicine in Anglo-Saxon England*. Manchester: Centre for Anglo-Saxon Studies, 9–40.

MIGNE, J.-P. (ed.) (1880). *Burchardi Vormatiensis Episcopi Opera Omnia*, Volume 1. Patrologia Latina 140. Paris.

MILNER-GULLAND, R. R. (2000). 'An interior journey: on the secular and sacred dynamic of the northern Russian landscape', in J. Renwick (ed.), *L'Invitation au Voyage*. Oxford: Oxford University Press, 23–30.

PRICE, N. (2002). *The Viking Way: Religion and War in Late Iron Age Scandinavia*. Uppsala: Department of Archaeology and Ancient History.

SCHAEFER, S. B. (2002). *To Think with a Good Heart: Wixárika Women, Weavers and Shamans*. Salt Lake City: University of Utah Press.

STARK, L. (2002). *Peasants, Pilgrims, and Sacred Promises*. Helsinki: Finnish Literature Society.

STORÅ, N. (1971). *Burial Customs of the Skolt Lapps*. Helsinki.

CHAPTER 38

SACRED SPACES AND PLACES IN PRE-CHRISTIAN AND CONVERSION PERIOD ANGLO-SAXON ENGLAND

SARAH SEMPLE

INTRODUCTION

The pagan spiritual topography of early medieval Europe has long been visualized in terms of sacred groves, hilltops and fields, holy wells and springs, trees and stones (Grimm 1888: 69; Stenton 1941; Gelling 1978: 158–61; Hines 1997: 385). Scholarship over the last century has fully accepted this, but has simultaneously adopted a reluctant standpoint regarding pre-Christian religion, considering it too vague to be researched with any real clarity (Stanley 1975: 122; see Hines 1997 for contra argument).

Significant theoretical advances have, however, allowed us to change how we research 'pagan' religion and belief. The integration by medieval archaeologists of prehistoric methodologies (e.g. Williams 1998; 1999; Brookes 2007) and an increasing adoption of the interdisciplinary methods and cognitive post-processual approaches developed in Scandinavian and European scholarship (see for example the work of Brink 2001; Price 2002; and Andrén *et al.* 2006) have all had a positive impact. The physical landscape and the archaeological record are now considered more readily as a source of evidence for ideological and religious change (Carver 2001; 2002). The act of raising new monuments and using old monuments, drawing on the power of the ancient and the natural, is conceived as an active process of physical myth-making, with the landscape both adopted and used afresh to add emphasis to the legends and beliefs of communities (Williams 2006: 145–78).

The landscape has come to the forefront of theoretical approaches hinging on the belief that changes in religious or political ideology can result in physical alterations to settlement, land use and division, burial practices, and administrative arrangements (Turner 2006: 4; Hoggett 2007). The attention of researchers has thus moved towards a search for what has recently been termed the *signals of belief* within the material record of the early medieval period (Carver *et al.* 2010). In a search for Anglo-Saxon pre-Christian beliefs and practices, it is a composite approach that is proving successful: with archaeological and artefactual evidence contextualized by integrating a wide variety of complementary sources (e.g. Hamerow 2006; Pluskowski 2006; Carver 2003; Carver *et al.* 2010).

This chapter presents a summary of a lengthier exploration of the numinous and sacred qualities of the natural world in pre-Christian England, published as a paper in the edited volume *Signals of Belief* (Carver *et al.* 2010), and thus represents a general introduction to the relevant ideas, themes, and source materials interrogated and pursued at greater length elsewhere. Types of natural locale considered to have held sacred or superstitious importance are reviewed below, with evidence drawn from an interdisciplinary aggregate of sources, but with place-names often at the fore. Topographic observation and archaeological evidence are used alongside historical sources and accounts, in a review of evidence for special natural places in the Anglo-Saxon psyche. The second part of the chapter focuses on the human-altered landscape, with monument re-use and new monumentality reviewed as evidence for sacred places and religious structures. The chapter concludes with some thoughts on three overarching themes: accessibility, identity, and the importance of the *longue durée*.

SACRED NATURAL PLACES

Natural places have an archaeology because they acquired significance in the minds of people in the past, and although the appearance of such places may not be outwardly altered, one way of recognizing the importance of these locations is through the evidence of human activity that is discovered there (R. J. Bradley 2000: 35). This could comprise material culture such as votive deposits, or structures built to enhance the site or natural location. However, natural places may also attract activity in the wider landscape around them—monuments, burial grounds, etc. (ibid.). It is perhaps a modern construct, informed by the European classical past, to look for designated sacred locales—a grove, a temple, a shrine, etc. It is clear in recent research that past societies often interacted with extended sacred landscapes, containing focal points of activity such as monuments and cemeteries created and used, and of course ancient monuments adopted and re-used, to structure how people viewed, experienced, and even moved through the landscape (Tilley 1994; 1996; R. J. Bradley 2000; Williams 2006: 179–214; Brookes 2007). Sacred places might be important, too, because of how they were reached—their accessibility or indeed inaccessibility, visibility or invisibility, were just as significant as their immediate and wider landscape context (Mulk and Bayliss-Smith 1999; R. J. Bradley 2000; Scarre 2002a, 2002b). Place-names offer some of the most important evidence for our understanding of 'sacred landscapes' (Gelling 1998: 75, 97). They reference supernatural creatures such as elves, monsters, demons, or giants, associating them with fissures and hollows, openings in the ground, pools and wetplaces, ancient monuments and ruins (Semple 2002: 286–7; Blair 2005; Hall 2006). On rare occasions they describe sites linked with, or dedicated to, pagan deities (Gelling 1978; Hines 1997: 386, table 12-1), and sometimes seem to name temple and shrine sites of the pre-Christian past (Blair 1995; Meaney 1995; Semple 2007).

Fields and groves

The existence of fields and groves dedicated to specific deities is attested by a range of place-names reviewed by John Hines (1997). *Feld* (field) and *lēah* (grove) occur several times in combination with god's names such as Thunor or Tiw (Hines 1997: 386, table 12–1). Few of these sites are locatable today, but we assume these names refer to places of belief, or cult locations where sacred activities might have been carried out.

As discussed elsewhere, in greater length, the place-name terms can offer some speculative evidence for the ways in which sites were interacted with and perceived (Semple 2010). *Feld* is a term that was used regularly as early as the sixth and seventh centuries AD and seems to have been applied indifferently to land that might or might not be under the plough, not marsh or woodland or hills, but pasture, particularly unencumbered land with unrestricted access (Gelling and Cole 2000: 269–71). In its earliest application, *feld* may have designated open areas of communal rough pasture for groups of settlements, and in the north could denote land that separated the upland from the cultivated lowland (Gelling and Cole 2000: 272).

Lēah, in contrast, has variously been interpreted as 'forest, wood, glade and clearing' (Gelling and Cole 2000: 237) and may have initially been used in reference to especially ancient and long-established woodland, copses, and woodland clearings (Rackham 1976: 56; Gelling and Cole 2000: 237). It is perceived as an active term, often indicative of settlement in cleared areas, within or at the fringes of the wooded environment (2000: 220; and Gelling, this volume), providing some emphasis that *lēah* might be applied to areas of actively managed or maintained woodland clearance. Indeed Della Hooke has very recently argued for its usage in relation to 'wood—but a wood of a characteristic open type—or wood pasture rather than clearing' (2009: 376). We can perhaps visualize places such as Thursley (*Thunor's-lēah*) as defined and maintained and actively managed areas of open wood or wood pasture.

These English place-names suggest locales with specific qualities: visual and sensory contrast with their surroundings, and differing degrees of accessibility and liminality. Both types of locale (*lēah* and *feld*) are likely to have been subject to periodic management, by traditional means such as grazing and coppicing, and as a consequence, perhaps such places acquired a distinctive quality in terms of their flora and fauna through their sporadic usage.

Hilltops

This notion of peripheral yet accessible and visited places is found, too, in the topographic profile of several hilltop sites considered to be of pre-Christian sacred significance. Hilltops are widely accepted as an indisputable aspect of pre-Christian sacred topography; Tishoe, Surrey, for example, is often cited as a distinctive spur dedicated to the god Tiw (Gelling 1978). Sir Frank Stenton firmly believed the place-name term OE *hearg* 'temple/shrine' referred in many instances to some form of hilltop sanctuary (1941).[1] This interpretation is upheld by the frequent association of surviving *hearg* place-names with distinctive hilltops or whale-backs of land e.g. Harrow-on-the-Hill, Middlesex (Fig. 38.1). The types of hilltop associated with *hearg* place-names vary, however: dominant and distinctive examples such as Harrow-on-the-Hill contrast with low and rounded rises such as Wood Eaton, Oxfordshire. The landscape surrounding Harrow Hill in Sussex provides a natural screen hiding the dramatic hilltop (Semple 2007). These sites, if sacred places, were visited and used. A hidden location would have increased the visual impact of the approach to a site, just as a steep climb to a spur or hill could have served to enhance the spiritual aspect of journeying.

---

[1] It should be noted, however, that place-names containing the element *harrow* are now being extensively reviewed and it is an emerging possibility that at least in some instances Harrow place-names traditionally accepted as attestations of 'heathen temples or shrines' by Stenton, Gelling, and Meaney, may have had an entirely different meaning and identity as components of the natural landscape (Briggs forthcoming).

Figure 38.1 A landscape view of Harrow-on-the-Hill, Middlesex, London (from Lysons 1762–1834: 560)

Fissures, hollows, and pits

Belief in supernatural inhabitation of the landscape is attested both in highly evocative and problematic texts such as *Beowulf* and again within the Anglo-Saxon place-name record, with elves, water spirits, and monsters or goblins mentioned in association with a range of topographic features (Semple 2002; Hall 2006). Perhaps for obvious reasons, the dark places of the world—clefts, pits, hollows, fissures, and caves—were especially evocative. In the tale of St. Cuthman, an old woman who cursed the saint was picked up by the wind and blown across the downs, before being swallowed into the earth at a place later known as Fippa's pit (Blair 1997). Such openings in the earth and rock were dangerous places, reminiscent in the minds of late Anglo-Saxon Christian communities of the persecution by demons and beasts that awaited those unlucky enough to fall into the cracks and fissures of Hell (Semple 2003a) (Fig. 38.2). Such a fate befell the drowned sinners described in the late-tenth-century text *Andreas*, who were swallowed by a fissure in the earth (Vercelli XIV, ed. Scragg 1992). Place-names attest to popular superstitions which associated this type of feature with supernatural creatures: for example, a *þyrs pytt* is recorded in Marlcliffe, Worcestershire in AD 883 (Sawyer 1968: S 222) suggesting late Anglo-Saxon local beliefs in a pit-dwelling beast or demon (discussed more extensively in Semple 2010).

The existence of long-lived and widely-held folk-superstitions or popular beliefs relating to fissures, pits, or caves is evident, but little in the way of material evidence

Figure 38.2 Detail showing a stylized rocky cleft as a place of torment or entrance to hell (London, British Library, Harley 603, 73r). © British Library Board. All rights reserved

for active ritual or votive practices has been found. In the Anglo-Saxon mind, a range of fearful supernatural creatures existed and lived in, or were to be encountered at, certain places in the landscape, including pits, nooks, and hollows. It is possible these beliefs emerged within and after the Conversion period, reflecting new attitudes to landscape influenced and developed by Christian texts and teachings on hell and damnation. The place-name evidence, however, alongside the unusual motifs within some of the *Vitae*, point to these folk-superstitions comprising long-running beliefs surviving beyond the arrival of a new Christian theology, and perhaps even continuing to influence the mentality and imagination of Christian writers and artists (Jolly 1996: 6–34; Blair 2005: 471–9).

Rivers, pools, springs, wells, and wetlands

Watery places were also significant topographic features for Anglo-Saxon populations. They were often equated with dangerous gateways to other-worlds, occupied by less than welcoming inhabitants: 'The monster must dwell in the fen, alone in his realm.' (*Maxims* II, lines 42–3; see S. A. J. Bradley 1995 for translation). The *nicor* or 'water spirit/demon', referred to in the field-names Nikerpole, Mildenhall, Wiltshire (1272) and aqua de Nikerpoll, Sussex (1263) (see Mawer and Stenton 1939: 499 and Mawer and Stenton 1930: 562), evokes an image close to that captured by the creator of *Beowulf*, of terrifying monsters, lurking below the surface of the water (*Beowulf*, lines 702–824; see Alexander 1973 for translation). Nonetheless, springs, wells, rivers, and lakes attracted activity of a ritual or religious nature in the pre-Christian and Conversion period. This is attested by finds of metalwork retrieved from rivers, and the establishment of churches, standing crosses, and the application of Christian dedications to river crossings, springs, and wells, not to mention the appropriation of watery sites for baptism.

Votive deposits in wetlands and rivers

The ritualized hoarding or deposition of metalwork in water is a phenomenon generally associated with late prehistoric communities (Levy 1982; R. J. Bradley 1998; Blair 1994: 99; Hines 1997: 381; Halsall 2000). Evidence for similar activity in the Roman, early medieval, and later historic periods implies such practices continued or re-emerged in later periods. Excavations in 1981 at Fiskerton, Lincolnshire, produced evidence for late prehistoric and Roman deposition of metalwork and organic material associated with a timber causeway crossing wetlands and a tributary leading to the River Witham (Parker Pearson and Field 2003). Early medieval finds from the River Witham include weaponry and pins dating to the late eighth century. Stocker and Everson have shown that depositional ritual practices took place at six such causeways along the Witham Valley into the late medieval period, where metalwork finds of the fourteenth and fifteenth centuries, including several items of weaponry, have been recovered (2003: table 17.1). Such finds are traditionally explained as casual losses, although researchers have increasingly questioned this assumption, pointing to the possibility of intentional rites (D. M. Wilson 1965). Stocker and Everson emphasize the pre-Christian 'sacred' nature of the Witham river valley, suggesting deposition rituals may have been used to facilitate the periodic appropriation of the causeways as access points to the river, or the marshy areas adjacent, or to boats for crossing or travelling the Witham. Such rituals might have included acts associated with safe passage across liminal or supernaturally charged locations, made at the onset or safe completion of long journeys (Lund 2005 and 2010). Equally, these deposits could also relate to decision-making, boundary disputes, or oath-taking rituals (Blair 1994: 104; Halsall 2000).

Springs and wells, tidal zones and islands

The Christianization of wells and springs has been discussed at greater length elsewhere, and will thus only be summarised here. Sam Turner, in his review of western British evidence, argues for a twofold process: the Christianization of wells and springs with pre-existing significance, and an emerging, newly applied sanctity around some natural phenomenon, associated with the establishment of an early medieval or medieval Christian foundation (2006: 132–3). The former type of development is relevant here for, as John Blair has outlined, the survival of pre-Christian cult foci after the Conversion represents continuity and survival in popular belief (Blair 2005: 226–7, 472–3; Turner 2006: 132–3). Blair notes that this appropriation could certainly happen at minster level (Rattue 1995: 55–61) but also postulates a 'much humbler level' of adoption, taking account of less formally developed landmarks (Blair 2005: 226, see too 477–8). Locations such as Barton-on-Humber attest to such early appropriations (Rodwell and Rodwell 1982: fig. 6).

Watery locations with indeterminate topographic status or identity, such as seasonal islands, tidal islands, inter-tidal zones, marshes, and fens subject to seasonal inundations, were also of special significance (see for example the discussion of the ritual or spiritual importance in prehistory of inter-tidal zones and islands in Scarre 2002a and b). The seasonal quality of the fenland isle inhabited by the hermit Guthlac, amid marshes subject to winter and spring inundations, describes precisely the type of liminal qualities communities seem to have recognized and valued (*Vita Guthlaci* XXV; trans. Colgrave 1956: 89). In the early medieval period, water courses were used as places of assembly. Islands, bridges, rivers, and streams often functioned as territorial divisions and boundaries (Cohen 2003), but in addition they provided natural barriers, crossing-places, and routes of communication. These 'liminal' and contrastingly 'accessible' qualities may have been particularly valued for assembly locations (see Pantos 2002; 2003). Royal assemblies, such as the inauguration rituals for King Edgar in 973, were held on the River Dee (Barrow 2003: 81–93), a free-flowing river without ownership or claim (Pantos 2002), and of course at the inter-tidal section of the river—again a location perhaps particularly favoured for public rituals (Barrow 2003).

ANCIENT MONUMENTS AND STRUCTURES

A range of special natural locations have been reviewed here. Within and adjacent to these fields, groves, hilltops, and watery places, made places—the monuments created in a more ancient time by past communities—were also important to Anglo-Saxon populations. The great variety of purposes to which prehistoric and Roman monuments were put by fifth- to eleventh-century people attests to their interest and curiosity, their intimate knowledge and understanding of their environs, and the significance of human-made structures in the processes of ideological display and identity creation by communities across this period. Ancient remains can be argued as potent symbols of real, mythic, and imagined pasts: components within a landscape charged with meaning and imbued with beliefs and myths—a landscape absorbed into and changed by the Conversion.

Monuments and burials

It is clear that cemeteries, whether cremation or inhumation, were places of special importance that were frequented by the living, and were used as arenas for ceremonies and assemblies (Williams 2006). They were created as political and spiritual markers (Carver 2002; 2005), as signals of identity, and as complex reflections of social relations within and between communities (Lucy 2002; Devlin 2007). We now understand that cemeteries functioned as far more than just places of disposal for the dead: some may have been used as theatres for rituals, meetings, and ceremonies (Härke 2001; Carver 2005; Williams 2006), with graves and monuments arranged to structure access and use of the cemetery as sacred locales, e.g. Street House, Yorkshire (Sherlock and Simmons 2008). Cemeteries are discussed in this volume by Howard Williams and are not covered here in depth; however, the relationship of cemeteries and burials with prehistoric and Roman remains does need some exploration, as this aspect of re-use offers compelling evidence for the special value placed on ruins and monuments from the pre-Anglo-Saxon past.

Cemeteries and individual burials were frequently associated with prehistoric and Roman relict monuments and the diversity and variability in how communities used them is extensive (Williams 1997) and appears to have changed across the Conversion Period (Williams 1998; 1999). Barrows were preferred, particularly Bronze Age round barrows; but long barrows, earthwork enclosures, and hillforts were chosen too, along with the ruins of villas and forts and other Roman structures (Williams 1997; 1998; Semple 2003b; 2008).

The use of ancient remains for burial accounts for over 25 per cent of the known early medieval funerary record, and rises in frequency in the late sixth to seventh centuries AD (Williams 1997). A more regionally varied scene is becoming apparent, however, in terms of the choices and trends in monument re-use made by individual communities and regional populations (Brookes 2007; Semple 2003b; 2008). This diversity suggests that, from the fifth century onwards, people and communities used the visible, local past in processes and actions designed to fix themselves in the landscape, signalling their identity and land ownership (Williams 1998; Lucy 2002). By the seventh century, the use of ancient remains had become largely the preserve of aristocratic groups, seeking to legitimate new hereditary systems of control over enlarged kingdoms, particularly within frontier zones and other contested areas of the landscape (Semple 2003b; Williams 1999; 2006). Ruins, ancient sepulchres, tombs, and enclosures, became significant for early medieval communities as sites that evoked the ancestral past, and were perhaps even considered the homes of ancestors.

Churches, settlements, and ancient monuments

Whilst the relationship between burials and ancient remains has been revisited several times in recent years, the more diverse and varied uses of prehistoric remains in the pre-Christian and Conversion eras remain under-explored. In 1989 Richard Morris drew attention to the incidence of medieval churches located in association with hengiform monuments, Roman buildings, prehistoric standing stones, and barrows. Citing the letters of Pope Gregory that asked the Christian missionaries to adopt and incorporate pagan sacred places (Bede, *HE* I.30, ed. McClure and Collins 1994), Morris argued that the juxtaposition of church and monument, seen for example at Rudston, Yorkshire, or Stanton Drew, Somerset, reflected the significance of these ancient monuments in pre-Christian worship and belief (Morris 1989: 46–92, 71–4).

Ancient remains, prehistoric and Roman, were certainly appropriated by the Christian church during and after the Conversion Period (ibid. and Blair 1992). Anglo-Saxon churches sometimes incorporated re-used Roman stone and brick, and were sited within, or close to, standing Roman remains (e.g. Escomb, Co. Durham and Corbridge, Northumberland). Although this might reflect the practical advantages of re-using material, in ideological terms it can also be seen as an attempt to symbolically rebuild Roman authority, and draw on the potency of those Roman structures that continued to be revered as sacred places, long after the Roman military withdrawal (Bell 2005). In addition to the use of Roman fabric and remains, a wide variety of prehistoric monuments were brought into use by the Christian Church, and in these instances functional motivations are often less plausible; indeed it is difficult to ascribe any single interpretative framework to this wide variety of sites and exemplars. Churches can be found next to standing stones and stone circles (e.g. Awliscombe, Devon, and Avebury, Wiltshire: Fig. 38.3); adjacent to and on top of prehistoric round barrows (e.g. Fimber, Yorkshire, and Bampton, Oxfordshire) (see Blair 2005: 186); within ancient enclosures (e.g. Tetbury, Gloucestershire, and Breedon-on-the-Hill, Leicestershire); and on occasion within a palimpsest of remains, using and appropriating an array of ancient structures (e.g. Knowlton, Dorset). Interpreting all such juxtapositions as evidence of a 'de-paganizing' act is too simplistic. We might instead consider that a church and barrow reflect the appropriation, and even 'conversion' of ancestors; the adoption of a stone or well could attest to the absorption of a place of healing or medicinal virtue within the auspices of the church; whilst a hilltop enclosure would not only offer a useful boundary, but also a means of legitimizing and underlining the new power of the church by placing it in a superior position to the surrounding

Figure 38.3 Avebury, Wilts, from the air (© English Heritage)

landscape. Only through the examination of each site's particular biography can the reasons for any re-use of such monuments within a Christian locale be determined.

Temples, shrines, and idols

In addition to the open-air sites discussed above, place-name evidence, notably the OE terms *hearg* 'temple', and *weoh* 'holy place, idol, altar' (see Meaney 1995: 29), can also refer to places conceived in the Anglo-Saxon mind as temples and altars. The OE term *hearg* occurs in an eighth-century charter (Sawyer 1968: S 106), and in ninth-century texts (Meaney 1995: 31), whilst the word *weoh* can be found in an authentic late-seventh-century charter (Sawyer 1968: S 235; Whitelock 1955: 484, no. 58).

Written evidence for built structures includes Bede's description of the heathen temple at *Godmundingham* (Goodmanham, East Yorkshire), where reference is made to sacred enclosures (*HE* I.30, completed in AD 731: *templa et altaria* 'temples and altars', *aras et fana idolorum cum septis quibus erant circumdata*, 'altars and temples of idols with the fences/hedges with which they were surrounded', *fanum cum omnibus septis suis*, 'the temple with all its fences/hedges'; translation from Blair 1995). Similarly, a reference in a letter written by Aldhelm in the 680s, recognized by John Blair, refers to pillars or posts and shrines: 'let us raise a hymn... that where once the crude pillars (*ermula cruda*) of the same foul snake and the stag were worshipped with coarse stupidity in profane shrines (*fana profana*), in their place dwellings for students, not to mention holy houses of prayer, are constructed skilfully by the talents of the architect' (Letter V to Heahfrith, translation from Lapidge and Herren 1979: 143–6, 160–4, 201 n. 25). Later laws occasionally mention the worship of springs, stones, or trees (see for example II Cnut V, 1020–1: Wormald 1999: 345), and in one rare instance the setting up of sanctuaries at such places 'if there is on anyone's land a sanctuary [*friþgeard*] round a stone or a tree or a well [=spring] or any such nonsense' (*Northumbrian Priests Law*; see Whitelock et al. 1981: 463). These sources imply that, although religious activity might well take place in open spaces and in relation to natural phenomena, such sites might be enhanced by the addition of man-made, often small structures which functioned as religious buildings or temples.

This chapter has emphasized the importance of the natural landscape and ancient remains within the beliefs and spiritual perceptions of early medieval communities, before and after the Conversion. The locations associated with place-names, suggestive of shrines and temples, may themselves have been special because they were sites where natural phenomena and ancient monuments attested to the long-term significance of the place. Elsewhere, I have suggested that places with names incorporating the term *hearg* were naturally distinctive locations with material evidence for long-lived activity. Whether driven by the attraction of monumentality, or natural features, or through memory of past activities, archaeological evidence at a few of these sites can be argued to attest to repeated activity from late prehistory to the post-Roman era (Semple 2007). We cannot say with any certainty that each of these sites continued in use; they may have been renegotiated and re-used at different points in time, and had different meanings to each successive audience.

Whether natural places or sites enhanced with structures, there has been a tendency to envisage the temples or sacred places of the Anglo-Saxons as spatially removed from settlements and cemeteries (Wilson 1985; Meaney 1995: 37), although Audrey Meaney has recently pointed to potential associations with hundred meeting-places and, at the end of the pagan period, with royal estates (1995: 37).

Ritual or religious buildings and structures are, however, attested at the well-known site of Yeavering, Northumberland (Fig. 38.4). Building D2 has long been

Figure 38.4 Yeavering, Northumberland: an aerial view showing Yeavering Bell and the palace site in the foreground (© The Gefrin Trust)

considered a type of temple or cult structure (Hope Taylor 1977; Blair 1995; 2005; although see Hamerow 2006). However, there are at least five possible 'religious' structures in the lifespan of this part of the site: the square shrine imposed on the western ring ditch (see below); the standing post imposed on the eastern ring ditch; building D2; Structure E and building B (considered a Christian church); and six if we include the great hall, which could have performed a significant ritual or cult function (Walker 2010; see, too, analogous Continental halls and *hofs*, e.g. Fabech 1994 or Larsson 2007). Not only does the evidence at Yeavering provide an insight into how the integration and ritual orientation of settlements relates to ritual structures, combining functional and spiritual elements, but the settlement sits within, and makes reference to, an extraordinary array of prehistoric and late prehistoric remains (Hope Taylor 1977; R. J. Bradley 1987). Yeavering can therefore be understood to further corroborate the idea that places re-used over time accumulated special meaning. These were places relevant to the processes of identity creation and consolidation: spiritually potent precisely because they were well-used, ancient and set at the heart of long-term patterns of land-use; linking community to landscape and the living to the past.

Shrines, beams, poles, and totems

The existence of more ephemeral cultic structures or foci is suggested by a complex range of evidence, including square enclosures, standing posts, and shrine-type buildings, from settlement and cemetery excavations. The square enclosure imposed on the western ring ditch at Yeavering, which has long been identified as a type of cultic structure or shrine (Hope Taylor 1977), was positioned around a central post, itself a focus for a radial arrangement of burials (Hope Taylor 1977; Blair 1995 and Lucy 2005). The enclosure continued to attract burials before a shift in focus occurred, and D2, again with a square enclosure/annexe around a central post, took over as a ritual focus for burial. Square enclosures seem to have had a long duration. There are well-evidenced Iron Age and Roman examples; however, there are also many undated instances, such as the grouping at Harford Farm, Norwich, Norfolk, which attracted a small series of early medieval cemeteries (Penn 2000; Pestell, this volume, Fig. 29.6), and the example at Windmill Hill in Wiltshire (Smith 1965). Some, like Yeavering or Slonk Hill, Sussex, can be dated to the sixth to seventh centuries AD (Blair 1995; Hartridge 1978). These are occasionally superimposed on, or adjacent to, prehistoric round barrows or ring ditches, or situated in relation to extensive complexes of prehistoric remains. At least two are associated with Anglo-Saxon settlements (ibid.: fig. 11). Whilst caution is needed in assuming that any of the ubiquitous undated examples are early medieval, the evidence implies a type of ritual monument or structure with a lifespan bridging the Iron Age and Roman periods, still actively in use in pre-Christian England. It is also clear from funerary enclosures at Tandderwen, Wales, and Garton Slack, Yorkshire, and numerous square-ditched funerary enclosures and barrows from Scotland and the borders, that in the early medieval period this type of ritual enclosure had a wide repertoire of uses and did not hold any particularly Anglo-Saxon ethnic association.

John Blair has collected together evidence for standing orthostats or pillars functioning as cultic foci, complimenting what we know about the three standing posts at Yeavering: those in the square enclosure and its later replacement; and another within the eastern ring ditch. The place-names which include the OE elements *stapol* and *bēam* may evidence sacred trees, tree trunks, wooden posts, or stone pillars, whilst the seventh-century letter by Aldhelm, mentioned above, refers to the worship of crude pillars of the 'foul snake and stag' (see Gelling 1978; Blair

1995; Meaney 1995). A handful of documented assembly sites seem to have made use of places associated with standing posts or monuments, e.g. Thurstaple, Kent, is a lost example of a hundred meeting-place apparently associated with the *stapol* or post of Thor (Meaney 1995). This again is a monument with varied uses: markers for graves, barrows, cemeteries, and ancient barrows, foci for settlements, and elements structuring the orientation of both burials and buildings. A final connection worth emphasizing, however, is with the sacred importance of living trees (Blair 1995; 2005), which are considered a key element of northern European, pre-Christian belief and forming an almost universal element in world religion (Russell 1979). Well-known Continental accounts attest to the felling of pagan sacred trees in the eighth century (Talbot 1954: 45–6), and a small group of written accounts also suggest some trees were held sacred in England before the Conquest (see Blair 2005: 476–9 for a synopsis account of other sources).

Discussion

This chapter has summarized some of the wide variety of evidence for pre-Christian sacred landscapes and ritual foci, providing an introduction to the topic, which lies at the interface of a range of disciplines (archaeology, place-name studies, history, art history, linguistics, etc.). What emerges from this overview is the rich array of evidence for the significance of the natural world and the ancient Roman and pre-Roman monuments and remains to the communities of the fifth to eighth centuries and after—indeed the relevance of landscape as a whole to the beliefs of pre-Christian populations. Several themes have emerged which need further exploration, but are summarized briefly here as potential avenues for future researches.

Accessibility and visitation

Some of the places discussed here were accessible and some were not; similarly some places and monuments were visible and others hidden. Burial sites in particular seem to be important, or at least retained importance, because of their accessibility and proximity to major routes of communication through the landscape (Williams 1999; Semple 2008). Some 'sacred' hilltops were highly visible, topographic features, e.g. Harrow-on-the-Hill, Middlesex; watery places were important if they were fording-places or bridging points, e.g. the Witham Valley. In contrast, it is clear that other locales were significant because they were hidden, inaccessible, and liminal—enclosed within surrounding curtains of hills, or by marsh, water, or sea, or lying at the edge of cultivated land. Periodic accessibility seems to have been especially meaningful. Sites that were accessible at low tides, or within dry seasons, acquired a similar level of significance. Islands were valued, as too were caves and fissures, precisely because they were potentially difficult to access and represented a removed element within the expanse of known landscape: places at the limits of everyday/ commonplace human experience.

The way in which people experienced localities and places in sensory and psychological terms is as relevant to their meaning as any natural resource or human-altered monument present on the site. Although surviving from a later Christian period, several elf remedies record very specific rituals for the collection of herbs—for example at dawn and dusk, in silence, avoiding other living creatures, etc. (*Leechbook* III: lxii; see Jolly 1996: 160 for recent translation). This emphasizes how accessing and engaging with the sacred—the journey, the approach, the collection—was relevant to its significance. We need, therefore, to explore our evidence for special places in the Anglo-Saxon landscape with more of an eye for how these sites would have been experienced in sensory terms. Researching their accessibility, visual presence, perhaps even their acoustic properties or ancient faunal and floral profiles, may offer new insights into how early medieval communities interacted with and revered the natural world, and why certain places, hills, trees, cemeteries, stones, and ancient remains took on special meaning and importance as sacred locales.

The *longue durée*

A second running theme throughout this chapter has been the long-term relevance of places. Making associations between the sacred places of the Neolithic and their later importance to medieval communities may, for some, be taking ideas of long-term spiritual and religious belief too far, but one cannot underestimate the evidence for continuity of activity at sites such as Yeavering or Fiskerton, where locations, wet or dry, marked by hills, rivers, springs, or pools, become a focus for prolonged trajectories of activity running from prehistory into the Roman and later periods. Continuity is an incorrect term for these types of site: instead one must assume that the repeated renegotiation of such places changed to suit new ideologies, changing communities, and shifts in political and social structures across time. However, to dismiss these as simply coincidental junctures where early medieval activity overlaps with prehistoric ritual is to dismiss the overwhelming evidence that early medieval communities had a strong and nuanced, knowledgeable, and aesthetic appreciation of their surroundings. They perceived remnants of the ancient past, used them for a variety of purposes, and wove them into their understanding of past, ancestry, and landscape, making them the physical markers on which to hinge memories and myths.

Natural, untouched and hidden locations were also important, however. This chapter opened with the use of fields, groves, and woods as sacred places, and identified them as locations with spiritual meaning to pre-Christian and Conversion period communities. Such sites contrast with the powerful locales dominated by ancient remains and were likely chosen for their natural and untamed beauty, for their isolation and secret position. The rare mentions of the need to meet outdoors away from bounded or roofed spaces underpins the idea that open and natural spaces may have been important for their untouched, unaltered states. As Insoll has shown, however, the 'natural' may become the human-altered or created (2007). A vast array of repeated processes, collection or gardening of natural materials, fencing, grazing, enclosing, or delimiting of sites—difficult to discern in archaeological terms—should perhaps now be looked for. Such details might assist our exploration of the long-term relevance of the natural landscape alongside the human-altered palimpsest.

Identity and belief

Entwined with the idea that places may have been remembered and used over long time periods is the broader concept that people's community identity, both in local and regional terms, may have been bound up with the ways in which they used and perceived the landscape. The repeated use of ancient remains for burial, for the positioning of palace sites, and for assembly, is as much about people's need to forge an identity rooted in past and present, linking people to landscape, as it is about active statement-making, about legitimacy, authority, and ownership. Sites like Yeavering attest to the need in communities to use the visible past to confirm and reaffirm a common local identity, intimate to the landscape, often over extended time scales. Key sites, locales, and land-marks, natural, human-altered, and ancient, may have been integral to the framing and development of community perceptions of origins, rootedness, identity, and ancestry.

The numinous landscape offers a rich and relatively uncharted territory for further research. The regional preferences and choices which are now being revealed in funerary topography (e.g. Semple 2003b; Lucy 2005; Brookes 2007; Semple 2008), could extend above and beyond the funerary theatre. Such preferences might extend to, and be discernible in, a wider 'landscape of belief'. Perhaps we should begin to look for regionally, or even locally, distinct 'sacred' landscapes, within which palimpsests of significant natural or man-made features were woven, using stories, land claims, genealogies, memories, and legends, into distinctive mythic and sacred topographies, resonant to particular groups or communities inhabiting that space and locale.

Concluding remarks

The combined concepts of the sacred natural place and the numinous landscape have been sustained in modern scholarship despite changing perspectives, and have been particularly emphasized within prehistoric research on phenomenological and aesthetic approaches to material remains within their landscape (Tilley 1994; R. J. Bradley 2000; 2002). This chapter has identified just some of the types of locale that seem to have been significant within early medieval mentalities, beliefs, and superstitions. Even from such a cursory overview, however, it is clear that such places did not exist in isolation—their wider relationship with the landscape, the communities inhabiting it, and the people moving through it, seem to have added to or enhanced their special and attractive qualities.

Christopher Tilley argued that the natural was equally as important as the man-altered landscape, and that the two should be read together: the natural world was used to frame and guide human experience of human-altered landscapes (1996). Richard Bradley added that absence of evidence is just as important, and that we need look at the apparent inactivity as well as activity within extended areas (2000). To understand the sacred pre-Christian and Conversion period landscape in Anglo-Saxon England, we need to build on these ideas, and explore 'belief' not just in terms of individual sacred locations—natural or human-altered—but also in terms of the movement and experience of the medieval population in the landscape as a whole, with a keen eye for regional and local distinctiveness in activities, perceptions, and beliefs, rooted in the land.

Acknowledgements

I would like to thank Professor Howard Williams and Professor Martin Carver for comments on a variety of early drafts of this paper and Ms Gwendoline Dales for her detailed commentary and suggested changes in the final stages of production.

References

ALEXANDER, M. (1973). *Beowulf: A Verse Translation*. Harmondsworth: Penguin Books.
ANDRÉN, A. et al. (2006). *Old Norse Religion in Long-Term Perspectives: Origins, Changes and Interactions*. Lund: Nordic Academic Press.

Barrow, J. (2003). 'Chester's earliest regatta? Edgar's Dee rowing revisited'. *Early Medieval Europe* 10(1): 81–93.
Bell, T. (2005). *The Religious Reuse of Roman Structures in Early Medieval England*. British Archaeological Reports British Series 390. Oxford: Archaeopress.
Blair, W. J. (1992). 'Anglo-Saxon minsters: a topographical review', in W. J. Blair and R. Sharpe (eds.), *Pastoral Care before the Parish*. Leicester: Leicester University Press, 226–66.
—— (1994). *Anglo-Saxon Oxfordshire*. Stroud: Alan Sutton Publishing.
—— (1995). 'Anglo-Saxon pagan shrines and their prototypes'. *Anglo-Saxon Studies in Archaeology and History* 8: 1–28.
—— (1997). 'Saint Cuthman, Steyning and Bosham'. *Sussex Archaeological Collections* 135: 173–92.
—— (2005). *The Church in Anglo-Saxon Society*. Oxford: Oxford University Press.
Bradley, R. J., (1987). 'Time regained: the creation of continuity'. *Journal of the British Archaeological Association* 140: 1–17.
—— (1998). *The Passage of Arms*. 2nd edition. Oxford: Oxbow Books.
—— (2000). *An Archaeology of Natural Places*. London: Routledge.
—— (2002). *The Past in Prehistoric Societies*. London: Routledge.
Bradley, S. A. J. (1995). *Anglo-Saxon Poetry*, London: J.M. Dent.
Briggs, K. (forthcoming). 'Harrow'. In consideration for the *Journal of the English Place-Name Society*.
Brink, S. (2001). 'Mythologizing landscape, place and space of cult and myth', in M. Stausberg (ed.), *Kontinuitäten und Brüche in der Religionsgeschichte: Festschrift für Anders Hultgard zu seinem 65. Geburtstag am 23.12. 2002*. Ergänzungsband zum Reallexikon der Germanischen Altertumskunde 31. New York: Walter de Gruyter, 76–107.
Brookes, S. (2007). 'Walking with Anglo-Saxons: landscapes of the dead in early Anglo-Saxon Kent', in S. Semple and H. Williams (eds.), *Early Medieval Mortuary Practices*. Anglo-Saxon Studies in Archaeology and History 14. Oxford: Oxbow Books, 143–53.
Carver, M. O. H. (2001). 'Why that, why there, why then? The politics of early medieval monumentality', in A. Macgregor and H. Hamerow (eds.), *Image and Power in Early Medieval British Archaeology: Essays in Honour of Rosemary Cramp*. Oxford: Oxbow, 1–22.
—— (2002). 'Reflections on the meaning of Anglo-Saxon barrows', in S. Lucy and A. Reynolds (eds.), *Burial in Early Medieval England and Wales*. Society for Medieval Archaeology Monograph 17. London: SMA, 132–43.
—— (ed.) (2003). *The Cross Goes North: Processes of Conversion in Northern Europe, AD 300–1300*. Woodbridge: Suffolk.
—— (2005). *Sutton Hoo: A Seventh-Century Princely Burial Ground and its Context*. London: British Museum.
—— Sanmark, A., and Semple, S. (eds.) (2010). *Signals of Belief in Early England: Anglo-Saxon Paganism Revisited*. Oxford: Oxbow Books.
Cohen, N. (2003). 'Boundaries and settlement: the role of the river Thames'. *Anglo-Saxon Studies in Archaeology and History* 12: 9–20.
Colgrave, B. (ed.) (1956). *Felix's Life of St. Guthlac*. Cambridge: Cambridge University Press.
Devlin, Z. (2007). *Remembering the Dead in Anglo-Saxon England: Memory Theory in Archaeology and History*. British Archaeological Reports British Series 446. Oxford: Archaeopress.
Fabech, C. (1994). 'Reading society from the cultural landscape. South Scandinavia between sacral and political power', in P. Nielsen, K. Randsborg, and H. Thrane (eds.), *The*

Archaeology of Gudme and Lundeborg. Copenhagen: Institute of Prehistoric and Classical Archaeology, 169–83.

GELLING, M. (1978). *Signposts to the Past.* Chichester: Phillimore.

—— (1998). 'Place-names and landscape', in S. Taylor (ed.), *The Uses of Place-Names.* St. John's House Papers No. 7. Edinburgh: Scottish Cultural Press, 75–100.

—— and COLE, A. (2000). *The Landscape of Place-names.* Stamford: Shaun Tyas.

GRIMM, J. (1888). *Teutonic Mythology,* Volume 1. Trans. J. S. Stallybrass. London.

HALL, A. (2006). 'Are there any elves in Anglo-Saxon Place-names?' *Nomina* 29: 61–80.

HALSALL, G., (2000). 'The Viking presence in England? The burial evidence', in D. Hadley and J. Richards (eds.), *Cultures in Contact: Scandinavian Settlement in England in the Ninth and Tenth Centuries.* Turnhout, Belgium: Brepols, 267–8.

HAMEROW, H. (2006). '"Special deposits" in Anglo-Saxon settlements'. *Medieval Archaeology* 50: 1–30.

HÄRKE, H. (2001). 'Cemeteries as places of power', in M. De Jong and F. Theuws with C. van Rhijn (eds.), *Topographies of Power in the Early Middle Ages.* Leiden, Boston and Cologne: Brill, 9–30.

HARTRIDGE, R., (1978). 'Excavations at the prehistoric and Romano-British site on Slonk Hill, Shoreham, Sussex'. *Sussex Archaeological Collections* 116: 69–141.

HINES, J. (1997). 'Religion: the limits of knowledge', in J. Hines (ed.), *The Anglo-Saxons from the Migration Period to the Eighth Century.* Woodbridge: Boydell Press, 375–401.

HOGGETT, R. (2007). 'Charting conversion: burial as a barometer of belief?'. *Anglo-Saxon Studies in Archaeology and History* 14: 28–37.

HOLLIS, S. (1998). 'The Minster-in-Thanet foundation story'. *Anglo-Saxon England* 27: 41–64.

HOOKE, D. (2009). 'Early medieval woodland and the place-name term *léah*', in O. J. Padel and D. N. Parsons (eds.), *A Commodity of Good Names: Essays in Honour of Margaret Gelling.* Donnington: Shaun Tyas, 365–76.

HOPE TAYLOR, B. (1977). *Yeavering: An Anglo-British Centre of Early Northumbria.* Department of the Environment Archaeological Reports No. 7. London: HMSO.

INSOLL, T. (2007). '"Natural" or "human" spaces? Tallensi sacred groves and shrines and their potential implications for aspects of northern European prehistory and phenomenological interpretation'. *Norwegian Archaeological Review* 40: 2, 138–58.

JOLLY, K. (1996). *Popular Religion in Late Saxon England.* Chapel Hill: University of North Carolina Press.

LAPIDGE, M., and HERREN, M. (1979). *Aldhelm: the Prose Works.* Cambridge: D.S. Brewer.

LARSSON, L. (2007). 'The Iron Age ritual building at Uppåkra, southern Sweden'. *Antiquity* 81: 11–25.

LEVY, J. (1982). *Social and Religious Organisation in Bronze Age Denmark: An Analysis of Ritual Hoard Finds.* BAR International Series 124. Oxford: British Archaeological Reports.

LUCY, S. (2002). 'Burial practice in early medieval eastern England: constructing local identities, deconstructing ethnicity', in S. Lucy and A. Reynolds (eds.), *Burial in Early Medieval England and Wales.* Society for Medieval Archaeology Monograph 17. London: SMA, 72–87.

—— (2005). 'Early medieval burial at Yeavering: a retro-spective', in P. Frodsham and C. O'Brien (eds.), *Yeavering: People, Power and Place.* Stroud: Tempus.

LUND, J. (2005). 'Thresholds and passages: the meanings of bridges and crossings in the Viking age and early Middle Ages'. *Viking and Medieval Scandinavia* 1: 109–37.

—— (2010). 'By the water's edge', in Carver *et al.* (eds.), *Signals of Belief.*
MAWER, A., and STENTON, F.M. (1930). *The Place-Names of Sussex, Part II.* English Place-Name Society Volume 7. Cambridge: English Place-Name Society.
—— —— (1939). *The Place-Names of Wiltshire.* English Place-Name Society Volume 16. Cambridge: English Place-Name Society.
MCCLURE, J., and COLLINS, R. (eds.) (1994). *Historia ecclesiastica gentis Anglorum.* Oxford: Oxford University Press.
MEANEY, A. L. (1995). 'Pagan English sanctuaries, place-names and hundred meeting-places'. *Anglo-Saxon Studies in Archaeology and History* 8: 29–42.
MORRIS, R. (1989). *Churches in the Landscape.* London: J. Dent & Sons Ltd.
MULK, I., and BAYLISS-SMITH, T. (1999). 'The representation of Sámi cultural identity in the cultural landscapes of northern Sweden: the use and misuse of archaeological knowledge', in P. Ucko and R. Layton, *The Archaeology and Anthropology of Landscape: Shaping Your Landscape.* One World Archaeology 30. London: Routledge.
PANTOS, A. (2002). *Assembly-Places in the Anglo-Saxon Period: Aspects of Form and Location.* Unpublished DPhil thesis, University of Oxford.
—— (2003). '"On the edge of things": The boundary location of Anglo-Saxon assembly sites', in D. Griffiths, A. Reynolds, and S. Semple (eds.), *Boundaries in Early Medieval Britain.* Anglo-Saxon Studies in Archaeology and History 12. Oxford: Oxbow, 38–49.
PARKER PEARSON, M., and FIELD, N. (2003). *Fiskerton: An Iron Age Timber Causeway with Iron Age and Roman Offerings.* Oxford: Oxbow.
PENN, K. (2000). *Excavations on the Norwich Southern Bypass,1989–91, Part 2: The Anglo-Saxon Cemetery at Harford Farm, Caistor St. Edmund, Norfolk.* East Anglian Archaeology 92. Dereham: Archaeology and Environment Division, Norfolk Museums Service.
PLUSKOWSKI, A. (2006). *Wolves and the Wilderness in the Middle Ages.* Woodbridge: Boydell.
PRICE, N. (2002). *The Viking Way: Religion and War in Late Iron Age Scandinavia.* Uppsala: Uppsala University Press.
RACKHAM, O. (1976). *Trees and Woodland in the British Landscape.* London: Dent.
RATTUE, J. (1995). *The Living Stream: Holy Wells in Historical Context.* Woodbridge: Boydell.
RODWELL, W., and RODWELL, K. (1982). 'St. Peter's Church, Barton-upon-Humber'. *Antiquaries Journal* 62: 283–315.
RUSSELL, C. (1979). 'The tree as a kingship symbol'. *Folklore* 90: 2, 217–33.
SAWYER, P. H. (1968). *Anglo-Saxon Charters: An Annotated List and Bibliography.* London Royal Historical Society Guides and Handbooks No. 8.
SCARRE, C. (2002a). 'Coast and cosmos: the Neolithic monuments of northern Brittany', in C. Scarre (ed.), *Monuments and Landscape in Atlantic Europe.* London: Routledge, 84–102.
—— (2002b). 'A place of special meaning: interpreting prehistoric monuments through landscape', in B. David and M. Wilson (eds.), *Inscribed Landscapes: Marking and Making Place.* Honolulu: University of Hawaii Press, 154–75.
SCRAGG, D. (1992) (ed.) *The Vercelli Homilies and Related Texts.* Oxford: Oxford University Press.
SEMPLE, S. J. (2002). *Anglo-Saxon Attitudes to the Past: A Landscape Perspective.* Unpublished PhD Thesis, Oxford University.
—— (2003a). 'Illustrations of damnation in late Anglo-Saxon manuscripts'. *Anglo-Saxon England* 32: 31–45.
—— (2003b). 'Burials and political boundaries in the Avebury region, North Wiltshire'. *Anglo-Saxon Studies in Archaeology and History* 12: 72–91.

—— (2007). 'Defining the OE *hearg*: a preliminary archaeological and topographic examination of *hearg* place names and their hinterlands'. *Early Medieval Europe* 15(4): 364–85.

—— (2008). 'Princes and polities in the South Saxon Kingdom: a landscape perspective'. *Oxford Journal of Archaeology* 24(4): 407–29.

—— (2010). 'In the open air', in Carver *et al.* (eds.), *Signals of Belief*, 21–48.

SHERLOCK, S., and SIMMONS, M. (2008). 'A seventh-century royal cemetery at Street House, north-east Yorkshire, England'. *Antiquity* 82, gallery.

SMITH, I. F. (1965). *Windmill Hill and Avebury, Excavations by Alexander Keiller 1925–1939*. Oxford: Clarendon Press.

STANLEY, E. G. (1975). *The Search for Anglo-Saxon Paganism*. Cambridge: Brewer Ltd.

STENTON, F. M. (1941). 'The historical bearing of place-name studies: Anglo-Saxon heathenism'. *The Transactions of the Royal Historical Society*, 4th Series, 23 (1941): 10–11.

STOCKER, D. and EVERSON, P. (2003). 'The straight and narrow way: Fenland causeways and the conversion of the landscape in the Witham valley, Lincolnshire', in Carver (ed.), *The Cross Goes North*, 271–88.

TALBOT, C. H. (1954). *The Anglo-Saxon Missionaries in Germany*. London: Sheed and Ward.

TILLEY, C. (1994). *A Phenomenology of Landscape: Places, Paths and Monuments*. Oxford: Berg.

—— (1996). 'The power of rocks: topography and monument construction on Bodmin Moor'. *World Archaeology* 28(2): 161–76.

TURNER, S. (2006). *Making a Christian Landscape: The Countryside in Early Medieval Cornwall, Devon and Wessex*. Exeter: Exeter University Press.

WALKER, J. (2010). 'In the hall', in Carver *et al.* (eds.), *Signals of Belief*.

WHITELOCK, D. (1955). *English Historical Documents*, Volume 1: *c. 500–1042*. London: Eyre and Methuen.

—— BRETT, M., and BROOKE, C. N. L. (1981). *Councils and Synods with Other Documents Relating to the English Church*, Volume 1: *AD 871–1204*. Oxford: Clarendon Press.

WILLIAMS, H. (1997). 'Ancient landscapes and the dead: the reuse of prehistoric and Roman monuments as early Anglo-Saxon burial sites'. *Medieval Archaeology* 41: 1–32.

—— (1998). 'Monuments and the past in early Anglo-Saxon England'. *World Archaeology* 30(1): 90–108.

—— (1999). 'Placing the dead: investigating the location of wealthy barrow burials in seventh century England', in M. Rundkvist (ed.), *Grave Matters: Eight Studies of First Millennium AD burials in Crimea, England and Southern Scandinavia*. BAR International Series 781. Oxford: Archaeopress.

—— (2006). *Death and Burial in Early Medieval Britain*. Cambridge: Cambridge University Press.

WILSON, D. M. (1965). 'Some neglected Late Anglo-Saxon swords'. *Medieval Archaeology* 9: 32–54.

WILSON, D. R. (1985). 'A note on O.E. *hearg* and *weoh* as place-name elements representing different types of pagan worship sites'. *Anglo-Saxon Studies in Archaeology and History* 4: 179–83.

WORMALD, P. (1999). *The Making of English Law: King Alfred to the Twelfth Century*, Volume 1: *Legislation and its Limits*. Oxford: Blackwell.

CHAPTER 39

THE ARCHAEOLOGY OF PAGANISM

ALEKS PLUSKOWSKI

DEFINING PAGANISM

In the fourth century, Christians invented the term *paganismus* to collectively define and singularize the beliefs of non-Christians, including Jews (Dowden 2000: 3). This of course concealed an incredible diversity of beliefs and practices, and until relatively recently, scholars have accepted this polar opposition between what were envisaged as effectively two pristine states of faith (Kilbride 2000: 8). Indeed, the Anglo-Saxon bishop Asser presented King Alfred's wars against the Vikings as a struggle between *pagani* and *Christiani* (Abrams 2001: 32). But the term 'pagan' continues to be useful for understanding processes of religious conversion in northern Europe. What has changed is the recognition that pagan belief systems existed on many levels: they could be shared by a specific social group over a wide geographic area, held by a particular community at a particular time, transformed, re-asserted, and constructed with little local precedent (see Pluskowski and Patrick 2003). Moreover, these systems are inseparable from other aspects of contemporary life, although some elements are more visible than others, such as the cultic aspects of warfare in pagan Scandinavia (Price 2002). As the ethnic and socio-political composition of the 'Anglo-Saxons' is seen as increasingly complex—reflected in the regional variation of their material culture and burial rites—it is possible to suggest the existence of multiple Anglo-Saxon 'paganisms', arising from the re-shaping of identities which took place in England from the fifth to eighth centuries.

Incoming Anglo-Saxon groups came to control areas with populations holding mixed religious beliefs: a combination of Christian communities in towns, villas, and forts—almost certainly a minority group—and the polytheistic hybrids of indigenous British and Roman cults which dominated the countryside (Watts 1991: 216–21). As the Anglo-Saxons came to dominate much of England, Christian communities appear to have shrunk into obscurity, whilst the incomers brought with them a new cosmology. Their world-view was broadly shared with other 'pagan' societies in Scandinavia, north Germany, and the eastern Baltic, within which variation arose from local complexity: the interaction between political, social, and environmental contexts, as well as responses to external influences such as missionary activity or trade. But the material traces of religious practice are difficult to untangle from other aspects of life, and this has made understanding the nature of Anglo-Saxon paganism—by isolating it—very difficult. It is impossible, for example, to reconstruct the cults of specific deities with the limited evidence available, and traces of cultic buildings remain elusive and tantalizing (see Semple, this volume). The clearest material expressions of paganism in Anglo-Saxon England are found in cemeteries (Hutton 1991: 275): the foci of elaborate funerary rituals where new social and cosmological identities were physically constructed for the dead (see Williams, this volume). Here, animals were sometimes interred with people, and it is the relationship with animals, also expressed in the zoomorphic art of Styles I and II (see Webster, this volume) and the popular use of animal elements in personal names recorded in later literature, which can be used as a point of departure for exploring pagan Anglo-Saxon spirituality.

There are, of course, inherent methodological problems concerning the identification of diagnostically 'pagan' and even 'Christian' material culture, which we are reminded of in virtually every treatment of the topic. Firstly, it is useful to highlight the varied pace of religious conversion itself: from Augustine's mission to the kingdom of Kent in 597, to the official acceptance of Christianity by all English kings, following the conversion of Sussex and the Isle of Wight by the end of the seventh century (Blair 2005: 9), the adoption of Christianity was slower in some regions than others. Indeed, most of the Anglo-Saxon kingdoms relapsed into a brief period of paganism following the death of the first converted king (Yorke 1990: 173; D. R. Wilson 1992: 174–5). In the earlier seventh century, aristocratic barrow burials were constructed in large numbers, some of which included artefacts decorated with Christian symbols (Williams 2006: 147); an understanding of Anglo-Saxon paganism must go hand in hand with an understanding of the process of religious conversion, since we see most of traditional Anglo-Saxon religion as it overlaps, formally and chronologically, with Christianity (Hines 1997: 396). In the relatively short time-span of its existence, the character of

Anglo-Saxon paganism can therefore best be described as mutable: its material culture potentially ambiguous and inseparable from other aspects of society.

Virtually every book that offers a snapshot of Anglo-Saxon archaeology has treated the topic of paganism, typically subdivided into thematic sections concerned with the evidence for cult sites, burials, artefacts, written sources, and so on, and concluding with the establishment of Christianity. Numerous studies of Anglo-Saxon funerary archaeology or other aspects of the conversion period in England touch on the topic of paganism and how to define its material culture. Echoes of pagan belief are preserved in later Christian written sources (Jolly 1993), and these have been explored by numerous scholars, with more comprehensive analyses by Glosecki (1989) and North (1997). The most important interdisciplinary synthesis remains David Wilson's *Anglo-Saxon Paganism* (1992), which comprehensively outlined the state of knowledge at the time, and has been very influential in shaping subsequent research agendas. The aim of this chapter is not to replace Wilson's synthesis, nor to rehash succeeding summaries of the evidence, but to suggest how the archaeology of early Anglo-Saxon religion can contribute to understanding variety within a pre-Christian world-view where many elements were shared by societies across the North Sea and Baltic.

The Material Traces of Cultic Practice

What did the early Anglo-Saxons actually *believe in*? This is impossible to reconstruct, but it is possible to explore their spiritual preoccupations and the degree to which cultic practices were institutionalized. The conceptual leap from material culture to practice to belief is far from straightforward, but the physical enactment of cult and its environmental foci remain fundamental starting points in the absence of contemporary texts (Hines 1997). In the search for Anglo-Saxon paganism, cues are invariably taken from Christian texts and edicts. The use of shrines and temples containing idols and altars, as well as the existence of priests, is attested in a number of sources. The first edicts against idols appear in 640, when according to Bede, Eorcenberht, king of Kent, ordered their abandonment and destruction throughout his realm (D. R. Wilson 1992: 29), but references to idolatry continue into the tenth century (North 1997: 88–90): a coalition of Scots and Welsh kings and the Earl of Northumbria was obligated to renounce 'idol-worship' (most likely referring to the activities of their Scandinavian associates) as part of an agreement with Æthelstan in 927 (Abrams 2001: 39). Idols had been singled out in the earliest Christian attacks on paganism, and idol-construction remained a source of anxiety for Western Christian authorities throughout the

Middle Ages (Camille 1989). Potential cultic images shaped from wood, stone, and metal have been recovered from sites in Poland, north Germany, and Scandinavia (Słupecki 1994; Price 2002), and there is possible evidence for the deliberate burial of cultic images in, for example, Roman London, perhaps to 'spiritually cleanse' a pagan site or alternatively to protect them from Christian iconoclasts (Rodwell 1993: 92). But no comparable examples are known from Anglo-Saxon sites, perhaps because they were largely constructed from wood which has simply not survived. A small number of early Anglo-Saxon anthropomorphic images have been found, mostly in Kent and dating to the first half of the seventh century, typically interpreted as having an amuletic function (Dickens *et al.* 2006: 76). Unfortunately, identification of representations of deities—whether anthropomorphic or zoomorphic—is partly hampered by the fact that whilst the names of at least some Anglo-Saxon gods are known (North 1997), their contemporary attributes remain elusive and we rely on later Christian commentaries, as well as the rich corpus of Old Norse material for analogies. But, removed from their specific contexts, neither can be taken as accurate documentation of early Anglo-Saxon polytheism.

Christian sources tend to isolate pagan cultic foci, and this is perhaps why archaeologists have traditionally searched for traces of cult divorced from the sphere of daily life. There is certainly a consistent relationship between religion and landscape, but again it is difficult to isolate 'pagan' elements, since these were 'imaginatively compounded' environments (Hines 1997: 390). Evidence for paganism in Old English place-names has been traditionally used to reconstruct the topography of belief in early Anglo-Saxon England (D. R. Wilson 1992: 5–21; Blair 1995; Meaney 1995); however, only recently has this information begun to be tested with an archaeological investigation of such sites (see Semple, this volume).

In England, it is likely that cemeteries were important foci for some form of cultic activity (Arnold 1997: 150). Certainly there are structures within their bounds that could be potential shrines (Blair 1995); the best known example is structure D2 at Yeavering, interpreted as a 'temple' because of its association with burials and a pit layered with ox skulls (Ware 2004: 156). The diversity of burial rites evident within and between Anglo-Saxon cemeteries from the fifth to seventh centuries has been linked to complex socio-political and ethnic fragmentation (Williams 2006: 24; see also Williams, this volume). But is it also possible to read diversity in cultic praxis and religious beliefs associated with mortuary rites? John Hines (1997: 408) has argued there is no evidence for any widespread concept of the afterlife in Anglo-Saxon 'paganism', and that many explanations may be sought for the deposition of various combinations of objects in graves. Whilst this is a fair criticism of stereotypical interpretations of grave-goods, the idea that belief in an afterlife did exist cannot be readily dismissed. Grave-goods interred with the body are typically linked to a variety of 'statements' regarding the identity of the deceased, but least explored in recent scholarship is their cosmological significance.

This is perhaps because it is extremely difficult to untangle religious identity from other aspects of an individual's social status (Arnold 1997: 149): is a horse sacrificed and buried with a person to accompany them to the otherworld, as a ritualistic gesture to a specific deity, or as a display of the deceased's ranking in their community, or all of these?

A recurring complaint in Christian sources, alongside the worship of idols, is the sacrifice of animals. The widely distributed evidence for the use of meat as funerary offerings and whole animals killed for deposition in burials suggests this was a regular and well-established practice in early Anglo-Saxon society (Bond and Worley 2006). Whilst food offerings to the dead by various Christian communities have been documented in recent ethnographies, the idea of killing an animal for the primary reason of interment with a human characterizes select pre-Christian burial rites across northern Europe. In later Anglo-Saxon England, an unusual exception is the occasional interment of animals with humans in execution cemeteries: perhaps the end result of prosecutions of bestiality. However, these examples have a clear judicial context (see Reynolds 2009). Audrey Meaney (1995: 29) has highlighted unusual treatments of animal remains in Anglo-Saxon cemeteries as evidence of sacrifice, such as the careful positioning of an ox skull at Soham (Cambridgeshire), or a pig's skull at Frilford (Berkshire).

The range of species used in the mortuary theatre was limited, with the most diverse combinations found at cemeteries where cremation was practised (e.g. Spong Hill). In the cremation rite practised around the Humber and Wash estuaries as well as north Norfolk, horses stand out as particularly important sacrificial animals, occurring with as much as 10 per cent of the buried population (Fern 2005: 46; Carver and Fern 2005: 298–301). Thirty-one inhumations of horses have also been discovered: in the sixth century whole animals or simply their skulls were deposited in the same grave accompanying (largely) adult males, and from the early seventh century, in separate graves (Fern 2005: 43–4). The comparison between the horse inhumation and cremation rites is interesting, and when combined with the use of other animals, particularly dogs (Crabtree 1995), it may suggest that something more than social status was being expressed in the killing of these animals. After the end of horse burial in the early seventh century, horse harnesses continue to be deposited, perhaps as a symbol of equestrian status (Fern 2005: 44). Although Christian commentators naturally linked sacrifice with devotion to a deity, the end of animal interment (but not furnished burial) suggests it may have had a strong religious dimension, rather than conceptualizing deposited fauna as 'equipment' (Carver and Fern 2005: 299). The variety and selection of animal deposition may therefore reflect very specific cultic practices, as much as expressions of social status. Indeed, for the archaeologist, the symbolic use of animals is one of the most visible aspects of early Anglo-Saxon religion.

ANIMALS AS PORTALS TO THE HIDDEN

Zoomorphic forms characterize Anglo-Saxon applied art (Speake 1980): an aesthetic milieu also found in Scandinavia, where its persistence from the fifth to eleventh centuries contrasted with Christian figural and narrative art (Wicker 2003). But there are few examples of complex zoomorphic decoration: most Anglo-Saxon jewellery is relatively basic, suggesting the most elaborate pieces were exclusive. The use of applied zoomorphic ornament into the eleventh century cannot be accounted for under a single explanation (Schutz 2001: 219; Thompson 2004: 132–3). But even if this is the case, is there any evidence for a sacral function alongside the more obvious associations with wealth and social ranking? David Leigh (1984) suggested that Style I square-headed brooches almost universally exhibit a theme of animal masks, which when viewed from a 90° angle become human masks—brooches were 'visual riddles', an aesthetic ambiguity which mirrors the later poetic tradition relying on literary devices conveying multiple and hidden meanings. The similarities with Christian allegorical exposition may have facilitated the process of conversion, and bridged the use of zoomorphic and asymmetrical art in pagan and Christian contexts (Rosenblitt 2005: 113). Human–animal hybridization and ambiguity has been seen as evidence for an 'ideology of transformation' within Anglo-Saxon cosmology (Williams 2001). Moreover, where complex and intricate representations were applied to objects, their details would not have been recognizable without very close scrutiny. On this basis it is likely that such objects had an apotropaic aspect. Whilst this cannot be linked to any cultic praxis per se, the power conferred by the animals in question would have been situated within a broader cosmology. As with the use of animals in mortuary rites, a select group recurs in zoomorphic art.

The raptor is one of the main distinguishing features of Style II animal ornament and features on a range of objects from the late sixth and seventh centuries, interpreted as belonging essentially to the upper strata of Anglo-Saxon society (Dickinson 2005). The predatory bird is found throughout the Germanic world, but there are significant regional differences—and the closest analogies occur in Scandinavia, leading George Speake (1980: 85) to conclude that the significance of the animal in the two areas was the same. More recently, Karen Høilund Nielsen (1999: 200) suggested that Kentish Style II developed as a result of Frankish influences in the sixth and seventh centuries, whereas East Anglian Style II developed probably from a Danish connection with the royal house: in both regions the style was used by the elites to legitimate their authority. With these strong links between certain animal representations, artefacts, and social groups, it is possible to suggest the raptor (along with animals such as the wolf, wild boar, and serpent) was used in the context of social identification, and in a religious system preoccupied with the boundary between humans and animals, its use may have had a strong cosmological dimension (Hedeager 1998).

Raptors feature amongst some of the most elaborate examples of early Anglo-Saxon animal representations on artefacts from Sutton Hoo. This site can be regarded as an unusual concentration of impulses found elsewhere in England. In Mound 1, for example, the boar is represented on artefacts ten times, but elsewhere it can be found dispersed across the country: on the crest of the Benty Grange helmet (Derbyshire), stamped on a sword blade from the River Lark (Cambridgeshire), on jewellery from a number of sites in Kent as well as at Womersley, Yorkshire (Speake 1980: 78–81); perforated boar tusks have also been found in a range of (predominantly female) graves with no clear regional pattern (Meaney 1981). The specific role of the boar in these diverse contexts cannot be determined, but like other animals, its form and body parts were plausibly employed for amuletic or apotropaic purposes. It is likely that the multiple uses of the boar, as suggested by varied contexts, revolved around its flexible association with protection, aggression, fertility, and identity (Glosecki 2000: 14). The remains of wild boar are rarely found in Anglo-Saxon sites, and there is no evidence that this animal was frequently encountered—indeed, on the basis of the representation of wild species in faunal assemblages, hunting seems to have been extremely limited before the ninth century, with communities relying almost exclusively on livestock for meat and secondary products (Crabtree 1989; also see Sykes, O'Connor, this volume).

This ecological context is important, because it parallels the limited representation of wild animals in applied art and funerary ritual, both regionally and within any given cemetery. As already suggested, this may be because ownership of such artefacts—and any resulting associations—was exclusive. It may also imply that an understanding of their complex roles was also restricted. Similar exclusivity can be attributed to the use of early Saxon runic inscriptions, which were added to artefacts largely, if not entirely, associated with high-status ownership (Hines 1991: 72). As with applied zoomorphic ornament, runic inscriptions on artefacts would be difficult to use in visual display given their small size, their obscure location, and their indecipherability for the majority of the population. Evidence for secret religious knowledge has been used to support an interpretation of pagan Scandinavian spirituality as 'shamanic' (Price 2002), a term that is being increasingly applied to early Anglo-Saxon religion.

Anglo-Saxon paganism as 'shamanism'

The use of animals as active (rather than simply metaphorical) mediators between the natural and supernatural worlds is a characteristic of shamanic religious systems (Eliade 1989). Stephan Glosecki (1989) has argued for a shamanic view of early Anglo-Saxon society on the basis of traces of totemism and ecstatic techniques found in later Anglo-Saxon literature, whilst Howard Williams (2001) has proposed a similar interpretation of Anglo-Saxon paganism, grounded in the evidence of animal use and representation in fifth- and sixth-century funerary rites. More specifically, Glosecki and Williams have argued for an animistic pagan Anglo-Saxon society, where the spiritual was accessible through the natural.

There is very little direct evidence for the actual veneration of animals as deities in England, although the practice is attested in other regions of northern Europe. A letter written by Aldhelm of Sherborne (d. 709) mentions shrines which had been converted to Christian uses, where previously the 'crude pillars of the accursed snake and stag' had been worshipped, perhaps referring to an image of a stag or hybrid stag-deity (Filotas 2005: 144), or to a representation of a sacrificial animal (Meaney 1995: 30). Such examples are exceptional. On the other hand, the centrality of zoomorphic ornament, the incorporation of animals into funerary rites, personal display, and hints in later literature of their original totemic functions, such as their use in personal names, all point to a paradigm where animals played a key role in social and cosmological organization (Pluskowski 2006: 135–6). Here the conceptual boundary between human and animal could be readily blurred, and desirable qualities associated with some species, particularly wild animals, could be tapped and controlled. In the case of Iron Age Scandinavian society, there is convincing evidence for the existence of specialists directly involved in this process, with distinctive material culture (Price 2002). Is there any evidence for such specialists in early Anglo-Saxon England? Is there evidence of traditional, albeit local, 'shamanism'?

The process of religious conversion in England, as elsewhere in Europe, was facilitated by the aristocracy (Fletcher 1997: 162). Aside from the political aspects of the conversion, it is likely the pagan aristocracy played key roles in the organization of cultic activity. William Chaney (1970) argued for the fundamental roles of kings as cultic leaders in pagan Anglo-Saxon England with continuity into the Christian period: individuals who traced their descent to the god Woden, mediated with the divine, and whose burial mounds became communal meeting points. Alongside the role of kings in the organization of cult, there is tentative evidence for the existence of burial specialists directing the complex process of a funeral. Focusing on a few unusual female graves as a point of departure, Helen Geake (2003) has proposed the existence of an entire class of female ritual specialists or 'cunning women', with clear parallels in Scandinavia (Price 2002).

If the 'visual riddles' of zoomorphic art required special knowledge to construct and interpret, as has been proposed for Scandinavian runic art (Andrén 2000), this is perhaps evidence of the existence of spiritual specialists, or at least groups who possessed and transferred knowledge concerning the metaphysical relationships between humans and animals. When all of this indirect evidence is coupled with

Christian sources referring to pagan 'priests', as well as a basic necessary level of organization in cultic activity, it is likely that spiritual specialists existed in pagan Anglo-Saxon society, although to the archaeologist they remain intangible. However, perhaps the select few linked with animals or birds in death represent such a group and, irrespective of social and political boundaries, all sharing the closest identification with the natural world.

IN THE SHADOW OF SCANDINAVIA

Comparisons and contrasts between north German and southern Scandinavian and early Anglo-Saxon paganisms have coloured the study of north European pre-Christian religion, although virtually every time such links are brought together a disclaimer is issued concerning the problems in relative chronology, as well as over-generalization on the basis of very fragmentary evidence. More recently, there has been increasing interest in the mutability of Anglo-Saxon paganisms in response to religious systems *within* Britain: for example, existing Romano-British paganisms influencing Anglo-Saxon cultic practice, as John Blair (1995: 21) has argued in the context of the persistence of Roman- and British-type shrines in the late sixth and early seventh centuries, and as Michael Enright (2006) has argued for the pre-Christian Celtic cultic origins of the whetstone sceptre buried at Mound 1 in Sutton Hoo. Certainly the Anglo-Saxons incorporated prehistoric monuments into their ritual landscape (see Semple, this volume). In turn, Christianity may have influenced Anglo-Saxon ritual—as proposed for the explicit 'paganism' at Sutton Hoo (Carver 1998) (although the idea that the Sutton Hoo burials represent paganism has been rejected by Blair (2005), especially in the light of the Prittlewell burial) or the suggestion that Anglo-Saxon square shrines may have taken their cue from the monumental sacral architecture of Christianity (Blair 1995: 22). Inter-influence between the ritual activities of the Picts and the north Saxons also appears to have taken place (Meaney 1995: 30; Foster 2004: 90). Christianity could have played a role in another way of course, by accommodating practices such as those found in Sutton Hoo and resulting in the abandonment of furnished burial for other reasons (Hines 1997: 382).

Nonetheless, there are important links evident in the material culture of pagan societies in the North Sea region. Anglo-Saxon cemeteries established in the fifth century included burial rites which exhibited close similarities with those in southern Scandinavia and northern Germany, particularly in the case of cremations (Williams 2006: 24). Aside from comparable mortuary rites and the shared use of zoomorphic decoration, there are more specific examples of what may be potential supra-regional religious motifs. On a buckle from Finglesham and on the Sutton Hoo helmet, 'dancing warriors' wear helmets which bear horns terminating in zoomorphic beaked heads, perhaps representing birds circling overhead (Price 2002: 388; see also Blackwell 2007). These are the best-known English examples paralleling images of horned figures in southern Scandinavia and on the Continent, which in the case of a helmet plate-die from Torslunda and pressed mounts from Gutenstein and Obrigheim are accompanied by wolf-coated or lupine hybrid warriors. These and related motifs can be convincingly linked to the cult of Óðinn (ibid.: 372–3), which appears to have derived from the cult of Mercury as it developed in Roman Gaul. Given contemporary etymological links between Anglo-Saxon Woden and Scandinavian Óðinn, their cults appear to have been expressed in the symbolic repertoires of both regions in comparable ways, although the regal traits of the deity appear to have been adopted in Scandinavia from the West Saxons (North 1997: 78). In this instance the use of dancing warriors and birds in both England and southern Scandinavia may have alluded to a personal affinity with the deity or his cult.

Moreover, comparisons of pre-Christian references in Old Norse and Old English literature have resulted in some interesting conclusions. Richard North (1997), for example, in his study of paganism in Old English literature suggested that Anglo-Saxons were familiar with the type of sorcery associated in Scandinavia with Óðinn and the Vanir, but what we are left with is a 'literary cult of Woden', echoing earlier beliefs. Judith Jesch (2002) compared the use of the beasts of battle—the wolf, raven, and eagle—in both literary groups and concluded that although the two regions shared a mutual understanding of their meaning, Old English poets used the animals to highlight the horror and tragedy of war, whereas Scandinavian audiences recognized their role in exalting the heroism of warriors in battle. The divergence in the roles of deities and other entities in Anglo-Saxon England and Scandinavia can partly be understood as a process of religious transformation directly resulting from the migration—adapting to new socio-political and ecological circumstances—and partly as the product of separate conversion histories (Pluskowski forthcoming). After all, Scandinavians remained pagan for a significantly longer period of time and despite the Viking incursions into England in the ninth and tenth centuries, Anglo-Saxon Christianity had become established enough to resist a national religious relapse. Instead, manifestations of Anglo-Scandinavian paganisms can be seen as localized responses to specific socio-political circumstances. As with the earlier Anglo-Saxon migration, religion was intimately associated with identity.

The Viking impact

In the latter decades of the ninth century, Scandinavians colonizing parts of the British Isles brought their beliefs and cultic practices with them, resulting in a brief introduction of paganism into parts of northern Britain. As with material traces of Anglo-Saxon paganism, this is largely visible in the introduction of mortuary rites. Heath Wood, Ingleby, close to the Anglo-Danish frontier, represents one of two known intrusive Scandinavian cemeteries found to date in England, the other recently discovered near Cumwhitton in Cumbria. A relatively short-lived cremation barrow cemetery (which included deposited artefacts and sacrificed animals), Ingleby has been interpreted by Richards (2001: 98; and this volume) as an expression of authority, reflecting the need to re-enforce an overtly Scandinavian 'paganism'—a fusion of religious, political, and military identity—at a time of protracted conflict and instability. It is also possible that two equestrian burials combining skeleton, horse, and sword—at Leigh-on-Sea and Reading—may be Scandinavian (Graham-Campbell 2001: 112), or perhaps a continuation of earlier Anglo-Saxon rites. The only other examples of clear Scandinavian burials are found in the northern and western isles of Scotland, and on the Isle of Man, where mound burials were combined with cremation, boat burial, weapon deposition, animal sacrifice, and in two instances (at Ballateare and Balladoole), potential human sacrifice. However, given the range of burial rites in contemporary Scandinavia, and the fact that the presence or absence of grave-goods cannot be used as an indicator of religious allegiance, it is possible that many Scandinavians simply adopted local burial customs (Halsall 2000: 270). In northern England, some Scandinavian lords also took advantage of native stone sculptural traditions to express elements of their pagan world-view, almost certainly within the context of adopting Christianity (Bailey 1980: 101–42).

There is no evidence that Anglo-Saxons living within the Danelaw adopted this new belief system; indeed the very opposite process happened and Scandinavians appear to have converted to Christianity within a few decades of settling (Abrams 2001). The fusion of pagan Scandinavian and Christian imagery evident on some of the north English sculptures hints at how—despite the documented episodes of military conflict—the acceptance of Christianity was at times as much reflective as it may have been confrontational (Pluskowski 2004). At Sedgeford in Norfolk, a female skeleton buried with a horse in an otherwise Christian mid-late Saxon cemetery may suggest the presence of an Anglo-Scandinavian community (Graham-Campbell 2001: 112). Like Anglo-Saxon zoomorphic ornament, Scandinavian animal styles—even if they had once been recognizable expressions of a distinctly northern 'pagan identity' (Wicker 2003)—continued to be used by Christian Anglo-Scandinavians, even being adopted outside the colonized area (D. M. Wilson 1984: 146). The period of Scandinavian settlement highlights the problems associated with attempting to isolate evidence for pre-Christian beliefs: very few actual Scandinavian burials in England are identifiable, and Scandinavian elements in place-names alluding to cult practice, the adoption of personal names of pagan deities, and the use of objects such as Thor's hammers (Abrams 2000: 140–1) mask a religious system or systems as mutable as early Anglo-Saxon paganisms, and as closely interwoven with local socio-political circumstances and the construction of personal and group identities.

Conclusion: Anglo-Saxon paganisms

Before the widespread acceptance of Christianity in England, Anglo-Saxon religion is difficult to perceive because it is entangled with other aspects of daily life. This does not mean that religion can be ignored as a fundamental motivator of behaviour during this time (Kilbride 2000: 12), and instead of attempting to isolate 'paganism', an alternative approach aims for an integrated view of early Anglo-Saxon society. Of course, there are inherent methodological problems: for example, if cultic sites were located at ephemeral places in the landscape, they will be extremely difficult to locate archaeologically. But since the worship of deities and the specifics of cultic activity would have been linked to the construction of local identity (Yorke 2006: 109), variation in Anglo-Saxon culture arising from the processes of migration, settlement, and kingship formation invariably resulted in a multitude of 'paganisms'.

Yet all of these paganisms shared some common elements. The organization required to run and maintain cultic sites, including cemeteries, presupposes some level of local institutionalization. This notion may be supported by the fundamental roles played by the regional aristocracies in the process of conversion. There is also some evidence for inter-regional standardization, at least in terms of semiotics—the use of a limited group of animals as symbols appears to have crossed ethnic and political boundaries. If we accept the argument that Christianity influenced the character of Anglo-Saxon paganisms in the seventh century, it is also interesting that different groups chose to respond in similar ways. In conclusion, early Anglo-Saxon religion can be understood on many levels, with variation arising as a result of local responses to changing social and political situations; however, for archaeologists the most visible indicators of Anglo-Saxon spirituality are in the symbolic roles played by animals. In this respect, by exploring the ecological contexts of religious conversion in England (and elsewhere in Europe) further, we can continue to advance our understanding of pre-Christian paganisms.

References

Abrams, L. (2000). 'Conversion and assimilation', in D. M. Hadley and J. D. Richards (eds.), *Cultures in Contact: Scandinavian Settlement in England in the Ninth and Tenth Centuries.* Turnhout: Brepols, 135–53.

——(2001). 'The conversion of the Danelaw', in Graham-Campbell *et al.* (eds.), *Vikings and the Danelaw*, 31–44.

Andrén, A. (2000). 'Re-reading embodied texts: an interpretation of rune-stones'. *Current Swedish Archaeology* 8: 7–32.

Arnold, C. J. (1997). *An Archaeology of the Early Anglo-Saxon Kingdoms.* London: Routledge.

Bailey, R. N. (1980). *Viking Age Sculpture in Northern England.* London: Collins.

Blackwell, A. (2007). 'Notes', *Medieval Archaeology* 51: 165–72.

Blair, J. (1995). 'Anglo-Saxon pagan shrines and their prototypes'. *Anglo-Saxon Studies in Archaeology and History* 8: 1–28.

——(2005). *The Church in Anglo-Saxon Society.* Oxford: Oxford University Press.

Bond, J. M., and Worley, F. L. (2006). 'Companions in death: the roles of animals in Anglo-Saxon and Viking cremation rituals in Britain', in R. Gowland and C. Knüsel (eds.), *The Social Archaeology of Funerary Remains.* Oxford: Oxbow, 89–98.

Camille, M. (1989). *The Gothic Idol: Ideology and Image-making in Medieval Art.* Cambridge: Cambridge University Press.

Carver, M. (1998). *Sutton Hoo: Burial Ground of Kings?* Philadelphia, PA: University of Philadelphia Press.

——(ed.) (2003). *The Cross Goes North: Processes of Conversion in Northern Europe, AD 300–1300.* Woodbridge: Boydell.

——and Fern, C. (2005). 'The seventh-century burial rites and their sequence', in M. Carver (ed.), *Sutton Hoo: A Seventh-Century Princely Burial Ground and its Context.* London: British Museum, 283–314.

Chaney, W. A. (1970). *The Cult of Kingship in Anglo-Saxon England: The Transition from Paganism to Christianity.* Manchester: Manchester University Press.

Crabtree, P. (1989). 'Sheep, horses, swine and kine: a zooarchaeological perspective on the Anglo-Saxon settlement of England'. *Journal of Field Archaeology* 16: 205–13.

——(1995). 'The Symbolic Role of Animals in Anglo-Saxon England: evidence from burials and cremations', in K. Ryan and P. Crabtree (eds.), *The Symbolic Role of Animals in Archaeology.* Philadelphia: University of Pennsylvania; MASCA, 21–6.

Dickens, A., Mortimer, R., and Tipper, J. (2006). 'The early Anglo-Saxon settlement and cemetery at Bloodmoor Hill, Carlton Colville, Suffolk: a preliminary report'. *Anglo-Saxon Studies in Archaeology and History* 13: 63–79.

Dickinson, T. (2005). 'Symbols of protection: the significance of animal-ornamented shields in early Anglo-Saxon England'. *Medieval Archaeology* 49: 109–63.

Dowden, K. (2000). *European Paganism: The Realities of Cult from Antiquity to the Middle Ages.* London: Routledge.

Eliade, M. (1989). *Shamanism: Archaic Techniques of Ecstasy.* London: Arkana.

Enright, M. J. (2006). *The Sutton Hoo Sceptre and the Roots of Celtic Kingship Theory.* Dublin: Four Courts Press.

Fern, C. (2005). 'The archaeological evidence for equestrianism in early Anglo-Saxon England, c.450–700', in A. G. Pluskowski (ed.), *Just Skin and Bones? New Perspectives on*

Human–Animal Relations in the Historical Past. BAR International Series 1410. Oxford: Archaeopress, 43–72.

FILOTAS, B. (2005). *Pagan Survivals, Superstitions and Popular Culture in Early Medieval Pastoral Literature*. Toronto: Pontifical Institute of Mediaeval Studies.

FLETCHER, R. (1997). *The Conversion of Europe: From Paganism to Christianity 371–1386 AD*. London: Harper Collins.

FOSTER, S. (2004). *Picts, Gaels and Scots: Early Historic Scotland*. London: Batsford.

GEAKE, H. (2003). 'The control of burial practice in Anglo-Saxon England', in Carver (ed.), *The Cross Goes North*, 259–69.

GLOSECKI, S. O. (1989). *Shamanism and Old English Poetry*. New York: Garland.

——(2000). 'Movable beasts: the manifold implications of early Germanic animal imagery', in N. C. Flores (ed.), *Animals in the Middle Ages*. New York: Routledge, 3–23.

GRAHAM-CAMPBELL, J. (2001). 'Pagan Scandinavian burial in the central and southern Danelaw', in Graham-Campbell *et al.* (eds.), *Vikings and the Danelaw*, 105–23.

——HALL, R., JESCH, J., and PARSONS, D. N. (eds.) (2001). *Vikings and the Danelaw*. Oxford: Oxbow.

HALSALL, G. (2000). 'The Viking presence in England? The burial evidence reconsidered', in D. M. Hadley and J. D. Richards (eds.), *Cultures in Contact: Scandinavian Settlement in England in the Ninth and Tenth Centuries*. Turnhout: Brepols, 259–76.

HEDEAGER, L. (1998). 'Cosmological endurance: pagan identities in early Christian Europe'. *European Journal of Archaeology* 1(3): 382–96.

HINES, J. (1991). 'Some observations on the runic inscriptions in early Anglo-Saxon England', in A. Bammesberger (ed.), *Old English Runes and their Continental Background*. Heidelberg: Carl Winter, 61–83.

——(1997). 'Religion: the limits of knowledge', in J. Hines (ed.), *The Anglo-Saxons from the Migration Period to the Eighth Century: An Ethnographic Perspective*. Woodbridge: Boydell, 375–410.

HØILUND NIELSEN, K. (1999). 'Style II and the Anglo-Saxon elite'. *Anglo-Saxon Studies in Archaeology and History* 10: 185–202.

HUTTON, R. (1991). *The Pagan Religions of the Ancient British Isles: Their Nature and Legacy*. Oxford: Blackwell.

JESCH, J. (2002). 'Eagles, ravens and wolves: beasts of battle, symbols of victory and death', in J. Jesch (ed.), *The Scandinavians from the Vendel Period to the Tenth Century: An Ethnographic Perspective*. Woodbridge: Boydell, 251–80.

JOLLY, K. (1993). 'Father God and Mother Earth: nature-mysticism in the Anglo-Saxon world', in J. E. Salisbury (ed.), *The Medieval World of Nature*. New York: Garland, 221–52.

KILBRIDE, W. (2000). 'Why I feel cheated by the term "Christianisation"'. *Archaeological Review from Cambridge* 17(2): 1–17.

LEIGH, D. (1984). 'Ambiguity in Anglo-Saxon Style I art'. *Antiquaries Journal* 64: 34–42.

MEANEY, A. L. (1981). *Anglo-Saxon Amulets and Curing Stones*. BAR British Series 96. Oxford: Archaeopress.

——(1995) 'Pagan English sanctuaries, place-names and hundred meeting-places'. *Anglo-Saxon Studies in Archaeology and History* 8: 29–42.

NORTH, R. (1997). *Heathen Gods in Old English Literature*. Cambridge: Cambridge University Press.

PLUSKOWSKI, A. G. (2004). 'Lupine apocalypse: the wolf in pagan and Christian cosmology in medieval Britain and Scandinavia'. *Cosmos* 17: 113–31.

——(2006). *Wolves and the Wilderness in the Middle Ages*. Woodbridge: Boydell and Brewer.

——(forthcoming). 'Animal magic', in M. Carver, A. Sanmark, and S. Semple (eds.), *Signals of Belief in Early England: Anglo-Saxon Paganism Revisited*. Oxford: Oxbow.

——and PATRICK, P. J. (2003) '"How do you pray to God?" Fragmentation and Variety in Early Medieval Christianity', in M. Carver (ed.), *The Cross Goes North*, 29–58.

PRICE, N. S. (2002). *The Viking Way: Religion and War in Late Iron Age Scandinavia*. Uppsala: Uppsala University, Dept. of Archaeology and Ancient History.

REYNOLDS, A. (2009). *Anglo-Saxon Deviant Burial Customs*. Oxford: Oxford University Press.

RICHARDS, J. (2001). 'Boundaries and cult centres: Viking burial in Derbyshire', in Graham-Campbell *et al.* (eds.), *Vikings and the Danelaw*, 97–104.

RODWELL, W. (1993). 'The role of the Church in the development of Roman and early Anglo-Saxon London', in M. Carver (ed.), *In Search of Cult: Archaeological Investigations in Honour of Philip Rahtz*. Woodbridge: Boydell, 91–9.

ROSENBLITT, J. A. (2005). 'The Lindisfarne Gospels and the aesthetics of Anglo-Saxon art'. *Anglo-Saxon Studies in Archaeology and History* 13: 105–17.

SCHUTZ, H. (2001). *Tools, Weapons and Ornaments: Germanic Material Culture in Pre-Carolingian Central Europe, 400–750*. Leiden: Brill.

SŁUPECKI, L. (1994). *Slavonic Pagan Sanctuaries*. Warsaw: Institute of Archaeology and Ethnology, Polish Academy of Sciences.

SPEAKE, G. (1980). *Anglo-Saxon Animal Art and its Germanic Background*. Oxford: Clarendon Press.

THOMPSON, V. (2004). *Dying and Death in Later Anglo-Saxon England*. Woodbridge: Boydell.

WARE, C. (2004). 'The social use of space at Gefrin', in P. Frodsham and C. O'Brien (eds.), *Yeavering: People, Power and Place*, Stroud: Tempus, 152–60.

WATTS, D. (1991). *Christians and Pagans in Roman Britain*. London: Routledge.

WICKER, N. L. (2003). 'The Scandinavian animal styles in response to Mediterranean and Christian narrative art', in Carver (ed.), *The Cross Goes North*, 531–50.

WILLIAMS, H. (2001). 'An ideology of transformation: cremation rites and animal sacrifice in early Anglo-Saxon England', in N. Price (ed.), *The Archaeology of Shamanism*. London: Routledge, 193–212.

——(2006). *Death and Memory in Early Medieval Britain*. Cambridge: Cambridge University Press.

WILSON, D. M. (1984). *Anglo-Saxon Art*. London: Thames & Hudson.

WILSON, D. R. (1992). *Anglo-Saxon Paganism*. London: Routledge.

YORKE, B. (1990). *Kings and Kingdoms of Early Anglo-Saxon England*. London: B. A. Seaby.

——(2006). *The Conversion of Britain: Religion, Politics and Society, c. 600–800*. London: Pearson.

CHAPTER 40

THE MATERIAL CULTURE OF THE ANGLO-SAXON CHURCH

ELIZABETH COATSWORTH

INTRODUCTION

What constitutes the material culture of the church could be interpreted very broadly, for an era in which the church was a major landowner and landlord; a major builder in stone and wood for both religious and domestic use (and indeed of workshops and farm buildings indistinguishable from those on secular sites); and was possibly as involved as any secular lord in the development of trade and market centres. It is a fact that many types of production (textile working, metalworking) were carried on at both secular and ecclesiastical estates, in cases where their status can be established. There is, however, an ongoing discussion both as to how 'high status' sites are to be distinguished and which of these can then be identified as ecclesiastical sites, monastic or other: the presence of items indicating literacy, such as styli, are no longer regarded by many as adequate evidence of monastic status on their own (see for example Loveluck 2001; Pestell and Ulmschneider 2003; Cabot et al. 2004; Naylor 2004). Others have come to the opposite conclusion, however. John Blair, for example, has argued strongly for styli as evidence of monastic identity (Blair 2005: 204-12). He has pointed to the richness of sites with styli in comparison with known *wics*; however, the problem of distinguishing rich monastic sites from royal or aristocratic sites has not yet been satisfactorily answered.

Numerous examples of everyday objects, including tools and metal utensils, dress fittings, pottery, shoes and other leather goods, objects of bone and horn (and very often the means to produce them), and other indicators of economic activity, such as coins, are certainly found on excavated monastic sites, sometimes in abundance. Such considerations were outlined briefly in Cramp (1976), a survey of monastic sites excavated to that time. The increased importance given to all categories of material finds, including the ways in which they reflected the status of a monastic site, or showed interaction with the contemporary secular economy, is demonstrated in Cramp (1993), in her re-assessment of the monastery at Whitby. Since then there have been a number of major monastic excavation reports (for example Hill 1997; Hardy et al. 2003; Cramp 2007) as well as interim reports promising more (for example Hull 2002), so that material for the assessment of material culture in relation to economy and status is not lacking.

There are problems with approaching the depiction of the church through its material remains, however. One is that the discussion of the surviving remains as outlined above does not necessarily distinguish items specifically related to the church's liturgical and mission function. It is also necessary to remember that churches and monasteries will have varied greatly in material terms, proportionate to their landed endowments and other evidence of high-level, including royal, patronage. It is also true that monasticism can imply an ascetic lifestyle, and that the material world of those who lived in them might also be relatively invisible, or that there may even have been a tension between the requirement for high-level economic activity in certain spheres—in the production or acquisition of objects in the liturgy or to beautify worship or to demonstrate the glory of God, for example—and that life as lived. This was apparently the case at Lindisfarne, where a specialized production site was identified, with quantities of juvenile cattle remains, possibly for the production of calf skins for the monastic scriptorium, while among the archaeological finds there was an apparent lack of personal possessions such as dress fittings (O'Sullivan 2001).

If one looks at documentary sources for items specifically related to the church's function, there is a huge mismatch between the evidence in these sources and the surviving material, which one can say with confidence as they have been largely collected for the Anglo-Saxon period (Lehmann-Brockhaus 1955-60; Dodwell 1982). These sources are very rich for objects in precious materials, including ivories and textiles: the picture they present is of a church spectacularly endowed with costly material objects, but of course it is the value of the objects in the worldly sense which has determined their inclusion in the records, and their celebration too in works of contemporary literature. Relatively few textiles or metalwork objects which specifically relate to church function survive, however. The opposite problem occurs with other categories of material, such as stone sculpture. These are usually found in association with church buildings, and in the case of sculpture in some areas in considerable quantity, but contemporary or near-contemporary references to them are very rare. I have tried to take this imbalance into account in my discussion below.

Textiles

The best survey of documentary sources for Anglo-Saxon textiles generally is that in Dodwell (1982: 129–87), in which a large proportion of the references are to textiles made for or donated to churches, and thus provide a glimpse of this important facet of early medieval life and worship which can no longer be achieved so easily through a study of the few remains. Most modern readers would expect textiles in the form of ecclesiastical vestments, but many of these references are to church furnishings. For example, there are numerous records of wall-hangings devoted to churches: King Oswald is said to have presented churches he founded early in the seventh century with wall-hangings of silk interwoven with gold; according to Alcuin, Archbishop Egbert presented silk hangings with exotic forms or figures to his church in York in the mid eighth century (Godman 1982: 26–7, ll. 278–9; 98–9, ll. 1267–8); and at the end of the tenth century, Sigeric, Archbishop of Canterbury, gave altar cloths decorated with white lions to Glastonbury (William of Malmesbury 1981: 136–7). A verse history of an unidentified cell of a Northumbrian monastery (possibly Crayke in North Yorkshire rather than Lindisfarne—see Lapidge 1990; Lapidge *et al.* 1999: 6; Michael Lapidge in his paper on Æthelwulf and *De abbatibus* argues that there is nothing in the text, and no other reason, to suppose that this unidentified minster was a cell of Lindisfarne), written in the first quarter of the ninth century, is one of the few to mention textiles with a specifically Christian subject matter. It briefly describes hangings woven with red metal, and showing the miracles of Christ (Æthelwulf 1967: ll. 633–5). Skeuomorphs of such textile objects appear in sculpture: an example is a grave cover from Kirkdale in Yorkshire, with its embroidered surface and its fringed and tasselled edge, and a cross-base from Lindisfarne, which seems to have a cover with girdle-like ties (Coatsworth 2008b).

Donations to churches could include textiles originally made for secular use: the most famous example is probably the hanging woven or embroidered with the deeds of the Ealdorman Byhrtnoth, killed at the Battle of Maldon, which was donated to Ely by his wife, Ælfflæd (*Liber Eliensis* 1962: chap. 63, p. 136).

King Edgar gave Ely a gold-embroidered cloak to be made into a chasuble (*Liber Eliensis* 1962: 117). Wall hangings were also used to create domestic comfort within ecclesiastical contexts: for example Goscelin (a Flemish monk of St Bertin), who came to England in 1058, wrote about how he transformed a hovel into acceptable living quarters with curtains, hangings, and seat covers (*Goscelin* 1955: 102; see also Coatsworth 2007a: 5–6). Ælfwold, bishop of Crediton (1008–12) left wall-hangings, seat-covers, and bed-gear to a kinsman and a sister in his will (Napier and Stevenson 1895: 10, pp. 23–4, ll. 15–16, 21–2; see Coatsworth 2007a: 6–9, to see how this fits with secular elite practice of the time). The letters of St Boniface and his circle demonstrate that ecclesiastics in the eighth century sent each other gifts including textiles: some clearly rich examples of vestments and church furnishings, others quite humble items such as towels and rugs (Coatsworth 2007a: 10–11).

It might, therefore, appear to be difficult to distinguish secular from ecclesiastical textiles; in practice, however, the most substantial textile remains from Anglo-Saxon England have all been preserved within ecclesiastical contexts, either tombs or church treasuries (in some cases in treasuries outside England, in Belgium, France, and Italy). There have been a few possible fragmentary examples, discovered in the course of modern excavation (Coatsworth and Owen-Crocker 2007: 10). For example, a grave found beneath the Norman refectory floor at Worcester Cathedral contained a skeleton with the remains of gold brocading at the back of its neck: from the position of the grave this could have been an ecclesiastic, and from the position of the textile within the grave, it was possibly from the centre of an ecclesiastical stole. This grave was first radiocarbon-dated broadly to the fifth to seventh centuries (Barker and Cubberley 1974), with C. A. R. Radford writing within the same article favouring the earlier end of this dating, suggesting a sub-Roman rather than an Anglo-Saxon context. However a recent analysis has indicated that the seventh century is much more probable (Baker and Holt 2004: 146–7). A skeleton with elaborate gold thread decoration on the skull, with braids hanging down over the right clavicle and onto the right shoulder, was found in what was probably a ninth-century grave in Winchester Cathedral (Biddle 1965). The position of the gold braid does not lend itself so readily to identifications as an item of ecclesiastical dress here, but this was certainly a person of high status. Gold foil from gold thread found near the displaced skull of a skeleton from Monkwearmouth has been suggested as an indication of a high-status female burial, lay or religious, during the late seventh to ninth centuries (Cramp 2007, 2: 229). More certainly, silk fragments with lions, griffins, and foliage embroidered in silver-gilt thread in the underside couching technique were recovered from the grave of William of St Calais, Norman bishop of Durham 1081–96, when it was opened in 1795: these deserve serious consideration as being among the last remains of Anglo-Saxon ecclesiastical embroidery, although it is not known to what textile or vestment they belong (King 1963; Ivy 1992; Coatsworth 2005). Occasionally archaeological evidence will coincide satisfactorily with art or documentary evidence: for example the leaf embroidered in gold on the garment of a man at Repton (Biddle and Kjølbye-Biddle 2001) is neatly paralleled by a gold embroidered leaf on the shoulder of an ecclesiastic depicted in the Benedictional of St Ethelwold (British Library MS Additional 49598, folio 118v; see Dodwell 1982: pl. 50 for other examples of ecclesiastical dress with this feature).

The most important example of an ecclesiastical burial with textiles is, however, undoubtedly that of St Cuthbert, a Northumbrian monk and bishop who died in 687. This is an important record not only of the textile remains themselves, which include textiles which might have been used for hangings as well as vestments, but also, from the varying dates of the textiles and from documentary sources, because it provides an excellent illustration of the practice of rich textile donations to the shrines of saints. St Cuthbert's tomb was opened on a number of documented occasions when gifts, especially luxury textiles, were placed in the reliquary coffin (Coatsworth 1989). The remains of these were recovered by excavation in the nineteenth century. The account of the nineteenth-century discovery and of the modern examination of the surviving remains is still essential reading on all the objects recovered, both for its text, especially its detailed technical studies, and for its close-up photographs of details (Battiscombe 1956). This has been augmented (though not superseded) by a more recent study of both the history of St Cuthbert and his community, and the tomb finds (Bonner et al. 1989).

The textiles include several vestments. One was a possible dalmatic of c.800 (Granger-Taylor 1989a), thought however to be more likely a richly decorated *casula* of the same date (Larratt Keeffer 2007: 32 n. 70). In addition, there was a stole and maniple with inscriptions and figures (Hohler 1956; Plenderleith 1956; Coatsworth 2001; Coatsworth 2005; Coatsworth 2007b; Coatsworth 2007c); and a second item with plant decoration traditionally called 'maniple 2'. Robert Freyhan (1956) thought it was a girdle cut in two with the two pieces joined side by side; but an alternative explanation is that 'maniple 2' was almost certainly a secular piece, possibly a girdle, but more likely a pair of ribbons possibly originally depending from a headdress, or as ties for a garment such as a cloak: both types were shown in contemporary illustrations of secular figures (Coatsworth 2001). It is thus an example of an item of originally secular use donated to the church. The donor inscriptions on the stole and maniple 1 and the style of these and 'maniple 2' convincingly suggest that these pieces were made in southern England, quite probably Winchester, and that it is probable though not ultimately provable that these were the gifts given to St Cuthbert by King Æthelstan c.934 and described as a stole, maniple, and girdle (*Historia de Sancto Cuthberto* 1882–5, 1: 196–214, chap. 26).

The abbey church of Aldeneik, founded by the sister Anglo-Saxon saints Harlindis and Relindis in the early eighth century, housed two important early medieval textile groups which were preserved there until 1571, when they were moved to St Catherine's church, Maaseik (Budny and Tweddle 1984; 1985). They were preserved because of their association with the founder saints, but they are in fact of later date. Part of their importance, as with the even more varied finds from the tomb of St Cuthbert, is that they offer a glimpse of the contents of the early medieval saint's shrine. The first group comprises several pieces of embroidery identified as Anglo-Saxon influenced by southern English or Mercian work of the late eighth to early ninth century, put together at some later but still probably medieval date into a composite object as a relic in its own right: this is the so-called *casula* of SS Harlindis and Relindis, which implies it was a chasuble or at least a garment, but the suggestion that the main pieces probably originally decorated an altar frontal is more convincing (Coatsworth 2007b; 2007c). The group consists of four pieces of gold and silk embroidery on linen: four on narrow rectangular strips decorated with continuous series of arcades or roundels; and four on appliqués in the form of monograms which were painted as well as embroidered. The backing cloths include an unusual, possibly western-made silk with the enthroned figure of King David identified by inscription.

The second group, also a composite textile, known as the *velamen* of St Harlindis, which convincingly represents a cloak- or veil-like garment, is made of red and purple brocaded silk, with a probable seventh- to ninth-century date range. It has appliqués of purple and green silk of a similar date, forming two crosses and two squares. These are edged with silk tablet-woven braids brocaded with gold. An inscription on a red and beige braid edges the squares, and because of this the *velamen* has been dated to the eighth or ninth century on epigraphic grounds, but it is impossible to show where this was made, or that it had any other connection with Anglo-Saxon England apart from being associated in the same treasury as the *casula*. A woven, probably Anglo-Saxon girdle with an inscription was found in the tomb of a bishop in Sant' Apollinare in Classe, Ravenna (Coatsworth 2007c: 198–9).

The most famous textile associated with Anglo-Saxon England is the embroidery known as the Bayeux Tapestry, which, it is worth repeating, is the largest surviving early medieval object apart from a building. It was commissioned by a churchman, Bishop Odo of Bayeux, and was preserved in the church treasury there, but was probably made for a secular setting such as a hall. It has a very extensive literature, as indicated by its bibliography (Brown 1988; 2004). The modern researcher is well-advised to start with that and with the most up-to-date survey (Bouet *et al.* 2004).

Metalwork and Ivories

Ecclesiastics needed many of the same type of metalwork objects as seculars. Cwicwine, a monk in the early-ninth-century poem *De Abbatibus*, is portrayed working as a blacksmith at a forge to produce humble iron objects, and working copper to make vessels for the brothers' table (Æthelwulf 1967: ll. 278–81, 302–5). Elsewhere in the poem, lead for roof repair and copper vessels with 'clappers ringing in hollow rattles' (?bells) which 'resound to the delight of the brothers' would probably also be the work of the monk-smith (ibid.: ll. 452–3, 36–7). The need for objects for dress and other domestic use is borne out in excavation reports from monastic sites. It is clear from documentary sources and archaeological evidence that large monasteries could have fine metal workshops producing some of the vessels and other objects such as figures of saints and crosses required in the liturgy or in the church. There is also evidence for goldsmiths in these establishments, both clerical and lay (Coatsworth and Pinder 2002: 207–26; Dodwell 1982: 188–215).

Surviving items which had or might have had a liturgical function, however, are relatively few. Richard Bailey (1974: 141–50, pls. XXVa, XXVIa–c) pointed to the difficulty of assessing the function of some finds in the case of a small, elaborately decorated bucket found at Hexham, though noting that buckets are frequently mentioned in church inventories, and are depicted in use by figures on the cover of the Drogo Sacramentary (Paris, Bibliothèque Nationale, MS lat. 9428: Hubert et al. 1979: pls. 214–15).

Objects of recognizable church plate are rare survivals indeed, possibly because many of them would have been in recyclable valuable materials such as gold and silver. One such, a chalice, gold with markings of silver and covered in gems, donated by a pious priest, is described in the poem *De Abbatibus* which also featured the more practical products of the smith Cwicwine, mentioned above (Æthelwulf 1967: ll. 448–51, 36–7). Bailey (1974: 150–5, pl. XXIXa) noted a possibly eleventh-century chalice in gilded copper alloy, also from Hexham: the only other example, in silver, discovered in Anglo-Saxon England, appears to be that from the Trewhiddle hoard. This hoard, discovered at a site near St Austell in Cornwall in 1774 (Wilson 1964: cats. 90–103; Webster and Backhouse 1991: cat. 246 a–j) is believed to have been deposited c.868: it is a mixture of ecclesiastical and secular objects, and it is the secular objects which have given the find's name to an art style of the late ninth century. Leslie Webster and Janet Backhouse (1991: 272) noted a possible Anglo-Saxon example from Lough Kinale, Co. Longford, Ireland. The richly decorated eighth-century Tassilo chalice (so-called because its inscription commemorates Tassilo, the last Duke of Bavaria, who presumably gave it to the monastery he founded in 777 at Kremsmunster in Austria where it still is) is relevant because it is believed to be derived from an Anglo-Saxon model (Webster and Backhouse 1991: cat. 131). The other object of ecclesiastical significance in the Trewhiddle hoard is the silver scourge in trichinopoly chainwork: this has a glass bead at one end, while the other end has an elaborate knot fastening four tails. Its use must have been symbolic of penance rather than actually painful.

There are at least two surviving portable altars. One is from the tomb of St Cuthbert at Durham (see under 'Textiles' above). This is basically a small wooden block with five crosses and an inscription dedicating it 'In honour of St Peter', which, it seems possible, actually dates from the seventh century. It is covered in silver with a seated figure of St Peter and plant ornament of eighth- to ninth-century date, and a roundel of tenth- to eleventh-century work. This piece illustrates a feature also found in textiles and sculpture, in which a venerated object is at least partly remodelled or added to at a later date or dates (Coatsworth 1989: 296–301, pl. 38; Webster and Backhouse 1991: cat. 99). Portable altars were an important item in the early medieval period, especially in the period before the development of the parish church. There is another Anglo-Saxon example in the Musée de Cluny, Paris, in this case a porphyry slab with an oak base, edged by nielloed and gilded silver plates decorated with the Crucifixion with Saints Mary and John, the Agnus Dei, and the symbols of the four evangelists (Backhouse *et al.* 1984: cat. 92).

There are a number of house-shaped reliquaries from the eighth to the ninth centuries: one from Sussex Street, Winchester, with plant ornament; another in a different style with an inscription and figures of Christ and the archangels Michael and Gabriel, preserved at Mortain in France (both in gilded copper alloy on a beechwood base); and a whalebone casket (the Gandersheim casket) with framing edges in copper alloy patterned with twist, interlace, and other motifs (Webster and Backhouse 1991: cats. 136–8; Backhouse *et al.* 1984: cat. 12; and see Webster, this volume). In addition, there are a small number of examples of decorated metalwork, some of which have been convincingly identified as fragments of the decoration of portable altars, reliquaries, or of the similar decoration applied to the backs of books: see for example a silver plaque from Hexham with its nimbed figure (Bailey 1974: 155–8, pl. 29b,d).

Other items may have been fragments of larger items than dress accessories, but are less certainly from objects with a religious function, such as a circular mount of late-eighth-century date, from Mavourne Farm, Bolnhurst, Bedfordshire; another discovered in Scotland but plainly eighth-century Northumbrian work; a small head, perhaps a mount from a shrine or reliquary (Webster and Backhouse 1991: cats. 102–3, 185); another small head for a shrine or reliquary from Winchester (Coatsworth and Pinder 2002: 85, 107, 109, 158, 267 and pl. VIb; this volume, Fig. 48.1); and various tenth- to eleventh-century mounts which could have come from caskets, or in one case even furniture (Backhouse *et al.* 1984: cats. 100, 102–3). Even fine metalwork found within the area of important monastic complexes, like the Ripon jewel (Hall *et al.* 1999), cannot with certainty be attributed to an object of ecclesiastical use (though it bears comparison with, for example, the cross of St Cuthbert discussed below, and features of its construction are also imitated on eighth-century Northumbrian stone sculpture) since it is also typical of seventh- to eighth-century gold and garnet cloisonné jewellery generally.

Pendant crosses for personal wear, or brooches with religious themes, could of course have belonged to secular individuals: there are early examples of crosses from early (seventh-century) archaeological, mainly burial contexts (see for example Webster and Backhouse 1991: cats. 10–13). The cross found in the tomb of St Cuthbert, however, though related to other examples which are all from the south and have Kentish connections, was certainly in the possession of the Northumbrian saint at his death, and its repairs suggest it was a well-worn item (Coatsworth 1989: 287–96). Cuthbert lived a life of notable piety and, when he was able, of ascetic withdrawal: it seems his possession of this valuable item (which might of course have been part of his dress as a bishop) was not seen as inconsistent by those who buried him. Brooches such as the late ninth-century Fuller brooch with its complex iconography around the Five Senses and the Creation, which required considerable knowledge of Christian exegesis in its design, could however have been made for a pious, and wealthy, secular patron; and the same applies to the related 'Alfred Jewel' and a number of mounts intended to tip a small rod-like implement, although if these were indeed pointers for books (not always accepted now) they could equally have belonged to wealthy or important ecclesiastics (Pratt 2003; Webster 2003).

Larger, though still portable, crosses are likely to have belonged to altars, however. Two such crosses from Anglo-Saxon England have survived. One, the Bischofshofen (Rupertus) cross, of gilt copper alloy with polychrome glass inserts over a maple base, has survived in Austria: its decoration, which has strong affinities with Northumbrian and Mercian sculpture of the eighth to the ninth centuries but also with Carolingian art, has caused some to suggest it was not necessarily made in England but possibly by an Anglo-Saxon craftsman working for a Continental patron (Webster and Backhouse 1991: cat. 133). The early-eleventh-century cross from Brussels, however, with its Anglo-Saxon inscription, is undoubtedly Anglo-Saxon (Backhouse *et al.* 1984: cat. 75).

Another indubitably liturgical object type to have survived is the censer, of which there are a number of examples, including a sixth- to seventh-century example from Glastonbury Abbey, Somerset (though the provenance of this find is not secure); the three surviving from late Anglo-Saxon England all have an architectural form (Wilson 1964: cats. 9, 44, 56; Backhouse *et al.* 1984: cats. 73–4). Of these, the Pershore censer-cover is perhaps the most interesting, since its inscription, 'Godric made me', might indicate a metalworker at the nearby Abbey of Evesham (Coatsworth and Pinder 2002: 209, 225, 237). A small gilded copper alloy jug with a snake handle and an animal head spout decorated with relief ornament has been identified as a cruet, a vessel which held the wine or water before these were poured into the chalice during the Mass (Backhouse *et al.* 1984: cat. 72 and pl. XXII). This interpretation has not been accepted by all, the problem partly being that there is no overtly Christian symbolism in the decoration.

OTHER INTERIOR DECORATION: PAINTING, GLASS, TILES

Painting is mentioned far less often in documentary sources than metalwork and textiles, although there are occasional references to items because they were donated by significant persons, or perhaps because they were remarkable in some other way. For example, Bede decribes in some detail the programme of two sets of panel paintings brought by Benedict Biscop to the churches of the twin monasteries he had founded at Monkwearmouth and Jarrow (Bede 1896: 6, pp. 369–70; and 9, p. 373). Bede was concerned to demonstrate the function of such paintings—to enlighten those who could not read—and to make some points about the interpretation of the particular scenes chosen. These rare mentions are important to those interested in the figural sculpture and manuscript paintings which do survive, as probable sources of their iconography. In general, however, paintings and painters are rarely mentioned, and this indifference probably arises from the fact that they did not have the value of costly arts like metalwork and textiles.

No panel-painting of the period has survived. Painted plaster has, however, been recovered in the course of excavation from a number of sites—Monkwearmouth and Jarrow, and the Old and New Minsters, Winchester, for example—and a painting of four angels upholding a mandorla *in situ* at Nether Wallop has been recognized as Anglo-Saxon. There is also considerable evidence for the painting of architecture and sculpture. The majority of evidence to date is gathered in Cather *et al.* (1990), which brings together papers on all these topics and others on their context in documentary sources and comparative material from Europe. Also useful, however, is the recent publication of the Monkwearmouth/Jarrow material, in which for example the decoration at Jarrow with its compass-drawn ornament was shown to relate to contemporary seventh- to eighth-century Northumbrian art, and which also usefully brings together the few other early Anglo-Saxon examples (Cramp 2007, 2: 2–18). Painted plaster is one area where new discoveries are sometimes made in churches still standing, as recently at St Mary's church, Deerhurst, Gloucestershire (Bagshaw *et al.* 2006), where a tenth-century painting was discovered in 1993: the architectural context suggests it flanked a feature such as an altar. Traces of paint on sculpture are noted where they exist in each volume of the *Corpus of Anglo-Saxon Stone Sculpture* as they come out (see section on stone carving below).

Window glass seems to have been used only in church buildings from its first appearance at the beginning of the period, when Bede recorded the import of workers with the technology for Monkwearmouth/Jarrow (Bede 1896: 5, p. 368), and where indeed many examples of stained glass, and the lead cames which held the cut pieces in place, have been found. Rosemary Cramp (2007, 2: 56–161) demonstrated the range of colour and shape found there, and showed the possibility of reconstructing the glass into small square and circular windows, including, in one case, a conjectural but suggestive restoration of a small arched panel incorporating a possible figure. The same paper lists all other examples of sites which have produced evidence of glassworking to date, including sites such as Brandon, Suffolk (which was a high-status site, possibly monastic); Whitby, North Yorkshire (see Webster and Backhouse 1991: cats. 66y and 107j); and Winchester at the end of the period (Biddle and Hunter 1990).

Tiles are rare finds from the pre-Conquest period, all associated with major minsters and cathedrals, from Bury St Edmunds, St Albans, Winchester, and York. Examples and a bibliography can be found in Backhouse *et al.* (1984: cats. 142–4). There are a number of literary references which could suggest they also appeared in rich secular contexts, however (Coatsworth 2005). An earlier type of flooring is found at Monkwearmouth/Jarrow: *opus signinum*, an originally Roman technique in which crushed terracotta was mixed with mortar. In the Roman period this was usually covered by tesserae or marble slabs but in the Anglo-Saxon examples the terracotta was merely concentrated on the surface to provide an acceptable finish (Cramp 2007, 2: 18–19). Other early Anglo-Saxon churches had the same type of flooring (see Taylor 1978: 1061).

CARVING IN IVORY, WOOD, AND STONE

Dodwell (1982: 188–215) noted that some of the documentary sources for precious objects of church furnishing specifically mention ivory as well as gold, silver, and precious stones, as for example a crucifix of gold and ivory given to the shrine of St Cuthbert at Chester-le-Street in 934 (Simeon of Durham 1882–5, II: 211). An Anglo-Saxon crucifix reliquary of *c.* AD 1000, in gold, ivory, and enamels on a wooden core, survives (Backhouse *et al.* 1984: cat. 118, pl. XXVI). There are fairly numerous survivals under the general heading of ivory (whether elephant ivory, walrus ivory, or whale bone), relative to objects in gold and silver. Their iconography and decoration indicates that many of the most finely carved of these definitely or probably belonged to objects of liturgical function or devotional use (many have clearly been torn from their more valuable and re-usable settings). For example, a high proportion of the ivories in the exhibition catalogue *The Golden Age of Anglo-Saxon Art* (ibid.: cats. 112–34) can be identified as panels from shrines or book-covers, including a large number with the crucifixion scene, and scenes of the Nativity and the Baptism of Christ. Other survivals include a reliquary cross, and part of a possible pendant cross; subsidiary figures from a crucifixion group (Fig. 25.9c); crozier heads; and one probable pyx (a box for holding the sacrament intended for future use). There are some very fine examples from the earlier part of the period, such as the Gandersheim casket, already referred to because of its metalwork decoration, which is a complete reliquary casket in whalebone. There are also some very fine fragments of panels from book covers (see for example Webster and Backhouse 1991: cats. 138–41). The most famous Anglo-Saxon whalebone casket, the Franks casket, with its connections with eighth-century Northumbrian manuscript art, has juxtaposed scenes drawn from Jewish, Roman, Christian, and Germanic history and traditional themes, placed in such a way that meaningful parallels were certainly intended, and is probably therefore also a reliquary casket, though its precise meaning continues to be debated (ibid.: cat. 70; Lang 1999; Webster 1999). For a general survey of medieval ivories in England, Beckwith (1972, but re-published in 1990) is still a useful guide.

The Anglo-Saxon building tradition before the coming of Christianity was in wood, and there is plenty of evidence for wooden church buildings, but little to suggest their appearance or their construction details above ground level. One stone gable finial survives from Lastingham, north Yorkshire (Lang 1991: pls. 610–13), probably comparable to similar gable finials in wood. There is, however, what is clearly a fragment of wood panelling with edge mouldings from Iona (Karkov 1991: 32–4 and fig. 2), and while there is no direct evidence of such detail from any Anglo-Saxon church, the influence of such panelling appears manifest in the panelled layout of many Northumbrian crosses, with their relatively broad edge, and finer inner mouldings. I have mentioned a probable relationship between panel-paintings and the iconography of stone crosses (above), and the way the sculptured panels are treated supports the hypothesis of a framed wooden prototype: see for example the flat edge mouldings with inscriptions on the Ruthwell cross and the arched panels and fine inner mouldings of the Bewcastle cross (see Cassidy 1992: pls. 11–32 and 49–52). A very finely carved panel from Monkwearmouth has multiple fine mouldings which look indicative of a fine woodworking style (Cramp 1984: pl. 656). Examples of stone furniture, such as a chair from Hexham, Northumberland (ibid.: pls. 1028–32); parts of chair arms from Bamburgh, Northumberland (ibid.: pls. 812–16); and octagonal supports for reading desks or other items requiring a stand, from Jarrow, Co. Durham and Melsonby, North Yorkshire (Cramp 1984: pls. 527–35; Lang 2001: pls. 654–61), all give some idea of church furniture generally, which of course would have been in wood more commonly perhaps than in stone.

The major survival, however, is the late-seventh-century coffin of St Cuthbert, so rare a survival it has been studied from every possible aspect, including its construction and the iconography of its incised carvings (Kitzinger 1956; Cronyn and Horie 1985; 1989). It is not too much to say that this is one of the most important figured items from the early Christian phase of Anglo-Saxon England, because of its material, its style, and its iconography, which is interesting in itself as an indicator of the theological preoccupations of the monastic community at

Lindisfarne, and for its influence, or the influence of its models, on other Northumbrian work in painting and sculpture.

Otherwise, the main survivals are in the wooden bases of many metalwork pieces already mentioned. However, at least one eleventh-century, boxwood, house-shaped casket, carved with scenes from the life of Christ, has survived. Although its lid and base turned up separately in Uttoxeter (Staffordshire), and Nelson (Cheshire) respectively, the two parts are linked stylistically to each other and to two manuscripts with miniatures by the same mid-eleventh-century artist (Backhouse *et al.* 1984: cat. 128, cf. cats. 70, 71). Writing tablets could also be backed with wood: there is an eighth-century example from Blythburgh, Suffolk (Webster and Backhouse 1991: cat. 650), but although such items must have been in use in ecclesiastical circles, in monastic schools, for example, the presence of one, like that of a stylus, would not itself confirm a site as ecclesiastical.

Stone sculpture is scarcely mentioned in documentary sources, but forms the largest category of objects expressing religious observance to have survived, and the greatest majority has survived preserved in and around the fabric of later churches. Some sculpture has been discovered in excavation, especially of monastic sites; much more from the dismantling of church walls at periods of rebuilding or restoration. As with paintings, new discoveries are made in this area through excavations and studies of the fabric of churches: a recent example has been the discovery of the figure of an angel at Lichfield Cathedral. This was discovered in 2003 in the excavation of the east end of the nave, and is thought to have formed part of a shrine chest of *c*.800 (Rodwell 2003–5 and Fig. 25.7g).

Sculpture is not quite evenly spread across the country, with the bulk from areas with a locally available supply of suitable stone; nevertheless, it is found in all areas of Anglo-Saxon England, with some famous examples, like the Ruthwell cross, coming from what is now Scotland. The majority of the sculptures date from the late ninth to the eleventh centuries rather than from the earlier centuries. Most of the earlier sculpture is associated with monastic and other high-status ecclesiastical sites. Surviving carvings represent the full range: architectural sculpture including wall panels; decoratively pierced slabs for window openings; string courses; imposts; capitals; columns and column bases; door jambs; dedication slabs (once or still *in situ* in church buildings); furniture (mentioned briefly above); cross-shafts and cross-heads; and a variety of upright and recumbent grave-markers, including stele, house-shaped shrines, and their Viking-age successors the hogbacks. Figural sculpture and inscriptions are found on a minority of the surviving corpus, but some very major examples of these occur on stonework from pre-Viking sites, some of which have iconographic programmes of great importance for their links with exegetical, liturgical, or other contemporary literary texts. Within this early period, also, some scholars have detected a move from early simplicity—in Northumbria, for example, at sites such as Lindisfarne, Northumberland, and at Whitby, north Yorkshire, where the influence of early wooden prototype crosses has been suggested—to a more decorated style and the use of figural scenes possibly dating from the acceptance of the Roman Easter at the Synod of Whitby in 664 and the increased influence of the Roman church thereafter. The more highly decorated sculpture is certainly a feature of St Wilfrid's foundations at Hexham (Northumberland) and Ripon (north Yorkshire); and also at Monkwearmouth and Jarrow with their Roman connections. However, patterns of distribution vary according to the ecclesiastical history and connections of each area, so that one would expect to see such connections represented in the art styles everywhere, as we do for example at Bradford-on Avon, Wiltshire, where a slab reflects the seventh-century taste for Insular types of ornament (Cramp 2006: pls. 407–9); and at Reculver, Kent, where there are fragments of seventh-century columns and a major cross of the ninth century, made before the development of the Winchester style of the tenth century (Tweddle et al. 1995: pls. 11–20).

The later part of the period is interesting because of the great increase in the use of stone sculpture, in some areas more dramatic than others. A much higher proportion of this sculpture is funerary, and there is evidence that much of this was not only for ecclesiastics, but also for (presumably wealthy) laypeople, and therefore presumably made under their patronage. The appearance of new art styles and monument types in this period is an important indicator of the movement of peoples of Scandinavian origin into England, either directly or via Ireland or Scotland. These questions and many others are addressed volume by volume in *Corpus of Anglo-Saxon Stone Sculpture* as they appear, along with a full bibliography for each piece (Cramp 1984; Bailey and Cramp 1988; Lang 1991; Tweddle et al. 1995; Everson and Stocker 1999; Lang 2001; Cramp 2006; Coatsworth 2008; Bailey forthcoming). Information on later volumes can be obtained from the *Corpus* website (http://www.dur.ac.uk/corpus/index.php3).

The study of this aspect of the material culture of the Church, and what it represented, has been strong since the nineteenth century, but it has never been livelier or healthier. It is impossible to cover all recent publications in this area. Probably because of the access to material provided by the *Corpus*, there has been a huge increase in interest in the study of sculpture and its iconography, for example: its meaning to the church; to seculars; in the landscape; in gender studies; and indeed from a range of theoretical viewpoints. Some of these developments have been explored in recent work, of which the papers in Karkov and Orton 2003 are a good example, and provide a summary bibliography of recent work in the field. However, the related field of palaeography as applied to inscriptions (which can of course occur on other materials) is especially important in elucidating the significance of sculptures, even if inscriptions occur in a minority of them. The work of David Parsons (on runic inscriptions) and John Higgitt (on non-runic inscriptions), appears in volumes of the *Corpus* already mentioned; the work of Elisabeth Okasha in this area is also essential reading, from Okasha 1971 to several supplements in *Anglo-Saxon England* vols. 11, 21, and 33, and many other papers.

REFERENCES

ÆTHELWULF (1967). *De Abbatibus*. Ed. A. Campbell. Oxford: Oxford University Press.
BACKHOUSE, J., TURNER, D. H., and WEBSTER, L. (1984). *The Golden Age of Anglo-Saxon Art 966–1066*. London: British Museum Publications Ltd.
BAGSHAW, S., BRYANT, R., and HARE, M. (2006). 'The discovery of an Anglo-Saxon painted figure at St Mary's Church, Deerhurst, Gloucestershire'. *The Antiquaries Journal* 86: 66–109.
BAILEY, R. N. (1974). 'The Anglo-Saxon metalwork from Hexham', in D. P. Kirby (ed.), *Saint Wifrid at Hexham*. Newcastle upon Tyne: Oriel Press, 141–67.
—— (forthcoming). *Corpus of Anglo-Saxon Stone Sculpture*, Volume 9: *Cumberland, Westmorland and Lancashire-North-of-the-Sands*. Oxford: Oxford University Press.
—— and CRAMP, R. (1988). *Corpus of Anglo-Saxon Stone Sculpture*, Volume 2: *Cheshire and Lancashire*. Oxford: Oxford University Press.
BAKER, P. A., and HOLT, R. (2004). *Urban Growth and the Medieval Church: Gloucester and Worcester*. Aldershot: Ashgate.
BARKER, P. A., and CUBBERLEY, A. L. (1974). 'Two burials under the refectory of Worcester Cathedral'. *Medieval Archaeology* 18: 146–51.
BATTISCOMBE, C. F. (ed.) (1956). *The Relics of St. Cuthbert*. Oxford: Oxford University Press.
BECKWITH, J. (1972). *Ivory Carvings in Early Medieval England*. London: Harvey, Miller and Medcalf.
BEDE (1896). *Historia Abbatum auctore Baedae*, in C. Plummer (ed.), *Venerabilis Baedae Opera Historica*, I. Oxford: Clarendon Press, 364–87.
BIDDLE, M. (1965). 'Excavations at Winchester, 1964, third interim report'. *The Antiquaries Journal* 45: 230–64.
—— and HUNTER, J. (1990). 'Early medieval window glass', in M. Biddle (ed.), *Object and Economy in Early Medieval Winchester*. Winchester Studies 7.2: *Artefacts from Early Medieval Winchester*. Oxford: Oxford University Press, 350–86.
—— and Kjølbye-Biddle, B. (2001). 'Repton and the "great heathen army" 873–874', in J. Graham-Campbell, R. Hall, J. Jesch, and D. N. Parsons (eds.), *Vikings and the Danelaw: Select Papers from the Proceedings of the Thirteenth Viking Congress, Nottingham and York, 21–30 August, 1997*. Oxford: Oxbow, 45–96.
BLAIR, J. (2005). *The Church in Anglo-Saxon Society*. Oxford: Oxford University Press.
BONNER, G., ROLLASON, D., and STANCLIFFE, C. (1989). *St Cuthbert, his Cult and his Community to AD 1200*. Woodbridge: Boydell.
BOUET, P., LEVY, B., and NEVEUX, F., (eds.) (2004). *The Bayeux Tapestry: Embroidering the Facts of History*. Caen: Presses Universitaires de Caen.
BROWN, S. A. (1988). *The Bayeux Tapestry: History and Bibliography*. Woodbridge: Boydell.
—— (2004). 'The Bayeux Tapestry: a critical analysis of publications 1988–1999' and 'Bibliography of Bayeux Tapestry studies 1985–1999', in Bouet *et al.* (eds.), *The Bayeux Tapestry*, 27–47, 411–18.
BUDNY, M., and TWEDDLE, D. (1984). 'The Maaseik embroideries'. *Anglo-Saxon England* 13: 65–96.
—— —— (1985). 'The early medieval textiles at Maaseik, Belgium'. *The Antiquaries Journal* 65(2): 353–89.
CABOT, S., DAVIES, G., and HOGGETT, R. (2004). 'Sedgeford: excavations of a rural settlement in Norfolk', in J. Hines, A. Lane, and M. Redknap (eds.), *Land, Sea and Home:*

Proceedings of a Conference on Viking-Period Settlement, at Cardiff, July 2001. Society for Medieval Archaeology Monograph 20. Leeds: Maney, 313–23.

CASSIDY, B. (ed.). (1992). *The Ruthwell Cross.* Index of Christian Art Occasional Papers 1. Princeton, NJ: Princeton University Press.

CATHER, S., PARK, D., and WILLIAMSON, P. (1990). *Early Medieval Wall-painting and Painted Sculpture in England.* BAR British Series 216. Oxford: British Archaeological Reports.

COATSWORTH, E. (1989). 'The pectoral cross and portable altar from the tomb of St Cuthbert', in Bonner *et al.* (eds.), *St Cuthbert, His Cult and Community*, 287–302.

—— (2001). 'The embroideries from the tomb of St Cuthbert', in J. Higham and D. H. Hill (eds.), *Edward the Elder 899–924.* London and New York: Routledge, 292–306.

—— (2005). 'Stitches in time: establishing a history of Anglo-Saxon embroidery', in R. Netherton and G. R. Owen-Crocker (eds.), *Medieval Clothing and Textiles* 1. Woodbridge: Boydell, 1–27.

—— (2007a). 'Cushioning medieval life: domestic textiles in Anglo-Saxon England', in R. Netherton and G. R. Owen-Crocker (eds.), *Medieval Clothing and Textiles* 3. Woodbridge: Boydell, 1–12.

—— (2007b). 'Inscriptions on textiles associated with Anglo-Saxon England', in A. R. Rumble (ed), *Writing and Texts in Anglo-Saxon England.* Woodbridge: Boydell and Brewer, 71–95.

—— (2007c). 'Text and textile' in A. Minnis and J. Roberts (eds.), *Text, Image, Interpretation: Studies in Anglo-Saxon Literature and its Insular Context in honour of Eamonn Ó Carragáin.* Turnhout: Brepols, 187–207.

—— (2008a). *Corpus of Anglo-Saxon Stone Sculpture*, Volume 8: *Western Yorkshire.* Oxford: Oxford University Press.

—— (2008b). 'Design in the past: metalwork and textile influences on pre-Conquest sculpture in England', in C. Karkov and H. Damico (eds.), *Aedificia Nova: Studies in Honour of Rosemary Cramp.* Kalamazoo, MI: Medieval Institute Publications.

—— and OWEN-CROCKER, G. R. (2007). *An Annotated Bibliography of Medieval Textiles of the British Isles, 450–1100.* British Archaeological Reports British Series 445. Oxford: Archaeopress.

—— and PINDER, M. (2002). *The Art of the Anglo-Saxon Goldsmith.* Woodbridge: Boydell.

CRAMP, R. J. (1976). 'Monastic sites', in D. M. Wilson (ed.), *The Archaeology of Anglo-Saxon England.* Cambridge: Cambridge University Press, 201–52.

—— (1984). *Corpus of Anglo-Saxon Stone Sculpture*, Volume 1: *Durham and Northumberland.* Oxford: Oxford University Press.

—— (1993). 'A reconsideration of the monastic size of Whitby', in R. M. Spearman and J. Higgitt (eds.), *The Age of Migrating Ideas: Early Medieval Art in Northern Britain and Ireland.* Edinburgh and Stroud: Alan Sutton Publishing, 64–73.

—— (2006). *Corpus of Anglo-Saxon Stone Sculpture*, Volume 7: *South-West England.* Oxford: Oxford University Press.

—— (2007). *Wearmouth and Jarrow Monastic Sites.* 2 volumes. Swindon: English Heritage.

CRONYN, J. M., and HORIE, C.V. (1985). *St Cuthbert's Coffin: The History, Technology and Conservation.* Durham: Dean and Chapter, Durham Cathedral.

—— —— (1989). 'The Anglo-Saxon coffin: further investigations', in Bonner *et al.* (eds.), *St Cuthbert, His Cult and Community*, 247–56.

DODWELL, C. R. (1982). *Anglo-Saxon Art: A New Perspective.* Manchester: Manchester University Press.

EVERSON, P., and STOCKER, D. (1999). *Corpus of Anglo-Saxon Stone Sculpture*, Volume 5: *Lincolnshire*. Oxford: Oxford University Press.

FREYHAN, R. (1956). 'The place of the stole and maniple in Anglo-Saxon art of the tenth century', in Battiscombe (ed.), *The Relics of St Cuthbert*, 409–32.

GODMAN, P. (1982). *Alcuin: The Bishops, Kings, and Saints of York*. Oxford: Clarendon Press.

Goscelin (1955). *The Liber Confortatorius of Goscelin of St Bertin*. Ed. C. H. Talbot, in *Analecta Monastica*. 3rd Ser. Studia Ansemiana fasc. 37. Rome: Herder, 1–117.

GRANGER-TAYLOR, H. (1989a). 'The weft-patterned silks and their braid: the remains of an Anglo-Saxon dalmatic of c. 800?' in Bonner et al. (eds.), *St Cuthbert, His Cult and Community*, 303–28.

—— (1989b). 'The Inscription on the Nature Goddess Silk', in Bonner et al. (eds.), *St Cuthbert, His Cult and Community*, 339–42.

HALL, R., PATERSON, E., and MORTIMER, C. (1999). 'The Ripon Jewel', in J. Hawkes and S. Mills (eds.), *Northumbria's Golden Age*. Stroud: Sutton Publishing, 268–80.

HARDY, A., DODD, A., and KEEVILL, G. D. (2003). *Ælfric's Abbey: Excavations at Eynsham Abbey, Oxfordshire, 1989–92*. Thames Valley Landscapes 15. Oxford: Oxford University School of Archaeology.

HILL, P. (1997). *Whithorn and St Ninian: The Excavation of a Monastic Town 1984–91*. Stroud: Sutton Publishing.

Historia de Sancto Cuthberto (1882–5) in T. Arnold (ed.), *Symeonis Monachi Opera omnia*. 2 volumes. London, Rolls Series 75ii.

HOHLER, C. (1956). 'The Stole and Maniple: the Iconography', in Battiscombe (ed.), *The Relics of St Cuthbert*, 396–408.

HUBERT, J., PORCHER, J., and VOLBACH,, W. F. (1970). *Carolingian Art*. London: Thames and Hudson.

HULL, G. (2002). 'Barkingwic? Saxon and medieval features adjacent to Barking Abbey'. *Essex Archaeology and History* 33: 157–90.

IVY, J. (1992). *Embroideries at Durham Cathedral*. Durham: The Dean and Chapter of Durham.

KARKOV, C. (1991). 'The decoration of early wooden architecture in Ireland and Northumbria', in C. Karkov and R. Farrell (eds.), *Studies in Insular Art and Archaeology*. American Early Medieval Studies 1. Oxford: American Early Medieval Studies, 27–48.

—— and ORTON, F. (2003). *Theorising Anglo-Saxon Stone Sculpture*. Morgantown: West Virginia University Press.

KING, D. (1963). *Opus Anglicanum: English Medieval Embroidery*. London: Arts Council, Victoria and Albert Museum.

KITZINGER, E. (1956). 'The coffin reliquary', in Battiscombe (ed.), *The Relics of St Cuthbert*, 202–304.

LANG, J. T. (1991). *Corpus of Anglo-Saxon Stone Sculpture*, Volume 3: *York and Eastern Yorkshire*. Oxford: Oxford University Press.

—— (1999). 'The imagery of the Franks Casket: another approach', in J. Hawkes and S. Mills (eds.), *Northumbria's Golden Age*. Stroud: Sutton Publishing, 247–55.

—— (2001). *Corpus of Anglo-Saxon Stone Sculpture*, Volume 6: *Northern Yorkshire*. Oxford: Oxford University Press.

LAPIDGE, M. (1990). 'Ædiluulf and the School of York', in A. Lehner and W. Berscin (eds.), *Lateinische Kultur im VIII. Jahrhundert: Traube-Gedenkschrift*. St. Ottilien: E.O. S. Verlag, 161–78.

—— Blair, J., Keynes, S., and Scragg, D., (1999). *The Blackwell Encyclopaedia of Anglo-Saxon England.* Oxford: Blackwell.

Larratt Keefer, S. (2007). 'A matter of style: clerical vestments in the Anglo-Saxon church', in R. Netherton and G. R. Owen-Crocker (eds), *Medieval Clothing and Textiles* 3. Woodbridge: Boydell, 13–40.

Lehmann-Brockhaus, O. (1955–60). *Lateinische Schriftquellen zur Kunst in England, Wales und Schottland vom Jahre 901 bis zum Jahre 1307.* 5 volumes. Munich: Prestel.

Liber Eliensis (1962). Ed. E. O. Blake. London:Royal Historical Society.

Loveluck, C. (2001). 'Wealth, waste and conspicuous consumption: Flixborough and its importance for mid and late Anglo-Saxon settlement studies', in H. Hamerow and A. MacGregor (eds.), *Image and Power in the Archaeology of Early Medieval Britain: Essays in Honour of Rosemary Cramp.* Oxford: Oxbow Books, 79–130.

Napier, A. S., and Stevenson, W. H. (1895). *The Crawford Collection of Early Charters and Documents (Analecta Oxoniensia).* Oxford: Oxford University Press.

Naylor, J. (2004). *An Archaeology of Trade in Middle Saxon England.* BAR British Series 376. Oxford: Archaeopress.

Okasha, E. (1971). *Hand-list of Anglo-Saxon Non-runic Inscriptions.* Cambridge: Cambridge University Press.

O'Sullivan, D. (2001). 'Space, silence and shortages in Lindisfarne. The archaeology of asceticism', in H. Hamerow and A. MacGregor (eds.), *Image and Power in the Archaeology of Early Medieval Britain: Essays in Honour of Rosemary Cramp.* Oxford: Oxbow Books, 33–52.

Pestell, T., and Ulmschneider, K. (2003). *Markets in Early Medieval Europe: Trading and 'Productive' Sites, 650–850.* Macclesfield: Windgather.

Plenderleith, E. (1956). 'The stole and maniples, the techniques', in Battiscombe (ed.), *The Relics of St Cuthbert,* 375–96.

Pratt, D. (2003). 'Persuasion and invention at the court of King Alfred the Great', in C. Cubitt (ed.), *Court Culture in the Early Middle Ages: The Proceedings of the First Alcuin Conference.* Turnhout: Brepols, 189–221.

Rodwell, W. (2003–5). 'Lichfield Cathedral: archaeology of the sanctuary', *Church Archaeology* 7–9: 1–6.

Simeon of Durham (1882-5). *Historia de Sancto Cuthberto,* in *Symeonis monachi Opera omnia.* Ed. T. Arnold. 2 volumes. London: Rolls Series 75ii.

Taylor, H. M. (1978). *Anglo-Saxon Architecture,* 3. Cambridge: Cambridge University Press.

Tweddle, D., Biddle, M., and Kjølbye-Biddle, B. (1995). *Corpus of Anglo-Saxon Stone Sculpture,* Volume 4: *South-East England.* Oxford: Oxford University Press.

Webster, L. (1999). 'The iconographic programme of the Franks casket', in J. Hawkes and S. Mills (eds.), *Northumbria's Golden Age.* Stroud: Sutton Publishing, 227–46.

—— (2003). '*Aedificia nova*: treasures of Alfred's reign', in T. Reuter (ed.), *Alfred the Great: Papers from the Eleventh-Century Conferences.* Aldershot: Ashgate, 79–103.

—— and Backhouse, J. (1991). *The Making of England: Anglo-Saxon Art and Culture AD 600–900.* London: British Museum Press.

William of Malmesbury (1981). *The Early History of Malmesbury.* Ed. and trans. J. Scott. Woodbridge: Boydell.

Wilson, D. M. (1964). *Anglo-Saxon Ornamental Metalwork 700–1100 in the British Museum: Catalogue of the Antiquities of the Later Saxon Period,* I. London: Trustees of the British Museum.

CHAPTER 41

THE ARCHAEOLOGY OF THE ANGLO-SAXON BOOK

RICHARD GAMESON

The phrase 'the archaeology of the book' is normally taken to mean the successive stages in the manufacture of a manuscript and the perceptible traces that each may leave in the fabric of the finished volume; in the present essay, however, we shall be stressing rather the ways in which the processes of book-making, along with the resources and implements that were required, fitted into the material culture of an early medieval society. Whilst many details are hazy or debatable owing to inadequate or ambiguous evidence, the date at which our topic starts and its immediate social setting are not: books reached Anglo-Saxon England with the first Christian missions; they were central to the beliefs, ceremonies, and systems of the church, and, notwithstanding some limited lay patronage and ownership, remained largely its prerogative. Accordingly, the making of manuscripts was principally the domain of ecclesiastics, though the infrastructure needed to support the operation spread well beyond the church.

The basic material from which the pages of Anglo-Saxon books were made was, of course, animal skin.[1] Identifying by non-destructive means the type of creature

---

[1] As celebrated in *aenigmatum* V by Tatwine: Glorie 1968, p. 172; no particular animal is specified as the source (nor in the analogous riddle of Eusebius, no. XXXII; Glorie (ed.) 1968: 242).

that was used for a particular manuscript or sheet is extremely difficult and few hard facts are currently available; nevertheless, it is logical to assume that calf, sheep, and goat, the farm animals with suitable hides, were the staple of the industry. As calf gave the finest quality product (vellum), it was presumptively favoured for most if not all high-status volumes; while since the sheep was the most numerous (as documented in our one and only pre-Conquest farming memorandum and underlined by the Domesday survey of 1086[2]), it would be reasonable to suppose that its skin was the most commonly used for 'ordinary' books. In the early days of Anglo-Saxon Christianity, ecclesiastical communities requiring parchment will have had to make it themselves or organize tenants to do so for them: the quantity of cattle-remains found around the complex of buildings in the dunes at Green Shiel on the northern shore of Holy Island, raises the possibility that this was where the Lindisfarne community processed its vellum (O'Sullivan 2001: 41–3). More persuasive evidence, incidentally, has been found in Pictland, where a fuller and hence more compelling collocation of relevant finds has permitted the plausible identification of a parchment-making site associated with the monastery of Portmahomack, Easter Ross (Carver and Spall 2004). By the end of the Anglo-Saxon period, professional parchment-makers based in or near urban centres may have played a role in supplying demand: Winchester had a *Taennerstret* (Tanner Street) by the late tenth century, the tradesmen of which might have made parchment as well as leather; and at the very beginning of the twelfth century, the abbot of Abingdon could designate tithes 'for *buying* parchment for restoring the books of the church'.[3] Whether accomplished in monastic out-buildings, on ecclesiastical estates, or in towns, parchment-making stood alongside the longer-established leather-working and tanning trades in the exploitation of skins, all relying in turn upon animal husbandry.

The manufacture of parchment involved soaking the flayed skin, possibly in a solution with fermenting vegetable remains, perhaps in one fortified with lime, in order to loosen the hairs and the fatty tissue, which would then be stripped away from the dermis (corium); this would subsequently be washed clean, scraped smooth, and allowed to dry while held under tension pegged to a frame. The simultaneous drying and stretching was essential for transforming a limp hide into a tauter yet still supple support for writing. Further paring, to achieve as smooth and even a surface as possible, might be carried out while the skin was on the frame. Alongside butchers' knives for the initial flaying and a ready supply of fresh water, parchment-making required troughs or tubs for soaking (there was a pit

---

[2] The inventoried holdings of a farmstead in Ely in the early eleventh century included 15 calves, 47 goats, and 250 sheep: London, British Library, Add. MS 61735. Reproduced in Backhouse *et al.* 1984: 147, no. 150; edition: Robertson 1939: 252–7 (Appendix 2, no. ix). Overview of livestock recorded in Domesday: Darby 1977: 162–70.

[3] The Winton Domesday: Biddle 1976: 60, 235, and 247. *Historia Ecclesie Abbendonensis* II.219: Stevenson 1858, 2: 153; Hudson 2002: 216.

at Portmahomack), frames for stretching ('herses'), pebbles, twine and pegs for attaching the skin to the frame, curved blades for scraping and smoothing, and bone, chalk, or pumice for pouncing. While bone and chalk were readily available in England, pumice (a type of lava) only tends to be washed up on the northern and western shores of Britain: most Anglo-Saxon scriptoria were presumably, therefore, dependent upon trade and exchange for their supplies. The nature of stretching frames is well known from depictions and descriptions; although these date from the twelfth century onwards, the forms that they record remain remarkably stable and there is no reason to think that early medieval equivalents were any different.[4] The device consisted of a wooden rectangle or circle—its dimensions necessarily larger than those of the biggest skin—punctuated at regular intervals with tightening pegs (at Portmahomack, appropriately-worked cattle metapodials may have fulfilled this function), to which the pelt was fastened, either by clips or by turning the edge of the membrane over pebbles and wrapping twine around the resulting 'bulge'. The images invariably also show the stretched skin being scraped with a rounded or lunar knife: a curved blade was essential if the worker was to avoid slitting the membrane as it 'gave' under the exerted pressure. One Anglo-Saxon tool of the requisite shape was found at Flixborough, and a similar item came to light at Portmahomack (Leahy 2003, fig. 48; Carver and Spall 2004).

The sheets of parchment were cut and folded according to the size of the book that was desired, and gathered into quires. The ways in which this might be done—which varied according to time and place, not to mention the quality of the material, but would not require any special equipment beyond a knife and, perhaps, a straight edge—need not detain us here. Defining a balanced textblock, however, did imply a measure of technical preparation. The first stage of the process consisted in marking up the sheets with prickings to map out the position and proportions of the area that would receive writing in relation to those of the page as a whole, and to establish the parameters of a grid that the scribe would in due course follow. Almost all such prickings, arranged in pairs, were subsequently joined up with ruled lines; there would inevitably be many more holes running down the sheets (to guide the numerous horizontal lines of writing) than across them (to define vertical boundaries). One of the advantages of doing the preliminary marking in this way was that the punctures could go through several sheets simultaneously, both expediting the process and (assuming the sheets in the pile were all properly aligned) ensuring that the ruling grid would be identical throughout. One can only speculate concerning how exactly this crucial task was done, and procedures doubtless varied. The nature of the little holes that survive on many pages shows that the pricking might be effected with an awl (giving rounded punctures) or the tip of a knife (resulting in slits). The straight

---

[4] The earliest representation seemingly appears in Bamberg, Staatliche Bibliothek, Misc. Patr. 5 (Ambrose; mid-twelfth century), fol. 1v: Evans 1969, pl. 1; Suckale-Redlefsen 1995, no. 30, ill. 71.

lines of prickings observable in some manuscripts were evidently made against a firm ruler or frame; the curving courses of certain other runs suggest either that the ruler slipped or that a non-rigid guide, such as twine, may sometimes have been used. Whatever form the rule or frame took, it was presumably itself marked at regular intervals to ensure that the worker would space the prickings evenly. One could imagine the spacing being indicated on the guide-rule with chalk, charcoal, or lead for short or one-off exercises, and with incisions or holes if the run was to be repeated many times; in the absence of surviving examples, however, this is necessarily speculative.

Early medieval depictions of writing figures generally show them with a knife in one hand—or amongst their tools nearby (see Fig. 41.1). Varying considerably in form, the blades of these implements might be rounded, or sharp and pointed (Biddle 1990: 738–9 and 747–53 with fig. 213). Any example of the latter type could in theory have served to make the pricking slits observable in the manuscripts. Equally, any awl-like tool (*punctorium*) could have been responsible for the rounded holes. Small bone implements with a ball-like head and a sharp metal point are sometimes identified as 'parchment prickers'; however, predominantly associated with the later Middle Ages, these objects do not seem well-suited to the task of driving long series of neat holes through piles of four or more sheets of animal skin, and the traditional interpretation of them as styli seems more plausible.[5] Altogether more practical, by contrast, is the type of *punctorium* (if such it be) featured in the mid-twelfth-century 'portrait' of Laurence of Durham which has a larger, more bulbous grip and a longer point.[6]

The folios of Anglo-Saxon manuscripts were generally pricked and ruled not as open sheets but rather folded into their quires: consequently, there are normally two sets of prickings on each page to guide the horizontal rulings. In a few cases, however, although the quires were clearly folded when they were treated, there is but one set. The obvious implication is that the ruling (which is still perfectly aligned) was here done with the aid of a set-square as opposed to just a ruler. In point of fact, a set-square could also have been useful at the pricking stage, enabling the worker to establish that the rows of punctures were properly aligned with the centre-fold of the quire. Accordingly, it seems reasonable to add it to the range of tools that certain scribes may have had.

At the very end of the Anglo-Saxon period, the lines were occasionally ruled in plummet or lead, and writing-leads suitable for this task have been recovered from eleventh-century contexts (as also, indeed, from earlier ones: Biddle 1990: 735–8, 743–6; Hardy, Dodd, and Keevill 2003: 265–6, fig. 9.6 (no. 55)). Normally, however, it

---

[5] MacGregor 1985: 122–5; Biddle 1990: 733–5; and Egan 1998: 272 (favouring use on wax tablets). Colour plate: Kyriacou *et al.* 2004: 84.

[6] Durham University Library, MS V.iii.1, fol. 22v: Zarnecki *et al.* 1984, no. 58. Rosenfeld 2003: 347 suggests instead that this is a lidded inkpot.

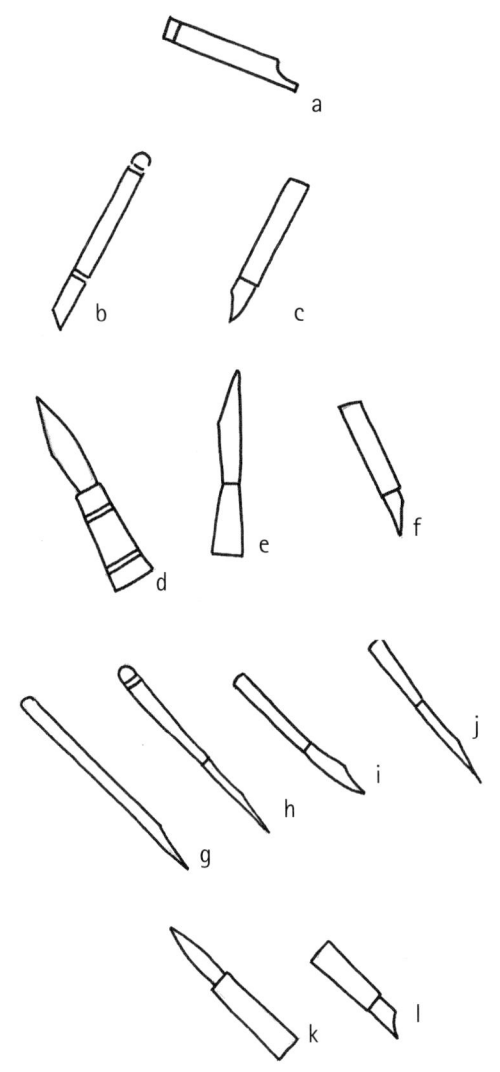

Figure 41.1 Knives associated with writing figures depicted in a cross-section of Anglo-Saxon manuscripts (drawings: RGG): (a) Cambridge, Corpus Christi College, 389; (b and c) Vatican City, Biblioteca Apostolica Vaticana, Barberini lat. 570 (Barberini Gospels); (d and e) Hannover, Kestner-Museum, WM XXIa 36 (Eadwig Gospels); (f) London, British Library, Add. 34890 (Grimbald Gospels); (g and h) Monte Cassino, Archivio della Badia, BB 437 (Gospels of Judith of Flanders); (i) New York, Pierpont Morgan Library, M 709 (Gospels of Judith of Flanders); (j) New York, Pierpont Morgan Library, M 708 (Gospels of Judith of Flanders); (k and l) Cambridge, Pembroke College, 302 (Hereford Gospels)

was effected with a hard point: that is, the lines were scored into the sheets with a tool that had a fine, hard but rounded (as opposed to sharp and pointed) tip—some form of smooth-tipped stylus or possibly the back of a rounded knife. Certain of the knives represented in early medieval scribal 'portraits' do have appropriately rounded tips; while one twelfth-century image which actually depicts the act of hard-point ruling shows the scribe wielding a very blunt implement more akin to a ruler than a knife.[7]

Two late Anglo-Saxon written sources, the *Monasteriales indicia* (monastic sign-language) and the *Colloquies* of Ælfric Bata, list the implements that might be needed by an Anglo-Saxon scribe. The former include hand-signals for styli, wax-tablets (large and small), a ruler, an ink-well, and a quill; while the monks in the latter state that they need wax tablets, styli, pen-knives, other knives, awls and ruler, parchment and (?scrap-) sheets, ink, razors, whetstones, and 'plenty of pens for writing and decorating' (Banham 1991: 44–6; Gwara and Porter 1997: 110–16). The various knives and razors, along with the whetstones, underline the role of cutting and scraping, pricking and ruling in the preparation of the sheets to receive text; they also reflect the importance of such tools both in the making and maintenance of pens, and during the act of writing, when the scribe would use a knife to hold down the sheet and to erase errors. The plentiful pens 'for writing and decorating' reflect the fact that much artwork, and not just script, was accomplished by pen rather than brush (which, it will be noted, neither text mentions).

Various written sources note the use of wax tablets for the drafting of works and even for the transmission of texts,[8] and metal styli, with a pointed tip for incising wax and a broad flat triangular end for smoothing it for re-use, have been recovered from several Anglo-Saxon sites. Typical of the genre are those from Barking, which measure between 12 and 20 cm in length and are made of iron or copper-alloy (Webster and Backhouse 1991, nos. 67i, j, k; cf. Biddle 1990: 729–32; and Pestell 2004: 40–8). However, more elaborate examples are also known: nearly a dozen bear ornamental motifs (generally on the eraser), one copper-alloy specimen from Whitby was adorned (on its eraser) with silver foil, while two (one from Flixborough, the other from Bawsey) were actually made of silver (Webster and Backhouse 1991, nos. 69 and 107c; Leahy 2003: 93–4). Styli of the same basic form are depicted in the eighth-century Vespasian Psalter from Kent, in the tenth-century Benedictional of Æthelwold from Winchester, and in the eleventh-century Caligula Troper.[9] The figure in the Benedictional writes on a single wax tablet

---

[7] With a rounded tip: New York, Pierpont Morgan Library, M 709, fol. 122v: Ohlgren 1992: 439. The blunt implement: Manchester, John Rylands University Library, MS 11, fol. 14v: James 1921, pl. 30; Rosenfeld 2003: no. 13.

[8] E.g. Orderic Vitalis, *Historia ecclesiastica*, VI, c. 3: Chibnall 1968–80, III: 218; and Baudril de Bourgueil, Carmen 9: Tilliette 1998: 34.

[9] London, British Library, Cotton Vespasian A. i, fol. 30v (Alexander 1978, ill. 146); Add. MS 49598, fol. 92v (facsimile: Prescott 2001); Cotton Caligula A. xiv, fol. 20v (M. Brown 2007, pl. 134).

whose frame incorporates a handle at the bottom; those in the Psalter and the Troper inscribe one leaf of a diptych or multi-tablet set. A single rectangular bone leaf from a writing diptych or tablet-set of eighth-century date was found at Blythburgh in Suffolk: measuring just over 9x6 cm, it is decorated on the outside with a simple incised knot motif; its inner face has a recessed area which once contained the wax; while the two holes drilled through the inner edge took the thongs by which it was formerly strung to its neighbour(s).[10] When Aldhelm of Malmesbury (d. 709) wrote of the 'stiff leather shoes' of a writing tablet, he was conceivably alluding to such straps; however, he was equally if not more likely to be referring to a leather cover or slip-case of the sort known from later, medieval survivals.[11] For an extant set of early medieval tablets one must turn to the suite of yew-wood examples of seventh-century date that was recovered from Springmount Bog in County Antrim; the handled form of writing tablet is also paralleled in the archaeological record, albeit at a later date.[12]

Two Old English riddles seem to describe ink-pots; both indicate that the receptacles in question came from the antlers of stags (Krapp and Dobbie 1936: 239–40 and 241–2 (nos. 88 and 93)). By contrast, the ink horn evoked in a Latin *aenigmatum* (riddle) of a certain 'Eusebius' (perhaps Hwætberht, the eighth-century abbot of Wearmouth-Jarrow) is said to come from a bull (no. XXX: Glorie 1968: 240); and the horns of sheep may also have been used. Items of the requisite form are shown, slotted into furniture, in the eleventh-century Trinity and Hereford Gospels (Fig. 41.2 c, g).[13] To make a receptacle, the sheath of the horn had merely to be separated from its bony core—however, these depicted examples have clearly been fitted with a metal rim, sensible protection for their brittle upper edge (MacGregor 1985: 364–6). The ink-horns shown in the Hereford Gospels seem rather larger than those in the Trinity Gospels; if such capacious horns were used— and there are plentiful later images that show examples of similar if not greater size—then they may also have been equipped with a smaller internal reservoir, since scribes would surely not in general wish to fill so large a vessel with ink, nor would it be particularly convenient just to fill the tip and so be obliged to dip deep

---

[10] Webster and Backhouse 1991, no. 65; MacGregor 1985, fig. 66 (showing both faces). For a wooden set of eleventh-century date from France (Angers), both leaves of which are preserved, see Gaborit-Chopin et al. 2005: 149.

[11] Aenigmatum XXXII: Ehwald 1919: 111. Mid-fourteenth-century e.g. from York: find no. 1989.28, 57; Kyriacou et al. 2004: 86–7.

[12] Springmount Bog: Webster and Backhouse 1991, no. 64; M. Brown 2007: pl. 1 (there are, of course, older examples from Roman Britain). For a handled tablet see, e.g., the thirteenth-century one from Cologne, Gross St Martin: Legner 1985, I: 287, no. 69.

[13] Cambridge, Trinity College, B. 10. 4, fol. 17v; Cambridge, Pembroke College, 302, fol. 38r: Temple 1976, ills. 214 and 292. The fact that inkhorns went right though the writing board is confirmed by later three-dimensional representations of writing figures, such as those at the four corners of the mid-twelfth-century portable altar of Stavelot: Bruxelles, Musées royaux d'art et d'histoire, inv. 1590: Van Noten 1999, no. 2.

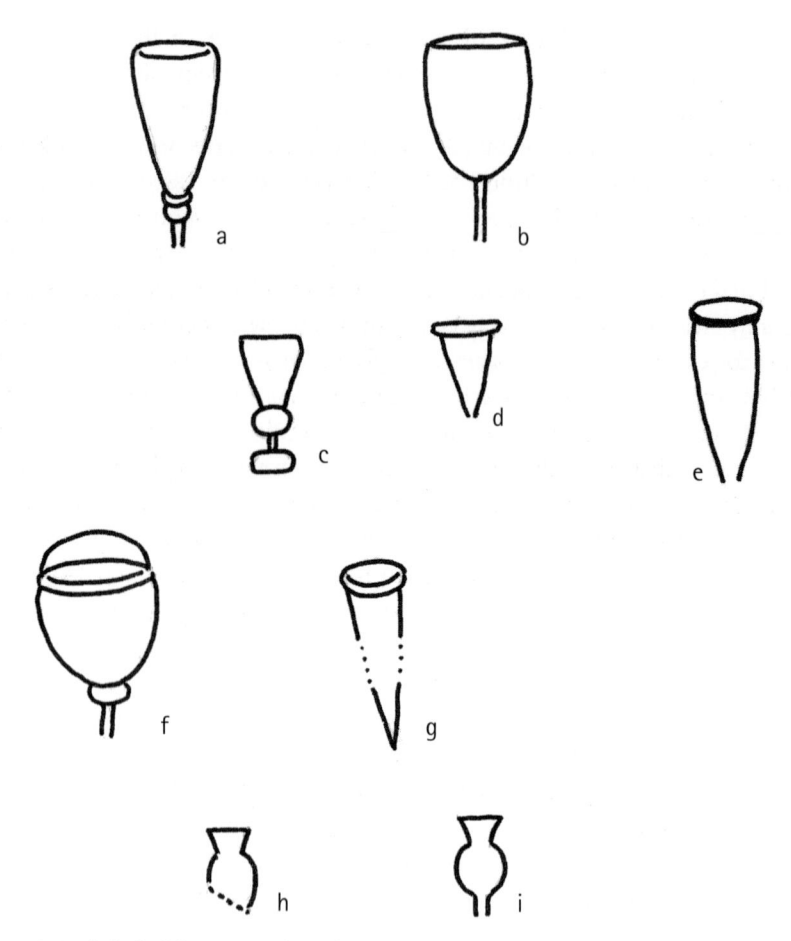

Figure 41.2. Ink-holders associated with writing figures depicted in a cross-section of Anglo-Saxon manuscripts (drawings: RGG): (a and b) Biblioteca Apostolica Vaticana, Barberini lat. 570; (c) Cambridge, Trinity College, B.10.4; (d and e) London, British Library, Add. 34890; (f) Hannover, Kestner-Museum, WM XXIa 36; (g) Cambridge, Pembroke College, 302 (partly hidden). (h) New York, Pierpont Morgan Library, M 709 (partly hidden). (i) New York, Pierpont Morgan Library, M 708.

into the long curving shape. Cup-like receptacles also appear in the visual record: St Mark in the eighth-century Barberini Gospels is equipped with a prominent goblet-shaped ink-holder, and similar forms reappear in the eleventh-century Eadwig and Grimbald Gospels, the shape of those in the latter being more akin to that of champagne flutes (Fig. 41.2 a, b, e, f).[14] Such designs, with the added

[14] Vatican City, Biblioteca Apostolica Vaticana, Barb. lat. 570, fol. 50v (Alexander 1978, ill. 174); the receptacles used by Luke, John, and Matthew are less obviously goblets and could be horns mounted

versatility of an integral stem and/or foot, seem eminently plausible and could have been made of pottery, metal, wood, or indeed an assemblage of different materials.[15] The same is true of the compact types (consisting of a small spherical or egg-shaped body, capped with a funnel-like top) that are depicted in two of the Anglo-Saxon manuscripts associated with Judith of Flanders (Fig. 41.2 h, i).[16] Leather might also have been used to craft ink-pots, and later medieval *cuir-bouilli* examples are known.[17] Mention should also be made of the dish with separate compartments for black and red ink which features in the depiction of Ezra in the Codex Amiatinus, the giant one-volume Bible made at Wearmouth-Jarrow sometime before 716; on the floor nearby are two small flasks, seemingly holding further supplies of the two inks.[18] Notwithstanding debates about the nature of its precise source, the image is unquestionably based on a late antique model, and this portrait-type, complete with the bipartite ink dish and other implements, was to have a long life in Byzantine art. In the absence of corroborating evidence we should hesitate to accept as part of the Anglo-Saxon corpus of tools something which is so redolent of the antique and Byzantine, rather than the early medieval western, world.

The standard medieval implement for writing was the quill-pen. The relationship between the tool and the feathers of birds was teased out in Latin *aenigmata* composed by Aldhelm of Malmesbury and Tatwine of Canterbury (d. 734), as also in an Old English Riddle (Ehwald 1919, no. LIX; Glorie 1968, no. VI: 173; Krapp and Dobbie 1936: 51). Later medieval texts such as Caxton's *Vocabularius* specify swans and geese as the source, and modern experimentation teaches that the best plumes for the purpose are the outer flight feathers of these large birds, perhaps supplemented for particularly fine work by those of a crow.[19] They had to be cleaned of their waxy coating and hardened in order to permit the creation of a firm nib; this was presumably achieved simply by leaving them for some years to dry out, though it is conceivable that the process was occasionally accelerated, as happened in later ages, by soaking then tempering. Medieval depictions indicate that the tip of the feather was regularly sliced off and most or all of the barbs were trimmed away (Fig. 41.3). The nib could then be cut to the optimum shape for the type and size of the

---

on stands. London, British Library, Add. MS 34890 (Temple 1976, ill. 215). Hannover, Kestner Museum, WM XXIa 36 (Temple 1976, ills. 226–7).

[15] Pottery, bronze, and glass examples survive from Roman Britain.

[16] New York, Pierpont Morgan Library, M 708, fol. 26v; M 709, fols. 2v and 77v: Ohlgren 1992: 444, 433, and 437.

[17] E.g. London, Museum of London, A28570: Ward-Perkins 1940: 198, pl. XLV. That the Anglo-Saxons made other vessels from leather is shown, e.g., by the cup found at Benty Grange: Meaney 1964: 72.

[18] Florence, Biblioteca Medicea Laurenziana, Amiatino 1, fol. Vr: Weitzmann 1977, pl. 48; general comment: Rosenfeld 2003, no. 1.

[19] 'George the book-seller has...ink and parchment, pens of swans, pens of geese...' (Oates and Harmer 1964: 46). Aldhelm optimistically or artistically specified the Pelican ('onocrotalus'), conceivably thinking of the cormorant.

script, not to mention the user's personal ductus. In addition to the initial preparation, regular trimming was required to keep the nib well formed and its ink-slit tight and effective: the various depictions that show writing-figures contemplating or paring their pen doubtless often evoke such trimming rather than the initial cutting.[20] As for storage, one Anglo-Saxon evangelist is shown with his pen tucked behind his ear, while another has quills in a horn on the side of his writing-desk;[21] from the twelfth century onwards the implements are sometimes shown protruding from holes hollowed into the scribe's desk, or held by various types of grips fixed to its side.[22] One ornately-carved walrus-ivory box and one decorated and inscribed wooden box lid, both of eleventh-century date, are of the right dimensions to have been Anglo-Saxon pen cases.[23]

The immediate working environment of the early medieval scribe necessarily included: a broad, smooth surface, its angle adjustable, across which to spread sheets of parchment; a chair; places within easy reach for lodging inkwells and other tools; and somewhere to prop the exemplar, plus a means of keeping it open. In addition there must have been a source of good light. Depictions of all periods regularly show scribes with their feet on rests or stools, a practice that may have done something to aid circulation in the lower limbs, enhancing comfort and hence stamina and performance. It also raised up their knees to a more suitable height to work on. Now, a couple of early Anglo-Saxon depictions do show the scribe writing across his knees or on a lap-desk.[24] This was standard practice in Antiquity, but how long it—as opposed to the influence of antique pictorial models—continued into the early Middle Ages is a contentious issue (Rosenfeld 2003: 322–30, with summary of earlier views). Certainly, we should not reject such approaches out of hand: offering the advantages of portability, flexibility, and control, the knees may have suited certain early medieval practitioners, practices, or circumstances. When in 970 Aldred of Chester-le-Street made additions to a manuscript in the tent of a bishop, as his colophon records, he is unlikely to have had more than a portable table or lap-desk on which to press, and may just have

---

[20] E.g. Cambridge, Pembroke College 302, fol. 38r. Colour ill.: Panayotova 2007, pl. IV.

[21] Cambridge, Pembroke College 302, fols. 9r (Panayotova 2007: 61, ill. 3 and (enlarged) 74, fig. c) and 38r (Rushforth 2006, fig. 18). Compare the pen-holder shown in the portrait of St Mark in the late antique Rossano Gospels: Weitzmann 1977, pl. 33 (the date of this page—whether contemporary with the rest of the book or a Romanesque addition—has become a matter of contention).

[22] Cambridge, Corpus Christi College 4 (Dover Bible, made at Canterbury), fol. 64v; New York, Pierpont Morgan Library, M 777 (gospel-book): Kauffmann 1975, ill. 58.

[23] London, British Museum, MLA 1870, 8–11, 1: Backhouse et al. 1984, no. 132, col. pl. XXV. Lund, Kulturen, KM 53436/1125: Graham-Campbell 1980, no. 317; Okasha 1984. Compare the thirteenth-century example in Cologne, Schnütgen-Museum, inv. nr. B.10: Legner 1985, I: 284 (B71).

[24] E.g. Codex Amiatinus, fol. Vr; Lindisfarne Gospels (London, British Library, Cotton Nero D. iv), fols. 25v, 137v; Barberini Gospels, fols. 11v, 50v, 79v, 124v: Mark, Luke, and John directly on their knees, Matthew on a lap-desk.

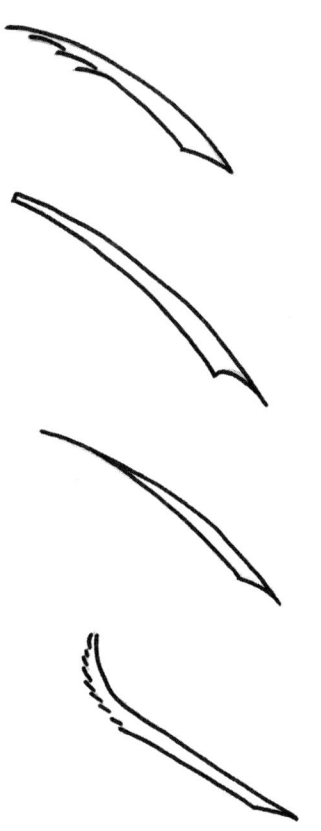

Figure 41.3 Quill pens associated with writing figures depicted in a cross-section of Anglo-Saxon manuscripts (drawings: RGG): (a) Cambridge, Corpus Christi College, 389; (b) Biblioteca Apostolica Vaticana, Barberini lat. 570; (c) London, British Library, Add. 34890; (d) New York, Pierpont Morgan Library, M 708

had his knees.[25] Moreover, not only is the practice depicted in a range of early medieval Continental manuscripts and other media but, more telling, a carefully-drawn, 'non-formulaic' mid-twelfth-century illustration shows the apprentice-illuminator Everwinus drawing on a sheet or board spread over his knees; and altogether more 'realistic' later medieval images with many credible details occasionally immortalize similar procedures.[26]

---

[25] Durham Cathedral Library, A. IV. 19 (Collectar, etc.): Corrêa 1992; Gameson 2002, no. 15.

[26] Prague, Metropolitan Library, A. XXI/1, fol. 153v: Alexander 1992, ill. 18. A mid-twelfth-century ? English example appears in Le Mans, Bibliothèque municipale, MS 263 (Pliny): Avril, Barral I Altet, and Gaborit-Chopin 1983, ill. 181. Other examples include Modena, Biblioteca Capitolare, O. I. 2, fol. 154v; Brescia, Biblioteca Queriniana, A. II. 18, fol. 86r (Zanichelli and Branchi 2003, ills. 42 and 45); the lower register of the 'Gregory' ivory, Vienna, Kunsthistorisches Museum, Inv. Nr. 8399 (Goldschmidt 1914, no. 122; Lasko 1994, ill. 149); Paris, Bibliothèque nationale de France, lat. 4915, fol. 1r (mid-fifteenth-century): Alexander 1992, ill. 49.

If pictures of scribes writing on their knees should occasionally then be given the benefit of the doubt, some depicting writing desks ought probably to be regarded with scepticism. The first figure in a western manuscript to be shown writing at a table is seemingly St Mark in the Lindisfarne Gospels.[27] The table-top is circular. Whilst not wholly implausible as a piece of furniture, the fact that its two-dimensional form exactly matches that of the evangelist's halo with which it is juxtaposed suggests that it was rendered thus for artistic and symbolic effect—to signal the sanctity of the text alongside that of the evangelist. Late Anglo-Saxon images of evangelists and authors often show them working at what looks more like a lectern than a board or desk. Again, whilst obviously not impossible, this—like the bound codex which is invariably displayed thereon—suggests artistic licence with the aim of presenting their book as a resonant and revered object, rather than a serious attempt to evoke the realities of its production with disbound sheets supported on a suitably large surface.

More credible details occasionally appear in other contexts. A drawing in a ninth-century Frankish copy of the Pauline and Catholic Epistles presents Titus in a high-backed chair, his feet on a footstool, a large board across his lap (possibly resting on a hidden part of the chair); his tools (including knife, stylus, inkpots, penholder and pumice) are on or set into the board (Fig. 41.4). Also on the board is a single bifolium on which he writes. A stand in front of him supports an open book at eye-level.[28] Similarly, the scribe pictured in a twelfth-century homiliary from Saint-André du Câteau works in an open bifolium on the angled desk across his knees (it is unclear whether this actually rests on his upper legs or is part of the chair); an ink horn is attached to the desk; the scribe looks across to an open exemplar supported on a separate stand beside him.[29] Other twelfth-century images provide more coherent views of 'writing stools' which (like a baby's high-chair) are equipped with an adjustable desk supported by a pair of arms that slotted into either side of the frame; while later medieval images show various arrangements of weights and strings steadying the sheet on which the scribe works and holding the exemplar open.[30]

Where might such an operation have been located? In England, the first apparent reference to a scriptorium in the sense of a communal writing-room relates to the abbey of Saint Albans in the time of Abbot Paul (1077–93) (*Gesta abbatum*: Riley 1867: 57–8). Now even if the source does accurately record the situation at the end of the eleventh century (as opposed to the mid-twelfth century when it was reputedly composed, or the mid-thirteenth when the version that we have was

---

[27] London, British Library, Cotton Nero D. iv, fol. 93v. The design is echoed in the Copenhagen Gospels (Kongelige Bibliotek, G. K. S. 10 (2°)) whose iconographical relationship to the Lindisfarne Gospels has never been satisfactorily explained (see, e.g., M. Brown 2003: 350–5).

[28] Düsseldorf, Universitätsbibliothek, A. 14: Gattermann 1989, no. 4; Rosenfeld 2003, no. 3.

[29] Cambrai, Médiathèque, 528, fol. 1r: Molinier 1891: 194–6.

[30] E.g. Durham University Library, Cosin V. iii. 1, fol. 22v; Cambridge, Corpus Christi College, MS 48 (second half of the twelfth century), fol. 7: Kauffmann 1975, ills. 215, 278.

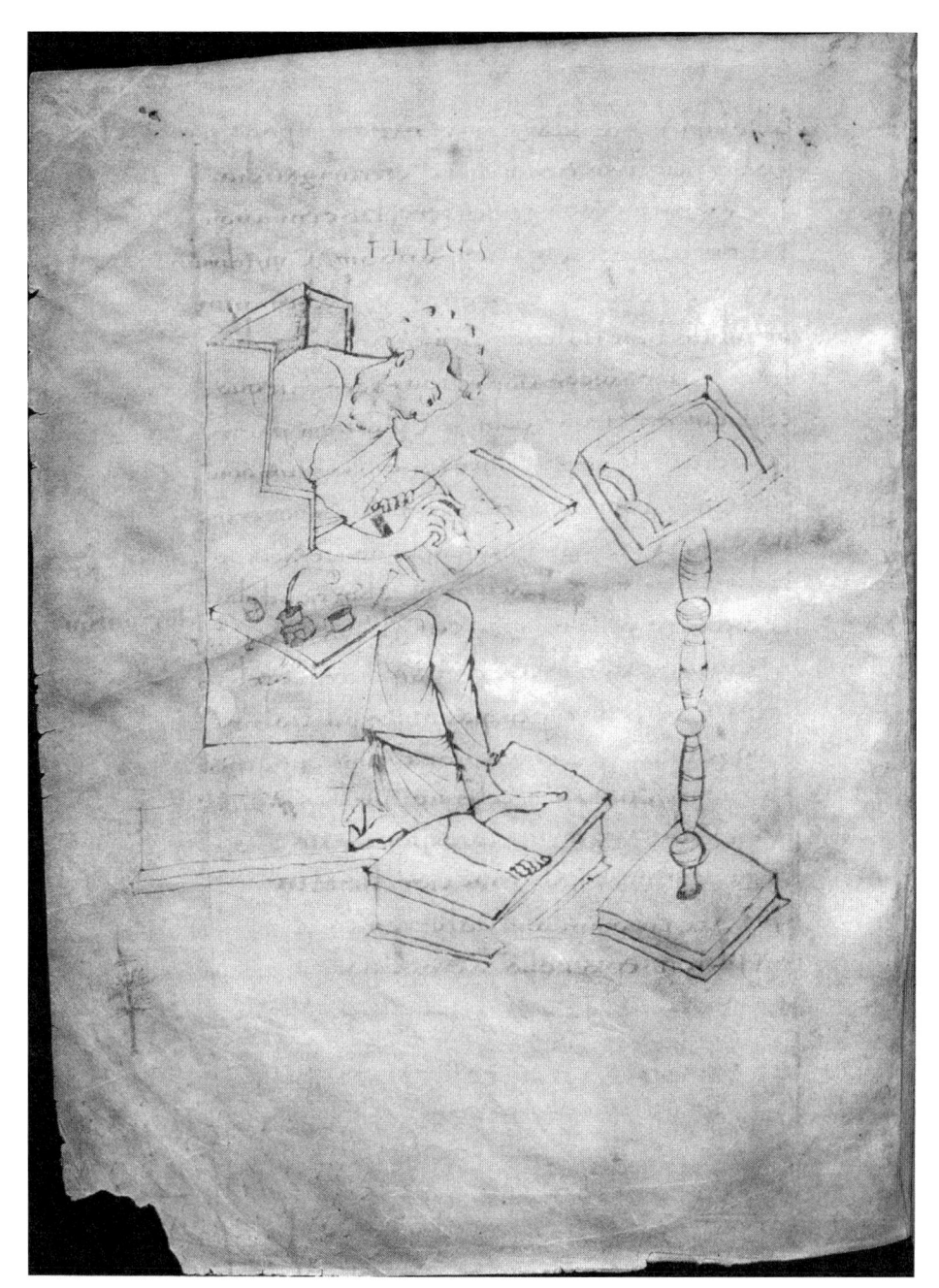

Figure 41.4 Düsseldorf, Universitätsbibliothek, A.14, fol. 119v. Pauline and other Epistles; Northern Francia; early ninth century. (Photograph: Düsseldorf UB)

actually penned) it reflects very particular circumstances. The transcription, we are told, was in fact being done by hired scribes, funded from tithes provided by a local knight: thus to preserve the seclusion of the monks and the integrity of the monastery, a designated working space had to be created for this group of non-monastic professionals. A famous text from Tournai, penned in the mid-twelfth century but purporting to describe the situation half a century earlier, paints a vivid picture of more than a dozen young monks seated in the cloister of Saint Martin's Abbey there, silently writing at ingeniously-constructed boards or tables—the archetypical image of monastic book production.[31] However, as the first proper cloister to be constructed in England is believed to have been that of Edward the Confessor's Westminster Abbey in the mid-eleventh century, while prior to that date it is only at Glastonbury, Canterbury, and Eynsham that there is evidence for ranges of buildings around a courtyard approximating to such a form (Fernie 1983: 90–111; Hardy et al. 2003: 487–92), we should hesitate to imagine cloisters *per se* as the setting for much scribal activity during the Anglo-Saxon period as a whole. The early-ninth-century monastery plan at St Gallen features a designated chamber for scribal work (*sedes scribentium*) below a library room, abutting the eastern apse of the abbey church; it is equipped with tables or desks along the north and east sides, each beside a window (Price 1982: xii and 19; Horn and Born 1986). A very damaged image in the late tenth-century Beatus Commentary from Tábara shows various stages of manuscript-making (cutting parchment, and writing or decorating) being carried out in a first-floor chamber adjacent to the monastery's bell-tower; the book's colophon, which specifies that the second scribe laboured in a tall stone tower, provides corroboration for the arrangement.[32] The St Gallen plan and the Tábara image are manifestly idealized and have no particular connection with Anglo-Saxon England; nevertheless, it is notable that neither locates scribal work in a cloister. Moreover, some of the English centres with which scribal work can be associated were communities of canons (not of monks) for whom claustration—however that may have been conceptualized and realized—was irrelevant.

In point of fact there is a general dearth of clear archaeological and architectural evidence for designated writing rooms among early medieval monastic (and other) complexes (Horn and Born 1986). In the absence of hard evidence for such facilities prior to the Norman Conquest, we should probably envisage Anglo-Saxon scribes working in divers locations—chambers, halls, even open or semi-open spaces—wherever the light was suitable. The references in early sources, English and

---

[31] *Herimanni liber de restauracione Sancti Martini Tornacensis*, c. 80 (Waitz 1883: 313): '... si claustrum ingredereris, videres plerumque XII monachos iuvenes in cathedris sedentes et super tabulas diligenter et artificiose compositas cum silentio scribentes'.

[32] Madrid, Archivio Historico Nacional 1097B: Williams 1977, frontispiece; Williams 1994, no. 5, ill. 257; Rosenfeld 2003, no. 3.

Continental alike, to the deleterious effect of cold weather on such work suggest that the places in question were poorly heated, if at all.[33] Scribal work was as movable as its implements, and the different stages of book production were probably spread around a monastic complex as was logistically most convenient. Though we should avoid placing too much weight on the evidence of chance losses and finds, the circumstance that the writing implements recovered from ecclesiastical sites such as Whitby (Cramp 1976: 223–9) tend to be scattered around them rather than focused in one building or range is compatible with this interpretation.

Concerning the inks and pigments used by individual Anglo-Saxon scribes and illuminators, specific data are limited since few relevant manuscripts have undergone non-destructive scientific investigation to identify the composition of their colours. On the other hand, the evidence supplied by early medieval treatises (none of English origin) along with recent analysis of selected manuscripts means that it is possible to review the types of pigment that were in general use and to indicate some of their properties.[34]

Black or brown ink, the *sine qua non* of writing, also extensively used in artwork, was made from vegetable extracts containing gallo-tannic acid, combined with iron salt (thus creating a black precipitate) and gum (to give the liquid viscosity). The gallo-tannic acid could be extracted from oak galls or from oak or hawthorn bark (which was also used for tanning), while iron salt was obtained by the evaporation of water from ferrous earths. Possible local sources of gum were trees of the prunus family (almond, cherry, plum).

Colour stuffs may conveniently be classified into three general types according to whether they were primarily based on vegetable matter, on minerals, or were developed from a manufactured substance. As examples of the first we may cite the greens based on flora such as aquilegia flowers, woodbine berries, elder leaves, and buckthorn berries, and the blues derived from imported indigo or locally-available woad (the cultivation of which is documented in the Old English text, *Gerefa* (Liebermann 1886)). Typically, colours derived from vegetable sources were stable chemically but could be fugitive. Commonly-used mineral pigments included red ochre (an earth formed by the weathering of iron ores such as hematite, of which there are plentiful deposits in Britain), azurite blue (widespread in Britain albeit often in small quantities, but widely available on the Continent), malachite green (with a distribution akin to azurite), orpiment yellow (a trisulphide of arsenic which occurs in the oxidized parts of arsenic-bearing veins, not found in Britain but scattered across mainland Europe), and chalk, bone, and shell whites.

---

[33] E.g. the letter of Cuthbert of Jarrow to Lul of Mainz (Tangl 1916, no. 116: 250–1); colophon to Rouen, Bibliothèque municipale, A. 225 (from Jumièges); and Orderic Vitalis: Chibnall 1968–80, II: 360.

[34] A convenient conspexus of recipes and collections: Clarke 2001. Recent scientific analyses: K. Brown *et al.* 2003; K. Brown and Clark 2004; and Clarke 2004.

From around the millennium, lazurite (the blue mineral within the complex limestone, lapis lazuli) was more widely used, having presumably travelled all the way from the distant quarries of Badakshan, Afghanistan (Plesters 1993). The most opulent mineral pigment was of course gold, which could be applied to manuscripts in leaf form or turned into an ink. Although the metal occurs in small quantities in many places in Britain, there is no evidence that local sources were being exploited during our period; on the contrary, the Anglo-Saxons would seem to have been reliant upon imports. It is surely no coincidence, then, that prior to the Viking Age, chrysography (writing in gold) and the use of leaf seem to have flourished above all in Kent, the area with easiest access to Continental bullion.[35]

Indispensable manufactured pigments, prized for their fine rich tones and good covering properties, included lead white, lead red, and verdigris greens. Lead (galena) is widespread in Britain—indeed Bede lists it among the materials in which the country was rich (*Historia ecclesiastica*, I, 1: Colgrave and Mynors 1969: 16)—and the Peak District was the focus of a lead 'industry' that is documented from the ninth century onwards and may be even older. When exposed to acetic acid vapour and carbon dioxide in a warm environment (one twelfth-century recipe recommended placing thin sheets in a hollow piece of wood and covering them with warm vinegar or urine in order to effect this (Theophilus, *De diversis artibus*, I, 37: Dodwell 1961: 33)), it eventually develops a white crust of lead carbonate. Removed and rinsed clean of salts, the white crust could be ground to form a workable pigment. The red equivalent, a lead tetroxide, could be manufactured directly from galena or by roasting white lead while stirring with an iron rod. Another manufactured red, possibly used towards the end of our period, was vermilion, a mercuric sulphide made by combining and heating metallic mercury and sulphur, then allowing the vapour to condense on a colder surface (though sulphur itself is rare in Britain, it was easily synthesized from pyrites which is common here). The bright and intense verdigris was a range of pigments based on copper (of which Britain had rich deposits): thin plates of this metal exposed to vinegar in warm conditions (as for lead) would eventually 'grow' a blue or blue-green crust, the colour of which could then be purified or modified by such means as dissolving it in wine, apple-juice, euphorbia sap, or acetic acid, or by adding parsley juice, stale urine, or even malachite. In addition to the extra labour involved in their creation, the disadvantages of manufactured pigments included being unstable (prone to discolouration), aggressive (the verdigris range was corrosive to parchment), or, in the case of the leads and vermilion, toxic to those making them.

---

[35] E.g. Stockholm, Kungliga Biblioteket, A.135 (Codex Aureus); London, British Library, Cotton Vespasian, A. i (Vespasian Psalter); Royal 1 E. vi (Royal Bible). That chrysography was practised in Minster-in-Thanet is documented by Boniface's letter to Abbess Eadburgh (Tangl 1916, no. 35). The small quantities of gold in the Northumbrian Lindisfarne Gospels, Codex Amiatinus and the Wearmouth-Jarrow Gospel fragment are insignificant in comparison. St Wilfrid's now-lost gold and purple gospel-book (see note 40) is often assumed to have been imported.

Even this very cursory survey highlights several important points. Illumination with a varied palette required access to a range of materials, some of which had to be acquired from far afield, doubtless at appreciable direct or indirect expense. Converting the materials into pigments presupposed time, labour, specialist skills, and, in some cases, significant hazards; turning the pigments into optimal inks and paints was a further task that also required experience—not to mention a slab, ideally of marble, on which to grind them, plus implements such as spatulas for melding and mixing. Pictorial evidence from the twelfth century onwards suggests that illuminators kept the paint they were actually using in horns, little dishes or shells, and it seems reasonable to presume that their Anglo-Saxon predecessors had done likewise.[36] The earliest paint-stained palette-shell that has so far been recovered from a medieval English context (Guildhall Yard, London) is ascribed to the later eleventh or earlier twelfth century; it contained vermilion (Howard 2006). Behind every illuminated manuscript stood the early medieval equivalent of a chemical factory whose essential equipment—based merely on the items that are mentioned in passing in a single early twelfth-century treatise as necessary for processing a basic range of colours—included: barrels, beating tools, cauldrons, earthenware pots, copper pots, teeth (of beavers, boars, and bears), glass jars, grinding stones, metal hammer and anvil, scales, wooden receptacles and boards, parchment bags, horn tablets, shells, scissors, a wooden mallet, a pestle and mortar made of copper and tin, a paintbrush, straining cloths, and 'a slender curved iron rod fitted at one end with a wooden handle' (Theophilus, *De diversis artibus*, I, 1–2 and 12–37: Dodwell 1961: 5, 20–33).

The final stage in the manufacture of a book was sewing together into a binding structure the many folded sheets of parchment that had remained as loose-leaf quires throughout the lengthy process of writing and decorating. Owing to the fact that most Anglo-Saxon books have almost inevitably been rebound (often several times) in subsequent centuries, this is another aspect of our subject for which we have very little primary evidence (Clarkson 1996, refining Pollard 1975). Few Anglo-Saxon manuscripts preserve a significant portion of their 'original' binding structure, and only a couple are in a near-pristine condition. The two in question are the Stonyhurst (or Cuthbert) Gospel of St John made at Wearmouth-Jarrow around 700, and a volume containing the Song of Songs, the Pauline Epistles, and the Apocalypse that was put together at Saint Augustine's Abbey, Canterbury, at the end of the eleventh century (Fig. 41.5).[37] The twelve quires of the little gospel were link-stitched to each other via two pairs of sewing stations, one near the head

---

[36] See, e.g., Alexander 1992, ills. 18 (from a Bohemian sacramentary, showing three dishes), 25 (Weissenau legendary; four horns and two dishes), and 26 (Dover Bible; one shell), all manuscripts of twelfth-century date.

[37] London, British Library, Loan MS 74 (T. J. Brown 1969, esp. 13–23, with Powell and Waters 1969); Canterbury Cathedral Library and Archives, Add. MS 172 (Gameson 2008, no. 15).

of the spine, the other near its tail; the ends of the sewing thread (flax) were then lodged into single holes in the birchwood boards, close to the spine edge. With a dearth of coeval western European material, the parallels for this ancient technique appear in the Near-East (where, incidentally, it was to have a long life (Szirmai 1999, part I)). The boards were then covered with red goatskin; a raised plant-scroll motif was created by fixing to them a cord arranged in the requisite pattern and then moulding the goatskin over it. Other early Anglo-Saxon covers may have been adorned with metal mounts of the sort that survive on a re-made binding at Fulda and which, embellished with interlace, are both decorative and protective (Wilson 1961).

With improved technique, the quires of the late eleventh-century Canterbury book are sewn not to their neighbours but onto two sewing-supports, the ends of which are laced into wooden boards.[38] This flat-spined structure was covered with whittawed skin and originally had endband tabs (one survives), plus a single fastening strap. Tawing skins white involved immersing them in a solution of aluminium potassium sulphate—at Portmahomack the casings of locally available tubeworms may have been used as a substitute—in warm conditions (20–30°) in a process that could last up to a year. During the eighth to tenth centuries (judging by Continental material) a binder working with sewing-supports would start by fixing them into one of the boards, would then sew the quires to them, and would finally lodge their exposed ends into the second board. From the eleventh century, by contrast, the binder is likely to have had the supports strung up on a separate frame while he sewed all the quires onto them; when this had been accomplished, he would then have fixed the ends of the supports into both boards. Thus in addition to drawing on the skills and tools of leatherwork, woodwork, and metalwork, such a binding required a specific piece of equipment in the form of a sewing frame; the earliest known representation of one appears in a mid-twelfth-century German manuscript.[39]

High-status volumes might be further adorned with goldsmiths' work. The final stage in the manufacture of the Lindisfarne Gospels (according to the account that was added to it in the tenth century) was that 'Billfrith the anchorite forged the ornaments which are on it on the outside and adorned it with gold and with gems and also with gilded-over silver, pure metal'; while for the deluxe gospel-book that he presented to Ripon, Bishop Wilfrid (d. 709) 'ordered jewellers to make a case entirely of the purest gold and adorned with the most precious gems'.[40] Such

---

[38] For scientifically-identified cases of hemp and, above all, flax as the thread used in early medieval continental binding structures: Szirmai 1999: 117. The Fleury Custumal of *c*.1000 spells out the use of 'twisted thread' (doubtless flax or hemp) 'for the sewing of books' and deer skin for covering them: 'ad conpingendos codices fila retorta, cervorum coria que sunt librorum tegmina': *Consuetudines Floriacenses Antiquiores*, c. 9: Davril and Donnat 2004: 184.

[39] Bamberg, Staatliche Bibliothek, Misc. Patr. 5 (see n. 4 above). See further in general Szirmai 1999, ch. 8.

[40] London, British Library, Cotton Nero D. iv: Kendrick *et al*., 1960, Bk II, ch. 1. *Vita Wilfridi*, c. 17: Colgrave 1927: 36.

Figure 41.5 Canterbury Cathedral Archives and Library, MS Add. 172. Pauline Epistles and other texts; Canterbury, Saint Augustine's Abbey; late eleventh century. (Photograph: Canterbury Cathedral A&L)

gospel-books were thus elevated to the status of physical as well as metaphysical treasures, their external appearance matching other precious metalwork of the church. Though only one treasure binding which might conceivably preserve Anglo-Saxon work has come down to us,[41] various metalwork mounts and little ivory plaques that could have adorned the English equivalents are known: the golden plaque from Brandon with a nielloed image of an eagle-headed St John is a possible early example, various small-scale morse ivories carved with New Testament figures or scenes are late ones (Webster and Backhouse 1991, no. 66a; Backhouse *et al.* 1984, nos. 117, 119, 122, 126–8). These fragments, considered

---

[41] The front of New York, Pierpont Morgan Library, M 708 (Needham 1979, no. 8, col. pl. on p. xxi; McGurk and Rosenthal 1995: 297–8); sometimes ascribed to England, it is just as likely to be Flemish.

alongside better-preserved Continental examples (Steenbock 1965; Laffitte and Goupil 1991), not only demonstrate how elaborate such work could be, they also indicate the range of techniques involved. Panels of gold or gilt-silver, plain or patterned, might clothe the boards, while figural imagery in metal could be incorporated either as repoussé work or cast separately and then soldered or pinned into place. If ivory plaques were to be included, recesses might be hollowed into the wooden board into which they could be set, being secured by small rivets, 'claws' or an overlapping metalwork rim. Surfaces without imagery might be enlivened with golden filigree or set with gems.

Another precious item that was directly associated with books was the *æstel* that King Alfred (d. 899) distributed alongside his vernacular translation of Gregory the Great's *Pastoral Care*. Often assumed (on etymological grounds) to have been a type of pointer—whose handle is then sometimes identified with the Alfred Jewel—this otherwise undocumented object resists analysis; however, stated to have been worth fifty mancuses, it was clearly extremely valuable.[42] Precious bindings were the prerogative of the goldsmith or jeweller, whose workshops and tools were thus also deployed in the finishing of certain books. One of the relatively few late Anglo-Saxon goldsmiths to feature by name in documentary sources—doubtless because of his station—was Mannig, abbot of Evesham 1044–58; celebrated as a skilled cantor, scribe, painter, and gold-worker, he could in theory have accomplished every stage in the manufacture of a high-status book, including the creation of a treasure binding.[43] Communities that had men like Mannig in their midst would presumably have undertaken the relevant precious metalwork 'in house', but elsewhere the task was doubtless 'contracted out' and presumably accomplished 'externally'. Such may have been the case for the Thorney Gospels whose lost Anglo-Saxon binding is recorded in an eleventh-century inscription added to the start of the manuscript; this notes that the 'two oras of weighed gold which is wired on the outside of this same book' had been given by a certain Ælfric and Wulfwine who, moreover, are described as the 'goldsmiths of Eadgifu'.[44]

Specific information on the storage of Anglo-Saxon books is predictably exiguous. Some high-status volumes would have been kept on or around the altar or near to the shrine of a saint, but even here there are uncertainties. We know, for instance, that Ceolfrith of Wearmouth-Jarrow (d. 716) 'placed [great one-volume Bibles] in the churches of his two monasteries so that it should be easy for all who wished to read any

---

[42] Alfred's Preface: Sweet and Whitelock 1967, no. II. The Alfred Jewel (Oxford, Ashmolean Museum, inv. no. 1836, 371): Webster and Backhouse 1991, no. 260; also more generally, Hinton 2005: 129–31.

[43] *Chronicon abbatiae de Evesham*, c. 149: Macray 1863: 86; Sayers and Watkiss 2003: 156. See further in general Coatsworth and Pinder 2002.

[44] London, British Library, Add. MS 40000, entry on fol. 4r: Ker 1957, no. 131; Coatsworth and Pinder 2002: 222–3. Although this is the obvious and generally accepted sense, the grammar seems flawed.

chapter of either Testament to find what they wanted' (*Vita Ceolfridi auctore anonymo*, c. 20: Plummer 1896, I: 395), but no details are given about the furniture on which these gigantic volumes must have rested. A lectern is, however, allusively evoked in one of Tatwine's *aenigmata*, where it is described as having a pair of wings and a single foot (no. X: Glorie 1968: 177). By the twelfth century (for which we have more documentary and physical evidence) many volumes were kept in *armaria*, an ambiguous word which could imply free-standing chests or cupboards, as well as shelving set into wall recesses (Gameson 2006: 13–21). The earlier existence of similar furniture can safely be assumed; indeed, one of Aldhelm's *aenigmata* describes a book-chest.[45] A magnificent book cupboard dominates the background of the illustration of Ezra in the Codex Amiatinus. One should avoid generalizing from an image which, as we have seen, was copied from a late antique exemplar and seems more relevant to Antique and Byzantine than to medieval western tradition; nevertheless, the basic elements of this book cupboard are concordant with later western evidence, and the circumstances that the volumes are stored flat (lying on their sides), and that there are not many of them, are certainly sound.

In point of fact, most Anglo-Saxon book collections, even institutional ones, will not have been very large. The greatest 'libraries' of grand, wealthy, and ancient foundations like those in Canterbury will, at their peak, have attained a maximum total of several hundred volumes (doubtless kept in distinct caches in different locations according to their nature and function). More modest cathedrals and monasteries are likely to have numbered their books in tens rather than hundreds: at the end of our period a solid 'foundational' collection for a major community associated with a bishopric, as represented by the donations of Bishops Leofric (d. 1072) to Exeter and William Carilef (d. 1096) to Durham, comprised around sixty volumes (Lapidge 1985, list X; Turner 1918). A list from Bury St Edmunds in the time of Abbot Leofstan (1046–65) documents a collection of some fifty items, dispersed around the foundation: nine service books and a copy of the *Vita Edmundi* were kept in the abbey church, eleven liturgical books were in the possession of seven named individuals, while a further thirty volumes were in the care of Leofstan himself; a single chest or cupboard would have sufficed for storing these (Lapidge 1985, list VII). Minsters and parish churches would doubtless have had even smaller holdings: the fact that priests were exhorted to have a minimum of eight to ten titles essential for their duties suggests that some may have had rather fewer, as other evidence tends to confirm.[46]

In conclusion, three general points are worth underlining. First, far from being a single skill, book production involved a series of distinct operations, as we have

---

[45] No. LXXXIX, 'Arca libraria': Ehwald 1919: 138. 'Now my inwards are filled with divine words and all my insides hold sacred books.'

[46] Haddan and Stubbs 1871: 417; Fehr and Clemoes 1966: 13–14, 51–2, 126–7. It is difficult to imagine that the 'half-educated man who knows all too little' whose ordination is envisaged in a Wulfstanian text (Whitelock *et al.* 1981, I: 425) would have had many.

seen. If the practical details of several of these processes now elude us, it is nevertheless clear that each was specialized, time-consuming, and had particular requirements in terms of raw materials, tools, and training. Now, while certain of these activities were specific to manuscripts, others drew upon the expertise and equipment of pre-existing crafts. Accordingly, some of the 'archaeological' evidence for book-making is likely to be concealed within the deposits of other trades.

Second, book production presupposed long-distance contacts. First practised in Anglo-Saxon England by Italian and Irish missionaries (according to different conventions), its continuation invariably presupposed both the borrowing of textual exemplars from other centres, sometimes overseas, and the acquisition of materials, some of which (notably certainly pigments) must have been imported. Quite aside from the issue of local talent, the variables of supply chains necessarily affected what was possible in a particular centre at a given time. It is no accident that the finest books tend to be associated with well-connected major ecclesiastical centres at times of comparative affluence. Correspondingly, alongside their practical functions and spiritual value, such high-grade manuscripts advertise the prosperity and cosmopolitan connections of their owners as overtly as other luxury goods.

Third and finally, there is the methodological point that reconstructing the elusive realities of Anglo-Saxon book production requires an holistic approach to the available evidence, such as it is. Codicology can provide invaluable guidance concerning the processes and sequences of making a manuscript but cannot define with precision the tools that were used, and sheds little light on the settings and infrastructure for such endeavours. Contemporary illustrations may offer further clues about tools and procedures of writing. Stylized and variously indebted to visual models, early medieval art is generally of questionable value as a source for the 'real world' of Anglo-Saxon England; however, in relation to the field of manuscript-making—of which every illuminator will, by definition, have had first-hand knowledge—its potential value is higher, so long as each example is considered on its own merits, its stylization decoded, and its ambiguities and limitations recognized. Recovered artefacts are, of course, invaluable witnesses, but the range of what is currently available is restricted, and the identity of some of it debatable. In relation to an era with few 'writing rooms' as such and with equipment made of perishable organic matter or that was not exclusive to manuscript-making, recognizing possible traces of book-related activities in the fragmentary archaeological record requires a keen awareness of the practicalities and variables of the processes. In sum, it is essential to take codicological, documentary, art-historical, and archaeological evidence together, along with the experience of modern scribes, testing each against the others. If the present sketch, based on such principles, should foster a greater mutual awareness between these fields, it will have achieved its purpose.

REFERENCES

ALEXANDER, J. J. G. (1978). *Insular Manuscripts 6th to 9th Century*. London: Harvey Miller.
—— (1992). *Medieval Illuminators and their Methods of Work*. New Haven and London: Yale University Press.
AVRIL, F., BARRAL I ALTET, X., and GABORIT-CHOPIN, D. (1983). *Les Royaumes d'Occident, Le monde roman 1060–1220*. Paris: Gallimard.
BACKHOUSE, J., TURNER, D. H., and WEBSTER, L. (eds.) (1984). *The Golden Age of Anglo-Saxon Art*. London: British Museum.
BANHAM, D. (ed.) (1991). *Monasteriales indicia: The Anglo-Saxon Monastic Sign Language*. Pinner: Anglo-Saxon Books.
BIDDLE, M. (ed.) (1976). *Winchester in the Early Middle Ages: An Edition and Discussion of the Winton Domesday*. Oxford: Clarendon Press.
—— (1990). *Object and Economy in Medieval Winchester*. Oxford: Clarendon Press.
BROWN, K. L. and CLARK, R. J. H. (2004). 'Analysis of key Anglo-Saxon manuscripts (8th–11th centuries) in the British Library: pigment identification by Raman microscopy'. *Journal of Raman Spectroscopy* 35: 181–9.
—— BROWN, M. P., and JACOBS, D. (2003). 'Analysis of the pigments used in the Lindisfarne Gospels' in M. P. Brown, *The Lindisfarne Gospels*, 430–51.
BROWN, M. P. (2003). *The Lindisfarne Gospels: Society, Spirituality and the Scribe*. London: British Library.
—— (2007). *Manuscripts from the Anglo-Saxon Age*. London: University of Toronto Press.
BROWN, T. J. (1969). *The Stonyhurst Gospel of St John*. London: the Roxburghe Club.
CARVER, M., and SPALL, C. (2004). 'Excavating a parchmenerie: archaeological correlates of making parchment at the Pictish monastery of Portmahomack, Easter Ross'. *Proceedings of the Society of Antiquaries of Scotland* 134: 183–200.
CHIBNALL, M. (ed.) (1968–80). *The Ecclesiastical History of Orderic Vitalis*. 6 vols. Oxford: Clarendon Press.
CLARKE, M. (2001). *The Art of All Colours: Medieval Recipe Books for Painters and Illuminators*. London: Archetype.
—— (2004). 'Anglo-Saxon manuscript pigments'. *Studies in Conservation* 49: 231–44.
CLARKSON, C. (1996). 'Further studies in Anglo-Saxon and Norman bookbinding: board attachment methods re-examined', in J. L. Sharpe (ed.), *Roger Powell, the Compleat Binder: Liber amicorum*. Bibliologia 14. Turnhout: Brepols, 154–213.
COATSWORTH, E., and PINDER, M. (2002). *The Art of the Anglo-Saxon Goldsmith*. Woodbridge: Boydell.
COLGRAVE, B. (ed.) (1927). *The Life of Bishop Wilfrid by Eddius Stephanus*. Cambridge: Cambridge University Press.
—— and MYNORS, R. A. B. (eds.) (1969). *Bede's Ecclesiastical History of the English People*. Oxford: Clarendon Press.
CORRÊA, A. (ed.) (1992). *The Durham Collectar*. Henry Bradshaw Society 107. London: Boydell & Brewer.
CRAMP, R. (1976). 'Monastic sites', in D. M. Wilson (ed.), *The Archaeology of Anglo-Saxon England*. London: Methuen, 201–52.
—— Bettess, G., Bettess, F., et al., (2005). *Wearmouth and Jarrow Monastic Sites*. 2 volumes. London: English Heritage.

DARBY, H. C. (1977). *Domesday England.* Cambridge: Cambridge University Press.
DAVRIL, A., and DONNAT, L. (eds.) (2004). 'Le Coutumier de Fleury: Consuetudines Floriacenses Antiquiores par Thierry d'Amorbach'. *L'Abbaye de Fleury en l'an mil.* Sources d'Histoire médiévale 32. Paris: CNRS Editions, 145–251.
DODWELL, C. R. (ed.) (1961). *Theophilus, The Various Arts.* Edinburgh: Nelson.
EGAN, G. (1998). *Medieval Finds from Excavations in London 6: The Medieval Household. Daily Living c. 1150–c. 1450.* London: HMSO.
EHWALD, R. (ed.) (1919). *Aldhelmi Opera.* Monumenta Germaniae Historica, Auctores Antiquissimi 15. Berlin: Weidmann.
EVANS, M. W. (1969). *Medieval Drawings.* London: Hamlyn.
FEHR, B., and CLEMOES, P. (eds.) (1966). *Die Hirtenbriefe Ælfrics in altenglischer und lateinisher Fassung.* Darmstadt: Wissenschaftliche Buchgesellschaft.
FERNIE, E. (1983). *The Architecture of the Anglo-Saxons.* London: Batsford.
GABORIT-CHOPIN, D. et al. (2005). *La France romane au temps des premiers Capétiens (987–1152).* Paris: Hazan.
GAMESON, R. G. (2002). *The Scribe Speaks? Colophons in Early English Manuscripts.* Cambridge: Dept. of Anglo Saxon, Norse and Celtic, University of Cambridge.
—— (2006). 'The Medieval Library (to c. 1450)', in E. Leedham-Green and T. Webber (eds.), *The Cambridge History of Libraries in Britain and Ireland* I. Cambridge: Cambridge University Press, 13–50.
—— (2008). *The Earliest Books of Canterbury Cathedral.* London: The Bibliographical Society.
GANZ, D. (2006). 'Anglo-Saxon England', in E. Leedham-Green and T. Webber (eds.), *The Cambridge History of Libraries in Britain and Ireland* I. Cambridge: Cambridge University Press, 91–108.
GATTERMANN, G. (ed.) (1989). *Kostbarkeiten aus der Universitätsbibliothek Düsseldorf: Mittelalterliche Handschriften und Alte Drucke.* Wiesbaden: Reichert.
GLORIE, F. (ed.) (1968). *Collectiones aenigmatum Merovingicae aetatis.* Corpus Christianorum Series Latina 133. Turnhout: Brepols.
GOLDSCHMIDT, A. (1914). *Die Elfenbeinskulpturen aus der Zeit der karolingischen und sächsischen Kaiser VIII–XI Jahrhundert* I. Berlin: Bruno Cassirer.
GRAHAM-CAMPBELL, J. (1980). *Viking Artefacts: A Select Catalogue.* London: British Museum Publications.
GWARA, S., and PORTER, D. (eds.) (1997). *Anglo-Saxon Conversations: The Colloquies of Ælfric Bata.* Woodbridge: Boydell.
HADDAN, A. W., and STUBBS, W. (eds.) (1871). *Councils and Ecclesiastical Documents relating to Great Britain and Ireland,* vol. III. Oxford: Clarendon Press.
HARDY, A., DODD, A., and KEEVILL, G. (2003). *Ælfric's Abbey: Excavations at Eynsham Abbey, Oxfordshire 1989–92.* Oxford: Oxford University School of Archaeology.
HINTON, D. A. (2005). *Gold and Gilt, Pots and Pins: Possessions and People in Medieval Britain.* Oxford: Oxford University Press.
HORN, W., and BORN, E. (1986). 'The medieval monastery as a setting for the production of manuscripts'. *Journal of the Walters Art Gallery* 44: 16–47.
HOWARD, H. (2006). 'Shells as palettes and paint containers in England', in J. Nadolny (ed.), *Medieval Painting in Northern Europe: Techniques, Analysis, Art-History.* London: Archetype, 202–14.

HUDSON, J. (ed.) (2002). *Historia ecclesie Abbendonensis: The History of the Church at Abingdon II.* Oxford: Oxford University Press.

JAMES, M. R. (1921). *Catalogue of the Latin Manuscripts in the John Rylands Library at Manchester*, 2 vols. Manchester: Manchester University Press.

KAUFFMANN, C. M. (1975). *Romanesque Manuscripts 1066–1190.* London: Harvey Miller.

KENDRICK, T. et al. (1960). *Codex Lindisfarnensis*, vol. II. Olten and Lausanne: Urs Graf.

KER, N. R. (1957). *Catalogue of Manuscripts Containing Anglo-Saxon.* Oxford: Clarendon Press.

KRAPP, G. P., and DOBBIE, E. V. K. (eds.) (1936). *The Exeter Book.* The Anglo-Saxon Poetic Records III. New York: Columbia University Press.

KYRIACOU, C., MEE, F., and ROGERS, N. (2004). *Treasures of York.* Ashbourne: Landmark.

LAFFITTE, M.-P., and GOUPIL, V. (1991). *Reliures précieuses.* Paris: Herscher.

LAPIDGE, M. (1985). 'Surviving booklists from Anglo-Saxon England', in M. Lapidge and H. Gneuss (eds.), *Learning and Literature in Anglo-Saxon England: Studies Presented to Peter Clemoes.* Cambridge: Cambridge University Press, 33–89.

LASKO, P. (1994). *Ars Sacra 800–1200.* 2nd edition. New Haven and London: Yale University Press.

LEAHY, K. (1999). 'The middle Saxon Site at Flixborough, North Lincolnshire', in J. Hawkes and S. Mills (eds.), *Northumbria's Golden Age.* Stroud: Sutton, 87–94.

—— (2003). *Anglo-Saxon Crafts.* Stroud: Tempus.

LEGNER, A. (ed.) (1985). *Ornamenta ecclesiae: Kunst und Künstler der Romanik.* 3 volumes. Cologne: Schnütgen-Museum.

LIEBERMANN, F. (1886). 'Gerefa'. *Anglia* 9: 251–66.

MACGREGOR, A. (1985). *Bone, Antler, Ivory and Horn.* London: Croom Helm.

MACRAY, W. D. (ed.) (1863). *Chronicon abbatiae de Evesham.* Rolls Series. London: Longmans.

MCGURK, P., and ROSENTHAL, J. (1995). 'The Anglo-Saxon gospelbooks of Judith, countess of Flanders: their text, make-up and function'. *Anglo-Saxon England* 24: 251–308.

MEANEY, A. (1964). *Gazetteer of Early Anglo-Saxon Burial Sites.* London: Allen & Unwin.

MOLINIER, A. (1891). *Catalogue général des manuscrits des bibliothèques publiques de France: Départements XVII—Cambrai.* Paris: Plon.

NEEDHAM, P. (1979). *Twelve Centuries of Bookbindings 400–1600.* New York and London: Oxford University Press.

OATES, J. C. T., and HARMER, L. C. (eds.) (1964). *Vocabulary in French and English.* Cambridge: Cambridge University Press.

OHLGREN, T. H. (1992). *Anglo-Saxon Textual Illustration.* Kalamazoo, MI: Medieval Institute Publications.

OKASHA, E. (1984). 'An inscribed Anglo-Saxon lid from Lund'. *Medieval Archaeology* 28: 181–3.

O'SULLIVAN, D. (2001). 'Space, silence and shortage on Lindisfarne: the archaeology of asceticism', in H. Hamerow and A. MacGregor (eds.), *Image and Power in the Archaeology of Early Medieval Britain: Essays in Honour of Rosemary Cramp.* Oxford: Oxbow, 33–52.

PANAYOTOVA, S. (ed.) (2007). *The Cambridge Illuminations: Conference Proceedings.* Turnhout: Brepols.

PESTELL, T. (2004). *Landscapes of Monastic Foundation: The Establishment of Religious Houses in East Anglia c. 650-1200.* Woodbridge: Boydell.

Plesters, J. (1993). 'Ultramarine Blue, natural and artificial', in A. Roy (ed.), *Artists' Pigments: A Handbook of their History and Characteristics* 2. Washington: National Gallery of Art, 37–54.

Plummer, C. (ed.) (1896). *Venerabilis Bedae opera historica*. 2 volumes. Oxford: Clarendon Press.

Pollard, G. (1975). 'Some Anglo-Saxon bookbindings'. *The Book Collector* 24: 130–59.

Powell, R., and Waters, P. (1969). 'Technical description of the binding', in T. J. Brown, *The Stonyhurst Gospel*, 45–55.

Prescott, A. (2001). *The Benedictional of St Æthelwold: A Masterpiece of Anglo-Saxon Art*. London: British Library.

Price, L. (1982). *The Plan of St Gall in Brief*. Berkeley: University of California Press.

Riley, H. T. (ed.) (1867). *Thomas Walsingham, Gesta Abbatum*, Rolls Series. London: Longmans.

Robertson, A. J. (ed.) (1939). *Anglo-Saxon Charters*. Cambridge: Cambridge University Press.

Rosenfeld, R. (2003). 'Iconographical sources of scribal technology: select catalogue of non-formulaic depictions of scribes and allied craftsmen (Western Europe, s. vii^{ex}–xiv^{in})'. *Mediaeval Studies* 65: 320–63.

Rushforth, R. (2006). *St Margaret's Gospel-Book*. Oxford: Bodleian Library, University of Oxford.

Sayers, J., and Watkiss, L. (eds.) (2003). *Thomas of Malborough, History of the Abbey of Eynsham*. Oxford: Oxford University Press.

Steenbock, F. (1965). *Der kirchliche Prachteinband im frühen Mittelalter von den Anfängen bis zum Beginn der Gotik*. Berlin: Dt. Verl. für Kunstwiss.

Stevenson, J. (ed.) (1858). *Chronicon monasterii de Abingdon*. 2 volumes. Rolls Series. London: Longman.

Suckale-Redlefsen, G. (1995). *Die Handschriften des 12. Jahrhunderts der Staatsbibliothek Bamberg*. Wiesbaden: Harrassowitz.

Sweet, H. and Whitelock, D. (1967). *Sweet's Anglo-Saxon Reader in Prose and Verse*. Rev. edition. Oxford: Clarendon Press.

Szirmai, J. A. (1991). *The Archaeology of Medieval Book-Binding*. Aldershot: Ashgate.

Tangl, M. (ed.) (1916). *Die Briefe des heiligen Bonifatius und Lullus*. Monumenta Germaniae Historica, Epistolae Selectae 1. Berlin: Weidmann.

Temple, E. (1976). *Anglo-Saxon Manuscripts 900–1066*. London: Harvey Miller.

Tilliette, J.-Y. (ed.) (1998). *Baudri de Bourgueil, Poèmes* I. Paris: Les Belles Lettres.

Turner, C. H. (1918). 'The earliest list of Durham manuscripts'. *Journal of Theological Studies* 19: 121–32.

Van Noten, F. (1999). *La Salle aux Trésors, Chefs-d'Oeuvre de l'Art Roman et Mosan, Musées royaux d'art et d'histoire, Catalogues des collections* I. Turnhout: Brepols.

Waitz, G. (ed.) (1883). *Herimanni liber de restauracione monasterii Sancti Martini Tornacensis*, Monumenta Germaniae Historica, Scriptores 14. Hannover: Hahn, 274–317.

Ward-Perkins, J. B. (1940). *London Museum Medieval Catalogue*. London: HMSO.

Webster, L., and Backhouse, J. (eds.) (1991). *The Making of England: Anglo-Saxon Art and Culture AD 600–900*. London: British Museum Press.

Weitzmann, K. (1977). *Late Antique and Early Christian Book Illumination*. London: Chatto and Windus.

WHITELOCK, D., BRETT, M., and BROOKE, C. N. L. (eds.) (1981). *Councils and Synods with other Documents relating to the English Church 871–1204.* 2 volumes. Oxford: Clarendon Press.

WILLIAMS, J. (1977). *Early Spanish Manuscript Illumination.* London: G. Braziller.

—— (1994). *The Illustrated Beatus II: The Ninth and Tenth Centuries.* London: Harvey Miller.

WILSON, D. M. (1961). 'An Anglo-Saxon bookbinding at Fulda'. *The Antiquaries Journal* 41: 199–217.

ZANICHELLI, G. Z., and BRANCHI, M. (2003). *La Sapienza degli Angeli: Nonantola e gli Scriptoria Padani nel Medioevo.* Modena: Franco Cosimo Panini.

ZARNECKI, G., HOLT, J., and HOLLAND, T. (1984). *English Romanesque Art 1066–1200.* London: Weidenfeld and Nicolson.

CHAPTER 42

CHRISTIAN SACRED SPACES AND PLACES

HELEN GITTOS

INTRODUCTION

I have just visited every part of this monastery in turn: I have examined their cells and their beds, and I have found no one except you concerned with his soul's welfare; but all of them, men and women alike, are sunk in slothful slumbers or else they remain awake for the purposes of sin. And the cells that were built for praying and for reading have become haunts of feasting, drinking, gossip, and other delights; even the virgins who are dedicated to God put aside all respect for their profession and, whenever they have leisure, spend their time weaving elaborate garments with which to adorn themselves as if they were brides, so imperilling their virginity, or else to make friends with strange men.

(Bede, *HE* IV.25 = Colgrave and Mynors 1969: 425–7)

This condemnation of the nunnery at Coldingham (Northumberland) makes it sound more like a royal palace than an austere house of prayer. What Bede reports here are conventional criticisms made throughout the history of monasticism, but they do reflect how inseparable the secular and sacred worlds were in late-seventh- and eighth-century Northumbria (Wormald 1978; Blair 2005: 84–91, 100–8). The extent of interdependence, throughout the Anglo-Saxon period, has been one of the most striking themes to emerge from recent research. It results in significant archaeological problems, not least in terms of identifying whether or not a particular site was ecclesiastical; after all, the material remains of these nuns, metal objects like dress pins and tweezers, would have looked just like those of their secular sisters. Research on the archaeology of Christian sacred spaces and places has transformed our understanding of Anglo-Saxon society because the Church interconnected with so many aspects of it.

CHRONOLOGICAL OUTLINE OF MAIN THEMES

This is a field in which there has been a long history of cooperation between archaeologists and historians, and the results that come from integrating material and written evidence are exemplified by John Blair's book *The Church in Anglo-Saxon Society* (2005). The scope of this work is such that future debate on many topics relating to Anglo-Saxon church history is likely to be defined by it for some time, and I make frequent reference to it in this chapter. In order to consider as much as possible of a huge field I will begin by outlining key themes in the ecclesiastical history of this period and then discuss some particular issues.

The Britons who practised Christianity during the fifth and sixth centuries have now been rescued from Bede's mostly derogatory depiction of them. The evidence for the Church during this period remains scrappy, but Blair proposes a helpful framework for characterizing it. He suggests thinking of Britain as divided into three different zones (Blair 2005: 8–34, fig. 2). In the far west there is considerable evidence for Christianity: for monasteries, priests, and a hierarchy of bishops. The evidence for this comes largely from inscriptions, place-names, and the sixth-century writer Gildas. The publication of all the early medieval stone sculpture from Wales (Edwards 2007; Rednap and Lewis 2007; Edwards forthcoming) and the completion of the Celtic Inscribed Stones Project (www.ucl.ac.uk/archaeology/cisp/database) means this material is now more accessible. At Whithorn (Wigtown), part of a monastery that had been founded by the mid sixth century has been excavated and interpreted as revealing zoned areas of burial and settlement (Hill 1997). By contrast with the west, in much of the eastern half of what would become England there is very little evidence for Christianity. There were, however, some areas in which it was practised, most notably around St Albans, where excavation in the vicinity of Roman *Verulamium* has uncovered parts of the extra-mural cemetery in which the cult of the martyred Alban was venerated (Biddle and Kjølbye-Biddle 2001). St Albans is interesting because of the evidence for its repeated use for large-scale ritual gatherings from the mid first century AD, though unbroken continuity has not been proven (Niblett 2001; Niblett and Thompson 2005). In between these two broad zones on the eastern and western sides of Britain was a central region where there is some evidence for interaction between Christian and pagan communities.

That, broadly, was the situation when the Augustinian mission arrived. Eric Cambridge's (1999) reinvestigation of the churches associated with the Roman missions is one of the most interesting pieces of recent research on them. In particular, he argues that the earliest churches, notably SS Peter and Paul, Canterbury, were built by masons from Gaul, but those built later in the seventh century, notably Reculver, were constructed by masons from northern Italy. A new fieldwork project at Lyminge (Kent), which is being led by Gabor Thomas, is intended to reveal more about the environs of one of these early foundations (Thomas 2009).

From the mid seventh century onwards, when archaeological and literary sources become more plentiful, debate has focused on what is often, though erroneously, called 'the minster system'. An awareness that this was a controversial topic (Cambridge and Rollason 1995; Blair 1995; Rollason 1999) and a lack of clear understanding about precisely what was being debated led to a general, though largely not publicly stated, discomfort with the issue, and some avoidance of engagement with it. That should now change thanks to clarification of what the word 'minster' is being used to describe and of the ideas themselves (Blair 2005: esp. 2–5 and for what follows). The use of the term 'minster' derives from two observations: that 'a simple classification of ecclesiastical sites as "monasteries" or "parish churches" is anachronistic for Anglo-Saxon England' (Blair 2005: 3); and that contemporaries used Latin *monasterium* and Old English *mynster* almost indiscriminately to describe any sort of ecclesiastical place. By using a modernized form of the Old English word used by contemporaries, historians can usefully avoid making judgements about the nature of the places they describe when they usually do not know what they were like but do know most were *not* like what the word 'monastery' normally denotes. Put simply, 'minster' is used to describe any sort of place where there was a religious community, whether of priests, monks, nuns, or laity and of whatever size. Confusion has arisen because some historians have used the same word to refer to the appearance in later sources of mother-churches to which other local churches owed their allegiance.

One of the fundamental arguments to emerge during this debate is that most churches in Anglo-Saxon England from *c.*650 to *c.*850 were the focus for communities of religious people, numbering from perhaps only a handful to perhaps several hundred. Blair (2005: 75, 118–21, 212–16) thinks few, if any, local churches were established by local landowners during this period, although he does acknowledge that there were hermitages and outlying chapels on minster estates. If his contention is right, then the situation was different in the English kingdoms from that in Frankish Gaul. This view is not universally accepted (Cubitt 2005; S. Wood 2006: 30–2).

The general trend in the fortunes of churches in the middle Anglo-Saxon period is not controversial. From about the 670s to perhaps the 740s, a huge number of minsters was founded and a massive amount of land was granted to them. It has been suggested (Blair 2005: 84, 100–8) that initially this was made principally by royal families but that towards the end of this period a wealthy tier of society beneath that level were also investing in minsters. This is the world in which the Franks Casket, the Lindisfarne Gospels, and the Codex Amiatinus were produced. The results were no less impressive in the landscape, as it is still possible to see in places like the Vale of Pickering and the Tyne valley: 'The experiment of drawing circles of three- to five-mile radius around the minsters of some sample areas suggests that by 800 most people who lived in England, outside the highland zone, were within what they would have considered a reasonable walking distance from a minster' (Blair 2005: 152; Cubitt 2005: 280–1; I. Wood 2008). Even if eighth-century oxherds never satisfied their curiosity by peering into a church they would have struggled to avoid being aware of them. This was not a world in which the church was detached from all but the wealthiest and most educated in society.

One subject that remains contentious is precisely the extent to which minsters involved themselves in the lives of the people who lived around them. Did minsters provide pastoral care and in return did the local community support them financially? Blair (2005: 153–65) and Sarah Foot (2006: ch. 7) contend that many minsters did provide pastoral care, that this was the ideal as conceived by Bede, and that many also received payments of various kinds in return. John Nightingale (2006) suggests it may be better to think less of priests going out to perform pastoral care from minsters than of the churches 'maintaining shrines to which people flocked for help in personal and collective crises'. (Certainly, the extent of pilgrimage activity throughout the Anglo-Saxon period is a topic which deserves more study: Rollason 1989: 186–8; Halpin 1997; Foot 2006.) It remains to be seen whether previously dissenting voices (e.g. Rollason 1999: 59–67) will be convinced; Catherine Cubitt appears not to be. She cautions that 'the monkish lens of modern scholars has tended to over-emphasize the monastic at the expense of the clerical'. She does, though, agree that most of the clergy lived in communities but asks whether some of the clergy 'were in charge of village churches' (Cubitt 1992; quoted, 2005: 277, 286).

A separate but also problematic issue is that whilst it has been clear for some time that there were networks of minsters (Monkwearmouth-Jarrow, Hexham-Ripon-Oundle are famous examples) it is not known quite how they operated. It has also been suggested they were more widespread than has been thought (Morris 2005: 13–21; Foot 2006: ch. 6; Morris 2008: 22–3 and n. 150). If true, this is likely to be reflected by similarities in their material remains (Morris 2008: 23 and n. 154).

Archaeologically, one of the biggest challenges has been to recognize minsters on the ground, especially those not recorded in written sources. This problem has been discussed since at least the 1970s (Rahtz 1973) but debate has intensified in recent years in relation to the interpretation of three sites: Northampton, Brandon (Suffolk), and Flixborough (Lincolnshire). All were considered by their excavators to be wealthy settlements, with Northampton a putative royal palace, but Blair has argued strongly that all are more likely to be minsters (Williams *et al.* 1985; Carr *et al.* 1988; Loveluck 2007; Blair 2005: 204–12). He has identified a 'consistent set of attributes' which documented minster sites tend to have: 'a preference for hills, promontories, peninsulas, and confluences; enclosedness; groups of churches, often axially aligned; structured and stable settlements; and an unusually rich material culture', especially one containing styli (Blair 2005: 204). He contends that sites which match most of these characteristics are likely to be minsters. This view has met with some opposition (Pestell 2004: 40–8; Loveluck 2007: ch. 8). At root, this is due to unease about the apparent ubiquity of minsters, which appear to be used as an explanation for almost everything. It is also due to the difficulty of disproving the argument. If all stable, wealthy, planned settlements are minsters how could a royal estate centre which was not associated with a minster be identified? In Blair's most recent discussion of the issue, where the relevant section contains very limited comparison with other sorts of places, it is acknowledged that 'some of these characteristics occur also at secular sites, but it is the minsters which recurrently combine several of them' (Blair 2005: 204–5). A more specific comparison is made between the almost complete absence of styli from the coastal emporia in contrast to the frequency with which they have been found at documented minster sites (Blair 2005: 209–10 n. 116). But the lack of more detailed comparisons between minsters and other places has fuelled a reluctance to accept that in the eighth and ninth centuries wealthy places with complex settlements tended to be minsters. Loveluck (2007: 148–9, 159) suggests that one defining characteristic of a secular aristocratic settlement is the comparatively high consumption of wild animals, especially birds, indicative of hunting.

A related argument concerns the role of minsters in the development of towns. Blair thinks that in the mid Saxon period, minsters were the central places within the landscape and that not only did they 'look more like towns than any other kind of pre-Viking settlement; they also showed a strong tendency to become real towns as the economy developed between the ninth and twelfth centuries' (2005: 290, 262). Royal palaces, where they existed, were temporary, short-lived settlements like Yeavering (Northumberland). The coastal emporia such as Hamwic (Hampshire) were certainly key centres of trade and production but otherwise minsters were at the top of a settlement hierarchy with which the centres of local estates struggled to compete. The difficulty of disproving this view is likely to encourage the sceptics: how could one conclusively prove that a site was not a minster? Would one be able to do so even if in the unusual position of being able to excavate a site in its entirety? Questions also remain about how much of these settlements was under the control of the minsters or whether villages simply grew up adjacent to them. Should we interpret a site like Bishopstone (Sussex) where areas of settlement and craft production were found next to an Anglo-Saxon church (Thomas 2005; forthcoming) as part of a minster precinct or as a thegnly residence adjacent to a church?[1]

I do not agree with the view that we would be better off thinking more carefully about the evidence we do have than beginning new projects because there have been so few modern research-led excavations of Anglo-Saxon ecclesiastical sites. The publication of Jarrow and Monkwearmouth (Cramp 2005) is a milestone. But one big problem is that in most cases only small parts of a site have been excavated and it is often not clear what their relationship is to the whole, which makes interpretation difficult. There is, though, considerable work to be done on old excavations. The state of our knowledge about, for example, St Augustine's, Canterbury, Barking, Glastonbury, and Whitby is inadequate, although a project led by Roberta Gilchrist and Cheryl Allum to analyse and publish the excavation archive for Glastonbury is promising. A long series of excavations over the last twenty years by the Canterbury Archaeological Trust to the north of St Augustine's Abbey has produced evidence for extensive iron-working and some settlement from the mid-late Saxon period. This contains some of the best evidence for Anglo-Saxon metalworking in the country and is currently being written up by the Canterbury Archaeological Trust (Hicks and Bennett 1995; Jarman 1997; Houliston 1999; Helm 2006).[2] Despite these difficulties, some patterns have emerged (what follows is based on: Rodwell 1984; Blair 1992: 231–46, 258–64; Blair 2005: 135–41, 196–9, 201–4, 255–61, 282 with references). In the pre-Viking period, minster precincts tended to be between 150 and 300 metres in diameter, were probably separated from surrounding land, either by man-made banks, ditches, and fences, or pre-existing features such as Roman walls, streams, or slopes, which were perceived as boundaries. Within that area, in addition to a church or churches there may have been other religious foci like springs, trees, specially venerated graves, and stone crosses. There will have been places for burial, for the religious as well as their extended community, in some cases communal buildings for eating and sleeping, in others perhaps family houses, and both would have needed kitchen gardens. There were also areas for craft working (such as carpentry, weaving, stone-carving, the working of bone and metals). Additionally, there were sometimes wharves for shipping, open spaces where market stalls could be set up, and buildings where visitors, pilgrims, and patrons could be housed. It is not surprising that the excavated areas of the minsters at Hartlepool, Whithorn, and St Augustine's, Canterbury were extremely densely occupied (Daniels 2007; Gem 1997; Hill 1997).[3] It is, though, vital to remember that the fortunes of foundations fluctuated

---

[1] This problem has also been raised in relation to work north of St Augustine's, Canterbury (Houliston 1999: 2).

[2] I am grateful to Gabor Thomas for drawing these sites to my attention.

[3] Note also the recent excavations at Portmahomack, north-east Scotland (Carver 2004; 2006).

and there was always a spectrum of wealth. Some could have been mistaken for a small farm, others perhaps for a Carolingian palace.

In the second half of the eighth century and into the ninth century, the fortunes of minsters appear to have declined significantly. Precisely when this happened, and for what reasons, is uncertain. Blair (2005: 132–4, ch. 6) prefers explanations based on changes in attitudes towards them. But the degree to which a very significant economic decline was responsible needs further investigation. The amount of coinage in circulation dropped dramatically *c.*750. It has been suggested that this reflects a shortage of silver and that there was no decline in the quantity of other metalwork being produced during this period (Blackburn 2003: esp. 32, 34–5; Blair 2005: 133) but this does need to be more firmly established. During the period from *c.*700 to *c.*750 there was an exceptionally large amount of coinage being produced but such a rapid ensuing decrease may have had significant economic consequences. Whether fashion or poverty is to blame, the Vikings had such an impact on the church because they aggravated what was already happening; Alfred's comments to that effect were not simply rhetoric (Sweet 1871: 2–9). The nunneries seem to have been especially affected but it is not certain whether this was because the Vikings exacerbated a decline in interest in nunneries that had already been happening (Foot 2000, 1: ch. 3), or whether it was a result of more widespread secular appropriation of ecclesiastical wealth (Blair 2005: 323–9), or changes in royal power (Yorke 2003: ch. 2). Targeted archaeological investigation may help resolve some of these questions of chronology and causation.

What happened to the nunneries was unusual. There has been a growing recognition that although the Vikings had a significant impact on churches throughout Britain, institutions were rarely wiped out. Instead, there is often evidence for some sort of ecclesiastical life occurring at the same sites in the tenth century. It is rarely possible to prove continuity, though, and in most cases the churches were much less wealthy, and their nature had often changed. There was substantial regional variation and the patterns are unsurprising: those areas most affected by Viking political takeover and settlement are broadly those where there was greatest discontinuity (Blair 2005: 291–323 with references; Hadley 2006: ch. 5).

Although less wealthy and less powerful than in their heyday, minsters survived as institutions right through to the end of the Anglo-Saxon period (Blair 2005: 341–67). That is to say that in the tenth and eleventh centuries, there were still considerable numbers of churches run by communities of secular clergy, or by monks, although varying wildly in size and in the nature of the communal lives they led. Blair (2005: 291, 323-41) brings together a disparate body of evidence to argue for a long-term trend towards the secularization of minsters as kings and aristocrats eroded their autonomy, appropriated their estates, and adopted them as places for their own residences, for defence and administration. He predicts that one should find evidence for the construction of noble houses at earlier minsters (Blair 2005: 328).

In the second half of the tenth century, a small but powerful group of reforming bishops with the support of King Edgar founded and re-founded no more than forty monasteries and nunneries whose communities were to follow a strict life of poverty and chastity based on the Benedictine Rule. This reform, as reforms tend to, generated a considerable number of texts which have distorted its impact and significance and considerable work continues to be undertaken to re-assess it (Yorke 1988; Ramsay *et al.* 1992; Brooks and Cubitt 1996; Robertson 2005; Scragg 2008). Amongst these studies are a few which redress the emphasis on the reform by focusing on the continued existence of large numbers of clerical communities: 'Given that some hundreds of secular minsters were probably still functioning, it is unlikely that the reformed communities ever comprised much more than 10 per cent of the total. This numerical measure is in a way misleading...but it puts the local impact of the reform into perspective' (Blair 2005: 351; see also Lenker 2005). The reformers did have a real impact but their strident voices should not be allowed to drown out those who made less noise.

There are indications that the reformers' ideals led to alterations within monastic precincts. There is some evidence for the construction of cloisters and of domestic buildings (Gittos forthcoming). There is also a great deal of discussion about the importance of enclosure; in the case of Winchester, it is clear that re-planning did take place on a significant scale. Æthelwold constructed separate precincts around each of the three minsters and had to redistribute parcels of land in the process. The subsequent creation of the enclosures with their boundary walls or hedges 'caused the stopping or diversion of watercourses, the closure of streets, the demolition of houses, and the ruin of some established mills' (Rumble 2002: 25). This was not simply reformers' rhetoric. It looks rather as though reformed monasteries, some of which were also cathedrals, proclaimed the changes within them by the construction of perimeter boundaries which helped to differentiate them from other types of churches.

The construction of hundreds, if not thousands, of small, local churches in the later Anglo-Saxon period had a far more lasting impact than the reform. Once again it is Blair (2005), building principally on the work of Richard Morris (1989), who has transformed our understanding of the processes by which these churches were created. He argues that small, local churches were uncommon until the later tenth century (Blair 2005: 70–1, 118–21, 385–96). They do not start to be mentioned in the surviving sources until the 960s when King Edgar's law code refers to the churches of thegns and contains legislation to ensure that minsters did not lose out financially to such churches (Blair 2005: 442–4). A consistent pattern has emerged in excavations that the earliest phase consisted of a tiny wooden church that was subsequently rebuilt in stone and often enlarged at the same time. So far, few of these wooden buildings have been precisely dated and our understanding of precisely when they began to be built in large numbers remains obscure. They appear not to have been present in the seventh and eighth centuries but are certainly around from the mid tenth century. Quite when in the intervening period they began to be fashionable is hard to gauge. The written sources are unhelpful because they are consistently conservative about the growth of local churches, only acknowledging change long after it had taken place (Blair 2005: 426–7). It would be useful to have a better regional chronology and also a clearer understanding of whether or not there was a relationship between growth in the provision of local churches and the 'village moment' (Lewis et al. 2001: 191–201).

The period in which these flimsy structures, which probably looked little different from domestic buildings, were transformed into permanent stone churches, with stone fonts within them, and endowed with land to support them, is better understood, not least because there is so much surviving physical evidence. It 'can be conceived as a tide which rose in eastern and southern England around 1000, rolled slowly but steadily westwards and northwards through the eleventh century, but failed to spread far into the highland zone until after' *c.*1100 (Blair 2005: 420–1).

Churches: identification and dating

The churches built during the period of rebuilding and endowment which took place during the eleventh century make up a substantial part of Taylor and Taylor's corpus of Anglo-Saxon buildings (Taylor and Taylor 1965–78). There is now an orthodoxy that many of these date from after 1066 (Fernie 1983: 162–73; Gem 1988; Fernie 2000: 208–19; Blair 2005: 411–17) but it is desirable that more research should be done to understand the chronology of later Anglo-Saxon and Anglo-Norman buildings. Is it right to say that 'the stylistic arguments do now seem to be pushing all but a small minority of our standing "Anglo-Saxon" local churches into and beyond the last eighty or so years of Anglo-Saxon history' (Blair 2005: 412)? It would be helpful to have a better understanding of diagnostic features which could provide guidance to the dating of these buildings, not least because of the very large number of parts of buildings which have been recognized as late Anglo-Saxon or early Romanesque since Taylor and Taylor's work. Few of those observations have been published and one way of doing so would be to produce some form of updated Taylor and Taylor in electronic format, preferably in association with the Corpus of Anglo-Saxon Stone Sculpture (www.dur.ac.uk/corpus/).

In the wake of the publication of *Anglo-Saxon Architecture*, a series of pioneering case studies were undertaken aiming to understand particular buildings and develop methodologies for their study. (The best current guides to the study of medieval churches are Rodwell 2005 and Parsons 1998.) At Barton-on-Humber (Lincs.) and Rivenhall (Essex), Warwick and Kirsty Rodwell demonstrated the importance of excavating churches, how much information could be gained from recording the standing fabric, and how complex their building history often is (1982; 1985–93). At Brixworth (Northants), stone-by-stone drawings were employed onto which different stone types were marked as a means of trying to distinguish between building campaigns and repairs (Sutherland and Parsons 1984; Parsons and Sutherland forthcoming). In some cases, notably at Deerhurst (Glos.) (Rahtz and Watts 1997), detailed study revealed so much complexity that it became extremely difficult to untangle the sequence of events. Frustratingly, dating of standing structures still usually relies on art-historical judgements, and comparison with a handful of more or less securely dated buildings. There has been some success with dendrochronology. The wooden church at Greensted (Essex) has been dated to between c.1063 and c.1100 (Christie *et al.* 1979; Hewett 1980: 5–13; Tyers 1996). And a door, which currently leads from the chapter house vestibule at Westminster Abbey, was almost certainly re-used from Edward the Confessor's building (Miles and Bridge 2005). Techniques for obtaining radiocarbon dates from lime mortar have now been refined but have not yet been applied to Anglo-Saxon buildings (Hale *et al.* 2003; Lindroos *et al.* 2007). This method is currently expensive but a carefully designed project could produce dramatic results. Sophie Blain (forthcoming), working as part of a project to investigate the use of luminescence for dating medieval bricks, has been very successful in assessing whether or not bricks were re-used or manufactured anew in a group of early medieval churches in Normandy and south-east England. In addition to these methods, recent research on early medieval churches in Ireland (Ó Carragáin 2010), on English Romanesque architecture (Fernie 2000; Thurlby 2003), and new research in progress by David Petts on the early church in western Normandy, mean there is now far greater potential to consider Anglo-Saxon buildings within their regional and chronological context.

CHURCHES: FUNCTIONS

Unravelling the history of the fabric of a church is only the beginning of trying to understand it. How Anglo-Saxon churches were designed to be used and how their functions changed over time has long been of interest, yet we are far from an adequate appreciation of the subject. In most cases research involves using surviving literary sources in conjunction with the buildings themselves. This is more difficult than it sounds, because relevant documentary sources mostly relate to cathedrals and reformed monasteries of which very little physical evidence survives. Some conclusions are possible, however, such as the use made of multiple churches during processions (Gittos forthcoming). Mark Spurrell (1992) and Arnold Klukas (1984a,b,c) have both made use of the *Regularis Concordia*, the adaptation of the Benedictine Rule promulgated for use in English monasteries *c.*973, though many other sources also survive (Gittos 2005a, b). A study of the uses made of upper spaces in churches is of wider interest than its title might suggest (Huitson 2009). The report on an archaeological survey of the early medieval religious site at Inishmurray (Sligo) is a model of how much can be gained in terms of interpretation by drawing on a wide range of sources including ethnographic ones, even where contemporary evidence for the function of a site is lacking (O'Sullivan and Ó Carragáin 2008). Tomás Ó Carragáin's (2009; 2010) combination of the thorough architectural investigation of many buildings and the combing of written sources is also creating exciting results.

Much can be gained from looking very carefully at the buildings themselves for clues to their function. This is often extremely difficult because churches have usually been repeatedly and radically altered, often only fragments of them survive, and their internal fittings rarely do. Recently, though, a pioneering study by Paul Everson and David Stocker (2006; Stocker and Everson 2006) on a group of late-eleventh-century towers in Lincolnshire has produced considerable results. They observed that the many towers built during this period in the area had a certain set of characteristics, and they have proposed a specific explanation for this relating to changes in the burial rite promoted by Archbishop Lanfranc and Remigius, bishop of Lincoln. Whilst detailed examination of individual buildings is always necessary, the investigation of a particular feature found in several buildings may yield more results, not least because whilst huge numbers of bits of churches survive, almost none do so in their entirety. What one can say on the basis of one particular structure may be limited; asking questions about the function of a feature found in several churches may be more profitable.

The regional characteristics of Anglo-Saxon buildings deserve more study, not least because Blair (2005) explicitly seeks to identify regional patterns throughout and makes a whole series of suggestions that could usefully be tested further. Is he right, for example, to say that the 'thegnly tower-naves of central and eastern England exemplified by Earls Barton, may...reflect distinctive tastes of the Norse and Anglo-Danish nobility' (Blair 2005: 425)? Some regional patterns must be related to the use of particular materials though it would be helpful to have some corroboration of that. Is the widespread use of wood, because of the lack of building stone, the reason why so little post-850 stone sculpture survives from Kent and East Anglia? Regional patterns are sometimes affected by the distinctive practices of nineteenth-century restorers. Some proudly displayed the carved stones they discovered, others discarded them. As Thomas Pickles (pers. comm.) has suggested, a better understanding of the attitudes of key restorers may help us interpret patterns in the surviving buildings and sculpture.

CHURCHES: SYMBOLISM

Church architecture was influenced by tradition, fashion, and the properties of available materials but also by ideas about what these buildings symbolized. The extent to which these concepts affected the physical form of buildings, and how some people thought about them, is the subject of ongoing research. One example, which emerges from reading the late Anglo-Saxon rituals for dedicating churches, is the emphasis they place on the symbolism of church floors. It is possible that in high-status Anglo-Saxon buildings this found a tangible expression in polychrome relief tiles. There is also an unusual late Anglo-Saxon ritual for blessing a pavement moved from elsewhere which suggests they were considered precious (Gittos 2005b: 100; forthcoming). The significance of church floors and how they were interpreted is emerging particularly clearly in the work of Lucy Donkin (2009).

There has been a growing awareness that exclusively functional explanations of observed behaviour are rarely adequate ones. It has been argued that the re-use of Roman masonry was a deliberate statement of *Romanitas* rather than simply being pragmatic (Eaton 2000). The symbolism of using red Roman tiles, an arch as at Escomb, individual inscriptions, or even entire buildings, would have been readily apparent. Tyler Bell's (2005) thorough study of the religious re-use of Roman buildings has increased our understanding of this issue and there is probably more to be gained from studying the sites he has brought together.

The well-known preference of Anglo-Saxon architects for retaining older buildings, incorporating them within newer structures rather than rebuilding from scratch, demonstrates a reverence for the buildings themselves as well as the relics they contained. By contrast, it has been suggested that sometimes the deliberate burial of objects is also indicative of veneration. Stocker (1997) proposes that old fonts were sometimes carefully buried beneath their replacements because they were considered too holy to be disposed of in another way.[4] A comparable example from the Anglo-Saxon period has been discussed by Warwick Rodwell at Lichfield where he discovered some fine pieces of late-eighth-century sculpture which have been interpreted as parts of a shrine. Rodwell (2006: 3) suggests part of the shrine was purposefully buried beneath the church floor within 200 years of its having been carved (see Fig. 25.7g).

Attending to such ideas makes one aware quite how difficult it is to understand how buildings were experienced by individuals in the past. What does it mean to say that one part of a building was symbolic of something? To whom and at what

---

[4] There may be an additional example to the ones he cites at St Laurence, Upwey, Dorset, where a font had been incorporated into one of the piers of the north arcade. I am grateful to Moira and Brian Gittos for this information.

times was that symbolism apparent? When were those individuals mindful of it? Mary Carruthers (1998: 272–6) has plausibly suggested that medieval cloisters were designed and used as aids to meditative thought. It is challenging to try to think about Anglo-Saxon buildings in this way because almost none of the grandest survive above ground and so few humbler buildings remain in anything approaching completeness. Yet the potential of the physical and written sources has not been exhausted. In Gittos forthcoming, I attempt in a case study to consider the implications of the repeated use of a building for how it was understood and experienced, though I would be the first to admit this is highly conjectural. Another topic that could usefully be explored further is the afterlife of Anglo-Saxon holy places. It is often harder to consider buildings in contexts subsequent to their initial construction rather than as first intended. At Wells, Warwick Rodwell (2001, 1: 87–98, 114, 161) suggests that the oddly orientated Lady Chapel deliberately preserved the site of the pre-Conquest Marian chapel. At St Augustine's Abbey, Canterbury (Kent), the incoming Norman abbots destroyed most of its long line of pre-Conquest churches, but the easternmost of them, St Pancras, was maintained throughout the life of the monastery. In the later medieval period it served as a cemetery chapel (Tatton-Brown 1991: 77): an incontrovertible sentinel of the abbey's antiquity.

Sacred places in the landscape

Holy places need to be considered not only as places in themselves but also within their wider geographic context. Research over the last twenty or so years has greatly helped to clarify the sorts of places in which churches were located. A huge amount of fieldwork is helpfully synthesized in Blair (2005: 191–3). A more difficult question to ask is why particular types of places tended to be chosen as the locality for a church. In the Witham valley (Lincs.) Stocker and Everson (2003) discuss its high concentration of churches in relation to extremely long-term continuity of ritual activity. Dominic Powlesland (2003: 5 and pers. comm.) has suggested the Vale of Pickering (Yorks.) is exceptionally rich in sacred sites of all periods because of the peculiarity that its river, the Derwent, rises only a few kilometres from the sea and yet flows inland: the vale was numinous because its river flows backwards.[5] This explanation is compelling but difficult to prove. Elsewhere, others have discussed the impact of biblical exegesis on the

---

[5] For another, not mutually exclusive, explanation: I. Wood (2008).

interpretation of the landscape (Morris 2005: 10–11; Pickles 2006: ch. 3; Pickles forthcoming; Gittos forthcoming).

The proximity of many Anglo-Saxon churches to certain naturally occurring features, notably springs, has long been recognized (Rodwell 1984: 16–18; Blair 2005: 377–80). So far, few of those springs have received any archaeological investigation and it is difficult to be sure whether any were venerated. Were structures sometimes built around them? Were ritual deposits made in them? Was access to them controlled? Whilst some springs were located within ecclesiastical precincts, it has traditionally been thought that the Anglo-Saxon landscape was not dotted with what Blair (2005: 374) has termed 'undeveloped' holy places. He is referring here to features which were considered holy but where behaviour and access was not controlled by an institution and usually where there were no churches or chapels at the site, as was common in Ireland, Cornwall, Wales, and parts of Scotland. There is now, however, considerable evidence for the veneration of natural features such as wells, springs, trees, and stones in Anglo-Saxon England (Blair 2005: 51–65, 226–8, 374–83, 471–89). It has been argued (Blair 2005: 377 n. 32, 478 n. 234) that the apparent contrast between the 'Celtic' west, where holy wells are plentiful, and the 'Anglo-Saxon' east, where they are rarer, is the product of later events rather than early medieval patterns. The archaeological exploration and identification of such natural features is extremely difficult, but, as Richard Bradley (2000) has demonstrated in prehistoric contexts, it is not impossible and can reap significant rewards. It would be good to see Anglo-Saxonists take up that challenge.

Conclusion

The study of Christian sacred places in Anglo-Saxon England is a dynamic field in which huge progress has been made during the last forty or so years. Success has come from true interdisciplinary study where all types of available evidence are considered on their own merits, the audacity to undertake excavations as substantial as that at Winchester, syntheses based on detailed local topographical studies, and by looking sideways at parallels in Europe, prehistory, and anthropology. Yet we are still a very long way from answering key questions about, for example, the extent of popular participation in the church before *c.*1050, whether certain areas of the landscape were considered sacred over a very long time span, or even what a minster precinct actually looked like. In the preface to his *The Early History of the Church of Canterbury* (1984: xiii), Nicholas Brooks thanks the schoolmaster who advised him to '"tackle the big subjects"'; there are plenty of them left.

Acknowledgements

John Blair and Andy Hudson kindly read the text and offered helpful suggestions. Moira and Brian Gittos, Lucy Donkin, Tomás Ó Carragáin, and Tom Pickles patiently answered questions, checked references, and allowed me to read unpublished work, for which I am extremely grateful.

References

Bell, T. (2005). *The Religious Reuse of Roman Structures in Early Medieval England.* British Archaeological Reports British Series 390. Oxford: Archaeopress.

Biddle, M., and Kjølbye-Biddle, B. (2001). 'The origins of St Albans Abbey: Romano-British cemetery and Anglo-Saxon monastery', in M. Henig and P. Lindley (eds.), *Alban and St Albans: Roman and Medieval Architecture, Art and Archaeology.* The British Archaeological Association Conference Transactions 24. Leeds: British Archaeological Association, 45–77.

Blackburn, M. (2003). '"Productive" sites and the pattern of coin loss in England, 600–1180', in T. Pestell and K. Ulmschneider (eds.), *Markets in Early Medieval Europe: Trade and "Productive" Sites 650–850.* Macclesfield: Windgather Press, 20–36.

Blain, S. (forthcoming). *The Use of Ceramic Building Material in the early Medieval Period in North-West France and South-East England: A Luminescence Dating Approach.* Unpub. Ph.D. thesis in progress, Universities of Durham and Bordeaux III.

Blair, J. (1992). 'Anglo-Saxon minsters: a topographical review', in J. Blair and R. Sharpe (eds.), *Pastoral Care Before the Parish.* Leicester: Leicester University Press, 226–66.

——(1995). 'Debate: ecclesiastical organization and pastoral care in Anglo-Saxon England'. *Early Medieval Europe* 4.2: 193–212.

——(2005). *The Church in Anglo-Saxon Society.* Oxford: Oxford University Press.

Bradley, R. (2000). *An Archaeology of Natural Places.* London: Routledge.

Brooks, N. (1984). *The Early History of the Church of Canterbury: Christ Church from 597 to 1066.* London: Leicester University Press.

——and Cubitt, C. (eds.) (1996). *St Oswald of Worcester: Life and Influence.* London: Leicester University Press.

Cambridge, E. (1999). 'The architecture of the Augustinian mission', in R. Gameson (ed.), *St Augustine and the Conversion of England.* Stroud: Sutton, 202–36.

——and Rollason, D. W. (1995). 'The pastoral organization of the Anglo-Saxon Church: a review of the "minster hypothesis"'. *Early Medieval Europe* 4.1: 87–104.

Carr, R. D., Tester, A., and Murphy, P. (1988). 'The middle-Saxon settlement at Staunch Meadow, Brandon'. *Antiquity* 62 (235): 371–7.

Carruthers, M. (1998). *The Craft of Thought: Meditation, Rhetoric, and the Making of Images, 400–1200.* Cambridge Studies in Medieval Literature 34. Cambridge: Cambridge University Press.

Carver, M. (2004). 'An Iona of the east: the early-medieval monastery at Portmahomack, Tarbat Ness'. *Medieval Archaeology* 48: 1–30.

——(2006). 'A Columban monastery in Pictland'. *Current Archaeology* 205: 20–9.
CHRISTIE, H., OLSEN, O., and TAYLOR, H. M. (1979). 'The wooden church of St Andrew at Greensted, Essex'. *Antiquaries Journal* 59: 92–112.
COLGRAVE, B., and MYNORS, R. A. B. (1969). *Bede's Ecclesiastical History of the English People*. Oxford: Clarendon Press.
CRAMP, R. (2005). *Wearmouth and Jarrow Monastic Sites*. 2 volumes. Swindon: English Heritage.
CUBITT, C. (1992). 'Pastoral care and conciliar canons: the provisions of the 747 Council of *Clofesho*', in J. Blair and R. Sharpe (eds.), *Pastoral Care before the Parish*. Leicester: Leicester University Press, 193–211.
——(2005). 'The clergy in early Anglo-Saxon England'. *Historical Research* 78 (201): 273–87.
DANIELS, R. (2007). *Anglo-Saxon Hartlepool and the Foundations of English Christianity*. Hartlepool: Tees Archaeology.
DONKIN, L. (2009). 'Pavimenti decorati come luoghi di memoria', in A. C. Quintavalle (ed.), *Medioevo: Immagine e Memoria, Atti del XI Convegno Internazionale di Studi*. Milan: Electa, 408–14.
EATON, T. (2000). *Plundering the Past: Roman Stonework in Medieval Britain*. Stroud: Tempus.
EDWARDS, N. (2007). *A Corpus of Early Medieval Inscribed Stones and Stone Sculpture in Wales*, Volume 2: *South-West Wales*. Cardiff: University of Wales Press.
——(forthcoming). *A Corpus of Medieval Inscribed Stones and Stone Sculpture in Wales*, Volume 3: *North Wales*. Cardiff: University of Wales Press.
EVERSON, P., and STOCKER, D. (2006). 'The common steeple? Church, liturgy, and settlement in early medieval Lincolnshire'. *Anglo-Norman Studies* 28: 103–23.
FERNIE, E. (1983). *The Architecture of the Anglo-Saxons*. London: Batsford.
——(2000). *The Architecture of Norman England*. Oxford: Oxford University Press.
FOOT, S. (2000). *Veiled Women*. 2 volumes. Aldershot: Ashgate.
——(2006). *Monastic Life in Anglo-Saxon England, c. 600–900*. Cambridge: Cambridge University Press.
GEM, R. (1988). 'The English parish church in the eleventh and early twelfth centuries: a great rebuilding?', in J. Blair (ed.), *Minsters and Parish Churches: the Local Church in Transition 950–1200*. Monograph 17. Oxford: Oxford University Committee for Archaeology, 21–30.
——(1997). 'The Anglo-Saxon and Norman churches', in R. Gem (ed.), *English Heritage Book of St Augustine's Abbey, Canterbury*. London: Batsford/English Heritage, 90–122.
GITTOS, H. (2005a). 'Is there any evidence for the liturgy of parish churches in late Anglo-Saxon England? The Red Book of Darley and the status of Old English', in F. Tinti (ed.), *Pastoral Care in Late Anglo-Saxon England*. Anglo-Saxon Studies 6. Woodbridge: Boydell, 63–82.
——(2005b). 'Architecture and liturgy in England c. 1000: problems and possibilities', in N. Hiscock (ed.), *The White Mantle of Churches: Architecture, Liturgy, and Art around the Millennium*. International Medieval Research 10: Art History Subseries 2. Turnhout: Brepols, 91–106.
——(forthcoming). *Liturgy, Architecture, and Sacred Places in Anglo-Saxon England*. Medieval History and Archaeology. Oxford: Oxford University Press.
HADLEY, D. M. (2006). *The Vikings in England: Settlement, Society and Culture*. Manchester: Manchester University Press.
HALE, J., *et al.* (2003). 'Dating ancient mortar'. *American Scientist* 91.2: 130–7.
HALPIN, P. A. (1997). 'Anglo-Saxon women and pilgrimage'. *Anglo-Norman Studies* 19: 97–122.

HELM, R. (2006). 'New Grange House, King's School, St Augustine's Abbey'. *Canterbury's Archaeology* 29: 8–13.

HEWETT, C. A. (1980). *English Historic Carpentry*. London: Phillimore.

HICKS, M., and BENNETT, P. (1995). 'Christ Church College'. *Canterbury's Archaeology* 18: 1–7.

HILL, P. (1997). *Whithorn and St Ninian: the Excavation of a Monastic Town, 1984–91*. Stroud: Sutton Publishing.

HOULISTON, M. (1999). 'Christ Church College'. *Canterbury's Archaeology* 21: 1–4.

HUITSON, T. (2009). *The Medieval Ecclesiastical Staircase, Galley and Upper Chamber: Design, Form and Function in Romanesque and Early Gothic East Kent c. 1000–1230*. Unpublished PhD thesis. University of Kent.

JARMAN, C. (1997). 'Christ Church College'. *Canterbury's Archaeology* 20: 2–4.

KLUKAS, A. W. (1984a). 'Liturgy and architecture: Deerhurst Priory as an expression of the Regularis Concordia'. *Viator* 15: 81–106.

——(1984b). 'The continuity of Anglo-Saxon liturgical tradition in post-Conquest England as evident in the architecture of Winchester, Ely, and Canterbury Cathedrals', in *Les mutations socio-culturelles au tournant des XIe–XIIe siècles: études anselmiennes (IVe session)*. Paris: Éditions du Centre national de la Recherche scientifique, 111–23.

——(1984c). 'The architectural implications of the *Decreta Lanfranci*', *Anglo-Norman Studies* 6: 136-71.

LENKER, U. (2005). 'The rites and ministries of the canons: liturgical rubrics to vernacular gospels and their functions in a European context', in H. Gittos and M. B. Bedingfield (eds.), *The Liturgy of the Late Anglo-Saxon Church*. Subsidia 5. London: Henry Bradshaw Society, 185–212.

LEWIS, C., MITCHELL-FOX, P., and DYER, C. (2001). *Village, Hamlet and Field: Changing Medieval Settlements in Central England*. Revised edition. Macclesfield: Windgather Press.

LINDROOS, A., et al. (2007). 'Mortar dating using AMS C14 and sequential dissolution: examples from medieval, non-hydraulic lime mortars from the Åland Islands, SW Finland'. *Radiocarbon* 49.1: 47–67.

LOVELUCK, C. (2007). *Rural Settlement, Lifestyles and Social Change in the Later First Millennium AD: Anglo-Saxon Flixborough in its wider Context*. Excavations at Flixborough 4. Oxford: Oxbow.

MILES, D., and BRIDGE, M. (2005). *The Tree-Ring Dating of the Early Medieval Doors at Westminster Abbey, London*. Centre for Archaeology Report 38/2005.

MORRIS, R. (1989). *Churches in the Landscape*. London: J. M. Dent & Sons Ltd..

——(2005). '"Calami et iunci": Lastingham in the Seventh and Eighth Centuries'. *Bulletin of International Medieval Research* 11: 3–21.

——(2008). *Journeys from Jarrow*. Jarrow Lecture 2004. Jarrow: St Paul's Church.

NIBLETT, R. (2001). 'Why *Verulamium*?' in M. Henig and P. Lindley (eds.), *Alban and St Albans: Roman and Medieval Architecture, Art and Archaeology*. The British Archaeological Association Conference Transactions 24. Leeds: British Archaeological Association, 1–12.

——and THOMPSON, I. (2005). *Alban's Buried Towns: An Assessment of St Albans Archaeology up to AD 1600*. Oxford: Oxbow Books.

NIGHTINGALE, J. (2006). 'Review of *The Church in Anglo-Saxon Society*, by John Blair'. *Reviews in History* 520. <www.history.ac.uk/reviews/paper/nightingale.html>.

O'SULLIVAN, J. and Ó CARRAGÁIN, T. (2008). *Inishmurray: Monks and Pilgrims in an Atlantic Landscape*, Volume 1: *Survey and Excavations 1997–2000*. Cork: Collins Press.

Ó Carragáin, T. (2009). 'The architectural setting of the mass in early-medieval Ireland'. *Medieval Archaeology* 53: 119–54.

——(2010). *Churches in Early Medieval Ireland: Architecture, Ritual, and Memory.* New Haven, CT: Yale University Press.

——(forthcoming). 'The architectural setting of baptism in early medieval Ireland', *Peritia*.

Parsons, D. (1998). *Churches and Chapels: Investigating Places of Worship.* 2nd edition. York: Council for British Archaeology.

—— and Sutherland, D. (forthcoming). *The Anglo-Saxon Church of All Saints Brixworth, Northamptonshire: Survey, Excavation, and Analysis.*

Pestell, T. (2004). *Landscapes of Monastic Foundation: the Establishment of Religious Houses in East Anglia c.650–1200.* Anglo-Saxon Studies 5. Woodbridge: Boydell.

Pickles, T. (2006). *The Church in Anglo-Saxon Yorkshire: 'Minsters' and the Danelaw, c. 600–1200.* Unpublished DPhil. thesis, University of Oxford.

——(forthcoming). 'Scriptural exegesis and the topography of monasticism in Anglo-Saxon England', in P. Thomas and J. Sterrett (eds.), *Sacred Text – Sacred Space.* Leiden: Brill.

Powlesland, D. (2003). *25 Years of Archaeological Research on the Sands and Gravels of Heslerton.* n. pl.: The Landscape Research Centre.

Rahtz, P. (1973). 'Monasteries as settlements'. *Scottish Archaeological Forum* 5: 125–35.

——and Watts, L. (1997). *St Mary's Church, Deerhurst, Gloucestershire: Fieldwork, Excavations and Structural Analysis 1971–1984.* Woodbridge: Boydell.

Ramsay, N., Sparks, M., and Tatton-Brown, T. (eds.) (1992). *St Dunstan: His Life, Times and Cult.* Woodbridge: Boydell.

Rednap, M., and Lewis, J. M. (2007). *A Corpus of Early Medieval Inscribed Stones and Stone Sculpture in Wales,* Volume 1: *Breconshire, Glamorgan, Monmouthshire, Radnorshire, and geographically contiguous areas of Herefordshire and Shropshire.* Cardiff: University of Wales Press.

Robertson, N. (2005). 'Dunstan and Monastic reform: tenth-century fact or twelfth-century fiction?' *Anglo-Norman Studies* 28: 153–67.

Rodwell, W. (1984). 'Churches in the landscape: aspects of topography and planning', in M. Faull (ed.), *Studies in Late Anglo-Saxon Settlement.* Oxford: Oxford University Department for External Studies, 1–23.

——(2001). *Wells Cathedral: Excavations and Structural Studies, 1978–93.* 2 volumes. London: English Heritage.

——(2005). *The Archaeology of Churches.* 3rd edition. Stroud: Tempus.

——(2006). 'Lichfield Cathedral: archaeology of the nave sanctuary'. *Church Archaeology* 7–9: 1–6.

——and Rodwell, K. (1982). 'St Peter's Church, Barton-upon-Humber: excavation and structural study, 1978–81'. *Antiquaries Journal* 62: 283–315.

—— ——(1985, 1993). *Rivenhall: Investigations of a Villa, Church and Village, 1950–77.* CBA Research Report 55, 80. York: Council for British Archaeology.

Rollason, D. W. (1989). *Saints and Relics in Anglo-Saxon England.* Oxford: Basil Blackwell.

——(1999). 'Monasteries and society in early medieval Northumbria', in B. Thompson (ed.), *Monasteries and Society in Medieval Britain: Proceedings of the 1994 Harlaxton Symposium.* Harlaxton Medieval Studies, new ser. 6. Stamford: Paul Watkins, 59–74.

Rumble, A. R. (2002). *Property and Piety in Early Medieval Winchester: Documents Relating to the Topography of the Anglo-Saxon and Norman City and its Minsters.* Winchester Studies 4.3: The Anglo-Saxon Minsters of Winchester. Oxford: Clarendon Press.

SCRAGG, D. (ed.) (2008). *Edgar, King of the English 959–975: New Interpretations*. Woodbridge: Boydell.

SPURRELL, M. (1992). 'The architectural interest of the *Regularis Concordia*'. *Anglo-Saxon England* 21: 161–76.

STOCKER, D. (1997). 'Fons et origo: the death, burial and resurrection of English font stones'. *Church Archaeology* 1: 17–25.

——and EVERSON, P. (2003). 'The straight and narrow way: Fenland causeways and the conversion of the landscape in the Witham Valley, Lincolnshire', in M. Carver (ed.), *The Cross Goes North: Processes of Conversion in Northern Europe, AD 300–1300*. Woodbridge: York Medieval Press/Boydell, 271–88.

————(2006). *Summoning St Michael: Early Romanesque Towers in Lincolnshire*. Oxford: Oxbow Books.

SUTHERLAND, D. S., and PARSONS, D. (1984). 'The petrological contribution to the study of All Saint's Church, Brixworth, Northamptonshire'. *Journal of the British Archaeological Association* 137: 45–64.

SWEET, H. (ed.) (1871). *King Alfred's West Saxon Version of Gregory's Pastoral Care*, Volume 1 of 2. Early English Text Society, orig. series 45. London.

TATTON-BROWN, T. (1991). 'The Buildings and topography of St Augustine's Abbey, Canterbury'. *Journal of the British Archaeological Association* 144: 61–91.

TAYLOR, H. M., and TAYLOR, J. (1965–78). *Anglo-Saxon Architecture*. 3 volumes. Cambridge: Cambridge University Press.

THOMAS, G. (2005). 'Bishopstone: in the shadow of Rookery Hill'. *Current Archaeology* 196: 184–90.

——(2009). 'Uncovering an Anglo-Saxon monastery in Kent: interim report on University of Reading excavations at Lyminge, 2008'. Unpub. report: <www.reading.ac.uk/archaeology/research/projects/arch_lyminge.aspx>.

——(forthcoming). *A Downland Manor in the Making: the Archaeology of a Later Anglo-Saxon Settlement at Bishopstone, East Sussex*. York: Council for British Archaeology.

THURLBY, M. (2003). 'Anglo-Saxon architecture beyond the millennium: its continuity in Norman building', in N. Hiscock (ed.), *The White Mantle of Churches: Architecture, Liturgy, and Art Around the Millennium*. International Medieval Research 10: Art History Subseries 2. Turnhout: Brepols, 119–38.

TYERS, I. (1996). *Tree-ring Analysis of Timbers from the Stave Church at Greensted, Essex*. Ancient Monuments Lab Report 14/96.

WILLIAMS, J. H., SHAW, M., and DENHAM, V. (1985). *Middle Saxon Palaces at Northampton*. Northampton: Northampton Development Corporation.

WOOD, I. (2008). 'Monasteries and the geography of power in the Age of Bede'. *Northern History* 45.1: 11–25.

WOOD, S. (2006). *The Proprietary Church in the Medieval West*. Oxford: Oxford University Press.

WORMALD, P. (1978). 'Bede, *Beowulf* and the conversion of the Anglo-Saxon aristocracy', in R. T. Farrell (ed.), *Bede and Anglo-Saxon England: Papers in Honour of the 1300th Anniversary of the Birth of Bede, given at Cornell University in 1973 and 1974*. BAR British Series 46. Oxford: British Archaeological Reports, 32–90.

YORKE, B. (ed.) (1988). *Bishop Æthelwold: his Career and Influence*. Woodbridge: Boydell.

——(2003). *Nunneries and the Anglo-Saxon Royal Houses*. London: Continuum.

PART IX

SIGNALS OF POWER

PART IX

SIGNALS OF POWER

CHAPTER 43

OVERVIEW: SIGNALS OF POWER

MARTIN O. H. CARVER

The early Middle Ages saw much social change in England. In the earlier period (fifth and sixth centuries) documents and place-names lead us to imagine groups of affiliated peoples, such as Britons, Angles, North Folk, Hwicce, Meonware, and Paecsaetan, some of them immigrants and all conscious of a local and a communal identity. In the seventh and eighth centuries, we believe these groupings to have rearranged to form a series of kingdoms, such as Mercia, Bernicia, Elmet, Dyfed, Kent, and Wessex, some of them predominantly English-speaking and others speaking British (which the Anglo-Saxons knew as Welsh). From the time of Alfred in the ninth century, larger polities were being formed: England in the south, Wales in the West, and Alba in the north. Throughout these seven centuries there is a strong impression of increasing social control. Allegiance is transferred from a kin to a folk to a single male leader in ever larger blocks of territory. The kingdoms are state-like, in that they have hierarchies and property and laws, but they still depend on older systems of loyalty to kin and tribal leaders.

The archaeological agenda is intended to illuminate the way that power was exercised and how it changed. Our raw materials are burials, settlements, artefacts, and landscapes, all of which display marked and variable characteristics between the fifth and eleventh centuries, and at least some of these characteristics are held to reflect power relations. England is rich in furnished burials of the early period (fifth and sixth centuries), the diversity of which—some sparsely furnished, some with astonishing wealth—should indicate differential access to resources. Chris Scull sees the contents of graves as the relics of a system of gift exchange which provides evidence for unequal social relations and the emergence of kingdoms. In the seventh century, the burials reached their apogee of wealth, as the memory of fewer individuals was celebrated more extravagantly. At the same time, settlements, for long small and dispersed in character, began to flourish in new forms: so called palace-sites, such as Yeavering, monastic sites such as Jarrow, and *emporia*, such as *Hamwic, Lundenwic,* Ipswich, and *Eoforwic.* Scull sees these *emporia* as special-purpose sites through which surplus from estates could be directed towards foreign exchange partners. Since the beneficiaries of this exchange were the estate owners themselves, their relative wealth would have greatly accelerated.

While the increasing social control of the sixth and seventh centuries is widely accepted, it may be that burials do not reflect it directly. I suggest, in my contribution to this Part, that furnished graves, especially rich ones, actually represent a political opinion expressed at the time of burial—thus more of an aspiration than a social commentary. Changes in the degree of investment in burial may not indicate changes in social structure so much as the need to signal it. In other words, the social structure of life may have always been hierarchical but the need to emphasize such ranking in death changes with ideology.

For Märit Gaimster, artefacts, their ornament and imagery, are also powerful markers of ideology and politics. She shows how the metalwork can be deconstructed and read in terms of displayed belief—and these beliefs are complex. The brooches and bracteates make multiple references to Rome and to Odin in a vivid material language that brings us closer to the way people actually thought. Women are prominent in communicating ideas not only as wearers of insignia but as spiritual leaders who were determinant in the implementation of Christianity. Much of Gaimster's inspiration comes from Scandinavia, and is a reminder of how impossible it is to study our subject without Scandinavia, and of the relative poverty of Anglo-Saxon England in comparison. Temples, or centres of institutionalized pre-Christian religion of some kind, have long been postulated but never found. But the *guldgubber* of Gudme on Fyn and the first convincing temple in Scandinavia at Uppåkra are only finds of recent years. Such things must surely await discovery in Britain too (see Semple, Pluskowski, this volume).

Andrew Reynolds shows how landscapes also carry the imprint of power and focuses on one of its most severe manifestations—capital punishment. Hanging, decapitation, and exposure on gibbets can all be detected among the skeletal remains of execution victims, and occasionally the post-holes of the gallows themselves, as at Sutton Hoo. The victims are mostly young men, but occasionally men and women were buried together. Dated by radiocarbon, the human remains seem to belong to the seventh to eleventh centuries. Reynolds's research is perhaps the most vivid demonstration yet of the degree of personal control brought in with the Christian era, control that no doubt extended to sexual behaviour as well as loyalty to the new regime and the elimination of dissidents.

Modern archaeologists therefore are more confident that their material reflects on power relations, ideology, and allegiance, rather than on ethnicity or migration. Nevertheless, ethnicity and demographic movement were not unknown to the Anglo-Saxons and must have been highly significant at some periods. I tackle the problem from the premise that material culture, whether artefacts, sites, or landscapes, do not report on ethnic reality, but are always rich in references to cultures and ideas. Taking four sites as examples—Wasperton, a cemetery of the fifth–seventh centuries; Sutton Hoo, a cemetery of the seventh–tenth centuries; Portmahomack, a monastery of the sixth–ninth centuries; and Stafford, a *burh* of the tenth and eleventh centuries—I show that in each case, but to different degrees, the agents that created the sites, their assemblages and sequences, make references to the commanding influences in a current mindset. Among those that always seem to be present and important is the prehistoric landscape from which the English read the past of the land—their 'green Bible'. This is an area of research still in its infancy, but the prehistoric experience is suggested to lie behind regional identities and even the way Christianity was practised. Another permanent force in the intellectual theatre was Rome, present and imitated, but in quite different ways, at all four examples. Other aspects of the mindset are barely explored and in my paper I propose that in this period many variations of religion are possible, and that a simple dichotomy between Christian and pagan is inappropriate.

The process of archaeological inquiry therefore leads us not so much to what happened in early England, but rather into what the early English were thinking. The neutral scientific role that archaeologists have adopted with respect to the past has been moderated by the realization that everything made by humans—artefacts, buildings, and graves, as well as texts—is potentially skewed by optimism, fear, and aspiration. This puts us on the same footing as our colleagues in history and language, and under the same obligations to assess and deconstruct our sources. And as a result we have more to say to each other, and a greater number of shared objectives.

CHAPTER 44

SOCIAL TRANSACTIONS, GIFT EXCHANGE, AND POWER IN THE ARCHAEOLOGY OF THE FIFTH TO SEVENTH CENTURIES

CHRISTOPHER SCULL

THIS short contribution examines some structures and dynamics which may have contributed to the development of social and political hierarchies in England in the fifth to seventh centuries, and some of the problems associated with this field of research. In particular, it examines how some social dynamics and institutions, and the relationships between economic and social dynamics, may be seen to have promoted structures of power—that is, reproducible social and economic inequalities which reinforce the ability of an individual or group to force, coerce, persuade, or influence others—in ways that conditioned the development of dynasties wielding local, regional, and eventually supra-regional power by the beginning of the seventh century. It draws on, and develops, previously published models and critiques (Scull 1992a; 1993; 1999). Length does not permit a detailed or systematic treatment of the archaeological evidence but it is hoped that a sketch of some issues and questions will have some value.

The existence of kingdoms in England by the seventh century, ruled by kings who claimed continental Germanic ancestry, is securely attested by insular documentary sources of the seventh century and later (Yorke 1990; Kirby 1991). Aspects of the archaeological record from the late sixth century, which are consistent with a new degree of social differentiation and political centralization, suggest that this threshold of historical visibility genuinely coincides with a significant threshold of social and political development. The strongest signals are seen in princely burial; in the development of a settlement hierarchy which indicates territorial authority and formalized surplus extraction; and the existence from the early seventh century of special commercial or trading settlements—the *wics* or *emporia*—which may be linked to the centralization of economic and political power (Hodges 1982; Arnold 1988; Carver 1989; Scull 1993; 1999; Carver 2005: 497–9). There is, however, little or no reliable contemporary documentary evidence relating to the fifth- and sixth-century societies from which these polities emerged. The study of the fifth to seventh centuries in England therefore straddles the divide between history and pre- or proto-history for which archaeological material is the prime source. Integrating the two perspectives is desirable but can be complex and problematic. The limitations of early written sources for society and economy in fifth- to seventh-century England, and the ideological nature of much early history, are widely accepted and understood (Yorke 1993; 1999). Historical retrospection risks anachronism; archaeological models derived from historical retrospection risk circularity; and generalizing archaeological approaches, if applied insensitively, may mask significant variation and complexity (Scull 1993: 65–7).

Nonetheless, source-critical approaches which recognize the limitations, potential, and applicability of different data-sets, and which explicitly apply appropriate models drawn from the wider social sciences as well as medieval history, can successfully integrate archaeology and textual sources, both historical and literary, to deliver a new or deeper understanding of early medieval societies and the contexts of social action (cf. Hedeager 1992; Herschend 1998: 9-62; Carver 2000; Blair 2005: 182–245). In the absence of reliable contemporary accounts this contribution therefore adopts such an approach, using generalizing social and economic models to identify and interpret aspects of the archaeological record which may reflect, or have been deliberate statements of, power relations. It does so within the broader explanatory framework provided by evolutionary models of state formation which have been applied to early medieval England, but focuses on individual action and agency. It recognizes that cultural systems are not a fixed arena, independent of the social actors who perform in them, but are themselves constructs, negotiated and renegotiated (Bourdieu 1977; Giddens 1979). Social, economic, and political transformations are the aggregates of innumerable individual interactions and relationships; social structures may be seen as epiphenomena, the products of individuals' social strategies (Barth 1967).

Substantivist perspectives in cultural anthropology have emphasized the embedded nature of social, political, and economic relationships in many pre-industrial societies; the importance of ties of obligation and reciprocity in maintaining social and political relations; ways in which a deliberate tipping of the balance of reciprocity may be used as a strategy to build power through obligation; and the importance of gift exchange in embodying and articulating such relationships (Mauss 1965; Polanyi 1944; 1957; Sahlins 1974; Layton 1997: 98–126; cf. Grierson 1959; Charles-Edwards 1976). These are echoed in the heroic literature which has conditioned our view of elite male roles and relationships in migration-period Germanic society (Bazelmans 1999). The ideal relationship between lord and retainer in a military society hinged on loyalty unto death in exchange for material reward and prestige: gifts which defined and were commensurate with the retainer's worth. The retinue, based on such ties, provided leaders with the means to extend their power through military adventure. Conversely, in politically fissile and segmented societies, the need to attract and retain followers may have acted to fuel competition through military adventure. Such dynamics may have been one of the factors that helped precipitate population movement from North Germany and South Scandinavia to Britain in the fifth century (Scull 1995: 75–6). If so, it may be presumed that the institution of the retinue, and the reciprocal ties that it embodied, were also a feature of insular Germanic societies in the fifth and sixth centuries. Elements of this ideal were certainly important in Bede's England, and reciprocity—often mediated through gift-giving—was of a wider fundamental importance to kinship and social relations in contemporary society (Campbell 1979: 8–10; Charles-Edwards 1997).

Gift exchange creates and transforms relationships between living contemporaries but may also extend into the realms of gods and ancestors (Dumont 1980; Bazelmans 1999). Ethnography has focused on material exchange, but in focusing on social interactions in migration-period societies in England it may also be useful to consider non-material or permissive transactions such as allowing access to skills, networks, or opportunities that may have been socially controlled, conferring permanent privileges, or rendering labour within the context of reciprocal or constrained social relationships (cf. Charles-Edwards 1997: 195–200). Inheritance as a distinct mode of exchange may also have been a significant element in some strategies of social reproduction and competition. The formal distinction normally drawn between commodity and gift exchange remains useful at some levels. However, it appears likely both that the commodity exchange apparent in the archaeological record from the seventh century developed from earlier socially-embedded elite exchange networks, and that it was controlled by elites (Scull 1992b; 1997; Saunders 2002). Boundaries between modes and spheres of exchange may therefore appear blurred in a tributary or redistributive economy where access to commodity exchange, or its benefits, may have been constrained and embedded in social relations.

Acts of giving and exchange in the past are not directly observable, but when material which has been exchanged enters the archaeological record through deliberate deposition, loss, or discard, it does so as the end product and fossilization of a chain of human actions. Analysis of context, provenance, distribution, character, and inherent value or investment in an item will then allow judgements to be made about the likely mechanisms and modes of acquisition and exchange, and the economic and social spheres in which these took place. Archaeological models of such past dynamics are by their nature forensic, and depend (implicitly or explicitly) on historical or anthropological models.

In theory any item or property might be given as a gift. The reward of landrights to a retainer for his lifetime might be seen as the peak of the exchanges which characterized the ideal retainer–lord relationship (Charles-Edwards 1976: 181–3). This is not, however, something that we are likely to recognize often, if at all, in the archaeological record (although burials associated with the excavated settlement at Carlton Colville, Suffolk, which may represent a short-lived episode of tenure or lordship in the later seventh century, perhaps indicate how such a gift might be recognized archaeologically: see Scull 2009a). Archaeological evidence for gift-giving is therefore usually seen, or sought, in the recognition of material culture items with apparent symbolic qualities, and/or of high value and scarcity in the sphere in which they circulated and were deposited. It is important to emphasize the point, which also underpins ranking approaches to social identity in early medieval mortuary studies, that items which appear invested with value or significance in one context or social sphere may not carry the same charge in another.

In practice, therefore, assemblages from furnished burials (inhumations and cremations) constitute the main archaeological source for considerations of gift exchange. Social identities and circumstances may have many dimensions, and how these are expressed in burial may transform rather than simply reflect their importance in life. The issues this poses for archaeological interpretation have been exhaustively discussed and remain a central area of debate (Ucko 1969; Leach 1979; Pader 1982; Dickinson, this volume). There is, nonetheless, a consensus that consistencies in the provision of grave-goods and other aspects of mortuary practice in the fifth to seventh centuries in England demonstrate a concern to express or assert aspects of the identity of the deceased, both as an individual and as a member of family, kin, household, or lineage. Mortuary practice provided common symbolic vocabularies at local, regional, and inter-regional level, within which individual provision might be almost infinitely nuanced; some aspects of variation also indicate social and economic inequalities (Shephard 1979; Pader 1982; J. Richards 1987; Härke 1992a; Brush 1993; Lucy 1998; Stoodley 1999; Carver 2005: 312–13, 490–3; Scull 2009a; 2009b).

The expression of identity in burial was fashioned by those who buried the dead and, while appropriate to the social roles and personas of the deceased, the symbolic message also conveyed the circumstances, aspirations, and identities of the survivors. Material items in burials do not constitute direct evidence for gift exchange, but the burials in which they occur symbolize the social spheres in which they circulated and had significance. If the identities expressed in burial are to some extent idealized, then the symbolic language of the burial assemblages may amplify ideals of identity and social relationships. Items embodying such social identities, relationships, roles, and obligations may therefore be deliberately selected for inclusion in grave assemblages. We may acknowledge the complexities of inferring social reality from burial evidence, and the biases arising from differential preservation and recovery, but the fact that these are symbolic deposits structured by social practice and intention may actually enhance our ability to identify social spheres and the items deemed significant within them. Archaeology should therefore allow an evolutionary perspective which is also sensitive to the local and individual.

Power and unequal social relations operated, and their material correlates may be observed in the fifth- to seventh-century archaeology of England, at different scales and at different social levels. The symbolic expression of social distance in burial also changed in character and intensity over time. It is argued here that the fundamental social structures, constraints, and expectations that governed the behaviour of paramount dynasties in regional or inter-regional political arenas of the late sixth and seventh centuries were founded in structures and relationships that also operated at the level of the household, kin, and clan, and that these had promoted the development of social and political inequalities through the fifth and sixth centuries.

Archaeological evidence for community and social structure over much of southern and eastern England in the fifth and sixth centuries is consistent with a model of internally-ranked descent groups exploiting ancestral territories. The mortuary evidence allows the identification of social and economic inequalities which, when amplified and reproduced between lineages over time through processes of peer-competition and competitive exclusion, would lead to the establishment of local hegemonies (Bassett 1989; Scull 1993; 1999). The fact that there is little clear archaeological evidence for regional or paramount elites before the later sixth century may be explained by the proposal that the local chieftaincies established through such peer-competition were personal and impermanent. Thus some accentuation of social ranking might be expected, but no marked social stratification until one group was able to establish a more stable paramount status. This provides a plausible context for princely burials, whose appearance in the archaeological record in the late sixth century is broadly contemporary with other indications of emergent social stratification and political centralization. These may be attributed to attempts by new paramount elites to consolidate and perpetuate new configurations of power and authority and to legitimize a new status. Such transitions might be effected in a number of ways, all of which might become axes of competition: manipulation of external political and exchange contacts; manipulation of symbolism and ideology; manipulation of the past, descent, and ethnic or cultural identity; and manipulation of the means of production through changes in landholding and territorial organization (Scull 1993: 76–7; 1995: 77–9; 1999: 20–3).

The archaeology of the later sixth and seventh centuries may thus be read as indicating increasing social distance between elite groups and other segments of society, and the centralization of political and economic power. This is consistent with the emergence of increasingly powerful dynasties able to consolidate regional or inter-regional hegemony, and the emergence of the historically-attested kingdom structure may therefore be linked plausibly to archaeological indications of a change from a ranked to a stratified social hierarchy, the territorialization of power, and increasing elite control of agrarian surplus and long-distance exchange.

Processual archaeological models, developed from long-term social evolutionary perspectives, have emphasized external factors, and in particular competition for access to prestige goods through long-distance exchange, and peer-polity dynamics, as critical stimulants of the internal social and political developments which culminated in the kingdom structure of the seventh century (Hodges 1982; 1986; Arnold 1988; Hodges 1989). A limited number of material culture types and raw materials which might be seen as the fossils of embedded or socially-restricted exchange contacts with continental Europe or Scandinavia have been identified in burials of the late fifth to early seventh centuries (P. Richards 1983; Arnold 1988: 51–73; Huggett 1988). Distributional analysis suggests at least two major axes of overseas contacts with Kent having a primary or near-monopolistic role in the articulation of exchange with the Merovingian continent in the sixth century through which, it is argued, Kentish elites were able to establish a political dominance in south and east England. The occurrence of items such as cast copper-alloy vessels from the east Mediterranean and crystal balls and amethyst beads in graves outside Kent may therefore be seen as evidence for socially-embedded transactions with Kentish elites, and the items themselves as the objects of gift exchange. The coincidence of evidence for contacts with the Merovingian continent (including the acquisition of continental gold coinage) and indications of an early emergence of royal authority in Kent, and to a lesser extent in the Upper Thames Valley, appears at a general level to support the hypothesis that external exchange contacts helped precipitate or amplify trends towards the development of a permanent social and political hierarchy (Hawkes 1982; Scull 1992b).

The general usefulness of such processual models is undeniable but among the criticisms that may be levelled at their specific application to England in the fifth to seventh centuries are that these have taken insufficient account of the internal structures and dynamics of insular societies; that they have tended to underestimate the sophistication and complexity that might be expected of societies with their roots in the continental Roman Iron Age; and that they over-emphasize the significance of long-distance external exchange contacts at the expense of the fundamental social and economic resource: land (Scull 1993; 1999). The possibility that fissile political and social structures leading to military adventure may have been one factor in the fifth-century migrations, and that the noble retinue or warband would have been a key institution in such ventures, has already been noted. It is important to emphasize that the fundamental structures which allowed their parent societies to maintain social hierarchies and local and regional hegemonies were embodied in the first Germanic communities in England, that migration may have acted to accentuate some structures of power, and that this may have been one motivation to migration in politically fissile societies (Scull 1995: 75–9; cf. Anthony 1990).

It is therefore argued here that the major fault-line of peer-competition in migration-period society in England, whether at a local level or in the regional dynastic conflicts recorded by Bede, was between kindreds or lineages, and that both the motivation and capacity for competition and conflict (which fuelled the processes of competitive exclusion whereby higher levels of social differentiation, political integration, and territorial hegemony were established by the seventh century from the smaller-scale and more fragmented political groupings of the fifth and sixth centuries) were a feature of Germanic society in England from the outset (Scull 1992a; 1993; 1995; cf. Charles-Edwards 1997; Härke 1997). The range of social and political transactions articulated by gift exchange are thus placed in the spectrum of strategies of competition, of which aggressive organized violence was the most extreme and potentially the most rewarding.

Viewed in this way it is possible to shift perspective from regional and inter-regional spatial distributions and to focus instead on how items which might have been acquired through gift exchange were used in the construction of statements of identity and aspiration in burial, and what in turn this might tell us of the relationships and transactions they articulated, and the social spheres within which these took place. As noted above, attention has focused on foreign exotica which may be interpreted as indicating the circulation of prestige goods within elite social spheres. However, gift exchange and its correlates (access to expertise or craft skill, or privilege) would in segmentary societies have operated at a variety of social, economic, and spatial levels, not only between the elite individuals and kindreds who wielded local or regional hegemony, but also within and between households, kindreds, lineage groups, across generations, and across the boundaries between the spheres of the living and those of gods and ancestors.

The material culture assemblage from the Mound 1 ship burial at Sutton Hoo may be read as a highly complex symbolic statement of the social identities, roles, and relationships that sustained power and status at the level of the paramount elite in the early seventh century. At one level it demonstrates the wide geographical range of the contacts enjoyed (directly or indirectly) by elite lineages, and the scale of the portable wealth they could accrue from which items for burial might be selected. Some components of the assemblage, notably the Byzantine silver, may be explained plausibly as having been acquired as diplomatic gifts; the hanging bowls, east Mediterranean copper-alloy vessel, the gold coinage, and even the drinking horns embody elite contacts with western Britain and the Continent; weapons and textiles may also embody links with Scandinavia (Bruce-Mitford 1975; 1978; 1983; Carver 1986: 102–10; Hinton 2005: 58–62).

Among the statements asserting authority and dominance that were intended in this burial are those of wealth, worth, and reward. The burial assemblage as treasure (Carver 2000) embodies or asserts the worth of the deceased, and the kin that buried him; symbolizes the range and value of the elite relationships from which he benefited; and makes an emphatic statement about the ability or potential of the lord, or lordly kin, to reward followers and retainers. The treasure is at least in part composed of gifts, and has been selected from the store from which gifts might in turn be given to the worthy: the implicit offer of wealth and reward may have been an important component of the message to an audience which might have included those whose personal obligations to the lordly kin had been ruptured by the death. Other less spectacular elements of the grave assemblage may also be read as symbolizing reciprocal social relations. In particular, the drinking vessels, tub, cauldron and other containers, the lyre, and gaming pieces may have symbolized the lord's obligation of hospitality to his followers (Bruce-Mitford 1983; Werner 1982). One of many interlocking readings of the grave, therefore, is that it presented to the audience of the burial a symbolic microcosm of social relationships, symbolizing the place of the elite individual within the networks of reciprocity and obligation—both peer and subordinate—by which he, his kin, and his peers and competitors sought to structure society and reproduce power to their advantage.

Although none is as spectacular as Sutton Hoo Mound 1, the same symbolism, mediated through the deposition of the same material culture types, can be seen in other princely burials of the late sixth and early seventh centuries, as at Taplow, Broomfield, and Prittlewell. It may also be possible to discern in some of these graves a specific and personal relationship embodied in particular items. The great buckle and other elements of the assemblage from Taplow may have been a gift from a Kentish overlord to a subordinate or sub-king in the Thames Valley (Webster 2000: 55–6). The silver spoons from Sutton Hoo Mound 1 and Prittlewell have been interpreted as baptismal gifts (Bruce-Mitford 1983: 132–46; MoLAS 2004). Given the evidence for a link between the power of a Christian overlord and the conversion of kings (Campbell 1973), and the relationship between convert and baptismal sponsor, such an interpretation of these items would identify them as symbolizing a relationship with an overlord, making a statement about the nature of power and what sustains it, and place them firmly in the context of gift exchange in the ideological and political spheres. At a lower social and political level, sword-rings, in England a feature of sixth-century burials in east Kent, have been interpreted as gifted symbols of rank or favour, evoking the role of lord as ring-giver (Evison 1967: 63; Fischer 2007: 23–4). Their occurrence in graves has been interpreted as indicating that the deceased enjoyed a special rank or favour, possibly a place in an administrative or jurisdictional as well as a social and political hierarchy (Evison 1987: 120–1; Scull 1992b). These factors, and the apparent concern among higher-status kindreds to symbolize in burial a subordinate relationship, are consistent with interpretations which would see an early establishment of paramount regional authority in east Kent in the sixth century.

The princely graves of the late sixth and early seventh centuries are extreme statements but they employ the same broad symbolic language as contemporary furnished graves of a lower social status and those of the later fifth to mid sixth centuries. The proposition that furnished burial, as a vehicle for statements about identity of the deceased and the kindred, symbolized as well the place of the deceased within contemporary social networks of reciprocity and obligation, is also equally applicable. This focuses attention on the extent to which the material culture items through which social identities were constructed in burial carried plural or multiple symbolic charges, and how their deposition at death may have related to their ownership, acquisition, and circulation during the lifetime of the deceased.

It is possible to examine this through the example of weapon burial. The provision of weapons was a primary symbol of masculine identity. It is argued convincingly that it was appropriate to individuals who had the right or duty of recourse to violence, and that the warrior status it symbolized was a widely-shared ideological construct for which one qualified by age and descent rather than by necessary participation in combat (Härke 1992a: 182–95; Stoodley 1999: 106–8). Within the segment of the male population entitled to weapon burial, differential provision of grave goods and the provision of specific weapon types and combinations indicate status distinctions which may be equated with membership or leadership of a free family at one end of the scale to individuals of a local or regional importance at the other (Härke 1992b). Deposition of weapons in burial does however appear to have been strictly constrained by age at death, expressing age categories which cut across other social identities. It is possible to identify—at the ages of around 3 years, 12–14 years, and 18–20 years—age-thresholds in the life of the individual at which the giving and receipt of weapons, or the right to bear weapons, affirmed individual social identity and the relationships between individual, kin, peers, lord, and subordinates, all of which in turn were embodied in the aspects of identity at death which were symbolized by the provision of weapons as grave goods.

Heroic literature identifies the bestowal of arms by king or lord upon follower or retainer as the pivotal transaction in the idealized elite sphere (Bazelmans 1999). In the archaeological record, sword-rings may be the clearest echo of such ideals in the real world. There is no reason to doubt that such social transactions took place in the fifth to seventh centuries in England, and that some weapons known from burials were given and received in this way. We may question, however, whether every adult entitled to bear arms, or to be buried with them, obtained them as a member of a noble retinue. It is inherently probable, especially in the context of the relatively small-scale and local political structures of the later fifth and earlier sixth centuries, that rites of passage of puberty and adulthood were effected within the household, kindred, or lineage, or within a local network of alliances. (Rites of passage associated with weaning are by definition almost certain to have been marked within the nuclear family.) Articulating such rites of passage by gifting weapons, if undertaken outside the immediate kin or family, would create a relationship of obligation which might create or cement an alliance. If undertaken within the immediate family or kindred, it might serve to conserve group resource and focus ties of authority and obligation upon the immediate social group. Both strategies would reinforce and reproduce structures of power and authority, and both would have social and political advantages and disadvantages (in the former case obligation may cut across family or kin interests, in the latter case internal group strength is emphasized at the expense of external support). In both cases resource is invested in social reproduction.

Whether or not the weapons selected for burial are those which were gifted, the burial of a male with weapons would thus signal not only the individual masculine social identity but also the social roles, relationships, and obligations which the deceased had accrued through the social rituals that confirmed his right to the status that they symbolized. Equivalent significances may be proposed for the provision of grave goods which symbolized feminine identities, in particular dress jewellery, which also appears to have been structured by age at death (Stoodley 1999: 106–12). For adults some symbolism of the social transactions surrounding marriage, essential for biological and social reproduction and itself a social transaction creating and cementing kin alliances, is to be expected. In both male and female spheres consideration of the material resource invested in social reproduction should also be extended to include socially-embedded constraints on the raw materials and craft skills needed to create the socially-restricted items through which identities were articulated.

Furnished burial may be considered an extension of gift-giving into the realm of the ancestors, and giving gifts to the dead in the form of grave goods should not necessarily be seen as alienating individual or kin property. Rather, it may be interpreted as a reciprocal transaction intended to reinforce the identity and status both of the deceased and of the living kin: gifts to the ancestors enhanced the worth of the ancestral lineage and thus the status of the living descendants, and may indeed have been intended to transform aspects of kin identity.

Manipulation of descent and identity have been identified as strategies of legitimation. The phenomenon of princely burial is best interpreted in this light and similar motivations may be read in the assemblages placed in other and earlier graves. An example is the inclusion of material culture items of South Scandinavian origin or South Scandinavian type, in particular D-bracteates and silver relief brooches, in the graves of higher-status Kentish women in the earlier sixth century. Sonia Hawkes (1981: 324–28; 1982: 70–4) has argued that the relief brooches were the ancestral heirlooms of a South Scandinavian (Jutish) aristocracy, disposed of at a time when connections with Merovingian Gaul were of paramount importance for Kentish elites and so when their currency both as dress accessories and as signals of social and political affiliation had come to an end. Rather than simple disposal, however, using and burying such items in assemblages of dress jewellery otherwise composed of contemporary Frankish types might be read as affirming simultaneously the link between status and descent and identification with a new social and cultural identity. Another possible reading is suggested by the work of Fischer (2007), who argues that South Scandinavian descent was a fictive identity adopted by Kentish elites in the face of Merovingian cultural and political hegemony. The circulation and use—in life and in burial—of objects of South Scandinavian type may therefore be seen as an element of strategies of distinction within a broader symbolic acknowledgement of Merovingian Frankish cultural and political hegemony.

Burial was thus an arena of social and political competition. It provided a powerful medium for assertions of status and identity, assertions that might be used to reinforce claims to dominance or authority through appeal to the past or by setting up inequalities through competitive consumption and display. In addition to investment in the burial assemblage, ties of social obligation might also be deployed to provide the labour investment seen in mound burial, and there is a strong likelihood that other aspects of burial practice, such as a funeral meal, may also have functioned to reinforce and symbolize ties of obligation and dependence.

Inheritance, as a mode of exchange between generations, is in many ways the antithesis of gifting items to the dead through furnished burial. Where followed by gifts to the ancestors, however, it may also be viewed as the initial action in a reciprocal relationship. Because inheritance involves retaining material in the sphere of the living it leaves few direct traces in the archaeological record except where recognizably curated items occur in direct association with later material. Consideration of antique material in early medieval burials has often centred on the re-use of Roman materials or cautionary tales about the effect of the heirloom factor on chronological models, with interpretation favouring magical or amuletic significance, symbolic substitution, scrap, or simply disposal of the outmoded. All of these may be valid approaches and interpretations, but it is also important to recognize that heirlooms, as items which embody and symbolize past actions and present identities, may act as powerful media for social cohesion and reproduction both when retained in the sphere of the living through inheritance and when gifted to (or retained by) the ancestors—that is, in our case, buried as grave-goods (Bazelmans 1999; Härke 2000).

Curated material, when selected for burial, was part of the contemporary assemblage circulating in the sphere of the living and had contemporary significance. In some cases, therefore, the burial of heirloom material (genuine or fictive) should be seen as an emphatic statement of identity with a sacrificial element and intended to unite ancestors and the living. Contexts for such actions might include the assertion of new status or circumstances, or a response to threat. The burial of a sword with an old Sjörup-style scabbard mouthpiece in what may be regarded as the founder burial of the small inhumation cemetery at Spong Hill might be an example of the former: a statement of special identity and an appeal to Continental warrior descent by a lineage who had established some local status and authority and who sought to signal this through differentiation in burial (Hills *et al.* 1984; Scull 1992a: 18–19). The presence of material culture items of South Scandinavian type in sixth-century Kentish graves, referred to above, may be an example of the latter.

The evidence of the *emporia* indicates the development of larger-scale and more overtly commercial long-distance exchange from the early seventh century and there are strong arguments that the power of regional elites was reinforced by their ability to channel and control exchange with the Continent and the benefits—in revenue, prestige, and authority—that flowed from it. The seventh-century *emporia* may be seen as special-purpose sites through which surplus from networks of elite-controlled estate holdings and obligations could be directed towards foreign exchange partners (Scull 1997; 2002; Saunders 2002). These overseas contacts represent a development from the smaller-scale socially-embedded elite exchange networks of the sixth century, but the change in the scale and organization of activity suggests a threshold of development in elite ability to extract and redeploy the surplus of the land at about the time that assertions of paramount social and political status are being made in princely burial.

This emphasizes that any consideration of the relationship between exchange and power structures in fifth- to seventh-century England must take into account the fundamental importance of land as the basis of social, economic, and political capital. Following Charles-Edwards' discussion of links between the territorialization of authority and changing relationships between status and landholding in pre-Viking England, it is possible to model ways in which inheritance, landholding, and pressure on land as a social as well as an economic resource acted to promote social and political stratification (Charles-Edwards 1972; Scull 1993: 77–9; 1999: 22).

He argued that in early Anglo-Saxon society status as a free man (which may be taken to include the household) depended upon a minimum landholding and that if this was not available status by birth could not be perpetuated. If this was the case among the fifth-century Germanic settlers of eastern Britain then over time any population increase within the higher-status segments of the population would drive a social imperative towards territorial expansion as individuals in each generation required sufficient land to maintain and pass on their status by birth. Any limit on territorial expansion—physical or political—would lead to pressure on land as a social resource. One result of this might be external conflict. Another, internal to kindred or local polity, might be to increase the number of higher-status individuals dependent upon a local chieftain or leader in a client–lord relationship, a process which would concentrate political power and control of land (directly or indirectly) in fewer and fewer hands. Either would enhance or accelerate the social and political dynamics whereby a group or individual might establish a local or wider regional hegemony, and in the long run convert temporary hegemony to permanent overlordship. Consolidating control of the land's wealth would provide new paramount elites with the economic and political capital to consolidate their new status and exploit external exchange contacts in new ways and on a larger scale.

Finally, in considering social transactions and power it is appropriate to refer briefly to the importance of ideological endorsement and legitimation. It is not impossible that the critical factor which consolidated the seventh-century kingdom structure as we know it was the influence of divine support through the Christian (and Roman) church. Gift exchange is a tangible expression of reciprocity but reciprocity may also operate with intangibles: ideological sanction for a new level of hierarchy and overlordship repaid in turn by elite support for conversion. In this context it is worth considering the possibility that tension between furnished burial and inheritance as different modes of exchange between generations, perhaps amplified by Churchmen's views on the proper recipients and dynamics of gifts and rewards and a corresponding shift in perceptions of the relationship between the living and the ancestors, was one factor which contributed to the abandonment of furnished burial by the end of the seventh century.

Social change is complex and its study must consider both the internal structures and dynamics of society and economy, and the external contacts and circumstances that may have triggered new trajectories or accelerated the pace of change. The issues and models discussed above indicate how a generalizing archaeology which is sensitive to the local and specific, and to human agency, has the potential to integrate understanding of social and political dynamics at different scales, and to illuminate at some level the circumstances, opportunities, and choices facing individuals in what was sometimes a brutally competitive social and political environment.

REFERENCES

ANTHONY, D. (1990). 'Migration in archaeology: the baby and the bathwater'. *American Anthropologist* 92: 894–914.

ARNOLD, C. (1988). *An Archaeology of the Early Anglo-Saxon Kingdoms*. London: Routledge.

BARTH, F. (1967). 'On the study of social change'. *American Anthropologist* 69: 661–9.

BASSETT, S. (1989). 'In search of the origins of Anglo-Saxon kingdoms', in S. Bassett (ed.), *The Origins of Anglo-Saxon Kingdoms*. London: Leicester University Press, 1–27.

BAZELMANS, J. (1999). *By Weapons made Worthy: Lords, Retainers and their Relationship in Beowulf*. Amsterdam: Amsterdam University Press.

BLAIR, J. (2005). *The Church in Anglo-Saxon Society*. Oxford: Oxford University Press.

BOURDIEU, P. (1977). *Outline of a Theory of Practice*. Trans R. Nice. Cambridge: Cambridge University Press.

BRUCE-MITFORD, R. (1975). *The Sutton Hoo Ship Burial*, Volume 1. London: British Museum Press.

——(1978). *The Sutton Hoo Ship Burial*, Volume 2. London: British Museum Press.

——(1983). *The Sutton Hoo Ship Burial*, Volume 3. London: British Museum Press.

BRUSH, K. (1993). *Adorning the Dead: the Social Significance of Early Anglo-Saxon Funerary Dress in England (Fifth to Seventh Centuries AD)*. Unpublished PhD thesis, University of Cambridge.

CAMPBELL, J. (1973). 'Observations on the conversion of England'. *Ampleforth Journal* 78: 12–26.

——(1979). *Bede's 'Reges' and 'Principes'*. Jarrow Lecture.

CARVER, M. (1986). 'Sutton Hoo in context'. *Settimane di Studio del Centro Italiano di studi sull'alto medioevo* 32: 77–123.

——(1989). 'Kingship and material culture in early Anglo-Saxon East Anglia', in S. Bassett (ed.), *The Origins of Anglo-Saxon Kingdoms*. London: Leicester University Press, 141–58.

——(2000). 'Burial as poetry: the context of treasure in early medieval graves', in E. Tyler (ed.), *Treasure in the Medieval West*. York: York Medieval Press, 25–48.

——(2005). *Sutton Hoo: A Seventh-Century Princely Burial Ground and its Context*. Reports of the Research Committee of the Society of Antiquaries of London 69. London: British Museum Press.

CHARLES-EDWARDS, T. (1972). 'Kinship, status and the origins of the hide'. *Past and Present* 56: 3–33.

——(1976). 'The distinction between land and moveable wealth in Anglo-Saxon England', in P. Sawyer (ed.), *Medieval Settlement: Continuity and Change*. London: Edward Arnold, 180–90.

——(1997). 'Anglo-Saxon kinship revisited', in Hines (ed.), *The Anglo-Saxons*, 171–210.

DUMONT, L. (1980). *Homo Hierarchicus: The Caste System and its Implications*. London: University of Chicago Press.

EVISON, V. (1967). 'The Dover ring-sword and other sword-rings and beads'. *Archaeologia* 101: 63–118.

——(1987). *Dover: the Buckland Anglo-Saxon Cemetery*. HBMCE Archaeological Report 3. London: Historic Buildings and Monuments Commission England.

FISCHER, S. (2007). *Les Seigneurs des Anneaux*. Bulletin de Liaison de l'Association française d'Archéologie mérovingeienne Hors Série 2. Condé-sur-Noireau: AFAM.

GIDDENS, A. (1979). *Central Problems in Social Theory: Action, Structure and Contradiction in Social Analysis.* London: Macmillan.

GRIERSON, P. (1959). 'Commerce in the Dark Ages: a critique of the evidence'. *Transactions of the Royal Historical Society,* 5th series, 9: 123–40.

HÄRKE, H. (1992a). *Angelsächsische Waffengräber des 5 bis 7 Jahrhunderts.* Zeitschrift für Archäologie des Mittelalters Beiheft 6. Cologne: Rheinland-Verlag.

——(1992b). 'Changing symbols in a changing society: the Anglo-Saxon weapon burial rite in the seventh century', in M. Carver (ed.), *The Age of Sutton Hoo: the Seventh Century in Northwestern-Europe.* Woodbridge: Boydell, 149–65.

——(1997). 'Early Anglo-Saxon social structure', in Hines (ed.), *The Anglo-Saxons,* 125–70.

——(2000). 'The circulation of weapons in Anglo-Saxon society', in F. Theuws and J. Nelson (eds.), *Rituals of Power: From Late Antiquity to the Early Middle Ages.* Leiden: Brill, 377–99.

HAWKES, S. (1981). 'The gold bracteates from sixth-century Anglo-Saxon graves in Kent, in the light of a new find from Finglesham'. *Frühmittelalterliche Studien* 15: 316–70.

——(1982). 'Anglo-Saxon Kent c. 425–725', in P. Leach (ed.), *Archaeology in Kent to AD 1500.* CBA Research Report 48. London: Council for British Archaeology, 64–78.

HEDEAGER, L. (1992). *Iron Age Societies: From Tribe to State in Northern Europe 500 BC to AD 700.* Oxford: Blackwell.

HERSCHEND, F. (1998). *The Idea of the Good in Late Iron Age society.* Uppsala: Uppsala University Department of Archaeology and Ancient History.

HILLS, C., PENN, R., and RICKETT, R. (1984). *The Anglo-Saxon Cemetery at Spong Hill, North Elmham,* Part 3: *Catalogue of Inhumations.* East Anglian Archaeology Report 21. Gressenhall: Norfolk Archaeological Unit.

HINES, J. (ed.) (1997). *The Anglo-Saxons from the Migration Period to the Eighth Century: an Ethnographic Perspective.* Woodbridge: Boydell.

HINTON, D. (2005). *Gold and Gilt, Pots and Pins: Possessions and People in Medieval Britain.* Oxford: Oxford University Press.

HODGES, R. (1982). *Dark Age Economics: the Origins of Towns and Trade AD 600–1000.* London: Duckworth.

——(1986). 'Peer-polity interaction and socio-political change in Anglo-Saxon England', in C. Renfrew and J. Cherry (eds.), *Peer-Polity Interaction and Socio-Political Change.* Cambridge: Cambridge University Press, 69–78.

——(1989). *The Anglo-Saxon Achievement: Archaeology and the Beginnings of English Society.* London: Duckworth.

HUGGETT, J. (1988). 'Imported grave goods and the early Anglo-Saxon economy'. *Medieval Archaeology* 32: 63–96.

KIRBY, D. (1991). *The Earliest English kings.* London: Routledge.

LAYTON, R. (1997). *An Introduction to Theory in Anthropology.* Cambridge: Cambridge University Press.

LEACH, R. (1979). 'Summary', in B. Burnham and J. Kingsbury (eds), *Space, Hierarchy and Society.* British Archaeological Reports S 59. Oxford: British Archaeological Reports, 119–24.

LUCY, S. (1998). *The Early Anglo-Saxon Cemeteries of East Yorkshire: an Analysis and Reinterpretation.* British Archaeological Reports 272. Oxford: British Archaeological Reports.

MAUSS, M. (1965). *The Gift: Forms and Functions of Exchange in Archaic Societies.* Trans. I. Cunnison. London: Cohen and West.

MoLAS (Museum of London Archaeology Service) (2004). *The Prittlewell Prince: The Discovery of a Rich Anglo-Saxon Burial in Essex*. London: Museum of London Archaeology Service.

Pader, E.-J. (1982). *Symbolism, Social Relations and the Interpretation of Mortuary Remains*. British Archaeological Reports S130. Oxford: British Archaeological Reports.

Polanyi, K. (1944). *Origins of our Time: the Great Transformation*. New York: Holt, Rinehart and Winston.

——(1957). 'The economy as instituted process', in K. Polanyi, C. Ahrensberg, and H. Pearson (eds.), *Trade and Market in the Early Empires*. New York: Free Press, 243–70.

Richards, J. (1987). *The Significance of the Form and Decoration of Anglo-Saxon Cremation Urns*. British Archaeological Reports 166. Oxford: British Archaeological Reports.

Richards, P. (1983). *Byzantine Bronze Vessels in England and Europe: the Origins of Anglo-Saxon Trade*. Unpublished PhD Thesis, University of Cambridge.

Sahlins, M. (1974). *Stone Age Economics*. London: Tavistock.

Saunders, T. (2002). 'Early medieval *Emporia* and the tributary social function', in D. Hill and R. Cowie (eds), *Wics: the Early Medieval Trading Centres of Northern Europe*. Sheffield: Sheffield Academic Press, 7–13.

Scull, C. (1992a). 'Before Sutton Hoo: structures of power and society in early East Anglia', in M. Carver (ed.), *The Age of Sutton Hoo: the Seventh Century in Northwestern-Europe*. Woodbridge: Boydell, 4–23.

——(1992b). 'Scales and weights in early Anglo-Saxon England'. *Archaeological Journal* 147: 183–215.

——(1993). 'Archaeology, early Anglo-Saxon society and the origins of Anglo-Saxon kingdoms'. *Anglo-Saxon Studies in Archaeology and History*, 6: 65–82.

——(1995). 'Approaches to material culture and social dynamics in the migration period of eastern England', in J. Bintliff and H. Hamerow (eds.), *Europe between Late Antiquity and the Middle Ages: Recent Archaeological and Historical Research in Western and Southern Europe*. British Archaeological Reports S 617. Oxford: Tempus Reparatum, 71–83.

——(1997). 'Urban centres in pre-Viking England?', in Hines (ed.), *The Anglo-Saxons*, 269–310.

——(1999). 'Social archaeology and Anglo-Saxon kingdom origins'. *Anglo-Saxon Studies in Archaeology and History* 10: 17–24.

——(2002). 'Ipswich: developments and context of an urban precursor in the seventh century', in B. Hårdh and L. Larsson (eds.), *Central Places in the Migration and Merovingian Periods*. Uppåkrastudier 6; Acta Archaeologica Lundensia Ser 8, 39. Stockholm: Almqvist and Wiksell, 303–16.

——(2009a). 'The human burials', in J. Tipper, S. Lucy, and A. Dickens, *The Anglo-Saxon Settlement and Cemetery at Bloodmoor Hill, Carlton Colville, Suffolk*. East Anglian Archaeology 131. Cambridge: Cambridge Archaeological Unit.

——(2009b). *Early Medieval (late 5th Century AD—early 8th Century AD) Cemeteries at Boss Hall and Buttermarket, Ipswich, Suffolk*. Leeds: Society for Medieval Archaeology.

Shephard, J. (1979). 'The social identity of the individual in isolated barrows and barrow cemeteries in Anglo-Saxon England', in B. Burnham and J. Kingsbury (eds), *Space, Hierarchy and Society*. British Archaeological Reports S59. Oxford: British Archaeological Reports, 47–80.

STOODLEY, N. (1999). *The Spindle and the Spear: A Critical Enquiry into the Construction and Meaning of Gender in the Early Anglo-Saxon Burial Rite.* British Archaeological Reports 288. Oxford: British Archaeological Reports.

UCKO, P. (1969). 'Ethnography and archaeological interpretation of funerary remains'. *World Archaeology* 1: 262–77.

WEBSTER, L. (2000). 'Ideal and reality: versions of treasure in the early Anglo-Saxon world', in E. Tyler (ed.), *Treasure in the Medieval West.* York: York Medieval Press, 49–59.

WERNER, J. (1982). 'Das Schiffgrab von Sutton Hoo. Forschungsgeschichte und Informationsstand zwischen 1939 und 1980'. *Germania* 60: 193–228.

YORKE, B. (1990). *Kings and Kingdoms of Early Anglo-Saxon England.* London: Seaby.

——(1993). 'Fact or fiction? The written evidence for the fifth and sixth centuries AD'. *Anglo-Saxon Studies in Archaeology and History* 6: 1–6.

——(1999). 'The origins of Anglo-Saxon kingdoms: the contribution of written sources'. *Anglo-Saxon Studies in Archaeology and History* 10: 25–9.

CHAPTER 45

IMAGE AND POWER IN THE EARLY SAXON PERIOD

MÄRIT GAIMSTER

THE early Saxon period has always been characterized by its burials, and above all by the decorated metalwork deposited as grave goods. Brooches, belt buckles, weaponry, and horse fittings—but also objects such as amuletic pendants, drinking vessels, and musical instruments—were decorated with a zoomorphic and highly stylized art. Defined as Styles I and II, a terminology introduced by the Swedish scholar Bernard Salin in 1904, the appearance of this characteristic animal-style art in Britain was associated with the *adventus saxonum* of Bede and the arrival of settlers from southern Scandinavia and northern Germany. The decorated objects could be seen either as evidence of a Scandinavian ethnicity or—later in the sixth and seventh centuries—as heirlooms or the reflection of continuous cultural contacts with the Scandinavian homelands (see for example Hines 1984 and Speake 1980.) Besides its Scandinavian associations, the animal-style art has also been seen as an expression of pagan mythology and, through its appearance on prestigious objects, an indication of high social status (for earlier discussions of a mythological content in animal-style art, see Leigh 1984 and Speake 1980: 77–92.)

In spite of its potential as a source for illustrating early medieval society, studies of animal-style art have been mainly concerned with questions of origin and chronology. Analyses have continued to employ the methods developed by Salin, approaching the imagery as a set of stylistic details where animals and other recognizable motifs are rarely afforded any deeper meaning.[1] As a result, the main social context ascribed to the animal-style art has been the neutral field of fashion. More recently, however, research has begun to explore the connection between imagery, mythological beliefs, and power in early medieval metalwork (see Dickinson, Pluskowski, this volume). New approaches are painting a different picture of early medieval Europe, moving away from linear histories of nations and ethnically defined peoples, towards a more complex understanding of societies at this time.[2] The period following the fall of the Roman Empire in the west is recognized as a time of profound transformation of social and ideological structures, and this is reflected in the material culture. New forms of dress accessories and personal belongings appear, and a new burial ritual where the dead are put to rest in richly furnished graves. Behind these changes, a new form of community has been recognized: one that was political rather than ethnic or tribal (Hedeager 1992b: 280–2). These communities have been described as warrior societies, led by kings and chieftains, often volatile, sometimes short-lived, but with a common lifestyle reflected in objects, rituals, and values.

In this context, the understanding of art has changed, too: instead of being seen as a general expression of fashion, or as an ethnic marker, the imagery may be explored as a conscious and meaningful articulation of religious, political, and social ideas. Figural representations within the animal-style art have been the subject of new methods of understanding early medieval imagery, but studies of the wider context where the decorated metalwork was used and produced have also generated models of regional organization in the late fifth and sixth centuries. Research has been complemented with studies of precious-metal and symbolic objects as political media; here amuletic pendants, in particular, may also offer an insight into the role played by women in the creation of early medieval kingship.

New research has shifted the perception of the Scandinavian character of the animal-style art in Anglo-Saxon England away from explanations based only on economic and cultural contacts, to include conceptual meanings that were consciously used to express social and political power in a regional context. Such ideological functions have also been explored in the decorated metalwork from princely burials of the early seventh century, but in this context conceptual aspects of the imagery have rarely been discussed. Here, the view of animal-style art as an expression of northern traditions and ideas needs to be complemented by a broader recognition of formative influences from the Christian Continental culture.

---

[1] Today, Salin's stylistic method is still used and adapted to computer analyses; see for example Høilund Nielsen 1999.

[2] Much of the new research has been generated within the European Science Foundation-funded project 'Transformation of the Roman World AD 400–900'; see in particular Webster and Brown 1997; Theuws and Nelson 2000; de Jong et al. 2001.

Animal-Style Art and Scandinavia

South Scandinavia is broadly recognized as a central region for the appearance of Style I animal art. Developing in the course of the late fifth century, its main source of inspiration can be seen in late Roman military belt buckles and weapon accessories, decorated with carved and punched geometric designs and with moulded animal features. Such influences can be seen in a range of Germanic metalwork, on the Continent and south-east Britain as well as in Scandinavia.[3] Against this background, however, Style I appears as a highly developed art where the late Roman elements have been transformed into a distinct and original Germanic imagery (Fig. 45.1). This can be seen in hybrid creatures developed from antique models into new forms, with four-legged animals replacing sea creatures, and in the appearance of new representations combining human and animal features (Haseloff 1986). Characteristic of the new style is also the sophisticated manner in which human and animal motifs are broken down into elements and arranged in complex designs (Erä-Esko 1965; Dickinson 2002; Webster, this volume).

Besides objects such as decorated brooches and weapon accessories, a new form of amuletic pendants was also produced. These thin gold discs, known as gold bracteates, were embossed with figural representations, symbolic signs, and, sometimes, runic inscriptions, framed with stamped borders and furnished with loops for suspension (see Fig. 45.2–3). Like Style I, the gold bracteates show how Roman imagery was adapted to express Germanic mythological ideas. However, the inspiration for their motifs was not the metalwork and military equipment; instead, they were closely modelled on late Roman precious-metal coins and medallions. Today over 900 Scandinavian gold bracteates are known, with the vast majority from south Scandinavia (all gold bracteates found before 1989 are catalogued in Axboe *et al.* 1985–9).

Style I decorated objects and gold bracteates are known from many regions in northern and western Europe, with the largest concentration of finds outside Scandinavia from Anglo-Saxon England (Haseloff 1981: Abb. 359; Hedeager 1992b: fig. 52). The English finds of gold bracteates, today comprising over fifty issues, are concentrated in Kent and East Anglia (Gaimster 1992; for more recent English finds, see Axboe *et al.* forthcoming); here, as in other regions outside their core area, they were usually deposited as grave-goods in burials. In south Scandinavia, however, these pendants were instead placed in wetlands or in the ground as sacral offerings (Gaimster 1992: fig. 2). Besides bracteates, such hoards may include precious-metal and prestigious objects such as gold arm- and

---

[3] The connection between late Roman art and Style I is still best described by Günther Haseloff in his monumental work from 1981; for an English summary of this, see Haseloff 1974. For Continental and British metalwork, see Böhme 1986 and Suzuki 2000.

Figure 45.1 Style I decorated brooch of gilt silver from Vedstrup, Zealand, East Denmark; actual size 135mm (after Salin 1904)

neckrings, brooches, glass beads, and Roman coins, and, more rarely, decorated sword-sheath mounts (Hines 1989: 198–9; Hedeager 1991). These offerings have been the subject of much research in the past fifteen years, where Scandinavian archaeologists have focused their interest on studies of regional organization in the early Middle Ages, and on the social and political context where animal-style art was used.

Art and Regional Organization

In south Scandinavia, the depositions of gold and precious objects in the late fifth and early sixth centuries appear to reflect a change in ritual practices. For a long time, offerings were associated with lakes and wetlands, but now they begin to take place on dry land, where they can frequently be associated with settlements of a special character. These settlements have been identified as 'central places', settlements or conglomerates of sites characterized by wealth, far-reaching contact or trade networks, specialized craft production, and evidence of ritual practices in offerings, cult objects, and sacral place-names (Fabech 1999; 2006). The trend becomes particularly clear by the seventh century, when wetland sacrifices seem to have been completely abandoned. Ritual activities are now reflected in minute gold foils embossed with or clipped into human representations. These small votive offerings are normally found in direct connection with buildings, deposited in post-holes or preserved in floor layers. Their presence has been seen as an indication of ritual activities associated with the *hov*, the cult focus within the hall, or with specially designated pagan cult buildings (Watt 1999; Lamm 2004).

The most extensively researched example of this development is the Gudme-Lundeborg complex on Funen in central Denmark.[4] Here a settlement with a sequence of remarkably large halls and evidence for import of luxury goods as well as craft production and specialized workshops, including both bronze and precious-metal objects, was excavated in the 1980s and early 1990s. The site dates back to the late Roman period, but it appears to have flourished during the migration period (*c.* AD 400–600). Nearby, at the coastal site of Lundeborg, further evidence of production and far-reaching trading contacts was revealed. In the area surrounding these sites, cult activities are represented both in sacral place-names and numerous gold finds, among them Denmark's largest gold hoard with seven gold bracteates and thirty-five gold rings along with bullion and a gold brooch (Munksgaard and Thrane 1978). Bracteates are also known from a further large hoard of nine bracteates, and several single finds (Axboe 1987). At Lundeborg,

---

[4] Nielsen *et al.* 1994 includes a range of papers on the finds from Gudme and Lundeborg; see also Randsborg 1990. For an interesting interpretation of Gudme as a sacral centre, see Hedeager 2001.

more than 100 votive gold foils were recovered during the excavations (Hauck 1992: 511–57).

More recently, an early medieval high-status settlement and cult site has been investigated at Uppåkra in south-west Sweden (Hårdh and Larsson 2002; Larsson 2004). Here also, the site dates back to the Roman period, and indeed continues until the present day; however, as at Gudme, it is the migration-period phase that has yielded the mixture of finds characteristic of a central-place settlement with high-status finds, ritual activities, large-scale craft production and long-distance or exotic contacts (Hårdh 2002). At the centre of the site an unusually large hall or cult building yielded over one hundred votive gold foils and numerous deliberately bent spearheads; among the unusual finds from this building were also an exotic glass bowl and a metal vessel decorated with gold-foil panels embossed with Style I motifs (Larsson and Lenntorp 2004; Hårdh 2004). Finds from the site included patrices for the production of gold-foil figures and two gold bracteates (Watt 2004; Pesch 2002a).

The new ritual and political landscape has been interpreted as the result of profound changes in early medieval society which saw the emergence of a new form of political authority, separate from the old tribal community and lying instead in the hands of powerful individuals (Fabech 1999: 38; cf. Hedeager 1992a: esp. 80–1). The establishing of new sacral rituals and cult places played a crucial part in this development, but also the creation of a visual imagery and a distinct animal-style art. Among its important functions would have been to convey mythological ideas and a cosmology that served to legitimize power and social organization. The framework for this has been recognized in the Old Norse religion and its pantheon of Asir gods, preserved in much later written sources. During the migration period this new, or re-invented, cosmology has been related to the rise of a cult centred on Odin, the king of the Asir, and his powerful magical knowledge and healing skills (Hedeager 1997; 1999).

A PAGAN COSMOLOGY

The idea that Old Norse religion could be traced back to the migration period is not new. Here the gold bracteates have played a central role; they were early on recognized as mythological representations and many attempts were made to interpret these directly from the later Scandinavian documentary sources.[5] A more systematic approach was taken by the German historian Karl Hauck, in a

---

[5] Gaimster (1998: 22–36) gives a brief overview in English of the early research history of the bracteates.

lifetime of studying the bracteate imagery and other figural representations from the early medieval period. In contrast to earlier interpretations, based on identifying the Old Norse gods through their attributes, Hauck developed a contextual iconography where the representations were understood as motifs, visualizing in compressed and symbolic form an oral tradition of well-known mythological stories.[6]

Like earlier scholars, Hauck's work relies heavily on later written sources for any interpretation of the imagery. However, his interest was also based on an appreciation of how these amulets reflect a conscious adaptation not only of the motifs, but also the concepts behind the late Roman coins and medallions upon which they were modelled. The bracteates were not simply copies of existing coins, but can be shown to draw on numerous individual coin types and their details. This suggests an intimate understanding of the Roman coin representations, where iconographic elements were carefully chosen and adapted to express Germanic mythological ideas (Axboe and Kromann 1992; Gaimster 1996).

Some bracteate motifs and their details concur well with the known Norse mythological tradition, in particular the god Tyr's adventure with the Fenris wolf (Axboe *et al.* 1985–9, IK 190; Gaimster 1998: 30 with further references), and a scene that appears to show the god Baldr who was shot with an arrow made of mistletoe (see Axboe and Kromann 1992: 292–3 and Gaimster 1998: 30–1 with further references). However, the most commonly recurring motif on the gold bracteates, represented on nearly half of the over 900 known gold bracteates, features a human head, modelled on the imperial image, placed above a horse. Hauck showed how this motif—rather than the misunderstood rendition of a horse and rider—can be interpreted as a representation of the god Odin and his healing powers (for a discussion in English of this interpretation, see Behr 2000: 36–7 and Gaimster 1998: 43–8, both with further references). One particularly large and detailed bracteate in this group of so-called C-bracteates carries the runic inscription "houaR"—the High One—known as an epithet for the god (Axboe and Kromann 1992: 290) (Fig. 45.2a). Even if the motifs include other gods and mythological figures known from the literary sources, Hauck has identified Odin as the central god behind the bracteate art; their principal themes are above all concerned with the god's magical and healing powers. Modelled on the portrait on late Roman coins and medallions, Odin appears as a Germanic reflection of the divine emperor.

Besides the C-bracteates, a second major motif group is represented by depictions of snake-like animals. Known as D-bracteates, their imagery shows many similarities to the complex and broken-down animal motifs found on the Style

---

[6] Hauck wrote numerous long articles on the iconography of the gold bracteates and other early medieval figural representations. For broad overviews of his method and interpretations, see Hauck 1983; 1986; 1988. For a discussion in English of Hauck's iconographic method, see Gaimster 1998: 21–48 with further references.

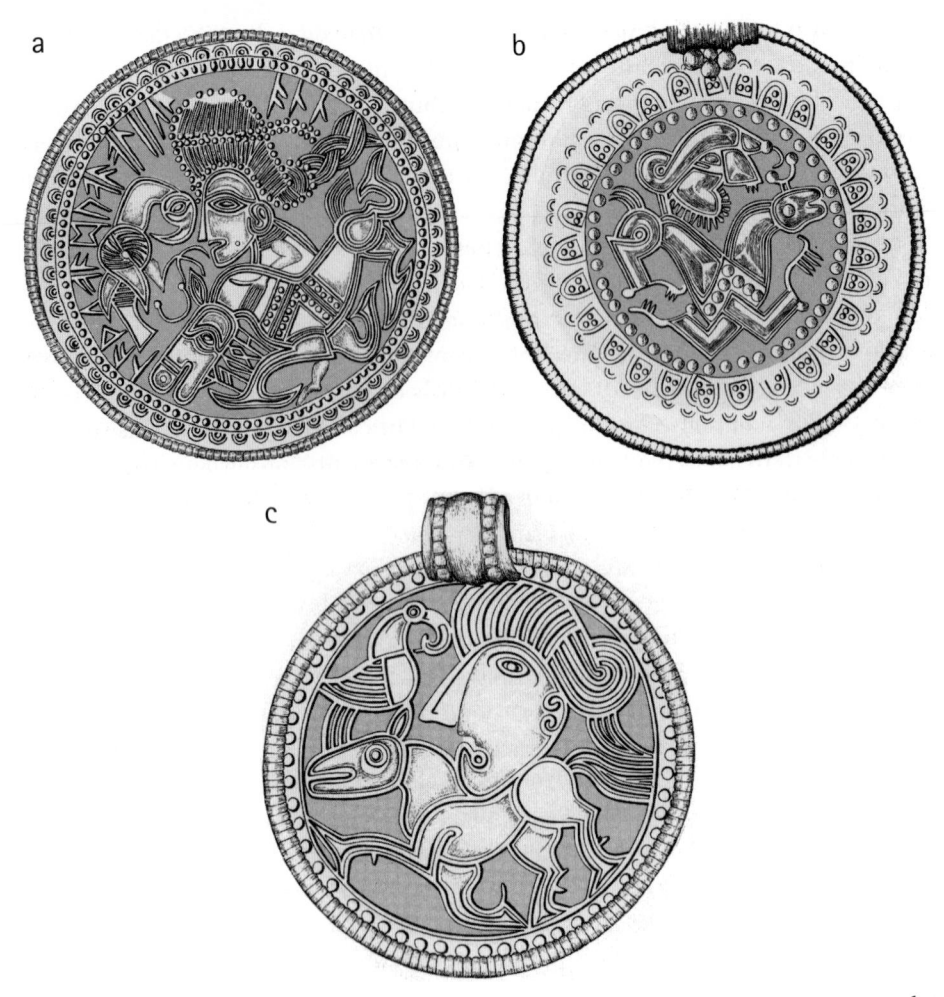

Figure 45.2 (a) C-bracteate from Funen, Denmark; actual size 37mm diameter (IK 58); (b) C-bracteate from Øvre Tøyen, Norway; actual size 39mm diameter (IK 137); (c) C-bracteate from Sletner, Norway; actual size 28mm diameter (IK 172)

I brooches. Like other bracteate motifs, however, iconographic details suggest the D-bracteates represent abbreviated versions of a mythological theme. A common motif includes human details such as an ear, a foot and a hand, and has been interpreted as a representation of Odin fighting against monsters (Fig. 45.3). (For a brief discussion in English of Hauck's interpretation of the D-bracteates in English, see Gaimster 1998: 33–6 with further references.) The same monsters are sometimes included also within other bracteate motifs, supporting the existence of a common mythological tradition behind these pendants.

While Hauck's detailed interpretations of their motifs remain controversial, the recognition of the gold bracteates as iconographic representations is significant in its own right.[7] It was recognized early on that the bracteates display a limited number of motifs;[8] however, while the same motifs occur in many of the areas where bracteates were used, local and regional issues show variation in small details or in the specific design of identifiable motifs (Fig. 45.2a–c). These groups of design-related bracteates have been the focus of more recent research (Pesch 2002a: 56–65; Pesch 2004; cf. Behr 2007). In a similar way to the adoption of motifs from the Roman coins, they show that bracteates were not simply copied from existing models, but represent different ways of visualizing established mythological themes. The existence of a recurring and limited set of representations suggests that bracteates were made in a small number of workshops, most likely situated at central places and cult centres such as Gudme and Uppåkra. At the same time, the distribution of gold bracteates reveals a network of contacts across many regions, where ideas and concepts were shared and exchanged among the social elite.

Figural representations and motifs occur also on Style I decorated objects other than bracteates, above all on large decorated relief brooches, and have been interpreted within the mythological framework of the bracteate iconography (cf. Hedeager 1999; Magnus 2001a). Here the recent work by Tania Dickinson (2002: 178; 2005; Parfitt and Dickinson 2007) on Anglo-Saxon Style I is of particular interest, emphasizing representations with direct parallels in bracteate motifs. Such parallels may be identified not only on brooches, but also on embossed mounts for drinking vessels and on animal-style decorated shields.

BRACTEATES AS A POLITICAL MEDIUM

An important aspect of the gold bracteates is that they do not only show how religious ideas and expressions were translated from the late antique world to

---

[7] The problems in identifying mythological content behind the imagery of pre-literate societies, particularly through the use of later texts, are discussed by Hines (1997) and Hawkes (1997). The understanding of pre-Christian religion as a uniform, continuous, and organized cult has been criticized by Callmer (2006). For comments on the problems of interpreting imagery, see Dickinson 2005: 111–12.

[8] Since the nineteenth century, gold bracteates have been divided into four categories on the basis of their motifs; A-bracteates show a human head, closely based on Roman prototypes, B-bracteates show one or more complete human figures, C-bracteates show a human head above a horse, and D-bracteates show one or more animals.

express Germanic mythological ideas. They also show the adoption of new ways of expressing social and political power through symbolic objects. The central figure on these pendants is sometimes shown carrying imperial insignia, such as the pearl diadem or the shoulder brooch, but also displays Germanic symbols of power; on some bracteates the image is portrayed with long plaited hair, known as a symbol of kingship among the Merovingians (Fig. 45.2a). This should not be taken to imply an individual king behind the motif, but reflects the tradition, known also in Christian art, of representing deities dressed as kings or emperors (Axboe and Kromann 1992: 287–90).

The imagery shows that these symbols of power were well understood, but the bracteates themselves also embody political functions inherent in their models. The late Roman gold medallions were an important means for the emperor, through gifts and donatives, to demonstrate his power and to establish personal and political alliances; the value of such gifts can be seen in the transformation of these large and valuable coins into prestigious jewellery (Gaimster 2001: 148; cf. Andrén 1991: fig. 1). This phenomenon can also be seen in the many late Roman medallions that made their way across the borders where they were framed and looped for suspension, and sometimes imitated, by Germanic goldsmiths. These coin pendants are found in eastern and central Europe, as well as south Scandinavia, and the strong similarities in their loops and frames across the area where they are found suggest they were distributed through systems of gift exchange. The function of the medallions was adopted by Germanic leaders and chieftains, who may have used them to demonstrate and legitimize their own power (Bursche 2001). However, south Scandinavia appears to be the only region where the idea behind the late Roman gold medallions led to the development of a genuinely Germanic form of this medium.

The use of precious-metal and symbolic objects as social and political media is today recognized as a fundamental aspect of early medieval societies (see Scull, this volume). Such special-purpose money is particularly well reflected in arm- and neckrings; they appear frequently in Anglo-Saxon and Old Norse poetry, and form a significant inclusion in precious-metal hoards from the late Roman to the Viking periods (for a general discussion of precious-metal hoards from this perspective, see Gaimster 1992 and 2007). When compared with the rings, however, the bracteates provide an unusually rich source of information regarding the mechanisms of gift exchange; the distribution of closely related designs and die-linked bracteates can be seen as the reflection of a political geography where these pendants were used to maintain friendship and political alliances (Andrén 1991: fig. 8; Gaimster 1992: fig. 4). In this context the runic inscriptions on bracteates may give us an insight into the situations where politics were acted out. It has been suggested that these also may be understood in light of adaptations from the Roman medallions, where the most frequently occurring words may be related to the terms *dominus*, *pius*, and *felix*. While the Latin inscriptions refer to personal attributes within the

Figure 45.3 D-bracteate from Finglesham, Kent, Grave 203; actual size 20mm diameter (IK 426,2)

emperor cult, the words *laþu* (invitation), *alu* (ale) and *laukaR* (leek, onion) can be associated in a more concrete way with the medium through which ideals and normative behaviour were expressed: the great feasts where acts such as gift-giving, oath-taking, and offerings would have taken place.[9]

Similar political functions have also been suggested for the finds outside Scandinavia, where both gold bracteates and brooches decorated with Style I were regionally produced (Pesch 2004 demonstrates that Scandinavian-style gold bracteates were regionally produced to a far greater extent than previously assumed). In contrast to conventional explanations of Scandinavian-style objects as ethnic markers or a reflection of trading contacts, Lotte Hedeager (1993: 123–4; 2000) has seen the adoption of Scandinavian animal-style art as evidence of a shared cosmology which served to create identity and self-perception among Germanic peoples. She has particularly drawn attention to the use of Style I and bracteates in areas where Scandinavian origin myths were part of upper-class

---

[9] Andrén (1991), who also sees these inscriptions as a Germanic translation of the inscriptions on Roman coins, suggesting the bracteates depicted actual kings and chieftains modelling themselves on the emperor; for a critical comment on this, see Axboe 2001.

ideology and claims to kingship. Such genealogies are known from the Goths and the Lombards, but also from the Jutes in Kent. While they were written down later, in a context when Christian kings found it useful to legitimize kingship through pagan origin myths, the bracteates and the animal-style imagery may be seen as evidence of their roots in long-established mythological traditions.

This aspect has been particularly illuminated in a study of the gold bracteates from Kent. Here, Charlotte Behr (2000) has argued that it may be possible to identify similar regional developments as in south Scandinavia, in spite of differences in archaeological finds and research traditions. Using Gudme as a model, the Kentish bracteates could be seen to reflect a concentration of power and the existence of central places; they are associated with high-status burials and cemeteries characterized by a wide range of cultural contacts, particularly with the Franks, and frequently in close proximity to places with royal connections. Two of the cemeteries with gold bracteates are also in close vicinity to the only documented sacral place-name in Kent associated with the veneration of Odin/Woden. Previously, the Kentish gold bracteates have been interpreted as heirlooms, testifying to the historical migration of Jutes described by Bede in the early eighth century (Chadwick Hawkes and Pollard 1981: 320–6). However, the articulation of a Scandinavian identity through gold bracteates and a select choice of brooches could instead be understood from a political perspective: rather than indicating the actual Scandinavian descent of Kentish kings, bracteates may be seen as evidence of sixth-century mythological concepts of power and kingship.

Bracteates and Powerful Women

The political ideas and actions that held early medieval societies together have often been discussed from the perspective of men and warfare. Here the central role is played by the king or chieftain and his *hird* of warriors, where politics are acted out in feasting, gift-giving, and heroic tales (cf. Halsall 1989; Alkemade 1997; Theuws and Alkemade 2000). In this picture, strongly coloured by poetry and later written sources, women seldom feature beyond a supporting role. In contrast, during the sixth and seventh centuries women are highly visible in the grave finds. A focus on the female sphere is reflected in the choice of dress accessories like brooches as the dominant medium for the animal-style art (see, however, Dickinson 2005 for weapon accessories decorated in Style I), but also in the gold bracteates, which appear to have been almost exclusively worn by women. This is clear not only from their use as pendants on necklaces, testified in burials, but also from the composition of sacral deposits in Scandinavia, where bracteates are frequently associated with beads, other pendants, and brooches (Behr 2000: 35; Gaimster 2001). In Scandinavia, this may represent a transfer of some of the political functions associated with the late Roman medallions to the female sphere, as the earlier medallion imitations appear in both male and female burials (Gaimster 2001: 144–5).

The female context of the gold bracteates presents a challenge to the current understanding of early medieval kingship based on warrior ideologies. It suggests a more complex picture where women, through their responsibilities within the ritual and political sphere, could play a more active part in the creation and legitimization of power. The political role of women has mainly been seen in their function as representatives of family and kin, above all in the context of political marriages; here women are rarely portrayed as active or powerful individuals, and have even been described simply as a medium for gift exchange (see Gilchrist 1997 for a critique of the conventional view of early medieval women). However, the gold bracteates and the necklaces where they were worn show their owners as individuals of prestige and social standing. This has been further highlighted when the bracteates are related to other contemporary high-status necklaces. Such parallels are particularly obvious for coin pendants, which were displayed in a similar way (Gaimster 2001; forthcoming).

As pendants, bracteates were worn on necklaces hung with glass beads and frequently additional precious-metal and prestigious pendants. More often than simply fastened round the neck, they were strung across the chest between pins or brooches and were sometimes incorporated in multi-strand arrangements (Fig. 45.4). The development of these elaborate chest decorations has been related to the emulation of Byzantine fashion, visible among Frankish high-status women from the sixth century (Schulze 1976; Vierck 1981: 88–94). Through their composition of bracteates with different motifs, some Scandinavian finds give an impression of how spectacular such displays could be. This can be seen in the large bracteate hoard from Gudme in Denmark where nine bracteates, together with a looped Roman silver coin and other pendants, have been reconstructed into a two-strand chest decoration (Fig. 45.5). The Gudme necklace can be compared with a find from a richly furnished church burial in Cologne dating from around AD 530. Here a female member of the Merovingian royal family was laid to rest wearing a necklace composed of eight looped coins together with a further thirty pendants and beads of gold, garnet, and glass. The coins comprise a series of gold *solidi* stretching from the late fourth and into the early sixth centuries, and a further *solidus* of Theodosius II, contemporary with the burial, hung singly on a gold chain suspended between two brooches (Doppelfeld 1960; Müller-Wille 1996: 216 and figs. 153–4).

Figure 45.4 Reconstruction of two-strand necklace from Finglesham, Kent, Grave 203 (after Chadwick Hawkes and Grainger 2006)

The Cologne pendants reflect the continuous function of precious-metal coins as political media and they recall hoards of late Roman medallions, which were sometimes accumulated over a long period by their Germanic owners.[10] The implications behind these coins suggest some of the social and political mechanisms that helped constitute power, and it is easy to understand why they were important to display on a necklace. The sequence of coins reveals a long and continuous contact with the Roman empire and shows their owner and her family as important people, on equal or friendly footing with the emperor. The single solidus of Theodosius II may even have been a personal gift to the princess.[11] For a Christian woman, however, the close and continuous contact with Rome, symbolized in the medallions, must also have had important religious connotations.

The spectacular finds from Gudme and Cologne reveal something of the symbolic meaning of necklaces and the social position of the women who wore them.

[10] This is particularly reflected in the find from Szilágy Somlyó in Hungary, discussed by Gaimster (2001: 149 with further references).
[11] Gregory of Tours describes such a gift of from the emperor Tiberius II to the Frankish king Chilperic in AD 581; see Gaimster 2001: 151 with further reference.

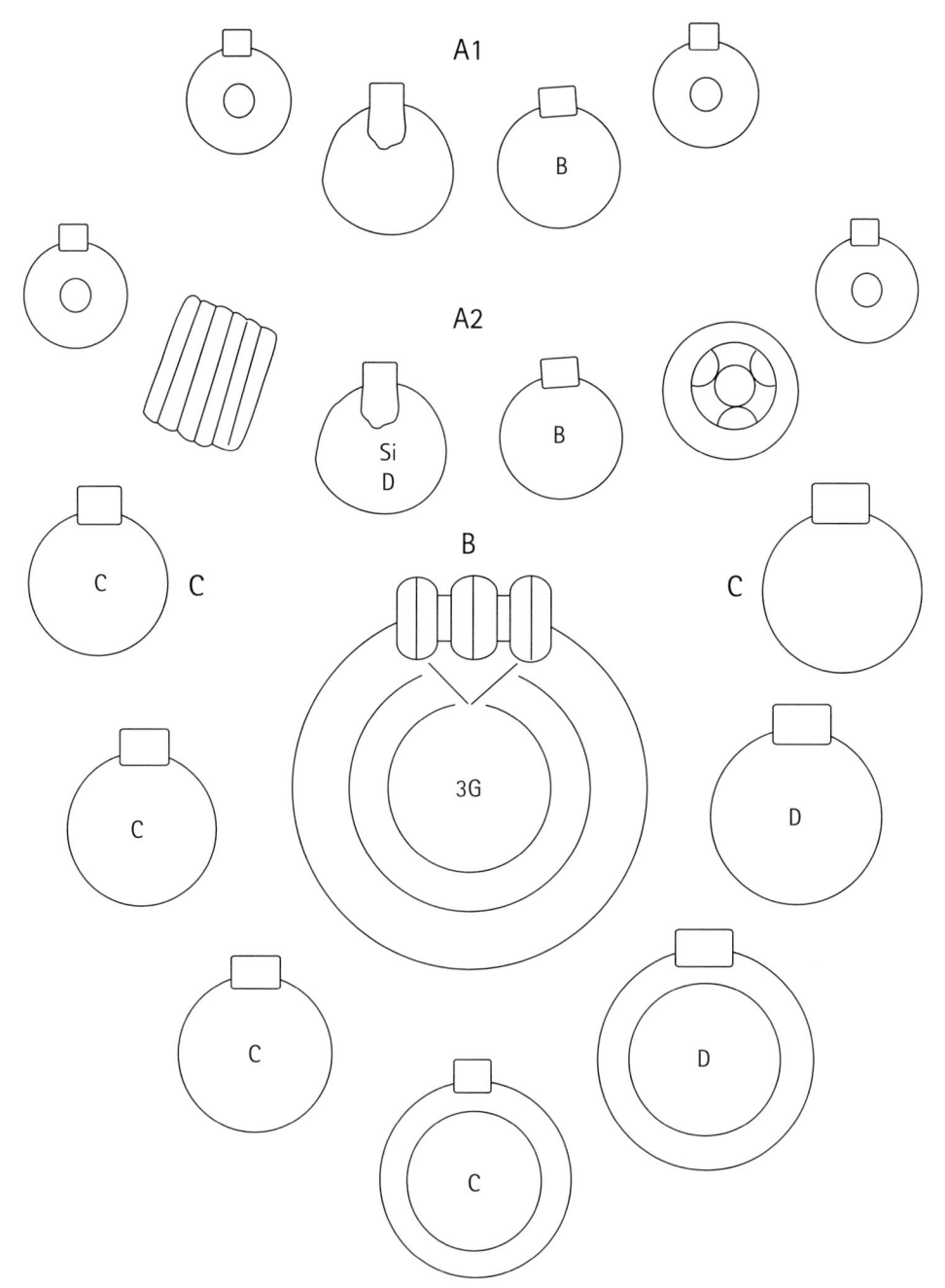

Figure 45.5 Reconstruction of two-strand necklace from Gudme, Funen, Denmark (after Hauck 1992)

Both the gold bracteates and the coin pendants incorporate multiple functions as amulets, status markers, and symbols of power. The necklaces, therefore, were not a simple display of wealth, but embodied a complex sphere of religious, political, and ideological messages.

Women as cult specialists

The bracteate imagery tells us little about the position women had in early medieval cult. With few exceptions they portray male gods; only one motif, known from a handful of issues, features a female representation.[12] The motif appears to be modelled on the Christian image of the spinning Mary, and has been interpreted as a representation of the Norse goddess Freya (Enright 1990; Pesch 2002b). This corresponds well with the metaphorical image of spinning in terms of prophecy in the Scandinavian literature, and the important role played by women in the *seiðr*, the ability to transcend into a state of ecstasy which allowed the soul to travel in time and space (Ellis Davidson 1993: 136–8; Hedeager 1999 with further references). Freya also features in the Lombard origin myth, written down in the seventh century; uniquely, in this tradition, it is women who play a decisive role in establishing the identity of their people (Wolfram 1994: 21–4; Behr 2000: 51). However, more direct parallels to the role sixth-century women may have played in the creation of kingship have also been explored in the active involvement of Anglo-Saxon women during the conversion period (see Staecker 2003 for a similar discussion of the role of high-status women during the conversion period in Scandinavia).

The powerful position held by high-ranking women in the religious sphere has long been recognized in the role of royal women as abbesses and founders of nunneries. However, the historian Barbara Yorke has argued that their influence stretched beyond the image of piety given by contemporary chroniclers, to include an active political role in the legitimization of kingship. This can be shown in their involvement in the Anglo-Saxon double houses, established during the late seventh century and normally headed by an abbess of royal birth. Yorke has drawn attention to the secular context of these monasteries and their function in promoting dynastic interests and identities: among their tasks were the creation and nurturing of cults of royal saints. Such interests are reflected in the rapid spread

---

[12] Female representations occur also among the gold foils, mostly in representations of male–female couples; for recent interpretations see Lamm 2004: 120–2. Some single female figures have been interpreted as representations of Freya; see Arrhenius 1962.

of the double house across the Anglo-Saxon kingdoms, and by the fact that all appear to have had more than one foundation, established by members of competing royal houses (Yorke 2003a: esp. 17–46 and 147–50).

The study of these religious women explored in particular their secular identity, and how this was expressed in dress and jewellery. This is most poignantly reflected in the late-seventh-century shroud of Queen Balthilde, founder of the nunnery at Chelles, embroidered with an elaborate three-strand necklace arrangement including a pectoral cross and at least nine gold and enamel medallions with Christian motifs (Vierck 1978; Yorke 2003a: 149). An earlier example is the Christian coin necklace which may be identified among a hoard of pendants retrieved from Canterbury in the nineteenth century. Dating from the late sixth century, this included a gold medalet or coin of Bishop Liudhard, the chaplain of King Æthelbert's Frankish Queen, Bertha, along with four looped Continental coins worn as pendants (Webster and Backhouse 1991: 23–4; Gaimster forthcoming). Like the earlier necklace from Cologne, the coins and medallions can be seen as symbols both of social standing and Christian associations; this is further emphasized in the chest arrangement on the shroud from Chelles and its overt Byzantine ideals.

Yorke has also considered the role of women in light of more profound changes in power and kingship in the face of conversion (Yorke 2003b). This would have included necessary re-adjustments of kings who had been both secular rulers and leaders of cult, which was no longer acceptable in Christian doctrine. After unsuccessful attempts to retain their traditional role, reflected in a brief phase of monastic and saintly kings, the double task of cult specialist and guardian of the sacral aspect of kingship appears to have been taken over by royal women. This solution would have been acceptable for the church; however, it may also have been successful because it followed a tradition of powerful women in this sphere. Evidence of this may be seen in the gold bracteates as symbols of both secular power and mythological concepts, and in the continuing display by Christian women of coins and symbolic and religious pendants on elaborate necklaces.

IMAGE AND POWER IN THE SEVENTH CENTURY

The Scandinavian gold bracteates were only produced during a few generations, and perhaps no later than the mid sixth century (Axboe 1999). A unique source for a period of dynamic development in early medieval Europe, they were part of an elite culture that expressed itself in new ritual practices, cosmological ideas, and manifestations of power. With their iconographic representations and models in precious-metal coins and medallions, these gold pendants provide an insight into the mythological and political ideas that helped shape the identities of Germanic societies in the late fifth and sixth centuries.

If the gold bracteates shed light on the mechanisms behind power and the emergence of kingship, the contexts of seventh-century animal-style art, since the discovery in 1939 of the richly furnished ship burial at Sutton Hoo, have played a role in the debate about 'real' kings. The burial (published and discussed by Bruce-Mitford 1978, 1983), possibly that of the East Anglian king Rædwald, contained an unrivalled wealth of decorated high-status weapon equipment; together with other symbolic objects they were interpreted early on as symbols of royal power. Some of the objects, in particular the decorated mounts on the shield and the helmet, have parallels in finds from Scandinavia; others, including the shoulder clasps and the possible sceptre and standard, were seen as having been modelled on late Roman symbols of office. Still other elements revealed Continental contacts and influences. The gold-and-garnet sword and its accessories, the purse filled with Merovingian coins, and the numerous Mediterranean silver vessels, some of which were at least a hundred years old when buried, were suggestive of contacts, above all with the Frankish court.

Earlier research saw the Sutton Hoo finds in a rather uncomplicated way as the accoutrements of a pagan Anglo-Saxon king; they could be seen as a complement to the documentary evidence of a known king, but also as an illustration of the heroic Germanic warrior culture described in the Anglo-Saxon poem *Beowulf*. Because the story of Beowulf is set in Scandinavia, the Swedish parallels among the finds played an important role in interpretations as evidence of close contacts with a Swedish court, or even as Swedish products.[13] Today, scholars have begun to take a more critical view of the finds: together with other princely burials they have been explored as a means of understanding ideologies of power and kingship in the late sixth and seventh centuries. Thus Martin Carver has seen the Scandinavian elements at Sutton Hoo, along with other East Anglian burials employing the northern tradition of ship burial, as an ideological statement by pagan kings, for whom allegiance to Scandinavia was a means of expressing independence from encroaching Christian kingdoms (Carver, this volume).

Other archaeologists have focused on the late Roman and Byzantine elements, and the adoption of Roman insignia, as a key source to understanding seventh-century ideas of kingship (Webster 1992; Filmer-Sankey 1996). Already an established tradition among Continental kings, such ideals are particularly emphasized at Sutton Hoo, where the personal attire—the shoulder clasps, the helmet, and the decorated belt buckle—appears to show a man who above all modelled himself on

---

[13] Wilson (1992) offers a critical comment on the earlier publications and interpretations of the Sutton Hoo ship burial.

the image of an emperor. In this, the finds from princely burials like Sutton Hoo, Taplow, and the recently discovered chamber grave at Prittlewell in Essex reveal how social and political power was expressed through symbolic objects, but they also show a visible shift in the use of animal-style art to the male sphere where weapon accessories, harness mounts, and belt buckles appear more frequently as a medium for decoration. Here the symbolic meaning of the belt buckle, in particular, has been recognized: from late Antiquity and throughout the Middle Ages it functioned as a symbol of authority and a medium for negotiating friendship and loyalty (for the most recent study of Anglo-Saxon belt buckles, see Marzinzik 2003: 4–6). Like the earlier gold bracteates, the buckle could also carry a double significance as a religious object and a symbol of secular power.

Unlike the bracteates, however, the imagery of seventh-century decorated metalwork has played a marginal role in discussions of power and regional organization. Both patterns and animal features may have had a symbolic meaning which is difficult for us to interpret or understand, but there is also a small group of figural

Figure 45.6 Design on embossed mounts of tinned copper alloy, decorating the helmet from Sutton Hoo, Mound 1; actual size c.40 by 56mm (after Bruce-Mitford 1978)

and iconographic representations depicting riders and warrior figures (Fig. 45.6). While above all associated with the decorated helmets from Sutton Hoo and the Swedish boat burials at Vendel and Valsgärde, the representations belong to a series of motifs that also appear, in the form of sword sheath mounts and harness pendants, on prestigious warrior equipment in Continental finds. Hauck has shown that these motifs may be interpreted within the mythological tradition of the earlier gold bracteates, where the seventh-century iconography represents a shift of focus from the mythological themes concerned with healing and shamanistic knowledge in the bracteate art.[14] However, he also drew attention to influences from Christian motifs behind this pagan warrior mythology. Heiko Steuer, too, has seen the appearance of helmets and other symbols of power decorated with pagan motifs in the light of warrior equipment with Christian symbols (Steuer 1987; see also Hedeager 1992b: 290). Like Hauck he has interpreted this phenomenon, not only in terms of emulating powerful Christian kings, but as an expression of rivalling cosmologies.

While broadly associated with Scandinavian or Germanic mythological ideas, the seventh-century decorated metalwork has also provided an important source for discussing early Christian art, where parallels in the use of animal-style art in sculpture and manuscripts have been recognized (see for example U. Roth 1987; Hawkes 1997). In this sense, the seventh-century animal-style art has come to occupy two separate but parallel worlds; it is not without significance that, unlike the earlier Style I, the cultural context of Salin's Style II has been far more debated. Characterized by the integration of Germanic animal-style elements with complex interlace motifs from Mediterranean art, it appears across the cultural area where Style I was used. Some scholars have claimed an origin in Lombard Italy, others among the Alemans in south-west Germany; more controversially, the impetus behind Style II has also been seen in the Christian culture of the Franks.[15] An argument for this is that, on the Continent, Style II was not only used on secular objects such as brooches, belt-buckles, weapons, and horse equipment; it was also used in an ecclesiastical context, on reliquaries, chalices, altar stones, and funerary monuments. In spite of this debate, Style II has continued to be accepted as a Scandinavian innovation by most scholars.

If we want to explore the cultural and conceptual milieu behind the seventh-century animal-style art, however, a wider perspective may be advantageous. This is indicated in the figural motifs, but is also supported in some of the decorated metalwork itself. Recent studies of Style II suggest that Continental motifs and ideas were more influential on the new style than previously thought, including on

---

[14] See for example Hauck 1980 and 1982; for a discussion of these interpretations in English, see Gaimster 1998: 1–20 and 48–70.

[15] For a Lombard origin, see Åberg 1945; for an Alemannic origin, see Haseloff 1981: 647–73; a Frankish origin for Style II has been argued by Holmqvist (1939) and Arrhenius (1986); for a compilation of ecclesiastical objects with Style II, see Wamers forthcoming.

objects produced in Scandinavia (cf. Gaimster 1998). English finds, too, indicate that a focus on northern traditions and influences may be too narrow. Among the objects from Sutton Hoo the great gold buckle, decorated in high-quality Style II, has long been recognized by Continental scholars as a reliquary buckle. Hollow and with a hinged back plate, it has a close parallel in a Frankish royal burial at St Denis (Werner 1982: 198–201; U. Roth 1987: 26). Continental influences can be seen also in a group of Style II decorated gold bracteates from Kent; their designs cannot be related to the iconographic representations on the earlier Scandinavian bracteates, but appear instead to be modelled on pendants and bracteate brooches from the Rhineland.[16]

Broadening the view from Scandinavia to a more Continental perspective may offer a better position to understand the animal-style art also in the context of Christian elements in princely burials, actualized in the recent Prittlewell find (Hirst et al. 2004). It provides an opportunity to approach the seventh-century decorated metalwork, not simply as evidence of Christian beliefs, but as a conscious articulation of and response to the social and political developments of its time.

REFERENCES

ÅBERG, N. (1945). *The Occident and the Orient in the Art of the Seventh Century*, Volume 2: *Lombard Italy*. Stockholm: Kungliga Vitterhets Historie och Antikvitets Akademien, Handlingar 56:2.

ALKEMADE, M. (1997). 'Elite lifestyle and the transformation of the Roman world in Northern Gaul', in Webster and Brown (eds.), *Transformation of the Roman World*, 180–4.

ANDRÉN, A. (1991). 'Guld och makt—en tolkning av de skandinaviska Guldbrakteaternas function/Gold and power—the function of the Scandinavian gold bracteates', in Fabech and Ringtved (eds.), *Samfundsorganisation*, 145–54.

——JENNBERT, K., and RAUDVERE, C. (eds.) (2006). *Old Norse Religion in Long-Term Perspectives: Origins, Changes and Interactions*. Vägar till Midgård 8. Lund: Nordic Academic Press.

ARRHENIUS, B. (1962). 'Det flammande smycket'. *Fornvännen* 57: 79–101.

—— (1986). 'Einige christliche Paraphrasen aus dem 6. Jahrhundert', in H. Roth (ed.), *Zum Problem der Deutung frühmittelalterlicher Bildinhalte*, 129–51.

AXBOE, M. (1987). 'Die Brakteaten von Gudme II'. *Frühmittelalterliche Studien* 21: 76–81.

---

[16] Gaimster 1998: 116–17; cf. Høilund Nielsen 1999: 194. A Scandinavian source for the imagery on the Style II bracteates was argued for by Speake (1980). For the Continental brooches and pendants, see the catalogue by Klein-Pfeuffer (1993).

—— (1999). 'The chronology of the Scandinavian gold bracteates', in J. Hines, K. Høilund Nielsen, and F. Siegmund (eds.), *The Pace of Change: Studies in Early Medieval Archaeology*. Oxford: Oxbow Books, 126–47.

—— (2001). 'Amulet pendants and a darkened sun', in Magnus (ed.), *Roman Gold*, 119–35.

—— and KROMANN, A. (1992). 'DN ODINN P F AUV? Germanic "imperial portraits" on Scandinavian gold bracteates'. *Ancient Portraiture: Image and Message. Acta Hyperborea* 4: 271–305.

—— DÜWEL, K., HAUCK, K., and VON PADBERG, L. (1985–9). *Die Goldbrakteaten der Völkerwanderungszeit: Ikonographischer Katalog* (IK Vols. 1–3). Münstersche Mittelalterschriften 24. Munich: Wilhelm Fink Verlag.

—— —— —— —— (forthcoming). *Die Goldbrakteaten der Völkerwanderungszeit: Ikonographischer Katalog* (IK Vol. 4). Münstersche Mittelalterschriften 24. Munich: Wilhelm Fink Verlag.

BEHR, C. (2000). 'The origins of kingship in early medieval Kent'. *Early Medieval Europe* 9: 25–52.

—— (2007). 'Using bracteates as evidence for long-distance contacts', in A. Harris (ed.), *Incipient Globalization? Long-Distance Contacts in the Sixth Century*. Reading Medieval Studies 32. BAR International Series 1644. Oxford: British Archaeological Reports, 15–25.

BÖHME, H. W. (1986). 'Das Ende der Römerherrschaft in Britannien und die angelsächsische Besiedlung Englands im 5. Jahrhundert'. *Jahrbuch des Römisch-Germanischen Zentralmuseums Mainz* 33: 469–574.

BRUCE-MITFORD, R. L. S. (1978). *The Sutton Hoo Ship-burial*, Volume 2: *Arms, Armour and Regalia*. London: British Museum Publications.

—— (1983). *The Sutton Hoo Ship-burial*, Volume 3: *Silver, Hanging-Bowls, Drinking-Vessels, Containers, Musical Instrument, Textiles, Minor Objects*. London: British Museum Publications.

BURSCHE, A. (2001). 'Roman gold medallions as power symbols of the Germanic élite', in Magnus (ed.), *Roman Gold*, 83–102.

CALLMER, J. (2006). 'Ornaments, ornamentation and female gender. Women in Eastern central Sweden in the eighth and early ninth centuries', in Andrén et al. (eds.), *Old Norse Religion*, 189–94.

CARVER, M. (ed.) (2003). *The Cross Goes North: Processes of Conversion in Northern Europe, AD 300–1300*. The University of York: York Medieval Press.

CHADWICK HAWKES, S., and GRAINGER, G. (2006). *The Anglo-Saxon Cemetery at Finglesham, Kent*. Monograph 64. Oxford: Oxford University School of Archaeology.

—— and POLLARD, M. (1981). 'The gold bracteates from sixth-century Anglo-Saxon graves in Kent, in the light of a new find from Finglesham'. *Frühmittelalterliche Studien* 15: 316–70.

DICKINSON, T. M. (2002). 'Translating animal art. Salin's Style I and Anglo-Saxon cast saucer brooches'. *Hikuin* 29: 163–86.

—— (2005). 'Symbols of protection: the significance of animal-ornamented shields in early Anglo-Saxon England'. *Medieval Archaeology* 49: 109–63.

—— and GRIFFITHS, D. (eds.) (1999). *The Making of Kingdoms*. Anglo-Saxon Studies in Archaeology and History 10. Oxford: Oxford University Committee for Archaeology.

DOPPELFELD, O. (1960). 'Das fränkische Frauengrab unter dem Chor des Kölner Domes'. *Germania* 38: 89–113.

ELLIS DAVIDSON, H. (1993). *The Lost Beliefs of Northern Europe*. London and New York: Routledge.

Enright, M. (1990). 'The goddess who weaves'. *Frühmittelalterliche Studien* 24: 54–70.

Erä-Esko, A. (1965). *Germanic Animal Art and of Salin's Style I in Finland*. Finska Fornminnesföreningens tidskrift. Helsinki: Oy Weilin & Göös AB.

Fabech, C. (1999). 'Organising the Landscape. A matter of production, power and religion', in Dickinson and Griffiths (eds.), *The Making of Kingdoms*, 37–47.

—— (2006). 'Centrality in Old Norse mental landscapes', in Andrén *et al.* (eds.), *Old Norse Religion*, 26–32.

—— and Ringtved, J. (eds.) (1991). *Samfundsorganisation og Regional Variation. Norden i romersk jernalder og folkevandringstid*. Aarhus: Jysk Arkaeologisk Selskabs Skrifter 27.

Farrell, R., and Neuman de Vegvar, C. (eds.) (1992). *Sutton Hoo: Fifty Years After*. American Early Medieval Studies 2. Ohio: Miami University, Department of Art.

Filmer-Sankey, W. (1996). 'The "Roman emperor" in the Sutton Hoo ship burial'. *Journal of the British Archaeological Association* 149: 1–9.

Gaimster, M. (1992). 'Scandinavian gold bracteates in Britain: money and media in the dark ages'. *Medieval Archaeology* 36: 1–28.

—— (1996). 'The Scandinavian gold bracteates', in E. Björklund, L. Hejll, and L. Franchi dell'Orto (eds.), *Roman Reflections in Scandinavia*. Exhibition catalogue, Malmö Museums. Rome: L'erma di Bretschneider, 218–21.

—— (1998). *Vendel Period Gold Bracteates on Gotland: On the Significance of Germanic Art*. Acta Archaeologica Lundensia series altera in 8°, No. 27. Lund: Almqvist & Wiksell International.

—— (2001). 'Gold bracteates and necklaces', in Magnus (ed.), *Roman Gold*, 143–55.

—— (2007). 'Viking economies: evidence from the silver hoards', in J. Graham-Campbell and G. Williams (eds.), *Silver Economy in the Viking Age*. UCL Institute of Archaeology Publications. Walnut Creek, CA: Left Coast Press, 123–33.

—— (forthcoming). 'Coin pendants and gold bracteates: an amuletic perspective of early medieval coins', in M. A. S. Blackburn and K. Bornholdt (eds.), *Gods, Graves and Numismatics: Interpreting Early Medieval Coin Finds of Northern Europe in Sacred Contexts*. Leiden: Brill.

Gilchrist, R. (1997). 'Ambivalent bodies: gender and medieval archaeology', in J. M. Moore and E. Scott (eds.), *Invisible People and Processes: Writing Gender and Childhood into European Archaeology*. Leicester: Leicester University Press, 42–58.

Halsall, G. (1989). 'Anthropology and the study of pre-conquest warfare and society. The ritual war in Anglo-Saxon England', in S. Chadwick Hawkes (ed.), *Weapons and Warfare in Anglo-Saxon England*. Oxford: Oxford University Committee for Archaeology, 155–77.

Hårdh, B. (2002). 'Uppåkra in the migration and Merovingian periods', in Hårdh and Larsson (eds.), *Central Places in the Migration and Merovingian Periods*, 41–54.

—— (2004). 'The Metal Beaker with Embossed Foil Bands', in Larsson (ed.), *Continuity for Centuries*, 49–91.

—— and Larsson, L. (eds.) (2002). *Central Places in the Migration and Merovingian Periods: Papers from the 52nd Sachsensymposium Lund, August 2001*. Uppåkrastudier 6. Acta Archaeologica Lundensia series in 8°, No. 39. Lund: Almqvist & Wiksell International.

Haseloff, G. (1974). 'Salin's Style I'. *Medieval Archaeology* 18: 1–15.

—— (1981). *Die germanische Tierornamentik der Völkerwanderungszeit: Studien zu Salin's Stil I*, Volumes 1–3. Berlin, New York: de Gruyter.

—— (1986). 'Bild und Motiv im Nydam-Stil und Stil I', in H. Roth (ed.), *Zum Problem der Deutung frühmittelalterlicher Bildinhalte*, 67–110.

Hauck, K. (1980). 'Gemeinschaftstiftende Kulte der Seegermanen (Zur Ikonologie der Goldbrakteaten XIX)'. *Frühmittelalterliche Studien* 14: 463–617.

—— (1982). 'Zum zweiten Band der Sutton-Hoo Edition'. *Frühmittelalterliche Studien* 16: 319–62.

—— (1983). 'Text und Bild in einer oralen Kultur (Zur Ikonologie der Goldbrakteaten XXV)'. *Frühmittelalterliche Studien* 17: 510–600.

—— (1986). 'Methodenfragen der Brakteatendeutung. Erprobung eines Interpretationsmusters für die Bildzeugnisse aus einer oralen Kultur (Zur Ikonologie der Goldbrakteaten XXVI)', in H. Roth (ed.), *Zum Problem der Deutung frühmittelalterlicher Bildinhalte*, 273–96.

—— (1988). 'Zwanzig Jahre Brakteatenforschung in Münster/Westfalen (Zur Ikonologie der Goldbrakteaten XL)'. *Frühmittelalterliche Studien* 22: 17–52.

—— (1992). 'Frühmittelalterliche Bildüberlieferung und der organisierte Kult' (Zur Ikonologie der Goldbrakteaten XLIV), in K. Hauck (ed.), *Der historische Horizont der Götterbild-Amulette aus der Übergangsepoche von der Spätantike zum Frühmittelalter*. Abhandlungen der Philologisch-Historischen Klasse der Göttinger Akademie der Wissenschaften. Göttingen: Vandenhoeck & Ruprecht, 433–564.

Hawkes, J. (1997). 'Symbolic lives: the visual evidence', in J. Hines (ed.), *The Anglo-Saxons from the Migration Period to the Eighth Century: An Ethnographic Perspective*. Woodbridge: Boydell Press, 311–38.

Hedeager, L. (1991). 'Gulddepoterna fra aeldre germanertid—forsøg på en tolkning/ Migration period gold hoards—an attempt at interpretation', in Fabech and Ringtved (eds.), *Samfundsorganisation*, 203–12.

—— (1992a). *Iron Age Societies: From Tribe to State in Northern Europe, 500 BC to AD 700*. Oxford: Blackwell.

—— (1992b). 'Kingdoms, ethnicity and material culture: Denmark in a European perspective', in M. Carver (ed.), *The Age of Sutton Hoo*. Woodbridge: Boydell Press, 279–300.

—— (1993). 'The creation of Germanic identity', in P. Brun, S. van der Leeuw, and C. R. Whittaker (eds.), *Frontières d'empire. Nature et signification des frontiers romaines*. Actes de la Table Ronde Internationale de Nemours 1992. Nemours: Mémoires du Musée de Préhistoire d'Ile de France no. 5, 121–31.

—— (1997). *Skygger af en anden virkelighed: Oldnordiske myter*. Denmark: Samlerens Universitet.

—— (1999). 'Myth and art: a passport to political authority in Scandinavia during the Migration Period', in Dickinson and Griffiths (eds.), *The Making of Kingdoms*, 151–6.

—— (2000). 'Migration period Europe: the formation of a political mentality', in Theuws and Nelson (eds.), *Rituals of Power*, 15–57.

—— (2001). 'Asgard reconstructed? Gudme—a "central place" in the north', in de Jong et al. (eds.), *Topographies of Power*, 467–508.

Hines, J. (1984). *The Scandinavian Character of Anglian England in the pre-Viking Period*. BAR British Series 124. Oxford: British Archaeological Reports.

—— (1989). 'Ritual hoarding in migration-period Scandinavia: a review of recent interpretations'. *Proceedings of the Prehistoric Society* 55: 193–205.

—— (1997). 'Religion: the limits of knowledge', in J. Hines (ed.), *The Anglo-Saxons from the Migration Period to the Eighth Century: An Ethnographic Perspective*. Woodbridge: Boydell Press, 375–401.

Hirst, S., Nixon, T., Rowsome, P., and Wright, S. (2004). *The Prittlewell Prince: The Discovery of a Rich Anglo-Saxon Burial in Essex*. Museum of London Archaeology Service.

Høilund Nielsen, K. (1999). 'Style II and the Anglo-Saxon elite', in Dickinson and Griffiths (eds.), *The Making of Kingdoms*, 185–202.

Holmqvist, W. (1939). *Kunstprobleme der Merowingerzeit*. Stockholm: Kungliga Vitterhets Historie och Antikvitets Akademien, Handlingar 47.

Jong, M. B. De, Theuws, F., and van Rhijn, C. (eds.) (2001). *Topographies of Power in the Early Middle Ages*. Transformation of the Roman World no. 6. Leiden: Brill.

Klein-Pfeuffer, M. (1993). *Merowingerzeitliche Fibeln und Anhänger aus Pressblech*. Marburger Studien zur Vor- und Frühgeschichte 14. Marburg: Hitzeroth.

Lamm, J. P. (2004). 'Figural gold foils found in Sweden: a study based on the discoveries from Helgö', in B. Gyllensvärd, P. Harbison, M. Axboe, J. P. Lamm, T. Zachrisson, and S. Reisborg (eds.), *Exotic and Sacral Finds from Helgö*. Excavations at Helgö XVI. Motala: Almqvist & Wiksell International, 41–142.

Larsson, L. (ed.) (2004). *Continuity for Centuries: A Ceremonial Building and its Context at Uppåkra, Southern Sweden*. Uppåkrastudier 10. Acta Archaeologica Lundensia series in 8°, No. 48. Lund: Almqvist & Wiksell International.

—— and Lenntorp, K.-M. (2004). 'The enigmatic house', in Larsson (ed.), *Continuity for Centuries*, 3–48.

Leigh, D. (1984). 'Ambiguity in Anglo-Saxon Style I art'. *Antiquaries Journal* 64: 34–42.

Magnus, B. (2001a). 'The enigmatic brooches', in Magnus (ed.), *Roman Gold*, 279–95.

—— (ed.) (2001b). *Roman Gold and the Development of the Early Germanic Kingdoms: Aspects of Technical, Socio-Political, Socio-Economic, Artistic and Intellectual Development, A.D. 1–550*. Kungl. Vitterhets Historie och Antikvitets Akademien, Konferenser 51. Stockholm: Almqvist & Wiksell International.

Marzinzik, S. (2003). *Early Anglo-Saxon Belt Buckles (late 5th to early 8th Centuries AD): Their Classification and Context*. BAR British Series 357. Oxford: Archaeopress.

Müller-Wille, M. (1996). 'Königtum und Adel im Spiegel der Grabfunde', in A. Wieczorek, P. Périn, K. von Welch, and W. Menghin (eds.), *Die Franken: Wegbereiter Europas; Vor 1500 Jahren: König Chlodwig und seine Erben*. Exhibition catalogue, Reiss-Museum, Mannheim. Mainz: Verlag Philipp von Zabern, 206–21.

Munksgaard, E., and Thrane, H. (1978). 'Broholm'. *Reallexikon der Germanischen Altertumskunde* (Hoops) volume 3, 2nd edn: 469–70.

Nielsen, P. O., Randsborg, K., and Thrane, H. (eds.) (1994). *The Archaeology of Gudme and Lundeborg*. Arkæologiske Studier 10. Copenhagen: Akademisk Forlag.

Parfitt, K., and Dickinson, T. M. (2007). 'The Anglo-Saxon cemetery at Old Park, near Dover, revisited', in M. Henig and T. J. Smith (eds.), *Collectanea Antiqua: Essays in Memory of Sonia Chadwick Hawkes*. British Archaeological Reports International Series 1673. Oxford: Archaeopress, 111–26.

Pesch, A. (2002a). 'Uppåkra im Licht der Formular-Familien der völkerwanderungszeitlichen Goldbrakteaten', in Hårdh and Larsson (eds.), *Central Places in the Migration and Merovingian Periods*, 55–78.

—— (2002b). 'Frauen und Brakteaten—eine Skizze', in R. Simek and W. Heizmann (eds.), *Mythological Women: Studies in Memory of Lotte Motz 1922–1997*. Studia Medievalia Septentronalia. Vienna: Fassbaender, 33–80.

—— (2004). 'Formularfamilien kontinentaler Goldbrakteaten', in M. Lodewijckx, *Bruc ealles well: Archaeological Essays Concerning the Peoples of North-West Europe in the*

First Millennium AD. Acta Archaeologica Lovaniensa, Monographiae 15. Leuven: Leuven University Press, 157–80.

RANDSBORG, K. (1990). 'Beyond the Roman empire: archaeological discoveries in Gudme on Funen, Denmark'. *Oxford Journal of Archaeology* 9: 355–66.

ROTH, H. (ed.) (1986). *Zum Problem der Deutung frühmittelalterlicher Bildinhalte: Akten des 1. Internationalen Kolloquiums in Marburg a.d. Lahn, 15. bis 19. Februar 1983*. Veröffentlichungen des Vorgeschichtlichen Seminars der Phillips-Universität Marburg a.d. Lahn. Sonderband 4. Sigmaringen: Jan Thorbecke Verlag.

ROTH, U. (1987). 'Early Insular manuscripts: ornament and archaeology, with special reference to the dating of the Book of Durrow', in M. Ryan (ed.), *Ireland and Insular Art A.D. 500–1200*. Dublin: Royal Irish Academy, 23–9.

SALIN, B. (1904). *Die Altgermanische Thierornamentik*. Stockholm: Almqvist and Wiksell.

SCHULZE, M. (1976). 'Einflüsse byzantinischer Prunkgewänder auf die fränkische Frauentracht'. *Archäologische Korrespondenzblatt* 6: 149–63.

SPEAKE, G. (1980). *Anglo-Saxon Animal Art and its Germanic Background*. Oxford: Clarendon.

STAECKER, J. (2003). 'The cross goes north: Christian symbols and Scandinavian women', in Carver (ed.), *The Cross Goes North*, 463–82.

STEUER, H. (1987). 'Helm und Ringschwert. Prunkbewaffnung und Rangabzeichen germanischer Krieger Eine Übersicht'. *Studien zur Sachsenforschung* 6: 189–236.

SUZUKI, S. (2000). *The Quoit Brooch Style and Anglo-Saxon Settlement*. Bury St Edmunds: Boydell Press.

THEUWS, F., and ALKEMADE, M. (2000). 'A kind of mirror for men: sword depositions in Late Antique northern Gaul', in Theuws and Nelson (eds.), *Rituals of Power*, 401–76.

—— and NELSON, J. L. (eds.) (2000). *Rituals of Power: from Late Antiquity to the Early Middle Ages*. Transformation of the Roman World no. 8. Leiden: Brill.

VIERCK, H. (1978). 'La chemise de Sainte-Balthilde à Chelles et l'influence Byzantine sur l'art de cour mérovingien au VIIe siècle'. *Actes du Colloque International d'Archéologie Rouen 1975/* 3: 521–64.

—— (1981). '*Imitatio imperii* und *interpretatio germanica* vor der Wikingerzeit', in R. Zeitler (ed.), *Les Pays de Nord et Byzance*. Acta Universitatis Upsaliensis. Figura Nova Series 19. Uppsala: Almqvist & Wiksell International, 64–113.

WAMERS, E. (forthcoming). 'Behind animals, plants and interlace. Salin's Style II on Christian objects', in J. Graham-Campbell and M. Ryan (eds.), *Anglo-Saxon/Irish Relations before the Vikings*. British Academy.

WATT, M. (1999). 'Kings or gods? Iconographic evidence from Scandinavian gold foil figures', in Dickinson and Griffiths (eds.), *The Making of Kingdoms*, 173–83.

—— (2004). 'The gold-figure foils ("Guldgubbar") from Uppåkra', in Larsson (ed.), *Continuity for Centuries*, 167–221.

WEBSTER, L. (1992). 'Death's diplomacy: Sutton Hoo in the light of other male princely burials', in Farrell and Neuman de Vegvar (eds.), *Sutton Hoo*, 75–81.

—— and BACKHOUSE, J. (eds.) (1991). *The Making of England: Anglo-Saxon Art and Culture AD 600–900*. London: British Museum Publications.

—— and Brown, M. (eds.) (1997). *The Transformation of the Roman World AD 400–900*. London: The British Museum Press.

WERNER, J. (1982). 'Das Schiffsgrab von Sutton Hoo. Forschungsgeschichte und Informationsstand zwischen 1939 und 1980'. *Germania* 60/1: 193–209.

WILSON, D. (1992). 'Sutton Hoo—pros and cons', in Farrell and Neuman de Vegvar (eds.), *Sutton Hoo*, 5–12.

WOLFRAM, H. (1994). '*Origo et religio*. Ethnic traditions and literature in early medieval texts'. *Early Medieval Europe* 3: 19–38.

YORKE, B. (2003a). *Nunneries and the Anglo-Saxon Royal Houses*. Leicester: Leicester University Press.

—— (2003b). 'The adaptation of the Anglo-Saxon royal courts to Christianity', in Carver (ed.), *The Cross Goes North*, 243–57.

CHAPTER 46

CRIME AND PUNISHMENT

ANDREW REYNOLDS

INTRODUCTION

Traditionally, archaeologists have charted the rise of secular elites in Anglo-Saxon England through the remains left by their burial customs and settlements. A series of spectacular discoveries, particularly of later-sixth- and seventh-century date, indicate the emergence of an increasingly polarized social structure developing from the apparently kin-based communities of the fifth and sixth centuries. Indeed, much has been written in recent years regarding the development and nature of early kingship as an institution and of kingdoms as social and political entities during this period (Bassett 1989; Carver 1992; Scull 1993). Much has been made of the abilities of Anglo-Saxon elites to control the procurement of rare or exotic commodities, wage war against their neighbours, marry off their sons and daughters to form alliances, and impose taxes on their subjects. High-status burials with evidence for international contacts, notably Sutton Hoo, and pretentious residences representing a command of substantial local resources, such as Yeavering, however, tell us little about the formal mechanisms of social organization or processes of early governance and administration. While developing systems of social organization may be reasonably inferred from the presence of prestige goods in elite contexts and the development of central places with impressive buildings, it nevertheless remains possible to interpret such evidence purely as a function of the ability of a warrior elite to maintain authority as much by force as by formal negotiation, dispute settlement, and other processes characteristic of more complex societies.

Expressions of secular power in the early Middle Ages, however, can be approached in a wider range of contexts. Several historians have, in recent years, placed increasing emphasis on the importance of limiting feud and maintaining fora for dispute settlement as a key element of the emergence and maintenance of successful kingship (Hudson 2006; Hyams 2001, 2003). Archaeology, in the form of execution cemeteries, is now making a major contribution to our knowledge of judicial activity. One of the principal advantages of studying archaeological material is that it provides a standpoint, independent of written evidence, for assessing the chronology and landscape context of punitive practice and, importantly, a means of assessing the reality of the intent expressed in written law codes.

While there is a substantial body of archaeological information from pre-Christian community cemeteries for the burial of individuals who were deemed social 'others' by their peers, this material is beyond the scope of this chapter and is treated in detail elsewhere (Reynolds 2009a). Although certain traits of outcast burial can be followed across the pagan/Christian transition in England, this chapter covers the seventh to eleventh centuries, from the conversion of the Anglo-Saxons to Christianity up to a century or so after the Norman Conquest, when essentially 'Anglo-Saxon' practice for dealing with social miscreants disappears from the archaeological record. The chronological starting point for this chapter is marked by a distinct change in the archaeological record whereby from the later seventh century onwards, the burials of social outcasts are found outside community cemeteries rather than within them and a fundamental shift in social practice can be observed.

A brief sketch is provided of judicial behaviour as it is understood from a variety of documentary sources, and this material is considered in relation to the developing administrative landscapes of the period. The evidence from execution cemeteries is then presented, examining aspects such as their location and relationship to existing landscape features, and the range of burial types encountered within them. Further evidence for non-churchyard burial, such as isolated burials including those at crossroads, is also taken into account and related to our central theme.

The evidence of written sources

Although substantial advances have been made with regard to our understanding of early written sources for the rise of powerful families, including genealogies, regnal lists, and charters, the earliest law codes remain difficult to interpret, while written sources more generally present significant difficulties for historians, as they do for archaeologists (Dumville 1977; Yorke 1993). No single contemporary source describes Anglo-Saxon judicial procedure in its entirety and what follows outlines what is known of the way that state-administered justice worked, drawn from a range of texts. It is important to note, however, two of the principal failings of much general work on judicial practice, namely a neglect of chronological change and of regional variation. More recent work has approached the written laws with a much keener eye on developments over time (Wormald 1999a).

The Anglo-Saxon laws

Over the last 150 years scholars have pondered whether the surviving law codes, along with other forms of documents, represent only a fraction of the actual volume of written legal prescriptions, or, alternatively, if they are a sizeable, if not near-complete, assemblage (Wormald 1991a: 25–6). It seems likely that the surviving laws do represent the majority of such material and it is pertinent here to note Patrick Wormald's comment that Anglo-Saxon law codes are better seen as minutes of much more extensive discussions at councils, while earlier commentators have noted how the material assumes a wide knowledge on the part of the reader of existing, orally-transmitted, custom and practice (Wormald 1978: 48; Pollock and Maitland 1923: 26). An indication that the written laws do not represent the full body of Anglo-Saxon law is further demonstrated by the fact that there is not one instance of a written law being quoted in a lawsuit, charter preamble, or any other source relating to the legal process beyond the copying of earlier laws by later kings (Wormald 1999a: 143).

The earliest English law code is that of the Kentish King Æthelberht produced c. AD 600, which is a long and detailed tariff of offences and (largely) monetary fines for their atonement. It is worth noting that the very first clause of English legislation committed to vellum relates to keeping the peace at a meeting-place (OE M[æthl] friþ)(Abt 1; Attenborough 1922: 4 and n. 2), the context, of course, for dispute settlement and arbitration. Three further sets of laws emanated from the Kentish court during the seventh century: the lost laws of Earconberht (640–64) noted only by Bede (*HE* III.8), those of the joint kings Hlothere (673–85) and Eadric (685–6); and, finally, dated 685, the laws of King Wihtred. Wihtred's laws are broadly contemporary with the first of the West Saxon legal codes issued by King Ine, probably between 688 and 694 (Wormald 1999a: 103, n. 358), and direct points of comparison can be drawn between the two, for example clauses stating the need to sound a horn if travelling away from a known route (W 28; I 20). Of particular significance is the fact that Ine's code is the first to refer to capital punishment, a chronological development supported by archaeological evidence. It is not until the later ninth-century code of King Alfred that the issue of legal codes became commonplace in Anglo-Saxon royal courts. Even Alfred's code leant heavily on its predecessors, including a reference to Æthelberht's legislation, a full rendition of Ine's laws and an acknowledgement of the 'laws' of King Offa, the last now recognized rather as a 'capitulary' produced in 789 by papal legates at the Mercian and Northumbrian courts than as a legal code in the traditional sense (Wormald 1991a). Following Alfred, as Wormald has noted, each of the succeeding Anglo-Saxon kings (with the exception of three short reigns) issued at least two codes, with those of Cnut's reign (1016–35) ending the series (Wormald 1999b: 279).

As noted above with regard to Æthelberht's laws, by far the most common penalties in the whole series of Anglo-Saxon laws are monetary fines. Despite popular perceptions of early medieval societies as unduly harsh, with people's lives being a cheap commodity, even the written sources indicate that capital punishment was a last resort reserved only for the most severe offences or for repeat offenders. Fines rather than execution also served to limit the development of blood-feud between the families and associates of perpetrator and victim (Wormald 1991b: 11). A further indication that execution was relatively uncommon is provided by the observation that only six of the 178 surviving Anglo-Saxon lawsuits record capital punishment as the outcome (Wormald 1988; Reynolds 2009a). Again, archaeological evidence can throw interesting light on the frequency of capital punishment in cases where execution cemeteries are completely excavated and well-dated (see below).

A remarkable tenth-century document known as the Fonthill letter describes the career of an Anglo-Saxon serial offender named Helmstan who, although a landowner, committed theft on two occasions, firstly of a belt (presumably one with valuable fittings), and subsequently of cattle; despite two legal hearings and forfeiture of his estates, Helmstan emerged a freeman with his lands intact (Boynton and Reynolds 1996). Although personal connections might have aided Helmstan's eventual freedom, his guilt was 'proven' in the second instance by an early example of the presentation at court of evidence in the form of scratches to his face, evidently acquired whilst in flight. This case further indicates that capital punishment was the exception rather than the rule.

In Anglo-Saxon England, cases were heard at public assemblies, normally at meetings of the hundred court, the hundred being a self-contained local territory below the level of the shire, at least from the tenth century when it is described explicitly in a document probably of King Edgar's reign (959–75) known as the Hundred Ordinance (Wormald 1999a: 378–9). Among other situations, the Ordinance describes procedures for raising a posse in pursuit of cattle thieves and the obligations of populations of individual districts to assist each other. Hlothere and Eadric's laws refer specifically to judicial assembly, while the early-tenth-century code of the West Saxon king Edward the Elder (899–921) is the first to note that hearings were to be held every four weeks, presumably dictated by the lunar cycle. In an age prior to the use of forensic evidence (with the notable exception of Helmstan!), and unless caught red-handed, innocence was 'established' by the ability of the accused to assemble credible 'oath-helpers' to swear to his or her good character.

There is a substantial body of field remains relating to sites of judicial assembly. Hundreds shared their names with their assembly sites and many of the latter can still be located in the modern landscape. Hundred courts commonly met at distinctive locations, often marked by pre-existing monuments such as Bronze Age barrows or standing stones, while other meeting-places included bridges and fords, trees, and, much less commonly, settlements (Meaney 1995; 1997; Pantos and Semple 2004). Assembly sites were normally located centrally within their districts, but often at the meeting points of boundaries of lesser importance, presumably to ensure the neutrality of the place (Pantos 2003). The origins of public assembly as a means of dispute settlement are obscure. Although the existence of hundreds named after pagan deities, such as Woden and Thor, and the co-incidence of certain hundred meeting-places with early Anglo-Saxon burial sites (for example Heane, Kent; Loveden Hill, Lincolnshire; and Moot Hill, Driffield, Yorkshire) suggests a pre-Christian communal origin for certain meeting-places, others might result from later Anglo-Saxon administrative planning determined by elites (Meaney 1995; Reynolds in press). While aspects of the place-name evidence for assembly sites have been explored, the field archaeology of such places is effectively unknown. About a dozen sites have been investigated by excavation, in each case barrows, but the use of assembly sites must have incorporated a wider range and tantalizing glimpses of possible sites of periodic assembly have been recorded at a few locations, such as Dorney, Berkshire and Saltwood in Kent, the latter the site of the meeting-place of Heane Hundred in Kent noted above (Adkins and Petchey 1984; Foreman *et al.* 2002; Reynolds in press).

In the event that an individual was caught in the act of committing an offence or judged guilty at trial, then a range of punishments could be enacted. As we have observed, the majority of atonements comprised monetary fines, but for a range of offences from the reign of Ine onwards, courts could impose the death penalty, of which more shortly.

Non-capital punishments found in the late Anglo-Saxon laws include exile, forfeiture of land, and mutilation. Banishment from society is prescribed in King Athelstan's Exeter law code of AD 935 (IV As 3; V As 1–3) and it has been suggested that communities of outcasts may have been a feature of the late Anglo-Saxon landscape (Tallon 1998–9). Forfeiture of land appears in the laws from the reign of King Alfred (871–99) (Wormald 1999a: 149). Mutilation varied from effectively state-sponsored grievous bodily harm, then casting out mutilated offenders to die in the fields (Edward and Guthrum 10; Wormald 1999a: 389–91), to more specific wounding, such as the removal of a hand for theft or on account of counterfeiting by moneyers, where the severed extremity was to be 'fastened over the mint' (II As 14.1). Scalping and the removal of ears, noses, eyelids, and tongues is known from the tenth century, notably in legislation of King Edgar's reign preserved only in Lantfred of

Winchester's *Translatio et Miracula St Swithuni*, and such practice is thought to have developed as a result of the increasing influence of leading churchmen on the moral and ideological tenor of the law (Wormald 1999a: 125–7).

Capital punishments prescribed by the laws largely comprise hanging and decapitation, although other means related to social rank are also recorded. Anglo-Saxon society in the Christian centuries was highly stratified, but based on an essential distinction between the free and unfree. Slaves (OE *thralls*) were valued according to their abilities and to whom they belonged, while ordinary freemen (OE *ceorls*) had a monetary value, known as OE *wergild*, literally 'man money', recognized in the eyes of the law as 200 shillings. Thegns, direct servants of the king in the earliest Christian centuries and local lords by the end of our period, had a *wergild* of 1,200 shillings. In King Athelstan's fourth law code, female slaves could be burned for theft, while free women might be thrown from a cliff or drowned; male slaves could be stoned to death (IV As 6.7, 6.4, and 6.5).

Other Written Sources

The later law codes contain a few remarks noting either the good conduct of the people or, alternatively, the king's disappointment that the laws are not being upheld (Keynes 1991). Otherwise, beyond the lawsuits and charters, archaeology provides our only means of assessing the degree to which offences of the most serious nature occurred.

Poetry and prose sources provide both indirect and direct information that aids reconstruction of the judicial process. While the putatively eighth-century epic poem *Beowulf* (lines 2444–6 and 2940–2) contains references to people hanging from gallows, the tenth-century OE *Life of St Juliana* records how the saint is taken 'close to the border of the country' to be slain by a slash of the sword (Bradley 1982: 317), a territorial location exhibited by places of execution, as we will see. The OE poem *The Fates of Men*, from the tenth-century collection known as the Exeter Book, includes a graphic description of an executed corpse:

One shall ride the high gallows and upon his death hang until his soul's treasury, his bloody bone-framed body, disintegrates. There the raven black of plumage will pluck out the sight from his head and shred the soulless corpse—and he cannot fend off with his hands the loathsome bird of prey from its evil intent. His life is fled and, deprived of his senses, beyond hope of survival, he suffers his lot, pallid upon the beam, enveloped in the mist of death. His name is damned.

(Mackie 1934: 29)

Anglo-Saxon land charters supply a range of material related to our theme. Charters frequently open with a written statement of the circumstances for the change in ownership of an estate, known as a preamble, and a particularly noteworthy example dated 963 x 75 records how a Northamptonshire widow was drowned on account of witchcraft at (a) London bridge (probably in her home county) for sticking iron pins into an effigy of her husband (S1377). By far the most valuable contribution of charter evidence, however, is provided by the evidence of boundary clauses, written descriptions of the physical features delimiting estates in largely rural but also urban contexts. Prior to the ninth century, boundary clauses are mainly written in Latin, but after that date they are produced in the vernacular. While the earliest reliable charters are of later-seventh-century date, the central decades of the tenth century saw what can only be described as an explosion in the granting of parcels of land, mainly by kings to private individuals (D. Hill 1981: 26, table 36).

For our purposes, boundary surveyors used a wide variety of terminology to describe places of execution and burial. The earliest charter to describe a place of execution is a document of AD 778, preserved in a tenth-century copy, that records *gabuli* (L. 'gallows') in the bounds of an estate at Little Bedwyn in Wiltshire (S264). The site lay on what by Domesday was the northern boundary of the hundred of Kinwardstone, perhaps indicating the significance of that boundary from a much earlier period. The mass of information from charters is of tenth-century date, but rather than viewing this feature as describing a proliferation of execution sites during this period, it is instead a function of the increased production of such documents. The distribution of charters is also uneven geographically and thus attempting to establish regional patterns in the terminology of execution sites must be approached with caution. Nevertheless, and with these caveats in mind, it is possible to observe the use of the term *wearg* (wrongdoer) in combination with terms such as 'barrow' and 'rood' (meaning cross/gallows in this context) evenly across southern England. The OE term *heaðenan byrgels* 'heathen burial(s)', long considered to refer to disused pagan burial grounds by late Anglo-Saxon land surveyors, has now been argued on both archaeological and topographical grounds to relate instead to the burial places of social outcasts of the Christian period (Reynolds 2002). Interestingly, the 'heathen burial' terms exhibit a marked concentration in south-central England, particularly in the counties of Berkshire, Hampshire, and Wiltshire (ibid.: 176, fig. 1). Other terms include OE *Þeof* 'thief' and *sceacere* 'robber' in combination with topographical or other features which are also exhibited variously by the series of excavated execution sites.

A literal description of a place of execution can be found in the three instances of the OE term *cwealmstow* 'killing place', while certain of the dozen or so references to OE *heafod stoccan* 'head-stakes' may refer to the display of heads on poles (see Winchester below). A striking feature of many of the places of execution and outcast burial mentioned in charters is that they lie on the boundaries of Domesday hundreds, as opposed to more local territories (see Reynolds 2009a for a full discussion of the charter evidence).

A dynamic judicial landscape?

We have noted so far that places of judgement and execution were distinct from each other in a landscape context, but that individual hundreds contained all of the administrative apparatus necessary for the maintenance of the judicial process. Prior to a court hearing, the accused could be confined and there is evidence from Ine's laws (I 36) that this could be the responsibility of an ealdorman (an official of the king), while Mercian charters of c. AD 800 note that wrongdoers should be delivered to a royal manor (S179; S1861). By the reign of King Alfred, explicit reference to the maintenance of prisons at royal estate centres is provided by the king's own writings, for example in Books I and III of his translation of Augustine's *Soliloquies*.

In difficult cases an individual might be subject to judicial ordeal, although there is limited evidence for this practice actually being carried out in Anglo-Saxon England. Ordeal is first referred to in Ine's laws (I 37), its conduct explicitly described in a tenth-century text known as *Ordal*, while a few minster churches, for example Canterbury, Northampton, and Taunton, are known to have possessed the right to conduct the ritual (Wormald 1999a: 373–4; Blair 2005: 448). Altogether, it can be seen that the progress of a capital offender from apprehension to execution might lead him or her on a protracted and highly ritualized journey throughout their local district ending up ultimately at its limits.

ANGLO-SAXON EXECUTION CEMETERIES

Besides the remains of assembly sites noted above, archaeological evidence for judicial activity largely comprises excavated execution cemeteries of which about thirty have been identified, mainly in southern and central England (Fig. 46.1), with only one known cemetery in northern England at Walkington Wold in East Yorkshire just north of the River Humber (Buckberry and Hadley 2007). Given that the majority of known execution sites are associated with pre-existing features, predominantly barrows, it is remarkable that the extensive barrow digging campaigns by eighteenth- and nineteenth-century antiquarians across large tracts of English upland landscapes did not reveal sites. The vigorous activities of antiquaries such as Greenwell and Mortimer in Yorkshire, Faussett in Kent, and (William) Cunnington in Wiltshire failed to reveal a single Anglo-Saxon execution site, although it is possible that their method of sinking a trench through the summit of burial mounds might well have failed to locate execution burials, which are normally located on the southern and eastern sides and away from their associated mounds. Even so, it may well be the case that the known distribution of sites broadly reflects the reality and there may well have been

Figure 46.1 Distribution of excavated execution cemeteries in England: 1 Dunstable, 2 Galley Hill, 3 Abingdon, 4 Castle Hill, 5 Bran Ditch, 6 Chesterton Lane, 7 Wandlebury, 8 Wor Barrow, 9 Meon Hill, 10 Old Dairy Cottage, 11 Stockbridge Down, 12 Staines, 13 South Acre, 14 Crosshill, 15 Wallingford/Crowmarsh, 16 Sutton Hoo, 17 Ashtead, 18 Eashing, 19 Galley Hills, 20 Guildown, 21 Hog's Back, 22 Burpham, 23 Malling Hill, 24 Bokerley Dyke, 25 Old Sarum, 26 Roche Court Down, 27 Walkington Wold

distinct regional differences in the ways that miscreants were despatched and disposed of according to customs which were never recorded in documents and which have left no currently discernible archaeological trace. As noted above, the distribution of terms for places of execution and burial in Anglo-Saxon charters exhibits patterns which must be a function of either local practice or dialect, yet a lack of charter references to such places or excavated cemeteries is a marked feature, for example, of Kent, despite extensive charter coverage, and intensive antiquarian activity there.

Location

One of the most remarkable aspects of Anglo-Saxon execution sites is their consistent location on territorial boundaries, in the main of major administrative significance such as shire, hundred, royal estate, and borough. Anglo-Saxon territorial geography can be at least partially reconstructed using the evidence of the Domesday Survey of 1086, which groups individual holdings by hundreds, while extant boundary clauses in many cases facilitate a mapping of more local territories. Indeed, one of the major debates in early medieval archaeology over the last forty years or so has concerned the antiquity of the territorial framework of the English landscape as visualized by the Domesday Survey; execution cemeteries with radiocarbon dates bring an important new perspective to the problem. The prevalent view that local estates and the hundreds within which they were grouped are products of the late Anglo-Saxon period (cf. Hooke 1998) can now be challenged (at least outside the Danelaw) by the fact that a series of execution sites with origins scientifically dated to the seventh and eighth centuries indicate a much earlier recognition of territorial limits, particularly at the scale of units that became explicitly termed hundreds by the tenth century (Reynolds 2009a).

The realization that a series of execution cemeteries are to be found on the boundaries of Anglo-Saxon boroughs, such as Cambridge, Eashing, Guildford, Steyning, and Winchester, and probably Old Sarum, Staines, and Wallingford among others, reveals two of the defining characteristics of Anglo-Saxon towns long considered beyond the reach of the archaeologist, those of a judicial role and legal autonomy, both key features of Martin Biddle's influential list of urban criteria published in his classic essay on Anglo-Saxon towns (Biddle 1976: 100). Importantly, the archaeological evidence for the judicial function of each of these towns is not to be found at the town itself, but on major approach roads where they cross borough bounds. At Cambridge, the execution cemetery at Chesterton Lane Corner lies on the Roman road approaching the town from the north-west and lies on the boundary of the Domesday Hundred of Cambridge; radiocarbon dates demonstrate beyond doubt a later seventh- or an eighth-century origin for the cemetery, perhaps coinciding with a period of urban regeneration during the reign of King Offa of Mercia (Cessford *et al.* in press). On the approach to Winchester, again from the north-west and along a Roman road, is a cemetery with many decapitated individuals at a location on the Domesday Hundred and borough boundary known today as Harestock, derived from OE *heafod stocc*. Three separate sets of Anglo-Saxon charter bounds (for the estates of Chilcomb, Easton, and Headbourne Worthy) describe the spot in those very terms. Radiocarbon dates from the Winchester cemetery confirm its existence by the second half of the ninth century, precisely the period when the town began to grow rapidly as a centre of occupation and commerce (Reynolds 2009b).

In rural locations execution cemeteries lay on the boundaries of hundreds, presumably with the responsibility for their maintenance shared by the districts either side of the boundary. Rural cemeteries as well as urban ones also frequently lay beside major highways as illustrated by the cemeteries of Meon Hill and Stockbridge Down in Hampshire, and Roche Court Down on the Hampshire/Wiltshire border, all of which lay beside the highway linking Old Sarum (where yet another excavated cemetery is known) with Winchester; a later Anglo-Saxon traveller between the two towns would thus have seen at least five places of execution leaving no doubt about the presence of royal power in the landscape (Liddell 1933; N. G. Hill 1937; Stone 1932; Blackmore 1894). A highly distinctive feature of Anglo-Saxon execution sites and cemeteries is their visibility. They are frequently placed either immediately adjacent to or within prominent view of routes of communication either by road or water. How such prominence in the landscape was perceived is difficult to judge, but surely attitudes varied according to the social, moral, and political perspective of the individual observer. While one person may have read the message of the gallows as one of royal protection and a clear sign of the king's concern for public security, others may equally have found the spectacle of heads on stakes and rotting corpses, potentially of children as young as 12, hanging from gallows an intimidating and depressing manifestation of an overbearing moralizing state.

The re-use of earlier features

One of the more intriguing aspects of the location of execution sites and cemeteries is their overwhelming tendency to re-use pre-existing monuments, largely Bronze Age barrows but also linear earthworks (Fig. 46.2). To a degree this pattern can be explained by the fact that both monument types were used as boundary markers in the Anglo-Saxon period, but their specific re-use as execution sites indicates both conscious choice and a broader cultural acceptance of such places as suitable for the burial of individuals literally cast to the margins of society. Literary sources and place-names suggest that attitudes to ancient monuments, particularly barrows and dykes, became negative following the conversion to Christianity (Semple 1998; 2003), while a more nuanced approach suggests that a sense of place was a fundamental consideration and that in certain contexts ancient monuments might be positively viewed and in others not; liminality was surely a key factor. The life of the early-eighth-century St Guthlac, for example, reports how, following a life of ill ways, the saint set up his hermitage in the chamber of an ancient burial mound where he was tormented by the devils and demons who lived there (Colgrave 1956; Semple 1998). While this is an oversimplification of a complex debate relating to (changing) perceptions of the Anglo-Saxon landscape, the fact that virtually every known execution site references a pre-existing barrow or linear earthwork must be significant. Indeed, linear earthworks were frequently given

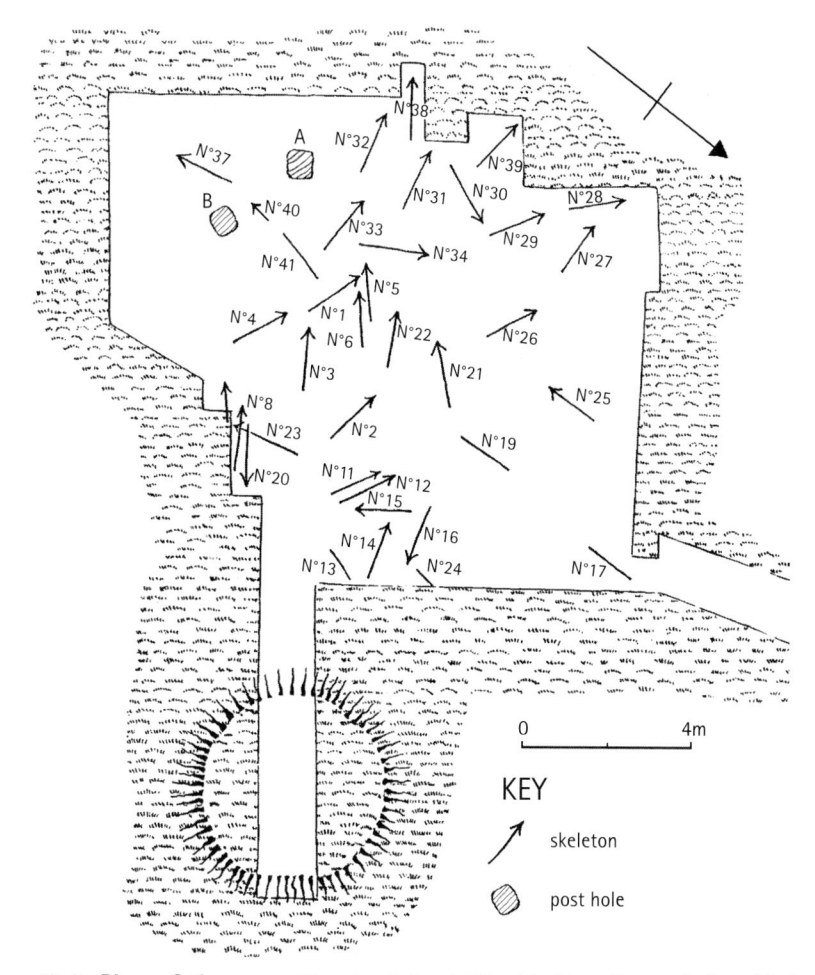

Figure 46.2 Plan of the execution burials at Stockbridge Down (after N. G. Hill 1937: pl. 3; reproduced by permission of the Hampshire Field Club and Archaeological Society)

grim names, alluding to Woden (Gelling 1988: 149), and in other cases named in ways emphasizing their liminal character, for example the Fleam Dyke in Cambridgeshire (from OE *fleming*, 'fugitive').

Dating

Perhaps the most significant aspect for the study of execution cemeteries has been the application in recent years of radiocarbon dating. Before radiocarbon dating became a widely applied technique, and before execution sites were studied in detail, three excavations—at Guildown, Surrey (Lowther 1931), Meon Hill, and

Stockbridge Down, Hampshire (Liddell 1933; N. G. Hill 1937)—undertaken in the early part of the twentieth century, had revealed burials associated with coins of Edward the Confessor (1042–66). This dating evidence appeared to confirm, at least broadly, that organized judicial activity was indeed a feature of the late Anglo-Saxon period as indicated by written evidence. A series of sites, however, have now revealed burials dated potentially as early as the seventh century and certainly the eighth century: Cambridge, Staines, Sutton Hoo, and Walkington Wold (Cessford *et al.* in press; Hayman and Reynolds 2005; Carver 2005; Buckberry and Hadley 2007; Reynolds 2009b). Dates from Staines and Sutton Hoo indicate the use of such sites into the twelfth century. Low-status dress-fittings, such as iron and copper-alloy buckles and the occasional simple hooked-tag, are sometimes found with execution burials and fit with the date-range provided by other means. The relative abundance of such objects, which imply clothed burial, compared to ordinary cemeteries indicates a lack of preparation of the body for burial as would be expected in a normative context.

Burial practices

The range of burial practices found at execution cemeteries is surprisingly broad. In contrast to the view of many commentators over the years who have characterized execution burials as hasty and careless (cf. Dickinson 1974: 23), careful study reveals considerable variety. While alignment of graves with the head to the west is the most common in execution cemeteries, it is also characteristic of pagan and Christian cemeteries and thus it is not possible to assume, as many have done, that it is exclusive to Christian burials. At most execution cemeteries a wide range of orientations is observed, although at sites where linear ditches are appropriated, the course of the earthwork determines both the linear arrangement of the burials and the orientation of the corpses, although heads and feet may be reversed. Bran Ditch in Cambridgeshire provides a case study of an extensively, if poorly, excavated example of such a site (Lethbridge and Palmer 1929). Where individuals have been decapitated, the head is often found placed between the legs, as seen in several cases at Meon Hill in Hampshire (Fig. 46.3).

Again in common with most 'normative' cemeteries, the most frequently encountered body position in execution cemeteries is for the corpse to be placed lying on the back, with the hands either by the side or crossed over the pelvis or a variation of the two. In other cases, however, bodies might be found lying on their side, often in the flexed or 'crouched' position, while a series of burials has been recorded where the corpses appear to have been bound or trussed, for example at Sutton Hoo, where burial 38 from Group 1 of the two groups of execution victims appears to have been bound with the knees drawn tightly towards the chest (Carver 2005: 330, fig. 147). Other instances are documented where the individual

Figure 46.3 South-facing view of execution burials at Meon Hill; note the position of skulls (after Liddell 1933: pl 5; reproduced by permission of the Hampshire Field Club and Archaeological Society)

concerned appears to have been despatched while kneeling in a shallow grave. At South Acre in Norfolk and Roche Court Down in Wiltshire, the lower legs of two individuals are clearly bent at the knees and underneath the upper legs; presumably the corpses were simply pushed backwards into the grave which was then backfilled (Wymer 1996: 73, pl. 19; Stone 1932: pl. 1). The nature of the latter kind of burial suggests a desire for a rapid execution and burial, and that there was no wish on the part of the executioners or authorities to display the corpse as a sign of secular authority in the way suggested by the *Fates of Men* excerpt quoted above. In plenty of other cemeteries, however, there are examples of partial corpses committed to the ground apparently having lost extremities while hanging from a gallows. We have already noted the 'head stakes' recorded in certain Anglo-Saxon charters, but at Walkington Wold in Yorkshire, skulls, some lacking their mandibles, indicative of weathering, were found buried separately from corpses over the Bronze Age mound which had been re-used as an execution site (Buckberry and Hadley 2007).

Besides these various modes of burial, and other minor variations, three further features of execution cemeteries require comment. Prone, or face-down, burials are found, if in low numbers, at the majority of execution sites. Rather than indicating hasty or careless burial they suggest a conscious and purposeful mode of burial and in a number of cases they are found in deep, well-cut graves in contrast to the normally shallow burials otherwise encountered. A striking example is Grave 159 from Guildown in Surrey (Fig. 46.4), where the prone burial of a man with his hands tied behind his back had been carefully laid in a well-cut grave nearly one metre deep (Lowther 1931). The motivation to bury a corpse in this way is most likely due to a genuine fear that particular individuals might return from the graves to haunt the living. Measures such as prone burial and decapitation appear to have been viewed as an effective means by which to render a corpse 'safe' (see for example the twelfth-century life of [the Anglo-Saxon] St Modwenna where decapitation is employed for just such a purpose: Bartlett 2002).

Burials with tied hands are frequently found in execution cemeteries and present circumstantial evidence that the individuals were hanged. The only illustration of a judicial hanging from an Anglo-Saxon manuscript, from BL MS Cotton Claudius BIV f. 9v, shows a man being hanged from a two-post gallows with his hands clearly secured behind his back (Booth *et al.* 2007: 405). Burials are also known with the hands tied to the front of the body and, in a very few instances, excavators have recorded flexion of the hands (in one case at the neck—presumably a result of trying to free a noose), an indicator of a highly stressful death experience.

A final notable aspect of execution cemeteries is that they often contain multiple burials, most frequently two individuals but also triple burials and occasionally more. These burials are worthy of comment in several respects. At the most basic level, instances of multiple burials might be read as the outcome of the cutting down of several individuals who happened to be hanging from a gallows or who had been otherwise executed around the same time, the digging of a single grave simply an exercise in efficiency. A more nuanced approach might suggest that the individuals so found are related more closely, perhaps even intimately. Three factors tend towards the latter view. The first is the disposition of the bodies as found. Several instances of double and triple burial, for example from Staines, exhibit what are best described as sexually suggestive positions (Fig. 46.5). The second aspect is that female burials are rare at execution cemeteries, yet there are several cases where women have been found in multiple burials, at Galley Hill, Bedfordshire (Dyer 1974); South Acre, Norfolk; and Sutton Hoo. The third indicator, repeated multiple burial at one specific location, is present only at Staines, although that site serves to illustrate all three aspects particularly well (Hayman and Reynolds 2005: 224, illus. 5).

The geography of burial

Brief mention should be made here of the fact that churchyard and execution cemeteries represent the two extremes of burial location in the Anglo-Saxon

Figure 46.4 Prone burial 159 with the hands tied behind the back from Guildown (after Lowther 1931: pl. 22; reproduced by permission of the Surrey Archaeological Society)

Figure 46.5 Double burial S441/S442 (left) and triple burial S432/S433/S434 (right) from Staines. Note the entwined position of the double interment and the placing of the hands of the central interment (after Hayman and Reynolds 2005: pls. 7 and 8; reproduced by permission of the Royal Archaeological Institute and the Surrey County Archaeological Unit)

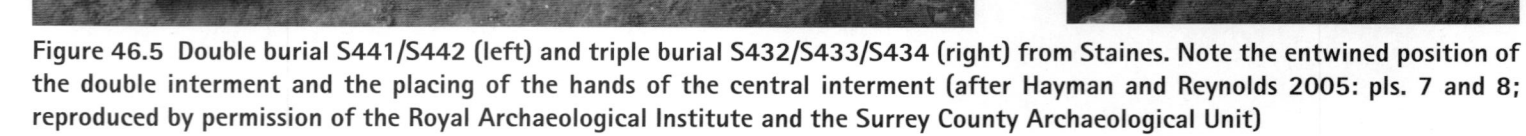

landscape between the seventh and eleventh centuries. While it is possible to observe a developing concept of liminality in the context of early Anglo-Saxon cemeteries, whereby prone or other unusual burials were often placed at the edges of community cemeteries, the range of burial contexts encountered in the Christian centuries is really quite extraordinary. Field cemeteries lacking churches but associated with rural settlements are an increasingly recognized class of 'normal' cemeteries, while excavation and radiocarbon dating has revealed a series of isolated burials on local boundaries that appear to begin in the seventh and eighth centuries (Reynolds 2009a). Many are associated with routeways, including crossroads, and provide an archaeological manifestation of the named individual burials found in a number of Anglo-Saxon charter bounds (Reynolds 2002). This latter type of burial is perhaps the longest-running individual burial type found in England as it was still being enacted in local situations for suicide burials into the nineteenth century.

Conclusions

Judicial activity and its outcomes are not simply a reflection of the prescriptions of secular authorities in a climate of state formation and consolidation, but instead represent a complex melding of pre-Christian practice with regard to individual burial rites, secular administration with regard to the use of administrative boundaries, folk belief in terms of the re-use of barrows and linear earthworks and concepts of liminality, and, later in the period, ecclesiastical influence relating to exclusion from consecrated ground and an increasingly overbearing moral codification of Anglo-Saxon law.

What processes explain the development of judicial behaviour in Anglo-Saxon society? It seems most logical to view the need for formal judicial practice against the background of kingdom formation. While kingdoms might conquer their neighbours by military force, such territorial expansion necessitated the domination and protection of social groups unrelated by kin to their conquerors (Reynolds 2009a). Given that radiocarbon dating places the earliest execution cemeteries within the period of the origins of Anglo-Saxon kingdoms, formalized judicial activity can be seen as part of a package of social and economic phenomena, such as the widespread use of coinage and development of mercantile centres, that characterized the growth and consolidation of the major early Anglo-Saxon kingdoms. Prior to this major phase of developing social complexity, individual communities of the fifth and sixth centuries, perhaps with a supra-local element, appear to have negotiated their own ways of determining social 'otherness', although interestingly with apparently universally understood modes of signifying such a status (prone burial and decapitation).

Although the populations of execution cemeteries vary by quite some measure, the average size is about fifty individuals. If such cemeteries could be used for periods of 500 years, as the radiocarbon determinations indicate, a crude reckoning, and that is all it can ever be, indicates one execution every ten years, while, if individual hundreds shared places of execution and burial, capital punishment at twenty-year intervals within individual hundreds is indicated, making such events remarkable rather than commonplace. The infrequency of capital punishment fits with the impression gained from the surviving laws and lawsuits and serves to underscore a contemporary appreciation of the severity of the ultimate penalty.

Ultimately, this chapter shows how archaeological evidence can make a substantial contribution to debates about aspects of society only usually approached using written evidence. It also attempts to show that rather than emphasizing divisions between the disciplines of archaeology and history, much can be gained by focusing on points of contact in a positive way.

Acknowledgements

I am grateful to the volume editors for their invitation to contribute to this volume and subsequently for their forbearance. The subject matter of this chapter represents a summary of the book from which it is drawn (Reynolds 2009a).

References

Adkins, R. A., and Petchey, M. R. (1984). 'Secklow Hundred Mound and other meeting place mounds in England'. *Archaeological Journal* 141: 243–51.

Attenborough, F. L. (ed.) (1922). *The Laws of the Earliest English Kings*. Cambridge: Cambridge University Press.

Bartlett, R. (ed. and trans.) (2002). *Geoffrey of Burton: Life and Miracles of St Modwenna*. Oxford: Oxford Univerity Press.

Bassett, S. (ed.) (1989). *The Origin of Anglo-Saxon Kingdoms*. Leicester: Leicester University Press.

Biddle, M. (1976). 'Towns', in D. M. Wilson (ed.), *The Archaeology of Anglo-Saxon England*. Cambridge: Cambridge University Press, 99–150.

BLACKMORE, H. P. (1894). 'On a barrow near Old Sarum'. *Salisbury Field Club Transactions* 1: 49–51.
BLAIR, J. (2005). *The Church in Anglo-Saxon Society*. Oxford: Oxford University Press.
BOOTH, P., DODD, A., ROBINSON, M., and SMITH, A. (2007). *Thames Through Time: The Archaeology of the Gravel Terraces of the Upper and Middle Thames; The Early Historical Period: AD 1–1000*. Oxford: Oxford University School of Archaeology.
BOYNTON, M., and REYNOLDS, S. (1996). 'The author of the Fonthill letter'. *Anglo-Saxon England* 25: 91–5.
BRADLEY, S. A. J. (1982). *Anglo-Saxon Poetry*. London: J.M. Dent and Sons Ltd.
BUCKBERRY, J. L., and HADLEY, D. M. (2007). 'An Anglo-Saxon execution cemetery at Walkington Wold, Yorkshire'. *Oxford Journal of Archaeology* 26(3): 309–29.
CARVER, M. (ed.) (1992). *The Age of Sutton Hoo*. Woodbridge: Boydell Press.
—— (2005). *Sutton Hoo: A Seventh-Century Princely Burial Ground and its Context*. Reports of the Research Committee of the Society of Antiquaries of London 69. London: The British Museum Press.
CESSFORD, C., DICKENS, A., and REYNOLDS, A. (in press). 'An Anglo-Saxon execution Cemetery at Chesterton Lane Corner, Cambridge'. *Archaeological Journal* 164.
COLGRAVE, B. (ed.) (1956). *Felix's Life of St Guthlac*. Cambridge: Cambridge University Press.
DICKINSON, T. M. (1974). *Cuddesdon and Dorchester-on-Thames*. BAR 1. Oxford: British Archaeological Reports.
DUMVILLE, D. N. (1977). 'Sub-Roman Britain: history and legend'. *History* 62: 173–92.
DYER, J. (1974). 'The excavation of two barrows on Galley Hill, Streatley'. *Bedfordshire Archaeological Journal* 9: 13–34.
FOREMAN, S., HILLIER, J., and PETTS, D. (2002). *Gathering the People, Settling the Land: The Archaeology of a Middle Thames Landscape; Anglo-Saxon to Post-Medieval*. Oxford: Oxford Archaeology.
GELLING, M. (1988). *Signposts to the Past*. 2nd edition. Chichester: Phillimore and Co. Ltd.
HAYMAN, G., and REYNOLDS, A. (2005). 'A Saxon and Saxo-Norman execution cemetery at 42–54 London Road, Staines'. *Archaeological Journal* 162: 115–57.
HILL, D. (1981). *An Atlas of Anglo-Saxon England*. Oxford: Basil Blackwell.
HILL, N. G. (1937). 'Excavations on Stockbridge Down 1935–36'. *Proceedings of the Hampshire Field Club* 13: 247–59.
HOOKE, D. (1998). *The Landscape of Anglo-Saxon England*. Leicester: Leicester University Press.
HUDSON, J. (2006). 'Faide, vengeance et violence en Angleterre (ca 900–1200)', in D. Barthélemy, F. Bougard, and R. Le Jan (eds.), *La Vengeance 400–1200*. Rome: École Française de Rome, 341–82.
HYAMS, P. (2001). 'Feud and the state in late Anglo-Saxon England'. *Journal of British Studies* 40(1): 1–43.
——(2003). *Rancor and Reconciliation in Medieval England*. Ithaca, NY and London: Cornell University Press.
KEYNES, S. (1991). 'Crime and punishment in the reign of King Aethelred the Unready', in I. N. Wood and N. Lund (eds.), *People and Places in Northern Europe 500–1600*. Woodbridge: Boydell Press, 67–81.
LETHBRIDGE, T. C., and PALMER, W. M. (1929). 'Excavations in the Cambridgeshire Dykes. VI. Bran Ditch. Second Report'. *Proceedings of the Cambridge Antiquarian Society* 30: 78–93.

LIDDELL, D. M. (1933). 'Excavations at Meon Hill'. *Proceedings of the Hampshire Field Club* 12: 126–62.

LOWTHER, A. W. G. (1931). 'The Saxon cemetery at Guildown, Guildford, Surrey'. *Surrey Archaeological Collections* 39: 1–50.

MACKIE, W. S. (1934). *The Exeter Book Part II: Poems IX–XXXII*. Early English Text Society Original Series 194. London, New York and Toronto: Oxford University Press.

MEANEY, A. (1995). 'Pagan English sanctuaries, place-names and hundred meeting places'. *Anglo-Saxon Studies in Archaeology and History* 8: 29–42.

—— (1997). 'Hundred meeting-places in the Cambridge region', in A. R. Rumble and A. D. Mills (eds.), *Names, Places and People: An Onomastic Miscellany in Memory of John McNeal Dodgson*. Stamford: Paul Watkins, 195–239.

PANTOS, A. (2003). 'On the edge of things: the boundary location of Anglo-Saxon assembly sites', in D. Griffiths, A. Reynolds, and S. Semple (eds.), *Boundaries in Early Medieval Britain*. Anglo-Saxon Studies in Archaeology and History 12. Oxford: Oxford University School of Archaeology, 38–49.

—— and SEMPLE, S. (eds.) (2004). *Assembly Places and Practices in Medieval Europe*. Dublin: Four Courts Press.

POLLOCK, F., and MAITLAND, F. W. (1923). *The History of English Law Before the Time of Edward I*. 2nd edn. 2 vols. Cambridge: Cambridge University Press.

REYNOLDS, A. (2002). 'Burials, boundaries and charters in Anglo-Saxon England: a reassessment', in S. Lucy and A. Reynolds (eds.), *Burial in Early Medieval England and Wales*. Society for Medieval Archaeology Monograph 17. London: Society for Medieval Archaeology, 171–94.

—— (2009a). *The Emergence of Anglo-Saxon Judicial Practice: The Message of the Gallows*. The Agnes Jane Robertson Memorial Lectures on Anglo-Saxon Studies 1. Aberdeen: The Centre for Anglo-Saxon Studies.

—— (2009b). *Anglo-Saxon Deviant Burial Customs*. Oxford: Oxford University Press.

—— (in press). 'The Anglo-Saxon and medieval archaeology: burial, settlement and the structure of the landscape', in H. Glass, P. Garwood, T. Champion, P. Booth, A. Reynolds, and J. Munby, *Tracks Through Time: The Archaeology of the Channel Tunnel Rail Link*. Oxford: Oxford Archaeology.

SCULL, C. J. (1993). 'Archaeology, early Anglo-Saxon society and the origins of Anglo-Saxon kingdoms'. *Anglo-Saxon Studies in Archaeology and History* 6: 65–82.

SEMPLE, S. J. (1998). 'A fear of the past: the place of the prehistoric burial mound in the ideology of middle and late Anglo-Saxon England'. *World Archaeology* 30(1): 109–26.

—— (2003). 'Illustrations of damnation in late Anglo-Saxon manuscripts'. *Anglo-Saxon England* 32: 231–45.

STONE, J. F. S. (1932). 'Saxon interments on Roche Court Down, Winterslow'. *Wiltshire Archaeological and Natural History Magazine* 45: 568–82.

TALLON, P. (1998–9). 'What was a caldecote?'. *English Place-Name Society Journal* 31: 31–54.

WORMALD, P. (1978). 'Aethelred the Lawmaker', in D. Hill (ed.), *Ethelred the Unready: Papers from the Millenary Conference*. BAR British Series 59. Oxford: British Archaeological Reports, 47–80.

—— (1988). 'A handlist of Anglo-Saxon lawsuits'. *Anglo-Saxon England* 17: 247–281.

—— (1991a). 'In search of King Offa's lost law code', in I. Wood and N. Lund (eds.), *People and Places in Northern Europe 500–1600*. Woodbridge: Boydell Press, 25–45.

—— (1991b). 'Anglo-Saxon society and its literature', in M. Godden and M. Lapidge (eds.), *The Cambridge Companion to Old English Literature*. Cambridge: Cambridge University Press, 1–22.

—— (1999a). *The Making of English Law, King Alfred to the Twelfth Century*, Volume 1: *Legislation and Its Limits*. Oxford: Basil Blackwell.

—— (1999b). 'Laws', in M. Lapidge, J. Blair, S. Keynes, and D. Scragg (eds.), *The Blackwell Encyclopaedia of Anglo-Saxon England*. Oxford: Blackwell Publishing, 279–80.

WYMER, J. J. (1996). *Barrow Excavations in Norfolk, 1984–88*. East Anglian Archaeology 77. Dereham: Norfolk Museums Service.

YORKE, B. A. E. (1993). 'Fact or fiction? The written evidence for the fifth and sixth centuries AD'. *Anglo-Saxon Studies in Archaeology and History* 6: 45–50.

CHAPTER 47

WHAT WERE THEY THINKING? INTELLECTUAL TERRITORIES IN ANGLO-SAXON ENGLAND

MARTIN O. H. CARVER

Over the past 150 years the study of the material culture of south-east Britain between AD 400 and 1100—the study we call Anglo-Saxon archaeology—has largely focused on the illustration of a historical model based on written documents, inscriptions, and place-names. This model sees the arrival of unspecified numbers of Germanic incomers during the fifth century into an area occupied by partially Christianized Britons and Roman citizens of diverse origin. During the fifth to seventh centuries, the incomers became culturally and linguistically dominant and created new kingdoms (Kent, East Anglia, Northumbria, Wessex) within broad tribal affiliations (Angles, Saxons, and Jutes). The creation of the kingdoms was coincident with political pressure from the Continent and the arrival of a new Christian mission from the south, although it is not clear which of these initiatives was primary or determinant. The instruments of the Christian kingdoms were kings, operating from palaces (*villae regales*) and stimulating trade through market centres (*wics*), and the ruling families were closely allied to a Christian network based on monasteries (*monasteria*).

Through the seventh and eighth centuries this confederacy built up alliances and exchanges with other Christian kingdoms on the Continent and in Mediterranean lands. But in the early ninth century it suffered widespread disruption when Scandinavian marauders targeted monasteries either out of ideological revulsion or economic exclusion, or both. Their initial reign of terror subsided into settlement and the governance of the country was divided between the Danelaw (north) and the kingdom of Wessex (south). In the late ninth/early tenth century Alfred of Wessex and his successors Edward and Æthelflæd set about the conquest or reconquest of the greater part of Britain, using a new type of fortified town (*burh*). This resulted in the creation of a kingdom of England which was broadly located within its modern boundaries. During the tenth and eleventh centuries the church was institutionalized so as to mobilize the full framework of diocese, parish, reformed monastery, and secular college. However, ambition to control the wealthy island of Britain and collect its revenues was prosecuted by the south Scandinavians, the Normans, and later the French well into the Middle Ages (Chadwick 1905; Levison 1946; Whitelock 1954; Bassett 1989; Higham 1995; Fletcher 1997; Blair 2005).

Anglo-Saxon archaeology has been highly successful in illustrating this narrative. The large-scale excavation of more than a hundred cemeteries has shown that burial assemblages and rituals noted in the south-east parts of Britain correlate well with Germanic practice in northern mainland Europe and with pagan ideas that survived in later medieval Scandinavian literature. Archaeologists have excavated convincing examples of palace sites, *wics*, and monasteries belonging to the mid Saxon period, and *burhs* of the later Saxon period, enlarging and refining their economic and symbolic roles through studies of finds assemblages and the use of space. The Christian liturgy and its development are recognizable in church buildings, sculpture, and illuminated manuscripts, all of which also contribute to an enhanced picture of the metaphysics and artistry of the Anglo-Saxon people (Hodges 1989; Carver 1992; Welch 1992; this volume, *passim*).

With such a record of achievement, it would be understandable if scholars of an interdisciplinary persuasion were content to continue to celebrate and research the Anglo-Saxons through the discussion of objects, buildings, and sites which are already linked to their world through Latin or Old English literature. But, as this handbook shows, the twenty-first century presents us with a new agenda and new principles for Anglo-Saxon archaeology. These can be attributed to three different forces, the first of which is the rise of theoretical archaeology and its increasing influence on the early medieval period, something not unconnected with its administrative academic grouping with prehistory rather than history departments (Andrén 1998; Carver 2002b; Hills 2007). Archaeologists applied the study of process to the emergence of the Anglo-Saxon kingdoms (e.g. Carver 1989; Scull, this volume) and structuralism to the complexity of metalwork styles in the early period (Gaimster, this volume). Post-structuralist thinking invited us to consider the effects of the current political climate on our own research, and this has led, directly or indirectly, to the questioning of assumptions about ethnicity, gender, and religion—particularly the degree to which they are signalled in graves (for histories of thinking see Rahtz et al.. 1980; Lucy 2000: ch. 1; and Williams 2005).

As Heinrich Härke (2007) has pointed out, this is not an evolving topic, but a cyclical one. In an article published posthumously in 2005, Bartholomew expressed the conviction that through the archaeological tracking of migrations (which he sees as coming from Frisia) 'it is possible to recover, once again, a true understanding of the mighty movement of peoples which took place in the early fifth century and which transformed the Britannia of the Late Roman empire into the land of the Angles, the Engla-land in which we live today' (2005: 28). Härke (2002: 147) puts it bluntly: 'The few historical sources depict the process of settlement in terms of what would now be called "ethnic cleansing" of the native Britons by large-scale immigration of Anglo-Saxons.' Alex Woolf, writing around the same time, comments: 'Rejection of the obviously legendary accounts of the fifth-century invasions dates back to Kemble, but more recently it seems as if some scholars believe that proving that the invasions did not happen as they were described in later sources is the same thing as proving that they did not happen at all' (2000: 99). Myres in 1936 felt that these were times 'whose quality cannot be portrayed without serious distortion in those broad and rational sequences of cause and effect so beloved by the historian. The conflicts are too complex, the issues too obscure, the cross-currents too numerous, and the decisions too local, to make possible the application of any single formula to their solution; and it is at least reassuring to remember that, if we found such a formula, we should unquestionably be wrong' (Myres in Collingwood and Myres 1936: 455–6). The earliest of these authorities is thus perhaps closest to the scepticism of today.

In the critique of their historical model, recent Anglo-Saxon archaeologists have shown some aversion to the acceptance of overwhelming Germanic immigration and pagan thinking, preferring to promote the influence of Britons or British culture (Lucy 2000; Hills 2003). The evidence for British continuity on the ground is still elusive and indirect—the continuation of farming on the same piece of land, the proximity of Roman settlements and Anglo-Saxon cemeteries, or the presence of stones and planks in an unfurnished grave (Rahtz et al. 2000). Moreover the initial scholarly reservations have been inflated in cavalier hands into a generalized negativity in which there were no invasions and Britain was always continuously occupied by Britons throughout pre- and proto-history (e.g. Pryor 2004: 176). Moreland (2000: 50) comments 'Given the lack of evidence for a massive rupture in the countryside of Late Roman Britain, however, we must assume that the vast majority of the population was not of Germanic origin/descent.' The irony of such assertions is that one ethnic assumption is simply replaced by another. Meanwhile the massive culture shifts that took place in the fourth to seventh centuries remain unexplained.

A second key influence is provided by new tools in the scientific toolbox which to some extent have allowed archaeologists to break free of traditional documentary and artistic forms of dating and provenance, with their unfortunate propensity for circular argument. Radiocarbon dating, assisted by Bayesian analysis, offers a date of death for a buried person, whether inhumed or cremated, to within fifty years (Buck *et al.* 1996). Correspondence analysis brings greater precision to the typological progression of both objects and assemblages (Hines *et al.* 1999; Brugmann and Penn 2007). Stable isotope analysis has begun to report on the likely birthplaces of buried persons, so contributing to the migration debate, if only anecdotally. At West Heslerton, for example, four out of twenty-four individuals had oxygen values suggesting a childhood in 'eastern continental Europe or, more likely, Scandinavia'. These were also the only females to be buried without brooches, in poorly furnished graves. Of the twenty others (fourteen females, five males) seven were local and thirteen originated west of the Pennines (Budd *et al.* 2004; though see Hull and O'Connell, this volume). These results raise fresh, and perhaps more interesting, questions than those of migration. Who were these westerners, and what made them seek (or fail to escape) a life in Yorkshire? Population mobility, while it certainly involves settlers from overseas, must also reflect marriage, slavery, conscription, the hire of agricultural labour, and every other form of human trafficking. Stable isotope analysis is more likely to give us a hundred small stories than one big one—although none the worse for that. DNA analysis, once it is reliably applicable to ancient material, will also help to group ancient peoples; it is currently a blunt instrument using the modern population as its point of departure (Thomas *et al.* 2006; Hills 2003).

The third element of the new agenda is more positive in outlook and is the subject of the rest of this chapter. It combines three aspects of recent theory as its foundation. In Braudel's layered history, the ecological and environmental circumstances (the *longue durée*), social circumstances, and personal circumstances all change at different rates (Braudel 1972). Peer Polity Interaction (PPI) assumes that social groups have an equal chance of influencing each other, as compared to core and periphery in which one group is dominant (Renfrew and Cherry 1986). Thus PPI may be thought particularly appropriate to the period between the Roman Empire and the Middle Ages, in which, during a period almost unique in European history, no overarching authority succeeded in holding sway. These two frameworks of ideas have been found very helpful in the interpretation of material culture. The third, a relative newcomer to the party, takes as its underlying basis the assumption that material culture can be ranked in terms of its investment, such that the greater the investment, the greater will be the intended expression. In any community, objects of relatively high investment—defined as 'monuments'—have messages that relate to the community's view of itself at a particular moment. Thus monuments do not report on a specific social structure, ethnicity, or religion, which indeed they are hardly in a position to know; but they do offer an epitome of a contemporary, short-lived, and local thinking. It may well be possible one day to collate examples of these encapsulated thoughts into a narrative history, just as it would be possible in theory to write a general history from a thousand pages torn from individual diaries. But for the present the archaeological inquiry mainly chronicles the results of encounters with a wide range of individuals and records their opinions and aspirations (Carver 2001; 2003; Frazer in Frazer and Tyrrell 2000: 4).

This kind of study requires a different kind of analytical language to the one that gave us the historical model with which this chapter began. We now accept that we cannot declare a grave to be Christian or Saxon, but we can recognize that it makes references or allusions to cultural material that we already know. Unfortunately, the material concerned has already been ethnically pre-labelled during decades of study, so we may be obliged to use terms such as 'culturally Saxon', 'culturally female', or 'culturally Christian' to show we are talking about a type of object, a type of burial, or a way of thinking, but not about a type of person. The mixed cultural messages that are features of early medieval monuments and led to the questioning of ethnic and religious attributions in the first place are here seen as a strength. The underpinning assumption is that the messages are not mixed because of confusion or unfamiliarity, but because early medieval people were dextrously employing a common vocabulary to say something creative and original. The aim of the archaeologist is to record and interpret myriad local voices, without expecting them to bear directly onto a pre-existing historical framework—although they may. In our analysis of sites and monuments we find we cannot often reliably distinguish migration, trade, diplomacy, proselytization, sex, rank, or documented forms of religion or ethnic groups. But we can use the detected references and allusions to define *identities* and *ideologies*, which signify *allegiance* or *defiance* to contemporary forces. Given that we are dealing with the construction of objects or graves or buildings or sites, what we observe is the active signalling of adherence to a world view and a future programme, in other words, politics. In this line of reasoning, what the larger monuments mainly signify is *political alignment*.

To show this kind of approach in action, or rather to illustrate its potential, there follow four case studies of sites, one from each early medieval sub-period, which attempt to break down monuments into their political alignments. A second group of case studies considers how artefacts may be used to define territories, and what these territories might mean. Some attempt will then be made to compare and contrast these archaeological alignments and territories with those known from documents. It will be found that while archaeology cannot always endorse the historical record in the way we might wish, it can open its own window onto the Anglo-Saxon experience.

Wasperton: an intellectual frontier of the fourth to seventh centuries

The cemetery at Wasperton was in use from the fourth to seventh centuries and lay within a prehistoric landscape, ten hectares of which were excavated (Fig. 47.1). A programme of radiocarbon dating and stable isotope analysis indicated likely dates of death and regions of birth for a handful of examples, and the combination of radiocarbon dating, stratification, and grave alignment allowed the construction of a sequence in which all graves, furnished and unfurnished, could be included. The prehistoric landscape in the immediate vicinity included a Neolithic earthwork, a Bronze Age round barrow, and Bronze Age, Iron Age, and Roman enclosures and field boundaries, many of which were visible to the users of the cemetery. The first burials are those of members of a third- to fourth-century agri-business who commandeered a Romano-British enclosure for the purpose. These burials were well spread out so as to imply family plots, and diagnostic burial rites of the period included decapitation, north-south orientation, and inhumations dressed with neck-rings, bracelets, and hobnails. Of five fourth-century individuals, three grew up locally and two can be assigned a Mediterranean childhood.

Throughout most of the fifth century, graves were unfurnished and aligned north-south or west-east; a significant number included stones and planks, and there was a notable plot in the south-east quadrant of the enclosure in which this type of burial predominated. Of nine burials assigned to the fifth century and analysed for stable isotopes, five grew up locally, three were from the West Country, and one was raised in a Mediterranean land. During the fifth century a group of cremations made its appearance. One urn was buried in a Neolithic earthwork, but the majority was clustered in the western half of the enclosure and demarcated by an arc of postholes. Their cremation urns were paralleled in East Anglia and in north Germany.

The first furnished inhumations of Germanic type appeared at much the same time, while during the sixth century, furnished, gendered inhumation—equipped with weapons or lavish ornamental dress items—was the diagnostic and dominant burial rite. In the earlier sixth century the artefacts appeared to reference East Anglia and the upper Thames valley; but in the later sixth century, the references were more southerly, to the Thames Valley as a whole and to the territory of Wessex beyond (Fig. 47.2). In the mid sixth century, burial for certain individuals, male and female, moved outside the enclosure on its northern side, where they were placed around or within one pre-existing and one newly-built mound. Of five burials assigned to the early seventh century, four were relatively well-furnished and placed at the north, east, west, and south sides of the now almost erased enclosure. A fifth grave, dated to the early seventh century by radiocarbon, was lined with planks and stones and placed in the south-east quadrant of the enclosure. This individual had a Mediterranean provenance (Carver *et al.* 2009).

4th century

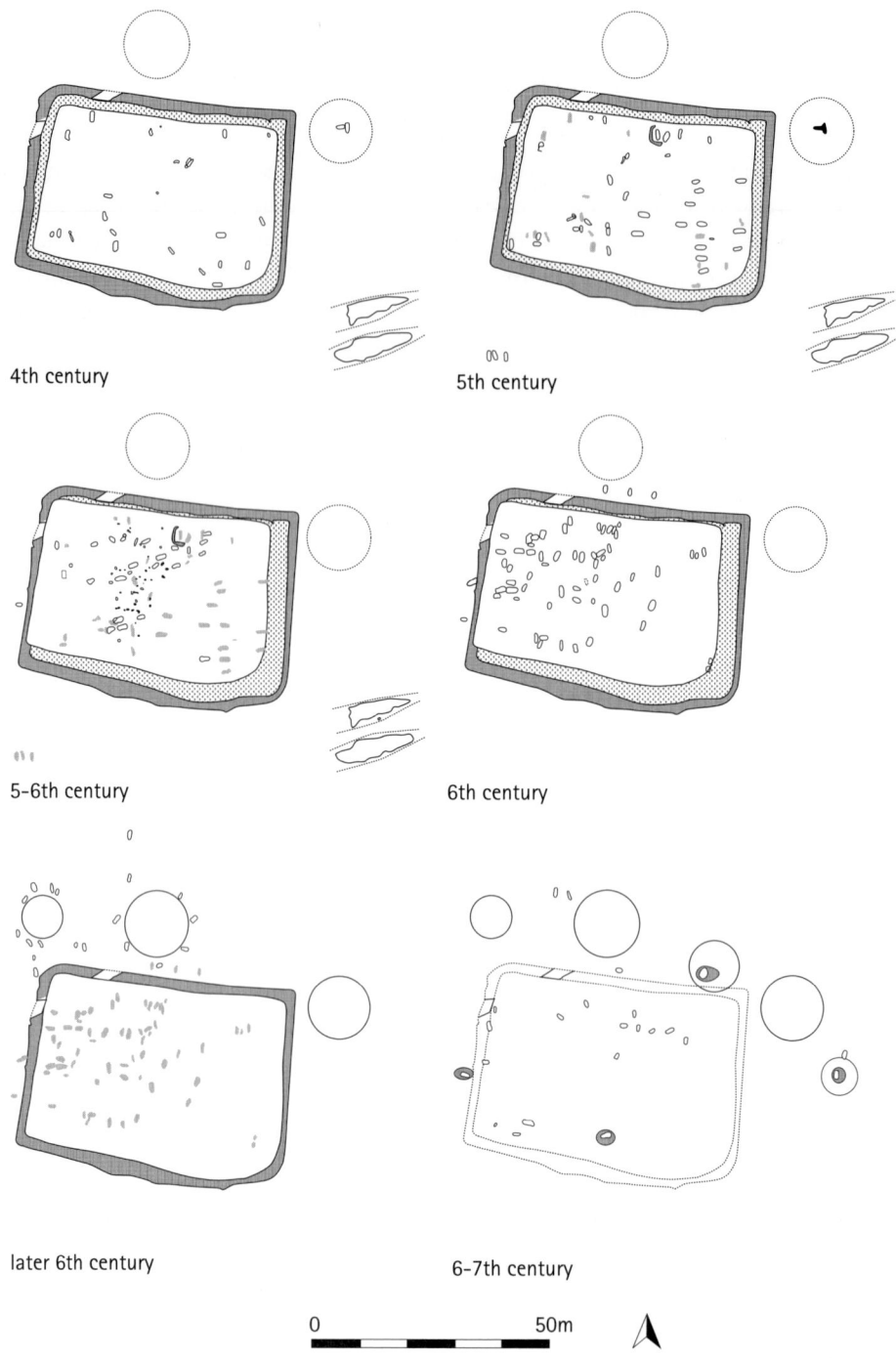

5th century

5-6th century

6th century

later 6th century

6-7th century

0   50m

Figure 47.1 Cemetery evolution at Wasperton, fourth to seventh centuries (Carver et al. 2009: fig. 1.2)

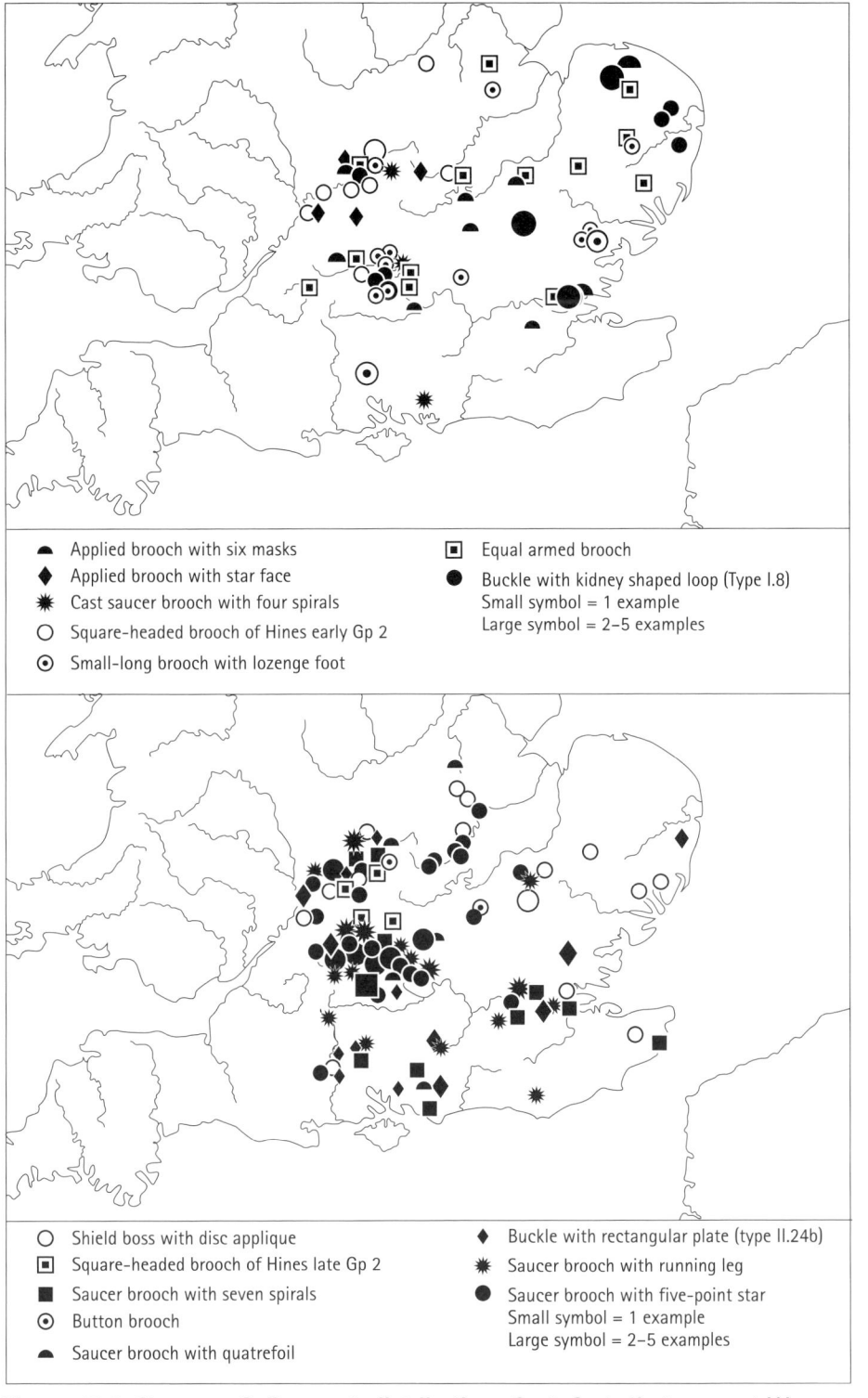

Figure 47.2 Changes of alignment: distribution of artefacts that occur at Wasperton (a) in the earlier sixth century and (b) the later sixth century (Carver *et al.* 2009: figs. 4.22–3)

This sequence can be read without recourse to immigration, ethnicity, or Christianity, without denying that such attributes may one day be recognizable. For the time being we can note that during the fourth century a cemetery was established in family plots to serve an ideologically mixed population. Some aspects of burial rites (the hobnails and decapitation) reflect the wider Roman world, but others, such as north-south and west-east orientation, are following a local preference. Whereas we are not entitled to assume that all, some, or none of these burials reflect a Christian community, we may certainly claim the presence of a variety of ideologies that we do not otherwise know. This is also true of the west-east fifth-century burials with planks and stones, about which we can note that they include westerners and reflect not only practice in contemporary western Britain but a fainter echo of previous prehistoric burial. By contrast, the type and location of the fifth-century cremations strongly indicate an intrusive group, and the allusions they make are to East Anglia or to northern continental Europe. The inhumations were acculturated into the former cemetery plots, presumably as a result of marriage, but the accentuation of gender and the signals of alignment with the northern continent grow stronger. Barrow burial from the mid sixth century may or may not imply an increase in ranking, but it does imply a new fealty to the still visible prehistoric landscape. This is unlikely to imply a 'past regained' or a legitimation of land (already firmly possessed), but rather an ideological swing towards whatever meaning barrows were then thought to have (cf. Bradley 1987; Carver 2002a; Müller-Wille 1992, 1993). We can also note that the development of the cemetery always included unfurnished graves in every plot, but the furnished burial rite barely intruded into one conservative corner, where the west-east plank burials continued from the Roman period to the seventh century.

On the face of it, this is a Roman, British, and Anglo-Saxon cemetery and it displays versions of Christianity and other religions running alongside each other, as expressed in burial practice. The archaeology is really reporting the way people were thinking, rather than the way they were acting. Thus, the political alignment turns this way and that, but even in this small group of fewer than fifty persons alive at the same time, they never spoke with a single voice. This cemetery, like others, is not a fuzzy expression of migration, or of acculturation between pre-defined religions or ethnic groups, but a rather precise expression of complex ideological identities not yet in the history books, ideas that we have only just begun to study.

SUTTON HOO: CHANGES IN ALIGNMENT DURING THE SIXTH TO TENTH CENTURIES

The earliest Anglo-Saxon burials defined at Sutton Hoo belong to a sixth- to seventh-century cemetery excavated in the year 2000 in advance of the construction of a visitor centre (Carver 2005: ch. 13). The burial rites there include small earth mounds and a cremation in a bronze bowl, a harbinger of the earliest rituals at the better known aristocratic burial ground which lies 300 m to the south (Fig. 47.3). Here, traces of prehistoric earthworks (actually field systems) were visible on a promontory overlooking the River Deben, where up to eighteen mounds were subsequently erected, the earliest at the corners of the Iron Age earthworks. In the hectare excavated, the burials began with the cremations of men, originally well furnished, accompanied on the pyre by sheep, horse, and cattle in around AD 590 (Fig. 47.4; Mounds 5, 6, 7). Next, a young man was buried in a coffin, with his horse in a separate pit beneath the same mound (Mound 17). Then, in the 620s came two ship burials, the first in which the ship was placed over the top of a well-furnished chamber (Mound 2) and the second where the chamber was constructed inside a ship placed within a trench underground. The horse-and-rider burial and the two ship burials were all wealthy weapon graves, provisioned also with feasting equipment. The Mound 1 chamber also famously contained a helmet, shield, standard, and sceptre all richly ornamented with symbolic images. This was the apogee of the princely burial ground, but there was sporadic late use in the form of modest graves for three young persons and the chamber grave of a high-status woman bedecked with silver (Mound 14).

The princely burial ground only endured for some sixty years (c.590–650). It was, however, re-used almost immediately for the burial of execution victims who had been hanged on a gallows or displayed on a gibbet at one site to the east of the mounds and another on top of Mound 5. The princely burial ground was used as a place of execution, at a time which radiocarbon dates place between the eighth and the tenth centuries, by which time a Christian governance of East Anglia is not in doubt. Whether it represents the dispatch of villains, dissidents, sinners, or non-conformists, this ritualized killing field was the work of Christian kings (Carver 1998; 2005: 315–59).

The Sutton Hoo burial ground has been reconciled with the exiguous written records to tell a story of kingship and conversion—and it may be so. However, the type of archaeology considered in this chapter focuses on the history of the intellect. During its short life, the princely burial ground was the scene of investment of outstanding intensity. The cremations in bronze bowls refer not only to the family cemetery a few hundred yards upriver, but to earlier burial practice in north Germany. Horse-and-rider graves begin in the Rhineland where they have been suggested to originate with a Frankish warrior group (Müller-Wille 1970–1; 1998). Ship-burials of this and earlier periods are known from the Baltic and the Continental North Sea coast (Müller-Wille 1974, 1995; Carver 1995). In England all these burial rites, which refer to an earlier period overseas, are confined to the same part of the country, namely the Sandlings of Suffolk, which also features most of the known lyre burials (Lawson in Filmer-Sankey and Pestell 2001: 215–23). Whatever this flowering of special celebration might mean, we can at least be certain that it was in no sense traditional, or a 'final phase' (see Geake 1997). These are new burial

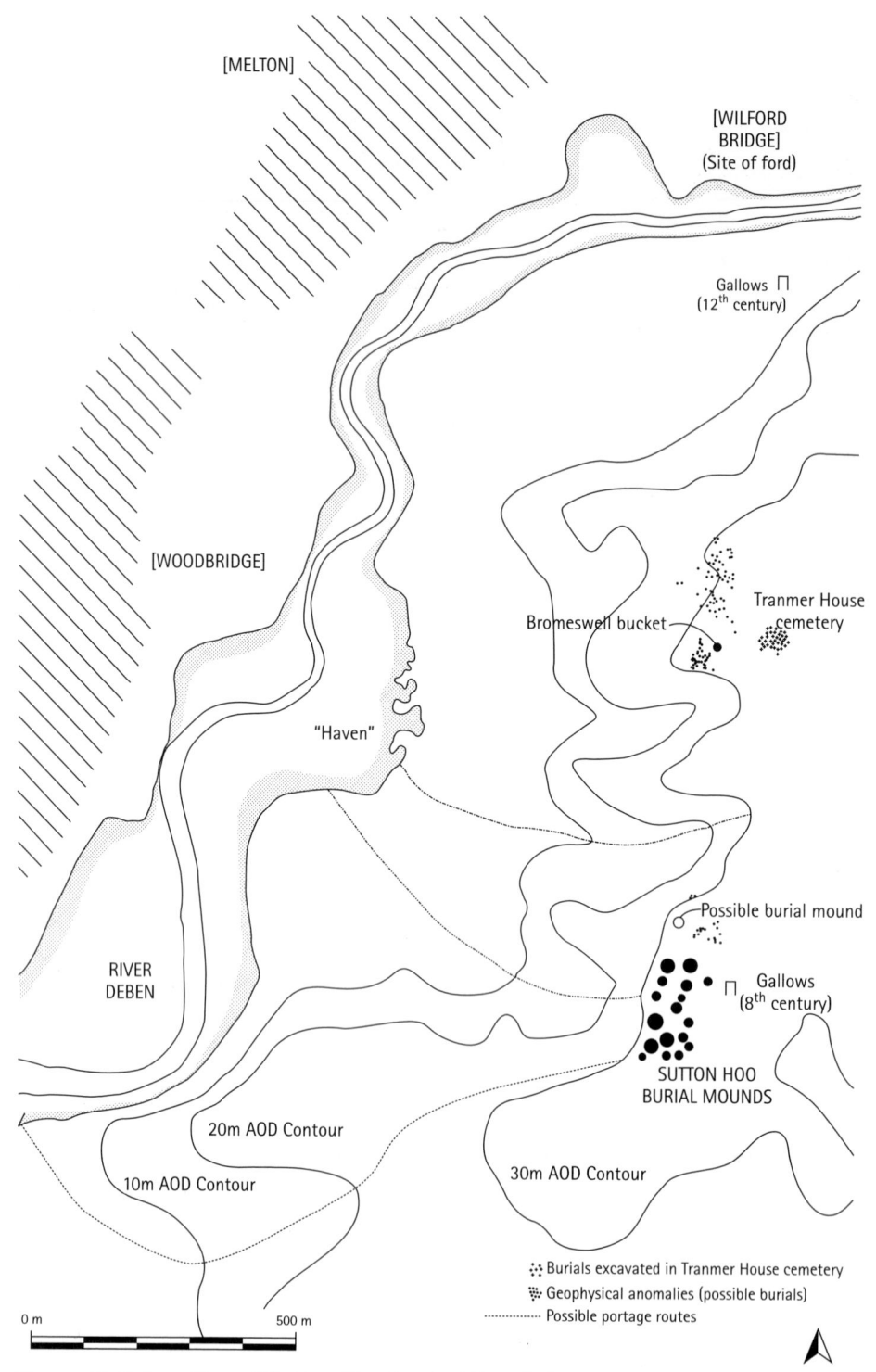

Figure 47.3 Location of Sutton Hoo by the River Deben in Suffolk. Tranmer House cemetery marks the site of Sutton Hoo's sixth- to seventh-century predecessor. (Carver 2005: fig. 220)

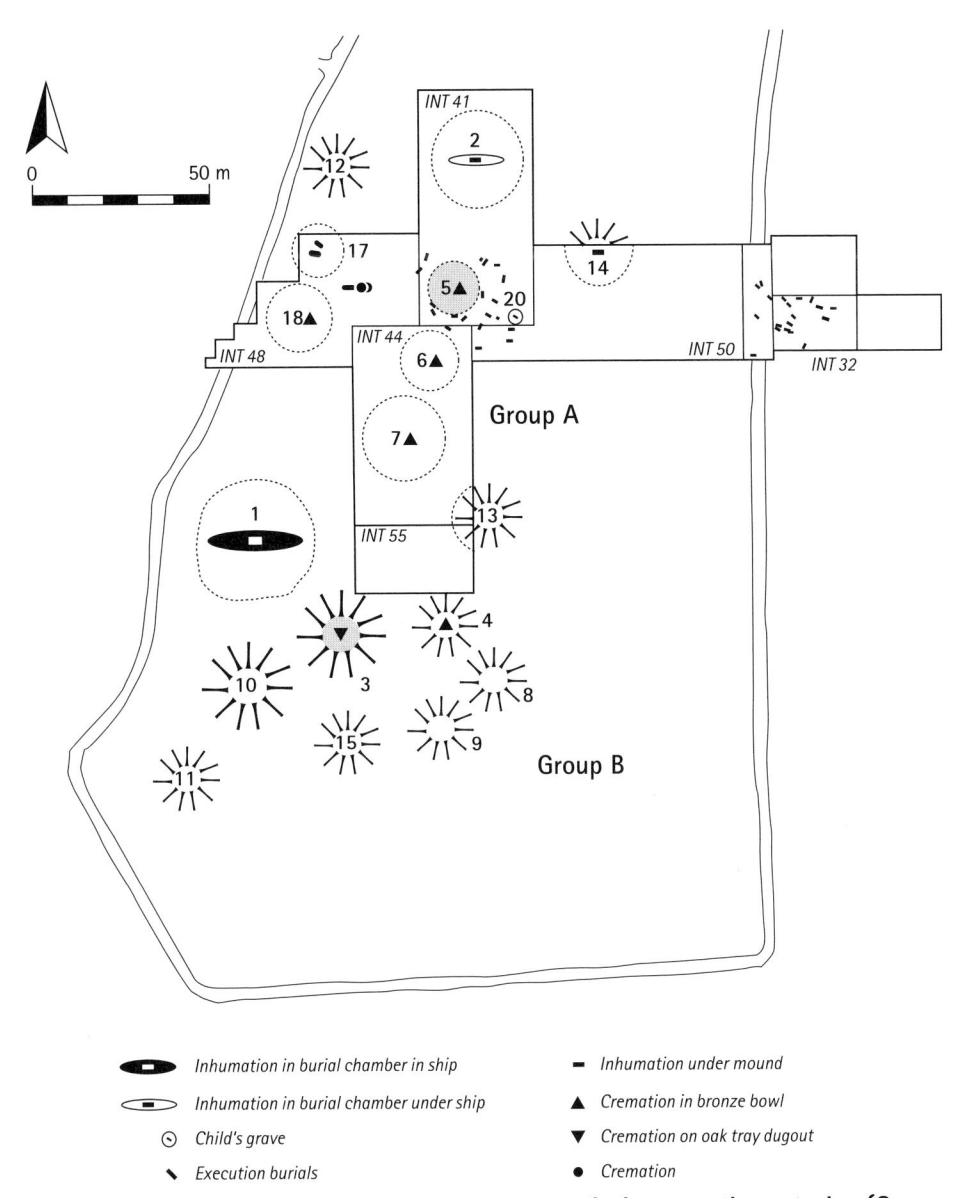

Figure 47.4 Plan of the Sutton Hoo cemetery, sixth to tenth centuries (Carver 2005: fig 219)

rites with a new message that obtained only in a specific part of England at a particular time. It may of course also refer to other processes such as kingship, or apprehension at the approach of the Christian missions, but we are not offered direct access to such historical matters, any more than there is information on whether any documented figures lie buried there (Carver 2001; Bruce-Mitford 1975: ch. 10; Carver 2005: 502–3 for critique).

In this reading, the Mound 1 ship burial is neither the last of a great tradition nor a template for the burial of Anglo-Saxon kings. It is a 'palimpsest of allusions', allusions to the Roman empire, to Scandinavian heroes, to the island of Britain, to the Northern gods, to the Celtic gods, to Christ, and so forth. In this it resembles a poem in which the hopes and fears of the day were reified as appropriate to one place, person, and occasion (Carver 2000; cf. Frank 1992). In this sense the properties of the burial are not even cultural; they are original.

It must be admitted that to produce a convincing reading of such a poem, as with Beowulf, will take much more study. The link with history is not hopelessly unreadable, but it must be refined. Looking at ship burial, for example, we cannot trace it as an adoptive practice relayed from one place to another. It comes from a shared intellectual inheritance, and while we may not be in a position to decide what ship burial means, we can perhaps discover why it was suddenly adopted (Carver 1995). The right questions to ask of Mound 1 are therefore not 'is it Roman?', 'is it Swedish?', or 'is it Christian?', but why that, why there, and why then? One day it seems likely that our answers to these questions will become more informative and more subtle than they can be today. They will also reinforce history where this period most needs it, in the affairs of the mind.

Sutton Hoo begins with the optimistic expressions of a local warrior class whose political alignment is towards the east: pagan, maritime, and autonomous. By the early seventh century the need for extravagant monumentality becomes pressing and must betray anxieties about threats to intellectual freedom. The complexities, eclecticism, and depth of conjecture revealed by the ship burials are as metaphysical in their way as any Mediterranean codex and possibly more original. That these fears were well grounded is indicated by the subsequent use of the burial ground of kings as a *cwealmstow* (killing place) for criminals (Carver 2005: chs. 8, 9, 14).

Portmahomack: choices of the Picts, sixth to ninth centuries

The third case study is not in Anglo-Saxon England at all but at Portmahomack in the north-east of Scotland (Carver 2008a; Fig. 47.5). It is included to emphasize that the 'Anglo-Saxons' were only one group of many expressing ideas in early medieval Britain (see below), and it might be instructive to look at parallel processes and different ideas emerging at the same time as Sutton Hoo but at the other end of the island. At Portmahomack an excavation of 0.75 hectares has unearthed a Pictish settlement which has been designated as monastic, although it is documented by nothing except (somewhat obscurely) an association with St Colman of

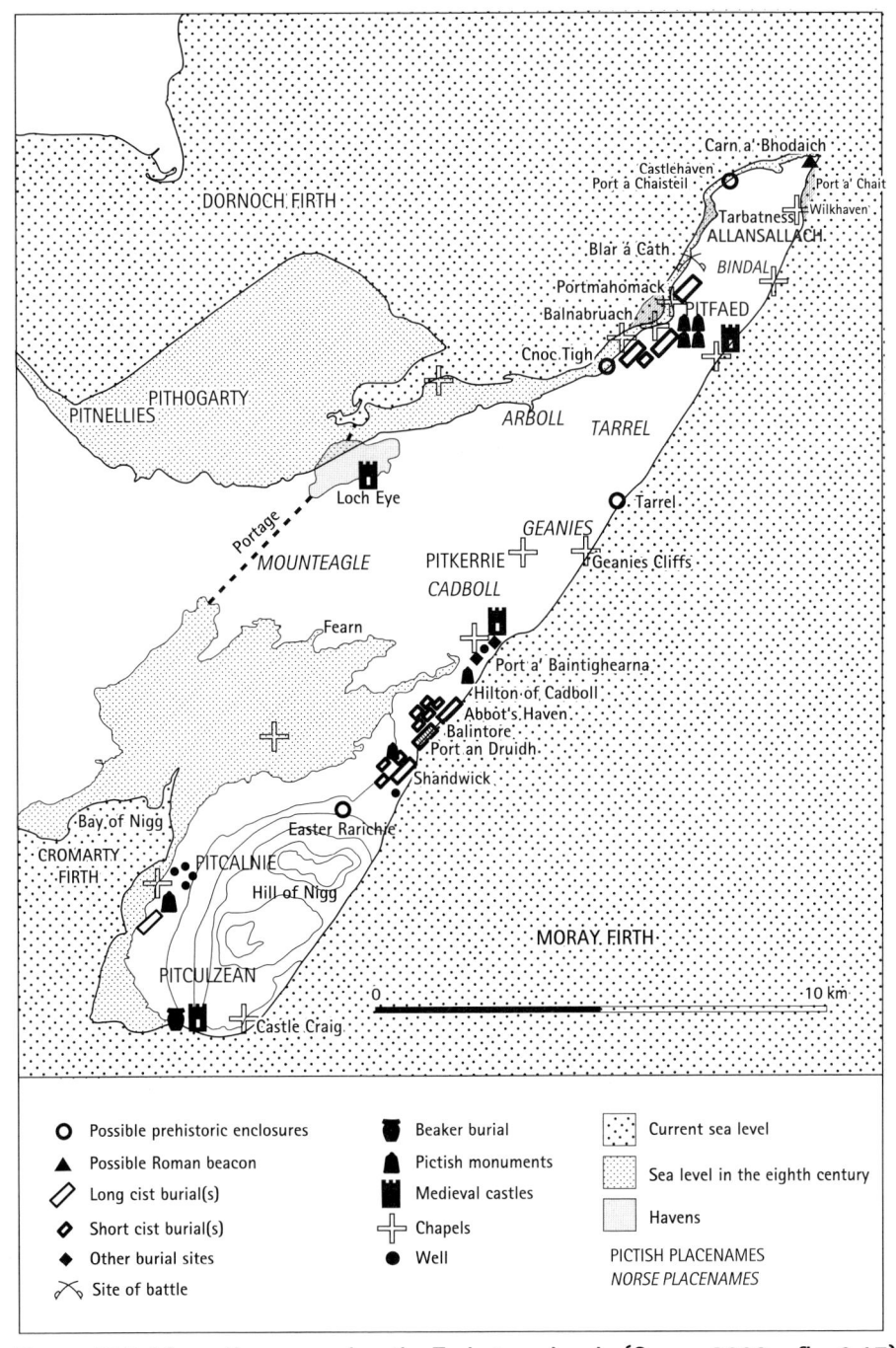

Figure 47.5 Monastic geography: the Tarbat peninsula (Carver 2008a: fig. 3.17)

Lindisfarne, preserved in the Middle Ages and later in its place-name and church dedication. But it has produced a wealth of sculpture paralleled in Iona and the west coast, in southern Pictland, and in Northumbria, at least as far south as Yorkshire. One piece carried a Latin inscription in insular majuscules, close to Lindisfarne in type, while another carried Pictish symbols.

The settlement began in a small way on top of a hill between the Firth and a marsh in the later sixth century, and its occupants were mainly concerned with obtaining fresh water. At this time the principal investment was in burials, unfurnished but lined with large slabs of stone, a practice that was not specifically Christian but had begun in the local Iron Age. Indeed there were already burials of this kind on the Tarbat peninsula before the first Christian community arrived. In the late seventh or early eighth century the settlement underwent a major development. Large quantities of soil and stones were moved to create a new landscape, with a paved and stone-kerbed road running down the hill to a pond formed by building a dam across the valley. On either side of the road were workshops processing cattle and making leather and vellum. Across the valley a building as geometrically perfect as any brooch or gospel book was used by metalsmiths engaged in making church vessels of silver, bronze, and glass. The monastic establishment, as indicated by workshops and sculpture that was radiant with Christian symbolism, endured through the eighth century. By the later eighth century, both the Portmahomack churchyard and the Tarbat peninsula as a whole were marked out as sacred spaces with large standing stone crosses. At the end of the eighth century the monastery was burnt down, but revived as a farm and workshops, at first recycling precious metals and latterly (in the ninth to eleventh centuries) as a smithy (Fig. 47.6).

The documentary evidence is poor throughout, and particularly for the ninth to eleventh centuries, but a passable attempt can be made at reconciling it with the archaeology. The monastery was probably founded in the late sixth century on a pre-existing Iron Age 'holy island' in association with Columba's visits to the northern Picts. The monastery only exhibited its truly diagnostic parameters in the eighth century when it functioned also as a centre of manufacture, presumably for the equipping of more monasteries. The levels of investment were massive at this time, the standing carved stone monuments erected on the Tarbat peninsula being among the largest and most elaborate known from early medieval Europe. They appear to mark out the monastic territory in the manner known in monastic Ireland (Fig. 47.5; Carver 2008a, b). The destruction of the workshop and its subsequent revival can be placed in the context of the Viking raids and the war that followed between the earls of Orkney and those of Moray, culminating in a major battle in about 1035 at Tarbat Ness itself.

However, the intellectual story offered by the archaeology is more interesting than this. In the sixth and early seventh centuries, while the communities of Wasperton and the aristocracy of Sutton Hoo were lavishly burying portable

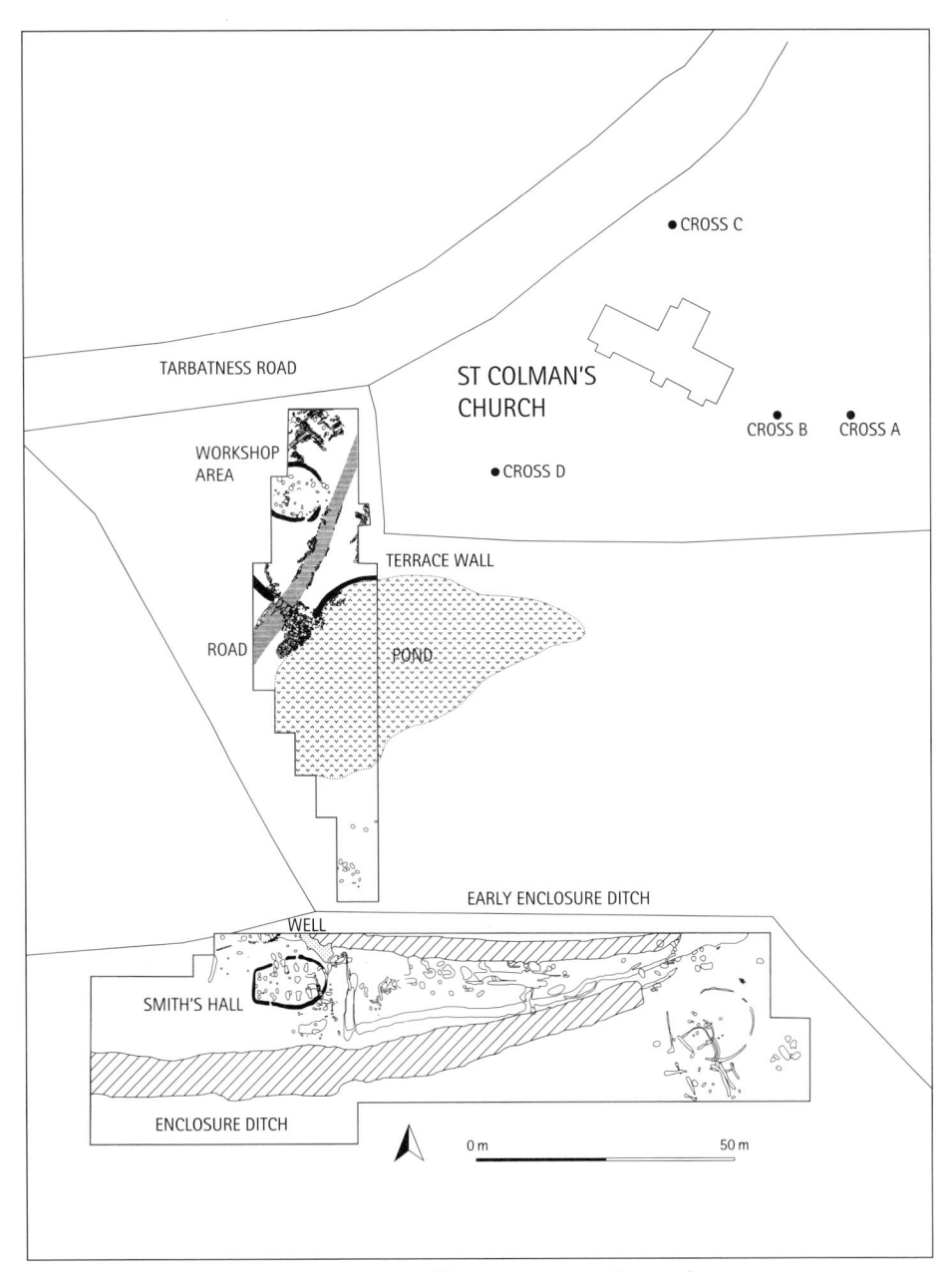

Figure 47.6 The Tarbat excavations (Carver 2008a: fig. 9.1)

wealth, the contemporary ideology of Portmahomack was referencing imported Christian ideas moderated by local prehistoric thinking (Carver 2008b), resulting in minimal monumentality. But in the eighth century an expansionist phase can be seen in the flowering of monastic industry producing vellum and church plate and the multiplying of cross-slabs. The references of the sculpture are to Ireland and

Northumbria, of the symbols to Pictland, of the road to the Romans, of the waterworks to the Irish, of the iconography to the Christian Levant, of the inscription to Northumbria. It would be impossible, archaeologically, to assign a primary influence. The sculpture portrays local ornament, animals, and people with a famous mastery of line, but it also offers metaphysical symbolism and detailed knowledge of the life of King David and the meeting of Anthony and Paul in the desert. On the Tarbat peninsula in the far north-east of Scotland in the eighth century there is no trace of the kind of ignorance or confusion that has earned the dismissive soubriquet 'syncretism'. These are independent thinkers who are aware of the broad repertoire of contemporary philosophy and chose to give to it their own emphasis. But the thinking and ambition is very different from that of their contemporaries further south.

STAFFORD: INTIMATIONS OF ROMANITAS IN THE TENTH CENTURY

The last case study takes to us a *burh* of the tenth century, providing an example from the more formalised Christian Anglo-Saxon nation (Carver 2010). The site of Stafford was a peninsula of cultivated land surrounded by marsh, with a ford across the river Sow. It was the subject of a research campaign from 1975 to 1985 (Fig. 47.7). Excavation at a site in the centre of the town just north of St Mary's, the principal church in Stafford, showed that grain had been processed there intermittently from the Iron Age through to the twelfth century and beyond. Four tenth-century ovens were found, two for drying and two for baking wheat and oats on a large scale (Moffett 1994). Experiments showed that one of these ovens could produce twenty loaves an hour. To the east was an industrial site, also of the tenth century, producing pottery, the so-called Stafford Ware, with a range of products which included lamps, bowls, and cups (Fig. 47.8). This pottery looks like the local Roman pottery made 700 years earlier in the same place, and no doubt frequently dug up by Anglo-Saxons; indeed they are so alike, that there is little doubt that the craftsmen were deliberately copying Roman pottery. Severe penalties were imposed on the Stafford potters who got it wrong: amongst the pottery wasters were found three human skulls. The most common form of pot and the only type to be found outside Stafford was the jar, and its numerous examples seem to be all the same size, implying a standard measurement.

The context of tenth- and eleventh-century Stafford was the reconquest of Britain by Alfred's son Edward who took the eastern route, and Edward's sister Æthelflæd, Lady of the Mercians, who was in command of the left flank. She

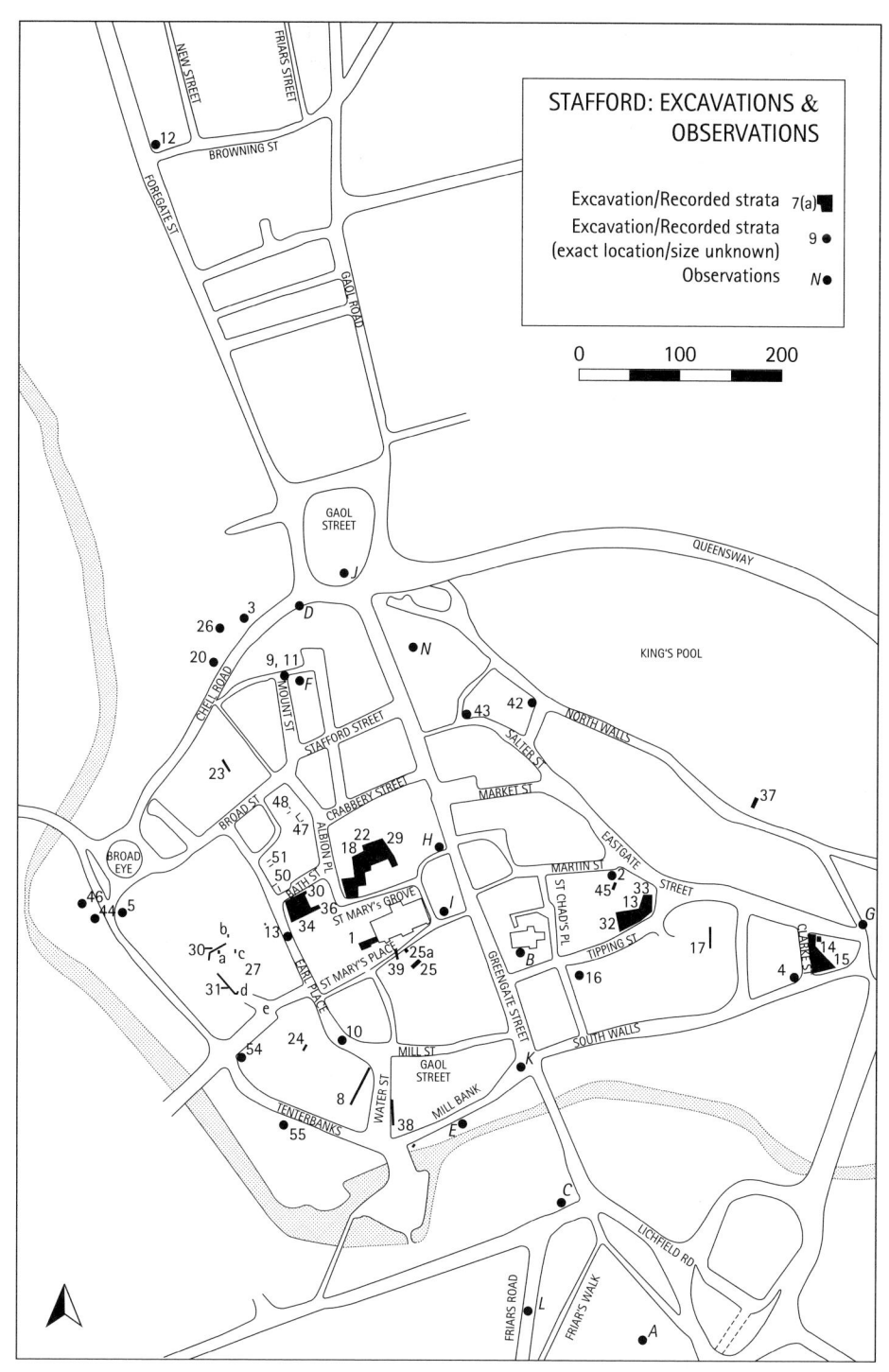

Figure 47.7 Plan of Stafford town, showing the sites of excavation to 1990 (Carver)

Figure 47.8 Stafford Ware (Carver)

fortified Bridgenorth in 912, Tamworth and Stafford in 913, Hereford in 914, and Runcorn in 915, as well as repairing some old Roman forts. Hereford has provided an excavated example of *burh* fortifications, an earth bank eventually revetted in stone. Its rampart lay over a corn-drier dated to the eighth to ninth century, and it is very likely, as H. M. Chadwick suggested 100 years ago, that *burhs* were sited on places which were already tribute-collecting points; in fact it is most probably the collecting of tribute and storage of food rent that is to be protected by the *burh* (Chadwick 1905: 255: 'In earlier times most of the places mentioned in the Burghal Hidage must have been merely royal estates or villages'; cf. Campbell 1986: 109: 'An English *villa regia* . . . was the centre of a fairly wide area all or most of whose people owed something to it'). The distribution of Stafford Ware spreads to the rest of Mercia and its fringes, but mostly to other *burhs* (see below; Vince 1985; McCarthy and Brooks 1988: 200). In the marsh at the edge of the Stafford *burh*, piles of animal bones were found, suggesting the centralized processing of meat. We have here glimpsed a system of the control of resources through a network of *burhs*, each no doubt with a garrison which was protecting tribute delivered from the estates. The pottery was probably made as a container which formed part of the provisioning strategy, as did the production of loaves.

The *burh* system pioneered by Alfred erected defensive enclosures at twenty-mile intervals in Wessex, and the northward advance of his successors was punctuated by new *burhs* in a manner that bears more than a passing resemblance to the Roman conquest (Carver 1993: 73). The idea of linked forts was once thought to have been taken, along with many other ideas and works of art, from Carolingian France. But the results from Stafford point rather to an inspiration of the Wessex kings' own vision of the Roman Empire, and particularly the province of Britannia. Anglo-Saxon kings seem to have noticed the ruins of Roman Britain and the pots that were dug up on old Roman sites when they went there to rob stones to build churches. They became archaeologists themselves. Where we have seen them, the *burhs* look like Roman forts, both in their shape and distribution. One Wessex *burh*, Cricklade (1,500 hides, so 2,000 yards around the edge) has been extensively excavated without finding anything inside the defences, suggesting that it never evolved beyond the first stage of a tented encampment with a 'minster' (Haslam 1981: 29).

Alan Vince, re-examining the archaeological evidence, has shown that the development of the *burhs* followed a three-phase trajectory (1994). The places fortified in the late ninth and early tenth century have little evidence for manufacture and seem to be military in function. There is a proliferation of mints in the late ninth century, but this can be associated with the conversion of tribute into silver. Winchester is planning its streets in the early tenth century, but even there manufacture does not seem to begin until the mid tenth century. After that we have plenty of evidence for shoe-making, cobbling, pottery-making, glass-working, working precious metals, and iron-smithing. In Wessex at least, the distribution of pottery now suggests a large amount of traffic between the *burh* and countryside. It is the early eleventh century which sees the flowering of international trade and, incidentally, of deep sea fishing, as suggested by hooks.

So, following and elaborating the Vince model, the late ninth- and early tenth-century *burh* foundations were forts, which protected taxation points and only developed as manufacturing centres in the mid tenth century. They did not participate in international trade, even in London, until the early eleventh century. Stafford is interesting in that it never reached that latter stage of development before the Norman Conquest closed the place down for a century. Archaeologically, that means we can see more clearly the ruthless 'Roman' programme of the kings of Wessex, uncluttered by the more open market town that came later. Stafford may be seen as essentially a fort, protecting the delivery of tribute, with a *vicus* on the east side where pottery was manufactured and cattle were processed.

READING ALIGNMENT

The presentation of these four case studies in summary form shows that early medieval sites in Britain can be assigned a number of intellectual properties. The builders of cemeteries, monasteries, and *burhs*—we could extend this to palaces and *wics*—could draw on a number of different models of civilization with which they could then declare or deny alignment. Among these we can identify first the prehistoric landscape, an open book from which the Anglo-Saxons could recite, using a commonly understood and inherited vocabulary including chambers, mounds, and ship burials (Williams 1998, 2006). Next, the occupants of southeast Britain could hardly fail to be knowledgeable about the inheritance of the Britons. Although reference here is notoriously elusive, we may find it in the use of certain practices, such as the inclusion of stones in graves, which has a different emphasis countrywide (Carver *et al.* 2009: chs. 3, 6). Next, the Scandinavian neighbours can be assumed to have had a permanent intellectual presence in eastern Britain, although as with all political alignments there were times when it was embraced and times when it was strenuously rebuffed. It seems likely, although it is less well documented even in Northumbria, that a similar force made itself felt from Ireland. The monastic design, with its water management schemes and the type of territory marked by crosses that declared itself at Portmahomack, may yet prove to underlie Anglo-Saxon monasteries too. The Roman project, of which the Anglo-Saxons were permanently aware, may have acted as the antithesis to the Scandinavian. It can be seen even from this very brief review that archaeology reveals a series of Roman 'renaissances' of different kinds in the seventh, eighth, later ninth, and tenth centuries.

In attempting to deconstruct the thinking behind our monuments, we may choose to summarize their elements as Roman, Scandinavian, Christian, or non-Christian. But it will be important to return frequently to the starting point—namely the originality of minds and creative artists at work in the first millennium, who, while they had all these ideas in reach and within their repertoire, need not have surrendered their allegiance to any. Writing of the Iron Age, Barry Cunliffe remarks: 'The iconography of Britain before the Conquest, reflected largely in the Roman formalisation of the situation, shows that an immense number of local or tribal gods existed, each known by a regional name and each endowed with specific qualities' (2005: 575–6); at the end of the Roman period, he sees the clock turning back to the Middle Iron Age (2002: 136) so presumably some of this diversity returned. Diversity is certainly implied by the repertoire of pre-Christian burial practice; even for Christianity James Campbell sees it as a 'safe generalization' that 'England and its church contained much diversity' (1986: 84; see Brown 2003 for the general phenomenon). Only with the institutionalization of Christian governments and the successful imposition of wide social control would it become possible for these diverse minds to be successfully closed. In Anglo-Saxon England this was probably not achieved or achievable before the eighth century.

It will also be noted that if we intend to use archaeology to write an intellectual history of the Anglo-Saxons, it is important that the area of study is not confined to Anglo-Saxon England itself, or even to Britain. Britain is an island that faces onto three seas, each of which had been regularly crossed since the Bronze Age. Each of these seas can be regarded as a thoroughfare, not a barrier (Carver 1990; Cunliffe 2001; 2002: 117). The starting assumption is therefore that, unless prevented from doing so by politics, people and ideas could and did cross them. The references discovered in Anglo-Saxon archaeology require us equally to know the archaeology of British prehistory, the northern Roman Empire, and early medieval Ireland, France, and Scandinavia.

Regional allegiance: territories, of the land, of the mind

Archaeologists can therefore attempt to define which kinds of identity and ideology are being expressed by deconstructing references and allusions in the material culture of artefacts, graves, stone monuments, and settlements. It is not expected that one definition will prevail, any more than an interpretation of *Beowulf* need command consensus. But we can at least agree to the proposition that the builders of monuments expressed allegiance to a number of different ideas at the same time, even if we cannot agree about the relative emphasis of each.

Allegiance to territories is harder to deconstruct since the effect of agency, of expressed intention, is much less certain. Even in modern times, territories cannot easily be created, but emerge out of a claimed 'natural' or 'ethnic' cohesion. Nevertheless, the expectation should be, as with sites, that the territories represent the resolution of a number of competing claims. They will be strongly influenced by prehistoric and Roman predecessors, as well as by contemporary government. Documented Anglo-Saxon territories still survive today (East Anglia, Kent, Wessex, Northumbria) so we will not be surprised if these also represent territories of some antiquity. At the same time, by using archaeological evidence, we shall hope to discover otherwise hidden territories, to which people gave their allegiance in some way. We can already anticipate that these different types of territorial allegiance will not always coincide.

The historical framework suggests that the early Anglo-Saxon period should map into zones for Angles, Saxons, and Jutes, the middle period into kingdoms and sub-kingdoms as described in the Tribal Hidage, and the late period broadly into the counties and dioceses that survived into the twentieth century. However, although no boundaries are known with precision, it can be noted that all these territories map more convincingly onto the Roman and Iron Age territories which preceded them (Fig. 47.9). Kent was the Roman *civitas Cantiaci* and before that the tribal territory of the *Cantii*. Mercia, a marchland or border territory, was the border between Britannia Prima and Britannia Secunda, as well as (later) between

Figure 47.9 Four territorial mosaics for Britain: (a) Iron Age tribal areas (Cunliffe 2005); (b) Roman *Civitates* (Wacher 1974: 28); (c) Anglo-Saxon and British kingdoms (Hill 1981: 76, modified); (d) Truce terms used in twentieth-century school playgrounds (Opie and Opie 1982: 169)

England and Wales (Thomas 1981: 200). The territorial divisions of Anglo-Saxon England are basically Iron Age, even if they can sometimes skip several generations. The *civitas* of the Iceni re-emerges as the diocese of Elmham, although it had been 'Norfolk' in between. The mid Saxon kingdom of East Anglia is remembered as Harold's possession at the Conquest, and Northumbria as Siward's, although both had been incorporated into the Danelaw in the interim (Hill 1981: 89, 96, 105). Perhaps owed to the geography of language, whether Iron Age or English, these territories and their subdivisions can still come to the surface in unexpected ways, as in Peter and Iona Opie's famous map of the truce terms used in school playgrounds in the 1950s (Opie and Opie 1982). These exclude the private-school term for fending off attack—*pax*, a Latin word (like *cave*) that had survived countrywide but confined to a particular social group.

This mapping exercise reinforces the perception that all territories, perhaps in Europe as well as in Britain, are simply the products of the *longue durée*. Andrew Gillett (2002: 120) sees terms such as 'Goths' as artefacts of late Roman popular geography, nicknames of territories that stuck, 'with no ethnic connotations whatever'. Sebastian Brather feels that the territories that artefacts map onto are merely the previous Roman territories: 'the differences between Frankish and Alammanian is actually the difference between Roman Gaul and the barbarian lands adjacent to the *limes*' (2002: 156–7). Not only does the distribution of material culture have no ethnic content, but neither do terms such as Goth, Angle, or Pict at their time of use. They are simply late Roman nicknames given to the current residents of pre-existing long-lived territories. Such territories may have an environmental rationale that political will is powerless to erase.

The archaeological investigation not only hopes to endorse these territories but aims to recover hidden ones: popular trends that are working beneath the political radar. The method it uses is primarily the distribution map, which fell out of favour in Britain in the 1960s to such an extent that the production of the excellent Ordnance Survey maps and all its imitations virtually ceased. The reason given was that since all areas of the country had not been investigated to an equal degree of intensity, all distribution maps were 'misleading' (Hurst 1976: 288). There has been no such coyness on the Continent and there are at least four good reasons why it would be a shame now to rob ourselves in Britain of this invaluable method of pattern-seeking. First, total representation is impossible for any map and always will be, but that is no reason for not using them, if only to point to areas where further investigation might be desirable. Second, pattern-seeking is what we do; if a pattern fails to survive for more than a few years so be it: nothing is lost except a little vanity. A map is a basis for argument rather than a fact. Third, we have digital mapping technology as never before, so it seems sensible to make use of it. Fourth, we have had twenty years of unparalleled data gathering from CRM mitigation (archaeological investigation in advance of development); not only have we failed to make much use of its distribution to date, but we are presently on the threshold of a data-gathering revolution which will make the previous acquisition look distinctly sparse—namely the advent of the Portable Antiquities Scheme. The distribution mapping that is possible now will reveal and enhance secret systems of allegiance and communication far beyond the tentative exercises given here.

Various cultural items have already been mapped and used. Cruciform brooches, square-headed brooches, and pottery have all indicated territories. Old English (but not Latin) inscriptions, sceattas, stycas, and pennies all map territories of use which reflect the relations of Anglo-Saxons and their partners in trade or gift exchange. In sculpture, the ongoing analysis of the *Corpus* is beginning to discern schools of practice, for example in the concentration of hog backs, or preference for particular kinds of cross, within the general pan-insular dictionary (Cramp 1984). These exercises do not map exactly onto those of the documented territories, so we must at least entertain the possibility that they are following a logic of their own. In the space remaining, I use two examples to explore these themes, both of the late Saxon period.

The first example is the late Saxon pottery industry, which John Hurst already warned us not to map (see above); it will nevertheless be worth a try (Fig. 47.10). The territories are to some degree exclusive, so that the supplies relate to a particular zone. Hurst noticed the 'strong Roman influence' in late Saxon pottery and assumed it was due to traditional potters migrating from the Low Countries (1956: 48). But the references can be more local than that. Just as Stafford Ware seems to reflect the same cheerful orange ware of the Trent Valley (or Severn Valley) potters, the Thetford Ware potters echo the dark Roman fabrics of the local Nene Valley. Some of these factors may have their rationale in the local clays. But like the documented territories, the pottery zones may have even deeper roots than the Roman. Some of the Iron Age pottery zones of the sixth to fourth centuries BC published by Barry Cunliffe (Fig. 47.11) prefigure those of the tenth and eleventh centuries AD, for example Darmsden–Linton = Thetford Ware; All Cannings Cross–Meon Hill = Cheddar E; Chinnor–Wandlebury = St Neots Ware. The St Neots 'territory' is prefigured by the early-sixth-century East Anglian contact zone at Wasperton (Fig. 47.2), which may provide a clue to its identity. The distribution actually follows the locus of the Icknield Way, so relating to no political, cultural, or ethnic territory, but simply an ease of communication. The same may be said of Late Saxon Shelly Ware which follows the Thames Valley. Vince (1985: 30) might express surprise that these potters exclusively supplied London, but it is logical if they were bringing their wares downstream by boat. For the late Saxon potters we can therefore discern a zonation that depends, to different degrees, on transport, political investment, and a potting tradition that can lie dormant from the Roman period or even from the Iron Age—up to a thousand years or more.

A second example uses an artefact that should not have any prehistoric technical antecedent: the buildings of the Christian church. Although he wrote a large book breaking down Anglo-Saxon architecture into its elements, Taylor was cautious

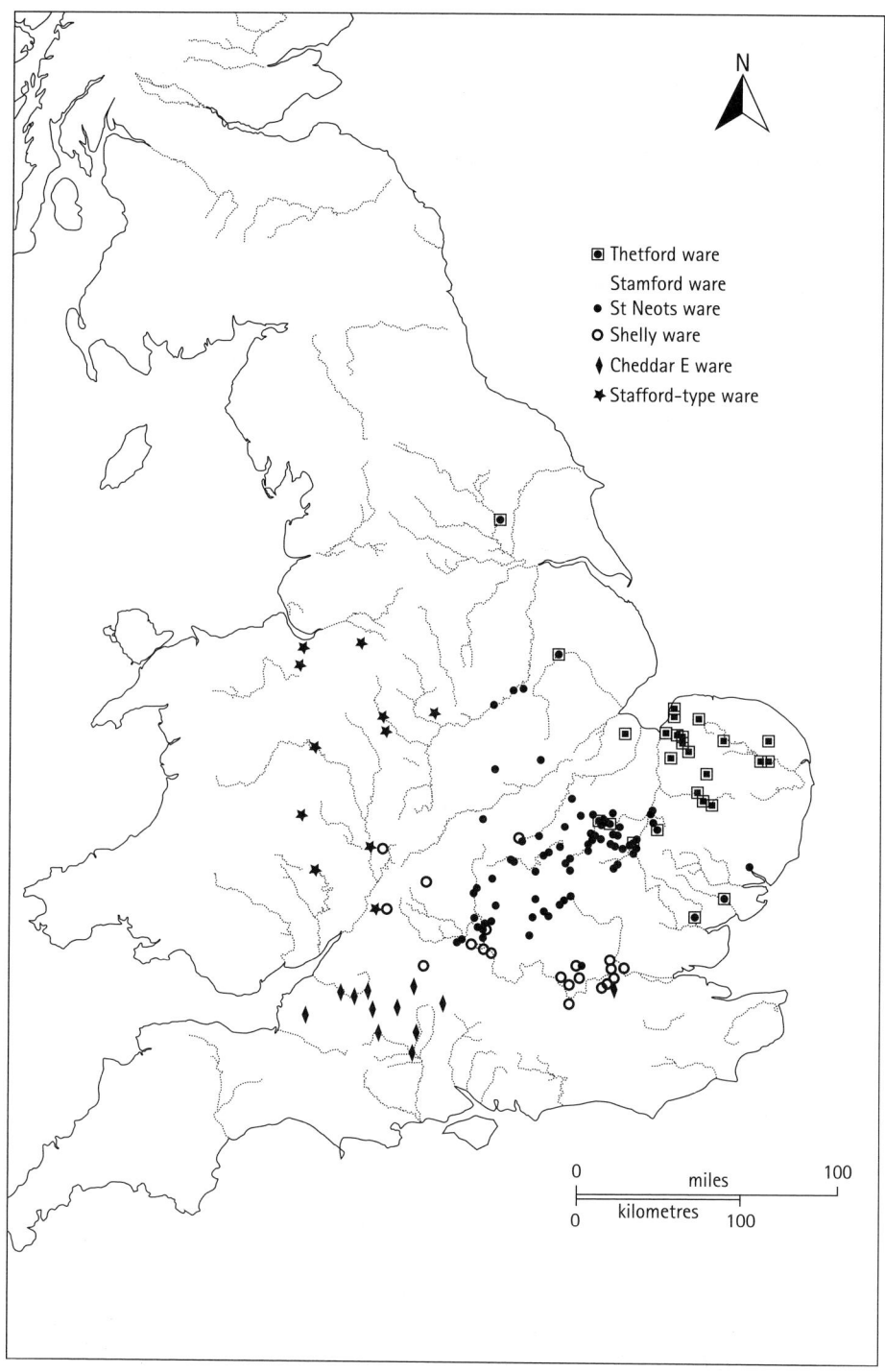

Figure 47.10 Late Saxon pottery distributions, tenth and eleventh centuries (Carver after Hurst 1956; 1957; 1958; 1976; Kilmurry 1980; Vince 1985)

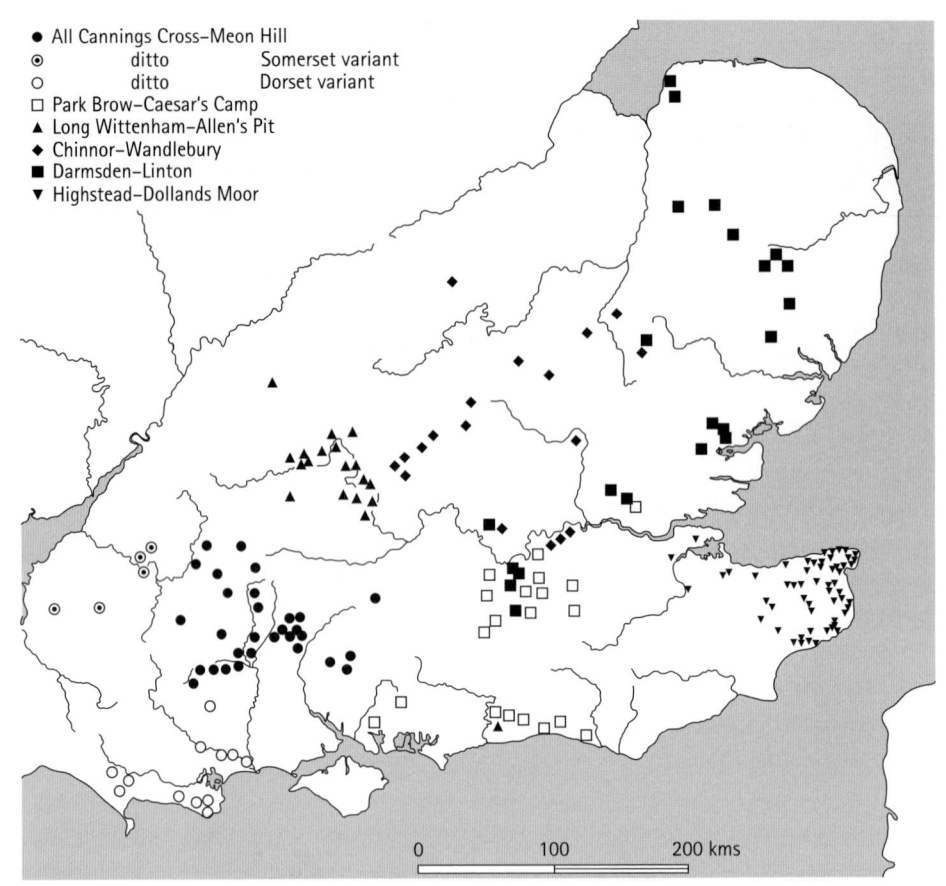

Figure 47.11 Iron Age pottery zones, sixth to fourth centuries BC (Cunliffe 2005: 98)

about the significance of their distribution (Taylor 1978: 774). The survival of churches and the survival of the elements themselves were subject to the random forces of later rebuilding. He was thus confident in the regionality of only a few of his architectural attributes, noting the concentration of round towers in Norfolk, the absence of long-short quoins from Northumbria, the stripwork confined to the east coast, apsidal east ends confined (with one exception) south of the Fosse Way, and the clusters of pilaster strip types in Kent, Essex, and Norfolk (Fig. 47.12). These examples show that there is some regional variation in tenth- and eleventh-century churches, but do not easily explain it. In some cases, the character of the local stone is a factor (as with the flint pilasters, and possibly the round towers). In others, the ease of communication is probably paramount (as with the east-coast distribution of stone pieces for stripwork). More cultural groupings may emerge with closer analysis, since Taylor's categories were quite coarse. 'Stripwork', for example, includes the gable-headed hoods for windows and doorways that provide such a distinctive aspect of thirteen churches in Norfolk. It is also possible that church-builders, like manuscript-makers, belonged to extensive multi-regional cooperatives in which ideologies and practices were shared. In any event, if the distribution of some elements (building stone) can have a geological explanation, other preferences (types of opening) probably betray a more intellectual confederation.

Conclusion

There are therefore at least two kinds of territories for which future early-medieval archaeologists may be disposed to hunt: the one traditional, stable, geographically logical, and probably ancestral, which is reflected in artisan industries; the other innovative, varied, and intellectual, expressed in monumentality. There will be moments when these coincide and moments when they do not; times when only ancestral territories show, and times when these are obliterated by an overwhelming orthodoxy. Up to now, archaeology's interests have been almost exclusively attracted by the orthodox and imperial, the Christian and the Roman archetypes with their obtrusive and repetitive 'culture'. Perhaps now is the moment to start listening to the dissident voices.

Anglo-Saxon archaeology should not be a private matter for English archaeologists to indulge in. At the scale of the site and of the territory, its new agenda looks to the evidence of prehistory and to the neighbours, both on the island and overseas, to determine the references and allusions being made. We note that the 'expressivity', the degree of agency, varies with the kind of material culture. The expression of identity and ideology is strong in high-investment graves and sculpture, lower in pottery and architectural elements. Artefactual territories reflect ancient usage—particularly of routes of communication and prehistoric territories; they seem to say little about documented ethnic groups, and when they do, the documentary labels and the archaeology are often out of synchrony with each other. In the fifth century, when the Angles, Saxons, and Jutes are supposed to have partitioned the country, there is little demarcation of the graves. It becomes marked only in the following generations, during the sixth century (Hills 2003: 106). In the seventh century, when the Anglo-Saxon zone is theoretically divided into kingdoms, the grave goods not only take on a distinctly Roman or Byzantine quality, but proclaim a united territory which equates with later England (Geake 1997: 1999; cf. Campbell 1986: 67). But when we arrive in the English kingdom of the tenth century, the increase in prosperity and in material engagement lights up the local taste, and reveals artefactual zones that are variations on those of the mid Saxon period or its Roman and prehistoric predecessors.

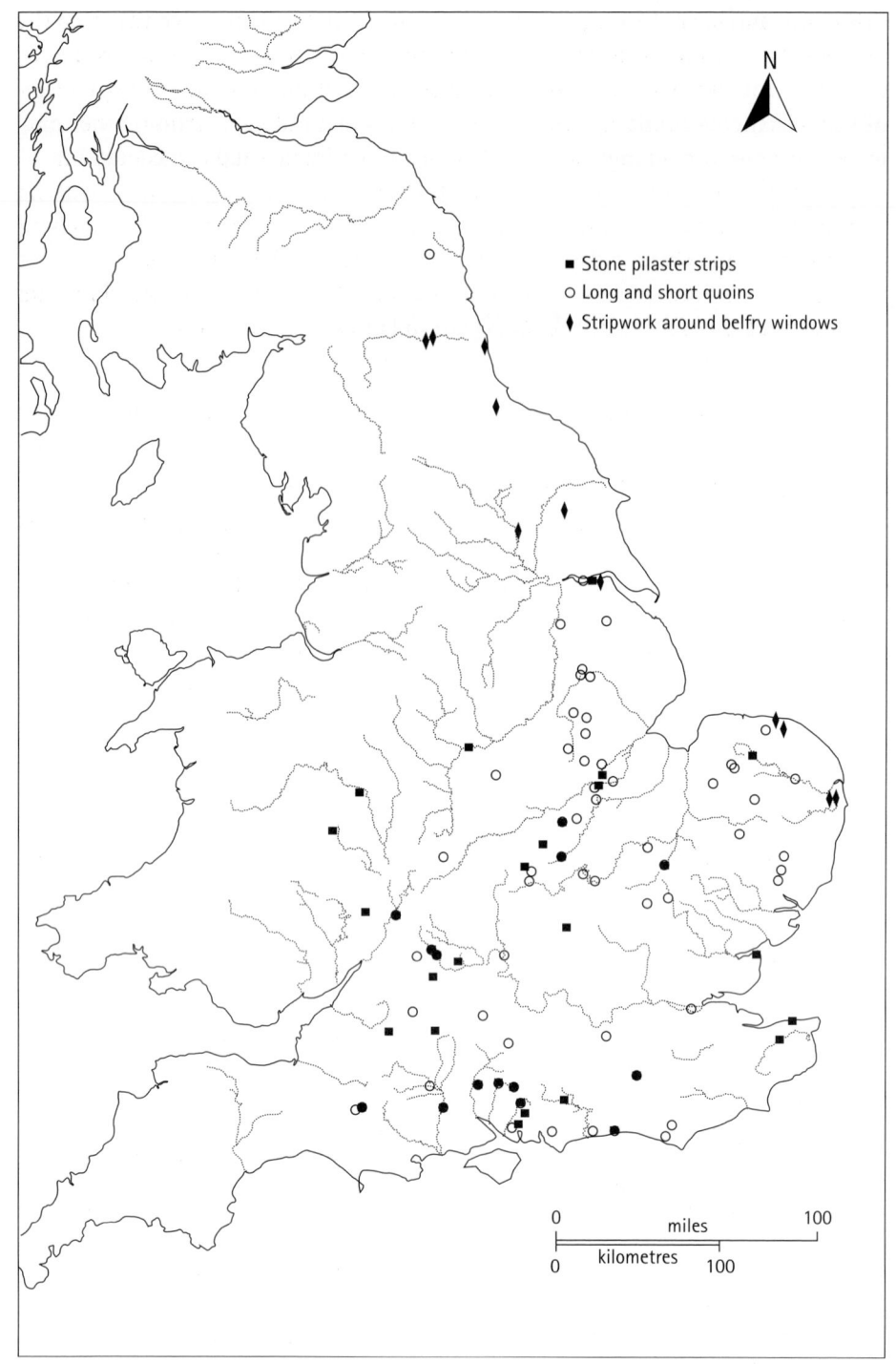

Figure 47.12 Architectural preferences in Anglo-Saxon churches, tenth and eleventh centuries (Carver after Taylor 1978: 890, 920, 930, 945)

For the thinking expressed in sites and monuments, territory, real and perceived, is one of the wells on which creative monumentality can draw. Stafford was aware of its Iron Age function as a processor of tribute, but acknowledged the previous Roman territory and the supply zone of the Roman potters as well as the contemporary territory of Æthelflæd's conquest. This is a highly intellectual agenda of some complexity, but it is not impenetrable or even forbidding. The Anglo-Saxons were an intellectual and complex people. They deserve more from their archaeologists than superficial explanations based on race, social structure, and Christianity. Our business is to release and celebrate the diversity of the times, its promises and menaces, as the earliest English themselves felt it to be.

Acknowledgements

The basis for selecting the case studies discussed here is only that the author knows them well. There are surely better ones and will be still more in the future. I am grateful to Nicky Toop of FAS Ltd for making the maps.

References

Andrén, A. (1998). *Between Artifacts and Texts: Historical Archaeology in Global Perspective*. New York: Plenum Press.

Bartholomew, P. (2005). 'Continental connections: Angles, Saxons and others in Bede and Procopius'. *Anglo-Saxon Studies in Archaeology and History* 13: 19–30.

Bassett, S. (ed.) (1989). *The Origins of Anglo-Saxon Kingdoms*. London and New York: Leicester University Press.

Blair, J. (2005). *The Church in Anglo-Saxon Society*. Oxford: Oxford University Press.

Bradley, R. (1987). 'Time regained: the creation of continuity'. *Journ. Brit. Archaeol. Assoc.* 140: 1–17.

Brather, S. (2002). 'Ethnic identities as constructions of archaeology: the case of the Alamanni', in A. Gillett (ed.), *On Barbarian Identity: Critical Approaches to Ethnicity in the Early Middle Ages*. Turnhout: Brepols, 149–75.

Braudel, F. (1972). *The Mediterranean and the Mediterranean World in the Age of Philip II*, Volume 1. London: Collins.

Brown, P. (2003). *The Rise of Western Christendom: Triumph and Diversity AD 200–1000*. 2nd edition. Oxford: Blackwell.

Bruce-Mitford, R. L. S. (1975). *The Sutton Hoo Ship Burial*, Volume 1. London: British Museum.

BRUGMANN, B., and PENN, K., with K. HØILUND NIELSEN (2007). *Aspects of Anglo-Saxon Burial: Morning Thorpe, Spong Hill, Bergh Apton and Westgarth Gardens.* East Anglian Archaeology 119. Gressenhall: Norfolk Museums Service.

BUCK, C. E., CAVANAGH, W. G., and LITTON, C. D. (1996). *Bayesian Approach to Interpreting Archaeological Data.* Chichester: Wiley.

BUDD, P., MILLARD, A., CHENERY, C., LUCY, S., and ROBERTS, C. (2004). 'Investigating populations movement by stable isotope analysis: a report from Britain'. *Antiquity* 78: 127–41.

CAMPBELL, J. (1986). *Essays in Anglo-Saxon History.* London and Ronceverte: Hambledon Press.

CARVER, M. O. H. (1989). 'Kingship and material culture in early Anglo-Saxon East Anglia', in Bassett (ed.), *Origins*, 141–58.

—— (1990). 'Pre-Viking traffic in the north sea', in S. McGrail (ed.), *Maritime Celts, Frisians and Saxons.* CBA Research Report 71. York: Council for British Archaeology, 117–25.

—— (ed.) (1992). *The Age of Sutton Hoo.* Woodbridge: Boydell Press.

—— (1993). *Arguments in Stone: Archaeology and the European Town in the First Millennium.* Oxford: Oxbow Books.

—— (1995). 'Ship burial in early Britain: ancient custom or political signal?', in O. Crumlin-Pedersen and B. Munch Thye (eds.), *The Ship as Symbol in Prehistoric and Medieval Scandinavia.* Copenhagen: The National Museum, 111–24.

—— (1998). *Sutton Hoo: Burial Ground of Kings.* London: British Museum.

—— (2000). 'Burial as poetry: the context of treasure in Anglo-Saxon graves', in E. Tyler (ed.), *Treasure in the Medieval West.* Woodbridge: Boydell, 25–48.

—— (2001). 'Why that, why there, why then? The politics of early medieval monumentality', in A. MacGregor and H. Hamerow (eds.), *Image and Power in Early Medieval British Archaeology. Essays in Honour of Rosemary Cramp.* Oxford: Oxbow Books, 1–22.

—— (2002a). 'Reflections on the meanings of monumental barrows in Anglo-Saxon England', in S. Lucy and A. Reynolds (eds.), *Burial in Early Medieval England and Wales.* Society for Medieval Archaeology Monograph Series 17. London: Society for Medieval Archaeology, 132–43.

—— (2002b). 'Marriages of true minds: archaeology with texts', in B. Cunliffe, W. Davies, and C. Renfrew (eds.), *Archaeology: The Widening Debate.* London: The British Academy, 465–96.

—— (ed.) (2003). *The Cross goes North: Processes of Conversion in Northern Europe, AD 300–1300.* York: York Medieval Press.

—— (2005). *Sutton Hoo: A Seventh-Century Princely Burial Ground and its Context.* Reports of the Research Committee of the Society of Antiquaries of London 69. London: The British Museum Press.

—— (2008a). *Portmahomack: Monastery of the Picts.* Edinburgh: Edinburgh University Press.

—— (2008b). *The Pictish Monastery at Portmahomack.* Jarrow Lecture.

—— (2010). *The Birth of a Borough. An Archaeological Study of Anglo-Saxon Stafford.* Woodbridge: Boydell Press.

—— HILLS, C., and SCHESCHKEWITZ, J. (2009). *Wasperton: A Roman, British and Anglo-Saxon Cemetery in Central England.* Woodbridge: Boydell Press.

CHADWICK, H. M. (1905). *Studies on Anglo-Saxon Institutions.* Cambridge: Cambridge University Press.

COLLINGWOOD, R. G., and MYRES, J. N. L. (1936). *Roman Britain and the English Settlements*. Oxford: Oxford University Press.

CRAMP, R. J. (1984). *A Corpus of Anglo-Saxon Stone Sculpture*. Oxford: Oxford University Press.

CUNLIFFE, B. (2001). *Facing the Ocean: The Atlantic and its Peoples*. Oxford: Oxford University Press.

—— (2002). 'Tribes and empires c.1500 BC–AD 500', in P. Slack and R. Ward (eds.), *The Peopling of Britain: The Shaping of a Human Landscape*. The Linacre Lectures 1999. Oxford: Oxford University Press, 115–38.

—— (2005). *Iron Age Communities in Britain*. 4th edition. London: Routledge.

FILMER-SANKEY, W., and PESTELL, T. (2001). *Snape Anglo-Saxon Cemetery: Excavations and Surveys 1824–1992*. East Anglian Archaeology 95. Gressenhall: Norfolk Museums Service.

FLETCHER, R. (1997). *The Conversion of Europe: From Paganism to Christianity 371–1386 AD*. London: Harper Collins.

FRANK, R. (1992). 'Beowulf and Sutton Hoo: the odd couple', in C. B. Kendall and P. S. Wells (eds.), *Voyage to the Other World: The Legacy of Sutton Hoo*. Minneapolis: University of Minnesota Press, 47–64.

FRAZER, W. O., and TYRRELL, A. (eds.) (2000). *Social Identity in Early Medieval Britain*. Leicester: Leicester University Press.

GEAKE, H. (1997). *The Use of Grave-Goods in Conversion-Period England, c. 600–c. 850*. BAR British Ser. 261. Oxford: British Archaeological Reports.

—— (1999). 'Invisible kingdoms: the use of grave-goods in seventh-century England'. *Anglo-Saxon Studies in Archaeology and History* 10: 203–15.

GILLETT, A. (ed.) (2002). 'Was ethnicity politicised in the earliest medieval kingdoms?', in A. Gillett (ed.), *On Barbarian Identity: Critical Approaches to Ethnicity in the Early Middle Ages*. Turnhout: Brepols, 85–121.

HÄRKE, H. (2002). 'Kings and warriors. Population and landscape from post-Roman to Norman Britain', in P. Slack and R. Ward (eds.), *The Peopling of Britain: The Shaping of a Human Landscape*. The Linacre Lectures 1999. Oxford: Oxford University Press, 145–75.

—— (2007). 'Ethnicity, "race" and migration in mortuary archaeology: an attempt at a short answer'. *Anglo-Saxon Studies in Archaeology and History* 14: 12–18.

HASLAM, J. (1981). 'Cricklade', in J. Schofield and D. Palliser (eds.), *Recent Archaeological Research in English Towns*. York: Council for British Archaeology, 28–30.

HIGHAM, Nick (1995). *An English Empire: Bede and the early Anglo-Saxon Kings*. Manchester: Manchester University Press.

HILL, D. (1981). *An Atlas of Anglo-Saxon England*. Oxford: Blackwell.

HILLS, C. (2003). *Origins of the English*. London: Duckworth.

—— (2007). 'History and archaeology: the state of play in early medieval Europe'. *Antiquity* 81: 191–200.

HINES, J., HØILUND NIELSEN, K., and SIEGMUND, F. (eds.) (1999). *The Pace of Change: Studies in Early-Medieval Chronology*. Oxford: Oxbow Books.

HODGES, R. (1989). *The Anglo-Saxon Achievement*. London: Duckworth.

HURST, J. G. (1956). 'Saxo-Norman pottery in East Anglia'. *Proceedings of the Cambridge Antiquarian Society* 49: 43–70.

—— (1957). 'Saxo-Norman pottery in East Anglia. Part II. Thetford Ware with an account of Middle Saxon Ipswich ware (with S E West)'. *Proceedings of the Cambridge Antiquarian Society* 50: 29–60.

—— (1958). 'Saxo-Norman pottery in East Anglia Part III. Stamford Ware'. *Proceedings of the Cambridge Antiquarian Society* 51: 37–65.

—— (1976). 'The pottery', in D. M. Wilson (ed.), *The Archaeology of Anglo-Saxon England*. London: Methuen, 283–348.

KILMURRY, K. (1980). *The Pottery Industry of Stamford, Lincolnshire c AD 850–1250: Its Manufacture, Trade and Relationship with Continental Wares, with a Classification and Chronology*. BAR British Series 84. Oxford: British Archaeological Reports.

LEVISON, W. (1946). *England and the Continent in the Eighth Century*. Oxford: Clarendon Press.

LUCY, S. (2000). *The Anglo-Saxon Way of Death: Burial Rites in Early England*. Stroud: Sutton Publishing.

MCCARTHY, M. R., and BROOKS, C. M. (1988). *Medieval Pottery in Britain AD 900–1600*. Leicester: Leicester University Press.

MOFFETT, L. (1994). 'Charred cereals from some ovens/kilns in late Saxon Stafford and the botanical evidence for the pre-*burh* economy', in J. Rackham (ed.), *Environment and Economy in Anglo-Saxon England*. CBA Research Report 89. York: Council for British Archaeology, 55–64.

MORELAND, J. (2000). 'Ethnicity, power and the English', in Frazer and Tyrrell (eds.), *Social Identity in Early Medieval Britain*, 23–51.

MÜLLER-WILLE, M. (1970–71). 'Pferdegrab und Pferdeopfer im frühen Mittelalter'. *Berichten v.d. Rijksdienst v.h. Oudheidkundig Bodemonderzoek* 20–21: 119–248.

—— (1974). 'Boat-graves in Northern Europe'. *International Journal of Nautical Archaeology* 3: 187–204.

—— (1992). 'Monumentale Grabhügel der Völkerwanderungszeit in Mittel- und Nordeuropa. Bestand und Deutung', in W. Paravicini (ed.), *Mare Balticum: Beiträge zur Geschichte des Ostseeraums im Mittelalter und Neuzeit. Festschift zum 65. Geburtstag von Erich Hoffman*. Kieler Historische Studien, Band 36, 1–20.

—— (1993). 'Burial mounds and burial practices', in P. Pulsiano (ed.), *Medieval Scandinavia*. New York and London: Garland, 58–60.

—— (1995). 'Boat-graves, old and new views', in O. Crumlin-Pedersen (ed.), *The Ship as Symbol in Prehistoric and Medieval Scandinavia*. Studies in Archaeology and History 1. Copenhagen: The National Museum, 101–10.

—— (1998). 'Zwei religiöse Welten: Bestattungen der fränkischen Könige Childerich und Chlodwig'. *Abhandlungen der Akademie der Wissenschaften und Literatur*. Mainz–Stuttgart: Steiner: Geistes- und sozialwissenschaftliche Klasse 1: 3–45.

OPIE, I. and OPIE, P. (1982). *The Lore and Language of Schoolchildren*. Granada.

PRYOR, F. (2004). *Britain AD*. London: Harper Collins.

RAHTZ, P., DICKINSON, T. M., and WATTS, L. (eds.) (1980). *Anglo-Saxon Cemeteries 1979*. BAR British Series 82. Oxford: British Archaeological Reports.

—— HIRST, S., and WRIGHT, S. M. (2000). *Cannington Cemetery*. Britannia Monograph Series 17. London: Society for the Promotion of Roman Studies.

RENFREW, C., and CHERRY, J. F. (eds.) (1986). *Peer Polity Interaction and Socio-Political Change*. Cambridge: Cambridge University Press.

TAYLOR, H. M. (1978). *Anglo-Saxon Architecture*, Volume 3. Cambridge: Cambridge University Press.

THOMAS, C. (1981). *Christianity in Roman Britain to AD 500*. London: Batsford.

THOMAS, M. G., STUMPF, M. P. H., and HÄRKE, H. (2006). 'Evidence for an apartheid-like social structure in early Anglo-Saxon England'. *Proceedings of the Royal Society B*. doi:10.1098/rspb.2006.3627: 1–7.

VINCE, A. G. (1985). 'The Saxon and medieval pottery of London: a review'. *Medieval Archaeology* 29: 25–93.

—— (1994). 'Saxon urban economies: an archaeological perspective', in J. Rackham (ed.), *Environment and Economy in Anglo-Saxon England*. CBA Research Report 89. York: Council for British Archaeology, 108–19.

WACHER, J. (1974). *The Towns of Roman Britain*. London: Batsford.

WELCH, M. (1992). *Anglo-Saxon England*. London: English Heritage.

WHITELOCK, D. (1954). *The Beginnings of English Society*. Harmondsworth: Penguin.

WILLIAMS, H. (1998). 'Ancient landscape and the dead: the reuse of prehistoric and Roman monuments as early Anglo-Saxon burial sites'. *Medieval Archaeology* 41: 1–32.

—— (2005). 'Heathen graves and Victorian Anglo-Saxonism: Assessing the Archaeology of John Mitchell Kemble'. *Anglo-Saxon Studies in Archaeology and History* 13: 1–18.

—— (2006). *Death and Memory in Early Medieval Britain*. Cambridge: Cambridge University Press.

WOOLF, A. (2000). 'Community, identity and kingship in Early England', in Frazer and Tyrrell (eds.), *Social Identity in Early Medieval Britain*, 91–110.

PART X

THE PLACE OF ARCHAEOLOGY IN ANGLO-SAXON STUDIES

PART X

CHAPTER 48

HISTORICAL SOURCES AND ARCHAEOLOGY

JAMES CAMPBELL

So little is known of the history of Britain for long after the Romans left that understanding can hardly go beyond speculation about possibilities. The few thousand words of the main written sources are difficult indeed. The usual dating of Gildas' diatribe to the mid sixth century has to be tentative and the work itself contains no dates (Winterbottom 1978). The *Anglo-Saxon Chronicle* must contain valuable material, but the text as we have it is of *c.*891 and it is such that the reliable and the unreliable are hardly distinguishable (Whitelock *et al.* 1965). An example of its value and difficulties is this. For 577 the *Chronicle* refers, most interestingly, to three British *ciningas* in association with three *ceastra*: Gloucester, Cirencester, and Bath. This annal (of unknown origin) is the only evidence for possible post-Roman city states. Among the difficulties are these. If there was such a system there is no telling how prevalent it was. And there is no telling whether the *ciningas* were independent rulers or sub-kings. Another characteristic example of the patches of information which are nearly all the written sources give is this. By fortunate chance evidence survives which has been powerfully argued to demonstrate the survival in south-eastern Wales of a society using Latin documents into and beyond the sixth century (Davies 1978). There are no means of determining whether similar conditions prevailed elsewhere, for example in the British kingdom of Elmet surviving, east of the Pennines, until the very early seventh century.

If the written sources are scarce and sometimes ambiguous, they have major value in demonstrating inadequacies of the 'archaeological record'. That 'record' in relation to Anglo-Saxon invasion and settlement is chiefly from burials, though evidence from settlements is increasingly available. Comparison with Gaul is important here. There, better written sources indicate how incomplete a guide graves can be to the course of events. For example, as Hawkes pointed out more than fifty years ago (1956), Franks did not normally deposit grave-goods until the sixth century, considerably after their possible initial involvement in Britain.

The shortfalls of burial evidence are plain enough in approaching the central problem: that of the fate of the Britons (Higham 2007; Loveluck and Laing, this volume). The debate on this relates to wider discussion on the role (or non-role) of invasions. If we consider whether the Anglo-Saxon invasions could fall into the class of those which should be seen as essentially transfers of culture rather than as (on a major scale) of population, the evidence of the written sources is important. This relates to the possibility of genocide, which has achieved a more vivid, and horrible, prominence in the light of recent events in, in particular, Rwanda. In praising the Northumbrian king Æthelfrith (c.592–616) Bede says that no ruler had subjected more lands to the English people, making them tributary or habitable, having subjugated or exterminated the inhabitants (*exterminatis vel subjugatis indigenis*) (Colgrave and Mynors 1969: 116–17). (The ambiguity of the verb *exterminare* is a reminder that massacre and migration could go hand in hand.) In describing Penda of Mercia's campaign of 655 Bede says of him that 'he was determined to destroy and exterminate the whole [i.e. Northumbrian] people from the greatest to the least' (ibid.: 290–1). The possible genocidal element in the Anglo-Saxon invasions may have been exaggerated in the nineteenth century, but underestimated in the twentieth.

Another important determinant which comes to light, not least in late Irish sources, is the possibility of a politically and socially dominant group becoming demographically dominant also (Nicholls 1972: 10–12). The likely association of the leading elements in Anglo-Saxon society with polygyny and established concubinage suggests how they might have out-bred lower orders (Clunies Ross 1985: 4–8). Superior chances of survival in recurrent famines and entrenched legal advantages would also have strengthened the cumulative demographic gain of groups whose number had originally been disproportionate to their authority (Woolf 2007: 127–9). Such developments would have had major effects on the DNA record (if it can be extracted: Hedges, this volume).

Strangely, the organization and leadership of Anglo-Saxon incursions is little discussed. So far as written sources take us (which is anything but all the way) the story in Britain seems to contrast with what appears on the Continent. The *Chronicle*'s account is that of war under organized if divided leadership on several fronts. Gildas' account in terms of the ebb and flow of conquest is consonant with this and seems to indicate stronger 'native' resistance than was met by invaders elsewhere in the former empire. Only in Britain did Roman collapse leave certain areas in the long-lasting power of peoples who had been there before the Romans came. This may be related to Gildas' strong emphasis on British as opposed to Roman identity (Lewis 2007).

When Bede writes of invasion by Angles, Saxons, and Jutes, is he referring to no more than perception of ethnicity, which could be a vague or fluid concept? Or did he (or the sources of his information) have in mind polities, entities nearer to what earlier writers could have envisaged in mentioning Goths or Vandals? Germanic peoples, however mobile, could have sophisticated organizations, known to us only in incidental references in written sources, such as that which Ammianus makes to the Alemanni in the fourth century (Rolfe 1971: 264–5), or Bede to the continental Saxons in the seventh (Colgrave and Mynors 1969: 480–3). The problems of organization and leadership in the early period of incursion are put into focus by current views on the appearance of rich graves from about the mid sixth century onwards and most dazzlingly represented by that in Mound I of Sutton Hoo. It is suggested that such burials indicate the appearance of a newly rich group of nobles and have bearings on a positive process of 'state-formation' (e.g. Carver 1998: 104–5). This argument, that they represent more than a change in burial customs, has to skirt round a number of problems and possibilities. How does it accommodate the existence of apparently powerful leaders (surely not all fictional) such as are mentioned in the *Chronicle*? It has to cope with the absence in Northumbria of burial evidence which could suggest wealth such as that known to have been enjoyed by at least one Northumbrian nobleman by the later seventh century, Benedict Biscop. It would be a large assumption that his wealth did not come from pagan ancestors (Campbell 2000: 74). There is a paradox in the association of rich burials with state formation. Might not a newly rich nobility, if there was one, have been an influence for the division rather than the extension of power?

In guessing about political structures in the early period it is well to begin with what is known of the position by 800. There were four kingdoms: Mercia, Wessex, Northumbria, and East Anglia. Three of these were the product of merger or absorption. Mercia, the most powerful of them under Æthelbald (716–57) and Offa (757–96), appears to have incorporated a number of polities, the most conspicuous that of the Hwicce in the West Midlands. Northumbria was the product of a merger between two English kingdoms and the acquisition of British lands including the kingdom of Elmet. Wessex had incorporated the former kingdoms of Sussex and Kent and the larger part of the British kingdom of Dumnonia. To consider East Anglia is to be given a bracing reminder of cold ignorance, largely because the only written sources are a genealogical king-list and passing references.

The 'archaeological record', as normally, raises more questions than it answers. It has been argued in fine detail that the evidence of grave-goods suggests quite widespread and early German fifth-century settlement there, with unknown political consequences (Böhme 1986). The early-seventh-century burials at Sutton Hoo and related finds can suggest a strongly concentrated authority in south-east Suffolk; but it is impossible to know how to interpret this. Was this area that of a formerly distinct polity which had acquired wider power, or does it represent one of several areas of special significance in an always united East Anglia, the others such not having been discovered, or the relevant evidence not having survived? We simply do not know whether there had been a united early kingdom of East Anglia, and, if so, what it was like. There is, however, just a little evidence: the two great dykes which run across the Icknield Way defending approaches to East Anglia from Mercia. They probably antedate the ninth century and, if so, speak for extensively organized power in East Anglia though, necessarily, they can give no more than limited evidence on the boundaries of that power.

It is indeed earthworks which tell us most about power. It has been rightly observed that 'the hillforts of the South West reveal a powerfully centralized élite able to mobilize labour to repair hundreds of metres of fortification' (Hodges 1989: 32). (They are indeed the only evidence for any kind of administration there.) Above all consider Offa's Dyke, over a hundred miles of mighty bank and ditch. Written sources indicate that King Offa was responsible, or largely responsible, for the immense feat of organization involved. In explanation of such a feat the relevant documents take us straight to assessment in hides. Our earliest land-grants, 'charters', beginning in the late seventh century, almost always give assessments in Latin terms agreed to be equivalents of 'hide'. What is more, some of these show that such assessments could apply not only in large sums to extensive areas, but in smaller numbers to particular places or estates. From the eighth century many charters emphasize that there could be no exemption from, *inter alia*, fortress building. It is highly probable that such clauses tell something about the origin of great dykes.

Assessment, extensive and regular assessment, in hides (or similar units) is a key factor in Anglo-Saxon history from Offa's Dyke to Domesday. Its origins are little studied. They could be Roman. Undeniably Britain's departure from the empire had caused 'systems collapse'. But that need not apply to all systems. Roman taxation to the extent that it was in kind, or by conscription, could perhaps have survived the evaporation of a cash economy. The Roman system in Britain may indeed have gone back to the Iron Age kingdoms which at the time of the Roman conquest were more developed than their Anglo-Saxon successors half a millennium later. On the other hand such a hidage assessment system might possibly have been imported from Germany by Anglo-Saxon invaders. Later evidence shows corresponding units being employed there at various levels of assessment and description. If there was such an importation this would tell something very weighty about the organization and capacity of the invaders. Any serious consideration of the system of hidage assessment in early England demands willingness to accept the likely possibilities of either the survival of Roman systems, or the complex power of imported Germanic ones, or both.

Hidage problems come to a difficult focus in consideration of the 'Tribal Hidage', a text (probably seventh or eighth century) listing thirty-three units with assessments varying from a hundred thousand hides for Wessex to three hundred for minor units in the Midlands. 'Tribal' in the title is a nineteenth-century introduction on the assumption that the names attached in the genitive plural to assessed areas of land in the list are those of 'tribes'. This assumption neglects the fact that 'people' names could be used to denote administrative areas. The 'tribal' interpretation of the text envisages the Anglo-Saxon conquest as having been such as to create perpetuate 'tribes' whose little polities later became merged or submerged into kingdoms. Later evidence indicating the existence of relatively small units with a possibly early name has been used to support this theory. There is no evidence that such units were ever independent; but one must beware of confusing the absence of evidence with the silence of evidence. Maybe there was justification for such a comment as that made by Henry of Huntingdon (in the early twelfth century) on the conquest of Mercia and East Anglia. 'Many men often came from Germany...but these had not yet been brought under united rule. Many leaders contended for the possession of districts and so innumerable wars came about. Because these leaders were many they are not known by name' (Greenway 1996: 98–9, cf. civ). However, he almost certainly lacked a source for this statement and so it is an early example of comment on this period such that the author's intelligence outruns his information.

The 'Tribal Hidage' as a tribute list directs attention to relations between kingdoms, a theme on which archaeology offers little beyond theories based on the movement of valuable goods, although an effort has been made to link grave patterns to hegemony (Myres 1969: 116–19). Discussion here has centred on Bede's account of seven kings who enjoyed (discontinuous) *imperium* over most of the other kingdoms between the late fifth century and the mid seventh, and whom a ninth-century author calls '*bretwaldas*'. It is a question of dispute as to how far at least some of the rulers concerned had an 'institutionalized' position or whether there is no more involved than a vocabulary and rhetoric of occasional power. There could be something of a false dichotomy here because historians have tended to underestimate the complexity, even sophistication, of relationships between polities, greater and lesser, in early England. The rulers concerned came from societies with long traditions and conventions of complicated interaction, and overlordships may have had different weights and have been expressed in varied ways which related to this without there being a distinctly defined 'office' of *bretwalda*.

On the ordering of society the most immediate guides are the seventh-century laws. Their message is not pellucid. But they indicate that in both Kent and Wessex there were more free Anglo-Saxon classes than one: in Kent at least two, in Wessex at least three. In addition there were Britons in Wessex with wergelds set at half those of their Anglo-Saxon equivalents. The size of the wergelds indicated varied from 100 shillings (probably gold tremisses) to 300. It is impressive and would suggest either that members of the free classes were not numerous or that these were very wealthy societies (Campbell 2000: 69–72). The presence of unfree classes is shown, but, of course, not their number.

Another view of the social landscape has been provided by scholars researching into overall patterns of landholding and estate organization. They have of necessity to schematize and largely on the basis of late sources. What seems to emerge, with all due reservations made, is that over much of Britain there was a pattern of 'extended estates': areas of up to, say, 100 square miles, each with a centre of authority, commonly royal, with which would be associated a small number of 'unfree' settlements providing labour and services, and a larger number of free ones whose inhabitants had lighter obligations of a largely 'public' nature. The extended estate system presents numerous problems. Three of the most pressing are these. How far were such estates coincidental with the 'small shires', units of authority into which at least large areas of early England were divided? How far are we looking at a system which, though appearing in various forms in late sources, had a degree of uniformity over much of Britain? Could it have been one which went back to or beyond the Roman period? In short, could it be that the Anglo-Saxons in some considerable measure took over an existing landscape of power and exploitation? A key question/difficulty is 'Indo-European': how far did systems of a similar kind prevail over much of Europe?

There is a major factor to which the written sources draw attention, but which is not explicit in the 'archaeological record' though it could well have done much to affect its nature. The factor concerned is plague. There is good reason to believe that there was a major and extensively fatal epidemic—it may well be of bubonic plague—in and after 664 (Maddicott 1997). If so it could have been as determinative in many ways as was the Black Death in the later Middle Ages. For example, the Black Death had important effects on patterns of settlement, yet a major study of early Anglo-Saxon settlement can allow no place for plague (Beresford 1954; Hamerow 1991). If a leading archaeologist is willing to contemplate, though hesitatingly, the possibility that between the fourth century and the late sixth the population declined from about one million to about a quarter of a million, then it must be suggested that, if so, disease would have been important (Hodges 1986: 72).

Written sources and archaeology meet in the search to identify places of authority. Bede gives an explicit account of Canterbury as Ethelbert's capital: '*imperii sui totius... metropolis*' (Colgrave and Mynors 1969: 74–5). Archaeology has not identified the physical focus of power in Ethelbert's Canterbury, though it has done so in Edwin's York. Other Roman towns probably retained a similar role. Royal vills were other main centres of power. Yeavering is the most remarkable, but also the only one excavated, and it may well be an unusual example. Consideration of discoveries made at the Danish centre of authority at Lejre demonstrates the great advances which might be made if comparable sites other than Yeavering could be found and investigated in England (Niles and Osborn 2007). Lejre has a special relationship to a written English source, *Beowulf*. While one may be more interested than convinced by discussion of the possibility that Lejre was in some meaningful sense the locale of the poem, such discussion has brought out the way in which the poem may provide somewhat detailed information about a royal hall. Itinerant power may often have been exercised from transitory accommodation. Major meetings could be held at places such that the great men there, with their entourages, would have been sheltered in ways almost defying archaeological investigation: under canvas (more likely leather) or wattle. One might think of the wattle palace put up for Henry II at Dublin (Orpen 1911: 267).

Most important elements in the early Anglo-Saxon economy were war and law. The narratives of Bede and the *Chronicle* show how far the economy of kings and nobles was one of predation. Kings raided one another's lands, sometimes at great distances. Royal treasures, *ornamenta regia*, were the currency of power (Colgrave and Mynors 1969: 290–1). References to treasures in charters show that in nature and scale they would go well beyond even those found at Sutton Hoo (Campbell 2000: 233). The capture of slaves was an important fruit of military success (Pelteret 1995). Indeed the slave trade could have been a key factor. Bede's account of the aftermath of a battle in 679 is crucial here. He tells of a captive who was sold to a Frisian slave merchant (apparently ready at hand) who took him in chains towards London, no doubt for export (Colgrave and Mynors 1969: 294–5). Enslavement came not only through war. A father could sell his children, provided they were under the age of 8 (McNeill and Gamer 1938: 211). It is likely that enslavement was the fate of those who could not meet legal penalties.

The legal system was in a sense very commercial. It was not for nothing that the laws abound in values, penalties, and compensations expressed in terms of gold 'shillings' though probably often paid in kind. Every part of the human body had its determined value, down to the very toes. The system was one such as to require the frequent use of quantifiable exchange media: a need best met by coin. It is likely that by the early decades of the eighth century over wide areas such a need was being well met. In the last quarter of the seventh century the gold coin which had been struck in England was replaced by silver 'sceattas', which became a currency common to Frisia and much of England. Many millions of these coins were produced, indicating a burgeoning North Sea and Channel economy (Op den Velde and Metcalf: esp. 1–3, 74–5, 160–1; Blackburn, this volume). Intrinsic to it were big trading places. The application to them of the term *emporium* is interesting. It means simply 'trading place'. Bede said London was an *emporium* for 'many peoples coming by land and sea' (Colgrave and Mynors 1969: 142–3). The term has been taken up by scholars when they refer to such places as Hamwic and Dorestad: chiefly because they are afraid to call them towns. There are probably other such places to be discovered. An example is Norwich where a place-name with the palatalized 'wich' element is an important clue (Ekwall 1964). The size of these identified *emporia* indicates that they must have been involved in trade in goods in bulk and quantity. What goods? As exports, slaves certainly. One may wonder about cattle or, not least, that fundamentally important commodity, leather (Maddicott 2000: 32–7). Cattle could well have been a normal currency, not least for the collection of tribute. One can envisage how the *emporia* may have been part of an economy in which tribute-taking, slave-catching, and plunder played a considerable part (Thacker 2005: 493).

An economic revolution was accompanied by (and partly related to) a religious one. It is interesting, even sobering, to consider how far the conversion of England in the seventh century could be identified by entirely archaeological means. Not easily, if at all. The study of possibly pagan temples has not progressed far enough for their fate to be brought with confidence into archaeological argument. No difficulty would be found in disassociating the discontinuance in deposit of grave-goods from Christian conversion (Halsall 2005: 81–2). The only modern research excavation of major monastic sites, those of Jarrow and Monkwearmouth, would not have been undertaken had not Bede demonstrated their importance. It is only our written sources which indicate, indeed prove, the great number, scale, and wealth of the monastic foundations of the religious revolution; and indicate the possibility of political and social bouleversements brought about by conversion.

The tempting wealth of the monastery of Lindisfarne attracted the traumatic Scandinavian raid (793) which begins the story of the invasions which transformed—in a way created—England. When Alfred became king of Wessex in 871 Danish leaders were very well on the way to subduing most of Northumbria. The last Anglo-Saxon king of East Anglia had been killed in 869. Wessex was in dire straits. Alfred fought hard. The tide turned with his victory in 878. When he died in 899 he was secure in dominions which he had largely extended, not least because he and the Dane Guthrum had carved once great Mercia up between them.

How did Alfred succeed? His dynasty was already rising. His grandfather Ecgberht (802–39) had extended its authority over most of England south of the Thames. Alfred was able to deploy an administrative system based on flexible hidage assessment, so he could organize a powerful range of fortified places along the frontiers of Wessex (Hill and Rumble 1996). One may ask why the Mercians could not have emulated this. After all, the construction of their mighty western dykes had, very probably, depended upon a hidage-based organization. Part of the explanation for the contrast between West Saxon success and Mercian failure may be dynastic. Until the accession of Alfred's father Æthelwulf (Ecgberht's son) in 839 royal succession in Wessex seems to have been open to a large number of potential claimants with some share of royal blood. But from 839 until 1015 every king of Wessex (and later England) was the son, brother, or half-brother of his predecessor. No such regularity prevailed in ninth-century Mercia or Northumbria. Alfred's success must also have been aided by his effort to show himself as the leader of all Christian Anglo-Saxons. The *Anglo-Saxon Chronicle* presents him in a strong heroic light, probably considerably justified, but also somewhat distorted. His biographer Asser presents him as concerned for learning no less than war. The remarkable series of translations published from his court bears this out; and indicates him as a ruler who, somewhat like Charlemagne, integrated pursuit of learning and pursuit of power.

How much could be learned of Scandinavian invasion or of Alfred's endeavours from archaeology alone? Little. Thus, although the forts of the Burghal Hidage have been identified, few, if any, of them could be dated solely on archaeological evidence. The debate on the scale of Scandinavian settlement in the north and east turns very largely on the interpretation of place-name and institutional evidence. Archaeology plays no major part in the discussion of such settlement in the countryside, but does make an urban contribution.

Alfred's son and heir Edward ('the Elder', 899–924) and his grandson Æthelstan (924–39) made their West Saxon dynasty kings of England. Edward conquered the Danish-ruled lands in East Anglia and the Midlands. Æthelstan showed himself the most fearsome ruler in Britain when at Brunanburh in 937 he defeated rulers and forces from Danish Ireland, Scotland, and Strathclyde. The middle years of the century were tense politically. But 954 was a year of key achievement, when King Eadred replaced the last Scandinavian king in Northumbria. The reign of Edgar (957–75) marked an apogee of power, piety, and even peace. The years which followed brought defeat, and, paradoxically, in defeat showed singular evidence of English power. During the reign of Ethelred II (978–1016) Danish assaults, increasingly and powerfully successful, were such as to enable the Dane Cnut to become king of England in 1016 (a little later he gained Denmark also). Rather surprisingly Ethelred's son, Edward ('the Confessor') became king in 1042. His death in 1066 was followed by two problematical successions: that of Harold, not a prince, but the greatest nobleman in England, and a few months later by William ('the Conqueror'). William's claim was not by birth, but was secured by brutal victory and the death of Harold at Hastings in October 1066.

The successes, indeed aspects of the failures, of the English kings speak of the wealth and administrative power of a formidable state. The repeated, repeatedly successful, campaigns of Edward the Elder show powerful organization in the deployment of armies and in a complementary programme of fortress building. One might imagine that *per contra* the decline and defeats of Ethelred II showed the weakness of his regime. Paradoxically, it had notable strengths. The *Anglo-Saxon Chronicle* states sums paid to buy off Danish invaders (Danegeld), or to pay Scandinavian troops between 991 and 1018, totalling 240,500 pounds of silver. Examination shows these sums as plausible indications of orders of magnitude, and quite possibly approaching true figures (Lawson 1984; 1989; 1990). Only a powerfully centralized state could have raised such sums in years of stress and turmoil. The defeat of 1066 tells the same tale in a different way. It has never been usual for a kingdom to be overcome in and taken over after just one battle. Why was Hastings so decisive? Because England was so centralized: nothing of the kind could have happened had England been so decentralized as feudal France or like the Ireland of many kings.

That England was an elaborately ordered kingdom is not a matter of speculation or theory. It is demonstrated by the record of the Domesday survey of all England south of the Tees and the Ribble, ordered by William the Conqueror in 1086. No other part of Europe has anything distantly comparable to the amazing Domesday Book. If it did not exist one would hardly believe it could have done. It describes 13,418 settlements including a large majority of the villages and towns of later and modern England. The very scale and scope of Domesday proves the capacity of the state which produced it. It shows that most of the territory of this state was carefully divided and defined. The thirty-three shires had clear boundaries (a large number of these retain administrative importance even today). Every significant landholding had an assessment in 'hides' or 'carucates'. Everywhere there is order, method, definition. The compilation and maintenance of a 'Domesday archaeology' recording remains and discoveries from later eleventh-century England would be a major service to learning. It would not only provide a methodical complement to Domesday, but also would enable Domesday to be used as a control on the 'archaeological record' otherwise impossible to find.

The evidence of Domesday is reinforced by that of the coinage. The standard coin was the silver penny, which had replaced the 'sceatta' in the later eighth century and was coined in many millions. The tenth-century kings of the house of Wessex maintained a monopoly of currency. Its system was organized into one such that the whole currency was withdrawn at intervals, one type of penny being replaced by another. The intervals between changes approximated to six years until the reign of Edward the Confessor. Evidence provided by numismatists is no less astonishing than convincing. The coinage was abundant. It is calculated that for what was probably the largest issue, one of Cnut's, something over forty million coins were minted (Metcalf 1981: 63). Mints were numerous: over sixty in the earlier eleventh century. The kings' control was tight: foreign coin was not allowed to circulate in their dominions; the changes of coin type were made with considerable efficiency.

Two themes resound through the two volumes of Domesday and all the silver pennies: powerful administration and serious wealth. The history of Anglo-Saxon administration is long, important, surprising, and unclear. Consider the pattern, the complete and rather orderly pattern, of the shires. Five, those of 'old' Wessex, were certainly there by the ninth century and could well be older. Four (Kent, Sussex, Essex, and Cornwall) were former kingdoms. Most of those of the Midlands had been laid out on an orderly plan at some unknown date in the tenth century. East Anglia and Yorkshire were special cases. One, though divided in two shires, retained some administrative unity. Yorkshire had been divided into three subordinated entities ('ridings'), segments, whose points converged on York. With so much diversity a key element was nevertheless major uniformity in shire organization. The shire system was the stable framework of English government for about a thousand years.

The shires were divided into clearly defined sub-units: 'hundreds' or 'wapentakes'. Indicative of integrated Anglo-Saxon administration was that these divisions served both fiscal and judicial purposes: each was a unit in tax assessment, and each had its own law court. Shire and hundred courts formed the higher tiers of local jurisdiction. It is characteristic of the limitations on our knowledge that the distinction between these layers is unclear. It may have depended on status: shire courts dealing with more important people, hundred courts with less.

We have contemporary laws associated with all Anglo-Saxon kings who reigned for more than a year or so between Alfred and Edward the Confessor (though not including the latter). These 'codes' (so-called) varied in content and intention. They very largely exclude such a major element as land law. But they play the major part in defining our knowledge: of determining elements in the system. It was royal, public, and participatory. Although some great ecclesiastics enjoyed major jurisdictional authority within the royal system, there was little or no private jurisdiction comparable to what had been established by the time of Domesday in lands across the Channel. Most justice was exercised in relation to defined units within the royal system. Intrinsic to that system was an assumption of direct relationship between the king and the freemen whose silver pennies bore his picture. Probably from the time of Alfred, and probably earlier, all had to take an oath of loyalty to the king (Wormald 1999b). Society was considerably regimented, not least in systems of suretyship to ensure maintenance of the peace and that men appeared before the law as required (Wormald 1999a).

Kings displayed a harsh urge to keep the peace. Savage penalties could be inflicted not only on individuals but on districts also. England was not only a disciplined country, but also a comparatively peaceful one. There were, indeed, succession disputes which involved violence. Edward the Elder's invasions of the Danish-held areas cannot have been painless or bloodless. The Scandinavian invasions in Ethelred II's time must have been fearsome for many. All the same England saw longer periods of internal peace than did other parts of Europe. This was specially true of the reign of Edward the Confessor (1042–66). Through much of the tenth century and up to the Conquest great noblemen had been entrusted with considerable authority (under the king) over wide areas, as 'ealdormen', later 'earls'. Such office was confined to a limited number of families (new ones coming to favour under Cnut), but earldoms were not hereditary in a strict sense. In the Confessor's reign there were two dominant earlish families: those of Godwin and of Leofric. Their ambitions and rivalry could have caused civil war, and nearly did so; but the tensions were confined to stand-offs in 1051–2 and 1065. No other European area had so long a run of internal peace as did England. (Though, of course, when Godwin's son Harold seized the throne in 1066, this led to trouble.) It is an interesting element in our knowledge, or lack of knowledge, of late Anglo-Saxon England that although the great noblemen must have had important dwellings, focuses of power, not one of these has been archaeologically investigated.

The history of the English church in the later Anglo-Saxon period unites many themes. The great monastic foundations and re-foundations of the tenth century, product of the 'tenth-century reformation' under the auspices of three great prelates Dunstan, Oswald, and Æthelwold, were endowed not only with tens of thousands of acres of lands but also, and importantly, with great treasures. For example, the shrine for the body of St Swithun at Winchester required 300 pounds of gold and silver; Ely was given statues of Jesus and of saints, life-size and covered in gold and silver (Dodwell 1982: 198, 211). Such marvels are known from written sources alone. Only a tiny surviving fragment such as a little silver-gilt head from Winchester provides material evidence (Fig. 48.1; Lasko 1990). A fundamentally important change was the introduction of the 'parochial system'. In the early days of Christianity in England large areas had been served by monastic or quasi-monastic communities. By the time of the Confessor a system of a church for each village was far established which probably bore reference to the break-up of 'extended estates' (Blair 2005). There survive approaching three hundred churches whose stone buildings contain at least fragments dating from the Conquest or not long after (Taylor and Taylor 1965–78). Written sources indicate that village churches were far more numerous than this. This was a society which could invest in numerous churches as it could in numerous water-mills. It was God-conscious and God-directed. Late Anglo-Saxon kings were anointed when they were crowned. Ordeal, resort to divine judgement, played a major role in the legal system. Fundamental to the parochial system was the payment of tithe. From the tenth century on that was enforced by the king.

Law, order, and (comparative) internal peace were important in establishing the context of English wealth. That wealth was gloated over by such a contemporary commentator as William the Conqueror's biographer William of Poitiers. 'This kingdom is many times richer than Gaul in its wealth of precious metals; it seems as if it should be called the granary of Ceres because of the abundance of its corn, and the treasury of Arabia because of its richness in gold' (Davies and Chibnall 1998: 174–5). Domesday Book brings out important elements of this wealth. Not least it shows how strongly capitalized was English agricultural production. Thus it demonstrates the presence of 6,082 water-mills, the most elaborate machines then known. The dazzling power of Domesday shines when one considers that other written sources reinforced by archaeological discovery would be very hard put to demonstrate the presence of a dozen mills in England in 1086. Just as impressive is Domesday's record of plough-oxen in England: 673,472, an enormous amount of tractive power. If one accepts calculations based on Domesday data which put England's population at somewhere between 1,200,000 and 1,600,000 then there was an ox for every two or three men, women, and children (Darby 1977: 89, 336).

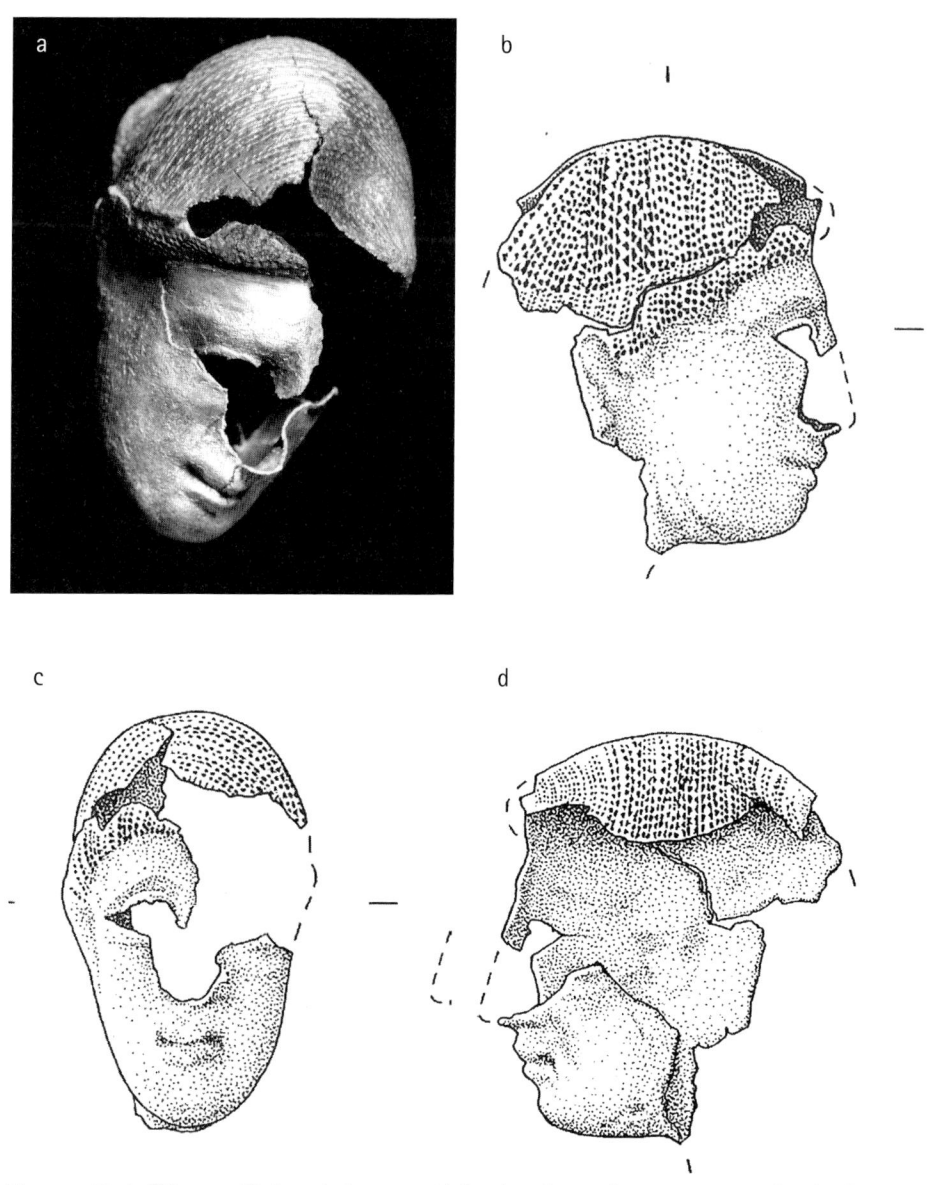

Figure 48.1 Silver-gilt head, late tenth/early eleventh century, probably from a plaque, excavated at the Cathedral Green, Winchester: actual height 22 mm (reproduced by kind permission of the Winchester Excavation Committee)

The estimate of population could well be too low. But, thanks to Domesday, we do have reliable minimum figures such as are not available for any earlier part of British history, or for any comparable area elsewhere in Europe.

One conspicuous element in Domesday's population indications is the high proportion of the population living in towns. It seems that at least 8 per cent of the population lived in places with a population of over four hundred and did Domesday cover London and Winchester (as it does not) the proportion would be higher (Campbell 2000: 189). It seems likely that major provincial towns had populations of the same order of magnitude in the later eleventh century as in the later fourteenth. (Though the list of major towns in 1400 differs from what it had been in 1100.) Among the commonplace suggestions or questions which must arise in relation to such urban prominence, two are especially prominent. First, how far were towns centres of manufacture? The key evidence here is that from archaeology. No written source mentions, for example, the extensive production of pottery, especially in eastern towns. Pottery leaves more tangible evidence than other small goods, but others were probably more important. Biddle made the significant discovery of an apparent important increase in the availability of manufactured goods at Winchester in the late Anglo-Saxon period (Barclay et al. 1990). Important in the English economy was lively trade in small manufactured goods and the production and distribution of these must have been important in towns, and socially significant.

What of larger-scale, more distant, trade? There are many doubts and problems, as in the leading example of wool. It was importantly observed by Sawyer that the extent of the export of English silver in the time of Ethelred II could have been such as to have diminished the supply of silver in England. Yet the great production of coin early in Cnut's reign suggested that this apparent contrast might be explained by the export of wool creating a favourable balance of trade (Sawyer 1965; Metcalf 1981: 56). A difficulty here is that there are no references to such a trade until the early twelfth century. But one of these is impressive. Henry of Huntingdon says that there was abundance of German silver in Britain, so much so that the wealth of silver there seemed greater than in Germany and that it came in return for agricultural exports including 'most precious wool' (Greenway 1996: 10–11). Could wool have been a major export generations before his time? Here one should bear in mind that in the thirteenth and fourteenth centuries, when the written sources prove the great scale and the importance of the export of wool, there is no direct archaeological evidence for such export, even though there is some for wool production.

The most important things about the England which William conquered are that it was a nation-state, was ordered and organized in such a way that strong royal power was integrated into regular systems of local organization requiring participation by the numerous free elements in the population. Ordericus Vitalis, writing two generations after the event, attributes strongly royalist views to the numerous English who he says volunteered to help William Rufus suppress the rebellion of 1088: 'Study the pages of English history: you will find that the English are always loyal to their princes' (Chibnall 1973: 176–7). Or consider how the early-twelfth-century author of *Leges Edwardi Confessoris* describes the Conqueror as summoning twelve 'wise and learned' English nobles from each shire so that he might consult them on the customs and laws of the country (O'Brien 1999: 158–9). It is unlikely that any such thing happened. But, even in a myth, participatory and representational emphasis is importantly interesting. Such passages support the views of—for example—William Stubbs, who saw the origins of a free constitution in the Anglo-Saxon past. Archaeology can illuminate institutions no more than very imperfectly and can give no insight into values. Written sources from Anglo-Saxon times have just about nothing to tell us about wide areas of life and activity. All students of those times have to bear in mind that little is known and, worse, how little can be known. Were it not for Domesday Book and the silver thread of numismatic history our notions of late Anglo-Saxon England would be misconceived. Maybe the limits on our knowledge of early Anglo-Saxon England tend to lead to broad misconceptions on that period. There is no doubt about the intellectual weight of the English church, at least for a generation or so around 700. We may underestimate the extent of deployed secular intellect present and fail to see a society as sophisticated in its government as in its treasures.

Select bibliography

Good general works on Anglo-Saxon history and sources are:

Campbell, J., John, E., and Wormald, P. (1982). *The Anglo-Saxons.* Oxford: Phaidon (Paperback 1991, London: Penguin Books).

Fouracre, P. (2005). *The New Cambridge Medieval History,* Volume 1: *c.500–c.700.* Cambridge: Cambridge University Press (especially the chapters by Halsall, Hamerow, and Thacker).

Hill, D. (1981). *An Atlas of Anglo-Saxon England.* Oxford: Basil Blackwell.

Hinton, D. A. (2005). *Gold and Gilt, Pots and Pins: Possessions and People in Medieval Britain.* Oxford: Oxford University Press.

Hodges, R. (1989). *The Anglo-Saxon Achievement: Archaeology and the Beginnings of English Society.* London: Duckworth.

Keynes, S. (2004). *Anglo-Saxon England: A Bibliographical Handbook for Students of Anglo-Saxon History.* Cambridge: Department of Anglo-Saxon Norse and Celtic, University of Cambridge.

Lapidge, M., Blair, J., Keynes, S., and Scragg, D. (1999). *The Blackwell Encyclopaedia of Anglo-Saxon England.* Oxford: Blackwell.

Stenton, F. M. (1971). *Anglo-Saxon England.* 3rd edition. Oxford/New York: Oxford University Press.

Whitelock, D. (ed.) (1979). *English Historical Documents c. 500–1042.* 2nd edition. London/New York: Eyre Methuen and Oxford University Press.

References

Barclay, K., Biddle, M., and Orton, C. (1990). 'The chronological and spatial distribution of the objects', in Biddle (ed.), *Object and Economy in Medieval Winchester,* 1: 42–73.

Beresford, M. (1954). *The Lost Villages of England.* London: Lutterworth Press.

BIDDLE, M. (ed.) (1990). *Object and Economy in Medieval Winchester.* Winchester Studies 7.2. Oxford: Clarendon Press.
BLAIR, J. (2005). *The Church in Anglo-Saxon Society.* Oxford: Oxford University Press.
BÖHME, H. W. (1986). 'Das Ende der Römerherrschaft in Britannien und die angelsächsische Besiedlung Englands im 5. Jahrhundert'. *Jahrbuch des Römisch-Germanischen Zentralmuseums Mainz,* 33(2): 449–574.
CAMPBELL, J. (2000). *The Anglo-Saxon State.* London/New York: Hambledon and London.
CARVER, M. (1998). *Sutton Hoo: Burial Ground of Kings?* London: British Museum Press.
CHIBNALL, M. (ed.) (1973). *The Ecclesiastical History of Orderic Vitalis,* Volume 4. Oxford: Clarendon Press.
CLUNIES ROSS, M. (1985). 'Concubinage in Anglo-Saxon England'. *Past and Present* 108: 3–34.
COLGRAVE, B., and MYNORS, R. A. B. (eds.) (1969). *Bede's Ecclesiastical History of the English People.* Oxford: Clarendon Press.
DARBY, H. C. (1977). *Domesday England.* Cambridge: Cambridge University Press.
DAVIES, R. H. C., and CHIBNALL, M. (eds.) (1998). *William of Poitiers: The Gesta Guillelmi.* Oxford: Clarendon Press.
DAVIES, W. (1978). *An Early Welsh Microcosm.* London: Royal Historical Society.
DODWELL, C. R. (1982). *Anglo-Saxon Art: A New Perspective.* Manchester: Manchester University Press.
EKWALL, E. (1964). *Old English 'wic' in Place-Names.* Acta Universitatis Upsaliensis Nomina Germanica. Arkiv för germansk namnforsknig 13. Uppsala: A-b. Lundesquistka bokhadeln.
GREENWAY, D. (ed.) (1996). *Henry, Archdeacon of Huntingdon: Historia Anglorum, the History of the English People.* Oxford: Clarendon Press.
HALSALL, G. (2005). 'The sources and their interpretation', in P. Fouracre (ed.), *The New Cambridge Medieval History,* Volume 1. Cambridge: Cambridge University Press, 56–92.
HAMEROW, H. J. (1991). 'Settlement, mobility and the "middle Saxon" shift. Rural settlement patterns in Anglo-Saxon England'. *Anglo-Saxon England* 20: 1–18.
HAWKES, C. F. C. (1956). 'The Jutes of Kent', in D. B. Harden (ed.), *Dark-Age Britain: Studies Presented to E. T. Leeds.* London: Methuen, 91–111.
HIGHAM, N. J. (ed.) (2007). *Britons in Anglo-Saxon England.* Woodbridge: Boydell Press.
HILL, D., and RUMBLE, A. R. (eds.) (1996). *The Defence of Wessex: The Burghal Hidage and Anglo-Saxon Fortifications.* Manchester/New York: Manchester University Press.
HODGES, R. (1986). 'Peer polity interaction and socio-political change in Anglo-Saxon England', in C. Renfrew and J. E. Cherry (eds.), *Peer Polity Interaction and Socio-Political Change.* Cambridge: Cambridge University Press, 69–78.
—— (1989). *The Anglo-Saxon Achievement: Archaeology and the Beginnings of English Society.* London: Duckworth.
LASKO, P. (1990). 'Silver-gilt head', in Biddle (ed.), *Object and Economy in Medieval Winchester,* 761–2.
LAWSON, M. K. (1984). 'The collection of Danegeld and Heregeld in the reigns of Æthelred II and Cnut'. *English Historical Review* 99: 721–38.
—— (1989). '"These stories look true": levels of taxation in the reigns of Æthelred II and Cnut'. *English Historical Review* 104: 951–61.
—— (1990). 'Danegeld and Heregeld once more'. *English Historical Review* 105: 385–406.
LEWIS, C. P. (2007). 'Welsh territories and Welsh identities in late Anglo-Saxon England', in Higham (ed.), *Britons in Anglo-Saxon England,* 130–43.

MADDICOTT, J. R. (1997). 'Plague in seventh-century England'. *Past and Present* 157: 7–54.
—— (2000). 'Two frontier states: Northumbria and Wessex, *c.* 650–750', in J. R. Maddicott and D. M. Palliser (eds.), *The Medieval State: Essays Presented to James Campbell*. London/Rio Grande: Hambledon Press, 25–46.
MCNEILL, J. J., and GAMER, H. M. (eds. and trans.) (1938). *Medieval Handbooks of Penance*. New York: Columbia University Press.
METCALF, D. M. (1981). 'Continuity and change in English monetary history *c.* 973–1086, pt. 2'. *The British Numismatic Journal* 51: 52–90.
MYRES, J. N. L. (1969). *Anglo-Saxon Pottery and the Settlement of England*. Oxford: Clarendon Press.
NICHOLLS, K. (1972). *Gaelic and Gaelicised Ireland in the Middle Ages*. Dublin: Gill and Macmillan.
NILES, J. D., and OSBORN, M. (eds.) (2007). *Beowulf and Lejre*. Tempe, AZ: Arizona Center for Medieval and Renaissance Studies.
O'BRIEN, P. R. (1999). *God's Peace and the King's Peace*. Philadelphia: University of Pennsylvania Press.
OP DEN VELDE, W., and METCALF, D. M. (2007). *The Monetary Economy of the Netherlands and the Trade with England: A Study of Sceattas of Series D*. Jaerboek voor Munt en Penningkunde 90 (for 2003). Utrecht: Koninklijk Nederlands Genootschap Munt-en Pennigkunde.
ORPEN, G. H. (1911). *Ireland under the Normans*, Volume 1. Oxford: Clarendon Press.
PELTERET, D. A. E. (1995). *Slavery in Early Medieval England*. Woodbridge: Boydell Press.
ROLFE, J. C. (ed.) (1971). *Ammianus Marcellinus, with an English translation*. London/Cambridge, MA: Heinemann and Harvard University Press.
SAWYER, P. (1965). 'The wealth of England in the eleventh century'. *Transactions of the Royal Historical Society*, 5th series, 15: 145–64.
TAYLOR, H. M., and TAYLOR, J. (1965–78). *Anglo-Saxon Architecture*, 3 vols. Cambridge: Cambridge University Press.
THACKER, A. (2005). 'England in the seventh century', in P. Fouracre (ed.), *The New Cambridge Medieval History*, Volume 1. Cambridge: Cambridge University Press, 462–9.
WHITELOCK, D., DOUGLAS, D. C., and TUCKER, S. L. (eds.) (1965). *The Anglo-Saxon Chronicle*. 2nd (corrected) imprint. London: Eyre and Spottiswoode.
WINTERBOTTOM, M. (ed.) (1978). *The Ruin of Britain and other Works*. London/Chichester: Phillimore.
WOOLF, A. (2007). 'Apartheid and economies in Anglo-Saxon England', in Higham (ed.), *Britons in Anglo-Saxon England*, 115–29.
WORMALD, P. (1999a). 'Frankpledge', in M. Lapidge, J. Blair, S. Keynes, and D. Scragg (eds.), *The Blackwell Encyclopaedia of Anglo-Saxon England*. Oxford: Blackwell, 192–3.
—— (1999b). 'Oaths', in M. Lapidge, J. Blair, S. Keynes, and D. Scragg (eds.), *The Blackwell Encyclopaedia of Anglo-Saxon England*. Oxford: Blackwell, 338–9.

CHAPTER 49

LITERARY SOURCES AND ARCHAEOLOGY

JOHN HINES

A specialist in any period of English literature will normally argue that his or her particular field is of especial interest. In the case of the Anglo-Saxon period, however, the importance of this phase of literary history involves the place of literacy within the wider cultural history of the era in a quite fundamental way. The period was constituted by a set of radical transitions, of which the genesis of the English language itself was amongst the first. Over the period there was a gradual shift in practical life from circumstances in which communication, recording, and performances using language were almost entirely oral experiences to a situation in which physical, written texts had become both familiar and essential components of social life.

Twentieth-century scholarship saw intense discussion, particularly amongst anthropologists and psychologists, of the extent to which literacy appears to take control of human thought-processes and behaviour. It was suggested that the 'literate mind' is a real and distinctive element of human cognitive history that creates a critical difference between the literate and the non-literate (Ong 1982; Goody 1987). While the most recent, empirically-based research concerned with such phenomena has tended to move away from a strongly determinist position to a scheme more interested in measuring the influence of language and literature upon our concepts and actions (J. Lucy 1992a, b; Clanchy 1993: 253–78), whatever we compare with a mentality profoundly shaped by literacy must comprise not only the exclusively oral mode—in which language is encountered only as speech: spoken, heard, remembered, or recalled—but also a culture in which material objects and actions served functions that in literate contexts are served by texts (Andrén 1998). A notion that is essential to an understanding of the actual relationship between the literature and archaeology of the Anglo-Saxon period is that material items did not just exist alongside texts, as a quite separate category of things that might be referred to or described. Rather they themselves regularly participated in discourses that truly 'mattered' in the original circumstances of their production and reception. The integrated study of archaeology and literature thus has a key role to play in attempts to characterize and understand the Anglo-Saxons.

THE LITERATURE OF ANGLO-SAXON ENGLAND

Alongside many features of material culture with their immediate sources around the eastern shores of the North Sea, from the Low Countries right round to western Norway, the wide-ranging changes between Roman Britain and Anglo-Saxon England included the introduction of the Germanic language that was to become English. There should have been 'dialectal' differences in language between the groups of settlers, but the extent of those—as, of course, the nature and level of their colonization of Britain—is far from clear (Nielsen 1981; Hines 1995a). In its earliest recorded, 'Proto-Old English' phase, the language of the Anglo-Saxons diverged rapidly from the West and North Germanic of the neighbouring Continent and Scandinavia through a series of changes in its sound system. Dialectal divisions appeared within English from the outset, but these owe nothing to detectable pre-settlement divisions within Germanic. The principal dialects we are able to trace in the Old English period (the fifth–twelfth centuries AD) are labelled politically, with some justification, according to the major kingdoms (Toon 1983): Northumbrian, Mercian, and West Saxon, plus Kentish. With the unification of the kingdom of England under the West Saxon dynasty, and the concomitant Benedictine Reform in the Anglo-Saxon Church, a 'Late West Saxon' standardized literary language was widely adopted from the second half of the tenth century (Blake 1996: 75–104).

In the 730s, the Venerable Bede was familiar with five languages in Britain: his own English; indigenous British, the Irish Gaelic, and Pictish; and Latin (*HE* I.1). Varieties of the p-Celtic British language, the ancestor of Breton (apparently), Cornish, and Welsh, remained in use in western England throughout the Anglo-Saxon period, although over large areas they were gradually replaced by English. For Bede, Latin was the language of the Church, a super-national community, but Vulgar Latin would have been a language of some of the population in southern and eastern England at least in the transitional period between Roman and Anglo-Saxon. How many people would have habitually used Latin in what circumstances we cannot tell, but the inclusion of Latin words in southern English place-names—e.g. *funta*, 'spring', in Bedfont and Chalfont; *crocus*, 'saffron', in Croydon—provides firm evidence of this situation (Gelling 1978: 63–86).

For practical reasons, this chapter will concentrate selectively on aspects of the relationship between literary sources in the Old English vernacular language and Anglo-Saxon archaeology; but any impression that Anglo-Saxon England was a monolingual culture must be exploded. In literary terms, Latin was of the greatest importance. As the language of the Church it was also the language of communication between England and a wider world. It was the language of a prestigious and dominant ideology, and the influence of Latin literature on Old English has proved to be deep and diverse. Greek was of at least equal importance in the early medieval Church as a whole; some Anglo-Saxon churchmen knew Greek, but this knowledge was much less widespread and influential than that of Latin. The establishment of Christianity in England starting in the very late sixth century produced in the later seventh and eighth centuries an outstanding flourishing of Anglo-Latin literature, both poetry and prose. The leading authors of this period were Aldhelm, of Wessex, and in Northumbria Bede, at Jarrow, and Alcuin of York. There were several further, able authors whose identities are now lost to us (Lapidge 1993; 1996; Orchard 1994).

One other language, with its own rich literary culture, was introduced to England after the time of Bede. The Norse of the Scandinavian Vikings could begin to lay down roots after Viking raiding gave way to land-taking in the middle of the ninth century. By the end of that century we see the first signs of the ultimately massive Norse influence on the English language, in the form of Norse words being used in English texts (Townend 2002). This was reinforced by a later wave of Scandinavian attacks and colonization under the Danish kings Sweyn, Cnut, and Harthacnut from the 980s to the 1040s. Norse literature was cultivated and produced within England. Some of this survives; in many important contexts, strata of Insular influence have been detected in the medieval Norse literature ultimately written down in Iceland (Dronke 1997: 93–8, 202–8, 269–86). There are significant correlations to be drawn between such literary works and, *inter alia*, the archaeology of Anglo-Scandinavian York (Hines 1995b), or the art of Anglo-Scandinavian sculpture and metalwork (Bailey 1980).

In this chapter, the term 'literature' is used in a broad sense: it is defined as art in the medium of language. The earliest English and Norse literatures were evidently *oral*. When those languages were used to recount narratives, for instance, memorized or re-created stories would have been presented in an extemporized version, following a range of acquired formulae for composition (Lord 1960; Finnegan 1977). The evidence of an oral-formulaic background surviving in written Old English literature has been well explored (Renoir 1988; O'Brien O'Keeffe 1990).

Meanwhile the history of the writing of Old English is itself a complex one. A few, extremely brief runic inscriptions provide evidence of the form of the language from as early as the fifth century, but the extensive writing of texts in English was a reflex of the establishment of the Church and the adaptation of the Roman script used for writing Latin. Around the beginning of the seventh century, England's first Christian king, Æthelberht of Kent, had a law code written in English (Bede, *HE* II.5). Remarkably, this text survives—not in its original spelling, but the style and vocabulary of the text appear to preserve ancient forms (Lendinara 1997). The seventh to ninth centuries saw a gradual increase in the writing of English in Roman script in utilitarian documents such as law codes, charters, and wills. As part of a general diffusion of literacy through society at this time, it appears that the practice of writing English in runes also became more widespread, at least in the eighth century (Parsons 1999). It is likewise from the eighth century that we have our few, earliest examples of written Old English poetry, in both runic and Roman script.

In the late ninth century, as his kingdom was recovering from the worst of the Viking onslaught of the 860s and 870s, King Alfred the Great composed a reflection upon the state of 'wisdom' in England, which he correlated specifically with the state of *literacy* in England (Keynes and Lapidge 1983: 124–6). He alleged that Latin learning had collapsed almost completely, implying at the same time that literacy in English had recently been common. To start to remedy the situation, he announced a programme of translations of the works 'most necessary for all people to know': a policy that has left us Old English versions of a series of Christian Latin works—Pope Gregory the Great's *Dialogues* and *Pastoral Rule*, Orosius' *Histories Against the Pagans*, Boethius' *On the Consolation of Philosophy*, the *Soliloquies* of St Augustine, and Bede's *Ecclesiastical History of the English People*. The corpus of Old English translations of such scholarly prose continued to grow into the eleventh century, with, for instance, a *Martyrology*, tales of Alexander the Great and Apollonius of Tyre, a tract on *The Wonders of the East*, and original works such as Byrhtferth of Ramsey's *Enchiridion*. The earliest extant version of the *Anglo-Saxon Chronicle* was compiled in the late years of Alfred's reign, to be copied in the tenth century into a manuscript along with our first surviving version of the Old English law codes of King Alfred and his late-seventh-century predecessor Ine (Keynes and Lapidge 1983: 275–81, 303–4).

The Late West Saxon literary language referred to above is particularly associated with the collections of homilies equally composed in response to the general circumstances of political and ecclesiastical change of the very late tenth and early eleventh centuries by two leading churchmen: Ælfric, successively of Cerne Abbas and Eynsham, Wessex, and Wulfstan, Bishop of Worcester and Archbishop of York. These proved highly influential collections of texts as they—along with the law codes—were those still most persistently read, copied, modified, and even imitated well into the twelfth century, after the Norman Conquest (Swan and Treharne 2000). A peculiarity of the prose-style, especially in the writings of Ælfric, is the employment of metrical features of traditional Old English poetry, such as alliteration; this is in turn plausibly to be identified as a significant factor in a later medieval English revival of this poetic style (Hanna 1999).

It is only from the second half of the tenth century at the earliest that we have extensive surviving manuscript collections of Old English poetry: four volumes in total (Krapp and Dobbie 1931–53; Scragg 1991). During the last three decades it has been a matter of keen debate how much earlier than their surviving manuscript copies the composition of some of this poetry may be. That the majority of what we find here is of tenth-century origin—or, if written earlier, is now available only in a distinctly tenth-century version—is not in question; nevertheless a group of scholars—the present author included—believes that a significant number of poems can be assigned an original date of composition in the eighth or ninth centuries, and that the process of transmission has not completely transformed them (see Chase 1980; Lapidge 2000; Bjork 2001: 3–56; Hines 2004: 41–5).

If we define literature as the artistic use of language, literary texts can be distinguished from non-literary texts by reference to *form*. A simple and practical test is that of whether the style of wording and presentation is or is not a significant aspect of the functioning of the text. If I want instructions on how to mix cement, it does not matter to me if they are written in plain or flowery English, in prose or verse, as long as they tell me what to do; with a play by Shakespeare, conversely, even minor editorial interventions will affect my perception of the work of art as such. This also means that texts whose sense and contents are explicit and unambiguous belong at one end of an important spectrum of types. It is not the case that such explicit texts cannot count as literature; however, experience reveals that the combination of archaeological understanding with critical reading of literature is most revealing when the significance—the 'message' or 'moral'—of the text is implicit: something for the reader or listener to think about, to discover for themselves, and to appreciate as a personal insight. This justifies restricting our attention to certain works of Old English poetry in what is necessarily a brief, introductory essay. What must be emphasized, though, is that this is a very selective approach, not only in relation to the whole range of literature from Anglo-Saxon England, but also in respect of the potential scope for integrating the study of literary sources with Anglo-Saxon archaeology (cf. Schwyzer 2007: 36–71, 174–204, for some quite different approaches).

Literature and archaeology

Methodologically, an obvious way to start to correlate the literary records and the archaeology of Anglo-Saxon England with one another is to look for specific correspondences between the two: to identify features and objects in archaeological reports or museum collections for which we also have textual references. Such do exist; and there are cases where the evidence in one medium adds significant insight and understanding to the other. At a very particular level, for instance, we should never have had more than a vague notion of what the *wīrum bewunden wala* ('*wala* wound around with wires') on a helmet presented to Beowulf (*Beowulf*: 1030–1) actually was without a find such as the Sutton Hoo helmet with its crest apparently perfectly fitting this description (Bruce-Mitford 1974: 210–13). At a broader categorical level, our archaeological knowledge of deviant, socially excluded, and execution cemeteries primarily of the late Saxon period gives both a special, concrete perspective, and a heightened emphasis, on literary accounts of burial and the use of funerary imagery in, *inter alia*, the poems *Andreas* and *The Wife's Lament* (Semple 1998; Hines 2004: 61–2; and Reynolds, this volume). This can profoundly modify our insight into what the poems are about.

Simultaneously, textual sources in these circumstances can corroborate and extend, or just vivify, the archaeologist's appreciation of the motivation and meaning of past practices that are reflected in the material record. In *The Ruin*—and in several other Old English literary works—we can read an account of an archaeological encounter with the material past within the Anglo-Saxon period itself: a representation of what appears to be the ruined Roman town of Bath, and a moral reflection upon the lessons that offers. Since the poem is found in the Exeter Book, which is dated to *c.*950–975 (Conner 1993: 54–94; cf. Muir 1994: 1; Gameson 1996), it is almost certain that this poetic meditation was first composed before King Edgar's decision to stage a coronation ceremony for himself in the *burh* (formerly a Mercian royal vill) of Bath in 973; immediately followed by a voyage, down the Avon and the Bristol Channel and then north through the Irish Sea, to Chester, where another imperial ceremony of submission by Irish, Scots, Norse, and Welsh kings—who rowed him on the River Dee—was staged (A. Williams 2004). We do not know what the circumstances of the composition of *The Ruin* were. What is certain, though, is that, copied at this time, the poem must embody some of the ideological attitudes that would have been factors in the decision to use these major Roman centres as the stages for King Edgar's dramatic ceremonies. That the sites of former Roman towns were used in substantial and diverse ways in the Anglo-Saxon period is well known; those particular acts of monument re-use, however, would be unknown to us were it not for the fact of their being recorded for posterity both in verse and historical prose (*Anglo-Saxon Chronicle*, MS A *s.a.* 974; MS E *s.a.* 972).

The scope for this sort of illustrative relationship between literary accounts and material practices in the Anglo-Saxon period is limited, however. A literary source typically offers an individual, reflective, and often quite imaginative response to real events or situations. *Beowulf* does not record for us in any precise or comprehensive way what fifth- to eighth-century Anglo-Saxons either did when burying their dead or what their reasons were for the customs they practised. Nor does *The*

Battle of Maldon give us anything but the most selective glimpses of the reality of military practice and experience in a battle between an Anglo-Saxon *fyrd* and a Viking force in the 990s (Scragg 1993). The Anglo-Saxon archaeology of the later fifth to the mid seventh centuries is particularly rich, but that is a period from which we have *no* literary sources. Mid and late Saxon archaeology is now receiving much greater attention than hitherto, but putting a date and provenance to works of literature before the late ninth century remains a difficult matter in most cases, often a controversial one.

What might seem the most restrictive circumstance of all is the fact that realism is a literary mode rarely to be found in any Anglo-Saxon literature. There is, however, one generic group of verses in both Anglo-Latin and Old English for which reference to everyday and recognizable phenomena is essential. These are the *enigmata*, or riddles: usually just a few lines of verse which present a series of clues—either from a speaking subject, or describing an object—from which a solution is to be identified. These poems belong to a learned tradition. A few of the ninety-six Old English riddles collected in the Exeter Book are translations of known Latin originals: most famously, the bizarre sketch of a 'one-eyed garlic seller'. Nevertheless, the great majority of the riddles demonstrate a keen eye for and dramatically imaginative appreciation of the real world in which the authors and readers lived: both its natural and its manufactured components. Several of the riddles are pious and devotional; more than one has the suggested solution of 'God's Creation'. Conversely there are a few that exploit blatantly bawdy *double-entendres*, usually by including the handling of the mystery object by a woman: for instance the onion (Riddle 25), whose stem is steep and high and which stands in a bed, and makes a girl's eyes run. It is a matter of broader significance that, scurrilous or not, the ambiguities essential to the riddle depend upon recognition of the fact that language can be used—in game, in this case—to represent more than one reality. The riddles in fact provide us with some glimpses of real life in Anglo-Saxon England that we simply do not have in any other form.

A more demanding but ultimately the most rewarding approach to the correspondences between literature and archaeology is to relate both modes of expression—whether, superficially, they coincide or not—to a deeper level of cultural structure and practice. The strongest justification for interdisciplinarity as a crucial strategy for understanding human behaviour and experience is that interdisciplinarity is *the* precondition for a history of culture that overrides and is in fact indifferent to the modal divisions between the types of evidence that are reflected in the disciplinary specializations of history, textual and literary criticism, art history, archaeology, philology, and so on. As aspects of cultural history, literary sources and material remains must always fall into a meaningful relationship with one another. A practical way of demonstrating what this can mean is to consider a topic in respect of which both these forms of evidence reflect deep-seated and persistent attempts in the Anglo-Saxon past to define and realize ideals and objectives. At the same time, the literary and material forms of practice both had to negotiate tensions between tradition and innovation. There are no given, fixed points anywhere amongst these phenomena. As mutable aspects of real Anglo-Saxon cultural life, all of these swirled around one another, in an endless dance. But the performance and adaptive choreography of that dance were thoroughly meaningful.

Culture and death

The archaeological evidence for the treatment of the dead is voluminous: a feature of material practice that all but constantly demands attention. A considerable range of Old English literary sources also had to deal with the profound topic of death. Put together, the two fields of information not only lead us to a fuller understanding of how death was apprehended and responded to in Anglo-Saxon England (Thompson 2004; Lee 2007), but also point to fundamental structural patterns in Anglo-Saxon culture.

One point upon which the evidence of the epic poem *Beowulf* proves unproblematically congruent with the archaeology is in respect of the use of material artefacts as a medium of discourse (cf. above; Hines 2008). In early Anglo-Saxon burials, of the fifth to seventh centuries, it was common practice to include artefacts in graves with the body—which might be either cremated or inhumed unburnt. There has been much argument over when *Beowulf* as we know it can be considered to have been composed. The poem survives in a single copy made around the year 1000. Nobody, however, would argue for a date of written composition before the very late seventh century, which is precisely when the traditional burial practice with grave-goods was coming to a complete end. Despite that, the text of the poem was evidently composed with an awareness of that burial practice, even if as something rather alien and different (Owen-Crocker 2000, and review by Hines 2001).

Beowulf seems to have retained a significant level of continuity with earlier Anglo-Saxon material culture in its thorough understanding of the autonomous discursive power of objects. As a means of expression, artefacts in the poem are not simply symbols: that is, objects as signs which either stand for or refer to some quality but are intrinsically quite distinct from whatever they denote. We might at first read the fact that Beowulf and his men arrive in Denmark ostentatiously equipped with a full range of weaponry and armour in order that they should be recognized as noble warriors primarily in such symbolic terms. In these scenes the equipment is worn to be seen and interpreted, rather than to be used in battle.

There was of course a practical relationship between war-gear and elevated social status in this period. However, the poem also reveals that there was a definite but surprising hierarchical contrast between weapons and body armour (mail-shirt and helmet), which the visiting warriors retain in the Danish hall, Heorot, even after they were prepared to put aside their swords, spears, and shields.

Common-sense explanations of this distinction miss the profound connotations of the full sequence enacted in the hall. Of course it is a different matter to put down portable objects than to take off items of costume—although not, perhaps, a heavy and uncomfortable helmet. It is also pragmatically understandable that visiting warriors in an alien hall should be made to leave their offensive weapons at the door, but prefer to keep their own armour on. However, no such practical logic explains why Beowulf, warmly received, keeps his helmet on all through the evening's drinking and speeches, only to remove all of his armour precisely at the point when he settles himself to await Grendel's night-time attack (lines 669–74). Up to this point his accoutrements, and the different things he does with them, have shown us how social identity is subject to achievement and construction using these objects, and is recognized by others in precisely this way. The body armour and helmet emerge, then, not just as status symbols but rather as an embodiment of that constructed identity. Beowulf divests himself of that social and cultural identity in order to assume a new character. He declares his actions to be an act of submission to God's will (675–87). His weapons and armour are the artefacts of a technically higher culture than is available to Grendel, so he will wrestle with his adversary, body against body.[1] God will grant victory where He thinks fit.

It would be a distinctly modern view to claim that this dramatic sequence represents a critique of materialism—implying an ideological assertion that there is some essential, abstract, or spiritual truth that is distorted or disguised by human material culture. The alternative, which should not be a very startling idea, is that Beowulf's body itself has now become a significant object: the artefact of the divine creator and ruler of the world. This idea is precisely what makes sense of the striking sequence of exchanges of body parts as tokens that maps out and motivates the following stages of the drama. Beowulf tears off Grendel's hand and arm, to be displayed over Heorot as a trophy and as a token of victory. Grendel's mother attacks the next night, retrieving her son's arm, and carrying off the warrior Æschere, whose head she leaves behind as her own token of defiance, and of revenge achieved, on the path leading to the mere in which she dwells. Beowulf, now depending totally on armour and weaponry, enters the mere, battles with and kills her, and brings back two truncated trophies: Grendel's head, and the hilt of the sword he used to decapitate Grendel's body, the blade of which melted upon contact with Grendel's venomous blood.

---

[1] We can leave to one side here the uncertain issue of whether Grendel is subsequently said to have used protective magic to render himself immune to human weaponry: lines 801–5.

For all the evidence we have that swords were prestigious objects—status symbols for the male social elite (Ellis Davidson 1962; Härke 1992)–the melting of this sword-blade is one of a series of incidents in this poem which demonstrate how the sword, like the human body, could break, fail, and decay. Remarkably, but not inappropriately, this sword-hilt bears its own tale of pride and fall: representing, perhaps both iconographically and in an inscription, the semi-apocryphal tale of God's defeat of the giants (Genesis 6:4; Wisdom 14:6; *Beowulf* 1687–93). Hrothgar reads the sword-hilt as a text—not by telling the story, but by interpreting its significance in the present circumstances. With all Beowulf's newly achieved glory, this is a warning to him to be wary of *oferhygd*: 'over-ambition'. Beowulf's response to the whole situation is then tested in the final episode of the epic: his battle with the dragon over the dragon's hoard. One of the most challenging interpretative questions for any readership or audience of *Beowulf* is how to regard the ethical ambivalence of Beowulf's struggle to win the dragon's hoard: is it an act of foolhardy arrogance and greed, or the self-sacrifice of an ageing king, ridding his people of a scourge and winning valuable treasure for them?

Another Old English poem, *The Seafarer*, expressed an explicitly Christian critique of the pre-Christian tradition of burying artefacts with the dead as spiritually useless (lines 98–102). The dragon's hoard is interred in a barrow with Beowulf's dead body, and it is directly stated that there this treasure is as useless as it was before (3163–8). Again, rather than a merely—or a distinctly modern—anti-materialist ethos, it is more appropriate to interpret this in terms of the implicitly non-Christian Geats (Beowulf's people) not knowing how to use the treasure properly. The positive use they can make of it is to sacrifice it, thus marking Beowulf's greatness and providing a concrete measure of their own desolation at his death. Within the grave it also marks his achievement, but there is little emphasis on any such positive perspectives within the poem. The contemporary Church had a well-established and relevant doctrine that heathen valuables and treasure could be appropriated and converted to Christian use and the service of God (Augustine, *De doctrina Christiana* II.60). Thus the Israelites fleeing Egypt despoiled the Egyptians of their treasures, even though they were soon to use some of these to make the Golden Calf; awareness of this moral fragility hangs ominously over the final lines of the Old English poetic version of this episode, *Exodus* (580–9).

It is nothing new to observe that early Anglo-Saxon grave-goods correlate in various ways with the identity of the individual they were buried with. The last two decades of archaeological research, significantly aided by detailed and comprehensive osteological studies on the human skeletal remains, have added an awareness of how age at death seems to have been a factor in an individual's material associations—and thus implicitly in their recognized social role immediately prior to their death—to complement the increasingly detailed examinations of the sex and gender nexus, gradations of wealth represented in both the quality and the quantity of the objects in the grave, connections of kinship, and wider group identities (Stoodley 1999; S. Lucy 2000). Identity was truly complex, but all of these facets can be shown to find a material correlation in the artefacts buried with the individual. In many respects it is entirely reasonable to adopt essentially pragmatic explanations for these correlations, preferring to interpret them in terms of simple cause and effect rather than any deep ideological significance. Men and women between their late teens and late thirties are most likely to be buried with larger artefact-assemblages, for instance, because that age-group would normally have provided the fittest and thus the dominant members of the community. Geographically discrete distributions of artefact-types coincide with demographic groups because both represent practical networks of contact and exchange. In hand-to-hand combat men usually made better warriors than women.

It is nevertheless considerably more productive, not least in relation to the breadth of variation in burial practice across the Anglo-Saxon period, for our interpretations to incorporate and build upon the notion that, like the body armour in *Beowulf*, clothing was effectively understood to embody the person's identity. What we conventionally refer to as the 'furnished' burials of the early Anglo-Saxon period are in fact the inhumation burials that in most cases would more appropriately be described as 'clothed' (Walton Rogers 2007). The more richly dressed women went into the grave in a costume that—with regional and chronological variations—might include metal brooches, belts or chatelains with buckles, keys, and other attachments, necklaces, pendants, and bracelets. From these remains it can be possible to reconstruct original costumes in great detail. Men, contrastively, rarely had a costume comprising more than one buckle as a costume-fitting which would survive. There is nevertheless adequate evidence to show that they too went into the grave in costumes that could vary in fabric and finish; and indeed that we can also assume that those who were buried with no surviving dress-accessories at all had been buried in a completely organic suit of clothing (Walton Rogers 2007: 199–223).

The most ostentatious man's outfit we have is that from Sutton Hoo Mound 1, where besides helmet, mail-shirt, and weaponry, the costume-fittings included shoulder-clasps, strap-ends and -mounts, and several buckles. The principal buckle, the 'great gold buckle', was made of an amount of gold that corresponds very closely indeed to the quantity of three hundred of the contemporary gold coins known as tremisses: a coin almost certainly known to seventh-century Anglo-Saxons as the 'shilling' (Grierson and Blackburn 1986: 157; Blackburn, this volume). This buckle, then, did not just *represent*, but actually *was* the wergild, the quantity of gold that was the life-price of a nobleman, as specified in laws of the seventh century (Attenborough 1922: 18–19). A man who could appear with that possession on his belt was manifestly constructed as a figure of supreme power in the social hierarchy: as a king.

Let us postulate, then, that not only the practice of clothed burial but even (and simultaneously) the practice of inhumation itself reflects a deep-seated motivation to maintain the social personhood of the individual throughout the funerary rites and into his or her final resting-place in the grave. In the Roman period, these

Germanic peoples cremated their dead, almost without exception; inhumation came increasingly to be practised alongside cremation in the fifth century, and steadily superseded it in the sixth. If our interpretative hypothesis is a valid one, the shift in practice was more than just an ideological response symptomatic of social pressures, which themselves would then be the essential historical explanation required. To identify this inferred motivation as a core aspect of Anglo-Saxon culture is not to imply that it was a priority shared by all. As in the fictional example provided by *Beowulf*, the stripping off of one culturally constructed identity can be concomitant with the making or adoption of a new one. The assertion of a religious identity, as Christian, is a particularly clear instance of that, both in the poem and archaeologically: grave-goods and, so far as we can tell, clothed burial disappear completely from the end of the seventh century—despite, rather than because of, the Church's rather laissez-faire approach to burial practice at this date (Blair 2005: esp. 58–65; Effros 2002: 41–68).

This perspective simultaneously highlights the rich potential for interpretation that resides within the contrasting early Anglo-Saxon cremation rite. Cremation is of course destructive; nevertheless, the remains of dress-accessories that have been collected from the pyre are surprisingly few. Conversely, but perhaps fittingly in light of the deeper issues concerned, the inclusion of implements for bodily grooming—tweezers and combs—is at a very much higher level than amongst contemporary inhumations (H. Williams 2002; 2006: 90–6). Combs became more frequent as grave-goods in seventh-century inhumation burials precisely when cremation had effectively disappeared (Geake 1997: 63–4). As a method of handling the dead body, the crucial attribute of cremation that contrasts constructively with inhumation is that the cremators take control of the process of bodily decomposition by accelerating it, spectacularly. Once again, then, the contrast between clothed inhumation and cremation is not one between an awareness and a cult of personhood and an individual's social identity in the former case and their absence in the latter. Unless we dismiss the practice of incinerating bodies as merely a form of waste-disposal, the cremation rite implicitly embodied a different sense of humanity and personality. The social composition of the major cremation cemeteries is also very different from that of any contemporary inhumation cemeteries. It is entirely valid, then, to hypothesize that cremation positively embodied a more aesthetic sense of general human nature than the particular sense of human identity implicit in inhumation.

With any particularly rich archaeological complex of associated finds, such diverse lines of evidence and interpretation may be drawn together to elucidate and to read the knot of traditions and aspirations that material construct made manifest. The Prittlewell chamber grave discovered late in 2003 (MoLAS 2004; Fig. 15.1) has rightly attracted great interest. With two gold-foil crosses placed by the head of the dead man (Fig. 49.1a), this is probably our earliest Anglo-Saxon burial with an overt expression of an allegiance to the then very newly introduced Christian religion. The pre-eminent social position and identity of the dead man were reflected in his costume: he had an elegant gold buckle (Fig. 49.1b) and was apparently clothed in a gold-braided tunic. His weaponry, by contrast, does not differ in any significant way from other men's graves in the same cemetery, and he was buried with no armour.

What the Prittlewell burial definitively has in common with the other broadly contemporary Anglo-Saxon 'princely' graves (at Sutton Hoo in Suffolk, Broomfield in Essex, and Taplow in Buckinghamshire) is the recreation of the lordly hall in its burial chamber: with a large provision of equipment for hospitality—feasting and musical entertainment (cf. Bruce-Mitford 1974: 1–72). The idealized nature of such a social milieu is, of course, clearly reflected in *Beowulf* (Herschend 1997; 1998; 2003). Here, though, we may draw attention to some apparent peculiarities of the man's personal equipment and costume within this special structural setting. His gold buckle is of a familiar form, but strikingly plain (cf. Marzinzik 2003: 50 and 448–51, figs.). With no decoration or embellishment it looks incomplete but not unfinished; particularly through its position in the grave it calls attention to its counterparts, as gold objects, in two continental tremisses, the gold braid on the tunic, and at the head two gold crosses. Might a process of the dissolution and redistribution of material statements of identity and ideals already be incipient here, with the buckle, in a sense, completed within the grave by the pair of crosses? As of yet, no pommel has been found for the sword in this grave, which seems a remarkable omission in a burial of this rank. At this stage, it must be emphasized that these can only be points for consideration. But in the full cross-disciplinary perspective, this archaeological find perfectly illustrates the fact that the significance of material objects resides not just in what they are, but much more in their context, and most of all in what is done with them.

Conclusion

What is the relevance of literary sources to archaeology in the Anglo-Saxon period? There is no single answer to the question; nor any one formula for putting literary scholarship and archaeology together properly. One reason for this is that the potential interfaces between these two modes of cultural life are so multifaceted and multivalent. Another reason, no less significant, is that the six centuries and more of the Anglo-Saxon period saw profound change, not least in the semantic role of the material world and in the relative roles of speech and text. Those role-changes were parts of a single set of processes, and none is fully comprehensible without reference to the others.

In the end, this implies that a full archaeological understanding of a literate society must pay attention to the art and artefacts produced by literary creativity in that

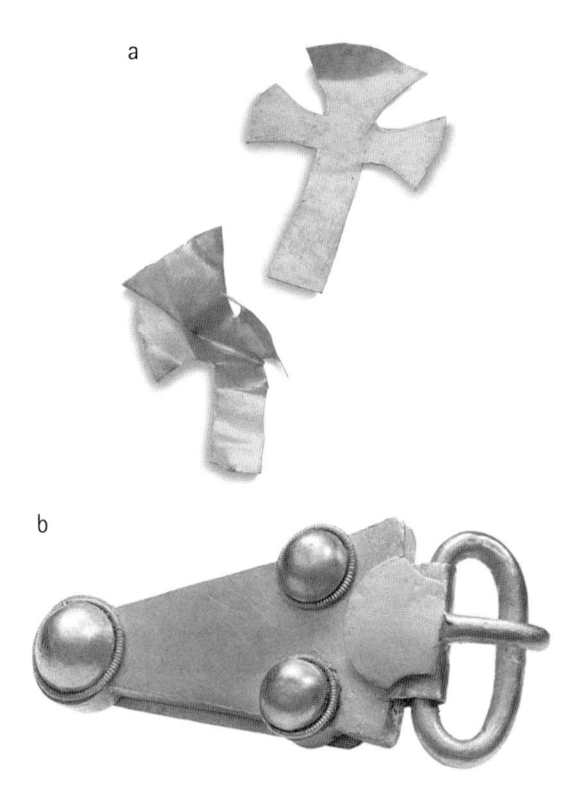

Figure 49.1 Artefacts from the Prittlewell, Essex, chamber-grave, excavated in 2003 (MoLAS site EX-PRO 03): (a) gold-foil crosses: lengths c.30 mm; (b) gold buckle: length 72 mm (reproduced by kind permission of the Museum of London Archaeological Service)

society. Equally, the critical and historical study of that literature ought to include informed consideration of the circumstances of its production in the real world. These conclusions undoubtedly increase the challenge that the study of the past poses, but the objectives are realizable, and the results that ensue can be very rich indeed.

BIBLIOGRAPHY OF PRIMARY SOURCES

GENERAL ANTHOLOGIES AND COLLECTIONS

BRADLEY, S. A. J. (ed. and trans.) (1982). *Anglo-Saxon Poetry*. London: Dent.
CROSSLEY-HOLLAND, K. (ed. and trans.) (1982). *The Anglo-Saxon World: An Anthology*. Woodbridge: Boydell.

KRAPP, G. P., and DOBBIE, E. VAN K. (1931–53). *The Anglo-Saxon Poetic Records.* 6 volumes. New York: Academic Press.

INDIVIDUAL TEXTS AND TRANSLATIONS

Anglo-Saxon Chronicle: J. Earle and C. Plummer (eds.) (1892). *Two of the Saxon Chronicles Parallel.* 2 volumes. Oxford: Clarendon Press.
——: D. N. Dumville (gen. ed.) (1986). *Anglo-Saxon Chronicle.* 10 volumes to date. Woodbridge: Boydell.
——: M. Swanton (trans.) (1996). *The Anglo-Saxon Chronicle.* London: Dent.

Bede, *Historia Ecclesiastica Gentis Anglorum* [*HE*]: B. Colgrave and R. A. B. Mynors (eds. and trans.) (1969). Oxford: Clarendon Press.

Beowulf: An Edition: B. Mitchell and F. C. Robinson (eds.) (1998). Oxford: Blackwell.
——: M. Swanton (ed. and trans.) (1978). *Beowulf.* Manchester: Manchester University Press.
——: Bradley (ed. and trans.) (1982), *supra*: 408–94; Crossley-Holland (ed. and trans.) (1982), *supra*: 74–154.

Exodus: P. J. Lucas (ed.) (1977). *Exodus.* London: Methuen. (Repr. 1994, Exeter: Exeter University Press.)
——: trans. Bradley (ed. and trans.) (1982), *supra*: 49–65.
Old English *Riddles*: B. Muir (ed.) (1994). *The Exeter Anthology of Old English Poetry.* 2 volumes. Exeter: Exeter University Press. Volume 1: 287–330, 355–6, and 362–82.
——: (selections) Bradley (ed. and trans.) (1982), *supra*: 367–81, 397, and 403–4; Crossley-Holland (ed. and trans.) (1982), *supra*: 236–50.

The Ruin: R. F. Leslie (ed.) (1961). *Three Old English Elegies.* Manchester: Manchester University Press. (Repr. 1988, Exeter: Exeter University Press.)
——: Bradley (ed. and trans.) (1982), *supra*: 401–2; Crossley-Holland (ed. and trans.) (1982), *supra*: 59–60.

The Seafarer: I. L. Gordon (ed.) (1960). London: Methuen. (Repr. 1997, Exeter: Exeter University Press.)
——: Bradley (ed and trans.) (1982), *supra*: 329–35; Crossley-Holland (ed. and trans.) (1982), *supra*: 53–6.

REFERENCES

ANDRÉN, A. (1998). *Between Artefacts and Texts: Historical Archaeology in Global Perspective.* New York: Plenum.

ATTENBOROUGH, F. L. (1922). *The Laws of the Earliest English Kings*. Cambridge: Cambridge University Press.

BAILEY, R. N. (1980). *Viking Age Sculpture in Northern England*. London: Batsford.

BJORK, R. (ed.) (2001). *The Cynewulf Reader*. London: Routledge.

BLAIR, J. (2005). *The Church in Anglo-Saxon Society*. Oxford: Oxford University Press.

BLAKE, N. F. (1996). *A History of the English Language*. Basingstoke: Macmillan.

BRUCE-MITFORD, R. L. S. (1974). *Aspects of Anglo-Saxon Archaeology: Sutton Hoo and Other Discoveries*. London: Victor Gollancz.

CHASE, C. (ed.) (1980). *The Dating of 'Beowulf'*. Toronto: University of Toronto Press.

CLANCHY, M. T. (1993). *From Memory to Written Record: England 1066–1307*. 2nd edition. Oxford: Blackwell.

CONNER, P. W. (1993). *Anglo-Saxon Exeter: A Tenth-Century Cultural History*. Woodbridge: Boydell.

DRONKE, U. (1997). *The Poetic Edda*, Volume 2: *Mythological Poems*. Oxford: Clarendon Press.

EFFROS, B. (2002). *Caring for Body and Soul: Burial and the Afterlife in the Merovingian World*. University Park, PA: Pennsylvania University Press.

ELLIS DAVIDSON, H. R. E. (1962). *The Sword in Anglo-Saxon England: Its Archaeology and Literature*. Reprinted 1994, Woodbridge: Boydell.

FINNEGAN, R. (1977). *Oral Poetry: Its Nature, Significance and Social Context*. Cambridge: Cambridge University Press.

GAMESON, R. (1996). 'The origin of the Exeter Book of Old English poetry'. *Anglo-Saxon England* 25: 135–85.

GEAKE, H. (1997). *The Use of Grave Goods in Conversion Period England, c.600–c.850*. BAR British Series 261. Oxford: British Archaeological Reports.

GELLING, M. (1978). *Signposts to the Past*. London: Dent.

GOODY, J. (1987). *The Interface between the Written and the Oral*. Cambridge: Cambridge University Press.

GRIERSON, P., and BLACKBURN, M. (1986). *Medieval European Coinage*, Volume 1: *The Early Middle Ages (5th to 10th Centuries)*. Cambridge: Cambridge University Press.

HANNA, R. (1999). 'Alliterative poetry', in D. Wallace (ed.), *The Cambridge History of Medieval English Literature*. Cambridge: Cambridge University Press, 488–512.

HÄRKE, H. (1992). *Angelsächsische Waffengräber des 5. bis 7. Jahrhunderts*. Cologne: Rheinland-Verlag.

HERSCHEND, F. (1997). *Livet i Hallen*. Opia 14. Uppsala: Institutionen för arkeologi och antik historia, Uppsala Universitet.

—— (1998). *The Idea of the Good in Late Iron Age Society*. Opia 15. Uppsala: Institutionen för arkeologi och antik historia, Uppsala Universitet.

—— (2003). 'Material metaphors—some Late Iron Age and Viking examples', in M. Clunies Ross (ed.), *Old Norse Myths, Literature and Society*. University Press of Southern Denmark, 40–65.

HINES, J. (1995a). 'Focus and boundary in linguistic varieties in the late North-West Germanic continuum', in Volkert F. Faltig et al. (eds.), *Friesische Studien II*. NOWELE Supplementary Vol. 12. Odense: Odense University Press, 35–62.

—— (1995b). 'Egill's Hǫfuðlausn in time and place', *Saga-Book* 24: 83–104.

—— (2001). Review of Owen-Crocker (2001). *Notes and Queries* 48: 319–21.

—— (2004). *Voices in the Past: English Literature and Archaeology*. Cambridge: Brewer.

—— (2008). '*Beowulf* and archaeology—revisited', in C. E. Karkov and H. Damico (eds.), *Aedificia Nova: Studies in Honor of Rosemary Cramp*. Kalamazoo, MI: Medieval Institute Publications, 89–105.
Keynes, S., and Lapidge, M. (1983). *Alfred the Great*. Harmondsworth: Penguin.
Krapp, G. P., and Dobbie, E. van K. (1931–53). *The Anglo-Saxon Poetic Records*. 6 volumes. New York: Academic Press.
Lapidge, M. (1993). *Anglo-Latin Literature 900–1066*. London: Hambledon.
—— (1996). *Anglo-Latin Literature 600–899*. London: Hambledon.
—— (2000). 'The archetype of *Beowulf*'. Anglo-Saxon England 29: 5–41.
Lee, C. (2007). *Feasting the Dead: Food and Drink in Anglo-Saxon Burial Rituals*. Woodbridge: Boydell.
Lendinara, P. (1997). 'The Kentish laws', in J. Hines (ed.), *The Anglo-Saxons from the Migration Period to the Eighth Century: An Ethnographic Perspective*. Woodbridge: Boydell, 211–43.
Lord, A. B. (1960). *The Singer of Tales*. Cambridge, MA: Harvard University Press.
Lucy, J. A. (1992a). *Grammatical Categories and Cognition: Case Study of the Linguistic Relativity Hypothesis*. Cambridge: Cambridge University Press.
—— (1992b). *Language Diversity and Thought: A Reformulation of the Linguistic Relativity Hypothesis*. Cambridge: Cambridge University Press.
Lucy, S. (2000). *The Anglo-Saxon Way of Death*. Stroud: Sutton.
Marzinzik, S. (2003). *Early Anglo-Saxon Belt Buckles (Late Fifth to Early Eighth Centuries AD)*. British Archaeological Reports British Series 357. Oxford: Archaeopress.
MoLAS (2004). *The Prittlewell Prince: The Discovery of a Rich Anglo-Saxon Burial in Essex*. London: Museum of London Archaeology Service.
Muir, B. (ed.) (1994). *The Exeter Anthology of Old English Poetry*. 2 volumes. Exeter: Exeter University Press.
Nielsen, H. F. (1981). *Old English and the Continental Germanic Languages*. Innsbrücker Beiträge zur Sprachwissenschaft 33. Innsbrück: Institut für Sprachwissenschaft der Universität Innsbrück.
O'Brien O'Keeffe, K. (1990). *Visible Song: Transitional Literacy in Old English Verse*. Cambridge: Cambridge University Press.
Ong, W. (1982). *Orality and Literacy: The Technologizing of the Word*. London: Methuen.
Orchard, A. (1994). *The Poetic Art of Aldhelm*. Cambridge: Cambridge University Press.
Owen-Crocker, G. R. (2000). *The Four Funerals of 'Beowulf'*. Manchester: Manchester University Press.
Parsons, D. (1999). *Recasting the Runes: The Reform of the Anglo-Saxon 'Futhorc'*. Runrön 14. Uppsala: Institutionen för nordiska språk vid Uppsala Universitet.
Renoir, A. (1988). *A Key to Old Poems: The Oral-Formulaic Approach to the Interpretation of West-Germanic Verse*. University Park, PA: Pennsylvania University Press.
Schwyzer, P. (2007). *Archaeologies of English Renaissance Literature*. Oxford: Oxford University Press.
Scragg, D. G. (1991). 'The nature of Old English verse', in M. Godden and M. Lapidge (eds.), *The Cambridge Companion to Old English Literature*. Cambridge: Cambridge University Press, 55–70.
—— (ed.) (1993). *The Battle of Maldon AD 991*. Oxford: Blackwell.
Semple, S. (1998). 'A fear of the past: the place of the burial mound in the ideology of middle and later Anglo-Saxon England'. *World Archaeology* 30:109–26.

STOODLEY, N. 1999. *The Spindle and the Spear: A Critical Enquiry into the Construction and Meaning of Gender in the Early Anglo-Saxon Burial Rite.* BAR British Series 288. Oxford: British Archaeological Reports.

SWAN, M., and TREHARNE, E. M. (eds.) (2000). *Rewriting Old English in the Twelfth Century.* Cambridge: Cambridge University Press.

THOMPSON, V. (2004). *Dying and Death in Later Anglo-Saxon England.* Woodbridge: Boydell.

TOON, P. (1983). *The Politics of Early Old English Sound Change.* New York: Academic Press.

TOWNEND, M. (2002). *Language and History in Viking Age England.* Turnhout: Brepols.

WALTON ROGERS, P. (2007). *Cloth and Clothing in Anglo-Saxon England, AD 450–700.* CBA Research Report 145. York: Council for British Archaeology.

WILLIAMS, A. (2004). 'An outing on the Dee: King Edgar at Chester, A.D. 973'. *Mediaeval Scandinavia* 14: 229–43.

WILLIAMS, H. (2002). '"Remains of pagan Saxondom"? – the study of Anglo-Saxon cremation rites', in A. Reynolds and S. Lucy (eds.), *Burial in Early Medieval England and Wales.* Society for Medieval Archaeology Monograph 17. Leeds: Maney, 47–71.

—— (2006). *Death and Memory in Early Medieval Britain.* Cambridge: Cambridge University Press.

CHAPTER 50

PLACE-NAMES AND ARCHAEOLOGY

†MARGARET GELLING[1]

PLACE-NAMES are one of the three main sources of information which can be drawn upon in attempts to chart the course of events in post-Roman Britain. There are a few historical records, and there is a vast though unevenly distributed quantity of archaeological material. Place-names differ from the other two by being both abundant and ubiquitous; and while they do not provide firm answers to the problems they must be taken into account in all discussions about the period from AD 400 to AD 600. No suggested scenario for these two centuries can be convincing if the place-name evidence tells against it. Perhaps their most important function is that of keeping people away from the lunatic extremes of the wide arc of Dark Age hypothesizing.

METHODOLOGY

Before considering the contributions which place-names can make to understanding the Anglo-Saxon past it is desirable to give a brief account of the method by which they are studied. In England the basis of the study is the assembling of Old English and

[1] The late Margaret Gelling had only submitted the first draft of her paper for consideration before she was overtaken by her last illness, and that first draft is essentially what has been published here. Readers will therefore be aware that it does not necessarily represent her final intentions for this contribution. The editors are most grateful to Dr Ann Cole for advice and additional help in preparing this text for publication.

Middle English spellings. Old English spellings of place-names become available after the coming of Roman Christianity in the latter part of the seventh century. They become abundant in the eighth century and very abundant in the tenth. England is extremely fortunate in possessing these written sources from the Anglo-Saxon period which provide a large number of pre-Norman Conquest name spellings. These form a scientific basis for the study of the much larger number of names first recorded in Domesday Book or later. Philologists can observe the development in Middle and Modern English of names which are recorded in pre-Conquest sources, and this makes it possible for them to ascertain the Old English forms of names for which records begin at a later date. The county volumes of the English Place-Name Society (eighty-four to date) provide an ample base for what is essentially a comparative study of names which contain the same sequences of sounds. If place-name material is to be used for any academic purpose two principles must be accepted:

1. the oral transmission of names prior to their appearance in written records is reliable;
2. sound-developments and the representation of them in writing are recognizable and consistent processes.

If these principles are not accepted it is not legitimate to use the material in historical, geographical, or archaeological studies.

THE HISTORICAL SIGNIFICANCE OF PRE-ENGLISH NAMES

Since a place-name is a linguistic phenomenon, two basic questions can be asked about it: what language is it in and what does it mean? The first question is particularly important in the consideration of the bearing of place-name evidence on theories about the course of events in Britain in the immediate post-Roman period.

The transformation of Roman Britain into Anglo-Saxon England between the early fifth and the late seventh century presents archaeologists with what is arguably the most interesting and certainly the most obscure problem in English history. The abundant and sometimes spectacular grave-goods deposited with burials from this period are overwhelmingly Germanic, and these attest the coming into the country of non-Christian people from northern Europe. There are widely divergent opinions about the extent to which the immigration of these people transformed the ethnic composition of the population. Perhaps the only totally indisputable fact is that their coming caused a replacement of the spoken language from the Celtic one known to philologists as British, which is the ancestor of modern Welsh, to the Germanic one, Old English, which (with the admixture of some Scandinavian, many French, and other borrowed words) became Modern English. Most philologists would agree that their coming also led to a replacement of most of the stock of Celtic place-names by Germanic ones, and such a replacement is potentially more significant than the change of spoken language; but because massive place-name replacement is difficult to explain without massive immigration, attempts are sometimes made by believers in minimum immigration to dispute the Old English nature of the place-names. It is important that all students of this period understand the evidence for this place-name replacement.

The decades following the Second World War saw a great swing of opinion in the debate about continuity versus change after the collapse of Roman rule in Britain. The lunatic extreme of nineteenth-century opinion—'It is enough that [the Britons] were exterminated, got rid of in one way or another, within what now became the English border' (Freeman 1888: 76)—was recognized as untenable when scientific place-name study demonstrated the survival of a substantial number of British place-names. The incoming Germanic settlers would not, while engaged in a policy of extermination, have ascertained from their victims the names of rivers or hills, memorized them carefully, and rendered them into a form compatible with the sound system of their own language, a process which was demonstrated by Professor Kenneth Jackson in an important book published in 1953 to have been widespread in the Anglicized part of Britain. Nevertheless, a refined version of the 'clean sweep' theory, the belief that the continuous history of settlement, land-use, and administrative geography in England began with the Anglo-Saxon settlement, was promoted into the middle decades of the twentieth century by extremely influential historians, notably Sir Frank Stenton (1939) and Professor Dorothy Whitelock (1952), both of whom were closely associated with place-name studies. There was a vigorous revolt against this attitude in the 1950s and 1960s, which led to the promotion by some scholars of the opposite, and equally untenable, extreme, which is the assertion that the Anglo-Saxons were a small warlike elite whose coming did not cause any substantial change in the ethnic composition of the inhabitants of Britain: 'I firmly believe myself that the predominant element in the population of England is Celtic' (Chadwick 1963: 111).

Place-names constitute the buffer into which this last hypothesis crashes. Language change could be ascribed to the prestige and political power of an elite, but how could the members of this elite impose new names on so many settlements? Nothing of this kind happened as a result of the Roman Conquest or the Norman Conquest. The names recorded from Roman Britain, which number between 350 and 400, are predominantly in the Celtic language which was spoken throughout Britain. These names were adopted easily by Latin speakers because the sound systems of the two languages coincided closely. There is a handful of Latin coinages, like *Castra Exploratorum* and *Salinis,* but there is no doubt that, even for the forts on Hadrian's Wall, the stations along Watling Street, and the new *civitas* capitals, the Romans used names which they learned from the Britons.

Any assessment of the historical significance of the survival of Brittonic place-names depends on correct identification. A great many are beyond dispute, especially among river-names which can be matched in Wales and Scotland and in parts of Europe, and there is no doubt about names which embody part, or occasionally the whole, of those recorded from Roman Britain, such as London, Manchester, York, Wroxeter, and Penkridge. The modifications made by speakers of Old English to these firmly identified pre-English names were analysed in Jackson 1953 and found to be consistent and explicable in terms of the sound systems of the two languages. Evidence for rationalization or substitution of Old English words in this material is negligible, possibly non-existent, and this disproves the suggestion that many apparently Old English names are really Brittonic names which were misheard, mispronounced, or rationalized by Anglo-Saxons. This suggestion is made occasionally in attempts to minimize the number of immigrant settlers: 'It may well be that the apparent absence of settlement-names derived from Primitive Welsh is proof only that the Englishman's traditional inability to pronounce a foreign language correctly is a trait of very long standing' (Alcock 1971: 194–5). It is an absurd anachronism to suggest that Old English speakers might have treated Brittonic names in similar fashion to twentieth-century soldiers who called Ypres 'Wipers', and the training camps at Trawsfynnydd and Tonfanau 'Trousers' and 'Aunt Fanny'. The whole vast corpus of English place-names makes sense in a way which would be impossible if English speakers were, for instance, substituting *cot* for *coed*. Three generations of philologists have studied these names since the early twentieth century, and a fourth generation of scholars is studying them now. If they were the random results of mispronunciation and substitution of English words for Welsh ones it is very unlikely that they could have been interpreted as showing a consistent use of Old English terms for settlements and landscape features.

By refusing to believe in the ability of Old English speakers to hear Primitive Welsh names correctly and to employ systematic modifications where necessary to render them easier to pronounce, the advocates of this theory deprive themselves of the precious evidence which genuine name survival provides for peaceful cohabitation between the descendants of Romano-British people and the immigrant Anglo-Saxons. The identification of these names depends on the ability of philologists to recognize the systematic adjustments to them made by the Anglo-Saxons in the same way as they can recognize Old English names which were modified by speakers of Norman French.

The search for pre-English names has become much more diligent since the 1960s, and a major role in this has naturally been taken by toponymists whose main expertise is in the Celtic languages. In a lecture published in 1963, the great Celticist Kenneth Jackson gave a witty account of the discrediting of the 'clean sweep' theory which, he said, 'was pretty well abandoned now', and went on to say that: 'nowadays the difficulty for the Celtic scholar is rather the reverse, to restrain some historians from putting up Celts from every bush' (Jackson 1963: 73). Now, forty years later, it is specialists in Celtic languages rather than historians who may be suspected of excessive zeal in identifying hitherto unnoticed British place-names.

There has been a trickle of reliably identified items (one example being Professor Richard Coates' analysis of Leatherhead as 'grey ford' (Coates 1980), which is a valuable addition to the cluster of names which indicate substantial contact between Saxons and Britons in an area south-west of London; but there have been many suggestions which have not gained general acceptance. A recent collection of studies by Richard Coates and Andrew Breeze (2000) should be taken as an assemblage of suggestions rather than as a generally accepted corpus.

The distribution pattern of pre-English names which remained in use after the Anglo-Saxon settlement is of interest to archaeologists and historians. In very general terms the number increases to the west and north of the parts of England where Anglo-Saxon remains are found, but there are anomalies in this pattern. Two such anomalies are a cluster of names indicative of a British presence in the Croydon region of Surrey (Leatherhead, Penge, and possibly Caterham, supported by Croydon, Addiscombe, West Wickham, Walton on Thames, Walworth, and Wallington, the relevance of which is discussed below), and the virtual absence of such names in the area of Shropshire which was the hinterland of Wroxeter.

Study of distribution patterns requires maps, and when the subject of study is pre-English place-names difficulties arise because of the varying degrees of certainty and probability in the material. It is, however, possible to deal with this problem, as even in the areas where they are best evidenced, the number of pre-English names to be mapped is never so dense that they cannot be written against the symbols or along the rivers, allowing the user of the map to discard any which seem insufficiently reliable. Maps of this kind, on a relatively large scale, are a useful adjunct to Dark Age studies in any area of England.

NAMES WHICH REFER TO BRITISH PEOPLE

In addition to identifiable pre-English names, there are several categories of names in the Old English language which are considered to be evidence for contact between immigrant Anglo-Saxons and descendants of Romano-British people. The most important of these comprises names which contain the words *walh* and *cumbre*, both of which are Old English terms for British people.

Names containing *walh*, in the genitive singular (e.g. Walsall), the nominative plural (as in Wales, both the country and a settlement in the West Riding), and in the genitive plural (e.g. numerous Walcots and Waltons and several Wallingtons), were examined in great detail in a paper by Professor Cameron published in 1980. This developed the case made in a 1975 paper by Dr Margaret Faull for regarding *walh* as a specifically ethnic term in Old English before it became a general term for a slave, a development which seems to have taken place between c.800 and c.950. Care must be taken in mapping Walcot and Walton names because other Old English words (*wælle* 'spring', *wald* 'forest', *wall* 'wall') occur in some of them, but these can be distinguished in early spellings, and the corpus established in Professor Cameron's paper can be used with confidence. There has not yet been a comprehensive study of names containing Old English *cumbre*, which is much less common than *walh*. It is an Old English version of Welsh *Cymro*, so is perhaps a politer term for Welsh speakers than *walh*, which originally meant 'foreigner'. Both terms occur sometimes as personal names, as in Walsall, Staffordshire, and Cumberwood, Gloucestershire, and here they may be nicknames equivalent to modern *Taffy*.

Professor Cameron's 1980 paper includes a map of names containing *walh* which shows that they are widespread across the country from the east coast to the Welsh border and from the south coast as far north as Lancashire and Yorkshire. They may well signify a recognition by English speakers of settlements where Welsh speech survived into the eighth century.

NAMES WHICH CONTAIN LOAN-WORDS FROM LATIN

Another category of Old English names which may be evidence for continuity from Roman Britain consists of those which contain words derived from Latin. The name Wickham with its variants Wykeham, Wycomb, Wykham, was studied in Gelling 1967 and was found to have a remarkable correspondence with major Roman roads and minor Roman settlements. This led to the suggestion that in this compound (though not, of course, in its widespread use in other place-names) Old English *wic*, which is a loan-word from Latin *vicus*, was used by people who knew the meaning of the Latin word and applied it to settlements which were still, in the immediate post-Roman period, inhabited by people who were leading a recognizably Romanized life, or to recently deserted Romano-British settlements the remains of which were still clearly visible. Archaeologically this suggestion was a success. Coates in a paper published in 1999 said: 'There are several newly-noted instances of Wickham and the like, and the coincidence of these with known Roman settlements proves to be as striking as those established in the first years of the hypothesis.' It could be that the ultimate Holy Grail of Dark Age archaeology, the discovery of firm evidence for continuity between late Roman and Anglo-Saxon activity, will be found at a *wīchām* site.

A further study (Gelling 1988) of the use in English place-names of the Latin loan-words *camp*, *funta*, and *port* revealed another suggestive distribution pattern with close links to that of *wīchām*. In Kent and Sussex, *camp* names have subsequently been shown to occur with significant frequency in the vicinity of Roman villas. It was hoped that *funta* ('spring'), which occurs in nineteen place-names, might be a reference to springs which had the remains of Roman stonework, causing this word to be used in preference to the ubiquitous *well*. This has so far received no support from archaeological evidence, but these names deserve note as possible indicators of contact between Anglo-Saxons and some Latin speakers.

Some of the *funta* names are heavily disguised in modern forms, such as Chadshunt, Bedmond and Fovant, and in *camp* names the more familiar -*combe* has often been substituted for -*camp*; but reliable lists of all the relevant names are provided in the articles cited.

A similar significance could be claimed for 'one-off' names containing words of Latin origin, such as Croydon (Latin *crocus*), Faversham (*faber*: 'smith'), Dovercourt (*cohors*: 'enclosed yard').

Names containing the Old English form, *eccles*, or British *eglēs* ('Christian centre'), which is the ancestor of Modern Welsh *eglwys* ('church'), and which was borrowed into Welsh from Latin *ecclesia*, were studied by Cameron in a paper published in 1968. These are heavily concentrated in the West Midlands, with a few instances in Lancashire, Cumberland, and Yorkshire. Two instances in Norfolk and one in Kent are widely separated from the West Midland group, and it is possible that these should be classified with the *camp*, *funta*, and *port* names as very early borrowings directly from Latin *ecclesia*, but in the West Midlands and in Lancashire and Yorkshire the borrowing was clearly a later one of British *eglēs*.

In a field called Eccles in Stanbury in the West Riding of Yorkshire an aerial photograph, which was brought to Cameron's attention by Faull, shows a rectangular enclosure of about an acre with square and circular huts similar to the structures on Irish monastic sites (Cameron 1968: 7). More archaeological evidence is needed before the archaeological significance of *eccles* names is established, but it is probably safe to say that the occurrence of the term in place-names shows an awareness, and probably tolerance, by pagan Anglo-Saxons of religious practices different from their own.

The nature of British settlement-names

In their rearguard action against the growing belief in substantial Celtic survival, Whitelock and Stenton used the absence of British place-names which make specific reference to a habitation site. Whitelock observed that 'no place-name supplies a certain instance of a British habitation name' (Whitelock 1952: 18), and Stenton said 'among the numerous names of woods, streams and hills adopted by the

English settlers there might be expected to occur at least a few unmistakable habitation-names' (Stenton 1939: 260). This is a false argument. These two great scholars were led into error by their failure to consider the corpus of names which are recorded from Roman Britain (Gelling 1988: ch. 2). They are saying, in effect, 'where are the British equivalents of Edgbaston and Didcot?'. The evidence from Roman times shows that the people of Roman Britain did not use names of that sort for their farms and villages, so the absence of such names is not evidence that the Anglo-Saxons established a completely new settlement pattern. Romano-British Celts most frequently defined their settlements by giving them the names of adjacent topographical features such as hills and rivers (Gelling 1988: 50–1). Many surviving Celtic names for settlements, such as Malvern and Penn, were probably applied to the settlements as well as to the hills. Many rivers with pre-English names have towns and villages on their banks which use the river-name, and if these can be considered as evidence for survival of pre-English settlement-names the body of evidence which can be adduced for continuity is considerably enhanced. Such an enhancement would be particularly welcome in Devon.

Another point to be noted when assessing the historical significance of pre-English names which remained in use is that names for relatively insignificant features should be accorded a higher rating than those referring to major rivers such as Thames, Trent, Severn, to massifs like the Malverns, or to major Roman towns like London and York. There is a correlation between the number of people using a name and its chances of survival, and some of the names used in Roman Britain would be widely known to Continental as well as to Insular people. In areas where small streams keep their pre-English names, however, it is reasonable to postulate prolonged contact between Welsh- and English-speakers. There is one such area in north-west Worcestershire, where two tributaries of the River Severn flowing through the Wyre Forest have the Celtic names Dowles and Lem. There cannot have been widespread knowledge of these names, which are accompanied by some hybrid Welsh/English compounds. Here also is the remarkable name Pensax, coined by Welsh speakers to denote a 'hill' where there were some 'Saxons'. The order of elements in Pensax, with the qualifying term 'Saxons' placed after the main element, contrasts with that in the older Celtic name Malvern, 'bare hill', where Welsh *moel* comes before the hill-term *bryn*. This change in the manner of forming compounds occurred in the Welsh language after the Roman period.

The chronology of English place-names

Pre-English names adopted by Anglo-Saxons can be placed in an historical context. It is more difficult to establish a chronological framework for the great mass of English names, although much thought has been, and still is being, given to this problem.

Scholars who were concerned in the initiation of organized English place-name studies believed that certain types of name could confidently be ascribed to the earliest years of Anglo-Saxon settlement. Symbols for these names were sometimes plotted on maps together with symbols for Anglo-Saxon burial sites, and they were for several decades regarded as part of the evidence for the course of the movement which led to the dominance of the Anglo-Saxons over the south and east of Britain. In the 1960s and 1970s, however, increasing scepticism about the significance assigned to these names turned into outright disbelief. The two main classes of names were:

1. Those in which the suffixes -*ingas* and -*ingahām* were added to a man's name, giving place-names like Reading, Hastings, Gillingham, Wokingham. These compounds, which mean 'the followers of Rēad (or Hāsta)', and 'the homestead of the followers of Gylla (or Wocca)', were supposed to represent, in the case of the -*ingas* names the first land-takings of the immigrant Anglo-Saxons, in the case of the -*ingahām* names the immediate second stage of the settlement.
2. Those which refer to the sites of pagan religious worship (like Harrow and Wye) or to Germanic gods (like Wednesbury and Thundersley).

Papers published in 1961 (Gelling) and 1966 (Dodgson) challenged the accepted belief in these names. There was initial hostility from senior historians and archaeologists to the suggested removal of these items from the body of evidence for early Anglo-Saxon settlement, but eventually the glaring discrepancies between the situation of the names and the sites of early Anglo-Saxon burials became widely perceived, and the new suggestions for likely historical contexts for the names gained the general acceptance which they enjoy at present. John Dodgson suggested that the Reading/Hastings type, which probably referred originally to groups of immigrants, was more likely to be used for settlements on the boundaries of the territories eventually dominated by these groups than for their original or main settlement; and Margaret Gelling suggested that the 'heathen' names were most likely to refer to places where the Germanic gods continued to be worshipped after most people had accepted Christianity.

These developments led to a demand from archaeologists for the identification of other English names which could be regarded as dating from the earliest years of the settlement. It is, however, unlikely that any category exists which should be treated, as the -*ingas* and 'heathen' names were, as suitable for representation by the dots on a distribution map on which are also shown the find-spots of fifth-century artefacts. Place-names differ from archaeological finds. It may be possible to use the general character of names in a fairly wide region as evidence for earlier or later Anglo-Saxon infiltration or colonization, but (with the possible exception of the Latin-loan-word category) no type can give a positive indication of early Anglo-Saxon presence such as that given by a burial containing a fifth-century brooch. Moreover, although arguments can be mustered for earlier or later use of name-forming terms, most English place-names could, on linguistic grounds, have been coined at any time from the first arrival of English speakers to the tenth or eleventh centuries. In this they differ greatly from artefacts bearing Anglo-Saxon decorative styles which can be dated to quarter-centuries, perhaps to decades. However, while it would be unwise to assert that any single place-name must have been coined in the earliest years of English speech in Britain, studies undertaken since the demolition of the -*ingas* and heathen-name hypotheses have established some broad probabilities about 'earlier' and 'later' types of settlement-name.

Before the revisionist work of the 1960s and 1970s it was frequently, perhaps generally, assumed that the 'habitative' type of settlement-name, in which the main component is a word for a settlement, is likely to be earlier than the 'topographical' type, which defines the settlement by reference to a feature of the geographical environment without reference to buildings. This assumption has been shown to be at variance with several types of evidence. An analysis of names recorded between AD c.670 and c.730 (Cox 1976) showed that topographical names were more numerous in this small corpus. Topographical names have also been shown to predominate in some areas, notably north-west Berkshire and south-central Essex, where a very early Anglo-Saxon presence is archaeologically attested (Gelling 1988: 116–23), and in these areas they are much more frequently the names of parishes, while the habitative names more often belong to subsidiary settlements.

In north-west Berkshire and south-central Essex the topographical names often refer to particularly advantageous settlement-sites. These were not likely to have been unoccupied when the first Anglo-Saxon settlers saw them, and it is possible that immigrants gave to long-established settlements names in their own language which acknowledged the special advantages of the sites. In the hinterland of Mucking the predominant term is *dūn*, which describes the low hills overlooking the estuary marshes; Basildon is one of six *dūn* names here. In the valley of the Berkshire River Ock the most frequent terms in parish-names are *īeg* 'island' and *ford*, noting the slightly elevated areas which determine sites of settlements in this wetland area and the stream-crossings and causeways essential for communication. There are also a number of settlements which are named from small tributaries of the River Ock. These streams, insignificant to the modern eye, were important to drainage, and some can be shown from boundary surveys in Anglo-Saxon charters to have been canalized. Wantage, for instance, is named from a stream called *Wanating*, and a survey of AD 968 mentions both *wanating* and *ealdan wanating*.[2] Such names reflect a concern with environmental factors which might be expected in farmers infiltrating a new area. They differ clearly from names like Buckland ('estate granted by charter') and Fyfield ('estate assessed for taxation at five hides'),

---

[2] The spelling with an 'e' (*Waneting*) is just as common. The reference in PN Berks p. 734 in the survey of 968 is actually to '*ealdan wanatiting*', which seems to have been a scribal error for '*waneting*'.

in the same area, which clearly came into use at a later stage in the organization of the West Saxon kingdom.

The association of early Anglo-Saxon archaeological finds with a group of topographical names which have a coherent theme is noteworthy in the two examples detailed above, and valuable as demonstrating the unsatisfactory nature of hypotheses about *-ingas* and heathen names and the supposed primacy of habitative names. The model is not, however, universally applicable. It is not evidenced, for instance, in the Croydon region of Surrey, where the habitative terms *hām* and *stede* are particularly common.

The search for a clearly identifiable category of names which could be recommended unequivocally to Dark Age archaeologists as indicators of early settlement was unsuccessful. This was demonstrated in 1986 in a publication by Dr G. J. Copley, which contains a list of fifth- and sixth-century archaeological sites in Saxon and Jutish areas of settlement, with a study of the place-names in a ten-mile radius of each fifth-century site. The complex conclusions of this study are summarized in Gelling 1988: 254.

It would be useful to have a historical context for the two words which are by a very large number the commonest terms in English settlement-names. These are *tūn*, which is the commonest of many habitative names, and *lēah*, which occurs with a quite different frequency from any other topographical term. An environmental context can certainly be established for them. It was recognized from the earliest years of place-name study that *lēah* is a term associated with woodland. More recently it has been demonstrated that *tūn* is the most frequent term in areas which were not wooded, and that it is, in fact, rare or absent in those where *lēah* names are dense (Gelling 1974: 64–9).

These two words do not predominate in place-names over the whole of England, but they do so in a broad belt running south-west from Northumberland to Devon, broadening in the Midlands so that it extends from Offa's Dyke to The Wash, but excluding some north-western and south-eastern areas. In this belt the distribution of *tūn* and *lēah* names gives an excellent guide to the extent of woodland at whatever date the names were coined. It is remarkable, in view of their enormous frequency, that both words make a poor showing in Dr Brian Cox's list of names recorded by *c.*730, which has six instances of *tūn* and seven of *lēah*. A suggestion that this indicates that the terms only came into very frequent use after *c.*750 (Gelling 2000: 237–8) has been countered by studies which suggest that *tūn* was in frequent use at a much earlier date, Baker 2004 being the most recent of these. The suggestion, also in Gelling 2000, that the widespread use of *tūn* for a settlement in open country and *lēah* for one in a woodland environment may have ceased *c.*950 has not, however, been challenged. This is likely because by the mid-tenth century both words had developed meanings different from their earlier ones of 'enclosure, farm' and 'wood, woodland clearing, wood pasture'.

Many *tūn* names have as qualifier an Old English personal name, and in most cases the relationship of the man or woman named with the settlement is a matter for conjecture. In a few cases, however, records are available which show that the person concerned obtained overlordship of an estate in the tenth or eleventh centuries. The Wulfric of Woolstone, Berks., was a king's thegn who obtained an estate here by royal grants in 944 and 958. The Æffe of Aughton, Wilts., was a widow given this estate by her husband's will, which is dated *c*.931. More instances of this 'manorial' relationship are revealed in Domesday Book. East Garston, Berks., for instance, was Old English *Esgarestūn*, and Esgar was an official of Edward the Confessor. Other instances are cited in Gelling 1988, chapter 7. This relationship is quite different from that which was sometimes suggested in early place-name literature, where these personal names were seen as potentially those of pioneering founders of new settlements. It cannot be proved that the 'x's *tūn*' type of name never dates from the early years of the Anglo-Saxon settlement, but it seems reasonable to envisage most of them as referring to overlordship of long-established settlements with their supporting land, the earlier names of which were replaced by these 'manorial' ones. It is certain that Wulfric's holding under the White Horse was one of several land-units here known as *Æscesbyrig*, the Old English name of Uffington Castle, that East Garston was one of a number of such units named from the River Lambourn, and Aughton was one of a similar group called Collingbourne.

In these tenth- and eleventh-century instances, *tūn* clearly has the sense 'estate' rather than 'farm'. Recent work on the other predominant term, *lēah*, by Dr Della Hooke (2008) suggests that it meant 'wood-pasture', which might be anything from fairly open woodland to trees widely spaced in grassland. This might explain the earlier belief amongst place-name specialists that the meaning of *lēah* shifted from 'woodland' to 'pasture, meadow'. This was considered by Bosworth (1898) to be the only sense evidenced in the very sparse literary occurrences of *lēah*, but it is no longer necessary to believe, for example, that *butere* 'butter' was an oblique reference to good pasture in names like Butterley, particularly as Dr Harold Fox (2008) has shown that *butere* and *smeoru* usually refer to places where butter was made. Names like Shipley 'sheep pasture' make better sense if *lēah* means wood-pasture rather than 'woodland'.

Despite many queries and qualifications it can be suggested that some topographical names date from the first coming of the English speakers to a region, that -*ingas* and -*ingahām* names may result from an expansion of Anglo-Saxon dominated territories between *c*.500 and *c*.600, that references to heathen practices may date from *c*.AD 700 on, when such practices were becoming rare, and that the overwhelming popularity of the generics *tūn* and *lēah* probably belongs to the period *c*.750 to *c*.930.

'Late' settlement-names

As regards settlement-names dating from the last two centuries of the Anglo-Saxon period, there is one large class which can be firmly identified: those which are in the Old Norse languages or which contain Old Norse words or personal names. This category is not discussed here, as it has to be linked with historical evidence for the Viking invasions, rather than with the sparse archaeological evidence for a Norse presence in eastern and northern England. Arguments about the extent to which Norse place-names indicate Norse colonization of some sparsely settled areas have produced a great deal of literature, an excellent summary of which can be found in Abrams and Parsons 2004, together with a valuable re-assessment of the evidence. The significance of Norse names is in the main a historical study, but there will sometimes be a direct link with archaeology. One such link is explored in Appendix I to Volume IX of the Wharram Percy reports (Gelling 2004).

There are some English place-name elements which can be considered indications of relatively late encroachment on areas of pasture or rough grazing: these are *feld*, *æcer* (Old Norse *akr*), and *land*. The word *feld*, modern 'field', underwent a semantic development from 'open country' (equivalent to Latin *campus*) to 'communally cultivated arable' and finally to 'enclosed piece of ground'. Settlement-names with *feld* as generic must have been coined while the first sense was operative. These were listed and mapped in Gelling and Cole 2000: 269–79. This analysis shows that a large proportion of such names are found in one of two situations. They frequently occur at the junction of high and low ground, usually at about the 500-feet contour (as Sheffield and Huddersfield on the east edge of the Pennines and Macclesfield on the west), or at the junction of forest and open land (as in the eleven adjacent parishes, Bradfield, Englefield, Burghfield, Shinfield, Wokefield, two Stratfields, Swallowfield, Arborfield, Heckfield, Sherfield, which lie between Windsor Forest and the downland of Berkshire and Hampshire). In others the contrast may be between marsh and firm ground or between heath and cultivated land. There are some isolated examples, but names with -*feld* as generic most frequently occur in belts or clusters, and it is possible to envisage a scenario in which such areas were reserved for pasture in the early Anglo-Saxon period (and perhaps earlier) but were brought into cultivation with settled occupation when there was need for more arable.

Settlement-names in -*æcre* and -*land* are also analysed and mapped in Gelling and Cole 2000 (263–6, 279–84). Reasons are given there for considering both terms to have been used with the connotation 'newly-broken-in'. For Old English *æcer*, Old Norse *akr*, the translation 'marginally cultivated land of limited extent' was suggested (cf. Muker, by the Pennine way, an Old Norse name meaning 'narrow acre'). Both terms have in place-names a clear relationship to reclamation of high moorland, heath, and marsh, and the frequency in northern counties of the Old

Norse qualifiers with both terms indicates a likely date of coinage later than the Viking wars. In the recurrent Newland(s), the reference may sometimes be to land brought into cultivation after the Norman Conquest. The above observations about *feld* and *land* only apply to their use as generics in settlement-names: their use in district-names is a different matter.[3]

REFERENCE BOOKS

Since the upheavals of the 1960s and 1970s, which resulted in a radical reappraisal of the historical bearing of place-name evidence, there has been a relatively small amount of controversy on that topic. The debate about the significance of Norse names remains lively, but on other aspects the account given in Gelling 1988 is still broadly accepted. There has, however, been a great increase in challenges to long-accepted interpretations of individual names, and this causes serious problems for the users of place-name dictionaries. It is axiomatic that anyone wishing to draw conclusions from the meaning of place-names must first look them up in a reliable reference book, but at present no available dictionary can be recommended as wholly reliable. Eilert Ekwall's great work, *The Concise Oxford Dictionary of English Place-Names*, first published in 1936, dominated the subject for several decades, and the fourth edition of 1960 is still valuable, though users should take account of changes in opinion since 1960. Also it is important to note that no credence is now given to Ekwall's belief that the large category of names ending in -*ington* belong to the -*inga*- category, with the genitive of a folk-name. In these names, with very few exceptions, -*ing*- is a connective particle, so that Kensington, for instance, is 'estate associated with a man named Cynesige', not, as Ekwall 1960 has it, 'the *tūn* of Cynesige's people'. (The varied uses of the particle -*ing*- are outlined in Gelling 1988: 109–10, 177–8).

The Cambridge Dictionary of English Place-Names (Watts 2004), which was planned as a replacement for Ekwall, suffered from the tragedy of the sudden death of the editor in 2003. The final stages of preparation for publication were not competently carried out and the dictionary has many flaws. There are no unsound etymologies, but users may find it confusing because the county sections in which it was compiled were amalgamated without attention to the slightly varying phrasing used for identical names which occur in several counties. Also, it was not practicable in the twenty years over which the dictionary was compiled to

---

[3] One category of place-names about which Margaret Gelling made no mention in this draft of her text were place-names that may indicate features of interest to archaeologists, which no doubt she would have discussed in fuller detail had she had time to revise her contribution. She deals with these in chapter 6 of her *Signposts to the Past* (1988).

incorporate the suggestions for revised etymologies which were being put forward in increasing numbers.

In a highly successful series of dictionaries by A. D. Mills (1991/1998/2003) account is taken of revised etymologies, but without noting that some of those offered in 2003 differ radically from those in the earlier books, and without indication of where the new ones come from. Some of these latter have only the status of suggestions, not of generally accepted solutions to difficult names. The Mills dictionaries, while excellent for the purposes of the general reader, are not entirely adequate for historians and archaeologists.

The English Place-Name Society's series of annual county volumes, which began in 1924 with Buckinghamshire, continued on much the same lines until it was interrupted during the Second World War. The hiatus in publication lasted from 1943 to 1950, and surveys since 1950 have been much fuller, usually requiring a number of volumes for each county. These volumes are an essential resource for students and scholars, but note should always be taken of the date at which they were compiled and allowance made for developments in the subject since that date. There is not yet complete coverage of the country, but a number of county editors have issued dictionaries of the 'major' names in their counties in advance of the main survey. There are also numerous county-based books by authors not associated with the English Place-Name Society, and these vary enormously in quality, some being excellent, but others being seriously misleading.

In view of all these reservations it is extremely difficult to offer advice to students and scholars who wish to access reliable place-name evidence. It is advisable to consult more than one reference book and to seek further information if serious discrepancies are noted. The best advice is probably to consult a place-name specialist, most of whom are easily contactable and very willing to help. For an archaeologist wishing to assess the place-name evidence which is relevant to excavation results or field studies a good option is to ask a place-name scholar to contribute a section to the report.

The English Place-Name Society is based in the Institute for Name Studies at Nottingham University. Staff there will answer queries and give advice about reference books and scholars who may be consulted

REFERENCES

ABRAMS, L., and PARSONS, D. N. (2004). 'Place-names and the history of Scandinavian settlement in England', in J. Hines, A. Lane, and M. Redknap (eds.), *Land, Sea and Home: Proceedings of a Conference on Viking-Period Settlement*. Leeds: Maney, 379–431.

ALCOCK, L. (1971). *Arthur's Britain: History and Archaeology, AD 367–634*. London: Allen Lane.

BAKER, J. (2004). 'The distribution of *tun* place-names in Hertfordshire, Essex and neighbouring areas'. *Journal of the English Place-Name Society* 36: 5–22.
BOSWORTH, J. (1898). *An Anglo-Saxon Dictionary*. Oxford: The Clarendon Press.
CAMERON, K. (1968). 'Eccles in English Place-names'. *Place-Name Evidence for the Anglo-Saxon Invasion and Scandinavian Settlements*. Nottingham: English Place-Name Society, 1–7.
—— (1980). 'The meaning and significance of Old English *walh* in English place-names'. *Journal of Early Place-Name Studies* 12: 1–53.
CHADWICK, N. (1963). *Celtic Britain*. London: Thames and Hudson.
COATES, R. (1980). 'Methodological reflexions on Leatherhead'. *Journal of the English Place-Name Society* 12: 70–4.
—— (1999). 'New light from old wicks: the progeny of Latin *vicus*'. *Nomina* 22: 75–116.
—— and BREEZE, A. (2000). *Celtic Voices, English Places*. Stamford: Shaun Tyas.
COPLEY, G. J. (1986). *Archaeology and Place-Names in the Fifth and Sixth Centuries*. BAR British Series 147. Oxford: British Archaeological Reports.
COX, B. (1976). 'The place-names of the earliest English records'. *Journal of the English Place-Name Society* 8: 12–66.
DODGSON, J. McN. (1966). 'The significance of the distribution of English place-names in -ingas, -inga- in South-East England'. *Medieval Archaeology* 10: 1–29.
EKWALL, E. (1960). *The Concise Oxford Dictionary of English Place-Names*. 4th edition. Oxford: Clarendon Press.
FAULL, M. L. (1975). 'The semantic development of Old English *Wealh*'. *Leeds Studies in English*, New Series 8: 20–44.
FOX, H. (2008). 'Butter place-names and transhumance', in Padel and Parsons (eds.), *A Commodity of Good Names*, 352–64.
FREEMAN, E. A. (1888). *Four Oxford Lectures*. London: Macmillan and Co.
GELLING, M. (1961). 'Place-names and Anglo-Saxon paganism.' *University of Birmingham Historical Journal* 8(i): 7–25.
—— (1967). 'English place-names derived from the compound *wīchām*'. *Medieval Archaeology* 11: 87–104. (Reprinted in 1987: *Place-Name Evidence for the Anglo-Saxon Invasions and Scandinavian Settlement*. Nottingham: English Place-Name Society, 8–26.)
—— (1974). 'Some notes on Warwickshire place-names'. *Transactions of the Birmingham & Warwickshire Archaeological Society* 85: 59–79.
—— (1988). *Signposts to the Past: Place-Names and the History of England*. 2nd edition with addenda. Chichester: Phillimore.
—— (2000). *Place Names in the Landscape: The Geographical Roots of Britain's Place Names*. London: Phoenix Press.
—— (2004). 'A regional view of place-names', in P. Rahtz and L. Watts (eds.), *Wharram: the North Manor Area and North-West Enclosure*. York University Archaeological Publications 11. York: English Heritage, 347–51.
—— and COLE, A. (2000). *The Landscape of Place-Name*. Stamford: Shaun Tyas. (Reprinted with corrections 2003, Donington: Shaun Tyas.)
HOOKE, D. (2008). 'Early medieval woodland and the place-name *lēah*', in Padel and Parsons (eds.), *A Commodity of Good Names*, 365–76.
JACKSON, K. H. (1953). *Language and History in Early Britain: A Chronological Survey of the Brittonic Languages, First to Twelfth Century A.D.* Edinburgh: Edinburgh University Press.

—— (1963). 'Angles and Britons in Northumbria and Cumbria', in H. Lewis (ed.), *Angles and Britons: O'Donnell Lectures*. Cardiff: University of Wales Press, 60–84.

MILLS, A. D. (1991/1998/2003). *A Dictionary of British Place-Names*. 1st/2nd/3rd editions. Oxford: Oxford University Press.

PADEL, O. J., and PARSONS, D. N. (2008). *A Commodity of Good Names: Essays in Honour of Margaret Gelling*. Donington: Shaun Tyas.

STENTON, F. M. (1939). 'The historical bearing of place-name studies: England in the sixth century'. *Transactions of the Royal Historical Society*, fourth series, 21: 1–19. (Reprinted in D. M. Stenton (ed.), *Preparatory to Anglo-Saxon England, being the Collected Papers of Frank Merry Stenton*. Oxford: Oxford University Press (1970), 253–65.)

WATTS, V. (2004). *The Cambridge Dictionary of English Place-Names*. Cambridge: Cambridge University Press.

WHITELOCK, D. (1952). *The Beginnings of English Society*. London: Penguin Books.

CHAPTER 51

ANTHROPOLOGY AND ARCHAEOLOGY

CHRIS GOSDEN

The societies of Early Medieval Britain have no direct ethnographic analogy. For a comparativist this is the source of much of its interest and stimulus to thought. Even amongst the provinces of the former Roman Empire, Britain was unusual in seeing quite such a complete collapse of political and economic structures, as well as through the fairly thorough-going replacement of part of its population (Wickham 2005: 306–10; see also Brugmann, this volume). Any role anthropology might play in providing insights into the period from the fifth century onwards is not through pointing out cases which are directly comparable or analogous, but rather through a more general stimulus to thought about societies unlike our own and the human or material forces that work to shape them. But the relationship is not one-way. Anglo-Saxon England has material to offer the anthropologist, extending the range of human societies to be understood, especially those in profound transition whereby identity, hierarchy, gender, religious belief, relations with landscapes and with objects, notions of power, law, and kinship were all thrown into doubt and reformulated.

I should make clear at the outset that I am not an anthropologist, but rather an archaeologist with a reasonable knowledge of a sister subject. My interest in anthropology arose from working in Papua New Guinea, first on archaeology of earlier periods, but then on issues of colonial change, which involved charting changes in settlement patterns, material culture, and shifts in cosmologies. Later

I worked in the Pitt Rivers Museums on the entangled history of museum collections and their role as historical and intellectual documents not only of the original makers and users of objects but of all people who have held and transacted them on their way to the museum, together with curators and conservators (Gosden and Larson 2007). Because of this nexus of interests in materials, relationships, identities, and colonial change and power I have been drawn to what is known as 'cultural' anthropology, in distinction to social anthropology. In some ways the two are now converging, but social anthropology has generally been interested in kinship and social relations, exchange, belief systems, forms of knowledge, and modes of representing the world. Social anthropology has been seen historically as a British approach to the subject, whereas cultural anthropology has more American roots. This branch of the discipline concentrates not only on social relations themselves, but on the cultural materials through which social relations are produced. Objects, houses, landscapes, art forms, and the human bodies that interact with these are the main subject matters of cultural anthropology, which is also more prone to a historical orientation than its social counterpart. Cultural anthropology and archaeology are allied through common interests in materials, landscapes, and bodies. Both also link into broader forms of cultural theory which are discussed below.

Complex historical currents run through the relations between archaeology and anthropology, particularly on both sides of the Atlantic. For much of the twentieth century in north America (cultural) anthropology, archaeology, physical anthropology, and linguistics came together in the broad field of anthropology charting the range, nature, and histories of human variety. The post-modernist turn hit cultural anthropology with more force than most areas of archaeology, which maintained a more processual, evolutionary framework. This difference in theory has led to tensions in many American departments, leading to new separate departments forming in places like Stanford.

In Britain, by contrast, post-modern and post-colonial thought has had a more equal impact on archaeology and anthropology. Some measure of agreement over theory created a rapprochement with the result that in Britain archaeology and anthropology are now close, being almost indistinguishable in their treatments of the last few hundred years. In branches of British archaeology where classics and history have been important elements, such as Roman and medieval archaeology, post-modern and post-colonial thought is less well known, so that links with anthropology and indeed with prehistoric archaeology have been fewer. In the pages that follow I shall give a brief and inevitably idiosyncratic account of elements of current anthropology which might be useful when studying early medieval archaeology, a subject to which I have always been attracted. I have mentioned my route into anthropology in order to make clear that my account here will focus on aspects of the discipline that I know about. My account is generally framed within the ambit of recent post-modernist theory and those with dispositions resistant to such approaches might find it best to look away now.

I shall focus on four areas key to contemporary anthropology which might prove to be useful if pursued further by Anglo-Saxonists. These include two broad orientations—relational thought and practice theory—as well as the two topic areas of materiality and identity. I won't dwell on topics such as gift exchange or kinship structures, which to some degree have already seen considerable discussion in the Anglo-Saxon literature (Hodges 1982; Wickham 2005). Underlying any anthropological attitude is a commitment to understanding, appreciating, and respecting difference. It is not just the past which is a foreign country, but other contemporary cultural forms represent terrains unfamiliar to Western commonsense and sensibility. Practices or ideas that at first sight seem exotic, odd, or dangerous—eating dead relatives or a belief that stones can move—are always part of a broader cultural logic which is more or less internally consistent, coherent, and able to sustain life in a healthy and practical manner. Many of our practices—including a veneration of pop, film, and sports stars or our ability to tolerate homelessness as a major condition of society—bear little real examination by the rational criteria we think we live by. To adopt an anthropological attitude requires a degree of unlearning, of questioning our own tacitly held commonsense views, which does not mean we can or should step out of our world-view. Rather, we have temporarily to suspend a belief in everything we take for granted, suspending disbelief in other ways of doing, thinking, and feeling. The sheer strangeness of an Anglo-Saxon world needs to be accepted and embraced.

I shall start with two broad dispositions to thought common in anthropology: relational thought and practice-based approaches.

Relational thought

Relational thought critiques essentialism, holding that there are no essential or core attributes to aspects of life, such as gender, class, or identity. Instead human life unfolds as a complex set of changing relations which are constantly giving new values to objects, people, and groups. In this view people do not have relationships; rather they are composed of relations. There is no self-sufficient or self-defined person who exists prior to relationships who can then enter into them, but we are shaped and formed by each new connection we enter into. We can get a sense of how far we are given an identity through relations from the fact that we are a slightly different person with our parents, our friends, or our children.

Relational thought stresses change, mutability, and instability. Lying behind these views as an ultimate inspiration is the work of the fiendishly difficult French writer, Gilles Deleuze, whose philosophy has emphasized the idea that life has no set or easily discerned directions working instead like a rhizome through the soil (Deleuze and Guattari 1988; 1994). Of more immediate influence is the equally difficult writing of the anthropologist, Marilyn Strathern, whose book *The Gender of the Gift* (1988) has had an immediate influence in a range of disciplines, including archaeology (see Strathern 1999 for a further development of her argument and Fowler 2004 for an explication of her ideas and an attempt to apply them in archaeology). When looking at Melanesia, principally Papua New Guinea, Strathern felt that gender was not a property which derived from biological sex, but rather that maleness or femaleness emerged from the situation. In this view, everyone has both male and female characteristics, so that the male characteristics of women or the female characteristics of men could be brought out in certain situations, and vice versa. This could happen at an overt symbolic level, when in certain male initiation rites men played a female part, or in a more generalized fashion through male nurturing of children and in the domestic sphere. In political leadership or war women played what might be seen as a male role, so that these heavily gendered societies were much more fluid beneath the surface.

Strathern's most infamous concept is that of the dividual (an idea deriving from Marriott 1976, working in India) where a biologically separate person can be seen not as socially separate, but as a divided element of a social whole. Dividuals share identities and social reactions with others, being parts of a broader entity rather than being genuinely separate. Extremely productive discussions resulting from Strathern's work have pointed out (LiPuma 1998) that rather than there being some societies which emphasize social linkages and the dividual, and others principally in the West in the last few centuries that privilege the individual, all societies swing between individual and dividual elements. Even in the heavily individualistic West there are moments when our reactions are identical to those of others—in the audience of a compelling film, for instance. But equally in Melanesia there are times, such as fronting a big exchange event or standing for parliament, when people pick themselves out from the mass. The analytical question then becomes: under which circumstances in a particular society do people become individuals and under which circumstances are they more immersed in the group? Such questions have considerable importance for an understanding of leadership, the nature of power, of gender and identity. Before considering briefly how these questions might be posed of Anglo-Saxon evidence, let us look at one other thinker whose relational approach has also been widely influential: Bruno Latour.

Latour's most famous concept or method (it is hard to know which) is actor-network-theory, which Latour (1993, 2005; Latour and Woolgar 1979) has at different times both proselytized for and disavowed. Latour stresses networks rather than Strathern's relations, but the effect is similar in emphasizing the changeable, flowing, and unpredictable nature of human life. Latour's subject matter differs from Strathern's and he is interested in science and technology, looking at how people and things together lead to conclusions about the way the world works. Latour criticizes the twin poles of science and technology studies around which arguments have been marshalled. On the one hand lies objectivism, which says that proper observations and experimental procedures will make it obvious how the world works. The world has a structure we work to comprehend. On the other hand is social constructivism which holds that all scientists and technicians work within social and cultural values which lead them to pick out certain aspects of the empirical world as salient, ignoring others. We create the world in thought and action according to social norms and conventions. Indeed, according to this view, the notions of science, experiment, objectivity, or technology are socially and historically recent, not self-evident procedures or attributes for understanding the world correctly. The dichotomy between objectivism and social constructivism is a false one, Latour argues. In real life we are able to live and work in the world in skilled ways observing how it works, but we are also children of our time and hold current cultural values which influence what we do and see.

At a larger intellectual scale Latour would like to do away with the distinctions between culture and nature. There is little in nature that has not been altered by people, and equally the observations and interventions we make in the world are socially directed and influenced. Rather than existing in a world divided between a realm of culture and of nature, human beings are entangled in a series of material and social networks, in which the material properties of things and people have complicated influences on how they relate socially and culturally. We have to take seriously the material properties of things, but equally the cultural directions of people. A key term for Latour is the assemblage, in which human societies are made up of houses, settlements, landscapes, artefacts, bodies, histories, values, and politics all jumbled up together and causing complex and multi-directional outcomes. As analysts our job is to trace through a complex network of people and things, together with their mutual influences. Ultimately everything will connect up with everything else, so that analysis involves a deliberate and somewhat arbitrary cutting of a network to pick out the things and connections of interest, leaving others out of consideration. Latour is interested in political forms and how political decisions are made, bringing both social and material matters of concern into account. He has commented on political bodies, especially the Icelandic *Thing* (or *Thingvellir*) in which the characteristics of place and of the social body were not clearly distinguished, a complication which was sometimes useful blurring in his view.

There are considerable overlaps in the thought of Strathern and Latour, with the former discussing the latter (Strathern 1999). The difference, at least in the earlier manifestations of Strathern's work, was her lack of stress on materials, something she came to emphasize later, partly as a result of a series of discussions she had with Alfred Gell, whose book, *Art and Agency* (1998) is important in its own right. In this book Gell was concerned with the anthropology of art, looking at how objects help create and give force to social relations. His key move was away from the question

'What does this mean?' to 'What does this do?'. His key examples were artefacts which could enchant, overwhelm, or undermine the will of people in their vicinity. One of the most famous of all anthropological case studies is that of the kula ring in the islands of the Massim province at the eastern tip of Papua New Guinea. Here people sail from one island group to another exchanging armshells and necklaces. An armshell can only be exchanged for a necklace, so that the former move clockwise and the latter anti-clockwise around the kula ring. People's prestige and social standing depend to some considerable degree on their ability to organize exchanges, with especially famous objects having names and biographies which then contribute to the fame of their temporary possessors. The exchange of these valuables helps produce and maintain systems of social relations which can then act as conduits for more utilitarian exchanges, for example of food.

Islanders travel in canoes with lavishly carved and painted decorations on their prows. These, Gell argues (1998: 68–72), have an important influence on exchanges. A truly accomplished carving can only be carried out by people who tap into the broader creative powers of the universe and is hence a signal of this larger power. Someone who is well-placed with divine and spiritual forces in one area of their lives, such as carving, is also likely to be difficult to resist in other areas, such as exchange. Intricately carved canoes can then change the conditions of exchange, making those who see them less likely to resist bargaining. A highly decorated canoe is not, in his view, just a backdrop to the exchange, but a key part of it, altering the attitudes various parties have about each other.

In some ways Gell's ideas parallel Latour's in that both focus on the mutual influences of people and things, with Gell sharpening the focus on the sensory, emotional, and hence social impacts that objects have. The enchantment that objects possess implies some form of agency on the part of things, where the effects of objects come from their formal qualities, decorations, and materials in ways that are over and above, or indeed different to, the intentions of their makers. If objects have qualities that do not derive solely from human intentions, coming from the object itself in some way, objects should perhaps be seen as agents, as active presences shaping and changing human actions. Gell slightly equivocated on this, calling objects 'secondary agents' refracting and bearing the primary agency of intentional humans. Others, such as the art historian W. J. T. Mitchell, go further in attributing agency to things, as shown by his famous title *What do Pictures Want?* (2005), a title I have reprised (Gosden 2005; see also Freedberg 1989 and Mitchell 1994 for more art-historical work exploring the power of objects and images; even closer to the Anglo-Saxon period is Zanker's 1988 consideration of Rome). Implicit in Latour's notion of a network charting the mutual influence of people and things is the influence that things may have in their own right, although as far as I know he has never highlighted the impacts of objects in terms of their agency.

Gell and Strathern's discussions (see Gell's essay 'Solving Strathernagrams', 1999) had a considerable influence on both. In her earlier formulations of the nature of relational personhood, Strathern included some consideration of objects but these tended to act as bearers of social relations. A key term for Strathern was 'partibility' by which she meant parts of persons that could be broken off and circulated socially. An axe, a string bag, or a pig containing the labour of one person or many can be passed from hand to hand in exchanges, both creating and paying off debts and obligations (Strathern 1988: ch. 8). Gift exchange is socially transformative partly because gifts are inalienable: they always bear a connection to, and the impact of, the maker and previous transactions of an object. A gift is part of a person circulating socially. Gift exchanges set up deep skeins of connection, linking all the individuals who have been party to transactions of one object. An object, the objectification of a person or group's labour, represented part of them circulating out in the world. This idea led to another for Strathern, the notion of distributed personhood. A person's influence, biography, and being are not all to be found located in or near their body, but circulate out in the world. If you are reading this now it is an aspect of my agency circulating out in the world, at a distance from me and largely out of my control. A relational person is a distributed person, whose being and influence flows through the world in multiple ways, at a distance from them and at a temporal remove too, continuing even after their death. Such a picture of what it means to be a person is extraordinarily complicating, but is realistic and necessitates complex modes of mapping and analysis.

Strathern did not at first highlight the form of objects, but Gell and others started to point out that the qualities of objects change social relations, so that the Trobriand canoe prow was not just a bearer of its author's agency, but became something of an agent in its own right. In the last two chapters of *Art and Agency*, Gell (1998) develops in parallel the old anthropological (and archaeological) concept of style and Strathern's view of distributed personhood. In cultures where strongly expressed styles are found (Gell uses the Marquesan islanders in eastern Polynesia as a prime example), the objects which circulate as parts of people have strong imperatives of their own, influenced by the canons of style. A newly made object, such as a Marquesan carving, is created through what Gell calls the 'principle of least difference' through a tiny modification of the style which makes it unique and different, but still allows it to stay well within the rules and forms of the style. Pushing these ideas to a polemical point, Gell talks about the 'inter-artefactual domain' (1998: 216) where objects influence each other, almost as if humans need to obey the rules set down by a panoply of existing objects, so that a craft worker can give their new object the right degree of similarity and of difference from others existing in the same style. What Gell refers to as 'the extended mind' (1998: ch. 9) is made up of the distributed agency of people and of objects simultaneously—people do not understand the world using purely mental apparatus, but through objects and the actions, emotions, and reactions surrounding objects.

There is more that can be said about human practical action and objects, the reader may now be dismayed to know, but before developing some of these ideas, let us pause to think of the possible implications of the foregoing discussion for Anglo-Saxon archaeology, using my privileged position as an outsider peeking in.

Relational thought and the Anglo-Saxons

The key intent behind relational thought is to destabilize existing categories of persons, things, and entities, showing in the process that there are other ways to think of social wholes and the smaller elements, groups and people, that make them up. The early world of the post-Roman period is one of great instability and change, perfect for the interests of a relational approach.

In comparison to other parts of the Western Empire, Britain shows very little continuity between the structures of the Roman and early medieval worlds. Esmonde Cleary (1989: 200) suggests there might have been a gap between the final evidence of Romano-British structures around AD 430–40 and the first phases of Anglo-Saxon settlement. This is perceptible in eastern England where the gap is least and likely to be longer further West. This breaks any formal continuity from one period to another, but also makes it less likely that Romano-British institutions and forms of economic organization persisted for long into the fifth century. Even when large-scale migration started the scale might not have been all that large—'the number of Anglo-Saxon migrants to Britain was probably of the order of tens of thousands, as against an indigenous population probably numbered in the millions' (Esmonde Cleary 1989: 204 and this volume). We are dealing with a situation through the whole of the fifth century and beyond where all the key elements of life—identity, language, kinship, exchange, attachment to land—were all up for grabs as people became first post-Romano-British and then Anglo-Saxon. If there was continuity it might have been at the level of the organization of the agricultural community and the relations deriving from that.

A premise of relational thought is that, as one aspect of relations changes, it has a ramifying effect through all others. Such a view helps nuance the opposed possibilities of continuity versus change. The rapid and total collapse of Romano-British institutions indicates how fundamentally these were predicated on broader connections to empire rather than to local conditions. A set of fluctuating and dynamic long-distance links and relations existed through the fourth century, with continual movement and changes as a norm. Once long-distance contacts were withdrawn many of the energies that sustained towns, villas, and the more impressive aspects of material culture went with them, leading to a solely agrarian society, which, in some areas, saw depopulation and abandonment of the land. The virtual disappearance of Latin and many elements of material culture would have had profound implications for power and identity, newly and briefly configured in a post-Roman, pre-Anglo-Saxon world, to take on new dimensions in the later fifth century.

The fascinating world from *c.* AD 350 to 650 was a period of continually shifting dynamisms, rather than one which can only be discussed in terms of continuity or change. Quite what the dynamisms were is a key question. The emerging view, convincing in many ways, is of institutional and elite change but of some basic structural continuity in terms of local kinship groups, land holding, and land use. A new picture which is emerging of the late Iron Age in Britain, prior to the Claudian invasion, is one of instability, population movements, and re-colonization of lightly populated areas. Rather than seeing the power centres in Britain that existed immediately prior to the Conquest as having grown up over some centuries, J. D. Hill (2007) has put forward the idea that many of the areas in which *oppida* grew up were only thinly populated prior to the first couple of decades AD. Rapid re-colonization then took place by people embracing newly Romanized forms of material, larger more-or-less urban settlements, and some form of kingship. In this view the late Iron Age emerges as a volatile, unstable world where large-scale population movements were possible. This is not a social universe in which long-term links to land provided the basis for enduring kinship groups inherent in many of our notions of peasant societies anywhere and in places like England in particular.

Pushing speculation to, and probably beyond, its limits we might see the 350 years of the Romano-British period as one where populations were maintained in an unusually stable state by a network of forts, towns, villas, and roads. Once these disappeared in the early fifth century volatility became again the norm, until held in check by new forms of manorial and parochial structures. Stable populations with fairly fixed boundaries and kinship structures that we start to see again from the later Anglo-Saxon period might be historically unusual, preceded by another unusual period in the form of Roman Britain. Without overarching structures of states and urban centres people did not stay fixed in all areas.

Following such a train of thought, the fifth to later seventh centuries look more like later prehistoric Britain with the added destabilizing factors of the withdrawal of Roman power and the influx of German speakers from across the North Sea. My picture of instability echoes the theory, with relational thought encouraging us to think in terms of change, flux, and a lack of essential qualities in identity.

Chemists make a distinction between a mixture and a reaction. In the former, two or more chemicals mix to form a new solution in a process which can be reversed, so that the original chemical components can be separated out. The formation of a reaction is irreversible, with the component chemicals coming together to form something new. The early Anglo-Saxon period has often, it seems to me, been seen as a mixture, with arguments over how much continuity can be seen from the fourth to the fifth centuries in cemeteries like Wasperton and Frilford, or individual burials with mixed materials like those at Dorchester-on-Thames (Meaney 1964; Hawkes 1986; Scheschkewitz 2006). Key questions have been how far (Romano-) British practices and deities carried on into the fifth century, under what sorts of circumstances, and with what consequences? This assumes some fixity to (Romano-) British identity, given to it above all by the continuing use of older objects. But if we start from the opposite assumption, that identity has always been in a state of flux due to its relational nature, then new sets of relations will change the nature and direction of the flux, not move from one set of stable relations to another. Fifth- and sixth-century Britain, at least in the south and east, changed from being embedded within the Roman Empire (itself a far from static entity) to being orientated towards North Sea links. This brought about complex and irreversible changes, such that one could neither entirely separate out the (Romano-) British and Anglo-Saxon components nor reverse the process. Continuity as against basic change in post-Roman Britain appears a false dichotomy, as change occurs throughout. Looking for the nature of new relations, their consequences and dynamics is more productive in the transition from one form of state power to another. We should also bear in mind that we cannot take for granted the nature of individuals and groups, as Strathern and others have pointed out: the conditions of the modern possessive individualist are historically unusual, growing up in the last few centuries, as are the groups that support our hyper-individual state. Documents deriving from a newly stabilizing world in the seventh century may well be a misleading guide to groups and ownership 150 years earlier.

Relational thought lying behind much modern anthropology is often known as deconstructive. We need to be aware that ideas of person, property, and group which make sense to us may prove misleading when looking at other worlds, especially those undergoing massive and rapid change.

Anthropologies of practice and materiality

There are further dominant strands in anthropology, separable but not truly separate from relational approaches, which are of considerable interest to archaeologists.

Anthropologies of practice focus on everyday, habitual, unthought actions which are culturally learned, but so deeply ingrained in us that they are invisible. Much of this approach goes back to a short, brilliant essay by Marcel Mauss (1979) on the techniques of the body (Mauss being better known amongst archaeologists for his book *The Gift*, 1969). Mauss asks a series of beguilingly simple questions: Why do Americans walk differently to French people? Why do armies vary in their marching styles? Why did French and British soldiers find it hard to use each other's tools when digging trenches in the First World War? His answer was not that people were anatomically different, but that they had learned to use their bodies in a variety of ways in tune with culturally developed norms of action. Different walking styles were not symbolic or subject to direct interpretation in terms of meaning, but they did provide the basis for cultural differences and these were generally learned in an informal way in the first few years of life. Mauss appropriated the term 'habitus' to designate structures of habit arising in various cultures, which are learned but invisible to an insider because they are so deeply taken for granted. The term habitus was taken up by the sociologist and anthropologist Pierre Bourdieu to form the basis of his anthropology of practice. Bourdieu argued (in infamously complex prose) that anthropology and other disciplines had ignored everyday life and its forms in favour of an analysis of symbolism, meaning, exchange, and kinship structures. Bourdieu did not argue that such issues should be ignored, but rather that they could not be understood fully without taking everyday forms of cultural action into account. Habitus is something that we are, not something that we know, but such non-discursive aspects of life (non-discursive because they are so deeply taken for granted we find it hard to put them into words) form the basis for conscious, verbal knowledge of the world.

Habitus derives not from the body alone, but from the body in its material settings and this is where theories of practice become interesting to the archaeologist. In a famous exposition of the Kabyle house (the Kabyle are a Berber people living in the highlands of north-eastern Algeria) Bourdieu (1990: Appendix) looked at how patterns of activity around the house in food preparation and cooking, weaving, stabling and feeding animals underlay gender distinctions and a host of positive and negative associations key to Kabyle cosmology. Bourdieu showed how the rectangular form of the house, the passage of light and dark within it in the course of the day, and the position of fixed or movable objects within the house were linked to social roles and relations, as well as the values attached to these. Bourdieu's approach has been so widely imitated that some of its force is lost (see Parker Pearson 1990 for an Iron Age example) and was conceived within a series of structuralist oppositions (light:dark, good:evil, etc.) which many now see as mechanistic, including Bourdieu himself in later life. Nevertheless, he showed in this and other works how a distinction between the everyday and the intellectual or symbolic realms is false, with even the most practical of actions being the source for broader social values. There is great possibility here for the archaeologist looking at house plans, settlement layouts, or the landscape as a whole (see Hamerow, this volume).

Bourdieu's work on the house has helped maintain a strand of research on so-called 'house societies' in which the house acts as the centre of the domestic social group. Revising Claude Lévi-Strauss's idea that the noble houses of medieval Europe were part of a much broader physical, social, and symbolic phenomenon, Janet Carsten and Stephen Hugh-Jones (1995) look at house societies in South-East Asia and South America to explore the mixture of the physical structure, levels of production and consumption, as well as political factions that make up house societies. In a subsequent work, Carsten (2000) revisited the central anthropological issue of kinship, using both relational and practice-based approaches. Utilizing the latter, she showed that kinship and genealogy were often a gloss given to people who worked together closely, so that patterns of practice helped influence to whom people felt most closely related and which relations were emphasized over others. Along the way, she and her contributors throw doubt on the separate nature of the biological and social aspects of kinship, part of a broader critique of distinctions between culture and nature to which I will return.

Influences emanating from Bourdieu feed into a general interest in material culture which has grown over the last twenty years, an interest which arises from thinking about how practices are inculcated into human bodies partly through the objects that surround people and help channel action. One area of especial influence is through the work of Catherine Bell (1992; 1997) on ritual. There is a fair bit of fruitless discussion about how far ritual is a separate category of human activity. Bell tries to sidestep these problems of definition by looking not at ritual, but ritualization. Ritualization looks at general patterns of practice to see which are formalized in some way—such formalization is equivalent to the process of ritualization. Rituals concerning birth, marriage, death, intercession with the gods, and so on are important subjects of study in their own right, but are even more important as diagnostics of the cultural process more broadly. If people put time, effort, and materials into formalizing and ritualizing some element of their lives it must be because this aspect is a key element in the way they live.

Bell and others make a useful distinction between performative and prescriptive rituals. In the former case the key question is 'did it work?'; in the latter the issue is 'did we do it right?'. Performative rituals aim to ensure a particular result—to conjure spirits to aid one community or harm another; to ensure fertility of people, animals, and crops; or to avert looming disaster. Prescriptive rituals need to be carried out in accordance with liturgy or other rules and have a general effect of confirming human or cosmological order, rather than being aimed at a definite result. The re-emergence of Christianity in England in the seventh century could have seen a greater emphasis on prescriptive ritual through the medium of Christian worship, although this did not mean performative rituals died away (see e.g. Hamerow 2006). The ritual landscape suddenly became more complex and variegated.

All practice-based approaches emphasize the actions of the human body, as carried out in the first few years of life, making childhood and early forms of socialization (and perhaps 'culturization') important topics of study. An interest in the body leads directly to material culture. Bourdieu's work has been an important influence on the resurgence of material culture studies since the 1980s. Many intellectual routes have led to the interactions between bodies and objects, a key statement being Arjun Appadurai's (1986) edited volume *The Social Life of Things*, in which Appadurai emphasized that aspects of life like gift or commodity exchange could not be understood without taking seriously the material and formal qualities of the items exchanged. In the same volume, Igor Kopytoff developed the idea that objects could have biographies in similar ways to people, so that the stages and changes objects have gone through are key to their present significance (Gosden and Marshall 1999 develop an archaeological approach to biography). An old item of gift exchange, such as a necklace or armshell of the Kula ring in Papua New Guinea, has its own name which is then connected to the names of all the people who have transacted the item. Human biographies and object biographies are mutually influential, with the values attached to people and to things linked (Munn 1986; Hoskins 1998).

A further key influence on material culture studies is the anthropology of art, which takes issues of colour, form, complexity, and skill seriously in looking at how objects influence people and their social relations. Earlier post-war manifestations of the anthropology of art developed within a concern for meaning, itself part of a broader symbolic or structuralistic approach. Danny Miller (1987) and others have argued that only language is truly meaningful and that objects cannot be read as texts, but should be seen rather as having more general sensory and emotional effects. An intermediate position between those emphasizing the symbolism or meaning of objects and those emphasizing the physicality of things is developed by Howard Morphy (1991) who looks at systems of knowledge in Australian aboriginal communities and how those are supported by paintings. These have aesthetic effects, but also specific symbolism acting as prompts to stories concerning ancestors and present-day spirits, focusing on how humans should best act towards them.

Another strand in the intertwined set of approaches to material things might be called ecological, developed most forcefully by Tim Ingold (2000). Ingold, like many others, has been influenced by the ideas of the psychologist J. J. Gibson who put forward what he called an ecological approach to perception. The basic idea is that humans only rarely perceive the world from a static position, but more usually perceive and know the world through processes of action. Gibson's ideas parallel Bourdieu's to some extent in taking the active, intentional subject as the basic human condition, with the material world showing up not in a valueless or objective manner but as a series of landscapes and things potentially of use for human purposes. What is important about people is not their genetic inheritance or the inherent characteristics of their bodies but the total set of relations within which they develop, be these environmental or social relations. Indeed, Ingold refuses to make any distinction between the environmental/natural on the one hand and the social or cultural on the other, going back to a point touched on above.

The material world of plants, animals, and even the features of the landscape have been profoundly altered by people so as not to be easily seen as natural. People growing up in a rainforest, desert, or temperate western European landscape become cultural beings through developing skills of making, using, and appreciating objects in ways influenced by what is available to them. To say where culture stops and nature starts is pointless because it is impossible. Furthermore, many cultures do not distinguish between culture and nature, a distinction key to Western thought but few others (see Descola 1994). The distinctions we make, for instance, between what is animate (living things) and what not (landscape features, metals, clay, etc.) is relatively unusual whereas animism, which holds that rocks can move or animals behave like persons under certain circumstances, is common. Practices that we call magical, using spells, incantations, or physical interventions, can be seen to be effective in many cosmologies constructed around a less mechanistic universe than our own. Quite what Anglo-Saxon conceptions of cause, effect, and magic were is hinted at in texts such as *Beowulf*, but could be explored more fully by archaeologists.

Ingold has become a fierce and insightful critic of an emerging orthodoxy, around the new term materiality. This is surprising in some ways as the notion of materiality designates an approach close to Ingold's own, stressing the active aspects of material things in shaping human reactions and interactions (Ingold 2007). Most important to me is the idea that materials are active presences in human lives, with different material worlds helping to produce different human beings. People have intents and purposes, but material things provide them with a sense of the possible or desirable, and sometimes send their actions off in unexpected directions (Gosden 2008). Material engagement (Malafouris 2004; Renfrew 2007) helps focus attention on the human senses and the emotions, which give content, direction, and values to human life in particular cultural contexts.

Ideas around material culture form a fertile and fast-developing area of debate, sketched here briefly. How relevant are these ideas to the study of the Anglo-Saxons?

Material cultures of the Anglo-Saxons

In the period following Britain's incorporation into the Roman Empire, peoples' senses, bodily habits, aesthetic values, and social relations were radically recalibrated or newly attuned. The linear took over from the circular or irregular in roads, town layouts, and domestic interiors. Interior space became lighter through lamps and windows, with light reflecting from glass and the glossy surfaces of pots, and illuminating new colours in pottery, jewellery, and dress. These changes were most keenly felt in elite contexts, but had some impact throughout society. These changes were reversed after AD 410, with the decline of so-called 'carpentered' environments. The fifty year period after AD 410 saw one of the most massive changes in material circumstances in British prehistory or history. The mass production of pottery, metal, brick, and tile fell away rapidly as money supply through markets and taxation ceased. Agriculture was aimed more at meeting subsistence needs than at producing surpluses to underpin high levels of production or impressive modes of display. It is certainly true that a child born in AD 390 would have been habituated into a very different world to a grandchild born in AD 430, and the notion of habitus might help us understand the social and individual effects of new interior spaces and less highly coloured material culture.

The object world requires of us at least two sets of skills. The skills of making (e.g. Leahy 2003; and this volume) saw a shift, for instance, from (often crude) handmade pots in the early Anglo-Saxon period to wheel-turned, high-fired wares from the eighth century. Much less discussed, but ultimately more important, are the skills of use and discrimination which can judge colour, texture, form, or purpose, assigning to them social value. New materials and styles of objects required changed forms of bodily action or sensory appreciation. Bodily responses to the material world around us become elements of what we are, rather than aspects of what we know, to paraphrase Bourdieu. A different set of responses and actions would make us different people, so that daily interactions with things become a profound element of our identity. The regionalization of pottery and dress styles (see Owen-Crocker, this volume) in sixth-century Anglo-Saxon England may demonstrate varieties of identity, all fast-changing and malleable. This period saw radical changes in the shift from Roman forms and styles, but also localized variations complicating broader patterns. A combination of practice-based approaches stemming from Bourdieu coupled with more recent ideas on materiality and the requirements things place on us has a lot to offer in grasping the complexity of change.

As already emphasized, artefacts should not be understood purely through a political–economic paradigm, emphasizing structures of production and exchange, but also as contributing to the constitution of persons (Bazelmans 1998). Jos Bazelmans draws on theory from Mauss and Strathern to consider how early medieval leaders and followers were made as social beings through the giving or the receiving of horses, weapons, rings, and bodily adornments. Such giving and receiving also links into broader conceptions of power and its ultimate root in cosmological considerations, designating the generative powers of the universe (ibid.: 468–9). In poems such as *Beowulf*, artefacts and actions are linked, so that the possession of weapons or personal ornament is only truly socially effective if used in the right style or with requisite bravery. Right action is in turn concerned with battles between good and evil or the effective actions for maintaining the solidarity of the group.

Such views outlining how things help constitute people are extremely useful as a more general analytical stance when thinking through the richness and changing nature of material culture from the fifth century onwards. As Tania Dickinson (1991) points out, from the late fifth century onwards there is a proliferation of brooch types in Britain which ultimately derive from the Continent, but which are given new details of form and material. Her careful study of saucer brooches shows some of the complexity of the movements and changes. The example of the five-spiral brooch has an ornament stemming from late Roman male belt assemblages. Some of these belts were deposited in German graves beyond the boundaries of the Empire. The five-spiral design then moved from male belts to female saucer brooches. Dickinson (1991: 62) sees this move as men displaying their status through women, but this is to ignore both the possibilities of female appropriation of the ornament and the importance of the statement made by having a formerly male ornament deployed in a female realm. Parenthetically it would be interesting to trace this ornament back through the Roman world, with the possibility existing that it might derive from so-called Celtic art, making for an even greater depth of transformation.

Saucer brooches were then introduced into Britain, where ornament from the late Roman world might have taken on new significance within the former Empire. They became most common in central England where incomers would have been in obvious contact with the former Roman authorities and the indigenous population. Five-spiral saucer brooches have variable associations with other classes of artefacts, such as toilet equipment and bronze (but not iron) belt buckles. It is not quite clear what these artefactual relationships indicate, but they are part of complex means of creating differences in gender, identity, and status, which are themselves interlinked categories. Additional complexities can be added through burials such as those from Dyke Hills in Dorchester, which appear to combine late Roman and Germanic artefacts (Blair 1994: 5).

We can potentially follow chains of artefacts, linked by motif and material across much of western Europe and from the late Roman period onwards. These are likely to lead us to conclusions not about simple migrations of peoples or other groups, but about tangled sets of connections and of transformations. Scholars of the early Anglo-Saxon period have been obsessed with issues of identity—who moved into Britain from the fifth century onwards, where did they come from, how far did they form discrete groups and how did these groups influence later political and ethnic identities? Such questions and approaches have been much questioned and critiqued (e.g. Moreland 2000), but little coherent has been put in place of a broadly migrationist perspective. Following artefacts and their transformations will provide a useful corrective to any simple models of movement or stasis of populations, issues which are complicated by considerable change through time. For instance, detailed studies such as Nick Stoodley's (1999) and Sam Lucy's (1998) have shown from an analysis of grave goods that a masculine kit of weaponry was found in burials from the fifth century, at a time when male graves outnumbered female ones. The feminine assemblage of ornaments emerged more slowly through the sixth century, by which time women were buried with more material than men. But in the late sixth and early seventh centuries this pattern was reformed as fewer people were buried with any sort of grave goods and women were buried with artefacts that seem to indicate more definite roles (Stoodley 1999). This might indicate first a less well-defined form of femininity followed by a period when women became key to newly established kindreds in the sixth century (Dickinson 2002: 84). Means of constituting persons were not always clear or unambiguous, although they do show interesting trends.

Artefacts, landscapes, and settlements were not only tied up with the constitution of persons but also with the constitution of the cosmos. The scientific divisions of the world into physics, chemistry, and biology did not exist for Anglo-Saxons. What we often call magic held a position structurally equivalent to what we call science, concerned as it was with cause and effect and human beings' abilities to influence this. People had a fine and effective appreciation of how to work with clay, wood, wool, or metal, but such appreciation often blurs the distinctions between people and things, what was animate and what not, with spirits taking the place of our forces and dangers coming from ghosts and monsters, not just the fierce heat of the forge or pottery kiln. *Beowulf* provides a wonderful window onto this world, where halls and swords had names and ancient spirits could be evoked at 'pagan shrines' to help save them from Grendel, a demon envious of the feasting and gold in the hall named Heorot. Alchemical traditions known from later medieval and early modern periods may well have their roots in this world, so that what we call magic was integral to the making, use, and abuse of things. The warnings of Ingold and others that we cannot always divide culture from nature, so that ideas of animism and totemism might be appropriate, are potentially useful here. The sheer foreignness of many elements of the Anglo-Saxon world needs accepting and emphasizing, rather than simply feeling that this was a world in which language, institutions, and identity are directly ancestral to our own and therefore accessible to us. Hamerow's (2006) article on special deposits starts to show how people used the bodies of animals or people, together with material culture, to play with issues of fertility, protection, and procreation. There is obviously much more to be gained in pursuing these topics which take us to the heart of how different life was then compared to now.

FINAL THOUGHTS

There is much from contemporary anthropology that I have not considered here, for instance discussions of globalization, because they are less relevant to understanding the Anglo-Saxons, but in other cases, such as considerations of memory and history, because they have already been brought into analyses of Anglo-Saxon material (Semple 1998; Williams 2006). Contemporary anthropology can be difficult because of the language used, but also because it is trying to deal with difference, challenging and undermining our preconceptions of how the world works.

Relational thought is usually deployed in situations which are stable. The Anglo-Saxon situation was anything but and was one in which identity, gender, sexuality, and hierarchy must have changed rapidly. However, relational thought could be modified to help gain an understanding of rapid change. Few periods exemplify quite such massive changes as the early Anglo-Saxon one, and there is a clear affinity between this difficult body of theory and the evidence from the first few centuries of post-Roman Britain. Later sets of relations of course keep changing, but within more prescribed limits as state forms and their attendant hierarchies reassert themselves.

Bourdieu's notion of habitus might provide an analytical anchor here, calling for a detailed understanding of the practices carried out in domestic space or the landscape more generally and the sets of cultural values they help create. Ideas of materiality have an ultimate root in work like that of Bourdieu, but focusing more fully than he did on the material requirements objects have of the human body. Here archaeological evidence can come more fully into its own, working at a variety of scales, from that of individual objects to their use and deployment in physical settings, to explore the sensory and emotional worlds of the past. It is hard to think about social relations without focusing on the content given to these relations by our senses and emotions. Ideas such as Gell's notion of the technology of enchantment are especially powerful when considering a rather dull sensory world of browns and greys, thrown into relief by splashes of colour from jewellery, textiles, and wall painting or the intricacies of pattern on early Anglo-Saxon burial urns. Such items and the actions that surrounded them would have been powerful in exciting strong reactions and analytically vital in providing us with pointers to social and cultural hot spots.

The process of entering the Roman Empire and of coping with its fall may have interesting parallels. In both cases, we may be dealing with fluid sets of relations within Britain, with mobile populations, as well as connections across the Channel. In both the late Iron Age and Anglo-Saxon periods people made use of Roman material culture in ways that transformed it. The use of materials from a new and expanding empire in the first centuries BC and AD had a very different set of resonances from that which occurred after its end. But there might be some surprising similarities, such as the proliferation of forms of personal ornament in the first century BC and the fifth century AD, in periods where identity was being reformulated. In both periods too, people made links to the prehistoric past a marked trait—notably by means of burials around Bronze Age barrows—as if to create an anchor in times of massive change.

The theory I have sketched here leads to an emphasis on instability, fluidity, and transformation, so that we should be aware of seeing the world as theory leads us to. We also need to acknowledge, however, that an older paradigm which assumed populations were stable as a norm and moved exceptionally had its own, rather conservative biases. We might indeed be inclined to reverse these assumptions—late prehistoric populations and relations may well have been unstable, as Hill (2007) has emphasized, with new areas colonized in the late Iron Age. In southern Britain this instability was held in check after AD 43 by imperial forms of governance and control, again to be released after AD 410. This ushered in several centuries of unstable connections, which were gradually damped down again with new state forms of control from the eighth century onwards to produce a high medieval world which became the epitome for later scholars of insularity, and of a peasantry weighed down by feudal and ecclesiastical relations. This image, in itself clichéd, is unhelpful when cast back into earlier periods. The small-scale societies we are dealing with may have had latitude to reformulate connections and identities relatively rapidly and easily. The stability seen in the Roman period is quite unusual when viewed from the long-term perspective of prehistory. The Roman world offered a set of cultural resources people could draw on to reformulate their identities both before and after incorporation into the Empire. Quite how these resources were used and combined with other areas of life is a rich area of study.

What it means to be a modern Westerner has developed over the last few centuries. An important element of a developing self-image has been a conscious contrast with the Roman and medieval past. Indeed the notion of modernity has come about due to a Renaissance-inspired break from a hidebound, superstitious medieval past. Archaeology and anthropology are important, if small, outgrowths of modernity, which solidified the idea of the modern in contrast to the primitive. The othering of our ancestral selves from the prehistoric, Roman, and medieval worlds was a means by which people are made more contentious and less stable. A less solid and stolid version of the past will make the modern look less energetic, mobile, and inventive. Transformations of views about the Anglo-Saxon period are well under way. It is important to embrace current theory to engage in broader and more contemporary sets of debates. But theory can be even more useful to crack apart some of the more basic models of identity, productivity, and relationship that have been applied to the Anglo-Saxon world, allowing the incredibly rich data to be seen in new ways. Ideas current in the social sciences, including anthropology, can be of use in this endeavour.

Acknowledgements

I am grateful to Helena Hamerow for asking me to write this chapter, although readers might not share this feeling. Judy East typed the manuscript and helped in other ways.

References

Appadurai, A. (ed.) (1986). *The Social Life of Things: Commodities in Cultural Perspective.* Cambridge: Cambridge University Press.

Bazelmans, J. (1998). 'Geschenke', in H. Beck, H. Steuer, and D. Timpe (eds.), *Reallexikon der Germanischen Altertumskunde.* Berlin: Walter de Gruyter, 466–70.

Bell, C. (1992). *Ritual Theory, Ritual Practice.* Oxford: Oxford University Press.

——(1997). *Ritual: Perspectives and Dimensions.* Oxford: Oxford University Press.

Blair, J. (1994). *Anglo-Saxon Oxfordshire.* Stroud: Sutton Publishing.

Bourdieu, P. (1990). *The Logic of Practice.* Cambridge: Polity.

Carsten, J. (ed.) (2000). *Cultures of Relatedness: New Approaches to the Study of Kinship.* Cambridge: Cambridge University Press.

——and S. Hugh-Jones (eds.) (1995). *About the House: Lévi-Strauss and Beyond.* Cambridge: Cambridge University Press.

Deleuze, G., and Guattari, F. (1988). *A Thousand Plateaus: Capitalism and Schizophrenia.* London: Athlone Press.

————(1994). *What is Philosophy?* London: Verso.

Descola, P. (1994). *In the Society of Nature: A Native Ecology in Amazonia.* Cambridge: Cambridge University Press.

Dickinson, T. (1991). 'Material culture as social expression: the case of Saxon Saucer Brooches with running spiral decoration'. *Studien zur Sachsenforschung* 7: 39–70.

——(2002). 'Review article: What's new in early Medieval burial archaeology?' *Early Medieval Europe* 11: 71–87.

Esmonde Cleary, A. S. (1989). *The Ending of Roman Britain.* London: Routledge.

Fowler, C. (2004). *The Archaeology of Personhood: An Anthropological Approach.* London: Routledge.

Freedberg, D. (1989). *The Power of Images: Studies in the History and Theory of Response.* Chicago: University of Chicago Press.

Gell, A. (1998). *Art and Agency: An Anthropological Theory.* Oxford: Clarendon Press.

——(1999). *The Art of Anthropology: Essays and Diagrams.* London: Athlone Press.

Gosden, C. (2005). 'What do objects want?' *Journal of Archaeological Method and Theory* 12: 193–211.

——(2008). 'Social ontologies'. *Philosophical Transactions of the Royal Society B* 363: 2003–10.

——and Larson, F. (2007). *Knowing Things: Exploring the collections of the Pitt Rivers Museum 1884–1945.* Oxford: Oxford University Press.

——and Marshall, Y. (1999). 'The cultural biography of objects'. *World Archaeology* 31: 169–78.

HAMEROW, H. (2006). 'Special deposits in Anglo-Saxon settlements'. *Medieval Archaeology* 50: 1–30.

HAWKES, S. (1986). 'The Early Anglo-Saxon period', in G. Briggs, J. Cook, and T. Rowley (eds.), *The Archaeology of the Oxford Region*. Oxford: Oxford University Department of Educational Studies, 64–108.

HILL, J. D. (2007). 'The dynamics of social change in Later Iron Age eastern and south-eastern England *c.* 300 BC–AD 43', in C. Haselgrove and T. Moore (eds.), *The Later Iron Age in Britain and Beyond*. Oxford: Oxbow Books, 16–40.

HODGES, R. (1982). *Dark Age Economics: The Origins of Towns and Trade A.D. 600–1000*. London: Duckworth.

HOSKINS, J. (1998). *Biographical Objects: How Things Tell Us the Stories of People's Lives*. London: Routledge.

INGOLD, T. (2000). *The Perception of the Environment: Essays in Livelihood, Dwelling and Skill*. London: Routledge.

—— (2007). 'Materials against materiality'. *Archaeological Dialogues* 14: 1–16.

LATOUR, B. (1993). *We Have Never Been Modern*. London: Prentice Hall.

—— (2005). *Reassembling the Social: An Introduction to Actor-Network-Theory*. Oxford: Oxford University Press.

—— and S. WOOLGAR. (1979). *Laboratory Life: The Construction of Scientific Facts*. Beverly Hills, CA: Sage Publications.

LEAHY, K. (2003). *Anglo-Saxon Crafts*. Stroud: Tempus.

LIPUMA, E. (1998). 'Modernity of forms of personhood in Melanesia', in M. Lambek and A. Strathern (eds.), *Bodies and Persons: Comparative Perspectives from Africa and Melanesia*. Cambridge: Cambridge University Press, 53–79.

LUCY, S. (1998). *The Early Anglo-Saxon Cemeteries of East Yorkshire: An Analysis and Reinterpretation*. British Archaeological Reports British Series 289. Oxford: Archaeopress.

MALAFOURIS, L. (2004). 'The cognitive basis of material engagement: where brain, body and culture conflate', in E. DeMarrais, C. Gosden, and C. Renfrew (eds.), *Rethinking Materiality: The Engagement of Mind with the Material World*. Cambridge: The McDonald Institute for Archaeological Research, 289–302.

MARRIOTT, M. (1976). 'Hindu transactions: diversity without dualism', in B. Kapferer (ed.) *Transaction and Meaning*. Philadelphia: ISHI Publications, 109–42.

MAUSS, M. (1969). *The Gift: Forms and Functions of Exchange in Archaic Societies*. London: Routledge and Kegan Paul.

—— (1979). *Sociology and Psychology: Essays*. London: Routledge and Kegan Paul.

MEANEY, A. (1964). *A Gazetteer of Early Anglo-Saxon Burial Sites*. London: Allen and Unwin.

MILLER, D. (1987). *Material Culture and Mass Consumption*. Oxford: Basil Blackwell.

MITCHELL, W. J. T. (1994). *Picture Theory: Essays on Verbal and Visual Representation*. Chicago: University of Chicago Press.

—— (2005). *What Do Pictures Want? The Loves and Lives of Images*. Chicago: University of Chicago Press.

MORELAND, J. (2000). 'Ethnicity, power and the English', in W. Frazer and A. Tyrrell (eds.), *Social Identity in Early Medieval Britain*. London: University of Leicester Press, 23–52.

MORPHY, H. (1991). *Ancestral Connections: Art and an Aboriginal System of Knowledge*. Chicago: Chicago University Press.

Munn, N. (1986). *The Fame of Gawa: A Symbolic Study of Value Transformation in a Massim (Papua New Guinea) Society.* Cambridge: Cambridge University Press.

Parker Pearson, M. (1990). 'Food, sex and death: cosmologies in the British Iron Age with particular reference to east Yorkshire'. *Cambridge Archaeological Journal* 9: 43–69.

Renfrew, C. (2007). *Prehistory: The Making of the Human Mind.* London: Weidenfeld and Nicholson.

Scheschkewitz, J. (2006). *Das spätrömische und angelsächsische Gräberfeld von Wasperton, Warwickshire.* Bonn: Habelt.

Semple, S.J. (1998). 'A fear of the past: the place of the prehistoric burial mound in the ideology of middle and later Anglo-Saxon England'. *World Archaeology* 30: 109–26.

Stoodley, N. (1999). *The Spindle and the Spear: A Critical Enquiry into the Construction and Meaning of Gender in the Early Anglo-Saxon Burial Rite.* British Archaeological Reports British Series 288. Oxford: Archaeopress.

Strathern, M. (1988). *The Gender of the Gift: Problems with Women and Problems with Society in Melanesia.* Berkeley: University of California Press.

——(1999). *Property, Substance and Effect: Anthropological Essays on Persons and Things.* London: Athlone.

Wickham, C. (2005). *Framing the Middle Ages: Europe and the Mediterranean 400–800.* Oxford: Oxford University Press.

Williams, H. (2006). *Death and Memory in Early Medieval Britain.* Cambridge: Cambridge University Press.

Zanker, P. (1988). *The Power of Images in the Age of Augustus.* Ann Arbor: University of Michigan Press.

CHAPTER 52

ANGLO-SAXON ARCHAEOLOGY AND THE PUBLIC

SONJA MARZINZIK

There is today a new and wider audience for archaeology—including Anglo-Saxon archaeology—than ever before thanks to television, re-enactment societies, and metal-detecting. This survey highlights certain aspects of the dynamic relationship between Anglo-Saxon archaeology and this wider public and focuses in particular on the question of whether formal education has kept pace with these new developments. Historical overviews of antiquarians and later historians and archaeologists interested in Anglo-Saxon archaeology, their interpretations, and the reception of their findings have been published elsewhere (e.g. Hills 2003, esp. 35–8; H. Williams 2006: 6; MacGregor 2007, 30–2) and will therefore not be discussed here.[1]

EDUCATION

Primary and secondary education

The introduction of the National Curriculum in 1988 brought about a unified approach to the teaching of history at school level in England and Wales. Archaeology was embedded within particular study units such as Ancient Greece and was

---

[1] This article was submitted in January 2008. Developments that took place afterwards could not be integrated and only minor revisions were possible after submission (cf. note 7).

available as a separate subject at GCSE and A-level. The teaching of history became less focused on imparting knowledge of dates and events, and more on fostering transferable skills (Cooper 2000: 34) and archaeology was seen as an ideal vehicle to help achieve this goal (cf. Corbishley and Stone 1994: 394).

Key Stage 2, i.e. seven- to eleven-year-old school children, is where Anglo-Saxon archaeology comes into play. Within the framework of British History, the impact on society of movement and settlement of different peoples prior to the Norman Conquest is examined.

The Anglo-Saxons are one of three detailed case studies from which teachers can choose to address the question why 'people [have] invaded and settled Britain in the past' (QCA 2007). Archaeology and artefacts, as well as their use in gathering information, are used to convey an understanding of migration to Britain, both past and present, and of the impact of the Anglo-Saxon arrival. Factual knowledge about early medieval England and archaeology in general, in addition to transferable skills such as carrying out research and using 'terminology appropriate to the period', are further goals of this course unit. Suggested teaching activities include depictions of Anglo-Saxon life, scenes that should be sorted 'into invasion and settlement groupings', and the compilation of dictionary definitions of the terms 'invade' and 'settle' (QCA 2007). The implicit scenario of organized, large-scale military movements is alarming, as is the false dichotomy drawn up between 'invaders' and 'settlers'. It appears that academic debate, which long ago moved on to other models to understand the *adventus saxonum*, has not penetrated the twenty-first-century classroom.

This might partly be a reflection of what teachers and those designing the curriculum themselves were taught at school, but it also reflects the need for a straightforward, comprehensible narrative which can be used to illustrate points, not only about the past, but also about current debates (Hills 2003: 37f., 110–13).

Conversely, information packs for teachers, such as those provided by the British Museum or the Ashmolean Museum's 'Anglo-Saxon Discovery' online quiz aimed at school children are developed by educators and curators and are one way of sharing current knowledge and debates with people outside the academic community (http://anglosaxondiscovery.ashmolean.org/teachers_resources/quizzes.html).

The Anglo-Saxons and their archaeology do not play a major role at either GCSE or AS/A-Level. Of the three exam boards setting GCSEs for England, namely AQA, Edexcel, and OCR, only the latter two include the Anglo-Saxons at all. Both offer an optional unit on Anglo-Saxon versus Norman law within their Schools History Projects for History GCSEs (Edexcel 2007; OCR 2007). For the final two years of school education, both AQA and OCR's AS and A-Level specifications include the Norman Conquest and the transition from Anglo-Saxon to Norman England, while the earliest option that Edexcel offers is the Tudors (AQA 2007a; OCR 2007; Edexcel 2007).

Where Anglo-Saxon archaeology is likely to feature most prominently is the A-Level in Archaeology, offered by AQA, England's largest exam board, even though the Anglo-Saxons are not mentioned at all in the fifty-seven-page specifications. Students taking the exam are expected to be familiar with archaeological methods and theory. These, as well as the modules on 'Settlement and Social Organization' and 'Material Culture, Technology and Economics' may all be taught and illustrated with both British and foreign examples of the teacher's choice. The personal study candidates have to conduct should normally be based on 'their local environment' (AQA 2007b: 25). There is therefore ample scope to introduce the Anglo-Saxons, although teachers and candidates may of course choose other periods as their focus.

To summarize, Anglo-Saxon archaeology has a low profile on the Curriculum, compared to, for example, the Romans or modern history. Even the A-Level in archaeology does not explicitly refer to it. In general, much depends on the interests and initiative of teachers as well as on the individual local setting and its archaeology. One question that arises here is whether this low profile has an influence on sparking an interest in the subject in students from economically deprived backgrounds and ethnic minorities. Both groups are traditionally under-represented, for instance, among museum professionals.

Higher and Continuing Education

As is to be expected with the specialization that university degrees represent, Anglo-Saxon archaeology features more prominently in the higher education sector. HEFCE (Higher Education Funding Council for England) funds 88 universities, 44 specialist institutions and general colleges, and 143 further education colleges in England. (<http://www.hefce.ac.uk/unicoll/, accessed 14 July 2007). UCAS (the University and Colleges Admissions Service) is the central organization through which undergraduate courses at these universities and colleges are processed.

The undergraduate course search provides fifty-two universities offering a total of 454 archaeological, combined, and closely related courses for 2008. Only two institutions, the universities of Cardiff and of Wales, Lampeter, offer 'medieval' as an explicit component of one of their course options. The UCAS site does not contain any references to Anglo-Saxon archaeology and many of the general course links do not provide any further information on whether it is part of a course or not. 'Anglo-Saxon' per se does not feature in the UCAS subject listings, nor does it bring up any results when used in the general search.

It would be unrealistic to expect an undergraduate degree specifically concentrating on the Anglo-Saxons and perhaps even a wider European and Mediterranean early-medieval degree would not be viable. It is, nonetheless, worth observing that while those interested in archaeology have a wide online selection to entice them—ranging from Archaeology and Scottish Ethnology (Edinburgh), to Archaeology and Multimedia Technologies (Chester), and Marine Archaeology (Bournemouth)—there is nothing at this point to engender a specific interest in the Anglo-Saxons or the early medieval period (www.ucas.com/search/index.html, accessed 14 July 2007).

The Anglo-Saxons certainly feature in many general archaeology courses and in related disciplines such as history, linguistics, and history of art, and there is no doubt the possibility to tailor course options to individual interests, as, for instance, within the framework of the history-, language-, and literature-based Anglo-Saxon, Norse, and Celtic tripos of Cambridge University. But nevertheless potential candidates for the subject may well be drawn into other areas at this stage.

On the evidence of *Prospects*, billed as 'the UK's official graduate careers website' (<http://www.prospects.ac.uk>, accessed 22 July 2007), the picture is not dissimilar at postgraduate level.[2] Out of ten courses retrieved by a keyword search on 'Anglo-Saxon', only two are MAs in Medieval Archaeology which include a specific focus on the Anglo-Saxons (at the Centre for Medieval Studies, University of York, and at the University of Nottingham) and one is a degree in archaeological conservation at Cardiff University, which mentions specifically that expertise on the Anglo-Saxons is available in the department. The six courses provided by a search on 'early medieval' concentrate on the wider early medieval world and do not specifically address the Anglo-Saxons (http://www.prospects.ac.uk/cms/ShowPage/Home_page/Find_courses_and_research/p!eacge?mode=Main, accessed 22 July 2007).

Again, as in the case of undergraduate degrees, Anglo-Saxon course options are available, but perhaps simply not via *Prospects*. An example is the Medieval option of the Masters degree in Archaeology offered by UCL's Institute of Archaeology (<http://www.ucl.ac.uk/archaeology/masters/summary/MAarchaeology.htm>, accessed 22 July 2007).

The continuing education sector presents a slightly different picture, presumably catering to a demand from those who would like to gain a deeper knowledge of Anglo-Saxon archaeology. The University of Bristol offers such a diploma or certificate and the Cardiff University website lists a course on 'Life and Death in Anglo-Saxon England'.[3] Cambridge University's continuing education section runs a diploma in Anglo-Saxon studies. The Open University, on the other hand, concludes the European section of its World Archaeology option with the end of the Roman Empire (<http://www3.open.ac.uk/courses/bin/p12.dll?C01A251>, accessed 28 December 2007).

---

[2] I am much indebted to Charlotte Behr for a very stimulating discussion of the topic and for drawing this website to my attention.

[3] This 10-week course listed for autumn 2006 was, however, cancelled. No information about the current status of the course was available.

This brief, web-based survey suggests that, as far as the higher education sector is concerned, Anglo-Saxon archaeology has only low prominence. Those with an interest in the subject, while faced with a plethora of specialist archaeological subjects, may find it difficult to identify a course catering specifically for their interest. Given that the internet is now a first point of contact and a major source of information on educational offers, there is a significant opportunity here to raise the profile of Anglo-Saxon archaeology. This only became clear during the research for this chapter and resulted in the decision to provide web-based references—as yet uncommon in this field—wherever possible, in the hope of making the material referred to available to a wider audience.

An important additional channel for promoting the subject and getting prospective students interested are open days and schools visits, which are run by many archaeology departments. It is even likely that the current high profile of early medieval topics on TV programmes influences student choices (cf. below).

Entertainment and leisure

The Museums and Galleries Yearbook for 2007 lists some 2,300 institutions in its index (Museums Association 2007: 311–20),[4] although it is difficult to ascertain how many of them feature Anglo-Saxon archaeology. Many local museums have at least a few relevant objects on display and schools visits are a first point of contact with the Anglo-Saxon period.

A few museums are specifically dedicated to the period such as West Stow Anglo-Saxon village in Suffolk (www.stedmundsbury.gov.uk/sebc/play/weststow-asv.cfm), Bede's World in Newcastle (www.bedesworld.co.uk), and the National Trust's visitor centre at Sutton Hoo (Fig. 52.1) (www.nationaltrust.org.uk/main/w-vh/w-visits/w-findaplace/w-suttonhoo.htm). Thanks to the involvement of professionals and academics in their conception and administration, they are far more than historical theme parks. They may have a research aspect, such as in the reconstruction and maintenance of Anglo-Saxon buildings. At all three sites, an indoor exhibition space is complemented by an outdoor experience. At Sutton Hoo this is a country walk around the burial mounds, while West Stow and Bede's World include reconstructed Anglo-Saxon villages. In addition, all sites also offer themed events where Anglo-Saxon craft demonstrations and costumed re-enactors give first-hand insights into early medieval England. Coupled with the substantial visitor numbers, at Sutton Hoo over 90,000 in 2006/7 (K. Sussams, pers. comm.),

---

[4] I am grateful to Kira Hopkins for diligently making her way through the index.

they are important ambassadors for the subject and are places where archaeology comes alive.

'Living history' is a key factor in the interest that many re-enactors have in the Anglo-Saxons. Individuals may choose to be independent or attached to local societies or museums. The two largest organizations representing the Anglo-Saxon period are Anglecynn (no current website) and Regia Anglorum (www.regia.org). The spectrum of re-enactors is wide, ranging from those wearing 'fantasy' dress to those who undertake painstaking research into their costumes, accessories, and even their hairstyles. Costumed interpretation at historical sites has been shown to be a highly effective means of conveying knowledge to the public (Souden et al. 2006: 75) and are hence more than just a means of attracting visitors (Fig. 52.2). The fact that such events are highly memorable makes it all the more important that re-enactors and costumed interpreters provide a well-informed picture of the past, emphasizing not only similarities, but also the differences between ourselves and the Anglo-Saxons (cf. Planel 1994).

Interpretations of the past also manifest themselves in temporary exhibitions with an Anglo-Saxon theme. Internationally important exhibitions such as *The Golden Age of Anglo-Saxon Art* and *The Making of England* brought the Anglo-Saxon period to the attention of wide audiences and attracted over 60,000 visitors each (BM 1987: 64; 1993: 43, 86). Moreover, their catalogues (Backhouse et al. 1984;

Figure 52.1 The visitor centre at Sutton Hoo (courtesy of the National Trust)

Webster and Backhouse 1991) and that of a third, closely related, show on Celtic metalwork (Youngs 1989) are still seminal.

Today, even smaller events, such as the temporary exhibition staged each summer at Sutton Hoo, can attract some 70,000 visitors (K. Sussams, pers. comm.). In addition, temporary exhibitions usually offer a supporting programme of events, lectures, or activities, designed to engage visitors and encourage participation, already at a young age, and to complement the information conveyed in the displays.

It has been suggested that television is the most important source of information about archaeology for those who visit museums little or not at all (Kulik 2006: 76) and series such as 'Time Team' appear to have an impact on student interest (K. Giles, University of York, pers. comm.). This would not be surprising, as archaeology programmes can achieve viewer figures in excess of 5 million (Kulik 2006: 82). This new brand of 'infotainment' has been on the rise since the 1990s (Holtorf 2003: 125; Kulik 2006: 75) and today is seen as a means for museums to reach new

Figure 52.2 A re-enactment tableau featuring a replica of the seventh-century hanging bowl from Oliver's Battery, around which a temporary exhibition was conceived (courtesy of Winchester City Museums)

audiences, as demonstrated by a collaboration between the British Museum and Channel 4 on the 'Codex' game show series, which featured an episode dedicated to the Anglo-Saxons. The involvement of professionals in Anglo-Saxon archaeology is of key importance as they constantly strive to reconcile media interest in the unusual, spectacular, and eye-catching with a reasonably accurate and current picture.

The most recent medium to be discovered by Anglo-Saxon archaeologists is the internet. One early project was the Ashmolean Museum of Oxford's Potweb (<http://potweb.ashmolean.org/HomePage.html>), which has a dedicated section on the Anglo-Saxons. Here, visitors can look at enlargeable images of early medieval ceramics and access some basic information about them.

PASt explorers (<http://www.pastexplorers.org.uk/>) is aimed specifically at children and was developed by the Portable Antiquities Scheme (PAS, see below). Apart from information about various periods, there is the virtual Anglo-Saxon village of West Mucking. The reconstructed cartoon village contains easily-accessible information about the Anglo-Saxons and, through connecting the past with the current appearance of the site, also teaches users about archaeological methods. For adults, the PAS has a learning section which includes detailed information, e.g. on good practice in metal detecting and on recording techniques. Sharing information in this format has led to an increase in data quality, which in turn benefits those using PAS data in their research (see below).

The internet and powerful databases have exponentially increased the amount of information about the Anglo-Saxons available to anyone. The databases of the PAS (www.findsdatabase.org.uk/hms/home.php?publiclogin=1), the Archaeological Data Service (http://ads.ahds.ac.uk), the University of Oxford *Novum Inventorium Sepulchrale* (http://web.arch.ox.ac.uk/archives/inventorium), and the University of Strathclyde's BUBL (http://bubl.ac.uk/link/a/anglo-saxonarchaeology.htm) are some of the major British, academic web portals leading to raw data or other information and take-up of these resources is steadily on the increase. Metal detectorists themselves have also started a database, cross-linking their entries to PAS entries (<http://www.ukdfd.co.uk/>). Moreover, many counties are now making their Sites and Monuments Records available electronically.

This selection partly presents data generated by those who have traditionally done so, i.e. professionals and academics, but through PAS and UKDFD the public can for the first time make a major contribution, potentially altering the way we see the Anglo-Saxon period (see below).

Recently, the internet has even been used for raising funds for cultural institutions such as Bede's World. As part of the 'TopLots' auction on eBay, bidders could win a handling session of the largest collection of seventh-century window glass from Europe. In addition to generating funding, this was an excellent outreach activity, showcasing the museum's collection (www.bedesworld.co.uk/newsevents-news.php, accessed 2 November 2007). As with the higher education sector, the importance of the internet as a tool for communication, information, education, and entertainment in connection with Anglo-Saxon archaeology is readily evident.

Young Archaeologists' Club and Archaeological Societies

Unlike many other European countries, the UK has a strong grass-roots tradition of public involvement in archaeology. This finds expression, for example, in the Young Archaeologists' Club and in the large number of archaeological and historical societies (cf. Darvill and Russell 2002: 48f. and 69, ref. to Appendix E). In areas such as Kent, where the Anglo-Saxons feature prominently in the archaeological record, the latter are particularly important in the context of this chapter. For instance, the 150th anniversary of Kent Archaeological Society in 2007 was celebrated with an exhibition at Maidstone Museum and Bentliff Art Gallery, re-uniting key finds from the county, including much Anglo-Saxon material. The Sutton Hoo Society has over the years not only sponsored excavations, research on the site's environs, and publications, but also organizes conferences on the Anglo-Saxons and trains volunteers to provide site tours.

Both cases illustrate well how important a contribution local, often volunteer-run, societies have made in the past and continue to make through raising awareness of archaeology, providing training in excavation techniques, sponsoring excavations and scholarship, publishing journals and monographs, and, last but not least, generating enthusiasm and rallying volunteer power.

Government initiatives and legislation

Metal detecting

Another facet of amateur involvement in archaeology is metal detecting. This is now a major leisure time pursuit in England, with an estimated 30,000 detectorists in Britain (Copping 2007). High-profile early medieval discoveries, such as the Viking Hoard from the Harrogate area and celebrity endorsement (Treasure Hunting 2007: 79) contribute further to its popularity. From initially wary positions on both sides (cf. Dobinson and Denison 1995: 61f.), the relationship between archaeologists and detectorists has now moved on to one of better understanding and collaboration. This is partly a result of the realization that engagement with, and education of, the public is a better way of ensuring the protection of the archaeological heritage than a prohibitive and hostile stance.

Many detectorists are members of local clubs and the two major organizations are the National Council of Metal Detectorists (NCMD: <http://www.ncmd.co.uk>) and the Federation of Independent Detectorists (FID: <http://fid.newbury.net>). Both websites feature codes of conduct for responsible detecting and refer to the Treasure Act.

Although the majority of detectorists observe legislation by getting permission from the landowner, staying clear of scheduled monuments, and reporting treasure, and moreover register their finds with the local Finds Liaison Officer (see below), 'nighthawking', i.e. illicit detecting, often coupled with illegal sales of archaeological finds via the internet, is persistent. Anglo-Saxon sites, notably early cemeteries with their plethora of metal costume accessories and weapons, are at particularly high risk from looting. A national survey has been launched under the title 'Nighthawks and Nighthawking: Damage to Archaeological Sites in the United Kingdom and Crown Dependencies caused by illegal searching and removal of antiquities'. The project aim is not only to gather data on the negative impact of nighthawking on the archaeology of the UK and Channel Islands, but also to 'foster a climate of opinion within all sectors that the illegal search, removal and sale of antiquities is unacceptable' (<http://nighthawking.thehumanjourney.net/prd.htm>, accessed 29 October 2007). Results of this eighteen-month survey, which was initiated by English Heritage, are expected in late 2008 (K. Spandl, pers. comm.) and may have an impact on legislation against illegal detecting.

The Treasure Act

In September 1997 the Treasure Act 1996 came into effect, replacing the Treasure Trove law then current in England, Wales, and Northern Ireland (DCMS 1998b: 2). Under the Act, there is a legal obligation to report all finds of treasure. For the Anglo-Saxon period, the chief criterion which defines treasure is that the object contains more than 10 per cent of gold or silver by weight. Coins only qualify if they were found in a closed group that usually represents either a hoard, a group of coins lost together, e.g. in a purse, or a votive deposit. Each coin should contain at least 10 per cent precious metal or, if that is not the case, at least ten of them must have been found together. Any objects that are associated with a treasure object are treasure as well, irrespective of their material. This is relevant, for instance, in the case of grave groups or of coin hoards and their containers. Natural, unworked objects, including human and animal remains, do not qualify as treasure (PAS 2006a: 10f.). A Code of Practice was published by the Department for Culture,

Media and Sport (DCMS) for England and Wales (<http://www.finds.org.uk/documents/treasure_act.pdf>), with a separate Code available for Northern Ireland.

Any finder is obliged to report treasure within fourteen days either of discovery or of realizing that the object constitutes treasure. Reports to the Coroner will now in most cases take place through a local Finds Liaison Officer. The reward payable for the object, should a museum wish to acquire it, is determined by the independent Treasure Valuation Committee (TVC), which comprises representatives of the antiquities trade, metal detectorists, and museums. Both the finder, unless he or she is an archaeologist, and landowner are entitled to half of the payment. If no public institution wishes to acquire it, the find is disclaimed and returned to the finder unless the landowner, who is notified by the Coroner, objects. All finds which have gone through the system are published in the Treasure Annual Report, which is not only available in paper form, but also electronically (<http://www.finds.org.uk/news>). Information on the treasure process is available from the DCMS, the Department of Treasure and Portable Antiquities at the British Museum, from metal detector organizations, and from local museums and Finds Liaison Officers. It can also be downloaded from the Portable Antiquities Scheme webpage (<http://www.finds.org.uk/treasure>).

The number of early medieval treasure objects has been steadily increasing since September 1997. While the first year of the new treasure law saw the report of nineteen Anglo-Saxon objects and eleven coins (DCMS 1998b: 4), the calendar year of 2004 brought seventy-two early medieval objects and three coins. Over 90 per cent of metalwork finds are now discovered through metal detecting and just under 5 per cent come from archaeological excavations, as these, too, are subject to the Treasure Act (DCMS 2004: tables 1, 2). The latter has potentially far-reaching consequences for any excavation involving Anglo-Saxon cemeteries, as the landowner will be entitled to half the reward for treasure finds, which would have to be funded by any museum wishing to keep all the finds from a site together.

As many treasure finds are acquired by regional museums, the profile of Anglo-Saxon archaeology has been increasing on a local level, with treasure cases highlighting the importance of the period through press coverage of finds and through displays. The amount of data becoming available through metal-detector finds has also had an impact on how academics see and interpret the Anglo-Saxon past. For instance, Anglo-Saxon high-class metalwork of the finest craftsmanship, such as the Market Rasen sword hilt fittings (DCMS 2002, cat. no. 58), has come to light outside southern and eastern England, where such finds have traditionally been concentrated. Perhaps more importantly, a new layer of society is slowly becoming visible between the large number of more or less well-furnished Anglo-Saxon graves and the 'princely' stratum of a few outstanding burials (Evans 2007). Likewise, settlements or 'productive' sites with access to luxury goods and coinage may be more widespread than previously thought (cf. G. Williams 2006: esp. 170

and 172f.). This information, partly resulting from data generated by the public, will in turn influence the narrative about the Anglo-Saxon era that scholars present to that public.

The Portable Antiquities Scheme

The Portable Antiquities Scheme (PAS) was established in 1997, in connection with the launch of the Treasure Act. As it records all kinds of archaeological finds up to and including the twentieth century, the remit of PAS is much wider than, and complements, the Treasure Act.

Following extensive consultation with both archaeologists and metal detectorists, the pilot project was designed as a voluntary scheme to record archaeological finds from five counties and regions in England, sponsored by the Department for Culture, Media and Sport (DCMS) and the British Museum (DCMS 1998a: 4–6). Additional funding for another five posts, including Wales, was provided from 1999 through a successful bid to the Heritage Lottery Fund, coordinated by the Museums, Libraries and Archives Council (DCMS 1998a: 4; Batt 2004). Today PAS provides complete coverage of England and Wales through a network of local Finds Liaison Officers and six finds advisers, two of whom specialize in the medieval period (PAS 2006b: 126f.). Since 2006, PAS has been funded by DCMS (PAS 2006b: 9) and is led by the British Museum's Department of Portable Antiquities and Treasure.

From the outset, the public featured prominently. Express aims of the Scheme are not only the 'advance [of] knowledge of the history and archaeology of England and Wales by systematically recording archaeological objects found by the public', but also the promotion of heritage awareness and, explicitly, an increase in 'opportunities for active public involvement in archaeology and [to] strengthen links between medal-detector users and archaeologists' (PAS 2006b: 9). The latter is essential as metal detectorists form a substantial proportion of those who pursue archaeology as a hobby in England and Wales.

Finds Liaison Officers (FLOs) are often based in local museums and record objects brought in by the public, including treasure finds. In 2005/6 over 57,500 records were added to the PAS finds database (<http://www.finds.org.uk>), many of them with images, and the website received more than 53 million hits (PAS 2006b: 7). FLOs also play an active role in schools, higher and further education programmes, finds days, events such as National Archaeology Week or Museum and Galleries Month, and community archaeology projects (PAS 2006b: 10–18). The annual Portable Antiquities conference held at the British Museum features, among others, FLOs and scholars talking about Anglo-Saxon archaeology. Like, for instance, the Sutton Hoo Society conferences or those held by the Oxford University Continuing Education Department, its aim is not only to address the academic community, but to attract participants from the interested general public as well.

The potential for promoting Anglo-Saxon archaeology to a wide, largely non-academic, audience is clear.

Most FLOs also attend meetings of local metal detector clubs (PAS 2006b: table 7b) and metal detector rallies. The latter present unique opportunities to record a detailed archaeological biography of a site in a short time-span through the finds which are metal-detected or otherwise picked up during a rally over one or more days (cf. Daubney *et al.* 2007). Identification of previously unknown Anglo-Saxon sites may be the result of such meticulous recording. Examples include an early Anglo-Saxon cemetery site in mid Norfolk and a largely ninth-century 'productive' site at Studley Roger, North Yorkshire (PAS 2006b: 63 and 75f.). Therefore, although early medieval material constitutes only some 3.5 per cent of all finds recorded by the PAS in 2005/6 (PAS 2006b: table 5), it has led to significant discoveries.

In addition, public involvement via finds reported under the Treasure Act or to the Portable Antiquities Scheme can significantly augment our knowledge of the Anglo-Saxon era, for instance, by rounding out the picture still biased towards highly-visible cemeteries for the early Saxon period. For example, distribution maps based only on known cemeteries, and those which include finds recorded on the PAS database can be strikingly different, as new research on Kent demonstrates (Richardson and McLean 2007). Equally important is the contribution PAS has made to improving our grasp of the mid Saxon period. Due to the lack of grave goods and the low number of excavated and published settlements, metal-detected finds play a crucial role, extending our knowledge not only of metalwork from the period but also of settlements and productive sites that would otherwise have gone undiscovered (cf. Leahy 2003: 10).

Thus, the public, whether as metal detectorists, field walkers, gardeners, or anyone who finds archaeological material, now has a significant impact on the research community. Instead of the traditional one-way dissemination of data and knowledge, a feedback cycle has begun, with both sides generating data and information, with the mutual aim of increasing our understanding of the past.

PPG16 and resulting discoveries

In addition to ancient monuments legislation, PPG16, a Planning Policy Guidance note on Archaeology and Planning published by the then Department of Environment in 1990, was the major tool in preserving the archaeological and historical heritage of England and in extending our knowledge of it. Crucially, PPG16 established the consideration of archaeological issues as a fixed component of the 'decision-making process for both development control and strategic planning' (Darvill and Russell 2002: 3). Consequently, archaeological concerns are now built into the planning process for any building project from the outset. Despite discussions of the quality and quantity of excavations generated as a result of PPG16, its impact has been huge, with close to 90 per cent of fieldwork in the late 1990s and early new millennium generated in response to it (Darvill and Russell 2002: 3f.). Relevant development work might include anything from road and railway schemes to mineral extraction or woodland planting (Darvill and Russell 2002: 40 and ill. 23).[5]

Archaeological remains from the early medieval period featured below the 5 per cent mark in both planning-related and non-planning-related investigations in England during the period from 1990 to 1999 (Darvill and Russell 2002: figs. 27, 29). In fact, the early Middle Ages lagged behind the other periods investigated, but it should be noted that some of the planning-related Anglo-Saxon discoveries of recent years have been of major importance. Two examples are the princely burial found in advance of road improvement works at Prittlewell, Southend-on-Sea, Essex; and the Anglo-Saxon cemeteries uncovered in Kent ahead of the construction of the Channel Tunnel rail link between London and Folkestone.

In both cases, the archaeological work resulted not only in scholarly discussions and unpublished assessment reports, but also in plans for a more popular output. The success of the Museum of London's Prittlewell Prince book (MOLAS 2004), its website (<http://www.molas.org.uk/pages/siteReports.asp?siteid=pro3&section=-preface>), and the temporary exhibition of some key objects from the grave proves that there is a strong public interest in this outstanding discovery.

Developers funding large-scale investigations are interested in acknowledgement of their sponsorship and presentation of findings to an audience beyond the academic community. Union Railways and Rail Link Engineering, the companies behind the Eurostar high-speed link from London to the coast, were keen for an accessible publication to showcase the excavations. Its appearance is expected in 2011 with a scholarly publication as a further goal (I. Riddler, pers. comm.). Among other periods, two early Anglo-Saxon cemeteries at Cuxton and Saltwood, some with arguably high-status grave-goods, were identified and assessment reports, data, and images were made available online through the Arts and Humanities Data Service (see Kilbride 2004 with links).

The impact on the public of PPG16 is hence both direct, via the influence it might have on the planning process of any given project, and indirect, via new modes of dissemination. The latter bring detailed accounts at least of high-profile finds from the early Saxon era to a much wider audience than was previously possible. Unlike press coverage alone, popular publications, whether in print or via the web, allow for contextualization and thus become a vehicle for promoting interest in and understanding of the period.

---

[5] PPG16 has since been replaced by Planning Policy Statement 5: Planning for the Historic Environment (PPS5), published on 23 March 2010.

PUBLIC INTEREST IN AND KNOWLEDGE OF ANGLO-SAXON ARCHAEOLOGY

Together with the large number of supporting programmes for exhibitions and schools packs, media coverage will continue to improve public knowledge of Anglo-Saxon archaeology. Although there is an indisputable interest, it is difficult to assess knowledge of the period. There does not seem to be any dedicated research on general understanding of the early Middle Ages, but visitor evaluations carried out by both the Museum of London and the Victoria & Albert Museum for their respective new medieval galleries suggest that knowledge of early medieval England is hazy. Visitors are, for example, confused over the difference in terminology between historians, who generally speak about the medieval period, and archaeologists, who specify that the Anglo-Saxons were *early* medieval. On the whole, there seem to be 'few solid preconceptions' about the Middle Ages (Bartlett and Clark 2002: 7). Knowledge of the Middle Ages is impressionistic and coloured by prejudice about poor living conditions and the plague, while there is little understanding of what life looked like on a day-to-day basis (Fisher 2002: charts 11, 13, 33). Any Anglo-Saxon archaeologist working with the public should therefore be wary of overestimating the amount of background his audience may have, even though it is difficult to generalize.

Archaeologists have an important role to play in current debates to which Anglo-Saxon archaeology is directly relevant. These may concern questions of identity and heritage, as for instance the recent unveiling of two public sculptures of Æthelberht of Kent and Bertha illustrate. The project was initiated by the Canterbury Commemoration Society and it was hoped that the statues would 'evoke a major event in Kent's history and become a focus for civic pride in Canterbury' (*Kent on Sunday*, 9 February 2003: 12).[6] Academics were involved from early on in the project to advise on the appearance of dress and costume accessories.[7]

Although currently not a major concern, neo-heathen movements may in future try to influence debates on Anglo-Saxon excavations, especially of human remains. The sometimes polemic nature of debates led by exponents of the neo-pagan (i.e. prehistoric) scene shows how important it may become for Anglo-Saxon archaeologists to engage in an informed discourse and to provide the public with a well-founded picture of this era, rather than cede the field to fantasy versions that may be used to lay claim to

---

[6] I am grateful to B. Ager for providing me with a copy of the article and background information on the project.

[7] As the editors make clear in their Preface, the papers in this volume were submitted before the discovery in July 2009 of the Staffordshire Hoard. The public interest in that extraordinary material can be measured by the number of people who queued for hours (some 42,000 at Birmingham and over 52,000 at Stoke-on-Trent; D. Symons and D. Klemperer, pers. comm.) to see it when it first went on display, and by the individual donations both from Britain and abroad amounting to nearly £1 million that contributed significantly to raising its purchase price.

archaeological sites and finds and even political debate (cf. Arnold 2006, esp. 175f.; Blain and Wallis 2006). The arguments surrounding the case of the 'Prince of Bling' and the squatters' camp founded at Prittlewell to prevent further excavation (<http://www.sacredsites.org.uk/news/campbling.html>) are only one aspect of debates around the ownership of the past, which previously centred on the prehistoric period.

Future perspectives

A significant proportion of funding for Anglo-Saxon archaeology (including research projects, excavations, and museum acquisition of objects) now has to be generated through grant-giving bodies or from private sources, as local authority and government funding is decreasing. Private sponsors may be seen as representing the public at large and will be keen for a dissemination of results in a widely accessible form, acknowledging their contribution. Charitable organizations such as the Heritage Lottery, Heritage Memorial, and Art funds also consider the public outcome, and not only the academic or intellectual merit of applications, as imperative in their decision-making process. Even the Arts and Humanities Research Council stipulates a summary 'accessible to a variety of readers, including the general public' on its grant forms and encourages public outreach in addition to scholarly goals of projects.

The previous government had an interest in archaeology and it accepted responsibility for continuing the Portable Antiquities Scheme after Heritage Lottery funding ended in March 2006 (PAS 2006b: 9). The future of PAS once more looked uncertain in 2008 (Heyworth 2008), but the Labour government also had a clear agenda which saw archaeology as a means to benefit the public and improve people's lives (cf. Lammy 2006) and further funding was secured.

Acknowledgements

The author wishes to thank the following for valuable discussions, information, or images: Alex Sanmark, Angus Wainwright, Barry Ager, Charlotte Behr, Elisabeth O'Connell, Helen Rees, Ian Riddler, John Clark, Kate Giles, Kate Sussams, Kira Hopkins, Lyn Blackmore, Stuart Frost, Tania Dickinson. Katharine Hoare, of the British Museum, kindly commented on a draft of the section on primary and secondary education. The author takes responsibility for any remaining errors.

References

AQA (Assessment and Qualifications Alliance) (2007a). 'Qualifications'. <http://www.aqa.org.uk/qual/>. Accessed 27 October 2007.

—— (2007b). *General Certificate of Education: Archaeology 6011/5011, 2008.* Version 1.0, 0506. Downloaded from <http://www.aqa.org.uk/qual/>. Accessed 11 June 2007.

Arnold, B. (2006). 'Pseudoarchaeology and nationalism: essentializing difference', in G. G. Fagan (ed.), *Archaeological Fantasies.* Oxford: Routledge, 154–79.

Backhouse, J., Turner, D. H., and Webster, L. (eds.) (1984). *The Golden Age of Anglo Saxon Art: 966–1066.* Bloomington: Indiana University Press.

Bartlett, S., and Clark, J. (2002). *Medieval London: Report on a Pilot Evaluation Exercise.* Unpublished Museum of London report.

Batt, C. (2004). 'Preface'. MLA (Museums, Libraries and Archives Council), *Portable Antiquities Scheme Annual Report 2003/04.* London: MLA, 5.

Blain, J., and Wallis, R. J. (2006). 'Pasts and pagan practices: moving beyond Stonehenge'. *Public Archaeology* 5/4: 211–22.

BM (The British Museum) (1987). *Report of the Trustees 1984–1987.* London: The Trustees of the British Museum.

—— (1993). *Report of the Trustees 1990–1993.* London: The Trustees of the British Museum.

Cooper, H. (2000). *The Teaching of History in Primary Schools.* 3rd edition. London: David Fulton. (Repr. 2005.)

Copping, J. (2007). 'Night metal detectors "looting Britain"'. *Sunday Telegraph,* 7 July 2007.

Corbishley, M., and Stone, P. G. (1994). 'The teaching of the past in formal school curricula in England', in P. G. Stone and B. L. Molyneaux (eds.), *The Presented Past: Heritage, Museums and Education.* One World Archaeology 25. (Repr. 2003.) London: Routledge, 383–97.

Darvill, T., and Russell, B. (2002). *Archaeology after PPG16: Archaeological Investigations in England 1990–1999.* School of Conservation Sciences Research Report 10. Bournemouth and London: Bournemouth University and English Heritage.

Daubney, A. et al. (2007). 'A word from the Midlands Region'. *Treasure Hunting,* August 2007: 45.

DCMS (Department for Culture, Media and Sport) (1998a). *Portable Antiquities Annual Report 1997–98.* London: DCMS.

—— (1998b). *Treasure Annual Report 1997–1998.* London: DCMS.

—— (2002). *Treasure Annual Report 2002.* London: DCMS.

—— (2004). *Treasure Annual Report 2004.* London: DCMS.

Dobinson, C., and Denison, S. (1995). *Metal Detecting and Archaeology in England.* London and York: English Heritage and Council for British Archaeology.

Edexcel (2007). 'Qualifications'. <http://www.edexcel.org.uk/quals>. Accessed 27 October 2007.

Evans, A. C. (2007). 'A Golden Age? Shifting perspectives in early Anglo-Saxon archaeology'. Unpublished paper delivered at the 'Wonderful and Precious Treasures' symposion, British Museum, 10 May 2007.

Fisher, S. (2002). 'What do Medieval and Renaissance really meant to people?' Unpublished report for the Victoria & Albert Museum.

Heyworth, M. (2008). 'Portable Antiquities Scheme too good to become history'. *British Archaeology* 101 (July/August 2008): 30–1.

Hills, C. (2003). *Origins of the English*. Cambridge: Duckworth.
Holtorf, C. (2003). 'Has Archaeology never been so much fun?'. *Public Archaeology* 3: 125–7.
Kilbride, W. (2004). 'Light from the end of the Tunnel'. *AHDS Newsletter Autumn/Winter 2004*. <http://ahds.ac.uk/news/newsletters/autumn-2004/index.htm#top>. Accessed 4 August 2007.
Kulik, K. (2006). 'Archaeology and British television'. *Public Archaeology* 5: 75–90.
Lammy, D. (2006). 'Foreword'. *PAS 2006*: 2–3.
Leahy, K. (2003). *Anglo-Saxon Crafts*. Stroud: Tempus.
Macgregor, A. (2007). 'E. T. Leeds and the formulation of an Anglo-Saxon archaeology of England', in M. Henig and T. J. Smith (eds.), *Collectanea Antiqua: Essays in Memory of Sonia Chadwick Hawkes*. BAR International Series 1673. Oxford: Archaeopress, 27–44.
MoLAS (2004). *The Prittlewell Prince*. London: Museum of London Archaeology Service.
Museums Association (2007). *Museums and Galleries Yearbook*. London: Museums Association.
OCR (Oxford, Cambridge and RSA Examinations) (2007). 'Qualifications'. <http://www.ocr.org.uk/qualifications/index.html>. Accessed 27 October 2007.
PAS (Portable Antiquities Scheme) (2006a). *Advice for Finders of Archaeological Objects, including Treasure*. Edition 6/2006. London: Portable Antiquities Scheme.
—— (2006b). *Portable Antiquities Scheme Annual Report 2005/6*. London: PAS.
Planel, P. G. (1994). 'Privacy and community through medieval material culture', in P. G. Stone and B. L. Molyneaux (eds.), *The Presented Past: Heritage, Museums and education*. One World Archaeology 25. (Repr. 2003.) London: Routledge, 206–15.
QCA (Qualifications and Curriculum Authority) (2007). Schemes of Work, Unit 6B. <http://www.standards.dfes.gov.uk/schemes2/history/his6b/>. Accessed 27 October 2007.
Richardson, A., and McLean, L. (2007). 'Early Anglo-Saxon brooches in southern England: the contribution of the Portable Antiquities Scheme'. Unpublished paper delivered at the 2007 Portable Antiquities Scheme conference, British Museum, 18 April 2007.
Souden, D., Jones, C., and Crawford, I. (2006). 'The dressing-up box'. *Heritage 365* 3: 74–9.
Treasure Hunting (2007). 'Product Report: Bill Wyman Signature Detector'. *Treasure Hunting September 2007*: 73.
Webster, L., and Backhouse, J. (eds.) (1991). *The Making of England: Anglo-Saxon Art and Culture AD 600–900*. London: British Museum Press.
Williams, G. (2006). 'The circulation and function of coinage in conversion-period England c. AD 580–675' in B. Cook and G. Williams (eds.), *Coinage and History in the North Sea World, c. AD 500–1250: Essays in Honour of Marion Archibald*. The Northern World 19. Leiden and Boston: Brill, 146–92.
Williams, H. (2006). *Death and Memory in Early Medieval Britain*. Cambridge: Cambridge University Press.
Youngs, S. (ed.) (1989). *The Work of Angel: Masterpieces of Celtic Metalwork*. London: British Museum Press.

GENERAL INDEX

Note: pages numbers in *italics* refer to figures and tables.

Abdy, R. 427, 592
Åberg, N. 223
Abrams, L. 49, 57
  paganism 766, 767, 773–5
acculturation 32, 33, 35, 38, 40, 53, 72, 548
  Anglo-Scandinavian 53
  in burials 74, 543, 545
  educational 37
  intermarriage 35, 39, 41, 48, 49–50, 55
  stone sculpture and 74
  in Wales 548
Adams, K. A. 181
Addyman, P. 120 n.1, 129, 131, 132, 138
  field systems 200, 381
adults and adulthood
  burials 649, *650*, 655–6, 660–1
  grave goods 649, 655–6, 660–1
  interpretation of terms 644
  passage into 644
Ælfflæd 781
Ælfric Bata: *Colloquies* 338, 802
Ælfric of Eynsham 302, 971
  Colloquy 95, 336, 668
Ælfwold, bishop of Crediton 782
aerial photographs 120
Æthelbald of Mercia 547, 557, 605
Æthelberht of Kent 894, 896, 971
Æthelberht II of Kent 333
Æthelflæd 65, 101, 607, 609–11, 930–3
Æthelred 582
Æthelred II 48, 65, 67, 594, 961, 964
Æthelred of Mercia, Ealdorman 607, 608
Æthelstan 65–6, 490, 766, 783, 959
  hospitals 717
  law codes 67, 610, 897
Æthelweard, king 582
Æthelwold 831
Æthelwulf 484, 582, 785, 958
age and ageing 641–64
  grave goods and 644–5, 648–9, 657
  growing up/old 643–5
  life cycle 644–57

Blacknall Field, Pewsey 651–4, *652*, 653–4
Mill Hill, Deal 646–51, *647*, *648*, *649*, *650*
Norton 654–7, *657*, *658*, *659*, 660–1
significance of 642
see also children
Ager, B. 465, 1040
agriculture 964
  common-field system 189–92, 317–18, 377–9, *379*
  crop rotation 317, *318*
  early Saxon arable 382–3
  fallowing 386, 393
  hay meadows 386
  infield-outfield system 317, 322, 380, 383, 384
  mid Saxon arable 383–6
  mouldboard ploughs 385
  open-field system 321–3, 324, 377–8, *378*, 390
  soil fertility 385, 386
  strip systems 318–19, 391–2
Aird, W. M. 273
Albarella, U. 363, 677
Alcock, L. 120, 547, 615, 989
Alcuin 47, 728, 781, 970
Aldhelm of Malmesbury, bishop of Sherborne 732, 753, 771, 803, 805 n.19
Aldred of Chester-le-Street 806
Alexander, J. J. G. 476, 479
Alfred, king of Wessex 10, 65, 67, 105, 199, 432, 486, 958–9
  burhs 605, 608
  coinage 581–4
  law code 896–7
  prisons 899
  translations 971
Alfred Jewel 434, 485, 487, 787
Aliortus of Elmet 547
Allen, M. 593
Allen, T. 212
Allerston, P. 393
Allison, E. 333
altars 110, 490, 752–3, 766
altars, portable 786

altar cloths 781, 784
amber 73, 93, 98, 106, 250, 417, 434
Ambrose, S. H. 670
Ambrosiani, B. 48, 559
Amundsen, D. W. 716
anaemia 708, 712
ancient DNA 717
Anderson, J. G. 705, 714
Andreas (poem) 746, 973
Andrén, A. 771
Andrews, P. 149 n.8, 414, 432
Angel of the Annunciation 480, *481*
Anglecynn 1030
Anglo-Saxon Chronicle (ASC) 64–5, 516, 524, 528, 951, 958, 959, 973
  on Alfred 958–9
  burhs 602, 611, 614
  coinage and 582
  five boroughs 52
  King Edgar 64–5
  Scandinavian raids 46, 47
  tribute payments 585
  Viking attacks 605–6, 609, 614
Anglo-Saxons
  Britons and 534–48
    eastern and southern England 537–9
    Mercia and Northumbria 539–44
    paradigms of interaction with Britons 534–6
    Scotland and Wales, relations with 544–8
  end of era of 62–75
Anglo-Scandinavian identity 46–58
  burials 52, 55–8
  costume and dress accessories 53–5
  documentary sources 47–9
  place-names and linguistic evidence 49–50
  settlement archaeology 50–3
animal husbandry 361–73
  husbandry 368–70
  livestock 364–8
  NISP data 364–6, *365*, *366*
  role and value 370–3
  source material 362–4
animals
  in burials 245, 251–3, 269, 768
  and paganism 769–70, 773
  and religion 735, 736
  see also art, animal-style
ankylosing spondylitis 707
Anonymous Life of St Cuthbert 718
anthropology 1003–21
  Anglo-Saxon material cultures 1016–19
  materiality 1016–19
  practice theory 1016–19
  relational thought 1005–12, 1020
apartheid 41, 88
Appadurai, A. 1015
Appelbaum, S. 392
Arbon, A. 393
Archer, S. A. 362, 367
Archibald, M. M. 594
Ardener, E. 628
Armstrong, P. 418
Arnold, C. J. 853
  burials 224
  diet 669
  on elite migration 38–9
  paganism 767, 768
  strip fields 392
art, animal-style 865–85
  bracteates
    as political medium 873–6
    and powerful women 876–80
  and Christianity 105–6, 884–5
  pagan cosmology 870–3
  regional organization 869–70
  Scandinavia and 867–9
  7th-century image and power 885–9
  Style II: 885
  women as cult specialists 880–1
Ashby, S. P. 54
Asser 609
  paganism 775
  Vita Aelfredi 338, 606, 608, 609, 959
assimilation 41
  Anglo-Saxon/Scandinavian 46, 48–9
  material culture 54
  see also acculturation
Astill, G. 69, 352, 414
  trade, exchange and urbanization 503–12
Aston, M. 387, 511
Atkin, M. A. 387
Atkinson, D. 174
Audouy, M. 174, 179, 207
aurochsen 331
Austin, D. 210
Axboe, M. 453, 463, 470, 874, 881
Aybes, C. 333
Ayers, B. 427, 615
Ayre, J. 296

Backhouse, J. 417, 475, 476, 815
  burials 270, 271, 273, 274, 277, 281
  church furnishings 418, 785, 786, 791
  jewellery 276, 472
Badeslade, T. 175

badgers 329
Bailey, R. N. 57, 474, 774, 785, 786
　burials 291, 301
　Gandersheim Casket 483
　Ruthwell Cross 476
Baker, J. 26
Baker, N. 174, 175, 509, 607, 608
Baker, P. A. 782
Bakka, E. 480
Bald's *Leechbook* 717, 757
Baldwin Brown, G. 31, 34–5, 223, 542
Balthilde, queen 881
Banham, D. 318, 354–5, 802
Barberini Gospels 479, *481*
Barker, P. 19, 23, 121, 519, 529, 782
barley (*Hordeum vulgare* L.) 351, 385
barns and granaries 144–5, *145*
Barrett, J. 334, 336, 337, 677
Barrow, J. 509, 749
Bartel, R. 266
Barth, F. 850
Bartholomew, P. 916
Basil of Caesarea 716
basketry 444
bass (Dicentrarchus labrax) 330–1
Bassett, S. 167, 382, 391, 607
Bately, J. 47–8
Bateman, N. 301
Batey, C. 50
Battiscombe, C. F. 273, 490, 783
Battle of Maldon, The 493, 973–4
Baxter, J. E. 630
Bayeux Tapestry 95, 338, 493, 784
Bayley, J.
　craft production 418, 429
　jewellery 409, 427
　metalworking 412, 427, 453, 594–5
Bayliss, A. 471
Bazelmans, J. 271, 850, 857, 859, 1017
bead ornaments 98–100, 277–8
　in burials 245, 250
　crystal 434
　as healing magic 106
beans (*Vicia faba* L.) 352
bears 329, 331, 332, 333
Beatus Commentary 810
beavers 332–3
Bédat, I. 95
Bede 10, 156, 159, 185, 279, 331, 516, 522, 953
　on Æthelfrith 952
　on Canterbury 956
　on languages 969
　Letter to Ecgberht 733

　on London 557, 957
　on paganism 766
　on panel paintings 788
　on Penda of Mercia 952
　on window glass in churches 788
　see also Historia Ecclesiastica
Bede's World 1029
Behr, C. 876, 880
belief: dress and identity and 106–10
Bell, C. 1014
Bell, R. D. 174
Bell, T. 24, 25, 174, 751, 835
Bellamy, B. 425
bells 51, 178, 418
belt-fittings, *see* buckles
Benedictine Reform Movement 417–18
Benedictional of St Æthelwold 491, 783, 802–3
Benedictow, O. 718
Beowulf 106, 156, 271, 748, 882, 973, 975–7
　crime and punishment in 897
　hunting 334
　Lejre and 957
　Sutton Hoo burial and 973
Beresford, G. 51, 131 n.1, 143, 146, 166, 210, 212
Beresford, M. 174, 382
Bernicia 540–5, 601
Biddle, M. 55, 74, 511, 520, 522, 559, 600, 611
　Anglo-Saxon books 799–800
　burhs 508
　church furnishing 418
　clothed burial 299
　coinage 593
　defended sites 605
　pottery 964
　religion 825
　textiles 782–3
　towns 901
Bidwell, P. 19
Biggam, C. P. 430
Bimson, M. 435, 456
birds 333
Birbeck, V. 569
Blackburn, M. 48, 427, 557, 562–3, 830
　coinage 580–96
Blackmore, L. 614
Blain, S. 833
Blair, J. 71, 137
　burials 181, 267, 273–5, 290, 299, 706
　cemeteries 255, 279, 304, 305
　Christianization of wells and springs 749
　Church as landowner 561
　churches 173–9, 182, 184, 189, 779–80, 834, 962
　late Saxon settlements 199

Blair, J. (*cont.*)
  long ranges 206
  metalwork 413
  minster system 826–8, 830, 831
  paganism 772
  place-names 746
  religion 727–40, 825
  sacred places 191, 746, 836
  settlement hierarchy 161–3, 165, 167
  and shrines, beams, poles and totems 755, 756
  transport of goods 505–6
Blake, N. F. 969
Blinkhorn, P. 161, 164, 268, 406
block demesnes 390
Blockley, K. 71
Blockley, M. R. 65
Blunt, C. E. 301
Blythburgh tablet 336
Boddington, A.
  burials 231, 268, 290–1, 294–5, 299–300
  cemeteries 180, 280, 281, 302, 304
  churches 174
  grave goods 300
  infectious diseases 710–12
body and life course 625–37
  biology, social context of 633–5
  grave goods, significance of 635–6
  life course and mute groups 627–31
  osteo-archaeology 626, 631–2
  social archaeology 626, 631–2
  Boethius *488*, 490, 971
Bogaard, A. 677
Böhme, H. W. 229–30, 953
Boisseau, S. 333
Boldon Book 143 n.5
Bolton, J. 505
Bond, J. 245, 332, 768
Bonner, G. 783
Bonney, D. 280
Bonser, W. 716, 718
Book of Durrow 475–8, *477*
books, Anglo-Saxon 797–818
  animal skins 797–9
  æstels 816
  binding 813–14
  collections 817
  high status volumes 814–17
  implements 802, 813
  ink-pots/inkhorns 803–5, *804*
  inks and pigments 811–13
  knives 799, 800, *801*, 802
  pens 802, 805–6, *807*
  pricking 799–800

  ruling 800–2
  storage 817
  styli 802
  wax tablets 802–3
  writing boards 806–8, *809*
  writing rooms 808–11
Boon, G. C. 520
Born, E. 810
boroughs 52, 601
Borre Style 51, 52, 54–5, 73, 491
Bosworth, J. 997
Boulter, A. 152
Bourdieu, P. 138, 849–50, 1013, 1020
Bourdillon, J. 368, 432
bow-sided buildings 51
Bowsher, D. 424, 432, 605, 614
Boyle, A. 242, 248, 278, 632
bracteates, *see under* pendants
Bradley, J. 382–3, 391
Bradley, R. 150, 296, 743–4, 759
Brassica species 355, 356
Brather, S. 937
Braudel, F. 917
bread wheat (*Triticum aestivum L.*) 349–50, 351, 385
breastfeeding 678, 708–9, 713
Breeze, A. 990
Brennand, M. 48
Bretwalda 955
Bridge, M. 833
Briggs, D. E. G. 669
Briggs, K. 745 n.1
bristle oats (*Avena strigosa Schreb.*) 351–2
Britnell, W. J. 174
  Britons 952
  and Anglo-Saxons 534–48
brooches 96, 98–100, 101, 463, 1018
  Borre Style 54
  Christian decorations 106–7
  in burials 245, 250
  cruciform 454, *469*
  disc 51, 53–4, 522
    Anglo-Saxon 54
    Christian decorations 106–9
    composite 36, 277, *408*, *408*, 546, 570, *571*
    convex 53
    gold 471
  and ethnic identity 689
  Jelling Style 51, 53, 54
  jewelled 277
  lead alloy 416
  oval 54
  pagan decorations 106, *107*

pennanular 25, 526, 538, 541
plate 277
quadrangular openwork 53
Quoit Brooch Style 24–5, 463–5
Roman Britain 24–5
saucer brooches 1018
Saxon Relief Style 466
Scandinavian 51, 53
square-headed 468, 769
strap-end 51
Style I: 769, 868, 873
trefoil 53, 54
Trewhiddle Style 483–4, 485
Urnes Style 492–3
Brookes, S. 568, 572
Brooks, C. 71
Brothwell, D. 713
Brown, A. E. 381, 382, 391
Brown, K. 410
Brown, M. P. 430, 461, 475, 480
Brown, N. R. 200
Brown, P. 524, 528
Brown, T. 318, 321
Browne, T. 222
Brownsword, R. 409
Bruce-Mitford, R. 210, 223, 274, 405, 855, 973
Brugmann, B. 469–70
 burials 227, 231, 250, 257, 267, 646
 migration 30–42
Brush, K. 241, 248, 692
Bryant, R. 174, 294
Buckberry, J. L. 631–2
 burials 291, 293, 294, 296, 299
 cemeteries 181, 304
 churches 174
 grave goods 299
buckets 251, 278, 424, 444, 785
buckles 96, 278, 462, 469, 560, 545–6, 1018
 Borre Style 51
 in burials 250, 271, 272
 Crundale 276
 as expression of political power 883
 gold 471, 473, 884–5
 possible Christian emblems 107, 109
 Roman Britain 24–5
 Scandinavian 51
 triangular 281
Budd, P. 696
Budny, M. 93, 430, 783
Bullough, D. 291
Burch, M. 614
Burchard of Worms 736
Burghal Hidage document 511–2, 606, 932

burhgeats 51, 167, 199–200, 615
burhs (enclosures) 52, 65, 67, 69, 200, 508–9, 600–16
 5th–8th-century 601–5
 9th-century and 10th-century Viking/Scandinavian/Anglo-Scandinavian 610–3
 9th-century and later defended sites 605–7
 10th-century and 11th-century 613–6
 as defensive refuges 508
 development of towns 607–10
 minting-places 616
 Stafford 930–3, *931*
burial taxes 291
burials 239, 241, 541
 adults 649, 650, 655–6, 660–1
 Anglo-Saxon 34
 Anglo-Scandinavian 52, 55–8
 animals in 245, 251–3, 269, 768
 armour in 269–70
 barrows 33, 160, 269, 274–5, 540, 922
 bronze vessels in 244, 269, 274, 278
 buckles in 250, 271, 272
 chamber graves 253, 269, 270, 271
 children 257, 628–30, 648, 649, 651, 652, 654, 658, 659–61, 693
 Christian 26, 271, 273, 283, 290
 Christian symbols in 271
 churchyard burial 290–1, 305, 706–7
 cist graves 542
 clerical 273
 clothed 250, 267, 299–300, 691–3
 coffins 294, 297–9, 443, 790–1
 cremation burials 241–9, 244, 255, 645, 680, 693–4, 696, 979
 cinerary urns 243–7, 247, 255, 546, 693
 female 274, 277–8, 648, 649, 651, 659, 662
 funerary monuments 56–7, 74, 75
 gender and gender roles 694–8
 grave markers 56, 301, 302
 guilds and 291
 and identity 3, 10, 48
 infant burials 294, 295, 657–8, 706
 inhumation burials 24, 241–2, 243, 249–55, *251, 252*, 560, 680, 978–9
 jewellery in 656, 662, 857, 858
 liminal burials 729, *730*
 lyre burials 923
 male 278, 294, 651, 662–3, 676
 mortuary practice 851–2
 mortuary rituals 221–32
  current research issues 225–8
  developing study of 222–5

burials (*cont.*)
    outline of 228–32
  mound burials 48, 55
  multiple burials 709, 906
  practices 692
  princely 269, 852–3, 858
  prone 249, 296, 678, 714, 905–6
  provenance of ornaments 37–8
  Roman Britain 24, 25
  royal 271–3
  Scandinavian 48
  shroud burials 283, 284
  stones/pebbles in 300–03
  symbols of authority in 269–71
  unfurnished inhumation 538
  wooden houses for 738, 738–9
  youth group 648, *649*, 652, *654*, 654–6, *659*, 662
  see also cemeteries; grave goods; weapon burials
Burnell, S. 274, 280
Bursche, A. 874
buzzard 333
Byhrtnoth, Ealdorman 493, 781

Calberg, M. 93
Callmer, J. 317
Cambridge, E. 826
Cameron, E. A. 432
Cameron, K. 990–992
Camille, M. 767
Campbell, E. 546
Campbell, G.
  cereals 350, 351, 356, 357
  fallowing 386
  fruits and nuts 354
  hay meadows 386
  legumes 352
Campbell, J. 729–31
  Christianity 934
  historical sources 951–65
  signals of power 850, 855–6
  transport of goods 505
cancer 713–4
Canterbury Commemoration Society 1039
Capelli, C. 87, 683
  capital punishment 846, 894–7
caprines 362
carbon-14 dating, *see* radiocarbon dating
carburization 451
Carnicelli, T. A. 199
Carr, R. 137, 174, 362
carrots (*Daucus carota* L.) 355
Carruthers, M. 836

Carruthers, W. J. 352, 353, 356, 669
Carsten, J. 1014
Carver, M. 111
  Anglo-Saxon books 789
  burials 225, 230, 269, 274–5
  cemeteries 750
  cremation practices 244, 248
  inhumation practices 253
  intellectual territories 914–43
  mortuary change 241
  mortuary process 239
  paganism 768, 772
  public executions 275
  religion 743
  signals of power 855
Cather, S. 788
cattle 362, 367, 369–71, 958
cellared buildings 52
cemeteries 98, 180, 181, 280, 281, 301, 304, 305, 750–1
  dating of 275–6, 903–4
  early Anglo-Saxon 255–8
  mixed-rite 242
  orientation of 279
  Roman Britain 22
censers 787
Ceolfrith of Wearmouth-Jarrow 476, 816
cereals 347, 348–52, 356–7, 384–5, 387, 677
  storage of 144–5
cess pits 145–6
Cessford, C. 904
Chadwick, H. M. 932
Chadwick, N. 988
chalices 273, 483, 785
Chambers, R. 24, 230
Champion, T. 138 n. 4
Chaney, W. 771
Chapman, A. 203, 207
charcoal-burning 424–5
Chardonnes, L. 715
Charles, B. 145
Charles-Edwards, T. 850, 851, 859–60
Charnwood pottery 410
Charters, S. 669, 670
chatelaine fittings 277, 278, 651
Cherry, J. 432, 917
Cherryson, A. K. 302, 337
chickens/domestic fowl 667
children
  burial of 257, 628–30, 648, *648*, 649, 651, 652, 653, 654, *658*, 659–61, 693
  Christianity and 643
  grave goods 648, 649, 651, 654, 657

inhumation practices 250, 251
interpretation of term 632, 633, 643–4
invisibility of agency 628, *629*
Mill Hill burials 646–51, *651*
chip-carving 413, 461, *462*, 465
Christianity 105
  animal-style art and 885
  burials 26, 271, 273, 283, 290
  and children 643
  conversion to 699
  and healing and health care 716
  influence on art 474–9
  introduction of 106
  parochial system 962
  Roman Britain 16, 26
  sacred spaces and places 824–37
    chronological outline of main
      themes 825–32
    churches, functions of 833–4
    churches, identification and dating
      of 832–3
    churches, symbolism of 835–6
    in the landscape 836–7
    minster system 826–31
Christie, H. 833
Christie, N. 178
chrysography 812
churches 172–92, 509–10, 516–7, 779–92
  annexes and 136–7
  bells 178, 418
  burial arrangements 180–3
  chronology 176–80
  fonts 178
  functions of 833–4
  furnishings 418, 781, 782, 789
  identification and dating of 832–3
  ivories 784–7
  longitudinal history 187–92
  mapping territories 937–8, *939*
  material culture of 779–92
  metalwork 784–7
  minster system 826–31
  painting, glass, tiles 788–9
  sculpture 188–9
  shrines 182–3
  steeples 178
  stone carvings 790–1
  symbolism of 835–6
  textiles 781–4
  towers 178–9, *180*
  wood and stone 183–7
  wood carvings 790–1

churchyard burial 290–1, 305, 706–7
Cigaar, K. 110, 112
cinerary urns 243–7, *247*, 255, 546, 693
civitas 518, 520, 527, 557, 572, 604, 935
Clapham, A. J. 351, 352, 353, 356
Clarke, H. 559
Cleere, H. F. 426
cleft palates 713
Cleveland Casket 493
clothed burials 299–300, 691–3
clothing, *see* dress
Clunies Ross, M. 952
Cnut, king 55, 74, 971
  coinage 63, 594
  law code 140, 715, 895
Coates, R. 990, 991
Coatsworth, E. 94, 96, 98, 111, 407
  burials 273, 299
  churches 189
  craft production 418
  goldsmiths 414
  jewellery 409, 411
  makers' inscriptions 415
  material culture of churches 779–92
  monastic crafts 417
cod *(Gadus morhua)* 330–1, 334, 336–7
Codex Amiatinus 476, 477, 817, 827
Codex Aureus 479, 544
Coenwulf of Mercia 557
coffins 253, 291, *292*, *293*, *294*, 297
  St Cuthbert 273, 443, 783–4
Coggins, D. 50, 132 n.2, 211
Cogitosus 559
coinage 63, 523–4, 960
  as artefacts 584–5
  bronze 591
  coin loss 587, *588*
  in context 580–96
  Cotswolds' silver coin-hoards 23
  counterfeiting 16, 18
  as dating evidence 589–91
  dies 584–5, 593–5, *594*
  Edgar and 65
  Edward the Elder *180*, *180*, 586
  Egbert of Wessex 582–4, *583*
  evidence for minting 584–5, 593–5
  in exchange and trade 504–5
  future research 595–6
  gold 427, 557, 582, 589
  gold shillings 582, 589
  in graves 591–3
  as historical documents 581–4

coinage (cont.)
   Hywel Dda of Dyfed 66
   interpretation of finds 585–8
   in late Saxon graves 303
   mid Saxon 268, 561–2
   in mid Saxon graves 276
   Olaf Guthfrithson and 48
   Patching hoard 25
   possibly minted at monasteries 413
   recoinages 590
   reforms 615
   Roman Britain 16, 18, 22
   sceattas 268, 277, 504–5, 561–2, 568, 569, 570, 572–3, 957
   silver pennies 582, 583, 589, 592–3
   solidi 277, 463, 523, 570, 877–8
   stycas 268, 546, 563, 938
   thrymsas 434, 569
   and trade 574
   tremisses 569, 692
   as weights for use with balances 591–2
Cole, A. 744–5, 998
Coles, B. 333
Colgrave, B. 957
Collins, R. 331
Colloquies 95, 336, 338, 668, 802
combs 449, 979
   antler 54, 246, 250
   bone 54, 246, 432
commodity exchange 850–51
common-field system 189–91, 317–18, 377–79, 379
common oats (*Avena sativa L.*) 351–2
congenital dislocation of the hips 713
conger eels 330
Conkey, M. 695
Constantius: *Vita S. Germani* 516, 517, 522
Cook, A. 242, 257
Cool, H. 18
coopering 444
Copley, G. J. 996
Coppack, G. 174
copper 427–8
   copper alloy 564
   gilded chrismatory 481, 482–3
Corney, M. 527
Corpus of Anglo-Saxon Stone Sculpture (CASSS) 174
Correspondence Analysis 276, 917
Costen, M. 388
costume, *see* dress
costume jewellery 52, 53, 54
Cotton Tiberius calendar 338
Cowie, R. 413

cowrie shells 434–5
Cox, B. 995, 996
Cox, M. 695
   disease 707, 710, 712, 713–4, 717
   trauma 709
Coy, J. 331, 333, 368, 432
Crabtree, P. 329, 362, 367, 368, 369–70, 768
craft production and technology 405–18
   chronological overview 407–18
      5th-7th centuries 407–12
      8th-9th centuries 412–14
      10th-11th centuries 414–18
   sources/limitation of evidence 405–7
   see also crafts
crafts 413, 440–57
   antler-working 54, 246, 250, 418, 449
   bone-working 54, 246, 432
   glass 18–19, 73, 246, 251, 278, 27, 429, 456–7
   ironworking 449–51, 450
   metal objects, decoration of 455–6
   metalworking tools 455
   non-ferrous metalworking 451–4, 452
   sources of evidence 440–1
   wood and timber 417, 424, 441–4, 442
   see also jewellery; pottery; textiles
Cramp, R. 141–3, 535, 788
   burials 296
   churches 174, 780, 788
   coffins 297–299
   craft production 418
   flooring 789
   grave markers 301
   mapping territories 938
   Mercian Style 480
   stone and stones 433
   stone carvings 790, 792
   textiles 782
   Winchester Style 487–91, 490
   window glass 429, 474, 788
   wood carvings 790
   writing implements 811
cranes 333–4
Crawford, S. 715
   body and life course 625–37
   burials 240, 250, 271, 277, 294, 706
   children 643–4
   disease 297, 711
Creighton, O. H. 305
Crick, J. 184
cremation burials 680, 693–4, 696, 979
   cremation practices 241–9, 244, 255, 645
crime and punishment 892–910
   executions 275, 715, 895, 899–900, 923

exile 896
forfeiture of land 896
hundred courts 896, 961
judicial ordeals 899
monetary fines 895, 896
mutilation 715, 896–897
non-capital punishments 896–897, 899
prisons 899
written sources 893–9
Crockett, A. 149 n.8
Croft, R. 52, 207, 363
Cronyn, J. M. 790
crop rotation 317–18
Crosby, D. D. B. 434
crosses 56, 100, 107, 108, 110, 271, 273, 545, 787
Crowfoot, E. 94, 111
Crummy, P. 609
crystal 106, 434, 546
Cubberley, A. L. 782
Cubitt, C. 162, 831
Cuerdale hoard 586
cullet 429
cultivated vetch (*Vicia sativa* subsp. *sativa*) 352
culture: and death 975–80
Cummins, J. 338
Cunliffe, B. 141, 143, 301, 382, 526, 527, 606, 934
Currey, J. 449
Cuthbert, saint and bishop of Lindisfarne 273, 299, 783, 787
  coffin of 273, 443, 790–1
Cwicwine, monk 784–5
Cynewulf of Wessex 602

Dacre, M. 242, 257
Dallas, C. 71
Danegeld 490, 614, 959
Danelaw 48, 67, 586, 609, 915
Daniell, C. 297, 300–301
Daniels, R. 134, 138
Darby, H. C. 962
Dark, K. 525
Dark, P. 315
Darrah, R. 132, 135, 444
Darvill, T. 1037–8
daub 430
Daubney, A. 562–3
Davenport, P. 526
David, A. 121
Davies, D. J. 242
Davies, R. M. 418
Davies, R, R. 548
Davies, S. 120, 200–3
Davies, W. 547, 548, 951

Davis, A. 353, 356
Davis, S. J. M. 363
Davison, A. 381
Davison, B. K. 206
De Abbatibus (early-9th-century poem) 784–5
De diversis artibus (Theophilus) 443, 812, 813
De Excidio Britonum (Gildas) 31, 517
deafness 713
Dean, M. J. 248
death: culture and 975–80
deer 334, 335, 338, 339–340, 340
Deira 540, 541, 563
Deleuze, G. 1005–6
Dent, A. 333
dental diseases 707–8
Devlin, Z. L. 226, 248
Dickens, A. 767
Dickinson, S. 211
Dickinson, T. 468, 546, 715, 1018, 1019
  burials 266, 269
  cremation practices 284
  inhumation practices 251, 253
  mortuary ritual 221–32
  mortuary variability 240
  paganism 769
  religion 731
  Style I: 468, 470
  Wild animals 332
  wood-working 444
Dickson, C. 354
diet 667–684, 695–6
  age and 678
  chronological variations 681–3
  and disease 708–9
  floral/faunal evidence 668–9
  food preservation 668
  gender and 674–5
  geographic variations 679–81
  pottery analysis 669–70
  social differences in 674–8
  stable isotope analysis 670–674, 679
  wealth and 675–7
Dingwall, R. 704
disease 704–19
  detection and examination 704–7
  diet and 708–9
  disease–sin relationship 295
  epidemics 718, 956
  future research 717–18
  healing and health care 714–17
  gender, and incidence of 695
  specific diseases 707
    infectious diseases 710–12

disease (*cont.*)
    metabolic diseases 708–9
    other diseases 713–14
    physical impairment 295, 712–13
    trauma 709
DISH (diffuse idiopathic skeletal hyperostosis) 707
Dixon, P. 128, 136
DNA analysis 717, 917
Dobney, K. 174, 333–4, 363, 368, 370
Dodd, A. 71, 418, 607, 609
Dodgson, J. McN. 66, 994
Dodwell, C. R. 406, 407
    Anglo-Saxon books 813
    goldsmiths 414–15
    ivories 789
    monastic crafts 417
    place-names 417
    style 461
    textiles 781
Dolley, R. H. M. 590
Dölling, H. 140, 141–3
dolphins 335
Domesday Book 63, 184–5, 960, 962–4
    arable land 393
    fishing 337
    goldsmiths 415
    hunting 338–9
    iron ore smelting 427
    lead 428
    Norse personal names in 49
    wealth 962
    York 612
Donkin, L. 835
Donlon, D. 691
Doonan, R. 429, 595
Douglas, J. 33, 222
Dowden, K. 764
Down, A. 212, 248, 255, 257
Downham, C. 67
Down's Syndrome (trisomy 21) 713
dress *698*, 978
    artistic/documentary evidence 101, *102*
    in burials 250, 267
    in Christian art 105–6
    colours 105
    ecclesiastical vestments 110, 112, 490
    female *99*, *104*
    as gifts 112
    headdresses 101, 103–4, 105, 107, 110, 111
    and identity 4, 91–113
        Anglo-Scandinavian 53–5
        belief 106–10

    chronology 97–103
    ethnicity 104–6
    gender 103–4
    raw materials and manufacture 93–7
    status 111–12
    male 102, 104
    as marker of masculine authority 112
    reconstruction of 98–100, *99*
    shoes/footwear 97
dress accessories 98, 277, 278, 547
    in burials 274
    changes in 866
    fasteners 104
    of organic materials 96
    see also brooches; pins; strap ends
Drewett, P. 212
Drinkall, G. 276, 713
drinking horns 251, 331, 449, *469*, 469
Dronke, U. 970
Dudley, D. 210
Dumnonia 66, 538, 936, 953
Dumont, L. 805
Duncan, H. 709, 713
Dunning, G. M. 463
Dunstan of Glastonbury, St 110, 338, 417, 962
Dutour, O. 704, 705
dwarfism 713
dyeing 95, 430
Dyer, C. C. 199
Dyson, T. 609

Eadberht II of Kent 572
Eadred, king 67, 959
Eadric, Kentish king: law code 894, 895
Eadwald, king 528
eagles 332
Eagles, B. 279
Earconberht, Kentish king 894
earthfast timber buildings 128–46, *130*, *131*, *133*, *135*, *137*, 151–2
    annexes 136–40
    barns and granaries 144–5, *145*
    doorways 140
    form, function and configuration of internal space 136–46
    halls 139, 141–3, *142*, 144
    hearths 140–1
    kitchens and bakehouses 143–4
    latrines 145–6
    life cycle 134–6
    long halls 139, 142
    partitions 138–40
    relationship with Grubenhäuser 151–2

repair and rebuilding 134–6
  suggested chronological development 130
earthworks 954
East Anglia 959, 960
Eaton, T. 433, 835
ecclesiastical vestments 110, 112, 490, 783
Ecgberht, *see* Egbert of Wessex
Edgar, king 64–5, 488, 491, 973
Edmonson, G. 208
Edmund I, 66, 338
Edmund Ironside 67–8
education: archaeology in 1025–9
  higher and continuing 1027–9
  primary and secondary 1025–7
Edward the Confessor 110, 112, 961
Edward the Elder 65–6, 586, 959, 961
  burhs 615–6
  coinage 180, *180*, 602
  law code 897
Edwards, B. J. N. 48, 55
eels (Anguilla anguilla) 334, 335
Egan, G. 614
Egbert, archbishop of York 781
Egbert of Wessex 960
  coinage 596
Eglert, A. 47–8
Ekwall, E. 999
Elbern, V. H. 483
elephant ivory 432–3
Ellis Davidson, H. 880
embroidery 417, 461, 547–8
  Bayeux Tapestry 95, 338, 493
  ecclesiastical 781–4
Emery, P. A. 611
emmer (Triticum dicoccum Schübl) 348–50, 385
emporia 160, 334, 413–14, 508, 510–1, *558*, 568–9, 957–8
  definition 557–9, 560–1
  and signals of power 859
enamelling 456
enclosures 161, 200–3, *204, 207*, 323–4
enigmata (riddles) 974
Enright, M. 772, 880
Erä-Esko, A. 867
Erik Bloodaxe 67
Esmonde Cleary, S. 1010
  Roman Britain, end of 13–26
Ethelred II, *see* Æthelred
ethnicity
  dress and 104–6
  and identity 3–4, 104–6
  interpretation of 4–7
eutectic soldering 454

Evans, D. R. 527
Evans, J. A. 83–4
Evershed, R. P. 669
Everson, P. 56
  churches 174–5, 176, 187, 834
  monuments 305
  sacred places in the landscape 836–7
  votive deposits in wetlands and rivers 748
Evison, M. P. 56
Evison, V. 429
  burials 223, 227, 230, 248, 274, 279, 706
  cemeteries 242, 257, 275–6
  glass 429, 456
  Quoit Brooch Style 463
  signals of power 845
exchange and trade 504–6
execution cemeteries 296, 768, 899–909, 923
  burial practices 904–6
  dating 903–4
  geography of burials 906–9
  location 901–2
  re-use of earlier features 902–3
executions 275, 715, 897–8, 923
Exeter Book 897, 973, 974
exhibitions 1030–1, 1039
exile 896

Fabech, C. 869, 870
Fairbrother, J. 144–5, 200, 414, 453
Fairchild, H. P. 35
Fairnell, E. 336
Faith, R. 161, 167, 199, 388, 390
falconry 333, 337–8
Falkenberg, J. 642
fallowing 386, 393
Farke, H. 95
Fasham, P. J. 200, 212–13
Fates of Men, The (poem) 905
Faull, M. 242–3, 290, 535, 990–1
Faussett, B. 33, 222, 277, 279
Federation of Independent Detectorists (FID) 1034
Fell, C. 701
Fellows-Jensen, G. 417
Fen Drayton die 453
fer midboth 633–4
Fern, C. 239, 241, 245, 253, 768
Fernie, E. 178, 810, 832
Ferrante di Ruffano, L. 294
Field, N. 748
field systems 200, 377–94
  common-field system 189–91, 317–8, 377–9, *379*

field systems (*cont.*)
　early Saxon farming 380–3
　infield/outfield system 317, 322, 380, 383, 384
　late Saxon field layouts 392–3
　mid Saxon arable agriculture 383–6
　mid Saxon field layouts 387–92
　　enclosed 387–8
　　other layouts 390–2
　　unenclosed 389
　open-field system 321–2, 324, 377–9, 378, 390
　rectilinear 383
　strip systems 318–9, 391–2
field-walking 120–21
Filmer-Sankey, W. 269, 882
　cemeteries 255–8, 279
　inhumation practices 249–55
Filotas, B. 771
Finberg, H. P. R. 380, 388, 390
Finds Liaison Officers (FLOs) 1036, 1037
finger rings 101–3, 109, 250, 651
Fischer, S. 856, 858
fish 330, 668, 673, 677
Fisher, G. 697
fishing 337–8
Fishman, H. 625
Flammin, A. 474
Flanagan, J. F. 110
flatfish 330, 334
flax (Linum usitatissimum L.) 355–6, 385
Fleming, R. 70, 167, 336, 509
Fletcher, R. 771
Fleury, M. 269–71
Fleury Custumal 814 n.38
Florence (John) of Worcester 64, 66, 67–8
Foard, G. 318, 321, 381
Fogel, M. L. 678
folk medicine 716
Fonthill letter 895
food and drink
　in cremation burials 251–3
　in inhumation burials 249, 251
food plants 346–58
　cereals 144–5, 347, 348–52, 356–7, 384–5, 387, 677
　storage of 144–5
　dating of 348
　fruits and nuts 352–4
　legumes 352
　preservation of 347–8
　vegetables and flavourings 354–6
Foot, S. 827, 830
Ford, W. J. 319
Foreman, M. 276, 713

Foreman, S. 121, 162
Forestier's Disease 707
forts 19, 22–3, 24, 543, 547, 954
Foster, S. 772
Fowler, P. J. 213, 383
fowling 341–2
Fox, A. 210, 211–12
Fox, H. 318, 390, 393, 997
foxes 329
France-Lanord, A. 271–3
Franks Casket 335–6, 433, 479, 602, 827
Freeman, E. A. 988
Freestone, I. C. 406, 429, 435
Freyhan, R. 109, 783
Frithestan, bishop of Winchester 109
fruits and nuts 353–4
Fulford, M. 19, 520
Fuller, B. T. 678, 682
Fuller Brooch 485, 586–7, 787
furlongs 391, 393
furs 97, 331–2, 432

Gaffney, V. 19
Gaimster, M. 382–3, 392
　early Saxon image and power 865–85
Gameson, R.: Anglo-Saxon books 797–818
Gandersheim (Braunschweig) Casket 336, 481, 483, 786
Gannon, A. 413, 480, 582
Gardiner, M. 71, 131, 132, 134, 141, 143, 150 n.10
　enclosures 200
　fishing 337
　Franks Casket 335–6
　late Saxon settlements 198–214
Garmonsway, G. N. 336, 338
Garner, M. F. 296
garnets 96, 100, 109, 270, 273, 277, 408, 410–11, 434, 471, 472
　cutting 455–6
Gautier, A. 339
Geake, H. 111
　burials 231, 267, 268, 277, 290, 291, 299, 994
　cemeteries 180, 275–6, 304
　churches 174
　dress fashions 278–279
　gender associations in grave goods 707
　paganism 771
Geary, P. 42
Gell, A. 1007–9
Geller, P. 691
Gelling, M.: place-names 755–6, 970, 986–1000
Gem, R. 177, 178, 271, 283, 487
Gemuev, I. N. 736

gender and gender roles 688–701
    burial archaeology 694–8
    and diet 674–5
    disease, incidence of 711
    dress and identity 103–4
    previous perspectives 689–94
    settlement archaeology 699–701
    trauma, incidence of 695
genetic research 8, 717–18
geomagnetic surveys: Vale of Pickering 189–91, 192
geophysical surveys 121
Geþyncðo ('Dignities,' 11th-century text) 167, 199
Gerefa (11th-century text) 141, 199, 415
Germania (Tacitus) 317
Germanic peoples 5
Gerrard, J. 19, 524, 526
Gerritsen, F. 134
Gesta abbatum 808
Gibson, C. 241, 248
Gibson, J. J. 1015
Giddens, A. 849–860
gift exchange 851, 874, 1008, 1009
    as signal of power 850, 853, 856, 857–8, 860
Gilbert, J. 338
Gilchrist, R. 295, 301
Gildas 32, 825, 951, 952–3
    De Excidio Britonum 31, 517
Gillett, A. 937
Gillingham, J. 213
Gilmour, B. 290–1, 415–16, 517
Girault-Kurtzeman, B. 95
Gittos, H. 174, 180–1, 291, 305, 706
    Christian sacred spaces and places 824–38
glass 18–19, 73, 456–7
    beads 428–9, 456, 596
    in burials 246, 251, 278, 279, 537–8
    vessels 429, 537–8
    window glass 429, 474, 788–9
Glosecki, S. O. 770–1
Godman, P. 785
Goffin, R. 434
gold and gold objects 111, 417, 427, 454, 464, 470
    buckles 470, 979–80
    brooches 470
    clasps 473
    coinage 427, 573, 596, 615
    gold foil crosses 271, 273
    pendants 473, 571
Goldberg, P. J. P. 641–2
goldsmiths 414, 874
Goodburn, D. 424
Goodier, A. 280

Gordon, K. 296
Goscelin (Flemish monk) 782
Gosden, C.: anthropology 1003–1022
goshawks 337
Gould, J. 607
Gowland, R.
    age/ageing 642, 644–5
    burials 227, 661, 663
    grave goods 644
    mortuary change 240–1
    mortuary variability 239–40
Graham, A. H. 200–3
Graham-Campbell, J. 50, 55, 774
Grainger, G. 246, 255, 268, 281, 710
Granger-Taylor, H. 101, 112, 783
Grant, A. 365, 369–70
grave goods 37–8, 40–1, 246, 250, 299, 300–1, 977–8
    adults 649, 655–6, 660–1
    and age 644–5, 648–9, 657
    belt fittings 278
    children 648, 649, 651, 654, 658
    gender associations 663
    jewellery 651, 656, 662, 857, 858
    and paganism 767–8
    and reconstructions of clothing 98
    St Cuthbert 299
    significance of 635–6
    women 648, 649
    wooden chests 267, 278, 279
    youth group 648, 649, 654–6, 659
    see also cinerary urns
grave robbing 271
Graveney boat 505–6
Green, B. 246
Green, C. 120
Green, F. J. 349, 353, 356, 357
Greenwood, W. 338
Gregory of Tours 878 n.11
Gregory the Great, pope: Libellus Responsionum 517
Greig, J. 356
Grierson, P. 427, 586
Griffiths, D. 55
    Anglo-Saxon England, end of 62–75
Grubenhäuser 121, 134, 146–52, 147, 453
    grain storage in 144–5
    in Pictland 546
    relationship with earthfast timber buildings 151–2
    in Scotland 545
Gruffudd ap Llywelyn 548
Guido, M. 428–9

guilds 70, 291, 414
Guthlac, saint 902
Gwara, S. 802

habitus 1013, 1020
Hadley, D. M. 48, 50, 53, 55, 56, 57, 631–2
   burials 706, 707
   cemeteries 181
   churches 174
   late Saxon burial practice 288–306
hagas (land holdings) 607–8
Hagen, A. 337, 339, 668, 673
Hald, M. 97
Hall, A. 95, 353, 354, 356, 432, 613, 746
Hall, C. 381
Hall, D. 318, 381, 391, 393
Hall, R. A. 52, 54, 71
   burhs and boroughs 600–16
   burials 295, 297
   cemeteries 181
   jewellery 416
Hall-Torrance, M. 148–9
halls
   earthfast timber buildings 139, 141–3, *142*, 144
   late Saxon long halls 139, 142
Halsall, G. 55, 226, 229–30, 239, 240, 279, 774
Hamerow, H. 80, 156–9, 1019
   cemeteries 258
   changes in rural production 316
   field systems 382
   loom-weights 445
   religion 729
   rural settlement 119–26
   timber buildings 128–52
Hamilton-Dyer, S. 334
Hammon, A. 331, 333
hanging-bowls 278, 538, 567, *568*
Hanna, R. 971–2
Harald Bluetooth 51
Harald Hardrada of Norway 68
Harden, D. B. 230
Harding, A. F. 541
Hardy, A. 145, 174, 418, 810
hares 329, 338
Härke, H. 160, 240, 271, 444, 856, 916
   age/ageing 643, 644
   burials 224, 253, 645, 693
   cemeteries 255–8
   weapon burials 250–1, 856
Harley Psalter 490–1
Harold II 68, 959
Harrington, S. 250, 253
Harrison, D. 424, 505

Hart, E. 122
Harvey, M. 391
Hase, P. H. 570
Haseloff, G. 463, 467, 468, 471, 867
Haslam, J. 426, 605, 606, 933
Hatcher, J. 428
Hauck, K. 470, 870–1
Haughton, C. 249, 257
Hawkes, J. 182
Hawkes, S.C. 33, 100, 111, 246, 268, 876
   burials 223, 290
   cemeteries 255, 276, 278, 280, 281
   infectious diseases 710
   jewellery 276, 463
   military metalwork 461–3
   signals of power 853, 895
hawking 333
hay meadows 386
Hayman, G. 296
Heald, A. 454
healing and health care 634, 714–17
   Christianity and 716–7
   elf remedies 757
   folk medicine 716
   magic ornaments 106
   hearths 140–1
Heather, P. 269, 270
Heaton, T. H. E. 671
Hedeager, L. 472, 769, 866, 870, 875, 880
Hedges, R. E. M. 670
   Anglo-Saxon migration 79–89
hefting 122
Heighway, C. 174, 294
hemp (*Cannabis sativa* L.) 355–6, 385
Henderson, C. G. 210
Henig, M.: late Roman towns 515–30
Henry of Huntingdon 955, 964
Henry, P. A. 94, 432
herbs 354, 357
Hereford agreement 65–6
Hereford Gospels 493
Hereford Troper 493
herrings *(Clupea harengus)* 334, 337
Herring, P. 66, 213
Hesse, M. 393
Hetherington, D. A. 331
Hewett, C. A. 833
Hey, G. 121, 123, 145, 296, 381, 382, 386
Heywood, B. 19
Heyworth, M. P. 429
Hiberno-Saxon style 479
Higgs, E. 338
Higham, N. 39, 678, 680, 681

Hildebrandt, H. 317–18
Hill, D. 167, 413, 427, 937, 958
Hill, J. D. 1011, 1021
Hill, P. 300, 825
Hiller, J. 386
hillforts 24, 538, 606, 615, 954
Hillman, G. C. 350
Hills, C. 465, 468, 859, 916
   Anglo-Saxon identity 3–11
   burials 227, 242, 243, 253
   cemeteries 525
   mortuary change 240–1
hilltop sites 23–4
Hines, J. 49, 103, 409
   burials 226, 227, 229, 231, 268
   dating of cemeteries 276
   inhumation practices 249–50
   literary sources 968–81
   paganism 764–6, 770, 772
   place-names and sacred places 744
Hinton, D. A. 71, 74, 407–8, 411, 416, 509
   Alfred Jewel 485
   medieval trade 574
   metalwork 409, 415, 455
   raw materials 423–35
   signals of power 855
Hirschmann, C. 41–2
Hirst, S. 239, 240, 254, 255, 269, 296
Historia de Sancto Cuthberto 783
Historia Ecclesiastica (Bede) 31–2, 33, 42, 140, 281
   Æthelberht's law code 971
   Christian centres 517
   condemnation of nunnery 824
   heathen temples 753
   on London 523
   raw materials 836
   on wild animals 327
Hlothere, Kentish king 894, 895
Hobbs, R. 22
Hodges, R. 319–21, 392, 415, 559–62, 569, 853
Hoffmann, M. 93
Hogarth, A. C. 279
hogback tombstones 56–7
Hoggett, R. 743
Høilund Nielsen, K. 411, 471, 472, 769
Holbrook, N. 290, 300
Holloway, J. 297
Holmqvist, W. 409
Holt, R. 69, 174, 175, 509, 607, 608, 782
Hooke, D. 69, 211, 505
   field systems 381, 382
   place-names 339, 745, 997
   rural production 315–24

hooked tags 412, 568
Hope-Taylor, B. 135, 137, 138, 140–1, 143, 152, 160
   shrines, beams, poles and totems 755
   temples, shrines and idols 752–3
Horie, C. V. 790
horizontal stratigraphy 275
Horn, W. 810
horn-working 432
horse mackerel (*Trachurus trachurus*) 330–1
horses 364, 768
Horsman, V. 71, 609
hospitals 716–17
house societies 1013–14
Howard, H. 813
Howard-Johnston, J. 432
Howe, E. 480
Howell, R. 526
Huggett, J. W. 411, 434, 853
Huggins, P. J. 50
Hugh d'Avranches of Chester 64
Hugh-Jones, S. 1014
Hughes, M. J. 406
Hughes, R. 430
Hull, B.: diet 667–84
Humberht, local notary 540
hundred courts 896, 961
Hundred Ordinance 895
Huneberc of Heidenheim 557–9
Hunter, J. 418, 429
Hunter, K. 353, 356, 357
Hunterston Brooch 546
hunting 329, 337, 338–9, 341–2
Huntingdon, R. 239
Huntley, J. P. 353, 354
Hurcombe, L. 627
Hurst, J. D. 430
Hurst, J. G. 268, 382, 937, 938
Hutcheson, A. 565
Hutton, R. 765
Hyslop, M. 268, 278, 280, 281, 290
Hywel Dda of Dyfed 66, 333, 548

identity
   Anglo-Saxon 3–11
   Anglo-Scandinavian 46–58
   burials and 3, 10, 48
   churches and 57
   dress and 4, 91–113
      belief 106–10
      chronology 97–103
      ethnicity 104–6
      gender 103–4
      raw materials and manufacture 93–7

1058 GENERAL INDEX

identity (*cont.*)
    status 111–12
    ethnicity and 3–4, 689
    regional divisions/differences 10–11
idols 766–7
imagery in art 461, 471–2
immigration 696: *see also* migration
Ine, king of Wessex: law code 140, 335, 388, 390, 894, 895, 899
infant burials 294, 295, 671–2, 706
infectious diseases 710–12
infield-outfield system 317, 322, 380, 383, 384
Ingold, T. 1015, 1016
Ingrem, C. 339
inhumation burials 24, 569, 680, 978–9
    inhumation practices 241, 243, 249–55, *251*, 252
Inker, P. 463, 467
Innes, M. 48, 67
Insoll, T. 758
Insular Style 475–9
intermarriage 34–5, 39, 41, 48, 49–50, 55, 541: *see also* marriage
International Criminal Court: Rome Statute (2002) 41, 42
internet: archaeology on 1032–3
Ipswich ware 161, 164, 268, 362, 406, 445, 575
iron ore smelting 424–7
ironworking 449–51, *450*
ivories 490, 694
    in church furnishings 789–90
    diptych 475–6
    elephant 432–3
    figures *488*, 490
    on high status books 816
    walrus 432–3, 490, 806
Ivy, J. 782

Jackson, K. H. 988, 989
Jacques, D. 328, 333
Jakob, B. 708
James, E. 269–71, 274, 280
James, S. 130, 137, 141, 143, 161
Jelling Style 51, 53, 54–5, 491, 492
Jesch, J. 616, 773
Jessop, O. 329, 338
jet 73, 93, 434
Jewell, R. H. I. 480
jewellery 276, 409, 411–12, 416, 472
    bead ornaments 98–100
    in burials 671–2, 674, 680, 876, 881
    cloisonné 96, 475
    costume jewellery 52, 54
    crosses 100, 107, *108*, 271, 273, 547, 787

gilding 427–28
inscriptions on 96–7, 109
rings 101–3, 109, 250, 538, 874
wrist clasps 96, 97, 100, 103, 104–5
see also brooches; pendants
John (Florence) of Worcester 64, 66, 67–8
Johnson, P. 181
joint diseases 707
Jones, A. 239
Jones, G. 168, 351, 352, 356, 363, 365, 561
Jones, M. J. 174, 609
Jones, M. U. 453
Jones, R. 70, 322, 339, 381, 384, 393
judicial system 906–10, 961
    Alfred 894–5
    Anglo-Saxon laws 906–9
    Cnut 140, 715, 895
    hundred courts 896, 961
    Ine, king of Wessex 140, 335, 388, 390, 895, 896, 899
    other written sources 897–8
Judith of Flanders 805

Karkov, C. 790
Katzenberg, M. A. 671, 678, 682
Keefer, S. L. 112
Keen, L. 430
Keene, D. 608
Kemble, J. 34, 222
Kemp, R. L. 602
Kendrick, T. D. 36–7
Kenneth, king of Scotland 66
Kent, J. P. C. 592
Kent Archaeological Society 1033
Kenward, H. K. 353, 356, 432, 613
Keynes, S. D. 484, 491
Kilbride, W. 764, 775
Kilmurry, K. 52–3, 428, 431, 445
King, A. 50, 132, 211
King, D. 782
King, M. D. 591
King, V. 199
Kinsley, A. 243
Kinsley, G. 121, 132
Kipling, R. 294, 301
kitchens and bakehouses 143–4
Kitzinger, E. 790
Kjølbye-Biddle, B. 55, 520, 522, 600
    burials 291, 294, 297–9
    defended sites 605
    religion 825
    textiles 782–3
Klausner, D. N. 183

Klindt-Jensen, O. 491
Klukas, A. 834
Knight, J. 518
knitting 95
knives 246, 250, 282, 299, 416, 426, 441, 449
   length of blade, and age 643
Knüsel, C. J. 227
Kopytoff, I. 1015
Kornbluth, G. A. 434
Kromann, A. 463, 874
Krouse, H. R. 671
Kylie, E. 333

Lacnunga 716, 717
Ladle, L. 424–5
Laing, L.: Britons and Anglo-Saxons 534–48
land charters 897–8, 899, 900, 954
Lang, J. 56, 57, 73, 74, 182, 189, 453, 733, 790, 792
   churches 182, 189
   monuments 302, 305
language and languages 969–70
   literary language 970–2
   see also place-names
Lantfred of Winchester: Translatio et Miracula St Swithuni 896–7
Lapidge, M. 781
lapis lazuli 105
Larratt Keefer, S. 783
Latour, B. 1006–7
latrines 145–6
Laurence of Durham 799–800
law codes, see judicial system
Lawler, A. 672, 675, 676, 677
Lawson, A. 381
Lawson, M. K. 959
lead (metal) 428, 456
Leahy, K. 53, 54, 227
   Anglo-Saxon crafts 440–57
   cremation practices 242, 243, 247, 255
Leary, J. 569
leather-working 97, 417, 432, 449
Lee, C. 103
   disease 706–19
Lee, E. S. 40
leechbooks 712, 717
Leechdoms (10th-century text) 668
leeches (healers) 709, 711, 715
Leeds, E. T. 34, 35, 36, 37, 39, 465
   burials 223, 230, 231, 267
Leges Edwardi Confessoris 964
legumes 352, 385
Leigh, D. 138, 468, 769
Lemanksi, S. J. 339

Lendinara, P. 971
lentils (Lens culinaris Medik) 352
leprosy (Hansen's Disease) 711–12
Lethbridge, T. 37–8, 156, 267
Letts, J. 350
Lewis, C. 70, 208, 382, 953
Lewis, M. 630, 661, 708
Libellus Responsionum (Gregory the Great) 517
Liber Eliensis 781–2
LiDAR (Light Detection and Ranging) 315
Liddiard, R. 203, 339
Liebermann, F. 198, 199, 811
Life of St Dunstan 338
Life of St Juliana 897
Life of St Ninian 717
liminal burials 729, 730
limpets 330–1
Lindisfarne Gospels 475, 476, 477, 478, 814
linen 93, 431
linked estate model 320, 323
LiPuma, E. 1006
literacy 968–9, 971
literary sources 968–81
   Anglo-Saxon literature 969–72
   culture and death 975–80
   literature and archaeology 972–5
Lives of St Cuthbert 490
Lobb, S. J. 352
long ranges 203–206
longhouses 210–11
loom-weights 94, 149, 150, 430, 445, 447, 448, 636
Losco-Bradley, S. 121, 132, 382
Loseby, S. T. 159
Loveluck, C. 73, 124, 125, 134, 135, 140, 574
   animal husbandry 363
   Bernicia 542–5
   Britons and Anglo-Saxons 534–48
   churches 174, 828
   settlement hierarchy 163, 165
Lowther, P. 296
Loyn, H. R. 338
Lucy, S. 80, 174, 332, 916, 1018
   burials 224–225, 240, 259
   cemeteries 257
   gender and gender roles 688–701
Lund, J. 748
Luscombe, M. R. 274
lynxes 331
lyre burials 923

MacGregor, A. 336, 449
Mack, J. 426
mackerel *(Scomber scombrus)* 334

Mackie, W. S. 897
MacKreth, D. 145
Maddicott, J. 427, 428, 718
magic 106, 715, 736–7, 858–9, 1019
magnetometry 121
Magnus, B. 461, 470
Mahany, C. 426
Mainman, A. 416, 417, 602
Major, H. 136, 138, 141, 143, 145 n.6, 242, 257
malaria 712
Malcolm, king of Scotland 66
Malcolm, G. 424, 432, 569, 605
Malim, T. 276
Maltby, M. 330
Mammen Style 491, *492*
Manchester, K. 708, 710
Manco, J. 527
Mannig, abbot of Evesham 417, 816
manorial sites 200–4, *205*
manuscripts, decorated 417, 474–9, 480, 484, 490, 491
Margeson, S. 53, 54
marriage 57, 103, 465, 701, 857, 877: *see also* intermarriage
Marshall, A. 130, 131, 132, 138, 159
Marshall, G. 130, 131, 132, 138, 159
Marth, R. 483
Marvin, W. P. 334, 338
Marzinzik, S.: archaeology and the public 1025–40
Mason, D. J. P. 52, 71
material culture 17, 54
  Anglo-Saxon 13–14, 35, 1016–19
  changes in 8–10
  of churches 779–92
Maull, A. 207
Mauss, M. 1012–13
maxillary sinusitis 710
Maxims II: 747–8
Mayes, P. 248
Maynard, D. 426
Mays, S. 174, 177, 294, 671, 682, 707
McCann, B. 296
McCarthy, M. 71, 526
McClure, J. 331
McCobb, L. M. E. 669
McComish, J. 602
McCone, K. 633–4
McDonnell, G. 409, 425
McDowell, J. A. 110
McEvoy, B. 86–7
McKinley, J. 242, 243, 245, 248, 645, 715
McNeil, S. 296, 297

McOmish, D. 381, 382
Meadows, I. 274, 275
Meaney, A. 276, 332, 715, 716, 731, 756, 896
  burials 223, 290
  cemeteries 268, 276, 278, 280
  paganism 768, 769, 772
Meeson, R. 120, 443, 605
Mercia 65–6, 67–8, 557, 561, 939–41, 953
Mercian Style 483–7
Meredith, J. 427
metabolic diseases 708–9
metal-detecting 73, 561, 733, 1033–4, 1040–1
metalwork 409, 412, 413, 417, 418, 453, 594–5
  Anglo-Saxon influences in 559–60
  belt sets *462, 463, 464*
  Carolingian influences 484–7, 491
  churches and 784–7
  decoration of 455–6
  discs 867
  dress fittings 53, 73, 96, 98
  ecclesiastical 480–2, 490
  gold as prosperity marker 111
  military 461–3,
  non-ferrous 451–4, *452*
  pins 25, 96, 100, 101, 103–4, 109, 274, 277, 536
  secular: *see* jewellery; weapons
  strap-ends 51, 52, 54, 101, 413
  see also Borre Style; Ringerike Style; Style I; Style II; Urnes Style
Metcalf, D. M. 63, 239, 412, 574, 589, 615, 960
Metcalf, V. M. 527
Metzler, I. 714
Meyvaert, P. 476
Migne, J.-P. 736
migration 7, 32
  elite-migration hypotheses 41
  and endogenous change 30–42
  molecular evidence of 79–89
  methodologies and sample material 80–1
  molecular techniques 82–8
Miket, R. 137, 535
Miles, D. 381, 382, 833
Miles, T. J. 305
Miller, D. 1015
Millett, M. 80, 121, 135, 138, 140, 159, 527
  landed estates as lifetime gift 271
Mills, A. D. 1000
Milne, G. 71, 149 n.8
minke whales 335
Minter, E. M. 210
minting-places 610, 611, 615, *616*, 933, 960
Minuchin, S. 625
Mitchell, J. G. 434

Mitchell, W. T. J. 1008
Moffett, L. 930
  food plants 346–58
molecular evidence of migration 79–89
  methodologies and sample material 80–1
  molecular techniques 82–8
    DNA evidence of population shifts 84–5
    genetic evidence from living
      populations 85–8
    geographic evidence based on bone
      chemistry 82–4
Møller-Christensen, V. 711
Monasteriales indicia 802
monasteries 559, 560, 604, 831, 880, 928, 958
monastic crafts 417
Montgomery, J. 83, 717
Montserrat, D. 634
monuments 250, 307: *see also* sculpture
Moorhead, S. 592
Moreland, J. 161, 574, 575, 916
Morphy, H. 1015
Morris, C. A. 424, 444
Morris, C. D. 211
Morris, R. 186
  churches 509–10
    local 172–92
    minsters 827
    and settlements and ancient
      monuments 751
  location of cemeteries 304
Mortimer, R. 121, 167, 427
Morton, A. 584
mortuary rituals
  early Anglo-Saxon 238–59
    cemeteries 242, 255–8
    cremation practices 241–249, *244*
    inhumation practices 241–2, 243, 249–55,
      251, *252*
    mortuary change 240–1
    mortuary process 239
    mortuary variability 239–40
  mid Saxon Final Phase 266–84
    artefacts in 277–9
    dating burials and cemeteries 275–7
    elite burials 269–75
  late Saxon 288–306
    grave goods 297–304
    location of cemeteries 304–5
    mortuary variability 293–6
mouldboard ploughs 385
Mudd, A. 425
Müldner, G. 682
Müller-Wille, M. 923

Mulville, J. 335
Munby, J. 529
Murphy, K. 391
Murphy, P. 349, 353, 356, 357, 381
museums 1029
musical instruments 443–4
mussels 330
mute-group theory 628–9
Mutheisus, A. 110, 299
Myhre, B. 318
Mynors, R. A. B. 957
Myres, J. N. L. 223, 246, 916, 955

Naismith, R. 582
Napier, A. S. 782
Nash, A. 382
National Council of Metal Detectorists
  (NCMD) 1034
Naylor, J. 563, 565, 566
Neal, D. 19
Necklaces/necklets 100, 107–9, 277, 592, 648,
  648–50, 653, 655, 656, 659–61, 876, 877,
  879, 881, 1008, 1015
neo-paganism 1039–40
Neuman de Vegvar, C. L. 602
New Minster Charter *488*, 491
Newman, J. 164, 241
Niblett, R. *518*, 526, 825
Nicholls, K. 952
niello inlays 455
nighthawking 562, 1034
Nightingale, J. 827
Nitz, H.-J. 317
Nockert, M. 95
Noddle, B. A. 363
non-ferrous metalworking 451–4, *452*
Nordenfalk, C. 477, 478
Norse language 49
North, R. 780, 781, 787
Northover, J. P. 412
Northumbria 539–544, 970
nucleated settlements, 209, 538
nunneries 830, 831, 880

Ó Carragáin, T. 833, 834
obligation as signal of power 850, 857
O'Brien, C. 137
O'Connell, T. C.: diet 667–684
O'Connor, T. P. 334, 336
  animal husbandry 361–73
Oddy, W. A. 428, 434
Odo of Bayeux 64, 784
Offa of Mercia 511, 582, *583*, 605, 901

Offa's Dyke 547, 954
offerings 874–5
Oggins, R. 328, 338
Ogham inscriptions 547
Ogham stones 520, 521
Ohthere (Scandinavian merchant) 47–8, 105, 432
Olaf Cuaran 66–7
Olaf Guthfrithson 48
Oliver, T. 134
On Diverse Arts (Theophilus) 441, 812, 813
Ong, W. 968
Oosthuizen, S. 319, 321
　Anglo-Saxon fields 377–94
open-field system 321–2, 324, 377–9, 378, 390: see also common-field system
open grazing 211–12
Opie, I. 936, 937
Opie, P. 936, 937
opium poppies (*Papaver somniferum* L.) 355, 356
Ordericus Vitalis 964
O'Reilly, J. 476
organic materials 73
Origen 716
Orton, F. 175, 296, 792
osteitis 710
osteo-archaeology 631–2, 633
osteoarthritis 707
osteology 717
osteomyelitis 710
osteophytosis 707
O'Sullivan, A. 334–5
O'Sullivan, D. 432, 544–5, 780, 798
Oswald, king 543, 781
Ottaway, P. 426, 593–5, 440, 602–4, 613
otters 331–2
Otto, goldsmith 585
oval enclosures 387–8
Ovenden, P. J. 418
Owen-Crocker, G. R. 430, 432
　dress and identity 91–113
oxen 637
oysters 330

Pader, E.-J. 224, 240, 250, 643, 675, 392, 851–2,
Pagan, H. E. 301
paganism 105, 106, 107, 108, 109, 775
　animals and 787
　anthropomorphic images 767
　cosmology 874–7
　definition of 731–2
　grave goods 774
　material traces of cultic practice 766–8
　neo-paganism 1039–40

place-names and 775
Scandinavian influences 772–3
as shamanism 770–2
Viking influences 337, 363
zoomorphic images 467
Page, M. 70, 322, 381, 384, 393
Paget's Disease (*osteitis deformans*) 712
paintings
　panel paintings 788, 790
　wall paintings 430, 461, 487
palaeoepidemiology 704
palaeopathology 704, 705, 718
Palmer, J. B. O. 161, 163, 164, 165, 168
panel paintings 788
Pantos, A. 162, 749, 896
Pape, H.-W. 483
parchment 812–13
Parfitt, K. 250, 257, 267, 646
Park, D. 461, 487
Parker, S. J. 715
Parker Pearson, M. 748, 1013
Parry, S. 119, 207, 383, 384, 386, 393
parsnips (*Pastinaca sativa* L.) 355
Parsons, D. N. 49, 601
Passio Sancti Albani 517
PASt explorers 1032
Paterson, C. 53, 54
Patrick, P. 258, 715
Payne, S. 381
Peak District 539–40
Pearce, S. 538
peas (*Pisum sativum* L.) 352
Peer Polity Interaction (PPI) 917
Peirce, I. 415
Pelling, R. 145 n.6, 348–9
penannular brooches 25, 538, 541, 547
Penda of Mercia 952
pendants 54, 100, 274, 277, 281, 731
　bracteates 106, 462, 463, 469, 881, 883–5
　　C-bracteates 871
　　D-bracteates 858, 872, 875
　　Denmark 868–9
　　iconography of 472
　　Kentish 876
　　as offerings 867–9
　　and pagan cosmology 870–73
　　as political medium 873–6
　　and powerful women 876–80
　　Style II: 885
　Christian decorations 107, 108
　gold 462, 476
　in inhumation burials 248
　pagan decorations 106, 109

Riseley 282
silver 509
Style II: 412–13, 885
Penitential (Theodore) 716
Penn, K. 226, 227, 228, 231, 268, 279, 755
perch 330, 335
Percival, J. 350–51
peregrine falcons 333
Peri didaxeion 717
periostitis 710
periwinkles 330
Perkins, D. J. 429
Perring, D. 71, 522, 609
Pesch, A. 870, 873, 875, 880
Pestell, T. 169, 250, 251, 253, 254, 257, 483, 604, 779, 802, 828, 923
  markets, *emporia, wics* and 'productive' sites 556–74
Petts, D. 16, 290, 604, 833
  pewter 416
Pfeiffer, S. 678
Phillips, D. 19, 288, 289, 294, 297, 299, 301
Philpott, R. 24, 229, 240–1
physical impairment 295, 712–13
Pickles, T. 834, 836–7
pigs 364, 369–70, 372, 677
pike 330, 335
pin-beaters 94, 150, 446, 447, 448
Pinder, M. 96, 407, 409, 411, 414, 415, 417–418,
  craft production 417, 418
  jewellery 409, 411–12, 414
pins 96, 100, 101, 103–4, 109, 274, 277, 522
  bone 51
  decorated 25
Pinter-Bellows, S. 363
Pirenne, H. 573
Pirie, E. J. E. 593–4
place-names 504, 601, 986–90
  and Anglo-Scandinavian identity 49, 50
  British settlement-names 992–3
  burhs and 604
  cereals and 357
  and definition of sites 529
  enclosures and 388
  English, chronology of 993–7
  execution cemeteries 902–3
  and judicial system 896
  'late' settlement names 998–9
  methodology 986–7
  names containing loan-words from Latin 991–2
  names referring to British people 990–1
  Old English 461

and paganism 767
pre-English names, historical significance of 987–90
reference books 999–1000
and sacred places 744–7
and shrines, beams, poles and totems 755–6
and temples, shrines and idols 752–5
and wild animals 332–3, 339
plague 709, 718, 956
Planning Policy Statement 5: Planning for the Historic Environment (PPS5) 1038 n.5
Pleiner, R. 415–16
Plesters, J. 812
Plunkett, S. J. 413
Pluskowski, A. 333
  paganism 764–75
poliomyelitis 710–11
Pollard, M. 876
Pope, J. C. 302
porpoises 337
Portable Antiquities Scheme (PAS) 73, 547, 562, 733, 1032, 1035, 1036–7
Porter, D. 802
Porterfield, A. 716
portus 557
Postgate, M. R. 386
pottery 73, 415, 431, 445, 461, 964
  analysis of food residues 669–70
  Anglo-Saxon cremation pottery 55
  bar-lug 211
  in burials 223, 229, 275
  Ipswich Ware 161, 164, 268, 362–3, 445, 572
  mapping territories 938, *939*, 940
  Roman Britain 18, 25
  Stafford Ware 930, 932, *932*
  Stamford Ware 52–3
  Torksey Ware 53
  wheel-thrown 52–3
Powell, A. 335
Powlesland, D. 120 n.1, 121, 150, 151, 159, 189
  cemeteries 257
  inhumation practices 249–55
  landscape study 541, 836–7
PPG16 (Planning Policy Guidance note on Archaeology and Planning) 1037–8
Pratt, D. 486
Pressblech dies 452, 456
Price, E. 19
Price, L. 810
Price, N. 266, 731, 770, 771, 773
Prien, R. 32
prisons 899
Pritchard, F. 101, 432

Privat, K. L. 331, 671, 672, 673, 674–5, 676, 677
productive sites 160–1, 572
Prognostics 715
protector-spirits 735–6
Pryor, F. 123 n.3
punishments 715
pyres 247–8

quarrying 433
Quinnell, H. 65
Quoit Brooch Style 24–5, 463–5, *464*

racism 41–2
Radford, C. R. 128, 782
radiocarbon dating 227, 230, 277, 289, 919
Rahtz, P. 24, 138, 149, 150, 156–7, 916
  on bow-sided buildings 51
  burhs 632
  burials 271
  cemeteries 224, 290
  churches 174, 186, 833
  enclosures 200
  goldsmiths 419
  hunting 338
  settlements 119, 120, 122, 162, 165, 198, 207
  wood-working 461
Raistrick, A. 211
Ramsay, N. 414
Ramsey Psalter 490
Ravensdale, J. R. 381
Ravn, M. 224, 228, 246, 248, 696
raw materials 423–35
  glass, colourants, earth materials, salt 428–31
  metals 424–8
  stone and stones 433–5
  textiles and animal products 431–3
  timber and trees 423–4
Rawcliffe, C. 711
Ray, K. 319
re-enactors 1030
Rectitudines Singularum Personarum 198, 339
red deer 328–9, 301
red kites 333
Redknap, M. 547, 548
Reece, R. 592
Rees, W. 143 n.5
Regia Anglorum 1030
Regularis Concordia 834
relational thought 1009–14, 1020
religion 846
  animals and 735, 736
  idols 770–1
  local cults 182
  overview 731–44

paganism 768–79
  animals and 770–1
  definition of 768–70
  material traces of cultic practice 766–8
  Scandinavian influences 772–3
  as shamanism 770–2
  Viking influences 774–5
sacred spaces 742–63
  ancient monuments and structures 749–56
  natural places 743–9
  women and 881
  see also burials; churches
reliquaries 110, 278, 479, 484
  gold buckles 884–5
  St Cuthbert 461, 790
  see also Gandersheim Casket
Renfrew, C. 917
Ressler, C. 352
Reynolds, A. 161, 174, 206, 240, 291, 296
  crime and punishment 892–914
Rhodri Mawr of Gwynedd 547
Richards, J. 132 n 2, 149 n 8, 167, 412, 461, 604
  Anglo-Scandinavian identity 46–58
  burials 224, 695–6
  cremation practices 245, 246, 248, 645
Richards, M. P. 682
Richards, P. 853
Richardson, J. 373
Riddler, I. 414
Rigold, S. E. 592–3
Ringerike Style 54–5, 73–4, 491
rings 101–3, 109, 250, 538, 874
Ripon Jewel 786
Rippon, S. 124, 189, 381, 387, 391
rites of passage 857
ritualization 1014
rivet wheat (*Triticum turgidum* L.) 350–1
Roach Smith, C. 222
Robert d'Oilly 64
Robert of Rhuddlan 64
Roberts, B. 123, 189, 207, 321, 387, 390, 393
Roberts, C. 361, 709, 717
  disease 707, 708, 710–14, 717
  health 638
  trauma 709
Robinson, M. 348–349
Rodwell, K. 301, 302, 304, 305, 433
  churches 174, 179, 290, 837
Rodwell, W. 304, 305, 433, 791, 829, 837
  Angel of the Annunciation 481–2
  burials 288, 301, 302
  church symbolism 835–6
  churches 174, 179, 184, 837

roe deer 328–9, 339
Rogers, J. 707
Rogers, N. 416, 417
Rogerson, A. 71, 381, 568–9
Rollason, D. 303–4, 327
Roman Britain 13–26
  burials 24, 25
  cemeteries 22
  coinage 16, 18, 22
  elite (*rentier*) class 15–16
  forts 19, 22–3, 24, 529
  glass 18–19
  hillforts 24
  imperial/economic collapse 21–2
  peasantry 16
  pottery 18, 25
  state organs 15
  towns 15, 17, 22–3, 527–30
  villas 15–16, 17, 19, 22–3
Rosenblitt, J. A. 769
Roskams, S. P. 363
Rosser, G. 291, 510
round-houses 23
Royal Bible 484, 485
Ruben, I. 339
Ruin, The (poem) 973
Rumble, A. R. 167, 831, 958
rural production 315–24
  changes in time and place 315–21
  crop cultivation 321–3
  marginal landscapes 323–4
rural settlement
  enclosures 122–3
  overview 119–26
  settlement layout and buildings 122–4
  status, definition of 124–6
Russell, A. 258
Russell, B. 1037–8
Russell, C. 756
Russo, D. 508
Ruthwell Cross 476, 477, 546, 790, 791
Ryder, M. L. 93
rye (*Secale cereale L.*) 351, 357, 385

sacred spaces 742–59
  accessibility and visitation 756–7
  ancient monuments and structures 749–56
    churches, settlements and ancient monuments 751–2
    monuments and burials 750–1
    shrines, beams, poles and totems 755–6
    temples, shrines and idols 752–5
  Christian 824–38
    chronological outline of main themes 825–32
    churches, functions 833–4
    churches, identification and dating of 832–3
    churches, symbolism of 835–6
    in the landscape 836–7
  identity and belief 758
  longue durée 757–8
  natural places 743–9
    fields and groves 744–5
    fissures, hollows and pits 746–7, 747
    hilltops 745
    rivers, pools, springs, wells and wetlands 747–9, 869
  place-names and 744–6
Sadler, P. 337
Salin, B. 463: *see also* Style I; Style II
salmon 335, 337
salt 430
Salter, C. 425
Salter, H. E. 173
Samson, R. 299, 566
Sánchez Romero, M. 627
Saunders, A. D. 211
Saunders, S. 705
Saunders, T. 363, 561
Sawyer, P. 64, 301–2, 339, 752, 964
Saxon Relief Style 463, 465–7, 466
Sayer, D. 227, 240, 249, 255, 257
Schaefer, S. B. 737
Scheschkewitz, J. 24
Schön, M. 463, 465
Schulze, M. 877
Schutkowski, H. 680, 681
Schutz, H. 769
Scobie, G. 294, 296, 301
Scotland 56, 66, 544–8
Scragg, D. 746, 972
Scull, C. 132, 413, 471, 559, 592
  signals of power 848–60
sculpture 57, 479–83
  Angel of the Annunciation 481, 480–1
  Anglo-Saxon influences on 546–7
  Christianity and 57, 475
  churches 188–9
  funerary monuments 74, 75
  stone monuments 56, 74, 75, 791–2
sea bream (*Sparidae*) 330–1
Seafarer, The (poem) 977
Seebohm, F. 391
Semple, S. 257, 275, 304, 902
  sacred spaces 742–59

Senecal, C. 337
Senior, J. B. 186
Serjeantson, D. 337
settlement archaeology
    and Anglo-Scandinavian identity 50–3
    gender and gender roles 699–701
settlement hierarchy 156–68
    early Saxon period 157–160
    mid Saxon period 160–5
    late Saxon period 165–7
settlements, late Saxon 198–214
    high-status 199–207
    impermanent 211–13
    peasant 207–11
shamanism 729–31
    paganism as 770–2
    and weaving 737
Sharpe, R. 517, 522–3
sheep 362, 364, 367, 369, 371–2
Shelly Ware 938
Shephard, J. 224, 231, 254
Sheppard, J. 322, 382
Sherborne Pontifical 490
shields 55, 253, 274, 278, 341, 424, 444, 451, 467, 649, 651, 691, 692, 873, 976
shielings 122, 212
shires 69–70
shoes/footwear 97
Shoesmith, R. 605
Short, I. 74–5
shrines 744, 745, 827
    Christian 182
shroud burials 283, 284
Sidebottom, P. 74
Sigeferth, bishop of Lindsey 67
Sigeric, Archbishop of Canterbury 781
signals of power
    in burials 855–9
    emporia and 859
    overview 845–7
    social transactions and gift exchange 846–60
signet-rings 528
silk 93, 105, 431–2, 613
    ecclesiastical vestments 110, 781
    wall-hangings 781
silver 427, 964
    gilded 473
    coinage 22, 582, 583, 587, 591
    pendants 492
Silvester, R. 323, 391
Simeon of Durham 789
slaves and slavery 37, 636, 917, 957, 958

smallpox 709
Smith, N. 212
Smith, R. 223
smiths/smithies 409, 411, 415–16, 427
social archaeology 627, 631–2
Sofaer, J. *see* Sofaer Derevenski
Sofaer Derevenski, J. 630, 642, 694–5
Sørensen, M. L. S. 696
Souden, D. 1030
Spall, C. 799
sparrow hawks 333
Speak, S. 19
Speake, G. 248, 269, 471–3
    paganism 769, 770
Spearhafoc of Abingdon 417
spearheads 278
Spector, J. 689
Speed, G. 56
spelt (*Triticum spelta* L.) 348–50, 385
spindle whorls 93, 95, 150, 250, 430, 434, 447
spinning 93, 94, 408, 880
Spurrell, M. 834
St Brice's Day Massacre 48, 67
St Neots Ware 938
stable isotope analysis 24, 56, 671–4, 717, 919
    Anglo-Saxon cemeteries 680
    average animal/human values 674
    East Anglia 682
    male burials 676
    by region 679
    Weingarten cemetery, Germany 680
Stafford Ware 930, 932, *932*, 938
Stamper, P. 52, 207, 363
Stanford, S. C. 279
Stark, L. 739
Starley, D. 595
Steadman, S. 208
Stenton, Sir F. M. 65, 66, 745, 988, 992–3
Steuer, H. 884
Stevens, C. 352
Stevenson, W. H. 782
Stiff, M. 429
Stocker, D. 52, 56, 57, 189, 304, 305
    church symbolism 835
    churches 174–6, 185, 187, 189, 834
    churchyard burials 289–90
    sacred places in the landscape 748, 836
Stoerz, C. 120
Stone, J. F. S. 905
stones/pebbles: in burials 300–2
Stoodley, N.
    burials 224, 226, 230, 293–4, 694–5, 706, 857

cemeteries 257
childhood to old age 641–64
grave goods 691–2, 857, 1019
inhumation practices 249, 250
mortuary variability 240
Stout, M. 634
Stoves, J. L. 331–2
strap-ends 51, 52, 54, 101, 413
Strathclyde, kingdom of 544–5
Strathern, M. 1006–9
strip field systems 317, 391–2
Struth, P. 279
sturgeon 337
style 460–93
afterlife of 493
beginning of 461–3
Christian art 474–9
Insular Style 475, 476, 479
Mercian Style 479–83
Quoit Brooch Style 24–5, 463–5, *464*
Saxon Relief Style 463, 465–7, *466*
Style I: : 268, 467–71, 546, 769, 867, *868*, 875
Style II: 267–9, 470–4, 769, 884–5
Trewhiddle Style 73, 455, 483–4, 486
Wessex, rise of 483–7
Winchester Style 74, 487–93, *488*, *489*, *490*, *491*
Style I: 268, 467–71, 867
bridle fitting 546
decorated brooch *868*, 875
square-headed brooches 769
Style II: 267–9, 470–4, 769
animal-style art 884
bracteates 885
gold buckles 885
pendants 472, 885
Sutton Hoo Society 1036
Sutton Hoo Visitor Centre 1029, *1030*
Suzuki, S. 24, 465
Svein Forkbeard of Denmark 67
Swain, H. 522
Swanton, M. 198
swords 55, 278, 279, 415, 426, 546, 649, 651, 691, 692, 859, 976, 1019
Sykes, N. 64, 681
woods and the wild 327–42
Symonds, L. 53
Synod of *Clofesho* 605
Synod of Gumley 604–5
Szirmai, J. A. 814

Tacitus: *Germania* 317
Talbot, C. H. 756
Tallon, P. 896

tallow candles 433
tanning 432
taphonomy 705
Tassilo chalice 785
Tatham, S. 83
Tating Ware 431
Tatton-Brown, T. 433, 836
Tatwine of Canterbury 805
taxation 590, 933, 954
Taylor, C. C. 318, 321, 381, 382, 393
Taylor, G. 23, 123, 425
Taylor, H. M. 176, 177, 832, 962
Taylor, J. 176, 177, 453, 962
Tebbutt, C. 156
television: archaeology programmes 1031–2
textiles 445–8
in churches 780–4
dyeing 95, 430
embroideries 95, 417, 461, 480–1, 493, 547–8, 781–4
garment production 94–5
in inhumation burials 249–50, 253
manufacture 93–7, 415, 703
spinning 93, 94, 408, 450, 703
types of 94
washing 95–6
weaving 93–5, 408, 445–8, *446*, 737–8
woollen cloth 431
Thacker, A. T. 64, 515, 517, 522–3, 958
Theoderic, goldsmith 585
Theodore, archbishop of Canterbury 105, 337, 608, 781
Theophilus 418, 441, 826, 827
Thetford Ware 952
Theuws, F. 305
Thirsk, J. 393
Thomas, A. 290, 300
Thomas, C. 517, 936–7
Thomas, G. 53, 73, 74, 141, 145–6, 747, 832–3
craft production and technology 405–18
Thomas, M. G. 41, 42, 87–8, 697
Thompson, I. 825
Thompson, V. 302, 706, 769
burials 291, 297, 299
cemeteries 281
disease–sin relationship 295
grave goods 300–1
Thorn, C. 339
Thorn, F. 339
Thorney Gospels 816
Thurlby, M. 833
Tiberius Bede 484
Tiberius Psalter 493

tiles: in churches 788–9
Tilley, C. 759
timber buildings 120, 545
  foundation trenches 130–1
  plank-in-trench construction 131–2
  post-in-trench construction 131–2, 134
  sill-beam construction 131, 134
  social context 128–52
    earthfast buildings 128–46, *129*, *131*, *133*, *135*, 151–2
    Grubenhäuser 121, 134, 144–5, 146–52, *147*, 453
    stave-built wall construction 132
  two-square module 130
Timby, J. 135–6, 140, 243
tin 428, 429, 431, 813
Tinti, F. 291
Tipper, J. 146–7, 148, 149–50, 151, 159
Todd, M. 66
toilet implements 246, 250
tools/tool-kits 96, 100, 125, 246, *247*, 410, 411, 426, 428, 441–3, *442*, 455
Toon, P. 969
Töpf, A. L. 84
topochronology 275
Topping, P. 391
Tostig, Earl of Northumbria 68
Townend, M. 49, 970
towns 69–70, 71–2, 915, 973
  development of 607–10
  inter-relationship between 510–12
  late Roman 515–30
    definition of 541–2
    major towns 519–25
    smaller towns 525–7
  Roman Britain 15, 17, 22–3
Toynbee, J. C. M. 523
trade centres, pre-Viking 556–75
  early medieval trade, explanatory models 559–62
  productive sites 562–6
  trade and exchange 566–73
  see also *emporia*
Trafford, S. 49
Translatio et Miracula St Swithuni (Lantfred of Winchester) 896–7
trauma 631–2, 695, 709
Treasure Act 1996: 1034–6
Treasure Valuation Committee (TVC) 1035
trepanning 715
Treveil, P. 608, 614
Trewhiddle Hoard 428, 539, 785–6
Trewhiddle Style 73, 455, 483–4, 486, 546–7

tribal areas 935–7, *936*
Tribal Hidage 4, 537, 539–40, 935, 955
trout 335
Tsurushima, H. 328, 336–7
tuberculosis 361, 695, 705, 711, 717
Turner, S. 66, 174, 428, 743, 748–9
Tweddle, D. 93, 95, 110, 301, 406, 480–1, 792
Tyers, I. 185–6, 833
Tylecote, R. F. 415–16, 424–5, 434
Tyler, A. 242, 257
Tyler, S. 136, 138, 141, 143, 145 n.6

Uhtred, Earl of Northumbria 67–8
Ulmschneider, K. 562, 565, 574–5, 604, 779–80
  settlement hierarchy 156–68
Unwin, P. T. H. 381
Upex, S. 381, 382–3, 391
urbanization 503–12
Urnes Style 55, 73–4, 491, *492*

Vale of York Hoard 484
van der Veen, M. 349
Van Gennep, A. 642
van Houts, E. 299, 300
van Vuure, C. 331
vegetables and flavourings 354–6
vellum 432, 798, 894, 928, 929
Vespasian Psalter 479, 544, 802, 812 n.35
Vierck, H. 881
Vikings 609–10, 614
  Viking attacks 162, 490, 491, 614
  Viking Great Army 55
villas: Roman Britain 15–16, 17, 19, 22–3, 538, 729, 750, 1010–11
Vince, A. 410, 431, 445, 522, 604, 611–12, 932, 933, 938
Vita Aelfredi (Asser) 338, 605, 606, 608, 609, 764, 958–9
Vita Ceolfridi auctore anonymo 816–17
Vita Guthlaci 749
Vita S. Germani (Constantius) 516, 517, 520, 522

Wade, K. 362–3
Wade-Martins, P. 138, 140, 141, 145–6, 288, 295, 363
Wainwright, F. T. 66
Waldron, A. 174
Waldron, T. 288, 299–300, 707
Wales 547–8
Walker, J. 149, 754
wall-hangings 781–2
wall paintings 430, 461, 487
Wallis, S. 425

walrus ivory 432–3, 490, 789, 806
Walton, P. 95, 613
Walton Rogers, P. 56, 94–5, 97, 98, 100, 103, 105, 111
　burials 226, 228, 231, 267, 978
　dyeing 430
　gendered identities 697
　plant remains 348
　textiles 408, 430
Wamers, E. 416
Ward, S. 71
warfare 23–4
warlordism 20, 21, 22, 26
Warner, P. 321, 387
warrior crosses 56
Wasserschleben, F. H. 716
watermills 543, 605, 962
Wat's Dyke 547
Watson, J. 97, 424
Watts, D. 765
Watts, L. 174, 301, 833
Watts, V. 999
Waughman, M. 425
Wawn, A. 47
Weale, M. E. 87, 683
weapon burials 55, 56, 257, 269–70, 274, 278, 279, 649, 651, 652, 656, 662, 663, 856–7
　animals in 269
　in cremation burials 246
　in inhumation burials 250–51, 252, 253
weapons
　Mercian Style 480, 482
　spear heads 545
　swords 52, 415, 471, 472, 482, 486
　see also weapon burials
Weaver, S. 148–9
weaving 93–5, 408, 445–8, 446
　loom-weights 94, 149, 150, 430, 445, 446, 448, 636
　shamanism and 737–8
Webster, L. 276, 281, 413, 453, 785, 815, 882
　burials 231, 270, 271, 273, 274, 275, 277
　style 406, 460–93
Weddell, P. J. 210
weights and balances 591–2
Welch, M. 212, 229–30, 248, 255, 257, 411
　mid Saxon 'Final Phase' 266–84
wergelds/wergilds 897, 955–6
Werner, J. 855
Wessex 66, 120, 953, 955: see also Alfred, king of Wessex
West, J. 487–91
West, S. 140, 147–8, 149

West Stow Anglo-Saxon village 1029
whalebone 433
whales 337
Wheeler, H. M. 382
whetstones, decorated 270
Whitaker, C. R. 20
White, P. 319
White, R. 19, 518, 529, 537
White, S. 25
White, W. 300
Whitehouse, D. 560
Whitelock, D. 140, 335, 601, 607, 610
　Anglo-Saxon England, end of 64, 65, 66, 67–8, 69, 70
　place-names 988, 992–3
Whitfield, N. 463
whiting 330, 334
Whyman, M. 295, 297
Whymer, J. J. 296
Wicker, N. L. 774
Wickham, C. 505
wics 160, 334, 413–14, 417, 457, 602–4
　definition 557–9, 558
Wieczorek, A. 270–71
Wife's Lament, The (poem) 973
Wihtred, Kentish king 894
wild animal exploitation 327–342
　bird bone data 330
　early Anglo-Saxon period 328–32
　mid Anglo-Saxon period 332–6
　late Anglo-Saxon period 336–40
　mammal bone data 329, 338, 340
　place-names 332–399
　symbolism of animals 331–2, 341
wild boar 331, 332, 338, 770
wildfowling 330
William FitzOsbern 64
William the Conqueror 64, 68, 959
William Maldebeng 'Malbank' 64
William of Malmesbury 65, 781
William of Poitiers 962
William of St Calais 782
Williams, A. 51
Williams, D. 410, 431, 445
Williams, G. 592
Williams, H.
　burials 225, 226, 275, 294–5, 302, 305, 934
　cemeteries 181, 750
　early Anglo-Saxon mortuary practices 238–59
　paganism 765, 770–2, 772
　public executions 275
　religion 742–3
Williams, R. 145

Williamson, T. 70, 189, 318, 319
   field systems 323, 383, 389, 392
Wilmott, T. 294, 527, 528
Wilson, D. M. 96, 109, 110, 181, 406, 748, 814
   paganism 765, 774
   Winchester Style 490, 491
Wilson, D. R. 766, 767
Wilson, J. F. 86–7
Winchester Style 74, 487–93, *488*, *489*, *492*, *493*
witchcraft 897–8
Wolfram, H. 880
wolves 332, 333
women
   burials 274, 277–8, 648, 649, 651, 659, 662
   as cult specialists 880–1
   grave goods 648, 649
   powerful women, and bracteates 876–80
Wood, I. N. 174
wood and timber 441–4
woodworking and wooden objects 73, 417, 424, 441–4
   wooden chests 267, 278, 279
wool 93, 94, 95, 96, 101, 369, 371–2, 431, 448, 964
Woolf, A. 926, 952

Woolgar, C. M. 337
workboxes 267, 278, 279
Worley, F. L. 768
Wormald, F. 490
Wormald, P. 67, 894, 895, 896–7, 961
Worssam, B. C. 433
Wrathmell, S. 189, 207, 321, 387, 390, 393
Wright, T. 222
   wrist clasps 96, 97, 100, 103, 104–5, 689, 691
Wroe-Brown, R. 296, 608, 613–4
Wulfstan II, Archbishop of York 48, 65, 105, 199, 615, 971
Wymer, J. J. 200, 905

Yalden, D. 333
Yeates, S. J. 525
Yorke, B. 388, 765, 775, 830, 849, 880, 881
Young, G. 542
Young Archaeologists' Club 1033
Youngs, S. M. 526

Zadora-Rio, E. 180–1, 305
Zarnecki, G. 302
Zimmermann, W. H. 129

Index of Archaeological Sites

Note: pages numbers in *italics* refer to figures and tables.

Abbot's Worthy, Hampshire 669, 677
Abingdon, Oxfordshire 230, 417, 486, 713, 798
Addingham, Yorkshire 302–3, *303*
Adwick-le-Street, Yorkshire 56
Ailcy Hill, Ripon 295, *298*, 717
Alchester 527 n.
Alington Avenue, *see* Dorchester, Dorset
Alton, Hampshire 674–5, *676*
Alwalton, Cambridgeshire 246
Anderitum, *see* Pevensey
Andover, Hampshire 242, 253, 257
Apple Down, *see* Marden
Appleton-le-Street, Yorkshire 186, *188*
Aquae Sulis, *see* Bath
Aquemann, *see* Bath
Ardington, Berkshire 390
Ashley, Northants *191*
Asthall, Oxfordshire 248, 269
Aston Magna, Gloucestershire 387–8
Atlantic Trading Estate, *see* Barry
Avebury, Wiltshire: 275, *752*

Babraham, Cambridgeshire 682
Bamburgh, Northumberland 472, 542, 601, 614, 792
Banna, *see* Birdoswald; Carlisle
Banstead, Surrey 274
Bantham, Devon 330–1
Barking, London 802
Barrington, Cambridgeshire 250, 276
Barrow Hills, *see* Radley
Barry, Glamorgan 290
Barton Bendish, Norfolk 381, 383
Barton Court Farm, *see* Abingdon
Barton-on-Humber, Lincolnshire 713, 833
 burials 276, 299–300, *300*, 301, 302
 church 174, 179
Basingstoke, Hampshire 121, 159, 271
 timber buildings 135, 137, *137*, 138
Bath, Somerset 19, 301, 519, 526–7
Bawsey, Norfolk 558, 562–3, *564*, 569, 570, 802

Beckley, Oxfordshire 480, 574
Benty Grange, Derbyshire 106, 274–5, 449, 770
Bergh Apton, Norfolk 674–5, *676*, 681
Berinsfield, Oxfordshire 253, 331, 529, 674–6, *676*, 680
Bernuthsfeld, Germany 95
Bestwall, *see* Wareham
Beverley, Yorkshire 363, 369, 418
Bicester, Oxfordshire *139*, 143, 145 n.
Biddlesden, Whittlewood 381
Bifrons, Kent 108, 591
Biggleswade, Bedfordshire 557
Birdoswald, Cumbria 526–7
Bishopstone, Sussex 141, 145, 330, 339, *734*
Bitterne, *see* Southampton
Blacknall Field, *see* Pewsey
Bloodmoor Hill, Suffolk 699, *700*
Blythburgh, Suffolk 336, 791, 803
Bokerley Dyke, Dorset 24
Boksten, Sweden 95
Bolnhurst, Bedfordshire 786
Boss Hall, *see* Ipswich
Botal, Dumfries and Galloway 545
Botolphs, West Sussex 150 n. 10
Bourn Valley, Cambridgeshire 391
Bradford-on-Avon, Wiltshire 487, 527
Bran Ditch, Cambridgeshire 904
Brandon, Suffolk 136–7, 174, 333, 570
 animal-bone assemblages 362–3, 369–70
 Staunch Meadow 565–6
Brantham, Suffolk 586
Breedon, Leicestershire 480, 751
Brighthampton, Oxfordshire 22, 592
Brixworth, Northamptonshire 183, 833
Broomfield, Essex 269, 279
Bryant's Gill, Cumberland 50, 211
Buckland, *see* Dover
Burdale, Yorkshire 363
Burgh Castle, Norfolk 674, *680*, 681
Burnham, Norfolk 174

Burton Lazars, Leicestershire 389, 391
Bury St Edmunds, Suffolk 789, 817
Butler's Field, *see* Lechlade

Cadbury Castle, Somerset 538, 615
Cadbury Congresbury, *see* Congresbury
Caerleon, Newport 518, 527
Caerwent, Monmouthshire 517–8, 526, 528
Caistor-by-Yarmouth, Norfolk 675–6, *680*, 681
Caistor St Edmund (Caistor-by-Norwich) 279, 526, *572*, 755
  burials 246, 268, 571–2
  jewellery *408*, *571*
Caldecote, Cambridgeshire 382
Cambridge 901
Camerton, Somerset 718
Cannington, Somerset 24, 290
Canterbury, Kent 71, 417, 813, *815*, 836
  coins 523, *523*, 881
Capel Maelog 174
Carisbrooke, Isle of Wight 470
Carlisle, Cumbria 455, 544
Carlton Colville, Suffolk 473, 593, 674, 676–7, 851
Castle Eden, County Durham 542
Castle Mall, Norwich 85
Castledyke, *see* Barton-on-Humber
Castra Venta, *see* Caerwent
Catherington, Hampshire 382
Catholme, Staffordshire 132, *730*
Caxton, Cambridgeshire 382, 391
Chalton, Hampshire 121, 138, 384
Chamberlains Barn, *see* Leighton Buzzard
Chapel Street, *see* Bicester
Cheapside, London 608
Chelsea, London 608
Cheddar, Somerset 51, *139*, 143, 200, 338
  royal complex 138, 165–6, *166*, 206, 414
Chessel Down, Isle of Wight 468
Chester, Cheshire 71, 354, 511, 548
Chester-le-Street, County Durham 490
Chesterton Lane Corner, *see* Cambridge
Chichester, Sussex 529
Cirencester, Gloucestershire 524–5
Claughton Hall, Lancashire 48
Clausentum, *see* Southampton
Cleatham, Lincolnshire 243, 255, *452*
Cledemutha, *see* Rhuddlan
Coddenham, Suffolk 569
Codford St Peter, Wiltshire 486
Colchester, Essex 22, 381, 611
Collingbourne Ducis, Wiltshire 334
Cologne, Germany 878
Colonio, *see* Colchester

Colsterworth, Lincolnshire 189
Colton, Norfolk 54
Colyton, Devon 487
Compton Beauchamp, Oxfordshire 382
Congresbury, Somerset 120
Cook Street, Southampton 296
Coombe, Kent 244
Coppergate, *see* York
Corbridge, Northumberland 542–3, 751
Corinium, *see* Cirencester
Cornforth, County Durham 542
Coton Park, Warwickshire 207
Cottam, East Yorkshire 51, *558*, 563
Cottenham, Cambridgeshire 121, 123
Countisbury, Devon 606
Covent Garden, London 605
Cow Low, Peak District 274
Cowdery's Down, *see* Basingstoke
Crayke, Yorkshire 181
Cricklade, Wiltshire 933
Crickley Hill, Gloucestershire 23
Croydon, Surrey 242
Cumberworth, Lincolnshire 301–2
Cumwhitton, Cumbria 48, 55, 774
Cutcombe, Somerset 387
Cynuit, *see* Countisbury

Dacre 188
Dartmoor, Devon 210, 212
Deal, Kent 257, 646–51, *647*, *648*, *649*, *650*
Dean Moor, *see* Dartmoor
Deerhurst, Gloucestershire 174, 480, 788, 833
Desborough, Northamptonshire 273
Dinas Powys, Glamorgan 547
Doon Hill, *see* Dunbar
Dorchester, Dorset 22, 24, 120, 389, 391
Dorchester-on-Thames, Oxfordshire 188, 538
  burials 230, 518, 529, 538
  Queenford Farm 24, 230, 518, 529, 538
Dorcic, *see* Dorchester-on-Thames
Dorney, Berkshire 121n, 162, 383, 386
Dover *(Dubris)*, Kent 85, 527
  burials 29, 227, 257, 275, 277, 473
  weaving sword *446*, 447
Driffield, Yorkshire 541, 896
Droitwich, Worcestershire 430
Droxford, Hampshire 674–6, 680
Dublin 73
Dubris, *see* Dover
Dunbar, East Lothian 545
Durham, County Durham 273
Duxford, Cambridgeshire 382
Dyke Hills, *see* Dorchester-on-Thames

Earl's Barton, Northamptonshire 174, 179, *179*
East Boldon, County Durham 542
East Molesey, Surrey 149 n.
East Stour, Dorset *485, 487*
Eastbourne, Sussex 696
Eburacum, see York
Eccles, Kent 19, *272*, 713–4
Edix Hill, *see* Barrington
Elstow, Bedfordshire 480
Elton, Cambridgeshire 382
Ely, Cambridgeshire 188, 493, 688
   West Fen Road 123, 168
   Westfield Farm *690*
Eoforwic, see York
Exeter, Devon 19
Exmoor 381
Eynesbury, Cambridgeshire 334
Eynsham, Oxfordshire 174
   Eynsham Abbey 335, 418
   New Wintles Farm 137

Faccombe Netherton, Hampshire 9, 146
   hunting 337, 339
   manor site *144*, 200, 414
   workshop 453–4
Faversham, Kent 411 5, 429 1111
Faxton, Northamptonshire 381
Fen Drayton, Cambridgeshire *453*
Fetter Lane, *see* London
Finglesham, Kent 474, 773, *875*
   cemetery *256, 257, 268, 281, 878*
Fishamble Street, Dublin 73
Flaxengate, *see* Lincoln
Flixborough, Lincolnshire 174, 333–5, 415, 570, 604
   animal-bone assemblages 363, 367, 368, 370
   metalwork *446, 447*, 565, 802
   rural settlement 124–5, 132, 135, 138
   tools 441–4, 455
Flixton Quarry, Suffolk 152
Ford, Salisbury 274
Forest of Dean, Gloucestershire 427
Frocester, Gloucestershire 19, 392, 538
Funen, Denmark 869, *872, 879*
Fyfield Down, Wiltshire 382

Galley Hills, Banstead 274
Galsted, Jutland *462*
Garton-on-the-Wolds, Yorkshire 593
Genoels Elderen, Belgium 476
Gilton, Kent 592

Glastonbury, Somerset 296, 418
Glevum, see Gloucester
Gloucester 427, 524, 525, 608
   St Mary-de-Lode church 174
   St Oswald's 174, 418, 509, 713
Goltho, Lincolnshire 51, 146, 213, 339, 382, 391
   kitchens 131 n. 143
   long hall 138–40, *139*, 143
   long range 206
   manorial site 199, 203, *205*
Gosforth, Cumbria 57
Grantham, Lincolnshire 382–3
Great Chesterford, Essex 242, 257, 706
Green Shiel, Lindisfarne 432
Greensted, Essex 71, *72*, 185, 833
Guildhall, *see* London
Guildown, Surrey 903–4, 906, *907*

Haddon, Cambridgeshire 381, 382–3
Hadrian's Wall 15
Hales and Loddon, Norfolk 381
Halton Moor, Yorkshire 484
Hamwic, see Southampton
Hardingstone Hall, Northamptonshire 388
Hardwick, Cambridgeshire 382
   Harestock, Winchester 901
Harrogate, Yorkshire 484
Harrow-on-the-Hill, Middlesex 745, *746*
Hartford Farm, *see* Caistor St Edmund (Caistor-by-Norwich)
Hartlepool, Cleveland 134, 138, 453, 543
Haslingfield, Cambridgeshire 466
Hatch Warren, Hampshire 202
Heath Wood, Ingleby 774
Heckington, Lincolnshire 562–3, 569
Hereford 605
Heybridge, Essex 538
Higham Ferrers, Northamptonshire 145, *145*, 388
   cereals 339, 356–7
Hinton Hall, Suffolk 388
Hogbridge, East Lothian 545
Holderness, Yorkshire 391
Hordwell, Hampshire 391
Horton Kirby, Risely 281, *282*
Hound Tor, *see* Dartmoor
Hovingham, Yorkshire 182
Howletts, Kent *468*
Hoxne, Suffolk *464*
Hungate, Lincoln 611–2
Hungate, York *612, 613*
Hurst Park, East Molesey 149 n. 8

Ingleby 792
Ipswich, Suffolk 333
　animal-bone assemblages 363, 368, 369, 371
　Boss Hall 100, 109, *108*, 277, 570–1, *571*
　Buttermarket cemetery 570
　Gippeswic 567, 569–71, 602
　Whitehouse Road 200, *201*
Ixworth, Suffolk 273

James Street, London 356
Jarrow, *see* Wearmouth
Jorvik, *see* York

Ketton, Rutland *144*, 174
Kilham, East Yorkshire 362, 366, 369, 372
Kingston Down 277
Kingsworthy, *see* Winchester
Kinsley Cave, Yorkshire 331
Kirk Hammerton, Yorkshire *173*, 177
Kirkdale, Yorkshire 174, 301
Kislingbury, Northamptonshire 388

Lake End Road, *see* Dorney
Lankhills, *see* Winchester
Lastingham, Yorkshire 790
Launceston Castle, Cornwall 211
Lechlade, Gloucestershire 674
　animal bones 330
　burials 242, 250, *251*, 276, 278
　Butler's Field 250, *251*, 676
Ledsham, Yorkshire 188
Leicester 85
Leighton Buzzard, Bedfordshire 278, 280, 281
Lejre, Denmark 956–7
Lichfield, Staffordshire 382, 391, *482*, 480
Lincoln 517, 524, 594
　animal-bone assemblages 363, 366–7, 368, 369, 371
　coins 587, 594, 595
　Flaxengate 71, 594, 595, 609, 611
　Hungate 611–2
Lindisfarne 432, 780
Lindum Colonia, *see* Lincoln
Little Paxton, Cambridgeshire 200, 202, 207
Little Snoring, Norfolk 492
Llan-gors, Powys 101, 111, 547–8
Llanbedrgoch, Anglesey, Gwynedd, 547
Llandough, Glamorgan 290
Londinium, *see* London
London 71, 334, 587
　animal-bone assemblages 363, 369, 370
　burials 296, 301, 492, 522–3
　Cheapside 608
　Chelsea 608

Covent Garden 605
Fetter Lane *481*, 480
Guild Hall 74, 301
James Street 356
jewellery *416*, *571*
Londinium 522
Lundenburh 608
Lundenwic 356, 424, 432, 434, 561, 567, 571, 602
metalwork 74, *482*, 480
St Martin's in the Fields 522
St Paul's 492
Thames Exchange site 594, 595
Thames Street 522
waterfront sites 613–4
Westminster 188, 833
Lowbury Hill, Berkshire 274
Lower Brook Street, Winchester 22–3
Ludlow, Shropshire 472
Luguvalium, *see* Carlisle
Lundenwic, *see* London
Lydford, Devon 606, 614

Malham Moor, Lancashire 211
Malmesbury, Wiltshire 604
Marden, Kent 281–3
Marden, Sussex 212, 257, 708
Market Lavington, Salisbury 85
Marston Moretaine, Bedfordshire 208–10
Mavourne Farm, Bolnhurst 786
Mawgan Porth, Cornwall 120, 210–211, 213
Maxey, Cambridgeshire 381
Medehamstede, *see* Peterborough
Melbourn, Cambridgeshire 709, 713
Meon Hill, Hampshire 903–4, *905*
Micklemere, Suffolk 381
Middleton, Yorkshire 56, 189
Middleton-by-Pickering, Yorkshire *190*
Milfield, Northumberland 160, 391, 542
Mill Hill, *see* Deal
Mill Lane, Thetford 595
Milton Regis, Kent 273, *274*
Minster-in-Thanet, Kent 572, 812 n.
Monkwearmouth, *see* Wearmouth
Morningthorpe, Norfolk 675, 676
Mote of Mark, Kirkcudbright 545–6
Mucking, Essex 121, 134–5, 157–9, *158*, 453
　burials 230, 464, 466, 628
　field systems 381, 382
　metalworking 425, 452

Nazeingbury, Essex 713
Nether Wallop, Hampshire 487
Nettleton Top, Lincolnshire *447*, 448

New Wintles, *see* Eynsham
Newark, Nottinghamshire 243
Newark Street, Leicester 85
Newent, Gloucestershire 302
North Elmham, Norfolk 145–6, 295
  animal-bone assemblages 362
  buildings 51, 138, 140, 143, 208, *209*
North Marden, Sussex 212
North Shoebury Hall, Essex 200, *201*
Northampton 136–7, 426
Norton, Northumbria 85
  burials 654–7, *657*, *658*, *659*, *660–1*
Norwich, Norfolk 54, 85, 611
Nottingham 52, 609
Noviomagus, *see* Chichester

Odell, Bedfordshire 444
Old Byland, Yorkshire 184–5
Old Sarum, *see* Salisbury
Ormside, Cumbria 482–3
Orton Hall Farm, Cambridgeshire 145
Orton Longueville, Cambridgeshire 382–3, 391
Otley, Yorkshire 189
Outwell, Norfolk 568–9
Overton Down, Wiltshire 213
Oxborough, Norfolk 681
Oxford 71, 607, 609
Ozingell, Kent 592

Pakenham, Suffolk 381
Patching, Sussex 25, 427, 523–4
Pennyland, Buckinghamshire 145
Pentney, Norfolk *485*
Pershore, Worcestershire 417
Peterborough 483
Pevensey, Sussex 527–8
Pewsey, Wiltshire 651–4, *652*, *653–4*, *655–6*
Portchester, Hampshire 19, 143, *144*, 527, 528
  animal-bone assemblages 363, 368, 369
Portmahomack, Scotland 926–30, *927*, *929*
Portway, *see* Andover
Poundbury, *see* Dorchester, Dorset
Prittlewell, Essex 855
  chamber graves 100, 111, 138 n. 3, 269, *270*, *271*, 299, 979–80, *981*

Quarrington, Lincolnshire 23, 123, 425
Queenford Farm, *see* Dorchester-on-Thames

Radley, Oxfordshire 150, 356, 538
Ramsbury, Wiltshire 333, 425, 426
Raunds, Northamptonshire *144*, 166, 631–2
  burials 294–5, 299–300, 302

church 174, 185, 189
field layout 388, 392–3
Raunds Furnell, Northamptonshire 206, 207, 715
Reculver, Kent *558*, 573, 792, 826
Renhold Water End, Bedfordshire 135–136, *135*, 140
Repton, Derbyshire 55, 299, 605
Rhuddlan, Clwyd 65, 548
Ribblehead, Yorkshire 50, 211
Riccall Landing, Yorkshire 181
Richborough, Kent 527, 528, 529
Ripon, Yorkshire 188, 295, *298*, 717
Riseley, Kent 281, *282*
Rivenhall, Essex 174, 833
Riverdene, Hampshire 148–9
Roche Court Down, Wiltshire 905
Rockingham Forest, Northamptonshire 381, 425
Romsey, Hampshire 487, *488*
Rook Hall, Essex 425
Roundway Down, Avebury 274
Royston Grange, Derbyshire 319–20, 392
Runcorn, Cheshire 65, 511, 932
Ruthwell, Dumfriesshire *477*
Rutupiae, *see* Richborough
Ryedale, Yorkshire 56

St Albans, Hertfordshire 517, *518*, 522, 825
St Augustine's Abbey, Canterbury 836
St David's Head, Pembrokeshire 391
St Giles 682
St-Helen-on-the-Wall, York 710
St Martin's in the Fields, London 524
St Mary Bishophill Senior, York 54
St Ninian's Isle 480
St Paul's, London 524
Salisbury, Wiltshire 85, 274–5
  Swallowcliffe Down 274, 277, 444
Saltwood, Kent 896
Sancton, Yorkshire 243, 245, 332
Sandtun, Kent 334
Sarre, Kent *464*, 572, 592
Sarum, *see* Salisbury
Sawtry, Cambridgeshire 392
Sedgeford, Norfolk 774
Sewerby, Yorkshire 254
Shavard's Farm, Hampshire 673, 675, 676, 678, 680
Sheffield's Hill, Lincolnshire 449
Sherborne, Dorset 389, 391
Shrewsbury, Shropshire 338, 509, 519–520, 529, 610
Sibertswold, Kent *108*, 276
Silbury Hill, *see* Avebury

Silchester, Hampshire 19, 516, 520, *521*, 529
Simy Folds, County Durham 50, 211
Sleaford, Lincolnshire 468
Snape, Suffolk 253, 257–8
South Acre, Norfolk 296, 674, *680*, 681, 906
South Cadbury, Somerset 120, 511, 615
South Ferriby, Lincolnshire 54
South Kyme, Lincolnshire 182–3
South Newbald, Yorkshire 566
South Shields, Tyne and Wear 19
Southampton, Hampshire
  animal-bone assemblages 339
  Bitterne 522
  bone working 414, 474
  Clausentum 522
  Hamwic 296, 414, 432, 522, 568, 569, 570, 571, 602
    animal-bone assemblages 368, 371, 561
    coins 562, 587
    diet 334, 352, 353, 356, 357
    metalwork 426, 427, 428
Spofforth, Yorkshire 181, *182*
Spong Hill, Norfolk 673, 680, 681, 859
  burials 81, 227, 243, 245, 253, 680, 694
Springfield Lyons, Essex 138, 141, 143, 145 n., 242, 381
  diet 353, 356
Sprouston, Roxburghshire 542, 545
Stafford 357, 930–33, *931*
Staines, Middlesex 296, 906, *907*
Stamford, Lincolnshire 426, 428, *452*
Standlake Down, Oxfordshire 713
Staunch Meadow, Brandon, 565–6
Steyning, Sussex 132, 200, *202*, 206–7
Stockbridge Down, Hampshire 903–4, *903*
Stonegrave, Yorkshire 186, *187*
Stratfield Mortimer, Berkshire 301
Stratton Biggleswade, Bedfordshire 208–210, *209*
Streoneshalh, *see* Whitby
Strettington, Sussex 382
Studham, Bedfordshire 184
Sulgrave, Northamptonshire 51, *139*, 143, 206, 213
Sutton Bassett, Northants *191*
Sutton Courtenay, Oxfordshire 36, 382, *446*, 447
Sutton Hoo, Suffolk 244, 248, 922–6, *924*, *925*
  execution cemetery 275, 906, 923
  grave-goods 100, 111, 331–2
  helmet 106, *107*, 474, 773
  metalwork 96, 97, 106
  and paganism 770, 773
  ship burials 271, 279, 882–5, *883*, 923

  jewellery 472, 473, 884–5
  Mound I: 269–70, 273, 331, 424, 444, 472, 473, 592, 770, 855, 926, 978
  Mound II: 269, 331
  weapon burials 253
Sutton Walls, Herefordshire 382
Swaffham, Norfolk 675, 676, 681
Swallowcliffe Down, Wiltshire 274, 277, 444
Swinegate, York 292

Tamworth, Staffordshire 605
  mid-Saxon mill 120, 441, *442*, 443, 605
Taplow, Buckinghamshire 269, 304, 855
  barrow burials 100, 111, 275
  drinking horns 331, 469, *469*
  gold jewellery 472, 473
Tattershall Thorpe, Lincolnshire 409, *410*, 429, *450*, 455
Taverham, Norfolk 54
Teversham, Cambridgeshire 382
Thelwall, Cheshire 65, 511
Thetford, Norfolk 71, 363, 595
Thirlings, Northumberland 137
Thornton Steward, Yorkshire 181
Tidenham, Gloucestershire 337, 390
Tilbury, Essex 562
Towton, Yorkshire 682
Tredington, Warwickshire 388
Tresmorn, Cornwall 210
Trewhiddle, Cornwall 428, 539, 785
Trowbridge, Wiltshire 200
Tunley, Lancashire 387
Tyninghame, East Lothian 545

Uncleby, Yorkshire 267
Undley, Suffolk 462
Uppåkra, Sweden 870
Upper Bugle Street, Southampton 296
Upper Kentmere, Cumberland 211
Upwey, Dorset 835 n.

Venta, *see* Winchester
Venta Icenorum, *see* Caistor St Edmund (Caistor-by-Norwich)
Verulamium, *see* St Albans
Viroconium, *see* Wroxeter

Walkington Wold, Yorkshire 296, 899, 905
Wallingford, Oxfordshire 71
Wally Corner, Berinsfield 525, 529
Walpole St Andrew, Norfolk 391
Waltham Abbey, Essex 50
Wansdyke 24

Wareham, Dorset 424, 426
Warmington, Cambridgeshire 382–3
Warrington, Cheshire 682
Wasperton, Warwickshire 919–22, *921*
   burials 24, 227, 230, *920*
Water Eaton, Oxfordshire 391
Wearmouth, Sunderland 735, 788, 789, 792, 813–14
   burials 296, 301, 784
   religious houses 174, 406, 472–3, 474, 788, 960
Wells, Somerset 836
Wenhaston Old Hall, Suffolk 388
West Chisenbury, Wiltshire 382
West Cotton, Northamptonshire 206, 354, 363, 386
   enclosure and buildings 203, *204*, 206
West Fen Road, *see* Ely
West Heslerton, Yorkshire 83, 120, 121, 159, 538, 696, 917
   animal-bone assemblages 362, 366–7, 368–9, 372
   burials 253, 257, 691, 714
   Grubenhäuser 150, 151
West Hythe, Kent 212
West Runton, Norfolk 424–5, 426
West Stow, Suffolk 140, 329, 330, 381, 629, 677
   animal-bone assemblages 368, 369
   Grubenhäuser 147–8, 150
   loom-weights *446*, 447, 699
West Walton, Norfolk 391
Westbury, Buckinghamshire 208–210
Westfield Farm, Ely *690*
Westgarth Garden, Suffolk 675, *676*, 678, *680*, 681
Westley Waterless, Cambridgeshire 441
Westminster, London 188, 833
Weston-by-Welland, Northamptonshire *191*
Weston, Yorkshire 189
Wharram Percy, Yorkshire 207, 382, 412, 563, 682
   animal-bone assemblages 363, 366–7, 368, 369, 370, 372
   church 174, 177, 184, 189
   Grubenhäuser 149 n., 453
   South Manor 52, 361
Whitby, Yorkshire 174, 301, 566, 792
Whithorn (Wigtown) 825
Whitley Grange, Shropshire 19
Whittlesford, Cambridgeshire 393
Whittlewood, Northamptonshire 381, 393
Wicken Bonhunt, East Anglia 362–3, 366, 370, 372

Wigford, *see* Lincoln
Winchester, Hampshire 436, 493, 520, 786
   The Brooks 296
   burials 22–3, 246, *247*, 252, 278, 280, 296, 299, 521–22, 529, 710, 901
   Cathedral Green 520–21
   Harestock 901
   Lankhills 22–3, 529
   Lower Brook Street 22–3
   Old Minster 299, 418
   silver-gilt head 962, *963*
   street plan 608
   Venta 520
   Victoria Road 22–3
   Winchester Cathedral 782
   Winnall 278, 280, 675
   Worthy Park, Kingsworthy 246, *247*, *252*, 674, 675, *676*, 678, *680*, 710
Wing, Buckinghamshire 183
Winnall, *see* Winchester
Winster Moor, Peak District 274
Winterton, Lincolnshire 452
Witham Valley, Lincolnshire 187
Witton, Norfolk 381
Wollaston, Northamptonshire 106, 275, 388
Wolverton Turn, Buckinghamshire 334
Wolvesey, Hampshire 357
Worcester 613–14, 782
Worgret, *see* Wareham
Worthy Park, *see* Winchester
Wroxeter, Shropshire 19, 23, 516, 519, 529
Wylye, Wiltshire 382

Yarnton, Oxfordshire 121, 145, 356
   burials 296, 628–9
   field systems 381, 382
   hay meadows 123, 386
Yeavering, Northumberland
   annexes 136–7, 138
   burials 731, *731*
   doorposts 138, 140
   hearths 136–7, 143–5
   royal site 159–160, *160*, 162, 753–5, *754*
   timber buildings 135, 136–7, 138, 140–1, 143–4, 151–2
York 19, 52, 71, 570, 716
   animal-bone assemblages 363, 366–7, 368, 369, 370, 371, 372, 524
   burials 100, 289, 292, 293, 299, 301, 305, 710
   coinage 566, 593–4, *594*
   Coppergate 73, 95, 100, 371, 612–13, 614
      coin die 593–4, *594*
      craft production 416–17, 440, 444

York (*cont.*)
    diet 334, 353, 669
    metalworking 52, 54, 594–5
  diet 334, 353, 356, 669
  Eburacum 524
  Eoforwic 602–4
    plan of 568, 603
  Hungate 612, 614
  monuments 57, 301
  St-Helen-on-the-Wall 710
  St Mary Bishophill Senior 54
  Swinegate 292
  textiles 95, 110
  York Minster 289, 293, 299, 305